S0-ACN-229

THE FRENCH CANADIANS

THE FRENCH CANADIANS

1760–1945

by

MASON WADE

TORONTO

THE MACMILLAN COMPANY OF CANADA LIMITED

1955

MACMILLAN AND COMPANY LIMITED
London Bombay Calcutta Madras Melbourne

THE MACMILLAN COMPANY OF CANADA LIMITED
Toronto

PRINTED IN GREAT BRITAIN

For

J. B. B.

ABBREVIATIONS

AAQ: Archives of the Archdiocese of Quebec

APQ: Archives of the Province of Quebec

ASL: Archives seigneuriales de Lotbinière, Leclercville, Québec

Bib. St. Sulp.: Bibliothèque Saint-Sulpice, Montréal

Can. An. Rev.: The Canadian Annual Review

CAR: Canadian Archives Report

CHAR: Report of the Canadian Historical Association

CHR: The Canadian Historical Review

CJEPS: The Canadian Journal of Economics & Political Science

LOC: The Library of Congress

NYPL: New York Public Library

PAC: The Public Archives of Canada

PIB: Press Information Bureau, Montreal

QLHS: Quebec Literary & Historical Society

QLHST: Transactions of the Quebec Literary & Historical Society

RAPQ: Report of the Archives of the Province of Quebec

TRSC: Transactions of the Royal Society of Canada

PREFACE

THIS BOOK is essentially an attempt to explain why the French Canadians live, think, act, and react differently from English-speaking North Americans. It is also an account of what French Canadians call *le fait français en Amérique*—the French fact in North America—for only by tracing the intellectual and cultural history of French Canada from its beginnings can present-day Quebec be understood. French-Canadian culture is an intricate amalgam of the French heritage, the North American environment, and Roman, British, and American influences. The unifying thread in French-Canadian history is the spirit known as 'nationalism', which is actually an intense provincialism mingled with ethnic and religious factors. Therefore somewhat disproportionate attention will be devoted to the extremists of a generally placid and easy-going people, who possess a singular devotion to the golden mean as a rule of life; for this is an attempt to explain differences, not to stress resemblances.

This book is also the story of the ceaseless struggle of a minority group to maintain its cultural identity in the face of all manner of conscious and unconscious pressures to conform to the dominant civilization of other ethnic groups and another culture. The French Canadians are the *Sinn Feiners* of North America, for their strong group consciousness and cohesiveness arise from a basic loneliness and insecurity. It is the sense of 'ourselves alone' that motivates efforts at enhancement by stressing French Canada's peculiar ties with France and Rome. The attitudes of minority groups can often be explained only in psychological terms, and French Canada is no exception to this rule. Sir Wilfrid Laurier, one of the most eminent French Canadians, who had a profound understanding of both French and English Canadians,* once formulated this fact in the observation that 'Quebec does not have opinions, but only sentiments.' So this history will be in some measure a psychological study, whose findings may have some general validity for other minority groups.

Intellectual and cultural history is one of the broadest forms of non-specialized science. This book will be based on constitutional and political history, though by no means confined to it. It will use economic history and sociology, which do much to explain intellectual developments in this instance; it will employ literary and artistic

* These terms are used for 'French-speaking' and 'English-speaking' throughout, and do not necessarily refer to ethnic origin.

history for illustrative purposes. In so broad an attempt at synthesis in a field far from covered by adequate special studies, comprehensiveness or finality is not to be expected, but it is hoped that this book may lead to a better understanding of French Canada than previous histories largely concerned with political events unrelated to economic and social developments. So far as possible, this study is based upon primary sources, since many of the supposedly standard works proved inaccurate and unreliable upon detailed investigation. But it has not proved feasible to carry this policy as far as the author would have liked, largely because of the inadequacies of Canadian archives and libraries and the wide dispersion of materials. Considering its scope and the immense amount of work that remains to be done in the field, this book had to rely largely on the secondary sources which proved trustworthy. Crucial episodes have generally been investigated in the sources, and recourse has been had to the basic materials whenever the secondary works were obviously unsatisfactory. This method has provided a basis for critical judgment of earlier works, and the author has not hesitated to differ with them. This book could not have been written without critical use of previous work, for scholarship is a cumulative process, with an ungrateful tendency on the part of the laborer of the eleventh hour to disparage earlier workers in the vineyards. But historical truth can only emerge through continual sifting and winnowing of facts and theories in the light of new knowledge and new perspectives.

This process has been particularly necessary, for until very recently it has been the tradition in Canada to write history from a certain partisan position: French or English, Catholic or Protestant, Liberal or Tory. This tradition has had the unfortunate result of making the standard French and English histories of Canada so dissimilar as to suggest that they are the histories of two different countries. Such a situation, when members of the two chief Canadian ethnic groups are largely educated in separate school systems and different cultures, and are rarely thrown together until their minds are formed, can have and has had tragic consequences. It is hoped that this book will dispel some of the misunderstandings that are the basis of much needless friction between Canadians of different cultural backgrounds. The author has sought to use and correlate all available French and English sources, many of which are not available even throughout Canada, and as a disinterested outsider to interpret them objectively in a broader way than would be possible for a Canadian, subject to conscious or unconscious bias and preoccupied with the national scene.

The author is committed to neither side in the ancient ethnic conflict in Canada, and sympathetic to both, for his own ethnic and cultural heritage is Scots and English, while he shares the faith of

French Canada and is a native of New England, a region whose history has many analogies with that of Quebec and one which within the last century has become almost as French as Quebec has become English. He claims freedom from ethnic prejudice; and he believes that the Catholic historian's duty is best summarized by Leo XIII's dictum that the first law of history is not to lie, and the second not to be afraid to tell the whole truth. In the course of this book it has been necessary to state some hard truths; this has been done without malice and without any other design than to do justice to the facts. The ancient tradition of diplomatic relations between the the French and English in Canada has been outmoded by Canada's national development, and frankness is now the best and most useful approach to their differences.

It doubtless seems presumptuous of the writer to take it upon himself to write the history of a country of which he is not a native and whose mother tongue is not his own. There are advantages, however, in such a course; and perhaps particularly in this instance, where there has existed at times an almost unbridgeable abyss between two peoples with a common history, and where ancient quarrels have a fatal way of entering into the thinking of each group about the other. The writer has devoted ten years to this work; he lived in Quebec for two years, thanks to the Guggenheim Foundation, and has made many extended visits there for research purposes, thanks to the Rockefeller Foundation and the Carnegie Corporation of New York. The Corporation, through a grant to the Canada Foundation, has made publication possible. He has traveled through almost all parts of the province, which is larger than France and Britain combined, meeting and talking with all classes of its people, and learning some of the things which are not to be found in books. He has taught in a French-Canadian university and lectured on French Canada both in Quebec and the other provinces, and through discussion learned much of both French and English attitudes towards the matters with which this book is concerned. He is vastly indebted to many Canadians who undertook his education in their history, and is grateful for the light they have shed upon the problem with which he was concerned. He trusts that in these pages they will find no cause to regret their courtesy and kindness to a stranger in search of knowledge, who now seems to intervene in a family quarrel.

But the matters with which this book is concerned are not exclusively Canadian in nature. While there are 3,500,000 French Canadians in Canada, there are also some 2,000,000 Franco-Americans of Quebec and Acadian stock in the United States. While their history, and consequently their attitudes, like those of the French Canadians of the Maritime Provinces, Ontario, and the West, differ from those of the French Canadians of Quebec, the old province on the St. Lawrence remains to various degrees their cultural homeland, and they have deeply felt its influence. This book is primarily concerned with Quebec, the heart of French Canada; but it also deals with the history of the outlying groups when this has affected Quebec and the far-flung French-Canadian people have been re-united, regardless of provincial or international frontiers. It has been impossible for the author, with the time and means at his disposal, to tell this broader story in detail, or even to sketch it fully. But the history of Quebec is essential to the understanding of these outlying minority groups, which in the past have shown varying tendencies to follow the Quebec tradition of standing apart and preserving their separateness from English-speaking North Americans; and there are common patterns, as well as significant differences, in the behavior of all minority groups. These are of concern to all North Americans, whether citizens of Canada or the United States, and indeed to all mankind, for only by the acceptance of diversity, through the understanding and reconciliation of cultural differences, can the great world problem of our time be solved.

It is unfortunately impracticable for reasons of space to acknowledge in detail all the obligations incurred by the writer in the course of ten years' work. Among many libraries the Dartmouth College Library offered extraordinary facilities for research throughout the undertaking. The staffs of the Public Archives of Canada and of the Quebec Provincial Archives were unfailingly helpful. The author is particularly indebted for criticism of the first draft to Professors J. B. Brebner of Columbia University, and Jean-Charles Falardeau and Jean-Charles Bonenfant of Laval University, who read the entire manuscript. Others who criticized one or more chapters include Professors E. R. Adair, J. I. Cooper, and F. R. Scott of McGill University, A. L. Burt of the University of Minnesota, G. F. G. Stanley of the Royal Military College of Canada, Miss Elizabeth Armstrong, M. G. Ballantyne, Dr. Pierre Dansereau, the late J. K. Howard, and Major Gustave Lanctot. The late Paul Rainville, Gérard Morisset of the Quebec Provincial Museum, and A. J. H. Richardson of the Public Archives were of great assistance with the illustrations and maps. To these individuals and many others the writer wishes to express his gratitude, while absolving them of any responsibility for the views which he finally adopted after considering divergent points of view.

MASON WADE

Cornish, New Hampshire
April 1954

CONTENTS

LIST OF ILLUSTRATIONS

CHAPTER I

THE HERITAGE OF NEW FRANCE

(1534–1760)

NOWHERE in North America is the cult of the past stronger than in French Canada. Quebec's motto is '*Je me souviens*' ('I remember'), and this motto is no empty formula. French Canada has a sense of tradition unique in North America, and the French Canadians live in and on their past to a degree which it is difficult for English-speaking North Americans to appreciate. No real understanding of French Canada is possible without a realization of what its history—perhaps the most colorful, for its span of years, of any human record—means to the French Canadian, whose most popular historian has made familiar the phrase '*Notre maître, le passé*' ('Our master, the past') and established it as a principle for action in the present.[1]

What does '*Je me souviens*' mean to the French Canadian? Above all, it means that he remembers the days of New France, the heroic period of the French in America. The story of New France has been told too often and too well—most ably in English by Francis Parkman—to be retold once more at length, but its salient features must be recalled here because of their bearing on the subsequent periods with which this book is chiefly concerned. Some of the strongest forces in modern French Canada derive directly from the seventeenth century: the apostolic spirit of the Counter-Reformation or Catholic Revival, the cultural tradition of classicism, the political ideal of absolutism or benevolent despotism, and a semi-feudal hierarchical concept of society. To this golden age of French Canada its own historians have devoted disproportionate attention; every aspect of the French period (1534–1763) has been lovingly examined and re-examined, while many important phases of the English (1763–1867) and Canadian (1867 to the present) have been left untouched and unconsidered. The French Canadian consoles himself for an unhappy position in the present by dwelling upon the glories of his past. This very understandable psychological reaction also explains the tendency of the same historians to romanticize the history of New France, which is in itself so romantic as to need no added coloring. The staid Puritan Parkman is only one of many English-speaking writers to be moved by the same subject to excesses of romanticism. This general tendency has had the effect of beclouding the facts in a golden haze of glorious legend.

I

The discovery of America came at an epoch of great and profound changes in the European world. With the invasion of Italy in 1494 by Charles VIII of France, the Renaissance spread more rapidly from Italy to northern Europe. The classical humanism of the great artists and writers of the Italian Renaissance enlarged the intellectual horizons of the European mind, while Columbus gave mankind a new world and Copernicus a new heaven. The old closed European world was shattered into fragments, as a new epoch of restless intellectual curiosity began. The great age of discoveries and explorations followed inevitably, and in the exploration of North America the French took the leading role from the Italians and Spaniards who had led in discovery. This was also the period of the Reformation, when theological controversy and wars of religion racked the great nations of Europe. Bloody religious strife was carried across the sea from the Old World to New Spain, New France, and New England. Ribaut's French Protestants were massacred in Florida by Menendez' Spanish Catholics in the name of religion; while the French excluded Protestants from Canada, and the Puritans of New England barred Catholics from their colonies. In their infancy, the young colonies of New France and New England were opposed by religion; and the religious element was never absent from the long succession of wars which they waged against one another until the final downfall of New France. This fact has left its mark upon the mind of French Canada.

When New France was founded, France stood upon the threshold of its greatest age. Its population of some 14,000,000 was three times as large as that of England and Wales. Gibbon bears witness that Louis XIV was the master of a military establishment as great as that of the Roman Empire in its prime.[2] And then, as Macaulay puts it, 'France had, over the surrounding countries, at once the ascendency which Rome had over Greece, and the ascendency which Greece had over Rome,'[3] for French civilization was the model of all Europe. Latin at last yielded to French as the language of scholarship and diplomacy; the proud Spanish diplomat was forced to yield precedence to the Frenchman; French authority was supreme even in such minute matters as dress, cooking, and dancing. France was united as was no other European nation of the period; under the first three Bourbons—Henri IV, Louis XIII, and Louis XIV—the monarchy had become so absolute that Louis XIV could justly say—if he did—'I am the State,' and be supported in this position by Bossuet, the greatest French spokesman of the Church in his day.[4]

New France had an unequal share of the glories of France's greatest age. The absolutism and autocracy of the mother country affected every aspect of the life of the colony, but the needs of New France were often neglected by a monarch more concerned with Europe than America. A comparison of Quebec's Chateau Saint-Louis or Montreal's Chateau de Ramézay with the contemporary chateaux of the Loire reveals the pitiful inferiority of the colony to the mother country. The *seigneurs*, the much romanticized *petite noblesse* of New France, had little in common with the great nobles of France: in lineage, wealth, and power they were as nothing compared to the brilliant figures of the French court. The *haute noblesse* of France had little to do with Canada: some were fitfully interested in the fur trade and others lent the support of their names to the work of the missionaries, but few came to the colony themselves. Canada was commonly regarded in worldly France as the last resort of the ruined, the alternative to a prison cell, under both Louis XIII and Louis XIV, long before Voltaire dismissed it as 'several acres of snow.'[5] As with the great nobles, so with the kings: François I gave Jacques Cartier a ship and fifty crowns, and none of the Valois did more for New France. In the seventeenth century the Bourbons took a greater interest in Canada, but the colony still played only a minor part in their preoccupations.

The Bourbons, however, left a lasting mark on New France, and it was they and their ministers who shaped the development of the colony. Henri IV, the Protestant prince who became a Catholic king, gave France a degree of prosperity and national unity after the disruptive religious wars which permitted the founding of Port Royal and Quebec, the first settlements to be made after seventy-three years of regular voyages to the New World by French traders, explorers, and fishermen. Henri gave patents to develop New France to both Protestant and Catholic alike; if his example had been followed by later monarchs, the colony might have provided a refuge for the industrious Huguenots driven from France by the revocation of the Edict of Nantes and profited thereby; but Canada was destined by its founders to be a wholly Catholic land. Richelieu, through the Company of One Hundred Associates, tried to provide for the French traders of the northern seas the same support which the English and the Dutch had already given to their merchants of the Indies. Mazarin saved France from internal disruption and the loss of its European primacy, thus indirectly benefiting the colony, which was so dependent upon the mother country that in 1650 Marie de l'Incarnation, superior of the Quebec Ursulines, wrote home: 'Neither we nor all Canada can survive another two years without aid . . . if this aid is lacking, we must die or return to France, according to the opinion of the best thinkers.'[6] For seven years, from 1663 to 1670, Louis XIV gave the colony more support than it had yet received from the rulers of France; then European ambition replaced his zeal for colonization abroad. Colbert, the administrative genius behind the glory of the Sun King, left his mark on the colony, but with all his European concerns could never really give it the attention it deserved.

From the beginnings of the colony, the Church provided more support and encouragement than either crown or court. As the Puritans sought liberty of conscience in New England, so zealous priests, religious, and layfolk alike went forth from France to convert the savages and to build a new and more truly Catholic France in America. Missionary activity was not the primary purpose of the French in coming to America, and at first it was not their dominant concern, despite the claims of most French-Canadian writers; for New France was frequented by explorers and traders for nearly a century before the first missionaries came. The search for a Northwest Passage to the riches of the Indies; the lure of the flourishing fisheries of the Newfoundland and Nova Scotian banks; the hope that mines rivalling those of Spain might be discovered; the call of a continental treasure-house of furs—such were the motives which first brought the French to Canada. The fur trade remained the mainspring of the colony's life until long after the French period. Jacques Cartier paid lip service to the missionary motive, but his primary aims were exploration and the discovery of treasure. Champlain is the first writer on New France to stress a policy of Christianization; and he does not refer to it until his *Fourth Voyage* in 1613, and then as an afterthought: 'The desire that I have always had to make new discoveries in New France to the advantage, benefit, and glory of the French name, as well as to lead these poor peoples to the knowledge of God.'[7] But the missionary spirit was introduced into the life of New France early in the seventeenth century, and it has ever since remained a potent force in French Canada.

There is little truth, however, in the traditional opposition of a spiritual-minded New France to a materialistic New England. The French were first of all explorers and exploiters of the natural resources of the New World; and the great missionary effort of the seventeenth century was not unrelated to the necessity of winning the support of the Indians, whose goodwill was vital to the fur trade. Montreal was a fur-trading center long before Olier and Dauversière conceived the mission colony of Ville-Marie, and the Sulpicians placed the motto '*Hic evangelizabantur Indi*' ('Here the Indians were evangelized') above the entrance of their seminary in Montreal. Colonization, beyond the little necessary to assure the welfare of the fur trade, was discouraged by the great commercial monopolies who operated the trade. New France was ruled by transient Frenchmen for the benefit of France. On the other hand, the English colonists in the richer and milder region to the south had turned their backs upon their mother country, and they set about the creation of a New England upon a basis of permanent agricultural colonization. Only after that foundation had been firmly laid, by an effort which dwarfed that of New France, did they turn to trade by land with the Indians and by sea with the West Indies and with the French colonies themselves, neglected by a European-minded monarchy. These facts had an important bearing upon the conflict which soon developed between the rival empires of France and England in North America.

The destiny of New France was shaped by the fact that in the seventeenth century, the great age of the Catholic Revival in France, the renewed energy of the Church found in America an outlet from the restraint imposed at home by dominance of the state. The new religious spirit found heroic expression in the missionary activity of the Jesuits and Recollects* who saw to it that the Cross accompanied the *fleur-de-lis* from the Atlantic almost to the Rockies, from Hudson Bay to the Gulf of Mexico, as the French explorers bared the heart of the continent and traced out the principal waterways to which Jacques Cartier's '*grand fleuve de Hochelaga et chemin du Canada*,'[8] the 'river and road' of the St. Lawrence River system, led them. And while the missionaries made a continent familiar with their black and gray robes, devoted little bands of religious and pious layfolk cultivated the seeds of civilization on the banks of the St. Lawrence, where the fur traders had established only rude trading posts. Through these theocratic pioneers two great ecclesiastical disputes of the age of Louis XIV left their mark on the colony: the strife between Jesuit and Jansenist, and the struggle between Gallican and Ultramontane. The dominance of the Jesuits in New France gave short shrift to the doctrines of their enemies—the *Anti-Coton* was burnt at Quebec in October 1626—but nevertheless the ascetic and pietistic influence of Cornelius Jansen was felt through the close connections of the religious of Quebec and Montreal with their mother houses in France, which, like many of the pious lay supporters of the Canadian missions, felt the influence of the Port Royal movement. French-Canadian Catholicism has ever since had a strain of Jansenism in it, as American Protestantism has had a tinge of Puritanism.[9]

The strife between Louis XIV and Innocent XI over the relations of church and state was reflected in New France by bitter quarrels between bishop and governor and intendant, under the three-headed

* The Gray Friars, or Reformed Franciscans, a sixteenth-century foundation more devoted to asceticism and contemplation than the original order.

system of French colonial administration. But two of Bossuet's four fundamentals of gallicanism were reversed in the colony, where under the Jesuits and Bishop Laval the civil power came close to being considered subject to the spiritual one in temporal matters, and the Pope's authority was regarded as supreme and not subject to the usages of a national church. From the earliest days the leaders of the Church in New France had little use for Bossuet's reflection on the Papacy: 'Ocean itself, immense though it be, has its limits, and to break through at its own caprice would be to lay desolate the world.'[10] While gallicanism carried the day in Louis XIV's France, ultramontanism triumphed in New France under the championship of Bishop Laval, who vanquished the gallicanism of governor and intendant and established for himself a position which the Pope himself might have envied. Ever since, French Canada has remained a stronghold of clericalism, and very conscious of its spiritual dependence upon the Holy See.

2

It is appropriate that one of the three earliest written records of French Canada is Giovanni Battista Ramusio's *Navigationi e Viaggi* (1566), which contains Jacques Cartier's *Voyage au Canada en* 1534 and his *Bref récit . . . de la Navigation faite en MDXXXV et MDXXXVI*; for the rediscovery of America, after the Scandinavian explorations had been forgotten, was primarily the work of Italians: Columbus, the Cabots, Verrazano, and Amerigo Vespucci. Cartier is often credited by French-Canadian writers with the discovery of Canada, but John Cabot had touched at Cape Breton and planted the English flag on Newfoundland in 1497, while early in the sixteenth century Basques and Portuguese, as well as Frenchmen, were already swarming on the new fishing grounds discovered by searchers for a Northwest Passage to the Indies. In an age of faith and abstinence, when the European consumption of fish was far greater than in modern times, the rich Newfoundland fisheries were a discovery well worth exploiting, and the French fishermen of Brittany, the Bay of Biscay, and the Channel ports at first outstripped their rivals. When Jacques Cartier set out in 1534 from Saint-Malo with a crew of fishermen and a commission from François I to consolidate Verrazano's claim of 1523 to the northeastern American coast as Nova Gallia, he was following a route already familiar to fishermen of France and many other countries, and not, like Columbus, blazing a path to the unknown. That year Cartier merely charted the Gulf of the St. Lawrence, where he met other French craft, and Chaleur Bay, without entering the great river which the Indians called the 'road of Canada.' He was looking for either a passage to the Pacific or a route into the interior of Asia, and François I hoped he would forestall the Spaniards, who were already exploiting the riches of the New World in the southwest. At Gaspé Cartier raised a great cross which bore the *fleur-de-lis* and the words '*Vive le roi de France*,'[11] a fitting symbol of the close relationship between church and state in the New France thus claimed. Two Iroquoian Indians, kidnapped while fishing in Chaleur Bay and taken back to France, whetted François I's appetite for gain with their tales of the kingdoms of Hochelaga, Stadacona, and the Saguenay, which might be new Mexicoes, Perus, or the outposts of Cathay itself. Cartier found rich fisheries, fertile lands and a wealth of timber, but not the gold, silver, jewels, and oriental staples which his pre-mercantilist monarch desired.

In the following year Cartier made his way up the St. Lawrence, pausing at Tadoussac to marvel at the deep and mighty river which the Indians told him led to the Kingdom of the Saguenay, rich in copper, and touching at Ile-aux-Coudres before reaching the Mohawk settlement of Stadacona (Quebec). Then, despite the reluctance of the Indians to let him continue—the first instance of the enduring Quebec-Montreal rivalry—he went on up the river to the Huron or Onondaga center of Hochelaga (Montreal). There, from the summit of Mount Royal, he looked out over the great plain and saw the continental waterway stretching far beyond the Lachine Rapids[12] which had stopped his progress. He heard of the Ottawa River, leading to a land of silver and gold, from the Indians of Hochelaga, to whom he read the Gospel of St. John and gave gifts, after they had besought him to touch the sores of their sick, 'as if God had come there to cure them.'[13] Finding no treasure among the poverty-stricken northern Indians, whose bitter struggle for existence made European tools and trinkets all the more valuable to them, the French fell easily into the role of gods, which all the Indians assigned to the white newcomers, and did not outrage their hosts as the Spaniards did. In these few autumn months of 1535, Cartier traced out the lifeline of New France, the waterway which was long to be the limit of settlement. With a foreshadowing of that friendly relationship with the Indians which was to be the great buckler of New France in its struggle against the English, who long sought only to exterminate the savages, Cartier observed: 'By what we have seen and what little we have heard of this people, it seems that they would be easy to tame.'[14] Returning to Stadacona, he spent the winter there at the mouth of the Saint-Charles, losing twenty-five of his men to scurvy as the ships lay frozen up for five months under four feet and more of snow in a season whose severity appalled Frenchmen accustomed to a milder climate. In the spring he sailed back to France with Donnacona, the 'King of Canada.' He did not return until 1541, for François I was too involved in his struggle against encirclement by the Holy Roman Empire of Charles V to concern himself with North America.

In that year the most ambitious French effort in the New World for nearly a century was begun, with colonization and conquest of the 'outer limit of Asia' as its aim, but in the end it came to nothing. The Sieur de Roberval was made lieutenant-general of the king in the New World, with Cartier as his subordinate. Ten ships were to be laden with sailors, soldiers, artisans, and colonists; full equipment and stores for two years, and even livestock, were to be carried; and the expedition was to establish a colony, as a base for further search for the Northwest Passage and for the discovery of the riches of the mythical Kingdom of the Saguenay, which had appeared to be a new Peru in the tall tales told by Donnacona. But Roberval was detained in Europe, and Cartier set off in the spring of 1541 with only five ships. After going up the St. Lawrence, as far as the Lachine Rapids, he wintered at Cap Rouge near Quebec, and then returned to France with a cargo of false gold and jewels—Thevet's '*diamants de Canada*,'[15] meeting the belated Roberval with three more ships in June at St. John's, Newfoundland. Despite the latter's orders to accompany him back to Canada, Cartier continued on to France to get credit for his discoveries. Here he was joined by Roberval in the fall of 1543, after a winter exploration of the Saguenay and trouble with the Indians had frozen the colonizing spirit and revealed no treasure. Neither settlement nor new discovery resulted from this ill-starred expedition; and the discouraged court, preoccupied first with the Spanish conflict and then with religious and dynastic civil wars, lost interest in the New World. Montaigne summed up the prevailing French feeling about America when he remarked: 'I am afraid that our eyes are bigger than our bellies and that we have more curiosity than capacity, for we grasp at everything and catch nothing but air.'[16]

Meanwhile French fishermen frequented the waters which Cartier had carefully charted, and with the change from the green to the dry fishery, set up seasonal stations on the shores of Cape Breton, Nova Scotia, Gaspé, and the Gulf of St. Lawrence. The French were driven to the mainland, since the English had occupied the best portions of the Newfoundland coast for this purpose. Once contact had thus been established with the continent and its inhabitants, the fur trade became a profitable sideline of the fisheries. By the second half of the sixteenth century the trade came into its own; and Tadoussac, the Basque whaling post at the mouth of the Saguenay and at the head of the great waterway system used by the Algonkin tribes, became its center. The European demand for fur, a luxury which became a much desired staple after the discovery of the felting process, was as steady and as eager as the Indian demand for the iron weapons, tools, and utensils which were so superior to their traditional implements of stone, wood, bone, and bark. But monopoly was as essential to the fur trade as individualism was to the fisheries, and so the traders sought monopolies from the monarchy. As early as 1588 two nephews of Jacques Cartier petitioned the king to this effect, but not until ten years later did Henri IV grant the Marquis de la Roche a monopoly in Acadia, and soon after assign another in the Gulf and the Lower St. Lawrence to Pierre Chauvin, a Huguenot merchant of Honfleur. The monarchy was ruined by wars at home and abroad; the king had no money for colonization efforts but by obliging the monopolists to establish settlements, he hoped to gain his end at their expense. Colonization and the fur trade were incompatible, however, and the collapse of de la Roche's colony on Sable Island and the failure of Chauvin to establish a permanent post at Tadoussac supplied the first evidence of this fact.

In 1604 another monopoly was granted, with better results. The Sieur de Monts headed the new company, which included some of Chauvin's former associates, as well as the influential nobleman Poutrincourt, the literary lawyer Marc Lescarbot, and the trading associates Du Pont-Gravé and Samuel de Champlain, who had explored the St. Lawrence during the previous year in behalf of the colonization company of Aymar de Chastes. That spring an expedition of some 125 people set out from France. After exploring the Acadian coast, they settled on St. Croix Island, where Maine now meets New Brunswick. In the following year the settlement was moved across the Bay of Fundy to Port Royal on the Annapolis Basin. Here a trading post was established, which sheltered the banquets of the Order of the Good Time immortalized by Lescarbot in his *Histoire de la Nouvelle France* (1609), and where the same learned lawyer composed his *Muses de la Nouvelle France*, the first literary production of the French in America. More was accomplished than the writing of verses and the partaking of good cheer, however, for vegetables and grain were cultivated and some attempt at permanent settlement was made. But in 1607, at the instigation of other jealous traders, de Monts' monopoly was arbitrarily revoked by the minister Sully, and he abandoned the whole venture in disgust. Poutrincourt and his son Biencourt continued fur trading in Acadia, but at the suggestion of Champlain, who had already visited the St. Lawrence in 1603, de Monts was induced in 1608 to try his luck once more in the latter region. This move resulted in the lasting foundation of New France.

3

Samuel de Champlain was the true founder of French Canada. He started life as a Huguenot soldier in the wars of the League, but in

1598, after becoming a Catholic, he turned mariner and sailed to Cadiz with a shipload of Spanish soldiers who had served in France. While there he was offered the command of a vessel bound to the West Indies and Mexico. This two-year voyage gave him a first-hand knowledge of the Spanish colonies and moved him to the thought of a Panama canal. It also furnished him with the material for his *Bref discours des choses les plus remarquables . . . aux Indes occidentales*. Brought to the notice of Henri IV by this work, which is illustrated by sixty-two curious drawings of the Indians and of tropical flora and fauna, Champlain was named royal geographer. In 1603 he joined de Chastes' expedition to the St. Lawrence, which was under the command of Du Pont-Gravé of Saint-Malo, and was commissioned by the king to report on the expedition's discoveries. Thus he was formally launched upon his long career as an explorer and geographer. It is clear that his impelling motive was a love of discovery, for his explorations went far beyond the necessities of the fur trade in which he was nominally engaged, and his writings bear witness to the breadth of his curiosity. Champlain was a true man of the Renaissance, with a wide-ranging mind and a remarkable assortment of talents. He was at various times soldier, sailor, geographer, explorer, fur trader, historian, artist, architect, diplomat, governor, botanist, and gardener. But Lescarbot, the first historian of New France who was Champlain's companion at Port Royal, testifies that the latter's primary passion was discovery: 'Champlain promises never to cease his efforts until he has found either a western sea or a northern sea, opening the route to China which so many have sought in vain.'[17]

It was with this purpose that in the summer months of 1603 Champlain explored the Saguenay farther than any Frenchman had gone since Jacques Cartier discovered its mouth; that he followed the St. Lawrence up to the foot of the Lachine Rapids, and the Richelieu up to the rapids at Chambly. Thus convinced that there was no passage to the Indies by way of the great river, he inspected the Gaspé coast and Chaleur Bay in search of the elusive route which was the goal of all the great discoverers of the day. Laden with beaver skins and accompanied by some Indians, he sailed back to France, with his head full of the tales he had heard of great inland seas far up the St. Lawrence, beyond many rapids and a tremendous cataract. But his patron de Chastes had died during his absence, and de Monts, who succeeded to the monopoly, sought a milder climate than that which the traders had already experienced at Tadoussac and Quebec. So from 1604 to 1607 Champlain roamed along the seaboard from Nova Scotia to Martha's Vineyard, a coast which he was the first to map and name. So slowly and carefully did he do this work that he failed to reach the Connecticut and

Hudson Rivers, which led to richer and more naturally favored regions than that of the St. Lawrence.

In 1608 he came back to Quebec to stay. His reasons are revealed in his *Voyages* of 1613: 'So many voyages and discoveries vainly undertaken, with much labor and expense, have resolved we French these last years to try and make a permanent settlement in the land that we call New France, hoping more easily to accomplish this enterprise, since the voyage would begin in the land beyond the ocean, along which the search is made for the much sought passage.'[18] Thus, after almost seventy years, Cartier's work was resumed. Champlain left Du Pont-Gravé to barter with the Indians at Tadoussac, while he himself pushed on to the narrows of the St. Lawrence from which Quebec derives its name.[19] Here at the foot of the great rock he built the *habitation* of Quebec, the third settlement of the de Monts company and the one that was to endure. Of the twenty-eight white men who spent the winter there after Du Pont-Gravé sailed back to France, only eight survived. But the stout-hearted Champlain was not discouraged, unlike the earlier winterers at Quebec, and when summer came and Du Pont-Gravé brought support from France, he pushed on up the Richelieu to Lake Champlain, where not far from Ticonderoga he helped the Hurons and Algonkins of his party to defeat a band of Iroquois. He was forced thus to incur the lasting enmity of what proved to be the most powerful eastern savage confederation by the necessity of cultivating the friendship of the Indians who acted as his guides and furnished the French with furs. This motive comes out clearly in his account of the expedition against the Onondagas in 1615: 'It was very necessary to assist them both to put them the more under obligation to love us, and to facilitate my undertakings and discoveries which, as it seemed, could only be accomplished with their help, and also as this would lead to and prepare their conversion to Christianity.'[20] Here Champlain reveals the purposes of the founders of New France: first trade, then geographical curiosity, and finally missionary activity. This order is often reversed by French-Canadian historians, partly because history in French Canada has so largely been written by idealistic clerics.

Upon his arrival at Quebec in 1608, Champlain had found himself in the midst of a great Indian movement. The Algonkins and Montagnais, who were wandering hunters, were moving down from the north and replacing the sedentary, agricultural Iroquois whom Cartier had earlier encountered at Stadacona and Hochelaga. The corn culture of the latter had not flourished in the St. Lawrence Valley, while their enemies obtained superior iron tools and weapons from the French traders at Tadoussac and so the Iroquois retired into northern New York, and the Hurons to the Georgian Bay region.

The balance between the two groups became more even when the Dutch came to New York in 1609 and began to supply the Iroquois European arms in exchange for furs. This was the first known phase of a vast regional conflict based upon geography which has endured until the present day: a natural opposition of the St. Lawrence and Hudson-Mohawk river systems, the only eastern seaboard waterways which penetrated the mountain barriers and led to the heart of the continent. During the days of New France the two river systems were bitter rivals in the fur trade, for they provided the only channels of trade. Later, lumber and wheat were to replace fur as the staples of trade; canals to eliminate portages and carries; barges, steamers, and finally railroads to outmode canoes; but the opposition of the two systems remained, whether Indian, Frenchman, Dutchman, Englishman, or American controlled them.

Champlain, with his geographer's eye, was quick to appreciate the implications of the structure of the continent and to take action. In 1611 he cleared land for an establishment at Montreal, the meeting place of the two river systems and the predestined entrepôt of the St. Lawrence, because there ocean navigation ceased, interrupted by the Lachine Rapids, and all the traffic of the upper St. Lawrence, the Ottawa, and the Richelieu came together. In 1613 he went up the Ottawa in search of the mythical inland sea of which he had been told by a glib young Frenchman who had wintered with the Indians; and again in 1615 he followed the Ottawa to Lake Nipissing and Lake Huron, wintering with the Hurons of Georgian Bay, who served as middlemen for the French in the trade with the Western tribes. He went with them on an expedition against the Iroquois, who then fulfilled this same function for the Dutch, as they would later for the English. For commercial reasons the French had to incur the lasting enmity of the Five Nations, who already distrusted them as a result of Cartier's kidnapping exploits, and whose savage raids were almost to destroy New France in its infancy. The implications of geography and the relationship of the Indian tribes to the all-important trade overrode all other considerations, as the Recollect Frère Gabriel Sagard noted in his *Grand Voyage au Pays des Hurons* (1632): 'I had hoped to promote a peace between the Hurons and the Iroquois, so that Christianity could be spread among them, and to open the roads to trade with many nations which were not yet accessible, but some of the members of the Company advised me that it was not expedient, since if the Hurons were at peace with the Iroquois, the same Iroquois would lead the Hurons to trade with the Dutch and divert them from Quebec, which is more distant.'[21]

Champlain's activities were not confined to leadership in trade and war. In 1615 he brought the Recollects, or reformed Franciscans, to Quebec. Although the secular Abbé Jessé de Fléché had come to Port Royal in 1610 and the Jesuits Biard and Massé in 1611, these were the first priests in New France proper, and the only ones until the coming of the Jesuits ten years later. Of the first four Recollects, Pères Le Caron and Dolbeau went off immediately to missions among the Hurons of Georgian Bay and the Montagnais of the Saguenay-Lake St. John region—Le Caron was already established when Champlain reached Georgian Bay that fall—while the two others remained at Quebec in the convent which they built by the Saint-Charles River. With the coming of the Recollects, the mission of New France was born; with that of the Jesuits, the way was opened for the development of a theocracy such as France had never known. The energy and exaltation of the Catholic Revival in France found its fullest outlet in the colony, where the power of the king paled before the immediate power of the Church, whose heroic missionary effort and devoted social services at once gave it tremendous prestige and were essential to the life of New France.

The coming of the Recollects was the result of only one of the twenty voyages which Champlain made to and from France. He displayed no little statesmanship in maintaining the interest of king and court in the colony, despite contentions among the rival fur traders and the varying fortunes of the companies which held the monopoly of New France at different times. In 1617 he brought back from France the first true colonist, the Parisian apothecary Louis Hébert, and his family, which was the first to come to Quebec. Hébert had earlier shared the fortunes of Poutrincourt in Acadia and there, according to Lescarbot, had taken pleasure in working the soil. The Company was more interested, however, in his professional talents, and under the terms of his engagement Hébert had no chance to try his hand at agriculture for three years after his arrival. Then he was summoned to Tadoussac to act as de Caen's lieutenant, and in 1621 he was made royal procurator. But somehow in the midst of his official duties—no doubt with the aid of Champlain, who took an interest in gardens and knew their importance to the colony—Hébert managed to clear a bit of land atop the cliff at Quebec, high above the fort at its foot, and to grow peas and onions there. He had the farmer's love of land and obtained for himself the fiefs of Saut-au-Matelot and of the Saint-Charles River. But the actual pioneering of Hébert, the first Frenchman to attempt to settle in the New World, has been somewhat exaggerated in a Quebec which mistakenly considers itself to have been an agricultural region from the first. Only one and a half acres were cleared in the first twenty-two years of the colony, and no plow broke the soil of Quebec until 1628, the year after Hébert's death.[22] The successive companies which ruled the destinies of New France at this period made no effort to carry out the promises of colonization which they had given in exchange for a monopoly of the fur trade, since they would thus defeat their main purpose.

The first real colonization expedition to the St. Lawrence, sent out by Richelieu's powerful new Company of New France, was captured in the Gulf by two of the privateering Kirke brothers of Dieppe and London, while a third Kirke was demanding the surrender of Quebec from Champlain. The resolute governor concealed his pressing need for supplies and refused to yield, but after eking out another winter he was forced to capitulate on July 21, 1629. The Kirkes, who were half English and half Huguenot French, had the backing of both London and French Huguenot merchants and were supplied with letters of marque from Charles I of England. Their conquest thus marked the first round in that second Hundred Years' War between French and English which left a lasting mark on New France and finally brought about its downfall. It also marked the first assault of nationless capital upon French Canada. For three years the English flag waved over Quebec, until by the Treaty of Saint-Germain-en-Laye Charles exchanged New France and Acadia for the unpaid dowry of his wife, Henrietta Maria of France.

Then Champlain returned as governor and watched over the destinies of the colony until his death in 1635. But the great promise of the Company of New France had been blighted by the loss of almost its entire capital as a result of the Kirkes' activities. The company was forced to sublease its privileges and responsibilities, and so development of the colony continued in the old inadequate, hand-to-mouth fashion. By 1643 there were only 300 people in Quebec, instead of the 4,000 settlers that the company had promised to establish by that date. The most notable achievement in the field of colonization had been the granting of the fertile seigneury of Beauport to Robert Giffard in 1634, which established in a semi-feudal mold the pattern of settlement for the rest of the French regime. Aside from this beginning of real colonization, fur-trading posts were established at Trois-Rivières at the mouth of the Saint-Maurice in 1634 and at Fort Richelieu (Sorel) at the mouth of the Richelieu in 1642. Then, in the latter year, came the establishment of a colony at Montreal by a group of priests and pious folk, whose zeal for the conversion of the Indians was counted upon to secure this vital outpost of the trade.

It was the Church, rather than the monarchy or the trading companies, which gave the colony the support it needed during this difficult early period. The Jesuits, who came to New France in 1635 after the ill-starred Acadian mission of Biard and Massé in 1611–14, soon established a religious monopoly comparable to the commercial monopoly of the Company of New France. While their *Relations* served to arouse the mother country's interest in the colony and to bring a stream of missionaries and donations out from France, the Jesuits barred the Huguenots, who had thus far played a considerable part in New France, and soon crowded out their clerical rivals, the Recollects, who did not return until 1670, when the Jesuits had established a firm hold on the colony. The extent of that hold, and of the great missionary effort which is one of the most notable chapters in the history of the Society of Jesus, is revealed in the *Relations*, the annual reports of the mission of New France published in France from 1632 to 1673. The fact that the superior of the mission was responsible only to the general of the order in Rome set the ecclesiastical life of New France in an ultramontane pattern which differentiated it sharply from the mother country with its gallican-minded clergy dependent upon the monarchy.

The Jesuits sought to establish in Canada the closed theocracy which they later achieved in Paraguay. Their work among the Hurons of Georgian Bay was ended by the dispersion of that friendly nation by the Iroquois in 1649; but in the refugee Huron villages founded at Sillery near Quebec in 1637, and later on the Ile d'Orléans and at Lorette, they established the first of those theocratic Indian colonies where they sought successfully to christianize and gallicize the savages, while keeping them uncontaminated by the regrettably godless traders. After the downfall of the gentle Hurons, the Jesuits launched the mission to the Iroquois. Among this warlike people they had much less success in winning souls to Christianity—the little village of Caughnawaga, across the river from Montreal, easily held most of their converts—but they nevertheless served New France well by their influence on the bitterest enemies of the French. While the selfless heroism of the Jesuits has justly become legendary, their great work of learning and transcribing the Indian languages is less well known, though it played an important part in the development of the French empire in America.

Though the most notable work of the Jesuits was in the mission field, they were also the founders of the educational system of French Canada, for in 1635 they started a school at Quebec which eventually developed into a classical college with some of the attributes of a university. They were also instrumental in bringing out to New France Marie de l'Incarnation and her Ursuline nuns, whose school at Quebec for Indian girls was the humble beginning of a great tradition in the education of women in French Canada. The Jesuits also brought the Hospitalières, who came in the same ship with the Ursulines in 1639 to take charge of the Quebec hospital which had already been built by Père Le Jeune, who originated the project and obtained the necessary support from one of the pious ladies of the court. Similar backing permitted the realization of many another enterprise of the Jesuits in New France.

It was the Jesuit Père Vimont who accompanied the Society of Ville-Marie to their chosen mission field at Montreal in 1642, and it was the *Jesuit Relations* which inspired that foundation. The pious secret order known as the Company of the Holy Spirit also played an important part in the Montreal venture through its influence in high places at home. The leader in the New World of this group of dedicated priests and layfolk was the soldier Chomedey de Maisonneuve, who was driven by the fervor of a crusader in his determination to spread the Gospel among the Indians and to establish a bulwark against the Iroquois. With him was the devoted Jeanne Mance, who established a hospital at Montreal and ministered impartially to the sick, whether white or Indian, for the French had none of the English color prejudice. In 1657 Saint Marguérite Bourgeoys opened the first school at Montreal, and thus founded the great teaching order of the Congrégation de Notre-Dame, whose members were to play a major role in forming the character of French-Canadian women throughout the colony. From such small beginnings much developed: by 1663 there were at Quebec some 150 members of religious communities out of a total population of about 500 souls. From the early days of settlement, education and the care of the sick and needy were included in the province of the Church, whose missionaries already performed governmental functions as diplomatic agents among the Indians and as financial agents in France. Thus the Church won a firm hold on the life of New France and soon achieved an ascendency in the colony.

During these first crucial years of the colony, the fur trade upon which its economic life depended developed slowly and uncertainly. After one sub-company had shown a profit of 300,000 *livres* for five years' activity, another promptly lost a greater sum in three years. Reorganization was inevitable under such circumstances; and the evils of absentee control were in some measure remedied by the formation in 1645 of the Habitants' Company, which took over the monopoly from the Company of New France. Two years later all citizens of the colony were permitted to trade with the Indians, provided they sold their furs to the company's stores at government-controlled prices. The governor, solely responsible in the days of Champlain and his successor Montmagny to the company, was assisted in 1647 by an appointed council of three Quebec merchants. In the following year the Council was revised to consist of the governor and ex-governor of the colony, the superior of the Jesuits, two inhabitants of Quebec, and three syndics. Later, additional elected members were added to the Council. These were nominated by the Council itself, but the syndics, or representatives of the people, of Quebec, Trois-Rivières, and Montreal had a voice in their election. Thus a certain measure of representative government

François de Montmorency-Laval, Vicar Apostolic of New France (1659–74) and first Bishop of Quebec (1674–84)

Oil painting (c. 1671) by Claude François *dit* Frère Luc. This penetrating contemporary portrait reveals both the autocrat and the ascetic in Bishop Laval, who has been hailed both as a saint and as a tyrant (Inventaire des Oeuvres Artistiques de la Province de Quebec). (I.O.A.P.Q.)

France Bringing the Faith to the Indians of the New World

Oil painting by Frère Luc. The Recollet founder of the French-Canadian art here mixes the artistic traditions of the Old World and the scenes of the New. (I.O.A.P.Q.)

appeared for the first time in Canada. The colonists paid a high price for it, since no less than one quarter of the furs brought to the company's warehouses were taken as a tax to be applied to the support and defence of the colony. Meanwhile the supply of pelts was threatened by the attacks of the Iroquois upon both the French outposts and the villages of the Huron middlemen. The Iroquois set up a virtual fur blockade, which almost destroyed the French trading system by diverting the stream of pelts through their own hands into the Dutch warehouses of Orange (Albany) and New Amsterdam (New York). The Jesuits' mission to Onondaga, the very home of the Five Nations, and such exploits as Dollard's heroic stand in 1660 at the Long Sault on the Ottawa against the overpowering odds of an Iroquois war party, were defensive measures against this major threat to the survival of the colony.

4

At this crucial moment the rulers of France came to the rescue of the colony which they had so long neglected. Under Louis XIV and his great minister Colbert, the French colonial empire was given strong support by a paternalistic government under a mercantilist policy. In 1663 royal government was established at Quebec, and in the following year the great state corporation of the Company of the West Indies took over the monopoly of trade. In 1665 the Marquis de Tracy came with warships and soldiers, and in that same summer the new governor De Courcelles and the intendant Jean Talon arrived with shiploads of colonists and stores. Three forts were built to block the Iroquois warpath on the Richelieu; and in the following year de Tracy led the veterans of the Carignan-Salières Regiment, the *habitant* volunteers, and some Hurons and Algonkins deep into the Iroquois country. The expedition achieved little beyond the destruction of standing crops and grain stores—this was the first but not the last time that European soldiers found an Indian campaign in America like the pursuit of the will of the wisp—but the Iroquois, reduced in numbers by a generation's warfare, were impressed by the French show of force and sued for peace, which lasted for nearly twenty years.

This breathing spell was used to good advantage by the administrators of the colony. The old order was swept away and New France was made over in the image of Louis XIV's France. The element of representative government in the old Sovereign Council was abolished in the new Superior Council, composed of governor, intendant, bishop, twelve councilors appointed by the king, the attorney-general, and a secretary. Through this body, at once administrative, legislative, and judicial, the governor and intendant ruled the colony; while after 1726 they ruled virtually alone, as the Council lost most of its administrative power. These two officials, who represented in France the surviving authority of the great nobles of the district and the newer centralized power of the monarchy, often came into conflict; in New France a third head was added to the system, for François de Laval-Montmorency, the Jesuit-chosen bishop who arrived in 1659, had no sympathy with Colbert's gallican notions of the relations of church and state. Bishop Laval, who had risen under the regime of the ultramontane Queen Mother, was to cause the recall of no less than three governors and of the great intendant Talon himself under the gallican Louis XIV. The quarrels of the three leaders of the colony later imperiled its prospects, but for the moment the impetus of the new order carried all before it, and Talon's leadership was accepted.

Jean Talon was Colbert's chosen instrument for the remaking of New France. Colbert had decreed that 'the increase of the colony should be the rule and end of all the conduct of the intendant,'[23] and 2,000 settlers were sent out from France in the decade after 1663, many of them being soldiers who were induced to become colonists by liberal concessions. Practically all the provinces of France were represented in the emigration, although the greater number came from Normandy, Perche, Brittany, the Ile-de-France, and the western provinces. Colbert, through Talon, told the people of New France that 'their prosperity, their subsistance, and all that is dear to them depend upon a general resolution, never to be departed from, to marry youths at eighteen or nineteen years and girls at fourteen or fifteen.'[24] Early marriage and large families were rewarded by the state, while bachelorhood was penalized; and a paternalistic king sent over shiploads of his poor or orphaned wards, the *filles de roi*, to provide wives for veterans of the Carignan-Salières Regiment, and for the older colonists who had remained single in a land where white women were still rare. Thus was established the French-Canadian tradition of early marriage and large families, a tradition which has been one of the strongest forces in the tenacious survival and remarkable increase of this ethnic group. Large families were, of course, assets in the expanding agricultural economy of New France, though liabilities in the mother country.

Talon, too, was concerned about radically altering the way of life of New France, for Colbert had ordained that it was 'much more advantageous to the colony that the inhabitants devote themselves to cultivating and clearing the land, rather than to hunting, which can never be of any use to the colony.'[25] So Talon founded near Quebec the three model villages of Bourg Royal, Bourg la Reine, and Bourg Talon; but the nucleated village of ancient French tradition did not meet the needs of the colony, and the country parish was established as the basic unit of French-Canadian society. The necessity of close settlement for defence against the Indians, the use of waterways for transport and as a source of food, and the gregarious nature of the people combined to give the French-Canadian village its peculiar form. Land holdings were laid out in long narrow strips reaching back from the water, thus giving each settler access to the resources of river, fertile valley land, and forest; while the houses were set close together along first the river and then the single road which connected them with the church and *presbytère*. Early in the eighteenth century visitors to New France began to remark that the banks of the St. Lawrence resembled a continuous village.

Colbert believed in diversified economic activity and a measure of colonial self-sufficiency, so Talon encouraged shipbuilding, lumbering, tanning, flour milling, the salting of fish, and the extraction of oil from the porpoises and seals of the lower St. Lawrence. He investigated the iron deposits of Baie Saint-Paul and the Saint-Maurice, and the silver mines of Gaspé. He introduced the culture of hemp and flax, and encouraged home industry by importing wool for the domestic manufacture of cloth. Finding that the colonists were spending 100,000 *livres* a year for wine and brandy, and that the Church was up in arms against the ravages of strong drink among both the *habitants* and the Indians, Talon established a brewery, which checked both scandal and a considerable drain on the colony's slim resources.

Talon's vision was neither narrow nor dependent upon instructions from France. His mind was fascinated by the possibilities of the New World, and he dreamed great dreams, which sometimes alarmed the more cautious Colbert. Talon planned a road from Quebec to Acadia—now back in French hands in 1670, after an interlude of English rule for fifteen years and long negotiations which were part of Louis XIV's and Colbert's plan of empire. If his resources had been adequate to the task, the final fall of this first portion of New France to become English, half a century later, might have been prevented by its development along the same lines as the establishments on the St. Lawrence. He sent Saint-Simon and Père Albanel overland to Hudson Bay by way of the Saguenay, Lake St. John, and the Rupert in 1671–2, to offset the activities of the Company of Adventurers of England Trading into Hudson's Bay, which had just been formed in London by John Kirke, the youngest of the privateering brothers, on the strength of reports by the renegade *coureurs de bois* Groseilliers and Radisson. Then Saint-Lusson, backed by Jolliet, Perrot, and the Jesuit Allouez, was sent to Sault Sainte-Marie to claim the whole West for Louis XIV, as the French moved on to the Great Lakes to meet the Western tribes whose furs they had once received through the agency of the vanished Hurons. The existence of English and Dutch settlements along the coast to the south was no bar to Talon's dreams of empire. He wrote home that 'nothing can prevent us from carrying the names and arms of His Majesty as far as Florida, New Sweden, New Holland, and New England.'[26] To realize this dream, Lake Ontario was to be fortified, while the Iroquois were warned by the governor in 1671 to refrain from trading north of the lake. First Jolliet and Père Marquette, then La Salle, traced out the Mississippi waterway, which enabled the French to cut off the English advance and to monopolize the trade of the heart of the continent. The French empire in America soon stretched in a great crescent from the mouth of the St. Lawrence to that of the Mississippi, hemming in the other European settlements on the Atlantic seaboard.

But Talon had not heeded Colbert's significant warning of 1666: 'It would be better to restrict yourselves to an extent of territory which the colony itself will be able to maintain than to embrace so much land that eventually a part may have to be abandoned, with some consequent discredit to His Majesty's Crown.'[27] Talon was called back to France for good in 1672—he had once been briefly recalled because of his quarrels with Bishop Laval—and his successors lacked his genius. Then, in the same year, Louis XIV became involved in the long series of European wars which meant the waning of royal interest and support for the colony across the ocean, whose pleas for more colonists were rejected by Colbert on the ground that France would be depopulated. Despite the efforts of Talon, there were only 7,000 Europeans in Quebec and 500 in Acadia by 1675; there were not then, and never were to be, enough men to implement the French claim to the vast expanses labeled New France on the maps of North America. Between the Atlantic seaboard and the Appalachians were confined the much more numerous and substantial English settlements; and when the great struggle for the continent opened in 1689, 200,000 Anglo-Americans faced 10,000 French Canadians. When the final episode of the Seven Years' War opened in 1756, 1,500,000 Anglo-Americans were opposed to 70,000 French Canadians. The simple facts of population, plus the major factor of Britain's new sea power, settled the fate of New France.

The period of French expansion continued until the close of the seventeenth century, however, with energy and daring compensating for lack of manpower. Frontenac, the new governor, carried on the Western policy which Talon had launched. This proud and vigorous old soldier knew instinctively how to deal with the Indians by alternating presents and threats with a high hand, and under no other governor was the prestige of the French higher with their enemies the Iroquois. Frontenac built the fort at Cataraqui (Kingston) which Talon had conceived, and gave the land about it to La Salle as a seigneury. This chosen lieutenant of the governor was no sedentary colonist, but a restless explorer and promoter who dreamed of putting the fur trade on a basis of large-scale operations. He built the first ships on the Great Lakes; established forts and trading posts on the Illinois; and explored the Mississippi to its mouth, near which he was to meet his death a few years later in an attempt to establish a base for the conquest of the Spanish mines of Mexico. While the intendant Duchesneau called for limitation of the numbers of the *coureurs de bois*—in 1679 their number was estimated at 500–600—and Bishop Laval demanded the end of the brandy traffic with the Indians, and both joined forces to oppose Frontenac's expansionism, the *coureurs de bois* were blazing new trails all over the West, and brandy went with them. Liquor had become an essential article in the fur trade; if the French had no brandy to offer, the English got the best furs with their rum. The frontier moved on: Dulhut explored the country beyond Lake Superior; Nicolas Perrot roamed about the Great Lakes; Père Hennepin explored the upper Mississippi; Tonty pioneered in the Illinois country; and Cadillac established the trading posts at Detroit and Michilimackinac, which were to the West what Montreal was to the East. And with the explorers and the traders went the Jesuits, who established missions at the posts set up along the arteries of trade and empire.

This wave of expansion did not fail to arouse opposition from the Iroquois, whose trading territory had been invaded, and from their English allies. Governor Dongan of New York wrote with bitterness: "'Tis a very hard thing that all Countryes a Frenchman walks over in America must belong to Canada.'[28] But Frontenac was recalled in disgrace, along with the intendant with whom he had quarreled, and his successors La Barre and Denonville lacked both his skill in dealing with the Indians and his fierce aggressiveness. After the collapse of La Barre's expedition against the Iroquois in 1684, the Five Nations and the English traders moved into the lower Great Lakes region. During the next two years furs from Michilimackinac reached New York. The supremacy of the St. Lawrence system was again threatened by its aggressive rival.

The only answer was war, and a new French movement towards the two other gateways to the heart of the continent: the Mississippi and Hudson Bay. La Salle attempted to found a colony on the Gulf of Mexico, and Iberville captured the English posts on James Bay. Along the upper St. Lawrence Denonville launched a fruitless expedition against the Senecas, which only brought reprisals from the Iroquois, who not only harried the trading routes but in 1689 even dared to fall upon Lachine and massacre its inhabitants, almost under the walls of the French stronghold of Montreal. War between France and England broke out in Europe as this disastrous stroke threatened the colony's lifeline, and in the emergency Frontenac was called back to save New France. With his usual aggressiveness he carried the war to the English: raiding parties composed of Indians officered by Frenchmen suddenly issued from the winter woods and fell upon the frontier villages of New York, New Hampshire, and Maine. This was the sort of warfare the Indians understood and appreciated and the French stock went up again and the trade routes to the West were reopened.

But the English had been goaded into action. The massacres, ruthless destruction, and subsequent mistreatment of captives in the raids to which the French had instigated their Indian allies woke the old European religious hatreds between the English and the French colonists. A great Protestant crusade against the 'papists' who had loosed the savages upon their frontier settlements was undertaken by New England and New York. Samuel Vetch, a Scot allied to the Albany fur traders and interested in Boston's commerce with Acadia, evolved the plan of a joint attack by sea up the St. Lawrence and by land over the Hudson-Champlain-Richelieu route—this was to be the standard English strategy in the American Hundred Years' War, and after several failures was eventually to win it—but the colonists did not succeed in coordinating their efforts, for the liberty-loving English colonies lacked the military unity of absolutist New France. The land expedition came to nothing; while Sir William Phips with the fleet succeeded in capturing Port Royal—on which the Boston merchants long had had an envious eye—though he failed to shake Frontenac's hold on Quebec after a week's futile siege. The old soldier governor, now almost eighty, became more aggressive than ever, once this great threat had been averted. In the West his lieutenants goaded their savage allies to take the war-path against the Iroquois, while the Acadians led bands of Micmacs against the New England settlements. Frontenac himself devastated the western New York stronghold of the Oneidas and Onondagas in 1696, while Iberville ranged from Hudson Bay to the Gulf of Mexico in a brilliant one-man war against the English by sea and by land. Though the conflict in Europe ended in 1697, the struggle in America continued until 1701, when the humbled Iroquois made peace with the French and their Indian allies. Under the Treaty of Ryswick, France regained Nova Scotia and retained all but one of the Hudson Bay forts.

The St. Lawrence and the Mississippi river systems were now guarded by a stronger chain of French forts; and Iberville had founded the French base at the mouth of the Mississippi which La Salle had failed to establish. If there had been time for the consolidation of these gains, the French empire in America might have endured, but its slender resources were again called upon by the War of the

Spanish Succession (Queen Anne's War). In America the action was confined to Acadia, New England, and Newfoundland, and for the French consisted of privateering, attacks on fishing establishments, and raids on border villages in Maine, New Hampshire, and Massachusetts. In 1709 and 1711 Colonel Nicholson waited in vain at the head of the Hudson for news of the British fleet, which was to proceed up the St. Lawrence against Quebec while he attacked Montreal by the Champlain-Richelieu route; but first the need for ships in Europe and then a savage storm in the Gulf which wrecked the fleet again spoiled the scheme of joint attack. Port Royal was won once more from the French, and part of the first French settlement in the New World then passed permanently to England, which was to conquer the whole of New France in the next half century as its sea power eclipsed that of France. The outcome of the great colonial struggle was already indicated, for though New France had been saved and enlarged by Frontenac and his chosen band of daring explorers, adventurers, and *coureurs de bois*, it had been drained of much of its bravest and most enterprising blood by the years of war.

5

This period of expansion was also marked by a great development of the intellectual life of New France. In 1664 Pierre Boucher, who had come to the colony at the age of twelve and grown up to be the governor of Trois-Rivières, published his *Histoire Véritable et Naturelle des Moeurs et Productions du Pays de la Nouvelle France*. This first history of Canada by a Canadian was dedicated to Colbert and written at the request of Louis XIV, to whom Boucher had been sent by the governor-general to report on the state of the colony, as 'being better acquainted with Canada than any other.'[29] Boucher was given the first Canadian patent of nobility, and on his return from France brought a number of colonists, as befitted his conviction that all that Canada lacked was inhabitants. His simple and straightforward book differs from the earlier accounts of Lescarbot and Sagard in that it is not a travel book, telling of wonders and marvels, but a sober emigrant's guide. The theocratic character of the colony, and the beginning of a distinction between transient Frenchmen and those who had thrown in their lot with that of the colony, are revealed by Boucher's forthright statement: 'In one word, good people may live here very contentedly; but not bad people, because they are too closely looked after here; therefore I do not advise any such to come, because they might be expelled from the country, or at the best compelled to leave it, as many have done already; and it is precisely those who loudly decry the country, not having found in it what they expected.'[30]

How different New France had become from the mother country is revealed by the astonished comments of the clever and cynical Baron de Lahontan, a French Jonathan Swift, in 1683:

> One cannot have any pleasure, either at cards or in visiting the ladies, without the *curé* being told of it, and without his denouncing it from the pulpit. His indiscreet zeal goes so far as to name persons; and if he goes so far as to refuse Communion to noble ladies for wearing colored ribbons, for the rest you can judge for yourself. You can scarcely believe to what an extent the authority of these ecclesiastical seigneurs extends. I vow they are ridiculous in their actions: they excommunicate maskers, and even run to places where they are to be found, in order to unmask them and cover them with opprobrium; they watch over the conduct of the girls and women with more care than fathers and husbands. They persecute people who do not go to Communion monthly, and at Easter they oblige all sorts of people to carry tales to their confessors. They forbid and burn all books which are not concerned with devotion. I cannot think of this tyranny without protesting against the indiscreet zeal of the *curé* of this city. This cruel person, entering my host's house and finding some books on my table, threw himself bodily upon the romance of Petronius, which I regard more highly than my life because it is not expurgated. He tore nearly all the leaves out of it, with so little reason that if my host had not held me back when I saw the wretched remains, I should have hastened to the home of this turbulent pastor to pull out all the hairs of his beard in similar fashion. Not content with examining the actions of men, they wish even to search out their thoughts. Judge by this, Monsieur, what pleasure one has here.[31]

Lahontan burned to reform this theocratic society: 'One should commence by preventing clerics from making such frequent visits to the habitants, of whom they bluntly demand knowledge of their families' affairs down to the last detail, a practice which can often be contrary to the welfare of society, as you know.'[32] He noted the weariness of the colony under rule by excommunication, and the sad fate which befell governor or intendant who refused to accept clerical control. He paints a picture of every layman, from governor-general to simple officer, striving to keep on good terms with the clergy because of the power they wielded. Nevertheless, he admits that the people had great confidence in their priests, and that 'one is devout here in appearance.'[33] He summed up his impression of the French Canadians, whom he clearly considered a different people from his own, thus:

> The Canadians or Creoles are well built, sturdy, tall, strong, vigorous, enterprising, brave, and indefatigable. They lack only the knowledge of literature. They are presumptuous and full of themselves, putting themselves ahead of all the nations of the earth; and unfortunately they do not have the respect that they might for their relatives (the French).

Quebec Seminary *Procure* Wing

Constructed (1677–80) by Claude Baillif after the plans of Frère Luc, who was an architect as well as a painter. The top story was added after a fire in 1865. This is a fine example of the institutional building of the 17th century. The old elm in the centre of the court was treasured by all graduates of Laval until its recent loss. (I.O.A.P.Q.)

Montreal Seminary

Unsigned water color (c. 1826) attributed to John Drake, from Jacques Viger's *Album*. This is a view from the garden side of François Dollier de Casson's building of 1683, part of which still stands on Notre Dame Street. It was one of the many buildings designed and built by the great Sulpician. (I.O.A.P.Q.)

Villeneuve House, Charlesbourg

This late 17th century farmhouse is typical of the old dwellings in the Quebec district. (I.O.A.P.Q.)

Beauchemin House, Varennes

This farmhouse built in 1770 is typical of the Montreal style. Though in the country, it has the high stone gables which were required in Montreal as a protection against fire leaping from roof to roof. Houses of this type may still be found, usually behind a tin curtain of advertising placards, in downtown Montreal. (I.O.A.P.Q.)

The blood of Canada is very good; the women are generally pretty; brunettes are rare, the wise are common, and the lazy are found in great enough number; they love luxury dearly, and it falls to the one who best traps a husband.[34]

Lahontan is not the most reliable of witnesses, but he is the most outspoken; and some of his observations are supported by unimpeachable testimony.

The truly religious spirit of the theocracy is revealed in the *Jesuit Relations*, which continued to be published annually in France until 1673, and in the stream of letters which Marie de l'Incarnation sent to her correspondents in France until her death a year earlier. These are absorbing documents, which throw a flood of light on the life of New France. Their literary quality is best indicated by the fact that Parkman made extensive use of them to enliven his vivid narratives. The crusader spirit of the founders of Montreal, which differed somewhat from the missionary zeal and mystic preoccupations of the Quebec writers, is mirrored in Dollier de Casson's *Histoire de Montréal* (1672–3), the first local history and a richly revealing picture of the times. After serving as a captain of cavalry under the great Turenne, Dollier entered the priesthood and came to Canada in 1666. At once missionary, explorer, architect, and engineer, Dollier became the superior of the Sulpicians and as such the seigneur of Montreal, over which he ruled like a military monk of the Middle Ages. Another old soldier, Frontenac, who was a friend of Molière, revived the drama in Canada with garrison theatricals staged at Quebec by officers of the Carignan-Salières Regiment. The great plays of Corneille, Racine, and Molière were thus performed in the colony soon after they were first given in France, but Bishop Saint-Vallier, Laval's successor, first frowned upon this frivolity and then condemned it, as he did dancing and immodest or overly gay dress.[35] The theater was not a vigorous form of artistic expression in Quebec until recent years, because of the Jansenist element in French-Canadian Catholicism, which also gave a puritanical tone to the colony's society in other respects.

Other schools came into being to supplement the establishments of the Jesuits and Ursulines at Quebec, and of Marguerite Bourgeoys at Montreal. Before the end of the seventeenth century there were no less than twenty-four, of which fifteen were in Quebec, Trois-Rivières, or Montreal, where the bulk of the population of some 15,000 was to be found. In 1668 Bishop Laval established the Petit Séminaire of Quebec, whose students received instruction from the Jesuits, to supplement the Grand Séminaire created in 1663 to prepare candidates for the priesthood; and the bishop and Talon joined forces to inaugurate the Saint-Joachim school for artists and artisans at nearby Cap Tourmente. The bishop needed trained hands to build and decorate churches; while the intendant was intent upon making the colony self-sufficient. They succeeded in establishing a popular artistic tradition, which persisted for nearly two centuries, of simple craftsmen working in the classic style of Louis XIV, first simplified and then embroidered to meet the expanding needs of the colony. The medieval tradition of craftsmanship, of long apprenticeship, and of preoccupation with making a beautiful thing as well as possible regardless of the cost in time and trouble, was thus introduced into the French-Canadian way of life. This tradition almost perished between 1840 and 1920, in a colonial culture's passion for imitation of foreign models, but it has been revived in recent years; and the provincial arts and trade schools now scattered through Quebec derive from the foundation of St. Joachim. Modern Laval University at Quebec also traces its tradition back to this same period; for from 1655 onward the Jesuit school offered the complete classical college course of seven years, and shortly thereafter advanced instruction in mathematics, navigation, surveying, engineering, and map-making was added. Aside from this training in applied science under Martin Boutet and Jean-Baptiste Franquelin, there was the pioneer research work of Michel Sarrazin, who was at once physician, surgeon, zoologist, and botanist.

Sarrazin deserves the title of father of French-Canadian science, and in this field he was a worthy contemporary of Frontenac, La Salle, and Iberville. He was not the first of his profession to come to New France: the surgeon Bonnerme had accompanied Champlain; another named Duchesnes had been the first to hold title to the Plains of Abraham; while Robert Giffard was the physician of the Hôtel-Dieu of Quebec as well as the seigneur of Beauport. But Sarrazin played a more important part in the life of the colony than any of his predecessors. A year after his arrival in 1685 he was named surgeon to the troops, and soon found himself serving the hospitals of both Quebec and Montreal. Perhaps influenced by his close friendship with the cartographer Franquelin, the most scientific mind in the colony, Sarrazin returned to France in 1694, where in less than four years he completed the seven-year course in scientific and clinical medicine given by the School of Paris.

Thus furnished with the best training then available, Sarrazin returned to New France, where he was soon named royal physician, with governors, intendants, and bishops among his patients. His studies had given him a passion for research, and amid his daily duties he found time to correspond with the Academy of Sciences in Paris, to which he furnished notable reports on the beaver, the musk rat, the porcupine, the sea cow, and ginseng—the root whose discovery by the Jesuits had involved the colony in trade with China, where it was highly valued as a drug. Sarrazin's major work, however, was in botany. In five years he sent some 200 specimens of North American flora to Tournefort of the Jardin Royal, the great forerunner of Linnaeus. To accomplish this feat, Sarrazin enlisted the aid of officers at remote posts in the collection of specimens, which he then carefully studied and described. Tournefort gave the name of his zealous correspondent to the pitcher plant (*Sarracena purpurea*) to commemorate his painstaking work. With his studies of the sugar maple and the blueberry, Sarrazin paved the way for later exploitation of these Canadian natural resources, which were unknown in Europe. He even studied the mineral springs of Cap de la Madeleine, near Trois-Rivières, for which he over-optimistically foretold a future as great as those of the notable European spas. Concerned by the failure of French wheat to survive the Canadian winters, he imported the Swedish variety, which flourished and produced more satisfactorily than that on which the colonists had relied.

Correspondent of Réaumur, the Abbé Bignon, and Fontenelle, Sarrazin linked the colony with the great intellectual figures of the mother country. He became one of the notables of New France, and was named to the Superior Council and made keeper of the seals. The colony was not to see his like again until 1742, when Jean-François Gaulthier came out as royal physician, and under La Galissonnière, an associate of the Academy of Sciences of Paris and the founder of a Quebec Academy, revived the scientific tradition which Sarrazin had founded so brilliantly. After the English conquest that tradition was forgotten for a century, and did not again become a force in Quebec life until recent years.

Another medieval cultural tradition was established in Canada by the Ursuline nuns, who taught the art of embroidery to both their white and Indian pupils. Marie de l'Incarnation and Madame de la Peltrie, like all convent-bred French ladies of the period, were great needle-workers; and this art, along with religion and languages, figured largely in the Ursuline curriculum. The needlework was chiefly upon altar decorations and clerical vestments. The most noted pupil of the Ursulines was Jeanne Le Ber, a daughter of the wealthiest merchant of Montreal who became the most famed recluse of New France, spending nineteen years in a chapel opening off the church of the Congrégation de Notre-Dame, where she divided her time between her devotions and needlework. Wool, silk, and thread of gold and silver, woven into the traditional flower, leaf, fruit, and geometric patterns, went into the making of the richly colored and ornamented vestments and altar linens which she created. Examples of her art are still preserved in Montreal today, and modern French-Canadian work follows the same tradition. One curious result of the Ursulines' introduction of the art of embroidery was the development of a taste among the Indians for richly decorated costumes, which reached its peak in the nineteenth century. Such typical 'Indian' decorative motives as the swastika and other geometric patterns have been derived by some authorities from the Ursulines' instruction of Huron girls in the seventeenth century.

During the latter part of the same century the architectural tradition of Quebec was also established. The first buildings were '*en colombage*' (squared timber frames filled with short logs or rubble), '*pièce sur pièce*' (squared timber laid horizontally), or '*en pile*' (upright logs planted in the ground as in a palisade). The log cabin was only introduced into Quebec in the nineteenth century from the United States. None of these early buildings have survived, but detailed descriptions of them may be found in the writings of Champlain and Marie de l'Incarnation.[36] Towards 1650 or 1675 more building in stone took place, as the colony became a permanent establishment, but unfamiliar varieties of stone and mortar and a very different climate played havoc with the work of French masons. Some of the first stone churches fell in ruins only twenty or thirty years after their construction. The differences of environment and of materials at hand played a part in the gradual modification of the imported style, which was a peasant and provincial version of that of Louis XIV.

Houses were of two main types: the Montreal stone mansion, narrow, deep, and massive, flanked by chimneys and protected against fires by endwalls raised well above the roof line; and the Quebec house of stone, or wooden frame filled with stone, long and shallow, with a central chimney and a steep roof pierced by dormer windows, above low and solid walls. The first type derived from a Breton model; the second from a Norman. Both were roofed with cedar shingles, unknown in France; and later with sheet iron as a protection against fire. Thatched roofs were found only in the districts of Trois-Rivières and Charlevoix, and then only on barns and outbuildings. The penetrating northeast wind of Quebec, which quickly broke up mortar, resulted in the practice of facing that quarter of the dwelling with wood to protect the stone-work. For further protection against the weather the other walls were often covered with whitewashed plaster. Thick walls, small windows, steeply pitched roofs, and the extension of the roof well beyond the walls to form the distinctive bell-shaped gable, were all adaptions to the rigorous climate of New France, with its nine months of bitter cold and heavy snowfall. A covered gallery in front or around the house met the needs of the three hot months.

Ecclesiastical architecture was conceived in the same simple spirit. Monasteries, convents, seminaries, and hospitals were built in the form of vast two- or three-story stone rectangles, with dormer windows on a steep roof dotted with chimneys. Later additions took the form of wings to the original structure. Forts were built after the same general pattern, but with thicker walls and stronger roofs. Stone windmills, which also served as strongholds in case of Indian raids, were common along the St. Lawrence between Quebec and Montreal. They took the form of round towers with very steep, conical roofs. The churches were of two main types: the traditional cruciform type of the French countryside, with two transepts and a semi-circular apse, and a very steep roof and a tower with one or two lanterns; and another with a single nave, closed by a false vault and a square apse. This later style, known by the name of the Recollects who introduced it after their return to Quebec in 1670, flourished for a time in the towns, but eventually yielded to the structurally stronger transepted type. The chief survival of the Recollect style is the tradition of luxurious interior decoration, which was introduced by artists of the school of Frère Luc, who worked in Quebec after 1670. Most buildings were planned by master stonemasons and carpenters; but the religious orders numbered some trained architects, such as Frère Luc of the Recollects and his disciples, and Dollier de Casson and Vachon de Belmont of the Sulpicians. The Jesuits, curiously enough, considering their dominance, never introduced into New France the artificial style known by their name; and they built only some simple mission chapels, which were not architecturally noteworthy. Some of the military engineers—Villeneuve, Gédéon de Catalogne, and the two Chaussegros de Léry—drew up unrealized plans for public buildings in the Jesuit style, but most of their work was in the manner of Louis XIV and Vauban. Quebec's architectural tradition was fixed in a popular style which could be carried on by master craftsmen and whose charm was based upon its honesty, simplicity, and good proportions.

6

From the Peace of Utrecht in 1713 until the beginning of the War of the Austrian Succession in 1744, New France enjoyed thirty years of peace, or at least of armed truce, welcome after thirty years of warfare that had tried its slender resources. The population stood at only 18,000, despite all the efforts made to swell it; the company entrusted with the fur monopoly had collapsed, bringing down in ruins the trade upon which the economic life of the colony depended; and Canada was flooded with card money, which was redeemed in 1714 at half its value—a loss to the colony of 800,000 *livres*. New France's military strength was sapped by the absence of recruits from the mother country to fill up the royal regiments, and by the failure of immigration to swell the ranks of the colonial militia; while the allegiance of the Indian allies was strained when a shortage of trade goods developed. The Iroquois had come under the official protection of the English, who used them as a constant threat to the vulnerable Lake Ontario link in the French lifeline of trade and empire. Hudson Bay, Newfoundland, and Acadia, the outposts of New France, were now all in English hands. The colony was on the defensive, and in 1716 Governor Vaudreuil thus described its policy: 'To profit from the peace by fortifying Canada.'[37]

France was a good deal less interested in the colony at the close of Louis XIV's reign than at the outset of it. Only four or five thousand immigrants came in the next forty years to meet the colony's major need of more manpower. They were not all the best of citizens: some of them were young men of good family who had fallen into disgrace, and were sent out under *lettres de cachet*. They were loath to work with their hands and so lived by their wits. Many of them acted as itinerant schoolmasters. They amused themselves gallantly with the *habitants'* wives and daughters, and introduced scandalous songs; and their loose behavior did nothing to increase the prestige of education with the right-thinking simple country folk. Nonetheless they enriched French-Canadian folklore with many a gay song whose origin goes back to the Middle Ages. Another immigrant group consisted of poachers, smugglers, and counterfeiters, whose enterprise made them more welcome additions to the population, while there was little censure or opportunity in the colony for the exercise of the peculiar talents which had brought about their deportation from the mother country. A lack of civic consciousness and a certain willingness to sail close to the wind of the law may be in part considered the contribution to the French-Canadian tradition of these newcomers, though these characteristics may also be traced back to the lawless *coureurs de bois* and the profound individualism of the French temperament. The bulk of the threefold increase of the population during these thirty years—the total amounted to 55,000 in 1754—must be assigned to the extraordinary vitality of this ethnic group, triumphing over poverty, plague, and war.

The military question was acute. The royal troops had dwindled to a mere 600, many of that number being old men or boys; and reinforcements from France were refused. The militia organized by Frontenac became the principal force of New France under a policy of universal service which exempted only a few officials. Each parish had its company under a *capitaine de côte*, the exact equivalent of the Anglo-American militia captain, who became the local representative of the central government in civil as well as military affairs and as such a threat to the old dominance of the *seigneur* and the *curé*. The companies were grouped under the governments of Quebec, Trois-Rivières, and Montreal, the whole force being under the orders of the governor-general. Fortifications were clearly necessary to supplement the shortage of men; and so the countryside was dotted with rude wooden palisades with some stone forts at strategic points. The great fortress of Louisbourg, an American Gibraltar, was reared on Cape Breton Island to guard the mouth of the St. Lawrence, now threatened on either side by English Newfoundland and Acadia. But a naval base, no matter how powerful, is no stronger than the fleet which depends upon it; and in the absence of a powerful French fleet Louisbourg failed to fulfil its function and twice fell with astonishing ease when attacked by the English in 1745 and 1758.

In Acadia a passive resistance to English rule was maintained by the French farmers guided by their priests, while the Abenakis harried the expanding Maine settlements at the inspiration of their missionaries, who like their Acadian colleagues frequently confused religion and patriotism. In the West the French rebuilt Niagara to protect the line of communications between Canada, the Lake posts, and Louisiana; while at Crown Point on Lake Champlain they raised Fort Saint-Frédéric to block the traditional invasion path from the South. These fortifications were the work of the elder Chaussegros de Léry, an able disciple of Vauban. In the Illinois country the French fought a war of extermination—their first such Indian campaign—against the Foxes, who had been instigated to attack them by the English and the Iroquois. From 1731 to 1743 the La Vérendryes carried on the last great explorations of the French in America, reaching towards the Rockies in the last impulse of the old search for a passage to the Pacific and in the continuing effort to tap new fur territory.

During these years New France sought to evolve a sounder economy than it had yet known, with its sole reliance on the fur trade. Agriculture was encouraged by every device at the disposal of the governor and intendant, but it did not prosper and misery was often widespread. Commerce and industry fared as badly; the fur trade passed through its customary cycles of poverty and plenty; while inflation, shipwreck, and the profiteering of French merchants kept the prices of imports high, far beyond the means of most of the colonists. Local industry was alternately encouraged and then stamped out when it interfered with French manufacturing interests, under the mercantilist policy which prevailed at court; in 1702 it was still the king's view that 'The Colony of Canada is good only inasmuch as it can be useful to the Kingdom.'[38] Where noncompetitive industries could be established, they were encouraged with too lavish a hand, so that they never became self-sufficient. Corruption, the shortage of manpower and capital, the difficulties of communication and transportation, and absentee direction all combined to prevent New France from developing a strong and well-rounded economy.

Climate and the structure of society made the fur trade the major industry of New France: the long winters which hindered other enterprises favored this one; and soldier, gentleman, and unskilled laborer alike needed neither training nor capital to get rich quick in this wilderness trade. No less than 15,000 individuals left Montreal to engage in the trade during the seventeenth and eighteenth centuries; and they have left their mark in the French placenames scattered over the continent and in much mixed blood. But the free trader of the English colonies, with bétter and cheaper goods to offer in exchange for furs, and no rigid monopoly to hamstring his activities, soon drove the French trader farther and farther afield, or turned him into a dealer in contraband. As early as 1715, 50,000 pounds a year of beaver—a quarter or a sixth of the total yield—found its way deviously from Montreal to New York, while the French traders made increasing use of English trade goods, and more *coureurs de bois* deserted to the English. The transition had already begun from French monopoly to English control of the fur trade.

In the 1730's the first network of roads was built, and with this development colonization expanded and domestic commerce was liberated from six months of inaction while the waterways were frozen over. The colony supplied Louisbourg with part of its provisions, and this trade took on such proportions that when the fortress fell in 1745 the administrators of Canada sadly reported: 'The two colonies supported one another; today ours have no support.'[39] Louisbourg also served as entrepôt for a trade between Canada and the Antilles, which broke into but did not seriously threaten New England's long-established commerce in the Caribbean. These new developments brought about a great change in the colony's economic position. The land under cultivation increased from 63,000 *arpentes* in 1719 to 163,000 fifteen years later; the wheat crop was tripled in thirteen years; and Intendant Dupuy proclaimed that wheat was destined to replace beaver as the chief Canadian export. The copper of Lake Superior and the iron of the Saint-Maurice were exploited on a small scale, while the lumber industry founded by Talon took on new life, with the nineteen sawmills of 1719 becoming fifty-two by 1734. Shipbuilding increased, though it never reached the proportions attained in the English colonies. In general, the colony exported raw materials and imported manufactured goods, and was slowly developing a favorable balance of trade when the return of war destroyed the carefully built economy. All this economic development had been the work of French officials, for the feckless tradition of the discoverers and the *coureurs de bois* still was dominant among the French Canadians. The minister at home noted regretfully in his dispatches to the governor-general that the Canadians wished always to go farther afield, without bothering about building up settlements in the interior, because they earned more and enjoyed greater independence when they were away from the settlements.

7

During the seventy-two years of Louis XIV's reign, New France developed the institutions which it was to preserve with singular tenacity, even after the English conquest of 1760. It was the King's lifelong ambition to concentrate all the power of the state in himself, believing as he did that division of power among the great resulted in corruption and disorder. But Louis XIV also thought of himself as the father of his people, and therefore his absolutism was tempered with paternalism. His great churchmen Bossuet and Jurieu likened him to God so fulsomely that Madame de Sévigné was moved to write: 'One is not content to compare him to God; the comparison is made in such a fashion that it can be clearly seen that God is only the copy of the King.'[40] His successor Louis XV acted on the same principles, but lacked Louis XIV's greatness. There was a major flaw in this benevolent despotism as far as the colony was concerned: the King could not occupy himself with all the details of the administration of New France, and the corruption and disorder that had been feared from division of power flourished when absolutism was applied at long range and through a series of subordinates.

The minister of the marine was given complete direction of the affairs of the colony. He exercised this power through the governor-general, charged with military and diplomatic functions, and the intendant, charged with judicial, police, financial, and economic authority. The governor-general was the personal representative of the King; his prestige was greater than that of the intendant, but the latter had more power. The governor was a noble and usually an old soldier; the intendant was a civil servant of bourgeois or *noblesse de la robe* background, and usually a much younger man; it was evident that the two officials, with conflicting powers and very different mentalities, would clash. Indeed it had been so planned at court, in order that no colonial dictatorship should develop to threaten the royal authority. Both governor and intendant were creatures of the King and could be recalled at will; each year they received the royal instructions and further dispatches from the minister to guide their actions. Any suggestions from the men on the spot had to wait a year for approval or disapproval at home, since the St. Lawrence was closed by ice to the frail vessels of the day at least six months in the year. Here again absolutism and paternalism put the colony at a grave disadvantage, though continuity in administration was supplied in some measure by the minister's long tenure of office.

Beneath the governor and intendant was the Superior Council, of which the former was honorary president and the latter the functioning head, while the bishop was a potent member. The Council became the battleground of the three heads of New France, and was soon shorn of all powers save the judicial, in order to quell their disruptive disputes. The Council has been called a parliament, but it is difficult to concede it that name in the English sense when its members were appointed by the executive, and the King had flatly ordained in 1726 that it should 'in no fashion, either direct or indirect, concern itself with governmental affairs.'[41] To the governor-general, who was also governor of Quebec, were subordinated the governors of Trois-Rivières and Montreal; while the regular troops were distributed among all three districts, with the majority at Montreal where the danger of Indian attack was most acute. The intendant had a chief assistant, the commissary of the marine, who was stationed at Montreal and charged with the support of the troops, while other assistants were scattered among the settlements and trading posts. Each district had its own courts, while the Superior Council served as the highest court in the colony. All told, the administration was carried on by 208 officials, paid by the King and usually sent out from France, in order that their interests might not be those of the colonists. When the extent of territory they governed is considered, their number surely was not excessive; and Parkman's charge that New France was 'all head'[42] loses some of its force. Unfortunately these officials were poorly paid, and the temptation to supplement their income by graft was irresistible in many cases. In the last days of New France the administrative system became riddled through and through with corruption on a gigantic scale; but long before the days of the infamous Intendant Bigot, official graft represented a drain on the colony's finances.

The people had practically no share in the government; their role was simply to take orders. In the early days the Council, then significantly known as 'Sovereign' rather than 'Superior,' served in some measure to represent the interests of the colonists as well as those of the mother country; but this representative function was soon extinguished. Later the syndics, at first representatives of the merchants and then of the towns, could be heard by the government, while any person was free to present requests or complaints. But these were matters of privilege and not of right; any subject could appeal to the King in his own name, but no one and no group had the right to speak in the name of all. The militia captain was a representative of the people, but he was also the agent of the government. This situation no doubt lies at the base of the French Canadian's lack of civic consciousness. Under French rule he had no real share in the government; under British rule he first had to struggle for the unfamiliar rights of representative government, and then found himself exploited by compatriots who acted in his name, but often for their own benefit rather than his. Another factor was the growing love of independence, which may be considered a North American trait grafted upon the French tradition of individualism. From the early days of the colony French administrators and travelers noted an independence of spirit to which they were not accustomed in the absolutist mother country. Lahontan observed that: 'None must say *habitant*, for the title of peasant is no better received here than in Spain, whether because they pay neither *sel ni taille* and have the liberty to hunt and fish, or because their easy life puts them on a level with the nobles.' In 1725 Vaudreuil remarked a 'spirit of mutiny and independence' among all the *habitants*; while in 1736 Hocquart noted that the Canadians were 'naturally indocile.'[43]

The truth of the matter is that the old social institutions of France developed along new lines in the colony, where the environment was so different. The annals of the colony are full of quarrels over precedence and privilege among all classes; the society of New France was not stable but constantly evolving, and the social ladder was open to whoever had the energy and the will to climb it. Poverty was too general and too widespread for wealth to be the basis of the social structure. There was noble blood to spare in the colony—and nobility was blithely assumed by those who lacked it, like the humble Gascon Antoine Laumet, who came to call himself Antoine de Lamothe, Sieur de Cadillac. Some gentlemen of birth tilled the soil like peasants; and those who would not, from pride, entered the royal service, where they probably fared more wretchedly than the *habitant*, if more honorably by their lights.

The *seigneurs* were by no means all nobles; by the beginning of the eighteenth century *habitants* held a third of the seigneuries, and many others belonged to ecclesiastical bodies, officials, and merchants.[44] No *seigneur* could live in idleness on his small rents and feudal dues, and many of them labored beside their tenants. The seigneurial system was not established in Canada to create a privileged leisure class, but to encourage colonization. The *seigneur* might lose his fief if he did not succeed in establishing settlers upon it and in clearing the land. No less than one out of six seigneuries were thus withdrawn from their holders and reunited to the royal lands in 1741. The Jesuits, Sulpicians, and the Seminary of Quebec were the most successful *seigneurs*; for they carried on the work of settlement without interruption by warlike expeditions against the Indians or English, and they had the collective financial and intellectual resources to meet the problems of pioneering and cultivation under new and difficult conditions. The seignurial system as a whole, however, cannot be said to have proved itself a successful method of colonization in New France, for it was too decentralized and uncoordinated in its workings. The long dependence upon the rivers as the sole highways confined settlement to the banks of the St. Lawrence until roads were finally built in the 1730's; then a second and sometimes a third line (*rang*) of concessions was opened up behind those fronting on the river, while settlement pushed up the St. Lawrence and the Ottawa from Montreal, and up the Richelieu and the Chaudière. Before the outbreak of the final struggle between France and England in America, plans were even launched to make substantial settlements about Lake Champlain, and to expand those in the Illinois country and at Detroit. But the fur trade and constant warfare offered too many temptations to the *seigneurs* for colonization to be their main concern.

There is little basis for the common claim that the French Canadians displayed from the first a peculiar genius for agricultural pioneering. Agriculture did not really come into its own in Quebec until the fur trade was taken over by the English after the Conquest and the call of the *pays-d'en-haut* (hinterland) waned. Many of the founders of New France were soldiers and adventurers; more were artisans, whose traditions have been carried down in the various handicrafts for which Quebec is still renowned; it took time to turn them into sedentary farmers. Another factor in the late development of agriculture was the gregarious nature of the people, who insisted on clustering together in the towns rather than isolating themselves in the country. By 1754 almost a quarter of the population was urban, and the colonial administrators were trying by ordinance after ordinance to restrain a still growing movement towards the towns. The tendency was engrained in the nature of the people, however, and today highly industrialized Greater Montreal includes half the population of a province which likes to think of itself as primarily rural and agricultural. By the beginning of the eighteenth century Montreal had already become the commercial center of the colony, while Quebec maintained its position as the administrative center and the terminus of ocean shipping. No real bourgeoisie arose; commerce was too firmly monopolized by the mother country for many Canadian merchants to grow prosperous, while most of the chief administrative posts were held by transient Frenchmen. Lawyers were excluded from the colony in order that justice might be more speedy, less expensive, and less sought after. Doctors came out from France, as did artists and architects. There were really only two classes in New France: the ruling élite of administrators, clergy, and noble *seigneurs*; and the mass of the people. The élite was either French or French by assimilation; the people called themselves

Canadians and were jealous of Frenchmen. This social division was to survive tenaciously in French Canada, and to set it apart from the rest of North America, whose greatest strength lies in a dominant middle class which plays no part in the traditional French-Canadian scheme of things.

8

Parkman has justly stressed the fundamental importance of the Catholic Church in New France: 'More even than the royal power she shaped the character and the destinies of the colony . . . The royal government was transient; the Church was permanent. The English conquest shattered the whole apparatus of civil administration at a blow, but it left her untouched.'[45]. There can be little question that Bishop Laval had more influence on New France than Louis XIV during a long lifetime which appropriately paralleled Louis' reign. The development of the Church in New France may be said to be his work.

Laval came to the colony in 1659, having been named by Rome Vicar Apostolic of New France at the instigation of the Jesuits, who had maintained virtual ecclesiastical control of the colony since their arrival a quarter of a century before. The Abbé de Queylus, superior of the Montreal Sulpicians, had recently been appointed vicar of the Archbishop of Rouen, who claimed jurisdiction over New France. The Jesuits, who were barred from the bishopric by the rules of their order, nevertheless saw no reason why their rivals should have the office. The naming of de Queylus, who had likened the Jesuits to the Pharisees in a sermon preached in their stronghold of Quebec, was a definite threat to their dominance in the colony. With the aid of their powerful patron, Anne of Austria, Queen Mother and Regent of France, and of their influence at Rome, the Jesuits succeeded in having de Queylus supplanted by Laval, on the grounds that New France was a mission and that the naming of missionary bishops was a prerogative of the Papacy. Thus, at the moment of transition from mission to established church, the Church in New France was given an ultramontane rather than a gallican tendency. Under the regime of Laval, who had an inflexible will and an instinct for domination, ultramontanism was built into the very fabric of the Church in Quebec, which assumed a position very different from that which it held in gallican France.

From its foundation until about 1672, New France remained a mission in which the conversion of the savages was considered more important than the spiritual welfare of the colonists, except at Montreal, which was the parish as well as the seigneury of the Sulpicians. With the influx of immigrants under Colbert, the necessity of parish work became acute, for the new arrivals did not share the piety of the earlier settlers, and their behavior became a scandal to the Indian converts of the missionaries. The Carignan-Salières Regiment, fresh from long service in the Turkish war, introduced dissipations hitherto unknown in New France when they gave a ball at Quebec in 1667, the first in the colony, and staged theatricals. These innovations incurred the thunders of Bishops Laval and Saint-Vallier, who were singularly free with excommunications. The *coureur de bois*, descending upon the settlements after months in the wilderness, also upset the placid and pious colonists by his wild drinking, gambling, and wenching.

Laval had hardly disposed of the pretensions of his rival de Queylus when he tried to suppress the brandy traffic. Meeting opposition from the governors Argenson and Avaugour on this score, he returned to France and persuaded the government to recall the latter after he had disposed of the former. Laval came back with the new governor Mézy, who had been chosen on his recommendation but with whom he soon quarreled and had recalled in turn, over a question involving the bishop's position in the Council. This ascetic churchman who made a cult of personal humility belonged to one of the great families of France. By temperament and tradition he was inclined to stand upon the dignity of his office and the authority of the Church, which he considered to be lodged quite as absolutely in himself as Louis XIV considered the power of the state to lie in the monarchy. The bickering between bishop and governor went on until Laval went to France in 1672, returning clothed in the full dignity of Bishop of Quebec. There had been long negotiations between the Papacy and the French government on this score, and the latter had been forced to retire from its gallican position that the bishop should be named by the King. It was thus established that the Bishop of Quebec was to be in direct communication and dependence upon the Holy See; and this fact had important implications for the future.

Bishop Laval was no mere stickler for rank and rights; he was also a builder. Up to his time no Canadian had been ordained to the priesthood. Laval established the Séminaire de Québec in 1663 to prepare candidates for the priesthood. Meanwhile the Saint-Joachim School, also founded by Laval, trained craftsmen who helped to build the thirty churches reared between 1680 and 1730. Only 23 priests of Canadian origin came from the Quebec Seminary up to 1700, and 150 secular priests and 80 Jesuits from France supplemented them. Even after the growth of the colony had increased the number of candidates for the priesthood and provided for the support of a larger number of secular clergy—the Jesuit and Recollect missionaries were maintained by their orders—only 156 Canadian priests were ordained under the French regime, while 340 were brought from France to fill the gaps. Bishop Laval was an ultramontane centralizer, not a gallican or a believer in a national clergy. He was a churchman before he was a Canadian or a Frenchman; and under his guidance the Church in Quebec developed a tradition which it has preserved until today. Portraits of the Pope are found in French-Canadian homes more often than those of the Queen or of the prime ministers of Canada or Quebec, and the papal flag is displayed more frequently than at Rome.

Laval's centralizing tendencies found another outlet in his institution of *curés* who were re-assigned at the bishop's will, instead of being permanently fixed in one parish as in France. On this matter he had a long battle with the royal authorities who saw in this practice a dangerous extension of the episcopal power. Laval won this battle, as he won others with the state, and the secular clergy were controlled and supported by the seminary, which was headed by a superior chosen by the bishop. Laval's position in this matter was based upon local conditions, for few seigneuries were in a position to support a resident *curé*, as the king and Colbert wished. The first *curés* rivaled the Jesuit and Recollect missionaries in hardihood and devotion, as they made long journeys through the wilderness to visit their scattered flocks. The Seminary of Quebec was instituted as a branch of the Society of Foreign Missions of France, and the heroic labors of its first graduates validated this title. Bishop Laval retired to France in 1684 and resigned his charge, leaving his money, books, and furniture to the seminary; but he returned to Quebec in 1688, shortly after his successor Saint-Vallier had been installed in office. When the latter was captured at sea by the English, and was kept away from his diocese for thirteen years, the old bishop resumed office, which he held from 1700 to his death in 1708. In all, Laval guided the destinies of the Church in New France for thirty-four years, ruling in a more authoritarian and absolute fashion than any representative of the all-powerful Sun King. He left more of a mark upon the colony than any governor except the great Frontenac, with whom he had quarreled violently, as might have been expected when two autocrats were thrown together in a small settlement. There was no doubt to whom Frontenac was referring when he wrote to Colbert: 'Nearly all the disorders existing in New France have their origin in the ambition of the ecclesiastics, who wish to add to their spiritual authority an absolute power over temporal matters.'[46] The tradition of Bishop Laval has been a major force in the history of French Canada: his desire to subordinate state to Church, his authoritarianism, his Jansenism, his ultramontanism, have cropped up again and again in his spiritual heirs who have benefited from the prestige and ascendency which the first Bishop of Quebec won by his domineering will, his zeal, and his ceaseless effort.

After Laval's death the Church in Quebec was without a head for five years, before Bishop Saint-Vallier returned in 1713. He was then sixty, and though he maintained the prerogatives of the Church with a highly sensitive touchiness, he was unable to carry on where his predecessor had left off. After his death in 1727 the Church passed through evil days until the consecration of Bishop Pontbriand in 1741. Absentee bishops and a shortage of priests strengthened the hand of the seminary, which had already aroused the wrath of Bishop Saint-Vallier by 'the ideas it had formed of a new apostolic regime, where the seminary rather than the bishop led, and where all the ecclesiastics were to be subject to and dependent upon the seminary.'[47] The chapter of Quebec gave scandal by intrigues, idleness, and preoccupation with such worldly amusements as cards and good cheer, while it neglected its religious duties. The *curés* were seldom touched by such indictments; they continued their often arduous round of duties with zeal and devotion; they struggled to build churches; and as the only educated men in many districts, they gradually assumed a multitude of non-clerical functions, such as school-teaching and the drawing-up of notarial acts, which gave them an unequalled prestige and influence in their parishes. The theocratic tradition of early days was thus reinforced. Since the successors of Laval refused, despite constant pressure from the civil authorities, to establish fixed *curés*, the Bishop of Quebec had a stronger hold on the people than the governor, and the virtual local dictatorship of the *curé* was modified only by the fact that he was subject to recall at the bishop's will.

While the parochial and the hierarchical structure of the Church was built up and strengthened, missionary work was not neglected. In the Saguenay region the mission which had been abandoned in the seventeenth century while the colony was fighting for its life was resumed, and it was found that the Indians had handed down from generation to generation the tradition of the Mass and the hymns which the first Recollect missionaries had taught them. In Acadia the Jesuits continued their activity, which was both religious and political, for as Père Aubery frankly put it: 'Religion has been until the present the sole motive which has made the Abenaqui French, and when there will be no more missionaries there, they will become English and will alone be able to put the English in possession of the whole country at the first outbreak of war.'[48] Similarly the Abbé Le Loutre used his religious authority to keep French the Acadians of the peninsula, unwilling subjects of England since 1713, and lured them to the mainland and the French fortification on the Isthmus of Chignecto. In the West the missionaries accom-

Shipwreck at Lévis

Oil painting (c. 1754) attributed to Paul Beaucourt, presented to the Shrine of Saint Anne de Beaupré as a token of thanks ("ex-voto") by the three survivors of a party whose boat was upset in the St. Lawrence while crossing from Lévis to Quebec. This charming primitive is notable for the detachment of the masculine survivors with regard to the drowning "*creatures*". (I.O.A.P.Q.)

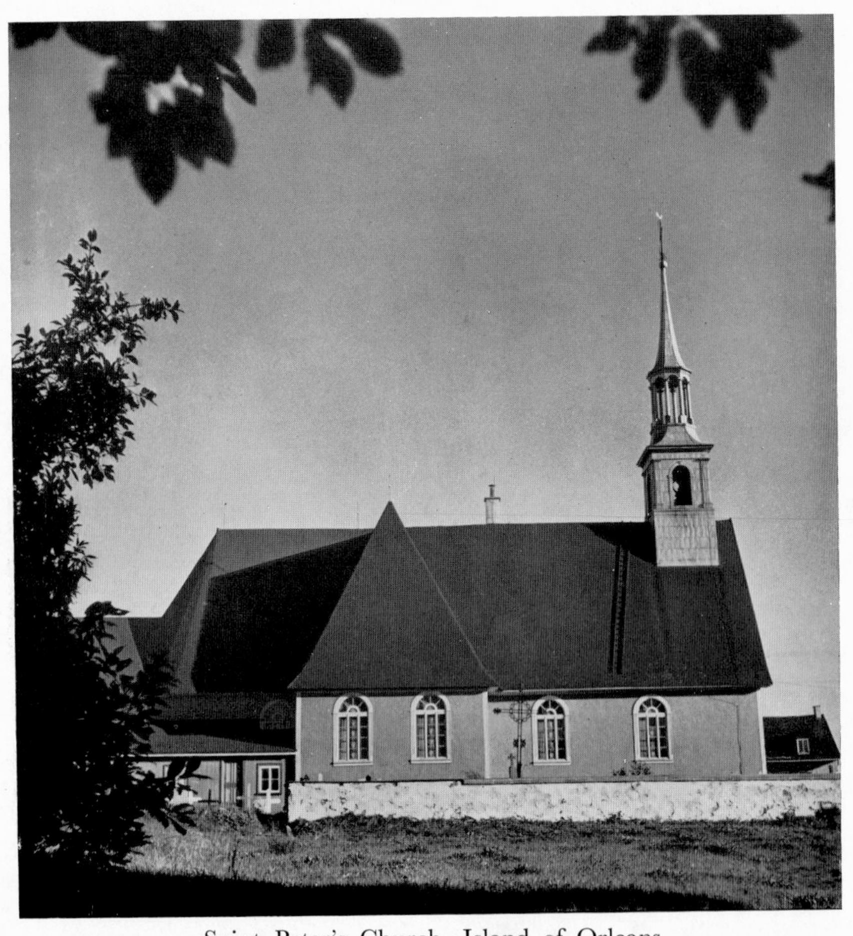

Saint Peter's Church, Island of Orleans

Constructed in 1716 by artisans trained at the Saint-Joachim School. This is one of the finest examples of the typical transept church on the Norman model. The spire was added in 1830. (I.O.A.P.Q.)

panied the La Vérendryes; and no less than forty-five Jesuit priests and lay brothers maintained the missions of the hinterland. At Lorette, Saint-François, Bécancourt, at Sault Saint-Louis, Lac des Deux Montagnes, and La Présentation, villages of Christian Indians were established close to French centers, where in peacetime religion reigned in apostolic purity and in time of war useful auxiliaries for the slim French forces might be found.

9

Such was New France, as it developed its definitive form. It has become very different from the mother country, as the comments of French visitors reveal. Père Charlevoix, the Jesuit who twice visited Canada early in the eighteenth century and taught for a time at Quebec, has left us the best picture we possess of the old regime:

Everyone has the wherewithal of existence here; one pays little to the King; the *habitant* knows not the *taille*; he has cheap bread; meat and fish are not dear; but wine, cloth, and all things that must come from France cost a great deal. The gentlemen and officers, who have only their pay and who are charged with families, are the worst off. The women usually bring no other dowry to their husbands than much wit, love, their charms, and a great fertility; for God bestows upon the marriages in this country the benediction that he gave to those of the patriarchs; to provide subsistence for such numerous families requires that one also lead the life of the patriarchs, but the time for that has passed. There is more noble blood in New France than in all our other colonies together. The King still maintains twenty-eight companies of troops of the Marine, and three staffs. Several families have been ennobled, and several officers of the Carignan-Salière Regiment have remained there, so that the country is peopled with gentlemen, of whom the greater part are not at their ease. They would be still less well off, if trade were not permitted to them, and if hunting and fishing were not here open to all.

After all, it is somewhat their own fault if they suffer misery; the soil is good almost everywhere, and farming is not degrading. How many gentlemen in all the provinces of France would envy the lot of the simple *habitants* of Canada, if they knew it? And those who languish there in shameful poverty, can they be excused for not embracing a profession which only the corruption of morals and of the most sane maxims has degraded from its ancient nobility? We know no healthier climate in the world than there; there is no special sickness, the countryside and forest are full of marvelous remedies, and the trees distill balms of great virtue. These advantages should at least retain those whom Providence has caused to be born there, but frivolity, aversion to assiduous and regular labor, and the spirit of independence have always made a number of young men leave, and have prevented the colony from peopling itself.

These are, Madame, the faults with which most often and most justly the French Canadians are reproached. They are also those of the Savages.

It seems that the air which one breathes in this continent contributes to it, but the example and the habit of its natural inhabitants, who put all their happiness in liberty and independence, are more than sufficient to form this character.[49]

Père Charlevoix adds avarice, conceit, lack of scientific knowledge, ingratitude, overweening pride, inconstancy, impetuousness, and lack of respect for parents to his list of Canadian faults; but on the other hand he finds the colonists pious, religious, brave, and clever. Elsewhere, he remarks upon the provincialism of a society which had no news of its own and received that of Europe once a year, when the ships came in the spring, so that 'one talks ancient politics and conjectures on the future, with science and art having their turn in a conversation which never ceases.' He noticed no trace of accent, and thought the French spoken in the colony as pure as that anywhere. It is clear that he found the easy-going life of Canada pleasant, with its card-playing; its excursions in summer by *calèche* or canoe, in winter by sleigh or on skates; its fine hunting and fishing, which provided more than sport, since 'many gentlemen have only this resource to enable them to live at their ease.' He paints a sharp picture of Canadian society:

There are no rich people in this country; and that is unfortunate, for there is a great fondness for keeping up one's position there, and nearly no one amuses himself by thrift. Good cheer is supplied, if its provision leaves means enough to be well clothed; if not, one cuts down on the table in order to be well dressed. Our Creoles have benefited by the change. Everyone here is of good stature, and the best blood in the world is to be found in both sexes; lively wits, gentle and polite manners, are common to all; and boorishness of manner or language is unknown even in the backwoods.[50]

Père Charlevoix traveled widely in North America, and he makes an interesting comparison of the French Canadian with the English colonist:

The English colonist amasses means and makes no superfluous expense; the French enjoys what he has and often parades what he has not. The former works for his heirs; the latter leaves his in the need in which he is himself, to get along as best they can. The British Americans dislike war, because they have so much to lose; they do not humor the Savages, because they see no need to do so. The French youth, on the contrary, loathe peace and get along well with the natives, whose esteem they easily win in war and whose friendship they always earn.[51]

Later travelers made more casual but nonetheless interesting comments on New France. In 1736 Hocquart found that all the Canadians were devoted to religion, and he repeated this observation ten years later.[52] Peter Kalm, the Swedish traveler who visited

America in 1749, remarked that the French Canadians gave much more time to prayer and religious observances than the English or Dutch settlers to the south, and stated flatly: 'All those who have traveled in France admit that the French Canadian is a more fervent Catholic than his European cousin. Unfortunately, religion seems to consist here only of external observances.'[53] Kalm was impressed by the love of science displayed by his host La Galissonnière and by Lusignan, and compared this taste among the élite for natural history and for literature with the general scorn for the sciences in the English colonies, 'where the sole preoccupation of everyone seems to be to get rich quickly.'[54] He was astonished by the extent of La Galissonnière's knowledge, finding this 'other Linnaeus'[55] as much at home in politics, philosophy, and mathematics as in natural history. Kalm noted luxury among the merchants of Quebec and poverty among the *habitants*; politeness and a certain spirit of equality he found among all classes. Since he was fresh from the English colonies when he came to Quebec, he made many comparisons, finding the differences much the same as existed between the mother countries in Europe.

Young Bougainville, who came to Quebec as Montcalm's aide in 1756, has left a no less interesting account of New France than Peter Kalm's, though it is not as well known. The extent of the difference which had developed between Frenchman and Canadian is revealed in his comment: 'It seems that we are of a different nation, even an enemy one.'[56] He considered the Canadian 'vainglorious, mendacious, obliging, kindly, honest; tireless for hunting, racing, and journeys to the *pays-d'en-haut*; lazy at cultivation of the land.' He noted that 'a very great deal of brandy was drunk here'; and that 'there was little concern for the education of youth, since one early devoted oneself to hunting and warfare . . . It must be granted that despite this lack of education, the Canadians have natural wit, speak with ease, although they do not know how to write; their accent is as good as at Paris; their diction is full of vicious phrases borrowed from the Indian tongues or of nautical terms used in ordinary style.'[57] He found the orthodoxy of Quebec somewhat oppressive: 'No Jansenist is to be found here; there is even suspicion attached to people who know what one is.'[58] He judged that a prevailing spirit of gain destroyed the spirit of honor; that the commercial spirit was dimming the luster of military glory; and he reported the assurance of the Grand Vicar of Quebec that most penitents thought it only a mere peccadillo to steal from the king. On July 29, 1758 he wrote the epitaph of New France: 'Woe to this land! It will perish the victim of its prejudices, of its blind confidence, of the stupidity or crookedness of its chiefs. "This oracle is more certain than that of Calchas!"'[59]

Bougainville was right. New France fell like an over-ripe fruit before the last English assault in the American Hundred Years' War. In the final struggle Montcalm was hampered by the stupidity and jealousy of the Canadian-born governor Vaudreuil, and by the reluctance of France to supply the force he needed. The economic structure of the colony was rotted through by the gigantic swindles of Bigot and his gang of boodlers; division and dissension between Frenchman and French Canadian reigned until the moment of disaster came; and Wolfe won New France for Britain on the Plains of Abraham in September 1759. The Battle of the Plains might not have been conclusive if France had sent support for the army of Lévis which defeated the English force, which it outnumbered three to one, at Sainte-Foy in the spring of 1760; but it was a British fleet which came up the St. Lawrence when the river opened, and thus the doom of New France was sealed. London had seen that the power of France might be broken on American battlefields as well as in Europe. Money and men had been poured across the ocean under the protection of British sea power; while France, fighting in Germany against Britain's allies, could spare few men and less money for the struggle in America. The old regime was dying and Voltaire celebrated the English victory at Quebec as the triumph of liberty over despotism, heralding the liberation of all America. The Reverend John Mayhew of Boston foretold that the Anglo-American colonies were destined to become 'in another century or two a mighty empire.'[60]

Parkman saw the great conflict which was concluded by the Treaty of Paris in 1763 as one between feudal, militant, and Catholic France and democratic, industrial, and Protestant England. Remove the religious terms from this equation, and it may better be restated as the conflict between the past and the future; for feudalism and military government in America were doomed by the mounting tide of democracy and industrialism, which soon made themselves felt in what had been the New France of Louis XIV and Bishop Laval.

Notes

[1] Canon Lionel Groulx, who has collected three volumes of historical studies under this title borrowed from the French writer André Beaunier (1869–1925), dramatic critic of *L'Echo de Paris* and literary critic of *La Revue de deux mondes*.

[2] Edward Gibbon, *The Decline and Fall of the Roman Empire*, Ch. I (Modern Library, New York, n.d.), I, 17.

[3] C. H. Firth (*ed.*), Macaulay's *History of England* (London, 1913), I, 387.

[4] C. W. Colby, *Canadian Types of the Old Regime* (New York, 1908), 21.

[5] Dom A. Jamet (*ed.*), Marie de l'Incarnation, *Ecrits spirituels et historiques* (Paris, 1929–39), III, 195 n.; Voltaire, *Candide*, Ch. 23; *Oeuvres complètes* (Paris, 1826), LIX, 317.

[6] Marie de l'Incarnation, *Ecrits*, IV, 295.

[7] H. P. Biggar *et al.* (*eds.*), *The Works of Samuel de Champlain* (Champlain Society, Toronto, 1925–36), II, 241.

[8] H. P. Biggar, *The Voyages of Jacques Cartier* (Ottawa, 1924), 106.

[9] Jansenism was a Catholicism strongly tinged with Calvinism. It was condemned as heresy in 1653 and again in 1713, but found support among French Catholics until the middle of the nineteenth century. Its adherents held that Christ died only for the elect; and this belief is symbolized by the Jansenist crucifix on which the arms of Christ are represented close together, not fully extended to embrace all mankind. Such a crucifix is among the earliest relics of the French in Acadia, and others have been found on the Ile d'Orléans near Quebec. Cf. J. C. Webster, *Catalogue of Exhibits in the Ft. Beauséjour National Park Museum* (Ottawa, 1937), no. 9, and Commission des monuments historiques de la Province de Québec, *L'Ile d'Orléans* (Québec, 1927), 47.

[10] Bossuet's comment on the Papacy is cited by Colby, *Canadian Types*, 39.

[11] Biggar, *Cartier's Voyages*, 64–5.

[12] These rapids, originally known as Sault Saint-Louis, were nicknamed 'La Chine' by Dollier de Casson in mockery of La Salle's hope of finding a passage to the Orient in 1669. P.-G. Roy, *Les Noms géographiques de la Province de Québec* (Lévis, 1906), 232–3.

[13] Biggar, *Cartier's Voyages*, 165.

[14] *Ibid.*, 186.

[15] Fr. André Thevet, *Les Singularitez de la France Antarctique* (Paris, 1878), Ch. 80.

[16] J. Florio (*trans.*), *The Essays of Montaigne*, Bk. I, Ch. 30, 'Of Cannibals' (Tudor Translations, London, 1892), I, 218.

[17] M. Lescarbot, *Histoire de la Nouvelle-France* (Paris, 1866), Bk. III. This and other friendly references to Champlain were omitted in the 1617 edition, translated in the Champlain Society edition (Toronto, 1904–7).

[18] Biggar, *Champlain's Works*, I, 228–9.

[19] Roy, *Noms géographiques*, 328–31.

[20] Biggar, *Champlain's Works*, III, 31–2.

[21] F. Gabriel Sagard Theodat, *Histoire du Canada* (Paris, 1865), Bk. IV, Ch. III, 811.

[22] Biggar, *Champlain's Works*, V, 298; VI, 486–7.

[23] P. Clément (*ed.*), *Lettres, instructions et mémoires de Colbert* (Paris, 1865), III–2, 402, Colbert-Bouteroue, Saint-Germain, 5 avril 1668.

[24] Talon's ordinance was based on Colbert-Bouteroue, Saint-Germain, 5 avril 1668; Clément, *Lettres*, III–2, 405.

[25] Clément, *Lettres*, III–2, 639, Colbert-Duchesneau; trans. in E. B. O'Callaghan (*ed.*), *Documents Relating to the Colonial History of New York* (Albany, 1855), IX, 792.

[26] *RAPQ 1930–1*, 32, Talon-Colbert, Québec, 4 octobre 1665; trans. in O'Callaghan, *Colonial Documents*, IX, 30.

[27] *RAPQ 1930–1*, 43, Colbert-Talon, Versailles, 5 avril 1666; trans. in O'Callaghan, *Colonial Documents*, IX, 41.

[28] O'Callaghan, *Colonial Documents*, III, 514, Dongan-Denonville, 25 October 1687.

[29] J. G. Shea (*ed.*), *Charlevoix' History and General Description of New France* (New York, 1900), III, 52.

[30] P. Boucher, *Canada in the Seventeenth Century* (Montreal, 1883), II.

[31] R. G. Thwaites (*ed.*), *New Voyages to North America by the Baron de Lahontan* (Chicago, 1905), I, 89–90.

[32] *Ibid.*, I, 391.

[33] *Ibid.*, 385.

[34] *Ibid.*, 391.

[35] H. Têtu & C.-O. Gagnon, *Mandements, lettres pastorales et circulaires des évêques de Québec* (Québec, 1887), I, 170–2, 302–8, 413.

[36] R. Traquair, *The Old Architecture of Quebec* (Toronto, 1947), 5–17; C. W. Jeffreys & T. W. McLean, *The Picture Gallery of Canadian History* (Toronto, 1942), I, 116–17.

[37] APQ: Correspondence de Vaudreuil, 'Extrait du mémoire du M. Vaudreuil,' fevrier 1716; cited G. Frégault, *La Civilisation de la Nouvelle-France, 1713–1744* (Montréal, 1944), 33 *n.* 23.

[38] PAC: B 23: 85, 'Mémoire pour servir d'Instruction au Sr. de Beauharnois,' 6 mai 1702; cited Frégault, *Civilisation*, 72–3.

[39] PAC: C^{11} A, 83: 14, Beauharnois & Hocquart-Maurepas, 12 septembre 1745; cited Frégault, *Civilisation*, 102.

[40] *Lettres choisies de Mme de Sévigné* (Paris, 1934), lettre du 13 juin 1685; cited Frégault, *Civilisation*, 129.

[41] PAC: B 49–2, 386, 'Mémoire du Roy à Beauharnois & Dupuis,' 14 mai 1726; cited G. Lanctot, *L'Administration de la Nouvelle-France* (Paris, 1929), 111.

[42] F. Parkman, *The Pioneers of France in the New World* (Frontenac ed., Boston, 1899), I, xcvi.

[43] Thwaites, *Lahontan's Voyages*, I, 34–5; Hocquart, 'Détail de toute la colonie, 1736,' in *Collections des mémoires et de relations sur l'histoire ancienne du Canada*, 2; APQ: Corr. de Vaudreuil, Vaudreuil-Maurepas, 18 mai 1725; cited Frégault, *Civilisation*, 165. *CHAR 1940*, 98-9, A. L. Burt, 'The Frontier in the History of New France.'

[44] Frégault, *Civilisation*, 184.

[45] F. Parkman, *The Old Regime in Canada* (Boston, 1899), II, 203.

[46] P. Margry (*ed.*), *Découvertes et Etablissements des Français* (Paris, 1876), I, 302, Frontenac-Colbert, 1677.

[47] *RAPQ 1941–2*, 180: I. Caron, 'Inventaire des documents,' Saint-Vallier-Conseil de Marine, 3 novembre 1717 (?); cited Frégault, *Civilisation*, 245.

[48] PAC: C^{11} A, 49: 597–8, 'Canada, sur les Abénakis'; cited Frégault, *Civilisation*, 245.

[49] L. P. Kellogg (*ed.*), *Charlevoix' Journal of a Voyage to North America* (Chicago, 1923), I, 245–7.

[50] Kellogg, *Charlevoix' Journal*, 116–17.

[51] *Ibid.*, 117–18.

[52] PAC: C^{11} A, 85: 55, Hocquart & Beauharnois-Maurepas, 7 octobre 1746; cited Frégault, *Civilisation*, 272–3.

[53] A. B. Benson (*ed.*), *Peter Kalm's Travels in North America* (New York, 1937), II, 396, 544.

[54] *Ibid.*, I, 375–6.

[55] *Ibid.*, II, 504.

[56] Bougainville; cited L. Groulx, *La Naissance d'une race* (Montréal, 1919), 239–40.

[57] *RAPQ 1923–4*, Bougainville, 'Mémoire sur l'état de la Nouvelle-France, 1757,' 57–61.

[58] R. de Kerallain, *La Jeunesse de Bougainville* (Paris, 1896), 63, 68, 99–100, 110.

[59] F. Parkman, *Montcalm and Wolfe* (Boston, 1899), III, 169–70.

[60] F. Parkman, *Pioneers of France in the New World* (Boston, 1899), I, xcv–xcviii.

CHAPTER II

THE LEGACY OF CONQUEST

(1760–91)

When the French Canadian says '*Je me souviens*,' he not only remembers the days of New France but also the fact that he belongs to a conquered people. This fact is deeply embedded in his consciousness, although he may protest that New France was not conquered by the English but rather abandoned by the French; and it is an important factor in his psychological makeup—and in that of the English Canadian.[1] From it stem the persecution and inferiority complexes which underlie much French-Canadian thinking. These attitudes are mirrored in the work of certain French-Canadian historians,[2] who paint the early days of British rule in dark colors contrasting sharply with their brightly tinted pictures of New France.

It is still possible today to start bitter controversy in Quebec by pointing out that the first British rulers of Canada did not try to crush the French Canadians under the yoke of military government, but on the contrary actually befriended them against the pretensions of the swarm of campfollowers and commercial adventurers who descended upon the newly conquered land like a cloud of locusts.[3] Such, however, is the picture which emerges from sober study of the contemporary documents. In this age of ruthless oppression of conquered peoples the peaceful transition of Quebec from French to British rule is remarkable and noteworthy. The English conquest might well have meant the end of French Canada as a cultural unit in North America, and of the French Canadians as an ethnic group; instead the survival of both was assured by legislation adopted a decade after the peace treaty had been signed. The French Canadians benefited by the confusion of British politics from 1760 to 1774, when colonial affairs were almost completely neglected in George III's bitter struggle with the Whig majority. But their survival was not dependent, however, upon either British magnanimity or the force of circumstances; for French Canada possessed an indomitable will to live, witnessed in the first decade after the conquest by the attainment of the highest birthrate ever recorded for any white people.[4] The whole history of Quebec since 1760 reveals how completely the French Canadians concentrated their resources and devoted them to the struggle for survival. This effort still continues, long after survival has been assured.

I

When the struggle began, the position of the French Canadians was indeed desperate, and few contemporary observers would have risked much on their survival. The New France which had been so utterly dependent upon the mother country throughout its existence was now separated and isolated from the France which had supplied its rulers, its educators, and its apostles. If the French Canadians were to remain French, they had to do so on the strength of their own resources, under the aegis of a foreign power whose religion, language, laws, and customs were very different from their own. This foreign power had been the traditional enemy of the conquered people ever since the first seeds of French settlement had been sown in the New World. France and England had fought a second Hundred Years' War in North America, and when that war ended some 70,000 French Canadians and Acadians faced more than 2,000,000 British North Americans. The French Canadians had lost much of their boldest and bravest blood in the wars which had occupied half their history, and they were exhausted by the long battle against overpowering odds. Their economic position was equally sorry: France had left them a legacy of 41,000,000 *livres* ($8,200,000) of inflated paper money, on which payment had been suspended and which was only partially redeemed years after the conquest.[5] Merchant and farmer alike were ruined; Quebec stood shattered after two months' bombardment, and the lower St. Lawrence countryside had been systematically devastated by the conquerors as they advanced up the river.[6]

Brigadier James Murray, who became military governor of Quebec soon after Wolfe's victory, thus depicted the 'miserable situation of His Majesty's Canadian subjects' to Amherst, the commander-in-chief in North America, on January 1, 1761:

> . . . to describe it is really beyond my powers and to think of it is shocking to Humanity. It has afforded the King's British Subjects an opportunity of exerting that Benevolence and charity inseparable from the Sentiments which the freedom of our laws of church and state must ever inspire. The merchants and officers have made a collection of five hundred pounds Halifax currency and the Soldiers insist on giving one day's provision in a month for the support of the indigent, without these aids many must have perished and still I fear (in spite of all we can do) a famine unless a supply of corn is sent from Montreal or the British Provinces.[7]

Thus faced with common misery, British and French Canadians lived together, as Murray put it a few days later, 'in perfect harmony and good humour.'[8] Good relations had been established between the conquerors and the conquered soon after the Battle of the Plains in 1759. General Townshend lent Bougainville enough money to care for the French sick and wounded, though his own troops consequently went unpaid. All British officers, regardless of their sentiments about 'papistry,' were ordered to pay religious processions the 'compliment of the hat,' while the Ursulines knitted long woolen stockings for the kilted Highlanders during their first winter in Quebec.[9] The nuns of the Hôpital-Général and the Hôtel-Dieu, whose nursing had saved many British lives, were given special aid: the Hôpital-Général received £400 from Moncton, and all three communities were supplied with provisions and fuel during the first winter of British rule at Quebec.[10] The capitulations of Quebec and Montreal granted just and generous terms to the vanquished: the honor of the troops was preserved, while the people were assured the free exercise of their religion and of their civil and property rights.

Garneau and some later French-Canadian writers have been misled by the fact that Canada was governed by martial law from September 8, 1760 to August 10, 1764, and because of the traditional sternness of such government, have painted this period as one of tyrannical oppression. In fact, the military governments of Murray at Quebec, of Burton at Trois-Rivières, and of Gage at Montreal were all too tender to the French Canadians, at least in the minds of His Majesty's 'old subjects' who came flocking from Britain and the American colonies to exploit the conquest. No civil government could be set up until the peace treaty was signed in 1763, and after that, under the terms of the Peace of Paris, eighteen months were to elapse before British rule was officially established. Meanwhile the English military governors were supplemented by Swiss Protestant or Huguenot secretaries—Cramahé at Quebec, Bruyères at Trois-Rivières, and Maturin at Montreal, with Haldimand replacing Burton at Trois-Rivières in 1762—and so the strangeness of British rule was modified for the *habitant* by the fact that it was carried on in French.

There was little friction between the military and the French Canadians—the feudal structure of Quebec society appealed to the military mind—and Murray was justified in writing to his London agent early in 1764:

> No Military government was ever conducted with more disinterestedness and more moderation than this has been. Hitherto it has not been easy to satisfy a Conquering army, a Conquered People, and a set

of Merchants who have resorted to a Country where there is no money, who think themselves superior in rank and fortune to the Soldier and the Canadian, as they are pleased to deem the first Voluntary and the second born Slaves.[11]

He felt that he had won the 'affection and attachment of all the Canadian subjects,' and he protested his friendly sentiments towards the colony in a letter written in French to M. de Montesson, a prominent *seigneur*: 'I love it as much by inclination as by duty and my greatest pleasure will be to make its fortune, so far as that depends upon me.'[12] *Seigneurs* and British officers were soon upon the best of terms, and the intimacy of their personal relations is witnessed by the number of marriages contracted by British officers in the colony. Murray and Burton exchanged letters on the problems raised by the 'Matrimonial Distemper,' and the wife of the Quebec garrison chaplain remarked 'the extreme partiality for English officers' among the French-Canadian ladies.[13]

One of the best indices of good relations between English and French is the fact that '130 seigneurs, 100 gentlemen and bourgeois, 125 notable merchants, 25 legal authorities and lawyers (of whom several had belonged to the Superior Council), 25 to 30 doctors and surgeons, and nearly as many notaries'[14] remained in Quebec, instead of returning to France as they were permitted to do by the peace treaty. The French soldiers and officials, and some hundred of the colonial *noblesse*, deprived of their old opportunities for soldiering and fur-trading, were the only portion of the élite to emigrate. The clergy remained at their posts, and since their position alone among the élite was not affected by the conquest, their prestige as leaders of the people was strongly reinforced. The great mass of the population, the *habitants*, were little disturbed by the change of rule.[15]

To a singular degree the transition from French to British rule was unmarked by any radical changes. The new military governments continued the old administrative districts of Quebec, Trois-Rivières, and Montreal. The *curés* and the militia captains remained the agents of the central power, and through them the new oath of allegiance was administered in the rural parishes. The *habitants* objected more to giving up their arms than to taking the oath, and the regulations on this score were eased by the conquerors, who shared the *habitants*' passion for hunting. The militia captain became in some measure the magistrate of his parish, as well as its policeman. Murray revived the Superior Council of the old regime as the highest court of the colony, while British officers served as judges in cases appealed from the militia captain's jurisdiction. Some French Canadians were given office on the basis of their legal knowledge:

Jean-Claude Panet was made chief clerk of the Council, while J.-B. de la Fontaine was created attorney-general for the south shore and Joseph-Etienne Cugnet attorney-general for the north shore. The laws of the country were taken over and applied as they had existed under the French regime, and of necessity many Canadians found posts as clerks and assistants in the courts. In September 1761 an Englishman who was sued by a Canadian in the Quebec court had to get a copy of the charge against him translated into English. Furthermore, he was ordered to reply to it in French, for 'such was the language of the country.'[16] This was in a British court conducted by English officers under martial law. Notaries and land surveyers, like the militia captains, were recommissioned and continued in their functions. The military governors combined the roles of both governor and intendant under the old regime, and they did so in the same spirit of paternalism. Vicar-General Briand of Quebec paid tribute to them: 'Do not these noble conquerors succeed in forgetting that they have been our enemies, and concern themselves only with our needs and how to meet them?'[17]

The cherished laws, institutions, and customs of the French Canadians were thus early given toleration and a chance to survive. As regards their equally cherished religion, still more fundamental a part of French-Canadian culture, the situation was somewhat different. According to the capitulation of Quebec, 'the free exercise of the roman religion is granted, likewise safeguards to all religious persons, as well as to the Bishop, who shall be at liberty to come and exercise, freely and with decency, the functions of his office,' pending a treaty; and churches and convents were to be safeguarded.[18] According to the more comprehensive capitulation of Montreal, 'the free exercise of the Catholic, Apostolic, and Roman religion, shall subsist entire, in such manner that all the states and the people of the towns and countries, places and distant posts, shall continue to assemble in the churches, and to frequent the sacraments as before, without being molested in any manner, directly or indirectly' so far as the laws of England permitted, but the continuance of the tithe awaited 'the King's pleasure,' as did the privileges of the Jesuits, Sulpicians, and Recollects.[19] Vaudreuil had proposed, in good gallican fashion, that the French monarch should retain the right to name the Bishop of Quebec. This was refused by Amherst, and Quebec remained without a bishop, for Pontbriand had died four months before Montreal was surrendered, and no successor was named in the interval. The Church in Quebec was left without a head, and its future was imperiled. No new priests might be ordained without a bishop, and no recruits from France could supplement the numbers of the Canadian clergy, as in the past. Financial support from France was also withdrawn by the severance of relations with the mother country, while the tithe enjoyed no legal sanction.

The thorny question of the bishop was to drag on unsolved for six years, but for the rest the Church was treated with great tolerance by the conquerors, considering the Protestant prejudices of the time. It must not be forgotten that the frenzy of eighteenth-century hatred of 'papistry' reached its height during the French and Indian War.[20] But the American militiamen, who were most imbued with this fever, were sent home soon after the conquest, and the British regulars who remained were put under strict orders to show 'civility to the people who have chosen to live under our laws.'[21] To be sure, the Jesuits were turned out of their college in Quebec, which was the only undamaged building large enough to serve as barracks and government storehouse in the ruined Upper Town; and they, the Recollects, and the Sulpicians were forbidden to recruit their numbers; but at this same period even Catholic countries were expelling the Jesuits and prejudice against the religious orders ran high.

Though the conquerors were ordered by London to refrain from 'uncharitable reflections on the errors of that mistaken religion which they (the French Canadians) unhappily profess,'[22] and these orders were enforced, it is clear from Murray's correspondence that toleration was extended to Catholicism solely as a matter of policy and expediency. In June 1764 Murray, in writing to Lord Halifax about the renegade Jesuit Roubaud whom he had sent to London, revealed his private view that the French Canadians could be won from their religion:

He is a Man of extraordinary parts and great learning and is as Eloquent as Cicero. He is possessed of a thorough knowledge of the Views, Sentiments, & Faculties of the popish clergy of this province and perfectly sensible of the errors of their doctrine. He proposed Publickly renouncing the Roman Catholick Religion here, but such a measure would rather frustrate, than promote my schemes for the reform of the inhabitants of this colony. For that reason I send him to London where he may be useful and cooperate with me under the immediate direction of His Majesty's Servants in the great task I undertake of converting a great part of the Canadians.

I think I am not too sanguine in my hopes, I am at heart sure my attempt cannot be attended with any bad consequence, because nothing but mild and persuasive measures, the very reverse of persecution, shall be used, and therefore I rejoice to find Monsr. Charest has met with so favorable a reception at London, as I flatter myself that every indulgence that can be given will be granted these people. Great progress is already made; the National Antipathy is entirely got the better of on the side of the Canadians. I wish I could say as much of the British subjects, several from New England now established here are most inveterate fanaticks, a little address however may even make them of advantage, a proper contradiction of their insults will gain and strengthen the confidence of the Canadians to Govermt., which confidence being the Main Spring must be perpetually kept in order and cannot fail of perfecting the business I charge myself with, which is no less than the reformation of the greatest part of the inhabitants of this colony.[23]

Etienne Charest, *seigneur* of Lauzon and a notable Quebec merchant, had been sent to London in the fall of 1763 to present the petitions of the cathedral chapter of Quebec and of the Catholics of the whole colony for a bishop. The Abbé Montgolfier, superior of the Montreal Sulpicians, who had been named bishop by the chapter, left for Europe at the same time to have his nomination confirmed by the Holy See and to win the consent of the British government to his consecration. Murray opposed Montgolfier's nomination in a letter to Shelburne of September 14, 1763: 'If a priest as haughty and imperious, and so well connected in France, is placed at the head of this Church, he can later cause much trouble.'[24] So Charest was subjected to endless if polite delays in London, while Rome judged Montgolfier's election null, on the grounds that the canons had exceeded their powers in choosing a bishop. Under these circumstances Montgolfier withdrew and left the way clear for the nomination of Jean-Olivier Briand, Grand Vicar of Quebec and a friend of Murray, who praised his candor, moderation, and disinterestedness to Shelburne, concluding, 'I know no one of his cloth who more justly deserves the Royal favor.'[25]

Briand in turn departed for London, where he struggled for sixteen months against the ministry's reluctance to admit papal jurisdiction in a British possession—particularly when anti-Catholic feeling was running high at home. Finally he was informed unofficially that his consecration would be tolerated and that he could perform his episcopal functions in the colony, if he would content himself with the strange title of 'superintendant of the Romish church.' In June 1766 he returned to Quebec, where the Canadians congratulated one another happily and crowded the church to see their new bishop, 'Whom they regard as the support of their religion and as an earnest of the paternal kindness of the King towards them,'[26] according to the two-year-old bilingual Quebec *Gazette*, the first newspaper ever printed in Canada, where no press had been established under French rule.

Hardly had the foundation of French-Canadian survival been laid by Murray's military government when it was threatened by the institution of civil government according to the less liberal views of the Board of Trade, the forerunner of the Colonial Office of later days. These views were contained in the Royal Proclamation of October 7, 1763; Murray's commission as governor-general of

November 21, 1763; and his instructions of December 7. In accordance with the provisions of the peace treaty, Murray did not assume his new position until August 10, 1764, so the new order did not come into effect until that date. The proclamation gave the colony the name of the province of Quebec, and it sharply reduced its old boundaries. The Labrador coast as far west as the St. John River was placed under the naval government of Newfoundland, since it was uncomfortably close to France's last foothold in the islands of St. Pierre and Miquelon. The new southern boundary ran from Ristigouche Bay to the St. Lawrence, pretty much along the present Quebec provincial line, thus barring the Canadians from land which they had not yet settled and which might become more securely British if left to Nova Scotia and New England. The whole western hinterland was cut off from Quebec and turned into an Indian reserve, chiefly with the object of eliminating the causes of savage unrest, already evident in the conspiracy of Pontiac, the last great rising of the red man against encroachment by the white. The northern boundary ran from Lake Nipissing through Lake St. John; the eastern thence to the head of the St. John River; but at that time and until very recently the far northeastern portion of the continent was of no great concern to either Canada or England.

Much more important for the moment were the promises of a general assembly and of the laws of England which were made in the proclamation and implemented in Murray's commission and instructions. The tenor of the drastic new program of government has been admirably summed up thus: 'An old French colony was to be remade into an English colony.'[27] English laws and English courts were established; and provision was made for a large influx of British settlers, drawn either from old soldiers or from the crowded American colonies to the south. Assimilation was to be the order of the day; lands were set aside for the support of Protestant clergymen and schoolmasters, 'To the End that the Church of England may be established both in Principle and Practice, and that the said Inhabitants may by Degrees be induced to embrace the Protestant Religion, and their Children be brought up in the Principles of it.' The governor was even urged to report 'by what other Means the Protestant Religion may be promoted.'[28]

The outlook for the French Canadians would have been dark indeed if Murray had applied the ideas of the Board of Trade literally. He did not attempt to do so, however, because of their obvious impossibility, because of the sympathy he had formed for the French Canadians, and because of the quarrels in which he was already engaged with the English merchants and with General Burton, who was named commander of all the troops within the province and made absolutely independent of the governor's control. Murray poured out his woes to Elibank on September 16, 1764:

> It is by the Military force we are to Govern the lately Conquer'd Province in which there doeth not exist above fifty Protestant Subjects Exclusive of the Troops and by my instructions of these fifty protestants must be Composed the Magistracy: But what force, what weight can such a Magistracy have unless the Supme. Magistrate has Authority with the Troops? It is Evident the Brigadier must in fact be the Governor, that the people must be Oppress'd by the Soldiery. That the Civil Governor and his Magistrates must be Contemptable, and in place of being the means of preserving order and promoting the happiness of the Subjects, they must from the Natural Jealousie which such an establishment will produce become the Bane of Peace. And the Weak Effort they will of Course make to Exert their Authority, will be productive of Nothing but vexation and Confusion. The Reasons are so clear & simple they should not have escaped the ministry.
>
> It will be too hard a task for me to Govern in the Civil Way a great populated Country, of a different Religion, different language, different Manners & Customs, without the Aid of the Troops or the Assistance of the Law, for two (such) ignorant needy lawyers as are sent here from England to distribute Justice to the people were never sent before from any country.[29]

The 'two ignorant needy lawyers' were Chief Justice William Gregory, fresh from an English prison, and Attorney-General George Suckling, in search of new fields for his talents after a stormy political and legal career in Nova Scotia. Suckling knew some law; Gregory none; neither knew a word of French or much about human nature. Such were the legal advisors of a governor who was a military man without legal training, and yet was supposed to legislate for the colony, with the advice of his council, until an assembly should be summoned.

The Council was to be made up of the lieutenant-governors of Trois-Rivières and Montreal—who promply refused to serve under Murray, their former political equal and the military junior of Gage—of the surveyor-general of the American customs, who was seldom present; the chief justice; and eight members 'chosen from amongst the most considerable' of the residents in the province. The Council was at once a legislative, executive, and judicial body. Since the anti-Catholic form of oath of office required barred any French-Canadian Catholic from membership, its first members were Colonel Paulus Aemelius Irving, later administrator of the colony after Murray's departure; Captain Hector Louis Cramahé; Captain Samuel Holland, the engineer and surveyor-general; Walter Murray, a relative of the governor; Dr. Adam Mabane, an army surgeon; Benjamin Price and Thomas Dunn, English merchants; and François Mounier, a Huguenot merchant who had settled in Canada shortly before the conquest. These men were chosen by Murray, and despite the fact that they were largely drawn from the army, they were sympathetic to the French Canadians and came to be known as the 'French party.' As the council remained, although governors came and went, these men and their successors practically governed Canada until 1787.[30]

Their power was not confined to the Council, for the chief justice presided over the King's Bench, while Mabane and Mounier were two of the three judges of the court of common pleas, whose prevailing language they at least understood, if they were ignorant of law. Under the governor's instructions from London, the magistrates and jurors had to be chosen from among the English merchants and retired officers, while the militia captains were excluded as Catholics. The only contact between government and people which had been developed since the conquest was thus cut, with the result that the political life of the colony became largely a struggle between the French have-nots and the English office-holders. The way was thus paved for the development of a new ethnic feeling to replace that 'National Antipathy' which Murray had congratulated himself on eliminating during the period of military government.

To these measures Murray was forced by orders from London, but he refused to call an assembly in which only the English merchants could have sat because of the anti-Catholic oaths required, and he sent Cramahé to London to urge the need of revising the government's policy in the interest of the French Canadians. On October 27, 1764 he himself wrote to Eglinton:

> Mr. Cramahé has my Directions to lay everything before you, & I am sure You will do all in your power to assist him and a miserable People, who after having undergone the worst Calamities War can inflict, if not supported, must now either abandon their all or submit to the Persecution of the most cruel, Ignorant, rapacious Fanaticks who ever existed.
>
> For my part, My Dear Lord, I will with Joy undertake anything to distress & reduce to reason my Royal Master's Enemies, but I cannot be the Instrument of destroying, perhaps, the best and bravest Race on this Globe, a Race that have already got the better of every National Antipathy to their Conquerors, and could they be indulged with a very few Privileges, which the laws of England do not allow to Catholics at home, must in a very short time become the most faithful & useful Set of Men in this American Empire.
>
> If the Popular Clamour of England will not allow the humane Heart of the King to follow its own dictates & the [anti-] Popish Laws must be exerted with Rigour in Canada, for God's sake procure my Retreat, and reconcile it to Lord Bute, as I cannot be the Witness to the Misery of a people I love & admire.[31]

Such dispatches as this from the governor and the petitions from the people did much to help Cramahé bring about various modifications of the Board of Trade's policy. These changes led eventually to the Quebec Act and the utter overturn of the original policy. In 1765 the law officers of the Crown decided that the penal laws of England against Catholics did not apply in Quebec; and the Privy Council ordered that all discrimination against Canadians as jurors or lawyers should be abolished. In the following year a thorough revision of the judicial system was drafted, after the law officers of the Crown had condemned the administration of justice 'without the aid of the natives, not merely in new forms, but totally in an unknown tongue,' and the attempt to abolish 'all the usages and Customs of Canada with the rough hand of a Conqueror.'[32] Unfortunately this proposal was pigeon-holed at Whitehall when the elder Pitt replaced Rockingham as prime minister. The definitive solution of these vexing problems had to await the Quebec Act, while Murray tempered the English wind to the French-Canadian lamb as best he could.

Murray was having his own troubles, as the minority of English merchants—'the Licentious Fanaticks Trading here'[33]—grew more powerful and troublesome. Though only a small number of them had been born in the American colonies, most had spent some time there and had become infected with an unruly spirit of independence as well as anti-French sentiments. All claimed the right to be judged by English laws, and complained that their commercial operations were hindered by the unfamiliar French ordinances. These merchants were particularly numerous and influential in Montreal, the capital of the fur trade into which many of them forced their way soon after the conquest; and there was much friction between civilians who despised the military and an army which scorned shopkeepers. Murray observed in October 1764:

> At Montreal the Civilians & the Military are Inveterate Enemies, I am ashamed to say, from the most trifling Circumstances: Every Art is used to improve the least Accident which may augment Popularity with the Troops: Discipline of Command must be neglected, the Canadian deemed an Alien and an irreconcilable Enemy to England, the few settled there held cheap, and everything in a Furoure. The Contagion may reach Quebec, but it cannot exist long, where the commander is not infected.[34]

As this last remark suggests, Murray was embroiled with his colleague Burton, as well as with the merchants of Montreal.

The latter had strong connections in London, and eventually they brought about Murray's downfall. The three-cornered quarrels which marked the closing years of his government are reminiscent of those between bishop, governor, and intendant under the French regime. No stick was too small to beat the governor with, and finally he was recalled to London for an investigation of the province's affairs. Murray learned the unwelcome news from his enemies the merchants, whose commercial correspondence was speedier than the official dispatches. He returned home undaunted by the charge of tyranny which had been raised against him: 'The Canadians who have lived under my government six years Shall be the best Judges of the truth of that Aspersion. They will to a man Vouch that all the Malice & Clamour which have been exhibited in England against me proceed from the protection that I have given them, and the inflexible aversion I have on all Occasions Shewn to Oppression & the National English Prejudice.'[35] It was even so, but in later years French Canadians were to echo the charges of Murray's English enemies, without realizing that they were attacking a great friend.

2

Guy Carleton, who in 1766 replaced Murray with the temporary rank of lieutenant-governor, and Burton as commander of the troops, was an Anglo-Irish soldier whose career was to be closely bound up with that of Quebec until the close of the century. He lacked the easy friendliness and frankness of Murray, who had done much to father the great Quebec legend that the Scots are sympathetic friends of the French Canadian, while the English are racial enemies.* But Carleton was a statesman rather than a placeman, and he could not abide graft and corruption. These traits, plus the natural sympathy of a soldier and a member of the landed gentry for a semi-feudal society, were to make him quite as much of a friend to the French Canadians as his predecessor. Carleton was accompanied by a new chief justice, William Hey, a young lawyer whose promise was soon realized, and by a new attorney-general, Francis Maseres, a brilliant scholar whose Huguenot ancestry gave him a perfect command of French and a bigoted obsession against Catholicism.[36] All three entered upon their duties with a prejudice against Murray and all his works which had been instilled in them by the London agent of the Quebec merchants. Consequently they were opposed to the 'French party' in the Council, who still hoped for their leader's triumphant return after he had been heard at home. When this hope was extinguished and Carleton was confirmed as governor-in-chief, he found himself

* This legend was furthered by the settlement of the disbanded Highland battalions along the Lower St. Lawrence, notably at Murray Bay and Rivière-du-Loup, where they intermarried with the French Canadians and were largely assimilated by them.

gradually drawn to the 'French party,' which again became the 'King's party.'

But in the opening months of his administration Carleton struck hard blows at the old dominant faction and favoured the mercantile minority. He banished Irving and Mabane from the Council; and in his dispatches home he pleaded the cause of the Montreal fur traders, who were hampered by restrictions on the commerce of the Lake posts, and that of the Quebec merchants who carried on the seal fishery in the lower St. Lawrence. He also tolerated the refusal of the merchants to pay the old French customs duties which Murray had kept in force during the military regime, and which had been applied again in 1766. The merchants displayed a wholly American repugnance for paying taxes, with or without representation. When suits were brought against them by Maseres, juries made up of merchants refused to heed his arguments or the chief justice's instructions. This summary procedure gave the merchants a momentary victory, but it eventually cost them the right of trial by jury in civil suits, under the Quebec Act.

One of Carleton's major reforms was in the matter of fees, by which most of the public officials were remunerated in lieu of salaries. The scale of fees was based in theory upon that prevailing in colonies where the standard of living was much higher than in Quebec, and in practice unscrupulous officeholders charged what the traffic would bear. This was a source of great discontent among both French and English; for under the French regime justice had been free, while the English merchants revolted against the outrageous exactions of the officials, which surpassed anything they had ever known. At the outset of his administration Carleton launched his lifelong crusade against the system by dismissing some of the grossest offenders and by publicly renouncing his own perquisites.

Another major step, taken with the support of his legal advisors, both of whom opposed representative government in Canada, was Carleton's refusal of the old subjects' demand for an assembly in which no French Canadian could have sat. Before leaving England, Maseres had already placed on record his views on this question:

As to the erecting an assembly in that province, it is a measure which probably will not for some years to come be found expedient. If an assembly were now to be constituted, and the directions in the governor's commission, above alluded to, were to be observed, by which none of the members elected there are to be permitted to sit and vote in the assembly till they have subscribed the declaration against Popery, it would amount to an exclusion of all the Canadians, that is, of the bulk of the settled population of the province—An assembly so constituted, might pretend to be a representative of the people there, but in truth it would be a representative of only the 600 new English settlers, and an instrument in their hands of dominating over the 90,000 French. Can such an assembly be thought just or expedient, or likely to produce harmony and friendship between the two nations? Surely it must have a contrary effect.

On the other hand, it might be dangerous in these early days of their submission to admit the Canadians themselves to so great a degree of power. Bigotted, as they are, to the Popish religion, unacquainted with, and hitherto prejudiced against the laws and customs of England, they would be very unlikely, for some years to come, to promote such measures, as should gradually introduce the Protestant religion, the use of the English language, of the spirit of the British laws. It is more probable they would check all such endeavours, and quarrel with the governor and council, or with the English members of the assembly, for promoting them. Add to this, that they are almost universally ignorant of the English language, so as to be absolutely incapable of debating in it, and consequently must, if such an assembly were erected, carry on the business of it in the French language, which would tend to perpetuate that language, and with it their prejudices and affections to their former masters, and postpone to a very distant time, perhaps for ever, that coalition of the two nations, or the melting down the French nation into the English in point of language, affections, religion, and laws, which is so much to be wished for, and which otherwise a generation or two may perhaps effect, if proper measures are taken for that purpose.[37]

Carleton himself felt that 'the British Form of Government, transplanted into this Continent, never will produce the same Fruits as at Home, chiefly because it is impossible for the Dignity of the Throne, or Peerage to be represented in the American Forests.' Monarchy and aristocracy could not be forces in America, 'where all Men appear nearly upon a Level.' Carleton, with one eye on the colonies to the south, was convinced that democracy would become dominant in an assembly, and this was clearly to be avoided 'in a province so lately conquered and circumstanced as this is.' He agreed with Maseres that the Canadians did not desire an assembly, which was totally foreign to their traditions, and that it was sought most eagerly by some of the 'English adventurers,' for whom neither official had overmuch regard.[38]

Carleton was familiar with France—his wife had been brought up at the Court of Versailles—and he saw New France through eyes blurred by impressions of the old mother country. Aristocratic and autocratic himself, he regarded the *seigneurs* and the clergy as the real leaders of the French Canadians, and tried to restore a feudalism which had never existed in Canada. He pleaded for a revival of the royal bounty which had supplemented the slim purses of the *seigneurs* in the French period, and he urged that their sons be given commissions in the army. This latter measure he regarded as an important safeguard against a French war. Charged with the defence as well as the administration of the colony, he was not happy at the thought that his garrison of 1,500 regulars might be opposed to 9,000 Canadians who had served in the French forces, or that France could muster 170 officers who either were Canadians or had seen service in Canada. He recommended the construction of citadels at Quebec and New York, to be linked by strong fortifications at Crown Point, Ticonderoga, and Fort George—a measure that at once would cut the American colonies in twain if their current unrest ended in rebellion, and would also guard both colonies against possible French aggression.

To his mind it was clear that the Canadians must be 'inspired with a cordial attachment and zeal for the king's government,' and that their grievances on the score of laws, courts, and fees must be promptly redressed. He urged that 'three or four of their principal gentlemen' be added to the Council, and that some military units be raised amongst them, for 'as long as the Canadians are deprived of all places of trust and profit, they never can forget they are no longer under the dominion of their natural sovereign; tho' this immediately concerns but few, yet it affects the minds of all, from a national spirit which ever interests itself at the general exclusion of their countrymen.'[39] This 'national spirit,' or group consciousness, which Carleton remarked so soon after the conquest, has remained a vital factor in French Canada down to the present day. Once its existence was pointed out, London displayed an ability to make use of it by such measures as Carleton had suggested. Today, whenever Ottawa neglects this tradition of government, it is urgently reminded that Canada is made up not of one people, but of two.

As far as the Church was concerned, Carleton was confronted with two problems. Bishop Briand was anxious to prevent the recurrence of any such episcopal interregnum as had left the Church in Quebec leaderless for six years after the conquest; and so was seeking a coadjutor with the right of succession in case of his death. Carleton got wind of this activity, and went to the bishop, maintaining that it was one which concerned the government. Carleton favored the principle of a coadjutor, for it avoided the necessity of 'sending to foreign dominions' for the consecration of a new bishop; but he disliked the leading candidate for the office, the Abbé de la Joncaire, who had the fault of having lived twenty-seven years in France, though he was Canadian-born. Briand agreed to obtain the governor's consent before he exercized the right which Rome had given him of naming a successor; and for the moment the question went into abeyance. Just before Carleton returned to

England in 1770, he approved, without consulting anti-Catholic London, Briand's nomination as coadjutor of L.-P.-M. d'Eglis, the first Canadian-born bishop. Carleton had seen an opportunity to attach the Canadians to Britain by using his influence to reverse the old preference shown to priests of French rather than of Canadian origin. He also discouraged the coming of new priests from France by requiring that they procure passports from the Secretary of State's office in London. Thus the possibility of the continuation of French ecclesiastical domination in Canada, after French political rule had ended, was removed. The Church was left short-handed, but self-sufficient. Carleton also took one rather arbitrary and unjustified step when he refused to allow vacancies in the Quebec cathedral chapter to be filled; for this body, not so much under his control as the bishop on whose nomination he had passed, seemed to him an embarrassing source of independent ecclesiastical authority. The chapter became extinct with the death of the last canon in 1795.

Carleton thus did much in the interest of the *seigneurs* and of the clergy, the two groups to which he was drawn by his aristocratic and autocratic turn of mind. The masses of the people were neglected, however, until a new constitution for Canada was embodied in the Quebec Act of 1774, which was not his work, but that of many minds. Murray began the reform of the judicial and legal system of the Proclamation of 1763 soon after it went into force. The dispatches and petitions he sent home, interpreted by his agent Cramahé, led to the report of the law officers Norton and de Grey, to the effect that the penal laws of England did not apply to the Catholics of Canada. The Board of Trade drafted two further reports, which were added to by Charles Yorke at Cramahé's suggestion. The proposed scheme of reform, completed in June 1766, was pigeon-holed when the Rockingham ministry fell, and was not brought up again for a year. Then the opposition in the House of Commons carried a resolution that 'the Province of Quebec, for a considerable time past has wanted, and does now stand in need of, further regulations and provisions relating to its civil government and religious establishment.'[40]

For the next seven years a flood of reports, dispatches, petitions, and memorials ensued, upon which was based the legislation which gave Canada its first constitution. The petitions of old and new subjects; Carleton's reports and personal evidence; Maseres' innumerable writings on all sides of the subject; the representations of Chief Justice Hey and the *seigneur* Chartier de Lotbinière; and the reports of Solicitor-General Wedderburn, Attorney-General Thurlow, and Advocate-General Marriott all went into the making of the Quebec Act, which was railroaded through parliament at the end of the session, while revolt smouldered in the American colonies. The imminence of the American Revolution precipitated the Quebec Act, but it did not cause it, as the Americans immediately assumed when they learned that Labrador and the Ohio-Mississippi hinterland were restored to Quebec, thus hemming in the expanding population on the seaboard; that the French Canadians were granted the whole of their ancient civil law, almost to the exclusion of the English common law; and that the Catholic Church was virtually established in Quebec, while representative government was denied. All these measures in favor of their ancient enemies seemed to be as great blows to the economic, political, and religious liberties of the American colonists as the four penal laws directed against them, the 'intolerable acts,' which were jammed through parliament along with the Quebec Act. Great Britain strengthened her hold upon the portion of North America which was to remain British by allowing it to remain French and Catholic; but it revived the old sectional rivalry of the American Hundred Years' War. It was not wholly a coincidence that American unrest broke out into open rebellion at Lexington and Concord a few days before the Quebec Act came into effect on May 1, 1775.

Since the Quebec Act is virtually the Magna Carta of the French Canadians, its provisions must be examined in some detail. Its re-establishment in large measure of the ancient boundaries of New France restored the health of the northern economy, and once more made the St. Lawrence system a powerful rival of the Hudson-Mohawk route. The New York and Albany traders were indignant at the prospect of being excluded from the Niagara and Detroit trade, which they had shared with Montreal under the Proclamation of 1763; while the colony on the St. Lawrence, which had always felt the pull of the West, was once more given scope for expansion in that direction. As an aftermath of the Revolution, which delayed the immediate application of the Quebec Act, much of that westward expansion was English rather than French, however, for the majority of the American Tories or Loyalists who fled to Canada eventually settled not in present-day Quebec, but in the wilderness to the west which became Ontario.

Much more important at the moment to the French Canadians was the fact that the Act revoked the whole tenative system of civil, judicial, and ecclesiastical government which had been based upon the Proclamation of 1763, and which had aimed at the assimilation of the French Canadians into an English colony governed under English laws in an English spirit. Catholicism was no longer merely tolerated out of expediency; Catholics were assured the free exercise of their religion, which was no longer to be an obstacle to preferment to any office or position, since a new form of oath was provided which did not offend Catholic principles. The Catholic clergy were assured their rights and accustomed dues from Catholics, while the tithes of non-Catholics were to be applied to the support of a Protestant clergy. All future disputes as to property and civil rights were to be determined according to the 'Laws and Customs of Canada,'[41] the old French civil law, although the Crown retained the right to grant lands in free and common soccage rather than in fief, and wills might be made according to English law if so desired. On the other hand, the criminal law of England was to be retained as a whole, to the exclusion of the French criminal law. Since it was 'at present inexpedient to call an Assembly,' the power to legislate for the peace, welfare, and good government of the province was confided to a Council of not less than seventeen or more than twenty-three appointed members, acting with the consent of the governor. The Council was granted no power to tax except for public roads and buildings. Its ordinances were to be submitted to the Crown for approval or disallowance within six months, while no religious regulation at all and no punishment greater than fines or short imprisonment might be ordained without royal assent. A separate bill, the Quebec Revenue Act, established a schedule of duties and license fees which were to be applied to the support of the civil government and of the administration of justice.

The victory of the new subjects over the old was almost complete. The French Canadians, who outnumbered the English-speaking people in the colony by thirty to one, were granted their faith, laws, and customs, with the exception of the old criminal law. As a matter of fact, the original draft of the Quebec Act had provided for the revival of the French criminal law, except in cases of treason and other capital offenses. This provision had been supported by Maseres, Carleton, the *seigneurs*, and Thurlow; but Chief Justice Hey and Wedderburn had strongly attacked it, and their opinion had prevailed. Of the four cherished essentials of French-Canadian survival, only the question of language was left unsettled. It really had not yet arisen, save in the courts, for before the Quebec Act, as after it, 'all proclamations were published in both French and English, and ordinances were passed in the same manner.'[42] Since French was the only language understood by all the members of the new Council, debate was now carried on in French, although the minutes were kept in English. This fact, plus the increased power of the Council, added the last straw to the grievances of the merchants, who found themselves deprived of such traditional English rights as the *habeas corpus*, trial by jury, English mercantile law, and representative government.

For the withholding of an assembly, the unruly behavior of the American colonies was as much to blame as the lack of French-Canadian interest in representative government. Chief Justice Hey

Quebec from Lévis

Water color from George Heriot's sketch book for September, 1793. This Scot was the first of a long line of British watercolorists who were fascinated by Montreal and Quebec. (Public Archives of Canada.)

The Main Altar, Ursuline Chapel, Quebec

This is all that remains of the Recollet Chapel which was Frère Luc's masterpiece. The gilding, wealth of ornament, and handcarved wooden statues are typical of the best 17th and 18th century church decorations. (National Gallery of Canada.)

had testified to the Commons as they considered the Act that the French Canadians 'look upon the house of assembly as a house of riot, calculated for nothing but to disturb the government and obstruct public servants.'[43] The merchants' petitions for representative government had a tone which smacked to London of the sedition rife in the American assemblies. Finally there was the awkward fact that the French Canadians could not fairly be excluded from an assembly, and London was not inclined to risk entrusting power to a newly conquered people when colonies which had been British from the beginning were seething with revolt. It was intended that many of the merchants' grievances should be answered by gradual modifications of the French laws through ordinances of the Council, and such provisions were embodied in the governor's instructions. These secret instructions, of course, did not receive the publicity of the Act itself; and it is certain that the Quebec Act strengthened the old subjects' 'strong Bias to Republican Principles'[44] which Carleton had much earlier remarked. Their loyalty was soon to be tested and found wanting during the American invasion of 1775–6; while the gratitude of the clergy and the *seigneurs*, whose position was reinforced by the Act, was strikingly displayed in the part they played in resisting that effort to make Quebec the fourteenth American colony.

3

Although the Quebec Act was wholly satisfactory to neither French nor English in Canada, it did much to ensure that one portion of North America should remain British, while it contributed largely to the loss of the rest. For it was a red rag to the American colonial bull, already goaded into exasperation by the repressive trade ordinances. In an 'Address to the People of Great Britain' on October 21, 1774, the first Congress of the American colonies protested violently against this 'worst of laws,' which established a 'religion that has deluged our island in blood, and dispersed impiety, bigotry, persecution, murder, and rebellion throughout every part of the world.'[45] The old anti-'popish' frenzy—the spirit that had lent to the French and Indian Wars the air of crusades, though they were really wars of trade and empire—was roused once more in America. Desperate men are seldom oppressed by a need for consistency, however, and five days later the same Congress adopted an 'Address to the Inhabitants of the Province of Quebec,' which sought to convince the French Canadians that their true interest lay in uniting with the American colonies in the struggle for liberty, representative government, and freedom from economic persecution. In this remarkable document, which attempted to split the French-Canadian masses from the élite benefited by the Quebec Act, the following words were put into the mouth of the 'immortal Montesquieu,' whose ideas played a great part in the whole appeal:

Seize the opportunity presented to you by Providence itself. You have been conquered into liberty, if you act as you ought. This work is not of man. You are a small people compared to those who with open arms invite you into fellowship. A moment's reflection should convince you which will be most for your interest and happiness, to have all the rest of North America your unalterable friends, or your inveterate enemies. The injuries of Boston have roused and associated every colony, from Nova Scotia to Georgia. Your province is the only link that is wanting to complete the bright strong chain of union. Nature has joined your country to theirs. Do you join your political interests. For their own sakes they will never desert or betray you. Be assured that the happiness of a people inevitably depends on their liberty, and their spirit to assert it.[46]

And lest the difference of religion should prejudice the French Canadians against the Americans—though 'the transcendant nature of freedom elevates those, who unite in the cause, above all such low-minded infirmities'—the example of the Swiss confederacy, a peaceful union of Catholic and Protestant states which together defied tyranny, was carefully cited.

The American appeal was a moving one, but it ill befitted the men who had just evoked English religious prejudice in support of their cause. The clergy and the *seigneurs*, who were probably the only French Canadians on whom the exalted language of Congress was not largely wasted, did not fail to bring this hypocritical inconsistency to the attention of the *habitants* who listened to the American appeal, which was rapidly spread throughout the province by merchants who were British by origin but American by conviction, sentiment, or interest. The double-faced attitude of the Congress, which denounced Catholicism in England and praised freedom of conscience in Quebec, destroyed much of the effectiveness of its appeal, but nonetheless the new gospel of the *Bostonnais* caught the ear of the Quebec masses, who did not welcome a return to the old system of feudal dues and obligations. The French Canadians, a people just emerging from a feudal economy, got a startling lesson in revolutionary politics and *laissez-faire* economics, for Adam Smith's *Wealth of Nations* appeared almost simultaneously with the Quebec Act and the American Revolution, and its ideas were already widely spread. No French-Canadian delegates went to Philadelphia, as suggested by Congress, but during the winter of 1774–5 the *habitant* was willing to listen to the words of such American agents as John Brown of Montreal, and this gave his rulers considerable concern.

The immediate importance of the Quebec Act, like that of Magna Carta, has been overestimated. The French Canadians could hardly have been assimilated, even if there had been no such concession of their rights, for the ways of New France were more firmly fixed than the English realized then or later; and for more than half a century the French vastly outnumbered the English in Canada. Even without a Quebec Act, it is almost inconceivable that the French Canadians would have thrown in their lot wholeheartedly with the Americans, for the old tradition of ethnic enmity and sectional rivalry, nourished by bitter religious differences, was too powerful. In the last analysis, perhaps, it was the ever potent geographic factor of the Appalachian barrier, rather than the Quebec Act, which saved French Canada and prevented the British from making effective use of Quebec as a base for operations against the American colonies.[47]

The real importance of the Quebec Act was for the future, and its effect was not confined to Canada. A new principle of empire was laid down when it was conceded that the French Canadians could be British without becoming English. A precedent was thus established for the creation of multi-national empires. The British Commonwealth of Nations has been called an outgrowth of the Quebec Act; a realization of what Lord Acton considered to be a higher species of political organism, a greater achievement in civilized life, than the old national state. Then, in the virtual establishment of Catholicism in Canada, there was an anticipation of that ending of the old religious hatreds which did not come in England itself until the Reform Bill of 1829. Tolerance was a necessity of the new political order, as a modern student of the Quebec Act has pointed out: 'In the long run, the unity of the whole is all the deeper for the diversity of its parts, and . . . on fidelity to the old, deep loyalties of local or provincial or national life, and only indeed on that sure foundation, can be built, if men are wise and patient, a broader and more generous communion of human fellowship and service.'[48] The political lesson of the Quebec Act has not yet been thoroughly learned, as the warring nationalisms of our own times bear bloody witness.

The active agitation of John Brown, agent of the Boston Committee of Correspondence, and such Canadian-American merchants as Thomas Walker, during the winter of 1774–5 won many *habitants* to the interest of the Congress. Others, however, remembered the anti-Catholic fanaticism of the *Bostonnais*, and this deep-rooted heritage from the French and Indian Wars had much to do with keeping the majority neutral. The center of American sympathy was in Montreal, where the merchants talked of sending delegates to Congress, and where on the morning of May 1, 1775 the bust of

George III on the Place d'Armes was found with blackened face and decorated with a rosary of potatoes and the inscription: '*Voilà le Pape du Canada, ou le sot Anglois.*'*[49] More important than rebellious words or insults to statues were the melodramatic capture of Ticonderoga by Ethan Allen on May 10, and Benedict Arnold's subsequent seizure of Crown Point and St. Johns. As Carillon, Fort Frédéric, and Saint-Jean, these bastions of the traditional invasion route were all too well known in Canada, and their fall did much to increase American sympathies among the realistic French Canadians.

There was much searching of hearts in Canada over the question thus raised. Carleton summoned the militia on June 9, after urging Bishop Briand to call his flock to arms, which that prelate did with all the more willingness since England had just granted 'the practice of our laws, the free exercise of our religion, and the privileges and advantages of British subjects'[50] to the French Canadians. Threatened on the one hand by his spiritual leaders with the refusal of the sacraments if he refused to meet the obligation of defending his country; and urged on the other to throw off the renewed burdens of the tithe and seigneurial tenure, 'the irons of slavery which have been polished with so much care'[51] in the fine words of Congress, and to join with the Americans in the defense of liberty against British oppression, the French Canadian was undecided as to where to cast his lot.

Noting that the majority of old subjects at Montreal refused to enroll in the militia, he likewise refused, claiming a right of neutrality in what must have seemed an 'Anglo-Saxon' family quarrel to a very newly British people. The Montreal merchants did not neglect to point out to the perplexed *habitant* that he would be breaking the oath taken after the conquest if he bore arms against the Americans, who were lumped with the English as *les Anglois* in the popular speech. The contagion of Americanism was also evidenced in the fact that one of the *habitants*' chief objections to mobilization was an unwillingness to serve under the *seigneurs* who had become identified with the English, while another was popular disapproval of the active part taken by the clergy in the British interest. It was remarked with bitterness by good Catholic *habitants* that Bishop Briand's proper role was making priests rather than militiamen, while the overzealousness in recruiting of such *seigneurs* as Saint-Luc de la Corne, Rigauville, de Lanaudière, and de Tonnancourt defeated their object and brought on local revolts against mobilization at Terrebonne, Verchères, and Berthier.[52]

Meanwhile James Livingston, an American merchant of Chambly, spread word among the militia captains that the Americans would abolish the tithe and the seigneurial dues; and Ethan Allen launched

* 'Behold the Pope of Canada, or the English idiot.'

a rhetorical bombardment in favor of French-Canadian neutrality. An American army under Philip Schuyler and Richard Livingston's son-in-law Richard Montgomery, an Irishman who had served in Canada with Wolfe and Amherst, came down Lake Champlain and established itself at Ile-aux-Noix on the Richelieu in September 1775. With the exception of the forts at St. Johns and Chambly, besieged by the invaders, the whole district south of Montreal fell at once into American hands. Its *congrèssiste* sympathies were soon evidenced by the raising of one French-Canadian regiment under James Livingston, and later of a second under Moses Hazen, another American settler on the Richelieu. Sizeable groups in Montreal and Quebec were loyalist, while on the other hand the militia of the Trois-Rivières flatly refused to march against the Americans. The Ile d'Orléans and the region south of the river below Quebec were also disaffected.[53] The majority of the *habitants* tried to preserve a neutrality whose bias was influenced by the shifting fortunes of the contending parties. Bishop Briand bears witness that no more than 500 joined the American forces, though nearly all desired the capture of Quebec.[54] There were many factors involved in this situation: at the base of it was the fact that the French Canadians were a people worn out by a century of border warfare against heavy odds, and by the long effort to explore a continent and carry on a continental trade with a minimum of manpower. The greater number had become sedentary folk, deeply attached to their land, and wishing only to dwell on it undisturbed by war.

Even the bellicose character of the *congrèssistes* was subject to sudden change, as Ethan Allen found at Longue Pointe, at the cost of three years' imprisonment, when he brashly attacked Montreal on September 25 with thirty Americans and eighty French Canadians from Chambly. After a sharp skirmish with 30 British regulars, some 80–100 British volunteers (including Guy Johnson's Tory rangers from the Mohawk Valley), and 120 loyalist French Canadians, the hero of Ticonderoga, the 'Notorious New Hampshire Incendiary' as Governor Tryon of New York called him, was forced to surrender with the 31 men who had not run that they might fight another day.[55]

Allen had been assured that Montreal was ready to yield to the forces of liberty; and indeed Carleton was by no means certain of the ardor of the professed loyalists there. Great friend of the French Canadian as he was, Carleton wrote: 'I think there is nothing to fear from them while we are in a state of prosperity, and nothing to hope for while in distress.'[56] Though 1,200 *habitants* rallied to his standard in Montreal after the defeat of Allen, most of them developed a great interest in returning home for the fall plowing when Carleton refused to attack the Americans on the south shore of the St. Lawrence.

Simon Sanguinet, a hot loyalist of Montreal, who considered that Carleton's conduct showed lack of spirit, indicates another reason for the weakness of loyalist sentiment among the French Canadians: they suspected the *seigneurs*, whom Carleton trusted, of dealing secretly with the enemy. In at least one instance they were right, for Saint-Luc de la Corne secretly insured the neutrality of the mission Indians, and later went over openly to the Americans.[57]

Abandoning hope of defending Montreal, Carleton fled to Quebec on November 12, disguised as a *habitant* and guided through the American outposts at Sorel by the militiaman Jean-Baptiste Bouchette, skipper of a river craft and the founder of a notable French-Canadian family. Montreal capitulated to Montgomery, who had succeeded Schuyler in command, on the following day. Montgomery announced that his army had come 'to protect this province' and 'to accord it liberty and security.'[58] The *congrèssiste* inhabitants, with the Frenchman Valentin Jautard, three years later one of the founders of the Voltairean *Gazette littéraire de Montréal*, as their spokesman, sent Montgomery an address in which they rejoiced that 'our chains are broken' and declared that 'our hearts have always desired union, that we have always regarded and received the troops of the Union as our own.' The Montrealers were willing to join with their 'brothers of the colonies' in a permanent fellowship on the basis of the same laws, same rights, and proportional contribution.[59] Montgomery was not overly impressed by this eloquence; he judged the French Canadians much as Carleton had done and thought that they 'will be our friends as long as we are able to maintain our ground.'[60] Up to the walls of Quebec in late November the invasion was a triumphal progress for Montgomery, save for the heroic forty-five days' resistance of the garrison at St. Johns. Benedict Arnold, who led the other column of the American pincer movement against Quebec, and lost nearly half his command in the rigors of a march up the Kennebec and down the Chaudière at that season, was warmly welcomed and provisioned by the inhabitants of the Beauce when his men emerged from their epic battle with the wilderness.[61] He was already encamped before Quebec when Montgomery moved down the St. Lawrence from Montreal. The prospect of the rapid addition of the fourteenth colony to the rest was then at its brightest.

The tide soon turned. The defeat of Montgomery and Arnold's joint New Year's Eve assault on Quebec marked the first setback of the American fortunes in Canada. In it the leaders were lost—Montgomery was killed and Arnold severely wounded; and their successor's one triumph was a political one, when in February 1776 General David Wooster ordered elections in the parishes, in order that the holders of royal commissions might be replaced by those with authority from Congress. This measure introduced into Quebec the new idea of the people's right to choose its own chiefs, and the innovation was exceedingly well received throughout the province. The concept of popular government thus implanted in the French-Canadian mind was to bear fruit in later years. Wooster also distributed a letter from George Washington, addressed 'to the People of Canada' and calling for the co-operation of the French Canadians, since 'the cause of liberty and America is the cause of all virtuous American citizens, whatever their religion, whatever the blood from which they originate.'[62] But this appeal was not very effective in the face of growing friction between the invaders and the French Canadians. The seizure and sending southward as prisoners of loyalist French Canadians was resented bitterly, and so was the persecution which the clergy had largely brought upon themselves by their loyalist activities. Among many others, the Sulpician superior Montgolfier, who was vicar general of Montreal, and Grand Vicar Saint-Ours of Trois-Rivières were distinguished by their anti-American sentiments and activities, which did nothing, of course, to relieve the Americans of their traditional anti-Catholic prejudices.[63]

The tide of French-Canadian public opinion really turned against the invaders when cash ran out, and the Americans resorted to requisition or to payment in paper, which soon became inflated. Quebec remembered all too well the exactions of Bigot's regime and the still unredeemed French paper which was the mother country's legacy to her abandoned colony. It also was impressed by the prevalence of disease and desertion among the besiegers of Quebec, and it remembered that British sea power had been decisive in 1759 and 1760. Since the Americans had failed to take Quebec by storm when its defenders were isolated, the French Canadians argued that the invaders would surely be repulsed in the spring, when the opening of the St. Lawrence brought British ships and reinforcements to the hard-pressed garrison. Still, news of the success or the failure of the rebels in their own land was eagerly followed, while the mass of the French Canadians continued to traffic with either British or Americans as circumstances dictated.

Congress realized too late the seriousness of the Canadian situation. It addressed another letter to the Canadians, offering reassurance to the friends of liberty;[64] but not until the spring of 1776 did it send three commissioners—Benjamin Franklin, Charles Carroll, and Samuel Chase—to Montreal, after the *congrèssistes* Saint-Luc de la Corne, Thomas Walker, and James Price had gone to Philadelphia to urge the necessity of vigorous measures. The commissioners were accompanied by the French-educated Jesuit John Carroll, later the first American Catholic bishop, and by the printer of Congress's appeals to the *habitants*, Fleury Mesplet, a wandering Frenchman whom Franklin had picked up in London.

Mesplet had the distinction of establishing the first purely French press in Canada, since the bilingual *Quebec Gazette* established in 1764 was published by Britishers and was a government organ. But it is somewhat excessive to call Mesplet, as his biographer has done, 'the founder of the free press in Canada,'[65] for his first function was to propagate American ideas in French. Two years later, however, his press gave birth to the *Gazette littéraire de Montréal*, the French forerunner of French-Canadian journalism. In 1776 Mesplet was not ready for business in the basement of the Chateau de Ramézay until the American commissioners and the army of invasion had retired southward with marked precipitation. The father of French-Canadian journalism spent the latter part of June and the first days of July in jail—an omen of his future fate, and also of that of many French-Canadian editors for half a century to come.

The American commissioners themselves, hampered by the delays which occasionally make one despair of democratic procedure, had only reached Montreal on April 29, while British reinforcements arrived at Quebec on May 6. The francophile Franklin, who in this instance suffered one of his rare diplomatic failures, found that there was little to be done to save a bad situation, while Father Carroll was unable to win over the inflexibly royalist French-Canadian clergy, who greeted the raising of the siege with a *Te Deum* and later invoked harsh sanctions against *congrèssistes*.[66] The arrival of the British reinforcements at Quebec started an American retreat which soon degenerated into a panic-stricken rush for home and safety. The American Army was made up of amateur soldiers who had a healthy respect for British regulars; it was rotten with smallpox and dysentery; it lacked munitions, provisions, and credit; and it had dwindled away with the desertion of men who had volunteered for a quick and easy conquest which had not eventuated after nine months' hard service under miserable conditions. The Americans fell back along the St. Lawrence and the Richelieu, evacuating Sorel on June 14, Montreal on the 15th, Chambly on the 17th, and St. Johns on the 18th. They retired to Crown Point and Ticonderoga with 150 *congrèssistes* of Livingston's and Hazen's regiments, who constituted the second great exodus of French Canadians to what became the United States—the Acadian deportees of 1755 being the first.

Carleton did not press the pursuit vigorously or attempt an immediate counter-invasion. He was well aware that he had had a close escape, and that Canada stood in great need of being put in order after the American occupation had sapped its loyalty and set brother against brother. The British army spent the summer at Chambly and St. Johns, building boats in order to follow the Americans down Lake Champlain. The boats were not ready until early October, and then Carleton contented himself with destroying the American vessels on the lake and forcing the American defenders of Crown Point to burn the place and to retire to Ticonderoga.

Two thousand French Canadians had volunteered by the end of September, the greatest number to back their loyalism by action, but Carleton only accepted half of them, while he requisitioned the services of 1,200 *habitants* of the Richelieu for unpaid *corvées** in connection with the building and provisioning of the fleet. The army returned to Montreal for the winter, leaving the *habitants* of the Richelieu disgruntled and soon causing unrest in the city upon which it was quartered. No distinction was made by Carleton between those French Canadians who had been loyal and those who had sympathized with the Americans; and his conduct revealed more concern for American prisoners than for Canadian subjects.[67] Carleton's lack of energy in pursuing the campaign against the Americans and his attention to the prisoners may be explained by his conviction that these erring brethren might be led to see the error of their ways, while his confidence in the French Canadians had been badly shaken by their behavior during the invasion.

In any case he began to rule with a harsher hand. On March 29, 1777, the new Legislative Council, which had held few meetings during the difficult period through which the colony had just come, passed a Militia Act which imposed military service on all *habitants* from sixteen to sixty, and fixed heavy penalties for failure to comply. This act was even more unpopular with the people than the forced labor of the previous autumn, for fifteen years of freedom from military service, which had been compulsory under the French regime, made it seem an intolerable burden. In the enforcement of this law upon an unwilling people may be found a basis of the lasting French-Canadian dislike for compulsory military service.[68] Carleton was only able to raise 300 French-Canadian militiamen for Burgoyne's invasion force; and he realized 'how unwilling they were to engage in the affair.'[69] But *corvées* again rained upon the disgruntled *habitants*, in order that Burgoyne's unwieldy force might be launched upon its campaign; and friction between the British soldiers and their unwilling hosts did nothing to strengthen the loyalism of the people.[70]

Burgoyne's surrender at Saratoga in October 1777 at once raised the specter of a new American invasion; and, significantly enough, the articles of capitulation permitted Canadian prisoners to return

* Compulsory labor required under the feudal system.

home simply on their promise not to serve again. Congress had not yet despaired of the 'fourteenth colony,' for the Articles of Confederation of 1777 stipulated that Canada could be 'admitted into and entitled to all the advantages of this union.'[71] Quebec was once more on the defensive, and in February 1778 Carleton ordered the militiamen to hold themselves in readiness and provided payment for the *corvées* of the two previous years, as well as pensions for the volunteers who had seen service.[72] With the French alliance of that same month the chief result of Burgoyne's bungled campaign, Quebec was once more exposed to American intrigue and propaganda; and official kindness rather than sternness towards the French Canadians was clearly indicated. In the fall Lafayette's plan of a joint Franco-American expedition by land and by sea against Quebec was considered by Congress, while Admiral d'Estaing issued a resounding manifesto to his 'compatriots of North America' on the keynote: 'You were born French; you cannot cease to be so.'[73] Despite the effect of such appeals upon Canadian lovers of the old regime and sympathizers with the Americans, Canada profited by division among her enemies. First Washington opposed an enterprise which might restore Canada to a France whose ally Spain controlled Louisiana, and thus might revive the old encirclement of the American colonies; and then the French had no desire to see the Americans become self-sufficient and all-powerful on the North American continent. The scheme of 1778 was considered again in 1780 and 1781, but never carried into execution. The threat of invasion by the ancient masters of Canada remained strong enough, however, to contribute to differences between the old and new subjects in Quebec.

A modern French-Canadian historian has judged that 'perhaps no event has exercised so much influence upon Quebec, directly or indirectly, as the American Revolution.'[74] This verdict seems to be justified. The Revolution settled the fate of French feudalism and absolutism; it caused a split between the largely pro-British élite and the largely pro-American masses which had important and lasting results. It was a potent lesson in politics; and from this period onward democracy and liberty were forces in the French-Canadian mind. One of the immediate aftermaths of the Revolution was the introduction into Quebec of some 5,000 American Tories or United Empire Loyalists—professed Loyalists, at least, but undoubtedly the loyalty of many was merely to good farm land. Major André's executioner was discovered taking out land and provisions at Kingston as a Loyalist refugee.[75] The newcomers, however, numbered nearly a tenth of the French Canadians; they did not settle among the French, except at William Henry (Sorel), but along the unpopulated upper St. Lawrence and the southern Gaspé coast; and their resourceful energy made them even more of a force than their number indicates.[76] Their coming clinched Wolfe's victory; Canada was not to be French, but French and English. It also caused within some years the virtual repeal of the Quebec Act, the granting of the elements of representative government, and the division of British North America into Upper (English) and Lower (French) Canada. That terminology has long been dropped; but much bitterness and ill feeling in Quebec could have been avoided if the psychological attitudes of superiority and inferiority appropriate to it had also disappeared.

The day of Carleton, the friend of the French Canadians, had come to an end. He had been superseded in 1777 as military commander by Burgoyne; he had become embroiled with the new Chief Justice Peter Livius, a New Hampshire Tory, over his practice of arbitrary government through an inner circle in the legislative council, a body which was beginning to show signs of independence; and he had quarrelled with Germain, the Colonial Secretary. Finally the embittered Carleton, disappointed in his hopes both for himself and for Canada, resigned his post. He was replaced in June 1778 by Frederick Haldimand, the Swiss soldier of fortune who had served at Montreal under Gage from 1760 to 1762, and had then replaced Burton as governor of Trois-Rivières, where he had remained until his return to England in 1765. Haldimand was thus no stranger to Canada, but he judged its problems in a very different light than Murray or Carleton.

4

Haldimand was the ablest of the Swiss Protestants who played a vital but little-recognized role in Canada during the early years of British rule. Trained to his profession in the armies of Holland, Sardinia, and Frederick the Great, along with his friend Henry Bouquet, who saved the Alleghany frontier of the American colonies after Braddock's defeat, Haldimand raised a battalion of the Royal Americans from among the German and Swedish settlers of Pennsylvania and Maryland when he first came to America in 1754. In 1758 he was a member of Abercromby's ill-fated expedition against the French forts on Lake Champlain, and was wounded in the unsuccessful assault of Carillon (Ticonderoga). He commanded Fort Edward on the Hudson during that winter, and rebuilt Fort Oswego in the following summer. In the great campaign of 1760 he marched with Amherst against Montreal, and was charged with the occupation of the city and the negotiations with the Chevalier de Lévis, since he was far more at home with the French language than with English.

When called to Trois-Rivières as governor of the district, he displayed marked political and economic ability: regulating the fur trade, reopening the Saint-Maurice forges, building roads, and encouraging agriculture, to the general satisfaction of all concerned. When a French-Canadian contingent of 300 men was raised in 1764 to serve against Pontiac and the western Indians, Haldimand found it easy to enlist a company in his bailiwick. His secretary at Trois-Rivières, Conrad Gugy, another Swiss, took such a fancy to the region that he bought the nearby seigneury of Machiche and settled there, playing an active role as a loyalist during the American invasion. Haldimand himself acquired the seigneury of Grand Pabos in Gaspé and also land at Shipody in Nova Scotia, which gave him a firsthand knowledge of the problems of settlement, one of his chief concerns as governor-general. Haldimand also had had singular success in winning the people of Trois-Rivières to their new allegiance: only two women, two children, and a servant left his district for France under the terms of the Treaty of 1763. As for the rest, he wrote: 'I am persuaded that they would be in despair were they to see a French fleet and troops arrive in this country in any number whatsoever; they begin to taste too well the sweets of liberty to be the dupes of the French.'[77] The interval between his departure from Canada in 1765 and his return as governor had been filled with six years as governor in Florida, two at New York and Boston, and three at home, since London wisely prefered at first not to use foreigners to put down the rebellion in the American colonies. Haldimand was now given the difficult task of keeping Quebec British, while its ancient masters were striving to win it from its new allegiance by every sort of intrigue, and were threatening to invade the country.

Under such circumstances the neutrality of the French Canadians was clearly not to be counted upon, nor could the governor rely, as in 1775–6, on the loyalty of the *noblesse* and the clergy. Haldimand was conscious of the altered conditions:

> However sensible I am of the good conduct of the clergy in general during the invasion of the Province of the year 1775, I am well aware that since France was known to take part in the contest, and since the address of Count D'Estaing and a letter of M. de la Fayette to the Canadians and the Indians have been circulated in the Province, many of the Priests have changed their opinions, and in case of another Invasion would, I am afraid, adopt another system of conduct.[78]

The French priests who remained in the colony after the conquest still enjoyed a dominance over their Canadian colleagues, who had an inferior education. Under the altered circumstances, their loyalty to the government weakened, and they drew many of the native-born clergy with them.[79] Haldimand was obliged to make an example by deporting in 1778 a Sulpician, the Abbé Huet de la Valinière, who had come under suspicion during the American invasion and now openly advocated the return of Canada to France.[80] Despite this action the French proclamations still turned up on church doors, and the *presbytères* served as centers of seditious rumors. To Haldimand's mind, the only solution to a delicate problem was to import French-speaking priests from Savoy, who would be friendly to Great Britain, but London was slow to act on his advice.

The contagion of sedition was widespread among the élite, many of whom had relatives in France, and by no means confined to the French clergy.[81] Haldimand was obliged to arrest three prominent French citizens whose loyalty to Britain was more than suspect. The most notable was Pierre de Sales Laterrière, who had studied medicine in Paris under General Rochambeau's uncle, and had come to Canada in 1766 in the same ship with Hector Cramahé, Richard Montgomery, and the Jesuit La Jonquière. According to his *Mémoires*, a valuable if unorthodox picture of the period, Laterrière found Canada so agreeable that he thought himself in paradise. Since he was a gay young blade, the frivolity of 'my little new American Paris' was very much to his taste:

> Never have I known any nation so fond of dancing as the Canadians; they still practice the French square dances and the minuet, to which they add the English dances. During the winter, which lasts eight months, the nights are passed in feasts, suppers, dinners, and balls. The ladies are much given to cards before and after the dances. All games are played, but the favorite is an English game called *Wisk*. . . .
>
> . . . .
>
> One must admit that the Canadian ladies are beautiful; and that in general they receive more education by means of the schools and the nuns than the men; and that by their natural disposition they greatly surpass the men in *finesse*, in gentleness, and in manners. Demanding little, they do not take advantage of their superiority; and thus they attach the men to them, so that even strangers are obliged to give them credit. In general, the Canadian ladies are very economical, loving, and faithful spouses. It is very difficult for one who spends some years here to avoid marriage. The English felt this pressure after the conquest; many of them have married here, and at present the number has grown vastly.[82]

Laterrière became first the Quebec agent of the Saint-Maurice forges, and then the associate at Trois-Rivières of the manager, Christophe Pélissier. The latter was so thoroughly involved with the Americans, to whom he furnished bombs and tools during the siege of Quebec, that he was forced leave the country with them. Laterrière succeeded him both in the business and in the affections of Madame Pélissier, who remained in Trois-Rivières as his companion. This domestic situation, with its suggestion of the complete opposition of the two men, at first preserved Laterrière from arrest as an American sympathizer, but by February 1779 there was clear evidence that he was preparing the way for a new invasion and encouraging Canadians to join the Americans. He was clapped into a cell in the Quebec jail, and soon joined there by Valentin Jautard and Fleury Mesplet, the Voltairean founders of the *Gazette de Montréal*, who had indulged in too much freedom of the press for Haldimand's taste.

Traffic with the Americans was not confined to Frenchmen, however, for the journalists were joined in the fall of 1780 by the Scot Charles Hey, one of the British merchants of Quebec who had prudently taken up residence on the Ile d'Orléans during the American siege, and who was a brother and faithful correspondent of the American quartermaster-general at Albany. Most of the leading plotters, however, were Frenchmen like François Cazeau and Boyer Pillon of Montreal, and most notably Pierre du Calvet, whose vigorous pen has done much to give Haldimand the name of a tyrant. None of these political prisoners received a trial; but Laterrière was released in the summer of 1780 on his promise to leave the colony, and the others were set at liberty in May 1783, when the threat of American invasion was ended. They were held in light confinement, and du Calvet was even allowed to carry on his business and to pen his blasts against Haldimand in his prison cell. It is difficult to censure Haldimand for detaining these men, since there was considerable evidence against them in Canada and their names appeared in the list of traitors sent up from New York by General Clinton, to whom Benedict Arnold had revealed the Canadian plots after his treason.[83]

The mood of the people was uncertain. Soon after his arrival Haldimand deplored the 'sentiments which the French Alliance with the Rebels has undoubtedly raised up in numbers of them, who in regard of the Rebellion were unquestionably attached to Government.'[84] He hoped to awe them into loyal behavior by strengthening the fortifications of the Richelieu and by making a stronghold of Sorel, which commanded both that traditional invasion path and the St. Francis River, and also the approach to Quebec from indefensible Montreal. During the winters of 1781–3, when the threat of invasion was always imminent, he prepared to evacuate all provisions from the southern part of the province in order to hamper an American advance. Haldimand barred the loyalists from settlement along the American frontier, proposing to leave the

Eastern Townships as a forest barrier against invasion, and as a reserve for future expansion of the French Canadians. He thought it 'good policy that the frontiers should be settled by people professing a different language, and accustomed to other laws and government from those of our restless and enterprising neighbours of New England.'[85]

With vision unusual in a professional soldier, Haldimand saw that French and English might be drawn more closely together if their cultures were shared. With this object in mind, he established the first public library in Canada, half English and half French. When the difficulty of obtaining French books because of the war resulted in only English works being sent out from London, Haldimand refused to open the library until the other books arrived, 'to prevent any jealousy.' The library was established in the Bishop's Palace at Quebec, and its subscribers included French-Canadian priests and laymen as well as most of the English-speaking residents. In writing on March 1, 1779, to his Swiss friend General Buade in London, Haldimand gave an account of his enterprise:

> The few resources here, and the reason I have every day for perceiving that the ignorance of the people is one of the greatest obstacles that must be conquered to make them acquainted with their duties and their own interest, have given me the idea of establishing a public Library. I have led the Bishop and the Superior of the Seminary to see the advantage which would result from it. They have entered into my ideas, and I have had a subscription opened, which they have signed with me, as have several priests, almost all the British merchants and several Canadians. . . .[86]

According to the catalogue of 1785, this library included 1,000 French and 800 English books, mostly eighteenth-century works. This was a notable addition to the intellectual resources of Canada, for it has been estimated that there were only some 60,000 books there in 1765.[87]

During the French regime the most considerable libraries were in ecclesiastical hands. The important Jesuit collection at Quebec was dispersed by the suppression of the order, but the Sulpician library, perhaps the best and richest in the colony, remained available at Montreal. Some of the *curés* had notable collections—in the early years of the eighteenth century the Abbé Philippe Boucher of Saint-Joseph-de-Lévis possessed 400 volumes. The concentration of books in clerical hands naturally effected a somewhat rigorous selection, and books which might be considered dangerous or frivolous were exceedingly scarce in New France in the early days. There was, however, a relative abundance of religious works, of the Greek and Latin classics, and of legal works.

As the relations of the colony with the mother country increased during the prosperous first half of the eighteenth century, more books, and less discreet ones, were to be found. The catalogue of the library of the Sieur Joseph Fournerie de Vézon of Montreal in 1760 includes such items as *Gil Blas*, Voltaire, Montesquieu, Machiavelli, Mirabeau, Rousseau, Boccaccio, and the *Arabian Nights*. Vézon was a French officer who only came to Canada in 1757, but most of the books probably belonged to his wife's first husband, a Canadian.

The old legend that Quebec never felt the influence of Voltaire and the encyclopedists has been disproved by the discovery of their works in Canadian libraries both before and after the English conquest. The *Quebec Gazette* frequently printed selections from Voltaire after 1764, and a Voltairean academy flourished in Montreal in 1778. Voltaire and Rousseau were widely read in both England and America at this period, and their vogue in Quebec cannot be considered solely an English-inspired attempt to win the French Canadians from their faith. These men dominated the era everywhere that books were read, and their works were not strictly banned in Quebec until the middle of the nineteenth century, when a new tide of Jansenism set in, and the social consequences of their doctrines became apparent to the highly conservative religious leaders of the French Canadians.

Haldimand's reference to Canadian ignorance in his letter to General Buade reveals that this Swiss Huguenot did not share the high opinion of the French Canadians held by his English-speaking predecessors. Furthermore, he judged that 'no people in the world are more bigoted in their laws and usages,' and he considered that the clergy possessed an 'attachment for France, concealed under their zeal for the Preservation of their Religion.'[88] It is not unlikely that a certain confusion of a mild racism and nationalism with religion, which was to increase with the years, had already set in among the French Canadians, preoccupied as they were in this period of transition with insuring the survival of their faith, laws, customs, and language under the rule of men of another culture. But the Protestant Haldimand was no fanatical enemy of the French Canadians, as his resolutions upon taking office bear witness:

> To give protection and to have much regard for the orders and the religious houses; to be always polite and obliging but also to be always watchful; not to be adopted by either party; to ask time to consider things of any importance, but also to make it an inviolable rule to do whatever has been promised; not to become heated in conversation, rather to leave the room under any pretext, as was the case with a bishop, who prayed in order to give his blood time to cool; to return immediately, to listen with patience and take time for deliberation; to favour commerce and distinguish the merchants who deserve it; to have respect for the

officers which is due them, to associate with them at table and in parties with the Canadians, and to require from them good conduct and the regulation of their expenses; to have good manners and show confidence in the chief justice and procuror general and to consult them as occasion arises; to treat in the same way the Catholic clergy and make known to them the danger that their rights will be in if the rebels, and especially the *Bostonnais*, gain the upper hand, for it is these last who are the most interested in the reduction of Canada in order to people it with their own kind, assure their independence, and make themselves masters of commerce; their intolerance should be made known, the curés should speak to it.[89]

As can be seen from this entry in his journal, Haldimand's intention was to hold the balance more evenly between the French Canadians and the English merchants than had his predecessors; and this object he accomplished, so far as the grave peril of the colony permitted.

Haldimand has been called a persecutor of Catholicism because he banished the Abbé de la Valinière and two French Sulpicians who came to Canada disguised as laymen in 1783. But Vicar-General Montgolfier had himself proposed deporting La Valinière half a dozen years earlier,[90] and when England was at war with France Haldimand could hardly allow French priests to influence the Canadians against their rulers, as these three Sulpicians undoubtedly had done. He has also been denounced—Laterrière called him the 'cruel, hard, wicked Swiss'[91]—for making political prisoners and holding them without trial, but in the whole six years of his government, when British rule in Canada was put to its severest test, such arrests numbered only nineteen. The outraged Du Calvet's picture of jails bursting with innocent victims of the tyrannous governor is more than a little overdrawn. Then, after favoring the merchants at the outset of his administration, Haldimand gradually turned toward the 'French party'; and in the end both French and English combined to oppose him, demanding the repeal of the Quebec Act, the creation of an assembly with tax powers, and in short the establishment of Quebec as a British colony with British institutions and British rights. The effect of Haldimand's absolutist government and of the influence of American ideas upon the French Canadians was thus made evident.

The wartime governor was not the man to rule the colony in the postwar period of constitutional development; and Haldimand's long-standing request for leave was suddenly granted in 1784 by a London deluged with both French and English petitions against him. Guy Carleton, now Lord Dorchester, was sent out to replace him in 1786, and to finish the work begun in his earlier administration of making Canada secure as a loyal part of the British Empire.

5

Dorchester was not the same man as Carleton, however; he had lost his confidence in the French Canadians and in his understanding of their society. He was also old and ill. Under these circumstances the dominant figure in the new administration was the Tory Chief Justice William Smith, who had held the same office in New York when Carleton was commander-in-chief there during the Revolution. Both went to England in 1783, and were consulted by the government in its plans for consolidating what remained of British North America after the peace treaty of that year. Smith reported on the Canadian petitions of the following year and drafted an act to regulate the government of Canada. He also sketched out the new powers which should be given to Dorchester, whom he proposed as governor-general of all British North America.[92] Smith favored retaining the Quebec Act and setting up an assembly, while in his opinion the governor and legislative council could be counted upon to make all necessary adjustments of the system without recourse to the British parliament.

Smith wanted Dorchester to be a viceroy, but the ministry would only make him governor of Quebec, Nova Scotia, and New Brunswick, and commander-in-chief in all these provinces. Dorchester was also commissioned to report to the ministry in detail on the measures necessary to remedy discord in Canada. This compromise, with its limited anticipation of a united British North America, broke down through the force of geography and of transportation difficulties. After his arrival at Quebec in October 1786, Dorchester only once stirred from his seat of government, and then it was to visit the new 'United Empire Loyalist' settlements of American Tories on the upper St. Lawrence, while the lieutenant-governors of the Maritime Provinces reported direct to London as before.

Dorchester relied on Chief Justice Smith in all things save Loyalist matters, in which he followed the advice of Smith's influential disciple, Sir John Johnson, late master of the Mohawk Valley and now Superintendent of Indian Affairs for British North America. Quite apart from the influence of these advisers, Dorchester no longer saw only the French side of any question, for the behavior of the French Canadians under stress and the coming of the Loyalists to Canada had radically revised his outlook. Then Smith, who had seen peoples 'addicted to foreign laws and usages and understanding none but a foreign language'[93] absorbed to an English way of life in New York, New Jersey, and Pennsylvania, was confident that the French Canadians could likewise be assimilated in an English

Canada. He set about realizing this aim at once by a judicial decision which held that English civil law was in force in the province for old subjects. The 'French party,' already alarmed by the coming of the Loyalists and by the threat of anglicization, promptly launched a battle against Smith in the legislative council. Thanks to a six-hour attack by James Monk on the administration of justice, which was instigated by the merchants, a compromise bill, acceptable to both the chief justice and the 'French party,' was passed, while the governor was requested to investigate the courts. This investigation had no other immediate results than to reveal the chaotic confusion of judicial affairs, to discredit the judges of the 'French party,' and to bring about Monk's dismissal as attorney-general. But in the end its findings did much to support London's feeling that a new Canadian constitution must be drafted.

This feeling was also reinforced by the petitions of the merchants and the dispatches of the governor relating to the altered conditions of trade. The advance of the Spaniards up the Mississippi, and of the Americans into the western territory ceded (but not yet handed over to them) under the peace treaty, called for a liberation of the fur trade from the old restrictions. Then, despite the tenets of the old colonial system, the Richelieu trade with Vermont, which was still a republic independent of the American Union and flirting with annexation to Canada, was too valuable to be ruled out. The same question of commercial intercourse with the Americans in the case of the new settlements on the upper St. Lawrence and on the Great Lakes was likewise raised by the proposed division of the province, already being discussed in London. The Canadian merchants, anxious to replace the Americans as the source of supplies for Newfoundland and the British West Indies, also sought revision of the customs duties and of the Navigation Laws. Some half-hearted measures were taken by London, but the most vital decisions were put off until the question of a new constitution should be settled.

An investigation into the hitherto neglected question of education was also launched by Dorchester in 1787, when Amherst resumed his attempt to get, as a reward for his services in the conquest, the Jesuit Estates which had been confiscated in 1763. Under the French regime the Jesuits had acquired considerable property, which they used for the support of their Indian missions and for educational purposes. Forbidden to recruit new members under the terms of the capitulation of Montreal, the Canadian Jesuits had struggled on with dwindling numbers until suppression of the order in France in 1764 and the papal dissolution of the order in 1773 culminated the great upsurge of anti-Jesuit feeling which began as national phenomenon and ended as an international one supported by the Papacy.

The college at Quebec was closed in 1768, but the primary school survived there until 1776. The Jesuit Colleges in Quebec and Montreal were taken over by the English after the conquest for use as barracks, jails, and storehouses, but despite royal instructions in 1774 to suppress the order and to take over its property for the Crown, the Jesuits retained control of the rest, including ten seigneuries which brought in an annual revenue of eleven or twelve hundred pounds. By 1787 there were only four surviving Canadian members of the order, who used their income for poor relief, while the ultimate disposition of the property was still unsettled. Amherst's claim, first made after the conquest, had been delayed for almost twenty years by legal complications; now his renewed insistance raised a question which was not to be finally settled until 1888,* though the Crown took over the Estates in 1800 at the death of the last Jesuit.

At the moment, an order from London for a description of the Jesuit Estates raised a tumult in the colony, because both French and English Canadians felt that the revenue of the property should be used for its original purpose, the support of education, rather than handed over to Amherst. The sole secondary schools for boys were the seminaries of Quebec and Montreal, while girls were educated in the convents of Quebec, Trois-Rivières, and Montreal. There were six elementary Protestant schools in Quebec, two in Trois-Rivières, and four in Montreal, as well one each at Lachine, L'Assomption, and Sorel. These were small, inadequately staffed, and expensive by comparison with the Catholic schools, which were attended by many English children. Outside the cities and chief towns there were only a few small schools run by *curés* or nuns of the Congrégation de Notre Dame. The government supported four Protestant teachers, two in Quebec, one in Montreal, and one in Gaspé; the Catholic schools had to get along on their own resources.

The general ignorance was appalling; Hugh Finlay, the postmaster-general, who was in a good position to know the facts throughout the province, wrote home in 1784 that 'not one man in five knows how to read.'[94] Shortly after the conquest, Mrs. Frances Brooke, wife of the Quebec garrison chaplain, found the *habitants* 'ignorant, lazy, dirty, and stupid beyond all belief,' while she reported that 'all knowledge of language is confined to the sex, very few, even of the *seigneurs*, being able to write their own names.'[95] French-Canadian ignorance was a favorite theme of the English merchants, and it was said that the clergy deliberately kept the people ignorant in order to dominate them. Bishop Hubert denounced such statements in 1789, claiming that twenty-four to thirty people in each parish could read and write, and that the backwardness of his people was due to climatic and pioneering

* See Chapter VIII, pp. 423-9.

conditions. But his higher figure would give only some 4,000 literates out of a total French-Canadian population of 140,000.[96] To be sure, literacy was far from general in France or England at this period, but Canada was behind the more justly comparable American standard of the day.

Chief Justice Smith headed the committee on education and prepared the report which it issued in December 1789. It called for free parochial primary schools, with a system of free county secondary schools, whose curriculum would include such practical matters as bookkeeping and surveying. A university was to complete the educational structure. Theology was to be excluded, in order that both French and English might attend the same institution, whose governors were to include the Catholic and Anglican bishops, an equal number of prominent laymen of each faith, and the judges. Haldimand's library was to be taken over for the new university, which was to be housed in the Jesuit College at Quebec. A portion of the revenue of the Jesuit Estates was to serve as an initial endowment, to be completed by private contributions. Smith anticipated that such a university would make Quebec the intellectual capital of British North America, and that it might even attract American students, through the 'opportunity of acquiring one of the most universal languages of Europe.'[97] In contrast to the past, when education had been a monopoly of the Church, the new system 'would follow a single principle under the watchful eye of the Crown,' as Dorchester wrote to Grenville.[98]

This project, which was unanimously supported by the council, including the French Canadians J.-G. Chaussegros de Léry, François Baby, Charles de Lanaudière, and J.-B. Lecompte-Dupré, was opposed by both the Catholic and the Protestant bishops. The Anglican Bishop Inglis, who considered Quebec 'a French colony with an English garrison,' found the plan too kindly to the French Canadians and too indifferent to the rightful pre-eminence of his 'national church.'[99] The Catholic Bishop Hubert objected to it because of the difficulty of reconciling the educational interests of Catholics and Protestants, of French and English; while he blandly pointed out that if a university was urgently desired, nothing was simpler than to return the revenues of the Jesuits to their original purpose and to restore the Jesuit College of Quebec to its original function. For their part, the four surviving Jesuits offered to make over their revenues, less provision for themselves, to the Catholic bishop as an educational fund for the benefit of the Canadians.[100] But as discussion of the question dragged on, the establishment of a non-sectarian state university was supported by a petition of October 31, 1790, which bore the signatures of sixty French Canadians, including the coadjutor Bishop Bailly de Messein, the provincial of the Franciscans, and a director of the Quebec Seminary. Meanwhile the Montreal lawyer Simon Sanguinet left property worth four or five hundred pounds a year for the endowment of such a university. The Sulpicians applied for a charter for an affiliated institution in Montreal, to be known as Dorchester or Clarence College, which would teach the humanities, mathematics, engineering, and civil law, and which would be under the supervision of the Crown. All these projects were referred by the governor to London, which decided that they, like much else in Canada, must await the new constitution.

It is clear that Dorchester failed to perform his main function, which was to find a remedy for Canada's constitutional ills. In June 1787, when sending home reports at the request of London, he wrote: 'I confess myself as yet at a loss for any plan likely to give satisfaction.'[101] Sydney, the colonial secretary, writing to Dorchester on September 3, 1788, likewise confessed his perplexity: 'The variety of applications, which have from time to time been transmitted from thence upon this business, of so opposite a tendency to each other, render it extremely difficult to fix upon any Arrangements calculated to satisfy all the Parties interested in, or connected with it.'[102] But faced with a session of parliament and an unruly opposition, he called upon Dorchester for fuller information, to be supplied at once by an 'Extraordinary Packet Boat.' Dorchester's reply, which contained little if anything new, was drafted by Chief Justice Smith. It pointed out that an assembly was demanded chiefly by the English merchants of Quebec and Montreal, while the *habitants* were neutral in the matter, and the *seigneurs* opposed—in short that only one-fifth of the total population desired a 'change of the laws and form of government.'[103] The proposed division of the province was considered to be 'by no means advisable at present, either for the interests of the new, or the ancient districts.' While London delayed, the merchants filled the columns of the *Quebec Gazette* and the new *Herald* (founded, along with the French *Courier de Québec*, in 1788) with controversial correspondence on the needs of the colony, and their representative Adam Lymburner agitated at London in their interest.

In July 1789 the younger Pitt's cousin Grenville succeeded Sydney in the Colonial Office, and by the end of August he had drafted the basis of the Constitutional Act of 1791. He postulated an assembly on the grounds that the colony must stand on its own financial feet in the future, and that taxation without representation would lead Canada into the American Union. A single legislature was impossible for geographical and ethnic reasons; therefore an English province in the West must be cut out of the present province, 'rather than these two bodies of People should be blended together in the first formation of the new Constitution, and before sufficient time has been allowed for the removal of ancient prejudices, by the habit of obedience, to the same Government, and by the sense of a common interest.'[104] The legislative council was to be separated from the executive council, and to have the status of the House of Lords in the English system, with members holding their seats for life or during good behavior, and rewarded with baronetcies or some other mark of honor. The governor was to have both civil and military executive power and the right to dispose of the Crown lands. Grenville was inclined to believe that Canada would ultimately separate from the Empire, whatever constitution was given it; but he felt that the bestowal of a British constitution, in which the monarchic, aristocratic, and democratic principles were properly balanced, would delay that separation. In any case, a British constitution could no longer be denied to a large body of British subjects living in close proximity to the lost American colonies and at a great distance from England, while revolution was breaking out in France. The force of the geographical argument was evidenced by the fact that delays of navigation kept Grenville's proposal of 1789 from traveling out to Canada for comment and returning to London in time to be considered during the session of 1790. Dorchester's and Smith's contributions to the original draft were negligible, for Grenville acted on his own ideas, which were also those of the younger Pitt. The final bill, which was passed on June 10, 1791, was little affected by its passage through parliament, and the debate upon it was chiefly notable for the irrelevant clash of Burke and Fox on the French Revolution.

The Constitutional Act of 1791 did not repeal the Quebec Act, but only that portion of it which dealt with the form of government. The position of the Church and the status of the laws were left untouched. The actual division of the Province of Quebec into Upper and Lower Canada was embodied in a later order-in-council rather than in the Act itself, because Britain still held the Western posts ceded to the Americans in 1783. The project of a united British North America was abandoned, as Chief Justice Smith noted with sorrow: 'I miss in it, however, the expected Establishment, to put what remains to Great Britain of Her Antient Dominions in North America, under one general direction, for the united interest and safety of every Branch of the Empire.'[105] To his Tory satisfaction, however, Canada was not 'abandoned to Democracy' like the old colonies.

The Act really satisfied no single group in Canada except the Loyalists of Upper Canada, who were delivered from an uneasy dependence upon Quebec, their ancient enemy. The French-Canadian masses were indifferent to the change, as were the clergy.

The *seigneurs* found their position threatened by the prospect of a democratically elected assembly and of the granting of the Crown lands in freehold tenure. The merchants were the unhappiest of all: the combination of the division of the province and of the institution of representative government perpetuated their minority status under French-Canadian control. The long-sought English commercial laws were not to be theirs, unless the French Canadians decided to adopt them. Pitt, in his reply to Fox's objection to the division of the province on an ethnic basis, made the government's hopes on this score clear:

As the honorable gentleman has said, it would be extremely desireable that the inhabitants of Canada were united and universally led to prefer English laws and the English constitution. The division of the province is probably the best means to obtain that object. The French subjects will thus become convinced that the British government has no intention of imposing English laws upon them. Then they will consider with a freer spirit the operation and the effects of these laws, comparing them with the operation and effects of theirs. Thus, with time, they will perhaps adopt ours by conviction. That will happen more probably than if the government suddenly undertook to submit all the inhabitants of Canada to the constitution and laws of this country. It will be experience which will teach them that English laws are the best. But it must be admitted that they ought to be governed to their satisfaction.[106]

Macaulay mourned that Pitt had not died in 1792, when his name would have identified with these ideas of peace, freedom, philanthropy, temperate reform, and mild and constitutional government—the ideas of what a later historian has called the Second British Empire.[107] It is to the younger Pitt and to his cousin William Grenville that the French Canadians owe the forms of British self-government, which were so unfamiliar to them in 1791 that the grant was not appreciated, but which were shortly put to such good use that French-Canadian survival was assured for all time. A half century of constitutional conflict lay ahead, but thanks to London the French Canadians were armed to meet it.

Notes

[1] The marked preference by French Canadians for the term 'cession' rather than 'conquest,' when there would have been no cession without a conquest, is a psychological defence. The latent English-Canadian tendency to think of the French as a 'conquered people' is a similar defence mechanism on the part of a dominant minority concerned about maintaining its position against increasing odds.

[2] Notably Garneau and Groulx.

[3] Witness the reception of Abbé Arthur Maheux's *Ton Histoire est une épopée*, I, *Nos Débuts sous le régime anglais* (Québec, 1941). To be sure, there are indications in the Murray Papers (PAC) that Abbé Maheux, like Canon Groulx, approached the subject with a predetermined thesis, though with an opposite purpose. Both writers cite only such passages as suit their divergent ends.

[4] The birthrate from 1760–70 was 65.3 per 1,000. G. Langlois, *Histoire de la population canadienne-française* (Montréal, 1934), 262. On French-Canadian vitality in general, see J. Davidson, 'The Growth of the French Canadian Race in North America,' *Annals of the American Academy of Political and Social Science*, VIII (Sept. 1896), 213–35.

[5] T. Chapais, *Cours d'histoire du Canada* (Québec, 1919), I, 23–4*n*.

[6] 'A Journal of the Expedition Up the St. Lawrence,' by a British officer, *New York Mercury*, No. 385 (31 Dec. 1759); cited by J.-C. Bracq, *L'Evolution du Canada Français* (Paris, 1927), 50. A French translation of this journal was published as a pamphlet at Quebec in 1855. A. G. Doughty & G. W. Parmelee, *The Siege of Quebec and the Battle of the Plains of Abraham* (Quebec, 1901), VI, 173.

[7] PAC: Murray Papers, III, 'Letters to & from Murray, 1759–89,' 49–50, Murray-Amherst, 1 Jan. 1761.

[8] *Ibid.*, III, 53, Murray-Amherst, 11 Jan. 1761.

[9] *The Journal of Captain John Knox* (Champlain Society, Toronto, 1914), II, 260, 156*n.*; cited by A. L. Burt, *The Old Province of Quebec* (Minneapolis, 1933), 18.

[10] Burt, 19.

[11] PAC: Murray Papers, II, 'Letter Book, 1763–5,' 53–5, Murray-George Ross, 26 Jan. 1764.

[12] *Ibid.*, II, 47, Murray-de Montesson, 14 Jan. 1764.

[13] *Ibid.*, II, 104, Murray-Burton, 22 March 1764; F. Brooke, *The History of Emily Montague* (London, 1769), I, 38, Letter VI.

[14] Juge Baby, *L'Exode des classes dirigéantes à la cession du Canada* (Montréal, 1899). Cf. Abbé L. Groulx, *Lendemains de Conquête* (Montréal, 1919–20), 39–51.

[15] Abbé I. Caron, *La Colonisation de Québec* (Québec, 1927), I, 3–10.

[16] PAC: 'Registre d'Audience du conseil militaire de Québec, 1760–62,' II, 121; cited Burt, 35.

[17] H. Têtu & C.-O. Gagnon, *Mandements des évêques de Québec* (Québec, 1888), II, 169, Briand's mandement, 4 juin 1763.

[18] A. Shortt & A. G. Doughty, *Documents Relating to the Constitutional History of Canada 1759–1791, CAR 1905*, III (Ottawa, 1907), 6–7, Capitulation of Quebec, Arts. VI & IX.

[19] *Ibid.*, 25, Capitulation of Montreal, Art. XXVII.

[20] Sister Mary Augustina [Ray], *American Opinion of Roman Catholicism in the Eighteenth Century* (New York, 1936), 395.

[21] *Knox's Journal*, II, 260.

[22] PAC: B (Haldimand Papers), 37, 10, Egremont-Amherst, 12 Dec. 1761.

[23] PAC: Murray Papers, II, 'Letter Book, 1763–65,' 139–41, Murray-Halifax, 26 June 1764.

[24] PAC: CO 42, I,——,Murray-Shelburne, 14 Sept. 1763; cited Chapais, I, 45.

[25] PAC: Q I, 258, Murray-Shelburne, n.d.

[26] *Quebec Gazette*, 3 July 1766; cited Chapais, I, 53.

[27] Burt, 82.

[28] Shortt & Doughty, *Const. Docs., 1759–91*, 139–40, Murray's Instructions, 7 Dec. 1763.

[29] PAC: Murray Papers, II, 'Letter Book, 1763–5,' 154–7, Murray-Elibank, 16 Sept. 1764.

[30] Burt, 88.

[31] PAC: Murray Papers, II, 'Letter Book, 1763–5,' 170, Murray-Eglinton, 27 Oct. 1764.

[32] Shortt & Doughty, *Const. Docs., 1759–91*, Report of Attorney and Solicitor-General, 13 May 1766. See Caron, I, 18, for Chief Justice Mansfield's censure of the Proclamation.

[33] Shortt & Doughty, *Const. Docs., 1759–91*, 167, Murray-Lords of Trade, 29 Oct., 1764.

[34] PAC: Murray Papers, II, 'Letter Book, 1763–5,' 181, Montreal-Halifax, 30 Oct. 1764.

[35] *Ibid.*, 290, Murray-George Ross, 4 Dec. 1765.

[36] W. S. Wallace, *The Maseres Letters, 1766–1768* (Toronto, 1919), 9.

[37] Shortt & Doughty, *Const. Docs., 1759–91*, 185–6, Maseres, 'Considerations on the Expediency of Procuring an Act of Parliament for the Settlement of the Province of Quebec,' 1766.

[38] *Ibid.*, 206–7, Carleton-Shelburne, 20 Jan. 1768.

[39] *Ibid.*, 205–6.

[40] Cited Burt, 152.

[41] Shortt & Doughty, *Const. Docs., 1759–91*, 404, Quebec Act.

[42] Burt, 258.

[43] W. P. M. Kennedy, *Statutes, Treaties and Documents of the Canadian Constitution, 1713–1929* (Oxford, 1930), 128.

[44] Shortt & Doughty, *Const. Docs., 1759–91*, 207, Carleton-Shelburne, 20 Jan. 1767.

[45] *Journals of the Continental Congress*, I (1774), 88; cited G. Lanctot, *Les Canadiens-français et leurs voisins du sud* (Montréal, 1941), 98, 'Le Québec et les Colonies américaines.'

[46] Kennedy, *Docs.*, 146, 'Address of the General Congress to the Inhabitants of Quebec, 26 Oct. 1774.'

[47] *CHAR 1939*, 13, R. G. Trotter, 'The Appalachian Barrier.'

[48] R. Coupland, *The Quebec Act* (Oxford, 1925), 196.

[49] PAC: Q 11, 170–3; cited Burt, 209.

[50] Têtu & Gagnon, *Mandements de Québec*, II, 264–5, Briand's mandement, 22 mai 1775. This pastoral letter was sent only to the districts of Montreal and Trois-Rivières, those most open to American influence. L. Laurent, *Québec et l'église aux Etats-Unis* (Washington, 1945), 36*n*. Vicar-General Montgolfier of Montreal backed up Carleton's proclamation of June 9 with a circular to his *curés* on June 13. Têtu & Gagnon, II, 265–6. It is noteworthy that Bishop Briand stressed that the French Canadians were bound by their religion, as well as by their oath of allegiance, to defend their country and king, while discounting the possibility of foreign service. The traditional British loyalty of the French-Canadian hierarchy and the traditional aversion to foreign wars are here first exemplified.

[51] Archives seigneuriales de Lotbinière, MS. 'Lettre du Congrès Général aux Canadiens. Mai ou juin 1775.' Cf. *Journals of Congress*, II (1775), 68–70, 29 May 1775; cited Lanctot, *Voisins*, 104. Abbé François-Louis Chartier de Lotbinière, the former Recollect Père Eustache, became chaplain of James Livingston's French-Canadian regiment in 1776 after displaying American sympathies the previous year. Laurent, *Québec & l'église*, 54–6.

[52] Abbé Aug. Gosselin, *L'Eglise au Canada après la conquête* (Québec, 1917), II, 87; Abbé Verreau (*ed.*), *L'Invasion du Canada* (Montréal, 1873), 39, 54, 63.

[53] Verreau, 166; Caron, I, 101.

[54] Gosselin, II, 87.

[55] J. H. Smith, *Our Struggle for the Fourteenth Colony* (New York, 1907), I, 381–94; *E. Allen's Narrative of the Capture of Ticonderoga and of His Captivity and Treatment by the British* (Burlington, 1849), 12–13.

[56] PAC: Q 12, 188, Carleton-Germain, 28 Sept. 1776; cited by C. Martin, *Empire and Commonwealth* (Oxford, 1929), 140.

[57] Verreau, 55–6; *ibid.*, 51–3, 60, 101.

[58] *Ibid.*, 83.

[59] *Ibid.*, 85–6.

[60] Lanctot, 107.

[61] Smith, I, 598–607.

[62] J. C. Fitzgerald (*ed.*), *The Writings of George Washington* (Washington, 1931), III, 480.

[63] Verreau, 95.

[64] *Ibid.*, 99; quoted Caron, I, 103–4.

[65] TRSC, XII (1906), Sec. II, 197–309, R. W. McLachlin, 'Fleury Mesplet, the First Printer of Montreal.'

[66] Laurent, 45–9; Caron, I, 105; Têtu & Gagnon, II, 269–79, Briand's mandement, juin 1776. Cf. Briand's letter to his sister, 27 Sept. 1776, in *Revue canadienne*, VIII (1871), 441.

[67] Verreau, 135.

[68] C. P. Stacey, *Canada and the British Army, 1846–71* (London, 1936), 9.

[69] PAC: Q 13, 222, Carleton-Burgoyne, 29 May 1777; cited by Lanctot, 117.

[70] Verreau, 145–6, 155.

[71] *Journals of Congress*, 1777, 924; cited by Lanctot, 117.

[72] Verreau, 151–3.

[73] PAC: Q 16–1, 297, D'Estaing's proclamation, Boston, 28 Oct. 1778; Smith, II, 539. Cf. Caron, I, 109–10.

[74] Lanctot, 121–2.

[75] PAC: Q 16–1, 265; A. L. Burt, *The United States, Great Britain, and British North America* (New Haven, 1940), 121–2.

[76] Caron, I, 120–8.

[77] J. N. McIlwraith, *Sir Frederick Haldimand* (Toronto, 1906), 53.

[78] *Ibid.*, 128.

[79] Caron, I, 113–14.

[80] Laurent, 51–4.

[81] P. Aubert de Gaspé, *Mémoires* (Ottawa, 1866), 85, 90, 186.

[82] *Mémoires de Pierre de Sales Laterrière et de ses traverses* (Québec, 1873), 61–2, 52–3.

[83] Burt, *Old Prov.*, 296.

[84] PAC: Q 15, 268, Haldimand-Germaine, Sorel, 15 Oct. 1778; cited McIlwraith, 140.

[85] PAC: B 56, 204, Haldimand-North, 27 Oct. 1783; cited Caron, I, 123.

[86] QLHST 1887–9, 37.

[87] Benjamin Sulte's estimate, in A. Fauteux, *Les bibliothèques canadiennes* (Montréal, 1916), 13.

[88] McIlwraith, 13, 181.

[89] *Ibid.*, 179–80.

[90] AAQ: 'Vicaires Généraux,' V, 54, Montgolfier-Briand, 21 Oct. 1776; cited by Laurent, 53.

[91] McIlwraith, 277.

[92] NYPL: Smith Papers, 'An act for the regulation of the Province of Quebec—June 11, 1785,' 'An act to repeal part of an act entitled "An act for making more effectual provision for the government of the Province of Quebec in North America" and for the better regulating of the British colonies on that continent'; cited by Burt, 426.

[93] NYPL; Smith Papers, Smith-Dorchester, 7 Nov. 1788; transcript in PAC, Q 39, 117–21; cited by Burt, 432.

[94] Finlay-Nepean, 22 Oct. 1784; cited by Abbé L. Groulx, *L'Enseignement français au Canada* (Montréal, 1931), I, 48.

[95] Brooke, *Emily Montague*, I, 35, Letter VI.

[96] Groulx, *L'Enseignement*, I, 51.

[97] Burt, 465.

[98] Groulx, *L'Enseignement*, I, 67.

[99] PAC: Inglis Papers, I, 154, Inglis-Canterbury, Halifax, 27 Aug. 1789.

[100] Durham, *Report on the Affairs of British North America* (London, 1839), App. D, 100.

[101] Shortt & Doughty, *Const. Docs., 1759–91*, 646, Dorchester-Sydney, 13 June 1787.

[102] *Ibid.*, 653, Sydney-Dorchester, 3 Sept. 1788.

[103] *Ibid.*, 655, Dorchester-Sydney, 8 Nov. 1788.

[104] *Ibid.*, 664, Grenville-Dorchester, 20 Oct. 1789.

[105] *Ibid.*, 685–6, Smith-Dorchester, 5 Oct. 1780.

[106] *Parliamentary History*, XXIX, 113; cited by Chapais, II, 22.

[107] *Encyclopedia Britannica* (11th ed.), XXI, 673, Macaulay, 'William Pitt'; cited by Chapais, II, 12.

CHAPTER III

THE STRUGGLE FOR SURVIVAL

(1791–1834)

THE ERA of representative government in Canada opened under happy circumstances which contrast sharply with the gloomy picture of the period painted by some French-Canadian historians, who see 'secret thoughts' and 'unjust motives' behind Grenville's plan for Canada and consider it only a 'caricature of British parliamentary government.'[1] These writers fail to recognize the shattering effect of the outbreak of the Terror upon British official opinion, which had previously been somewhat sympathetic to the ideals of 1789, or at least had been confident that a revolutionary France was no longer to be feared. The tolerant attitude earlier shown to the French Canadians was replaced after 1793 by a fear of everything French, whether Continental or Canadian. As Britain struggled for its life against revolutionary, republican, and imperial France for the next twenty years, an ethnic tension hitherto unknown in Canada was created, which left its mark on the French-Canadian mind.

The fault lay largely with those Loyalists who had been rewarded for their losses in the United States by offices in Canada. Their fear of everything French, based upon their traditional hatred of French 'papists' and their bitter suspicion of French intrigues among the American republicans who had stripped them of their old homes and possessions, became almost hysterical. They furthered their new careers and feathered their nests by seeing 'French emissaries' everywhere, and finding 'French conspiracies' in the French Canadians' efforts to practice the self-government which Pitt and Grenville had granted. They were badly scared men, who had lived through one revolution in America and dreaded another in Canada as the old eighteenth-century order crumbled. Their nervousness led them to confuse a growing French-Canadian nationalism and North American republicanism with a loyalty to France which had died with the Terror. Like other revolutionary victims, their reaction was so violent as to further in the long run the very revolution they feared. Their efforts to deprive the French Canadians of the self-government embodied in the constitution of 1791 helped to bring on the Rebellions of 1837–8, for the 'unquestioned Democratik

Enthusiasm'[2] which they noted with alarm in the 1790's was not to be repressed.

But when the new constitution took effect on December 28, 1791, its advent was celebrated by public dinners in both the upper and lower towns of Quebec, where French and English alike sat down to feast and rose to drink such toasts as 'The French Revolution and true liberty throughout the universe,' 'The abolition of the feudal system,' 'May the distinction between old and new subjects be buried in forgetfulness, and may the title of Canadian subjects survive forever,' 'May liberty extend to Hudson Bay,' and 'May the event of the day be a mortal blow to the prejudices which are contrary to civil and religious liberty and to commerce.'[3] Representatives of the gathering in the lower town carried a letter to that in the upper town, proposing the toast: 'The Constitution, and may the unanimity among all classes of citizens cause all distinctions and prejudices to disappear, make the country flourish, and render it always happy.' This sentiment was drunk simultaneously at both gatherings amid general applause, and that night the capital was illuminated in honor of the new constitution. A Constitutional Club was formed by the 160 men who had dined together on this occasion, which was 'enlivened by the Prince's band of music,' while a *Club de Patriotes* at Montreal avidly discussed and cheered the news from France at this period.[4] The Prince in question was Edward, the soldier Duke of Kent and father of Queen Victoria, who was stationed with his regiment at Quebec from August 1791 to January 1794, fostered good feeling by his social talents, and made many friends among the French Canadians.[5]

I

The differences between French and English Canadians were not to subside, however, with the coming of representative government, but rather to increase. At the very outset the new subjects were offended by the division of the province into twenty-one counties, most of which were given incongruously English names. Then there were disorders involving ethnic differences at the elections held in June 1792.[6] The new assembly, whose members included *seigneurs*, lawyers, notaries, merchants, and *habitants*, numbered sixteen English-speaking members out of a total of fifty, though the English population numbered only some 10,000 out of a total of 156,000.[7] The French Canadians were in a distinct minority in the non-elective branches of the government: in the legislative council they had seven out of sixteen members, and in the executive council four out of nine.

At the first meeting of the new legislature the two ethnic groups came into conflict over the election of the speaker of the assembly:

Jean-Antoine Panet was nominated by the French members, while a choice among William Grant, James McGill, and Jacob Jordan was proposed by the English. A warm debate over the bilingual qualifications of the rival candidates sprang up, which was marked by the startling declaration of Pierre-Louis Panet, a cousin of the French nominee: 'It is absolutely necessary for the Canadians to adopt the English language in time, for this is the sole means to banish the antipathy and the suspicion which the diversity of language will maintain between two peoples united by circumstances and forced to live together. But while awaiting this happy revolution, I believe that it is only decent that the speaker whom we choose should be able to express himself in the English language when he addresses the representative of our sovereign.'[8] The notary Joseph Papineau made an eloquent rejoinder to the speeches of English members supporting this view, and when the vote was taken, Jean-Antoine Panet was elected speaker, despite the fact that his cousin Pierre-Louis Panet and the French-born François Dambourgès had joined the English-speaking bloc in opposing him.

This early conflict between French and English members was but a forewarning of a clash that soon followed over the question of which should be the official language of the legislature. Up to this date French had enjoyed no legal status, although it was commonly used for most of the colony's business, both public and private. Its dominance is indicated by the fact that all the English candidates for the speakership were bilingual, while Panet's qualifications in this respect were by his own admission imperfect. To the committee on rules, composed of four members of each group, Pierre-Amable de Bonne proposed that the journals of the assembly should be kept in both languages. John Richardson, the leader of the Montreal merchants, promptly offered an amendment that the English version be considered the legal text. A notable three-day debate followed, with Richardson, Pierre Panet, Grant, McGill, Lee, and Young opposed to de Bonne, Papineau, Bédard, de Lotbinière, Taschereau, and Rocheblave.

The most notable speech was made by Chartier de Lotbinière, who had upheld the rights of the French language before the British parliament when the Quebec Act was under consideration.[9] His desire was not to exclude English, but simply to provide that both languages should enjoy the same status. He pointed out that the Quebec Act insured to the French Canadians their religion, their laws, and their rights as citizens. To him it was clear that the division of the province into Upper and Lower Canada had been made 'in order that the French Canadians should have the right to make their laws in their language, according to their usages, their notions, and the present situation of their country.' He declared that the French

Canadians were loyal to the king, and that they were English at heart before they could speak a word of that tongue. Referring to France, then torn by the Revolution, he concluded: 'It is not by uniformity of language that nations are made more faithful or more united.' And Pierre Bédard, who soon became a parliamentary leader and was later to found the first French-Canadian newspaper, observed: 'If the conquered should speak the language of the conqueror, why don't the English still speak Norman? Is it not ridiculous to wish to make language the test of a people's loyalty?'[10]

Richardson's amendment was defeated by 26–13, with only Pierre Panet and Dambourgès crossing the ethnic line; a revised version was likewise defeated by 27–9, with two English members, Grant and McNider, voting with the French majority. The measure finally adopted by the assembly provided that all bills should be put into both languages by the clerk before being read, while members retained the right to bring in bills in their own language. It also ordained that the English text should be considered legal in the case of bills touching on the criminal law, which was of English origin, and the French text legal in the case of bills bearing upon the civil law, which was of French origin.[11] Thus the two languages were put upon a basis of equality, and both were given an official character, though English remained the language of the law at the insistence of London. Bilingualism was recognized in fact in 1792, if it was not to attain full legal status until 1867.[12] Thus representative government was used at the outset by the French Canadians to secure the last of the conditions of their national survival: official sanction of their language. Their religion, laws, and customs had already been secured by acts of the British parliament.

The English party soon became discontented with the assembly for which they had so long striven. Richardson, the leader of the opposition, confided his gloom about the new form of government to Alexander Ellice, the London partner of his great Montreal trading firm, in a letter of February 16, 1793:

> Unhappily the Session commenced with a determined spirit of Party amongst the French members, for they had a private meeting, at which it was decided that an Englishman should on no account be elected speaker.
>
> We wished to conciliate and be moderate, and that the choice should fall on whoever might be best qualified to fill the Chair, from ability, habits of public business, and knowledge in both languages, without distinction of Country. For this purpose three, Grant, McGill and Jordan, were proposed, of which they might select one, the most consonant to the general wish, but all was to no purpose, right or wrong, a Canadian must be the man, no matter how ill qualified; and the election fell on a Mr. Panet, a Quebec lawyer, whose ideas and talents were never

calculated for anything beyond the quibble routine and formality of a Court of Common Pleas, such as this Country has hitherto experienced.

The same principle which induced this first Out of Door Meeting has hitherto governed all their proceedings.

. . . . .

I fear there are Two Parties amongst the French—one obnoxious to the New Constitution, as they opposed our procuring it—the other more dangerous as being infested with the detestable principles now prevalent in France. These being my fears, my hopes of course are slender—still, as questions will arise on which they will split, it will give the English (who have no wish but the happiness of this country as a British Colony) a preponderance. . . . .

Nothing can be so irksome as the situation of the English members—without numbers to do any good—doomed to the necessity of combating the absurdities of the majority, without a hope of success—were I rid of it, no consideration would induce me again to accept of such a trust—but as I am in, I am determined to give my opinion boldly for such measures as in my conscience I shall think really calculated to do this province a service, under the relation it stands in as a part of the B.[ritish] Empire. I am persuaded—if this House is not dissolved—the English will in the end be the most popular—as facts will speak for themselves, and gradually remove prejudices, interestedly fomented.[13]

This letter reveals the outlook of one of the ablest British merchants in the colony, who resented French party spirit while he blandly assumed that only a member of his own group was qualified for the post of speaker; viewed his French colleagues with suspicion, and resented the dominance of the majority over the minority, although this was a basic principle of the British form of government which the merchants had so long desired.

To be sure, Lieutenant-Governor Sir Alured Clark, who represented the Crown in Dorchester's absence, also noted at the outset of the session a 'jealous spirit' and 'some animosity,'[14] which he blamed chiefly on the fear of the French Canadians that the English intended to control the assembly and to use it to change their ancient laws and customs. But by the end of the session he was pleased to find that distinctions of origin had disappeared almost entirely, and that all the members sat down together for a final dinner marked by 'the greatest harmony and the best mutual dispositions.'

2

Though it is extremely doubtful whether many members of the assembly were infected with the 'detestable principles now prevalent in France,' as Richardson thought, it is certain that French Canada did not wholly escape the influence of the French Revolution, despite the cherished Quebec legend to that effect. The turbulent Citoyen Genet, who represented the French Republic in the United States from April 1793 until early in the following year, was not uninterested in Canada, and his successors followed in his path in this respect. They used Vermont, then dominated by the 'Frenchified' Allen brothers—Ethan, who died in 1791, was the nominal author of a deist work, *Reason, the Only Oracle of Man* (Bennington, 1784) and Ira dealt with the Directory—as a base for intrigues against the colony. The busy channels of trade between the neighboring regions brought to the St. Lawrence the propaganda of the Enlightenment and the Age of Reason, as well as Vermont timber, pot and pearl ash, grain, and provisions. One of Genet's appeals, entitled 'The Free French to their Brothers of Canada,' which had been drawn up on the advice of a young Montreal revolutionary sympathizer, read thus:

> Imitate the examples of the peoples of America and of France. Break with a government which degenerates from day to day and which has become the cruelest enemy of the liberty of peoples. Everywhere one finds traces of the despotism, greed, and cruelty of the King of England. It is time to overturn the throne on which hypocrisy and imposture have sat too long. Fear nothing from George III, or from his soldiers, whose numbers are too small to oppose your valor. The moment is favorable, and insurrection is the holiest of duties for you. Remember that being born French, you will always be suspected and persecuted by the English kings, and that this title will be today more than ever a basis for exclusion from all employment . . . Canadians, arm yourselves; call the Indians to your aid. Count on the support of your neighbors and on that of the French.[15]

The old rumors of a French fleet bound for the St. Lawrence and of a new American invasion along the Richelieu passed once more through the province. There was foundation in fact for the first, and a possibility of the latter as the expansionist Vermonters reacted against a tightened frontier. The agitation reached its greatest heights in 1793–4 and 1796–7, when unrest and disorder were widespread. In May 1794 Dorchester called out the militia to repel the threat of invasion from Vermont, and the attempt to carry out this measure evoked new unrest, notably at Charlesbourg, near Quebec, where 300 armed men resisted 'in the name of the people, which is above the law.'[16] At Montreal there was an attempt to force the prisons, and messengers were sent out to raise the countryside against the government. In 1796 there was widespread unrest over the new Road Act, stimulated by French agents. In December Ira Allen, who had previously hoodwinked Haldimand in long negotiations for the union of Vermont with Canada, was captured by His Majesty's Navy in the English Channel aboard a vessel, inappropriately named the *Olive Branch*, which was laden with 20,000 muskets destined for French-Canadian use in case the French Revolution came to Canada. The agitation was brought to a close by the public execution for treason of David McLane at Quebec in July of the following year.[17]

The unrest was confined to the people, and it was opposed by the French-Canadian leaders, both lay and clerical. In November 1793 Bishop Hubert issued a firm circular letter to his clergy in which he declared that 'the bonds which attached them to France had been entirely broken, and that all the loyalty and obedience which they formerly owed to the King of France, they now owed to His Britannic Majesty.' It was their duty 'to drive the French from this Province.'[18] In the following year the Bishop headed the list of eminent French Canadians of Quebec who signed a loyalist manifest condemning 'with the greatest horror the seditious attempts lately made by wicked and evil-intentioned persons in circulating false and inflammatory writings, in exciting by false rumors the fears and doubts of our compatriots against the laws and the power of the government.'[19] A similar declaration was drawn up at Montreal by a committee headed by the leading French-Canadian citizens. In 1796 Bishop Hubert issued another circular to the clergy, in which he warned them against the 'mute and pernicious proceedings which tended to nothing less than to trouble entirely the peace, tranquility, and the happiness in which the inhabitants of the country rejoice under the government and protection of His Britannic Majesty.' He pointed out:

> It does not suffice that we be loyal and faithful subjects, if the *habitants* confided to our care allow themselves to be seduced by the enemies of peace and good order . . . we believe it to be more than ever our duty to impress upon the people, either in our public instructions or our private conversations, how closely they are obliged to maintain themselves in the loyalty which they have sworn to the King of Great Britain, in prompt obedience to the laws, and in the avoidance of any spirit which might inspire them with the ideas of rebellion and independence, which have caused such sad ravages in recent years, and from which it is so much to be desired that this part of the globe ever be preserved.[20]

The clergy, shocked by the revolutionary attacks upon the Church in France and fearful of American influence, was moved to a greater loyalty to Great Britain. In June 1794 the Abbé Joseph-Octave Plessis, then *curé* of Quebec and later bishop, pronounced at the funeral of Bishop Briand an oration which was permeated with a warm loyalism:

Our conquerors, regarded with a supicious and jealous eye, inspired only horror and a foreboding chill. We could not persuade ourselves that men strange to our land, to our language, to our laws, to our usages, and to our belief would ever be able to give to Canada that which she had just lost in changing masters. Generous nation, which has proved with so much evidence how false were these prejudices; industrious nation, which has brought to bud the riches which this land enclosed within its bosom . . . charitable nation, which has just rescued with such humanity the most faithful and most maltreated subjects of the kingdom to which we formerly belonged; kind nation, which gives each day new proofs to Canada of your liberality; no, no, you are not our enemies, nor those of our Holy Religion, which you respect. Pardon this early distrust in a people who still had not the happiness to know you; and if, after having learned of the overturn of the state and of the destruction of the true Faith in France, and after having tasted during thirty-five years the mildness of your rule, some amongst us are still found so blind or so evil-intentioned as to entertain the same suspicions and to inspire in the people criminal desires to return to their ancient masters, blame not on the whole what is only the vice of a small number.[21]

The Abbé Plessis even went so far as to impute to Bishop Briand the realization at the time of the conquest that 'the Faith itself might gain by this change of rule'—a statement still much contested by French-Canadian ultranationalists who use Catholicism to bolster their separatism.[22] In 1798, when Nelson defeated the French fleet at Aboukir, Bishop Denaut ordained public thanksgiving for the news which 'spread joy in all hearts,' and reminded his flock of 'the debt they owe to Heaven for having put them under the rule and protection of His Britannic Majesty.' His coadjutor, Bishop Plessis, in a sermon on this same occasion, exclaimed: 'Alas, where would we be, brethren, if this country, by an unfortunate reverse, should return to its ancient masters?'[23]

This new British loyalty was not confined to fine words; in 1799 the assembly offered to vote £20,000 to help England meet the expenses of the war with France, while in 1800 and 1801 a long list of French Canadians, headed by the clergy, subscribed to the patriotic fund raised to support British arms against France.[24] Thanks to the French Revolution, the break with France was almost complete; and the influence of the *emigré* French clergy, some fifty[25] of whom helped to relieve the shortage of priests in Quebec, did much to give the French Canadians an enduring distrust of modern France. On the other hand, the coming of the *emigrés* fortified the prestige of French culture, for they were highly educated men and some of them brought books and pictures which constituted a notable addition to the cultural resources of French Canada, largely cut off from its mother culture since the conquest. Their influence was greater than their number would indicate, since they took a leading role in the educational revival of the period, which saw seven new classical colleges established between 1802 and 1832, as well as many schools.[26]

More important, perhaps, than the influence of the French Revolution upon Quebec was the delayed effect of the American Revolution, though the two were intricately involved, thanks to the support given French agents by American republicans. The doctrine of liberty had been instilled into the French-Canadian mind during the invasion of 1775–6, and after the American Revolution British officials and French-Canadian élite alike were disturbed by its manifestations. Haldimand, Hamilton, and Holland all found the Canadians 'much tinged with Yankey Politics,' and François-Joseph Cugnet was scandalized that 'everyone here, even in the class of the third estate, considers himself entitled to make suggestions to the Councils.'[27] The people insisted upon maintaining the practice, established during the American invason of 1775–6, of electing the militia captains, who were now called upon to ascertain the opinion of the people; and for the first time petitions were circulated and signed by people of the lower classes rather than by members of the élite. This new popular spirit was nourished by some of the American sympathizers among the British merchants, 'secret enemies from within'[28] as Haldimand called them, and by many of the humbler newly arrived Loyalists, who sought 'a Government similar or Superior to that under which they were born, had lived, and were happy.'

The new spirit manifested itself in opposition to some of the measures adopted by the legislature, particularly the Militia Act of 1794 and the Road Act of 1796. The Loyalist Attorney-General James Monk blamed the disturbances of this period, which were directed against both government and clergy, on the ferment of French revolutionary propaganda among the populace, though Dorchester attributed the opposition to the Militia Act to the *habitants* having lost the habit of military service, rather than to disloyalty.[29] In 1796 the passing of a highway act which laid the burden of new *corvées* upon the people caused renewed unrest and resistance to the government. The Loyalist Attorney-General Jonathan Sewell considered that trouble-making French emissaries were responsible;[30] but some of the blame must doubtless be assigned to the unwillingness of the people to assume the burdens, as well as the privileges, of representative government, so different from any form of rule they had previously known.

3

The new legislature proceeded slowly about its work, passing an average of only eight bills a session during the first twelve years of its existence. Inexperience was one reason for this slowness in dealing with the important matters that pressed upon its attention; another was the fact that a quorum of thirty-four had been set, and many members found themselves financially unable to attend, since their services were unrewarded. One of the popular leaders, the notary Joseph Papineau, had to be brought to the bar of the assembly by the sergeant-at-arms, after failing to take his seat in 1802 and 1803; and then sought exemption from attendance, which was granted after long debate. Professional men and *habitants* gradually replaced the *seigneurs* in the assembly, while the latter found refuge in the legislative or executive council, allying themselves with the English ruling class after losing the confidence of the masses.

Among the principal measures adopted by the legislature were the Judicature Act of 1794, which established a system of courts that lasted for half a century; and the Revenue Acts of 1795, which added new import duties and increased those already established, while laying new taxes on peddlers and inn-keepers. In 1805 a measure providing for the construction and maintenance of public institutions brought about a sharp conflict between the merchants, who favored a tax on land, and the majority of the assembly, which favored further increases of the tariff and a sales tax. The principle of indirect taxation, supported by the popular representatives, triumphed and remained the basis of taxation in Quebec until modern times. The merchants took their defeat badly, and the critical editors of their organs, the *Montreal Gazette* (which had become English) and the new anti-French *Quebec Mercury*, were summoned to the bar of the assembly in 1806 for libel and contempt of that body. The cry of 'French domination,' already becoming well-worn, was raised once more in English circles.[31]

Surprisingly enough, considering the emphasis on cultural survival, the vital question of education was long left unsolved. There was a deadlock on this question between the English, who wanted state-controlled schools, and the French, to whom education was a religious matter which was a prerogative of the Church. In 1793 a measure providing for the establishment of parochial schools, to be supported by the revenues of the Jesuit Estates, was allowed to die after reaching a first reading, while Dundas postponed action on Dorchester's educational proposals until a Protestant bishop of Quebec was appointed.[32] In 1800, with the death of Père Casot, the last Jesuit in the province, the question of the disposition of the Jesuit Estates, and with it the question of establishing a new system of education, arose once more. The new lieutenant-governor Sir Robert Shore Milnes, who was to show more hostility to the French Canadians than any British administrator had yet revealed, promptly informed the assembly that he had been ordered to take possession of the Estates in the name of the Crown, and that this had already been done.

The education bill which the assembly was called upon to consider in 1801 was based upon the ideas of Jacob Mountain, first Anglican Bishop of Quebec. Appointed to that office in 1793 as a protégé of Pitt's tutor and secretary, he was appalled by the fact that the French-Canadian masses were 'deplorably ignorant,' and showed no progress 'in the attainment of the language of the country under whose government they have the happiness to live'; while he deplored the upper classes' practice of sending their sons to 'Foreign America' as one 'pregnant with alarming mischief.'[33] In 1795 he had proposed to Dorchester that English Protestant schoolmasters be placed in every parish to teach English free and writing and arithmetic at low fees. This measure would, he thought, break down the barrier between English and French, and induce the latter 'to embrace by degrees the Protestant Religion.' Nothing was done, however, along those lines, perhaps because Dorchester resented the appointment of Mountain rather than his own candidate for the see, but more probably because of Dorchester's lack of sympathy with anglicization and his reluctance to provoke further popular unrest in troubled times. In 1799 Bishop Mountain finally won approval by the executive council of a projected system of free primary schools, to be staffed by English teachers paid by the government.[34] If the government set aside funds for this purpose, as he had proposed to Dorchester in 1785, he foresaw that 'in a few years a new race of men, of subjects, and of Christians will be formed in this country; the surest and most peaceful means will have been found to make ignorance disappear, to stimulate industry, to confirm the loyalty of the people by the gradual introduction of English ideas, customs, and sentiments; the thick cloud of bigotry and prejudice which hovers over the country will be dissipated; and the wall which separates Canadians and English will be broken down.'[35] Bishop Mountain's project found favor with the anglifying governor and with the colonial secretary; and in 1801 the Speech from the Throne called upon the assembly to provide for its establishment by law.

The project involved the creation of a state system of education, to be known as the Royal Institution for the Advancement of Learning. Its controlling body was to consist of the governor, the lieutenant-governor, the Anglican bishop, the chief justice, and the speaker of the assembly. This body, naturally dominated by the governor, was to control all the resources of the Royal Institution, and was to be charged with the direction of the free primary and secondary schools to be set up under its supervision, as well as with control of the teachers and students. Its regulations were to be subject to the approval of the governor, who was given the power to establish primary schools in the parishes and townships, as well as two royal grammar schools in Quebec and Montreal, and to choose school commissioners to administer the school property. The teachers were to be named by the governor and commissioned by him. Herman Witsius Ryland, the governor's francophobe secretary, justly considered the measure 'an extremely powerful means to increase the executive power and to modify gradually the political and religious sentiments of the French Canadians'; while Denis-Benjamin Viger, a Montreal lawyer who was becoming a leading French-Canadian spokesman, thought it 'worse than the university system established in France by Bonaparte.'[36]

This highly autocratic scheme doubtless owed something to Governor Milnes' conviction that 'the Canadian Habitants are, I really believe, an industrious, peaceable and well disposed People; but they are, from their want of Education and extreme simplicity, liable to be misled by designing and artful Men, and were they only once made fully sensible of their own Independence, the worst Consequences might ensue.'[37] Milnes feared the opposition of the Catholic clergy, whose independence, he found, 'tends to lessen the Influence of Government in this Province.' But with the exception of a rival bill proposed by Joseph-François Perrault, the pioneer French-Canadian educational reformer, which failed on second reading, the government's measure passed through the assembly without incident or protest, except for the addition of amendments which secured the independence of all church schools or private institutions, and which made the creation of a Royal Institution school in any parish dependent upon the will of the majority of the inhabitants. The clergy, which had blocked the less objectionable scheme of Loyalist Chief Justice Smith, remained mute; Bishop Plessis later remarked to Sir James Craig: 'You say that our Church never sleeps, but you will allow, however, that we were asleep, and very profoundly too, when we suffered that bill to pass.'[38] But the anglicizers were also asleep, or too much concerned with land speculation, for the Act of 1801 long remained a dead letter, and the proposed land grants for the support of the Royal Institution were never made.[39]

The creation of the Royal Institution was the first step in a campaign of anglicization which endangered the basic elements of French-Canadian survival, and hence aroused vigorous French-Canadian resistance. This campaign was the work of the English or Loyalist placemen who filled the executive and appointive offices of the colony—the so-called 'Chateau Clique'—and it was supported by the British merchants. It even enlisted the backing of some of the *seigneurs* and other members of the French-Canadian élite* who had been attached to the official party by patronage, after they had

* Such men were called '*les chouayens*' or '*les vendus*' by the popular party. The latter term has ever since continued to be applied by French-Canadian nationalists to compatriots accepting office from '*les Anglais*,' whether English or Canadian.

been ousted from the French party by the rising class of lawyers and notaries. In constitutional terms it was a battle between the executive council and the assembly, as most of the reactionary-minded governors did their best to upset Pitt and Grenville's enlightened effort to give Lower Canada self-government adapted to the customs and the ideas of the French Canadians.[40] In religious terms it was a battle between the Anglican and Catholic Churches for supremacy as the established church of Quebec, with the Anglican bishop and governors natural allies. The campaign opened with Bishop Mountain's protests to the governor and to London that 'To authorize the Establishment of two Bishops of the same Diocese, of different religious persuasions, would be a solecism in Ecclesiastical Polity, which I believe never took place in the Christian world; to attempt the *union of different Churches* with the State would be, I hardly conceive, an experiment in the science of Government not less dangerous than novel.'[41]

The question of the position of the Catholic bishop dragged on until the eve of the War of 1812; but the political crisis came to a head in 1805, over the means of raising funds for the support of public institutions. The French majority, who represented agricultural interests, favored customs duties, while the English merchants wanted real estate taxes. Open warfare between the executive and the assembly ensued. The attacks of the *Montreal Gazette* and the *Quebec Mercury* on the assembly were followed by the establishment at Quebec of a French-Canadian organ, *Le Canadien*, on November 22, 1806. The rumor of this project was sufficient to induce one 'Anglicanus' to announce flatly in the *Mercury* of October 27: 'This province is already much too French for a British colony. To unfrenchify it as much as possible, if I may use the expression, should be our primary purpose.'[42] The reactionary spirit of the bureaucratic party was even more evident in another communication to the *Mercury*, on the day following the first appearance of *Le Canadien*:

> What remains to be done? Withdraw these privileges which are represented as too few, but which are in reality too many, and in which the conquered rejoice too freely; and order matters so that the administration of public affairs will be carried on in English, by Englishmen, or men of English principles. This will be the first step, and the most efficacious one, towards the anglicization of the province.[43]

Le Canadien, with its much-echoed motto '*Fiat justitia, ruat caelum*,' breathed the spirit of the times. It was founded by three lawyers, Pierre Bédard, Jean-Thomas Taschereau, and Joseph-Louis Borgia, and a doctor, François Blanchet, all members of the assembly. It based its stand on the principles of British constitutionalism, which some French Canadians with the aid of two or three

Englishmen or Scots had managed to master so well within fifteen years that they were already adept at the tactics of legislative obstruction. To the *Mercury* one 'Canadensis' replied in *Le Canadien* on December 6:

You say that, far from adopting the sentiments of those in whose footsteps you follow in order to prevent the Canadians from obtaining the same advantages as you from the constitution, the intention of His Majesty in dividing the province, as expressed by his prime minister, and that of his parliament, was to give the Canadians a large majority in Lower Canada, in order to relieve them from the tyranny which you would exercise on them. You say that the Canadians use their privileges too freely for a conquered people, and you threaten them with the loss of those privileges. How dare you reproach them for enjoying the privileges which the British Parliament has granted them? Was it not enough to have done all you could, to have made use of lies and calumnies, to prevent them from obtaining these privileges? . . . Ought you not finally to submit to what our sovereign and his parliament have ordained? What difference did they leave between you and the Canadians; from what right dare you derive this odious distinction of conquerors and conquered, when they wished to efface it forever? You ask absurdly whether the Canadians have the right to exercise these privileges in their own language. In what other tongue could they exercise them? Did not the parliament of Great Britain know what their language was?[44]

On January 31, 1807, *Le Canadien* deplored the alliance between the placemen and the English members of the assembly, which divided the legislature according to origin, and gave the English faction, which regarded itself as a privileged class to which all offices should be reserved, the appearance of 'being more concerned with conserving its advantageous position than with the interests of the inhabitants of the country.'[45] Such pronouncements seemed to be deplorably tainted with a Jacobin spirit to Attorney-General Jonathan Sewell, who rejoiced in an annual stipend of $12,688, or to the governor's secretary Ryland, who drew $5,000 from four offices. They were no less objectionable to Bishop Mountain, Receiver-General Henry Caldwell, Judges Alcock and Monk, and such pillars of the English party in the assembly as Richardson and Young.

This party of placemen and merchants—most of them up to their ears in speculation in the public lands, which were granted with amazing liberality to the Chateau Clique and its friends—was cheered by the appointment of Sir James Craig as governor in October 1807. Craig was a professional soldier whose ideas of colonial government were thoroughly eighteenth century in character, and who was singularly jealous of the royal prerogative, which he saw endangered by an independent-minded assembly. Shortly after his arrival, Craig reported to London that 'The disposition of mind seems to be excellent in all parts of the province.'[46] Such was not long to be his conviction.

In 1808 the assembly declared Ezekiel Hart, a Jewish merchant of Trois-Rivières, ineligible to sit or vote with it on religious grounds, while the English faction strongly dissented from this attack on one of their economic class. The assembly also raised the question of banning judges from its midst, in an attack on Judge DeBonne, who had gradually become a partisan of the placemen, and during the previous year had opposed with extreme vigor an attempt of the French party to introduce allowances for members of the assembly. He had also founded a middle-of-the road French paper, the second *Courier de Québec*, whose moderation under the editorship of Jacques Labrie had brought down upon it the thunders of *Le Canadien*. The bill declaring judges ineligible was passed by the assembly, but was promply rejected by the legislative council. The elections of 1808 were marked by the violent attacks of *Le Canadien* on the placemen, on the abuse of the royal prerogative, and on DeBonne, the leader of the '*Chouayens*.' Craig was moved by his advisers to cancel the militia commissions of the proprietors, on the grounds that he could have no confidence in the publishers of 'a seditious and libellous publication, that is actively disseminated through the province with great industry, and which is expressly calculated to vilify His Majesty's government, and to create a spirit of dissatisfaction and discontent among his subjects, as well as of disunion and animosity between the two parts of which they are composed.'[47]

War was now openly declared between the executive and the assembly, with Craig using his power of dissolution to counter French-Canadian obstructive tactics. Craig promptly prorogued the legislature in May 1809, when it again insisted upon expelling Ezekiel Hart, who had been re-elected, and the judges. But the elections of that fall returned much the same men to the assembly, and when the session opened in January 1810, a bill declaring judges ineligible was again quickly passed. The assembly also proposed to pay all the civil expenses of the government, thus attempting to weaken the control of the executive, and introducing a question which was to provide decades of discord. When the legislative council adopted the judicial ineligibility bill with an amendment protecting Judge DeBonne for the duration of the parliament, the assembly voted a resolution barring him. This was beyond its powers, and Craig promptly dissolved parliament the following day.

On March 17, a few days later, he seized the press of *Le Canadien* and jailed its printer; he filled the streets of Quebec with armed patrols; and he suspended the mail service. On March 19 he arrested Bédard, Blanchet, and Taschereau and jailed them without trial; while he followed these arbitrary acts with a curious proclamation in which he violently denounced these 'sowers of sedition' and querulously protested his innocence of any oppressive intentions.[48] The people were unmoved by protestations of good will accompanied by acts of tyranny; and in the elections which followed they re-elected the opponents of the placemen, including the prisoners Bédard and Blanchet. Upon this failure of his policy, Craig sent his secretary Ryland to London to discover how far the imperial government would back him in what promised to be an epic struggle with an unruly legislature. After his first arbitrary dissolution of the assembly, he had been warned by Castlereagh, the colonial secretary, to 'avoid any Expression which can be construed as touching in any degree upon their supposed Privileges and the general Freedom of Inquiry and Debate.'[49]

With Ryland to London went a long dispatch, in which Craig poured out all his woes to Liverpool, Castlereagh's successor, who encouraged him to get along without an assembly, drawing on the British Treasury for expenses. This document of May 1, 1810 affords a good picture of Canada at the outset of the agitation for responsible government, provided that Craig's prejudices are discounted. It was based upon a memorandum[50] prepared by the Loyalist Chief Justice Sewell, which postulated the eternal antipathy of French and English; the necessity of anglicizing the province if it were to remain British; a recourse to massive American immigration to swamp the French Canadians; the establishment of high property restrictions upon the franchise, to prevent French dominance in the assembly; the union of Upper and Lower Canada for more prompt and certain anglicization; and nomination of the *curés* by the Crown, in order to destroy the power of the Church. In short, Sewell called for a complete repudiation of the policy of 1791 and a return to that of 1763.

Craig began his dispatch[51] by insisting upon the fact that Canada was a conquered country, of whose total population of 250,000 only 20,000 were English or American. In his view the remainder were French: 'I use the term designedly, My Lord, because I mean to say that they are in Language, in Religion, in manner and in attachment completely French—bound to us by no one tie, but that of a Common Government, and on the contrary viewing us with sentiments of mistrust and jealousy, with envy, and I believe I should not go too far, were I to say with hatred.' Under the tensions of the Napoleonic Wars, Craig here expressed a view which has been echoed down to the present with less excuse by English-speaking people unable to differentiate between Frenchman and French Canadian, and which reflects the same xenophobia of which they accuse the French Canadian. Craig amplified his views on this basic point:

. . . the line of distinction between us is completely drawn. Friendship (and) Cordiality are not to be found—even common intercourse scarcely exists—the lower class of people, to strengthen a term of contempt, add *Anglois*—and the better sort, with whom there formerly did exist some interchange of the common civilities of Society, have of late entirely withdrawn themselves—the alleged reason is that their circumstances have gradually declined in proportion as ours have increased in affluence; this may have had some effect, but the observation has been made also, that this abstraction has taken place exactly in proportion as the power of the French in England (Europe?) has become more firmly established.

This division along ethnic lines into 'haves' and 'have-nots,' which lasted for nearly a century, arose largely from the fact that the commercial-minded English had the governmental influence and the access to British capital which enabled them to exploit the Canadian commercial revolution, which began with the Peace of 1783 and the coming of the Loyalists, and had reached its halfway mark by 1810. The products of farm and forest had become the major staples as the fur trade declined, and this new trade was largely in English hands. Napoleon's Continental Blockade of 1807, which cut Britain off from Baltic timber, was largely responsible for the revival of a commercial imperialism which flooded Canada with British capital. Canada suddenly was linked with the industrial civilization of Britain. The number of ships clearing from Quebec tripled between 1807 and 1810, with every branch of the timber and lumber trade showing a similar expansion. The French Canadians, long largely ousted from the management of the fur trade, had fallen back on the professions, petty trades, agriculture, and unskilled labor. The professional men and tradesmen were not commercial-minded. The *habitants* were deeply traditional; they practiced subsistance rather than commercial farming. Their insistance upon an outmoded feudalism and their economic self-sufficiency were matters of equal irritation to the commercial-minded Englishman. *Le Canadien* spoke for the French Canadians as a people, with a few rare exceptions, when in 1808 it deplored the new commercialism and characterized a mercantile aristocracy as 'equally prejudicial to the authority of the Crown, to the interests of landowners, and to the liberties of the people.'[52]

Craig, under the influence of Bishop Mountain like his predecessor Milnes, was distressed by the position of the Catholic Church and the influence of its clergy:

The Bishop, tho' unknown to our Constitution and confirmed, if not appointed by a Foreign Power, has been suffered to exercise every Jurisdiction incident to the episcopal functions; he nominates to all the benefices of the Province, and removes at his pleasure from one living to another . . . His Patronage is at least equal to that of the Government, & it is so perfectly at his pleasure, that Government has no other notice of it, than that he usually once a year delivers to the Governor a list of such changes as have taken place during the preceding twelve months. . . . In truth the Catholic Bishop tho' unacknowledged as such, exercises now a much greater degree of authority than he did in the time of the French Government, because he has arrogated to himself every power which was then possessed by the Crown . . .

With the Curés themselves, no direct communication from the Government exists in any shape; a numerous and powerful body, dispersed in every corner of the Country, and certainly possessing a very considerable weight and influence with the people, scarcely know, and are hardly known to the Government. . . .

Craig found, in the face of abundant evidence to the contrary, that the clergy's 'attachment to France is equally undoubted, and it is now even supposed to be not a little directed to the Person of Bonaparte, who since the concordat, is considered among them as the Restorer of the Roman Catholic Religion.' The source of this curious conviction may be surmised when Craig praises the legislative council in the next sentence as 'composed of everything that is respectable in the Province' and 'animated by the best intentions towards His Majesty's Service & the public good.' The respectable members of the legislative council were then engaged in loading themselves with a plurality of offices, in dividing the public lands among themselves, and in withholding from the British Treasury the royal revenue. But at least they were not French, and hence suspect of Bonapartist sentiments; and so they found favor in Craig's eyes.

Representative government was not at all to Craig's absolutist taste, especially when 'To a People circumstanced as I have described these to be, ignorant and credulous in the extreme, having no one common tie of affection or union, viewing us with Jealousy, mistrust and hatred, having separate & distinct Interests, it has been thought proper to give a share in the Government of the Country, by a House of Representatives in which they must ever have the Majority.' Craig railed against the absence of a property qualification for members, and he blamed their unruly behavior on ignorance rather than malevolence:

. . . at present they are completely in the hands of the party which leads the House, Debate is out of the question, they do not understand it, they openly avow that the matter has been explained to them the night before by such & such persons, and they invariably vote accordingly. It is in this manner, at their nightly meetings which are held for the purpose, that every question is previously decided, and it is impossible that these people can ever be set right, for those who judge right never meet them outside of the House; they do not associate with them.

In such a House, certainly 'the most independent Assembly that exists in any known Government in the world,' the governor could have no influence, even that arising from personal intercourse, for 'I can have none with Blacksmiths, Millers, & Shopkeepers; even the Avocats & Notaries, who compose so considerable a portion of the House, are generally speaking such as I can nowhere meet.'

It was clear to Craig's suspicious mind that this 'set of unprincipled Avocats and Notaries . . . having everything to gain and nothing to lose by any change that they can bring about,' had been encouraged by the revival of France under Napoleon, and were 'using every endeavour to pave the way for a change of Dominion and a Return under that Government.' Indeed, such was the general conviction 'of all ranks with whom it is possible to converse on the Subject.' In his own opinion, 'the great Mass of the people are completely infected,' and he reported that the leaders of the popular party 'publickly declare that no officer of the Crown is to be trusted, or to be Elected into the House. These, together with all English in general, and their own Seigneurs, are entirely proscribed.' *Le Canadien*, whose purpose was defined as 'to vilify and degrade the officers of Government under the title of *Gens en place*, and to bring into contempt His Majesty's Government itself,' linked leaders and people; and 'Every topick that is calculated to mislead & inflame the people has at times occupied the pages of this paper.' In view of the fact that 'no circumstance whatever has occurred to awaken their attachment to their Mother Country, nor have any pains ever been taken to produce such a change, their habits, language and religion have remained as distinct from ours as they were before the Conquest. Indeed it seems to be a favorite object with them to be considered as (a) separate Nation; *La Nation canadienne* is their constant expression, and with regard to their having been hitherto quiet & faithful subjects, it need only be observed that no opportunity has presented them an encouragement to shew themselves otherwise.'

Craig judged that the public welfare and general prosperity would never be promoted by the assembly: 'Religious prejudices, Jealousy, and extreme ignorance all forbid the expectation, and these, I am afraid, must prevail among the Canadian part of it for a long period to come.' As an example he cited the fact that the Canadians were 'loud in their Clamours' against the introduction of American settlers into the Eastern Townships, 'as having a tendency, which of all others they are most anxious to assert, to impede the complete Establishment of a Canadian Nation.'

Judging the situation thus, Craig proposed nothing less than the revocation of the Constitution of 1791, since 'that Spirit of independence, that total insubordination among them, that freedom of conversation by which they communicate their Ideas of Government as they imbibe them from their Leaders, all of which have increased wonderfully within these last five or Six years, owe their origin entirely to the House of Assembly, and to the intrigues incident to Elections.' As an alternative to this admittedly delicate and difficult measure, Craig suggested 'the Reunion of the Two Provinces, so as to Balance the Canadian Party in the House,' though he was 'more inclined to keep the Province of Upper Canada as a foreign and distinct population, which may be produced as a resource against that of this Country in case of necessity.' This latter policy of playing one ethnic group against the other has survived until the present as one of the basic principles of Canadian politics, both federal and provincial. As another alternative, Craig proposed a new division of the province, giving more representation to the Eastern Townships and thus offsetting the French Canadians.

But whatever measure should be favored by London, if the assembly were to be continued, the qualifications for membership must be raised, since 'it really, My Lord, appears to me an absurdity that the Interests of certainly not an unimportant Colony, involving in them those also of no inconsiderable portion of the Commercial concerns of the British Empire, should be in the hands of six petty shopkeepers, a Blacksmith, a Miller, and fifteen ignorant peasants who form part of our present House; a Doctor or Apothecary, twelve Canadian Avocats and Notaries, and four so far respectable people that at least they do not keep shops, together with ten English members, compleat the list; there is not one person coming under the description of a Canadian Gentleman among them.'

Having thus scornfully dismissed the fathers of Canadian self-government with typical Tory arrogance, Craig turned again to the question of the Catholic bishop. Since 'the Person who at present exercises the episcopal functions is not, I think, of a turbulent disposition, but he is a Man of great ambitions and some art,' Craig proposed that Bishop Plessis be bribed into submitting to nomination of the *curés* by the Crown, which would give the government 'not only the most extensive' but also 'the most powerful and useful influence.' He also proposed that the Crown should take over the Sulpician Estates, since 'the Majority of the present Members of the Institution are French emigrant Priests, and are not among the least dangerous persons in the Colony; the Person at the head of it is particularly of that description, a very able, but a very artful, designing Man, whose prediliction for France is not doubted.' He suggested that the Sulpicians should be left two-fifths of the revenue of their estates, and the Seminary of Quebec should be assured of its property; 'the two together form an ample provision for the Education of their Youth.'

These drastic proposals were backed by Herman Ryland's ardent advocacy in London, but the British government found it inex-

Morin College, Quebec

The old Prison of Quebec, built in 1808 after the plans of François Baillairgé, the greatest of the builders who combined the French and British traditions at this period. The building subsequently was converted for the use of Morin College, an English institution affiliated with McGill, and now houses the Quebec Literary and Historical Society. (I.O.A.P.Q.)

Masson House, Terrebonne

The Manor House of the Seigneurs of Terrebonne, built in 1848 in the English style from the profits of the fur trade by one of the few French-Canadian families which prospered under the new commercial system introduced after the Conquest. (National Gallery.)

pedient to launch a discussion of Lower Canadian affairs in parliament at that time. The question of the revocation or alteration of the Constitution of 1791 was thus put aside entirely, and the ministers delayed their opinion on the matters of the nomination of the *curés*, the disposition of the Jesuit and Sulpician Estates, and on the settlement of the Crown lands. The growing prospect of war with the United States discouraged the adoption of any measures which might arouse unrest in Canada; and once again the French Canadians won concessions affecting their survival from the British government, lest Canada should join the lost American colonies.

For London not only put aside Craig's recommendations, but also rejected the pretensions of the Anglican Bishop of Quebec. Bishop Mountain saw realized his fears of 1803 that 'unless some immediate and effectual remedy be applied to the abuses which have been gradually introduced . . . the Roman Catholic Church will be to all intents and purposes the established Religion of the Country; rapidly declining, as it should seem, in other parts of the world it will not only find here a safe asylum, but be raised to the preeminence and laid upon the broadest and most substantial Bases.' The early maneuvers of Bishop Mountain had been frowned on by the Colonial Secretary in 1804, when the latter advised the governor to discourage all differences between the two bishops.[53] The petition of Bishop Denaut for civil recognition of his office—made in 1805 at Attorney-General Sewell's instigation—likewise remained without response from London. Bishop Mountain, Sewell, and Ryland then joined forces to put the Catholic Church under the power of the Crown. Ryland's views on the Catholic clergy are clearly expressed in a letter of December 23, 1804:

> I call them 'Popish' to distinguish them from the Clergy of the Established Church, and to express my contempt and detestation of a religion which sinks and debases the human mind, and which is a curse to every country where it prevails. This being my opinion, I have long since laid it down as a principle, which, in my judgment, no Governor of this Province ought to lose sight of for a moment, that by every possible means which prudence can suggest gradually to undermine the authority and influence of the Roman Catholic Priests. This great, this highest object that a Governor can here have, might have been accomplished (I am confident) before now, and may by judicious management be accomplished before ten years more shall have passed over. . . . We have been mad enough to allow a company of French rascals to deprive us for the moment of the means to accomplish this [i.e., establishment of the royal supremacy, abolition of papal authority, and the Protestantizing of Canada].[54]

In 1807 Bishop Mountain went to London to press the Anglican case, and there Ryland wrote him, complaining of the promptness with which the administrator of the colony had received Bishop Plessis as the successor of Bishop Denaut, and had agreed to the nomination of Bishop Panet as coadjutor. The last had the misfortune to be the brother of the speaker of the assembly, who was in ill odor with Ryland and the Chateau Clique.

The appointment of Sir James Craig as governor strengthened the hand of Bishop Mountain, Sewell, and Ryland, for they found in him a man who shared their objections to the Catholic Church. Bishop Plessis suspected the danger which might arise when Ryland went to London in 1810 with Craig's report, for he wrote to Adam Lymburner, now retired to London:

> I should not be at all surprised if this occasion were used to calumny the clergy in the minds of the ministers. The revenues which our *curés* enjoy, the authority of the Catholic Bishop over them and the people, are long since the objects of jealousy. But I put all my hope in the Providence of the God I serve, and try to have served by my people, by inspiring them with the sentiments with which they should be permeated as Christians and as subjects.[55]

Somewhat unwisely at this crucial period, Bishop Plessis issued on October 25, 1810 a proclamation calling for public prayers for the Pope, in which he signed himself 'Bishop of Quebec by grace of the Holy Apostolic See.'[56] Ryland waved a copy of this document under the ministers' eyes in London, and called for criminal prosecution of the bishop for acknowledging a foreign jurisdiction in a British colony.[57]

After long delays the law officers of the Crown, to whom the proposals respecting the Church had been referred, finally reported that the King had the right of nomination of the *curés* and that the Sulpicians had no valid title to their estates. But they added that these matters had been so long neglected that rights of possession, difficult to upset, had arisen; and they entirely ignored the question of Bishop Plessis' proclamation. In December 1811, when the colonial secretary was about to send instructions to Craig covering the nomination of the *curés* and the disposition of the Sulpician Estates in accordance with the governor's views, the Lord Chancellor intervened, and Ryland went home disgruntled and empty-handed. Lord Chancellor Eldon was supported by Sir Robert Peel and Lord Castlereagh, the last of whom had, as colonial secretary some years before, thus dismissed Bishop Mountain's pretensions:

> The Canada Act assures to the Catholics of Canada the free exercise of their religion, and to their clergy the right to receive the tithes paid by those who belong to this faith, saving the supremacy of His Majesty as established by the Act of Supremacy. The Supremacy of the King, according to this act, is limited to preventing strangers from exercising

any spiritual jurisdiction in the possessions of the Crown. But the bishop of Quebec is not a stranger; he is chief of a religion which can be freely practiced by grace of the imperial parliament; he can claim and receive from Catholics the tithes and ordinary dues, and exercise upon them the rights which he had always enjoyed. It would be a very delicate business to intervene in the affairs of the Catholic religion at Quebec, or to force the titular bishop to abandon his titles and to act not as bishop, but only as superintendant.[58]

Sir James Craig's last effort as governor, in the spring of 1811, was an attempt to force Bishop Plessis to submit to his notion of the royal prerogative. Bishop Plessis has left an interesting account of the three interviews in which the governor tried without success by every means from threats to bribes to win the bishop to his way of thinking.[59] Then, thanks to the outstanding loyalty of the clergy in the War of 1812, the British government sent orders to the new governor, Sir George Prevost, that 'the salary of the Catholic Bishop of Quebec shall henceforth be increased to the sum recommended by you of £1,000 per annum, as a testimony to the sense which His Royal Highness entertains of the loyalty and good conduct of the gentleman who now fills that station and of the other Catholic clergy of the Province.'[60] Ryland, as secretary of the executive council, had to write with his own pen the words 'Catholic Bishop of Quebec,' after he had vainly tried to substitute 'superintendent of the Roman Church' for the phrase which the colonial secretary had used in his dispatch. The affirmation of the royal supremacy in the matter of the bishopric became a dead letter, and Bishop Plessis was justified in saying that a great danger had been averted and that the religious liberty of the French Canadians had been newly assured for the future.

4

Craig's 'Reign of Terror,' as French-Canadian historians call it, has tended to obscure the very important economic developments of the epoch, which underlaid the constitutional conflict between the Chateau Clique and the representatives of the people. The surrender to the United States in 1796 of most of the western trading posts marked the beginning of the decline of the Montreal fur trade; and the cannier merchants had already begun to turn their attention to new fields. The fur trade had been based upon a nomadic civilization, and was the enemy of colonization; the new economy was agricultural and based upon land ownership. Soon after the Loyalists settled along the Upper St. Lawrence, the Montreal merchants began dealing in wheat and flour from that region, as well as from the Richelieu Valley, and acting as middlemen for their Upper Canadian brethren in the London trade. They also took a hand in the growing commerce in American products, which were brought down the Richelieu from Lake Champlain and exported to England under colonial preference. The British fur traders, like their French predecessors, were finally conquered by the land, and acquired property in the neighbourhood of Montreal from the declining *seigneurs*. In many cases they established small industries on these seigneuries, flour and saw mills, potteries, and organized domestic industries, such as the production at L'Assomption of *ceintures flechées* or woven-worsted sashes for the North-West Company and later the Hudson's Bay Company. After the Crown Lands Proclamation of 1792[61] the British merchants began to indulge in land speculation on a considerable scale.

This land speculation centered in the vast empty expanses of the Eastern Townships, which first had been left unsettled as a barrier to American aggression, and then reserved by Haldimand for colonization by the French Canadians, whose difference in blood, language, and religion might be counted upon to act as a check to American expansion. But geography was not to be denied in this region, which is a natural extension of Vermont and New Hampshire; and immigrants from New England began to settle there, drawn by the richness of the land. At first this movement of squatters was frowned upon by the authorities; but when both French and English Canadians alike refused to take up land in the Townships, 'the most unlimited encouragement'[62] was given to Americans. The French were loath to leave their familiar world of the St. Lawrence for this remote region of vast virgin hardwood forests with a system of tenure new to them, and most of the English were more interested in trade or in office-holding than in the back-breaking work of pioneering.

As conflict between the English minority and the French majority in the new assembly developed, the coming of Americans to swell the numbers of the former was welcomed by the Chateau Clique, who were also interested in finding purchasers for the land grants which were one of their chief perquisites of office. Officially, grants were limited to 1,200 acres for a single individual, with 200 acres the normal amount; but these regulations were evaded by the speculators, who made use of many names to conceal their holdings. In 1795 one single partnership, composed of Sir John Johnson's son-in-law, Patrick Langan; the Postmaster-General Hugh Finlay; Captain David Alexander Grant, who had married the *seigneuresse* of Longueuil; and John Jacob Astor of New York, planned to take out grants on no less than 2,000,000 acres—twenty-four whole townships.[63] To obtain the number of names of 'intending settlers' required by law, advertisements offering 200 acres to anyone who could produce a certificate declaring himself to be 'an honest, industrious Person, and peaceable Inhabitant' were placed in the American newspapers.[64] The northward movement of New Englanders, some Loyalist in sympathies and more merely hungry for new land, began immediately after the Proclamation of 1792; in five years some 2,000 settlers came into the Townships; and by 1805 the population there numbered more than 5,000, mostly Americans. The fertile lands of the numerous well-watered valleys were soon cleared and put under cultivation by a people accustomed to pioneering in similar country; land values rose; roads were built; and the first coach route from Quebec to Boston was established in 1811, through what had been an almost impenetrable forest barrier between the province and New England only a few years before.

The newcomers demanded representation, and found the officials at Quebec well disposed to their plea. Craig was inclined to favor them as a counterweight to the French Canadians. Then, too, the governor was surrounded by Loyalist officials who had begun life in the American colonies and had a natural sympathy for the newcomers. It was the Massachusetts-born Chief Justice Sewell who produced the memorandum upon which Craig based his conclusions on the matter. The grounds for encouraging the American settlers and increasing their numbers with a view to swamping the French were thus stated by Sewell: the newcomers were 'of English stock, professing the same religion, speaking the same language, and would therefore be more easily assimilated and would become better subjects than those which we now possess.'[65] Quite naturally, this officially-encouraged immigration of foreigners into French Canada did nothing to check the growth of ethnic feeling among the old inhabitants of the province. *Le Canadien* thundered against the introduction of 'a half-savage people, whose forrays are as much to be feared in Canada as those made formerly by the Goths and Vandals into Italy,' while D.-B. Viger asked whether it was good policy for Britain to make 'an American province' out of Canada.[66]

But to the minds of the official class and of the merchants, panicky about French plots, irritated by their conflict with the French-Canadian majority in the assembly, and eager to profit by land speculation, an American Canada was better than a French one. The basic motive of the Chateau Clique in this instance was not hatred of the French but self-interest; the editor of the *Quebec Mercury* remarked: 'I have no particular personal friendship for the American; still less have I any enmity to the Canadian; but I must be permitted to have an anxious wish to see so large a portion of the British dominions in a superior state to wilderness.'[67] Another factor was also involved, as was indicated by an anonymous pamphleteer who railed against the failure of the French to exploit the resources of the country:

The population of this Province forms a small compact body inert in its nature, without one principle of percussion; and exhibiting its infant face, surcharged with all the indications of old age and decay. During a lapse of two centuries, little more than the borders of the St. Lawrence have been put under cultivation; in a few places only, have settlements slumbered forth, on the minor streams, with manifest reluctance and regret.[68]

To British merchants interested in booming trade, French-Canadian conservatism and adherence to an outmoded semi-feudal agricultural way of life were deplorable, in the face of the manifest opportunities of a new commercial and industrial era.

'Jeremy Cockloft, the Elder, M.A., P.C.,' whose *Cursory Observations* is one of the scarcest and most amusing Canadian books, paints a vivid picture of 'this dreary Province of Canada'[69] as seen through English commercial eyes in 1811 at the high tide of the Canadian economic revolution. 'Cockloft' is thought to have been a young Englishman sent out to Quebec in behalf of the London timber merchants. When not complaining about the prevailing dirt, the 'livid squalidness' of countenance, and the 'uncouthness' of dress among the French Canadians, he made some important economic observations. He found a general interest in the price of timber in England, which is not surprising, since timber exports had tripled between 1807 and 1810 and had become the basis of Quebec's prosperity, remaining such until the depression of 1833.[70] In Quebec he met an enterprising Bermudian, 'whose project was to make Bermuda a depot for the produce of both the other colonies' (Canada and the British West Indies), but the flaw in this scheme to him was that the West Indies could often get their provisions more cheaply from the United States, as they did according to Joseph Bouchette.[71] He also talked with Canadian gentlemen, who 'regretted the inert disposition of the 'Habitants, whom they said neither adversity nor prosperity could arouse from the torpid habits of their forefathers; that in general they planted no more now, although every species of provision had risen greatly in price, than they did four years ago when the trade was very trifling.' The go-ahead Englishman was appalled by the easy-going French Canadians: 'Their aversion to labor springs from pure, genuine, unadulterated *indolence*. Give a 'Habitant milk, a few roots, tobacco, wood for his stove, and a bonnet *rouge*, he works no longer;—like the native Savage, who seldom hunts but when driven by hunger.'[72]

'Cockloft' noted that Quebec imported cottons, woolens, hardware, bolt and bar iron, sheet lead, copper, tin, coals, salt, cordage, anchors, cables, sailcloth, mathematical instruments, earthen and glass ware, drugs, etc. from Britain; but that two-thirds of these imports went on to the United States. Quebec also imported rum, sugar, pimento, and coffee from the British West Indies; and codfish and whale oil from Newfoundland. Exports consisted of furs, timber, wheat, flour, oats, pot and pearl ashes, salted beef, pork, butter, hams, soap, lard, candles, and ships for the Britain–West Indies trade, but he observed that Quebec could not supply the West Indies. He found that the Quebec ships were not as well built as European ones, and that they were expensive because of the high cost of labor (double that in Europe); high freights, commissions, and insurance on all ingredients except timber; and the cost of sending out crews from England. With a mercantilist's regret he noted that the Canadians' consumption of imports was 'but trifling in comparison to the extent of their country, the 'Habitants in general manufacturing their own clothes, and in winter substituting skins for woolens. The wants of these people are very few; being perfectly free from any desire of luxury or finery . . . the 'Habitants seldom exert themselves to provide more than their immediate wants require; and if they sometimes get rid of their natural indolence, an exorbitant price is necessary as a stimulus for a continuance of their exertions.'[73]

'Cockloft' exempted the 'higher classes' from his general indictment of the *habitant*, but commented: 'In whatever place a paucity of natural enjoyment prevails, the mind of man is apt to descend to vulgar and idle, not to say criminal pleasure. This unfortunately is the case in Quebec. The liberal arts either have been frozen in some severe winter, have deserted to a more congenial clime, or perhaps have never visited the place.' The theater was encouraged chiefly by transients, while the two weekly newspapers seemed 'very weakly productions.' Instead of 'Newspaper animadversions, private gossips furnish an ample fund of anecdote and scandal, which circulates like the miasma of pestilence; and characters are stabbed in the dark, unconscious where the blow is derived, or by whom directed.' He briskly summed up the amusements of Quebec as 'gaming, scandal, licentiousness and drinking.'[74]

The insular 'Cockloft' was shocked to find that 'all the boys in Quebec speak English like Frenchmen, and indeed seldom speak it at all, when the French language will answer their purpose.' He noted an 'inveterate prejudice of the 'Habitants against the British.' He regretted that the Canadians had received 'the freedom of the British Constitution; which they did not at the time and I fear never will appreciate or rightly understand.'[75] Though most Englishmen of the trading class were strong mercantilist imperialists at this time, 'Cockloft' took a view more typical of the English Reformers after 1829:

Upon the whole, I think it very questionable, whether the Provinces of Canada are worth the expense of retaining under the British flag, even politically considered. The 'Habitants have certainly a strong predilection for the French, of which the universality of that language throughout the country must be admitted as a very presumptive proof,—more especially as it supersedes the English tongue in their legislature and courts of law, as well as in their private dealings with one another. The American people appear to have a great desire to possess the Canadas; and I really think the cession of the territory to them (especially if well paid for, as was the case with Louisiana) would be of great benefit to Great Britain, and an endless source of miseries and calamities to the Fredonians. . . .[76]

It is clear that 'Cockloft' remained too much of a traditional British imperialist to appreciate the workings of the new American economic imperialism which had already begun to invade Canada, regardless of sovereignty.

A new stage of the ancient rivalry of the St. Lawrence and Hudson trading systems had opened, and the American economy was beginning to push its Canadian rival to the wall. The old Canadian monopoly of the fur trade was broken forever when John Jacob Astor forced John Richardson and William McGillivray of Montreal into partnership with him in January 1811, and left only the Canadian North-West open to British traders. A flood of American manufactures was flowing into Canada under Jay's Treaty, as well as the timber for which the Continental Blockade had created such a demand in Great Britain. The Montreal and Quebec merchants benefited by the passage of American timber down the Richelieu and the St. Lawrence, but they found their monopoly of imported manufactured goods badly threatened. The American Embargo Act of 1807 could not stop the development of a north–south trade; the subsequent contraband traffic across a border which had become largely a legal fiction amounted to more than the previous legal trade.[77]

Hampered at home by the French majority's reluctance to protect commerce, the merchants sought relief in London by forming in 1809 the Committee of British North American Merchants, which served as a lobby at the seat of government for the commercial classes of Montreal and Quebec. In 1812 this body won the grant of imperial protection against the importation of commodities not the growth or manufacture of the United States, while American tariffs were to be adopted on American imports except in the case of natural products, from which the Canadian merchants benefited.[78] The War of 1812 gave the Canadian merchants some cheer, for it suggested the possibility of regaining the lost hinterland, and with it monopoly of the fur trade. Thus the traders and the Indians united to oppose the westward American movement and the settlement which followed in its wake, dooming the old economy.

5

Despite all the glorification by national historians of the French-Canadian part in the War of 1812, it was really a maritime and western war in which Quebec played little part. Though Joseph Bouchette, son of Carleton's guide in 1775, makes much of the 'insatiable desire for gain'[79] of the Americans—some of whom, like Massachusetts-born Philemon Wright, the founder of the Ottawa lumber trade, were displaying a most un-Canadian activity and industry—and Yankee designs on Quebec figure in many other French-Canadian accounts of the conflict,[80] it was really the American South and West that forced the war, and their interest in attacking Canada was a blow at Britain, not annexation. The Anglo-American maritime difficulties and the long delay in turning over the western posts, with consequent conflict between British traders and the Indians they controlled and the Americans, had irritated the swelling national pride of the United States, which was in a few more years to burst out in the eagle-screaming doctrine of Manifest Destiny. Federalist New England, however, was opposed to what it regarded as a republican war designed to aid Napoleon, and even threatened secession because of it. The nine thousand transplanted New Englanders of the Eastern Townships supplied six battalions to the British army in Canada, and Vermont and New York provided two-thirds of that army's supplies.[81]

The annexation of Quebec no longer figured in Yankee thinking: the economic relations between New England and its northern neighbour had become so close and so profitable that an American could write: 'we would regret much (between ourselves) that Quebec should not remain in possession of the English. They charge us no Duties upon Exports down the River, and our produce being shipped from Canada as the products of a British Colony, we obtain the Bounty or Discriminating Duties.'[82] Again, in 1808 the Governor of Vermont assured John Henry, the double renegade then serving as a secret agent of Craig, that in case of war his state would adopt a neutral attitude towards Canada. Although Henry's disclosure to President Madison of British designs, after he was repudiated by Craig, played some part in increasing war-mindedness in New England, this attitude of neutrality was the one followed in fact during the war by the states bordering upon Quebec.

As war came closer, French agents were active in trying to arouse French-Canadian unrest after Craig's 'Reign of Terror'; but their efforts were doomed to failure by the mild and conciliating conduct of his successor, Sir George Prevost, another Swiss professional soldier with the customary talent for handling French-Canadian sensibilities. The proposed alliance of Napoleonic France with the United States against Britain enlisted no sympathy in a Quebec which was now opposed to 'the enterprises of any power whatsoever in Canada.'[83] *Le Canadien* refered to Napoleon as the 'lawless leader of France'[84] and Quebec City had been illuminated in honor of Nelson's victory at Trafalgar; there was little left of the old bond between French Canada and France. The French Canadians had been irritated by American immigration into the Townships and injured in their pride by Jefferson's reference to the proposed invasion of Canada as a 'mere matter of marching.'[85]

When Vicar-General Deschenaux, in Bishop Plessis' absence, issued a circular letter calling the people to the defence of the country and of 'our good government' in the name of interest, gratitude, and religion,[86] the French Canadians embraced the British cause with singular unanimity. The assembly cheerfully voted $928,000 for military and civil purposes, and authorized the emission of paper currency for war purposes. It also passed a new militia law, under which 6,000 men were raised without difficulty. In April 1812, before the outbreak of the war, Lieutenant-Colonel Charles Michel de Salaberry, a Canadian who under the patronage of the Duke of Kent had seen long service in the British Army in many quarters of the world, recruited the first French-Canadian regiment of regulars, the *Voltigeurs Canadiens*. The ranks were filled in a few days.

Most of the War of 1812 was fought in Upper Canada, and with the exception of the part played by the French-Canadian *voyageurs* and *engagés* of the fur trade in the battles about the posts on the Great Lakes, Quebec had little opportunity to translate its loyalty and willingness to fight into action. As far as Quebec was concerned, there were only three campaigns. In 1812 Dearborn advanced on Montreal from Plattsburg. He halted at the border when warlike enthusiasm waned among his militiamen, and returned to his base with his homesick army after an utterly bloodless campaign of four days. On October 26 of the following year Hampton marched within fifteen miles of the St. Lawrence with a force of 4,000 men, but a night attack at Chateauguay by 800 Canadians, including De Salaberry's *Voltigeurs*, was enough to make him renounce the conquest of Canada. In 1814 Prevost's advance against Plattsburg, with 7,000 veterans of Wellington's campaigns, collapsed when his fleet was destroyed by Macdonough on Lake Champlain on September 11. One wonders where the ardent loyalist Bouchette found the 'depraved ferocity'[87] of which he accuses the Americans. But some verbal violence must be permitted to a fire-eater frustrated by the quite evident desire of the New England states to prevent war from interfering with business, and by Prevost's equal willingness to accept the situation. Despite recent disputes along the Vermont–New York frontier, so much in doubt that in 1818 it was found that the American fort at Rouse's Point had been built well within Canadian territory, no British move was made east of Lake Champlain.

The bellicose merchants of Montreal, who were constantly exhorting the government to greater effort, and whose traders, *engagés*, and the Indians they influenced made useful allies to the redcoats, did much to account for British successes in the West. Much of the old fur-trading empire was regained during the war, but once more British diplomacy, despite the merchants' insistence upon a new western boundary and the creation of an Indian barrier state, sacrificed the wartime gains in the Treaty of Ghent (1815). Astor's growing dominance in the fur trade was reinforced, while the Montreal traders found their last resource in the North-West threatened by Lord Selkirk's settlements after 1812 in the Red River country and by the expansion of the Hudson's Bay Company, which absorbed the North-West Company in 1821.

The War of 1812 weakened the British loyalty of the English in Quebec, while the French Canadians demonstrated much greater loyalty than they had shown in 1775. A new Canadian loyalty was beginning to spring up among both groups, who had fought together to repel invasion and whose doubts about the other had been dispelled by common effort. This new Canadianism was to be demonstrated in the years to come by a collaboration of members of both ethnic groups in favor of Canadian self-government and against British misrule.

6

This new spirit did not end the quarrels between the assembly and the executive; it merely altered the alignment of forces. Despite the mild and conciliatory attitude of the new governor, the assembly showed no disposition to forget its past grievances or to alter its intransigent attitude. Sir George Prevost had taken office when Britain, hard pressed on the Continent, was quite willing to make concessions to assure Canadian loyalty in the face of an American war. After a first examination of the situation, he had been struck by the prestige of the clergy in Quebec, and by his predecessor's error in alienating its support. It was at Prevost's request that Bishop Plessis prepared a memorial on the position of the Catholic bishop which served as the basis of the British government's grant of official recognition and support.[88] Prevost also attempted to conciliate the popular party by restoring to Pierre Bédard and Joseph Borgia the militia commissions which Craig had withdrawn as a penalty for their share in the publication of *Le Canadien.* A few months later he elevated Bédard to the bench. The francophobe Ryland was dismissed from his post as secretary to the governor; the executive council was given seven new members, of whom four were French Canadians; and several French Canadians were added to the legislative council.

Despite these conciliatory overtures, the assembly could not forget its past grievances. Though it gave the governor's war measures the fullest support in 1812, nevertheless it had formed a committee, composed of Bédard, Viger, Lee, Joseph Papineau, and his son Louis-Joseph Papineau among others, to enquire into the state of the province, the events of Craig's administration, and their causes. Nothing came of this move, which nonetheless indicated the unwillingness of the assembly to let bygones be bygones. The popular party also clashed with the legislative council over two wartime security measures, which consequently failed; and in 1813 it refused to grant the extended powers of martial law which the governor had specifically requested.

The most notable action of the assembly was its attempt to impeach its ancient Loyalist enemies, Chief Justice Sewell and his colleague Judge Monk. The instigator of this measure was James Stuart, a Nova Scotian Loyalist, who had been deprived of the attorney-generalship in 1809, as a result of his difficulties with Craig. He had seen Sewell's brother named to replace him, and doubtless personal feeling entered into his attack on the chief justice for his activities as adviser to Craig during the 'Reign of Terror.' Stuart acted as head of the popular party in the assembly, and thus for the first time in Canadian history was seen the spectacle of a man of one ethnic group leading a party dominated by the other. The governor refused to suspend the judges until the assembly's 'Heads of Impeachment,'[89] on which the legislative council had not been consulted and in which they did not concur, had been considered at London. As a result Prevost was promptly accused of violating the constitutional rights of the assembly; and then, after the legislators had had four days to cool off, was given a vote of confidence. The colonial secretary, Bathurst, disapproved the action of the assembly, which involved the new principle of ministerial responsibility in a colonial government, while in 1815 the Privy Council handed down a judgment favorable to Sewell, who had gone to London to plead his case. Meanwhile the assembly's attempt to send Stuart to England to support its charges had been blocked by the refusal of the legislative council to approve a vote of funds for this purpose. The council had also rejected the proposal of the assembly to send Judge Bédard to London to act as agent of the province. The old deadlock between the two houses of the legislature thus continued, despite Prevost's efforts to reconcile them.

This feud resulted in the refusal of the legislative council, despite Prevost's approval, to pass the assembly's bill for the establishment of parish schools under local control. The Royal Institution had remained virtually a dead letter, thanks to the unanimous opposition of the French Canadians, but its supporters in the council were opposed to this encroachment upon its domain. Ryland considered the assembly's bill nothing short of 'a most effectual means for insurrection and revolution.'[90] The council still included Sewell, Bishop Mountain, Monk, Ryland, and others of the old Chateau Clique, who showed little inclination to adapt themselves to the new regime of conciliation. In self-protection the council also rejected the attempts of the assembly to declare judges ineligible to sit in the upper house, and to place a heavy tax on the revenues of civil office and on pensions.

In proroguing the session of 1814, Prevost deplored such domestic strife while the country was at war, but in his dispatches to London he said of the assembly that he had 'no reason to distrust their loyalty or attachment to His Majesty's Person and Government.'[91] Prevost was a realist: he saw that the English party was too weak to serve as a support to the government, and that consequently the goodwill of the Canadians must be gained by taking into account their interests and claims. He believed that one solution of the recent difficulties was to admit Canadians to the offices which had hitherto been reserved to Englishmen: the leaders of the assembly were 'principally lawyers, who as it appears to me are merely seeking an opportunity to distinguish themselves as the Champions of the Public for the purpose of gaining popularity, and who are endeavouring to make themselves of consequence in the eyes of Government, in the hope of obtaining employment from it—some of them held Offices confered upon them by myself and all of them I have reason to think, was it necessary to purchase their Services, would be willing to barter them.'[92]

Unfortunately this governor who knew how to rule with moderation and by a judicious distribution of favors was called home in 1815 to answer charges based upon his exceedingly cautious military conduct during the War of 1812. The Chateau Clique used these charges to undermine Prevost's position in Canada, and he finished his term of office under a cloud which was never wholly cleared, since he died before his case was heard. He was temporarily replaced by the fire-eater Sir Gordon Drummond, who announced the Privy Council's decision in favor of Sewell to the assembly when it met in 1816, and promptly dissolved that body when it protested against the judgment. But the well-worn remedy of dissolution worked no cure of the ills of the body politic; the party of Stuart and his ally Louis-Joseph Papineau was returned in greater force; and when the new governor, Sir John Sherbrooke, arrived in July 1816 to take over from Drummond, he found a full-fledged political crisis raging. The placemen, cheered by Sewell's victory and the recall of Prevost, had celebrated the chief justice's return in triumph with a twenty-gun salute, an incident which had strengthened the popular party's conviction that the government was its enemy.

Sherbrooke, like Prevost, saw that continual dissolutions were no solution of the difficulty, and he was not inclined to follow the course suggested by Bathurst of governing without an assembly, although this was feasible, since the executive was not financially dependent upon that body. He reported to London that Sewell was anathema to all classes of the population and should have been induced to resign. But since the government had decided to reinstate him, a measure which would alienate popular support and prevent any harmonious development of the province, Sherbrooke proposed that the colony be given an agent at London to voice its grievances, and that Stuart be detached from the French party by the gift of office. As time went on Sherbrooke took other conciliatory measures which did much to reduce popular opposition to the executive: he named Bishop Plessis to the legislative council, and proposed that Louis-Joseph Papineau be added to the executive council. It was clear to him that 'the great evil of this country and the one most fruitful of discussions has been the lack of confidence in the executive government, not so far as regards the character of the governor but rather as regards the council, which has come to be considered as his adviser, and whose actions are regarded with a jealous suspicion which tends to hamstring all acts of government.'[93] Sherbrooke's policy was to win the confidence of the French Canadians and to reconcile them to the government by giving them a share in its responsibilities.

But neither Sherbrooke nor any governor until after 1840 was willing to let the prerogative of the Crown yield to the growing power of the assembly. Thus, when goodwill was lacking on the part of the governor and moderation on that of the assembly, the inevitable conflict of the two competing powers became acute. The Constitution of 1791 had established representative government with an irresponsible executive. It had left undefined the respective spheres of the British and provincial parliaments, thus providing two sources of friction between the Crown and the assembly. Then, as the Crown lost its financial independence based upon the Quebec Revenue Act of 1774 and became dependent upon votes of supply, the lines of conflict between the two powers became sharply defined.

7

Such was in brief the basis of the constitutional battles which culminated in rebellion in 1837. After the failure of Receiver-General Henry Caldwell, who in 1819 was found to be £97,000 short in his accounts, the chief issue was whether or not the government should be completely dependent upon the assembly for financial support.

The popular party was led by Louis-Joseph Papineau, son of the Montreal notary who had fought for the use of French in the first assembly in 1792, and who had carried dispatches for Carleton through the American lines in 1775–6. The younger Papineau, born in 1786 and educated at the Seminary of Quebec, became a lawyer after studying in D.-B. Viger's office, but he entered the assembly in 1808 and soon devoted his energies to politics. He early took a leading role, succeeding Panet in 1815 as speaker, a post which he held for the greater part of the next twenty years. Even as a small boy at the seminary he had revealed an oratorical talent which eclipsed that of his father, who was regarded, along with Pierre Bédard, as one of the most eloquent French-Canadian spokesmen of the day. This talent was developed by Papineau's wide reading, as was the natural independence of mind which made him one of the small group of members of the assembly who secretly met in 1812 to consider whether it might not be best to remain neutral in the coming conflict, and to let the British defend themselves from an American invasion. This course having been opposed by Bédard, Papineau cheerfully served as a militia staff captain during the three years of war. After his election as speaker, Papineau took no great part in party politics until 1820, but engaged in a study of history and constitutional law which later stood him in good stead.

The ideas of Papineau at the real beginning of his political career in that year are reflected in his eulogy on the death of George III, in which he compared 'the happy situation in which we find ourselves today with that of our ancestors when George III became their lawful monarch':

> George III, a sovereign respected for his moral qualities and his devotion to his duties, succeeded Louis XV, a prince justly despised for his debauches, for his lack of attention to the needs of the people, and for his senseless prodigality to his favorites and mistresses. Since that epoch the reign of law has succeeded to that of violence; since that day the treasure, the fleet, and the armies of Great Britain have been employed

to provide us with an effective protection against all foreign danger; since that day her best laws have become ours, while our faith, our property, and the laws by which they were governed have been conserved; soon afterwards the privileges of her free constitution were granted us, infallible guarantees of our domestic prosperity if it is observed. Now religious tolerance; trial by jury, the wisest guarantee which has ever been established for the protection of innocence; security against arbitrary imprisonment, thanks to the privilege of the *habeas corpus*; equal protection guaranteed by law to the person, honor, and property of citizens; the right to obey only laws made by us and adopted by our representatives—all these advantages have become our birthright, and will be, I hope, the lasting heritage of our posterity. In order to conserve them, we should act like British subjects and free men.[94]

It was this same insistence upon the rights of British subjects and free men which sent Papineau into exile with a price on his head within twenty years' time. The long battle over the right of the assembly to control the province's finances, a right essential to any real form of self-government and of representative institutions, began a few months after this patriotic utterance, with the coming of the arbitrary Lord Dalhousie, a governor whose name was to become associated in the French-Canadian mind with the hateful memory of Sir James Craig, despite the former's efforts to unite the two ethnic groups by founding the Literary and Historical Society of Quebec in 1824 and by setting up a joint monument to Wolfe and Montcalm at Quebec in 1827.[95]

Meanwhile the insistence of both the Lower and Upper Canadian assemblies on holding the purse-strings, and the quarrel between the two provinces over the division of import duties, seemed to offer to some minds an opportunity to settle both difficulties by a single measure, the reunion of Upper and Lower Canada into a single province—a measure often later revived and finally adopted in 1840. Thus the obstinate French-Canadian majority could be turned into a minority, and the financial difficulties of the young upper province could be assumed by the prosperous older one. This measure was favoured by the British ministers, weary of endless complaints from Canada; by the governing class in the colony, which saw its privileged position threatened by the rising power of the assembly; and by the Montreal merchants, who hoped thus to restore the commercial unity of the St. Lawrence system. They had long advocated the union of the Canadas, but now their pleas took on new force as the threat of the Hudson River system to its ancient rival became more acute with the completion of the Champlain Canal in 1822, which reversed the profitable Richelieu trade, and with the steady progress of the Erie Canal, which threatened to tap the commerce of the Great Lakes at the expense of the St.

Corpus Christi Procession at Quebec, 1821

Oil painting by Louis-Hubert Triand, professor of painting at the Ursuline Convent. This painting, still in the possession of the Quebec Ursulines, shows the Cathedral at the left, the old Jesuit College on the right, and the ancient houses on Buade Street (many of which are still standing) in the center. The spire of the Anglican Cathedral, built after Wren's plans by the Royal Engineers, towers in the background. (I.O.A.P.Q.)

Cathedral and Market Place, Quebec

Cromo-lithograph (1832) by C. Hullmandel after a drawing of W. Walton from a sketch of Robert Sproule. Another view of the same scene from the Jesuit College. (I.O.A.P.Q.)

Nicolet Seminary

Built 1827–32 by Jean-Baptiste Hebert from the plans of the Abbé Jérome Demers. This building, the handsomest example of institutional architecture in the Province, shows a perfect fusing of the French and British traditions. (I.O.A.P.Q.)

Lawrence system. While the growing commercial power of the United States thus threatened them at home, the merchants saw England begin to shift from mercantilism to free trade. The preferential timber duties were reduced in 1822, and the Reformer Huskisson was already well on his way to the presidency of the Board of Trade.

The merchants felt the necessity of immediate planning, revolutionary legislation, and vast public expenditures to enable the St. Lawrence system to survive this double threat; and yet they found themselves at the mercy of a legislature which was anti-commercial and utterly unmoved by their pleas for action. The governor alone was sympathetic to the merchants, for Dalhousie saw that Montreal was the logical center of the new commercial system: 'It is the heart of the country, and from it circulates the lifeblood of Canada.'[96] Yet Quebec remained the administrative center, and as always viewed its rival with suspicion and was jealous of its own power and prestige. The *Montreal Gazette* bitterly protested that 'Quebec affords an example of centralization of Military, Civil, Financial, Clerical, Commercial, and Marine power, worthy of the policy of the late Napoleon Bonaparte.'[97] Thus hampered at home, the merchants turned to London, where they had a friend at court in the person of Edward Ellice, son of one of the great Montreal merchants and son-in-law of Lord Grey, head of the Whig Party. Ellice was at once *seigneur* of Beauharnois near Montreal and a member of the British parliament; his friends were the leaders of the Montreal merchants, Richardson, Grant, and Molson. He brought their views to the ear of the ministers, and all but achieved the union of the Canadas which they so ardently desired.

Ellice's advocacy was supported by Judge Monk and Attorney-General Marshall, who found themselves in London to give advice on the question of customs duties; but the Attorney-General of Upper Canada, John Beverley Robinson, opposed the project of union in a memorandum which checked the growing resolution of the ministers in favor of union. He gave London the first statement of a new Canadianism, which was not dependent upon the ethnic background of its adherents:

> The French habitants of Lower Canada, I am firmly convinced, are as peaceably disposed, as submissive to authority, and as loyally attached to the British government as any portion of His Majesty's subjects; and whatever be the embarrassment that their representatives can cause in refusing to provide in a permanent manner for the civil list, or on the questions of revenues or other matters, whatever they may be, between them and the executive power, it must not be attributed to the preponderance of French influence on the English, but to the desire which all popular assemblies display to affirm and to exercise as much as possible

the segment of power which they believe granted to them by the constitution, and even to extend it, a disposition from which more inconveniences can be expected according to the degree of democracy of such a body. And I believe that the descendants of Englishmen, Irishmen, and Scots will be more inclined to persevere in such a course than the descendants of Frenchmen. If then the idea that the united legislature will be more reasonable on this score than the present legislature of Lower Canada seems perforce to render a union desirable, I do not believe that the result would justify the attempt.[98]

Robinson saw very clearly into the future, anticipating the collaboration of William Lyon Mackenzie with Papineau and of Robert Baldwin with Lafontaine in the achievement of responsible government for Canada—the natural outgrowth of the grant of representative institutions in 1791. But London was not yet ready to accept this development, and after receiving Robinson's opinion, which also sharply separated commercial matters from the project of political union, the government merely wavered in its resolution to join the two in a single bill. It was won back to its original intention by Ellice, and a bill 'to make more effective provision for the government of the provinces of Lower and Upper Canada, to regulate the trade thereof and for other purposes'[99] was consequently brought into the House of Commons in June 1822.

But there was also an anti-unionist group in parliament, whose spokesman was Sir James Mackintosh, a noted lawyer and social thinker and the chief orator of the opposition. When the bill was brought in, he protested against the introduction, at so late a stage in the session, of a measure which affected the most sacred rights of the Canadians, and declared his opposition to the project of union until the will of the people of Canada had been consulted. He was supported by Henry Bright, who objected to the injustice of a bill which had 'for its object to destroy the influence of Lower Canada and to give a certain superiority to the Protestant population over the Catholic population.'[100] Bright raised a telling question which served to generalize the debate: 'If Canada is deprived of its legislature, what security will the other English colonies have?' In the face of this opposition, the government cut the bill in two; the commercial provisions were passed as the Canada Trade Act, while the project of union failed of reconsideration before the end of the session. The Union Bill provided for a single legislative council and assembly, to be composed of the present members in both provinces. The power of naming new members to the legislative council was reserved to the governor, while the representation of Upper Canada in the assembly was increased from twenty-five to forty—that of Lower Canada remaining fifty—and the governor was authorized to erect new electoral districts in the Eastern Townships. The total future representation of either province was limited to sixty, and could not be altered without a two-thirds vote of both council and assembly. A property qualification of £500 was required of members. Four members of the executive council were to have the right to all the privileges of the assembly except that of voting. All records were to be kept in English, and after fifteen years English was to be the sole language of debate. *Curés* were to be named only with the consent of the governor.

Quite naturally, when news of this bill reached Quebec in September 1822, a tempest arose. The *Quebec Gazette*, the *Spectateur Canadien*, and the *Gazette Canadien* alike warned the people against this threat to their institutions, laws, and language. Public meetings were held at Montreal, where Denis-Benjamin Viger denounced the bill and its injustices. A committee of eighteen notable citizens drawn from both the bureaucratic and popular parties was formed, including Louis Guy, Charles de Saint-Ours, P.-D. Debartzch, L.-R. Chaussegros de Léry, C.-M. de Salaberry, L.-J. Papineau, Viger, Joseph Bédard, Augustin Cuvillier, and Louis Bourdagès. Similar protest meetings were held at Quebec, where the committee included L.-A. de Salaberry, J.-F. Perrault, L.-J. Duchesnay, I.-A. de Gaspé, F.-J.-P. Taschereau, Andrew Stuart, John Neilson, and F.-X. Blanchet. French Canadians and Britishers joined forces to oppose the union; the leaders of the protest movement included members of the legislative council and of the assembly, office-holders and leading spirits of the opposition, merchants and *seigneurs*, doctors and lawyers. The unionists also held a meeting in Montreal under the chairmanship of John Richardson, at which James Stuart, now won over to the cause of the oligarchy by the promise of office, maintained that any objections to the scheme were founded on prejudices which must be stamped out, or on local interests which should not enter into the question. To which the *Spectateur Canadien* replied: 'As if the language, laws, and institutions of a people could be considered mere prejudices; as if the particular interests of a country could be counted for naught in that very country!'[101] The two anti-unionist committees adopted a joint resolution of protest to London against any change in the established form of government. This was backed by a petition to the same effect signed by 60,000 individuals; and early in 1823 Papineau and John Neilson were sent to London by the committees to convey the petition to the ministers and Parliament. Thus began Papineau's partnership with Neilson, the first major collaboration of Canadians of different ethnic backgrounds in the common interest.

Neilson had come to Canada in 1790 from Scotland, imbued with radical Whig sympathies, and after seven years' apprenticeship on the newspaper founded by his uncle and inherited by his brother, became editor and proprietor of the *Quebec Gazette* in 1796, after weathering the witch-hunt of 1794 in New York. He combined the publication of this semi-official organ with bookselling, among his wares being the works of the French classical and romantic writers. He was elected to the assembly in 1818, where he sat until 1834. As a legislator he took a special interest in educational, agricultural, and land-grant questions, and soon espoused the cause of the popular party. In 1822 Dalhousie objected to the reflection of these views in the *Gazette*, and decided to found an official journal. Already faced with the competition of the *Mercury*, the organ of the English party, and of *Le Canadien*, that of the popular party, Neilson turned over the business management of the *Gazette* to his son Samuel, the King's Printer, and William Cowan; while the paper was edited by the Reverend John Charleton Fisher, who later composed the inscription for the Wolfe-Montcalm monument. But this compromise did not satisfy the governor, who set up a new *Gazette*, 'published by authority,' which was under the sole control of Fisher, and which lasted for several years.

This blow at Neilson's livelihood no doubt helped to throw him completely into the arms of the popular party, and he soon joined forces with Papineau, Bédard, and Viger. Neilson was a strong supporter of the Constitution of 1791; and in writing to Papineau on June 22, 1822 to warn him of the ministers' determination to revoke it, he remarked: 'This is a case of the only lamb of the poor man, which is seized by the rich man to add to the luxury of his feast. What fate have the inhabitants of this country to hope for from people who proceed in such fashion?'[102] He added his opinion that union would lead to annexation. The two men exchanged many letters before their departure for London in January 1823, and a still greater intimacy grew up between them during their mission. After their return Papineau paid his new friend this tribute: 'I know no one who has a greater right than you to the regard of my country, nor no one whom I esteem more than you.'[103]

When the two commissioners arrived in England, they sought out Wilmot Horton, under-secretary for the colonies, and Sir James Mackintosh, whom Papineau had mentioned to Neilson as a suitable London agent for Lower Canada as early as 1821. Mackintosh assured them that there was little likelihood of the government bringing in the union measure during the current session. At the request of the colonial secretary, Neilson, with Papineau's aid, drafted a memorandum which Garneau calls 'one of our best state papers.'[104] The commissioners pointed out at the outset of this document that only a small minority favored union, while the petition they bore carried the protests of seven-tenths of the adult population. The measure was open to objection on the grounds that it was impossible to set a common and convenient meeting place for two vast provinces whose joint extent was 1,500 miles and which even had different climates. The laws, customs, usages, religions, and dominant prejudices of the two regions were dissimilar, and each section was firmly attached to its own ways. The economic interests of the two provinces were actually opposed. There would be no saving brought by the measure, since the expenses of government would be increased by the difficulties of communication and transportation. In the matter of representation the bill unjustly favored Upper Canada, which would have more than twice Lower Canada's in proportion to population, while the latter province had five times as many inhabitants as Upper Canada.

On the language question the commissioners made this noteworthy observation:

> The common usage of two languages is embarrassing, but in many cases it is inevitable. It was thus in England after the Norman conquest, and the ill-advised measure of that barbarous epoch which proscribed the Saxon tongue suffered a deserved fate. The language of the majority of a nation whose elements have close mutual relations always ends by prevailing. The English language will inevitably become the dominant language in North America, with or without measures of law. There are probably not ten members of the present House of Assembly of Lower Canada who do not understand English; several speak it easily; and no citizen of the province having means or some notable situation neglects to have his children taught English. It is thus that things change with time and yield to circumstances. But the language of a father or mother, of family or friends, of first impressions and first memories, is dear to all. And this unjustified proscription of the language of the Canadian people has been violently resented in a country where this tongue did much to save the colony for Great Britain at the time of the American Revolution.[105]

The commissioners also pointed out that the article relating to the nomination of *curés* was an assault on the liberties which had been guaranteed to Catholics ever since the conquest. Such a measure, with its violations of the rights of the clergy as recognized even in English law, 'could not fail to arouse public opinion in Canada, and if ever applied, would inevitably cause those unfortunate differences between Catholics and Protestants which have desolated other countries and from which Canada has been so happily free under the benevolent and enlightened rule of His Majesty.' The commissioners concluded by urging that if the government was nevertheless determined to push through the bill, it should first order a complete census of both provinces, and authorize the governor to recommend to the legislature the appointment of one or more agents of the province, who could plead at London the case for the maintenance of the present constitution.

After submitting this memorandum, Neilson returned home, while Papineau remained in London until the end of the session, to guard against the surprise attack which Ellice threatened. The two rival spokesmen maintained social relations, however, and it was at Ellice's house that Papineau succeeded in winning over to his views Sir Francis Burdett, a noted Whig who felt his party would be compromised if it overrode the will of the Canadian majority by supporting the bill.

While the question of union was thus being argued in London, there was a lull in the conflict in Canada. But in 1824 it broke out once more, when the government found itself with an empty treasury, thanks to Receiver-General Caldwell's failure to make up the deficit in his accounts, and thus became dependent upon the assembly for a vote of funds. Papineau, who supported the Canada Trade Act when that piece of imperial legislation was attacked in the assembly on the grounds that British subjects could not be taxed without their consent, refused to support the vote of funds which the government demanded; and when the measure was nevertheless carried, he demanded that the salaries of officials be reduced by 25 per cent. On this last point he parted company with Neilson, whose deliberate calm often arrived at different conclusions from Papineau's passionate ardor. Believing that Canada was 'menaced by new injustices . . . on the part of the authorities in England,'[106] Papineau became more insistent on the appointment of Sir James Mackintosh as London agent of the colony, and on the necessity of making an alliance with 'the honest folk of Upper Canada to get from them more extensive information than we have and to encourage them to persist in their righteous resolutions.'[107] For William Lyon Mackenzie and the Reformers of Upper Canada were waging the same sort of constitutional warfare against the Family Compact of York as the followers of Papineau were engaged in against the Chateau Clique in Lower Canada.

In Lower Canada the conflict between the executive and the assembly had now clearly defined the issues: the government demanded a vote of the civil list for the life of the sovereign and control of the Crown revenue, while the assembly was only willing to approve the civil list annually and claimed the right to control the whole revenue. During the absence of Dalhousie in 1825 a clash was averted on this matter, for the administrator, Sir Francis Burton, agreed to the views of the assembly on the budget; but Burton's action was censured by the colonial secretary and repudiated by Dalhousie upon his return. There was a head-on collision between the executive and the assembly on this score in 1826; and when the assembly persisted in its stand the following year, Dalhousie promptly prorogued the legislature with a sharp speech to the effect that 'nothing likely to promote the public interest can now be expected from your deliberations.'[108] Papineau and six followers censured this address in a manifesto marked by violent indignation—he had already described Dalhousie's administration to Neilson as that of 'birds of prey and passage, who call enrichening themselves governing us'[109]—and the elections which followed were stormy. At the beginning of the new session Dalhousie refused to accept Papineau as speaker of the assembly; and when that body persisted in its choice, he dissolved it two days after it had met. Parliamentary government was virtually paralyzed, and popular indignation was so strong that there was no difficulty in getting 87,000 'signatures'—of which 78,000 were marks, which led the bureaucrats to refer scornfully to the popular party as 'Knights of the Cross'—on a new petition to London for the redress of Canadian grievances. In January 1828 Neilson, Viger, and Cuvillier took ship for England with this document,[110] while at the same time 10,000 inhabitants of the Townships forwarded another petition which complained of their particular wrongs.[111]

Before Neilson's departure Papineau wrote him a letter which reveals the strength of their friendship and his own bitter disillusionment with the form of government which he had eulogized six years before:

> So many private losses, so many public difficulties render wretched the state of our society. You are worth much more than me, for you have the same sensitiveness as I have, and the strength that I have not. There is no one that I like to see as much as you; more than once you have stiffened my weakening courage. The loss of my friends makes me melancholy to the extent that I am nearly reduced to a complete and stupid inaction, which is my wretched dominating inclination. The injustice done to my country destroys me and agitates me to such a degree that I am not always capable of taking counsel only of an enlightened patriotism, but rather of anger and hatred against its oppressors. . . . The descendants of the French have no right to equal rights with their masters of British origin. Some political arrangement must be found by which the privileged minority may govern the majority without being disturbed by the latter's complaints. . . . The history of no other colony presents a similar spectacle of immorality.
>
> It is odious that when the laws do not exclude the Canadians from office, that practice should exclude them. They furnish nine-tenths of the revenue and receive barely one-tenth. Influence with the country is a title to persecution both for Europeans and natives. You are a European and persecuted because you have the regard of the country.[112]

Here Papineau in his discouragement reveals the temperamental instability which explains much of his later career, and which finally brought about his break with Neilson, after twelve years of close collaboration. He also shows a North American outlook reminiscent of that of the American revolutionary leaders, reacting against English misgovernment.

A new ministry headed by the Duke of Wellington had just taken office in England, and the colonial secretary to whom the delegates carried their complaints was William Huskisson, the Tory Reformer who made himself notable by supporting free trade and Catholic emancipation. After hearing the delegates and consulting with his colleagues, he suggested the appointment of a committee of the House of Commons to enquire into the state of the government of Canada. In proposing this motion, Huskisson singled out the financial question, calling for the establishment of a system 'which would give the Assembly the power to determine the application of all funds for the internal improvement of the province, and at the same time withdraw from its authority that which might be called the civil list.'[113] He found that the system desired by the assembly was 'not compatible with the independence and dignity of the representative of the Crown or of the judges.' In a debate marked by speeches by Sir James Mackintosh, Henry Labouchere, Wilmot Horton, Lord Stanley, and Joseph Hume, the motion was adopted.

The committee was made up of Huskisson, Wilmot Horton, Mackintosh, Labouchere, and seventeen other members. It sat for two months and heard the testimony of Neilson, Viger, Cuvillier, Samuel Gale, Ellice, Simon McGillivray, Wilmot Horton, and James Stephen. Neilson attacked the legislative council and demonstrated that eighteen of its twenty-seven members had accumulated so many offices that they annually divided $88,000 of the public revenue amongst themselves. Viger dealt with the judiciary, pointing out that only three of eleven judges, in a province composed of 400,000 French Canadians and 80,000 English, were French-speaking. He also arraigned the English judges as tools of a political faction, who did its work in the legislative and executive councils, thus at once making laws, ordering their enforcement, and rendering decisions on their observance or non-observance. Cuvillier dealt with financial matters, exposing the irregularities of the past. On the other hand Samuel Gale, the representative of the Eastern Townships, urged that English courts be established in his district, that English tenure be permitted in practice as it was in law, that the Townships be given representation in the assembly, and that English immigration no longer be discouraged. Gale, like Ellice and the old Montreal fur trader McGillivray, favored a legislative union of Upper and Lower Canada. These representatives of the commercial class also reviewed once more all the arguments against the French system of tenure and of law in general, and against duties on the trade between the United States and Canada. They called for the annexation of Montreal, the commercial capital, to Upper Canada, if the two Canadas were not united; and demanded the ascendency of British views and 'security for British capital.'[114] Huskisson and Wilmot Horton were won over to some extent to the views of the popular party during the proceedings, and the committee's report was regarded by Neilson, Viger, and Cuvillier as 'decidedly favorable to the desires of the petitioners,'[115] as they wrote home in triumph on July 22, 1828, the day it was made.

The report[116] recommended that representation should be based on territory as well as population, so that the Townships should have an equitable share in provincial affairs. It also favored the establishment of land registry and transfer offices in that region. As a remedy to the practice of conceding lands to officials who did not improve their nominal holdings, it recommended a tax on lands neither improved nor settled. It gave handsome recognition to French-Canadian rights:

> The committee cannot too strongly express its opinion that the Canadians of French extraction should be as little troubled as possible in their peaceful enjoyment of their religion, laws and privileges, as guaranteed by acts of the British Parliament, and far from demanding of them that they hold their lands according to English tenure, it is of the opinion that when the seigneurial lands shall be filled up, if the descendants of the first settlers still prefer the tenure *en fief et seigneurie*, it sees no objection against other portions of uninhabited lands in the province being granted to them in this latter tenure, provided that these lands be separated from the Townships and not contained therein.[117]

Most notably, the committee recommended that the receipt and outlay of the public revenue be put under the control of the assembly. Nevertheless it urged that the salaries of the governor, executive councilors, and judges be permanently assured and not left dependent upon an annual vote of funds. But all judges except the chief justice should be barred from the councils, while the majority of the legislative council was not to be dependent upon the executive for other offices. It recommended precautions against such financial disasters as the Caldwell failure, and suggested that the revenues of the Jesuit Estates be applied to education. The document's appearance coincided with the recall of Dalhousie, who was replaced by Sir James Kempt. The new governor promptly accepted Papineau as speaker of the assembly. The long drawn-out crisis was ended for the time being, with a virtual victory for the popular party.

8

During the two years of his administration Sir James Kempt played the role of conciliator with such success that the period was one of political truce. Without renouncing its claim to financial control, the assembly passed revenue bills which were acceptable to the legislative council. The electoral districts were redivided, and the Townships were given eight representatives. Despite the wails of the merchants, representatives of the English-speaking population, which was only one-sixth of the total, made up one-quarter of the assembly. The promised land offices were established in the Townships. But contention was not wholly dead: the assembly expelled Robert Christie, a Gaspé merchant, for contempt. He was four times re-elected, and four times re-expelled, to the detriment of his sympathy with the popular party in the *History of the Late Province of Lower Canada* which he later compiled. Kempt appointed leading members of the popular party, including Viger, Louis Guy, and de Beaujeu, to the legislative council, and even proposed that Papineau and Neilson should be added to the executive council. He was conscious, as he put it, that he was sitting on a barrel of gunpowder,[118] and he proceeded warily.

In the fall of 1830 Kempt was replaced by Lord Aylmer, who had been instructed by Goderich, the new colonial secretary, to follow a policy of conciliating the popular leaders. Aylmer named Papineau and Neilson to the executive council, but they refused office on the grounds that the regulations of the assembly did not permit them to accept a Crown appointment. A year later Aylmer included eight French Canadians among his eleven nominees to the legislative council. Reform was clearly in the saddle at Quebec as well as at London. In 1831 Aylmer offered the British government's solution of the financial question: it would renounce control of the revenue to the assembly in exchange for a permanent civil list covering the salaries of the governor and judges and certain pensions. The assembly refused this proposal, maintaining that it did not conform to the recommendation of the Commons Report of 1828, thus displaying the 'petty and spiteful spirit,'[119] which, along with a failure to exploit its successes, was to lead to disaster rather than to the responsible government it sought. John Neilson then proposed a moderate set of resolutions on Canadian grievances, which was passed after sharp attacks from the extremists.

From this time onward the popular party was divided into two groups, one headed by Neilson and the other by Papineau. The divergence of opinion between the two men was of some years' standing; Papineau defined it in a letter to Neilson on November 14, 1830:

> You are disposed to believe that the government can be pushed into the right path and will follow it passably well; I am disposed to believe that it goes from bad to worse. You complain loudly of the men who have led it; *ab hoc et ab hac* you are right: you have drawn on the public, which still keeps on when you wish to stop yourself. You believe that debased

men are no longer dangerous; that they will govern well because they no longer dare to do evil. The majority does not see that. It sees flagrant abuses which have not all been corrected, while their unpunished authors preserve the same principles as before, that is to say, the absence of all principle, indifference to the public welfare, the same ardor for conserving in their odious coterie the accumulation of offices which they have monopolized, the same means of vengeance that they have so unscrupulously employed, the same certainty of impunity so long as their phalanx is not broken. I cannot desist. The country is still the prey of determined and dangerous enemies, and the English ministry is more disposed to sustain them than to guide itself by the rules of justice towards us. . . . [I am convinced] that it is essential to the peace and good government of the province that its constitution be amended by suppressing the present Legislative Council and replacing it with an elective Council, in which each county will have a member.

That the courts of justice, badly constituted and not enjoying the least respect or public confidence, could not be reformed in the interest of the citizen while the judges controlled the Council and could not consent to increase their work and responsibility.

That the ungranted lands ought to be put under such regulations as the Legislature will adopt, and that the Jesuit Estates ought to be put at its disposition to aide the general education of the province. That we must not proceed to any other measure until these grievances have been satisfied, and request a prorogation of several months to await the response to the representations made to the King and to Parliament.[120]

Again, on May 11, 1831, Papineau playfully rallied his friend on his tendency to accept the conciliatory gestures of the government at their face value:

Cherrier tells me that you are to come in some weeks to see your Montreal friends. You have as much need as any other to see the wolves* in order not to forget how to howl. You are becoming too confiding, and too disposed to pardon the wrongs of the public and to forget the past. If it were from charity, nothing could be more edifying, but if it is weariness of fighting or confidence that the placemen here begin to wish to reform and to think of their salvation, it is a mistake. May God keep you in the holy resolution to come and see your Montreal friends.[121]

But the split between the two was not to be healed, despite Papineau's effort to remind his friend that he had always been '*tout bon canadien*,'[122] for Neilson was a moderate by nature and Papineau an extremist, and each attracted the support of the likeminded among the popular party.

In July 1831 Aylmer communicated to the assembly a long dispatch[123] from Goderich which offered remedies for the minor grievances contained in Neilson's resolutions and proposed to renounce control of the revenue in exchange for a civil list covering

* The Montrealers were popularly known as 'wolves,' Quebeckers as 'lambs.'

the salaries of the governor, his secretary, the provincial secretary, the attorney-general, and the solicitor-general. The assembly, grown somewhat overbearing with success, refused this virtual surrender to its demands since 1818. It also resumed its old quarrel with the legislative council over a motion of Bourdàges, which would have put the temporal possessions of the Church under the control of democratic parish councils—in effect, miniature local parliaments. This motion was carried in the assembly by Papineau's group over the opposition of Neilson's; but it was defeated, to the great joy of the clergy, in the legislative council at the instance of Sewell, who remarked: 'In destroying the discipline of the Church, one strikes at religion itself.'[124] Thus a militant anti-French Protestant gratified the Catholic clergy by opposing a bill supported by the French-Canadian majority. Such opposition explained in part why Papineau began to develop the anti-clerical attitude which later led to his complete break with the Church; in 1829, apropos of the question of the Seminary's estates, he had remarked to Neilson: 'If priests nevertheless sometimes tell the truth, I have long distrusted them.'[125] As Papineau became more radical in his ideas, he found himself in greater opposition to the clergy, who took their stand beside the other forces of conservatism.[126]

The era of political truce was broken on May 21, 1832 by the deaths of three French Canadians, shot by troops summoned by the magistrates to quell an election riot in Montreal. The commanding officers were arrested, but the indictment against them was quashed by the grand jury. Aylmer expressed to them his pleasure at the verdict, and his disapproval of the popular tumult directed against them. *Le Canadien* observed heatedly: 'Not content with having insulted a generous people, the representative of our sovereign must confirm the assassination of the subjects confided to him by his august master, and must compliment the murderers in a fashion most outrageous and contemptuous to the Canadian people.'[127] At the opening of the session a vote of censure was passed against the governor, and Dominique Mondelet, who had just been appointed by him to the executive council, was expelled from the assembly. The proposal to make the legislative council elective was taken up once more, and Papineau rallied a majority to its support, despite the opposition of his old allies Neilson, Quesnel, and Cuvillier.

The final stage of the struggle between the assembly and the executive now opened, over the issues of an elective council and of control of the revenue. The session adjourned without the adoption of a satisfactory revenue bill, and the government was forced to carry on by the old illegal expedients. For instance, £47,000 of the net revenues of £49,000 of the Jesuit Estates from 1801 to 1831—35 per cent of the receipts having been charged off to 'administrative costs' by the commissioners—were expended for general purposes, including the expenses and pensions of such notables of the Chateau Clique as Sewell and Ryland, while only £12,389 had been devoted to education—and confined, at that, to the anglicizing Royal Institution and the Royal Grammar Schools of Quebec, Montreal, and Kingston. In 1831 the government finally offered to devote the Jesuit Estates and their revenues to the benefit of the educational budget, which then amounted to only some £3,000, but the offer involved the provision of new barracks in return for renunciation of the old Jesuit College at Quebec. Since this would have absorbed the revenue for several years to come, and in addition set the precedent of contribution to defence in peacetime, the assembly refused the bargain, while education struggled along without adequate support.

Another matter envenomed the relations between the ethnic groups. Immigration, encouraged by the merchants of Montreal in order to people the Upper Canadian wilderness, to provide manpower for the great canal-building projects, and to offset French-Canadian preponderance, had risen steadily since 1825, reaching the figure of 50,254 in 1831. It was supported by the ministry in London as unemployment and distress increased in England, Scotland, and Ireland. The poverty-stricken migrants were packed into the unhealthy holds of the timber ships coming back to Canada in ballast. After a voyage which was more often than not a battle for survival, they were put ashore at Quebec and Montreal, often penniless and disease-ridden. Many, unable to proceed westward, became public charges; and in 1832 the assembly passed a bill establishing a head tax, to be paid by the captains of the emigrant ships, to offset the financial burden thus imposed. The merchants of Quebec and Montreal bitterly opposed this measure, and they were supported by interested Upper Canadians. Both saw in it an attempt 'to obstruct that influx of Europeans which by increasing the number of English inhabitants, threatens soon to merge the preponderance of the French Canadians in Lower Canada.'[128] There was no doubt something in this view, for the French Canadians, then as now, did not welcome a flood of British immigration which threatened to inundate them and to fill up the lands which they wished to reserve for their own descendents.

The real crisis of the immigration situation came in 1832 with an outbreak of Asiatic cholera, brought by the newcomers, which spread like wildfire along the St. Lawrence and decimated both immigrants and natives. Immigration became, to certain wild French-Canadian eyes, an English conspiracy to wipe them off the face of the earth. Edouard Rodier, a fiery spokesman of the extremist group, proclaimed:

It was not enough to send among us avaricious egotists, without any other spirit of liberty than that which could be bestowed by a simple education at the counter, to enrich themselves at the expense of the Canadians, and then to enslave them;—they must also rid themselves of their beggars and cast them by thousands on our shores; they must send us miserable beings, who, after having partaken of the bread of our children, will subject them to the horrors following upon hunger and misery; they must do still more, they must send us in their train pestilence and death."[129]

Even Neilson editorialized bitterly in the *Quebec Gazette* against immigration, describing its effect as 'similar to the passage of an immense army . . . leaving the inhabitants to take care of and provide for the sick, wounded, and disabled, and bury the dead.'[130] Papineau was confirmed in his melancholy view of the state of affairs as he wrote to Neilson during the height of the epidemic in August:

As for me, I have not had a moment of indisposition. I have great confidence in the merit of my temperament, which makes me indifferent enough about living or dying as a result of the indignation I feel against the policy under which each of our administrations in turn insults and tyranizes the country. The most wretched of all is that of today. Its fear of the merchants has let it permit the entrance of the plague into the country. Its fear of the military has let it permit the shooting of electors. Its fear of appearing to sympathize with them has assured impunity to their murderers. And all these crimes are the known fruits of the Governor's character, and of the position that he has taken from the outset of allowing himself to be guided by the counsels of the Solicitor. Nine-tenths of the Europeans have applauded the murders of the 21st. It is the most violent condemnation that can possibly be made of our detestable scheme of government. They well know that at their will armed force can be used against the Canadians, but not against them. What means is there to prevent a similar conviction being established in the minds of both populations? The sole means is to extend infinitely more than it has been the system of elections. Only by this arrangement may each consider itself equally protected by law.[131]

The organization in London in 1832 of the British American Land Company, which acquired over half a million acres in the Townships for British immigrants; the growing power of the chartered banks established in 1817 and 1818 by the English merchants; and the division of port revenues between the two provinces were other sources of irritation to the French-Canadian party, which like its counterpart in Upper Canada, grew more violent in its opposition to the oligarchy.

The mounting agitation and unrest came to a head in 1834. At the opening of the session the assembly was in a rebellious mood, and it did not receive in kindly fashion the censures of Stanley, the new colonial secretary, on its past proceedings. Papineau savagely attacked Aylmer, and was attacked in turn by Conrad Augustus Gugy, a great-nephew of Haldimand's aide. The temper of the times is best indicated by the Ninety-Two Resolutions, drafted by Papineau, Augustin-Norbert Morin, and Elzéar Bédard, and introduced in the assembly on February 17 by the latter. This was the manifesto of the popular party, which may well be compared with the declarations of principles which foreshadowed the American and French Revolutions. To the *Patriotes*, as they had begun to call themselves, it seemed that 'Liberty had both feet and one arm in bonds,'[132] and they called for reforms which went far beyond the goals of the English reformers of the day. The Resolutions also reflect a comparison of the British and American systems of government, and contain the first hint of annexationist sentiment in the popular party.

All of Papineau's ideas and all of his passion were evident in the Resolutions,[133] which were carelessly drawn up, repetitious, and of widely varying merit. The first eight were statements of loyalty and a recapitulation of the assembly's struggle for redress of its grievances. The ninth to the fortieth reviewed the arguments of the assembly against an appointive legislative council and in favor of an elective one. The forty-first to fiftieth singled out superior features of the American system of government, and concluded with a vague threat of seeking independence. The fifty-first to fifty-fifth summed up the rights and injustices of the French Canadians. The fifty-sixth to sixty-second dealt with the Canada Tenure Act and demanded its repeal. The sixty-third defended the assembly's expulsion of Christie and Mondelet. The sixty-fourth to seventy-fourth dealt with control of the revenue. The seventy-fifth complained that the French Canadians held only 47 out of 194 public offices, while they formed more than five-sixths of the population. The seventy-sixth to seventy-eighth dealt with judicial matters and grievances on this score. The seventy-ninth to eighty-third asserted the right of the assembly to all the powers, privileges, and immunities of the British Parliament. The eighty-fourth listed sixteen specific grievances not already mentioned. The eighty-fifth and -sixth called for the impeachment of Aylmer. The eighty-seventh and -eighth were declarations of gratitude and confidence to Daniel O'Connell and Joseph Hume for their support of the assembly's petitions in the British parliament. The eighty-ninth called for the formation of committees of correspondence at Montreal and Quebec to keep in touch with Viger, the province's agent at London since 1831, O'Connell and Hume, and likeminded persons in the other colonies, in the interest of concerted resistance to arbitrary oppression. The ninetieth begged Viger to remain at London in the public interest, and the ninety-first declared that the assembly would contract a debt of honor to the committees of correspondence for their expenses. The ninety-second called for the expunging from the record of the governor's message at the opening of the session, which contained Stanley's sharp comments on the assembly's petition in favor of the abolition or the making elective of the legislative council.

Papineau led the debate on the Resolutions, saying: 'We have to inquire if today we have not reached the period in which the first authority of the state should recover the respect it has lost, and in which honor, fortune, liberty, and existence should be assured, or whether we are to reconcile ourselves to see the latter fall to the last degree of abasement and the former rise to excesses.'[134] He attacked the 'vicious and imperfect' Quebec Act, and accused the clergy of being attached to the government because of it. To him it seemed that, neglecting the cause of the people, they had found that measure 'good because it was advantageous.' He traced the whole political history of the French Canadians: the early ignorance of constitutional rights and the struggle of the assembly since 1810 to attain them. He concluded with an indication of how far he had already gone in his own mind: 'It is certain that before long all America is to be republican. Meanwhile, ought a change in our constitution, if necessary, be guided by this consideration; and is it criminal to raise the question?' He summed up the Ninety-Two Resolutions, proclaiming them a bill of rights which must be adopted if French-Canadian liberties were not to perish.

Elzéar Bédard, Bourdàges, Sabrevoix de Bleury, George Vanfelson, and young Louis-Hippolyte Lafontaine all made supporting speeches. Neilson led the opposition of the moderate constitutional reformers, who feared that adoption of the Resolutions would block reform. Andrew Stuart pointed out that the grievances were really only those of a small group of professional men, the lay élite, while the masses were unconcerned. During the debate Quesnel and other followers broke with Papineau, but in the end the Ninety-Two Resolutions were adopted by a vote of 56–23, and an address to the British Parliament based upon them was sent to London in care of Morin, who was instructed to aid Viger in urging them upon the British ministry. While dissolving the assembly, Aylmer condemned the Resolutions, but popular agitation in their favor continued. In the elections of 1834 Papineau's followers emerged triumphant, while the opponents of the Resolutions, including Neilson, were defeated.

The English merchants of Quebec and Montreal, already made uneasy by the American financial panic of 1833 and by English attacks on the timber preference, were goaded into complete exasperation by the Ninety-Two Resolutions, which one of them termed 'the most insolent, disloyal, insane, and ridiculous productions that were ever submitted to the consideration of a deliberative body.'[135] They formed constitutional associations in their strongholds of Montreal, Quebec, Sorel, and in the Townships; and they contested the elections in militant fashion, denouncing the disloyalty of the popular party. Papineau countered in kind, suggesting a boycott of British goods and urging a run upon the banks, which were controlled by the merchants: 'The most efficacious and most immediate means which the Canadians have to protect themselves against the fury of their enemies is to attack them in their dearest parts—their pockets—in their strongest entrenchments, the Banks.'[136] In November there were runs on the Quebec Bank and the Bank of Montreal, and an alarmed Tory paper likened Papineau to 'a well-drugged Malay running a-muck.'[137] On November 17, when it became evident that they had lost the election, the Tories met at Tattersall's in Montreal, and protested that they would no longer 'submit to the domination of a party averse to emigration, to commerce, to internal improvements, and to all those interests which may be regarded as British.'[138]

Papineau and his fellow members of the Montreal committee of correspondence, already aroused by the Tory use in the elections of strong-arm squads of Irish canal-diggers, believed that still more violent plans had been made at this meeting, and for the first time they considered the possibility of reform by force rather than by constitutional means. On November 20 the Montreal committee wrote to its Quebec equivalent, which had complained of the Tories' electoral methods:

For the rest, like these last [the English party of Quebec] our adversaries in Montreal have also struck against all which is Canada and part of the liberties of the country; like them they have proclaimed European *ascendancy* by means of exclusion on one hand and terror on the other; like yours, they are going to have dinners whose end is to inflame against the security, the rights, and the very life of the people of the country those of their adepts who attend these gatherings. Today in their assembly at Tattersall's, these projects of oppression and these incendiary doctrines have been laid bare. Among other warmed-over plans discussed was that of a mission to Upper Canada to form among the people of the neighboring province associations of a sort to provide forces for the Montreal party of assassins, both to support the union of the provinces and the dismemberment of this one.

. . . We are so poor, so little organized to repel by force of arms a domination which has become so burdensome to us. Are we ready; are the people ready; are you ready? Should we take so great a responsibility upon ourselves? Have we authority to do so? Do there remain no more means of protection in constitutional legality, giving it all the extension which befits British subjects claiming their rights and free men living in America? Here are questions to which you, like us, must soon reply.[139]

But the committees of correspondence decided to confine themselves to implementing the Ninety-Two Resolutions, to protesting against the British American Land Company and the whole system of land granting and administration, to achieving an understanding with the popular leaders in Upper Canada and other neighboring colonies on common interests, and to adopting countermeasures against 'the system of industrial and commercial exclusion launched by our adversaries.'[140] Meanwhile the Tory constitutional associations in Montreal and Quebec adopted manifestoes protesting against persecution of other classes by the French Canadians, accusing them of republicanism, and making much of their own imperial loyalty.[141]

Both groups were conscious of the coming crisis, and the tension was not relieved by the sounding of appeals to ethnic solidarity. What had been a conflict of interests and of classes, brought to a head by the ruling class' attempt to repudiate the Constitution of 1791, was showing unmistakeable signs of becoming a war between English and French.

Notes

[1] Garneau, II, 431–2; L. Groulx, *Nos luttes constitutionnelles* (Montreal, 1915), II, 5. Garneau fails to recognize that there were two successive but very different attitudes on the part of British officialdom to the French Revolution. Whig sympathy with the ideals of 1789 and the belief of such men as Grenville that France was no longer to be feared were replaced after the execution of Louis XVI and the outbreak of the Terror by a panicky fear of everything French. The pamphlets published at Quebec by the closely supervised presses of Samuel Neilson and William Vondenvelden reflect this change of attitude, with Arthur Young giving way to the Bishop of Landaff. See M. Casey, *Catalogue of the Pamphlets in the Public Archives of Canada*, I, *1493–1877* (Ottawa, 1931), 109, 119. D. F. Mcquat has recently discovered that young John Neilson, who had high Whig sympathies, found it expedient to flee from Monk's witchhunt at Quebec in September 1794 and did not return from exile on Long Island until May 1795, when he declared that he had had the 'character of a Democrat and thought it prudent to avoid the charge.' PAC: Q 66, 5, Declarations of Aliens, J. Neilson, 30 May 1795; Q 66, 171, Dorchester-Dundas, 23 October 1793.

[2] PAC: Q 69–1, 4, Monk-Dorchester, 21 May 1794.

[3] Chapais, II, 42.

[4] *Ibid.*, 43; R. Christie, *A History of the Late Province of Lower Canada* (Quebec, 1848), I, 124–5; LOC: France, Archives des Affaires Etrangères, Correspondance Politique, Etats-Unis, Vol. 37, Pt. 6, 419–23 *verso*: Mezière-Genet, 12 juin 1793.

[5] Caron, II, 'Les Cantons de l'Est,' 14 n. 2; Christie, I, 116–8. P.-A. de Gaspé, *Mémoires* (Ottawa, 1866) 31, 62–4.

[6] Chapais, II, 43; Caron, II, 14–5. Such tongue-twisters as Buckinghamshire, Northumberland, and Effingham must have troubled the Canadians.

[7] Chapais, II, 45; Langlois, 267, gives the total as 161, 311.

[8] *Quebec Gazette* (20 December 1792); Chapais, II, 51–2.

[9] Shortt & Doughty, *Const. Docs, 1759–1791*, 399; Chartier de Lotbinière, 'Things which must be considered . . .' 1774.

[10] *Quebec Gazette*, 31 January, 14 February, 1793; Chapais, II, 69–70 & Caron, II, 17; N.-E. Dionne, *Pierre Bédard et ses fils* (Québec, 1909), 19–21.

[11] *Journal of the Assembly*, 1793, 167; Chapais, II, 76.

[12] PAC: Q 65, 324; Dundas-Dorchester, 2 October 1793; Chapais, II, 80–1 and *n*.

[13] W. P. M. Kennedy, *Statutes, Treaties and Documents of the Canadian Constitution, 1713–1929* (Oxford, 1930), 212–4; Richardson-Ellice, 16 February 1793.

[14] PAC: Q 63–2, 307; Alured Clark-Dundas, 3 July 1793; Chapais, II, 77–80.

[15] Excerpts in PAC: Q 69–2, 224–6; printed in W. Kingsford, *History of Canada* (Toronto, 1894), VII, 387–9 *n*. The full printed text, dated June 1793, in LOC: France, Archives des Affaires Etrangères, Correspondence Politique, Etats-Unis, XXXVII, 439–442 *verso*.

[16] PAC: Q 69–1, 4–25, Monk-Dundas, 29 May 1794; Chapais, II, 114.

[17] Chilton Williamson, *Vermont in Quandry* (Montpelier, 1949); *CHR* XXXI (Dec. 1950), 345–68: M. Wade, 'Quebec and the French Revolution of 1789: The Missions of Henri Mezière.'

[18] Têtu & Gagnon, *Mandements*, II, 471–2; Hubert's circular, 9 November 1793.

[19] PAC: S 44–5, 'Loyal Association Addresses, Lower Canada, 1794.'

[20] Têtu & Gagnon, *Mandements*, II, 501–2; Hubert's circular, 5 November 1796.

[21] AAQ: J.-O. Plessis, 'Oraison funèbre de Mgr Jean-Olivier Plessis, 27 juin 1796'; Chapais, II, 124–6 *n*.

[22] L. Groulx, *Notre maître, le passé*, IIIe série (Montréal, 1944), 125–64, 'La Providence et la conquête anglaise de la Nouvelle France.'

[23] Têtu & Gagnon, *Mandements*, II, 515–7, Denaut's mandement, 22 December 1798; PAC: Q 82, 211: Plessis' *Discours*, 10 January 1799; printed copies at Laval and Quebec Legislative Library.

[24] Christie, VI, 23–4; G. Lanctot, *Les Canadiens français et leurs voisins du Sud* (Montréal, 1941), 129. PAC: Q 83, 152–5, Souscription volontaire; Q 84, 158–67, List of Voluntary Subscriptions.

[25] N.-E. Dionne, *Les ecclésiastiques et les royalistes français refugiés au Canada*, (Québec, 1905), IX.

[26] L. Groulx, *L'Enseignement français au Canada*, I, *Dans le Québec* (Montreal, 1931), 181.

[27] PAC: CO 42, 17, Holland-Roberts, 9 November 1785; Lanctot, 126–7.

[28] Shortt & Doughty, *Const. Docs.*, *1759–1794*, 489, Haldimand-Germain, 25 October 1780; Lanctot, 125.

[29] PAC: Q 69–2, 254: Monk-Dundas, 30 May 1794; Q 71–1, 2: Dorchester-Dundas, 24 May 1794.

[30] *Ibid.*, Q 79–1, 19: Sewell-Prescott, 12 May 1797; printed in *CAR 1891*, 73–6: Note D, French Republican Designs on Canada, No. 17.

[31] Christie, I, 238–43; D. G. Creighton, *Commercial Empire of the St. Lawrence* (Toronto, 1937), 155–6.

[32] PAC: CO 42, 22, 258–9: Dundas-Dorchester, July 1793.

[33] Christie, VI, 39: Mountain-Milnes, 19 October 1799; E. A. Cruikshank, *Simcoe Correspondence* (Toronto, 1925) III, 91–4, Mountain-Dundas, 15 September 1794; PAC: Q 74–2, 207–13, Mountain-Dundas, 15 July 1795; T. R. Millman, *Jacob Mountain, First Lord Bishop of Quebec* (Toronto, 1947), 170–1.

[34] PAC: Q 84, 183–90: Letter of the Bishop of Quebec on Education, 19 October 1799; Millman, *Mountain*, 171.

[35] PAC: Q 74, 207–13, Mountain-Dorchester, 15 July 1795; Groulx, *Enseignement*, I, 76.

[36] Shortt & Doughty, *Const. Docs.*, 1791–1818, 349, Ryland's Observations, May, 1808; PAC: Q 220–3, 545–69, D. Viger, *Remarques sur l'Etat de l'Education en Canada en* 1831; Groulx, *Enseignement*, I, 78.

[37] PAC: Q 85, 228 Milnes-Portland, 1 November 1800; printed in Kennedy, 219, 218.

[38] Shortt & Doughty, *Const. Docs.*, *1791–1818*, 393: Graig-Liverpool, 1 May 1810; Groulx, *Enseignement*, I, 80.

[39] In 1816 two royal grammar schools were established in Quebec and Montreal, supported by the revenues of the Jesuit Estates and staffed by English teachers. Similar institutions had been established at Lévis in 1805 and at Saint-Nicolas in 1816. Fourteen teachers appeared on the public accounts in 1809; twenty-six in 1814, among them seven French Canadians serving in Catholic parishes. The efforts of the assembly to set up a rival educational system came to nothing in 1814, 1815, and 1817.

The Royal Institution finally came into official being in 1818, largely to take advantage of a bequest by James McGill of Montreal, who died in 1813, leaving his estate 'Burnside' to the Institution as the site of a college or university. If the will were not carried into effect within ten years, the property was to revert to McGill's heirs. The Montreal merchant also left £10,000 to be paid to the Royal Institution as soon as the college or university was established, to defray the expenses of launching and maintaining it. The bequest was prompted by the Reverend John Strachan, then missionary at York (Toronto), who married the widow of McGill's brother (*Montreal Gazette*, 3 September 1829: letter of P. Chartran; cited Millman, 173). Of the nine syndics who controlled the Royal Institution, only one was a French Canadian. The only other invited, Bishop Plessis, had refused. As Arthur Buller noted in his report on 'The State of Education in Lower Canada,' (Durham Report, App. D), the Royal Institution had an 'exclusively British and Protestant character,' and left the wants of the French Canadians 'virtually untouched.'

[40] H. T. Manning, *British Colonial Government, 1782–1820* (New Haven, 1933), 300, 337.

[41] PAC: Q 92, 253: Mountain-Milnes, 6 June 1805; printed in *CAR 1892*, 20: Note C, Ecclesiastical Affairs in Lower Canada, No. 2. However 'dangerous and novel' the experiment, such was the intention of London. Both Burke and Sewell considered that the Catholic Church had been established in Quebec by the Quebec Act. *A Letter from the Right Hon. Edmund Burke, M.P., to Sir Hercules Langrishe, Bart., M.P. on the subject of Roman Catholics in Ireland* (London, 1792), 83–4; QDA: Series C, 2, 29; cited Millman, 284 *n.* Burke spoke of his vote in 1791 as one "for the establishment of the Church of England *conjointly* with the establishment which was made some years before by Act of Parliament, of the Roman Catholics in the French conquered country of Canada."

[42] *Quebec Mercury*, 28 October 1806; Chapais, II, 179.

[43] *Ibid.*, 24 November 1806; Chapais, II, 180.

[44] *Le Canadien*, 6 December 1806; Chapais, II, 181.

[45] *Le Canadien*, 31 January 1807; Chapais, II, 185.

[46] PAC: Q 106–1, 5: Craig-Castlereagh, 9 November 1807; Chapais, II, 187.

[47] PAC: Q 107, 313–6, Ryland-Plante, Panet, Taschereau, Bédard, Borgia, Blanchet, 14 June 1808; printed in Christie, I, 276 *n.*

[48] Christie, I, 317–20 *n.*: Craig's proclamation, 21 March 1810.

[49] Doughty & McArthur, *Const Docs.*, *1791–1818* (Ottawa, 1914), 365, Castlereagh-Craig, 7 September 1809.

[50] *Ibid*, 400–5, Observations of Chief Justice Sewell on the Union of the Provinces.

[51] *Ibid.*, 387–400, Craig-Liverpool, 1 May 1810.

[52] *Le Canadien*, 22 November 1806; Creighton, 158.

[53] PAC: Q 92, 253, Mountain-Milnes, 6 June 1803; printed in *CAR 1892*, 20: Note C, Ecclesiastical Affairs in Lower Canada, No. 2; Q 92, 275, Hobart-Milnes, 9 January 1804; printed in *CAR* 1892, 22: Note C, No. 3.

[54] Christie, VI, 72–3, Ryland, 23 December 1804.

[55] Abbé Ferland, 'Mgr Plessis,' in *Le Foyer Canadien*, I, 140; Chapais, II, 156.

[56] Têtu & Gagnon, *Mandements*, III, 51, Plessis' Mandement, 25 October 1810.

[57] Christie, VI, 196–9, Ryland-Peel, 19 February 1811.

[58] Chapais, II, 161.

[59] Têtu & Gagnon, *Mandements*, III, 59–72: Plessis-Craig, May-June 1811. Cf. Plessis' conversations with Sewell in April and May 1805, Christie, VI, 74–82.

[60] Christie, VI, 312–3; Bathurst-Prevost, 2 July 1813; Ryland-Brenton, 28 October 1813; Brenton-Ryland, 2 November 1813; Ryland-Brenton, 5 November 1813.

[61] Doughty & McArthur, *Const. Docs.*, *1791–1818*, 60: Crown Lands Proclamation, 1792.

[62] PAC: Q 80–2, 278–9, Prescott-Portland, 13 August 1798; Lanctot, 131.

[63] Creighton, 122–3.

[64] PAC: Q 80–2, 279, 280, 299: Prescott-Portland, 13 August 1798; Lanctot, 131.

[65] Doughty & McArthur, *Const. Docs.*, *1791–1818*, 402: Sewell's Observations.

[66] *Le Canadien*, 12 December 1807; cited Creighton, 158; Viger, cited Lanctot, 132.

[67] *Quebec Mercury*, 3 April 1809; Creighton, 159.

[68] *An Apology for Great Britain* (Quebec, 1809), 22–3; Creighton, 160.

[69] J. Cockloft, *Cursory Observations, Made in Quebec, Province of Lower Canada, in the Year 1811* (Bermuda, n.d.), 3. Copy in QLHS.

[70] *Ibid.*, 4–6; Creighton, 150; H. Innis & A. R. M. Lower, *Select Documents in Canadian Economic History*, II, *1783–1885* (Toronto, 1933), 236, 247.

[71] Cockloft, 8–9; J. Bouchette, *A Topographical Description of the Province of Lower Canada* (London, 1815), 83–4.

[72] Cockloft, 11.

[73] *Ibid.*, 21–5.

[74] *Ibid.*, 30–2, 35, 37.

[75] *Ibid.*, 37, 42.

[76] *Ibid.*, 26–7.

[77] Innis & Lower, *Select Econ. Docs.*, 228–9.

[78] *Ibid.*, 235.

[79] Bouchette, *Topographical Description*, 186.

[80] *Ibid.*, ix. 9, 15; PAC: Journal de Labadie, 1794–1817, Cahier IV, Labadie-P. Bédard, 5 August 1811: 'Aujourd 'huy les Américains jaloux de notre liberté veulant nous la ravir.'

[81] PAC: Q 128–1, 185–6, Prevost-Bathurst, 27 August 1814; Lanctot, 138.

[82] Lanctot, 133–4.

[83] *Ibid.*, 135.

[84] *Le Canadien*, 24 September 1808; Chapais, II, 215. Labadie, '*comme canadien et bon anglois*,' produced a patriotic jingle on Napoleon: '*Ce consul implacable! Qui veut régner partout, Ce vautour redoubtable, Est en horreur chez nous.*' PAC: Journal, Cahier II, 1 February 1804.

[85] A. Shortt & A.G. Doughty, *Canada and Its Provinces*, (Toronto, 1814), III, 201: Jefferson-Monroe, 1812.

[86] Têtu & Gagnon, *Mandements*, III, 87: Deschenaux à MM. les curés, 29 juin 1812. Vicar-General J.-H.-A. Roux of Montreal issued a similar mandement on July 3 (Têtu & Gagnon, III, 88–91), while Deschenaux added two more circulars to the *curés* on July 20 and August 24 (*ibid.*, 91, 92) at the governor's suggestion.

Bishop Plessis expressed the governor's satisfaction and his own pleasure at the *curés*' assistance in a circular of October 6 (*ibid.*, 93), while on October 29 he issued a mandement encouraging the militia and ordaining a *Te Deum* for Wellington's victory over the French in Spain in July (*ibid.*, 94–8). The loyalist zeal of the clergy doubtless had a certain element of self-interest, with the question of the bishop's status still unresolved, but it expressed a sincere horror of Napoleonic France and of American sympathizers with it.

[87] Bouchette, 613.

[88] Têtu & Gagnon, III, 79–86, Plessis, *Mémoire*, 15 mai 1812.

[89] Doughty & McArthur, *Const. Docs.*, *1791–1818*, 445–50: 'Heads of Impeachment,' 1814.

[90] Christie, VI, 337: Ryland's 'A Brief Review of the Political State of the Province of Lower Canada during the last Seven Years,' May 1814.

[91] PAC: Q 127, 266: Prevost-Bathurst, 18 March 1814; Doughty & McArthur, *Const. Docs.*, *1791–1818*, 464.

[92] PAC: Q 128–1, 200, Prevost-Bathurst, 4 September 1814; Doughty & McArthur, 467.

[93] PAC: Q 143, 392; Sherbrooke-Bathurst, 21 April 1817; Chapais, III, 68–9.

[94] *Quebec Gazette*, July 1820; Chapais, III, 92–3.

[95] *The Centenary Volume of the Literary and Historical Society of Quebec* (Quebec, 1924).

[96] Creighton, 214.

[97] *Montreal Gazette*, 10 November 1828; Creighton, 213.

[98] PAC: Q 163–2, 553: Robinson-Bathurst, 23 April 1822; printed in *CAR 1897*, 39: Note A, 'Proposed Union between Upper and Lower Canada,' No. 20.

[99] Kennedy, 243: Union Bill, June 1822.

[100] Hansard, II Series, VII, 1708; Chapais, III, 117.

[101] M. Bibaud, *Histoire du Canada sous la domination anglaise* (Montréal, 1844), 235; Chapais, III, 117.

[102] Bib. St. Sulp.: Correspondence Papineau-Neilson (1819–23); Neilson-Papineau, 22 June, 1822; transcripts at PAC.

[103] *Ibid.*, Papineau Neilson, 29 November 1823.

[104] Garneau, II, 582 *n.* 23.

[105] PAC: Q 164–1, 113: Papineau & Neilson-Horton, 10 May 1823; Chapais, III, 134–5.

[106] APQ: Fonds Papineau, XI, 'Papineau à divers personnes, 1809–1844, 503: Papineau-Neilson, 13 September 1824.

[107] PAC: Neilson Collection, XIV, Papineau-Neilson, 13 September 1821; 30 April 1825.

[108] Kennedy, 251: Dalhousie's speech proroguing Assembly, 1827.

[109] Bib. St. Sulp.: Corr. Papineau-Neilson, Papineau-Neilson, 26 June 1826.

[110] *Imperial Blue Books*, *1820–1829*, 'Report of Committee of House of Commons 1828,' Ap.: Petition of 87,000 Inhabitants of Lower Canada, 1828.

[111] *Ibid.*, Petition of 10,000 from the Townships of the Lower Province, 1828.

[112] APQ: Fonds Papineau, XI, 509-A, Papineau-Neilson, 9 January 1828.

[113] *Hansard*, *II Series*, XIX, 300; Chapais, III, 207–8.

[114] Creighton, 257.

[115] *Affaires du Pays depuis 1828* (Quebec, 1834), 1; Chapais III, 214.

[116] Doughty & Storey, *Const. Docs.*, *1819–1828* in *CAR 1935*, Ap., 466–77: Report of Committee of House of Commons, 1828. Published as *Report from the Select Committee on the Civil Government of Canada* (London, 1828); republished in French at Quebec by Neilson & Cowan, 1828. Extracts in Kennedy, 254.

[117] Translated from Chapais, III, 216.

[118] PAC: Q 193–3, 377: Kempt-Murray, 2 March 1830; Chapais III, 229.

[119] Manning, 335.

[120] APQ: Fonds Papineau, XI, 516–7, Papineau-Neilson, 14 November 1830.

[121] PAC: Neilson Collection, XIV, 40, Papineau-Neilson, 11 May 1831.

[122] Bib. St. Sulp.: Corr. Papineau-Neilson, Papineau-Neilson, 20 August 1831.

[123] Chapais, III, 242: Goderich-Aylmer, 7 July 1831.

[124] *Le Canadien*, 12 January 1832; Chapais, III, 259.

[125] Bib. St. Sulp.: Corr. Papineau-Neilson, Papineau-Neilson, 12 November 1829.

[126] *Quebec Gazette*, 10 December 1831, Letter signed '*La Raison*' (Abbé C.-F. Painchaud): 'The Canadian clergy, having no longer anything to hope from the House of Assembly, would be wise to detach its hopes from it and attach them to the executive.'; Chapais, III, 257.

[127] Christie, III, 396–7, gives many of the documents; *Le Canadien*, Chapais, IV, 8.

[128] *Montreal Gazette*, 27 October 1832; Creighton, 275.

[129] *Ibid.*, 11 September 1832; Creighton, 275–6.

[130] *Quebec Gazette*, August, 11 November 1832; Christie, III, 355.

[131] APQ: Fonds Papineau, XI, 521, Papineau-Neilson, 11 August 1832.

[132] N.-E. Dionne, *Les Trois comédies de Status Quo* (Québec, 1909), 13.

[133] Kennedy, 274–90: Ninety-Two Resolutions, 21 February 1834; Chapais, IV, 18–25.

[134] *Précis des debats de la Chambre d'Assemblée* (Québec, 1834), 4–7; Chapais, IV, 27–9.

[135] PAC: Q 219–2, 216–31, letter from Montreal, 27 February 1834; Creighton, 289.

[136] *Montreal Gazette*, 11 December 1834; Creighton, 293.

[137] *Ibid.*, 6, 8 November 1834; Creighton, 293.

[138] PAC: Sec. of State's Papers, Lower Canada, Molson *et al.*-Craig, 22 November 1834; Creighton, 294.

[139] PAC: Neilson Collection, XIV, 48–9: Montreal Committee (Morin, Papineau, R. Nelson, O'Callaghan, Lafontaine, Perrault)—Quebec Committee (Vanfelson, Beserin, A. Berthelot, E.-R. Caron, Dubord, H.-S. Huot, J. Blanchet, A. Godbout, N. Boissonault, E. Bédard, *et al.*), 20 November 1834.

[140] *Ibid.*, 50.

[141] *The Patriot*, 16 January 1835; Creighton, 294. The Quebec Association under Neilson's leadership was more moderate and truly constitutional, opposing Union or the annexation of Montreal to Upper Canada.

CHAPTER IV

CRISIS AND CONFLICT

(1834–9)

THE REBELLION of 1837–8 in Lower Canda was neither a clear-cut conflict between the ethnic groups, as many French- and English-Canadian writers have considered it, nor a struggle between liberty-loving North Americans and reactionary Europeans, as Papineau saw it.[1] Many of Papineau's chief lieutenants were English Canadians,[2] and the *Patriotes* maintained close relations with Mackenzie's Reformers in Upper Canada.[3] In both sections the popular agrarian majority was in bitter conflict with the oligarchic minority of officials, placemen, and merchants; and in both sections rebellion resulted from the increasing frustration of the majority, whose odds in numbers were outweighed by their enemies' monopoly of power. Both Papineau and Mackenzie were publicly supported in the imperial parliament and privately encouraged by the English Philosophical Radicals;[4] and the agitation in the Canadas had much in common with the Chartist movement in England, which came to a head after the Canadian uprisings had been suppressed.[5]

Reform was the spirit of the age in both Canada and Britain; but Canada's proximity to the United States, and the time-lag between the Colonial Office and Parliament, brought matters to a head sooner in the colony than in the mother country. The rise of Jacksonian democracy in the United States reinforced the long-established influence of the American Revolution upon Canadian political thinking; the outmoded colonial system became more intolerable to the popular leaders, while the oligarchy was frightened into violent reaction by the crumbling of its wonted world. The political crisis was rendered more acute by the severe agricultural and commercial depression of 1833–8, which made both parties more intransigent and thus hastened the coming of open conflict.

I

In London, during April 1834, John Arthur Roebuck, a Radical M.P. who had been educated in Canada, savagely attacked the colonial administration of Lord Stanley and supported the Ninety-Two Resolutions. A month later another English Radical, Joseph

Hume, wrote Mackenzie a letter in which he referred to 'that crisis which is fast approaching in the affairs of the Canadas, and which will terminate in independence and freedom from the baneful domination of the mother country.'[6] But the Whig government was by no means of the same school of thought as these Radical spokesmen. In reply to Roebuck's attack, Stanley proposed a revival of the Committee of 1828 on Canadian affairs, and this course was followed. The committee heard the testimony of Viger, Morin, Sir James Kempt, Frederick Elliott of the Colonial Office, Ellice, James Stuart, and others. Finally on July 3 it turned in a terse, sibyline report, which maintained that the government had tried to act on the suggestions of 1828 and had been guided by the best interests of the colony. But difficulties had arisen between the assembly and the legislative council, and between the assembly and the executive, which had prevented the full achievement of the program of reform. The committee concluded its report by asserting its conviction that 'practical measures for the future government of Lower Canada may best be left to the mature consideration of the government responsible for their adoption and execution.'[7] In short, Grey's outgoing moderate Whig ministry left the problem to Peel's reformist Tory administration.

Just before handing over the Colonial Office to Thomas Spring-Rice, Stanley announced his intention of abrogating the law of 1831 which had renounced the government's claim to the Crown revenues, in anticipation of the grant of a civil list which had not been forthcoming. In addition to this old quarrel, Spring-Rice found himself confronted with new grievances in the form of resolutions against the British American Land Company and against Aylmer's appointment of the bureaucrat Samuel Gale to the bench in 1834. Spring-Rice scolded Aylmer for his lack of wisdom and tact in the latter matter, but sustained the land company. Meanwhile in Canada the assembly had met and chosen Papineau as speaker by a vote of 70–6 which indicated his decided dominance over that body. The now customary deadlock between the two branches of the government soon arose, and Aylmer prorogued the assembly after it had passed one bill.

London, weary of continual crises in Canada and moved by the spirit of reform then active at Westminster, appointed a royal commission to visit Canada and seek an end of the difficulties. In order to give the commission a free hand, Aylmer was recalled and replaced by Lord Gosford, who was named high commissioner as well as governor, with the Tory Sir Charles Grey and the Liberal Sir George Gipps as his colleagues. The commissioners arrived at Quebec on August 23, 1835. Gosford at once displayed a conciliatory spirit, and took pains to consult such *Patriote* leaders as Papineau,

L.-M. Viger, and Debartzch. In his speech from the throne at the opening of the session, he called for an end to dissension and promised redress of many grievances.

Meanwhile the commission set about its work. Its secretary, Frederick Elliott of the Colonial Office, found three opposed groups in Lower Canada: the Bureaucrats, jealous of their authority and privileges; the English party, made up of discontented merchants, *seigneurs*, and placemen, which he considered more likely to cut the tie with Britain than the French party, and more sympathetic to republicanism; and the French party, the majority in the assembly, made up of lawyers, doctors, and *habitants* and completely controlled by Papineau. The latter Elliott found personally charming, 'by nature, as much as by the position to which he has raised himself, the first of the French Canadians,'[8] but given to violence, lack of complete frankness, and bitter prejudice against the English. Elliott appreciated the uneasy position of the French Canadians, 'surrounded on all sides by millions whose language and customs are those whose influence they have so much reason to fear,' and he considered that their dread of the future extinction of their language and culture was well founded. He concluded that 'to reconcile the French Canadians and to guide them in the art of government is the surest and most convenient policy for the present, and also that which will lead to lasting and solid advantages in the future.' After arguing with the militant *Patriote* Etienne Parent, 'a little dyspeptic man, the editor of *Le Canadien*,' Elliott was surprised 'to see on what a friendly basis generally rest the ideas of the French Canadians, and how their understanding of political science is superior to that of the men by whom they have been so arrogantly despised.'

Gosford endeavored to further this friendly feeling. The high commissioner's display of conciliatory spirit was not confined merely to such social gestures as dining Papineau and Viger and showing special attention to Madame Elzéar Bédard, whose husband had sponsored the Ninety-Two Resolutions. When the ultra-loyalists of Montreal formed a British Rifle Corps, 'to preserve inviolate the connection which exists between Great Britain and Lower Canada,' the governor promptly suppressed it as being more apt 'to endanger the public tranquility' than to promote it.[9]

Under such temperate rule the split among the *Patriotes* was accentuated, with the moderates led by Elzéar Bédard and John Neilson acquiring such former followers of Papineau as Vanfelson, Berthelot, Caron, and Morin. By February 1836 Papineau could only muster a majority of one vote in the assembly. Indeed Gosford's mission was about to be crowned with success when the untimely disclosure of the instructions of the royal commission, made by Sir Francis Bond Head, the impetuous governor of Upper Canada, threw doubt on London's professed goodwill toward the colony. It was the Upper Canadian Reformer Mackenzie who sent damaging extracts from these instructions to Papineau, who promptly communicated them to the assembly.[10] Thanks to this incident, Papineau was put back in the saddle, for Gosford's communication to the assembly of a complete copy of his instructions, in order to remedy the harm done by a partial disclosure of their contents, did not restore his original favorable position. The suspicions of the *Patriotes* were also reinforced by the appointment to the bench of Bédard. The popular party had lost too many of its leaders in this fashion not to distrust the maneuver. Vanfelson succeeded Bédard as leader of the moderates, and called for a vote of confidence in Gosford and a truce in the long battle of the assembly with the executive. Papineau and his young disciple Louis-Hippolyte Lafontaine opposed this course in speeches of considerable violence, and the measure was defeated by eleven votes. The policy of conciliation had been rejected by those to whom it was directed; now coercion was to take its place, as an open break finally occurred.

A special twelve-day session in the fall of 1836, called by Gosford at the instigation of London in a last attempt to secure the support of the assembly, ended with that body announcing on September 30 its intention 'to adjourn our deliberations until His Majesty's government shall by its acts, especially by rendering the second branch of the Legislature conformable to the wishes and wants of the people, have commenced the great work of justice and reform, and created a confidence which alone can crown it with success.'[11] The intransigent attitude of the assembly in thus going on strike for an elective council, despite the governor's policy of conciliation, was in large measure due to the violent newspaper warfare of the period, which saw the publication of Adam Thom's savage 'Anti-Gallic Letters' in the *Montreal Herald*.

This Scottish school-teacher and lawyer made himself the journalistic spokesman of the hardshell Tory merchants, and poured scathing abuse upon French Canadians and governor alike. Thom upbraided Gosford in such terms as these: 'Good heavens, my lord of Gosford, are you mad enough to glory in your shame, hardened enough to rejoice in a delegated opportunity of doing evil, degraded enough to be "cheerful" under the double lash of a Frenchified cabinet and a French faction?'[12] The merchants were maddened to desperation by Gosford's policy of conciliating the French Canadians; in December 1835 the *Montreal Gazette* justified an appeal to force,[13] while in the following year Thom warned Gosford that the talk of a civil war to give scope to British capital and commerce was to be taken seriously: 'Your lordship may have been led to believe that the avowed determination of the constitutionalists, to resist the extension of French domination, was merely an empty threat; but they have not forgotten, that the glorious fields of Cressy, Poictiers, Agincourt and Minden were won by "miserable" minorities of Englishmen over vast majorities of Frenchmen.'[14] Under such provocation Papineau grew still more violent, despite counsels of patience and moderation from the English friends of the *Patriotes*, and he was supported by such disciples as Lafontaine, Augustin Morin, and Sabrevoix de Bleury. Even the moderate *Le Canadien* proclaimed: 'The Colonial Secretary has only words to offer an Assembly to which a long reign of corrupt abuse has given an ardent thirst for effective reforms. The immediate result of all this is not hard to anticipate.'[15]

The royal commission, less Gosford, who remained as governor, returned to England during the winter of 1836–7 and made its report.[16] On the whole the document was unfavorable to the claims of the assembly, which it thus summarized: a responsible executive council, an elective legislative council, complete and immediate cession to the assembly of control of all the revenue, the revocation of the Tenure Act and the British American Land Company Act, and basic control by the assembly over the administration and settlement of public lands. The commissioners considered that with two elective houses the Lower Canadian legislature would resemble too closely the American system of government and would be dominated by one party. They believed that a responsible executive council—the 'ministry' for which the French Canadians had long contended—was incompatible with the maintenance of the tie between the mother country and the colony. The commissioners recommended the retention by the Crown of a portion of the revenue, the grant of a civil list for the life of the sovereign or for at least seven years, the maintenance of the land company, a modification of the election law, and the abandonment of the project of uniting the two Canadas. They also singled out the abuses of naming the same individuals to both the executive and legislative councils, and of excluding the French Canadians from public office.

There was not much in the report to satisfy the assembly, which had taken its stand on the Ninety-Two Resolutions and refused to be conciliated by anything less than complete capitulation to its demands. To be sure, the abuses of which the Lower Canadian assembly complained were to be found in the other British North American provinces, and in Upper Canada, at least, produced very much the same reaction. But the situation was more dangerous in Lower Canada because of the division between a French majority and an English minority, although there were some English Canadians in the French party and some French Canadians in the English party. In the face of an ethnic conflict which embittered a political conflict, London sought to maintain the old doctrines of colonial government, while the Canadians demanded British responsible government with certain American features.

London was willing to reform but not to revise existing institutions—the same institutions which had produced the American Revolution. Some of the leading Bureaucrats were deprived of their offices under the reign of Goderich at the Colonial Office. Gosford's nominations to the legislative council in the spring of 1836, following those made since 1828, were designed to give that body a French-Canadian majority; by the same date the executive council numbered five French Canadians and three English Canadians; while four of the five new judges named since 1828 were French Canadians. But such concessions, particularly when they were used to deprive it of its leaders, did not satisfy the assembly, which held out for full control of the revenue, responsible government, and an elective legislative council. On the first point Gosford expressed the government's willingness to yield at long last. But London was not inclined to grant responsible government, when that meant putting power into the hands of Papineau and his party, nor an elective council, when such a concession would have made Papineau the master of both houses of the legislature, and left the English Canadians without protection.

The decision of the British government as to its Canadian policy was announced just four days after the report of the royal commission was made to parliament on March 2, 1837. Lord John Russell, the emancipator of the English Catholics and the proposer of the Reform Bill in 1832, presented his Ten Resolutions, based on the commission's report, which declared the creation of an elective legislative council inopportune but proposed to make it more popular, rejected the proposal of a responsible executive council, maintained the British American Land Company, offered hope of the revocation of the Tenure Act, authorized the governor to take the funds which the assembly had refused to grant from revenues in the receiver general's hands, provided for the cession of the Crown revenues to the assembly if the latter granted a civil list, and urged the legislatures of Upper and Lower Canada to settle their common interests.[17] The Resolutions evoked a three-day debate, in which O'Connell, Roebuck, and Hume opposed the government's proposals, and Labouchere, Peel, and Gladstone supported them. Young Gladstone, who was later to become the advocate of Home Rule for Ireland, proclaimed in the best Tory style: 'The question is not a question of party; it is simply whether one ought to consent to a virtual separation of Canada from England. . . . The question in dispute is not between the Assembly and the administration, but between the Assembly and the mother country, which has sanctioned all that the mother country has done.'[18] Except for the Radicals, the Commons supported the government's proposals; and in the House of Lords only Lord Brougham raised his eloquent voice against the measure. The Ten Resolutions touched off the explosive Canadian situation.

The Irish-born and French-educated Edmund Bailey O'Callaghan, a supporter of Papineau in the assembly and the editor of the three-year-old *Irish Vindicator* of Montreal, summed up the reaction of the popular party to the events in England thus:

> *A combined and dishonorable junction of Whigs and Tories, in a House of Commons 'reformed' but in name, may pass Resolutions to annihilate the last remnant of Liberty left in the Colonial Legislatures.* A House of Lords, the fundamental principle of whose Constitution is inimical to human freedom, may endorse the determination of the combined enemies of freedom in the Lower House, but neither the Resolutions, their authors, nor their supporters, can change the nature of things. *Robbery will be robbery still.* . . . Our rights must not be violated with impunity. A howl of indignation must be raised from one extremity of the Province to the other, against the robbers, and against all who partake of the plunder.
>
> *HENCEFORTH, THERE MUST BE NO PEACE IN THE PROVINCE —no quarter for the plunderers.* Agitate! *Agitate!! AGITATE!!!* Destroy the Revenue; denounce the oppressors. Everything is lawful when the fundamental liberties are in danger. 'The guards die—they never surrender.'[19]

And so the French-Canadian struggle for self-government abandoned constitutional means and had recourse to revolt, at the instigation of an Irish doctor quoting one of Napoleon's marshals. That revolt was an incident in the great struggle between the new and old orders launched by the American and French Revolutions, which had made 'liberty' and 'freedom' words capable of unleashing the energies of peoples against their rulers. Napoleon had risen to supremacy in Europe by using the social forces thus set in motion; it was not inappropriate that the proud words of one of his followers should serve to rouse the people of French Canada.

2

The Rebellion of 1837–8 in Lower Canada was a rebellion in spite of the intentions of its original leaders; like its counterpart in Upper Canada, it was a largely unpremeditated resort to arms to break the long constitutional deadlock between the people and the oligarchy, after much provocation from the latter. Looking back on his course of action after he had been forced to take refuge in the United States, Papineau proudly proclaimed: 'I offered constitutional opposition;

I did not offer any other. We did not conspire to overturn the government by force; we wished to cure it by [altering] its diet and way of life.'[20]

Thus the first form of resistance to Russell's Ten Resolutions was an attempt to dry up the sources of the revenue by boycotting imported goods, and by using only homemade or smuggled articles on which no duty was paid. In April 1837 Ludger Duvernay, the hotheaded *Patriote* who had founded the Saint-Jean-Baptiste Society in 1834, laid down the *Patriote* program in *La Minerve*:

> Friend Jonathan will supply us with the articles which we cannot make here. Therefore let us aid the smuggler; from now on he is a brave fellow whom each of us will encourage. Vigorous youths, determined and well organized, must be trained for this career. Smuggling must be done on a grand scale. No more circumspection or temporizing. Major remedies are needed for major evils. The sources of the revenue must be dried up. The vaults will empty; the thieves will find nothing more there. Then England will listen to reason. Never has a struggle been more just. We have withheld the subsidies; this weapon is now taken from us and we must seek others more efficacious.[21]

The *Patriote* leaders held public meetings to spread the gospel of economic revolt. They practiced what they preached: when the assembly was summoned in August, the appearance of the Montreal members aroused the humor of the government-controlled *Quebec Mercury*:

> Mr. Rodier's dress excited the greatest attention, being *unique*, with the exception of a pair of Berlin gloves, viz.: frock coat of granite colored *étoffe du pays*; inexpressibles and vest of the same material, striped blue and white; straw hat and beef shoes, with a pair of home-made socks, completed the *outré* attire. Mr. Rodier, it was remarked, had no shirt on, having doubtless been unable to smuggle or manufacture one.
>
> Dr. O'Callaghan's 'rig out' was second only to that of Mr. Rodier, being complete with the exception of hat, boots, gloves, and shirt [he *had* a shirt!] and spectacles.[22]

But as in the American Revolution, passive resistance to the arbitrary measures of the mother country soon led to more violent opposition. The general mood was highly explosive, since Canada was undergoing one of the worst depressions it had ever known—the wheat crop of the previous year had been a failure, and the farmers were hard-pressed during the spring and summer of 1837, while the business community was severely shaken by financial panic both in London and the United States. A resort to violence no longer seemed unthinkable, but rather the only solution of bitter frustration. The newspapers continued to fan the flames, and during the spring and summer great public meetings were held, particularly in the region of Montreal, that most sharply affected by the economic crisis. At these gatherings impassioned orators waxed more and more intemperate in their protests against British oppression and in their proposals of counter action. At Saint-Ours on the Richelieu on May 7 Wolfred Nelson, Cyrille Côté, and Siméon Marchessault—two doctors and a school-teacher—denounced the Ten Resolutions as a violation of the social contract and expressed regret that Canada had not made common cause with the Americans in 1775. This echo of Rousseau and the reference to the American Revolution are interesting in the light they shed upon the sources of *Patriote* ideas. Papineau was hailed as the Canadian Daniel O'Connell, a personification of the people.

This meeting of 1,200 persons adopted twelve resolutions prepared by the *Patriotes'* Permanent Central Committee, which corresponded to the first American Congress's declaration of rights and grievances in 1774 and to the French declaration of the rights of man in 1789. They read thus:

I. It is with feelings of the most lively indignation that we have seen the resolutions proposed for adoption by the House of Commons on March 6 last, resolutions of which the inevitable effect is to deprive us of any guarantee of liberty and good government in the future for this province.

II. The adoption of these resolutions will be a flagrant violation on the part of the Commons, and of the government which proposed them, of the Capitulation, treaties, and constitutional acts which have been granted to this country. These acts, and these treaties, carry reciprocal obligations, to wit, on our part, love and obedience; on England's part, protection and the assurance of liberty; and they would be virtually annulled by the violation of the promises of one of the contracting parties.

III. In these circumstances we can only regard the government which would have recourse to injustice, force, and a violation of the social contract as an oppressive power and a government of force, to which henceforth the extent of our submission should be measured only by our numerical strength, joined to the sympathies that we find elsewhere.

IV. The machiavelianism which has accompanied all the acts of the government since the cession, the bad faith which has characterized it until now, the feebleness revealed by every page of the commissioners' report and by speeches of the ministers, who did not blush to cite our division and our small numbers as reasons for refusing us justice; all this inspires us only with the most profound disgust and the most pronounced scorn for the men who rule one of the greatest and noblest peoples of the earth, or are attached to such a government.

V. The people of this country have long awaited justice from the colonial administration at first, and later from the metropolitan government, and always in vain; during thirty years fear has broken some of our chains, while an insatiable love of power has added heavier ones. The high opinion that we had of the justice and honor of the English people made us hope that the parliament which represented it would provide a remedy for our grievances. Disillusioned of this last hope, we have renounced forever the idea of seeking justice on the other side of the ocean, and we have recognized at last how much this country has been misled by the lying promises which made it fight against a people which offered it liberty and equal rights in behalf of a people who prepared to enslave it. Sad experience forces us to recognize that our true friends and natural allies were on the other side of the 45th parallel.

VI. We deny to the English parliament the right to legislate on the internal affairs of this colony without our consent, our participation, and our request, since the non-exercise of this right by England has been guaranteed to us by the Constitution, and recognized by the mother country when she feared that we would accept the offers of liberty and independence made to us by the neighboring republic. Consequently, we regard as null and void the Tenure Act, the Canada Trade Act, the act which incorporated the company known as the 'Land Company,' and finally the act which will doubtless be based upon the resolutions just adopted by the Commons.

VII. Regarding ourselves as no longer bound except by force to the English government, we shall submit to it as to a government of force, expecting from God, our valid rights, and circumstances a better fate, the favors of liberty and a juster government. Meanwhile, as our public funds which the home government dares to dispose of without any control are going to become in its hands a new means of pressure against us, we regard it as our duty, arising from our honor, to resist by all means now in our possession to a tyrannical power, in order to diminish as much as we can these means of oppression, and we resolve:

VIII. That we shall abstain, insofar as it may be in our power, from consuming imported goods, particularly those on which the higher duties are paid, such as tea, tobacco, wine, rum, etc. By preference we shall consume products manufactured in our country; we shall regard as deserving well of the homeland whoever establishes the manufacture of silk, cloth, sugar, spirits, etc. Considering the Trade Act as null, we shall regard as wholly lawful the commerce known as contraband; we shall judge this traffic as very honorable; we shall try to favor it by every means in our power, regarding those who devote themselves to it as deserving well of the homeland, and as infamous whoever denounces them.

IX. In order to render these resolutions more efficacious, this assembly is of the opinion that an association should be established in this country, with headquarters in Quebec or Montreal, whose purpose will be to bind its members to consume only products manufactured in this country, or imported without the payment of duties. . . .

X. In order to effect more efficaciously the regeneration of this country, all should rally around a single man, following the example of Ireland.

God has marked this man, like O'Connell, to be the political chief and the regenerator of a people. He has given him for that purpose an unsurpassed force of thought and word, a hatred of oppression, a love of country which no promise or threat of the powers-that-be can break down. This man, already singled out by the country, is L.-J. Papineau. This assembly, taking into consideration the happy results obtained in Ireland from the assessment known as 'O'Connell's Tribute,' is of the opinion that a similar assessment, called 'Papineau's Tribute,' ought to exist in this country. The committees of the association against importation would be charged with raising it.

XI. This assembly could not break up without extending its sincerest thanks to the orators, not numerous but zealous and able, who proclaimed the justice of our cause in the House of Commons, as well as to the honest and virtuous men who voted with them. The London workers, who with a spirit of liberty and of justice worthy of a free people presented a petition to the House of Commons in favor of this unhappy country, have an equal right to our profound gratitude. Our friends of the Political Union of Toronto also have a right to our thanks for the sympathy they manifested towards us in the resolution they adopted on April 17 against the ministers' measures of coercion.

XII. This assembly holds the conviction that in the general election with which the country is threatened at the instigation of weak and perverse men, as ignorant of public opinion in the present crisis as they are deprived of influence, the electorate will exhibit its gratitude to its faithful representatives by re-electing them and by rejecting those who have not fulfilled their promises and their duties, and who have betrayed the country either by siding with our enemies or by cowardly absence when the country expected from them an honest expression of their sentiments.[23]

This Declaration of Saint-Ours, a notable landmark in the development of French-Canadian nationalism, was spread through the province by publication in *La Minerve* and in the *Vindicator*. With its warning that the people might renounce their allegiance to Britain, and with its use of the threat of annexation to the United States, then in the throes of expansionism to the tune of Manifest Destiny, it went much farther than the Ninety-Two Resolutions of 1834, which were a parliamentary rather than popular expression of the same state of mind. It frightened the supporters of the government, and made such moderates as Etienne Parent, who characterized it as 'strange, absurd, and unrealizable,'[24] recoil before the prospect of either civil war or hopeless despair under new repression.

The vagueness of the Declaration's fine language was clarified and strengthened at the meetings which were held at Saint-Laurent, Chambly, Yamaska, Lachenaye, Quebec, Verchères, Saint-Hyacinthe, Sainte-Scholastique, and elsewhere in May and June. At Saint-Laurent on May 15 Papineau lashed out at 'the old enemies of the country: the governor, the two councils, the judges, the majority of the public servants, their creatures and their supports, whom your representatives have long denounced as forming a corrupt faction, hostile to the rights of the people and moved by self-interest alone to support a vicious system of government.'[25] He attacked Gosford as three times as detestable as Dalhousie and Aylmer and denounced the British parliament which wished 'to steal your money to pay your servants, whom your representatives have refused to pay because they have been lazy, faithless, and incompetent.' He hailed the example of the Americans, who had successfully resisted a similar attempt to oppress them in 1774; and proclaimed the sympathy of the American government and the British people with the Canadians in their struggle for justice.[26]

But in reality, despite expressions of sympathy in both quarters, financial panic and economic distress preoccupied both Britain and the United States at this moment. Papineau, who was an idealist thinking in purely political terms, did not realize this fact, nor did he see that such agitation as he was conducting, with constant appeals to systematic illegality, must end in violence. Yet he quoted Lord Brougham, who in the debate on the Ten Resolutions had warned the British ministry: 'Yes, if you attempt to consummate your iniquitous works, the Canadians have a moral duty to resist you. Yes, if the same blood ran in their veins as that which produced Washingtons, Franklins, and Jeffersons, they would chase you from their country as you were justly chased from the old colonies.'[27] Papineau claimed that he was not held back from rebellion by either fear or scruple, but by the conviction that constitutional resistance, which had won so many triumphs in the past for the French Canadians, would suffice once more, although he now envisaged for the first time the future necessity of stronger measures. The leaders of the agitation began to talk of free exchange with the United States and a general convention. The cooler-headed and more farsighted Etienne Parent, now denounced as a coward and a hypocrite by the *Patriotes*, warned the people that declarations of hostility to England were invitations for the use of force to crush a feeble Canada, unable to win its independence by arms.[28]

Outside of Montreal, the headquarters of the Permanent Central Committee of the *Patriotes*, which gradually dominated the county committees, the popular feeling was strongest in the Richelieu Valley, hard-hit by wheat-crop failures, and about Lac des Deux Montagnes. The districts of Trois-Rivières and Quebec were much calmer than that of Montreal, although Augustin-Norbert Morin and Robert Shore Milnes Bouchette held large meetings in May and June at the capital, whose Irish population first decided to make common cause with the *Patriotes* and then yielded to the inducements offered by the oligarchy. In June and July Papineau, Morin, Lafontaine, and

Girouard made a tour through the district of Quebec, whose *Patriote* fervor lagged behind the ever-swelling agitation in that of Montreal. In July, the opposition decided to fight fire with fire, holding constitutional assemblies at Montreal, Napierville, Trois-Rivières, and Quebec. But even the presence of the garrison troops at these gatherings could not swell their numbers to equal those of the *Patriote* meetings; and the fact that they were presided over by English Canadians, and that their chief speakers were either English- or French-Canadian bureaucrats, indicates that they were officially inspired and not true popular assemblies.

Both state and Church were alarmed by the growing unrest, and took steps to check it, without much success. On June 15 Gosford issued a proclamation denouncing the seditious assemblies and urging all public officials to oppose the measures proposed at them.[29] Several magistrates and militia officers who took part in the *Patriote* agitation were relieved of their commissions in August, when the meetings continued nonetheless. On July 25, at a dinner celebrating the consecration of Bishop Bourget as his coadjutor, Bishop Lartigue of Montreal informally advised his clergy that 'it is never permissible to revolt against legitimate authority or to violate the laws of the land; that absolution should not be given in the tribunal of penitence to anyone who teaches that it is permissible to revolt against the government under which we have the happiness to live, or that it is permissible to violate the laws of the land, particularly those which forbid smuggling.'[30] This résumé of the bishop's remarks—at a banquet attended by nearly all the clergy of the diocese—was published in *L'Ami du Peuple*, an anti-*Patriote* journal of Montreal, under the heading 'Catholicism against M. Papineau'; and was promptly disputed by the *Patriote* organ *La Minerve*, which denied that the bishop had condemned smuggling.[31] During the course of his pastoral visits in July, Bishop Signay of Quebec also recommended prudence to his clergy. But despite these restraining influences the agitation continued to mount, and scuffles and duels between the partisans of the popular and bureaucratic groups became more frequent in Montreal and the surrounding countryside.

The death of King William IV and the succession of Queen Victoria was used as a pretext by Lord John Russell, who was no doubt influenced by reports from Canada, to announce on June 23 the suspension of the program laid down in his Ten Resolutions, since the government was unwilling to blight the opening of a new reign by the application of coercive measures. On July 3 the British Commons voted a sum to meet the arrears of Canadian government costs. Gosford had already been ordered to call the assembly as soon as possible, in a final attempt to win its submission. Meanwhile London busied itself with taking action, after long delays, on the measures of conciliation which Gosford had earlier recommended. It was alarmed by a visit which the French minister to the United States, M. de Pontois, paid to Lower Canada, where he dined with Papineau and attended a *Patriote* assembly at Saint-Constant. With French Canadians greeting each other as *citoyen*, singing the *Marseillaise*, and displaying the Tricolor, Palmerston may be excused for his alarm.

But while a belated effort at conciliation was being made by the home government, the agitation in Canada continued to swell. Gosford's proclamation, with its attack on the *Patriote* leaders, had heightened rather than reduced the unrest; and in August congregations walked out on the traditional *Te Deum* which followed the proclamation from the pulpit of the new monarch.[32] Gosford himself still hoped to avoid serious trouble by liberalization of the two councils, and refused to call in troops from New Brunswick and Nova Scotia, as he had been authorized to do by London, despite growing disorder in the Two Mountains district northwest of Montreal. At the opening of the session on August 18, he announced the government's inclination to avoid recourse to the program of the Ten Resolutions, if the assembly consented to grant the needed funds. He also outlined the reforms which he had recommended and which had actually been decided upon in London as he spoke. If action had been taken upon them a month earlier, the course of history might have been changed.

But in its reply, which Papineau inspired and Morin—unaware that he had just been named commissioner of Crown lands—delivered, the unruly assembly announced:

> It is our duty, therefore, to tell the Mother Country that if she carries the spirit of these resolutions into effect in the Government of British North America, and of this province in particular, her supremacy therein will no longer depend upon the feelings of affection, of duty and of mutual interest which would best secure it, but upon physical and material force, an element dangerous to the governing party, at the same time that it subjects the governed to a degree of uncertainty as to their future existence and their dearest interests, which is scarcely to be found under the most absolute government of civilized Europe.[33]

The assembly decided to rest upon its old intransigent position, since no reform of the council had taken place. Meanwhile dispatches were actually on the way out from London with news of the appointment of seven French Canadians out of ten new legislative councilors. The bureaucratic delays of the Colonial Office, heightened by the varying policies of eight ministers in eleven years, brought about the breakdown of representative government in Canada. A moderate motion by Taschereau, supported by Huot and the now wavering Bleury, to grant the desired funds if reforms took place, was defeated by 46–18; and the Papineau-Morin reply was adopted by a majority of fifteen votes. On August 26 it was presented to Gosford, who expressed his regret that the assembly persisted in its determination to deprive the country of a local legislature; and when the members returned to their chamber, the last assembly of Lower Canada found itself dissolved by a proclamation placed on the seat of Speaker Papineau.

Gosford at last abandoned hope of conciliation. On September 2 he wrote to the colonial secretary:

> It is evident that Papineau's party will not be satisfied with any concession which will not put it in a more favorable position to realize its ultimate intentions, that is to say, the separation of this country from England and the establishment of a republican government. M. Papineau has gone so far that he must persevere, or submit to a defeat which would destroy all his influence; the plan that he follows shows that he has decided to risk everything to reach his goal. The violent and unjustifiable attacks which have been made by the ultra-Tories against the French Canadians in general have created an animosity of which M. Papineau has not failed to take advantage, and I attribute to this cause much of his influence on a great many members of the house. M. Papineau has emissaries in all directions, and although I do not know that there is reason to take alarm, there is need of much precaution and vigilance to prevent and check the disorders which might take place, as a result of the efforts made to excite discontent among the people by the most abominable representations. The government needs to be invested with the fullest power, and according to my present opinion, you may be under the necessity of suspending the constitution. It is with the most profound regret that I announce this opinion; but my duty forces me to do so.[34]

Gosford was right; the hot blood of the youngsters was carrying the *Patriote* movement out of the hands of staider elders. Late in August the New Brunswick-born and Vermont-bred Thomas Storrow Brown, André Ouimet, and Amédée Papineau, son of the *Patriote* leader, organized a *Fils de la Liberté* association in Montreal, in obvious imitation of the American Sons of Liberty of revolutionary days. The *Fils de la Liberté* met publicly for military training to the strains of George-Etienne Cartier's '*Avant tout, je suis Canadien,*' though they lacked arms. On October 1 they published a hotheaded manifesto in which they proclaimed their intention 'to emancipate our country from all human authority save that of the bold democracy residing within its bosom.'[35] The Tories of the disbanded British Rifle Corps, egged on by the *Herald*, had formed a rival organization, the British Legion or Doric Club, which masqueraded as a 'fraternal association' after Gosford had again frowned on their renewed proposal to form a volunteer military unit.[36]

Meanwhile the *Patriote* mass meetings continued, with the majority of the speakers more violent than ever. The Two Mountains committee decided on October 1 to elect its own justices of the peace and military officers by majority vote, to replace those deprived of office by Gosford, and did so at a meeting of *habitants* on October 15. The anti-*Patriote Le Populaire* hailed the news with: '*La Revolution commence!*' On October 23 5,000 people assembled at Saint-Charles on the Richelieu in the name of the Confederation of the Six Counties [of the Richelieu] to hear Papineau, L.-M. Viger, Dr. Coté, Rodier, Brown, and Amury Girod. Papineau, at last alarmed by the storm he had roused, advised against a recourse to arms, urging constitutional resistance and arguing that 'the best way to fight England is to refuse to buy anything from her.'[37] It was significant that Dr. Wolfred Nelson, the chairman of the meeting, interrupted the 'tribune of the people' to insist that the time for action had already come, that the moment 'to melt our spoons into bullets' was at hand. This assembly of the six counties of the Richelieu adopted thirteen resolutions, including a statement, clearly modelled on the American Declaration of Independence, of the rights of man, among which figured the people's right to change the form of government at will. The assembly called upon the citizens of the Richelieu to meet in December to elect judges and militia officers to replace those dismissed by the governor for their *Patriote* leanings. Military training and systematic resistance to officials appointed by Gosford were urged, and British soldiers were encouraged to desert. On the 24th the delegates called for the meeting of a convention to replace the 'nullified' legislature. This attempt to create a state within a state was inevitably the prelude to open rebellion.

The influence of the American and French Revolutions was more evident than ever: the organization of the *Fils de la Liberté* in Montreal was hailed as an example which each parish should follow, and a ceremony, modelled upon that of 1789 on the Champs de Mars in Paris, was held about a liberty pole, crowned with a Phrygian bonnet and bearing the inscription, 'To Papineau, his grateful compatriots, 1837.'[38] Young men took an oath, hand upon the pole, to be faithful to the fatherland and to conquer or die. The Saint-Charles meeting gave clear evidence that the movement was passing into more extreme hands than those of its original leaders: Papineau, the scheduled hero of the affair, was more moderate than at Saint-Laurent in the spring, but he was overruled by Dr. Nelson, as was his follower F.-X. Mailhot by the still more extreme Dr. Coté, who was echoed by Brown and Girod. Coté, the turbulent member for Lacadie and the circulator of Lamennais' *Les Paroles d'un croyant*, a revolutionary work condemned by Rome, concluded his fiery address with these words: 'The time for speeches has passed; we must now direct lead against our enemies.'[39]

On the day after this assembly at Saint-Charles, and a rival constitutionalist gathering at Montreal with Peter McGill as chairman, Bishop Lartigue issued a pastoral letter which *La Minerve* hailed, under the heading of 'More Politics in the Pulpit,' as a 'second edition of Gosford's proclamation.'[40] It was an attempt to avert the imminent danger of civil strife:

For a long time, brethren, we have heard only of agitation, even of revolt, in a country always renowned up to now for its loyalty, its peaceful spirit, and its love for the religion of its fathers. Everywhere brothers are seen arrayed against brothers, friends against friends, and citizens against their fellow citizens; and from one end of this diocese to the other discord seems to have broken the bonds of charity which existed between the members of one body, the children of one Church, of Catholicism which is a religion of unity.

We speak here on our own initiative, without any external pressure, solely from motives of conscience. We shall not give you our opinion, as a citizen, on the purely political question as to which is right or wrong among the diverse branches of the sovereign power (these are matters which God has left to the disputes of men: *mundun̄s tradidit disputationi corum*); but the moral question, i.e., what are the duties of a Catholic toward the civil power established and constituted in each state, this moral question, I say, is within our domain and competence . . .

Do not let yourselves be seduced if some one wishes to engage you in rebellion against the established government, under the pretext that you form part of the 'Sovereign People'; the all-too famous National Convention of France, although forced to admit the sovereignty of the people since its existence was due to it, took good care itself to condemn popular insurrections, by inserting in the Declaration of Rights at the beginning of the Constitution of 1795 the statement that sovereignty resides not in a part nor even in a majority of the people, but in the whole body of the citizens: adding, 'that no individual, that no partial union of citizens, can pretend to the "Sovereignty".' But who would dare say that in this country the whole body of citizens desire the destruction of their government.

Have you ever considered seriously the horrors of civil strife? Have you pictured brooks of blood flooding your streets and your countryside, and the innocent engulfed with the guilty in the same sequence of misfortunes? Have you reflected on the fact that, nearly without exception, every popular revolution is a bloody business, as experience proves; and that the philosopher of Geneva, the author of the *Social Contract*, the demagogue of the sovereignty of the people, says somewhere that a revolution would be bought too dearly, if it cost a single drop of blood?[41]

Bishop Lartigue based his exposition of the duties of the citizen particularly on Gregory XVI's encyclical of August 15, 1832, and the papal brief of July of the same year to the Polish bishops, in which the Polish patriots were reproved and the Czar was declared their lawful sovereign. These papal utterances, impregnated with the reactionary royalist sentiment of the period, had caused Lamennais' break with the Church and the publication of his *Les Paroles d'un croyant*, whose fervent denunciation of kings and priests found favor with the *Patriote* extremists.

Bishop Lartigue's intervention was greeted with anger, popular demonstrations, and anti-clerical counterblasts by the *Patriote* press. At Montreal, where 1,200 *Patriotes* paraded opposite St. James Cathedral at vespers, it was said that the pastoral letter would hasten the 'revolution,' while at Chambly three men left the church while it was being read and gathered a group who greeted Bishop Bourget and the clergy after Mass with cries of '*A bas le mandement!*' and '*Vive Papineau!*' Elsewhere *curés* were treated to the singing of the *Marseillaise* and the *Libera*. The popular feeling ran so high that Bishop Lartigue offered his resignation to Rome and planned to take refuge at the Seminary of Quebec against anti-royalist plots in what he called a 'civil war.' In November he published anonymously at Quebec a '*Défense du Mandement*,' refuting *Patriote* criticisms of his action in *La Minerve* and the *Vindicator*.[42]

On December 11 Bishop Signay, fearing the spread of the Montreal troubles, condemned recourse to revolt for the remedying of abuses as 'not only inefficacious, imprudent, and fatal to those who make use of it, but moreover criminal in the eyes of God and of our holy religion' and ordained prayers for peace.[43] Although the episcopal utterance was generally received with respect in the districts of Quebec and Trois-Rivières, there was opposition to it in the capital. Abbé Baillargeon, then *curé* and later bishop of Quebec, had already aroused a bitter storm of protest there when he counseled loyalty, prudence, and submission to lawful authority. The new *Patriote* organ of the capital, the bilingual *Liberal* edited by Robert Shore Milnes Bouchette, grandson of Carleton's guide in 1775 and son of the surveyor-general, and Charles Hunter, had then observed that 'It would be much better for the *curés* to receive quietly their tithes and the thousand other taxes raised on the ignorance of the people, as long as they can in return preach the moral doctrines of Christianity to their flocks, rather than for them to descend into the arena of political disputes, moved as they always are in these questions by their private interests.' Of the pastoral letters Bouchette remarked: 'The day is not far off when the bishops will regret having meddled in matters which did not concern them.'[44]

Etienne Parent's defense of the *curé* of Quebec caused *La Minerve* to censure both, and the Permanent Central Committee to denounce *Le Canadien* and Parent himself as one 'who has betrayed, and continues to betray, the interests of the country.'[45] In October Parent counseled the abandonment of illegal opposition by the *Minerve* group, and promised that all the French Canadians would rise as one man to demand or seek justice, if their opponents then indulged in excesses. But by that time the situation was already out of hand: disorders, directed chiefly against the English merchants, the *seigneurs*, and the '*Chouayens*' (as those French Canadians who would not join the *Patriote* movement were known), had already broken out in the Richelieu and Two Mountains regions near Montreal. Magistrates and militia officers favorable to the government were forced to resign their commissions, and even *curés* were troubled by assaults on their property. Apart from the spokesmen of the Church, Etienne Parent was now almost alone among French Canadians in raising his voice against the course the *Patriotes* were following. On November 22, the very eve of recourse to open rebellion, he delivered himself of a prophetic utterance in *Le Canadien:*

> If we emerge from our present plight without being crushed, let it be an eternal lesson to those who have not been able to learn from history, where it is written on every page, of the folly of agitating a people, of questioning the fundamental principles of the established social order, unless the oppression is directly felt by the governed and there remain no alternatives other than hard and dishonorable slavery or armed resistance. The agitation which has been aroused in this country has resulted in placing part of the population in open opposition to the government. But who would now say that the present government, with all its faults, is not preferable by far to the state of affairs which exists today in the district of Montreal? Would not the worst government be better than the anarchy which now grips the upper part of the province, even if anarchy were to be succeeded by a state of liberty; but no, it will be followed here as elsewhere by military despotism. That is not all. After the sword of the soldier has cut off the thousand heads of anarchy, then will come the law, which will arm the government with repressive measures that will necessarily retard the progress of the liberal cause . . . Thus we shall perhaps soon see the government vested with extraordinary powers which its creatures will certainly abuse. What will have caused that? The fatal agitation which has been imprudently aroused in this country, and which the leaders are no longer able to control. Once again, let this be at least a lesson for the future, if Providence reserves for us a future, which we must still hope.[46]

Parent had an observant as well as a prophetic soul: the *Patriote* movement had indeed run away from its original idealistic leaders and fallen into more violent hands.

The inevitable clash soon followed. Ethnic feeling was aroused by the boisterous parades of the rival *Fils de la Liberté* and Doric Club in Montreal, and on November 6 a street fight developed after the loyalists had been urged to 'crush rebellion in its bud,' which ended with the *Patriotes* breaking the windows of a magistrate's house and the Doric Club sacking the premises of O'Callaghan's *Vindicator* and assaulting Papineau's home. The troops were called out by the magistrates, a body which, along with the rest of Montreal's judicial organization, had just been purged by Gosford of all *Patriote* sympathizers. Armed guards, who tended to wink at the proceedings of the Doric Club, now patrolled the streets.[47] On the very day of the brawl in Montreal Gosford wrote home requesting power to suspend the *Habeas Corpus* Act and to proclaim martial law, while he also informed the colonial secretary that he had at last requested reinforcements from the Maritimes and Upper Canada.[48] Volunteer regiments, largely composed of Bureaucrats and gallophobes, were raised at Montreal, Quebec, and in the Townships.[49] Sir John Colborne, the commander-in-chief, who had long urged repressive rather than conciliatory measures, now obtained the governor's support. Public meetings and processions were prohibited on November 12, and warrants were issued on November 16 for the arrest for treason of twenty-six principal *Patriote* leaders. Papineau, O'Callaghan, Rodolphe Desrivières, T. S. Brown, and Ovide Perrault escaped arrest by fleeing from Montreal to the Richelieu, while André Ouimet, president of the *Fils de la Liberté*, and other minor *Patriote* figures of Montreal were clapped into jail. Morin, Bouchette, and a few others were arrested at Quebec, but later released on bail.

On the night of November 16 a troop of Montreal Volunteer Cavalry, sent to St. Johns with a constable to arrest Dr. Davignon and the notary P.-P. Demaray, was ambushed between Chambly and Longueuil by a force of *Patriotes* commanded by Bonaventure Viger* and Dr. Timothée Kimber, local chiefs of the movement.[50] Shots were fired and blood was shed; the volunteers fled, leaving their prisoners behind; and civil war had at last broken out, after a long prelude which contrasts sharply with the briefness of actual strife. But never has so little bloodshed been so well remembered, for ethnic division added to the bitterness of civil war.

3

The news of the successful skirmish at Longueuil heartened the *Patriotes*, driven to open rebellion by Tory provocation and by the government's adoption of repressive measures. They began to gather with such poor arms as they possessed at Saint-Denis and Saint-Charles on the Richelieu, where they were soon joined by the fugitives from Montreal. Those at Saint-Denis were commanded by Dr. Wolfred Nelson, an English-born local member of the assembly,

* A distant cousin of D.-B. Viger.

while the force at Montreal was commanded by Thomas Storrow Brown, a New Brunswick merchant of Montreal, who still bore scars from the fray between the Doric Club and the *Fils de la Liberté*, whose 'general' he had been.

Colborne had established, with the aid of the Montreal merchants and the *Chouayens*, an efficient intelligence service, and was well informed about *Patriote* doings. He promptly planned a joint expedition against the two centers of the disaffected Richelieu region, in order to nip the rebellion in the bud. One force under Lieutenant-Colonel Wetherall, consisting of a regiment of regular infantry, a troop of the Montreal Volunteer Cavalry, and two field guns, had already been sent to secure the lightly garrisoned fort at Chambly. This body was to advance down the Richelieu, and then to join forces at Saint-Denis with another force under Colonel Gore of five companies of regulars, a troop of mounted volunteers, and a field gun, which was to come up the river from the post at Sorel. It was thus hoped to round up the fugitive *Patriote* leaders and to disperse their followers. The plan was neatly conceived, but it made no allowances for the condition of rural roads in November, or for the military's unfamiliarity with the countryside and its language.

On the night of November 22, lashed by rain and sleet, Gore's force turned away from the main route along the river in order to avoid Saint-Ours, which was held by the *Patriotes*, and fell into difficulties on a muddy back road. His proposed surprise attack by night on Saint-Denis became a daylight attack by exhausted and half-frozen soldiers on a fully alert and strongly defended village, whose pealing bells alarmed the countryside and brought new defenders swarming to the scene. After five hours of inconclusive fighting, which resulted in the soldiers losing six killed and eighteen wounded, Gore retreated first to Saint-Ours and then to Sorel. One hundred and seventeen of his men failed to answer the roll call the evening after the battle. The *Patriotes*, who included some veterans of the War of 1812, lost eleven dead and seven wounded.[51] Among the dead was Ovide Perrault, a promising young lawyer and member of the assembly who was a devoted follower of Papineau. Young George-Etienne Cartier distinguished himself by bringing reinforcements across the river to the *Patriotes* under fire.

The great tribune himself, with Dr. O'Callaghan, had left early in the skirmish for Saint-Hyacinthe, another *Patriote* center, whence they later fled to the United States. Papineau declared that he adopted this course on the advice of Wolfred Nelson, who had said to him: 'Do not expose yourself uselessly; you will be of more service to us after the fight than here'; but Nelson later denied, after he had broken with his former chief, that he had ever made any such statement.[52] It may have been that Papineau, the undisputed chief of the movement, felt obliged to preserve himself from capture—it is said to have been agreed among the *Patriote* high command that Papineau should keep apart from all fighting, in order to be free to negotiate later with the government—or he may have been unwilling to participate in the open insurrection which he had always opposed. In any case his action at Saint-Denis, imitated later by most of the chiefs of the *Patriotes*, created a breach between the leaders and their followers which played no small part in the rapid collapse of the movement.

But a more important incident at Saint-Denis than Papineau's flight was the murder by the *Patriotes* of Lieutenant Weir, a dispatch carrier in civilian clothes who had missed Gore on the road from Sorel, thanks to the latter's detour, and who had been taken prisoner when he arrived at Saint-Denis before the troops. When the attack began, he was ordered off for safe-keeping to Saint-Charles, having given his word not to attempt escape. But, seeing the troops approach as he was being taken off, tightly bound, in a wagon, he leapt out and was promptly dispatched by the swords and guns of his guards and of the excited bystanders, whose traditional hatred of the English had been aroused. Weir's body was found lying in the Richelieu, weighted down by stones, when the British forces returned to Saint-Denis a week later; and the sight of the mutilated corpse so infuriated the soldiers that they sacked and burnt the greater part of the village. The slogan of the government forces during the rebellion became 'Remember Jack Weir,' and many later excesses on their part can be blamed on this incident.[53]

The savageness of *Patriote* feeling was not wholly ethnic in character, however, for on November 28 some *Patriotes* of St. Johns captured a French Canadian named Chartrand, who had enlisted in a loyalist volunteer corps and was reputed to be a government informer. After a drumhead court-martial, Chartrand was tied to a tree and shot.[54] Civil strife is rarely conducted according to the established rules of warfare, and the conduct of the unorganized *habitants* was not such as to either win the respect of the British professional soldiers or to calm the prejudices of the English-Canadian volunteers, excited by the Tory press and by wild rumors of *Patriote* outrages upon members of the English minority isolated in the countryside.

The initial victory at Saint-Denis was the sole battle which the insurgents won. The *Patriote* enthusiasm which it aroused was soon dampened by news from Saint-Charles. Colonel Wetherall left Chambly on November 22 about the same hour as Gore left Sorel. But according to Major Conrad Augustus Gugy, a Swiss-Canadian leader of the English party in the assembly who acted as a police inspector and intelligence officer during the rising and who accompanied Wetherall as guide and interpreter, 'not one of the Force knew anything of the roads or the people, nor do I believe that more than one spoke French.'[55] Through the same November rain and sleet, followed by frost, which beset Gore's force, Wetherall's detachment struggled on till he was persuaded to halt by Gugy's alarm at what might befall exhausted men 'in an enemy's country, surrounded by thousands of armed men.'[56] The column was still seven miles from Saint-Charles when Wetherall got word of Gore's reverse at Saint-Denis, and on Gugy's advice he sent back to Chambly for reinforcements. Awaiting their arrival took another day.

Meanwhile the *Patriotes* at Saint-Charles had fortified the manor house of the newly loyalist *seigneur* Debartzch, who had fled to Montreal. According to 'General' T. S. Brown, who had bruised some local feelings by assuming command, the *Patriotes* were less numerous there than the government supposed, a bare 200 men equipped with only 109 guns. The impossibility of any long-meditated recourse to rebellion is best witnessed by Brown's account of the *Patriote* armament:

> Of ammunition we had some half dozen kegs of gun-powder and a little lead, which was cast into bullets; but as the fire-arms were of every calibre, the cartridges made were too large for many, which were consequently useless. We had two small rusty field pieces, but with neither carriages nor appointments they were as useless as two logs.
>
> There was one old musket, but not a bayonet. The fire arms were common *fusils* [flintlocks], in all conditions of dilapidation, some tied together with strings, and very many with lock-springs so worn out, that they could not be discharged.[57]

The most active resistance encountered by the troops was waged by a force under Bonaventure Viger, which harried the advance of the column by destroying bridges and picking off skirmishers. Brown had placed pickets at the outskirts of the village, and these fell back from house to house as the troops slowly advanced, burning houses and barns as they came to rout out sharpshooters. Before launching an attack against the *Patriote* stronghold, Wetherall sent a message that the rebels would not be molested if they dispersed quietly. Brown dispatched a grandiloquent reply, offering free passage to the troops to Sorel, if they would lay down their arms. The engagement which ensued between Wetherall's fresh veterans and the *Patriotes*, whose enthusiasm and numbers had dwindled as they awaited the approach of the military, lasted less than an hour. The field pieces breached the rude log redoubt which had been raised about the manor house, and a bayonet charge soon cleared out the *Patriote* stronghold. Viger and some others escaped by swimming across the river; Brown tried vainly to rally fugitives at the village, whither he had gone in search of reinforcements, and then fled to Saint-Denis, a general without an army. The *Patriotes*, who were outnumbered by two to one, lost forty killed, thirty wounded, and thirty taken prisoner, while the soldiers reported three killed and eighteen wounded.[58]

This decisive defeat, which scattered the leaders and dispersed their followers, crushed the rebellion in the Richelieu region. The *Patriote* chiefs either went into hiding or fled across the frontier, hounded by search parties of French constables and English volunteers; their men disbanded, complaining of their leaders' conduct and of the lack of arms and ammunition. Wetherall, no doubt once more influenced by the alarmed Gugy, did not press on from Saint-Charles to Saint-Denis, but returned to Chambly and Montreal, as in fact an undelivered dispatch from Colborne had ordered him to do. He made a triumphal entry into Montreal, with thirty-two prisoners and the liberty pole from Saint-Charles.[59] Reinforced from Montreal, Gore revisited the scene of his defeat on December 1 and found all quiet. His men, goaded by the discovery of Weir's mutilated body, desecrated the church, looted and set fire to the village, whose people had taken good care, under Nelson's direction, of the British wounded left behind on November 23.[60] This action left a legacy of bitter anti-English feeling in the countryside, soon to be increased by other incidents.

Meanwhile the *Patriote* leaders who had fled across the Vermont and New York borders were hospitably received by the Americans, whose memories of their own struggle for liberty had been kept alive by impassioned Fourth of July orators, and who were affected by the same economic depression which had moved the *habitants* to rise in revolt. But benevolent neutrality rather than active aid was the part played in general by the people whom Papineau had so confidently hailed at Saint-Ours as 'our friends and our natural allies.'[61] In their schemes of a liberating invasion the French-Canadian exiles received little American assistance more substantial than that offered by the good ladies of Swanton, Vermont, who made the flags carried by the 200 armed men with whom E.-E. Malhiot and Robert Bouchette crossed the frontier on December 6, hoping to rouse the dispersed *Patriotes* once more. But just across the line, at Moore's Corners, the returning exiles, burdened with arms and ammunition for the force they hoped to rally, were met by a party of the Missiquoi Volunteers under Captain O. J. Kemp, who had been warned of their coming. In an evening ambush whose effectiveness was somewhat spoiled by the overeagerness of the loyalists whom Kemp had summoned from all quarters to supplement his force, the *Patriotes* were put to flight after a few minutes' fire. They retired hastily over the border, leaving one dead and three wounded behind them.[62] One of the wounded was Bouchette, who found himself once more arrested, as he had been earlier at Quebec. He was soon jailed at Montreal, along with Wolfred Nelson and Bonaventure Viger, who had been captured in the man-hunt now carried on in the disaffected region.

Most of the *Patriote* leaders found sanctuary beyond the frontier, however, and during the winter, spring, and summer of 1838 they foregathered in one border town or another in New York and Vermont. Their meetings were troubled by dissension between the peace party headed by Papineau, and the militant group led by Dr. Robert Nelson, the brother of the imprisoned leader at Saint-Denis, and including Dr. Côté, Rodier, Malhiot, Gagnon, and Duvernay. The confusion which followed the outbreak of open rebellion ended all coherence in the *Patriote* movement. So fervent a disciple of Papineau as Lafontaine had tried to calm the over-zealous at the last moment; and then upon hearing of the incident at Longueuil on November 18, had hurried to Quebec to beg Gosford to summon a sobered assembly. He turned against Papineau, and early in December journeyed again to Quebec with Leslie and other members of parliament to renew his request of the governor; but meeting refusal once more, he went to the States and thence to England, hoping to intercede with the authorities at London. Learning that a warrant had been issued against him for treason, he retired to Paris, where he kept in touch with the *Patriotes*' English friends.[63]

After Gosford had issued a proclamation on November 29 calling upon the population to return to its loyalty, martial law was declared on December 5 for the third time since 1760. On November 29 and December 1 Gosford put prices on the heads of the chief *Patriote* leaders.[64] The *habitants* were ordered to give up their arms, and the magistrates to re-establish peace; while pressure was brought to bear through Gugy upon the Richelieu *curés* to use the Church as a tranquilizing force. Many of the *curés* did not need prompting from government sources; their sentiments were those of Bishop Signay who condemned the insurrection in his pastoral letter of December 11. Indeed, one of them was reprimanded for his zeal in making himself 'a crier or herald for the state' by the *Patriote*-minded Bishop Bourget, whose superior Bishop Lartigue nonetheless formally ordered the clergy of the diocese of Montreal on January 8, 1838, to refuse the sacraments and Christian burial to unrepentant rebels, as he and his coadjutor had already done since the outbreak of the rising in several instances. The *curés* of the Montreal district were more sympathetic to the *Patriote* cause. Bishop

View in Montreal, Canada

)il painting (c. 1835) by W. H. B. Bartlett, showing the great Blondin walking the tight-rope cross Notre Dame Street between the Old Seminary Church and unfinished Notre Dame Church (Victor Spark Gallery, New York). (National Gallery.)

Saint Ferréol Falls

Oil painting (c. 1840) by Joseph Legaré, one of the most interesting early native painters of Quebe
(I.O.A.P.Q.)

Lartigue placed Abbé Etienne Chartier, who took an active revolutionary role, under interdict, but he protected two others, the Abbés Augustin-Magloire Blanchet* and F.-M. Turcot, who were 'arbitrarily imprisoned.'[66] Bishop Bourget urged the *curés* to follow the example of the clergy of France and Spain, but showed great sympathy with Chartier, Blanchet, and other *Patriote* prisoners.

Meanwhile the most serious encounter of the whole rebellion took place at Saint-Eustache on December 14. At the news of the victory at Saint-Denis the long turbulent county of Two Mountains, northwest of Montreal, boiled over in revolt. It was the constituency of William Henry Scott, one of Papineau's English followers, but the actual leader of the revolt there was a Swiss agronomist and adventurer, Amury Girod, whose plausible tongue had won him credentials from Papineau. His violence and audacity had enabled him to dominate the local *Patriote* leaders, Joseph Girouard and Dr. Jean Chénier. Girod had no high opinion of his colleagues, for in the secret journal which he kept in German and Italian he remarked: 'It is easier to prove to a Goose that it should not Cackle, than to make a Canadian hold his tongue.'[67] On the night of November 29 some two hundred *Patriotes* under the command of Girod and Chénier broke into the Hudson's Bay Company stores at the Indian mission of Oka, where they seized a few guns and ammunition. They also took an old three-pounder, the cherished possession of the superior, Abbé Dufresne. Girod failed to persuade the Indian chief to lend his people's arms to the insurgents. Upon their return to Saint-Eustache, the insurgents occupied a newly completed but empty convent in defiance of the loyalist Curé Jacques Paquin's orders, and made their headquarters there. Apart from guarding the Abord-à-Plouffe bridge, which connected this region with the Island of Montreal, Sir John Colborne ignored the northern insurrection until the Richelieu rising had been suppressed.

News of the defeat at Saint-Charles and the influence of Curé Paquin of Saint-Eustache dampened the ardor of some of the *Patriotes*, but not that of Chénier, who did not hesitate to put both the *curé* and his vicar under virtual arrest. In any case the inflammatory speeches of Abbé Etienne Chartier, *curé* of nearby Saint-Benoît and one of the few priests wholeheartedly to adopt the *Patriote* cause, offset the activities of the loyalist clerics. Girod succeeded in gathering together nearly 1,000 men, including Irish as well as French Canadians, though many of them lacked weapons and to his disgust the whole body passed its time in drinking, dancing, and quarreling, instead of drilling and making ready for the inevitable clash. He noted in his journal that 'Chénier is a lazy and foolish fellow—his Brother is a drunkard, and both cause a

* Later Bishop of Walla-Walla and Nesqually, Washington.

deal of confusion through their bad example.'[68] Girod had already quarreled with the moderate Scott and Girouard; and among the local leaders only the despised Chénier and the Abbé Chartier stood by him when he made himself unpopular by imposing discipline upon the disorderly assembly, which included much riffraff and many peaceably disposed persons who had been impressed into service by bellicose *Patriotes*. The numbers in the camp fluctuated widely, and on the eve of the conflict Girod was forced to set a guard about the village to prevent desertions.

On December 13 Colborne moved against this self-elected general and his disorderly following with three regiments of regulars and two of volunteer cavalry, as well as artillery—a force of more than 2,000 well-equipped men. On the following day this small army crossed the Rivière-des-Mille-Iles on the ice and reached Saint-Eustache, finding some 250 insurgents barricaded in the church, the rectory, the convent, and the house of Scott—the most substantial buildings of the place. The church was the chief *Patriote* stronghold, and against it the artillery was directed. While cannon balls scarred the façade, men of the Royals set fire first to the rectory and then to the rear of the church. Forced out by the flames, the *Patriotes* were shot down by the soldiers as they jumped from the windows. Chénier and seventy others were thus killed, while many charred bodies were later found in the ruins of the church. Over a hundred prisoners were taken, while the soldiers reported only one killed and nine wounded. Eye-witnesses, however, estimated the military losses as high as 150.[69] Among the wounded was the ubiquitous Major Gugy, who had led the way across the ice and distinguished himself in the attack on the church. Girod, who had fled to Saint-Benoît after disposing his men for the attack under the resolute Chénier, shot himself four days later, when threatened with capture near Montreal. Placed under interdict by Bishop Lartigue, the Abbé Chartier escaped to the United States, where after a voyage to France he later had parishes in New York, Indiana, and Louisiana before returning to Canada in 1845. Girouard and other *Patriote* chiefs of the region were soon rounded up and jailed.

Most of Saint-Eustache was devoured by flames, after it had been pillaged by the soldiers, some of whom paraded drunkenly through the streets in vestments taken from the church. On December 15 the troops set out for nearby Saint-Benoît, which on the advice of Girouard and the Abbé Defresne surrendered at their approach and that of a large body of volunteers from the Ottawa Valley, but the village was nevertheless sacked and burnt to the ground, while the church was abominably desecrated. According to one of the British officers, this inexcusable action was the work of the volunteers, who were 'not to be controlled, and who were in every case,

I believe, the instrument of infliction.'[70] Many of the volunteers were local men who had been ill-treated while the *Patriotes* were dominant. But Colborne, with 1,800 regulars at his command, can hardly be freed from blame for the devastation of a village whose inhabitants had surrendered to him and had offered no resistance whatsoever. The following day Colborne dismissed the unruly volunteers and returned quietly to Montreal with the regulars, while the volunteers looted and burnt their way home.

So ended the rebellion of 1837; for the rest of the province heeded the voice of the bishops and remained quiet, save for the village of Montmagny below Quebec, where Dr. Etienne-Pascal Taché was the mainspring of a minor disturbance. Thanks to the impromptu character of the revolt and to the irresolution of all the leaders save Chénier, who alone fought to the last, the resort to arms was a fiasco, like its counterpart in Upper Canada. But the authorities had had a bad scare, and Lower Canada soon became an armed camp. During December three regiments of regulars made an epic march overland to Quebec and Montreal from the Maritimes, and the cities and the military posts were soon strongly garrisoned, while parties of volunteers combed the countryside for the fugitive *Patriote* leaders. The conduct of the volunteers was such as to add to the bitter memories of Saint-Denis, Saint-Eustache, and Saint-Benoît, as was also the behaviour of the triumphant loyalist mob in Montreal when *Patriote* prisoners were brought to jail there. Gallophobia and anglophobia raged with new vigor in the uneasy province, though nominal peace had been imposed by force of arms.

On February 7, 1838, Bishop Signay issued a pastoral letter calling for thanksgiving at the return of peace and urging 'that Christian charity which ought to unite to one another the citizens of the same city, the dwellers in the same parish, and the subjects of the same province.' Bishop Lartigue followed suit, while both prelates encouraged their clergy to sign a petition to the Queen and British Parliament, protesting their loyalty, condemning the rising, and pleading against a union of Lower with Upper Canada and the loss of the French Canadians' rights and privileges. But this intervention of the clergy merely increased their unpopularity with the people, while the *Patriotes* remained convinced that union of the Canadas would lead inevitably to independence or annexation to the United States. Two days after thanksgiving had been duly made on February 26 for the return of peace, the *Patriotes* rose again.[71]

4

The rebellions in the Canadas had a profound effect in England, and at last brought the action which had so long been demanded.

Parliament met early in 1838 and on February 10 suspended the constitution of Lower Canada until November 1, 1840 and provided for the nomination by the governor of a council with legislative powers. Lord Durham was appointed governor-general and high commissioner to investigate Canadian grievances and to report on a remedy. On May 29 he took over from Sir John Colborne, who had become administrator of the colony when the ill and disheartened Gosford returned to England in February.

Colborne had appointed a special council of eleven English and eleven French Canadians—all Tories, Bureaucrats, or *Chouayens*[72]—that was given extraordinary powers under the proclamation of March 29 which suspended the constitution. The chief action of the council was to suspend the Habeas Corpus Act for three months, in order that the prisoners taken under martial law might still be held when the emergency measure was repealed in April. Colborne, who became the dominant force in Lower Canada after the rebellion broke out, governed with a hard hand, but not with brutality. Of the some 500 prisoners who had been taken during and after the rebellion, 200 were released by the end of January, and another hundred by the first of May. Seventy-two of the remaining 161 were considered by him to be important offenders, and he left their fate to be determined by Durham, who had been instructed to temper justice with mercy.

The new governor-general's first act was to dismiss Colborne's packed special council, so 'that his administrative conduct should be free from all suspicions of political influence or party feeling; that it should rest on his own undivided responsibility.'[73] In its place he appointed a new executive council of five members, three of whom were drawn from his own staff, while the other two, the provincial secretary and commissary-general, were non-political functionaries. On June 25 he appointed a new special council, made up of the senior military and naval officers and three members of his own staff. Charles Buller and Colonel George Couper served on both councils.

These acts were typical of the man, who combined a regal arrogance and strong dictatorial tendencies with Liberal and almost Radical opinions. He was the son of a wealthy colliery owner, who had been a member of parliament for the city of Durham. Educated at Eton, young Lambton had served for a year or two in the dragoons, and then succeeded to his father's seat in parliament, where he soon became a leader among the Whig Reformers and a bitter opponent of Liverpool, Castlereagh, and Peel. His second marriage to the daughter of Lord Grey, the leader of the Whigs, strengthened his political position; and he entered his father-in-law's cabinet as Lord Privy Seal in 1830, after having been elevated to the peerage in 1828. He was one of the committee of four which drafted the Reform Bill of 1832. Forced from the cabinet by ill health in the following year, he was given an earldom and sent on a special mission to Russia, where he pleaded the cause of the Polish rebels who were then being treated with great severity. Upon his return he took a leading role in the Liberal wing of the Whig party, and in 1835 he was made ambassador to Russia, chiefly to get him out of the more moderate government's way. The same motive played a part in his appointment to Canada, for he was the hero of both advanced Whigs and moderate Radicals, and was much spoken of as a future prime minister. His reports on Russia and Belgium, where he had played a part in the establishment of Leopold I as king, had given him a great reputation as a political analyst. His brilliant abilities were offset by temperamental instability and lack of tact; while his arrogance and love of pomp and circumstance contrasted strangely with his professed Liberal sentiments.

Quebec was dazzled by the splendor of Durham's regal retinue, numbering no less than eight aides-de-camp and so large that it took over the Legislative Buildings as well as the Chateau Saint-Louis. Popular confidence was in great measure won for Durham by the proclamation which he issued upon landing, expressing his desire to hasten the return of constitutional government and to be considered a friend and arbitrator, ready at all times to hear the people's will and griefs, and determined to act with the strictest impartiality.[74] His immediate dismissal of Colborne's council gave evidence that these were more than mere fine words. Etienne Parent at once displayed great friendliness to Durham, and on June 8 *Le Canadien* carried an ode to the new governor from the pen of the future historian Garneau, which closed with the assurance, later to become wearisomely familiar in patriotic orations, that 'Canada would be the last defender of old England on this great continent.'[75] Durham at once turned the bright young men of his entourage loose on an investigation of the state of the province, while he himself held a splendid court in the Chateau Saint-Louis, to which both French and English flocked to enjoy themselves and to win the governor to their respective ways of thinking.

The new governor's first great problem was the disposal of the imprisoned *Patriotes*. It would be difficult to obtain their conviction from a French-Canadian jury, and little less than judicial murder if they were tried by an English-Canadian jury. In any case their trial would reawaken the agitation which had happily subsided. In the columns of the *Montreal Herald* Adam Thom still demanded that the rebels be brought to the gallows, but there seemed to be no way to send them there except without trial. Faced with this situation, Durham determined upon an ingenious if arbitrary course of action. He obtained a signed confession of guilt from eight of the principal prisoners, including Wolfred Nelson, Bouchette, and Bonaventure Viger, who at his suggestion threw themselves upon his mercy and prayed that the public peace should not be troubled by their trial.[76] By an ordinance of June 28—Victoria's Coronation Day—Durham exiled these eight prisoners to Bermuda, under pain of capital punishment if they returned without authorization. Sixteen other leaders of the rebellion, who had fled abroad and were under indictment for high treason, were forbidden to return to Canada under pain of death. Those named were Papineau, Côté, O'Callaghan, Robert Nelson, Rodier, Brown, Duvernay, Chartier, Gagnon, Cartier, the two John Ryans, Perrault, Demaray, Davignon, and Gauthier.[77] Another proclamation of the same date extended a complete amnesty to all other prisoners and refugees, except those involved in the murders of Weir and Chartrand, on condition of future good conduct.[78] These merciful and wise—if illegal—measures received general acclaim in Canada, except in the pages of the *Montreal Herald*, and established Durham's position as a peacemaker.

Unfortunately, they also aroused a storm of protest in England, which was unaware of local conditions and somewhat obsessed with legality. Deportation without trial and the arbitrary decreeing of the death penalty had an ugly sound to liberty-loving English ears. Lord Brougham, a bitter political enemy of Durham, was not slow to launch a savage attack in the House of Lords upon these measures. Melbourne and Glenelg, who had already congratulated Durham unofficially upon his solution of a difficult problem, were forced to bow to the storm which Brougham raised and to disavow the governor's action. While this political battle went on in England, Durham was making a royal progress through Lower and Upper Canada, and sketching out his plans for administrative reorganization.

One of his first concerns had been to avert the threat of official or unofficial American intervention into the Canadian troubles. Both Upper and Lower Canadian exiles were then trying to achieve just such a step, and had won considerable sympathy in New York official circles. But President Van Buren protested to Durham's brother-in-law and unofficial envoy, Colonel Charles Grey, when his government was accused of favoring the rebels for its own purposes, that he judged annexation 'directly contrary to the interests of the United States.'[79] Colonel Grey met with similar assurances from the American Secretaries of State and War, and steps were taken by the authorities on both sides of the border to prevent the re-occurrence of the hit-and-run warfare previously carried on by both rebels and loyalists over the frontier. Durham himself publicly drank the President's health while visiting Niagara Falls, and extended special courtesy to all Americans he encountered. These acts, capping his clemency to the rebellion prisoners, did much to calm American public opinion, which had been aroused in favor of the insurgents by the refugees.

Apart from such diplomatic activity, Durham appointed sub-commissions to study the vital problems of public lands, education, and municipal institutions. Adam Thom was named to the municipal commission along with Dr. Taché, who refused to serve with him; and this appointment of their most notorious enemy made the French Canadians uneasy. Their confidence in Durham might have been further shaken if they had known that Thom also acted as liaison officer between the governor and the Tory merchants. Before he left England Durham had been approached by the merchants' representatives, for Edward Ellice happened to be his close friend. He did not hesitate to lay his plan for federating British North America before a committee of seven merchants chosen by Peter McGill of the Bank of Montreal, a month before the lieutenant-governors of the Maritime provinces were summoned to Quebec in August to consult officially with him on the project, which was further discussed by delegations from the Maritimes at Quebec in September.

Meanwhile members of Durham's suite sought information and opinion in all quarters. The chief figure among them was Charles Buller, a brilliant young Radical M.P., who was aided as chief secretary of the high commission by Thomas Turton, an able young Calcutta lawyer who had drafted the Reform Bill of 1821, but whose reputation was clouded by a sensational divorce case in which he had figured. William Kennedy, an expert on municipal reform, headed the commission on municipal organization. Another aide was Edward Gibbon Wakefield, a budding expert on colonial affairs who, after drafting the *Report's* section on public lands and emigration became a member of the Canadian parliament and ended his career as adviser of the Governor of New Zealand. Wakefield's appointment had also revived a scandal, that of his runaway marriage with a schoolgirl heiress, for which he had been imprisoned. Buller's brother, Arthur, the younger Edward Ellice, and a number of other bright young men also aided in the investigation of Canadian affairs. Durham's insistence upon the appointment of Turton and Wakefield had aroused criticism in England, as had the regal scale upon which he established his mission. The ground was thus well prepared for future attacks at home upon the high commissioner.

5

Durham's *Report on the Affairs of British North America*, which is generally considered one of the greatest studies of colonial government and the most epoch-making state paper in Canadian history, owes much to these aides of the governor. Charles Buller's informal account of the mission[80] has come to have an importance only second to that of the *Report* itself, but other documents which went into the making of the state paper are less well known.

Among the most interesting are the letters of Stewart Derbishire, a London lawyer and journalist who was employed as a confidential investigator by Durham and began his work in Canada before the latter's arrival at Quebec. On his way to Canada Derbishire interviewed W. L. Mackenzie, John Rolph, and Dr. O'Callaghan in New York, where Upper and Lower Canadian popular leaders had at last succeeded in achieving the close co-operation which had been lacking in 1837. In Montreal he cultivated the one-time London agent of Lower Canada, Denis-Benjamin Viger, whom he thought must be 'reckoned among the most intelligent of the Confederates (I fear I must so call him) of Papineau.'[81] After encountering considerable difficulty in getting French Canadians to speak freely with a stranger about the rebellion, Derbishire arrived at this conclusion:

> I am compelled to say that my impression at the present moment is, that the *habitants* up to the period of their revolt laboured under no practical grievances; and that their condition, social and political, was an enviable one, as compared with that of all other people upon the face of the globe. They knew not the sight of a tax-gatherer. Their imposts in the shape of rent were exceedingly light; and every man could obtain land in small or large quantities, or in addition to that which he possessed, according to his ambition or means of cultivation. . . . In his religion the french Catholic of Canada has enjoyed perfect freedom, the Catholic and Protestant contributing funds towards the creation of each other's ecclesiastical edifices, & the state of opinion and the laws so perfectly harmonizing as to religious toleration that there never has, so far as I can learn, been a ruffle to disturb the peace of society upon the score of a difference in creed. The freedom of person, of political opinion, and of the Press have been secured to the *habitant* by equal laws impartially administered.[82]

This glowing picture of conditions in Canada doubtless owes some of its rosy hues to the fact that Derbishire had been a special newspaper correspondent in the late Carlist Revolution and was contrasting the lot of the Canadian *habitant* with that of the unhappy Spanish peasant.

Derbishire judged, however, that the events of 1837 had altered matters considerably. He recounted the outrages of the loyalist volunteers, for whom he himself showed little sympathy and of whom Viger remarked that they 'had left wounds in the minds of the Canadians that could never be healed.'[83] Derbishire quoted a French-Canadian estimate that damage amounting to £85,000 had been caused in the six parishes visited by the military. They had burnt 297 buildings, including two churches, two rectories, and a convent—thus outraging the religious feelings of the people—twelve granaries, which were scarcely military objectives, and no less than eighty-nine houses at Saint-Benoît, where no resistance at all had been offered. Derbishire reported Papineau's advice that an amnesty for all political prisoners would do much to mend matters—Durham thus seems to have acted on a suggestion of the *Patriote* leader, which had also been made to him by Lafontaine before he left England[84]—and also Viger's comment that the rising had been 'no rebellion,' but an attempt to win justice. He also gave Viger's explanation of the ethnic animosity displayed by the *Patriotes*: 'The Scotch were disliked on account of their haughty, overbearing manners, & the Irish for their irregularities, violence, and bad faith.'[85] He cited as 'strictly true' Papineau's remark to an English gentleman—probably Roebuck, whom Derbishire had met before leaving England—about the French Canadians: '"Our people," he said, "don't want english capital nor English people here,—they have no ambition beyond their present possessions, & never want to go beyond the sound of their own Church Bells." '[86]

Thus supplied with a useful hint by the tribune of the people, Derbishire made a penetrating explanation of the popular unrest which had culminated in revolt:

> . . . with a people thus wedded to their own ways, & thus limited in their views, it may be readily understood that they would look with jealousy upon a race of more active and enterprising *habitants* who came to settle among them. The resistance offered to the English in this Country may be regarded as emanating from a kind of social or political *vis inertiae*. When to these feelings of aversion towards the intruder is added the alarm, oft sounded, of an intention on the part of the 'foreigners' to abolish the laws & language of the 'conquered nation,' to 'anglicize' the Province and destroy every vestige of a distinctive race in the original settlers,—notions diligently inculcated by the revolutionary leaders and ably seconded by the newspaper organs of the English party in the current of contemptuous abuse they have never ceased to pour down upon the *habitants*, & in their frequent demands to keep them down; and when the Papineau & his Confederates' appeals to the nationality of this vain people, to their gallantry, to their numbers, to the local and general advantages of emancipating themselves from

foreign thraldom & becoming masters of the soil are taken into consideration; and, above all, when due weight is allowed to the erroneous impression spread through the Country as to the conscious weakness of the Government by the tone of personal insult & scorn permitted Mr. Papineau towards the highest Functionary in the Province, the Representative of Majesty, the conduct of the people last Autumn will no longer appear extraordinary.[87]

He also reported the noteworthy observation of the Abbé Ducharme, *curé* of Saint-Thérèse: 'It was the educated men, the doctors, notaries, and lawyers, who were at the head of the rebellion & were the great seducers of the people, and he seemed to derive from it an argument against educating the lower orders.'[88] The professional class has always been the most liberal one in French-Canadian society and one which has produced many dissidents with the clergy's conservatism and their rivals for leadership of the people.

Derbishire attached considerable importance to the views of a *calèche* driver, recommended by Viger, who drove him about the countryside. These views, which he considered representative of the average French Canadian of the day, might well be those of a similar individual in one of the back-country districts of modern Quebec:

> . . . the french were the older inhabitants of the Country & the most numerous, & ought not to be subjected to the minority who cared nothing for them or the Country—but as they could make money out of it to carry away to spend elsewhere, and who for that purpose would '*fouler aux pieds les lois et les coutûmes des habitants* (trample under foot the laws and customs of the inhabitants)'.[89]

Derbishire also summed up the psychology of the French Canadians with some acuteness and considerable sharpness:

> The *habitants* are a sluggish race, fond of indolent pleasures, lighthearted and gay. They resemble the french in many of their qualities, & have all the national conceit of that people. They consider themselves superior to all the other peoples, and too good to mix with any other race. I believe that from the highest to the lowest they live in a perpetual atmosphere of self-adulation. They are, I believe, an innocent and virtuous race, have retained a character of primitive simplicity, & even in the lowest orders have that naturally good manner, mid-way between servility and familiarity, which distinguishes the same class among the natives of the old Country. The ambition of bettering their condition seems never to have visited their minds: Locomotive faculties they seem to have none. . . . There seems to be no decorative taste in the people, no active spirit of improvement, no ambition beyond the mere supply of the wants of nature.[90]

Though the investigator thus echoed some of the critical observations of the English party, he thought that 'the violence with which the British talk of the French here almost surpasses credence.' As one measure of improving relations between the two groups, he proposed the establishment of 'a Paper of moderate tone and liberal principles,'[91] since he found the English press entirely Tory.

Thanks to the wide range and informal nature of his contact with the French Canadians, this almost forgotten investigator achieved a more profound insight into French Canada in a few weeks than his exalted employer was to achieve in five months. It is also evident, from a letter Derbishire wrote to Charles Buller in August, after interviewing the exiled Dr. Côté at Rouse's Point, and in which he observed, 'To become *Masters* of the Country has, I fear, become a national sentiment with them,'[92] that Derbishire formed a more accurate view of the future than Durham, who thought that the French Canadians could be assimilated into a wholly English Canada. It is clear that Derbishire's initial report, written upon Durham's arrival in Canada in May had considerable influence at the outset in the high commissioner's course of action, though it was later supplanted by less impartial opinions. In its seventy-seven pages are outlined the chief elements of modern French-Canadian ultra-nationalism, which traces its origin to the Rebellion of 1837 and to the reaction to Durham's *Report*.

While his staff was still busy gathering material, Durham himself learned in September from an American newspaper that his ordinance on the rebellion prisoners had been disallowed, and that his 'despotic' action had been generally condemned in England. Humiliated and hurt, the sensitive Durham at once sent his resignation to the colonial secretary and, without waiting for its acceptance, made plans to leave Canada at once. Since extraordinary powers had been deliberately vested in him by the government, he wrote: 'I shall not blush to hear that I have exercised a despotism; I shall feel anxious only to know how well and wisely I have used, or rather exhibited an intention of using, my great powers.'[93] When news of his impending departure got about, Durham was deluged with sympathetic addresses from all camps, while the press echoed the popular regret that this well-disposed governor should leave and that his clement policy should be repudiated. In a remarkable farewell proclamation Durham explained the reasons for his resignation, and virtually appealed from the decision of the British government to Canadian public opinion.[94] This action resulted in *The Times* christening him the 'Lord High Seditioner.' Charles Buller, who remained behind in Canada to wind up the work of the commission, found, however, that the proclamation dispelled the unrest caused by Durham's departure: 'No disorder, no increase of disaffection ensued; on the contrary, all parties in the Province expressed a revival of confidence.'[95] After only five months in Canada, Durham left Quebec on a bleak November day, passing through streets lined by respectful crowds whose 'deep silence marked the general grief.'[96] The ship which bore him homeward was appropriately named the *Inconstant*.

6

Durham had hardly left the soil of Canada before the troubles which he had tried to remedy broke out once more, as they had before his arrival. Ever since the rising had been crushed in December 1837, the refugees, led by Robert Nelson and Dr. Côté, had been intriguing along the Vermont and New York border and in Canada itself, and their emissaries had ripened rebellion in the frontier counties of Lacadie, Laprairie, and Beauharnois. Robert Nelson, embittered by having been arbitrarily imprisoned for his brother Wolfred's acts in 1837, had joined forces with the turbulent Dr. Côté in organizing the frontier 'troublutions' of which Papineau disapproved, after breaking with the *Patriote* chief and Dr. O'Callaghan at an assembly of the exiles at Middlebury, Vermont, in January 1838.

The leaders had vainly sought aid and support from the officials of New York and Vermont, whose governors issued proclamations against aiding the rebels.[97] Papineau and O'Callaghan had even sounded out President Van Buren, who warned them that the United States, racked by financial crisis, had no intention of risking a war with Britain by maintaining anything but the strictest neutrality as far as the Canadian troubles were concerned. Van Buren issued a proclamation of neutrality on January 5, 1838, which was later implemented by the Neutrality Act of 1838. Papineau and O'Callaghan knew that without American support there was no hope for a Lower Canadian independence movement, and the old leader warned the undaunted Nelson that he would draw down new misfortunes upon their compatriots if he persisted. Nevertheless Nelson went ahead with his plans of provoking a new rising in Lower Canada by invading the province, timing his foray to coincide with those of the Upper Canadian rebels from Watertown, Ogdensburg, Buffalo, and Detroit.

Aided by some American sympathizers, and with 1,000 muskets from the arsenal at Elizabethtown, N.Y., Nelson crossed the border at Alburg on February 28, 1838; and under the self-assumed title of president of the Provisional Government of Lower Canada, he issued a declaration of independence announcing that the province had been relieved of its British allegiance and had become a republic.[98] This document decreed the separation of church and state, with the consequent suppression of the tithe; the abolition of seigneurial tenure, of the death penalty, except for murder, and of imprisonment for debt; and proclaimed freedom of the press, universal manhood suffrage (including the Indians, who were to be admitted to all rights of citizenship), and the secret ballot. The Crown lands and those of the British American Land Company were to be nationalized. A committee of delegates named by the people was to be charged with the drafting of a constitution subject to popular ratification. Both the French and English languages were to be used for all public affairs. A second proclamation appealed to the 'people of Canada' to rise against tyranny.[99] Though Nelson retreated across the frontier on the following day, when it became evident to him that the British and American authorities were co-operating to avoid border incidents,[100] this proclamation was spread abroad among the *habitants*, who in their discontent at the punitive measures adopted by the government after the 1837 rising, and at the repressive role played by the clergy, found much therein which appealed to them, particularly the prospect of liberation from seigneurial tenure and the tithe.

After a brief stay with Côté in an American jail for violating the frontier regulations, Nelson and his associates organized a secret society, the Hunters' Lodges or *Frères Chasseurs*, whose aim was the invasion of Canada and the achievement of independence. This semi-military organization, in which both Upper and Lower Canadian exiles made common cause and which enlisted some American adventurers, established itself during the summer of 1838 in the frontier states from Maine to Michigan and in both Upper and Lower Canada. Each district was commanded by a 'Great Eagle'—E.-E. Malhiot for the Richelieu—who had authority over the 'Eagles,' or company commanders, whose lieutenants, known as 'Castors,' directed the 'Raquettes,' who each commanded nine 'Chasseurs.' Each company had fifty men, commanded by five 'Raquettes' under a 'Castor.' There were horrendous secret oaths and ceremonies, and an elaborate system of signs and passwords by which the brethren recognized one another. The influence of Freemasonry was evident in the organization, whose French-Canadian centers were at Plattsburg, Montreal, and Quebec.

The leaders planned an invasion of Lower Canada five days after Upper Canada had been attacked, and the troops thus drawn off to the upper province. St. Johns, Montreal, and Quebec were to be assailed simultaneously under the command of three 'French generals,' recruited from among the European revolutionary exiles of 1830 in New York. Nelson was to exact £80,000 from John Molson, the Montreal merchant and banker, in reparation of the latter's wrongs against the province, while the banks, the Lachine Canal' and the customs station at St. Johns were to be confiscated to supply revenue for the new republic. All Jews were to be strangled and their goods confiscated. The minor centers of this conspiracy were at Chateauguay, Beauharnois, Napierville, and Laprairie, with a few in the Townships. As in 1837, the agitation centered in the region south of Montreal, but the *Chasseurs* were unable to evoke much enthusiasm in the stricken region north of the city which was still recovering from the devastation of the previous year. But Colborne, once more administrator of the province, after Durham's departure, estimated that the association had 200,000 members in Canada and the United States, with 3,000 in Montreal alone. This estimate is undoubtedly too high,[101] but the strength of the movement is evidenced by the fact that the *Chasseur* Félix Poutré, who later turned informer, was able to raise 3,000 men around St. Johns, though the majority were more eager to talk over their grievances than to bear arms.[102]

The conspiracy gained many new supporters when Durham's farewell proclamation of October 9, gave notice of his aim to 'elevate the Province of Lower Canada to a thoroughly British character,' 'to raise the defective institutions of Lower Canada to the level of British civilization and freedom, to remove all impediments to the course of British enterprise in this Province,' and to 'touch ancient laws and habits, as well as deep-rooted abuses.'[103] These remarks sounded all too much like the proposals of Adam Thom and the Montreal merchants, rephrased with elegance; at the prospect of national extinction many of the French-Canadian moderates joined with the extremists, and this time the clergy made no effort to check the agitation. Bishop Lartigue, who in June had objected to Durham's flooding the country with proclamations by the channel of the bishops, took refuge in Quebec against a Canadian Sicilian Vespers which was to involve 'a general massacre of Royalists.'[103a] In December he offered his resignation to Rome, since he had aroused the hatred of much of his diocese. The *Patriote* press had declared him guilty of high treason to the Canadian nation, for all his opposition to Durham.

The 1838 revolt began as planned on November 3, after the harvest was gathered, but little else went as the *Patriotes* had foreseen. The competent leadership and the supply of arms needed for so vast an uprising were lacking. Instead of the projected simultaneous risings at such key points as Quebec, Sorel, Chambly, Montreal, and Lac des Deux Montagnes, only the region southwest of Montreal revolted. Some 400 men seized the manor house of Edward Ellice at Beauharnois, while another 150 took possession there of the steamer *Henry Brougham*, which linked Lachine and the Cascade Rapids. By the morning of November 4, 600 men had gathered at Beauharnois, and the Bureaucrats of the region had been disarmed or taken prisoner. The *Patriotes* of Chateauguay succeeded in disarming the Scottish loyalists of the place, but came to grief when they tried to seize the arms of the Indians at Caughnawagha, and were themselves taken prisoners by the indignant savages. At Laprairie, where the local *Patriotes*, joined by a force from the United States, were to seize the barracks and the ferry linking the St. Johns railroad with Montreal, the revolt collapsed when no aid appeared, though some of the railroad was torn up. At Terrebonne the police and the *Patriotes* made a 'treaty,' after a few brushes. In the Richelieu parishes, less enthusiastic for revolt after the harsh repressive measures of the previous year, the *Patriotes* disbanded after they had vainly waited two days for the leaders and the arms which had been promised them.

Meanwhile Nelson had crossed the border and established himself on November 4 at Napierville, where 2,000–3,000 *Patriotes* had gathered under Dr. Côté. Nelson issued his declaration of independence of the previous February, and was proclaimed president of the new republic. But Nelson had only brought a handful of supporters with him, including two French soldiers of revolutionary views, Charles Hindenlang and one Touvrey, instead of the 'army' of which the *Chasseur* organizers had talked so confidently. Hindenlang found himself charged with the task of organizing into an army the mob which had gathered. Only 200–300 had any sort of guns, the rest being equipped only with pikes, pitchforks, or mere sharpened sticks. Thanks to the neutrality measures taken by the American government, Nelson had been able to secure in the States only 250 muskets and a single cannon, while the American membership of the *Chasseurs* had melted away. Several hundred more muskets and a cannon awaited the insurgents at Rouse's Point on the boundary, but the force under Côté which was sent to fetch them on November 6 was driven across the border the following day by loyalist volunteers, after a skirmish at Lacolle. Nelson was thus cut off from his American base and deprived of badly needed arms, which fell into loyalist hands.

On November 8 he learned that Colborne was advancing against him from Laprairie with a force of 5,000–6,000 men, including volunteers and Indians. Retreating to Odelltown, just north of the border, with about 1,000 men, Nelson was checked there the following day by the loyalist garrison of 200, strongly established in the village and making good use of the captured cannon. Some of his followers had already mutinied and attempted to turn him over to the volunteers. Nelson fled across the frontier on November 9, while his men retired to Napierville, having lost fifty dead and as many wounded. On the following day Colborne entered Napierville, and the panic-stricken *Patriotes* dispersed in small bands which were pursued by the troops.

Meanwhile another column of regulars and the Glengarry Volunteers scattered the insurgents at Beauharnois and set fire to the village. Throughout the disaffected region, but particularly in the county of Laprairie, the houses of known rebels were burnt down. As in 1837 the Volunteers entered with such zest into this work that even Adam Thom's *Montreal Herald* was moved to a curious display of humanity mixed with intolerance:

> Sunday night all the country back of Laprairie presented the frightful spectacle of a vast expanse of livid flames, and it is reported that not a single rebel house has been left standing . . . God knows what will become of the Canadians who have not perished, of their wives and families, during the winter which approaches, since they have in prospect only the horrors of hunger and cold. It is sad to reflect on the terrible consequences of the revolt, of the irreparable ruin of so great a number of human beings, whether innocent or guilty. Nevertheless the supremacy of the laws must be maintained inviolate, the integrity of the Empire respected, and peace and prosperity assured to the English, even at the expense of the whole Canadian people.[104]

For his part in permitting these excesses Colborne won the name of 'Old Firebrand,' though once again the devastation seems to have been largely the work of the volunteers, aroused to new heights of fury by the second rebellion.

Colborne, who warned his troops of the expected attack 'by a horde of rapacious brigands' on November 1, proclaimed martial law on November 4, while the *habeas corpus* was once again suspended by the special council on November 8.[105] Girouard, D.-B. Viger, Lafontaine, and Edouard Fabre were among those arrested on suspicion in Montreal. Colborne showed no inclination to trifle with the large number of prisoners who were taken during the single week of insurrection. By December 19, the prisoners numbered 753. One hundred and eight were promptly brought to trial before courts-martial, while three French-Canadian judges, Panet, Bédard, and Vallières de Saint-Réal, who regarded suspension of the *habeas corpus* as unconstitutional and attempted to force the government to give the prisoners civil trial by jury, were suspended by Colborne.[106] Ninety-nine of the accused were condemned to death, but only twelve of these were executed, while fifty-eight were deported to the Australian penal colonies, two banished, and twenty-seven freed under bond for good behaviour.[107]

The Tories protested at such mildness, while the French Canadians muttered against Colborne's 'bloodthirsty tyranny.' As Lady Colborne wrote on December 10, 1838, her husband was unable to please either group: 'As you will see by the *Herald* nothing can satisfy the ultra-British party, and with one party he must be content to be stigmatized as a tyrant, with the other as shamefully lenient.'[108] While Adam Thom and his colleagues of the Doric Club howled for more *Patriote* blood, the *Morning Chronicle*, a moderate Bureaucratic organ, reproved the *Herald* for losing sight of the purpose of punishment, 'which is to assure the safety of the community and not to arouse sympathy in behalf the sufferers and hatred against the government which permits such an effusion of blood.'[109] Since rebels were not allowed to defend rebels, French-Canadian lawyers were barred from the courts-martial. Lewis Thomas Drummond, a young Irish lawyer, and Charles Hart, the son of the much expelled Ezekiel, defended the Rebellion prisoners in the early trials, while Charles Mondelet, who was himself arrested on suspicion in 1838, a year later won from a French-Canadian jury the acquittal of those charged with the murder of Lieutenant Weir. Of the twelve executed men, two were the murderers of the loyalist Chartrand, four had killed an English settler in the Beauharnois troubles, and two more had benefited from Durham's amnesty for their actions in 1837, only to take up arms once more. None was a real leader of the insurrection, the most notable being the French 'General' Hindenlang, who refused to save his neck by turning state's evidence. A case can be made for the other five as innocent victims of enthusiasm aroused by impassioned politicians who left their followers in the lurch at the critical moment.

One of the curious features of the Rebellions of 1837–8 is that only the rank and file suffered penalties, while the leaders went almost scot-free and later rose to eminently respectable positions in Canadian or American life. After his futile negotiations with New York politicians for intervention in Canada, Papineau sailed for France in February 1839, hoping to interest the French press in Canada as he had been urged to do by M. de Pontois some months earlier. In Paris, during the following May, he began a *Histoire de l'Insurrection du Canada*, of which the first portion was published in the *Revue du progrès* there, and reprinted some months later by Ludger Duvernay's refugee *Le Patriote Canadien* press at Burlington, Vermont. This work was a hotly-worded assault on Durham's *Report*, and its errors of fact and interpretation were promptly refuted by Papineau's former follower Sabrevoix de Bleury. The latter's nomination to the legislative council in August 1837 had involved him in a duel with Duvernay, who accused him of abandoning the *Patriote* cause for the sake of office.

After reporting a remarkable—if true—conversation with Lord Bathurst in 1823, in which the colonial secretary anticipated the American Civil War and the European struggle between reform and reaction, Papineau professed his complete lack of faith in Durham's remedies, since they involved the union of the Canadas which he had always opposed, the absorption of the French Canadians, and the maintenance of monarchical institutions. Papineau was convinced that Britain might maintain for a time its 'military occupation' of Canada, but it could no longer govern the country by civil means. He saw the independence of Canada as the only solution of the problem, with separation from Britain being accomplished either by voluntary consent of the imperial government, or by the French intervention which he sought on the basis of the violation of the Treaty of 1763, or by the war between Britain and the United States which then seemed imminent to his American friends. Papineau still dreamed of American aid for the Canadian reformers and underestimated the restraint which Van Buren had placed upon the anglophobe warhawks at Durham's earnest behest. Charles Buller was justified in writing to John Stuart Mill on October 13, 1838, that one of his chief's greatest achievements was that he 'had re-established goodwill with the United States, and rooted out from that people all sympathy with Canadian rebellion.'[110]

In Paris, however, Papineau found more congenial company than that of his inconstant American sympathizers in the persons of Louis Blanc and the *Républicains rouges* who shortly were to launch the French Revolution of 1848. It was their ideas, and those of Lamennais and Béranger, that he brought back to Canada when he was permitted to return in 1845. Papineau also busied himself in Paris with researches into the French colonial history of Canada, and met his English Radical friends Hume and Leader, although Lord Brougham, now reconciled to Durham and his policy, refused to see him. After his return Papineau sat in the Canadian parliament from 1847 to 1854, but the lifelong leader of the opposition was lost in a new era in which a younger generation had taken the helm. His influence was no longer paramount in politics, but remained important in the intellectual world.

His young disciples of Rebellion days fared better than the old tribune in the new Canada. Lafontaine, Morin, Cartier, and Taché all became prime ministers. Wolfred Nelson was re-elected to parliament in 1844; Thomas Storrow Brown returned to his business and the writing of reminiscences in Montreal; and Robert Bouchette became collector of customs at Ottawa. A few exiles remained in the States: Robert Nelson practiced medicine in New York City and Dr. O'Callaghan became the state historian of New York, editing valuable works on the colonial history of the continent.

The chief aftermath of the rebellions, as far as the mass of the French Canadians was concerned, was on one hand a marked development of emigration across the frontier, from motives of discontent and unrest, and on the other a vague conviction that the *Patriote* cause was not dead and that a leader in Papineau's tradition would appear when the occasion demanded him. Like Napoleon, Papineau had captured the imagination of a people, and his memory has lingered long in Quebec. One group, echoing the refrain of a *Chouayen* ballad of the period—'*C'est la faute à Papineau!*' ('Papineau is to blame!')—lays all later French-Canadian difficulties to his account, while another cherishes his memory as that of the first great French-Canadian nationalist. Today it is clear to French and English alike that he was a great Canadian, who played an important role in the evolution of Canada as a nation by blending the political ideas of Britain, France, and the United States.

7

Before the echoes of the second rising had died down, Lord Durham presented his solution of the Canadian problem to the British government. The *Report* was published in February 1839 in both English and French, and was immediately greeted in London as a notable statepaper, before the party lines were drawn for its consideration in parliament. The London *Times* published a first instalment of the document before it was officially presented, and other English newspapers followed suit, giving the *Report* a wide circulation. In Canada Etienne Parent published the *Report* in French in *Le Canadien*, while Francis Hincks issued a pamphlet edition, dedicated to Robert Baldwin, at Toronto and Joseph Howe reprinted it in the Halifax *Nova Scotian*.

In both Lower and Upper Canada Durham's exceedingly plain speech grated on tender susceptibilities. Each of the *Report's* two main recommendations—union of the two provinces and responsible government—gratified one group and maddened the other. The Tories of both provinces were given the legislative union which they had long demanded, but they loathed the prospect of democratic responsible government which it recommended, and they were injured by Durham's castigation of the Chateau Clique and the Family Compact. The *Patriotes* and the Reformers received the long-sought prize of responsible government, but it was responsible government within the framework of imperial administration rather than an autonomy leading to the independent nationhood which both French and English radicals had lately come to favor. Upper Canadians in general were pained by the superficial, hasty, and ill-informed consideration given to their province, while the terms in which the recommendations of union and responsible government were made produced a sense of injustice and injury in French Canada which has survived in some measure to the present day.

Lord Durham's *Report* has a vastly lower reputation in French Canada than in English-speaking circles. For not only did it recommend the union of the Canadas, so long favored by the French Canadians' most bitter opponents, but it called for the absorption of the French Canadians into a wholly British North America. Far from showing sympathy with the *Patriote* doctrine of a '*nation canadienne*' whose needs were unique and peculiar and demanded independence, the opening paragraphs of the *Report* echoed Durham's predetermined conviction that confederation was the solution of British North American difficulties. Firsthand observation only reinforced his original view, for Durham remarked at the outset of the *Report* 'how inseparably connected I found the interests of Your Majesty's Provinces in North America, to what degree I met with common disorders, requiring common remedies.'[111] Federation of the British North American provinces had already been proposed by Roebuck in the Commons and advocated by him in a memorandum of which Durham made great use; it was approved by Durham's friends Edward Ellice and Lord Howick, the future third Earl Grey; it might be termed a Liberal if not a Radical idea.[112]

But another preconceived notion mirrored in the opening sentences of the *Report* was not at all Radical or Liberal: the idea that the solution of the Canadian difficulties should be based upon the mother country's interest. It was thus eloquently phrased by Durham:

> The country which has founded and maintained these Colonies at a vast expense of blood and treasure, may justly expect its compensation in turning their unappropriated resources to the account of its own redundant population; they are the rightful patrimony of the English people, the ample appanage which God and Nature have set aside in the New World for those whose lot has assigned them but insufficient portions in the Old. Under wise and free institutions, these great advantages may yet be secured to Your Majesty's subjects; and a connexion secured by the link of kindred origin and mutual benefits may continue to bind to the British Empire the ample territories of its North American provinces, and the large and flourishing population by which they will assuredly be filled.[113]

Such full-blooded imperialism, nourished by a sense of the divine right of the English, was worthy of a Tory rather than a Liberal leader, and offered short shrift to colonial notions of independent nationhood. Durham was no believer in the tenets of the Little Englandism which found so many disciples among his political friends and was becoming more and more dominant in the mother country at this period. The fundamental dichotomy of Durham's mind is reflected in the first pages of the *Report*, which reveal the mentality of a radical aristocrat and a benevolent despot.

Then Durham goes on to show a racist outlook which grated on a minority proud of its cultural differences from the Anglo-Americans, and which has ever vitiated the merits of the *Report* in the French-Canadian mind. He remarked that he had come to Canada expecting to find a dispute between the people and the executive, but instead 'found two nations warring in the bosom of a single state: I found a struggle, not of principles, but of races.' Durham stoutly maintained that: 'Our happy immunity from any feelings of national hostility, renders it difficult for us to comprehend the intensity of hatred which the difference of language, of laws, and of manners creates between those who inhabit the same village, and are citizens of the same state';[114] and assigned to personal experience in Canada his conclusion that the struggle was primarily a racial one. But his secretary Charles Buller bears witness that, on the voyage out to Canada, 'I used indeed then to think that Lord Durham had too strong a feeling against the French Canadians on account of their recent insurrection'; and that 'he had made up his mind that no quarter should be shown to the absurd pretensions of race, and that he must throw himself upon the support of British feelings, and aim at making Canada thoroughly British.'[115] This attitude hardly suggests that 'happy immunity' from racist feelings which Durham claimed as the heritage of Englishmen, and it reveals the influence that Ellice and the Montreal merchants had established over the governor-general even before he left England. Naturally this initial tendency was reinforced by Durham's association with Adam Thom and the group he represented in Canada.

In any case Durham observed: 'The national feud forces itself on the very senses, irresistibly and palpably, as the origin or essence of every dispute which divides the community; we discover that dissensions, which appear to have another origin, are but forms of this constant and all-pervading quarrel; and that every contest is one of French and English in the outset, or becomes so ere it has run its course.'[116] To his mind, the 'vicious system of government' had long concealed the racial quarrel, since the races were divided among both government and popular parties, and individuals could be found in the opposite camp from the majority of their national group. The national hostility had long been confined to Quebec and Montreal, while isolated groups of either race in the countryside were free from it. But year by year it had been increasing, and the insurrection had completed the division: 'Since the resort to arms the two races have been distinctly and completely arrayed against one another. . . . A few exceptions mark the existence, rather than militate against the truth, of the general rule of national hostility.'[117]

Durham reconciled his racism and his liberalism by remarking, with a measure of justice, that both French and English parties had been fighting under false colors: 'the French appear to have used their democratic arms for conservative purposes, rather than those of liberal and enlightened movement; and the sympathies of the friends of reform are naturally enlisted on the side of sound amelioration which the English minority in vain attempted to introduce into the antiquated laws of the Province.' He found it difficult to believe that 'the hostility of the races was the effect, and not the cause, of the pertinacity with which the desired reforms were pressed or resisted.' Hewing to his racist line, he maintained that 'the contest, which had been represented as a contest of classes, was, in fact, a contest of the races.' And in his opinion French and English were incompatible: 'It is scarcely possible to conceive descendants of any of the great European nations more unlike each other in character and temperament, more totally separated from each other by language, laws, and modes of life, or placed in circumstances more calculated to produce mutual misunderstanding, jealousy and hatred.'[118] Such sentiments were of course natural in a member of the English ruling class, a few years after the conclusion of the Second Hundred Years' War between Britain and France.

This last consideration also helped to shape Durham's view of the French Canadians. He saw them as the children of a 'central, ill-organized, unimproving and repressive despotism . . . calculated to repress the intelligence and freedom of the great mass of the people.' He pictured them thus:

. . . a race of men habituated to the incessant labour of a rude and unskilled agriculture, and habitually fond of social enjoyments, congregated together in rural communities, occupying portions of the wholly unappropriated soil, sufficient to provide each family with material comforts, far beyond their ancient means, or almost their conceptions; that they made little advance beyond the first progress in comfort which the bounty of the soil absolutely forced upon them; that under the same institutions they remained the same uninstructed, inactive, unprogressive people . . . The mass of the community exhibited in the New World the characteristics of the peasantry of Europe . . . They clung to ancient prejudices, ancient customs and ancient laws, not from any strong sense of their beneficial effects, but with the unreasoning tenacity of an uneducated and unprogressive people. . . . The Conquest has changed them but little. The higher classes, and the inhabitants of the towns, have adopted some English customs and feelings; but the continued negligence of the British government left the mass of the people without any of the institutions which would have elevated them in freedom and civilization. It has left them without the education and without the institutions of local self-government, that would have assimilated their character and habits, in the easiest and best way, to those of the Empire of which they became a part. They remain an old and stationary society, in a new and progressive world. In all essentials they are still French; but French in every respect dissimilar to those of France in the present day. They resemble rather the French of the provinces under the old regime.

Durham noted the 'remarkable equality of properties and conditions,' and the prevailing want of education among the *habitants*. He had kind words, however, for the secondary education of the province: 'I know of no people among whom a larger provision exists for the higher kinds of elementary education, or among whom such education is really extended to a larger proportion of the population.' This Old Etonian judged that the education provided by the classical colleges 'greatly resembles the kind given in the English public schools, though it is rather more varied.' But the existence of a highly educated class in a closed society created a great problem, since careers in the army, navy, and civil service were largely barred to French Canadians, and all must become priests, lawyers, notaries, or doctors, though these 'professions are greatly overstocked.' Since the educated man sprang from the people and was 'separated by no barrier of manners, or pride, or distinct interests, from the singularly ignorant peasantry . . . he combines, therefore, the influences of superior education and social equality, and wields a power over the mass, which I do not believe that the educated class of any other portion of the world possesses.'[119] To this state of affairs Durham attributed the extraordinary influence of the French-Canadian popular leaders, whom he called 'demagogues'—a term frequently applied to himself by his English political opponents.

Despite his racist prejudices, Durham was not overly kind to the English Canadians. He had some of the traditional English scorn for colonials, and his Liberal principles were outraged by the outdated Canadian oligarchy. He convicted the officials and army officers of forming 'a kind of privileged class, occupying the first place in the community, and excluding the higher class of the natives from society, as well as from the government of their own country.' He detected in them an 'exclusiveness of demeanour, which was more revolting to a sensitive and polite people than the monopoly of power and profit.' But he noted that 'the active and regular habits of the English capitalist drove out of all the more profitable kinds of industry their inert and careless competitors of the French race,' so that 'all felt yet more acutely the gradual increase of a class of strangers in whose hands the wealth of the country appeared to centre, and whose expenditure and influence eclipsed those of the class which had previously occupied the first place in the country.' He gave the English full credit for developing new fields of industry, as well as improving old ones:

The ascendency which an unjust favouritism had contributed to give to the English race in the government and the legal profession, their own superior energy, skill and capital secured to them in every branch of industry. They have developed the resources of the country; they have constructed or improved its means of communication; they have created its internal and foreign commerce. The entire wholesale, and a large proportion of the retail trade of the Province, with the most profitable and flourishing farms, are now in the hands of this numerical minority of the population.[120]

Consequently most of the French-Canadian workers found themselves in the employ of English capitalists; and the coming of British immigrants, who adopted the prejudices of their compatriots without the reservations imposed by education and prudence, divided along racial lines a working class whose interests were really common.

In discussing the basis of the conflict between the races, Durham spoke with frankness and penetration. He judged that the difference of language was the first factor in an inevitable collision. Then, contradicting his earlier assertion of English immunity from racism, he remarked: 'It is not anywhere a virtue of the English race to look with complacency on any manners, customs or laws which appear strange to them; accustomed to form a high estimate of their own superiority, they take no pains to conceal from others their contempt and intolerance of their usages.' The newcomers to Canada, conscious of being a chosen people, 'found the French Canadians filled with an equal amount of national pride.' As time went on, 'The French could not but feel the superiority of English enterprize; they could not shut their eyes to their success in every undertaking in which they came into contact, and to the constant superiority which they were acquiring. They looked upon their rivals with alarm, with jealousy, and finally with hatred. The English repaid them with a scorn, which soon assumed the same form of hatred.' Charges of arrogance and injustice on one side were countered by charges of meanness and disloyalty on the other, with evil results: 'The entire mistrust which the two races have thus learned to conceive of each other's intentions, induces them to put the worst construction on the most innocent conduct; to judge every word, every act, and every intention unfairly; to attribute the most odious designs, and reject every overture of kindness or fairness, as covering secret designs of treachery and malignity.' Separated by language, the two races also lacked the bonds of a common religion or a common education. The result was the development of two distinct mentalities: 'the arguments which convince the one, are calculated to appear utterly unintelligible to the other,' while the events of the day were seen in utterly different lights by each.

Intercourse between the two races was almost non-existent in either business or society, while racial animosities were played upon when French commercial energy belatedly awoke and founded the *Banque du Peuple* in 1835, to compete with John Molson's and Peter McGill's Bank of Montreal, established in 1817, and a rival steamship line to Molson's St. Lawrence service, begun in 1809. Citing the facts that he had 'heard of but one house in Quebec in which both races meet on pretty equal and amicable terms,' and that intermarriages, frequent in post-conquest days, had become rare, Durham multiplied his illustrations of the curious abyss between the French and English worlds in Canada, which remains one of the first and most striking impressions of the visitor even today.[121]

After giving his classic account of the fundamental cleft in Canada, Durham observed that political strife arising of such a situation was inevitable:

> The French regarded with jealousy the influence in politics of a daily increasing body of strangers, whom they so much disliked and dreaded; the wealthy English were offended at finding that their property gave them no influence over their French dependents, who were acting under the guidance of leaders of their own race; and the farmers and traders of the same race were not long before they began to bear with impatience their utter political nullity in the midst of a population, whose ignorance they condemned and whose political views and conduct seemed utterly at variance with their own notions of the principles and practice of self government.

It was clear to Durham that 'the superior political and practical intelligence of the English cannot be, for a moment, disputed,' while 'the greater amount of refinement, of speculative thought, and of the knowledge that books can give, is, with some brilliant exceptions, to be found among the French.' But he pointed out: 'That a race which felt itself thus superior in political activity and intelligence should submit with patience to a rule of a majority which it could not respect, was impossible.' And 'appeals to the national pride and the animosities of the French, became more direct and general on the occasion of the abortive attempt to re-unite Upper and Lower Canada in 1822, which the leaders of the assembly viewed or represented as a blow aimed at the institutions of their province,' while 'the anger of the English was excited by the denunciation of themselves, which, subsequently to this period, they were in the habit of hearing.'[122] The abuses of the executive power long postponed racial strife by aligning the have-nots, regardless of origin, against the haves; but the assembly was finally opposed by the whole English population because of its lack of interest in public works and in an alteration of the laws.

That body dominated by the French Canadians 'looked with considerable jealousy and dislike on the increase and prosperity of what they regarded as a foreign and hostile race; they looked on the Province as the patrimony of their own race; they viewed it not as a country to be settled, but as one already settled; and instead of legislating in the American spirit, and first providing for the future population of the Province, their primary care was, in the spirit of legislation which prevails in the old world, to guard the interests and feelings of the present race of inhabitants, to whom they consider the newcomers as subordinate.' Meanwhile the English 'regarded the policy of the assembly as a plan for preventing any further emigration to the Province, of stopping the growth of English wealth, and of rendering precarious the English property already invested or acquired in Lower Canada.' Thus grew up the 'singular alliance between the English population and the Colonial officials, who combined from perfectly different motives, and with perfectly different objects, against a common enemy.' The racial division thus begun was completed by the French-Canadian resort to arms in 1837–8: 'It is not difficult to conceive how greatly the evils, which I have described as previously existing, have been aggravated by the war; how terror and revenge nourished in each portion of the population, a bitter and irreconcilable hatred to each other, and to the institutions of the country.'[123]

Using to the full his powers of eloquence and psychological penetration, Durham painted a vivid picture of the respective outlooks of the two races on the morrow of the Rebellion—outlooks which still survive deep in the two folk memories today:

> [The French] brood in sullen silence over the memory of their fallen countrymen, of their burnt villages, of their ruined property, of their extinguished ascendency, and of their humbled nationality. To the Government and the English they ascribe these wrongs, and nourish against both an indiscriminating and eternal animosity. Nor have the English inhabitants forgotten in their triumph the terror with which they suddenly saw themselves surrounded by an insurgent majority, and the incidents which alone appeared to save them from the unchecked domination of their antagonists. They find themselves still a minority in the midst of a hostile and organized people; apprehensions of secret conspiracies and sanguinary designs haunt them unceasingly, and their only hope of safety is supposed to rest on systematically terrifying and disabling the French, and in preventing a majority of that race from ever again being predominant in any portion of the legislature of the Province.

Representative government, the militia system, the course of justice and of trade, all found themselves obstructed by this situation, for which Durham foresaw no solution within his lifetime. The French

Canadians wished to revenge themselves upon the English by forming a republic; or even by annexation to the United States, at the expense of preserving their nationality; while the English extremists stated that 'Lower Canada must be *English*, at the expense, if necessary, of not being *British*.'[124] Exasperated to the point of desperation with the government, the self-styled loyalist English were willing to conceive of annexation, which would involve both their immediate commercial advantage and the extinction of French-Canadian national pretensions. Here Durham singled out the first instance of a practice oft to be repeated in Canadian history, of annexation talk being used as a threat by either English or French Canadians against the other ethnic group, whenever relations between them reached a crisis, or the economic position of either group became too uncomfortable.

In summing up his survey of the problem, Durham observed: 'A jealousy between two races, so long habituated to regard each other with hereditary enmity, and so differing in habits, in language and in laws, would have been inevitable under any form of government'; but nevertheless he roundly condemned the old imperial policy of divide and rule. To his mind French Canada should either have been left to the French, or rapidly and completely been assimilated by the English. A start had been made in 1764 on the second 'and wiser' of the two policies, but it had been abandoned with the coming of the American Revolution. Then Canada had been divided into two provinces, one French and one British, but with grave inconsistency Lower Canada had not been left wholly to the French or under French institutions. 'The error, therefore, to which the present contest must be attributed, is the vain endeavour to preserve a French-Canadian nationality in the midst of Anglo-American colonies and States'; for: 'It will be acknowledged by everyone who has observed the progress of Anglo-Saxon colonization in America, that sooner or later the English race was sure to predominate even numerically in Lower Canada, as they predominate already, by their superior knowledge, energy, enterprize and wealth.' Durham also flayed the continued errors of the government: 'A policy founded upon imperfect information, and conducted by continually changing hands, has exhibited to the Colony a system of vacillation which was in effect no system at all. The alternate concessions to the contending races have only irritated both, impaired the authority of Government, and, by keeping alive the hopes of a French-Canadian nationality, counteracted the influences which might, ere this, have brought the quarrel to its natural and necessary termination.' Durham concluded his survey of the problem by stating: 'The struggle between the Government and the Assembly, has aggravated the animosities of race; and the animosities of race have rendered the political difference irreconcilable. No remedy can be efficient that does not operate upon both evils.'[125]

8

The remedy which Lord Durham proposed for the ills of Canada did indeed 'operate upon both evils.' His solution for the political difficulty owed much to the Upper Canadian Reformer Robert Baldwin of York (Toronto), who in August 1838 had won from Durham the hearing for his arguments in favor of responsible government which the Colonial Office had refused to grant him in 1836. At their meeting Baldwin gave Durham the memorandum which he and his father had drafted in 1828, and which now played a notable part in fixing Durham's ideas.[126]

Durham contended that representative government had long been established in Canada, and could not be revoked. Therefore, 'the Crown must submit to the necessary consequences of representative institutions; and if it has to carry on the Government in unison with a representative body, it must consent to carry it on by means of those in whom that representative body has confidence.' This was daring doctrine in application to colonial affairs at the time, but Durham pointed out that responsible government had long been considered an 'indisputable and essential part' of the British constitution; that its absence had been the cause of the collisions between the executive and representative bodies not only in the two Canadas, but in all the British North American colonies. In traditional Whig style Durham caustically criticized those 'who imagined that in any colony of England a body invested with the name and character of a representative Assembly, could be deprived of any of those powers which, in the opinion of Englishmen, are inherent in a popular legislature . . . To suppose that such a system would work well there, implies a belief that the French Canadians have enjoyed representative institutions for half a century, without acquiring any of the characteristics of a free people; that Englishmen renounce every political opinion and feeling when they enter a colony, or that the spirit of Anglo-Saxon freedom is utterly changed and weakened among those who are transplanted across the Atlantic.' To his mind, 'the Legislative Council was practically hardly anything but a veto in the hands of the public functionaries on all the acts of that popular branch of the legislature in which they were always in a minority.'[127]

Faced with this situation, the assembly fell into 'a constant warfare with the executive, for the purpose of obtaining the powers inherent in a representative body by the very nature of representative government.' Thus it was led to pervert the constitution by such practices as adopting temporary legislation, tacking measures it desired onto essential supply bills, and abusing the quorum. In the absence of local institutions of government and in the face of executive monopoly of patronage, it had developed a vast new field of patronage by grants for local improvements and for education, to make up for its long exclusion from places and privileges. Here Durham revealed his understanding of the vital role of patronage in parliamentary government.[128]

Misgovernment was thus general. Durham censured the absence of any real representative of the Crown in the colony, thanks to the subordination of the governor to a Colonial Office which was both constitutionally irresponsible and prone to dangerous delays. He condemned the executive council as irresponsible and 'composed of persons placed in it long ago,' so that a new governor was obliged to take the advice of persons in whom he had no confidence. There was no administrative system outside the three chief cities, and the French-Canadian population lacked both municipal institutions and the capacity for self-government developed through them. 'Accustomed to rely entirely on the Government, it has no power of doing anything for itself, much less of aiding the central authority.' The laws and judicial system of Lower Canada presented a chaotic picture, with no party feeling 'the slightest confidence in the administration of criminal justice' or 'in the honest administration of the laws.'[129]

In his observations and recommendations on education, Durham closely followed Arthur Buller's report on 'The State of Education in Lower Canada,' which was printed as an appendix to the *Report*.[130] In the absence of proper provision for education by the government, ignorance was general: 'The English are hardly better off than the French for the means of education for their children, and indeed possess scarcely any, except in the cities.' Though Durham had little hope of immediately establishing a sound general system of education, he found that 'there existed among the French population a very general and deep sense of their own deficiencies in this respect, and a great desire to provide means for giving their children those advantages which had been denied to themselves. Among the English the same desire was equally felt; and I believe that the population of either origin would be willing to submit to local assessments for this purpose.' But the clergy of most of the churches opposed non-sectarian education, while any other system 'would be particularly mischievous in this Province, inasmuch as its inevitable effect would be to aggravate and perpetuate the existing distinctions of origin.' Given the opposition of the laity of every denomination to 'these narrow views' of the clergy, Durham was confident that strong popular government would lead to the establishment of 'a liberal and general system of public education.'[131] He did not hesitate to censure the British government for not having done, or even attempted to do, anything for education; and for its misappropriation of the revenues of the Jesuit Estates.

Although Durham was opposed to clerical control of education, he was, as might be expected of an advocate of Catholic emancipation in England, by no means anti-Catholic. He noted that there was in Lower Canada: 'a degree of practical toleration, known in very few communities,' and added that 'the Catholic priesthood of this Province have, to a very remarkable degree, conciliated the good-will of persons of all creeds; and I know of no parochial clergy in the world whose practice of all the Christian virtues, and zealous discharge of their clerical duties, is more universally admitted, and has been productive of more beneficial consequences. . . . Intimately acquainted with the wants and characters of their neighbours, they have been the promoters and dispensers of charity, and the effectual guardians of the morals of the people; and in the general absence of any permanent institutions of civil government, the Catholic Church has presented almost the only semblance of stability and organization, and furnished the only effectual support for civilization and order.' To the Catholic clergy he also paid tribute for 'their eminent services in resisting the arts of the disaffected' during the Rebellion.

Durham blamed the failure of the French Canadians to expand beyond the limits of the crowded seigneuries on the absence of parochial institutions in the new settlements, and urged such provision by the government, 'in order to encourage them to spread their population, and to seek for comfort and prosperity in new settlements.' For, as he shrewdly observed, 'the religious observances of the French Canadians are so intermingled with all their business, and all their amusements, that the priests and the church are with them, more than with any other people, the centres of their little communities.' Finally he was convinced that 'the feelings and interests of the Catholic clergy and population should invariably meet with due consideration from the Government.'[132]

Durham's Liberalism was also revealed in his refusal to accept the official doctrine that 'the principles which are productive of harmony and good government in the mother country, are by no means applicable to a colonial dependency.' He proposed putting the management of internal affairs into Canadian hands, leaving to the mother country only control over the form of government, the regulation of foreign relations and trade, and the management of public lands and immigration; since 'A perfect subordination, on the part of the Colony, on these points, is secured by the advantages which it finds in the continuance of its connexion with the Empire.' He observed: 'The colonists may not always know what laws are best for them, or which of their countrymen are the fittest for conducting their affairs; but, at least, they have a greater interest in coming to a right judgment on these points, and will take greater pains to do so, than those whose welfare is very remotely and slightly affected by the good or bad legislation of these portions of the Empire.' Rejecting an old tenet of colonial government, he remarked: 'it surely cannot be the duty or interest of Great Britain to keep a most expensive military possession of these Colonies, in order that a Governor or Secretary of State may be able to confer colonial appointments on one rather than another set of persons in the Colonies.' He concluded that: 'The British people of the North American Colonies are a people on whom we may safely rely, and to whom we must not grudge power.'

But he did not believe that London could be restrained from 'injudicious interference' with the internal affairs of the colonies; 'while they remain the petty and divided communities which they now are.' Such interference or neglect would be avoided 'if these important and extensive Colonies should speak with one voice, if it were felt that every error of our colonial policy must cause a common suffering and a common discontent throughout the whole wide extent of British America.'[133] Here is vaguely reflected that initial conception of a united British North America with which Durham had begun his labors. It was first definitely formulated by Chief Justice William Smith in 1790, and had been urged upon Durham before his departure from England by Roebuck.

Its realization was to grow out of Durham's work, though the *Report* reluctantly abandoned the idea, on the grounds that the French Canadians could not be trusted with control of Lower Canada. Durham made only a few reservations in his recommendation of responsible government: the constitution of the form of government, the regulation of foreign relations and trade, and the disposal of public lands. He proposed that money votes should be subject to the consent of the Crown, as at Westminster, and that a system of municipal institutions should be established, since a 'general legislature, which manages the private business of every parish, in addition to the common business of the country, wields a power which no single body, however popular its constitution, ought to have; a power which is destructive of any constitutional balance.'[134] An appendix to the *Report* dealt with a proposed imperial system of land management, which remained a dead letter.[135]

But for the French Canadian the most notable recommendation of the *Report*—the proposal which vitiated the long-sought grant of responsible government and deprived the document of all merit in his eyes—was that Lower Canada should be made English by legislative union with Upper Canada. This was Durham's great error. The French Canadian can hardly be blamed for calling the *Report* a 'blueprint of assimilation' when Durham stated flatly:

I entertain no doubt of the national character which must be given to Lower Canada; it must be that of the British Empire; that of the majority of British America; that of the great race which must, in the lapse of no long period of time, be predominant over the whole North American Continent. Without effecting the change so rapidly or roughly as to shock the feelings and trample on the welfare of the existing generation, it must henceforth be the first and steady purpose of the British Government to establish an English population, with English laws and language, in this Province, and to trust its government to none but a decidedly English Legislature.

Durham, who had defended the Belgians against the Dutch and the Poles against the Russians, anticipated the objections to such a course: 'that this is a hard measure to a conquered people; that the French were originally the whole, and still are the bulk of the population of Lower Canada; that the English are newcomers, who have no right to demand the extinction of the nationality of the people, among whom commercial enterprize has drawn them.' He granted that: 'It may be said, that, if the French are not so civilized, so energetic, or so money-making a race as that by which they are surrounded, they are an amiable, a virtuous, and a contented people, possessing all the essentials of material comfort, and not to be despised, or ill-used, because they seek to enjoy what they have, without emulating the spirit of accumulation, which influences their neighbours.' He pointed out that: 'Their nationality is, after all, an inheritance; and they must not be too severely punished, because they have dreamed of maintaining on the distant banks of the St. Lawrence, and transmitting to their posterity, the language, the manners, and the institutions of that great nation that for two centuries gave the tone of thought to the European Continent.' And with a recognition of the great English principle of majority rule, Durham admitted that: 'it may be urged that justice demands that the minority should be compelled to acquiesce in the supremacy of the ancient and most numerous occupants of the Province, and not pretend to force their own institutions and customs on the majority.'[136]

But Durham had an eye both to the economic situation and to the future—two factors which the French Canadians, with their idealistic and traditionalist cast of mind, have always disregarded or underestimated—and so he replied thus to the objections he himself had raised:

But before deciding which of the two races is now to be placed in the ascendant, it is but prudent to inquire which of them must ultimately prevail; for it is not wise to establish today that which must, after a hard struggle, be reversed tomorrow. The pretensions of the French Canadians to the exclusive possession of Lower Canada would debar the yet larger English population of Upper Canada and the Townships from access to the great natural channel of that trade which they alone have created, and now carry on. The possession of the mouth of the St. Lawrence concerns not only those who happen to have made their settlements along the narrow line which borders it, but all who now dwell, or will hereafter dwell, in the great basin of that river. For we must not look to the present alone. The question is, by what race is it likely that the wilderness which now covers the rich and ample regions surrounding the comparatively small and contracted districts in which the French Canadians are located, is eventually to be converted into a settled and flourishing country? If this is to be done in the British dominions, as in the rest of North America, by some speedier process than the ordinary growth of population, it must be by immigration from the English Isles, or from the United States—the countries which supply the only settlers that have entered, or will enter, the Canadas in any large numbers. This immigration can neither be debarred from a passage through Lower Canada, nor even be prevented from settling in that Province. The whole interior of the British dominions must, ere long, be filled with an English population, every year rapidly increasing its numerical superiority over the French. Is it just that the prosperity of this great majority, and of this vast tract of country, should be for ever, or even for a while, impeded by the artificial bar which the backward laws and civilization of a part, and a part only, of Lower Canada, would place between them and the ocean? Is it to be supposed that such an English population will ever submit to such a sacrifice of its interests?

I must not, however, assume it to be possible that the English Government shall adopt the course of placing or allowing any check to the influx of English immigration into Lower Canada, or any impediment to the profitable employment of that English capital which is already vested therein. The English have already in their hands the majority of the larger masses of property in the country; they have the decided superiority of intelligence on their side; they have the certainty that colonization must swell their numbers to a majority; and they belong to the race which wields the Imperial Government, and predominates on the American Continent. If we now leave them in a minority, they will never abandon the assurance of being a majority hereafter, and never cease to continue the present contest with all the fierceness with which it now rages. In such a contest they will rely on the sympathy of their countrymen at home, and if that is denied them, they feel very confident of being able to awaken the sympathy of their neighbours of kindred origin. They feel that if the British Government intends to maintain its hold of the Canadas, it can rely on the English population alone; that if it abandons its colonial possessions, they must speedily become a portion of that great Union which will speedily send forth its swarms of settlers, and, by force of numbers and activity, quickly master every other race. The French Canadians, on the other hand, are but the remnants of an ancient colonization, and are and ever must be isolated in the midst of an Anglo-Saxon world. Whatever may happen, whatever government should be established over them, British or American, they can see no hope for their nationality. They can only sever themselves from the British Empire by waiting until some general cause of dissatisfaction alienates them, together with the surrounding colonies, and leaves them part of an English confederacy; or, if they are able, by effecting a separation singly, and so either merging in the American Union, or keeping up for a few years a wretched semblance of feeble independence, which would expose them more than ever to the intrusion of the surrounding population. I am far from wishing to encourage indiscriminately these pretensions to superiority on the part of any particular race; but while the greater part of every portion of the American Continent is still uncleared and unoccupied, and while the English exhibit such a constant and marked activity in colonization, so long will it be idle to imagine that there is any portion of that Continent into which that race will not penetrate, or in which, when it has penetrated, it will not predominate. It is but a question of time and mode; it is but to determine whether the small number of French who now inhabit Lower Canada shall be made English, under a Government which can protect them, or whether the process shall be delayed until a much larger number shall have to undergo, at the rude hands of its uncontrolled rivals, the extinction of a nationality strengthened and embittered by continuance.[137]

Durham thus admirably summed up the hard logic of geographic and economic facts over which French-Canadian ultra-nationalists have never ceased to stumble, in a rude awakening from their dreams of separatism and an independent French state.

But Durham, perhaps blinded by the very racism which he disowned, badly underestimated the French Canadians and their national will to live. The remedy which he proposed was brutal but merciful in his eyes, because of what he called their 'hopeless inferiority':

I know of no national distinction marking and continuing a more hopeless inferiority. The language, the laws, the character of the North American Continent are English; and every race but the English (I apply this to all who speak the English language) appears there in a condition of inferiority. It is to elevate them from that inferiority that I desire to give the Canadians our English character. I desire it for the sake of the educated classes, whom the distinction of language and manners keeps apart from the great Empire to which they belong. At the best, the fate of the educated and aspiring colonist is, at present, one of little hope, and little activity; but the French Canadian is cast still further into the shade, by a language and habits foreign to those of the Imperial Government. A spirit of exclusion has closed the highest professions on the educated classes of the French Canadians, more, perhaps, than was absolutely necessary; but it is impossible for the utmost liberality on the part of the British Government to give an equal position in the general competition of its vast population to those who speak a foreign language. I desire the amalgamation still more for the sake of the humbler classes. Their present state of rude and equal plenty is fast deteriorating under the pressure of population in the narrow limits to which they are confined. If they attempt to better their condition, by extending themselves over the neighbouring country, they will necessarily get more and more mingled with an English population: if they prefer remaining stationary, the greater part of them must be labourers in the employ of English capitalists. In either case it would appear, that the great mass of the French Canadians are doomed, in some measure, to occupy an inferior position, and be dependent upon the English for employment. The evils of poverty and dependence would merely be aggravated in a ten-fold degree, by a spirit of jealous and resentful nationality, which would separate the working classes of the community from the possessors of wealth and employers of labour.[138]

Durham thus foresaw a good measure of the future development of French Canada under the impact of the industrial revolution and capitalism, though he badly misjudged the strength of the national spirit. He saw, too, that the old closed agricultural system was doomed; and cited Andrew Stuart's report of 1826 which pointed out that since 1784 the population of the seigneuries had quadrupled, while the number of cattle had only doubled, and the amount of land under cultivation had only increased one-third. He predicted future developments with remarkable accuracy: 'If they wish to maintain the same kind of rude but well-provided agricultural existence, it must be by removing into those parts of the country in which the English are settled; or if they cling to their present residence, they can only obtain a livelihood by deserting their present employment, and working for wages on farms, or in commercial occupations under English capitalists.' In contrasting the depopulation and impoverishment of Canada with the rapid increase of population and wealth in the United States, Durham had already noted 'a large annual emigration of young men to the northern states . . . from which they generally return to their homes in a few months or years . . . a great many now take up their permanent residence in the United States.' Relying on the 'stationary habits and local attachments of the French Canadians,' Durham underestimated the future development of this trend, which was one result of the agricultural situation he described, and which he thought would put the French Canadians in a position 'similar to that of the poorest of the Irish peasantry.'[139]

Then, to justify his recommendation of national extinction, Durham wrote the words for which he has never been forgiven by the French Canadians, and which were taken as a challenge that became the impulse for a great intellectual awakening of French Canada and for a crystalization of its sense of nationality:

There can hardly be conceived a nationality more destitute of all that can invigorate and elevate a people, than that which is exhibited by the descendants of the French in Lower Canada, owing to their retaining their peculiar language and manners. They are a people with no history and no literature. The literature of England is written in a language which is not theirs; and the only literature which their language renders familiar to them, is that of a nation from which they have been separated by eighty years of a foreign rule, and still more by those changes which the Revolution and its consequences have wrought in the whole political, moral and social state of France. Yet it is on a people whom recent history, manners and modes of thought, so entirely separate from them, that the French Canadians are wholly dependent for almost all the instruction and amusement derived from books: it is on this essentially foreign literature, which is conversant about events, opinions, and habits of life, perfectly strange and unintelligible to them, that they are compelled to be dependent. Their newspapers are written mostly by natives of France, who have either come to try their fortunes in the Province, or have been brought to it by the party leaders, in order to supply the dearth of literary talent available for the political press. In the same way their nationality operates to deprive them of the enjoyments and civilizing influence of the arts. Though descended from the people in the world that most generally love, and have most successfully cultivated the drama —though living on a continent, in which almost every town, great or small, has an English theatre, the French population of Lower Canada, cut off from every people that speaks its own language, can support no national stage.

In these circumstances, I should indeed be surprised if the more reflecting part of the French Canadians entertain at present any hope of continuing to preserve their nationality. Much as they struggle against it, it is obvious that the process of assimilation to English habits is already commencing. The English language is gaining ground, as the language of the rich and of the employers of labour naturally will.[140]

This cultural indictment was largely true, though it was unjust in crediting the exceedingly lively press, the cradle of later French-Canadian literature, to the pens of Frenchmen from France, for that stage of cultural colonialism had been past for thirty years. It also neglected to note that the Jansenism of French-Canadian Catholicism frowned on the drama, which was thus reduced to an arid literary form. If Durham had cared to make similar observations about the English Canadians, he would have been forced to observe that such culture as they had developed was wholly colonial, with the British-born John Neilson and Adam Thom their leading journalists, and an English stage maintained by English touring companies. The Americans, whom Durham tended to lump with the English Canadians, were as yet not much farther on the way to cultural independence. But Durham's words spurred a young French-Canadian notary, François-Xavier Garneau, to write the epic of his people, and thus to lay the foundations of a nationalist literature obsessed with the history and the way of life of the French Canadians. The national pride was injured by Durham's frank indictment, and one of the unforeseen consequences of the *Report* was a strengthening of the instinct of national survival and the creation of more vigorous opposition to assimilative influences.

To his credit, Durham flatly rejected various plans for absolutist government of Lower Canada, 'constituted on an entirely despotic footing, or on one that would vest it entirely in the hands of the British minority.' Such a scheme would have the worst consequences, in his view, upon both the French and the English, and upon the United States, whose sympathy he thought it a matter of the greatest importance to preserve. Therefore he pronounced: 'The only power that can be effectual at once in coercing the present dissatisfaction, and hereafter obliterating the nationality of the French Canadians, is that of a numerical majority of a loyal and English population; and the only stable government will be one more popular than has hitherto existed in the North American Colonies.' He cited Louisiana as an example of the peaceful amalgamation of a minority group to the majority which could be achieved by such means; and then proposed a legislative union of Upper and Lower Canada to attain this object in the case of the French Canadians. Durham was unwilling 'to subject the French Canadians to the rule of the identical English minority with which they have so long been contending; but from a majority, emanating from so much more extended a source, I do not think that they would have any oppression or injustice to fear; and in this case, the far greater part of the majority never having been brought into previous collision, would regard them with no animosity that could warp their natural sense of equity.' Union would 'secure to Upper Canada the present great objects of its desire,' while 'the French, when once placed, by the legitimate course of events and the working of natural causes, in a minority, would abandon their vain hopes of nationality.'[141] But Durham fatally neglected the close connection between the political and cultural rights of minority groups.

Durham regretted that 'great practical difficulties' had forced him to abandon his initial idea of a federal union of all the British North American colonies:

> Such a union would at once decisively settle the question of races; it would enable all the Provinces to co-operate for all common purposes; and, above all, it would form a great and powerful people, possessing the means of securing good and responsible government for itself, and which, under the protection of the British Empire, might in some measure counterbalance the preponderant and increasing influence of the United States on the American continent. . . . If we wish to prevent the extension

of this influence, it can only be done by raising up for the North American colonist some nationality of his own; by elevating these small and unimportant communities into a society having some objects of national importance; and by thus giving their inhabitants a country which they will be unwilling to see absorbed even into one more powerful.

With another of his remarkable insights into the future, Durham observed that 'it would be the tendency of a federation sanctioned and consolidated by a monarchical Government gradually to become a complete legislative union; and that thus, while conciliating the French of Lower Canada, by leaving them the government of their own Province and their own internal legislation, I might provide for the protection of British interests by the general government, and for the gradual transition of the Provinces into an united and homogeneous community.'[142] But the morrow of armed rebellion was no moment for gradualism, and so the birth of modern Canada had to wait another quarter of a century.

The concluding pages of Durham's *Report* indicate how clearly he envisaged such a development. At the end of this eloquent and farsighted state paper, which stands as a great landmark in the development of colonial government, Durham protested his 'earnest desire to perpetuate and strengthen the connexion between this Empire and the North American Colonies, which would then form one of the brightest ornaments in Your Majesty's Imperial Crown.'[143] Though the purpose of the Union was defeated by its operation, and the French Canadians were not assimilated but came rather to hold the balance of power under responsible government, it cannot be gainsaid that the great Reformer, who was dying of tuberculosis as he wrote the *Report*, did much to attain his goal.

Notes

[1] Ever since Durham announced his conclusion that it was 'a struggle not of principles but of races,' English writers have tended to follow his lead. Kingsford (Vols. IX and X) is the leader of the racist authorities. D. G. Creighton (*Commercial Empire*, 310–20) upset the traditional racist interpretation by stressing the common economic factors behind both the Lower and Upper Canadian risings, despite his lack of sympathy with the French Canadians and with Reform principles. Garneau and Christie, writing while the ethnic cleavage brought about by the rebellions still persisted, are strongly affected by it. Groulx paints a battle of races, while the most detailed French-Canadian account, G. Filteau's *Histoire des Patriotes* (Montréal, 1938–42), is violently racist. A. Fauteaux's *Patriotes de 1837–38* (Montréal, 1950), a biographical dictionary with a prefatory historical summary by Félix Leclerc, is the most scholarly and objective French work.

[2] Notably Edmund Bailey O'Callaghan, Wolfred and Robert Nelson, Thomas Storrow Brown. Amury Girod was a Swiss.

[3] *Mackenzie's Own Narrative* (Toronto, 1838), 6–7; Christie, V, 110–11. W. S. Wallace, *The Family Compact* (Chronicles of Canada, Toronto, 1915), 117–18, 123, 125.

[4] Roebuck, Hume, O'Connell, and Brougham were the leading English spokesmen for the Canadian Patriots.

[5] See the reply of the Permanent Central Committee of the County of Montreal to the address of the Workingmen's Association of London, Christie, V, 57–63. This was sent previous to the risings in 1837, though only published in 1838. G.-E. Cartier and Chevalier de Lorimier were joint secretaries of the committee, which originated in 1834. Papineau was its leader and its headquarters were Edouard Fabre's bookstore. Filteau, II, 80–1.

[6] *Colonial Advocate*, 22 May 1834: Hume-Mackenzie.

[7] Christie, IV, 3–4.

[8] *CAR 1883*: Elliott's Letters, 160–7 and Notes A1 and A2; Chapais, IV, 63–9, 72. See also G. M. Fairchild, jr., *Lower Canada Affairs in 1836* (Quebec, 1910).

[9] Christie, IV, 142–50. The exasperated Tories belatedly dissolved the Rifle Corps after a proclamation had stamped it as 'unconstitutional and illegal,' but regretted that 'the day has arrived when, in a Colony conquered by British arms, a body of loyal subjects has been treated as traitors, by a British governor, for no other crime than that of rousing themselves to protect their persons and property, and to assist in maintaining the rights and privileges granted to them by the Constitution.' *Ibid.*, 145.

[10] Christie, IV, 155–7; Kennedy, *Documents*, 307–18, Gosford's instructions, 17 July 1835.

[11] Christie, IV, 341.

[12] 'Camillus' [A. Thom], *Anti-Gallic Letters* (Montreal, 1836), 129; cited Chapais, IV, 94.

[13] Creighton, *Commercial Empire*, 297.

[14] *Ibid.*

[15] Chapais, IV, 99.

[16] PAC: Q 232–5, Report of Royal Commission, 1837.

[17] Kennedy, *Documents*, 342–3, Russell's Ten Resolutions, 6 March 1837.

[18] *Hansard, IIIrd Series*, xxxiv, 95–6; Chapais, IV, 127.

[19] *The Vindicator*; Christie, IV, 351–2 *n.*

[20] APQ: Fonds Papineau, 530, Papineau-J.-G. Nancrède, 14 mai 1838.

[21] *La Minerve*, 27 avril 1837; Chapais, IV, 135.

[22] Christie, IV, 373–4 *n.*

[23] *La Minerve*, 11 mai 1837; Filteau, *Patriotes*, II, 83–7; Christie, IV, 352–6.

[24] *Le Canadien*, 15 mai 1837; Filteau, II, 103.

[25] *The Vindicator*, *La Minerve*, 16 mai 1837; Filteau, II, 106.

[26] Filteau, 108–11.

[27] *Ibid.*, 109–10.

[28] *Le Canadien*, 15 mai 1837; Chapais, IV, 137–40.

[29] *CAR 1922–3*, 270–1.

[30] *L'Ami du Peuple*, 26 juillet 1837; quoted Groulx, *Notre Maître*, II, 92–3.

[31] *La Minerve*, 27 juillet 1837; Filteau, II, 132–3; paraphrased in *CAR 1922–3*, 243. Cf. Groulx, II, 90–6, and L.-A. Desrosiers, 'Correspondence de Mgr Jean-Jacques Lartigue de 1836 à 1838,' in *RAPQ 1944–5*, 247: Lartigue-Mgr Signay, 29 juillet 1837; 255, Lartigue-Mgr Mai, 15 octobre 1837.

[32] Filteau, II, 134–6; Christie, IV, 391–2.

[33] Christie, IV, 384.

[34] PAC: Q 238–1, 71, Gosford-Glenelg, 2 September 1837; Chapais, IV, 166–7.

[35] Christie, IV, 395; Filteau, II, 172–6.

[36] Filteau, II, 171–2; Christie, IV, 398.

[37] Fauteux, 29; Filteau, II, 182.

[38] *The Vindicator*, 24 October 1837; Christie, IV, 400–10 *n.*; Fauteux, 29–30.

[39] Filteau, II, 182.

[40] *La Minerve*, 2 novembre 1837.

[41] *Mandements des évêques de Montréal* (Montréal, 1867), I, 14: Lartigue, 24 October 1837. Translation in Christie, IV, 415–9.

[42] *RAPQ 1944–5*: L.-A. Desrosiers, 'Correspondence de Mgr Jean-Jacques Lartigue de 1836 à 1838,' 257, Lartigue-Demers, 30 October 1837; 260, Lartigue-Superieur de Saint-Sulpice (Paris), 25 November 1837. *RAPQ 1945–6*: L.-A. Desrosiers, 'Correspondence de Mgr Lartique et de son coadjuteur Mgr Bourget de 1837 à 1840,' 142–3, Bourget-Sidyme (Turgeon), 26 October 1837; 143, Bourget-P. M.-Mignault, 6 November 1837; 144, Bourget-Sidyme, 13 November 1837. Cf. Groulx, 104–17.

[43] *Mandements de Québec*, III, 371: Signay, 11 December 1837.

[44] *The Liberal*, 3 November 1837; Chapais, IV, 173; Filteau, II, 195.

[45] *La Minerve*, cited without date by Chapais, IV, 175.

[46] *Le Canadien*, 22 November 1837; Chapais, IV, 183–4. For other extracts from Parent's writings at this period, see Chapais, 175–83.

[47] PAC: Q 239–1, 4; Chapais, IV, 195.

[48] Christie, IV, 426–37, gives the conflicting accounts of the *Montreal Herald, Montreal Gazette, L'Ami du Peuple, La Minerve*, and *Morning Courier* of the affair on November 6. Cf. Filteau, II, 217–24, which assigns the riot to a loyalist conspiracy.

[49] Christie, V, 2–3 *n.*

[50] PAC: Q 239–1, 98, Gosford-Glenelg, 22 November 1837; *RAPQ 1925–6*, 151–3, I. Caron, 'Les Evénements de 1837 et 1838,' Docs. 50–70; L.-O. David, *Les Patriotes de 1837–38* (Montréal, 1936), 25; Christie, IV, 448–50.

[51] Christie, IV, 461, quotes the official figures of six killed and eleven wounded among the troops. Filteau, III, 28–9, puts the military losses at 116. Christie puts the *Patriote* dead at thirteen, Filteau at ten dead and seven wounded.

[52] Christie, IV, 466–70 and *n.*, 507–40, gives many of the documents in the Papineau-Nelson dispute.

[53] *RAPQ 1925–6*, 166–7, Docs. 358–80; Christie, IV, 471–4, 511–16; Filteau, III, 14–15, 22–3.

[54] *RAPQ 1925–6*, 167, 168–70; Docs. 377–80, 381–440; Christie, IV, 474–5; Filteau, III, 50–1.

[55] Christie, V, 23, Gugy-Christie, 8 April 1853.

[56] *Ibid.*, 24.

[57] Christie, IV, 520, Brown-Nelson, 25 November 1851.

[58] Christie, IV, 465, gives the official return for the troops and quotes an estimate of more than 150 killed and more than 300 wounded for the *Patriotes*. Filteau, III, 44–5, estimates the *Patriote* losses as 40 dead, 30 wounded, and 30 prisoners, and states that the troops lost at least 30 men.

[59] Christie, IV, 466.

[60] *Ibid.*, 476–8, 513; Filteau, III, 58, 61–3.

[61] Lanctot, *Voisins*, 194; Papineau at Saint-Ours.

[62] Christie, IV, 481–3, Kempt-Colborne, 7 December 1837; 483–4 *n.*, Knowlton-Colborne, 7 December 1837; Filteau, III, 64–7.

[63] *CAR 1922–3*, 373, 'Giroud's Journal,' 22 November 1837; 167–8, Lafontaine-J. Parkes, 10 March 1838; Lafontaine-E. Ellice, 15 March 1838; 170, Lafontaine-Ellice, 17 April 1838; *CAR 1901*, Q 239–2, 291, 295, Gosford-Glenelg, 28 December 1837 and Lafontaine warrant. PAC: Q 239–2, Gosford-Glenelg, 6 December 1837.

[64] *CAR 1901*, 1011.

[65] Christie, IV, 486–9, Proclamation of November 29; 490–1 *n.*, reward of $4,000 for Papineau, 1 December 1837; 491–2, rewards of $2,000 for W. Nelson, T. S. Brown, E. B. O'Callaghan, C.-H.-O. Côté, J.-T. Drolet, J.-J. Girouard, W. H. Scott, E.-E. Rodier, A. Girod, J.-O. Chénier, and $400 for P.-P. Demaray, J.-F. Davignon, J. [L.] Gagnon, P. Amiot, L. Perrault, L. Gauthier, and R. Des Rivières, 29 November 1837; 492–3 *n.*, proclamation of martial law, 5 December 1837. Most of the proclamations offering rewards are reproduced in their English and French versions in *RAPQ 1925–6*, 160, 176, 208, 216, 224.

[66] *RAPQ 1945–6*, 151, Bourget-La Motte, 11 December 1837; *Mandements de Montréal*, I, 24, Lartigue's mandement, 8 January 1838; *RAPQ 1945–6*, 145, Bourget-Lefebvre, 4 November 1937; Bourget-Bellenger, 5 December 1937; 47, Lartigue-Blanchet, 27 January 1838; 145, Bourget-Quiblier, 20 November 1837; 151–2, Bourget-Chartier, 12 December 1837; 156, Bourget-Mousseau.

[67] *CAR 1922–3*, 375, Girod's *Journal*.

[68] *Ibid.*, 379.

[69] Christie, V, 6 *n.*; Filteau, III, 92.

[70] *RAPQ 1945–6*, 158, Bourget-Sidyme, 26 January 1838; A. Descelles, *The Patriotes of 1837* (Chronicles of Canada, Toronto, 1916), 101.

[71] *Mandements de Québec*, III, 374–7, Signay's mandement, 6 February 1838; 377–8, circular on petition, 7 February 1837; 378–81, text of petition. This petition was the idea of Abbé J.-C. Prince of the Seminary of Saint Hyacinthe, and Bishop Bourget had advocated it to Bishop Turgeon as early as November 20 as a means 'to satisfy the moderate *Patriotes* and protect the interests of the clergy without being the tool of M. Papineau.' He thought that it would restore the confidence of the people in the clergy (*RAPQ 1945–6*, 146, Bourget-Sidyme, 20 November 1837). A draft of the petition was drawn up by Bishop Lartigue in November before the fighting at Saint-Denis and Saint-Charles, which caused the project to be postponed (*RAPQ 1944–5*, 260). But Bourget's hopes were not realized, for after the petition was sent he noted that the people had turned against the clergy (*RAPQ 1945–6*, 167, Bourget-Belcourt, 24 April 1838).

[72] Christie, V, 51, lists the members, who included Neilson, James Stuart, and Peter McGill.

[73] Christie, V, 151 *n.*, Buller-executive councilors, 31 May 1838.

[74] Christie, V, 145–8, Durham's proclamation, 29 May 1838.

[75] Chapais, IV, 224–5, gives excerpts.

[76] Christie, V, 160 *n.* and 223–9, prisoners' letters of 18 and 26 June and Nelson and Bouchette's explanation of 19 October 1838.

[77] *Ibid.*, 161–6, ordinance of 28 June 1838.

[78] *Ibid.*, 174–7, proclamation of amnesty, 28 June 1838.

[79] *CAR 1923*, 315, Colonel Grey's Report, 22 June 1838.

[80] *Ibid.*, 341–69, Buller's 'Sketch of Lord Durham's Mission to Canada in 1838,' 1840.

[81] *CHR 1937*, 51, N. Storey (*ed.*), 'Stewart Derbishire's Report to Lord Durham on Lower Canada, 1838.'

[82] *Ibid.*

[83] *Ibid.*, 53.

[84] *Ibid.*, 52–3; P.-J.-O. Chauveau, *F.-X. Garneau et son oeuvre* (Montréal, 1883), ccxiii–iv.

[85] *CHR 1937*, 54, 55.

[86] *Ibid.*, 57.

[87] *Ibid.*, 57–8.

[88] *Ibid.*, 60.

[89] *Ibid.*, 57.

[90] *Ibid.*, 57.

[91] *Ibid.*, 62.

[92] *Ibid.*, 64.
[93] PAC: Durham Papers, II, 126, Durham-Glenelg, 28 September 1838.
[94] Christie, V, 211–21, Durham's farewell proclamation, 9 October 1838.
[95] *CAR 1923*, 361, Buller's *Sketch.*
[96] *Ibid.*, 363.
[97] Christie, V, 15–8, proclamation of Governor Jenison of Vermont, 13 December 1837; 83–4, proclamation of Governor Marcy of New York, 19 December 1837.
[98] Christie, V, 42–5, Nelson's proclamation, 28 February 1838.
[99] *Ibid.*, 45–6.
[100] Colborne continued martial law in the district of Montreal by proclamation on February 27, the day he took over the government from Gosford. On February 22 he had ordered the inhabitants of the counties of Laprairie, Chambly, and L'Acadie to give up their arms (Christie, V, 38–9). The official communiqué on the Caldwell's Manor episode clearly indicates that Nelson's invasion was anticipated (*ibid.*, 40–2). According to the *Burlington Sentinel*, Colonel John E. Wool, the U.S. commanding officer at Plattsburg, kept Colborne informed of the *Patriote* plans, and he was conveniently at hand to accept Nelson's surrender. Fauteux, *Patriotes*, 54; A. B. Corey, *The Crisis of 1830–1842 in Canadian American Relations* (Toronto, 1941), 41–2.
[101] TRSC 1926, III, 20, I, 17–34, I. Caron, 'Une Société Secrète dans le Bas Canada en 1838.' Corey, 75, estimates the membership at 40–50,000 members, with 107 lodges in Vermont, 283 in New York, 74 in New Hampshire, and 99 in Maine.
[102] Félix Poutré, *Echappé de la Potence: Souvenirs d'un Prisonnier d'Etat en 1838* (Montréal, 1869).
[103] Christie, V, 213, 217, 218, Durham's farewell proclamation, 9 October, 1838.
[103a] *RAPQ 1945–6*, 64, Lartigue-Turgeon, 6 June 1838; 80, Lartigue-Signay, 29 September 1838; 95, Lartigue-Provender, 21 August 1839.
[104] *Montreal Herald*, 14 November 1838; Chapais, IV, 218–19 *n.*
[105] Christie, V, 239–40, 263.
[106] *Ibid.*, 263–73, gives extracts from the loyalist and *Patriote* press.
[107] Fauteux, 75–9, identifies the prisoners and their fates.
[108] Chapais, IV, 224 *n.*
[109] Quoted in *L'Aurore*, 18 January 1839; Filteau, III, 208.
[110] *CAR 1923*, Buller-J. S. Mill, 13 October 1838.
[111] C. P. Lucas, *Lord Durham's Report* (Oxford, 1912), II, 9.
[112] *CHR 1939*, 128, C. New, 'The British Background of the Durham Report.'
[113] Lucas, II, 13.
[114] *Ibid.*, 16–17.
[115] *Ibid.*, III, 340.
[116] *Ibid.*, II, 17.
[117] *Ibid.*, 19–20.
[118] *Ibid.*, 22, 23, 27.
[119] *Ibid.*, 27, 28–31, 32, 33.
[120] *Ibid.*, 34, 35, 36–7.
[121] *Ibid.*, 38, 40, 43.
[122] *Ibid.*, 45–6, 47.
[123] *Ibid.*, 48–9, 51, 52.
[124] *Ibid.*, 52–3.
[125] *Ibid.*, 63, 70, 71, 72.
[126] *CAR 1923*, 326–8, R. Baldwin-Durham, 23 August 1838; 329–37, R. Baldwin-Glenelg, 13 July 1836; *CHR 1939*, 188, C. Martin, 'Lord Durham's Report and its Consequences.'

[127] Lucas, II, 278, 76, 82.

[128] *CHR 1938*, 22–30, J. B. Brebner, 'Patronage and Parliamentary Government.'

[129] Lucas, II, 110, 113, 128, 130.

[130] *Report on the Affairs of British North America from the Earl of Durham, Her Majesty's High Commissioner, &c. &c. &c.* (London, 1839), Appendix D.

[131] Lucas, II, 134, 135, 136.

[132] *Ibid.*, 137, 138, 139, 140.

[133] *Ibid.*, 280, 282, 282–3, 283, 285.

[134] *Ibid.*, 287.

[135] Report (London, 1839), Appendix B; Lucas, III, 34–130.

[136] Lucas, II, 288–9.

[137] *Ibid.*, 289–92.

[138] *Ibid.*, 292–3.

[139] *Ibid.*, 294. Emigration of French Canadians to U.S., 243, 262.

[140] *Ibid.*, 294–6.

[141] *Ibid.*, 296, 299, 307.

[142] *Ibid.*, 305.

[143] *Ibid.*, 333.

CHAPTER V

THE EMERGENCE OF A NATION—I

(1840–9)

THE FRENCH CANADIANS had lost their struggle for survival b resort to arms; they were to win it by resort to the arts c peace. Spurred by the direct attack on their culture whic Durham had made, and by the threat of the assimilation which h recommended, they soon overturned the political system which wa designed to effect it, and gave vigorous evidence of their cultura strength. The period between 1840 and 1867 is one of the mos notable chapters in the French-Canadian past.

Faced with the prospect of national extinction, the Frencl Canadians closed their ranks and won the peaceful victory whicl insured their national survival. They were favored by the curiou fatality which befell the first governors-general of United Canada– three of whom served a total of only seven years, and were overtake by death, while two were repudiated at home and two in Canada They were fortunate in their own political leaders, Louis-Hippolyt Lafontaine and George-Etienne Cartier, who displayed qualities c statesmanship as yet unrevealed by French Canadians: and the benefited by alliance with Robert Baldwin's Upper Canadia Reformers. They also profited by disunion among the English Canadian Tories, accentuated by economic disorders that were c less concern to a people as yet largely unconcerned with trade an commerce. Then French Canada produced a national historian François-Xavier Garneau, and a national poet, Octave Crémazie, a the very moment when a sense of nationality was necessary fo survival. A spirit of liberalism and progress infused new life into a ancient culture at the very period when it became essential that tha culture should change or perish. This notable era began wit French Canada deprived of representative government and con demned to extinction in a wholly British North America; it closed wit the duality of Canada recognized by a new constitution and with French-Canadian cultural tradition firmly established.

I

Such results were unthinkable at the outset of the period. Th union of the two Canadas had been decided upon by the Britis

overnment as a result of Durham's *Report*, but the grant of respon-
ible government was withheld. The first Union Bill proposed by the
ritish government in 1839 was withdrawn because of the protests
t aroused in Upper Canada. The Reformers in both provinces were
iven new hope by Durham's backing of the principle of responsible
overnment, while both groups of Tories united to denounce this
langerous suggestion. All parties were in some measure aggrieved
y Durham's frankness. A committee of the legislative council of
Jpper Canada declared that the adoption of Durham's plan 'must
ead to the overthrow of the great colonial empire of England.'[1]
Vith a singular anticipation of the Tory annexationist sentiment of
decade later, this body proclaimed:

> If England withdraw her influence, and leave her governors to be the huttle between colonial parties, no loyalty now existing among any of hese parties will prevent their seeking another influence in the neigh-ouring republic, to replace the one needlessly withdrawn; and as the 'rench of Lower Canada sought the alliance of their ancient enemies, he Anglo-American population of the neighbouring States, to give them he means of overwhelming the British population—for the time left vithout the countenance or support of the British government—so will he losing party, in either colony, seek some external influence to aid their ause. England refuses the umpirage, and there can be no doubt but hat it will be readily offered, before many years, to the United States.[2]

In the face of such provocative statements, the British government, vhich was not yet ready to consider parting with its colonies, sent ut Charles Poulett Thomson, a disciple of Durham, as governor-eneral, with instructions to gather further information on Canadian ffairs to serve in drawing up a new Canada bill. To him Lord John Russell, the colonial secretary and his close friend, expressed the overnment's anxiety 'to consult and, so far as may be possible, to lefer to public opinion in the Canadas on the subject of consti-utional changes,' and at the same time its great reluctance to depart rom the principles of 'a legislative Union of the two provinces—a ust regard to the claims of either province in adjusting the terms of hat Union—the maintenance of the three estates of the provincial egislature, the settlement of a permanent civil list for securing the ndependence of the judges, and to the executive government that reedom of action which is essential for the public good—and the stablishment of a system of local government by representative odies, freely elected in the various cities and rural districts.'[3]

In the face of continued Canadian agitation for responsible overnment, Russell further advised Thomson that he was to give o encouragement to the 'movement for what is absurdly called esponsible government.' He granted the existence of that system in England, but he did not favor its extension to the colonies:

> But if we seek to apply such a practice to a colony, we shall at onc find ourselves at fault. The power for which a minister is responsible i England, is not his own power, but the power of the Crown, of which he i for the time the organ. It is obvious that the executive councillor of a colon is in a situation totally different. The Governor under whom he serves re ceives his orders from the Crown of England. But can the colonial counc be the advisers to the Crown of England? Evidently not, for the Crow has other advisers, for the same functions, and with superior authority.
>
> It may happen, therefore, that the Governor receives at one and th same time instructions from the Queen, and advice from his executiv council, totally at variance with each other. If he is to obey his instruction from England, the parallel of constitutional responsibility entirely fails if, on the other hand, he is to follow the advice of his council, he is n longer a subordinate officer, but an independent sovereign.[4]

While objecting to the fundamental principle, Russell found none t 'the practical views of colonial government recommended by Lor Durham.' In short, he proposed that the fruits of Durham's plan b attained while the root was withheld. In his view this miracle wa to be achieved by the exercise of forbearance on the part of both th executive and the assembly: 'The Governor must only oppose th wishes of the Assembly where the honour of the Crown, or th interests of the empire are deeply concerned; and the Assembl must be ready to modify some of its measures for the sake of har mony, and from a reverent attachment to the authority of Grea Britain.'[5] Such an interest in harmony and such 'reverent attach ment' were hardly to be expected from those who had recently bee at one another's throats; only genius could make the policy briefl workable, and it was foredoomed to the failure which befell it withi a few years.

2

Poulett Thomson, who was shortly raised to the peerage as Baro Sydenham of Sydenham and Toronto—an appropriate title, sinc he was to govern in the interests of England and Upper Canada— was singularly well equipped for the difficult task thus set him c working out a practical implementation of Durham's policy. H was neither a Tory soldier, like most of the governors who had pre ceded him, nor a benevolent Liberal like Durham; but a business man who had been trained as a merchant and who had represente Manchester, the capital of the new industrialism, in Parliament for te years. He was at home with facts, figures, statistics and financial prob lems; he had served for five years as president of the Board of Trad and was considered a likely choice for chancellor of the exchequer.

It had been demonstrated that Upper and Lower Canada coul not exist economically separate; it seemed unlikely that they coul live politically united. But if any man could bring about a successful working of the Union, it was Thomson, who was both an able parliamentarian and an able businessman, though a businessman of a very different stamp from the Canadian merchants, since he was a Whig, a free-trader, and a former Baltic timber dealer, and thus triply anathema to them.

He was as much opposed to responsible government as they were, however, and as set upon the Union as a device by which bankrupt Upper Canada, with its debt of £1,200,000 (the interest of which the revenue did not suffice to pay), could be saved by amalgamation with the prosperous lower province, whose debt amounted only to £95,000. Though no mention was made of the matter in his official instructions, he had been secretly authorized by the Cabinet to grant at his discretion a British guarantee for a loan of a million and a half sterling to Upper Canada, to diminish the interest burden and to continue the canal and road program which was largely responsible for the upper province's debt.[6] It was no problem for the iron-willed and self-confident Thomson to win support for the Union project from the new special council of Lower Canada, made up of creatures of the government selected by Colborne; while the terms he offered of a permanent civil list, equal representation for each province, and the charging of the Upper Canadian debt upon the general revenue, won over the Upper Canadian legislature after some resistance.

The governor overcame by personal intervention opposition from members of the Tory Family Compact, who proposed that Lower Canada should have only fifty voices to Upper Canada's sixty-two in the new assembly, that the capital should be in the latter province, that English should be the sole language of legislation, and that a property qualification should be established for members. The city fathers of Toronto went one step farther by demanding in their address of welcome that the same rights and privileges given to the 'loyal British population of these provinces' should not be extended to 'that portion of the population which by education, habits, and prejudices is alien to our nation.'[7] Despite these excessively vigorous protestations of loyalty which a largely immigrant stock directed against the natives of their common country, Thomson confided to a friend that the reconciliation of Upper Canada to the Union was 'a more difficult matter' than that of Lower Canada, where 'The *Canadien* and the *Montreal Herald* lie down together upon this point. In short, the unanimity is wonderful.'[8] Thomson himself thought 'a despotism would be by far the best thing for Lower Canada for the next ten years,' but he recognized 'that cannot be.'[9] As for Upper Canadian loyalism, he commented dryly that 'The people have got into the habit of talking so much *separation*, that they begin to believe in it. The Constitutional party is as bad or worse than the other, in spite of all their professions of loyalty.'[10] Thomson was no gentler in describing the state of Lower Canada a few months later: 'They have only one feeling—the French hate the English and would cut all their throats if they could—the English hate the French and only desire to ride rough shod over them.'[11]

With Canadian consent obtained either by force or pressure exercised by the governor-general, the imperial parliament passed the Union Act[12] on July 23, 1840. The bill, introduced by Lord John Russell on March 23, established the Province of Canada, with a legislative council named for life and an elected assembly composed of forty-two members from Lower Canada and forty-two from Upper Canada. Any change in the number of representatives demanded a two-thirds vote of both houses. A property qualification of £500 was established. English was to be the only language of original record for the legislature,[13] but the existing laws of the two provinces were preserved. The revenues of the Crown were renounced to the new province in exchange for a civil list of £45,000, covering the salaries of the governor and judges, and of £30,000, covering the salaries of the principal civil servants. Thomson had urgently advised Russell: 'You must take a *large* civil list. Govt. in this country depends on your not being obliged to go to the Assembly for what you want.'[14] The governor was given the right to erect new counties or townships, and to name personal deputies. Bills relative to the rights of the clergy and of the Crown were to be submitted to the imperial parliament, which also retained power over the regulation of trade and navigation between Canada and other countries. The governor preserved the right of veto and the right to reserve legislation for the royal sanction, while the Queen could disavow any bill within a period of two years.

By giving the same representation to the 650,000 people of Lower Canada as to the 450,000 of Upper Canada, the bill violated one of Durham's major recommendations, that in favor of representation by population. By merging the revenues of the two provinces and their public debts, Lower Canada was saddled with the enormous debt of the upper province, largely contracted, to be sure, for the St. Lawrence canals which would be of mutual value in the future, though at present of benefit mainly to Upper Canada. The article establishing English as the sole official language was deeply resented by the French Canadians. It was the first official measure directed against an essential element of their survival, and the first step in Durham's proposed program of anglicization.

The bill was supported in the House by both parties, with Russell, Charles Buller, Gladstone, Peel, and Ellice backing it, while the only notable opposition was raised by Daniel O'Connell. He protested against the inequality of representation and the fact that the people of Lower Canada had not been consulted, seeing only disaffection and a weakening of the bonds between the two countries as the results of such a measure. But even Hume, long the champion of the Canadians, refused to vote against the bill, and it was carried with only six opposing voices in the House. In the Lords the opposition to the bill, led by Wellington, Gosford, Ellenborough, Brougham, and Hardwick, was more vigorous. Gosford protested that 'I do not believe that in any of our Colonies Her Majesty has more loyal subjects than the French Canadians of Lower Canada.'[15] Denouncing the inequality of representation and the merging of the debts, he exclaimed: 'There could be nothing more arbitrary and unjust.' But despite these objections of the former governor, and the petitions of 10,000 inhabitants of Quebec and of the bishops and clergy of Montreal and Quebec, the measure was carried.

One powerful force behind the Union Act was that of the banking firm of Baring Brothers, which had underwritten almost all the Upper Canadian securities whose value was now in question. One of the principals of this firm, Francis T. Baring, was chancellor of the exchequer in the Melbourne cabinet, and the Baring interests may have had something to do with the determination of the cabinet to shift the burden of Upper Canadian bankruptcy onto the shoulders of the prosperous lower province. Young Pierre Chauveau was moved to bitter verse by this banker's constitution:

C'est le jour des banquiers, demain sera notre heure.
Aujourd'hui l'oppression, demain la liberté;
Aujourd'hui l'on fustige un peuple entier qui pleure,
Demain l'on voit debout tout un peuple ameuté;
Aujourd'hui le forfait, et demain la vengéance,
Aujourd'hui c'est de l'or, et demain c'est du fer . . .
C'est le jour des banquiers, vous dis-je! c'est leur gloire
Que les placards royaux affichent sur nos murs;
L'Union que l'on proclame est leur chant de victoire,
Et tout devait céder à des motifs si purs! . . .
Ces vieux lords décrépits, ces ministres peureux . . .
Cependant, si Baring leur dit: moi, je le veux,
Enlacés comme ils sont aux filets de sa banque,
Ils n'ont rien à repondre et jamais il ne fait
D'inutile calcul, ni de projet qui manque.
Il voudrait l'univers, il leur demanderait
Le sang des nations pour verser dans sa caisse,
Que l'illustre Russell d'une tremblante main,
Jaloux de prévenir et d'écarter la baisse
Signerait aussitôt l'absurde parchemin. . . .*[16]

*It is the banker's day, tomorrow will be ours,
Today oppression, tomorrow liberty,

While the young poet thus inveighed in prosy verse against British economic conspiracy—which French Canadians were to suspect with more and more frequency in the years to come—the businessman governor-general lapsed into lyricism in proclaiming the establishment of the Union on February 10, 1841:

> Inhabitants of the Province of Canada: Henceforth may you be united in sentiment as you are from this day in name! Who can visit, as it has been my good fortune to do, the extensive regions which are now united in one common denomination, and fail to acknowledge the vast resources they present, for all that can conduce to the comforts and happiness of man? A part of the Mighty Empire of England—protected by Her arms—assisted by Her Treasury, admitted to all the benefits of Trade as Her citizens—your freedom guaranteed by Her Laws, and your rights supported by the sympathy of your Fellow-Subjects there—Canada enjoys a position unsurpassed by any Country in the world. It is for you, its Inhabitants, to cultivate these advantages—to avail yourselves of the new Era which now opens upon you.[17]

3

Though Sydenham was 'not a bit afraid of the responsible government cry,'[18] he was deeply disturbed by the home government's failure to establish under the Union Act a system of local government, which Durham had recommended and which he himself strongly favored. He wrote home:

> No man in his senses would think for a moment of the Union without its being accompanied by some sort of Local Government, in which the people may control their own officers, and the executive at the same time obtain some influence in the country districts. Without a breakwater of this kind between the Central Government and the people, Government with an Assembly is impossible in Lower Canada, and most

---

Today a weeping people is beaten,
Tomorrow a people will be up in arms,
Today the forfeit, tomorrow the vengeance,
Today is gold's, tomorrow steel's . . .
It is the banker's day, I say, it is their glory
Of which the royal placards give notice on our walls.
The Union thus proclaimed is their song of victory,
And all ought to yield to motives so pure! . . .
These decrepit old lords, these fearful ministers
If Baring says to them: 'I wish it';
Entrapped as they are in the meshes of his bank,
They have nothing to say, and never does he make
A useless calculation or a project doomed to fail.
If he wished the universe, he would ask of them
The blood of nations, to pour it in his safe;
Let the noted Russell, with a trembling hand,
Anxious to prevent and avoid a crash,
Sign at once the absurd parchment . . .

difficult in Upper Canada; and it is absurd to expect that any good system will be established by the Provincial Legislature, even if time admitted of its being proposed to them . . . not only has all chance of the Union Bill working well been destroyed, but also a change of system throughout all the Provinces . . . The establishment of Municipal Government by Act of Parliament is as much a part of the intended, scheme of Government for the Canadas as the union of the two Legislatures, and the more important of the two.[19]

There was some injured pride of authorship behind this indignation, for Sydenham himself had drafted the scheme which was omitted from the bill, at the insistence of Peel and Stanley, because of 'the want of Canadian authority.'[20]

It was easy to remedy the omission in the case of Lower Canada, for all Sydenham had to do was to have an ordinance establishing his scheme passed by the special council. He thought it particularly important to do so, for:

The Priest and the Lawyer return the member *now* and *that* without any control, or upon any ground except hatred to English Govt. and the English name. Establish a field in which the Inhabitants can discuss their own interests, and parties will soon be split in the different parishes and districts, and set there someone in the confidence of the Govt. who will expose the misrepresentations which are made, and you will either get different members or have a good check on them.[21]

But to get the measure through the first parliament of the Union required all his skill as a parliamentarian. An interesting light on the man and on his concept of his role in the new government is furnished by the account he gave of this episode to his brother:

My last feat has been to carry the Municipal District Bill for Upper Canada, word for word after my own ordinance for the Lower Province; thereby not only giving the complement to the Union (for you know I always declared that without such institutions the Union could not work), but setting up my own particular legislation by the sanction of the United Parliament. The bill has passed both houses, and I proceed to-day in state to give it the royal assent, in order to make perfectly sure of its being law, even if I were to quit this world the day after. But the trouble I have had to do this has completely justified all my anticipations of the next to impossibility of our getting such a measure through a Provincial Assembly, and the utter hopelessness of the effort, but for the course I followed of dictating it, while I was dictator, for one part of the province first. One party hated the measure because it was to give power to the people; another because it placed that power under wholesome control by the Crown; a third because it deprived the members of the Assembly of all their past power of jobbing. But I beat them all three, to the utter astonishment of the spectators; and at last carried my work, the Bill, the whole Bill, and nothing but the Bill, by a majority of forty-two to twenty-nine, or more than one third. I have now accomplished all I set much value on; for whether the rest be done now or some sessions hence, matters little. The five great works I aimed at have been got through—the establishment of a board of works with ample powers; the admission of aliens; a new system of county courts; the regulation of the public lands ceded by the Crown under the Union Act; and lastly, this District Council Bill.[22]

This letter reveals Sydenham's policy of being his own prime minister, and the success which crowned his energetic pursuit of the program of reconstruction on which he had decided.

But parliamentary government was at a different stage of growth in Canada than at Westminster or Washington. Lord John Russell knew what responsible government meant in England in 1839, but both he and the Canadian governors were puzzled by a concept of patronage which owed more to American than British precedents. For Papineau, Lafontaine, and Baldwin, under the influence of Jacksonianism, the spoils system was a cornerstone of their constitutional concepts. Their demands for the extension of the elective principle to the councils* and other public offices ran counter to the traditional eighteenth-century concept of patronage held by the governors, who sought to emulate George III. Metcalfe saw the conflict in Canada not as one about a principle of government but as to 'whether the patronage of the Crown should be surrendered to the Council for the purchase of Parliamentary support.'[23] But responsible government and patronage were inextricably linked in Canadian constitutional development, as the course of party politics from 1841 to 1847 gave evidence. Both Baldwin and Lafontaine made control of patronage the criterion of their taking office. The demand for a share of patronage was particularly strong among the now politically conscious French Canadians after their long exclusion from office by French and British placemen under the old imperial systems. Political office had special attractions for them, since other fields were largely dominated by English Canadians. Sydenham, and his successors until Elgin, ignored these facts, and their blindness cost them dear.

Sydenham named an executive council composed of four Tories and three Reformers, with not a single French-Canadian member. In explaining his action privately to Russell, the governor-general observed: 'The worst of it is, that there is really not a French Canadian to whom it is possible to give an office.'[24] To be sure, he had tried to induce Lafontaine to become solicitor-general of Lower Canada, promising in the future to call only Reformers to office from that section, but the latter had refused, not wishing to give his

* Baldwin, unlike his Lower Canadian friends, opposed an elective legislative council.

support to either the Union or to a government hostile to the French Canadians.

Since April 1839, when Francis Hincks had written him offering the co-operation of the Upper Canadian Reformers in achieving 'liberal institutions and economical government,'[25] Lafontaine had been in close touch with the leaders of that party. In 1840 he visited Robert Baldwin, and their acquaintance ripened into a lasting friendship and political alliance. Baldwin and Hincks preferred to join with men of their own political convictions rather than to accept the ethnic alliance offered by the British party in Lower Canada, for Baldwin held that 'There is, and must be, no question of races—It were madness on one side, and guilt, deep guilt on both to make such a question.'[26] Hincks kept urging Lafontaine to accept the Union and to act with the governor, assuring him that 'your brother Reformers in Upper Canada will meet you and your compatriots as Canadians, that no national animosities will be entertained, that we desire your friendship, esteem, and co-operation if we can obtain them consistent with our principles.'[27] When Baldwin accepted office as solicitor-general of Upper Canada, Hincks defended his course, and later urged Lafontaine to follow it, arguing that Reform influence in the government would thus be strengthened.[28]

Sydenham merely gathered in one cabinet representatives of the various factions whose support he needed to enact his policy; he did not choose a responsible ministry. He favored a dictatorship for Lower Canada, and he set about achieving the position of a dictator within the framework of the Union Act. The legislative council was in his power, since he named its members; the assembly offered more difficulties, since its members must be elected. But the governor took an active part in the elections held in the spring of 1841, talking freely of 'my candidates' and gerrymandering constituencies in order to achieve their election, notably at Montreal and Quebec:

> I shall reduce the limits of Montreal & Quebec to the Cities and cut off the suburbs, which will cause a great clatter with the French and their Allies, but you might just as well have given no representation at all to either city as far as the Trade and the British Mercantile Interest is concerned, as not to do so. *With* the suburbs, these towns are as much French Counties as the Counties of the same names.[29]

Where such tactics were not sufficient, he established the polling places in strongholds of the government, and winked at the intimidation of voters. By such means nineteen unionists were elected out of Lower Canada's forty-two representatives. Sydenham reported to Russell:

. . . considering that two years ago the people were cutting each other's throats and in arms against each other while the French Canadian press and leaders have been doing everything in their power to excite the passion of the People, I am quite surprised that they [the elections] went off so well.[30]

Lafontaine was defeated in Terrebonne, where several hundred strongarm men had been brought in from Montreal and Glengarry to support Sydenham's candidate. Faced with the prospect of involving his supporters in a murderous and hopeless battle at the polls, Lafontaine withdrew from the contest. At the outset of the election he had issued a manifesto which served as a new political program for the French Canadians. In it he pointed out that Canada was not only their ancestral home, but also the adopted home of the English who had established themselves there, and that the happiness and welfare of both groups were dependent upon social equality and political liberty. He defined the latter as:

The sanction by the popular will of the adoption of laws; it is its consent to vote taxes and to control disbursements; again, it is its effective participation in the action of its government; it is its legitimate influence in making the wheels of the administration turn and its effective and constitutional control on the individuals most immediately placed to make the administration function; it is, in a word, the great question of the day: responsible government, such as was avowed and promised to the Assembly of Upper Canada, in order to obtain its consent to the principal of Union, and not such perhaps as is now explained in certain quarters.[31]

Lafontaine had no confidence in Sydenham's promises of responsible government, and stated his belief that the governor would be guided in his actions by the character of the new assembly. He expressed his own faith in the principle of responsible government:

I see in its working the sole guarantees that we can have of good and effective government. The colonials should have the management of their own affairs. They should direct all their efforts to this end; and to succeed, the colonial administration must be formed and directed by and with the majority of the representatives of the people.

He condemned the Union of the two provinces:

An act of injustice and despotism, in that it is imposed upon us without our consent; in that it deprives Lower Canada of the legitimate number of its representatives; in that it deprives us of the use of our language in the proceedings of the legislature, against the spirit of the treaties and the word of the governor-general; in that it makes us pay, without our consent, a debt that we have not contracted; in that it permits the executive power to seize illegally under the name of a civil list, and without the vote of the representatives of the people, an enormous part of the revenues of the country.

Lafontaine flatly rejected the policies of French-Canadian abstention from public life or of a strong demand for the revocation of the Union Act; the representatives of Lower Canada 'should pause before adopting a decision whose immediate result might be to throw us back again under the liberty-killing rule of a Special Council and to leave us without any representation.'

His answer to the problem was an alliance with the Reformers of Upper Canada:

Our cause is common. It is to the interest of the Reformers of the two provinces to meet on the legislative ground in a spirit of peace, union, friendship, and fraternity. Unity of action is more necessary than ever. I have no doubt that, like us, the Reformers of Upper Canada feel the need of it, and that in the first legislative session they will give us non-equivocal proofs of it, which I hope will be the gage of a reciprocal and lasting confidence.

This statesmanlike policy was followed during the next eight years; it laid the foundation of that collaboration between French and English which ended in the achievement of responsible government. Lafontaine's manifesto was hailed by the Upper Canadian Reformers and published in full in Francis Hincks's *Toronto Examiner*, one of their chief organs. Etienne Parent and Augustin Morin of Quebec gave it their support, while embittered John Neilson opposed the Union Act without holding out any hope for the success of a joint alliance against it.

In the absence of Lafontaine, who published another letter to his electors in which he said he had been defeated by Sydenham himself and that 'there were defeats more honorable than victory,'[32] Morin was the leading French-Canadian representative in the new assembly. He was immediately questioned by Hincks on the disposition of the Lower Canadian majority. Morin expressed his hope that the Reformers of the two provinces would act together, 'even though there are among you those who approve of the Union because of the advantages that it gives to Upper Canada, while we are opposed to it because none of its provisions are either just or advantageous for us. But natural justice on one side, and common ideas and interests on the other, should lead to an entente even on this very delicate point.'[33] He rejected an alliance with the Tories of Upper Canada, who were opposed to the Union, but also opposed to the idea of responsible government; and concluded:

You, the Reformers, are our only natural friends. We have been too sincere in our aspirations after liberty and reform—however unknown and ill rewarded they have been—to join now with men of another political faith. Such, at least, is the idea that I conceive of the attitude that my fellow citizens will take; an attitude independent of the executive, but which is not hostile to it and which would even leave us ready to aid and support it, if it wished to hear our sincere opinions and to offer us the guarantee of men possessing the public confidence in its councils.

The ground was thus paved for a working alliance between the Reformers of the two provinces.

When the first assembly of United Canada met at Kingston on June 14, 1841, Sydenham had 'his' majority. Only eight of the twenty-four legislative councilors, named five days before the session began, were French Canadians, and only four or five were independent of the government. Sydenham wrote Russell: 'I wish there were more and better French names amongst them, but few are loyal, and of these some do not like the expense or trouble.'[34] Among the Upper Canadians in the assembly there were twenty-six Reformers favorable to the Union, six members favorable to the government, and only ten Tory anti-unionists. Etienne Parent, now member for Saguenay, was pessimistic about the prospects of the Lower Canadian representatives in his dispatches to *Le Canadien*: 'In the circumstances, all they can do is to protest vigorously against the injustices committed against their country, to submit their cause to the whole world and to appeal from the present to the future. God in His mercy has left hope to the oppressed, and it is all that remains to us.'[35]

Some immediate encouragement was found, however, in the election of Augustin Cuvillier, the former colleague of Papineau and D.-B. Viger, as speaker, and in the defeat of the Tory candidate for that post, Sir Allan MacNab. Then Robert Baldwin, the leader of the Upper Canadian Reformers who had set his face firmly against racial discrimination, resigned from the executive council on the opening day of the session, when Sydenham failed to meet his request to dismiss the Tory members of the council and to include some Lower Canadians in that body. The governor, who had considered Baldwin's appointment in 1840 'the greatest possible *coup*,' now dismissed him as 'the most crotchety impractical enthusiast I ever had to deal with.'[36] The way was thus cleared for a closer alliance between the English and French Reformers, since they had no representatives in the government and were left free to oppose it.

In the debate on the speech from the throne, the Reformers also wrung from the government spokesman an admission that the ministers would resign if unsupported by a majority, and John Neilson was able to win twenty-five votes, including those of Baldwin and Hincks, for his amendment protesting against the Union Act. Only five of the Upper Canadian Reformers joined their fellows from the lower province in this protest, for Sydenham had secured their support by his promise of an imperial guarantee for a loan of £1,500,000, two-thirds of which would be spent in Upper Canada on the vast program of public works which he proposed. The early part of the session justified Sydenham's letter to Lord John Russell of June 27, in which he declared his system of government: 'What I have seen and what I have had to do during the last three weeks, fortifies my opinion as to the absolute necessity of sending as my successor someone having parliamentary and ministerial experience, someone who will not be afraid of work and who will govern himself, as I do.'[37]

The most noteworthy event of the first session of the legislature under the Union was the adoption of the resolutions of September 3, 1841. These were proposed by Baldwin and contained the basic principles of the responsible government which he had long supported. Faced with the prospect of their support by the united Reformers, Sydenham avoided the appearance of defeat by having similar resolutions proposed by his spokesman and adopted. The principal resolution read thus:

> That in order to preserve that harmony between the different branches of the Provincial Parliament which is essential to the happy conduct of public affairs the principal of such subordinate officers, advisors of the representative of the Sovereign and constituting as such the provincial administration under him as the head of the Provincial Government, ought always to be men possessed of the public confidence whose opinions and policy harmonizing with those of the representatives of the people, would afford a guarantee that the well-understood wishes and interests of the people, which our gracious Sovereign has declared shall be the rule of the Provincial Government, will at all times be faithfully represented to the head of that government and through him to the Sovereign and Imperial Parliament.[38]

The passage of this resolution was one victory of the Reformers over Sydenham's maneuvers. This bill was rejected, of course, by the government-controlled legislative council. Sydenham's project of establishing a Canadian bank of issue was also turned down by the assembly, and one article of his cherished Municipal District Bill was carried by only one voice. The assembly had begun to feel its power, and the personal government system of Sydenham was already becoming untenable.

The only man who could make it function, by his willingness to 'breathe, eat, drink, and sleep on nothing but government and politics,'[39] died two days after parliament had been prorogued.

He had broken his leg in a fall from his horse two weeks before; the gout with which he was much troubled caused complications; and lockjaw ensued. Sydenham had created an efficient and economical administration for the new United Canada; he had launched a program of reconstruction and recovery which restored the credit of Canada and opened up its resources. He was not unworthy of the moderate Conservative Egerton Ryerson's epitaph: 'Lord Sydenham has done more in two years to strengthen and consolidate British power in Canada by his matchless industry and truly liberal conservative policy, than had been done during the past ten years by the increase of a standing army and the erection of military fortification.'[40] But if Sydenham saved 'millions to England,' as Ryerson said, he scarcely 'secured the affections of Canada.' Sydenham had not been the friend of the French Canadians —he informed Russell that 'any one district of it (Upper Canada) contains more real wealth and intelligence than all Lower Canada (exclusive of the Townships)' and that 'as for the French nothing but time will do anything with them. They hate British rule—British connexion—British improvement of all kinds whether in their Laws or their roads. So they sulk, and will try, that is, their Leaders, to do all the mischief they can.'[41] But Sydenham had made new allies for the French Canadians by his despotic policy of personal government.

4

It was ironic that Lafontaine was named a representative of York (Toronto) on the day before Sydenham was buried at Kingston. The man whom the late governor had kept out of the assembly now entered it through the courtesy of Robert Baldwin, who had been elected in both Hastings and York, and had asked his friends in the latter constituency to choose Lafontaine in his place. The incident was a proclamation of the alliance between the Reformers of the two provinces, and of that collaboration between French and English which was to create a different Canada than Durham had envisaged. A former lieutenant of Papineau, a man against whom a warrant for high treason had been issued four years before, a Catholic French Canadian, was elected from the stronghold of Protestant English Canada. The times had indeed changed. Etienne Parent hailed the electors of York in *Le Canadien*: 'It is on the principle of true equal justice that they intend to live with their brethren of Lower Canada, as the step they have officially taken indicates. They elect Mr. Lafontaine to show, they say, their sympathy for the Lower Canadians and their detestation of the ill treatment and the injustices to which we have been exposed.'[42]

A similar political revolution had also taken place in England, where the Whigs, who had held power for nearly eleven years, with but one brief interruption, fell before the Conservatives in the elections of June 1841. The new cabinet formed under Peel at the end of August restored Lord Stanley, who had been colonial secretary under Grey seven years before, to his old post. Sir Charles Bagot, a former undersecretary of the Foreign Office who had served as minister to Paris, Washington, St. Petersburg, The Hague, and Vienna, and had refused the governor-generalship of India, was named governor-general of Canada in October, but did not reach Kingston until the following January. He was chosen to fill Charles Buller's prescription of 'a humane just man who will have the liberality and good sense to raise up those whom we have been forced to put down in Canada.'[43]

Lifelong Tory that he was, Bagot nevertheless evinced from the moment of his arrival no such intention as Sydenham had displayed of identifying himself completely with one party and flatly opposing the other. Stanley's instructions to him were of a very different order.

> You cannot too early, and too distinctly, give it to be understood that you enter the Province with the determination to know no distinctions of National origin, or Religious Creed; to consult, in your Legislative capacity, the happiness and (so far as may be consistent with your duty to your Sovereign and your responsibility to her Constitutional advisers) the wishes of the mass of the Community; and, in your Executive capacity, to administer the Laws firmly, moderately, and impartially . . .
>
> In Civil matters, it must be your policy to seek to withdraw the Legislature, and the Population generally, from the discussion of abstract & theoretical questions, by which the Government of Canada, in former times, has been too often and too seriously embarrassed, to the calm & dispassionate consideration of practical measures for the improvement and advancement of the internal prosperity of the Province. In maturing measures of this description, you will endeavour to avail yourself of the advice and services of the ablest Men, without reference to distinction of local party, which, upon every occasion, you will do your utmost to discourage; and, in framing them for the consideration of the Provincial Legislature, you will endeavour to present them in the form in which they are most likely to be favourably received by the House of Assembly.[44]

Six weeks after his arrival in Canada, Bagot assured Stanley that there was 'scarcely anything to fear' from 'internal disaffection or disloyalty.'[45] Sydenham, suspicious of the French, had been somewhat disturbed by 'the great deal of uneasiness' which prevailed in Lower Canada, when the Anglo-French difficulties of 1840 over Egypt and Syria had caused the circulation of rumors of a French invasion of Canada.[46] But the new governor judged that there was much to dread from party feeling, and that 'the error of previous governments in Canada, has been the narrowness of the foundations on which they have been based . . . an attempt to govern by a sing party and to confer on them the whole patronage and power of th Government has invariably united all parties in opposition, and ha led to the defeat of the Government in the popular branch of th Legislature.' Thus:

> The chief opponents of the Government during the last Session wer first the French Canadians—secondly a portion of the (so named) Compact party, and thirdly the ultra popular Section of the Upper Canadian These parties, though differing entirely on all questions of principl repeatedly united for the purpose of defeating or obstructing the Government on individual measures.[47]

Bagot immediately set about breaking up this alliance by judiciou distribution of patronage. Morin, Huot, and Mondelet were mad judges, while Cherrier and Fisher were made Queen's Counse So much for securing the support of some leaders of the Frenc party; Bagot judged the masses could be brought around withou difficulty:

> So long as Lord Sydenham continued in the government the persona feelings which they cherished against him as the author of the Unior might probably have kept them in opposition—but that difficulty removed, the peculiarity of their position on this Continent, and thei habits and feelings would, I should think, lead them to ally themselve with the Government. Surrounded and outnumbered by a race of Britis descent, speaking a different language, following a different creed—bre up under a different system of law, and possessed at the same time of a energy of character and habits to which they can lay no claim, th French Canadians can scarcely avoid seeing that the natural Post is a alliance with the Government, and that by such an alliance alone ca they hope to maintain their peculiar laws and privileges.

Bagot thus foresaw the role the French Canadians were to play a fe years hence, when it was the English Canadians who sought t break the British connection, and also the reasons which still mak the French Canadians today more determined, in the last analysi to preserve that connection than their English-speaking fellov citizens, as insurance of their national survival.

In a later letter Bagot amplified his views of his own position an policy:

> When I left England, I had an opinion which five months residenc in this Country has much tended to confirm, that, as Governor of it, was about to be placed in a very peculiar position—a position in whic my Predecessor did not, and my Successor could not stand; but upo the careful maintenance of which, at this moment, might depend th

ıture well being and tranquillity of the Colony. I felt that, in fact, I ʼas the first Governor who was called upon to put practically into peration, and endeavour to give effect to the great measure of the Jnion, and to work out the experiment of fusing and identifying so far s might be possible, the very discordant elements to be reconciled by ıat irrevocable & unalterable Act—

The means which Lord Sydenham had resorted to, in order to carry nd complete the measure, may have been absolutely necessary—but ıey involved a public, and something very like a private quarrel on his art with the whole mass of the French Inhabitants of Lower Canada— nd it would have been totally impossible for *him* ever again to conciliate ıem, or indeed ever again to have met, with any prospect of success, nother Parliament in this Country.—He therefore could not have ffected the object.—I think that my successor would have quite as little hance of being able to do so.—He could not, as I accidentally can, treat *s* advent as a new starting point—a new era—and a new chapter in the istory of the Country.—When the time should come for his arrival, he ʼould most assuredly find that, if the opportunity had been lost upon ıe first establishment of the Union, of endeavouring to do away, all the ɩd-party exclusions and differences, which had existed previously to it, would be late too for him to make the attempt—that the Country had :lapsed into its old divisions and subdivisions—and that the moment ad passed, in which he could hope to extend, with safety, the patronage ; the Government to all parties equally without reference to past strangements, and to take from all sides the best and fittest men for the ublic service.[48]

Early in his administration Bagot set about taking 'from all sides ıe best and fittest men for the public service.' He named Vallières e Saint-Réal, the defender of the *habeas corpus* against Colborne, ıief justice of the district of Montreal, and the educational re- rmer Dr. Jean-Baptiste Meilleur as the first superintendent of ublic instruction for Lower Canada. These appointments did much make the new governor popular with the French Canadians, and agot's visits to Montreal and Quebec in the spring of 1842 both rengthened his position with the people and gave him some first- and acquaintance with French-Canadian opinion. He also visited oronto, and named Francis Hincks inspector-general of public :counts, a post for which the Upper Canadian Reformer had been lected by Sydenham, who admired his financial ability. Hincks ad gradually been won around to the government which he had iginally denounced, and so his appointment was criticized by oth Reformers and Tories. The Tories were given a sop of satis- ction by the nomination of Henry Sherwood as solicitor-general replace Baldwin.

But the government was still made up of heterogeneous elements, ıd it lacked the support of the assembly. The Tories were now more strongly opposed to the government than ever, since a Tory governo had made evident his failure to share their prejudices. The Re formers of both the French and English camps had increased i numbers, and under the leadership of Lafontaine and Baldwi they were more determined in their opposition than before. Th Lower Canadian Reformers now numbered twenty-five, formin part of a clear and well-disciplined majority, while Lower Canad was represented in the ministry by two Tories and one conviction less creature of the government, all of whom were English.

Bagot consulted with Harrison and Draper, two of the governmen leaders, and they both expressed the opinion that the support o the French Canadians must be obtained by giving them a large share in the administration. Confronted with this situation, Bago wrote to Stanley:

> I am nevertheless fast arriving at the persuasion, that the momen is come when this question must be determined one way or the other and this Government must be carried on, either in professed exclusion of, and defiance of the Canadians of French origin, or by their admission to such a share in it, as they may be contented to receive, and the Mothe Country may deem it safe and reasonable to give them . . .
>
> It is impossible to conceal from oneself that the French members o the Assembly possess the power of the Country and whoever directs tha power, backed by the most efficient means of controlling it, is in a situa tion to govern the Province most effectually.[49]

Bagot knew that the admission of the French Canadians to a share in the government was in opposition to Durham's ideas, Sydenham' practice, and Stanley's policy; but he found no other solution to the problem. The essential connection between patronage and parliamentary government had once more been demonstrated.

With the assembly meeting on September 8, there was no time to wait for Stanley's authorization to reverse the policy which had been followed since the Rebellions of 1837–8. Bagot summoned Lafontaine to two interviews on September 10 and 11, during a weekend adjournment of the debate on the speech from the throne and offered him the attorney-generalship of Lower Canada, a well as the right to nominate an English solicitor-general and a French commissioner of Crown lands. Lafontaine requested tim to consult with his friends, and insisted on the inclusion in th ministry of Baldwin, who had resigned the year before when th French Canadians were left out; on the naming of another French Canadian minister; and on the resignations of Draper and Sher wood, with whom Baldwin could not sit.

The debate was put off another day, and then opened on th 13th by Draper, who protested his belief in responsible governmen and in the inclusion of the French Canadians in the administration. The Tory leader revealed that under Sydenham, whom he could not win to his view, he had twice offered his resignation in order to further it; and that during the last forty-eight hours he had again offered to withdraw, in order to pave the way for a reconstruction of the government, which must necessarily include Baldwin, the ally of the French Canadians. His proposals to Lafontaine had been rejected, but he still hoped to see the day when the principle of government in accordance with the will of the people would be loyally followed. The speaker then read a letter from Bagot to Lafontaine,[50] delivered just before the meeting of the House, in which the governor offered him the attorney-generalship of Lower Canada, and the choice of a solicitor-general for Lower Canada, of a commissioner of Crown lands, and of the clerk of the executive council. Baldwin was to receive the attorney-generalship of Upper Canada, while the replacement of the solicitor-general of Upper Canada was left open for discussion. Ogden, the present attorney-general of Lower Canada, and Davidson, the present commissioner of Crown lands, were to receive pensions in return for resigning. Lafontaine had refused this last-minute offer, principally on the score of the pensions; and Bagot had decided to make it public, in order to embarrass Lafontaine and to make known his liberal intentions to the rank and file of the Lower Canadian Reformers.

The assembly was stunned by these revelations; but Baldwin attacked the ministry and reproached Draper for requiring eighteen months to reveal his belief in responsible government, concluding with a motion of no confidence in the government. The debate became vigorous. Finally Lafontaine rose and began to speak in French. One of the Upper Canadian ministers asked him to speak in English; and Lafontaine made his famous reply:

> I am asked to pronounce in another language than my mother tongue the first speech that I have to make in this House. I distrust my ability to speak English. But I must inform the honorable members that even if my knowledge of English were as intimate as my knowledge of French, I should nevertheless make my first speech in the language of my French-Canadian compatriots, if only to protest against the cruel injustice of the Union Act in trying to proscribe the mother tongue of half the population of Canada. I owe it to my compatriots; I owe it to myself.[51]

After this eloquent protest, Lafontaine went on to explain the negotiations with Bagot. Lafontaine stated that he had not given a flat refusal to the governor's offer, but had merely pointed out the obstacles to its acceptance. He paid tribute to Bagot's sense of justice and equity, and to Draper's public admission that his initial prejudices against the French Canadians had been overcome as he came to know them during the last session. Lafontaine joined with Draper in a demand for co-operation:

> The two populations of Upper and Lower Canada have common interests, and they will end by sympathizing with one another. Yes, without our active cooperation, without our participation in power, the government cannot function in a manner which will re-establish the peace and confidence which are necessary to the success of any administration. Placed by the Union Act in an exceptional position as a minority in the distribution of political power, if we are to succumb, we shall succumb while making ourselves respected. I do not recoil before the responsibility I have assumed, since in my person the governor-general has chosen the individual by whom he wished to make known his liberal and just views towards my compatriots. But in the state of bondage in which the iron fist of Lord Sydenham tried to hold the French population, in the presence of the deeds that were attempted in this end, I have as a Canadian only one duty to fulfil, that of maintaining the honorable character which has distinguished our fellow countrymen and to which our most bitter enemies are obliged to render homage. This character, Mr. Speaker, I shall never dishonor!

The governor's letter and Lafontaine's speech swayed the Lower Canadian Reformers. Negotiations between the two were resumed, and an agreement was reached on the basis of Sherwood's resignation, while the question of pensions remained open. Lafontaine and Baldwin became the attorneys-general of Lower and Upper Canada; Morin commissioner of Crown lands, and Etienne Parent clerk of the executive council; and the rest of the cabinet was revised so that only one Tory remained in it. The cornerstone of responsible government was thus laid on the foundation of control of patronage by the elected representatives of the people rather than by the appointees of the Crown. For the first time since the conquest the French Canadians were given their full share in the executive branch of the government.

Bagot broke the news to Stanley in a somewhat defensive letter which made much of the happy results of this action:

> I have united the voices of seven eighths of the House of Assembly in present support of the Government—some defection must be expected, but none by which the Govt. will be at all weakened. I have met the wishes of a large majority of the population of Upper Canada and of the British Inhabitants of Lower Canada. I have removed the main ground of discontent and distrust among the French-Canadian population; I have satisfied them that the Union is capable of being administered for their happiness and advantage, and have consequently disarmed their opposition to it. I have excited among them the strongest feeling of gratitude to the Provincial Government, and if my policy be approved by H.M.'s Govt. I shall have removed their chief cause of

hostility to British Institutions, and have added another security for their devotion to the British Crown.[52]

In a confidential dispatch of the same date, he contrasted his policy with that of Sydenham, who had rejected the same advice which Bagot had accepted from his councillors:

Towards the French Canadians his conduct was very unwise. He made enemies of them unnecessarily at a time when he should have propitiated them and diminished their objections to the Union. He treated those who approached him with slight and rudeness, and thus he converted a proud and courteous people, which even their detractors acknowledge them to be, into personal and irreconcilable enemies. He despised their talents, and denied their official capacity for office. In this respect he was mainly right; but there was the lesser reason for fearing their power when held in proper check, and for endeavouring further to weaken it by measures which will not stand the test of justice . . .

It was only by dint of the greatest energy, and I must add the unscrupulous personal interference of Lord Sydenham, combined with practices that I would not use, and Your Lordship would not recommend, in addition to the promise of the Loan and the bribe of the Public Works, that Lord Sydenham managed to get through the session.[53]

Faced with a *fait accompli* which appalled Peel and Wellington more than himself, Stanley sent a reluctant official approval of Bagot's action, coupled with private assurance that 'I do not mean to blame you for the step you have taken; on the contrary, I believe it to have been inevitable and that sooner or later it would have been found necessary to admit the leaders of the French party to a share in the government.'[54]

Bagot did not exaggerate the general satisfaction in Canada at his action. Parent reported in *Le Canadien* the friendly sentiments expressed by long-standing enemies of the French Canadians, and commented: 'I should not be surprised after that to see *La Minerve* embrace the *Herald*, *L'Aurore* embrace the *Montreal Gazette*, and the *Fils de Liberté* embrace the partisans of Captain Thom.'[55] Only the Tories were unhappy: they supplied three of the five dissenting voices to the assembly's resolution of approval; and their Toronto organ, the *Patriot*, referred to Bagot's letter to Lafontaine in the following bitter words: 'No public document since the triumph of Wolfe until this day has been read in the provinces of British North America by the faithful subjects of the Sovereign of Great Britain with such intense sorrow and humiliation.'[56] In England *The Times* expressed its astonishment that Bagot had called to the executive council 'known advocates of secession' and 'notorious traitors,'[57] while Charles Buller approved the governor's act in the London

Chronicle. Stanley had difficulty in winning Peel and Wellington over to Bagot's 'inevitable' course, but a ministerial crisis was avoided. In February of the following year, during a debate on the matter at Westminster, Buller paid tribute to Bagot: 'Sir Charles Bagot has adopted the surest and wisest policy; he has conducted himself in the most praiseworthy and best possible manner.'[58] Such words in the mouth of Durham's secretary and the reputed author of the *Report* carried great weight, since Bagot had reversed one of the fundamental proposals of that document.

The validity of another conclusion of Durham's *Report*, already shaken by Lafontaine's election by an English constituency, was shattered by the unanimous election of Baldwin as the representative of Rimouski in Lower Canada, after he had been defeated in his own Upper Canadian riding by the outraged Tories. A more united Canada could scarcely be imagined than that in which the two heads of the government were elected from each other's section, regardless of ethnic and religious differences.* During the short session of 1842 several ordinances of the special council or of Sydenham himself were upset, including those gerrymandering the constituencies of Quebec and Montreal and re-organizing the Lower Canadian judiciary. A new election law eliminated many abuses.

A few days after the assembly was prorogued, Bagot became severely ill with heart trouble. The place he had won in French Canada is indicated by the fact that many Masses were said for his intention. After one period of recovery, his condition grew worse and he died on May 19, 1843. He was widely mourned in Canada, and *La Minerve* regretted that his death had prevented the celebration of the anniversary of his first visit to Montreal with a great popular ovation: 'Only a memory remains to us now of the great man who was the regenerator of the French Canadians; but this memory, deeply marked on our grateful hearts, will be an eternal monument in the bosom of the people which posterity will contemplate when many others have crumbled and disappeared.'[59]

5

Bagot was replaced as governor-general by Sir Charles Metcalfe, an Anglo-Indian civil servant who had been governor-general of India and governor of Jamaica. He was offered the post by Stanley in January 1843, and took office in Canada on March 30. He

* A sidelight on the thoroughness of that unity is supplied by a letter of 1844 in which Baldwin consulted Lafontaine about a Quebec school for his son Willcocks: 'I must not expose him to the miserable embarrassment that I labour under myself for want of French.' Baldwin's daughters were already being educated by the Ursulines of Quebec. PAC, Lafontaine Papers, Baldwin-Lafontaine, 14 August 1844.

began his difficult task without eagerness and with premonitions of failure: 'I have never undertaken anything with so much repugnance, nor with as little hope of doing well. All my plans and my hopes of happiness are disappointed; and such little reputation as I have been able to acquire is, I fear, exposed to shipwreck in the agitated waters of Canada.'[60]

Metcalfe, an adherent of the old school of colonial rule, was struck soon after his arrival in Canada both by the doctrine of responsible government, which held that the policy and the conduct of the governor should conform to the party views and interests of the executive council, and by the violence of Canadian party feeling. He approved of Bagot's admission of the French-Canadian party to power, although he regretted the manner and the circumstances in which it had been done. He announced his determination to recognize no difference between French and English, but he commented on the dominant self-interest of the French party, which 'works ceaselessly for the maintenance and the extension of its power and for the interests of the French Canadians. It may be able to combine with other parties, on the principle of reciprocity, in giving support in exchange for support; but its views are purely French Canadian and have for object, among others, the conservation of the French language and laws. It opposes energetically any attempt to anglicize the French Canadian population.'[61] He also regretted the exclusion of the Tories, for he felt 'much more sympathy for those who have been loyal than for those who wished to shake off the yoke of the Mother Country.'

From these original dispositions he soon progressed to feeling no sympathy whatsoever for 'the anti-British bitterness of the French party, or the egoistical indifference of the republican party,'[62] with whom he had to co-operate. He then evolved the idea of 'freeing himself of exclusive relations with this or that party, and of adopting the best measures, rendering equal justice to all, with councillors chosen in all the parties.' In short he set out to follow the course of George III and Bute, creating a governor's party. It was inevitable that he should come into collision with Lafontaine, who threatened to resign when Metcalfe refused to accept the advice of the executive council. The governor, with his strong faith in his own views and a resolution which approached pigheadedness, saw the question simply as 'whether the governor will be purely and simply an instrument in the hands of his council, or whether he will have the right to exercise his own judgment in the administration of the government.'[63] It was a major conflict between the old and the new order in colonial administration; for the matter in question was the vital one of patronage, the appointment of Colonel de Salaberry, a French-Canadian Tory, as provincial aide-de-camp.

At the time Lafontaine was not even aware of the seriousness with which Metcalfe viewed the matter.

The irritated governor took a firm hand with the executive council, and revealed his curious concept of responsible government in a dispatch of June 25 to Stanley:

> I have not had any difficulties with the Council; I have been prudent, but without sacrificing what appears to be, in the present circumstances, the legitimate authority of the governor. I administer myself the affairs of the government by means of the secretaries; no order is given without my direction or my sanction. And only those matters are submitted to the Council which should be according to law or practice, or on which I wish to have the benefit of the advice or the local knowledge of the councillors. The Councillors have made no pretensions rendering necessary a counter exposition of principles, and it can almost be supposed that the unreasonable declarations previously made by some of them have been abandoned. I am not sure of it, however; and although I see no reason to anticipate an immediate rupture, I feel that it can happen any day.[64]

By August Metcalfe was finding even his version of Sydenham's system too confining, and was considering dismissing the council, 'chiefly because they are under the influence of party views, and would, if they could, drag me on with them in the same course . . . The meeting of the Legislature will probably allow me to see my position more clearly. It is at present far from certain that a change of councillors would produce any beneficial alteration in respect to the difficulty noticed, for any Council appointed on the principle of Canada Responsible Government would most probably have similar party views, and the same pressure on them from their partisans.'[65]

Metcalfe found himself faced with the highly distasteful prospect of party government:

> It seems to be inevitable in free and independent States where Responsible Government exists; and the same causes are likely to produce the same results everywhere; but there is a wide difference between an independent State and a colony. In an independent State all parties must generally desire the welfare of the State. In a colony subordinate to an Imperial Government, it may happen that the predominant party is hostile in its feelings to the mother country, or has ulterior views inconsistent with her interests. In such a case, to be obliged to co-operate with that party, and to permit party government to crush those who are best effected, would be a strange position for the mother country to be placed in, and a strange part for her to act. This ought to have been considered well before the particular system which has obtained the name of Responsible Government was established. It is now, perhaps, too late to remedy the evil.

The 'Sultan of India,' as Metcalfe had already been nicknamed by one of the Upper Canadian ministers, nevertheless sought to remedy the evil—and to console the Tories—by creating a governor's party through arbitrary disposition of patronage; he named the Tory Sherwood speaker of the legislative council, and another Tory to a clerkship which Baldwin desired for a supporter. Lafontaine and Baldwin demanded an interview with the governor, and for two days tried to win him to their concept of responsible government, which postulated that the royal prerogative should be used only on the advice of the ministers. But Baldwin had thought out the cabinet system more clearly than had yet been done in England. Metcalfe found their views untenable; and they and all their colleagues of the ministry, save one, resigned on November 26, 1843.

A twelve-day political crisis followed, during which the action of the retiring ministers was supported by a vote of 46–26 and the assembly refused to accept a message from Metcalfe requesting it to pursue its labors. In the face of this opposition the governor prorogued the assembly on December 9; and four days later named Denis-Benjamin Viger and William Draper to the executive council. Viger, the ancient champion of the people and of the assembly's privileges, was won from his life-long principles by the opportunity to play at last the leading role which had hitherto always escaped him. In the agitation previous to 1837 he had been thrust out of the limelight by his young cousin Louis-Joseph Papineau, and after the Rebellion he had been eclipsed by Lafontaine, a former student in his law office. But the seventy-year-old Viger was not destined now to play a notable role. Metcalfe contented himself with three ministers, who remained without portfolio or function, while he himself both reigned and governed, still curiously protesting his belief in responsible government.

For nine months, until August 1844, Canada lacked all save a token ministry. Then, after endless negotiations, Metcalfe succeeded in breaking down the refusal of Lower Canada to participate in his administration. After the attorney-generalship had been refused by six Lower Canadians, an English lawyer from Montreal was found who would accept it, while Denis-Benjamin Papineau, a brother of the great tribune, was persuaded to become commissioner of Crown lands. In his desperation Metcalfe had even thought of offering a place in the ministry to the exiled Louis-Joseph Papineau, in order to secure Lower Canadian support. This preposterous scheme had fallen through, but the great agitator's brother had been won over through his close ties with Viger. By September the ministry was formed, and on its advice Metcalfe dissolved the hostile assembly. The elections were bitterly contested, with Lafontaine's followers campaigning on the principle of responsible government, 'as understood by the ex-ministers.'[66] Lower Canada gave the Reformers twenty-eight out of forty-two seats, with Viger defeated in two constituencies and his follower John Neilson vanquished by young Pierre Chauveau, who had turned from verse to the hustings. In Upper Canada, where the governor had used the war cry of loyalty to the British connection, the situation was reversed, with Baldwin's followers winning only eleven seats. The result gave the governor an overall majority of six, won by the most vigorous intervention on his part in the elections.

The dubious quality of Metcalfe's victory was soon evidenced when the assembly met on November 28 at Montreal, which had been chosen as the capital at the last session. The government candidate for speaker, Sir Allan MacNab, was elected by only three voices. Baldwin's reply to the speech from the throne, in which he called for censure of Metcalfe's unconstitutional government during nine months, was warmly praised in the *Journal de Québec*, recently founded by Joseph Cauchon, a new member. Lafontaine parried Sherwood's condemnation of the French Canadians—for blindly following their leaders without understanding political questions—with the pointed remark that when his compatriots went to the polls, 'they vote for one of the candidates, and not for the governor-general, as in Upper Canada.'[67] Baldwin's resolution was defeated by just six votes.

Despite the near deadlock, the assembly passed a number of important bills, including one remodeling into its present form the plan of local government established by Sydenham. This measure had been drafted by Morin during the preceding session, and was now carried by Papineau. Another Morin measure established the school system of Lower Canada on a basis of voluntary contribution rather than direct taxation at the will of appointed municipal officials, as provided by Sydenham's Common Schools Bill of 1841, which had remained inoperative in the face of general opposition and had merely provoked the foundation of independent schools. The clergy were given the right to vote, and conversion of lands from seigneurial tenure was encouraged. A bill providing £40,000 for payment of indemnities for losses suffered during the Rebellion in Upper Canada was passed, but Lafontaine called in vain for a similar measure applying to Lower Canada. Nevertheless, at the opening of the session he had succeeded in obtaining unanimous approval of an address to the Queen praying for a general amnesty for the rebels of 1837–8. This measure was not adopted until 1849, but in practice the government began to act on it earlier in individual cases.

Lafontaine's maneuvers for repeal of the Union Act's provision against the legislative use of French were forestalled by Papineau's proposal of an address to the Queen on this subject, to which Metcalfe reluctantly consented as a tactical measure to disarm the opposition. The necessity of such action was proved in February 1845 when the speaker, Sir Allan MacNab, refused to accept a motion drafted in French by the member for Lotbinière, and his decision was supported by a single vote, after Lafontaine and Morin had made eloquent protests against a law contrary to natural right.

Dissension broke out among the ministerial supporters on the law establishing the University of Upper Canada, the forerunner of the University of Toronto. When the session closed at the end of March, Metcalfe found that 'the germs of division and of weakness have been sown in part by the divergence manifested on the university question, in part by personal dissatisfaction, and finally by the lack of popularity of the members of the Executive Council.'[68] Faced with this situation, he noted a tendency of some of the Upper Canadian Tories to join with the French Canadians, and remarked: 'If I saw a probability that this combination could be realized in conformance with just principles and in a manner to constitute a strong government, free of all anti-British sentiment, I should be disposed to encourage it.'

6

During the summer of 1845 Draper, the leader of the Upper Canadian Tories, opened negotiations with René-Edouard Caron, president of the legislative council, with a view to an alliance between the Lower Canadian Reformist majority and the Upper Canadian Tory majority. Under the proposed agreement Viger and Papineau were to retire from the ministry, leaving their places free for Morin as president of the executive council and another French Canadian as attorney-general. Lafontaine could not be admitted to the ministry, in view of Metcalfe's hostility to him, but he was to be given a place on the bench. Caron communicated these proposals to Lafontaine on September 8.

In reply Lafontaine condemned Draper's proposal as 'a repudiation of the principle of responsibility, in so much as it is a question of applying it to Lower Canada.'[69] Instead of forming a new administration for Lower Canada constitutionally, a few French Canadians were to be added to the ministry:

> From this moment those who enter thus into the ministry enter not as a result of constitutional right, not by the action of the opinion of their compatriots, but solely as a result of the favor, of the good will of the governor. From this moment, experience teaches us, they are without influence; they are no longer free agents, but only instruments in the hands of the governor, for evil as well as for good. If they possess some

capacity and talent, they will use them sooner or later to cause division amongst us . . . Above all, the French Canadians must remain united and make themselves respected in the Council and exercise there the legitimate influence which is their right. This will not happen when they are represented there only by passive instruments of the government, whatever their number, but rather when they are constitutionally represented there by a Lower Canadian administration formed in harmony with principles that public opinion does not disavow . . . In the administration Lower Canada should have what is granted to Upper Canada; nothing more, but also nothing less.

Lafontaine thus outlined his concept of the French-Canadian political position, calling for equal rights, equal justice, and equal influence. Beside this goal, mere places were to be despised, and he renounced all claim to personal consideration:

I have often said, and I repeat it again, no consideration for me should prevent my political friends from forming part of an administration organized for Lower Canada according to the constitutional principles which ought to guide our conduct. I shall never serve as a means to divide my compatriots. If an administration is formed which merits my confidence, I shall support it wholeheartedly. If this administration does not have my confidence, but possesses that of the majority of my compatriots, I, not being able to support it, shall willingly retire from the House rather than to throw division in our ranks. If under the system of accepting places at all cost, there are persons who for personal and momentary advantage do not fear to destroy the sole advantage which constitutes our strength, our unity, I do not wish to be and I shall never be of this number.

In his reply to Draper, Caron formulated the theory of double majority: 'It has been stated as a principle that the direction of affairs should be between the hands of the two dominating parties in each section of the province, that the administration should no more direct Lower Canada by means of an Upper Canadian majority than it should impose a law upon the Upper Canadian majority as a result of the aid received from Lower Canada, and that no administration should survive unless supported by a majority in each section of the province.'[70] Lafontaine had not gone so far; he had merely recognized the possibility of a coalition government for the two sections. Such a system had already been discussed in *Le Canadien*.

Lafontaine advised Baldwin of what was afoot, and the latter replied:

I consider the principle itself inadmissible and wholly impractical. I can conceive that in the practical labor of legislation a certain deference should be paid to the views of the respective majorities in each of the provinces, and that no measure should be imposed on one or the other against the will of a considerable majority of the representatives of the interested province. But this does not justify in any fashion the principle of having a double cabinet, of which half depends for its support upon the confidence of the representatives of Lower Canada and the other half upon the confidence of the representatives of Upper Canada. This principle, I am convinced, is absolutely incompatible with the very nature of our political institutions, and in the end it will be found impracticable.[71]

Baldwin expressed his opinion that Draper's negotiation indicated a weakness in the government and a fear of losing its majority. This opinion no doubt was affected by the consideration of the disaster which would have overtaken the Upper Canadian Reformers if the coalition had taken place. But it fell through, because of Draper's delays and Metcalfe's illness, which caused his resignation. The governor was afflicted with cancer, and the progress of the disease had already cost him the sight of one eye and soon made it almost impossible for him to speak or eat. On November 26, 1845, after a stubborn struggle against his illness, he handed over the government to Lord Cathcart, the military commander, and returned to England. He died nine months later, the third governor of Canada to whom the charge had proved fatal.

At the opening of the session in March 1846, Viger was savagely attacked during a debate on the reply to the speech from the throne, which contained a eulogy of Metcalfe to which Baldwin and the Reformers of both provinces took exception. At the request of the caucus of the Reformers, Lafontaine read the correspondence which had been exchanged between Draper and Caron and Caron and himself. The government was weakened by this revelation, and hardly managed to survive the session. The tension between England and the United States over the Oregon question made it easy, however, to pass a new militia bill, which evoked Etienne-Pascal Taché's much quoted phrase: 'The last cannon shot for the maintenance of English rule in America will be fired by a French-Canadian hand.' The Lower Canada school law of the previous year was revised at Dr. Meilleur's instance so as to rest upon a basis of obligatory rather than voluntary support, since the latter system had proved unworkable in the midst of the popular revolt against the new schools, known as the 'War of the Extinguishers.'[72] With subsequent amendments, notably in 1849, this statute (9 Victoria, Ch. 27) long remained the legal foundation of the Quebec school system. Another provision of the Union Act was eliminated when the imperial government agreed, in exchange for the assembly's vote of £70,000, to revoke the article enabling it to take a civil list of £75,000 from the Canadian revenues.

Viger and Papineau lost all popularity in debates on the Jesuit Estates and on financing of the administration of criminal justice in Upper Canada. Sherwood and Draper quarreled, and the government found itself in the minority more than once. After the prorogation in June 1846, Viger and Sherwood resigned, and during the summer efforts were made to constitute a stronger ministry. Caron and Morin were again offered portfolios, but refused them. Dissension and dissatisfaction were general in both Upper and Lower Canada when the Earl of Elgin was named governor-general in September 1846.

7

Lord Elgin, who was to have a greater influence than Durham on the development of Canada, was a descendent of Robert Bruce and the son of the British ambassador to Turkey who brought home the Elgin Marbles from the Parthenon, then threatened with destruction in the Greek Revolution. The new governor-general had gone in for gentleman-farming on his Fifeshire estates, after a brilliant career at Eton and Oxford, where he had been a member of a notable group which included Canning, Newcastle, Sidney Herbert, and Gladstone. He had studied law without practicing it, passed some time in France, and then entered politics in 1841 as a member for Southampton. He was a Tory, but not of the traditional type; he thus defined his Peelite politics: 'I am a Conservative, not because I am hostile to progress, not because I refuse to repair what is worn out or to modify what is defective in our political structure, but because I am convinced that in order to remedy effectively one must be determined to preserve religiously.'[73] When the death of his father elevated Elgin to the peerage of Scotland and barred him from the House of Commons in the same year as he entered it, Stanley offered him the governorship of Jamaica. He had a notable career there, though the climate cost him the loss of his first wife.

When he returned to England in 1846, the fall of the Tories seemed to leave him without prospects of office; but Grey, the new colonial secretary, who was as liberal a Whig as Elgin was a Tory, offered him the Canadian governor-generalship. Before leaving for Canada in January 1847, Elgin married Grey's niece, the daughter of Lord Durham. Elgin was very conscious of the heritage which had thus fallen upon him, and soon after he arrived in Canada, he wrote his wife, who at first remained in England:

I still adhere to my opinion that the real and effectual vindication of Lord Durham's memory and proceedings will be *the success of a Governor-*

eneral of Canada who works out his views of government fairly. Depend upon :, if this country is governed for a few years satisfactorily, Lord Durham's eputation as a statesman will be raised beyond the reach of cavil. I do ot indeed know whether I am to be the instrument to carry out this ork, or to be destined, like others, who have gone before me, to break own in the attempt; but I am still of the opinion that the thing may be one, though it requires some good fortune and some qualities not of the owest order. I find on my arrival here a very weak Government, almost s much abused by their friends as by their foes, no civil or private secre-ary, and an immense quantity of arrears of business. It is possible, herefore, that I may not be able to bear up against the difficulties of ny situation, and that it may remain for some one else to achieve that bject, which many reasons would render me so desirous to achieve.[74]

Like Durham, Elgin believed in the principle of responsible overnment, accepting party monopoly of patronage, and his faith in t was sufficiently sturdy to carry him through the trials which lay head. In July 1847 he outlined his concept of the proper role f a governor to Grey:

I give to my ministers all constitutional support, frankly and without eserve, and the best advice that I can afford them in their difficulties. n return for this, I expect that they will, in so far as it is possible for hem to do so, carry out my views for the maintenance of the connexion vith Great Britain and the advancement of the interests of the province.)n this tacit understanding we have acted together harmoniously up o this time, although I have never concealed from them that I intended o do nothing which may prevent me from working cordially with their pponents, if they are forced upon me. . . . It is indispensable that the ead of the Government should show that he has confidence in the oyalty of all the influential parties with which he has to deal, and that e should have no personal antipathies to prevent him from acting with he leading men.[75]

t was on this policy—very different from those of Sydenham and Aetcalfe—that Elgin intended to act, although it meant recon-iling himself 'to tread along a path which is somewhat narrow and lippery, and to find that incessant watchfulness and some dexterity re requisite to prevent him from falling, on the one side into the *éant* of mock sovereignty, or on the other into the dirt and confusion f local factions.'

Elgin was not alone in recognizing that he was the heir of Dur-am. At the opening of the session in June 1847, Baldwin and afontaine proposed an amendment to the address replying to the peech from the throne, which congratulated the new governor n his connection with Durham and expressed the hope that prac-ical application would be given to the principle of responsible government which had been recommended in the *Report*. This motion provided Baldwin with an opportunity to indict the ministry for its lack of principles. In reply Draper, who was resigning as attorney-general of Upper Canada and accepting an appointment to the bench, defended his role as leader of the government. He affirmed his belief in responsible government, and stated that he had conformed to this principle while serving under Metcalfe. He postulated that patronage should be dispensed only on the advice of the ministers. Since it was on these very matters that the Reformers quarrelled with his administration, it is evident that the same words held different meanings for Draper and for Baldwin and Lafontaine.

But the leaders of the Reformers had more love for their chief opponent than for his henchmen, particularly the Lower Canadian ministers, whom Lafontaine thus flayed: 'You have sacrificed honor to the love of office; you have been mere instruments in the hands of your colleagues, you have sacrificed the country, and you will soon have your reward. One of you has already been expelled from the Council, and the other soon will be.'[76] These merciless words referred to the fall of Viger, and the impending retreat of D.-B. Papineau, who now was the sole French Canadian in Sherwood's ministry. Baldwin's amendment was defeated by only two votes. While the government's power thus rested upon a precarious basis in the assembly, the legislative council manifested signs of revolt, with Caron supporting Neilson's attack on the government for its lack of French-Canadian representatives. Somehow the ministry staggered through the short session, but it was clearly doomed.

Elgin had recognized its weakness upon his arrival, and had favoured the fruitless negotiations to induce Caron and Morin to enter the ministry. He had written to Grey: 'If new elements of strength are required to enable the Government to go on, I think it very advisable to give the French a fair opportunity of entering the Ministry in the first instance.' And he added this significant comment, which was to become one of the basic principles of his governorship:

> I believe that the problem of how to govern Canada would be solved if the French would split into a Liberal and a Conservative Party and join the Upper Canadian parties bearing the corresponding names.—The great difficulty hitherto has been that a Conservative Government has meant Government of Upper Canadians which is intolerable to the French—and a Radical Government a Government of the French which is no less hateful to the British. . . . The national element would be merged in the political if the split to which I refer was accomplished.[77]

As Elgin foresaw, the ethnic conflict in Canada was to be greatly eased by the political collaboration of French and English.

The governor repeated his observation a month later, coupling with it a recognition of the indispensability of the French Canadians to any Canadian government: '. . . until the French break into political Parties and join British Parties with corresponding names, I do not think any strong and lasting administration will be formed. Their coherence enables them to organize a powerful opposition to any Ministry from which they are excluded, but it no less certainly provokes among the British both of Lower and Upper Canada a feeling of antagonism to one of which they form a part.'[78] At intervals down to the present L.-J. Papineau's concept of a 'national' or ethnic party has been revived in French Canada, but the results have been as unfortunate as Elgin predicted, for politico-ethnic division has been created without profit to the French Canadians. With such convictions, it cannot be doubted that Elgin encouraged the eventual decision of the tottering ministry to confront the country. Elections were held in December 1847, after a manifesto issued in the previous month by a Quebec Constitutional Committee of Reform and Progress, headed by Caron, had violently attacked the three-year-old government.

Unlike Sydenham and Metcalfe, the governor remained neutral in the electoral fray, not trying to form a governor's party. The ministry was roundly defeated. Only five or six of its supporters survived in Lower Canada, where Lafontaine was elected in two constituencies and the Reformers won a majority of thirty seats. In Upper Canada only sixteen supporters of the government were returned, while twenty-six adherents of Baldwin were victorious. From the Reformers' point of view, there was but one fly in the ointment: the old tribune Louis-Joseph Papineau, who had been permitted to return from exile in 1845 at Lafontaine's instance and who had been nominated in two counties and elected as member for Saint-Maurice, had issued an address to his electors in which he announced his support of the program of Lafontaine and Baldwin with certain reservations. This document discussed at length the constitutional issues for which Papineau had always fought and closed with the somewhat startling statement that he had been 'a disciple from my early youth of the school of Adam Smith, and ever the enemy of all monopoly and privilege.'[79] It was admirably summed up by Elgin, who transmitted it to Grey with these comments:

Considerable excitement has been produced by the appearance of a manifesto from the notorious L. J. Papineau who has been requested to represent two constituencies—This document is in a nolo episcopari strain—contains a pretty frank declaration of republicanism—expresses the writer's hatred of the British Government—his distrust of Responsible Government and concludes that the time has not come for his reappearance on the stage—Whether he will be elected or not is uncertain in the face of this quasi refusal—The French Liberals are a good deal disconcerted by the tone of this address—on the one hand they do not like to proclaim that their sentiments are at variance with those of this redoubtable chief who still has a hold on Canadian sympathies—on the other it is awkward to profess antimonarchical doctrines and a contempt for Responsible Government at the time when the said Responsible Government is likely to bring them into place—Besides it is doubtful whether Upper Canada liberalism may not be alienated by the assertion of such principles.[80]

After Papineau's election by acclamation, Elgin assigned his support to the 'considerable section of the French Canadians who take their political opinions from writers and speakers who derive their inspirations from the hoco[s]pocus of Yankeedom and democrats of France.'[81] And later in January 1848, after announcing his determination to call upon Lafontaine and Baldwin to form a government, Elgin suggested one difficulty which would beset them:

Notwithstanding the condemnation of my present council pronounced by the constituencies, I am far from thinking that their successors will have an easy task—M. Papineau who has more personal influence than any other individual in Lower Canada returns into public life with the avowed object of proving Lord J. Russell a deceiver, and Responsible Government a delusion and a snare. He hates Great Britain, and is believed to be somewhat jealous of those who have become the leaders of the French Canadians during his eclipse. If the system of Government established in this province works satisfactorily, his vocation is gone, and he is proved a false prophet. It will therefore be his object to prevent this result—on the other hand, I am disposed to believe, that with a certain class of the liberals of British origin, there exists a genuine preference for what they deem British or constitutional practise as opposed to Republicanism. Whether it will be possible to bring the views of these Gentlemen who look at our Institutions through an American medium into perfect harmony with those of British Statesmen sitting in Downing Street, may be doubtful—But there is obviously room for antagonism between those who hold that British Institutions rightly interpreted, are the best in the World, and those who are pledged to prove that they are among the worst.

Between these two political sections M. Lafontaine and his followers are now placed.—Circumstances, perhaps, conviction, will induce them for the moment to take rank with the latter——.[82]

The governor was no false prophet.

8

The session opened at the end of February, and the verdict of the people on the old government was immediately reflected in the election of the speaker. Sir Allan MacNab was rejected by a vote of 54–19, and Augustin Morin was then unanimously elected to the post. Baldwin proposed an amendment to the reply to the speech from the throne, declaring it to be essential that the government should have the confidence of the assembly and the people, and stating that the present advisers of the governor lacked this confidence. Elgin immediately replied that 'Always disposed to listen to the advice of the Parliament, I shall take without delay measures to form a new Executive Council.'[83] This answer proclaimed that responsible government had at last become a reality in Canada. Before Elgin's departure from England, he and Grey had agreed upon the extension to Canada of the system of full responsible government which had been worked out for Nova Scotia between the colonial secretary and Sir John Harvey. Its basic concepts, as laid down by Grey, were that 'any transfer which may take place of political power from the hands of one political party in the province to another is the result not of an act of yours but of the wishes of the people themselves,' and that 'it is neither possible nor desirable to carry on the government of any of the British provinces in North America in opposition to the opinion of its inhabitants.'[84] These instructions to the governor of Nova Scotia had been communicated officially to Elgin, and he had now acted upon them.

Lafontaine and Baldwin were called upon to form a cabinet and were given complete control of patronage. The new ministry included the two leaders as attorneys-general for their respective sections, Hincks as inspector-general of accounts, Taché as commissioner of public works, Aylwin and William Hume Blake as solicitors-general for Lower and Upper Canada, and Caron as president of the legislative council. Elgin observed to Grey that 'My present council unquestionably contains more talent and has a firmer hold on the confidence of Parliament and of the People, than the last. There is I think moreover on their part a desire to prove, by proper deference for the authority of the Governor General, (which they all admit has in my case never been abused), that they were libelled when they were accused of impracticability and antimonarchical tendencies.'[85] Grey, who had expressed his willingness to accept even L.-J. Papineau in the cabinet and who had been warned by Elgin that it might be necessary 'to accept as advisers persons who were denounced very lately by the Secretary of State and the Governor General as impracticable and disloyal,'[86] wholly approved Elgin's policy and actions, and added: 'It is most fortunate that you had a Ministry including some of the Leaders of the French party before the news of the French Revolution reached you.'[87] Elgin, some of whose family were in Paris when the disturbances of 1848 broke out and who as a Tory was appalled by the revolutionary fervor which was felt even in England at this time with the Chartist rising, agreed that it was just as well that a Canadian government with popular support had been formed before the European news arrived: 'There are not wanting here persons who might under different circumstances have attempted by seditious harangues, if not by overt acts, to turn the examples of France and the sympathies of the United States to account——'[88]

The veiled reference to Papineau, notoriously sympathetic to the French *Républicains rouges*, was not lost upon Grey. The old tribune had not been able to resist the strategic moment which had always summoned him to battle in the past, and when a vote of supply was called for at the end of the brief session, he protested against adjournment without taking measures to revise the system of representation upon the basis of population. In his first speech since re-entering the assembly, he developed the ideas contained in his address to the electors of Huntingdon in the previous December, stating his confidence in the new ministry and his willingness to support them in the full realization of responsible government, though he expressed his disbelief in this principle for Canada. The main measure he proposed was ill chosen, for the population of Upper Canada was rapidly overtaking that of Lower Canada and was soon to surpass it. But Papineau had been too long silent and too long out of the limelight which he loved almost as much as he loved to speak. After his return to Canada in the fall of 1845, loyalty to his brother Denis and his cousin Viger, then in office as Metcalfe's ministers, had kept him in obscurity. Before leaving Paris he had described Metcalfe's views and conduct as 'an undecipherable enigma,' but he had protested that 'agitation has never been a necessity for me; and it is less so than ever after the lapse of seven years.'[89]

Papineau's stay in France and his visits to Switzerland and Italy had made him highly sympathetic with the revolutionaries whose schemes bore fruit in the revolutions of 1848; he wrote to Roebuck shortly before leaving Paris: 'I am more than ever the impassioned friend of democratic liberties, the enemy of kings, nobles, and priests, everywhere leagued for the exploitation of the majority to the profit of their castes. With these sentiments I cannot live happily in Canada.'[90] Gloom had descended upon him, once he was back in Canada. In 1846 he found that 'the political state of the country

Merry-Making

Oil painting (c. 1860) by Cornelius Krieghoff. This Brueghel-like study of a gay evening at the celebrated inn of Jean-Baptiste Jolifou, much frequented by British officers driving out from the Quebec Citadel, provides an unmatched picture of French-Canadian *joie de vivre* (John T. Ross Collection, Quebec). (National Gallery.)

Notre Dame Church, Montreal

Built in 1824 (?) by John Ostell after plans by James O'Donnell of New York. This was the first Gothic church in Quebec and its influence was ruinous to the native architectural tradition. (I.O.A.P.Q.)

is more of a stench in my nostrils than it has ever been . . . Birthplace, old relatives, family interests chain me here like an oyster on the rock where I was born, but the intellectual life here is so lifeless, political life so detestable, that I shall live here unhappily.'[91] He met with Lafontaine in the fall of 1845, and the younger leader informed his old chief of all that had happened since their last encounter at Saratoga Springs in June 1838, when both were fugitives from warrants for high treason. Papineau approved Lafontaine's policies at that time, when the younger man was in the opposition, ever the favorite position of the elder. When chided by his ministerial brother for having delayed his return home by a day, Papineau had replied: 'I wanted to wait for an opposition boat; I love the opposition so much.'[92] The retirement of his cousin Viger in 1846 and of his brother Denis-Benjamin in 1847 at last freed him from the obligation of silence, and with a show of reluctance he re-entered political life.

Not all the Reformers viewed this step with pleasure; Joseph Cauchon commented thus:

> For my part, I should be glad to see M. Papineau in the House, because his talents, if his opinions were not extreme, could be useful to us. In the contrary case, in order to spare blood and oppression to our compatriots, we would be obliged to react against him and to isolate him. But then he would place us in a false position by making us appear men opposed to the democratic ideas which invade the new world.[93]

When Papineau's address appeared, Jacques Crémazie, brother of the poet and editor of the new *L'Ami de la Religion et de la Patrie*, defined the old tribune's program as 'war without mercy on the Tories and Reformers of Upper Canada who called for the Union Act; war on the mother country which granted it; blame for the Lower Canadian liberals who helped to make this mockery of responsible government function; and, finally, reproaches to the ex-ministers for having been too moderate.'[94] When congratulated by an English-Canadian friend upon his return on not having changed in appearance, Papineau had replied, 'I am always the same,'[95] and his political behavior indicated the truth of his remark. Under Grey and Elgin he adopted the same policy of implacable opposition which he had followed under Stanley and Aylmer; he was temperamentally incapable of any other attitude. Living in the past, he could not realize how much the situation had changed in his absence. In February 1848 he wrote gloomily to O'Callaghan: 'In a few years from now we shall stand in the same relation to Upper Canada as Ireland to England;' and again in April: 'All is glory, happiness, progress in the rest of the whole world; all is baseness, oppression, cowardly inaction or regression in Canadian society.'[96]

Papineau's first speech in the new assembly brought a vehement reply from his ancient enemy Colonel Gugy, the loyalist leader of 1837–8, and all the old quarrels and all the old wounds were reopened once more, to the joy of the surviving Tories. But the younger Lower Canadian Reformers censured Papineau's speech; and Cauchon wound up with the brutal comment: 'Once I much admired his brilliant harangues, but I admire them no longer, for they lead to nothing . . . There are men who are mighty in destruction, but who have never raised anything on the ruins they have made.'[97] Elgin judged the old popular leader 'a dangerous man' who has 'much influence among the French Canadians; who remember that he cheered them on to the fight, and forget that he left them in the thick of it.'[98] It was not consoling to the governor that Papineau should suggest to his Canadian electors that they should 'give themselves the pleasure of traveling to the United States, to see how much more at ease the farmers there generally are; how much more they harvest on bad land than we do on good; why their poor farms sell ten times more dearly than our richer ones,'[99] at a time when the jingoistic *New York Herald* was rejoicing in the prospect of acquiring Canada, Cuba, and the British West Indies through the aid of revolutionary France.

While Elgin struggled to maintain the British connection under these difficulties, Grey was writing to him: 'To us except the loss of prestige (no slight one I admit) the loss of Canada would be the loss of little but a source of heavy expense and great anxiety.'[100] With wry humor Elgin replied:

> I feel myself however, I must confess, somewhat in the position in which the master of one of those ricketty vessels which are sent to this quarter in quest of timber occasionally find himself. By dint of much labor and watching he succeeds in conveying ship and cargo safely through the tempests and icebergs which assail him on the voyage out and home, and he is not a little disappointed, poor simple minded man! when on reporting his arrival, he hears the owners mutter to one another 'It would have been better for us if the whole concern had gone to the bottom, as we should then have realized the Insurance.' Much in the same light are exertions made to maintain and perpetuate the connexion between this Province and the Mother Country, likely, I fear, to be viewed:—for Canada is beginning to be reckoned, I shrewdly suspect, by most English politicians, a bad bargain at any price.
>
> Nevertheless, so long as I am in charge, it is my duty, I presume, to steer by the old lights, and to endeavour to keep things together as best I can.[101]

Elgin was right about the attitude of the British government, despite Grey's disavowal of his personal belief in the new colonial doctrines, which were an outgrowth of the attempt to bring about what Elgin scornfully called 'the Free Trade Millenium.' The repeal of the Corn Laws and the Navigation Act had upset the old colonial theory; and 'Little Englanders' now dominated the House of Commons. The imperial government displayed a growing reluctance to carry the old colonial burdens, and proposed that Canada should bear the cost of its own defence and of the immigration which continued to pour into Quebec and Montreal thousands of sick and penniless wretches from Ireland, Scotland, and England itself. In discussing these matters Elgin had already observed to Grey:

> If you attempt to redress the balance by requiring the Colony to bear burdens which she does not choose to bear, you engage in a contest of which the issues are by no means certain. The position of Canada as respects British sympathies and antipathies is most anomalous and cannot be measured by ordinary rules.— . . . The question practically present to men's minds is not 'Do we hate England enough to renounce our allegiance and to affront all the inconveniences and perils of separation'—but rather, 'Do we love her enough, is her connexion sufficiently valuable to us to induce us to refuse to clasp the hand which is stretched out to us by a great neighbouring and kindred nation, with whose prosperity and rapid advancement as contrasted with our comparatively slow progress we are constantly taunted by British Statesmen.'[102]

In the face of continued efforts of the British government to cut its commitments in Canada, Elgin gave a sharper warning to Grey of the results that might be expected from such a policy:

> The present is not a favorable moment for experiments. British Statesmen, even Secretaries of State, have got into the habit lately of talking of the maintenance of the connexion between Great Britain and Canada with so much indifference, that a change of system in respect of military defence incautiously carried out, might be presumed by many to argue on the part of the Mother Country, a disposition to prepare the way for separation—Add to this, that you effected only a few years ago an Union between the Upper and Lower Provinces by arbitrary means, and for objects the avowal of which has profoundly irritated the French population—That still more recently you have deprived Canada of her principal advantages in the British markets.—That France and Ireland are in flames and that nearly half of the population of this Colony are French—nearly half of the remainder Irish![103]

Elgin detected a ground swell in Canada raised by foreign storms, and reported: 'M. Papineau is deeply chagrined by his present position and is doing all he can to create disaffection by evoking Irish and French sympathies.' In a later letter Elgin pictured 'Guy

Fawkes Papineau' waving a lighted torch among the 'combustibles' of French and Irish sympathies, also incited by Irish Americans against England. Elgin pleaded for revocation of the restriction on the official use of the French language, announcing his conviction of 'the impolicy of all such efforts to denationalize the French,' as 'causing the flame of national prejudice and animosity to burn more fiercely.' He also advanced a cogent political argument:

You may perhaps *americanise*, but, depend upon it, by methods of this description, you will never *anglicise* the French inhabitants of the Province. —Let them feel on the other hand that their religion, their habits, their prepossessions, their prejudices, if you will, are more considered and respected here than in other portions of this vast continent which is being overrun by the most reckless, self-sufficient and dictatorial section of the Anglo-Saxon race, and who will venture to say that the last hand which waves the British flag on American ground may not be that of a French Canadian?[104]

A revealing light on the rapid constitutional evolution of Canada is shed by a liberal Tory governor-general's echoing of the one-time rebel Taché's phrase.

With anti-British feeling increasing among the English Canadians as a result of the mother country's new trade policies, and the warhawk General Lewis Cass nominated as the Democratic candidate for the American presidency, Elgin developed a growing conviction that 'The sentiment of French-Canadian nationality which Papineau endeavours to pervert to purposes of faction, may yet perhaps if properly improved furnish the best remaining security against annexation to the States.'[105] He observed shrewdly: 'Was it, think you, love for England or hatred for these *sacrés Bostonais* which stirred the French-Canadian mind in the Revolutionary war and again in 1812?'

With such considerations in mind, Elgin gave official support to the colonization movement launched by Bishop Bourget of Montreal —at the inspiration of the Abbé Bourassa, a brother of Papineau's son-in-law—despite the fact that Papineau had 'pounced upon this association as a means of making himself of importance in the eyes of his countrymen and of gratifying his ruling passion by abusing England.'[106] The clergy had at last become alarmed by the ever-increasing emigration from Quebec to the United States, which had begun early in the century, grew considerably during and immediately after the Rebellions of 1837–8, and in 1849 was estimated to have amounted to 20,000 people in the last four years. Elgin defined the clergy's object in launching the colonization societies as 'being to prevent the sheep of their pasture, (who now, strange as it may appear, emigrate annually in thousands to the

States, where they become hewers of wood and drawers of water to the Yankees and bad Catholics into the Bargain) from quitting their fold.' The former gentleman-farmer sympathized with the colonization program:

No one object in my opinion is so important, whether you seek to retain Canada as a Colony, or to fit her for independence and make her instinct with national life and vigor, (a result by no means less desirable than the former in so far as the interests of Great Britain are concerned) as the filling up of her vacant lands with a resident agricultural population. More especially is it of moment that the inhabitants of French origin should feel that every facility for settling on the land of their Fathers is given them with the cordial assent and concurrence of the British Government and its Representative.

Elgin also judged it imperative to 'wrest from M. Papineau's hands a potent instrument of agitation,' to 'fill up the Frontier country with French—and the lands to the rear with British, who may retain their love of home and its institutions at a distance from American influences,' and to promote a movement sponsored by 'the Priesthood the most powerful influence in Lower Canada.'

The immediate results of Elgin's action were the retirement of Papineau to Montebello and the issuance by Bishop Bourget on June 17, 1848 of a pastoral letter, which closed thus: 'For we are all children of the same Father who is in Heaven; we all live under the same government which has no other end but the welfare of its subjects, and which must take its glory from ruling peoples speaking all the languages of the world; we all have the same rights; we are all members of the great family of the mighty British Empire; and finally we are all summoned to possess together the same land of the living, after we shall have finished our pilgrimage on this land of exile.'[107] From this time onward, the Church threw its full support behind colonization in the Eastern Townships, in the Saguenay-Lake St. John country where the first settlement of 1838 had been given new impetus by the lumber industry of William Price, and in the Saint-Maurice and Ottawa Valleys where the Baptist family and the Yankee Philemon Wright had founded a great timber trade in the opening years of the century. The French Canadians at last began to expand out of the original strip of settlement along the St. Lawrence, but the ever-increasing emigration to the States, where the industrial revolution caused continual calls for more labor, still was not checked.

Elgin was justified in depriving Papineau of any 'instrument of agitation,' for the latter continued to work upon the sympathies of both French and Irish Canadians, which were kept stirred up by sensational telegraphic reports from Europe of the doing of Lamartine in France, of the followers of O'Connell in Ireland, and of the Chartists in England. The old tribune addressed meetings at Montreal and Quebec, comparing the wrongs of Canada to those of Ireland and denouncing the Union Acts as the means of English oppression in both instances. He also published several manifestos in which he attacked the Reformers and Lafontaine. Splitting the party, he formed the *Parti démocratique*, a group of hotheaded young men, whose organ, the newly founded *L'Avenir* edited by Eric Dorion, echoed the old tribune's revolutionary views. A.-A. Dorion, L.-A. Dessaules, Rodolphe Laflamme, Labrèche-Viger, and J. Daoust were his chief disciples.

The group, known as the *Rouges*, urged repeal of the Union, the extension of the elective principle to every branch of the government, inclined towards annexation, and invoked the principle of nationality, which they saw threatened by the Union Act:

> Seduced, distracted after a fashion by its details, we have for a long time lost sight of the object of that measure, which, however, is every day recalled to our recollection by that invasion of ideas and institutions, foreign to our ideas and institutions, which renders each day the most desirable, in the midst of the confusion of institutions, that perfect labyrinth of laws, of manners and of language, which imposes upon us a double nationality, so as to render the one necessary, the other useless, that is to say, to make us lose ours and adopt the other . . .
>
> Nationality is the vital principle of a people, and someone has said with truth that the silence of a people, is its death . . . We pray you tell us, then, whether one hundred thousand should abandon their prejudices, rather than six hundred thousand should give up their just demands. We only wish for one thing, the preservation of our Institutions, our language, our laws, and our customs.[108]

In reply *La Revue Canadienne*, Lafontaine's organ, asked:

> Tell us, gentlemen of *L'Avenir*, you who weep so much over the ruins of the past, and over imaginary evils—tell us at what period of our history has the French-Canadian nationality been more brilliant, more honored, more respected, or has it occupied a higher position than it holds today? . . . Has it not been thanks to the ability, the tact, the firmness and the patience of its able representatives that it has gained more in a few years, than previously in half a century of combats?
>
> . . . The Union was brought about with the object of ruining us! But the Union has saved us, and after powerful and well-directed efforts, after having won a position which permits us to avoid its inconveniences and evil consequences, after having obtained the political rights for which we have struggled for fifty years, now it is, that the devoted and generous gentlemen of *L'Avenir* raise their voices against it . . .
>
> . . . But tell us, ye young and fiery apostles of French-Canadian nationality, what do you mean by the principle of nationality applied

to the management of public affairs? . . . Is it, perchance, that famous principle of public action which has excited the French lately to drive from France all workmen of English or foreign origin? . . . It is not after our party has recruited its ranks from men of all origins, when our friends, the liberals of Upper Canada and those of Lower Canada of foreign origin, have made prodigious efforts to carry the elections and that together we have gained the most signal victory—it is not now that your appeal to prejudices and passions will have the least echo in the country.[109]

Here are expressed for the first time the opposed principles of two great French-Canadian political factions, which have survived to the present day: the ultra-nationalist extremists, resisting all change and all outside influences, and lapsing into racism; and the much larger conservative group which is willing to collaborate with English Canada but is as determined as the nationalists upon the survival of the French Canadians and their language, laws, institutions, and customs. Almost all French Canadians are extreme nationalists in their youth, as English-speaking youth inclines to liberalism or socialism; almost all grow out of this frame of mind and adopt a more moderate position as they grow older; but some never do, and with these men this book will henceforth be largely concerned, because they personify the social forces which differentiate French Canada from the rest of Canada, and of North America.

Then as now, the ultra-nationalists were a minority, and they were bitterly criticized by the moderates. Only *Le Canadien* joined *L'Avenir* in supporting Papineau's idea, while Cauchon's *Journal de Québec*, *La Minerve*, and *Les Mélanges religieux* made common cause with *La Revue Canadienne* in condemning them. Dr. Wolfred Nelson, now back in the assembly as a Reformer, attacked Papineau for personal cowardice, and denied the story that he had urged the tribune to flee at Saint-Denis in 1837. Bitter controversy was widespread in the press, but not as much dissension resulted among the Reformers as might have been expected; Cauchon informed Lafontaine that 'the friends of M. Papineau in all the great parishes which he had recently visited were as rare as ears of corn after the harvest.'[110]

9

While the French Canadians were threshing over old political straw, a commercial revolution was taking place which profoundly affected most English Canadians and radically altered their political principles. Peel's budgets of 1842–6, particularly that of the latter year, which upset the old colonial system of privileged markets in Britain for colonial products at the expense of the British consumer, have been aptly described as 'the British Revolution from the

British Empire.'[111] Most of the preferential duties were abolished, crippling the wheat trade, ruining the new Canadian milling industry, and severely depressing the lumber trade. The American Drawback Acts of 1845–6, which permitted the duty-free passage of foreign imports to Canada and of Upper Canadian products through American territory, broke the monopoly of the St. Lawrence and gave New York a vast advantage over Montreal. What was left of the Navigation Acts kept St. Lawrence freights much higher than American ones. Canadian hopes of draining the products of both Upper Canada and the Middle West through the St. Lawrence system to the profit of Montreal and Quebec collapsed before the new canals were completed in 1848, despite successive relaxations of the Navigation Acts, which were finally abolished in 1849. An imperial loyalty which had thrived on privilege wavered and broke when loyalty was no longer profitable. In May 1846 the *Canadian Economist* was moved to ask: 'How far the adoption of Free Trade principles in Great Britain, and as a consequence in the colonies, is compatible with the nature of the connection subsisting between them?'[112] The Welland Canal miller Jacob Keefer supplied an answer in blunter language to W. H. Merritt in April 1848: 'The sooner the connection between Gt. Britain and Canada is dissolved the better.'[113] Reciprocity or annexation seemed the only solutions of their difficulties to the English-Canadian commercial classes, caught in a graver depression than that of 1836–7, and burdened with 100,000 cholera-stricken Irish immigrants dumped upon their shores in 1847. The Irish famine, which had hastened the repeal of the Corn Laws and caused this exodus, gravely tried English-Canadian imperialism.

Elgin, who had considered the danger from the Irish more serious than that from the French, now turned his attention to the English Canadians. He had already remarked that 'the only real discontent existing is to be found among the commercial classes,'[114] although the Canadian farmer also demanded the repeal of the Navigation Laws, 'not as favor but Justice,' since he had been deprived of protection on his products. Now Elgin pointed out: 'As soon as the navigation of the St. Lawrence is thrown open, and the barriers which check the entrance of Canadian products into the States removed, a large amount of American enterprize will be attracted hither. Whether the said enterprize and its accompaniments will or will not in the long run drag the whole concern first commercially and at last politically into the Union I do not now stop to enquire.'[115] In reply Grey sketched out the dilemma in which the British government found itself, and revealed a curious hope he had of its solution:

If we refuse to afford all the facilities we can for commercial intercourse between Canada and her powerful neighbour we must certainly create discontent inconsistent with our retention of the Colony—if on the other hand we encourage that intercourse there is every probability that Canada ere long will be Americanized by the influx of Yankees—between the two I have no hesitation in preferring the latter, and if ultimately it should lead to the separation of these Provinces from the British Empire let us hope that this may take place by amicable arrangement instead of by war, and may lead to a division of the Union—British America with some of the Northern States forming one Nation and the Southern States another—This would be no such bad result and in the mean time our trade would prosper and emigration would flourish.[116]

In disapproving arrangements for reducing the English garrison in Canada and inducing the colony to accept the burden of its defence, Elgin pointed out once more the drift towards annexation:

Canada is already gravitating pretty surely towards the United States.—A great deal has been done to strengthen that tendency by recent changes in the Commercial Policy of Great Britain—A little more and the onus probandi will be cast upon those who contend that the connexion with England should be maintained— . . . But I would be very cautious of announcing the principle that Canada was expected to defend herself—She owes it mainly to her connexion with you that she is pretty sure in the event of a war to have for an enemy the only nation on earth who could be formidable to her.[117]

Meanwhile the warhawks of the American press, unsatiated by the conquest of Texas and California, were talking of taking Canada when they pleased. Elgin anticipated trouble when the Irish sympathizers in the States were organized and strengthened by recruits drawn from 'the disbanded miscreants who are now returning in hordes from Mexico with appetites whetted for all deeds of rapine and blood.' In these difficult circumstances Canada was split into three groups, none of which offered much comfort to the anxious governor:

Firstly we have the Irish repeal body—I need not describe them—You may look at home—they are here just what they are in Ireland. Secondly we have the French population—Their attitude as regards England and America is that of an armed neutrality—They do not exactly like the Yankees but they are the *conquered oppressed subjects* of England.—To be sure they govern themselves, get all the places, pay no taxes, and some other trifles of this description—Nevertheless they are the victims of British *égoisme*. Was not the union of the Provinces carried without their consent and with the view of subjecting them to the British? Papineau, their press and other authorities, are constantly dinning this into their ears, so no wonder they believe it——

Again—our mercantile and commercial classes are thoroughly disgusted and lukewarm in their allegiance, if not disaffected— . . . It is easy to shew that as matters now stand the faithful subject of Her Majesty in Canada is placed on a worse footing as regards trade with the Mother Country than the rebel over the lines. The moral to be drawn from this fact is by no means encouraging to friends of the British connexion.[118]

Moved by 'much sullen discontent' among the commercial class, Elgin encouraged the schemes of William Hamilton Merritt, the promoter of the Welland Canal, for increasing Canadian prosperity, remarking that: 'He is considered sanguine, speculative and not very safe—but on the other hand he is unquestionably a man of large views and it is of great importance to kindle hope in the Public mind.'[119]

But the discontent of the merchants continued to increase. Elgin made a sound analysis of its causes:

Stanley's Bill of 1843 attracted all the Produce of the West to the St. Lawrence, and fixed all the disposable capital of the Province in Grinding mills, Warehouses, and Forwarding establishments—Peel's Bill of 1846 drives the whole of this Produce down the New York channels of communication, destroying the Revenue which Canada expected to derive from Canal dues, and ruining at once Mill owners, forwarders, and merchants. The consequence is that Private Property is unsaleable in Canada, and not a Shilling can be raised on the credit of the Province. We are actually reduced to the disagreeable necessity of paying all Public officers, from the Governor General downwards, in debentures, which are not exchangeable at par. What makes it more serious is that all the prosperity of which Canada is thus robbed is transplanted to the other side of the lines as if to make the Canadians feel more bitterly how much kinder England is to the children who desert her than to those who remain faithful. For I care not whether you be a Protectionist or a Free Trader, it is the inconsistency of Imperial legislation, and not the adoption of one policy rather than another, which is the bane of the Colonies. I believe that the conviction that they would be better off if they were annexed is almost universal among the commercial classes at present; and the peaceful condition of the Province under all the circumstances of the time is I must confess often a matter of great astonishment to myself.[120]

The merchants of Montreal began to hold meetings and formed an association to protect Canadian manufactures. Their organ, the *Gazette*, proclaimed: 'We hope that the Association, instead of looking any longer for commercial privileges in the English market, will regard English manufactures in the same light as foreign productions, and will sustain the interests of Canada in opposition to those of any other country. We are Canadians, let us regulate our trade for our own benefit alone.'[121]

But the ministry in London was finding it difficult to carry the repeal of the Navigation Laws which the Canadian merchants demanded; and was able to do little for the project, which Elgin strongly supported, of a Quebec–Halifax railway, which was expected to break the new American dominance of the carrying trade. The disaffection of the merchants grew steadily, and what had long been a smouldering fire flared up with the passage of the Rebellion Losses Bill by the assembly early in 1849.

10

That body met in January 1849, and the opening of the session was marked by Elgin's delivery of the speech from the throne in both English and French. The proscription of French in the Union Act had at last been repealed, and the French Canadians rejoiced at this official recognition of their cherished tongue. Papineau came into open conflict with Lafontaine in the debate on the address. In four three-hour speeches he displayed his old vituperative eloquence in attacking the ministry on every point of their legislative program. He concluded by exclaiming: 'Since I have been back in this country, I have been led to examine matters and to study men, and on one side I can say that the Tories are better than I thought, and on the other the Liberals are far from being what I thought them. This Tory ministry, which I thought so evil, and this Liberal ministry, of which I hoped so much, have both deceived my hopes and my fears.'[122]

Lafontaine replied, suggesting dryly that his own greatest fault had been to obtain permission for Papineau to return from exile. Papineau had condemned him for accepting power and for not following his own policy of last-ditch opposition. But in reply Lafontaine asked:

> Where would our compatriots be today? Where would be our language, which a governor proscribed by a clause of the Act of Union, against the spirit of the peace treaties? This tongue, the language of our fathers, would it be rehabilitated today, as it has just been in the most solemn manner in the House and the acts of the legislature? If in 1842 we had accepted the honorable member's system of exaggerated opposition, would we have been in a position to solicit, to press for, as we did, the return of our exiled compatriots to this country? If we had not accepted a place in the administration in 1842, would we have been in a position to obtain permission for the honorable member in question to return home? A permission to obtain which I did not hesitate to offer my resignation from the well-paid post that I then held, in order to overcome the reiterated refusals of Sir Charles Metcalfe. Yet here is a man who, obeying his ancient habit of pouring out outrageous insults, dares in the face of these facts to accuse me, as well as my colleagues, of

venality, of a sordid love of office, of servility to power! To hear him he alone is devoted to his country! I demand no gratitude from him I demand it from no one; but since he calls himself so virtuous, I ask him to be just, and nothing more. Is he capable of being so? If I had accepted the system of exaggerated opposition where would the honorable member be today? He would still be in Paris, doubtless fraternizing with the red republicans, or the white republicans, or the black republicans, and approving in turn all the constitutions which succeed one another so rapidly in France.[123]

Lafontaine also pointed out that his party had obtained the revocation of the most unjust clauses of the Act of Union, those which proscribed the use of French and appropriated the revenue without consent. He stressed that in fact and in law 'the Act of Union had not made one and the same province of the two Canadas, but had only reunited, under the control of one and the same legislature two provinces hitherto distinct and separate and which were to continue so for all other purposes; in a word, that there had been after the example of our neighbors a confederation of two provinces of two states.'[124] On this basis Lafontaine refused to accept the principle, which Papineau urged, of proportional representation. In concluding he attacked Papineau once more, and warned him that his day was past:

He has the modesty to think that he is authorized to threaten us with what he calls the anger of the people. Let not the honorable member be deluded by ancient memories. Let him learn that if he wishes to threaten us, I defy him to realize his threats, and that when the time comes, I shall be ready to meet him at any time and any place, this man who never ceases to vaunt his virtue and his courage![125]

It was Lafontaine's greatest moment as a parliamentary orator— he rarely attained eloquence—and it was the virtual end of Papineau's political career. Only one French Canadian and two English Tories joined Papineau in supporting the amendments he had proposed. His only triumph was to prevent by his own vote the two-thirds majority necessary to increase the representation of each province to sixty-five members, as Lafontaine proposed. The main outlines of the present judicial system were established by another ministerial measure, and the electoral laws were reformed. Baldwin's project of a non-sectarian University of Toronto was finally approved, while the government offered subsidies for the construction of railroads, and petitioned the imperial parliament to hasten the revocation of the Navigation Acts.

II

But the main business of the session was the passage of the Lower anada Rebellion Losses Act, a measure promised since Metcalfe's me. The bill aroused one of the most bitter debates in Canadian istory. The Tories, who while in power had adopted a similar ieasure for Upper Canada, now attacked the Reformers' proposal oth on principle and on the method of financing it from the general evenue. Sherwood fulminated: 'I know nothing in history so bominable as to address oneself to those who have taken arms for the efence of their country, and among whom a great number have lost ieir nearest and dearest relatives and friends, to recompense those ho have been the cause of murders and bloodshed all over the land! defy anyone to find a parallel in history . . . To admit the principle iat those who took arms or engaged in a rebellion must be paid, ould be an open invitation to revolt.'[126] Sir Allan MacNab roclaimed in a fine fury:

The Union has completely failed in its purpose. It was enacted with ie sole motive of reducing the French Canadians under English domination. And the contrary effect has resulted! Those that were to be rushed dominate! Those in favour of whom the Union was made are he serfs of the others! . . . I warn the ministry of peril, this ministry which reats me like a rebel when all the acts of my life show that I have striven o be loyal; I warn it that the course it takes is likely to throw the people f Upper Canada into despair, and to make them feel that if they are to e governed by foreigners, it would be more advantageous to be governed y a neighboring people of the same race than by those with whom it as nothing in common, neither blood, nor language, nor interests.[127]

The impassioned Tory went so far as to attack Lord Grey, whom he ccused of nepotism in appointing his nephew Elgin as governor.

In reply two Upper Canadian Reformers flayed the old Tory 'amily Compact which MacNab represented. Irish-born W. H. lake, the most eloquent orator yet heard in Canada, called MacNab nd his party 'the true rebels against the constitution and the counry,' and told them:

Your loyalty is the love of power . . . This loyalty which is always eady to extend and fortify the prerogatives of the Crown, in restraining nd limiting the liberties of the people, is not loyalty, but slavery. It annot result in fortifying the ties which unite this country to England; n the contrary, it can only weaken the allegiance of the people of this rovince by depriving them of the rights of British subjects . . . That is ot British loyalty; it is a bastard loyalty which in all epochs of history as provoked the revolt of humanity under the whip.[128]

MacNab challenged Blake to a duel; and the following day youn John A. Macdonald also sent him a challenge, as he continued t flay the Tories. But the speaker intervened and made the offendin members swear to keep the peace. Disorder outside the House coul not be repressed, however, and MacNab, Gugy, and other Torie agitated at public meetings, at one of which Lafontaine was burr in effigy.

Lafontaine attacked MacNab for calling the French Canadiar 'foreigners,' and asked: 'Would the honorable member who pride himself on being a native Canadian be such if the French Canadian at the time of the War of American independence, had not saved th Canadas for England by their valor and devotion? If it had not bee for the courage of the French Canadians in 1775 and 1812, Canad today would be part of the American confederation, and the honoı able member would not be here to play the role he plays.'[129] Th bill was finally carried in the House by a vote of 47–18, and in th legislative council by 20–14. There remained only the royal sanctio by Elgin, who was warned by the *Gazette* on March 30 that 'if h should commit the error of approving of this most unjust measure it will be the cause of such a movement as this province has neve witnessed since the first European placed his foot upon its soil.'[13 The Montreal *Courier* more forthrightly proclaimed: 'Let the parlia ment pass the bill, let the Governor sanction it if he pleases, *but whi there is an axe and rifle on the frontier, and Saxon hands to wield then these losses will not be paid.*'[131]

Meanwhile Papineau's followers condemned the measure fc excepting convicted or banished rebels from receiving indemnities

> Liberals, *Patriotes* of '37 and '38, have not blushed to declare legal th judgments of the most iniquitous court that ever existed; they have nc blushed to declare that their friends, in whose struggles they had pa ticipated, and who, less fortunate than they, could not escape vengeance that those men to whose principles they agreed, have been justly punishe that their blood has justly flown on the scaffold. Oh! if they have nc blushed, the whole country will blush for them.[132]

Again *L'Avenir* warned the Reformers that they were doomed in a age of democratic revolutions:

> 'Liberal' means in our day nothing but 'democrat'; if not, it is false or lying title, in which you muffle yourself up to deceive the peopl If you are not a 'democrat,' the people will repudiate you because yc are not one,—because you are striving to maintain monarchical an aristocratical institutions, in spite of democratic principles, which ha found a footing in America, which they will never give up; a fulcru from which they are raising Europe, which will have soon done justi

to those impious governments which for centuries have degraded humanity, crushed nations under the weight of tyranny. The people will repudiate you, because in America public men must be democrats first of all, because privileges, monopolies, despotism, are venomous plants to which the climate of America is deadly. A third party will form itself, stronger because it will leave convictions, purer because it will soak itself in the ideas of liberty, equality and fraternity; and one which will crush you, Tories, and self-styled Liberals, which will grind you like powder, because you have attempted to check it. The future belongs to democracy; this is a profound truth, and specially so in America, and you will perhaps grasp it when the people tell you, as the perjured King of France was told,—'It is too late!'[133]

Professing the hope that 'no power may ever be abused to the point of provoking reflecting men to the contemplation of an alliance with a foreign power,' the Montreal merchants formed the British American League and on April 19 issued a manifesto which stated: 'It is evident, from the known character of our race, that patient submission to any ascendency founded on feelings of nationality alone, and not actuated by any generous or progressive principle, never has been, and never will be for any length of time, endured by Britons.'[134]

Hoping the agitation would die down, Elgin delayed as long as possible the royal sanction to the Rebellion Losses Bill, but when he finally sanctioned it on April 25, 1849, he was booed in the House and exposed to a storm of rotten eggs and stones from a well-dressed English mob when he emerged from the Parliament Building. An extra of the *Gazette* termed him 'the last governor of Canada' and called for a racial uprising: 'Anglo-Saxons! you must live for the future; your blood and your race will be henceforward your supreme law, if you are faithful to yourselves. You will be English, if you no longer may be British.'[135] The meeting announced by the *Gazette* took place that evening on the Place d'Armes, and when the crowd of some 1,500 had been roused to fury by violent addresses, some one cried: 'To Parliament!' The mob burst in upon the assembly; some 'gutter Cromwell' proclaimed the dissolution of the 'French parliament'; another stole the mace; and the chamber was sacked and set on fire. Drafts from windows broken by a shower of stones whipped up the flames, and soon the whole building was ablaze. For several days Montreal was ruled by an English mob, which sacked Lafontaine's and Nelson's houses, damaged that of Hincks, and broke the windows of the *Pilot*, the sole English government organ.

Three days after the fire, the assembly, sitting under military protection, adopted an address to Elgin, expressing its indignation at the outrages. MacNab and Papineau both opposed the measure.

When the assembly's representatives went to the Chateau de Ramézay, which served as Government House, to present this address, it was necessary to read the Riot Act and clear the streets with bayonets. Elgin was stoned as he emerged to return to his residence at Monklands. He was also expelled from membership in many of Montreal's select social organizations by the outraged English Canadians. Petitions were circulated for his recall and for disallowance of the obnoxious bill.

The governor kept calm, despite all manner of provocation; he judged that 'The whole row is the work of the Orange Societies, backed by the commercial men who desire annexation and the political leaders who want place.'[136] He refused to make use of the troops or to swear in French Canadians, the only loyal part of the populace, as special police to keep order. He wrote Grey, 'Of course all French Lower Canada is with us but the great object is to keep them quiet and to prevent collision between the races.'[137] In this he succeeded, despite the raging violence of the Tory press, which did not scruple to attack him personally for cowardice and double-dealing. MacNab and another Tory leader went to England to seek Elgin's recall and the repudiation of the Rebellion Losses Act; but despite Gladstone's advocacy of their cause, Elgin's conduct and the act were approved by a large majority in the imperial parliament. Lord John Russell, who had opposed colonial responsible government in 1837, now championed it and was supported by the same Whigs who had opposed it twelve years before. Thus on June 14, 1849, the British House of Commons proclaimed Canada's full achievement of responsible government, thanks to Baldwin and Lafontaine, two former rebels, and Elgin, the Tory nobleman who had become anathema to Canadian Tories.

The ultra-loyalist English Canadians of 1837 and 1838 now leagued themselves with discontented French-Canadian radicals in an open annexationist movement; the British American League met in convention at Kingston in July; and early in October 1849 they published a manifesto calling for 'an amiable and peaceful separation from the British connexion and a union under equitable terms from the great North American confederation of sovereign States.'[138] This document bore 325 signatures, of which by far the greater part were those of the leading English merchants of Montreal, although there was a sprinkling of French names drawn from among the followers of Papineau and *L'Avenir*. Such was the final result, as Elgin had anticipated, of the '£.s.d. view' taken by the self-professed loyalist organizers of the Kingston Convention, who in July had advocated protection of native industry, administrative economy, and Confederation of the British North American provinces as the remedies for Canada's ills.

Notes

[1] Kennedy, *Documents*, 376, Upper Canada Legislative Council Committee's Report, 11 May 1839.

[2] *Ibid.*, 377.

[3] Kennedy, 416, Russell-Thomson, 7 September 1839.

[4] *Ibid.*, 421–2, Russell-Thomson, 14 October 1839.

[5] *Ibid.*, 423.

[6] P. Knaplund (*ed.*), *Letters from Lord Sydenham to Lord John Russell* (London, 1931), 31–2, Russell-Thomson, 2 September 1839.

[7] A. Shortt, *Lord Sydenham* (Toronto, 1908), 197.

[8] Kennedy, 427, Thomson-friend, 20 November 1839.

[9] Knaplund, 36, Thomson-Russell, 25 November 1839.

[10] Kennedy, 427, Thomson-friend, 20 November 1839.

[11] Knaplund, 52, Thomson-Russell, 13 March 1847.

[12] Kennedy, 433–45, Union Act, 1840.

[13] *Ibid.*, 440 *n.*1.

[14] Knaplund, 45, Thomson-Russell, 23 January 1840.

[15] Chapais, IV, 305.

[16] J. Huston (*ed.*), *Le Répertoire national* (Montréal, 1893), II, 216–24.

[17] Kingsford, X, 534–5.

[18] Kennedy, 430, Thomson-friend, 12 December 1839.

[19] *Ibid.*, 449–50, Sydenham-friend, 1840.

[20] *Ibid.*, 449, Russell-Sydenham, 25 October 1840.

[21] Knaplund, 94, Sydenham-Russell, 27 September 1840.

[22] Kennedy, 457, Sydenham-brother, 28 August 1841.

[23] Quoted in *CHAR 1938*, 28, J. B. Brebner, 'Patronage and Parliamentary Government.'

[24] Knaplund, 97, Sydenham-Russell, 12 October 1840.

[25] PAC: Lafontaine Papers (transcripts from Saint-Sulpice), Hincks-Lafontaine, 12 April 1839; R. S. Longley, *Sir Francis Hincks* (Toronto, 1943), 51–2.

[26] PAC: Lafontaine Papers, R. Baldwin-Lafontaine, 26 November 1840.

[27] *Ibid.*, Hincks-Lafontaine, 9 September 1839; Longley, 54.

[28] *Ibid.*, Hincks-Lafontaine, 23 August 1840; Longley, 68.

[29] Knaplund, 121, Sydenham-Russell, 24 February 1841.

[30] *Ibid.*, 130, Sydenham-Russell, 10 April 1841.

[31] L.-P. Turcotte, *Le Canada sous l'Union* (Québec, 1871), I, 58–61; Chapais, V, 12–18.

[32] *Le Canadien*, 2 April 1841; Chapais, V, 21.

[33] *CAR 1883*, 168, Note B, Morin-Hincks, 8 May 1841.

[34] Knaplund, 120, Sydenham-Russell, 24 February 1841.

[35] *Le Canadien*; Chapais, V, 33.

[36] Knaplund, 48, Thomson-Russell, 13 February 1840; 141–2, Sydenham-Russell, 12 June 1841.

[37] Sydenham-Russell, 27 June 1841; Chapais, V, 33.

[38] Kennedy, 458, Baldwin's Resolutions, 3 September 1841.

[39] Shortt, 339, Sydenham-brother, 28 August 1841.

[40] *Ibid.*, 347, Ryerson in *The Christian Guardian.*

[41] Knaplund, 91, Sydenham-Russell, 16 September 1840; 93, Sydenham-Russell, 27 September 1840.

[42] *Le Canadien*, September 1841; Chapais, V, 67.

[43] *CHR 1927*, 43, P. Knaplund (*ed.*), 'The Buller-Peel Correspondence Regarding Canada, 1841,' Buller-Peel, 9 September 1841.

[44] Kennedy, 459, Stanley-Bagot, 8 October 1841.
[45] *Ibid.*, 460, Bagot-Stanley, 23 February 1842.
[46] Knaplund, *Sydenham*, 97–100, Sydenham-Russell, 12 October 1840; 28 October 1840.
[47] Kennedy, 461, Bagot-Stanley, 23 February 1842.
[48] *Ibid.*, 463–4, Bagot-Stanley, 12 June 1842.
[49] *Ibid.*, 470, Bagot-Stanley, 28 July 1842.
[50] *Ibid.*, 473–4, Bagot-Lafontaine, 13 September 1842.
[51] Chapais, V, 89; Lafontaine's whole speech, Ap. IV, 289–99.
[52] Kennedy, 476–7, Bagot-Stanley, 26 September 1842.
[53] Kennedy, 478–9, Bagot-Stanley, 26 September 1842.
[54] Kennedy, 486, Stanley-Bagot (private), 3 November 1842.
[55] *Le Canadien*, 21 September 1842; Chapais, V, 101.
[56] Chapais, V, 103.
[57] *The Times* (London), 15 October 1842; Chapais, V, 107.
[58] *Hansard*, III Series, LXVI, 7 February 1843; Chapais, V, 111.
[59] *La Minerve*, 22 May 1843; Chapais, V, 130.
[60] Chapais, V, 139–40, Metcalfe-friend, 22 January 1843.
[61] Chapais, V, 143, Metcalfe-Stanley, 25 April 1843.
[62] Chapais, V, 149, Metcalfe-Stanley, 25 June 1843.
[63] Chapais, V, 150, Metcalfe-Stanley, 12 May 1843.
[64] Chapais, V, 158, Metcalfe-Stanley, 25 June 1843.
[65] Kennedy, 492–3, Metcalfe-Stanley, 5 August 1843.
[66] Chapais, V, 191.
[67] A. Gérin-Lajoie, *Dix Ans au Canada de 1840 à 1850* (Québec, 1888), 268.
[68] Chapais, V, 205, Metcalfe-Stanley, 13 May 1845.
[69] *Ibid.*, 210, Lafontaine-Caron, 10 September 1846.
[70] *Ibid.*, 214, Caron-Draper, September 1845.
[71] PAC: Lafontaine Papers, Baldwin-Lafontaine, 16 October 1845; Chapais, V, 215–16.
[72] *Le Journal de Québec*, 5 May 1846; Chapais, V, 226.
[73] Chapais, VI, 8.
[74] Kennedy, 501, Elgin-Lady Elgin, 1847.
[75] *Ibid.*, 500–1, Elgin-Grey, 13 July 1847.
[76] Chapais, VI, 17–18.
[77] A. G. Doughty (*ed.*), *Elgin-Grey Papers*, 1846–1852 (Ottawa, 1937), I, 20, Elgin-Grey, 27 March 1847. In this and subsequent quotations from the *Elgin-Grey Papers*, Elgin's informal shorthand has been expanded, since it is obstructive to the reader unfamiliar with his style.
[78] *Ibid.*, I, 28, Elgin-Grey, 26 April 1847.
[79] *Ibid.*, I, 114, Papineau's 'Addresse aux Electeurs des Comtés de Huntingdon et de Saint-Maurice, 1847.'
[80] *Ibid.*, I, 102, Elgin-Grey, 24 December 1847.
[81] *Ibid.*, I, 117, Elgin-Grey, 7 January 1848.
[82] *Ibid.*, I, 119, Elgin-Grey, 22 January 1848.
[83] Chapais, VI, 36–7.
[84] *Elgin-Grey*, III, 1022–3, Grey-Harvey, 3 November 1846.
[85] *Ibid.*, I, 135, Elgin-Grey, 17 March 1848.
[86] *Ibid.*, I, 123, Elgin-Grey, 5 February 1848.
[87] *Ibid.*, I, 138, Grey-Elgin, 14 April 1848.
[88] *Ibid.*, I, 139, Elgin-Grey, 27 March 1848.
[89] APQ: Fonds Papineau, XI, 544, Papineau- ——, 15 October 1844.
[90] *Ibid.*, 545, Papineau-Roebuck, 16 July 1845.
[91] *Ibid.*, 547, Papineau-O'Callaghan, 12 May 1846.
[92] Chapais, VI, 47.

93 *Le Journal de Québec*, 13 November 1847; Chapais, VI, 47–8.
94 *L'Ami de la Religion et de la Patrie*, 24 December 1847; Chapais, VI, 48.
95 Gérin-Lajoie, *Dix Ans*, 314–15.
96 APQ: XI, 547a, 548, Papineau-O'Callaghan, 22 February 1848; 19 April 1848.
97 Gérin-Lajoie, 481; Chapais, VI, 53.
98 *Elgin-Grey*, I, 134, Elgin-Grey, 17 March 1848.
99 *Ibid.*, I, 115, Papineau's Huntingdon address, 1847.
100 *Ibid.*, I, 125, Grey-Elgin, 22 March 1848.
101 *Ibid.*, I, 141–2, Elgin-Grey, 9 April 1848.
102 *Ibid.*, I, 12, Elgin-Grey, 2 March 1848.
103 *Ibid.*, I, 144–5, Elgin-Grey, 26 April 1848.
104 *Ibid.*, I, 149–50, Elgin-Grey, 4 May 1848.
105 *Ibid.*, I, 195, Elgin-Grey, 29 June 1848.
106 *Ibid.*, I, 191–2.
107 *Ibid.*, I, 200, Bourget's pastoral of 17 June 1848.
108 *Ibid.*, I, 152–3, *L'Avenir*.
109 *Ibid.*, I, 156–8, *La Revue Canadienne*.
110 PAC: Lafontaine Papers, Cauchon-Lafontaine, 23 June 1848; Chapais, VI. 4.
111 Innis & Lower, *Select Econ. Docs.*, II, 316.
112 *The Canadian Economist*, 30 May 1848; Innis & Lower, II, 347.
113 Innis & Lower, II, 357, J. Keefer-W. H. Merritt, 19 April 1848.
114 *Elgin-Grey*, I, 182 & *n.* 2, Elgin-Grey, 6 June 1848.
115 *Ibid.*, I, 204, Elgin-Grey, 5 July 1848.
116 *Ibid.*, I, 208, Grey-Elgin, 27 July 1848.
117 *Ibid.*, I, 217, Elgin-Grey, 2 August 1848.
118 *Ibid.*, I, 224, Elgin-Grey, 16 August 1848.
119 *Ibid.*, I, 250, Elgin-Grey, 19 October 1848.
120 *Ibid.*, I, 256, Elgin-Grey, 16 November 1848.
121 *Ibid.*, I, 285; *Montreal Gazette*.
122 Chapais, VI, 70.
123 *Ibid.*, VI, 74–5.
124 *Ibid.*, VI, 77.
125 *Ibid.*, VI, 79.
126 *Ibid.*, VI, 96.
127 *Ibid.*, VI, 97.
128 *Ibid.*, VI, 99–100.
129 Chapais, VI, 103.
130 *Montreal Gazette*, 30 March 1849; *Elgin-Grey*, I, 337.
131 *Montreal Courier*, ———; *Elgin-Grey*, I, 336.
132 *L'Avenir*, 24 February 1849; *Elgin-Grey*, I, 342.
133 *L'Avenir*, 3 March 1849; *Elgin-Grey*, I, 343.
134 *Elgin-Grey*, I, 348 *n.*
135 *Montreal Gazette*, 25 April 1849; Chapais, VI, 108.
136 *Elgin-Grey*, I, 350; Elgin-Grey, 30 April 1849.
137 *Ibid.*, I, 352, Elgin-Grey, 5 May 1849.
138 *Ibid.*, IV, 1490. The signatures, elsewhere usually omitted, are here given, as well as the document in full.
139 *Ibid.*, I, 441–3 *n.*, 'Address to People of Canada' of British American League, 31 July 1849.

CHAPTER VI

THE EMERGENCE OF A NATION—II
(1849–67)

IT HAD taken only ten years for the French Canadians to rall from the death sentence pronounced upon their nationalit by Lord Durham's *Report* and the Act of Union. Under th sage leadership of Lafontaine their constitutional resistance ha been so successful that they had gained undisputed politica power. The disgruntled francophobe press now railed agains French domination, protesting when the Eastern Townships wer brought under the same legal system as the rest of the provinc that 'the obvious intention of that majority, composed o Frenchmen, aided by traitorous British Canadians, is to forc French institutions still further upon the British minority i Lower Canada.'[1] The rebels of 1837–8, both English and French now held office and were supported by the British government while the former loyalists proclaimed their revolt: 'When Frenc tyranny becomes insupportable we shall find our Cromwell . . When we can stand tyranny no longer, it will be seen whethe good bayonets in Saxon hands will not be more than a match fo a mace and a majority.'

Both ethnic groups had now resorted to rebellion when dominate wholly by the other; the great achievement of the next two decade was to be the working out of a partnership of English and Frenc which guaranteed the rights of both. Thanks largely to Elgin' leadership, the threat of annexation to the United States was averte by the establishment of reciprocity of trade, which did much t cure the economic ills of Canada; thanks largely to George-Etienn Cartier,[2] the French Canadians were led to support the projec of the Confederation of British North America into a Canada whic was to be both French and English. Papineau's old lieutenant ha broken with his former chief on the question of republicanism an annexation: Cartier was convinced that the French Canadian were monarchists by religion, by customs, and by tradition. Thank largely to him, an English-French Canadian solidarity was achieved as a result of which it was definitely settled that the continent wa to be divided between two powers, rather than to be a politica entity; and that one power was to be bicultural.

I

The nature of the new Canada then in the making was foreshadowed by the decision of the legislature, after the Montreal riots, to meet alternately at Toronto and Quebec. After his Montreal experiences, Elgin favored the measure, for as he wrote Grey:

> You find in this city I believe the most Anti-British specimens of each class of which our community consists—The Montreal French are the most Yankeefied French in the Province—the British, though furiously anti-Gallican, are, with some exceptions, the least loyal—and the commercial men the most zealous annexationists which Canada furnishes—It must I think do great mischief to the members who come from the other parts of the Province to pass some months of each year in this hotbed of prejudice and disaffection——[3]

Though the self-styled loyalists had issued a proclamation to the 'Britons of the City of Toronto, Britons of the Home District,' urging them to 'let your eggs be stale and your powder dry' against the coming of Elgin, 'the political Judas Iscariot,'[4] it was decided that the legislature should go first to Toronto, to avoid the charge that the government was under French-Canadian influence.

Elgin travelled through Upper Canada during the autumn of 1849 on a courageous goodwill tour from which he returned with the firm conviction, as he informed Grey, that '*Canada cannot be saved unless you force the selfish scheming Yankees to concede reciprocity.*'[5] The annexationist English press of Montreal bewailed the loss of the seat of government, but the Tory *Daily British Whig* of Toronto told them to 'keep their breath to cool their porridge,' for it was:

> . . . the wretched selfishness of the Montrealers . . . caused the removal of the Seat of Government from Western Canada; from amid an Anglo-Saxon race, to place it within the control of French Oligarchists and their Helots. Had the Government remained at Kingston, or at any place within the limits of the upper province, the Franco-Canadians never would have attained and exercised that arbitrary power which has been the exciting cause of all the late political troubles and riots. A war of races might have existed, as it now does, but it would have been a defensive war on the part of the Eastern Canadians . . . From such evils the province, in future, will be protected, while legislation takes place in an educated land, and among free men. The Radicals may rule over us, and they will, but our rulers will be Anglo-Saxon Radicals, and not aliens to us in blood, language, and religion.[6]

It was to be a long time before the French Canadians would produce a racism as virulent as that which permeates this statement, which also reflects the powerful sectionalism that has remained almost a much of a factor in Canadian politics as the basic ethnic division

2

Elgin now put aside the ethnic question and turned his attentio to the economic matters which were of growing importance a Canada felt the impact of the industrial revolution. He was i close relations with William Hamilton Merritt, the promote of the Welland Canal and the advocate of reciprocity as a solu tion for Canada's ills, who had been president of the legislativ council and now became commissioner of public works. Elgi assured Grey that if reciprocity were obtained, 'Canada wil remain attached to England though tied to her neither by th golden links of protection, nor by the meshes of old-fashione Colonial office jobbing and chicane.' Otherwise, he feared tha 'the closing period of the connexion between Great Britain an Canada will be marked by incidents which will damp the ardo of those who desire to promote human happiness by strikin shackles either off commerce or off men.'[7] The repeal of th English Corn Laws and timber duties by the Little Englander now in the saddle at London had brought commercial disaste upon the English-Canadian merchants, who promptly abandone their traditional loyalism and sought a preferential market i the United States through annexation. Elgin thought a Britis preferential trade agreement with the United States was the onl means of saving Canada from annexation. This project did no find particular favor at the Colonial Office, for Lord Grey wa one of the new doctrinaire free-traders with little regard for th fate of the colonies.

Though the annexationist press continued to insult the governor Elgin contented himself with dismissing from office militia officer or magistrates who signed manifestoes calling for annexation to th States. Elgin refused to concur with Grey in making a distinctio between separation with a view to annexation and separation with view to independence. The colonial secretary considered the forme an act of treason, the latter a natural and legitimate step in progress Elgin protested: 'If you say that your great lubberly boy is too big fo the nursery and that you have no other room for him in your house how can you decline to allow him to lodge with his elder brethre over the way when the attempt to keep up an establishment fo himself would seriously embarrass him?'[8] The governor-genera also found it difficult to take strong measures against the annexa- tionists in Canada, when Lord John Russell was proclaiming a Westminster:

I anticipate indeed with others that some of the colonies may so grow in population and wealth that they may say—'Our strength is sufficient to enable us to be independent of England. The link is now becoming onerous to us—the time is come when we can, in amity and alliance with England, maintain our independence.' I do not think that time is yet approaching. But let us make them, as far as possible, fit to govern themselves—let us give them, as far as we can, the capacity of ruling their own affairs—let them increase in wealth and population, and whatever may happen, we have the consolation of saying we have contributed to the happiness of the world.[9]

Elgin judged that this anticipation of the severance of the British connection would have a deplorable effect in Canada, and he considered it unnecessary.

In a remarkable anticipation of the idea of the Commonwealth of Nations and the present status of Canada within its framework, he wrote:

Here for instance, where the vicinity of the U.S. exercises so great an influence, it is, I think, possible, that the time may come when it may be expedient to allow the Colonists to elect their own Governors, to reduce their civil lists to the starvation point, &c, England withdrawing all her forces except 2,000 men at Quebec and being herself represented in the Colony by an Agent—something like a Resident in India—If yr. agent was well chosen and had a good status I am not sure but that the connexion might be kept up under such an arrangement quite as well and as profitably for England as under the present—One thing is however indispensable to the success of this or any other system of Colonial Government—You must renounce the habit of telling the Colonies that the Colonial is a provisional existence.—You must allow them to believe that without severing the bonds which unite them to Great Britain they may attain the degree of perfection and of social and political development to which organized communities of freemen have a right to aspire.[10]

He reported that Robert Baldwin, whom he thought 'of more importance to the connexion than three regiments,'[11] was deeply moved by Russell's speech, and had remarked:

But is it not hard upon us while we are laboring through good and evil report to thwart the designs of those who would dismember the Empire that our adversaries should be informed that the difference between them and the Prime Minister of England is only one of time? If the British Government has really come to the conclusion that we are a burden to be cast off whenever a favorable opportunity offers, surely we ought to be warned.[12]

It is clear that Elgin echoed Baldwin's sentiments.

3

At the outset of the new session in May 1850, a motion in favor of breaking the tie with Great Britain was roundly defeated, with only Papineau and six diehard Tories supporting it. Sir Allan MacNab continued his intemperate attacks on Lafontaine and the ministry, and finally drew upon himself the reproaches of his fellow Tory, Colonel Gugy, who remarked that he could no longer follow the leadership which had led to the Montreal disorders: 'When I saw the House of Assembly in flames, I said to an influential conservative who was near me, "In these flames are consumed the hopes of the conservative party." In fact, I think this party will never return to power.'[13]

The ministry carried almost all before it, since the opposition was hopelessly divided among incompatible groups: some fifteen Tories, five or six dissident Reformers known as 'Clear Grits,' and the declared annexationists. The Clear Grits, who favored the application of the elective principle to all offices, universal suffrage, the secret ballot, biennial parliaments, free exchange, direct taxation, secularization of the clergy reserves, and other measures considered radical at the time, had broken away from the conservative Liberalism of Baldwin, as a similar Lower-Canadian group, the *Rouges*, was soon to do from that of Lafontaine. The ministry carried all its measures except Lafontaine's renewed proposal to increase the representation, which failed to win the necessary two-thirds vote. Free trade and reciprocity between the provinces of British North America were encouraged in one law which foreshadowed Confederation, while the vexed Upper-Canadian question of the clergy reserves was referred to the British parliament.

Of much more concern to Lower Canada were Lafontaine's resolutions leading to the abolition of seigneurial tenure. This measure, which had once been favored by the anti-French forces of the province, now had the backing of the *habitants*. A commission of enquiry had been appointed in 1841 and had made its report in 1843, but no action had as yet been taken. Lafontaine urged the abolition of seigneurial tenure with proper compensation to the landlords as a measure against revolution:

In justice to the two interested parties, it is time to destroy the evil which is so much complained of. I am convinced that the *seigneur* ought most to fear too long a delay of a remedy. Delay gives new occasions for the propagation of principles which tend to overturn society. There comes a time when the people say, 'It is too late.' In this case, as the *seigneurs* form the smallest number, they may expect to lose everything

> without compensation . . . But I hope never to see the day when society, when the whole country, will be demoralized. I see the march of events: it is the struggle of the masses against the few. The masses are beginning to become indignant. Time ought not to be lost. But if seigneurial tenure is to be effectively and really ended, let us all work together, *seigneurs* and *censitaires*, and if the *seigneur* gives the example of good will, it will be so much the better.[14]

But the question of seigneurial tenure was not settled at this session, though a committee was appointed to study the question and report upon it.

Oddly enough, the *seigneur* who did not display the goodwill for which Lafontaine called was none other than Papineau. The old champion of the rights of the people, the idol of the Lower Canadian democrats, whose organ *L'Avenir* denounced feudal tenure as a shameful relic of an abhorred past, was also the *seigneur* of Montebello and had no intention of renouncing his privileges. He rose to defend the wisdom and justice of seigneurial tenure, and denounced the demagogues who agitated the people in favor of its abolition. He proclaimed proudly: 'I am a great reformer in the matter of necessary political changes, but I am a great conservative in the matter of preservation of the sacred right of property.'[15] This curious mixture of political radicalism and economic conservatism was to become a tradition among French-Canadian leaders. Those who bewail most loudly the trampling underfoot of the rights of the people are often, like Papineau himself, members of the élite, aristocrats by temperament, taste, and appearance. The American democracy which Papineau preached was an exotic growth largely foreign to the French-Canadian tradition, reinforced at this period by renewed contact with France. Thanks to the intellectual reaction in Canada to the European revolution of 1848, American democracy never took root in French Canada, whose society still remains today a rigidly hierarchical structure, though lately somewhat shaken by movements from the long-submerged masses.

The course of the session, which closed in August, bore out Elgin's opinion that 'Bringing the French Canadian Members to this fine progressive well farmed Country, and placing them for a time in the midst of a British population who though they may have some John Bullish prejudices, do not cherish towards them the jealous antipathies of Montreal, gives in my opinion a chance to the Province and the Union which nothing else could have given—'[16] French and English acted together in coping with the most pressing questions of each section; annexationism lost strength as prosperity returned with a sudden rise of prices and trade, an increase of exports and imports, the freeing of the navigation of the St. Lawrence, the development of close economic relations with the United State the completion of the canals, the construction of railroads, th colonization movement, and an abundant harvest. Elgin pai tribute to the role played by the French Canadians: 'The Minist supported by the French (whose tendencies when they feel that the are treated fairly, not as aliens but as genuine subjects of the Quee are, as I always assured you, decidedly anti-revolutionary) have bee able to resist the destructives.'[17] He added, after assigning personal spite and selfishness the radicalism of the dissident Upp Canadians: 'Candor compels me to state that in these respects th conduct of the Anglo-Saxon portion of our M.P.P's, contrasts mo unfavorably with that of the Gallican.'

Elgin took this opportunity to review developments in Canad since the Rebellions and to make another of his accurate forecast

The result of the policy which I have pursued with yr. concurrenc and support has been briefly this—The French have been rescued fro the false position into which they have been driven, and in which the must perforce have remained so long as they believed that it was th object of the British Govt. as avowed by Lord Sydenham and othe to break them down and to ensure to the British race, not by trusting t the natural course of events but by dint of management and statecraft, predominance in the Province—To eradicate from the mind of a peop naturally prone to suspicion a belief of this kind when deeply engrained wa no easy task, but the startling events of last year and above all the furio assaults directed by the mob and Press of the so called British Party again the Queen's Representative have accomplished the object. The Frenc are restored to their normal condition and are therefore an essentiall conservative element in the Canadian compound. Accident, or rath I believe I should say the artifices of Imperial Policy have connecte them politically with the liberals of Upper Canada—They are unwillin to break this connexion and they will adhere to it as long as a modera liberal Party exists in this section of the province—If clear Gritism absorb all the hues of Upper Canadian liberalism the French, unless som interference from without checks the natural course of events, will fa off from them and form an alliance with the Upper Canadian Tories.[18]

In the fall of 1850 Elgin was troubled by the prospect of Lafontain abandoning public life at the end of the current parliament: ' do not altogether approve of a man of his age and with his influenc leaving public life, but the fact is that the French Canadians ar generally (with the exception of Papineau) quiet sort of people, an Lafontaine's health is not very good. His desire for retirement aris I think partly from health and partly from disgust at the worryin and turmoil of office—'[19] Elgin grew more and more convinced th the French Canadians would line up with the Upper Canadia Conservatives as the Clear Grits became more anti-French. Boulto one of the Grits' chief spokesmen, proclaimed at a public dinner that 'the negroes are the great difficulty of the States and the French Canadians of Canada,' a sentiment which Elgin correctly judged as 'likely to stick in the gizzard of a rather sensitive and suspicious people.'[20] This consideration has not prevented the sentiment from being echoed down to the present day.

4

The new session opened calmly in May 1851, and was notable only for the presence of William Lyon Mackenzie, the leader of the Upper Canada Rebellion in 1837–8, who had defeated George Brown of the *Toronto Globe* in an election in which the latter made vain use of the 'No Popery' cry, in connection with the re-establishment of the Catholic hierarchy in England. The legislature was more concerned with economic matters at home than religious ones abroad. The St. Lawrence commercial system, with its dangerous navigation, high insurance rates, and limited supply of grain and high freights, was still losing ground to the New York one, which enjoyed lower insurance and freight rates as the chief outlet for North American grain. Canada's trade with the United States increased more rapidly than that with Britain and became far more important than it had ever been before.

Since Canada found itself in the unhappy position of having completed some $20,000,000 worth of canals just as the rise of the railways lessened their importance, the legislature showed interest in Hincks' proposal to construct various roads, which were later consolidated as the Grand Trunk and the Intercolonial. In 1849 the annexationists mourned that Canada had only 50 miles of railway; but by 1854 2,000 miles were under construction and 800 already completed. $40,000,000 was spent on this program, and 20,000 men were given work in the summer of 1854. The railroads brought a large influx of foreign capital, mostly British. The legislature also turned its attention to the vexed question of the clergy reserves, which the imperial government had referred back for their decision. Lafontaine failed again to carry his project of increasing the representation, and it was still Papineau's vote which defeated the measure.

The far-sighted Merritt proposed a meeting of delegates of the British North American provinces to consider a constitution for a future confederation, but won only seven votes for this resolution. It was to be sixteen years before a majority would favor this project, proposed in the past by English administrators and now first brought to the attention of the Canadian parliament by a member of its government. The committee on seigneurial tenure made its report, and a group headed by its chairman Louis Drummond, the solicitor-general for Lower Canada, and including Cartier, Chauveau, and Cauchon, pressed for immediate action on the question. Lafontaine opposed a hasty settlement, and finally got his way, despite a sharp debate.

On June 30 Robert Baldwin, who had been able to defeat an attack on one of his judicial measures only with the aid of the Lower Canadian Reformers in the face of a revolt headed by Mackenzie, and who had also been embittered by the growing hostility of the Clear Grits, announced his resignation on the grounds that his party lacked confidence in him. Lafontaine declared that he, too, would resign after the session, and expressed his regret at Baldwin's action: 'I had at least hoped not to be separated until the end of my political career from my honorable colleague, to him I have been united not only by common principles but by the bonds of a close friendship.'[21]

Baldwin was only forty-nine; Lafontaine only forty-four, but they were both prematurely worn by their joint ten years' struggle to win responsible government for Canada, and so the great ministry resigned, closing one of the most notable epochs of Canadian parliamentary history. Grey wrote to Elgin: 'I am very sorry indeed you have lost Lafontaine from your Cabinet, he seems to me to have had more of the Gentleman about him than any other of the public men of Canada.'[22] Lafontaine himself, at a farewell public dinner in Montreal, gave some final advice to his compatriots: 'In retiring from public life I do not see without displeasure the attempts which are being made to divide those of my origin, and to array them against each other; but from my experience I may tell you that such efforts will not be successful. The common sense of our countrymen will prevent that; should it be otherwise, the fault and suffering will be theirs.'[23] Unfortunately this good advice was not taken, and much of the best of French-Canadian intellectual energy was long to be wasted in futile internecine bickering. Politics might well be considered the opium of the French-Canadian people, and over-indulgence in the vice has cost them dear.

5

The intellectual energy of the French Canadians was beginning, however, to find other outlets than politics. In the 1840's and 1850's there was a notable stirring in the cultural field which was not to be matched for almost a century, thanks to the tide of intellectual reaction which became dominant when Quebec found itself on the defensive in the new Confederation which it was only reluctantly brought to accept in 1867. French Canada responded vigorously to the challenge of Durham's contemptuous remarks about its culture in his *Report*, which merely echoed the long-standing opinion of the English merchants and officials of Quebec and Montreal.

In 1828, when young François-Xavier Garneau was a clerk in the Quebec law office of Archibald Campbell, he had been taunted by one of his English fellow clerks on the score of the constitutional struggle then raging in the assembly under the leadership of Papineau and Viger. The young Englishman had said: 'What is the use of all this quibbling, in this country conquered by our arms and which even has no history?' Garneau replied: 'I shall write the history which you do not even know exists. You will see that our ancestors yielded only when outnumbered. And then, "what though the field be lost, all is not lost." There are defeats which are as glorious as victories.'[24]

The son of a carriage-maker and innkeeper, Garneau had early attracted the notice of François-Joseph Perrault, the extraordinary ex-fur trader who became an educational reformer, establishing along Lancasterian lines the Quebec primary school which the boy attended, as well as writing legal and historical textbooks. Perrault, whose post as clerk of the Court of King's Bench enabled him to study and compile a manual of Canadian history, offered the boy, who lacked funds for the classical college course, a place in his office; and after two years there Garneau decided to become a notary. He apprenticed himself to Archibald Campbell, who did not allow his thriving practice and his extensive financial concerns to stop him from taking a lively interest in literature and science. Campbell opened his library to his serious young clerk, who thus became familiar with the chief English, French, and Latin poets and historians. After three years of self-education young Garneau accompanied a friend of Campbell on a journey to the Maritime Provinces, the United States, and Upper Canada, which helped to broaden his outlook. In 1830 Garneau passed his notarial examination, and having fulfilled his contract with Campbell by a year's further service in his office, set out for Europe in 1831 with $240 in his pocket, to visit, as he said, 'the cradle of genius and civilization to which America owes all that it is.'[25]

After passing a week in London seeing the sights, he went over to Paris, which was then celebrating the first anniversary of the accession of Louis-Philippe, the Citizen-King. It was the Paris of Lamartine, Victor Hugo, and Musset, of Thiers and Guizot, of Lamennais and Lacordaire—a very different world from that which Garneau had known in Quebec. Upon his return to London, he obtained the post of secretary to Denis-Benjamin Viger, then the assembly's agent in England. For a year Garneau drafted petitions to the colonial secretary, and correspondence to Papineau and Neilson, gaining an intimate knowledge of French-Canadian politics and also meeting such notables as William Lyon Mackenzie, Arthur Roebuck, and John McGregor, who came to call upon Viger. He also fell in with the Polish refugees whose meetings were frequented by O'Connell, the Irish patriot who was the friend of all oppressed peoples. With a natural sympathy for minorities under foreign rule, Garneau was drawn into the current of nationalism then undermining the old order in Europe. His studies in the British Museum were supplemented by visits to political meetings and the House of Commons, where he heard the debate on the Reform Bill. Thus Garneau obtained a thorough understanding of the workings of the British parliamentary system. This busy life was interrupted in the fall of 1832 by a two-weeks vacation in Paris with Viger and Amable Berthelot, and then resumed until May 1833, when Garneau took ship for Quebec. He returned greatly influenced by his two years in Europe: a democrat in politics, with a strong faith in the peaceful evolution possible under the English parliamentary system; a romanticist in literature, much influenced by Lamartine; and a Catholic of the liberal school of Lacordaire, Montalembert and Mgr. Dupanloup. He had resolved to serve his country with his pen.

Back in Quebec Garneau resumed practice as a notary to earn a living, but devoted much of his time to writing, first contributing verse to Etienne Parent's *Le Canadiene* and then launching, at the end of 1833, his own short-lived *L'Abeille Canadienne*. In the following year, that of Bédard's 92 Resolutions, Garneau abandoned literature for politics, and as secretary of the Quebec Constitutional Committee played an active role as a speaker and writer on the issues of the day. The next year saw little work from his pen, probably because of the illness and death of his mother, and his own courtship and marriage. But in 1836 Garneau, inspired by Guizot and Augustin Thierry, set about studying the history of Canada. During this and the following year he published in *Le Canadien* descriptions of the famous battles fought on Canadian soil. His avocation interfered with the demands of his profession, and to meet the needs of a growing family he gave up notarial work and became a cashier in an English bank. The Rebellion of 1837 enlisted his poetic talents in the *Patriote* interest, while the succeeding years of reaction drove him back to pure literature. He published the best French-Canadian verse of the period in *Le Canadien*, and then in 1840, with Etienne Parent and under the leadership of John Neilson and Edouard Glackmeyer, he threw himself into agitation against the Act of Union. In 1841, he launched another short-lived publication, *L'Institut*, devoted to science, industry, and literature.

After its collapse, he turned once more to his original determination to rally the French Canadians in this crucial hour by writing their history, in order 'to re-establish,' as he later wrote to Elgin, 'the truth which has been so often disfigured and to repel attacks and insults . . . on the part of men who wish to oppress and exploit them at the same time.' His aim, as he defined it for Lafontaine, was 'to impress upon this nationality a character which would make it respected in the future.'[26] Thus, at thirty-two, Garneau finally began his life work. He was a self-trained historian, but his masters were great men. Guizot taught him the importance of exact documentation. Thierry gave him the notions of atavistic survivals and of racial antagonisms; Montesquieu convinced him that environment and the popular will shape the evolution of a people. Raynal bolstered his liberalism; and Michelet taught him that the people constitute a collective being with an evolving soul. He was French Canada's first scientific historian, using original sources, analyzing and criticizing them, and declaring the truth as he found it.[27]

Garneau abandoned his cashier's position in favor of the post of French translator of the assembly, which gave him the leisure he needed for his researches. In 1842 he published a study on Jacques Cartier which appeared as his first book, after first being published in *Le Canadien.* In 1844 his friend Glackmeyer obtained for him a sinecure as Quebec City Clerk. Finally in August 1845 the first volume of his *Histoire du Canada depuis sa découverte jusqu'à nos jours* appeared. It was well received, although some ultramontanes criticized what they called its gallicanism as 'anti-Catholic and anti-Canadian,' and gave Garneau, as he himself remarked, a 'terrible reputation with vestrymen and sextons.'[28]

Before publishing his second volume in April 1846, Garneau made a trip to Albany to examine the Brodhead Papers, which were copies of official French documents in the Paris archives dealing with colonial history. These papers were under the care of Dr. O'Callaghan, Papineau's colleague in 1837, now historian of the State of New York, who was sympathetic to Garneau's purpose and gave him every aid. Soon after his return to Canada, Garneau consulted the transcripts which Papineau himself had brought back from Paris, in the hope of writing the history of the country in whose political development he had played such an active role. Papineau had one of the best historical libraries in Canada at his home at Montebello—Parkman took pains to consult it in 1856—and he had much in common with Garneau, whose 'love of historical truth' and whose 'independence in stating it' he admired.[29] For his part Garneau had nothing but respect for the great tribune, whose ardent supporter he had been up to 1837. The first great statesman and the first great historian of French Canada had frequent discussions after this first meeting, from which Garneau emerged with four precious volumes of Paris transcripts.

The third and final volume of his history, which stopped at 1792 appeared in 1848, arousing more attention in France than in Canada. It was reviewed most favorably in the *Revue Encyclopédique* of Paris by Isidore Lebrun, who considered Garneau a 'fellow Norman' and who had published a book on Canada in 1833.[30] The assembly then voted a grant of $1,000 to further Garneau's labors and in 1849 he was made a member of the Lower Canadian council of public instruction. Thus honored at home and abroad, he was less exposed to the criticism of the ultra-orthodox, who in any case had been largely won over by his affirmation in his third volume of the solidarity of religion and nationality in French Canada. Then Bishop Signay of Quebec completely disarmed the opposition by throwing open to him the diocesan archives, one of the richest sources for the history of New France. Garneau became one of the notables of French Canada, and was sought out by such distinguished visitors as the French academicians Marmier and Ampère in 1848 and in 1851. The French historian of Acadia, Rameau de Saint-Père, maintained a correspondence with him long after returning to France; and when Commandant de Belvèze came sailing up the St. Lawrence in 1855 in the frigate *La Capricieuse* on a goodwill mission one of his first requests was to be introduced to the historian of Canada.[31]

Despite the constant threat of epileptic attacks, Garneau did not rest upon his laurels, but continued his researches in order to revise the completed portion of his work and to carry the story down to 1840. Elgin opened the official correspondence of the governors-general to him, and in this pioneer period of American historical studies other great new stores of material were being uncovered from day to day by a host of students. A second edition of the *Histoire* was published in 1852, and was hailed by both Théodore Parie in the *Revue des Deux Mondes* and by Orestes Brownson in the *Quarterly Review* of Boston. Brownson congratulated the author on having written without bias or prejudice, and with a constant respect for principles and truth. This was high praise from the difficult doctor, a zealous Catholic convert who did not hesitate to lecture bishops on theology. Garneau became the leading spirit of the *Institut Canadien* of Quebec, which numbered among its members the poet Crémazie, whom Garneau inspired with his own love and knowledge of French-Canadian history, Pierre Chauveau, Jean-Charles Taché, and the elder Philippe Aubert de Gaspé, who favored the historian with his own rich recollections of three-quarters of a century. In 1854–5 Garneau published in *Le Journal de Québec*, an account of his youthful European tour, but his harsh words about former *Patriotes* who had become ministers under the Union and his evident republicanism aroused criticism, which made him suppress

La Pérade Church

ɜuilt in 1855, obviously under the influence of Notre Dame in Montreal. A disastrous ʋenture in a style foreign to Quebec's tradition, and an example of the *folie de grandeur* ʷhich was to burden many a small community with a cathedral instead of a church. (I.O.A.P.Q.)

Turtle Dove Hunt

Oil painting (1853) by Antoine-Sebastian Plaimondon, the first French Canadian to receive formal art education in Europe. Thanks to small boys' guns and farmers' flails, the once multitudinous turtle dove soon became extinct. (I.O.A.P.Q.)

the subsequent publication in book form of these *Voyages en Angleterre et en France (dans les années* 1831, 1832 *et* 1833).

As Garneau grew older and more conservative, and as he felt the powerful conformist influences of Quebec society, he decided to revise his history and modify its tone, as well as to incorporate in it the results of new researches and discoveries. In 1859 he published a third edition of the history, the last which he prepared himself, although he left materials for a fourth edition at his death in 1866. The 1859 edition was subjected to clerical censorship and lacks the ardor and the vigor of the earlier versions. Unfortunate as this revision was on literary and historical grounds, it cleared Garneau's name of the charges of anti-clericalism and free-thinking, and firmly established him as the national historian of French Canada. His history, which has never been surpassed by any French Canadian, though in part outmoded by time, became the 'national bible.' Its assertions of the essential relationship between 'our language, our laws, and our customs' and between faith and nationality have become French-Canadian dogmas. Garneau's preoccupation with ethnic and cultural survival, natural enough in the 1830's and 1840's, still haunts the French-Canadian mind, long after survival has been assured.

6

Garneau may fairly be considered the father of French-Canadian literature, although there had been isolated efforts before his time. The most notable of his precursors was Michel Bibaud, who edited a long series of short-lived periodicals, beginning with *La Bibliothèque Canadienne* in 1825, which provided a forum for Canadian writers. Bibaud's chief work was a history of Canada, intended as a reply to William Smith's ultra-Loyalist account, which first appeared serially in these magazines and was later brought out in three volumes in 1837, 1844 and 1878. A Bureaucrat, Bibaud was bitterly opposed to the *Patriotes* and biased in favor of the Chateau Clique. His ponderous history, which is often a mere undigested collection of documents, was completely put in the shade by Garneau's interpretive work.

Bibaud also tried his hand at poetry, producing in 1830 a volume of very dreary and pedestrian verse, whose classical inspiration is evident in its title, *Epîtres, satires, chansons, épigrammes*. This book, dedicated to Boileau and imitating him closely, is chiefly notable for the four satires against avarice, envy, laziness, and ignorance, which first appeared in the newspaper *L'Aurore* from 1815 to 1819. To Bibaud's mind these were the chief vices of the French Canadian, and he devoted his life to a crusade to banish at least one of them, ignorance, from Quebec. He began as a teacher, and then shifted in 1813 to journalism, which remained his chief occupation for thirty years. He founded no less than two newspapers and four reviews, all of which followed the same pattern: chapters of his history of Canada, articles on geography and scientific subjects, extracts from the European and American press, and comments on Canadian politics, education, and letters. Not content with this effort, he edited popular manuals, made translations, and encouraged his contemporaries to undertake similar labors for the enlightenment of the people.

Bibaud had a strong moralistic strain—the preface of his history begins: 'All men ought to desire to know the history of their country and their nation'[32]—and in his verse he set himself up as a Canadian Cato, condemning the faults of his countrymen. Bibaud's zeal and industry were greater than his talent: he himself admitted that he was 'more rhymer than poet.'[33] This self-judgment is surely just, since he found twenty-six rhymes for 'Quebec'. The much-revised history never became either readable or authoritative, despite his best efforts. His place is as a transition figure in the shift of French-Canadian expression from journalism to literature and history. Bibaud was a voice in the cultural wilderness, calling the French Canadians to greater creative effort.

One of Bibaud's most faithful collaborators was his schoolmate, the antiquarian Jacques Viger, who began his career as editor of *Le Canadien* in 1808–9. In 1810 he compiled his '*Néologie canadienne*,' a lexicon of Canadianisms. During the War of 1812 Viger served as a lieutenant in de Salaberry's *Voltigeurs*, keeping an interesting diary, '*Mes Tablettes de* 1813,' which Bibaud published in the second and third volumes of the *Bibliothèque Canadienne*. After the war Viger entered the municipal government of Montreal, becoming the first mayor of the city in 1833. He was an antiquarian by avocation and in the tradition of the *cahier*-keeping *philosophes* compiled a series of forty-four notebooks and scrapbooks, which he called '*Ma Saberdache*.' These contain copies of documents, reports, manuscripts, maps, plans, statistics, and other materials for the history of Canada, frequently annotated by Viger; as well as autographs, paintings, watercolors, and prints concerned with the same subject. Viger became an authority consulted by all concerned with the history of Canada, though he published only an account of the '*Régime militaire*' (1760–4) and two papers on Montreal history. He saved from destruction much valuable material which might well have perished before the belated foundation of Canadian archives. He was the first of a line of amateur archivists and antiquarians, tireless researchers rarely ready to write, who have done yeoman service for the cause of history in Quebec.

Viger's immediate successor in this role was his friend Georges-Barthélemi Faribault, a government clerk and translator from 1822 to 1855, who devoted his spare time to collecting books and manuscripts concerned with the history of Canada. In 1837 he published a pioneer bibliography of Canadiana, his *Catalogue d'ouvrages sur l'histoire de l'Amérique et en particulier sur celle du Canada, de la Louisiane, de l'Acadie et autres lieux ci-devant connus sous le nom de Nouvelle-France.* Faribault's first collection of more than 1,600 volumes was lost in 1849, when the Parliament Buildings at Montreal were burned by the mob. Two years later Faribault, who at sixty had promptly set to work to replace the loss, was sent to Europe by the government to complete his task. His second collection consisted of nearly 2,000 volumes, of which 700 were lost when the government building in Quebec burned in 1854. Having thus seen the fruits of his labor twice destroyed, Faribault retired in broken health to private life; but before his death in 1866 he had built up another collection of Canadiana, including 400 manuscripts, 1,000 books, and an album of maps, plans, and pictures.[34]

In 1837 appeared the first French-Canadian novel, the younger Philippe Aubert de Gaspé's *L'Influence d'un livre*, a romantic tale of black magic on the lower St. Lawrence. The rather thin plot is eked out by the inclusion of many legends of the region, which echo the beliefs and superstitions of the early settlers. In 1844 Joseph Doutre, later a leading *Rouge*, published his *Les Fiancées de 1812*, a highly melodramatic story in which true love triumphs over all obstacles. Doutre was only nineteen when his work appeared, while de Gaspé produced his at twenty-three. Both books have all the faults of youthful efforts, but they mark a considerable advance on the sketchy short stories and legends which began to appear in 1827 as the newspapers became more literary in tone, and which have been preserved in Huston's *Répertoire National*, the first anthology of French-Canadian literature, which was published in 1851. But the first really notable work in fiction was Pierre Chauveau's *Charles Guérin*, published anonymously in 1846 in the *Revue Canadienne* and then under its author's signature as a book in 1853. When his novel first appeared, Chauveau had just begun the political career which was to lead him to the premiership of Quebec. Since literature was then regarded as a mere pastime—a young man could be dismissed with a 'he does nothing—he writes'[35]—he deemed it best to conceal his connection with the work, lest he be branded as a ne'er-do-well. But the tale won acclaim in France, and as ever since in a provincial culture, this latter consideration was decisive as far as French-Canadian opinion was concerned.

Charles Guérin is a realistic novel on a theme which was to become all too familiar with the years: the plight of the classical college graduate faced by the congestion of the professions, the only role in life for which he was prepared. Chauveau's statement of the problem in 1846 has been echoed again and again down to the present day:

> In French Canada one must be doctor, priest, notary, or lawyer. Outside of these four professions it seems that there is no salvation for the young educated Canadian. If by chance one of us had an invincible distaste for all four; if it was too painful to him to save souls, mutilate bodies, or lose fortunes, there remained only one course for him to take if he were rich, and two if he were poor; to do nothing at all in the first case, to exile himself or to starve to death in the second.[36]

Charles Guérin plans to enter the priesthood; then, when financial ruin threatens his widowed mother, thanks to the machinations of an unscrupulous Protestant Channel Islander,[37] he turns to the study of law. During a country holiday he falls in love with a farmer's daughter. But once back in Quebec City and in his own world of the élite, he falls under the spell of the Channel Islander's daughter. While thus blinded by love, he is tricked by her father into signing away his heritage, so that his whole family is reduced to misery. His mother dies during a cholera epidemic, and he is forced to give up his studies. The once scorned country girl is now an heiress; she and Charles marry and become colonists in the undeveloped region of Quebec.

The tale is well constructed and moves rapidly; Chauveau's style, modeled on that of Chateaubriand, is pleasant. He makes skillful use of Canadianisms in the mouths of his rustic characters, without wearying the reader with them. But the great merit of the book is the clear picture of the times which it supplies, and its enunciation of certain themes which were to become traditional in French-Canadian literature. Such are the dilemma which confronts the young man educated only for the professions in a country where the professions are always overcrowded; the gulf between the élite and the *habitants*, often crossed of necessity because the superior commercial ability of cultural aliens forces members of the élite from their privileged position; the hymning of the rural life as the salvation of the French Canadians. In later life Chauveau became the second superintendent of public instruction, and like his predecessor, Dr. Jean-Baptiste Meilleur, he sought to liberalize the traditional educational system of Quebec in the light of European and American developments, giving more place to practical and vocational training. But the strength of tradition in Quebec and of French-Canadian resistance to change are evidenced by the fact that novels of recent years are still concerned with the same themes as *Charles Guérin*, though a century has passed.

7

Antoine Gérin-Lajoie was another of the early French-Canadian writers who helped to establish the tradition from which Quebec authors have not deviated until recent years. The eldest of the sixteen children of a *habitant* family of Yamachiche, young Gérin made his mark at the Collège de Nicolet, where at eighteen he wrote a three-act tragedy, *Le Jeune Latour*. This play, strongly inspired by the tradition of Corneille, was based upon a legend of the early days of Acadia, which was revived by Michel Bibaud in his *Histoire du Canada*. Its hymning of the faithfulness to France of the younger Latour, who refused to follow his turncoat father's course in the days of the privateering Kirkes, made it a great success when first performed at the college exercises, and won publication for it in 1844 in *L'Aurore des Canadas*, in *Le Canadien*, and finally in a brochure dedicated to the governor-general, Lord Metcalfe, who rewarded the young author with $25 and his compliments. While still a student, Gérin-Lajoie also wrote one of the most popular French-Canadian songs, *Un Canadien errant*, which admirably expressed the yearning homesickness of the political exiles of 1837–8. Upon his graduation from Nicolet in 1844, Gérin-Lajoie journeyed to New York to learn English, but failing to find employment as a teacher of French—the English-speaking prejudice, fostered by Frenchmen, against French Canadians in this capacity had already developed—he was forced to return ingloriously homeward after seventeen days, instead of the two years on which he had planned.

Back in Montreal he found that his literary reputation brought him only a $2-a-week position as Ludger Duvernay's assistant on *La Minerve*. In the spring of 1845 he became secretary of the Saint-Jean-Baptiste Society which his employer had founded; and several months later he was chosen president of the *Institut Canadien*, a literary and scientific society which served as a center for young intellectuals after its foundation in 1844. Gérin's health was unable to withstand the burden of his largely unremunerated patriotic labors, and in 1847 he resumed the study of law, his first choice of a profession. But his initiation into political life as a parliamentary correspondent soon led him back into politics as the secretary of Augustin-Norbert Morin, the founder of *La Minerve* and speaker of the assembly from 1848 to 1851. The violence of political debates in the era when Lafontaine's and Papineau's followers were at one another's throats soon disgusted the timid and scrupulous Gérin-Lajoie with political life. Failing to win success at the bar, to which he was admitted in 1848, he gladly accepted a post as copyist and paymaster in the Department of Public Works when the French

Canadians first received a share of patronage. With the exception of a few months, the rest of his life was passed as a civil servant in varying capacities.

But as early as 1849 he confided to his journal his disgust with the various white-collar occupations which had fallen to his lot, and his idealization of the rural life:

> I have returned to my project of going to live in the country as soon as possible . . . Oh, if only I were a farmer! . . . He does not become rich by beggaring others, as lawyers, doctors, and merchants sometimes do. He draws his wealth from the earth: his is the state most natural to man. Farmers form the least egotistical and most virtuous class of the population. But this class has need of educated men who can serve its interests. The educated farmer has all the leisure necessary to do good; he can serve as guide to his neighbors, counsel the ignorant, sustain the weak, and defend him against the rapacity of the speculator. The enlightened and virtuous farmer is to my mind the best type of man.[38]

Thus the atavistic call of generations of *habitants* was deeply felt while at the same time Gérin-Lajoie wrote a popular *Catéchisme politique* published in 1851, and in 1852 spent some months at Boston in order to improve his English and to prepare a study of the political, social, religious, and industrial development of the United States. The agrarian theme announced in his journal took more than a decade to ripen, while Gérin-Lajoie earned his living first as translator for the House of Commons and after 1856 as assistant parliamentary librarian. In the latter capacity he prepared the first catalogue of the Parliamentary Library, published in 1857–8. During the stay of the government at Toronto, Gérin-Lajoie became an intimate of Etienne Parent, then deputy provincial secretary of Lower Canada, and married his eldest daughter in 1858.

When the government moved to Quebec in 1859, Gérin-Lajoie fell in with the literary group which made Octave Crémazie's bookshop on the Rue de la Fabrique its headquarters. Here came Gérin-Lajoie's father-in-law, Parent; his professor of history at Nicolet, Abbé J.-B.-A. Ferland, then giving at Laval, the first French-Canadian university (1852), a popular course on the history of the French regime which was inspired by Garneau's work; and Garneau himself in all the glory of his last years. There were also the younger men who launched in 1860 the literary movement known as the Patriotic School of Quebec: Dr. Hubert LaRue, the brilliant young scientist just beginning his teaching career at Laval after studies at Louvain and Paris; Joseph-Charles Taché, the journalistic collaborator of Pierre Chauveau in the satiric *Les Guêpes Canadiennes* and the author of a study of the Confederation question (1850) and of a sketchy account of Canada, written for the Paris Exposition of

1855; and Abbé Henri-Raymond Casgrain, who had been inspired by Garneau's work to popularize Canadian history and to 'create,'[39] to use his own term, a Canadian literature.

In 1861 Gérin-Lajoie joined with LaRue, Taché, and Casgrain in launching *Les Soirées Canadiennes*, a monthly magazine announced as a 'collection of national literature.' The motto of *Les Soirées* was a quotation from Charles Nodier, the author of the original *Trilby*, 'Let us hasten to tell the delightful tales of the people, before they have been forgotten,' and the magazine sought to record the folklore of the pre-literary period in Quebec. LaRue was a man after Gérin-Lajoie's heart: a great popularizer of scientific knowledge who applied on his Ile d'Orléans farm the theories he taught at the university and expounded in a series of manuals for the common man; an intellectual who nonetheless shared Gérin-Lajoie's cult of the *habitant* as the best type of French Canadian. LaRue and Taché contributed folk-songs and popular legends to the magazine, thus continuing the vein opened by Abbé Casgrain in 1860 with his *Légendes Canadiennes*, which recounted old Canadian customs. Taché's specialty was the life of the lumberjacks and the tall tales told in their shanties (*chantiers*); while LaRue devoted himself to the *habitants* of his beloved Ile d'Orléans and Casgrain, the heir of an old seigneurial family of the Lower St. Lawrence, romanticized the rich folklore of that region. Under such influences Gérin-Lajoie wrote his *Jean Rivard, le défricheur*, which appeared in *Les Soirées* during 1862.

Gérin-Lajoie himself called this work 'a little tale which will scarcely please the young literary men, but which I have written for the public good.'[40] He was impelled by love of his country and concern for the future of the French Canadians to preach a return to the land, and the necessity of hard work and frugality guided by education. He evoked the great tradition of French-Canadian history in his epic of young Jean Rivard, who having finished his studies and having little capital beyond his robust health, his love of independence and of outdoor life, and a desire to serve his country, rejects the usual alternatives of seeking his fortune in the city or of emigrating to the States, and undertakes the hard life of a colonist in the wilderness of the Eastern Townships. Here Jean Rivard, with the aid of a single companion, clears a farm for himself, and establishes a home for his sweetheart. Thanks to his example, a new parish is born and an outlet is established for the surplus population of the old settlements along the St. Lawrence, from which a significant number of young men were already in the 1860's beginning to drift away to the mill towns of New England, there to be absorbed into the American melting pot and lost to French Canada. Gérin-Lajoie's book is at once a colonist's guide, an inspirational sermon, and a sociological treatise.

It is not a conventional novel, as the foreword makes clear: 'This is not a romance, and if anyone seeks marvellous adventures, duels, murders, suicides, or amorous intrigues, no matter how uncomplicated, I advise him in friendly fashion to seek them elsewhere. In this tale will be found only the true and simple history of a young man without fortune, born to a humble state, who knew how to raise himself by his own merit to an independent position and the first honors of his country.'[41] But despite Gérin-Lajoie's abandonment of the whole apparatus of romantic fiction, then the delight of the French-Canadian élite, the author's passionate sincerity and his ability to give an epic quality to his account of his hero's struggle with the wilderness made the book at once a classic. Far better than *Charles Guérin*, it succeeded in accomplishing the author's purpose of 'encouraging our Canadian youth to turn towards the agricultural career, instead of encumbering the professions of lawyer, notary, and doctor and the counters of merchants, as it increasingly does, to the great detriment of the public and national interest.'[42]

It met with such popularity that Gérin-Lajoie was urged to continue the tale, which he did in *Jean Rivard, économiste*, published in *Le Foyer canadien* (an offshoot of *Les Soirées*) in 1864. The second part of this epic of colonization carries on the history of Rivard's settlement as it develops into a prosperous town, while the hero becomes in turn mayor, militia major, justice of the peace, and finally member of parliament, from which exalted dignity he finally retires in order to find happiness again on his own land, after revealing the secrets of his success and laying down the principles of successful colonization. More clearly than in the first book, Jean Rivard is revealed as Gérin-Lajoie himself, no farmer but an intellectual in love with rural life. The author thus established a literary vein which was to be worked and reworked by many French-Canadian leaders in later generations, urban intellectuals themselves but sincerely convinced that the salvation of their people lay in the land. *Jean Rivard* remains essential reading today for those who would understand the French-Canadian mind, with its distrust of the urban industrial civilization of the rest of the continent, which it cannot reconcile with its own patriarchal rural tradition.

8

The role of Octave Crémazie in launching the Patriotic School of Quebec has been somewhat overshadowed by the fact that bankruptcy forced him into exile in 1862, just as the movement got well under way, while his colleague Abbé Casgrain remained in Quebec and became the leading spirit of the group and finally its historian. But Crémazie really shares with Garneau the fatherhood of French-Canadian literature, and the slim body of his work constitutes one of its corner stones. Casgrain, who maintained a correspondence with the exiled poet which reveals how great Crémazie's influence was upon his own critical ideas, and finally collected and published Crémazie's works in 1882, under the auspices of the *Institut Canadien*, himself judged that 'No one had a greater part in the literary awakening of 1860 than he.'[43]

Crémazie was descended from a Languedoc forebear who came to Canada in 1759, in the last days of New France. This heritage, in a land where genealogy is taken with tremendous seriousness, may have had something to do with the poet's preoccupation with the theme of faithfulness to France. Befriended as a student at Laval by the Abbé Jean Holmes, the great Vermont-born educational reformer and preacher of Quebec in the 1830's and 1840's, Crémazie early became a dweller in the world of ideas, as familiar with English, German, Italian, and Spanish literature as with French, and even learning Sanscrit. Of necessity he earned his living in the family bookstore, which after 1846 served the Upper Town of Quebec as a storehouse for the French Romantic writers of the school of 1830. His mind was less concerned with trade than with his studies and with the Hugoline verses which he composed mentally, long before he put them on paper. In latter years he regretted the way of life which had been forced upon him by the impossibility of earning a living in Canada as an intellectual, and complained bitterly that it had made him 'a bad merchant and a mediocre poet.'[44] But it is clear from Casgrain's biographical account that the attraction of Crémazie's astonishing erudition drew the literary men of Quebec to the dim backroom of the bookstores where this poet, physically disguised as a stolid bourgeois with 'all the virtues of an epitaph,'[45] held forth to his chosen friends, and made of the casual circle a coherent literary group.

Crémazie published his first verses in 1854, hymning the Anglo-French alliance in the Crimean War as an example for Canadians, 'children of these two races of which the whole world bears the noble traces.'[46] With ardent patriotism, he opposed annexationism and proclaimed that the French Canadians would revive the memory of Chateauguay and support the British flag if their country should be threatened by American ambition. In August of the following year, during the goodwill visit of the corvette *La Capricieuse*, which brought the French flag to the St. Lawrence for the first time since the Conquest, Crémazie wrote his 'Vieux Soldat Canadien,' one of his best known and most typical poems. It is based upon a legend of an old soldier of Montcalm who, remaining confident until his death that France would return to Canada, had visited the ramparts of Quebec during the great days of Napoleon, awaiting the sight of the French flag in the river, and had died expressing his belief that his son would see the great day when the French came back. Crémazie imagines this veteran and all the old Canadians roused from their graves by the sound of French cannon, and welcoming the display of the French flag from the ramparts of Quebec. In a final address to the sailors of *La Capricieuse*, the poet urges them to report that the Canadians had cherished the memory of France and conserved their heritage; that their heart still belonged to France, if their allegiance was to England.

It was long a carefully nourished legend in Quebec that the visit of *La Capricieuse* marked the resumption of cultural relations with France for the first time since the Conquest, and that romanticism then first crossed the seas and began to supplant the classicism of the eighteenth century French-Canadian tradition. This theory has been completely demolished by a close study of the French-Canadian press after 1800, which reveals that most of the Romantic authors and their books were well known in Canada only a few years after they made their mark in France. Rousseau was read in Canada as early as 1795; Bernardin de Saint-Pierre, the author of *Paul et Virginie*, as early as 1802; Chateaubriand by 1817; Béranger as early as 1829. Lamartine's and Victor Hugo's poems were first offered for sale in Canada in 1837, and the former, with his love of the country and his cult of the native heath, became the most popular of the Romantics with the French Canadians, and almost an obsession by the 1850's. The novels of Hugo, George Sand, the elder Dumas, Eugene Sue, and even Balzac were imported by the booksellers of Montreal and Quebec within a few years, and in some cases a few months, after their appearance at Paris.

It is true that the book-buying public in Canada was not large; but the Romantic authors reached a much greater audience, since they were put under contribution by the editors of the Canadian newspapers, which were also literary reviews. Lamartine and Victor Hugo were to be found in the pages of *La Minerve* by 1829 and 1831; Lamartine and Chateaubriand in *Le Canadien* by 1834. The editors picked and chose their selections carefully to avoid wounding the pious susceptibilities of their readers: the more indecorous features of Romanticism were slighted. French and French-Canadian literature were mingled from the outset. The youthful verses of Garneau appeared side by side with those of the great Romantics in the pages of Parent's *Le Canadien*, which more than any other newspaper of the period encouraged Canadian writers. In the 1840's the journals were full of Chateaubriand, Lamartine, and Hugo, as well as translations of Walter Scott; and in the late 1850's the early verses of Crémazie and Pamphile Lemay rubbed shoulders with those of their avowed masters.

The visit of *La Capricieuse*, then, did not introduce Romanticism to Canada, where since 1800 the authors most in demand in the bookstores had been, in order of popularity, Voltaire, Bossuet,

Bourdaloue, Fénelon, Fléchier, Massilon, Molière, Racine, La Fontaine, Corneille, Madame de Sévigné, Boileau, Rousseau, Bernardin de Saint-Pierre, and Chateaubriand, and where La Fontaine, Lamartine, Rousseau, Chateaubriand, Béranger, Voltaire, Bernardin de Saint-Pierre, and Victor Hugo, in that order, were most often pillaged by editors seeking to enrich their journals with borrowed jewels.[47] But *La Capricieuse* did bring to Canada a noteworthy collection of French books and pictures, with which Louis Napoleon endowed the *Instituts Canadiens* of Quebec, Montreal, and Ottawa, founded in 1847, 1844, and 1852. Thus the masterpieces of modern French literature were made available to a much larger audience than the small number who could afford to buy the books for themselves.

The coming of *La Capricieuse* and the great public demonstrations which everywhere greeted its captain, the Commandant de Belvèze, also ended the coldness which had existed between the ancient mother country and its former colony ever since the French Revolution. A distrust of the new France had been instilled into the French-Canadian mind by the considerable number of emigré clergy who settled in Quebec after the Revolution; and this distrust, coupled with the ultramontane tradition established in the days of Bishop Laval, had tended to make Rome rather than Paris the intellectual capital of French Canada. The Revolution of 1848, despite its influences upon the largely discredited Papineau and his disciples among the young republican *Rouges* of *L'Avenir* and *Le Pays*, did little to alter the sentiments of the masses, carefully guided by their conservative monarchist leaders, both lay and clerical. But the Anglo-French Alliance of 1854, sealed by the exchange of state visits by Queen Victoria and Louis Napoleon in 1855, opened a new era of good feeling between the ancient and modern mother countries of Canada.

Louis Napoleon, whose North American imperialism was to develop six years later into the tragic Mexican adventure of Maximilien, took the opportunity thus afforded to open relations with French Canada. These relations were professedly commercial, but Commandant de Belvèze was ordered not only to report on 'the commerce, transport, agriculture, and industry' of French Canada, but also on 'the political, moral, religious, and military situation'[48] of the country. The only portion of this report which has ever been made public was de Belvèze's description of his reception; and considering the coolness which developed between the British authorities in Canada and Belvèze, resulting in his reprimand by the French government at the request of London, it is possible that de Belvèze revealed the ambitions of his imperial master a little too clearly while in Canada.[49] Old seadogs are not the best diplomats—the commandant found making speeches to an English governor and a French and Catholic people 'an acrobat's job'—and in any case de

Belvèze's reception was so enthusiastic as to excuse some indiscretion. His role was made more difficult by the appearance of J.-G. Barthe's *Le Canada reconquis par la France* (Paris, 1855), with a preface by Enre de Carondel suggesting the cession of Quebec to France.

De Belvèze's own description of his visit, written to a friend in France from Cape Breton Island on his homeward voyage, is a curious document, revealing a cynicism which contrasts strangely with Crémazie's impassioned idealization of his mission:

Capricieuse, Sidney, Aug. 29, 1855.

My dear friend:

As you will not be obliged to answer this letter, I am pleased to recall myself to your memory and that of your good family, and to give you some details of my strange peregrinations. First of all, we are well, I as well as Waresquiel, and I think, with God's help, that towards the month of November favoring winds will bring us safe and sound to our beautiful France, the finest country in the world.

I arrive from Canada where I have made the most marvellous journey which can be described. Imagine the banner of France reappearing after a century's absence in our ancient colony and finding there the memory and the love of the old mother country dormant at the bottom of men's hearts, and the explosion of this sentiment bursting out everywhere, even among the English population, which, thanks to the alliance, also had to celebrate by frantic hurrahs the arrival of the representative of 'the mighty ally of their gracious sovereign' (such was their expression for your humble friend). Thus I made a princely progress across 800 leagues of rivers, lakes, and railroads, passing under I know not how many triumphal arches, finding night and day the civic fathers awaiting me at the entrance of their towns, address in hand, and finding myself, poor wretch, obliged to reply to all that by *beautiful* and *good* speeches that later must be paraphrased mercilessly at banquets, in toasts, etc., etc. What an excessive outlay of oratory I made in these three weeks!! Twenty addresses to reply to, more than fifty speeches to make, one of them on the Champs de Mars (at Montreal) before 10,000 people, while mounted on a carriage like Mangin of comic memory, and all to the accompaniment of saluting cannons, fireworks, etc. If I did not die of indigestion, I was apt to die of vanity; happily my stomach and my common sense saved me from both fates. When I read to Madame de Waresquiel the hyperbole-stuffed articles of the newspapers of Saint-Pierre with regard to my august person, I count on giving her one of those laughing fits with which I used to supply her in my best days. The fact is that I fulfilled there, as one of these worthy journals said, the function of a sovereign who visits his states, and I assure you it is a gruelling profession, and that I prefer that of the Parisian bourgeois.

I went from Quebec to Niagara Falls, following always the waterways; I returned by the river, descending the rapids, a marvellous spectacle of which one will never get an idea in Europe. I even descended one of the great rapids of the Saint-Maurice in a birchbark canoe, like an Iroquois. It would take a book to tell you the details of this marvellous voyage, and I have the materials with which to spin yarns to you during many evenings. I hope that your uncle will take some interest in these accounts, so different from what may be seen in our country. I have had an unhoped success from the political and commercial point of view, and I return from this country, where antagonisms always grate upon one another, without having indisposed anyone, a feat of which the difficulty was such that no one believed it could be accomplished. But, my very dear friend, no one is a prophet in his own country, and while here one exclaims, 'Fortunate France, which possesses such men!' (always hyperbole), at home batches of rear-admirals have been named and I am left aside. What's to be done? I have now behind me enough proof so that no one, not even myself, has the right to consider me an idiot. If then the Navy does not wish to make anything of me, or do anything for me, one must console oneself for it with: *Exegi monumentum* . . . I can do no more than rest on my laurels.[50]

The Commandant de Belvèze flattered himself somewhat unduly on the success of his mission, at least in one respect, for the U.E.L.-minded governor-general, Sir Edmund Walker Head, took offence at the enthusiasm which the visitor evoked among the French Canadians, and his protests to London had the effect of ruining de Belvèze's career. Crémazie flayed the governor's attitude in his poem 'Sur les Ruines de Sébastopol,' written at the close of the year, which hymned the Anglo-French victory in the Crimea and poured out an extravagant eulogy of France, 'home of glory and land of genius,'[51] whose joys and sorrows were always echoed on the shores of the St. Lawrence by her ever faithful sons. It is clear that the governor-general fell into the error, so frequently repeated since by ultra-loyal English Canadians, of taking the French Canadians' professions of sympathy with France too seriously and of conceiving that they were more French than Canadian. Belvèze urged his government to cultivate 'the remains of our nationality, not with an intent of absorption and conquest, but in the interest of our political and commercial relations,' but he thought independence or annexation would drown French-Canadian nationality. The France to which French Canadians profess loyalty perished in 1789, but the language barrier and the long survival of both French and British cultural colonialism in Canada have encouraged mistaken notions of the Frenchness of French Canada.

The true nature of French-Canadian faithfulness to France is revealed clearly in Crémazie's later work, which owed much of its inspiration to Garneau. It is best exemplified in his most famous poem, 'Le Drapeau de Carillon,'[52] which tells of an old soldier of Montcalm who cherished the white banner of Louis XV's France, after 'the Canadian heroes had been betrayed but not conquered,' and bore it to Versailles, in the hope of persuading the 'weak Bourbon' to come to the aid of his lost colony. But the Voltairean-minded courtiers asked of what value 'some acres of snow' were to the king, whose sole devotion was to pleasure; and the old soldier returned sorrowfully homeward, seeking his lasting place on the hill of Carillon (Ticonderoga), where he planted once more the banner which had there won eternal glory. In a powerful closing passage Crémazie hymned the old French flag as 'a living witness of the glorious exploits of a warrior race' and 'the radiant relic of a great epoch,' around which the French Canadians should rally, with the sacred tradition of its memories ruling their hearts and guarding their tongue and their faith from all attacks.

In another poem written in the same year (1858) on Canada, Crémazie formulates the French Canadian's love of his own land, on whose enchanted shores France had left an immortal mark. This lyric closes with a significant expression of French-Canadian isolationism:

> Happy he who knows this land, happier he who inhabits it,
> And, never leaving to seek other climes
> The shores of the great river where fortune bestows him,
> Knows how to live and to die where his fathers sleep.[53]

Crémazie might eulogize Napoleon in 'Un Soldat de L'Empire,' but it was as the hero who revived the great tradition of France in the days of Louis XIV's empire. As the poet's talent developed, he displayed a growing fondness for Canadian themes, turning from them only occasionally, as when he hailed French intervention in behalf of the Papacy in the Italian Revolution of 1859–60. His only two poems not devoted to his favorite themes of love of Canada and faithfulness to France are the melancholy 'Les Morts' and the morbid unfinished 'Promenade de Trois Morts,' which is more reminiscent of Théophile Gautier than of Victor Hugo, Crémazie's chosen model.

9

In the fall of 1862 financial catastrophe forced the poet-bookseller to flee to France. He wrote no poetry there, save a few occasional verses in honor of Hector Bossange, a former Montreal bookseller, and his wife, who befriended the exile, broken in both mental and physical health. But from time to time Crémazie wrote Abbé Casgrain, who sought him out when visiting Paris and once found employment for him as Parkman's copyist in the archives.[54] These letters constitute a notable literary testament which has been too much neglected. Writing to his mother and his brothers, Crémazie expressed his homesickness and his disillusionment with the France which he had hymned so lovingly while in Canada. He found the French peasant far less fortunate than the *habitant* of Quebec; he thought the expedients of Louis Napoleon's opposition would be ridiculous in America, where there was freedom of assembly and of the press; though he judged that the eloquence of Thiers threw that of the Canadian orators into the shade. In 1860 he remained confident almost to the end that France would overcome the Prussians—it is interesting to note that he thought that through religious bias England and even the French Protestants favored Protestant Prussia, and that the conquest of Catholic France would be 'the beginning of the end of the Latin race.'[55] He kept a 'Journal of the Siege of Paris' which bears witness to his gradual disillusionment in France's military might, and closes with the hope that, this hard lesson learned, it might once more be possible to speak of *Gesta Dei per Francos*.*[56]

With the establishment of the Commune at Paris in 1871, Crémazie completely lost his faith in the French. He considered them degenerate: 'Without religious beliefs, without fixed political principles, having respect neither for family or woman, having abused all material possessions during the twenty years of the Empire, which was an epoch of well being and richness previously unknown in the country, the French have lost all which constitutes the strength and honor of a country, all, even to the love of country.'[57] When his brother in Quebec informed him that a political charge of gallicanism had been made against the law faculty of Laval, he replied with bitterness: 'Here it is "liberty;" at home it is "true principles" which aid the ambitious to rise to power.' He found himself agreeing with Louis Veuillot that 'the immortal principles of '89 have caused more harm to humanity than all the tyrants whose names are consecrated by history to the malediction of their peoples'; and he vowed that if Louis XIV 'of despotic memory' should return to earth, he himself would cry with all his strength: 'Long live the great king! Down with liberty!' Like a true French Canadian, he was a monarchist sympathetic to republican principles, a contradiction in terms which can only be explained by the course of British constitutional development in Canada.

In his correspondence with Abbé Casgrain, Crémazie wrote the first noteworthy French-Canadian literary criticism. His critical sense was better developed than that of the enthusiastic propagandist of the Patriotic School of Quebec; and he was personally familiar, in a way that the socially-privileged Abbé could not be, with the obstacles which beset the path of the French-Canadian writer. He deplored the tendency evident in *Le Foyer Canadien* to print only established French-Canadian writers, and to give place to well known French authors instead of encouraging unknown young Canadians. When Casgrain published an ardent article on the literary movement in Canada, Crémazie checked him with some sober reflections:

* 'God's great deeds are done by the French.'

MM. Garneau and Ferland have already, it is true, supplied a granite base for our literary edifice; but if one bird does not make a spring, two books do not constitute a literature. All that has been produced by us, beyond these two great works, seems to me to have no chance of survival. Who will read ——— in fifty years? And if I may speak of myself, who will think of my poor verses in twenty years?

We have then only two noteworthy works, the monuments raised by MM. Garneau and Ferland. In poetry, in fiction, we have only second-class works. Tragedy, the drama, are still to be born. The cause of this inferiority lies not in the rarity of men of talent, but in the disastrous environment provided for the writer by the indifference of a population which has as yet no taste for letters, at least for works produced by native sons.

. . . . .

Canadian writers are placed in the same situation as those of the Middle Ages. Their pens, unless they engage in politics (and God knows the literature that we owe to the tirades of political pundits), cannot suffice for their least needs. When a young man leaves college, his greatest ambition is to have his prose or his verse inserted in some journal. On the day that he first sees his name emblazoned at the foot of an article of his making, he believes himself called to the highest destinies; and he dreams that he is the equal of Lamartine, if he devotes himself to poetry; of Balzac, if he has attempted the novel. And when he passes under St. John's Gate, he takes good care to bend, lest he bump his head. These foolish vanities of youth soon vanish before the daily cares of life. Perhaps he continues to work for a year or two; then one day his voice is silent. The need of gaining his daily bread has imposed upon him the harsh necessity of devoting his life to certain arid occupations, which will blight in him the sweet flowers of the imagination and break the intimate and delicate fibers of poetic sensibility. How many of your young talents have produced flowers which promised magnificent fruit; but their fate has been like those of certain fruits of the earth. A frost came which chilled forever the fire of their intelligence. This wintry wind which freezes sparkling spirits is the *res angusta domi* of which Horace speaks; it is the need of daily bread.

Under such conditions it is a misfortune to have received from heaven a portion of the divine fire. Since one cannot earn one's living by the ideas which boil in one's brain, one must seek employment, which is nearly always contrary to one's tastes. The most usual result is that one becomes a bad employee and a bad writer. Permit me to cite myself as an example. If I had not received at birth, at least the taste, if not the talent, for poetry, I should not have had my head stuffed with fancies which made me enter upon commerce as a means of existence, never as a serious end in life. I should have broken myself in entirely to business, and today I should have an assured future. Instead of that, what has happened? I have been a bad merchant and a mediocre poet.[58]

Crémazie criticized Casgrain for virtually giving away *Les Soirées Canadiennes*, while the review's writers went unpaid. He insisted upon the necessity of the artist being properly rewarded for his work, and urged the foundation of a joint stock company to underwrite a magazine which would pay its authors decently until it was established in the popular taste. He pointed out that capital was constantly poured into enterprises which were much more risky, and which lacked the merit 'of contributing to preserve our tongue, the second guardian of our nationality, since religion is the first.'[59] He singled out the lack of French-Canadian literary criticism, then represented only by the same sort of logrolling as was the lot of the hatter or dressmaker who bribed an editor. In urging Casgrain to deal out condemnation as well as praise when writing of French-Canadian literature, he observed: 'No one is better gifted than you to create literary criticism in Canada.' He summed up his views with the reflection that 'so long as our writers find themselves in the same situation as at present, Canada can indeed have, as in the past, literary accidents from time to time, but she will not have a national literature.'

In another letter Crémazie was roused to reflections on French-Canadian society by Casgrain's news that *Les Soirées Canadiennes*' circulation had dwindled to a few hundreds, while *Le Foyer* had had two thousand subscribers to start with. He denounced Quebec's 'society of grocers.'[60] By this term he meant the professional men whose intellectual interests were limited to their profession, for whom knowledge was only a tool: 'In such natures petrified by routine, thought has no horizon. For them, French literature does not exist after the eighteenth century.' The masterpieces of foreign literatures were completely unknown and of no concern to them; how should they be interested in an infant literature?

> Patriotism should perhaps take the place of a taste for letters in influencing them to encourage all which tends to preserve the language of their fathers. Alas, you know as well as I that our 'wealthy and educated gentlemen' understand love of their country only when it appears in the form of railroad and goldmining shares promising fat dividends; or again when it offers the prospect of political honors, appointments, and above all chances for 'jobs.' With such men you will make good fathers, having all the virtues of an epitaph; you will have aldermen, churchwardens, members of parliament, even ministers, but you will never succeed in creating a society which may be called literary, artistic, and I may even say patriotic, in the fine and larger sense of the word.[61]

As proof of his conclusion, Crémazie pointed out that in his bookselling days it was not these pillars of society but a few students and young priests who bought works of real value and devoted their slim savings to the masterpieces of literature. It seemed to him that there was nothing to do but await better days; and he suggested that the neglected young poet Fréchette might well paraphrase de Musset and write: 'I have come too soon into too young a country.'[62]

Though Crémazie thought himself finished as a poet at 39, he deplored the absence of Fréchette, Lemay, and Alfred Garneau, the poet son of the historian, from the pages of *Le Foyer*; and he criticized the custom of devoting each number to a single work instead of to a variety of material, although he praised Ferland's historical studies, Gérin-Lajoie's *Jean Rivard*, and Casgrain's biography of Garneau, which were thus published, as worthy of appearance in the great European reviews. He urged Casgrain not to fill up his pages, in default of native talent, with secondary, if doctrinally sound French writers; suggesting that it was better to let his readers suck the marrow bones of such 'lions' as Hugo, Musset, Gautier, Sainte-Beuve, Guizot, and Merimée, than those of such 'hares as' the Vicomte Walsh, the darling of the Bourbon-minded Faubourg Saint-Germain.[63]

In a noteworthy passage he treated the difficulties which beset the development of French-Canadian letters:

> The more I reflect on the destiny of Canadian literature, the less chance I find for its leaving a mark in history. Canada lacks its own language. If we spoke Iroquois or Huron, our literature would live. Unfortunately we speak and write, after a sufficiently pitiful fashion, it is true, the language of Bossuet and Racine. Say or do what we will, we will always remain only a simple colony from the literary point of view; and even if Canada became an independent country and made her flag shine in the sun of nations, we should remain nonetheless simple literary colonials. Look at Belgium, which speaks the same tongue as us. Is there a Belgian literature? Unable to compete with France in beauty of form, Canada might have conquered a place among the literatures of the old world, if among her sons had been found a writer capable of initiating Europe, before Fenimore Cooper, to the grandeur of our forests, to the legendary exploits of our trappers and voyageurs. Today, even if a talent as powerful as that of the author of *The Last of the Mohicans* were revealed among us, his works would produce no sensation in Europe, for he would commit the irreparable wrong to be second, that is, too late. I repeat, if we spoke Huron or Iroquois, the works of our writers would attract the attention of the old world. This masculine and nervous language, born in the forests of America, would have the native poetry which delights the foreigner. One would be overcome by admiration for a novel or a poem translated from the Iroquois, while one does not take the trouble to read a book written in French by a colonial of Quebec or Montreal. For twenty years translations of Russian, Scandinavian, and Roumanian novels have been published each year in France. If these same works had been written in French, they would not have found fifty readers.
>
> A translation has this to be said for it, if a work does not seem to deserve its reputation, one consoles oneself with the reflection that it must be magnificent in the original.

But what does it matter, after all, that the works of Canadian authors are not destined to cross the Atlantic? Are we not a million Frenchmen forgotten by the mother country on the shores of the St. Lawrence? Is it not enough to encourage all those who hold a pen to know that this little people will grow great, and that it will always guard the name and memory of those who have aided it to conserve intact the most precious of all treasures, the tongue of its fathers?

. . . . .

It should be thus with the Canadian writer. Renouncing without regret the beautiful dreams of echoing glory, he should regard himself as amply rewarded for his labors if he can instruct and charm his compatriots, if he can contribute to the conservation of the old French nationality on the young soil of America.[64]

Crémazie even had the ability, very rare among poets, of being able to criticize his own work soundly. He recognized that his widely hailed 'Drapeau de Carillon' had little literary value, and owed its success to its idea rather than to its form. With bitter truth he laid down the recipe for success as a French-Canadian poet: 'Rhyme "glory" with "victory" a certain number of times, "ancestors" with "glorious," "France" with "hope"; mingle with these rhymes some sonorous words like "religion," our "fatherland," our "tongue," our "laws," the "blood of our fathers"; warm the whole over the flame of patriotism, and serve hot. Everyone will say that it is magnificent.'[65] He recognized that his unpopular 'Les Morts' was a better poem than 'Drapeau de Carillon,' but remarked that only Chauveau had singled it out for notice. He confessed his literary creed:

As for me, while admiring the masterpieces of the seventeenth century, I love with all my heart the Romantic school which has given my soul the sweetest and purest pleasures it has ever known. And still today, when melancholy enwraps my soul like a mantle of lead, the reading of a meditation of Lamartine or of a *Nuit* of Alfred de Musset give me more calm and serenity than I should find in all the tragedies of Corneille and Racine. Lamartine and Musset are men of my time . . . Romanticism, after all, is only the legitimate son of the classics; but since ideas and customs are no more in the nineteenth century what they were in the seventeenth, the Romantic school has of necessity had to adopt a form more harmonious with modern aspirations, and it is in the sixteenth century that it has sought the elements of this new form . . . We should still be obliged to raise altars to Romanticism, if it had no other merit than to have delivered us from mythology and tragedy . . . This whole war that is declared on realism is absurd. What is this monster which makes so many worthy souls wroth? It is the 1789 of literature which necessarily followed the 1789 of politics; it is all the things scorned without reason by the privileged class of the classical school, which now come to claim their place in the literary sun; and be assured it will know how to wir that place just as well as the serfs and the proletarians in the political world.[6]

Despite Crémazie's protestations, Casgrain judged that the poet's patriotic verses alone were original; that such was the secret of hi success and his best claim to future fame, and that he would live a the father of French-Canadian national poetry. Casgrain was a bette prophet than critic, and his verdict has withstood the test of time Because of its nationalist content, Crémazie's verse, like Garneau's history, has survived, while the work of other pioneer French-Cana- dian writers has fallen into neglect. In a lyric passage Casgrair recalls the tremendous impression made upon him and his fellov students by the work of the two founders of French-Canadian litera- ture, which revived the memory of past glories and hymned th beauties of the land in which they dwelt: 'Those who then were o an age to appreciate the delights of literature can still reveal wha enchantment there was in the voice of this Canadian bard, standin on the rock of Quebec, and chanting in accents sometimes sonorou and vibrant like those of a trumpet in battle and sometimes plain- tive and tearful like the harp of Israel in exile, the glories and th griefs of our native land.'[67]

But despite the enthusiastic reception of Crémazie's work, onl a few interested themselves in him after his flight to France, chie among them being his clerical friends of the Seminary of Quebec A committee sought to appease his creditors so that he might retur home, but its efforts came to nought, and the exiled poet drudge out his life in France in such occupations as the kindness of friend provided for him. After sixteen years of an exile which weighe heavily upon him, Crémazie died at Le Havre in 1879. His las address was the Rue Bernardin de Saint-Pierre. It was not unfittin that the father of French-Canadian romanticism should perish in street which commemorated the author of *Paul et Virginie*.

10

The dominant figure in Canadian public life from 1855 to 186 was George-Etienne Cartier, who looked to the future rather tha to the past. Though he was loyally supported in Upper Canada b John A. Macdonald, Cartier as leader of the large Lower Canadia bloc was the real head of the Macdonald-Cartier ministries whic held power until 1862, and a major figure in the coalition governmen of 1864–7. Macdonald's own greatness became evident only a Confederation, and was not fully revealed until after the death o his colleague Cartier. From 1835 until his death Cartier played prominent role in the great movements of his time, and took a leadin part in the solution of all the great political questions after the attainment of responsible government in 1848. Cartier had greater influence in the assembly than any other political leader from 1855 to Confederation, both through his own driving energy and lobbying ability, and the weight of his well-controlled following when Upper Canadian political groups were badly split. Though Lower Canada was not much interested in the clergy reserves question, Cartier brought its support to the government in the settlement of the matter which so vexed Upper Canada; while the abolition of seigneurial tenure, the codification of Quebec law, and the judicial and administrative reforms of the period were peculiarly Cartier's achievements.

Confederation owed more to him, perhaps, than to any other single man; for without him it would have been impossible. The expansion of Canada to the West was largely his work, as was the settlement of the first Riel Rebellion and the extension of the language and school rights of the French Canadians to Manitoba in 1870; and he closed his parliamentary career, as he had opened it, by advocating the construction of railroads, the links of steel which bind Canada together. He was the third of the great line of French-Canadian statesmen, but unlike Papineau and Lafontaine, he was also a leader in the English-Canadian world, a world in which business loomed ever larger as the years passed. In the end, like so many French Canadians who have grown into a larger Canadianism, he lost much of his influence over his own people, but their debt to him is almost unreckonable.

Heredity probably played some part in Cartier's career as the first French-Canadian public man to think in economic terms and to assume a leading role in the industrial civilization which was beginning to develop in both Canada and the United States in the middle years of the nineteenth century. He was the offspring of three generations of merchants, who had successfully engaged in the import and export trade at Quebec and in the Richelieu Valley. Through his grandmother he was allied with the clergy, whose support played a vital part in his rise to political power as the golden mean between the 'no popery' Grits and the godless *Rouges*. The Cartiers had prospered so greatly in their dealings, first in salt and fish, and then in wheat, that his vivacious father, one of the founders of the Bank of Montreal and of the St. Lawrence and Lake Champlain Railway, was able to devote most of his time to pleasure and hospitality, rather than to the commercial pursuits for which he was trained. The Cartiers belonged to the comfortable merchant-*rentier* class of Quebec, living in the villages in almost as much state as the great seigneurial families but also closely tied to the *habitants*, since they were landowners as well as traders.

Young George-Etienne inherited from his father only a measure of gayness and fondness for song; his business sense can be traced back to his grandfather and great-grandfather, the founders of the family fortune; while from his pious mother he derived the religious and patriotic principles which were reinforced by his education at the Sulpician Collège de Montréal. He graduated from the *collège* in 1831, and at once entered upon the study of law in the office of Edouard Rodier, the noted advocate and *Patriote* orator. Admitted to the bar in 1835, he set about the creation of a practice, though a good measure of his time was devoted to patriotic activities in this period of political agitation. He was active in the Saint-Jean-Baptiste Society founded in 1834 by Ludger Duvernay, and was its first secretary and many years later its president. His deeply patriotic 'O Canada! Mons pays! Mes Amours!' was composed especially for the first banquet of the society, and was sung on that occasion by Cartier himself.

At twenty he opened his political career by supporting Papineau and Robert Nelson in the elections of 1834. His patron Edouard Rodier took a leading role in organizing the *Fils de Liberté* early in 1837, and if Rodier was one of their favorite orators, Cartier was their bard. His 'Avant tout je suis Canadien' was the marching song of the *Fils de Liberté*, and 'Petit Georges' was a familiar figure at their reunions. With Chevalier de Lorimer, who perished on the scaffold for his part in the 1838 Rebellion, Cartier was joint secretary of the Montreal Permanent Central Committee of the *Patriotes*. When the rebellion broke out at Saint-Denis, not far from Cartier's birthplace at Saint-Antoine, he served as Wolfred Nelson's aide and distinguished himself by his courage in crossing the Richelieu under fire to bring reinforcements to the victorious *Patriotes*. After the defeat at Saint-Charles and the collapse of the Richelieu rising, Cartier took refuge with friends at Verchères, while Nelson and other leaders fled over the border to the States. A convenient rumor, whose origin is sometimes assigned to Cartier himself, got about that he had perished of cold and hunger in the woods while seeking to escape. Etienne Parent mourned his passing in *Le Canadien* thus: 'He was a young man endowed in the highest degree with qualities of heart and mind and before whom a brilliant career opened,'[68] an observation which supports Parent's reputation for prophetic foresight.

Early in 1838, when Cartier's hiding place became known, he was forced to flee over the border, joining the other refugees first at Plattsburg, N.Y., and then at Burlington, Vt., where his associate in the Saint-Jean-Baptiste Society, Ludger Duvernay, launched *Le Patriote Canadien* on August 7, 1839, and printed Papineau's brief and tendentious *Histoire de l'insurrection*. Cartier, however, returned to

Montreal after the disallowance of Durham's amnesty, which had excepted him and twenty-three other leaders of the rising, and forbidden their return to Canada under pain of capital punishment. When Robert Nelson's ill-starred 'invasion' of November roused the *Patriotes* once more, Cartier was one of those upon whose head a price was put by Colborne. But he took no part in the second rising, having perhaps been led by his lifelong Sulpician friends to see that the clergy was right in condemning opposition to the constituted authorities, a view which he later recognized as 'the only one that offered some chance of salvation for the French Canadians.'[69] Cartier never apologized for his activity in 1837; years later he held that the cause of the *Patriotes* was just, though he censured the course of the political leaders of the time. To his mind the rising 'was caused by the actions of a minority which desired to dominate the majority and exploit the government in its own interests. . . . The events of 1837 have been misinterpreted. The object of the people was rather to reduce this oppressive minority to nothingness than to bring about a separation of the province from the mother-country.'[70]

Somewhat disillusioned by his early political experiences, Cartier devoted himself to his profession after his return to Montreal, and gradually won a notable position at the bar.[71] He became a constitutional Reformer and as such a follower of Lafontaine, but he refused his leader's requests to stand for parliament in 1841 and 1844. Though he devoted his energies chiefly to attaining an independent position in his profession, he nevertheless followed politics closely, taking heart at Lafontaine's appointment as attorney-general in 1842 and campaigning in 1844 against D.-B. Viger, the onetime *Patriote* who had become a pliant tool of Sir Charles Metcalfe. As a private citizen Cartier worked for the attainment of responsible government; and after being elected as member for Verchères in 1848, he supported Lafontaine in the latter's great duel with Papineau. Like his chief, he broke with the hero of the *Patriotes*, who now opposed the Union, denounced responsible government and came out for independence.

Papineau had lost all faith in Britain and monarchical institutions; while his former disciples Lafontaine and Cartier now upheld the British connection, and fought the annexation movement supported by the Montreal merchants and Papineau's ardent young *Rouge* followers. Lafontaine was the dominant figure of the transition period, but Cartier was a man of the future. In later years he expressed his belief that 'Papineau was justified in combatting the oligarchy then in power, but I have never approved the attitude that he took with regard to commercial affairs, nor his opposition to measures fit to favor the progress of the country.'[72] It was not without significance that Cartier's first speech in parliament was in support of a petition of the St. Lawrence & Atlantic Railway Co. for public aid in the completion of its proposed line linking Montreal and the ice-free harbor of Portland, Maine. Cartier's lifelong policy was to be 'a policy of railroads,'[73] and its fulfilment assured the creation of modern Canada.

His mind ran in the same grooves as those of the progressive English Canadians of the day, although in both person and temperament he was a true French Canadian. Small of stature, vigorous and lively of manner, terse and rapid of speech, quick in retort and tireless in labor, a man who did not suffer fools gladly but could be the soul of cordiality and urbanity, gifted with a charm and gaiety which drew his political enemies to him in leisure moments, Cartier was a human chameleon whose rapid changes of mood often hid from the casual observer his basic virtues of tremendous powers of work, courage, will power, and firmness of principle.

The commercial mind which he had inherited from his merchant forbears, no doubt developed by his legal practice in Montreal during the great transition period of the St. Lawrence trade, made him from the first the parliamentary spokesman of the transportation interests. When he entered the assembly, that body was considering the question of providing funds for the completion of the Welland Canal, begun in 1837. Cartier, who had perhaps devoted more study to such matters than any other public man of the period, supported the motion strongly, attacking the shortsighted local opposition to the project in Quebec:

> It is claimed that the expense will be for the benefit of Upper Canada and will bring to its door the agricultural products of the West which travel by Lake Huron and Erie; but it will do the like for Lower Canada! It will be the same with all the routes opened to communicate with distant parts. Remember that commerce always wishes to reach the sea. In our case all must end in the St. Lawrence. The Americans understand that. They have dug the Erie Canal across the land. Shall they surpass us? Yes, since we do not wish to compete with them. Nevertheless, the thing is simple for us. I say to Mr. William Hamilton Merritt that his creation of the Welland Canal is a monument which will perpetuate his memory and I urge the House to lend a final hand to the completion of this great national work.[74]

As late as 1864, when his forecast for the Welland Canal had been realized and the project of enlarging it was under discussion, Cartier not only supported the measure but urged the opening of the Ottawa River to navigation, with a Georgian Bay canal to shorten the Chicago–Montreal route and thus to offset the proposed New York ship canal.

But Canada had the fault of launching its canal program too late, and bringing it to a conclusion just as the American railroads rovided a new and more serious competition to the great waterway f Canada. Cartier was among the first in Canada to see that the oming age was to be that of the railroads. In August 1846, when Canada's sole railroad was the ten-year-old line running from Montreal to St. Johns, Cartier spoke at a public meeting in Montreal nder Lafontaine's chairmanship in favor of a line linking that city ith Portland. He called upon all classes to support the project as e did, by buying shares on that occasion:

In the present age it is impossible for a country to enjoy great prosperity without railways. . . . Well, let us resolve to have our railways in rder to join them to those of an enterprising people separated from us y an imaginary line, by a line which becomes only too visible, alas, when e contrast our apathy and our laziness with the incessant activity, the verish energy, and the enterprising spirit of our neighbors. The United tates can serve as an example to the peoples of America and even to hose of Europe. . . . I should point out also that each city which has he advantage of being the terminus of a railway sees the value of its property double; witness Buffalo, Albany, Boston, New York, Philadelphia, altimore, and a great many other cities. There is no doubt that the ame future awaits Montreal. . . . I shall not attempt to discuss whether his railway ought to be built, for this question has been treated by those ho spoke before me. I shall content myself with saying the prosperity f Montreal depends upon its position as entrepôt of the commerce of he West, that the changes in the Corn Laws have endangered this rade; and that we cannot conserve it if we do not have the best means f transport from the Western waters to the Atlantic by our canals and y this railway. . . . I then invite all those who are present to come and ake shares according to their means—first of all for their own profit, nd then out of patriotism, for love of our country ought to make us ork for its greater prosperity. I address myself to Canadians of all origins: Americans, French, and English, let us be united and march together owards our destiny. But above all let us not blush on this occasion to ake our enterprising neighbors for models. Our connection with them ill have a good effect; we shall know better their customs, habits, and heir civilization; we shall be in a better situation to concern ourselves ith the business relations that we will consequently have with them.[75]

Again at Montreal in 1849 Cartier spoke in favor of the railway:

We have an exceptional opportunity to attract foreign capital. . . . Look what New York has done. . . . She is at the head of American trade, ut to obtain this position, she has not feared to go into debt to the mount of $25,000,000. It was necessary for her to have faith in herself, n her spirit of enterprise, and to discount the future. . . . The time has ome to belie our reputation as apathetic men, without energy and pirit of enterprise. Let these epithets cease to be attributed to the Canadian name . . . Montreal is destined to become the great entrepôt f the West, but without railways and canals, it will be impossible for it to attain the glorious position which will make it one of the chief center of the continent.[76]

As a member of parliament he supported the Guarantee Act o 1849, which provided for government assistance to the Grea Western, St. Lawrence & Atlantic, and the proposed Halifax & Quebec line (soon known as the Intercolonial). Again in 1851 h backed the Hincks government's project of the Grand Trunk (Lévis Hamilton). Cartier sponsored the acts of 1852 which incorporated the Grand Trunk and provided government guarantees for it; in 1853 he fathered the bill for the Victoria Bridge at Montreal, and the Amalgamation Act which permitted the Grand Trunk to take over the local lines already constructed. Cartier was the storm center of this legislation, which roused furious protests from the cautious and the shortsighted; but firm in his faith in this 'nationa enterprise,' he triumphed over all opposition. He proclaimed publicly: 'I build for the future,' and privately this jingle was often in his mouth:

L'heure viendra. Sachons l'attendre.
Bientôt nous pourrons la saisir.
Le courage fait entreprendre
*Et l'adresse fait réussir.**[77]

Again in 1854–6, and 1861–2 he promoted the interests of the Grand Trunk, of which he became the legal adviser in 1853, through legislation which provided guarantees, loans, or reorganization for the great project which met with many difficulties not all unavoidable

Cartier's public part in aiding the construction of the Grand Trunk, of which he was admittedly the solicitor in Canada East (a Lower Canada was now known), was criticized at the time and ha been criticized since, but it is not always recognized that othe leading members of the successive governments of the time were more intimately involved with the company than he, and tha despite all criticism Cartier was maintained as chairman of the Parliamentary Railway Committee from 1852 to 1867. He was th ablest politician and the only French Canadian in the Hincks, Galt Merritt, Watkin, Keefer, Andrews group who created Canada's rail road system, without whose existence 'the union of British North America would have been a farce.'[78] Cartier played a notable par in increasing Canada's fifty miles of railroad in 1850 to more than 3,000 by 1869, with vast expenditures which stimulated industry gave employment to thousands, and attracted immigration. No

* The time will come. Know how to await it.
Soon we shall be able to seize it.
Courage leads to undertakings,
Cleverness makes them succeed.

only was he the strongest parliamentary supporter of the Grand Trunk and the Intercolonial schemes, but he also played a major role in the chartering of the Canadian Pacific in 1871. In fact his part in that enterprise brought on his political ruin. His interest in the development of transportation was not confined to railroads alone, for in 1860 he encouraged by a subsidy the establishment of the Allan Steamship Line, linking Quebec in summer and Portland in winter with Great Britain; and to the close of his career he remained an advocate of further development of the canal system. The communication network of modern Canada owes much to Cartier, who through the force of his leadership brought Lower Canadian support to the far-sighted projects of a few English Canadians. And without the ties which the railroads and the canals supplied between the provinces, Confederation would have been both unattainable and unworkable.

It is clear from Cartier's record in public life that he was primarily a statesman, and not, as his enemies often proclaimed, merely a spokesman of the great interests and a lobbyist. But if Papineau was an idealistic statesman who in the end was betrayed by his own idealism, Cartier was a practical politician who eventually fell victim to his practicality. Though Cartier was by temperament an autocrat who loved to exercise absolute power,[79] he knew how to restrain his political ambitions. Just as he twice refused Lafontaine's pleas to enter the assembly in the 1840's, so he twice refused cabinet posts in the Hincks-Morin government of 1851–4. He met offers of the solicitor-generalship and the commissionership of public works with the very 'Anglo-Saxon' response that the salaries were not adequate enough to justify him in abandoning his flourishing legal practice. In 1854 he was defeated by three votes for the speakership of the House as being 'too friendly to the Grand Trunk'[80] according to William Lyon Mackenzie. But though public office held no overpowering attraction for him, politics was in his blood. He took an active part in forming the alliance of the conservative Liberals of Lower Canada with the moderate Conservatives of Upper Canada in the MacNab-Morin government in that same year. And in 1855 he was induced to become provincial secretary of Lower Canada, when Etienne-Pascal Taché succeeded Morin as head of the Lower Canadian section of the ministry. While seeking the necessary new mandate from his electors of Verchères for this office, Cartier was bitterly attacked by the young *Rouges*, who regarded the conservative Liberals' alliance with the Upper Canadian Tories as a betrayal. But Cartier was re-elected by a slim margin, and launched an important program of educational reform before he became attorney-general for Canada East when the government was reorganized as the Taché-Macdonald ministry in 1856.

The great alliance of Macdonald and Cartier as the real leaders of Upper and Lower Canada was thus formed. The fact was recognized in the following year by the reorganization of the cabinet into the Macdonald-Cartier ministry. In the elections which followed Cartier won an overpowering majority in Lower Canada, being himself triumphantly re-elected in Verchères, though he lost the Montreal seat which he also contested. Macdonald was left in a minority in Upper Canada and thus dependent upon his colleague for the survival of the government of which he was the titular head. Until Confederation Macdonald had neither the support nor the influence which Cartier wielded in the assembly. Their government fell on July 28, 1858 when the Upper Canadian Liberal George Brown carried an anti-government motion against the adoption of Ottawa as the capital. The Brown-Dorion government which succeeded resigned on August 4 after a vote of non-confidence in the assembly, and Cartier was called to the prime ministership, with virtually the same cabinet as had held office under the Macdonald-Cartier regime.

This government took office on August 6, with the ministers exchanging portfolios, in order to avoid the necessity of seeking re-election under an act of the previous year. The following day, in what became known as the 'double-shuffle,' they resumed their old offices. This somewhat dubious proceeding, inspired by Macdonald, was frankly admitted by Cartier in the assembly to be designed 'to meet the requirements of the law and at the same time to prevent any unnecessary elections.'[81] The incident reveals Cartier's mastery of practical politics, for the government so questionably born was sustained against the objections of the opposition and had no difficulty in finding support for its program. Two notable items of its policy were the encouragement and protection of native industry and the consideration of a federal union of British North America. To Cartier's government belongs the distinction of first proposing administrative action on these two major matters, which A. T. Galt had made conditions of his entrance into the cabinet. Cartier showed such vigor and ability as prime minister that his government held office for nearly four years, an unusually long term in this disordered period of Canadian politics.

Though Cartier immediately took action on the question of Confederation, going to England that fall with Galt and John Ross to confer with the imperial authorities on the matter, that initiative bore no immediate fruit in the face of the apathy of the Maritimes. It was otherwise with other government measures. The future seat of government was fixed at Ottawa, thanks to Cartier's insistence, and A. T. Galt's protective tariff was adopted. Cartier's proposal of 1857, as attorney-general, of a measure for the codification of the civil law and civil procedure of Lower Canada was implemented by the formation in 1859 of a committee of jurists to perform the task, which was finally completed in 1864. At the same session in which this notable project was launched, Cartier had also sponsored legislation for judicial decentralization, the freer institution of new parishes, and the introduction of French civil law into the Eastern Townships, thus unifying the legal system of Quebec. And in 1859 Cartier passed the final measure in the long struggle to extinguish seigneurial tenure in Lower Canada, a struggle in which he had been active since 1850. Though credit for this reform belongs chiefly to Lafontaine and Lewis Thomas Drummond, Cartier took a prominent part in the final stages. The temper of his mind is well revealed by his comment when reviewing the whole question in April 1859: 'It has been said that the feudal system introduced by the kings of France, and later modified by special law, greatly contributed to assure the settlement of the country. I believe so, but this institution has had its day, and we have the satisfaction of being able to suppress it without the least trouble or the least effusion of blood.'[82] Here Cartier's essential conservatism and sense of tradition, coupled with a progressive outlook and a strong faith in gradual rather than revolutionary reform, are made clear.

Cartier's firmness in defending the rights of his own people, despite the fact that many of them regarded him as a traitor, is revealed by his vigorous opposition to the Upper Canadian Liberals' demand for representation by population. Like Lafontaine, Cartier held that the Union Act of 1840 was a compact or treaty whose basis could not be changed.[83] When the Union was established, each province had been given equal representation in the legislature, despite the fact that Lower Canada then had 600,000 inhabitants to Upper Canada's 400,000. This measure had been approved by English Canadians, though it had aroused much dissatisfaction among French Canadians. In 1852 the population of Upper Canada first surpassed that of the lower province, and agitation in favor of representation according to population was immediately launched in Upper Canada. This movement, whose most vigorous leader was the radical Liberal, or 'Clear Grit,' George Brown, grew rapidly. In 1856 it received the support of Antoine-Aimé Dorion, the chief of the Lower Canadian radicals, though he prefered formation of a federal union of the Canadas to reform of the existing order. In 1859 a great Reform Convention was held at Toronto, and a resolution was adopted to the effect that the Union was a failure and that only a government based upon 'Rep by Pop' would be acceptable to the people of Upper Canada. Appeals to London and even to Washington were threatened by the more hotheaded leaders. The agitation was stimulated by the revelation of the 1861 census that Upper Canada now had 300,000 more population than Lower Canada.

Cartier had fought the 'Rep by Pop' movement from the beginning, involving himself in many bitter brushes with George Brown, who spared neither French Canada nor its leaders in his attacks upon the government. In reply to the latter's war cry of 'No French domination,' Cartier observed in 1861: 'The Union in my view rests on the principle that the two provinces coexist with equal powers, and that neither should dominate over the other in parliament.'[84] Again he remarked: 'Lower Canada and Upper Canada are united by the St. Lawrence, by railways and canals, and each of the two sections is absolutely necessary to the prosperity of the other. I feel no hostile sentiment towards anyone; I am ready to render justice to Upper Canada as well as to Lower Canada, in maintaining the Union.'[85] He was already envisaging a greater confederation, but until it should be achieved, he believed in continuing the Union on the basis of equality. In this policy he was loyally supported by Macdonald, who had outgrown his youthful devotion to the rabid sectionalism of Sir Allan MacNab.

The Cartier government successfully resisted the Liberals' effort to make representation by population a panacea for Canada's ills and survived the bitter party warfare of the 1861 session, only to fall in May 1862 on the question of the reorganization of the militia system. The outbreak of the American Civil War and the *Trent* incident of 1861,[86] with its threat of a war between Great Britain and the United States which would probably be fought in Canada, caused the government to bring in a bill providing for an active force of 50,000 men and the expenditure of a million dollars. This measure, sponsored by Macdonald, was defeated by a majority of seven, with thirty-seven of the fifty-eight Lower Canadian members voting against it. Cartier for the first time thus lost the support of his province, with many of his closest followers objecting to the measure on the grounds of its cost. The ministry resigned, with Cartier consoling them with the face-saving reflection that 'we fall on a measure designed for the protection and defense of our country, a measure which we believe necessary to put Canadians in a state to enjoy freely their political institutions beneath the glorious flag of Old England.'[87] They were succeeded by the moderate Liberal government of John Sandfield Macdonald and Louis-V. Sicotte. This ministry survived reorganization in the following year as the Macdonald-Dorion government, only to collapse in March 1864. A Liberal-Conservative ministry was then formed under the leadership of Etienne-Pascal Taché and John A. Macdonald, but it lasted only three months.

The old double-majority system of the Union had completely broken down; four ministries had fallen in three years, two general elections had been held, and the parties still remained deadlocked with none able to maintain itself in office. Canada's constitutional difficulties were no nearer a solution, and all British North America feared that the massed strength of the Union Army might be turned against her after the defeat of the Confederacy, with which Great Britain and Canada had actively sympathized. The Confederate raid on St. Albans, Vermont, from the Eastern Townships, and the freeing of the participants after their arrest upon their return to Canada, awoke a wave of resentment in the North. The consequent war talk caused Henry Adams to write from London, where he was aiding his father in the American Legation, 'This Canadian business is suddenly found to be serious, and the prospect of Sherman marching down the St. Lawrence and Farragut sailing up it, doesn't just seem agreeable.'[88] Cartier, as attorney-general for Canada East, handled this delicate international case with great adroitness. But in February 1863, Bennett's *New York Herald* was calling for annexation: 'Peaceably if possible, forcibly if necessary.'

At this crucial moment George Brown startled everyone by combining forces with John A. Macdonald and Cartier in a coalition government under the neutral leadership of Taché. The coalition's purpose was to bring about Confederation as soon as possible. Brown paid public tribute to the part played by Cartier in making possible this alliance with his opponent of fifteen years' standing. Meanwhile New Brunswick, Nova Scotia, and Prince Edward Island had determined to hold a convention at Charlottetown in September to consider a union of the Maritime Provinces. This movement was British in origin, and it aimed both at strengthening the Maritimes against Canadian 'aggression' and increasing their bargaining power. For the leading spirit was Charles Tupper of Nova Scotia, who foresaw a union of all British North America in the not distant future. To Charlottetown the Canadian government sent a delegation composed of Macdonald, Cartier, Brown, Galt, D'Arcy McGee, Hector Langevin, William McDougall, and Alexander Campbell. Macdonald, supported by Cartier and Brown, proposed to the convention the advantages of a union of all the British North American Provinces. After two days the Canadian delegation retired, urging that the convention should suspend consideration of a Maritime union and adjourn to Quebec to consider the broader scheme.

This plan was adopted, and the Quebec Conference met on October 10, 1864, under the presidency of Sir Etienne Taché, the prime minister of Canada. The other French-Canadian delegates were Cartier, Langevin, and Jean-Charles Chapais. The meeting was held behind closed doors, and the minutes are scanty and unsatisfactory. But it is clear that Cartier played a major role in the gathering as the representative of Lower Canada, which numbered more than a third of the total population of the proposed confederation and which was the essential geographical and economic link in the scheme. It was Cartier, as the spokesman of French-Canadian particularism, who determined the initial decision that the union should take a federal rather than a legislative form. Macdonald, who presented to the conference an outline of the contemplated federation, himself favored a legislative union. But in discussion of the subject he found that both Lower Canada and the Maritimes wished to preserve their separate individualities, and so a federal union was decided upon. Macdonald carried his point, however, by following Galt's idea of 1858 in reserving to the federal government all powers not specifically granted to the separate provinces, so that in theory the Canadian federation was the exact opposite of the American one, then racked by civil war fought in the name of states' rights. In American constitutional terms Macdonald was a Hamiltonian, while Cartier was a Jeffersonian, as far as provincial autonomy and minority rights were concerned.

Cartier succeeded in establishing Quebec as the pivot of representation in the proposed federal parliament, while the principle of representation by population was at last consecrated by law. Both Upper and Lower Canada were made happy by settlement of the question, for Quebec was guaranteed a constant and fixed number of representatives, while the other provinces were to have as many representatives in proportion to their population as the number sixty-five bore to Quebec's population. After some difficulty in settling the financial basis of Confederation, the conference adjourned on October 28, having passed ninety-two resolutions which were to form the basis of the new constitution.

Cartier, who had already expressed his confident hope in the formation of 'a great confederation which will be to the benefit of all and the disadvantage of none'[89] in an address to a public dinner on September 8 after the Charlottetown meeting, and had evoked at a later Halifax banquet 'a great Anglo-American power,'[90] stretching from the Atlantic far westward, made a still more notable speech on October 28 at the banquet given by the citizens of Montreal to the delegates at the conclusion of the conference. He justified the final form of the project as the best assurance of commercial prosperity and the best insurance against annexation, and as supplying equal protection for both races and their interests:

> I have been told that in Lower Canada there exists a strong opposition to this project because the English-speaking population will find itself

at the mercy of the French population. Why, I answer, should the English born in Lower Canada yield to such arguments? Let them reflect that if the French have a majority in the provincial government, they will in their turn be in a large minority in the federal government. The French population, in confiding their interests to a federal government, give proof of their confidence in our English fellow countrymen. Is it too much to ask of the English that they should rely on the liberality and the spirit of justice of the French race in the local government? . . . For my part I am ready to admit openly today that the prosperity of the two Canadas is principally due to the spirit of enterprise of the English race. But why should they oppose the establishment of a provincial government in which the French-Canadians will be represented in accordance with their number? In any case I do not hesitate to proclaim that I will never suffer, as long as I am minister of the Crown, an injustice being done, under the constitution or otherwise, to my countrymen, whether English or Catholics. I will never permit that my compatriots, the French-Canadians, shall be unjustly treated, because they belong to a different race and religion from the people of Upper Canada.[91]

Cartier observed that the proposed central government would control all general interests, while the provincial governments would have power over local affairs and properties: 'Under the new system Lower Canada will have its local government and almost as much legislative power as formerly.'[92] He concluded by stressing that Confederation represented no destruction or even weakening of the tie with Great Britain: 'I am for confederation because I believe that the establishment of a general government will give even greater force to that tie which is dear to us all.'[93]

Meanwhile Eric Dorion, *Rouge* member from Drummond-Arthabaska, published the Quebec Resolutions in his newspaper, *Le Défricheur*, and campaigned vigorously against Confederation as a centralization of power which would be disastrous for Quebec and provincial autonomy. At Cartier's instigation *La Minerve* replied to Dorion's campaign, warning Quebec against dangerous isolation. Most of the leading Lower-Canadian papers supported Confederation, but with no great enthusiasm. French Canada's elder statesmen opposed the measure. Papineau saw in it 'the same defects as in preceding regimes, and additional ones which are particular to it.'[94] C.-S. Cherrier came out of retirement to oppose it before the *Institut Canadien-Français* at Montreal in February 1865. Public meetings and petitions against Confederation were organized by Médéric Lanctôt, the head of the law firm which employed young Wilfrid Laurier, and the founder of a secret society, the Club Saint-Jean-Baptiste, to fight the scheme. A host of pamphlets appeared, the most notable anti-Confederation one being the work of Charles Laberge, while Joseph Cauchon produced the strongest plea in its favor.[95]

Although the task of sponsoring action on the resolutions of the Quebec Conference fell to John A. Macdonald as leader of the government in the House when the legislature met in February 1865, while the nominal prime minister, Sir Etienne Taché, sponsored a similar bill in the legislative council, Cartier supported his colleague with a three-hour speech—one of the most notable efforts of a man who made no pretensions to oratory—on February 7, the day after Macdonald had introduced the measure. Outlining its provisions and advocating its advantages, Cartier traced the whole history of the Confederation movement, defending the measure itself and replying to the attacks which had been made upon him personally. He pointed out that the Cartier-Macdonald government of 1858 had proposed the project, which thus could hardly be called a surprise measure. The deputation to London in that year which he had headed had consulted with the imperial authorities, but of the Maritime Provinces only Newfoundland was then ready to confer on the subject. He traced his conflict with George Brown over representation of population, which he had opposed 'because of the danger of conflict between the two sections, . . . not with the intention of refusing Upper Canada justice, but simply to prevent Lower Canada from suffering injustice.'[96] Then he remarked: 'I do not fear that the rights of Lower Canada will in any way be placed in peril by the project of Confederation, even though in a general legislature the French-Canadians will have a smaller number of representatives than all other nationalities combined. The resolutions show that, in the questions which will be submitted to the Federal parliament, there will be no more danger to the rights and privileges of the French Canadians than to those of the Scotch, English or Irish.'[97]

Having thus reassured his countrymen, Cartier proclaimed that Confederation was the alternative to absorption in the United States. Disunited, the British provinces could not defend themselves against American aggression. Canada was the largest, wealthiest, and most populous province of British North America, but it lacked access to the sea during the winter, and for that vital necessity of its trade it was dependent upon the United States. He blamed the opposition among the English of Lower Canada to Confederation on their desire to throw Canada into the American union, and assigned the same aim to the *Rouges*. He traced the story of American efforts to win Canada in the past, and stressed the loyalty of the French Canadians in 1775 and 1778. Then he remarked: 'While the American union had divided against itself, the Canadians who have the advantage of seeing republicanism in operation for a period of eighty years, of perceiving its faults and vices, have been convinced that purely democratic institutions cannot assure the peace and prosperity of nations, and that we must unite under a federation so formed as to perpetuate the monarchical element.'[98] He pointed out that the 'five different groups inhabiting five separate provinces' had the 'same commercial interests, the same desire to live under the British Crown.'[99] But the unity brought about by Confederation would be a unity of diversity:

> If we unite we will form a political nationality independent of the national origin and religion of individuals. Some have regretted that we have a distinction of races, and have expressed the hope that, in time, this diversity will disappear. The idea of a fusion of the races in one is utopian; it is an impossibility. Distinctions of this character will always exist; diversity seems to be the order of the physical, moral, and political worlds. As to the objection that we cannot form a great nation because Lower Canada is chiefly French and Catholic, Upper Canada English and Protestant, and the Maritime Provinces mixed, it is completely futile. . . . In our confederation there will be Catholics and Protestants, English, French, Irish and Scotch, and each by its efforts and success will add to the prosperity, the might, and to the glory of the new federation. We are of different races, not to wage war among ourselves, but to work together for our common welfare.[100]

Fired by this noble vision, the practical Cartier for once was too idealistic as he looked to the future. He foresaw a 'happy spirit of emulation' arising from the contact of French and English, so that the 'diversity of races' would 'contribute to the common prosperity.'[101] With a Catholic minority in Upper Canada and a Protestant minority in Lower Canada, while the two communions balanced one another in the Maritimes, he foresaw no possibility of the arbitrary infringement of a minority's rights by either federal or provincial governments. He pointed out the strange bedfellows among the opposition to the project, with the *Rouges* lying down with English: '*The True Witness*, a Catholic journal which opposes the project, is of the opinion that if it is adopted the French Canadians will be annihilated, whilst its confrère in violence, the Protestant *Witness*, assured us that it will be the Protestants who will suffer.'[102] He brought the force of clerical support to bear: 'Those of the clergy who are high in authority, as well as those in humbler positions, have declared for Confederation, not only because they see in it all possible security for the institutions they cherish, but also because their Protestant fellow countrymen, like themselves, are also guaranteed their rights. The clergy in general are opposed to all political dissension, and if they are favorable to the project, it is because they see in Confederation a solution to the difficulties which have so long existed.'[103] He concluded by urging the necessity of seizing this favorable opportunity to adopt Confederation:

'We know that the approbation of the Imperial Government is assured. If, therefore, Canada adopts these resolutions, as I have no doubt it will, and if the other British North American colonies follow its example, the Imperial Government will then be called upon to accord us a central government established on a broad and solid basis, and provincial governments under whose protection will be placed the persons, the properties, and the civil and religious rights of all classes of society.'[104]

It was Cartier's great plea which finally won a slim majority of French-Canadian support for the project, by a vote of 27 to 21. His calm words of tolerance and practical logic were offset by the reply of Antoine-Aimé Dorion, the *Rouge* leader, who thought Confederation of all British North America premature at this time, though he had earlier favored a confederation of the Canadas to break the existing deadlock. He denounced the proposal of a nominated instead of an elected upper house and the support pledged to the construction of the Intercolonial Railway. The type of confederation he favored would give the largest powers to the local governments and only delegated authority to the central government. He considered the Confederation scheme as a plot of the Grand Trunk, and denounced the conservative tendencies of the whole project: 'With a Governor-General appointed by the Crown; with local Governors also appointed by the Crown; with Legislative Councils in the General Legislature and in all the provinces nominated by the Crown, we shall have the most illiberal Constitution ever heard of in any country where constitutional government prevails.'[105]

In the isolationist tradition Dorion saw no need for the creation of military or naval forces: 'The best thing Canada can do is to keep quiet, and to give no cause for war.'[106] It was absurd 'to speak as a means of defence of a scheme of Confederation to unite the whole country extending from Newfoundland to Vancouver's Island,'—this was the first reference to extension of Confederation to the Pacific—'thousands of miles intervening, without any communication, except through the United States or around Cape Horn.'[107] When Cartier interrupted to state that an interoceanic railway was to be built, Dorion denounced the suggestion as an extension of the Grand Trunk line for the benefit of English capitalists. He saw an intention to convert the proposed federal union eventually into a legislative union, which Lower Canada would never tolerate:

> The people of Lower Canada are attached to their institutions in a manner that defies any attempt to change them in that way. They will not change their religious institutions, their laws and their language for any consideration whatsoever. A million of inhabitants may seem a

small affair to a philosopher who sits down to write out a constitution. He may think that it would be better that there should be one religion, one language and one system of laws, and he goes to work to frame institutions that will bring all to that desirable state; but I can tell honorable gentlemen that the history of every country goes to show that not even by the power of the sword can such changes be accomplished. . . . I know that there is an apprehension amongst the British population in Lower Canada that, even with the small power that the local government will possess, their rights will not be respected. How, then, can it be expected that the French population can anticipate any more favorable result from the general government, when it is to possess such enormous powers over the destinies of their section of the country? Experience shows that majorities are always aggressive, and it cannot be otherwise in this instance.[108]

Finally, Dorion concluded, if the project of Confederation should be adopted 'without the sanction of the people, the country would never cease to regret it.'[109] He had put his finger on a weak spot, for the few farsighted statesmen who sponsored the measure were perfectly aware that there was no popular enthusiasm for it, and that if the scheme were to succeed under existing political conditions, it must be rushed through the legislature without the appeal to the people which Dorion urged.

Henri Joly, the Swiss-born deputy for Lotbinière who later became a Liberal premier of Quebec, supported Dorion's opposition to the measure. Oddly enough, considering his background, he stressed the historical weakness of federations, and denounced the project as fatal to the French-Canadian nationality.[110] He called Cartier a traitor who had sacrificed his people to his own ambition and interest. Another notable opposition speaker, J.-F. Perrault, reviewed the record since 1760 and predicted a constant French-Canadian struggle to maintain their rights and liberties under Confederation, which he considered 'the political suicide of the French race in Canada' and a 'scheme of annihilation specially prepared for our destruction.'[111] The arguments of the *Rouges* were not without effect. One of Cartier's followers, Henri Taschereau, was led to part company with his leader because to his mind the project lacked sufficient guarantees for the rights of the French Canadians.[112] Fear for a future in which French Canada would be at the mercy of an English majority broke down party lines. Throughout the consideration of the project in 1864 and 1865 Cartier was bitterly attacked on the platform and in the press of Lower Canada—with Eric Dorion's *Le Défricheur* reinforced by a paper called *L'Union Nationale*, founded by L.-O. David and L.-A. Jetté to campaign against both the project and Cartier personally. This onslaught fatally weakened Cartier's hold on French Canada, and he may be said to have made a greater personal sacrifice than any other father of Confederation in carrying the project through.

While Cartier was being attacked by his compatriots for sacrificing the interests of his province, he was also engaged in meeting the objections of the English minority in Lower Canada with a pledge to guarantee their rights. He reiterated his assurance 'as a Catholic and as a member of the Canadian Government, that when the measure for the settlement of the local government of Lower Canada comes before this House for discussion it will be such as to satisfy the Protestant minority of Lower Canada.'[113] John Rose, one of the English-speaking members for Lower Canada, had already paid tribute to Cartier's notable tolerance by saying that 'in the whole course of his public life there has not been a single act on his part, whether of executive, administrative, or legislative action, tinged with illiberality, intolerance, or bigotry.'[114] Cartier answered the objection that the French Canadians were left at the mercy of the English majority in the federal parliament by pointing out that in case of unreasonable opposition they could break up the administration by retiring: 'When the leader for Lower Canada shall have sixty-five members belonging to his section to support him, and command a majority of the French Canadians and British from Lower Canada, will he not be able to upset the government if his colleagues interfere with his nominations to office?'[115] Dorion replied that nobody would care if he did retire, since 'there would be a sufficient number of English members to carry on without him.'[116] But Cartier expressed his confidence that the spirit of fair play and justice of the English members of the government would assure fair treatment for the minority in the federal parliament, and pleaded for a similar confidence on the part of the English minority in Quebec. The language question under the new order was made clear by Macdonald's statement that the continued use of the French language was one of the principles of Confederation, while Cartier added that the rights of English in the Lower Canada legislature would also be guaranteed, so that 'the use of both languages would be secured by the Imperial Act.'[117]

Despite all the arguments and explanations of a month and a half of debate, A.-A. Dorion, who with his brother Eric, Holton, Joly, Dunkin, and J. S. Macdonald, led the opposition, remained firm in his position. The opposition took new heart when the pro-confederation government of New Brunswick was defeated early in March, while Nova Scotia and Prince Edward Island backed out of the project. Macdonald and Cartier pressed for a vote, despite the fact that it now appeared that the project would be merely a confederation 'of the two Canadas,'[118] as François Evanturel, the editor of *Le Canadien*, called it. The government's position in the face of these setbacks was that the measure should be passed and then the imperial government could be induced to bring pressure to bear upon the Maritimes to accept it. A.-A. Dorion summed up the gloomy state of mind of the *Rouges* and French-Canadian popular opposition to the project thus:

> I am opposed to this confederation in which the militia, the appointment of judges, the administration of justice, and our most important civil rights will be under the control of the general government, the majority of which will be hostile to Lower Canada, of a governor-general vested with the most ample powers, whilst the powers of the local government will be restricted first by the limit of the powers delegated to it, by the veto reserved to the central authority, and further by the concurrent jurisdiction of the general authority or government. Petitions with more than 20,000 signatures attached to them have already been presented to this House against the scheme of confederation. Numerous public meetings have been held in nineteen counties in Lower Canada and one in the city of Montreal. Everywhere this scheme has been protested against and an appeal to the people demanded; and yet in defiance of the expressed opinion of our constituents we are about to give them a constitution, the effect of which will be to snatch from them what little influence they still enjoy under the existing law. We are about, on their behalf, to surrender all the rights and privileges which are dearest to them, and that without consulting them. It would be madness—it would be more, it would be a crime. On these grounds I shall oppose the scheme with all the power at my command, and insist that under any circumstances it shall be submitted to the people before its final adoption.[119]

But Macdonald and Cartier succeeded in forcing the vote on March 10, 1865, when the House agreed to the Quebec Resolutions by a vote of 91 to 33, with 21 of the dissenting votes French Canadian. The measure had already been approved in the legislative council on February 20 by a 45–15 vote, with 6 French Canadians opposing it. The *Rouges*' campaign against Confederation was continued until the British North America Act was passed by the British parliament in March 1867. At the Westminster Palace Conference in London in December 1866 Galt secured a guarantee of minority educational rights in both Quebec and Ontario. But Dorion's and Perrault's objections to Confederation have often been re-echoed in French Canada through the years, and some of their dire predictions have come true, while some of Cartier's optimistic views have been discredited by developments. The greater Canada was not created without sacrifices by all who helped to make it, and its survival has been threatened by the failure of later leaders to live up to the liberal spirit of the fathers of Confederation.

Notes

[1] Kennedy, 502, Elgin-Grey, 30 April 1849. The quotations are from the *Montreal Courier*, as reprinted in the *New York Commercial Advertizer*, 5 April 1849.

[2] Cartier was named after George III. His signature usually follows the English spelling or is abbreviated to 'Geo.' See G. Malchelosse (*ed.*), *Sulte: Mélanges Historiques* (Montréal, 1919), 88, Ap., Note I.

[3] *Elgin-Grey*, II, 465, Elgin-Grey, 3 September 1849.

[4] *Ibid.*, II, 463, Proclamation to Britons of the City of Toronto, August 1849.

[5] *Ibid.*, II, 525, Elgin-Grey, 25 October 1849.

[6] *Ibid.*, II, 531, *Daily British Whig*, 26 October 1849.

[7] *Ibid.*, II, 534, Elgin-Grey, 8 November 1849.

[8] *Ibid*, II, 612, Elgin-Grey, 23 March 1850.

[9] *Ibid.*, II, 608 *n.*, *Hansard*, III Series, CVIII, 567, Russell, 8 February 1850.

[10] *Ibid.*, II, 609, Elgin-Grey, 23 March 1850.

[11] *Ibid.*, II, 585, Elgin-Grey, 28 January 1850.

[12] *Ibid.*, II, 610, Elgin-Grey, 23 March 1850.

[13] Chapais, VI, 152–3.

[14] *Ibid.*, VI, 169–70.

[15] *Ibid.*, VI, 172.

[16] *Elgin-Grey*, II, 670, Elgin-Grey, 31 May 1850.

[17] *Ibid.*, II, 706, Elgin-Grey, 2 August 1850.

[18] *Ibid.*, II, 707.

[19] *Ibid.*, II, 745–6, Elgin-Grey, 22 November 1850.

[20] *Ibid.*, II, 746.

[21] Chapais, VI, 205.

[22] *Elgin-Grey*, III, 900, Grey-Elgin, 2 October 1851.

[23] *Ibid.*, III, 904.

[24] G. Lanctot, *François-Xavier Garneau* (Toronto [1925]), 1–2.

[25] *Ibid.*, 12.

[26] *Ibid.*, 29.

[27] G. Lanctot, '*L'Oeuvre historique de Garneau*', in *Centenaire de l'Histoire du Canada de François-Xavier Garneau* (Montréal, 1945), 18–9.

[28] *Ibid.*, 24; Lanctot, *Garneau* (1925), 33.

[29] M. Wade (*ed.*), *Journals of Francis Parkman* (New York, 1947), II, 517–8; Lanctot, *Garneau*, 34.

[30] Lanctot, 36; *Garneau*, 'Voyage en Angleterre et en France,' in *La Litterature canadienne* (Québec, 1863), I, 250–1.

[31] Lanctot, *Centenaire*, 106.

[32] M. Bibaud, *Histoire du Canada* (Montréal, 1843), I, 2.

[33] C. Roy, *Nos origines littéraires* (Québec, 1909), 234.

[34] Faribault's collection, like Viger's '*Saberdache*,' is preserved in the Seminary Archives, Laval University, Quebec City.

[35] P.-J.-O. Chauveau, *L'Instruction publique au Canada* (Québec, 1876), 322.

[36] Chauveau, *Charles Guérin* (Montréal, 1853), 2.

[37] Large Channel Island firms, the Robins and Le Boutilliers, took over the fisheries of the Gulf of St. Lawrence after the Conquest and soon monopolized both them and the supply trade. Young Jerseymen, known as '*les Jersiais*,' were sent out to the Gaspé and Cape Breton coasts to serve as traders and company storekeepers, setting arbitrary prices for fish and supplies. They were disliked by French Canadians as foreign exploiters and French Protestants, like the earlier Swiss officials who were also allied with the English conquerors and cut across the

acial-religious line. On the Jersey monopolists, see Innis & Lower, *Select Econ. Docs., 1783–1885*, 700.

38 L. de Montigny, *Antoine Gérin-Lajoie* (Toronto, 1925), 13.

39 Abbé C. Roy, *L'Abbé H.-R. Casgrain* (Montréal, 1925), 1170.

40 A. Gérin-Lajoie, *Jean Rivard, le défricheur* (Montréal, 1874), Preface.

41 *Ibid.*, 2.

42 *Ibid.*, vii.

43 H.-R. Casgrain (*ed.*), *Les Oeuvres complètes d'Octave Crémazie* (Montréal, 1882), 10.

44 *Ibid.*, 22.

45 *Ibid.*, 13.

46 *Ibid.*, 100.

47 S. Marion, *Les Lettres canadiennes d'autrefois* (Ottawa, 1944), IV, 140–2.

48 Commandant de Belvèze, *Lettres choisies, 1824–75* (Bourges, 1882), 135.

49 Marion, IV, 110.

50 Belvèze, 150–2, Belvèze-Rohault de Fleury, 29 August 1855.

51 *Oeuvres de Crémazie*, 106; PAC: 173F, 88–9, 64, Belvèze, 'Mission de la Capricieuse au Canada,' 1 November 1855.

52 *Oeuvres de Crémazie*, 128, 136–7.

53 *Ibid.*, 138.

54 M. Wade, *Francis Parkman* (New York, 1942), 411.

55 *Oeuvres de Crémazie*, 234, 238, 244.

56 *Ibid.*, 469.

57 *Ibid.*, 508–9.

58 *Ibid.*, 20–2.

59 *Ibid.*, 24, 25.

60 *Ibid.*, 30.

61 *Ibid.*

62 *Ibid.*, 32.

63 *Ibid.*, 39.

64 *Ibid.*, 40–2.

65 *Ibid.*, 43

66 *Ibid.*, 51.

67 *Ibid.*, 62.

68 J. Boyd, *Sir George Etienne Cartier, Bart* (Toronto, 1914), 62.

69 Boyd, 64 *n.*

70 J. Tassé, *Discours de Sir Georges Cartier, Bart* (Montréal, 1893), 2.

71 *CHAR 1938*, 70–8, J. I. Cooper, 'G. E. Cartier in the Period of the 'Forties.' Cartier's first law partner was his brother Damien, who prepared the cases which Cartier argued in court. George declared that Damien had a much better head (Boyd, 416). Then Lafontaine and Amable Berthelot took George into partnership. After their return to the bench, Cartier was joined by F.-P. Pominville, who became the dominant figure in the firm of Cartier, Pominville, & Bétourney from 1855 to Cartier's death, as the latter became more preoccupied with political life. It was one of the first Montreal law firms to specialize in guiding English businessmen through the unfamiliar mazes of French civil law.

72 Tassé, 423.

73 *Sulte: Mélanges*, IV, 15, 'Les Oeuvres de Cartier.'

74 *Ibid.*, 12–3.

75 Tassé, 6–8.

76 *Ibid.*, 17–7.

77 *Sulte: Mélanges*, 15.

78 W. L. Grant, in *Canada and Its Provinces* (Toronto, 1914), V, 5–6; quoted Boyd, 167 *n.*

79 Tassé, 402.

[80] Boyd, 107.

[81] *Ibid.*, 117.

[82] *Ibid.*, 142; Tassé, 194.

[83] Boyd, 176.

[84] *Ibid.*, Tassé, 258

[85] *Ibid.*, 147; Tassé, 278.

[86] Two Confederate emissaries, Mason and Slidell, were seized on a British mail steamer intercepted by a U.S. warship. They were later released at the demand of Great Britain. See L. B. Shippee, *Canadian-American Relations, 1849–1874* (Toronto, 1939), 116, 126, 128.

[87] *Ibid.*, 129; Tassé, 309.

[88] W. Ford (*ed.*), *A Cycle of Adams Letters, 1861–65* (Boston, 1920), II, 238–9, H. Adams-C. F. Adams, Jr., 30 December 1864; *New York Herald*, 11 February 1865, cited J.-O. Mousseau, *Contre-Poison* (Montréal, 1867), 16.

[89] Tassé, 391.

[90] *Ibid.*, 395.

[91] *Ibid.*, 405–6.

[92] *Ibid.*, 407.

[93] *Ibid.*, 407–8; Boyd, 208–9.

[94] R. Rumilly, *Histoire de la Province de Québec*, I, 36.

[95] Joseph Cauchon, *L'Union des Provinces de l'Amérique Britannique du Nord* (Québec, 1865).

[96] *Parliamentary Debates on the subject of the Confederation of the British North American Provinces* (Quebec, 1865), 54.

[97] *Ibid.*, 54–5.

[98] *Ibid.*, 59.

[99] *Ibid.*, 60.

[100] *Ibid.*

[101] *Ibid.*

[102] *Ibid.*, 61–2.

[103] *Ibid.*, 62.

[104] *Ibid.*

[105] *Ibid.*, 255–6.

[106] *Ibid.*, 257.

[107] *Ibid.*, 263.

[108] *Ibid.*, 264.

[109] *Ibid.*, 268.

[110] *Ibid.*, 360–2.

[111] *Ibid.*, 613.

[112] *Ibid.*, 894.

[113] *Ibid.*, 932. Cartier's first pledge, *ibid.*, 411.

[114] *Ibid.*, 408.

[115] *Ibid.*, 571.

[116] *Ibid.*

[117] *Ibid.*, 944, 955.

[118] *Ibid.*, 71.

[119] *Ibid.*, 694–5.

CHAPTER VII

GROWING PAINS

(1867–96)

THE QUESTION of survival for the French Canadians was brought more to the fore by Confederation than at any time since the Conquest. Durham had counted on absorbing French Canada by uniting it with Upper Canada. His policy had failed because of the collaboration of French and English Reformers in the winning of responsible government. This collaboration greatly eased the tension between the two ethnic groups after the crises of 1837–8 and 1849. But with Confederation Quebec was united first to three and then to six English-Canadian provinces; and despite Cartier's arguments that the French Canadians' position was strengthened by a fixed federal representation and the attainment of their own Quebec legislature, both the *Rouges* and his own Conservative followers feared assimilation in the great English-speaking mass of which they had become a central part.

The French Canadians had outnumbered the English at the outset of the Union, and to their numerical strength some of their success in resisting the assimilative purpose of the Union must be assigned; but now they formed less than a third of the new Canada, a proportion which has declined slightly down to the present day.[1] The defensiveness aroused by this fact was enough to breed a strong spirit of reaction which contrasts strangely with the progressive spirit of the 1830's, 1840's, and 1850's; and the development of this reactionary spirit was greatly furthered by the immediate infringement and violation of Confederation's guarantees of minority rights and privileges. Confidence in the newly achieved partnership of French and English was undermined at the outset of the period, and in two decades' time the relations between the two groups had once more reached a state of major crisis.

The conflict was heightened by certain general trends, by no means confined to Canada, which were the legacy of the American and French Revolutions. In 1776 and 1789 the right of sovereignty was first attributed to the people. By 1848 this principle, and the derivative belief that each ethnic group or nation possessed the right of sovereignty, had wrecked the false reactionary European order established by the Congress of Vienna at the close of the Napoleonic wars. Nationalism was the most considerable political force in the nineteenth century, and the great historical process which began in 1776 has continued to our own day, which has seen nationalism locked in mortal combat with a new version of the older principle of internationalism. French Canada became involved in this historical process through two channels, one French and the other Roman. That the French Canadians had become North Americans and wholly distinct from the French of France was witnessed by the fact that far the more important channel was the Roman one. This fact affected the course of events in Canada during the first thirty years of Confederation, and involved the French Canadians in the European struggle between ultramontanism and liberalism, an outgrowth of the conflict between the old and new orders caused by the rise of nationalism.

For the first time since the days of Bishop Laval, Church and State were in open conflict in Canada. Among a people so religious and so politically-minded as the French Canadians, this struggle could not fail to be of extreme bitterness; and among a people who had confused, thanks to their history, racist and nationalist ideas with religious ones, it was inevitable that the major issues of the day, the ethnic conflict, the realignment of political parties to meet the new situation created by Confederation, and the relations of Church and State, should become intricately involved in a tangle which defied the talents of statesmen and canonists alike. The struggles of this period have left a deep mark on the French-Canadian mind, and out of them was born the ultranationalism which has attracted more attention outside Quebec than anything else connected with the French Canadians.

This nationalism, as befits the circumstances under which it arose, sometimes uses religion for political ends, and sometimes politics for religious ends, and in either case arouses the antipathy of English-speaking North Americans, whose cultural tradition is largely based upon the separation of Church and State. This antipathy in turn strengthens the French-Canadian minority complex which is based upon the acute consciousness of the fact that they constitute a political minority which represents only 30 per cent of the population of Canada, and a cultural minority which represents less than 2 per cent of the neighboring Anglo-American group. As in the case of the inferiority complex of the individual, whose feelings of inadequacy cause him to adopt the arrogant and aggressive attitudes which are a form of defence mechanism, so the minority complex produces similar manifestations which intensify the conflict between the majority and the minority. Thus the first thirty years after Confederation were crowded with racial, cultural, and religious conflicts. Yet the period ended with Canada governed for the first time by a French-Canadian Catholic who was the prophet of an unhyphenated Canadianism, blending the old loyalties into a larger one—a Canadianism whose attainment is not yet complete today, when even the larger nationalism must yield to internationalism if a troubled world is to find peace.

I

Since Confederation marked a new beginning for French Canada, an account of its state at this period is demanded. The census of 1871 gave Quebec a population of slightly over a million, of which more than three-quarters was French.[2] The French Canadians were thus numerically dominant in their homeland, but they were outnumbered two to one in the new Dominion of Canada, despite growing groups in Nova Scotia, New Brunswick, Ontario, and in the Red River colony in the West.[3] Their actual influence in Quebec was less than the population figure indicates: the countryside, occupied by 85 per cent of the population, was predominantly French; but the cities were more English than French, and the control of trade and industry was largely concentrated in the hands of the English who had launched them, while labor was predominantly French.

Quebec City, whose population of 59,699 was 40 per cent English, was on the eve of a decline from the peak of prosperity reached during the previous decade, for the old dominance of the St. Lawrence waterway had been shattered by the completion in 1860 of the Grand Trunk Railway, which ran south of the river from Rivière-du-Loup to Montreal and thence to Sarnia in Ontario. Quebec continued to rely on the river, and was only linked with this railroad at Lévis across the St. Lawrence in 1884. Until the north shore line linking Hull, Montreal, Trois-Rivières, and Quebec was opened in 1879, Quebec was left without direct rail connections to the east and west, although a Lévis-Richmond line, connecting with the Montreal-Portland route, was built in 1852. Even before the building of the railways, the port of Quebec had gone into decline with the deepening of the St. Lawrence channel. In summer the steamers which replaced sailing ships could easily continue on to Montreal instead of halting at Quebec, while in winter the railroad linked Montreal with the ice-free harbor of Portland when the St. Lawrence was closed for five months.[4] The changing times not only paralyzed the port of Quebec, but they ruined one of its oldest industries, shipbuilding, which had supported half the population; for ships were now built of steel and Quebec lacked both iron and coal. The square-timber trade, which in its heyday had filled the river at Quebec for ten miles on both shores with rafts of logs and the basin with as many as 350 ships in a single season, had fallen upon evil days with the loss of British preference and demand.[5] Ruthless cutting had also almost exhausted the best of the forests of the Saguenay and Saint-Maurice in sixty years, while Montreal better served the booming Ottawa Valley trade.

With the rise of Montreal, the down-river ports were eclipsed. Quebec was left with its small industries—35 tanneries, 8 foundries, assorted wood-working establishments, and several breweries—which employed at best a thousand men.[6] It was becoming a town which lived off Church and State, for it remained the administrative center of the Church and the provincial capital, though it lost the federal government in 1867 and the English garrison in 1871. Trois-Rivières, a town of 7,570 without any major industry since the exhaustion of the white pine timber of the Saint-Maurice, and left aside by the railroads, also stagnated. Ever since the days of the California gold rush in 1849, it had contributed a notable number of its enterprising young men to the swelling tide of emigration to the States. Sorel, with its 5,636 people, was in decline as the railroads reduced the importance of the Richelieu–Lake Champlain water route; but its shipbuilders, boatmen, and longshoremen could at least find employment in the foundry, brickworks, and other small industries which flourished there, relics of the industrial-minded Englishmen and American Loyalists who had made Sorel, or William Henry as they called it, the most Anglo-American of the old Quebec towns.

On the other hand, Montreal, profiting by the brisk development of Upper Canada, had a rapidly growing population which numbered 57,715 in 1851, 90,323 in 1861, and 115,000 in 1871.[7] Inspired by Cartier and his farsighted English business friends to meet the competition of New York, Boston, and Portland, and to maintain itself as the terminus of the Great Lakes–St. Lawrence trade, Montreal began to deepen the St. Lawrence ship channel to twenty feet in 1844. A port commission created in 1851 improved the harbor facilities, so that the first transatlantic ship reached Montreal in 1857 and the number of ships entering the port more than doubled in thirty years time, reaching 500 in 1867, while the value of imports rose from $19,000,000 in 1865 to $28,000,000 in the following year.[8] By 1867 Montreal had become the metropolis of Canada and its port completely eclipsed Quebec as the center of the British import and export trade. Agricultural exports exceeded forest products by 1861.[9] Five to six hundred new houses were built each year to shelter the growing population attracted by the sixty-odd manufacturing establishments beside the Lachine Canal. Linked to the south shore and the eastern section of the Grand Trunk by the Victoria Bridge, over which trains had run since 1861,

Montreal was becoming a great rail center as well as the natural hub of the waterway system. The Grand Trunk was the biggest business in the Canada of its day, and employed more men than any other Canadian enterprise. Its warehouses for grain and other freight, its shops, and its offices all were at Montreal, which also became the banking center of Canada after the failure of the two leading Ontario banks in 1866 and 1867.

But the men who held the reins of power in Montreal were largely English Canadians—indeed the population was still more English than French in 1861, and the squalid narrow streets of the old French quarter contrasted strangely with the magnificent English country estates built on the slopes of Mount Royal by the magnates of the fur trade, whose descendants had become merchants, bankers, and industrialists. The well-to-do English lived west of St. Lawrence Main, the well-to-do French to the east, between St. Catherine and Sherbrooke Streets; and each group gave a certain flavor of its own to these new quarters of the city. Working-class villages had grown up about the factories along the Lachine Canal, and in both these new settlements and in the old quarters filth and refuse, floating on a sea of mud from October to May, filled the streets. Montreal, like New York, was growing too rapidly to concern itself with the amenities, and the unshorn aspect of both cities shocked visiting Europeans, unaccustomed to new cities. In all the province Montreal's only rival in prosperity was Sherbrooke, where textile and paper plants and a host of small industries were giving this center of the Eastern Townships the same aspect as the booming New England mill towns on which it was modeled. Sherbrooke nearly doubled its population between 1871 and 1881.[10]

All this economic activity, which characterized the coming of the industrial revolution to Quebec, was reflected in an alteration of French-Canadian society. Yet that society, because of its traditional conservatism and a resistance to change bred by the struggle to preserve the French-Canadian way of life, was not as greatly affected as the English-Canadian world which welcomed the industrial age, while the French resisted it because its pioneers were cultural aliens. From 1851 to 1881 there was a decline in domestic employment, as the old self-sufficient rural world was invaded by the new products of the cities; a slight increase in the professional class which provided services for the industrial world; and a large increase in the agricultural, commercial, and industrial classes.[11] Agricultural competition from the American Middle West hit both Upper and Lower Canada about 1850 and eventually forced technical improvement and diversification of crops. The hide-bound tradition of Quebec agriculture led to much distress among the *habitants* and to the emigration of their sons before the system was finally changed.

Resistance to industralization at home and to emigration to th States led to strong support of the colonization movement launche in 1849, though with the development of large-scale grain culture i Ontario, Quebec turned in the 1870's from wheat to dairy farmin for a cash crop beyond the subsistence provided by its traditiona small-scale mixed farming. The old pull of the towns offset th increase of the agricultural class, and the exhaustion of the bes land of the St. Lawrence seigneuries was an obstacle which n amount of encouragement of colonization by Church and Stat could overcome until obsolete agricultural methods were abandone toward the end of the century. The province was glutted with chea labor, as the former employees of the shipbuilding and timber trade desperately sought new work in the midst of the Great Depressio which began in 1873; this situation and the absence of any govern ment control over wages and working conditions made gross ex ploitation of labor possible for the industrial pioneers.

An ever-increasing number of French Canadians, faced wit such conditions at home, passed over the border to the New Englan states where the industries launched during the first half of th century had swollen until their demands for labor were insatiable At first the migratory movement was seasonal, with the Frenc Canadians replacing at harvest time the native farming populatio which had been drawn to the mills by the lure of cash wages; the the French established a foothold in the brickmaking industr which was developed by the expansion of the mill towns; an finally they entered the mills themselves, where their large familie gave them an economic advantage in an industrial era founded o the wretchedly paid dawn-to-dusk labor of women and children a well as men.[12] A later movement of population followed the west ward course of the lumber trade which cut its way across the con tinent in record time, exhausting the forests as it went. Emigratio to the States remained at first largely transient, for most of th emigrants planned to return to Quebec after they had saved enoug money to free the family farm from debt or to establish themselve in comfort on new land; but more and more of them found the free way of life and the higher standard of living sufficiently attractiv to hold them permanently. They founded 'Little Canadas' whic were French-speaking islands in the New England towns.

Some of the most enterprising brought back to Quebec th knowledge of manufacturing processes which they had acquired i the States and established small industries in their native province This development was particularly marked in Quebec City in th 1860's, where French Canadians gradually became dominant a management as well as labor in the newly established shoe industry the foundries, the wood and metal-working shops, and the declinin shipbuilding trade. They maintained and increased their hold on the tanneries and lumber mills, as the keener English Quebeckers followed the movement of capital towards Montreal, and the remainder abandoned industry in favor of banking and other financial pursuits in which their access to English credit and capital favored them. The first French president of the Quebec Chamber of Commerce was elected in 1871, while two years later 7,300 workers were employed in industries dominated by French Canadians. The slack of unemployment caused by the decline of the timber and shipbuilding trades was thus largely taken up, but there was little further expansion during the great depression which afflicted Canada generally for the next two decades.

With the rise of the saw-log and lumber industries, there was a major displacement of population westward from the Quebec-Montreal region, and a minor one eastward along the lower St. Lawrence. The headquarters of the timber trade shifted from Quebec to Montreal, for steamships, railroads, and the greater transportability of the new staples eliminated the old seasonal drives down the river system to the Quebec timber coves. Despite the establishment of small sawmills at Montmorency in the 1860's and at Batiscan, Montmagny, and Chicoutimi in the 1870's, the great development was in the Ottawa and Gatineau Valleys at Hawksbury, Hull, and Chelsea. By 1881 the Ottawa timber and lumber trade, which at its peak in 1863 employed 15,000 men in the forests, 10,000 at the mills, and some 25,000 in exporting from Quebec, was petering out, as that of the Saint-Maurice had by 1873 and that of the Saguenay by the 1860's.[13] Towards the end of the century the new pulp and paper industry, which made use of forests already gutted of the best timber and lumber, was founded at Trois-Rivières and shortly afterward launched in the Saguenay-Lake St. John region and in the Ottawa Valley. This soon became the first industry of the province in which nearly all the wood was cut and half the paper made from it was manufactured.[14] The development was part of a shift from extractive industry to manufacturing which characterized the Quebec economy at the turn of the century, despite the continual exploitation of Chaudière River gold and of the Thetford asbestos deposits discovered in 1877 and developed after 1885.[15] Decentralization of manufacturing was fostered by the extension of the railroad network during the period. Trois-Rivières was linked to Arthabaska in 1865; Montreal to Sorel in 1882; Quebec to Lake St. John in 1888; and Gaspé to New Brunswick and Quebec in 1898.[16]

The economic development of this period was accompanied by a social development which held the seeds of a radical alteration in the character of French-Canadian society which is still being worked out today. French-Canadian labor, bred in the agricultural tradition of dawn-to-dusk work for little cash return, or in the hard life of the timber trade, was slow to follow the lead of English workers who organized unions soon after their arrival in Canada, though these were only legalized after long opposition in 1872. From the French regime the *Québecois* had inherited the guild tradition—there were guilds in the tanneries and among the carpenters of New France[17]—but being hard-working, thrifty, and accustomed to obey orders and to a lower standard of living than his English compatriots, he was slow to show interest in the aggressive Anglo-American unions which sprang up about the middle of the century. These were frowned on by the clergy as 'dangerous secret societies.'[18] In any case the former shipbuilder or lumberjack, faced with the prospect of starvation if he did not find a job, was not inclined to stand upon the rights of labor, while the newly industrialized *habitant* had lost none of his traditional individualism in the transition from rural to urban life.

Of the new national and international unions, only the Knights of Labor were conspicuously successful in penetrating Quebec, despite the differences of Anglo-American and French-Canadian mentalities; and after their initial success in 1881 they encountered determined opposition from the Church as a secret society of dubious principles and finally disappeared from Quebec after Cardinal Taschereau condemned them in 1886.[19] The Catholic syndicates, launched in the 1890's on the inspiration of *Rerum Novarum* and favoured by the deeply-felt need of the French Canadian for his own social organizations in order to avoid absorption into the Anglo-American world, checked the growth of Quebec locals associated with the Canadian Trades and Labor Congress established in 1886.

The union movement in Quebec was met by united opposition from the French-Canadian élite and the Anglo-American economic overlords: the Church opposed the materialistic and socialistic outlook of the labor leaders and their threat to its dominance in the social field; the politicians successfully appealed to ethnic loyalty to curb the political threat presented by the movement; the professionals benefited by acting as middlemen between the economic overlords and the masses; and the employers fought a development which threatened an industrial system based upon low labor costs.

The profound individualism of the French-Canadian character also did not offer a fertile field for development of the union ideal. Generally speaking, the French-Canadian worker was slow to turn against his traditional leaders and to lose his hierarchical view of society. He was willing to pay the price of being distinctively French and Catholic in an industrial system dominated by the Anglo-American Protestant world which encircled Quebec. Though he ometimes protested when exploitation was too flagrant, he was nuch more apt to rebel at attempted alterations of his traditional vays than at long hours, low wages, and poor working conditions. The French-Canadian worker was bred in a desperately hard school: he fur trade, subsistence agriculture, and lumbering had given him in endurance and a patience under hardship rare among North American workers, although poor nutrition and sanitary standards iad made him less productive than British or American workers.

2

These epoch-making alterations in the Quebec economy had a profound influence upon the French-Canadian mind, which tended hen as now to look at every new development primarily from an ethnic point of view, particularly when the changes were coupled vith English assertions of dominance in the political world. It is not without significance that the most bitter clashes of French and English opinion developed in Montreal and Trois-Rivières, where English economic influence was dominant, while French-dominated Quebec City remained serene and largely unaffected by the great conflicts of the period. The French Canadians, involved despite hemselves in an industrial economy alien to their tradition, tended o assert their Frenchness and to contest stubbornly any infringement of their rights under Confederation. This assertion of their separateness also involved an assertion of their Catholicism, since he concept of French-Canadian nationality had become inextricably nvolved with religion. This aggressive Catholicism was also excited by the effort after 1850 of English Canadians to break up the French-Canadian cultural group by a militant missionary effort centering n the Montreal region, and by attacks on the Catholic Church from sources outside Quebec. This Protestant onslaught merely ncreased the religio-ethnic cleavage which it sought to break down.

Cultural relations with France, which had been renewed in the 1850's and industriously cultivated by Napoleon III, were greatly strengthened by French intervention against the Italian nationalists n 1860, when Rome was held for the Pope by a French garrison, and when Garibaldi's renewed onslaught in 1867 was checked at Mentana by the Papal Zouaves, who were largely French. Two French Canadians and one English Quebecker served with the Zouaves in their early days, while in 1867 Bishop Bourget of Montreal decided to raise a contingent of Canadian Zouaves, although the Pope had only appealed for financial aid and not for volunteers. The Bishop's personal following of zealous priests and laymen, always to the fore in French and Catholic matters, preached a holy war from the pulpit and in the press. In February 1868, 135 volunteers, chosen from 564 with more regard for their moral tha military qualities, set out from Montreal after three days of publi ceremonies. Their flag, designed by Papineau's son-in-law, th artist Napoléon Bourassa, had been solemnly blessed; Bisho Laflèche of Trois-Rivières had preached them a stirring sermon o the Church militant and the Christian as a soldier; and Bisho Bourget had administered an oath by which the volunteers boun themselves to bring no stain upon Catholicism or their country with 'whose honor and glory you are charged.'[20] While at hom Bishop Bourget and the young Conservative orator Adolphe Chap leau continued to preach a crusade, the volunteers were greeted i Paris by the ultramontane journalist Louis Veuillot as a 'band c crusaders.'[21] The fact that they never saw action, thanks to th collapse of Garibaldi's movement, diminished none of the Zouaves fervor, and on the third anniversary of their departure they or ganized the Union Allet—named after their colonel—which becam a center of ultramontane activity and still persists today, while th Zouave uniform is affected by parish guards who add color t church celebrations.[22]

The effect of the Papal Zouave episode was to widen the ga between French and English in Canada, for Garibaldi was a her to the English-speaking world, and defending the temporal powe of the Papacy was not a popular course in North America outsid Quebec. Bishop Laflèche's discourse at the departure of the Zouaves which he had been unable to finish because of emotion, was late published. It opened the public phase of the ultramontane-libera conflict. For Bishop Laflèche added to the ancient battles of th Church against paganism, Arianism, Protestantism, and Voltairean ism, the contemporary struggle against rationalistic liberalism, bor of the principles of Voltaire and Rousseau and of the Frenc Revolution. He drew a black and white opposition between liberal ism and Catholicism, and called upon French Canada to fulfil it 'Providential mission of maintaining and spreading the Kingdon of God in the New World' by avoiding all contamination fron liberalism.[23] This discourse aroused considerable agitation amon the Liberals of Quebec, who were divided into a small and ver radical group known as the *Rouges* under the leadership of Louis Antoine Dessaules, Joseph Doutre, and Rodolphe Laflamme, an a larger and more moderate one made up of those who reconcile their politics with their religion, and relied upon the sympathie of pro-Liberal Archbishop Taschereau of Quebec and of Lava University, in the face of a general alliance of the clergy with th Conservative Party. The conflict thus opened was to continue o many fronts until the close of the century, leaving an indelibl mark on the French-Canadian mind.

3

Since the 1830's two radically opposed currents of ideas had been flowing through French Canada. They are commonly called ultramontanism and liberalism, although both are misnamed, for French-Canadian ultramontanism had a strong nationalist and even racist bent more characteristic of gallicanism than of its historical opposite, while French-Canadian liberalism was very different from its European namesake condemned by Pope Pius IX in the *Syllabus of Errors* (1864). The semantic confusion caused by applying European terms to North American movements of different origins and purposes envenomed the struggle between these two rival currents of ideas. The original leader of the ultramontane movement was Bishop Ignace Bourget, who became the second bishop of the new diocese of Montreal in 1840, after serving as vicar-general since its foundation. The Bishop sympathized with the *Patriote* movement of 1837–8; and in the diocese of Montreal the ecclesiastical authorities, with the exception of the Sulpicians, took a much less firm stand against the movement than did those of Quebec, with their tradition of strict loyalism which had won for the Church virtual establishment under English rule—a status far more favorable than that attained under the gallican French regime.

After the Rebellions, under the Union which was intended to deprive the French Canadians of their separate nationality, Bishop Bourget, a zealous, energetic, authoritarian, and very Roman-minded prelate, was the dynamic force in providing every bulwark for that nationality which came within the province of the Church. His enthusiastic followers did not always stop at these limits, which in any case were a matter of dispute at the time.

In the first decade of his possession of the see, Bishop Bourget established no less than ten religious orders in his diocese, bringing many of them from France and creating others in Canada. Among the teaching orders were the Jesuits, the Oblates, the Holy Cross Fathers and Brothers, and the Clerks of St. Viator, who exercized a strong conservative influence on the French Canadians in their reaction against the French Revolutions of 1830 and 1848. French support of the Papacy against the Italian Republicans of 1848 and 1860 strengthened the tendency of these clerics and their lay disciples to identify themselves with the French ultramontanes, whose spokesman was the zealous convert Louis Veuillot, editor of *L'Univers*. In particular the Society of Jesus, favored by Bishop Bourget and benefiting by the prestige of its achievements in New France, exercized a growing influence through its intellectual attainments and its identification with the promulgation of the dogma of the

Immaculate Conception (1854), with the condemnation of post-French Revolution ideas in the *Syllabus of Errors* (1864), and with the assertion of papal infallibility in matters of faith and morals (1870). The Jesuits were considered to be exceedingly close to Rome. Bishop Bourget befriended them and modeled his new cathedral on St. Peter's, while the more liberal Sulpicians fell out of favor and the vast single parish of Notre-Dame-de-Montréal, which they had held since 1657, was threatened with division by the bishop.

At this period many elements in the Catholic Church at large, in reaction to the blows dealt it by the French and Italian Revolutions, swung to a highly conservative position which clashed with the dominant ideas of the non-Catholic world, then deeply affected by the dynamic heritage of 1789. This Catholic conservatism hardened into reaction as a result of the plight of the Papacy, beset by successive nationalist assaults on its temporal power in Italy. Pius IX himself reflected this development by his gradual abandonment of his early liberal ideas for highly conservative ones. While ultramontanism was anti-nationalistic in Europe, it was combined with an aggressive nationalism in Quebec, in the fervor of French-Canadian reaction to the assimilative program of the Union.

The ultramontane doctrine of the supremacy of Church over State and the nationalist doctrine of vigorous defence of French-Canadian rights both held the seeds of religio-political conflict. This conflict was long postponed by the excellent personal relationship between the dominant figure of the hierarchy, Bishop Bourget, and the political master of Quebec, George-Etienne Cartier, both of whom were deeply conservative and authoritarian by nature. Then Cartier's legal advocacy of the cause of his old teachers, the Sulpicians, in opposition to the Bishop's desire to divide the parish of Montreal, brought about a coolness which favored subsequent open clashes between the two men. For all his reliance on clerical support in politics, Cartier was gallican-minded, and when in 1870 the Church became active in politics on its own account, Cartier fought the development as bitterly as any *Rouge*.

The opposing current of ideas, present in the French-Canadian mind ever since the American Revolution, was furthered by the writings of Lamennais and Lacordaire in 1830, which notably influenced *Patriote* thinking in 1837. When Papineau returned in 1845 from exile in France, he introduced the advanced democratic ideas which had subsequently been developed by these and other French intellectual leaders, who were ultramontanes in 1830 and radical liberals in 1848. Papineau himself, however, was rather more influenced by the tradition of English liberalism and by the development of that tradition in the United States. His democracy was always more North American than European, but many of his fiery young *Rouge* disciples mingled French and American doctrines in their thinking. After the split of the French Canadians in the late 1840's into Liberal-Conservatives and Liberals, the *Rouges*, in their republicanism, often flirted with annexationism. Like the English Canadians of 1849, who wanted to be English at the cost of being British, the *Rouges* were willing to cease being Canadian in order to remain French. As Lamennais broke with the Church because of what he considered to be a conspiracy of kings and priests against the people, while Lacordaire reconciled his republicanism with his Catholicism and died 'a penitent monk and an impenitent liberal,'[24] so the small group of *Rouges* who in 1847 launched the republican *L'Avenir* (named after Lamennais' and Lacordaire's organ of 1830) and its more moderate successor *Le Pays* in 1852, followed different paths. That of Lacordaire was made difficult for them by the rigid authoritarianism of Bishop Bourget and his still more inflexible disciple Bishop Laflèche. As the English-Canadian Tories had long supplied proof, a colonial culture is narrower than its model, and some French Canadians became more French than the French and more Catholic than the Pope.

The *Rouge* group, filled with the spirit of 1848, was not content with uphill political and journalistic action in a French Canada which was either becoming too preoccupied with business or too reactionary to care for new ideas. They became dominant during the 1850's in the *Institut Canadien* of Montreal, which in the absence of universities had been founded in 1844 to provide an intellectual center for French-Canadian graduates of the classical colleges. The *Institut* maintained a library and reading room; held debates and lectures; and provided a free forum for that fervent discussion of general ideas so dear to young French-Canadian intellectuals. Despite the foundation of two rival institutions, *L'Oeuvre de bons livres* and the Sulpician *Cabinet de Lecture*, whose establishment under clerical auspices was inspired by Bishop Bourget, the Montreal *Institut* and others modeled on it throughout the province grew rapidly until 1858, when the bishop first took formal steps against it. It numbered some 700 members in 1857.

The leading figures were Dr. Louis-Antoine Dessaules, a nephew of Papineau and like him a radical democrat of seigneurial background; Joseph Doutre, an able lawyer who was one of the editors of *L'Avenir* and one of the founders of *Le Pays*, a prophet of the Enlightenment and a mortal enemy of Cartier; Eric Dorion, the *enfant terrible* brother of Antoine-Aimé Dorion, the *Rouge* chief, and the founder of *L'Avenir* and *Le Défricheur*; and Charles Laberge, a lawyer who followed the elder Dorion in politics but broke with him over his alliance with the francophobe George Brown of Ontario. These radical-minded young men preached with various nuances the dawn of a new era of free speech and thought which was not at all to the taste of Bishop Bourget, who was disturbed by vigorous Protestant proselytizing in Montreal and by the *Institut's* tolerant attitude toward non-Catholic opinion.

So in the spring of 1858 the Bishop issued three pastoral letters, in the first of which he deplored the rise of irreligiousness in Canada as evidenced by 'bad books, lying publications, and irreligious discourses.' Members of literary societies were warned against 'books contrary to faith and morals.'[25] Now the *Institut's* library contained such books as Voltaire's works, Lamartine's *Voyage en Orient*, Pascal's *Provincial Letters*, Montesquieu's *Spirit of Laws*, Florente's *History of the Inquisition*, Montaigne's *Essays*, Sismondi's *History of the Italian Republics*, and Lamennais' *Paroles d'un Croyant*, while its sixty-odd journals ran the gamut from *Les Mélanges religieux*, the Bishop's organ, to the militantly Protestant *Witness*. After a meeting at which a majority of members decided that the *Institut* was capable of judging the morality of its library for itself, some hundred dissident members, headed by Edouard Fabre and Labrèche-Viger, resigned on the grounds that the *Institut*, which had been founded solely for French Canadians, now opened its library to all, and that it spread 'absurd moral, religious, and national ideas.' The dissidents, supported by the bishop, opened the short-lived *Institut national*, while the original body refused to recognize the authority of the *Index* on gallican grounds, and protested that its library was 'exclusively composed of moral books . . . suited to nourish the heart and to develop the intelligence,' and had never contained 'books of an obscene or immoral character.'[26] In reply Bishop Bourget issued another pastoral on March 30, invoking the authority of the Council of Trent on the question of episcopal jurisdiction in matters of censorship, and declaring that books listed in the *Institut* catalogue of 1852 had been condemned by the *Index*. Two months later he denounced 'bad newspapers,' defined as those 'whose belief and morality are contrary to those of the Faith.'[27] This utterance was clearly directed against *Le Pays*, the *Rouge* organ directed by Dessaules, then a dominant figure in the *Institut*. Dessaules later claimed that he twice wrote the Bishop for an explanation without receiving a reply.

Hostilities between Bishop Bourget and the *Institut* then lapsed for a few years, although the bishop threw his influence behind rival organizations under clerical control. Then in 1863 a committee, composed among others of Joseph Doutre and young Wilfrid Laurier, waited upon the bishop and in an attempt at reconciliation asked him to indicate the 'reprehensible works' in the library catalogue which they left with him. Bishop Bourget returned the catalogue without comment six months later, thus insisting upon formal submission to his authority before making peace. Meanwhile he had issued a pastoral letter on December 25, 1863, pointing out in apocalyptic terms the 'dangers of the times in which we live, the dangers from the men among whom we live, and the dangers of the errors in the environment in which we live.'[28] He also called for great vigilance lest impious books and bad newspapers should spread dangerous doctrines among Catholics. In March 1864 the *Institut* declared itself to be devoid of doctrine, although it carefully banned pernicious teachings and 'anything which might wound the religious sensibilities of some of its members.'[29] After another fruitless interview with the bishop, a group of members appealed to Rome and made charges against the bishop, who defended himself by sending to Rome a collection of pamphlets published under the *Institut's* auspices.

As a result of these steps, in 1868 the *Institut's* yearbook was put on the *Index*, an extraordinary measure, while the Provincial Council of the hierarchy again denounced impious and immoral books, libraries which contained both good and bad books, and certain harmful newspapers. The faithful were forbidden to own, edit, write for, or circulate the latter, while 'every true patriot' was called upon not to read them.[30] Meanwhile Papineau had emerged from his retirement at Montebello to contribute his prestige to be beleaguered *Institut* by giving a lecture under its auspices in December 1867, in which he maintained the thesis that solid convictions could only be arrived at by a free examination of the facts. This was taken as a declaration of open war by the bishop, and Montreal became the scene of a battle between the liberal and reactionary outlooks. Under the heavy pressure exerted by the bishop, Dessaules openly defied episcopal authority, while stoutly maintaining his Catholicism. Doutre declared himself an agnostic.

During these years the aging Bishop Bourget had received wholehearted support from the ardent young Grand Vicar of Trois-Rivières, Louis-François Laflèche, recalled from the Red River missions after twelve years to become first superior of the Séminaire de Nicolet and later administrator of the diocese, which he was to head from 1870 to 1898. After the papal defeat at Castelfidaro in 1860, Abbé Laflèche delivered a passionate sermon in favor of the temporal power of the Papacy, hymning Lamoricière and his Zouaves. In 1866 Laflèche, now grand-vicar, published his *Quelques considérations sur les rapports de la société civile avec la Religion et la Famille*. In this adaptation to French Canada of the ideas of Rohrbacher, who as an apologetic Church historian had dealt crushing blows to French gallicanism after parting company with the more radical Lamennais in 1832, his disciple laid down the basic principles of French-Canadian nationalistic ultramontanism:

I. A nation is constituted by unity of speech, unity of faith, uniformity of morals, customs, and institutions. The French Canadians possess all these, and constitute a true nation. Each nation has received from Providence a mission to fulfil. The mission of the French-Canadian people is to constitute a center of Catholicism in the New World.

II. Authority derives from God. The best form of government is a moderate monarchy (the Church and the family are examples of it); the most imperfect is democracy. Liberalism commits the fundamental error of seeking to build society on other than religious principles. Electors not only exercise a right; they fulfil a duty for which they are responsible before God. The priest thus has a right to guide them. 'It is an error condemned by reason, by history, and by Revelation to say that politics is a field in which religion has no right to enter, and in which the Church has no concern.'[31]

In a Saint-Jean-Baptiste Day address to the French Canadians of Ottawa in this same year, Grand Vicar Laflèche advanced the doctrine, destined to become a dogma of French-Canadian nationalism, that whoever lost his language lost his faith. He also referred to the necessity of learning English as 'the heaviest tax imposed upon us by the Conquest,' and urged his auditors: 'Let us pay it loyally, but let us pay only when necessary.'[32] He denounced the idea that only political states constituted nations, and maintained that the French Canadians, like the Irish and the Indians, remained distinct nations despite the fact that they were ruled by foreign governments. He insisted on the solidarity of family, nationality, language, and faith as the basis of French-Canadian nationhood; an analysis which is still the basis of nationalistic thinking in French Canada, despite the fact that the idea that faith is dependent upon language is totally foreign to true Catholicism, which is supranational.

Laflèche's doctrines were naturally opposed by the leading spirits of the *Institut*, who then dominated the Liberal Party in Quebec. Their position was gravely weakened when the *Institut* yearbook of 1868, containing an eulogy of free thought and annexationist speeches by Dessaules and Horace Greeley of the *New York Tribune*, was condemned by the Holy Office in July 1869 and put on the *Index*. In a pastoral letter issued from Rome, where he had gone for the Vatican Council, Bishop Bourget announced this decision and proclaimed that it was forbidden, under pain of being deprived of the sacraments, to be a member of the *Institut* while it taught perverse doctrines, or to read or possess the condemned yearbook.[33] Gonzalve Doutre, a Papal Zouave brother of Joseph Doutre and a professor of law at McGill, went to Rome in a vain effort to upset the condemnation and to invoke restraint of Bishop Bourget's high-handed ways. While Doutre was at Rome, the *Institut* met and protested its innocence, and its Catholic members accepted the condemnation. But the refusal of some members, led by the gallican-minded Dessaules, to bow to the storm provoked new episcopal thunders. The 1869 yearbook was in turn condemned by Rome in 1870, while the bishop again denounced 'promoters of such dangerous errors.'[34]

Then what had been hitherto a French-Canadian family quarrel became a national and international *cause célèbre* with the death in November 1869 of the printer Joseph Guibord, a member and former vice-president of the *Institut*. Bishop Bourget had decreed that those who persisted in membership in the *Institut* after its condemnation should be deprived of the sacraments and Christian burial. Some weeks before his death Guibord, who had not been a practising Catholic in recent years, had called a priest to his bedside, but refusing to renounce the *Institut*, had not received the last rites of the Church. In accordance with the bishop's order, the Sulpician *curé* of Notre-Dame refused to perform any religious ceremony for Guibord and stipulated that his body would be buried in the unconsecrated part of the cemetery, reserved for those who died outside the Church. In short, he expressed his willingness to grant civil burial, but refused Christian burial. Guibord died on a Thursday, and his funeral was set for Monday by his friends, fellow-members of the *Institut*. After their request for Christian burial had twice been refused by Curé Rousselot, the corpse was carried on Sunday afternoon to the Catholic cemetery of Côte-des-Neiges. When the caretaker refused to accept it without authority from the *curé*—Catholic burials were never performed on Sundays or in the afternoon—the funeral proceeded to the Protestant cemetery, where Guibord's body found a temporary resting place.

The following Wednesday suit was brought against the *curé* and churchwardens of Notre-Dame in the name of Guibord's illiterate wife, Henrietta Brown, who later gave evidence that she had had no desire to sue and that legal action was taken on the initiative of her husband's friends. Rodolphe Laflamme, one of the leading spirits of the *Institut*, appeared as her lawyer in the case, which was heard by Judge Charles Mondelet, the defender of the Rebellion prisoners in the 1839 trials whose independence of spirit was further indicated by the fact that he had married outside the Church. Louis-Amable Jetté, Laflamme's brother-in-law and a moderate *Rouge* though a fervent Catholic, was the advocate of Notre-Dame. Both lawyers were at the outset of brilliant legal and public careers which carried Laflamme to the federal cabinet and Jetté to the lieutenant-governorship of Quebec and membership in the Alaska Boundary tribunal. Laflamme was soon reinforced by Joseph Doutre, and Jetté by Francis Cassidy, an Irish Catholic founder of the *Institut*, and

F.-X.-A. Trudel, who was to become famous as the lay leader of the ultramontanes under the mocking title of 'Grand Vicar' Trudel.

With this array of legal talent, carefully chosen on both sides with regard to personal positions and views, the trial soon departed from the matter in question and became a public debate on gallicanism *vs.* ultramontanism, free speech *vs.* authoritarianism, French law *vs.* English law, canon law *vs.* civil law—in essence, State *vs.* Church. The lawyers wandered from the Council of Trent through the Inquisition to St. Bartholomew's Massacre, from the capitulations of the Conquest through the Quebec Act to the constitutions of 1791, 1840, and 1867. The whole conflict of the *Institut* with Bishop Bourget was fought once more in open court, and the attention devoted to the trial by both the French and English press made it a focus of the religio-political controversies of the day. Judge Mondelet, who exhibited during the trial a partisan attitude which made plain his gallican and liberal sympathies, delivered judgment on May 6, 1870, condemning the parish to provide burial within the Catholic cemetery within six days and to bear all costs of the trial.[35]

This sentence was reversed on September 30, 1870 by unanimous decision of the Court of Appeals, on the grounds that the civil courts had no jurisdiction in ecclesiastical cases; that gallican law had never been in force in Canada; and that priests of the Catholic Church were entirely independent of civil tribunals in the exercise of their ministry.[36] On December 2 an appeal was carried to the Queen's Bench Court, which on September 7, 1871 sustained the judgment of the Court of Appeals, after its English presiding justice had sharply rejected Doutre's motion that Catholic judges be barred from the bench for this case.[37] Appeal was then taken to the Privy Council in the name of the *Institut*—the widow Guibord having meanwhile died—and Doutre and Jetté went to London to argue the case. By a judgment rendered on November 28, 1874, the parish was ordered to bury Guibord in the Catholic portion of the cemetery and to pay costs amounting to $6,000. The Privy Council held that during the French regime canon law had been subject to the Gallican Liberties and that a right of appeal from ecclesiastical decisions to the civil courts had been recognized. It maintained that this right had been continued by the Quebec Act, and that since the *Index* had never been recognized in France or Canada, Guibord was free of any valid ecclesiastical sentence barring him from Christian burial.[38]

Thus, after six years of litigation and agitation, September 2, 1875 was set by Joseph Doutre for the burial of Guibord by court order in the Catholic cemetery lot already occupied by his wife's grave. The triumphant Doutre went beyond the terms of the judgment and demanded that burial be accompanied by the ordinary religious ceremonies, under pains of damages and interest. Al

Montreal and much of Canada was up in arms over the Guibord case, and both the mayor and chief of police were warned by Bishop Bourget to take measures against possible popular outbreaks on the day set for burial. While a turbulant crowd excited by the ultramontane press gathered at the Catholic cemetery, Guibord's body was exhumed from the Protestant cemetery and the coffin, covered with a British flag, was placed in a hearse surmounted by a cross. The funeral procession of a dozen carriages and some thirty people then proceeded to the open gates of the Catholic cemetery. Pushing aside the guards stationed there, the crowd closed the gates against the funeral procession. The caretaker, summoned by a bailiff to open the gates, declined to do so, protesting that he could do nothing against the opposition of the crowd. The mayor, summoned by telegram, arrived with police reinforcements after Doutre had retired to the Protestant cemetery with the body amid some stone-throwing and a growing hue and cry.

A few days later Bishop Bourget issued a circular letter urging the people to be calm and to offer no opposition to Guibord's burial. He added that the grave would be placed under interdict, and hence would be 'morally separated' from consecrated ground.[39] During the following month Doutre brought suit against *Le Nouveau Monde*, the ultramontane organ blamed for raising the agitation, and against the parish for refusing burial. Though both suits were thrown out of court, Doutre succeeded in extracting the costs of previous litigation from the parish, and these were paid under protest by the *curé*. Meanwhile an armed guard had been established over the Protestant cemetery, and a violent newspaper controversy broke out.

Finally, on November 16, after the *curé* of Notre-Dame had once more refused Christian burial and protested against this violation of the laws of the Church, the liberties of Catholics, and the sanctity of the cemetery by the enforced burial of Guibord in consecrated ground, the body was carried from the Protestant cemetery to the Catholic one under the protection of 1,235 soldiers, Mayor Hingston, and Judge Coursol. The *curé* assisted as a civil officer at the burial, but the only ceremony was a prayer by some of Guibord's friends. The grave was filled with cement and scrap iron as a precaution against desecration, and then guards were placed over the final resting place of the troubled corpse of Joseph Guibord. His epitaph was pronounced by Bishop Bourget in a pastoral letter published on the day of burial. The bishop rejoiced that calm had prevailed despite provocation; reaffirmed that the grave would be forever separate from consecrated ground; and concluded: 'There reposes a rebel who has been buried by force of arms.'[40]

4

The persecution of the *Institut Canadien* and the Guibord case cannot be understood without reference to the political history of the period. The *Institut* was not only a literary society; its leaders were also the leaders of the *Rouge* party, and they revolted against Bishop Bourget's authority in part because of the open alliance of the hierarchy with the Conservative Party. Since the *Rouges* believed in the new republican ideas which in Europe had endangered the position of the Church, the French-Canadian hierarchy was naturally inclined to ally itself with their political opponents. The new democracy of the nineteenth century had no appeal for the clergy, who were alarmed by the increase of official corruption and election disorders at home and by civil strife in Europe. Democracy was also tainted for them by its derivation from the suspect intellectual fathers of the French Revolution, and by the fact that its disciples went to still greater extremes than the leaders of the unsuccessful Rebellion of 1837–8, which had endangered the survival of French-Canadian nationality. The *Rouges* openly advanced the doctrine of the separation of Church and State—a doctrine repugnant to the Catholic tradition, which holds that such separation may be tolerated but not approved—and they gloated over the republican successes in Europe, which deeply distressed the innately conservative and monarchist French-Canadian clergy, who at this period identified themselves more closely with Rome than at any time since the days of Bishop Laval. The *Rouges* also were sympathetic to American ideas, ever distrusted by the clergy, and inclined to annexationism, which the clergy thought would doom French-Canadian Catholicism.

With the breakdown of the Union government in the early 1860's, the clerical leaders tended to throw their support behind Cartier in the project of Confederation, though not always enthusiastically—Laflèche, for instance, regarded repeal of the Union as impossible, legislative union as 'the extermination of our institutions and nationality'; and Confederation as the only solution 'which offers us a plank of safety.'[41] Possibly because of his difference with Cartier over the division of the parish of Montreal, Bishop Bourget contented himself with a neutral acceptance of Confederation, while the other bishops of the province supported it more warmly and thundered against the *Rouges* who opposed it. With the *Rouges* openly annexationist and opposed to the temporal power of the Church, it was easy for the bishops to view the political contest, as Laflèche did, simply as a 'struggle between good and evil.'[42]

Confronted with the prospect of an ever-diminishing minority position in Canada under Confederation, the French Canadians recoiled upon their own distinctive tradition, whose European bulwarks were also threatened at this period both in France and Italy. In 1870 Quebec was more French and Catholic than it had been since the heyday of New France. During the next thirty years French Canada turned more and more to the ancient mother country:

It established transatlantic contacts with France; it travelled in France for pleasure, for tourist and commercial purposes; it sent its sons to study in France; it read French periodicals and books; the textbooks which it used were for the most part published in France; it received Frenchmen as visitors, lecturers, preachers, and consuls; its newspapers cited the French press copiously; it sought French honors.[43]

One of the most notable French influences upon Quebec was that of *L'Echo de la France*, a review of science and literature founded by Louis Ricard in 1865, which familiarized Quebec with the writings of Mgr. Dupanloup, Montalembert, Père Félix, Père Hyacinthe, Lacordaire, Thiers, Berryer, Lamartine, Veuillot, Victor Hugo, Guizot, and Victor Cousin.

The renewal of ties between France and Quebec which had been fostered by Napoleon III in the 1850's and 1860's was furthered by the profound sympathy felt in Quebec for France when the Third Empire fell before the Prussian assault in 1870. In his unpublished memoirs Abbé Casgrain vividly describes the reaction in Quebec to the disasters of 1870:

The echo of these frightful disasters, brought by the telegraph and re-echoed by the newspapers, spread grief and consternation among the French population of Canada, which had remained profoundly attached to its mother country despite more than a century of separation. We were at first incredulous at the news of the first defeats; France, it was said, might suffer some reverses, but that she should fall, completely beaten down, demolished, and reduced to helplessness at the feet of an enemy whom she had already conquered, seemed implausible. The sad reality nevertheless had to be accepted. Stupor yielded to discouragement, to grief, to lamentation. It was as if each Canadian family mourned some of its members fallen on the fields of carnage where Frence left part of itself. The present generation cannot imagine the spiritual state in which we lived during this terrible year. We were hurt in the most sensitive and most intimate parts of national feeling. No more illusions were possible; we marched from humiliation to humiliation. Nevertheless, if we bent our heads at the sight of such great misfortunes, we raised them with pride to protest indignantly when cowardly detractors dared to raise their voices to insult conquered France.[44]

The Quebec clergy, which included some French emigrés of 1848, pronounced that France was undergoing the judgment of God for its sins, and the unusually vivid northern lights in the fall of 1870 were taken as divine portents of the disasters of which tidings continued to come from abroad. The news of the French surrender and Napoleon's capture, of the Paris Revolution and the proclamation of the Republic, was received by grief-stricken crowds in Quebec. Relief funds for French prisoners and refugees were raised with enthusiasm. Gambetta's determination to carry on the war, Thier's policies, and the rise of the Commune were opposed in a Quebec which followed the lead of the French clergy. Almost to a man the French Canadians espoused the cause of the Comte de Chambord, the royalist leader.

For all the intense sympathy felt in Quebec for afflicted France, a lasting distrust of the Republic became part of the French-Canadian mind, and from it stemmed a growing conviction, encouraged by royalist-minded French priests and nuns who emigrated to Quebec, that the French Canadians were a people chosen by Providence to carry on the true French and Catholic tradition, uncorrupted by liberalism and republicanism. After 1867 the Sulpician *Cabinet de Lecture*, which made more of French than French-Canadian literature and introduced Mgr. de Ségur's anti-Masonic tracts, helped to develop a tendency to blame France's woes and Quebec's prospective dangers on the influence of Freemasonry, an idea which by the 1890's became an obsession with ultramontane journalists. This trend reached its height in 1895 with the publication of Jules-Paul Tardivel's *Pour la Patrie*, a novel which foretold an Orange Order plot to seize the Dominion government and to exterminate French Canada.

The development of emphasis on Quebec's Frenchness was accompanied by an intensification of French-Canadian Catholicism during the same period. The ultramontane leaders of the Quebec hierarchy, Bishops Bourget and Laflèche, were among the most ardent supporters of the dogma of Papal infallibility, which was promulgated on July 18, 1870 by the Vatican Council. Bishop Laflèche wrote from Rome to his grand vicar that April: 'Protestantism has directly attacked the Church by rejecting its authority . . . Gallicanism, more hypocritical, has pretended to have a certain respect for the Church while exerting itself above all to attack it in its constitution.'[45] To him the providential moment had arrived to crush gallicanism—by which he meant any State opposition to the Church—and Protestant inroads on Catholicism. A month later he wrote again to Grand Vicar Caron: 'The dogmatic definition of the infallibility of the Sovereign Pontiff is the great remedy which God in His mercy has prepared to cure the frightful social evils of our time.'[46] Both Bishop Bourget and Bishop Laflèche returned from Rome with their ultramontane tendencies reinforced, and with new fervor to oppose the development in Canada of the political liberalism which had brought revolution to Italy and France. Both they and Bishop Taché of St. Boniface, who had been recalled from the Vatican Council by Cartier in January 1870 to aid the government in settling the Riel question,* evinced a tendency to extend Papal infallibility to the episcopate, while their zealous disciples extended it on down to the humblest *curé*. The way was thus paved for the bitter conflicts between Church and State which ensued for thirty years.

The old alliance between the hierarchy and the Conservatives was soon threatened by several developments. Bishop Bourget discovered that he could get little aid from Cartier, the political overlord of Quebec as well as the French-Canadian leader at Ottawa, in his campaign to divide the parish of Montreal. Cartier was loyal to his older teachers, the Sulpicians, whom he served as attorney in their legal proceedings in this matter, and he was too gallican-minded to take political orders from Bishop Bourget, who wanted legislative support for his plan. Then the federal government refused to disavow the New Brunswick law of 1871 which destroyed the separate schools of that province, where the French Canadians formed a large minority. Using as an excuse the danger of infringing provincial rights and thus setting a precedent which might later be turned against Quebec, the ever-temporizing Sir John A. Macdonald managed to resist French-Canadian pressure for remedial action by Ottawa as provided for in the B.N.A. Act (Sec. 93, 3 & 4), and instead suggested recourse to the courts. Thus the question dragged on for years, envenoming the relations between Church and State and arousing ethnic antagonism. The government's course in regard to the Riel question also weakened its alliance with the hierarchy.†

These differences played a major part in the formation of a 'Catholic Program' by a group of fervent ultramontane followers of Bishops Bourget and Laflèche before the provincial elections of 1871. This remarkable document opened with a declaration of allegiance in principle to the Conservative Party, 'the defender of social authority' and the 'only one offering serious guarantees to religious interests.'[47] But party loyalty should not prevail over religious interests in such questions as marriage, education, the establishment of parishes, and the keeping of vital records, and members of parliament considering such laws were obliged 'to change and modify them as the Bishops of the Province might request, in order to harmonize them with the doctrines of the Roman Catholic Church.' Therefore the elector should follow these rules in voting:

1. If the contest is between two Conservatives, it goes without saying that we shall support the one who accepts the program we have just outlined.

* Cf. Chapter VIII, p. 401. † *Ibid.*, 404–7.

2. If on the contrary it is between a Conservative of any shade whatever and an adept of the Liberal school, our active sympathies will be given to the former.

3. If the only candidates who come forward in a constituency are both Liberals or oppositionists, we must choose the one who will accept our conditions.

4. Finally, in the event that the contest is between a Conservative who rejects our program and an opportunist who accepts it, the position would be more delicate. To vote for the latter would be to imperil the Conservative Party, which we wish to see powerful. What decision should we make between these two dangers? In this case we would advise Catholic electors to refrain from voting.[48]

This attempt to set up a Catholic party within the Conservative Party was the work of a group of laymen which included F.-X.-A. Trudel, the defender of Notre-Dame in the Guibord case; Adolphe-Basile Routhier, an ultramontane writer and future judge; Testard de Montigny, the dean of the Zouaves; and Siméon Pagnuelo, Bishop Bourget's lawyer in the matter of the division of the parish. These were men of the bishop's 'New School,' and their model was Louis Veuillot. They met at the Montreal house of Alphonse Desjardins, owner of the ultramontane organ *Le Nouveau Monde* and host of the fugitive *Métis* leader Louis Riel, and in the presence of Canon Godefroy Lamarche, censor of that paper which had been established in 1864 at the instigation of the bishop. Bishop Laflèche's followers were represented by Magloire McLeod, editor of the *Journal de Trois-Rivières*, which reflected Laflèche's views as thoroughly as *Le Nouveau Monde* did those of Bishop Bourget. The Catholic program, written by Routhier, was approved by the two bishops and published in *Le Journal* on April 20, 1871.

The federal and provincial Conservative leaders, Cartier and Cauchon, immediately complained to the hierarchy about this attempt to form a Catholic party; and Archbishop Taschereau, the new bishop of Quebec, issued on April 24 a circular to his clergy and a statement to the press condemning the program as contrary to the regulation of the Fourth Council of Quebec against clerical intervention in politics, and as having 'the serious inconvenience of having been formulated without any participation of the episcopate.'[49] He persuaded his colleagues of Rimouski—Bishop Langevin was the brother of Cartier's aide Sir Hector—and of Saint-Hyacinthe to do likewise. This anti-ultramontane group of the hierarchy feared that the formation of a Catholic party in Quebec would provoke the formation of an inevitably stronger Protestant party in Canada at large, as well as a conflict between Church and State. But Bishops Bourget and Taché formally assured Trudel on June 6 that they fully approved the program, and thus the public was made aware of the disunity of the episcopate on the matter. In the provincial elections of June, only one programist, Trudel, was elected; and the Conservatives held their own by comparing their *Rouge* opponents to the *Communards* of Paris who had shot their archbishop and burnt the Tuileries, though a handful of new Liberal members, among them young Wilfrid Laurier, were elected.

Placed more strongly than ever under the disapproval of the Church, some of the moderate Liberals under the leadership of Louis Jetté attempted to get out of the impossible position in which the Catholic Program had forced them by forming a new *Parti National*, which was simply the old Liberal Party shorn of its extremist *Rouge* elements and its anti-clerical tradition. *Le National*, the organ of the new group, proclaimed:

> We are a national party because we are attached to our nation above all, and because we have pledged our unswerving loyalty to Canada above the whole world, Canada against the world . . . *Le National* will be a political and non-religious paper, but as the special organ of the Catholic population and in conformity with the opinions of the journal's directors, when occasion arises we shall concur with Catholic opinion; and we repudiate in advance anything which may inadvertently be overlooked in the hasty editing of a daily paper, in order to protest our entire devotion and our filial obedience to the Church.[50]

But the *Parti National* seemed as heretical to the obdurate ultramontane bishops as its forebear; and its only notable triumph was Jetté's victory over Cartier in Montreal East, despite the active aid of Sir Hugh Allan's brawny longshoremen and all the prestige and power of the Conservative leader.

Cartier, already much weakened by the Bright's disease which later brought about his death, was subsequently elected for Provencher in Manitoba, after Riel had been induced to give up the seat. But the older leader never regained his former power. His health drove him to London for medical care, and there he labored fitfully on the Manitoba Act. He died in April 1873, some months before the mounting rumors of Conservative corruption culminated in the Canadian Pacific scandal, which drove his colleague Macdonald from office. Clear proof was supplied that Sir Hugh Allan had furnished $350,000 to Conservative campaign funds, at the demand of Cartier and Macdonald, in hope of obtaining the contract for the proposed transcontinental railroad.

This downfall of the federal regime which had held power since Confederation was paralleled by that of the Conservative provincial government in 1874 after the Montreal tanneries scandal, but neither event did the Liberals much good in Quebec, for Boucher de Boucherville, a programist, formed the new provincial government and was supported by clerical influence in the 1875 election.

With the approval of Bishops Bourget and Laflèche, the ultramontanes hammered away at the Liberals as disciples of a doctrine condemned by the Pope and as Canadian counterparts of the French *Communards* who were now enacting anti-clerical legislation. When the Swiss Protestant Liberal leader, Henri Joly de Lotbinière, offered to resign to avoid embarrassing his colleagues because of his faith, his followers would have none of it, since the ultramontanes could be no more opposed to a Protestant Liberal than to a Catholic one.

5

What has been called the 'Holy War' in Quebec's political annals was now in full swing. On one side stood the ultramontanes, backed by Bishop Bourget, who had thus approved the Catholic Program in a circular to his clergy:

> I am very happy to see the formation of a group which is heartily attached to the teaching of the Holy See, which approves all that the Pope approves and condemns all that the Pope condemns; which consequently rejects liberalism, false philosophy, rationalism, indifferentism, and all the monstrous errors which like venomous serpents creep into the ranks of society. This group prides itself on following in all points the teaching of the Church, and its members prove by their deeds that they are sincere.
>
> This group is already composed of a good number of Catholics notable by their position in the various ranks of society, and above all of ardent and devout young men. We are happy to number among them several of our Zouaves, who consecrate their pens to the defence of the Holy See, since they are no longer able to use their swords to guard the Holy City. . . . These young men belong to good families . . . in several years they will be scattered through the legislature, the magistracy, and in other important positions. . . .[51]

At Bishop Bourget's right hand stood Bishop Laflèche, still more 'Roman' and rigid than the leader whose place he was to fill when illness and old age forced the elder man into retirement in 1876. Both men were conservative by nature; finding the Conservative or '*Bleu*' Party increasingly unresponsive to their influence as its power grew, they encouraged the ultramontane or '*Castor*' wing of that party which grew up under their domination.

The rest of the Quebec hierarchy took very different attitudes toward politics, with Archbishop Taschereau of Quebec, who possessed Liberal leanings, making no secret of his opposition to the proceedings of Bishops Bourget and Laflèche. This opposition in part reflected the ancient rivalry between Quebec and Montreal, for Quebec resented the rise of Montreal as the new center of the province. Bishop Larocque of Saint-Hyacinthe sought to remain neutral in the quarrel, while Bishop Langevin of Rimouski opposed the division of Conservative forces represented by the ultramontane development, out of loyalty to his brother, now Conservative leader after Cartier's death. Bishop Guigues of Ottawa favored strict neutrality in political matters. Aside from the major question of the relations of Church and State, another source of division among the hierarchy was the desire of Bishop Bourget, at the instigation of the Jesuits and with the backing of Bishop Laflèche, to establish a Catholic university at Montreal. This institution would destroy the educational monopoly enjoyed by Laval, of which Archbishop Taschereau had been rector before his elevation to the episcopate.

The rumored division of the hierarchy was made manifest at the celebration of Bishop Bourget's golden anniversary as a priest, which was marked by three days of tributes to the man who was already considered a saint by his devoted followers. For the moment his enemies were willing to relax their opposition and to pay honor to a distinguished career, and all his colleagues gathered in Montreal for the occasion. The climax of the celebration was a Pontifical Mass at Notre-Dame, where the ailing bishop, too ill to officiate himself, was enthroned on a dais which had served for the coronation of Charles X of France. This dais, like the sermon, was supplied by the Jesuits, who delighted to honor the bishop who had enabled them to regain so much of their ancient influence in Canada. The preacher was an Alsatian Jesuit, Père Braun, an extreme ultramontane theologian who was at loggerheads with the Abbé Benjamin Paquet, the leading Laval theologian.

Before a congregation which included all the bishops of Quebec and many from Ontario, as well as notables of the political world, Père Braun launched into a fervent promulgation of the extreme ultramontane position, framed in terms of eulogy for Bishop Bourget's war against gallicanism and liberalism:

> The Church can request the government to grant civil sanction to its laws, but this sanction adds nothing to the right of the law, but merely facilitates it.
>
> The Church does not submit bills, projected laws, to the government; but a law which is already an obligation of conscience. It is not for the government to revise these laws, to discuss them, or to change them; it has no jurisdiction.
>
> The Church alone possesses the right to judge ecclesiastical cases, to dispose of matrimonial cases, and to prescribe the formalities therefor. The Church enjoys these immunities, and whoever dares to interfere is guilty of sacrilege.
>
> Governments often aid in the establishment of parishes, but as a favor and not as a right, and they enjoy this right only when it is given them by the Holy Father. If the government should presume to aid in the

establishment of parishes without the permission of the Holy See, it would be guilty of an act of sacrilege.

Such are the truths which your pastor has caused to triumph. They assure the submission of the State to the Church, and the State dependent upon the Church will be submissive to God. . .

At the moment we may see throughout Europe Catholics vying with one another, with the encouragement of the Holy See, to fight those who seek to hamper the liberty of the Church, and to elect to office those right-thinking men who promise to defend the rights of the Church.

Similarly on many occasions the Bishop of Montreal has exhorted the faithful to vote for men who are determined to fight error and to protect the Church and its rights . . .

[The directors of *Le Nouveau Monde*] have accepted the task of defending the truth and serving as champions of the rights and liberties of the Church.

And may you, brethren, be always one with your bishop in the battles against error. As a general guides his army, your pastor leads you . . . Remember that he has caused to triumph the infallibility and independence of the Church, the subordination of the State to the Church.[52]

This discourse uttered in the church of the Sulpicians, whose struggle with the bishop over the division of the parish of Montreal was not yet ended, struck at Cartier and Langevin and the judicial proceedings in the Guibord case. It was an open declaration of war, and it was so taken by the supporters of Archbishop Taschereau and the other anti-ultramontane bishops, already irritated by an earlier sermon by the Abbé Alexis Pelletier, who had taken refuge in Montreal after being silenced for a Jansenist campaign against the teaching of unexpurgated classical literature at Laval.

A journalistic war promptly broke out, waged by clerics and laymen alike; and the skirmishing took on new vigor when a bill providing for the establishment of a Jesuit university at Montreal was introduced in the Quebec Legislature in November 1872. Bishop Bourget had already twice applied to Rome for sanction of this project. His request had twice been denied by the Congregation of the Propaganda at the instigation of Archbishop Taschereau, who opposed the plan on the grounds that the small number of students and the great expense involved justified only one university in the province. Quebec rejoiced at the spectacle of the 'Roman' Bishop of Montreal appealing from Rome to the legislature, while accusing the Quebeckers of gallicanism. Bourget and Taschereau exchanged correspondence, which the Archbishop closed by the terse comment: '*Roma locuta est, causa finita est*' ('Rome has spoken, the case is closed').[53] This correspondence was published, and every member of the legislature received copies of letters supporting Taschereau from the bishops of Rimouski, Saint-Hyacinthe, and Ottawa. The 'Holy War' had become a public issue. In December 1876 Archbishop Taschereau and the Rector of Laval left for Rome, where they were soon followed by Bishop Laflèche and Père Braun. Each party there urged its views on the vexed questions of the division of the parish of Montreal, of the university, and of the Catholic Program. Rome sanctioned the new parishes, maintained its opposition to a second university, and refrained from pronouncing on the religio-political question.

That question remained a cause of grave scandal and dissension. At the Provincial Council of the hierarchy in 1873 Archbishop Taschereau had opposed a motion by Bishops Bourget and Laflèche for a warning against liberalism with the comment that there were no liberals in the condemned Catholic sense in Quebec. Subsequently the Liberal Party won the federal elections of 1874 but lost the provincial ones of 1875, against the opposition of most of the clergy, who were disciples of the two ultramontane bishops and great readers of *Le Nouveau Monde*. Some of the defeated Liberals, represented by François Langelier of the Laval law faculty, applied to the courts for annulment of the elections they had lost, on the grounds of undue influence exercised by the clergy in the Conservative interest. The clergy closed ranks under this attack, which coincided with the last flare-up of the Guibord case and a new onslaught of sensational revelations by the renegade priest Charles Chiniquy, who had turned the evangelical fervor which had made him Quebec's apostle of temperance and a leader of the Illinois emigrants to the service of the Protestant Missionary Society's campaign against Rome and all its works.[54]

Thus, at the Provincial Council of the hierarchy in September 1875, Archbishop Taschereau was induced by his ultramontane colleagues to join in a joint pastoral letter which firmly supported Bishop Bourget on the Guibord question and pronounced a strong warning against Catholic liberalism:

> Distrust above all that liberalism which wishes to cover itself with the fine name of 'Catholic' in order to accomplish more easily its criminal mission. You will recognize it easily from the description which the Sovereign Pontiff has often given of it: (1) the endeavour to subordinate the Church to the State, (2) incessant attempts to break the bonds which unite the children of the Church with one another and with their clergy, (3) the monstrous alliance of truth with error under the pretext of reconciling all things and avoiding conflicts, (4) finally, the illusion, or at times the hypocrisy, which conceals a boundless pride under the mask of religion and of a fine assurance of submission to the Church. . . . No one, therefore, may in the future with good conscience be permitted to remain a Catholic liberal.[55]

The joint pastoral also condemned the views that religion had nothing to do with politics; that religious principles were not to enter into the discussion of public affairs; that the clergy's functions were confined to the church and the sacristy; and that in politics the people should practice moral independence. The bishops pronounced that priests had the same political rights as other citizens, and that there were political questions in which they might and should intervene in the name of religion. The Liberals, who had appealed to the courts against clerical intervention in the elections, were warned that it was for the Church to decide when it should thus raise its voice; and the Conservative press, which had attacked Laval for harboring such creators of scandal as Langelier and Flynn, was also warned that institutions under the protection of the bishops should not be called before 'the incompetent tribunal of public opinion.'[56] In both cases complaints should have been made to the hierarchy, rather than to the courts or in the press. In an accompanying circular letter, the clergy was warned against too free intervention in politics without consultation with the bishops. In his private circular Bishop Bourget added this bit of advice, which extended the new dogma of Papal infallibility to the lowliest *curé*: 'Let each say in his heart, "I hear my *curé*, my *curé* hears the bishop, the bishop hears the Pope, and the Pope hears Our Lord Jesus Christ."'[57]

Such counsels, coupled with ultramontane pamphlets which sought to demonstrate the perfect identity of Canadian and European liberalism, threatened the Liberal Party, then in power at Ottawa, with extinction in Quebec. Archbishop Taschereau was approached by moderate Liberals of the Jetté, Langelier, and Laurier school, who urged an official distinction between condemned Catholic liberalism and permitted political Liberalism. A collective pastoral was required to remedy the injustice done by a collective pastoral, but Bishop Laflèche flatly opposed such a step and was supported in his stand by other bishops. Meanwhile in two federal by-elections in Charlevoix in January 1876, Hector Langevin triumphed by announcing that he had the support of the clergy, by parading his pontifical decoration, and by stressing the fact that he was the brother of the bishop and of the grand vicar of Rimouski. Under the adroit management of Israel Tarte, the Conservative organizer who later became famous for his observation that elections were not won by prayers, but who for some years did not hesitate to make use of the spiritual arm in politics, the 'Holy War' was carried onto the electoral battlefields. Some *curés* told their congregation that a Liberal vote involved mortal sin. One observed that the Conservatives ('*Bleus*') carried the blue banner of the Pope, while the Liberals ('*Rouges*') bore the red flag of Garibaldi, and asked his auditors on whose side they wanted to be when they died. It was noted in reporting this incident that 'Garibaldi does not enjoy a good reputation in this parish.'[58]

The growing tendency towards clerical intervention in elections, which culminated in such incidents as these, had already provoked an attack on ultramontanism by Lucius Seth Huntington, the Liberal representative of the English Eastern Townships, who had bared the Pacific scandal. In a by-election at Argenteuil in December 1875 Huntington denounced his English Protestant fellows in Quebec for their blind support of the Conservative Party, and called upon them to make common cause with the French Liberals against the ultramontane threat to freedom. These words aroused comment in the House at Ottawa, where Prime Minister Alexander Mackenzie repudiated his supporter's action in raising the religious issue, while the Conservative Sir Alexander Galt endorsed it. Sir John Macdonald, as chief of the Conservative opposition, privately remarked that the best course was 'to use the priests in the next election, but be ready to fight them in the Dominion parliament,' and urged the outraged English Quebeckers to remember that 'ultramontanism depends upon the lives of two old men, the Pope and Bishop Bourget.'[59] In the end the English Protestants of Quebec wisely abstained from the French-Canadian family quarrel, but the English press of Montreal never failed to single out with alarm the more extreme ultramontane utterances.

Indeed, they alone in Quebec could do so with impunity in the prevailing intellectual climate. The moderate Liberal L.-O. David, after seeing his *Bien Public* banned in parish after parish, abandoned journalism and took refuge from the ultramontane storm as a translator at Ottawa in May 1876,* after criticizing the later pastoral letters of Bishop Bourget which 'stirred prejudices, encouraged bad faith, and excited a certain number of priests who needed to be restrained.' He added: 'There are parishes where since that time the pulpit has become nothing but a tribune for violent political harangues. It would appear that there is no longer but one crime in the world, but one mortal sin, that of voting for a Reform candidate, of receiving a Reform journal which questions the infallibility of Sir John and M. Langevin.' He warned that in the end such abuses would become intolerable to a Catholic people, 'and then indifference towards religion and hatred towards the priest [will] produce revolution.'[60] The still more moderate Laurier in December 1875 expressed to an English-Canadian colleague reluctance at his prospective elevation to the federal cabinet, for 'from that moment my quietness and happiness will be gone. It will be a war with the clergy, a war every day, every moment . . . I shall be denounced as anti-Christ. You may laugh at that, but it is no laughing matter to me.'[61]

*Thus establishing the subsequently well-worn precedent of French Canadians finding security from provincial pressures in federal employment. This tradition accounts for some of Quebec's chronic distrust of Ottawa.

The semantic confusion which identified English political Liberalism with Continental social liberalism seemed to be beyond clarification until Laurier addressed the *Club Canadien* of Quebec on 'Political Liberalism' on June 26, 1877. Laurier, who had been driven from Montreal to Arthabaska by threatened tuberculosis, had seen his newspaper, *Le Défricheur*, whose editorship he had taken over from Eric Dorion, forced to the wall by Bishop Laflèche, as he had seen the *Institut Canadien* collapse under Bishop Bourget's assaults. A veteran of the religio-political persecution waged by the ultramontanes, he well knew the prejudices which his party had to overcome if it were ever to win power in Quebec:

> I know that in the eyes of a large number of my fellow countrymen, the Liberal party is a party composed of men of perverse doctrines and dangerous tendencies, pressing knowingly and deliberately towards revolution. I know that in the eyes of a portion of my fellow countrymen the Liberal party is a party of men with upright intentions, perhaps, but victims and dupes of principles which are leading them unconsciously but fatally towards revolution. In short, I know that in the eyes of another and not the least considerable portion, perhaps, of our people, Liberalism is a new form of evil, a heresy carrying with it its own condemnation.[62]

Grouping all the charges against the Liberals in two principal propositions that 'Liberalism is a new form of error, a heresy already virtually condemned by the head of the Church,' and that 'a Catholic cannot be a Liberal,'[63] Laurier made his reply to the ultramontanes, which is one of the great landmarks of French-Canadian intellectual history.

At the outset he denied that political Liberalism was identical with condemned Catholic liberalism, and pointed out the consequences of this identification:

> Either we would be obliged to abstain completely from taking any part in the management of affairs of state, and then the constitution—that constitution which was granted to us for our own protection—would be no more than a dead letter in our hands; or we would be obliged to take part in the management of affairs of state under the direction and to the profit of the Conservative Party, and then, our action being no longer free, the constitution would again be a dead letter in our hands, and we would in addition have to bear the ignominy of being regarded by the other members of the Canadian family composing the Conservative Party as tools and slaves.[64]

He blamed the confusion of political Liberalism with Catholic liberalism on French Canada's lack of experience with representative institutions; and on the fact that Quebec studied the history of the Continent, where 'the history of liberalism has been written in letters of blood,' rather than that of England, 'the classic land of liberty.'[65] Condemning the popular attribution of the 'Conservative' label to everything good and the 'Liberal' one to everything bad—revolt, anarchy, and disorder—Laurier cited Macaulay's definition of the two opposed ideas:

> Everywhere there is a class of men who cling with fondness to whatever is ancient and who, even when convinced by overpowering reasons that innovation would be beneficial, consent to it with many misgivings and forebodings. We find also everywhere another class of men, sanguine in hope, bold in speculation, always pressing forward, quick to discern the imperfection whatever exists, disposed to think lightly of the risks and inconveniences which attend improvements and disposed to give every change credit for being an improvement.[66]

Dismissing the charge that Liberalism involved republicanism, Laurier remarked: 'the form matters little; whether it be monarchist or republican, the moment the people exercise the right to vote, the moment they have responsible government, they have the full measure of liberty.'[67] Citing Junius' remark that 'Eternal vigilance is the price of liberty,' Laurier commented that a representative monarchy lends itself better to this vigilance than a republic.

Then he went on to declare that both ideas which formed the basis of parties were theologically 'indifferent,' both 'susceptible of much good, as they are also of much evil.'[68] He made a moving confession of his own faith in Liberalism:

> I am one of those who think that everywhere, in human things, there are abuses to be remedied, new horizons to be opened up, and new forces to be developed.
>
> Moreover, Liberalism seems to me in all respects superior to the other principle. The principle of Liberalism is inherent in the very essence of our nature, in that desire for happiness with which we are all born into the world, which pursues us through life, and which is never completely gratified this side of the grave. Our souls are immortal, but our means are limited. We constantly gravitate towards an ideal which we never attain. We dream of good but never realize the best. We only reach the goal we have proposed for ourselves, to discover new horizons opening up which we had not even suspected before. We rush on towards them, and those horizons, explored in their turn, reveal to us others which lead us on ever further and further.
>
> This condition of our nature is precisely what makes the greatness of man, for it condemns him irrevocably to movement, to progress: our means are limited, but our nature is always perfectible, and we have the infinite for our arena. Thus there is always room for improvement of our condition, for the perfecting of our nature, and for the attainment of an easier life by a larger number. Here again is what in my eyes constitutes the superiority of Liberalism.[69]

Laurier contrasted the treatment of human aspirations in England, where reforms had been brought about without violence, with that on the Continent, where repression had produced social explosions. He cited the great English Liberals: Fox, O'Connell, Grey, Brougham, Russell, many of them aristocrats sacrificing their own privileges for the good of the people; and quoted Macaulay's triumphant account of the passage of the Reform Bill, which deprived him of his seat for a rotten borough.

Such were the models, the principles, the party of the Canadian Liberals, who were not to be identified with the liberals of France, Italy, and Germany, who 'are not Liberals; they are revolutionaries: in their principles they are so extreme that they aim at nothing less than the destruction of modern society. With these men we have nothing in common; but it is the tactic of our adversaries always to assimilate us to them.'[70] He then traced the history of the Canadian Liberal Party, pointing out that until 1848 all French Canadians had belonged to it. Then, when Papineau returned from European exile, 'a generation of young men of great talent and still greater impetuosity of character'[71] forsook Lafontaine's leadership for that of Papineau, and soon went farther than their leader did. Laurier characterized the program of *L'Avenir* as 'calling for a complete revolution in the province,' and remarked: 'The only excuse for those Liberals was their youth. The oldest of them was not more than twenty-two years of age.'[72] Their enthusiasm for the wave of revolution in Europe brought down upon them 'merciless war' from the clergy and opposition from the English Canadians—the latter being 'friendly to liberty, but also friendly to the maintenance of order.'[73]

The *Rouges* initiated all the reforms achieved during the next twenty-five years: the abolition of seigneurial tenure, judicial centralization, colonization; but they got no credit for these measures and no recognition was made that their youthful rashness had been replaced by 'calmer and more thoughtful ideas.' Meanwhile the Lafontaine Liberals merged with the Conservative Party and became the forebears of the ultramontanes of today. Of them Laurier remarked:

> If M. Cartier were to come back to earth today, he would not recognize his party. M. Cartier was devoted to the principles of the English constitution. Those who take the lead today among his old partisans openly reject the principles of the English constitution as a concession to what they call the spirit of evil. They understand neither their country nor their time. All their ideas are modeled on those of the reactionaries of France. They go into extasies over Don Carlos or the Comte de Chambord, just as the Liberals admired Louis Blanc and Ledru-Rollin . . . I accuse them of judging the political situation of the country not

according to what is happening in it, but according to what is happening in France. I accuse them of wanting to introduce here ideas which are impossible of application in our state of society. I accuse them of working laboriously and unfortunately all too efficaciously to degrade religion to the simple proportions of a political party.[74]

Laurier declared that he had 'too much respect for the faith in which I was born to ever use it as the basis of a political organization.' Then he went on to voice the first of his many warnings against parties organized on a religious or ethnic basis:

You wish to organize a Catholic party. But have you not considered that if you have the misfortune to succeed, you will draw down upon your country calamities of which it is impossible to foresee the consequences?

You wish to organize all Catholics into one party, without other bond, without other basis than a common religion; but have you not reflected that by that very fact you will organize the Protestant population as a single party, and that then, instead of the peace and harmony now prevailing between the different elements of the Canadian population, you throw open the doors to war, a religious war, the most terrible of all wars?[75]

To Laurier's mind the only justification for French-Canadian attacks on liberty was that 'liberty, as it has been generally understood and practised in France, has nothing very attractive about it. The French have the name of liberty, but they have not yet had liberty itself.'[76] Liberty in Canada was not the liberty of Auguste Barbier, but the liberty of Tennyson's 'In Memoriam.'

To the charge that the Liberals sought to relegate the clergy to the sacristy and to prevent them from teaching the people their duties as citizens and electors, Laurier gave this classic definition of his position on clerical intervention in politics:

I maintain that there is not one Canadian Liberal who wants to prevent the clergy from taking part in political affairs, if they wish to do so.

In the name of what principle should the friends of liberty seek to deny to the priest the right to take part in political affairs? In the name of what principle should the friends of liberty seek to deny to the priest the right to have and express political opinions, the right to approve or disapprove of public men and their acts, and to instruct the people in what he believes to be their duty? In the name of what principle should he not have the right to say that if I am elected, religion will be endangered, when I have the right to say that if my adversary is elected, the State will be endangered? Why should not the priest have the right to say that if I am elected, religion will inevitably be destroyed; when I have the right to say that if my adversary is elected, the State will go into bankruptcy? No, let the priest speak and preach as he thinks best such is his right, and no Canadian Liberal will dispute that right.

Our constitution invites all citizens to take part in the direction of the affairs of the State; it makes no exception of any person. Each has the right not only to express his opinion, but to influence, if he can, by the expression of his opinion, the opinion of his fellow citizens. This right exists for all, and there can be no reason why the priest should be deprived of it. I am here to speak my whole mind, and I may add that I am far from finding opportune the intervention of the clergy in the domain of politics, as it has been exercised for some years. On the contrary I believe that from the standpoint of the respect due to his character, the priest has everything to lose by meddling in the ordinary questions of politics; still his right to do so is indisputable and if he thinks proper to use it, our duty as Liberals is to guarantee it to him against all denial.

This right, however, is not unlimited. We have no absolute rights. The rights of each man in our state of society end precisely at the point where they encroach upon the rights of others.

The right of interference in politics ends at the point where it encroaches upon the elector's independence.

The constitution of the country rests upon the freely expressed wish of each elector. It intends that each elector shall cast his vote freely and willingly as he deems best. . . .

The law watches with so jealous an eye over the free expression of the elector's opinion as it really is that if in a constituency the opinion expressed by a single elector is not his real opinion, but an opinion forced upon him by fear, fraud, or corruption, the election must be annulled. It is therefore perfectly legitimate to alter the elector's opinion by argument and all other means of persuasion, but never by intimidation. As a matter of fact, persuasion changes the elector's conviction, intimidation does not. When by persuasion you have changed the elector's opinion, then the opinion he expresses is his own; but when by terror you force him to vote, the opinion he expresses is yours; remove the cause of his fear and he will then express another opinion, which is his own.

Now it will be understood that, if the opinion expressed by the majority of the electors is not their real opinion, but an opinion forced from them by fraud, threats, or corruption, the constitution is violated and you do not have government of the majority but government of a minority. Well, if such a state of affairs continues and is repeated, if after each election the will expressed is not the real will of the country, once more you do violence to the constitution; responsible government is no longer anything but an empty term; and sooner or later, here as elsewhere, the pressure will culminate in explosion, violence, and ruin.

But people are not wanting to say that the clergy have a right to dictate to the people its duties. I simply answer that we are here under the government of the Queen of England, under the authority of a constitution which was granted to us as an act of justice, and if the exercize of the rights which you claim is to have for effect the impeding of the constitution and our exposure to all the consequences of such an act, then the clergy themselves would not want it.

I am not one of those who parade themselves as friends and champions of the clergy. I say this, however: like most of my young fellow countrymen, I have been reared among priests and among young men who have become priests. I flatter myself that I have some sincere friends among them, and to them I can and do say: see if there is under the sun a country where the Catholic Church is freer or more privileged than it is here. Why then should you by claiming rights incompatible with our state of society, expose this country to agitations of which it is impossible to foresee the consequences?[77]

After this forthright demarcation of the rights of the clergy and of citizens, Laurier closed with an eloquent apostrophe to free British institutions which had enabled the French Canadians to remain French and Catholic under the British flag, 'which floats tonight over our heads, without a single British soldier in the country to defend it, its sole defence resting in the gratitude which we owe it for our freedom and for the security we have found under its folds.'[78]

It was this speech which made Laurier, an undistinguished minister without portfolio, a national figure; and adherence to the views expressed in it was to put him at the head of the Canadian government in 1896, after half a century marred by the bickerings of smaller men who made political capital of differences of origin and religion, and almost wrecked Confederation on those reefs which beset the course of a nation made up not of one people but of two.

6

Relief for the situation against which Laurier made his eloquent protest had already begun to come from several quarters. In May 1876 Archbishop Taschereau, realizing that the condemnation of Catholic liberalism threatened to provoke a serious anti-clerical movement, issued a pastoral letter in which he put the two parties on the same footing and urged the electors to make calm inquiry into the merits of opposing candidates.[79] Though the archbishop asserted that his new pastoral did not revoke the joint one of 1875, it was taken by both the Liberals and the ultramontanes as a repudiation of the latter. Bishop Laflèche and Canon Lamarche went to Rome to voice their differences with the archbishop on the religio-political difficulties in Quebec, on which Cardinal Franchi, the prefect of the Congregation of the Propaganda, had requested Taschereau's views. While Rome heard the rival arguments, Judge Routhier, the drafter of the Catholic program and Langevin's former political aide, dismissed Langelier's petition for the annulment of the Charlevoix by-election, on the ultramontane ground that the clergy were immune from questioning or control by the State of their actions on such moral questions as voting. Routhier made a distinction between temporal influence, which was forbidden by law and spiritual influence, which was legitimate. The case was appeale to the newly established Supreme Court of Canada, whose unanimou judgment, to the effect that undue influence had been exerted an that the election was consequently void, was delivered by M Justice Taschereau, brother of the archbishop, who threw ou Routhier's distinction.

While the appeal was in progress, the Superior Court of Quebe annulled an election in Bonaventure, where two *curés* had threatene to refuse the sacraments to Liberal voters. This judgment wa written by Judge Casault, a professor of law at Laval; and Bisho Langevin, whose diocese included the constituency, insisted t Archbishop Taschereau that Casault must either retract or b deprived of his academic position. This request was backed b Bishop Laflèche, and Archbishop Taschereau referred the questio to Rome, which eventually upheld the judge. To Rome the Liberal under Joseph Cauchon's leadership now also appealed for judgmen on the ultramontane charges against them. While this appeal wa under consideration, the bishops issued a joint declaration on Marc 26, 1877, protesting against the Supreme Court's decision an requesting a suitable remedy.[80] A telegram from Rome, warnin the hierarchy against a pronouncement on the question, was receive after the circular had been issued. There, after Canon Lamarch had offered the ultramontane arguments and the Abbé Benjami Paquet had refuted them as Archbishop Taschereau's representative it had been decided to send an apostolic delegate to Canada t investigate the situation which had filled the Vatican's offices wit petitions and counter-petitions.

Bishop Conroy of Ardagh, the Irish prelate appointed to thi mission, was instructed to eliminate the division among the Quebe bishops, the root of the troubles. It was likewise suggested to hin that another cause of the difficulties was 'interference of the clerg in politics without sufficient care for pastoral prudence'; and tha 'the Church, in condemning liberalism, did not intend to strike eac and every political party which happened to be called Liberal, sinc the decision of the Church applied to certain errors opposed t Catholic doctrine, and not to any political party, and that con sequently those did wrong who without further basis declared con demned by the Church one of the parties in Canada, i.e., the part known as Reformist, a party formerly warmly supported even b some bishops.'[81] Bishops were counseled to observe the greates reserve about politics, 'having regard particularly to the danger o provoking a violent war against the Church, when Protestants wer already uneasy and irritated against the clergy on the score of th latter's undue influence in political affairs.' The apostolic delegat arrived at Quebec in May 1877, visited Montreal and Ottawa, and then returned to Quebec, where he established himself—in order to preserve neutrality—in a country house on the Sainte-Foye Road, where he was besieged by ultramontane and Liberal spokesmen.

His views remained unknown until at his instigation the hierarchy issued a joint pastoral on October 11. This pronouncement made the distinction, as Laurier had done in his speech on 'Political Liberalism' in June, between political and Catholic liberalism, and declared that the Holy See's censures against Catholic liberalism were not to be applied to any particular political party.[82] In an accompanying circular to the clergy, they were reminded that 'The decree of the Fourth Council of Quebec forbids you implicitly to teach from the pulpit or elsewhere that it is a sin to vote for any particular candidate or party; even more is it forbidden to announce that you will refuse the sacraments for this cause. You are never to give your personal opinion from the pulpit.'[83]

Confronted with this ultimatum, Bishop Laflèche's organ, *Le Journal des Trois-Rivières*, bitterly observed: 'The year 1877 could be designated as the special epoch of concessions to liberalism and of cowardice, the epoch of the triumph of Catholic liberalism.'[84] In the like manner the *curés* who read *Le Nouveau Monde's* reflections on the circular viewed Bishop Conroy's mission as 'unfortunate for true principles.'[85] With that self-righteous fervor which sometimes makes French Canadians more Catholic than the Pope, the double rebuke by Rome of ultramontane pretensions through the Conroy mission and the Casault decision was not taken to heart. It was some years before the declaration which Bishop Conroy had inspired and which he hoped would restore peace to Catholic Quebec achieved its end.

The pronouncement did not immediately halt the use of religious means for political purposes. Forced to seek re-election by his elevation to the Mackenzie cabinet, Laurier was defeated in Drummond-Arthabaska—in Bishop Laflèche's diocese—on October 27, after a bitterly contested campaign in which his opponents made use of all the old ultramontane charges against the Liberals. The *curés*, somewhat checked in their Conservative zeal by the circular, followed a course which left the voters in a state of mind exemplified by one *habitant* who told his *curé*: 'I cannot vote for M. Laurier, for you tell me that if I vote for a Liberal, I shall be damned; I cannot vote for M. Bourbeau, for you tell me that if I do not follow my conscience, I shall be damned; I cannot vote for neither, for you tell me that if I do not vote at all, I shall be damned. Since I must be damned anyway, I'll be damned for doing what I like. I am going to vote for M. Laurier.'[86] Laurier was subsequently elected in Quebec East—in Archbishop Taschereau's diocese—in November, but his defeat in his own region left him with a certain bitterness against his opponents.

The same tactics were employed by the Conservatives in the provincial elections of May 1878 in which the Liberals under the Swiss Protestant Joly won a bare majority in the face of opposition from the *curés* in many counties. It was in this election that the memorable device was invented of indicating discreetly from the pulpit the right way to vote by the observation that Heaven was *Bleu* and Hell was *Rouge*.[87] And in the federal elections of September the Liberals went down to defeat in Quebec, where they were to remain in opposition until 1896. The obstinate self-righteousness of the ultramontanes, undaunted by Roman counsels of moderation and exploited by unscrupulous Conservative leaders, was so strong that the sudden death of Bishop Conroy on his way back to Rome was greeted as a clear intervention of Providence.[88]

7

The battle between ultramontanism and liberalism continued to rack French Canada for another twenty years. But essentially the outcome of that battle was determined by the election of Leo XIII to the Papacy in 1878. The new Pope's reign was to see the achievement of peace with the civil power, after the Catholic reaction under Pius IX against the new democratic nationalism. The duel between Archbishop Taschereau and Bishop Laflèche and between the two schools of thought they headed continued with the bitterness only possible in a deeply Catholic country, but each time that Rome was consulted, the decision went against the ultramontanes, whose obstinate conviction of the justness of their cause finally led them to the brink of rupture with that Holy See whose defenders and supporters they proclaimed themselves to be. The battle was fought on many fronts and produced such a wealth of literature, both public and private, that a book could be devoted to it alone. Only the main outlines of the endless bickering within the Church in Canada, which at this time gave Rome more trouble than the rest of Christendom combined, can be traced here.

One of the major quarrels was the question whether French Canada should have one university or two. Since 1843 there had existed at Montreal a medical school founded by English Protestants, which gradually became French and Catholic as the city did and as the rival McGill Medical School developed. It was known as the Victoria School because of its affiliation for degree-granting purposes with the Methodist Victoria University of Cobourg, Ontario. Bishop Bourget, under whose control the school was planned to make it part of the Catholic university which he wished to establish in Montreal. Its doctors supplied the medical service of the Hôtel-Dieu and other Catholic institutions. Its directors were ultramontane in outlook, and resisted Bishop Conroy's effort to affiliate the institution to the Montreal branch of Laval. They were moved both by the old rivalry between Montreal and Quebec, and by their pious suspicion of the Laval Medical School, whose faculty included several English Protestants rumored to be Freemasons, a damning disability in the eyes of Bishop Bourget's supporters.

The agreement worked out under the supervision of Bishop Conroy and confirmed by Rome broke down in 1879. The Montreal doctors then appealed to Rome, while Laval opened a rival medical school in Montreal. The Hôtel-Dieu remained loyal to Victoria, and closed its doors to students of the new school, of whose legal right to existence there was some doubt under the terms of Laval's royal charter. On this point the Victoria spokesmen consulted the federal minister of justice and the Crown law officers in England, the latter supporting their case. The university question inevitably became one of Montreal against Quebec, of Conservatives against Liberals, in the religio-political atmosphere of the day; and cries of liberalism, gallicanism, and insubmission were raised in the press and in pamphlets, despite the instructions of Bishop Fabre, Bishop Bourget's peace-loving successor, that the matter was not to be publicly discussed.

Thus the issue became involved in the 'Holy War,' which had been revived by the contesting of the Berthier election of 1878 on the grounds of undue influence. The Liberals now boasted a Montreal organ, *La Patrie*, founded in 1879 by the radical *Rouge* Honoré Beaugrand, in whose pages the poet Louis Fréchette hymned Republican France, despite the Republic's blatant anti-clericalism. The times were indeed changing, and further evidence of the fact was provided by the introduction into the federal house by a Quebec Conservative of a bill which liberalized the marriage laws. Bishop Laflèche, whose basic article of faith was that the State had no concern with schools, charitable institutions, marriage legislation, or differences involving a priest, ordered the sponsor of the bill to withdraw it. The latter refused, but the bill was stopped in the Senate by the ultramontanes Trudel and Bellerose. Then, after a trial rich in scandal, the Berthier election was annulled on November 30, 1880 by unanimous decision of the Supreme Court.

While radical Liberals rejoiced at having 'muzzled the clergy,' Bishop Laflèche—fresh from a visit to St. Boniface, where he had advised the French *Métis* that if they remained grouped around their clergy, no one could disturb them—wrote a series of articles on 'Undue Spiritual Influence' for *Le Journal des Trois-Rivières*.

These articles took high ultramontane ground on the relations of Church and State, and proclaimed that the law against the exercise of undue influence must be repealed or amended, since it attacked the liberties of the Church. L.-O. David, back in the provincial fray as editor of *La Tribune* of Montreal after the Liberal downfall at Ottawa, objected that recourse to the courts was the only remedy for a defeated candidate, since an appeal to the clerical authorities could not restore his lost seat. Bishop Laflèche republished his articles in pamphlet form, thus adding a new ultramontane text to the *Syllabus of Errors*, the Catholic Program, and the joint pastoral of September 1875.

Both Laval's attempt to obtain legal authorization for its Montreal branch and Bishop Laflèche's measure against the undue influence law were submitted to the provincial legislature in 1881. Bishop Laflèche refused to join the other bishops in supporting the Laval measure, while Archbishop Taschereau advised his colleagues after consultation with Premier Chapleau, who feared that such a measure would arouse Protestant feeling, that he felt it useless to insist upon revocation of the undue influence law. Bishop Laflèche's proposal was then dropped, despite complaints from some ultramontanes that the existence of a Catholic party would have prevented such cowardice on the part of the Conservative government.

But the 'Holy War' broke out again with renewed vigor on the university question, despite Bishop Fabre's demand that his diocesans submit to the twice-expressed will of Rome that the Laval Medical School be maintained in Montreal. *Le Nouveau Monde*, rigid in its pro-Montreal and anti-Laval views for all its ultramontane pretensions, presumed to question the bishop's right to halt discussion of public affairs. Bishop Laflèche authorized Senator Trudel, attorney for the Victoria School, to make public a letter in which he expressed his disagreement with the bishops who had endorsed the Laval School. From his retirement at Sault-au-Recollet, Bishop Bourget wrote an endorsement of the opposition measure which was published in *Le Nouveau Monde*. Archbishop Taschereau then accused Bishop Bourget of undermining the authority of his successor and of the other bishops—indeed, in so many words, of exercising 'undue influence'—and when the retired bishop replied, closed the correspondence with a sharp reflection on 'letters publicly addressed to the diocesans of Montreal, counselling them to resist the will of their bishop and of the Holy See.'[89]

Such an attitude towards the old ultramontane leader, already canonized in the minds of his followers, made for bitter feeling between his cohorts and those of the archbishop. Once more Laval was accused of tolerating dangerous principles, of neglecting philosophy for the natural sciences, and abandoning its traditions for 'pretended modern progress.'[90] The Laval bill was carried through the assembly and the legislative council with both Conservative and Liberal support, amid a rain of petitions and counter-petitions and scandalous personal reflections. No sooner was it passed than Senator Trudel departed for Rome to plead the cause of Victoria, where he was soon followed by eighty-two-year-old Bishop Bourget. Both emissaries attacked Laval as being under the influence of Freemasons. But they had already been forestalled at Rome by Bishop Racine of Chicoutimi and Grand Vicar Hamel of Quebec, supporters of the Archbishop. Both parties were received by the Pope, who sustained Laval after the case had been heard by the Propaganda.

The official communication of Rome's opinion on September 13, 1881 was accompanied by a renewed warning against confusing political and Catholic liberalism, and the bishops were instructed to consult the Holy See before seeking repeal of the undue influence law. This decision, loyally accepted by Bishop Fabre and accompanied by Archbishop Taschereau with a warning against 'discussions which excite men's minds to the detriment of religion and public affairs,'[91] was greeted with joy by the Liberals. *L'Evénement* of Quebec did not neglect to turn the sword in the ultramontane wound by observing:

> As to the Honorable M. Trudel, his religious mission seems to be ended. Rome decidedly does not wish a lay prelate among us. She does not desire that beside the orthodox Church a Church more orthodox still should establish itself. We must content ourselves with the religion of our fathers.[92]

When Archbishop Taschereau pressed his advantage and called for a joint declaration by the hierarchy against journalists who disobeyed the Holy See by attacking Laval, Bishop Laflèche first signed, then withdrew his signature and announced his departure for Rome to explain his objections. He was coldly received there by Leo XIII, who said that there was nothing further to be discussed and that his presence was not necessary at Rome, where the band of self-styled 'defenders of Montreal' had become wearisome to the Holy See. A communication to this effect from Cardinal Simeoni, the new head of the Propaganda, to Archbishop Taschereau was published at Quebec in January 1882.

Le Nouveau Monde took great offense, and did not scruple to blame both the Archbishop and the Cardinal for this insult to 'a bishop and priests whom the good Catholics of Canada have learned to venerate for their piety and devotion to the Holy See.'[93] Frédéric Houde, its proprietor, resigned rather than retract this statement at the request of Bishop Fabre. The ultramontanes had become so self-righteous, so full of a sense of mission, that they insisted upon going their own way regardless of the opposition of their bishop, of the hierarchy as a whole, of the Propaganda, and of the Holy Father himself. The Liberals did not fail to point out the humorous spectacle afforded by those who protested in the name of religion against complaints of clerical intervention in elections, but did not hesitate to make complaints against the Archbishop of Quebec and the Sacred Congregation of the Propaganda. On February 5 Archbishop Taschereau issued a pastoral which stressed the fact that the Propaganda had settled the university question once for all, and that no good Catholic could attack an institution protected by the bishops and the Holy See, particularly when such attacks were based on the fact that Laval had not condemned a political party which neither the hierarchy nor the Holy See wished to condemn. The freedom of electors to vote for either parties was again declared.[94]

Though the provincial elections of December 1881 had been contested by Conservatives and Liberals, in reality four parties were now involved. The Conservatives had with difficulty kept within their ranks the ultramontane group headed by 'Grand Vicar' Trudel, which threatened to revive the Catholic Program and to set up a Catholic party. Faced with this revolt, Chapleau was considering a coalition with the moderate Liberal Honoré Mercier, who found the radical Liberals headed by Beaugrand as embarrassing as Chapleau did the ultramontanes. The ultramontanes grew more and more discontented with Chapleau's dependence upon Senécal, the ex-Liberal railroad promoter who now footed the Conservative party's bills and was rumored to pay himself well for his pains; they did not hesitate to make political capital of the fact that Chapleau had a Protestant wife, and hence might be considered a Freemason. From the French monarchists whom they so much admired, the ultramontanes had adopted the practice of seeing Masons and Masonic plots everywhere, and no one in French Canada was more adept at this game than Jules-Paul Tardivel, who in 1881 launched his ultramontane *La Verité* at Quebec.

Tardivel, born of a French father and an English mother in the United States, had been educated at Saint-Hyacinthe, whose seminary he entered at the age of sixteen, not knowing a word of French. With the zeal of a convert to a heady doctrine, Tardivel espoused the ultramontane cause, serving as a sounding-board at Quebec for the views of Bishop Laflèche and Trudel. He tended to be more French than the Séminaire de Québec and more Catholic than Archbishop Taschereau. He pursued Laval with charges of Masonry borrowed from his idol Louis Veuillot, finding the dark hand of the Grand Orient not only in the medical and law schools, out in the very household of the archbishop. At the outset *La Verité* contented itself with a crusade against Sunday trains, but gradually it turned to heresy-hunting on a higher plane. So intoxicating was the ultramontane doctrine that Tardivel did not hesitate to point out that Rome could err, when the decision on the university question was announced:

> The Laval question is a question of fact, and without being a heretic or even a bad Catholic, one can say that the Pope is mistaken on this question. The question of indulgences is a question of doctrine, which is very different. In doctrine the Pope is infallible, he cannot err; but it is to expose our holy religion to the laughter of the impious to maintain that the Pope cannot err when it is a question of particular facts.[95]

And the still more official ultramontane organ, Bishop Laflèche's *Journal des Trois-Rivières*, proclaimed: 'It is certain that for one reason or another the Holy See can be led into error, above all for a certain time, on questions of fact and questions of doctrine.'[96] The Liberal press fell with glee upon such views in the mouths of those who had proclaimed themselves the best Romans of them all.

Bishop Laflèche, whose fighter's temperament was daunted neither by reverses nor rebuffs, remained at Rome despite the chilly atmosphere, compiling a memorandum on 'The Religious Troubles in Canada,' which was printed both at Rome and in Canada in 1882. Convinced as he was that gallicanism, liberalism, and nationalism were the 'fundamental errors of the epoch,' and that liberalism in particular was nothing short of a 'plague'[97] spread by the Masons, he summed up the history of the politico-religious struggle in Canada under three heads: the political question, the question of undue influence, and the university question. This sixty-page presentation of the thesis that 'Canadian liberalism, by its anti-social tendencies, by its hatred of the Church, and by its perverse principles, differed in no respect from European liberalism,' supported by a hundred pages of evidence and a rain of letters to Cardinal Simeoni, was little short of an indictment of Archbishop Taschereau and the Séminaire de Québec, where the 'subtle errors' of liberalism had penetrated 'like the serpent into the Garden of Eden.'[98] Bishop Laflèche concluded his memorandum: 'Thus all the most clear-sighted minds, both among the clergy and the laity, are frightened, and all agree that unless Providential aid enables us to check this fatal movement, we advance rapidly along the revolutionary paths of France and Belgium, and we shall fall sooner than is thought into the same abyss.'[99] To him it was clear that Freemasonry inspired the attack on the Church in Canada as elsewhere; and he viewed with alarm the influence of the French press on Quebec, whose native literature was still in infancy. This ultramontane preoccupation with Masonic intrigue and with the dangers of French cultural influences was to become a lasting part of the French-Canadian mind, thanks to twenty years' harping on the theme by Trudel and Tardivel in *Le Nouveau Monde* and *La Verité*.

Bishop Laflèche finally returned from Rome in May 1882. His friends Bishops Bourget and Taché endorsed the position he had taken in his memorandum, which Archbishop Taschereau refuted in a counter-memorandum which found favor in Rome. Bishop Moreau of Saint-Hyacinthe issued in November a circular to his clergy against encouragement of a new ultramontane organ launched by Senator Trudel with the support of Bishops Bourget and Laflèche, but against the desire of Bishop Fabre. Under this fire, the ultramontanes abandoned the proposed title of their new paper, but not the project itself. On January 23, 1883 the first number of *L'Etendard* appeared. It was to become the organ of the new Catholic party known as the '*Castors*' ('Beavers'), and its course was foreshadowed from the first by its campaign against the big three of the Conservative Party in Quebec, Chapleau, Senécal, and Mousseau. Chapleau was considered to be a Mason by Bishop Laflèche, and the ultramontanes complained that under his regime the interests of country and party had become secondary to those of 'The Great Man.'

Meanwhile there had been another epistolary battle between the archbishop and Bishop Laflèche, in which the former had summoned the latter to prefer his charges against Laval before the Superior Council of the university, while the latter refused to do so and rested upon his episcopal right to complain directly to Rome. The archbishop published the correspondence, having been assured by Cardinal Simeoni that Laflèche's charges were regarded in Rome as 'vague and without proof.'[100] A new decree of the Propaganda, accompanied by a pastoral letter from the archbishop, was read in all the churches of Quebec on March 25, 1883.[101] The former ordered that all attacks against Laval and its Montreal branch should cease, while the latter underlined the point that violation of the decree meant disobedience to the Holy See, of which an unfortunate example had been given for the last seven years elsewhere than in the diocese of Quebec.

While the irreconcilables of Victoria appealed once more to Rome, rumors came from thence that the diocese of Trois-Rivières was to be divided, with its richer portion south of the St. Lawrence to be established as the new see of Nicolet. Such a division was popularly regarded as a punishment and humiliation for Bishop Laflèche by his enemies. His friend Bishop Taché of St. Boniface wrote to Archbishop Taschereau a protest which he desired should be passed on to the hierarchy of Quebec. Replying that Bishop Taché eemed to regard Bishop Laflèche 'as a martyr whose executioners vere (1) the majority of the bishops of the province, (2) the Sacred Congregation of the Propaganda, (3) the Sovereign Pontiff him-elf,'[102] the archbishop refused to circulate the letter.

Bishop Laflèche set off once more for Rome, while his aroused sup-porters went so far as to accuse Grand Vicar Hamel of Quebec of ympathy with Masonry, on the grounds that when Rector of Laval e had informed Rome that the Masons on the medical school aculty were 'Protestant doctors, very worthy citizens, for whom reemasonry was in Quebec only a mutual aid society, without ostility to Catholicism.'[103] The ultramontanes of the Quebec *ercle Catholique*, headed by Dr. Landry, made much of this scanda-ous tolerance. Dr. Landry refused to retract his charges, and was leprived of his honorary professorship at the university, while Tardivel defended him in *La Verité*, which was promptly banned from he seminary, the university, and the archbishop's household. On une 1 the archbishop published a pastoral against secret societies in vhich he ordered that since membership in them carried the penalty f excommunication, accusations of being a Mason, made against Catholics to anyone except the ordinary of the diocese, were for-idden; and that violations of this regulation would be considered ases of conscience whose absolution was reserved to the archbishop, is grand vicar, or priests designated by him.[104] Dr. Landry's son hilippe promptly denounced this pastoral to Cardinal Monaco f the Inquisition. Rome, finding itself swamped by a flood of peti-ons, protests, and denunciations from Quebec, decided once more send an apostolic delegate to investigate the situation at first hand. ending his coming, the suppression of the Victoria School was to be ispended.

This success heartened the *Castors*, who fell upon Chapleau's uccessor Mousseau with renewed vigor when he sought a provincial eat that fall. 'The Great Man' was called to his follower's aid, and n September 6 at Saint-Laurent Chapleau broke definitely with the ltramontanes by making this formal attack upon them with all his ery eloquence:

> What is a *Castor*? Is it a question of that intelligent and industrious nimal who, along with the maple leaf, serves us as a national emblem? o, our opponents are not patriotic enough for that. What, then, is a *astor*? The urban worker calls by this name those who make great etensions and cannot do much, the braggarts and parasites of the trade. the country those little black beasts who live in bands upon the surface stagnant waters, spreading an odor than which there is nothing less greeable, the water skunks, are also called *Castors*.
>
> Are these typical of the tribe of *L'Etendard*? Political *Castors* are a ttle like that, and something still less good. Their party includes all

> the ambitious mediocrities who cannot come to power by the ordinar ways, all the disappointed ones, and a good number of hypocrites wh pretend to be religious and conservative in order better to ruin the grea Conservative Party and to destroy among the people true religious spirit whose fundamental basis is respect for authority and love of neighbor.
>
> For the rest, they have only one trait of resemblance to the true beaver They do their work with mud; they destroy the sluices of good mills t make their dens; and are useful only when their hides are sold.
>
> The opposition raised against us by these men would not be impor tant, if it were not for the character which they have given to wha they call their political mission. They have wrapped themselves in th mantle of religion, and in this disguise they have succeeded in deceivin a number of honest folk whom it is difficult to undeceive.
>
> . . . .
>
> It is time to rip off the mask. There is no worse exploitation tha religious exploitation. No one has the right to employ for his persona ends the great and powerful sentiment which dominates all others i this fine country of Canada.
>
> In a country where there are so many sincere Catholics, it is easy t win followers in the name of religion. But woe to him who uses religio as a footstool![105]

The indictment was a telling one, but the course of the *Castors* ha continued to be followed down to the present day by unscrupulou politicians who do not hesitate to make use of Quebec's profoun religious feeling for political purposes.

Back from Rome trooped the rival petitioners as the court c appeal was shifted to Canada by the arrival at Quebec in Octobe 1883 of the apostolic delegate, Dom Henri Smeulders, a Belgia Cistercian abbot. The ultramontanes were determined to win fror him a canonical inquest into all the religious difficulties. Dr. Landr took it upon himself to circulate a petition in favor of this step amon the clergy of the diocese of Quebec. The Christmas preacher at th Basilica of Quebec, the Grand Vicar Legaré, in the presence of th archbishop and Dr. Landry and Tardivel, who were wardens of th church, censured the latter:

> We shall have the desired peace when all laymen confine themselve to their roles. It is truly strange that here and there in our Canadia society men arise who take upon themselves the mission of lording over the Church. Do we not see them arrogate to themselves the righ to concern themselves with all the questions which are primarily th concern of the Pope, the bishops, and the clergy?[106]

The *Castors* replied to this discourse, which caused quite as muc excitement as Père Braun's ultramontane sermon of 1872, by pub ishing a pamphlet entitled '*La Source du mal de l'époque au Canada* credited to the Abbé Pelletier, which blamed the religious troubles on Archbishop Taschereau and his followers.

The delegate was overwhelmed with pleas, written and verbal, from the rival parties on the question of ultramontanism *vs.* liberalism, of Victoria *vs.* Laval, of the division of the diocese of Trois-Rivières, and of all the endless quarrels which had arisen between the adherents of two rival currents of ideas. The supporters of each sought to obtain exclusive control of the schools; and so the Victoria-Laval quarrel was duplicated on the secondary-school level by a bitter dispute between the Ecole Jacques Cartier of Montreal and the normal school which Bishop Laflèche, an opponent of lay instruction, proposed to establish at Trois-Rivières; and on the primary-school level by differences between the Christian Brothers and the Montreal School Commissioners. Dom Smeulders established himself at Montreal in the motherhouse of the Oblates; he visited Bishop Bourget in his retreat at Sault-au-Recollet, and he received the counsel of Archbishop Taché, who came east to defend his friend Laflèche. The latter was persuaded to renounce his request for a canonical inquest, and was then assured that the apostolic delegate regarded the division of his diocese as neither necessary or useful.

When this announcement was made, Bishop Laflèche took heart and insisted on a canonical inquest, while Archbishop Taschereau departed for Rome, where the ultramontane *Journal de Rome* was making much of lurid pictures of Masonic intrigue in Canada painted by the Jesuit Père Hamon ('Jean d'Erbrée') in *L'Etendard* and *La Verité*. French-Canadian pride was injured by unfavorable foreign comment, and Bishop Fabre denounced 'those who, moved by one knows not what motive, sow false alarms in our ranks.'[107] But the ultramontanes felt a new confidence, and Senator Bellerose flatly contradicted his bishop in the third of the anti-Masonic memoranda which he presented to Dom Smeulders, while Bishop Laflèche issued a circular to his clergy recommending sermons against the plague of Freemasonry. Archbishop Taschereau did not waste time at Rome; on May 31 the cardinal prefect of the Propaganda informed Dom Smeulders that the question of the division of the diocese had been reserved for decision in Rome.

Bishop Laflèche had already announced the decision of the delegate in his favor, and the position of Dom Smeulders was gravely weakened by this repudiation. Despite his dismay at the news from Rome, Bishop Laflèche made a fighting speech at the fiftieth anniversary of the Montreal Saint-Jean-Baptiste Society in June; it was on this occasion that he condemned the mania for speaking English and observed: 'I am well enough pleased to meet compatriots who speak English badly.'[108] Again on July 4, the 250th anniversary of the founding of Trois-Rivières, the Bishop discussed the close alliance between Church and State throughout Canada's history; called for the return to the Church of the Jesuit Estates; denounced Freemasonry and proclaimed once more the French and Catholic mission of his people. Meanwhile his supporters deluged Rome with petitions against the division of his diocese, maintaining that such a step would be a 'moral disaster . . . interpreted as the condemnation of the doctrine of the Bishop of Trois-Rivières.'[109] Laflèche himself requested of the Propaganda that full reparation be made by the Archbishop of Quebec and the Bishop of Chicoutimi for injustice done him and his diocese.

Rome finally spoke on the university question on August 23. Its decision was virtually a complete victory for Laval, since Laval, including its Montreal branch, was recognized as the sole Catholic university, which all bishops were directed to aid and support; the failure of the fusion of the Victoria and Laval medical schools was deplored, although Victoria was permitted to remain *in statu quo*; and Laval was to be aided by a province-wide ecclesiastical tax.[110] New trouble broke out in Montreal when Bishop Fabre ordered the submission of all parties to this decision, and an ultramontane representative of Victoria soon departed for Rome. But the ultramontane cause was failing fast; on October 5 Rome announced that the principle of the division of the diocese of Trois-Rivières was confirmed, though the actual division was not to take place until the coming of a new apostolic delegate.[111] In short, Dom Smeulders, who had been won over by the ultramontanes, was virtually repudiated by Rome. He somewhat pointedly left Quebec for Trois-Rivières the day Archbishop Taschereau returned from Rome, and in December he quit Canada after a mission of fourteen months. He was feted in defeat by the ultramontanes, although he had solved none of the difficulties which had brought him to Canada.

The ultramontanes continued to fight for control of education, but Bishop Laflèche's attempt to annex the normal schools to the classical colleges was defeated in the Council of Public Instruction at the instance of Archbishop Taschereau, who also succeeded in making his own candidate head of the Ecole Normale Laval. The Catholic Committee of the Council continued to reject the textbooks of the Christian Brothers, and the ultramontane press denounced the lay members of the Committee—viewed inevitably as Masons and friends of free-thinking France—for their efforts 'to destroy our old Christian usages and to substitute for them the principles of modern, that is to say revolutionary, pedagogy.'[112] Bishop Laflèche again opposed the provincial government's attempt to strengthen state medical control of the insane asylums as based on 'the fatal principle of the omnipotence of the State with which the Revolution overturned the religious institutions of our former mother country.'[113]

In May 1885 the nomination of Bishop Cameron of Antigonish, Nova Scotia, as the new apostolic delegate was announced. His function was not to investigate but to execute the decree of division. It was rumored that Bishop Laflèche would go to Rome once more to make a last effort against the division of his diocese. Archbishop Taschereau informed him that he had consulted Cardinal Simeoni, who had replied: 'It is inopportune that Bishop Laflèche come to Rome now.'[114] While the funeral of Bishop Bourget and the silver anniversary of the Séminaire des Trois-Rivières provided occasions for ultramontane rallies, it was announced that Archbishop Taschereau's Roman representative, Abbé Gravel of Saint-Hyacinthe, had been named bishop of the new see of Nicolet. Bishop Laflèche was assured by Cardinal Simeoni that the division of the diocese had not been provoked by any discontent with him at Rome, but kind words could not conceal the blunt logic of events. His followers made extravagant statements, saying among other things that Barabbas had been preferred to Jesus; but Bishop Laflèche himself submitted, though not with good grace, for he refused to assist at the enthroning of the new bishop. But on the urgent advice of Archbishop Taché, Laflèche's pastoral announcing the division of the diocese contained neither complaints nor reproaches. If there was any doubt in men's minds that the ultramontane cause was finished, it was remedied the following year when Archbishop Taschereau was made the first Canadian cardinal and Bishops Fabre of Montreal and Duhamel of Ottawa were named archbishops, while Bishop Laflèche was passed over.

He was to fight on for 'the true principles' as he saw them until the end of his life in 1898. As late as 1891 Laflèche was still capable of thundering with youthful vigor:

> Poor France! What remedy is powerful enough to cure her of the terrible revolutionary sickness which has crept even into the sources of her religious life? Great remedies are needed for great evils! She will continue to be the land of massacres so long as she does not vomit up the last drop of gallican and liberal poison and return squarely to the Catholic fold, socially, politically, as well as individually.[115]

The authoritarianism and apocalyptic sense of modern evils which Laflèche shared with Bishop Bourget were deeply rooted. The world was changing and the bishops were no longer listened to as they had been in the heyday of the 'Holy War.' While Laflèche dutifully accepted the new order which forbade clerical intervention in politics, he remained resolute in his lifelong principles:

> One must pray much for our poor people, who are prey to a crowd of demagogues who endeavor to inculcate them with revolutionary doctrines without even being aware of it themselves, because of their

ignorance of the questions with which they concern themselves. These are blind men, who will lead our people to the abyss, if the latter do not regard the guidance which their first pastors give them.[116]

But the divergence between the hierarchy and the French-Canadian people on the Riel question had weakened the traditional influence of the bishops and permitted the rise to leadership, despite their opposition, of such Liberals as Mercier and Laurier, whom Laflèche unquestionably regarded as 'demagogues.'

8

While the dominant literary school of this period devoted itself to piously hymning the French-Canadian past and the traditional values of Quebec society, certain new currents of thought became evident in the intellectual ferment of the 1860's, 1870's, and 1880's. A spirit essentially gallic but without precedent in French Canada, save for Lahontan and the elder Pierre de Sales Laterrière, began to examine the contemporary scene when Arthur Buies launched his weekly, *La Lanterne*, in September 1868. Born in Montreal of a Scottish father and a French-Canadian mother, Buies was early orphaned and was brought up by two aunts at Rimouski on the lower St. Lawrence, where he seems to have imbibed an overdose of the independence of spirit for which its people are noted. Educated at the seminaries of Quebec, Lévis, and Nicolet—all of which he left at the request of the authorities—Buies went to Paris to complete his studies. Finding that academic life palled upon his restless and undisciplined temperament, Buies left Paris to become one of Garibaldi's Redshirts in 1860, while most French Canadians were denouncing these revolutionaries with pious fervor. But military discipline was no more to his taste than the academic, and Buies soon deserted and returned home, imbued with republican and Bohemian notions very foreign to Quebec. He studied law and was admitted to the bar, but soon turned to journalism, serving as one of the editors of the *Rouge* organ *Le Pays*.

With a temperament that brooked no mastery, even his own, Buies then launched a series of shortlived personal organs which drew down upon him ecclesiastical censure, for his impatience with hypocrisy, conventionality, and reaction spared no one and nothing. In 1868 the prospectus of *La Lanterne*, whose title echoed both the cry of the French Revolution and Diogenes' search for honesty, announced flatly:

> I enter into open war with all stupidities, all hypocrisies, all infamies; that is, I take upon my back three-quarters of mankind, which is a heavy burden.

There are two sorts of imbecile: those who know it and those who do not. The latter are the worse; they write *La Minerve's* reports. As for the others, they console themselves with the prospect of the Kingdom of Heaven.[117]

Buies' chief targets were Conservatism and ultramontanism, the latter of which he flayed mercilessly with such comments as 'False piety always seeks to exhibit itself, because it is not what it appears.'[118] He remarked of one of Bishop Bourget's ceremonious progresses: 'I knew a time, which is not ours, when people were better Catholics than they are today, although they paraded it less.'[119] He spared neither cabinet ministers nor the influential Jesuits nor the Pope himself, commenting ironically on the spectacle of the Pastor of Christendom waging war. He attacked the clerical-Conservative alliance, clerical censorship, and clerical domination in general, blaming the reactionary tendency of close alliances between Church and State for the situation that 'in most Catholic states, revolution is permanently to be found beside the established order.'[120] Banned and persecuted by Bishop Bourget, *La Lanterne* succumbed in March 1869, to be succeeded by *L'Indépendant* (1870) and *Le Réveil* (1876), which were equally shortlived. Buies' talent was that of a pamphleteer and columnist, and his 'chronicles' for journals of such widely assorted opinions as *Le Pays*, *L'Opinion Publique*, *La Minerve*, and *Le National*, which were later collected in book form, provide a valuable commentary on the events of the time, whose satire is warmed by Buies' strong affection for French Canada.

In his own special way, which was that of the lone wolf and maverick, of the rebel against the established order, Buies was one of the Patriotic School of Quebec, although its godly members would have recoiled in horror at the thought. He was less blinded by sentiment than they, and by nature more keen-sighted and realistic. Buies is a serious writer beneath his mockeries and gibes at the great of his day, whose frailties he singled out unerringly. He had no love for pomposity and authoritarianism, whether found in such politicians as Cartier and Hector Langevin, or in such churchmen as Bishops Bourget and Laflèche; and he was a master of the witty and malicious gossip which is one of Quebec's little-celebrated but most notably French traits. Buies' matter was not limited to trivialities; as early as 1871 he deplored the misguided optimism dominant in the colonization movement, which resulted in tragedy for many colonists and vast waste of time and money in futile attempts to develop unsuitable regions, which had been chosen simply as blank spaces on the map which might be made French and Catholic. Not only did he describe the summer resorts of his beloved lower St. Lawrence, with sharply etched accounts of the social differences between French and English, but he explored the virtually unknown Saguenay, Gaspé, and Matapedia regions. He carried his patriotism even into the field of transportation: the railroads, particularly the Canadian Pacific, suffered from his attacks, while the largely French-operated St. Lawrence steamers found favor in his eyes.

As befitted a self-christened 'advanced *Rouge*,'[121] he delighted in the brilliant red wagons used to distribute *Le Pays* in the countryside, and he mourned over the death of Papineau in 1871. But his political thinking was not merely partisan. The perverse streak in him noted with ironic amusement that Canadian attachment to England grew as England showed an increasing willingness to free herself of Canada. In 1872, alone among the French-Canadian writers of the day, he was concerned with the rise of unions, wage problems, and emigration from the country to the cities, for he saw that Canada was becoming an industrial country, while his contemporaries preached a return to the obsolescent rural life. He also wrote intelligently on the plague of alcoholism in Quebec—he himself was not immune from it—but criticized the total abstinence movement which had been launched by the Church.

Writing a far more vigorous and lively French than most of his contemporaries, Buies deplored the corruption of his mother tongue by the anglicisms in use among lawyers and merchants, to whose growing cultural pretensions he opposed the fact that purer French was spoken in the country than among the urban élite. He considered that the genius of the language had been lost in Quebec, and many Frenchmen have since agreed with him. He censured the mania for 'having written a book, no matter what, no matter why,'[122] which developed in the self-conscious attempt to create a French-Canadian literature. To him, 'any real literature is impossible in a country where the sciences and arts are neglected,' and he added bitterly: 'Our people are not willing to do difficult intellectual work; they have not been trained for it.' In general he agreed with Abbé Casgrain's ideas on French-Canadian literature; though he singled out for particular praise only Garneau, Etienne Parent, Pierre Chauveau, the journalist Oscar Dunn, and Dr. LaRue.

Despite his interest in the advancement of his own people, whom he well served by drawing their attention to scantily-settled regions of the province, he deplored the narrow racist outlook. On Dominion Day 1877 he observed: 'While Canada is only a colony, there will be no Canadian nationality; there will be French, English, Scottish, Irish races, all hailing their respective mother countries, but they will never mingle under the common name of Canadians, because a Canadian nation cannot exist where there is no independent Canadian state.'[123] To him the French Canadians were the only true 'anadians; and this was in large measure true in a day when English 'anadians were hopelessly colonial-minded, and their leaders often eserted Canada for England after obtaining eminence or wealth 1 the New World.

Buies' lifelong difficulties were partly personal, the result of a :mperament not adapted to life in a closely knit and narrow society; ut they also arose in part because he was a man far ahead of his me. Only when his restless energy and graphic pen were enlisted y the dynamic Curé Labelle to publicize the colonization move-ent of the 1880's and 1890's did Quebec find a place for this ghly gifted son who refused to follow the ordained pattern of rench-Canadian life, and who added insult to injury by irreverent mments on that pattern. Buies' career was symptomatic of the eep ferments at work in French-Canadian life at this period.

Buies was anything but typical of the writers of this epoch, owever, most of whom devoted themselves to following the lead ' the School of Quebec and concentrated on history. In 1871 id 1872 Louis-Philippe Turcotte published *Le Canada sous l'Union*, history more notable for its minute detail than its penetration. rom 1870 onward Benjamin Sulte published a host of historical onographs, which were synthesized in his *Histoire des Canadiens ançais* (1882–4). Sulte was more of an antiquarian than a historian this period, and his works were carelessly written and constructed; it they have considerable charm and reflect a more independent oint of view than most writings of the period. Narcisse-Eutrope ionne was a meticulous researcher whose most notable productions ere a monograph on Champlain and a bibliography of Canadiana. -O. David produced a series of biographies and historical sketches hich are more lively than accurate. His *Les Patriotes de 1837–8*, ritten with the enthusiasm of an inveterate *Rouge* for the *Patriote* use, is his best work. Mgr. Cyrien Tanguay published an ex-haustive *Dictionnaire généalogique des Familles canadiennes*, which spite its errors is an invaluable compendium for historical workers d the forerunner of a flood of later genealogical studies. The obé Charles-Henri Laverdière admirably edited three classic storical texts in his *Oeuvres de Champlain*, *Relations des Jésuites*, and *urnal des Jésuites*. He was a pioneer of rigorously accurate historical ork. The Abbé Hospice-Anselme Verreau published many mono-aphs on Montreal history and edited a notable collection of docu-ents on *L'Invasion du Canada en 1775*, which appeared in 1873.

The most notable poet of the period, Louis Fréchette, reflected e main currents of the time in his work, and was involved in any of the main movements. He was born at Lévis, across the . Lawrence from Quebec, in 1839, but ran away from his step-other at the age of thirteen and found employment as a telegrapher in northern New York. He returned to Canada to finish his studi at the Quebec and Nicolet seminaries, and then studied law Laval. Meanwhile he became interested in poetry under the in fluence of Crémazie, then holding forth in his Quebec booksho Fréchette's first book, *Mes Loisirs* (1865), clearly reflects Crémazie influence. Fréchette set about the simultaneous practice of law journalism, and poetry in his native Lévis, but failing in all thre he sought his fortune in Chicago, where from 1866 to 1869 l published his annexationist *Voix d'un Exilé*, which included bitt attacks on the conditions which made it necessary for young Can dians to leave home for the States. This work was later bought u and burnt after Fréchette became the unofficial laureate of Quebe In 1871 Fréchette returned to Canada and entered politics. Aft twice having been an unsuccessful candidate, he was elected the federal parliament in 1874, where he served until the Liber downfall in 1878.

He published *Pêle-Mêle* (1877) and *Fleurs Boréales et Oiseaux Neiges* (1879), winning a prize from the French Academy in 188 for these poems on the themes of France and Canada, family an friendship. He was the first French-Canadian writer to be th honored by the Academy, and acquired enormous prestige Canada. His *Légende d'un Peuple* (1887) was published in Paris an dedicated to '*la France*.' Sounding as it did the patriotic chor which had made Crémazie famous, it reinforced Fréchette's standi as the laureate of French Canada. This eloquent evocation notable passages in the history of Quebec in the manner of Vict Hugo was probably his best work. In 1891 Fréchette publish another volume of verse, *Feuilles volantes*, but after that, with tl exception of the poetic drama *Veronica* he contented himself wi revising his early poems and writing casual prose works, such as h *Originaux et détraqués* (1892) and *La Noël au Canada* (1900), whi were popular studies in folklore. As dean of French-Canadi letters, he gave readings of his verse in Quebec and New Englan Installed in a comfortable mansion in St. Louis Square in Montre he waged polemical warfare with the ultramontane Judge Routhi and his rival William Chapman, who accused him of plagiarizi Hugo. A three-volume definitive edition of his works, illustrat by Henri Julien, was published at Paris in the year of his deat 1908. With Fréchette, literature finally became respectable Quebec.

Fréchette's most notable poetic rival was Pamphile LeMay, wh did not achieve the same popularity but produced better work his *Les Vengeances* (1875), a novel in verse, and *Les Gouttelettes* (190 a collection of sonnets. LeMay was a countryman by birth ar taste, and was the first French-Canadian poet to hymn rustic li founding the *terroir* school which has continued down to the present day. Librarian of the Quebec Legislature from 1867 to 1892, he found leisure to write his own poetry and to translate Longfellow's *Evangeline*, as well as to produce a series of undistinguished novels and a translation of William Kirby's *Golden Dog*, a sentimental romanticization of Quebec life in the days of New France which has given many English-speaking people a false picture of old Quebec. LeMay was a patriot as well as a lover of the countryside, and thus carried on the tradition of Crémazie. With William Chapman's first book, *Les Feuilles d'Erable* (1890), a younger poet carried the rhetorical tradition of Crémazie and Fréchette to the breaking point in writing on patriotic and religious themes. His attack on Fréchette in *Le Lauréat* (1892) shows his critical talents, as well as his polemical power. A contemporary, Nérée Beauchemin, published his first verses in *Les Floraisons matutinales* in 1897, but despite the immediate success of 'La Cloche de Louisbourg,' a poem in the tradition of Crémazie, remained silent until the publication of his *Patrie intime* in 1928 revealed that the poetic patriot of the '90's had become one of the finest French-Canadian lyricists writing in the *terroir* tradition.

Most of the prose writers of the period were less distinguished than the poets. Joseph Marmette and Napoléon Bourassa wrote popular romantic historical novels, while Faucher de Saint-Maurice, a Dumas musketeer who by some error of Providence found himself on the shores of the St. Lawrence, devoted himself to casual but well-written descriptive sketches of Quebec life and the retelling of old legends, after serving under Maximilien in Mexico as a young man and exploring the Lower St. Lawrence by boat. His *A la brunante*, a collection of legends, was the prose counterpart of Ernest Gagon's *Chansons populaires du Canada*, a collection of the old French folksongs which had survived in Quebec, as medieval English songs did among the mountaineers of Kentucky. The Abbé Léon Provancher carried on the popular scientific work of Dr. LaRue with his *Flore canadienne* (1862) and his *La Faune entomologique du Canada* (1877–89), compilations largely borrowed from American sources which helped to correct the French-Canadian tendency to confuse the North American environment with the European one of their French models. But as yet there was no true scientific writing in Quebec, and botany and geology were cultivated merely as avocations by a few amateurs.

The literature of 1860–1900 indicated a slow awakening to intellectual maturity of a people who had long lingered in a semi-primitive social state. So much intellectual energy was expended in the religio-political struggles of the period that there was little left for purely intellectual pursuits. The cultural colonialism produced by the renewal of close relations with France favored imitation rather than originality, while French-Canadian writers and painters were foredoomed to play second fiddle to those of France. The general preoccupation with religious and patriotic themes which characterizes the work of writers of the School of Quebec and their disciples reflects the fact that this literature was largely produced by members of the ecclesiastical and political élite, the only French Canadians who could afford to write when literature was an avocation rather than a profession. This élite was largely reactionary, and looked back at the past through romantic glasses, rather than forward to the future or closely at the present.

The enthusiastic reception given to the Bourbon pretender to the throne of France, the Comte de Paris, and his brother the Duc d'Orléans during the summer of 1890 indicates the temper of the times. Only three incorrigible *Rouges*, Fréchette, Honoré Beaugrand, and Raoul Dandurand, protested against the plans for a civic reception at Montreal, and the Conservative journalist Thomas Chapais dismissed them as 'the three Brutuses.' The ultramontanes outdid themselves in paying honor to the Bourbon princes, who were officially received at both Montreal and Quebec, and did not fail to pay homage to Bishop Laflèche at Trois-Rivières. Beaugrand redeemed republican honor by sending a telegram to President Carnot, and Dandurand was given the Legion of Honor, presumably for his legendary feat of crying '*Vive la République, Monsieur!*' as the Comte de Paris passed by.[124] A period of cultural colonialism was to end with Mercier almost succeeding in making Quebec an economic as well as a cultural province of France. It remained for Laurier to awaken French Canada to a larger Canadianism and for Henri Bourassa to spur its sense of particularism in the years to come.

Notes

[1] The population of Lower Canada in 1844 was 697,084, while Upper Canada's in 1840 was 432,159, according to the nearest comparable census figures, *Canada Year Book, 1922–23* (Ottawa, 1924), 142. The first census of the united Province of Canada in 1851 showed 60,000 more English-speaking than French Canadians, out of a population of nearly two millions. (Turcotte, *Canada sous l'Union*, II, 164). Massive emigration from Britain had strengthened the English-Canadian group—it is estimated that 428,000 emigrants from Ireland alone came between 1838–49 (Desrosiers & Fournet, *La Race française en Amérique*, 167)—though many of the newcomers continued on to the United States, immediately or after a short period. French-Canadian emigration to the United States from 1831 to 1844 is estimated by Sulte, *Histoire des Canadiens-français, 1608–1880* (Montreal, 1882–4), VIII, 132, at 40,000, and increased from that date onward. Although there are no U.S. census figures for French-speaking Canadians before 1890, when 302,496 were reported, it is probable that 50,000 had gone to the States by 1850, and

another 50,000 by 1860. R. H. Coats & M. C. Maclean, *The American-Born in Canada* (Toronto, 1943), 29–34. Langlois estimates 48,742 by 1851, and 86,615 by 1871. *Histoire de la Population canadienne-française* (Montréal, 1934), 174.

The French Canadians formed 31.07 per cent of the population in 1871, 30.03 in 1881, 30.71 per cent in 1901, 28.51 per cent in 1911, 27.91 per cent in 1921, 28.22 per cent in 1931, 30.27 per cent in 1941, and 30.8 per cent in 1951. *Canada Year Book, 1934–35*, 123; *ibid., 1945*, 104, *ibid., 1952–53*, 149. Their higher birthrate has been offset until recent years by massive immigration (see Langlois, 265–6, for annual totals, 1867–1933).

[2] Langlois, 168.

[3] *Ibid.*, 167. The outlying groups have steadily increased, and by 1941 almost a quarter of the French Canadians lived outside Quebec (Langlois, 169 and *Canada Year Book, 1945*, 105–6).

[4] R. Blanchard, *L'Est du Canada Français* (Montréal, 1935), II, 221–2.

[5] *Ibid.*, 202–3.

[6] *Ibid.*, 224.

[7] *Ibid.*, 219–20.

[8] Innis & Lower, *Select Econ. Docs., 1783–1885*, 489, 497.

[9] *Ibid.*, *Select Econ. Docs., 1783–1885*, 455–7; M. Q. Innis, *An Economic History of Canada* (Toronto, 1935), 185.

[10] *Canada Year Book, 1922–23*, 172.

[11] M. Q. Innis, 21.

[12] See E. Hamon, *Les Canadiens-Français de la Nouvelle Angleterre* (Québec, 1891).

[13] Innis & Lower, *Select Econ. Docs.*, II, 513.

[14] M. Q. Innis, 268.

[15] Innis & Lower, II, 583–4.

[16] *Ibid.*, 496.

[17] N. J. Ware & H. A. Logan, *Labor in Canadian-American Relations* (Toronto, 1937), vi.

[18] *Ibid.*, xviii.

[19] *Mandementsde Québec*, N.S., I, 554–7, Taschereau's pastoral, 19 April 1886; *ibid.*, IV, 633–5, joint pastoral of 4th Provincial Council, 14 May 1868.

[20] R. Rumilly, *Mgr. Laflèche et son temps* (Montréal, 1938), 43.

[21] Rumilly, *Histoire*, I, 138.

[22] *CHAR 1950*, 20–9: Léopold Lamontagne, 'Habits gris et chemise rouge.'

[23] Rumilly, *Laflèche*, 44.

[24] H. S. Lear, *Lacordaire* (London, 1899), 223.

[25] *Mandements de Montréal* (Montréal, 1887), III, 356, Bourget's pastoral, 10 March 1858; T. Hudon, S.J., *L'Institut Canadien de Montréal et l'Affaire Guibord* (Montréal, 1938), 58.

[26] Hudon, 59–60.

[27] *Mandements de Montréal*, VI, 38, Bourget's pastoral, 30 March 1858; Hudon, 60; *Mandements de Montréal*, III, 401, Bourget's pastoral, 31 May 1858; Hudon, 62.

[28] *Mandements de Montréal*, III, 427, Bourget's pastoral, 25 December 1863; Hudon, 64.

[29] Hudon, 65.

[30] *Mandements de Québec*, N.S., I, 628, 4th Provincial Council pastoral, 14 May 1868.

[31] Rumilly, *Laflèche*, 26–7.

[32] *Ibid.*, 28.

[33] *Mandements de Montréal*, VI, 48, Bourget's pastoral, August 1869; Hudon, 74.

[34] Hudon, 76.

[35] Hudon, 109–12.

[36] Hudon, 114.

[37] Hudon, 114–5.

[38] Hudon, 123–31.

[39] *Mandements de Montréal*, VI, Bourget's circular, 3 September 1875; Hudon, 135.

[40] *Ibid.*, Bourget's pastoral, 16 November 1875; Hudon, 147.

[41] Archives, Séminaire de Trois-Rivières, Fonds Laflèche, Laflèche-Boucher de Niverville, 2 March 1864.

[42] *Ibid.*, Laflèche-Abbé Boucher, 9 September 1867.

[43] *CHAR 1945*, 58–9, Abbé A. Maheux, 'Le Nationalisme canadien-français à l'aurore du XXe siècle.'

[44] *Ibid.*, 59.

[45] ASTR, Laflèche-O. Caron, 27 April 1870.

[46] *Ibid.*, Laflèche-O. Caron, 27 May 1870.

[47] Skelton, I, 129; Rumilly, *Histoire*, I, 177–8. Skelton's version is a poor translation.

[48] *Ibid.*,

[49] *Mandemenis de Québec*, N.S., I, 37, Taschereau's circular, 24 April 1871.

[50] *Le National*, 24 April 1872; Skelton, I, 131–2.

[51] Rumilly, *Laflèche*, 65–6, Bourget's circular, 19 March 1872.

[52] *Ibid.*, 69–70.

[53] *Ibid.*, 76.

[54] The career of Charles Chiniquy, one of the few apostate priests in French-Canadian history, has been neglected and deserves further study, for he was a great force for both good and evil in his two careers. Chiniquy was born at Kamouraska in 1809, the son of a notary and the grandson of the Basque pilot who guided Admiral Saunders' fleet upriver in 1759 in the expedition against Quebec. Orphaned at an early age, he was educated at Nicolet thanks to an uncle and to the director of the *collège*. After ordination in 1833, he served as vicar at Saint-Charles, Charlesbourg, and Saint-Roch, the working-class quarter of Quebec. He was named *curé* of Beauport in 1838, and of Kamouraska in 1842, after launching his crusade against strong drink. For this work he received a papal blessing in 1841 and encouragement from Mgr. Forbin-Janson, the peripatetic Bishop of Nancy. His *Manuel des Societés de Tempèrance* (Québec, 1844) sold 4,000 copies in six months—an unprecedented sale for a new book at this period in Quebec—and he became a great national hero.

Scandal involving a woman, however, forced his resignation from his parish and his departure from the diocese of Quebec in 1846. He then entered the newly opened Oblate novitiate at Longueuil, and after fourteen months resumed his temperance crusade in the diocese of Montreal. He was credited with inducing 2,300 to sign the pledge at Longueuil, and 10,000 more in other parishes. In eighteen months he covered one hundred and twenty parishes and converted 200,000 to temperance. The second edition of his *Manuel*, published at Montreal in 1847, sold 6,000 copies in a year and a half. But once more he fell into trouble with women, and after several warnings from Bishop Bourget, was deprived of his clerical faculties in 1851. He then went to the French-Canadian colony in the Kankakee country south of Chicago. Two hundred families from Canada followed him there in response to his letter in *Le Canadien* of September 22, 1851, which offered assurance that those who were forced to emigrate would not have to give up French-Canadian ways if they joined him there. In 1852 he returned to Canada to lead others to Illinois, and by 1856 he claimed that his parish numbered 6,000 souls. Chiniquy had become involved with difficulties with his bishop, however, and was put under interdict by Bishop O'Regan in 1856, and excommunicated shortly thereafter when he defied the interdict. The Bishop of Quebec sent his grand vicar, Mgr. Mailloux, to Illinois to combat Chiniquy and the schism he had created at St. Anne. Chiniquy sought reconciliation in 1856 and again in 1858, but further scandalous conduct called forth another excommunication in 1858.

He then became a Presbyterian, carrying some of his flock with him, and under the auspices of the Protestant Missionary Society visited Canada, England, Scotland, India, and Australia, preaching and lecturing against Catholicism. His best-known work of this second period is *The Priest, the Woman, and the Confessional,* a highly sensational work which appeared in the *Witness* of Montreal, as it served the purposes of the Protestant crusade against Catholicism. In a pastoral of March 19, 1875, Bishop Bourget forbade reading of the *Witness* and once more condemned Chiniquy (Rumilly, I, 345–6). The work was reprinted in Toronto in 1944 by Pastor Shields, the modern exponent of that tradition. Chiniquy died at Montreal in January 1899, publishing in the *Montreal Gazette* on January 10 his 'Testament,' which expressed his hatred and defiance of Catholicism once more. Le Jeune, *Dictionnaire générale du Canada*; biographical notice by Hector L. Langevin, in *Manuel des Sociétés de Tempèrance* (Montréal, 1849); M. L. Hansen & J. B. Brebner, *The Mingling of the Canadian and American Peoples* (Toronto, 1940), 129–30.

55 *Mandements de Québec,* N.S., I, 320–36, joint pastoral, 22 September 1875; Skelton, I, 135–6.

56 *Ibid.,* 330; Rumilly, I, 380.

57 *Mandements de Montréal,* VII, 299, Bourget's circular, 1 February 1876; Skelton, I, 136–7.

58 Skelton, I, 137; Rumilly, *Laflèche,* 95.

59 Skelton, I, 139.

60 *Ibid.,* 140–1.

61 *Ibid.,* 141.

62 U. Barthe, *Wilfrid Laurier on the Platform* (Quebec, 1890), 52.

63 *Ibid.,* 54.

64 *Ibid.,* 55.

65 *Ibid.,* 57

66 *Ibid.,* 59.

67 *Ibid.,* 59.

68 *Ibid.,* 60.

69 *Ibid.,* 61–2.

70 *Ibid.,* 67.

71 *Ibid.,* 68.

72 *Ibid.,* 69.

73 *Ibid.,* 70.

74 *Ibid.,* 71–2.

75 *Ibid.,* 72.

76 *Ibid.,* 73.

77 *Ibid.,* 75–8.

78 *Ibid.,* 79.

79 *Mandements de Québec,* N.S., I, 403–9, Taschereau's pastoral, 25 May 1876.

80 *Ibid.,* II, 10–13, joint circular, 26 March 1877.

81 Conroy's instructions published by Taschereau, *Mandements de Québec,* N.S., II, 271, Taschereau's circular, October 1881; Rumilly, *Laflèche,* 118–9.

82 *Mandements de Québec,* N.S., II, 52, joint pastoral 11 October 1877; L. David, *Histoire du Canada depuis la Confédération* (Montréal, 1909), 152; Simeoni-Taschereau, 13 September 1881; Rumilly, *Laflèche,* 123.

83 *Mandements de Québec,* N.S., II, 47, joint circular to clergy, 11 October 1877.

84 *Le Journal des Trois-Rivières*; Rumilly, *Laflèche,* 124.

85 Rumilly, *Laflèche,* 128.

86 Skelton, I, 212-13.

[87] *Ibid.*
[88] Rumilly, *Laflèche*, 133.
[89] Rumilly, *Histoire*, III, 75–80; *Laflèche*, 152.
[90] Rumilly, *Laflèche*, 156.
[91] *Mandements de Québec*, N.S., II, 265; Taschereau's circular, 7 October 1881.
[92] *L'Evenement*, October 1881; Rumilly, *Laflèche*, 161.
[93] *Le Monde*; Rumilly, *Laflèche*, 171.
[94] *Mandements de Québec*, N.S., II, 286–96, Taschereau's pastoral, 2 February 1882.
[95] *La Verité*; David, *Histoire*, 162.
[96] *Journal des Trois-Rivières*; David, *Histoire*, 161–2.
[97] ASTR: Fonds Laflèche, 'Diverses ouevres MSS,' Laflèche-Leo XIII on 'Humanum genus,' (1884). The encyclical was published by Cardinal Taschereau in May 1884, *Mandements de Québec*, N.S. II, 404–28.
[98] Rumilly, *Laflèche*, 176–7.
[99] *Ibid.*, 177.
[100] Simeoni-Legaré, 10 January 1883; Rumilly, *Laflèche*, 189.
[101] *Mandements de Québec*, N.S., II, 349–56, Taschereau's pastoral, 19 March 1883, Propaganda degree, 27 February 1883.
[102] Taschereau-Taché, 1 May 1883; Rumilly, *Laflèche*, 196.
[103] Rumilly, *Laflèche*, 198.
[104] *Mandements de Québec*, N.S., II, 366–70, Taschereau's pastoral, 1 June 1883.
[105] Rumilly, *Laflèche*, 208–9.
[106] *Ibid.*, 213.
[107] *Mandements de Montréal*, X, 5, Fabre's pastoral, 22 May 1884; Rumilly *Laflèche*, 225.
[108] Rumilly, *Laflèche*, 228.
[109] L. Desilets, *Exposé sommaire* (Rome, 1884); Rumilly, *Laflèche*, 232.
[110] Rumilly, *Laflèche*, 233.
[111] *Ibid.*, 235.
[112] *Ibid.*, 245.
[113] *Ibid.*, 249.
[114] Taschereau-Laflèche, 26 May 1884; Rumilly, *Laflèche*, 251.
[115] ASTR: Fonds Laflèche, Laflèche-Abbé Arcand, 21 October 1891.
[116] *Ibid.*, Laflèche-Curé Tessier, 5 March 1892.
[117] *La Lanterne* (Montréal, 1884), I, 'Aux Lectures.' This pamphlet was condemned by Archbishop Taschereau on 8 November 1886 (*Mandements de Québec*, N.S., II, 591–2).
[118] *La Lanterne*, I, 'Aux Lectures.'
[119] *Ibid.*, I, 4.
[120] *Ibid.*, I, 53.
[121] A. Buies, *Petits chroniques pour 1877* (Québec, 1878), VI.
[122] *Ibid.*, XI.
[123] *Ibid.*, 36.
[124] Rumilly, *Histoire*, VI, 163 *n.* 1.

CHAPTER VIII

RIEL, THE WEST, AND MERCIER

(1818–97)

THE STRIFE in Quebec in the years between 1867 and 1896 which was heightened by developments in the West, was remote at the outset of the period and dominated national life at its close. The same period saw the birth and death of hopes of building a new Quebec in the West, upon the foundations laid in the days of the fur trade, under both the French and English regimes.

I

The Red River colony had depended on Quebec for its religious organization since 1818, when Bishop Plessis answered Lord Selkirk's request for missionaries by sending out the Abbés Norbert Provencher and S.-J.-N. Dumoulin. With them went a few settlers from Quebec, also requested by the noble colonizer. These newcomers joined the French-Canadian and *Métis* (half-breed)[1] employees of the fur trade settled about the missions of St. Boniface and Pembina, after the absorption of the North-West Company by the Hudson's Bay Company in 1821 left many without work. At the outset the Selkirk colony was two-thirds Scottish, with the remaining third made up of German Swiss veterans of the Régiments du Meuron and De Watteville which had served in the War of 1812, French Canadians from Quebec, and veterans of the fur trade.[2] As the years passed, the French, who tended to follow a semi-nomadic hunting life, came to equal in number the Scottish and English settlers, who inclined more to agriculture. Because of this ethnic mixture the colony was described as 'a little Quebec.'[3] But the *Métis*, both French and English, increased far more rapidly than the pure-blooded whites, and developed a sense of nationality of their own, with Indian blood acting as a tie which offset ancient French and English differences.[4]

The West was more of a British frontier than a Canadian one at this period, since after 1821 it was controlled and supplied from Britain through Hudson Bay, rather than over the barrier of the Laurentian Shield north of the Great Lakes, or by the roundabout and difficult route from Canada through the States. The English group in the colony, including the Hudson's Bay Company men who dominated both trade and government, the Anglican missionaries, and a few settlers, was the most influential; the group of Scottish settlers the most homogeneous; and the French-Canadian and *Métis* group the most numerous.[5] Aside from the officials, the French Canadians had the closest economic relation to the Hudson's Bay Company, since they were largely nomadic trappers, *voyageurs*, and buffalo hunters who supplied the pemmican which was the basic ration of the fur trade. For this reason they were more restive under the company's monopoly than the agricultural Scots. Then from the North-Westers' bitter trade wars with the Hudson's Bay Company the French *Métis* had acquired a tradition of enmity to the latter; while from their Indian forbears they had inherited the belief that the West was their land, and that its natural resources were theirs, despite the company's strict regulations against unlicensed fur-trading. Gradually the *Métis*, both French and English, developed a sense of unity.

They called themselves the 'New Nation.'[6] Accustomed to choosing their own leaders, Indian-style, and to acting together with disciplined unity for the purposes of the buffalo hunt, the *Métis* grew increasingly restive under the regulations of the Hudson's Bay Company officials of Assiniboia, and in 1849 this unrest exploded into virtual rebellion.[7] When Guillaume Sayer was charged with illicit fur-trading before Recorder Adam Thom—who had been rewarded by Lord Durham for his services in 1839 with this office—a group of *Métis* under Scottish leaders invaded the courtroom and won the acquittal of Sayer by intimidation. Jean-Louis Riel, grandson of the famous *coureur de bois* Lagimonière and himself the miller of St. Boniface, was the most influential figure among the French *Métis*, thanks to the prestige of his two years as an Oblate novice and his later industrial training in Montreal. He was generally believed to be the leading spirit in the agitation over the Sayer case and in the demand for free trade which was then expressed though he remained behind the scenes of the courtroom drama in 1849.

The isolated little world of the Red River was gradually drawn into the life of the continent. There was an annexationist agitation in 1845–6, occasioned by the focusing of American expansionism on the Oregon boundary dispute, but its development was checked by a force of English troops who garrisoned the colony from 1846 to 1848.[8] In the West as in the East the Church threw its weight behind loyalty to the British connection, and the Abbés Blanchet and Demers were sent from the Red River to the Oregon settlement at the request of the imperial authorities to offset the influence of American missionaries in the latter regions. Again from 1857 to

861 a small force of the Canadian Rifles was stationed at Fort Garry to guard against Fenian raids and to offset the annexationist movement in Minnesota inspired by James Wickes Taylor, then a special agent of the United States Treasury, who reported to the Governor of Minnesota in 1860 that 'the frontier, hitherto resting upon the sources of the St. Lawrence and the Mississippi, is soon to be pushed far beyond the International frontier by the march of Anglo-Saxon civilization.'[9] During the 1840's and 1850's the Red River region, which had previously been tied to eastern Canada only by the dependence of its missionaries on Quebec and Montreal, gradually became a bone of contention between Upper and Lower Canada. George Brown, the francophobe and anti-Catholic editor of the *Toronto Globe*, aroused English-Canadian interest in the West and preached annexation of the Red River colony to Canada. In this cause he was aided by the like-minded William McDougall, whose *North American* was soon absorbed by the *Globe*. Both men wanted to make the West an extension of English Upper Canada, with a view to dominating French Canada.[10] Quebec, whose interest in the West had been stirred by the reports of the missionaries whom it supported and largely supplied, naturally opposed this program, which increased its chronic sense of insecurity.

With the project of Confederation already under discussion, Canadian pressure was brought to bear in London against the renewal of the Hudson's Bay Company charter in 1857; and in that same year a committee composed of George Brown and Joseph Cauchon was appointed by the Canadian legislature to consider Western affairs. Canada took the view that the Hudson's Bay Company title to the North-West was invalid,[11] and, as its own expansionism developed, became somewhat concerned at the extension of American economic influence in the Red River region, which was linked to the United States by steamer in 1859 and by rail shortly afterward, when the railroad reached St. Paul. The Hudson's Bay Company itself began to import supplies by this route rather than by the traditional York Factory one. The authority of the company declined after the renewal of its charter was refused in London. The company's officials were left in the forlorn position of a lame-duck American president, obliged to round out his term of office after defeat at the polls.[12]

In this situation Canadian and American annexationist parties grew up among the new settlers at Fort Garry, the English settlement about the Hudson's Bay post across the river from St. Boniface, the *Métis* and French Catholic center; while the older settlers agitated for Crown colony status. The American party received backing from Minnesota, and Taylor reported on December 17, 1861: 'The

Americanization of this important section of British North Americ is rapidly progressing. Unless the British Parliament acts promptl . . . I shall confidently expect a popular movement looking t independence or annexation to the United States.'[13] Two Canadians, William Coldwell and William Buckingham, founded in 185 the first newspaper, the *Nor'Wester*, which was the organ of th Canadian party.[14] In 1862 John Ross, a Scottish *Métis*, claime that the 'New Nation' wanted responsible government, while J.-L Riel denied it. Meanwhile the Canadian authorities, proceedin on their convenient view that Assiniboia had no legal government provided for the admission of the North-West Territories into Confederation at the Quebec Conference of 1864, without consultin the wishes of the people of the region.[15] When this news reache the Red River, it was proposed that one French and one Englis delegate should be sent to London to express the popular deman for Crown colony status.[16]

Resentment of highhanded eastern determination of the fate o the West continued to grow along the Red River. A short-live 'Republic of Manitoba' on the pre-annexation Texan model[17] wa set up in January 1868, with Thomas Spence, a newly arrive English-Canadian disciple of D'Arcy McGee as president, whil negotiations were still pending in London between the Hudson's Ba Company and the British and Canadian governments over dispositio of the territory. The move was probably intended to aid th Canadian case by proving that the company had lost control c the Red River colony.[18] A plague of grasshoppers produced considerable economic distress along the Red River that same year which sharpened the local opposition to the wholly illegal Canadia roadbuilding party under John A. Snow which had been sent int the region by William McDougall as a joint relief and politica measure.[19] The paymaster of this party was the poet Charles Mair whose Red River letters were published by the *Toronto Globe*. Th following summer Canadian surveyors under Colonel J. S. Denni proceeded to run their lines without regard to the river-strip holding of the old settlers, and with a show of racist contempt for th *Métis*. The population at this period numbered about 10,000, predominantly *Métis* and almost equally divided between English an French. Despite the urgent representations of Governor Mactavish Colonel Dennis, and Bishop Taché—who warned Cartier at Ottaw in July 1869 and Cartier and Hector Langevin at Quebec in September on the eve of his departure for the Vatican Council—tha trouble was brewing in the West, the land schemes of the Canadia government were deemed more important than the protests o 10,000 'half-castes,'[20] as Sir John Macdonald contemptuously calle the *Métis*.

The long negotiations carried on by Cartier and Macdonald with e Hudson's Bay Company finally came to an end. The company's ed of surrender of November 19, 1869, was to take effect with the ansfer of the North-West Territories to Canada on December 1, nen the latter was to pay £300,000, in addition to making land ants and other privileges to extinguish the company's claim. nder the Act for the Temporary Government of Rupert's Land, ssed in June 1869 without consultation of the Red River people, anada was to have both federal and provincial powers in the erritories, since the proposed governmental organization provided ly for an appointed governor and council, whose members did ot have to be residents. This was a backward step politically, for e old Council of Assiniboia had included local representation (on roughly equal French and English basis since 1855);[21] and further opular agitation against absentee control arose.

William McDougall, already unpopular with the colonists for his eavyhanded expansionist activities, was appointed lieutenant-overnor and dispatched by way of Chicago and St. Paul to the ed River, where he was to take office after the transfer of title on ecember 1. His council included Joseph-Norbert Provencher, ephew of the pioneer missionary bishop of the Red River and a rmer editor of *La Minerve*, Cartier's Conservative organ in Mon-eal; but for the rest was as militantly 'Anglo-Saxon' and Protestant McDougall could have wished. The new government was ankly despotic, for Macdonald wrote Charles Tupper that Mc-ougall 'will be for the time Paternal despot, as in other small rown Colonies, his Council being one of advice, he and they, owever, being governed by instructions from Headquarters.'[22] oseph Howe, shortly to become Dominion Secretary of State, paid n unofficial visit to the Red River to assuage the rising unrest there, nd found that discontent was general. The company officials felt at they should have received a share of the £300,000; the English ere dissatisfied at not being consulted about the transfer; and the rench were uneasy because of the appointment as governor of e francophobe imperialist McDougall.

2

The mounting unrest came to a head in October 1869. On the 1th, Louis Riel, the twenty-five-year-old son of the leader of the rench *Métis* in 1849, who like his father enjoyed great prestige mong his people because he had been educated for the priesthood Montreal, thanks to Bishop Taché and the Masson family of 'errebonne, broke up a survey party which was running its lines ithout regard to the holdings of the French settlers. On October

20 the *Métis* assembled and elected a provisional government model on their organization for buffalo-hunting, with the Scottish *Mé* John Bruce as president and young Riel as secretary. Their ai was to win recognition of their rights by Canada before the territo changed hands. Father J.-J. Lestanc, a Frenchman like many of tl Oblate missionaries in the West, who was acting as vicar-gener in the absence at Rome of Bishop Taché, refused to intervene wi Riel at the request of the old Council of Assiniboia, on the groun that the *Métis* were justified in urging their grievances upon tl government. Father Lestanc did not admire Riel, however, ar was opposed to any resort to violence or unconstitutional means protest; while the Canadian missionary of Rivière-Sale, Fath N.-J. Ritchot, was known to favor direct action by the movemer which he supported; and the Fenian seminarian William O'Don ghue of St. Boniface was for radical measures, even the annexatic to the States for which enthusiasm was being fostered in Minneso by James Wickes Taylor, who was now simultaneously an agent the State Department and of Jay Cooke.[23] The English settler though not threatened like the French on the score of langua and religion, met on October 19 and refused to adopt an addre of welcome to McDougall. But their attitude was one of willingne to wait and see how the new regime worked out, rather than resistance to the establishment of Canadian government.

Riel was summoned to appear before the Council of Assinibo on October 25, and there defended the actions of the *Métis* as bei in the interest of the whole colony. He expressed satisfaction wi the present government and objected to 'any government comi from Canada without their being consulted in the matter.' Behind this opposition lay the *Métis* fear of being crowded out their own country by the mass immigration from Ontario whic McDougall had been promoting in the *Globe*. On November Ambroise Lépine, the only other French *Métis* among the s officers of the provisional government, and a party of armed *Méti* escorted McDougall and two of his council out of the country whe he attempted to cross the frontier, after he had been warned on h arrival at Pembina on October 30 not to do so.[25] This incider has been responsible for the use of the term 'rebellion' in connectic with the *Métis* rising; but it is difficult to justify the term, sin McDougall was simply a private citizen and the Red River countr not Canadian territory until the anticipated transfer took plac On October 30 the acting governor of Assiniboia, Mactavish, ha written McDougall urging him to wait at the frontier.[26] On tl same day that McDougall was deported in the name of the provision government, Riel seized Fort Garry, thus forestalling a similar mov by the Canadian party headed by Dr. Schultz and Colonel Denni the head of the surveying party which included a number of hot-headed expansionists.[27] Colonel Dennis had written McDougall on October 27, warning him that trouble was brewing, and subsequently planned a *coup d'état* to bring him in by force.[28] On November 6 Riel called upon the eleven Scottish parishes to choose representatives to meet with the French *Métis* on November 16.

In the face of these developments the acting governor of Assiniboia, Mactavish, issued a mildly-phrased proclamation on November 16, protesting against the provisional government's actions and urging 'lawful constitutional' action.[29] He then advised McDougall to return to Canada. On November 22 A. B. Bannatyne recommended that the English settlers should combine with the French, and a joint plan was formed to supplant the old council by a new popular one, which would enter into negotiations with the Canadian government. Riel, who had become the dominant figure in the provisional government by this time, first agreed to this proposal and then rejected it, while on November 23 his followers seized the provisions and cash at Fort Garry and interrupted free communication in and out of the fort. Though the French *Métis* had so far taken the lead in the actions of the provisional government, by the end of November the English and Scottish half-breeds were drilling to defend their rights if need be against the Canadian authorities.[30] There was no need to do so, for the intimidated McDougall simply crossed the frontier once more on December 1, issued a proclamation[31] which was invalid since the transfer to Canada had not taken place as scheduled and he was unsworn as governor, and then promptly returned to the States. There he found a letter of November 20 from Macdonald instructing him that he was entering 'a foreign country' and that he was not to attempt to force his way in.[32] Colonel Dennis, who had constituted himself McDougall's advisor and who had been given a curious commission as 'Lieutenant and Conservator of the Peace,'[33] was characterized as 'exceedingly injudicious.' And finally Macdonald had refused on November 27 to accept transfer of the territory from the Hudson's Bay Company in its disturbed state when he learned of the resistance to McDougall.

Though Ottawa marked time, events along the Red River did not. Colonel Dennis, at the head of some seventy Canadians and as many more Indians, had planned a rising on December 2 which McDougall thought would succeed in putting down the provisional government of the *Métis*. This scheme advanced no further than the seizure of the Lower Fort on December 1, for the Colonel found his followers undependable. His movement broke up on the 9th, after Riel had issued on December 5 a 'List of Rights'[34]—most of which were conceded in the Manitoba Act of the following year—and had seized some leaders of the Canadian party at Dr. Schultz' house on the 7th and imprisoned them at Fort Garry. In defiance of McDougall's proclamation, the provisional government flew its own fleur-de-lis and shamrock flag from its headquarters at the fort. The Canadian party had already displayed a flag of their own—the Union Jack with 'Canada' embroidered on it.[35]

Macdonald, who had previously refused to take the *Métis* agitation seriously, reached late in November the correct conclusion that 'the resistance of the half-breeds evidently is not against the sovereignty of Her Majesty or the government of the Hudson's Bay Company, but to the assumption of the government by Canada.'[36] He promptly sent out two unofficial emissaries, Father J.-B. Thibault, a missionary with twenty-seven years' service in the region, and Lieutenant-Colonel Charles de Salaberry, the son of the hero of Chateauguay. Donald Smith, recommended to Macdonald by George Stephen as a good agent because of his experience in the region as a Hudson's Bay official, was also sent out to buy off the insurgent leaders. Riel was to be offered a post in the new territorial police; two *Métis* were to be included in the new council, two-thirds of which was to be elected from the settlement; land titles were to be adjusted; and secret funds were made available, as Macdonald blandly put it, 'to construct a Golden Bridge over which McDougall can pass into the country.'[37] But McDougall's actions of early December anticipated the arrival of the emissaries and compromised their efforts. Macdonald promptly repudiated the acts of McDougall and Dennis when he learned of their course and refused to accept title to the region when it was a state in insurrection. By a royal proclamation of December 6 the *Métis* were urged to lay down their arms, and an amnesty was promised to all who did so.[38]

Meanwhile Riel had become more highhanded with success. He assumed the presidency of the provisional government on December 29, two days after Donald Smith and Father Thibault reached Fort Garry, and made it difficult for them to get a hearing from the people. His sentiments remained distinctly British—there is evidence that he refused offers of aid in money, men, and arms from American annexationists[39]—but he was inclined to use the threat of annexation as a club to force the Canadian government to grant the *Métis*' demands.[40] Father Thibault and Colonel de Salaberry met with the council on January 13, but Smith, posing merely as an old Hudson's Bay man without official status, did not win a hearing from the suspicious *Métis* until after a split developed between Riel and another *Métis* leader Léveillé on January 19. Smith then read his instructions and the royal proclamation at public meetings of the settlers, calling for 'union and entire concord among all classes.'[41] The explosiveness of the situation had largely evaporated by this time. Most of the French *Métis* who had taken up arms dispersed by

Fort Garry

Photograph by Hine. This stronghold and base of the Hudson's Bay Company played the key role in the Riel rising of 1869–70. It was seized by Riel early in the struggle and served as his capital. Here Donald Smith and Bishop Taché made their appeals, here Thomas Scott was shot, and here General Wolsey made his headquarters. In six months the Fort flew five flags—those of the Hudson's Bay Company, of Riel, of the Fenians, of Canada, and of the United Kingdom. (Public Archives of Canada.)

Cathedral and Convent, Saint-Boniface

Photograph by Hine of the birthplace of Catholicism in the West. Saint-Boniface, across the Red River from Fort Garry, was the cultural center of the *Métis*. (Public Archives of Canada.)

anuary 22, while three days later a convention of twenty English nd twenty French representatives met and adopted a bill of rights, vhose nature was moderated through Smith's influence on January 9 and 31.[42] A formal provisional government headed by Riel was stablished on February 10, and by all the evidence it received *de acto* recognition from Ottawa pending the arrival of a new governor. This government appointed a three-man delegation to Ottawa, omposed of Father Ritchot representing the French *Métis*, Judge ohn Black for the English *Métis*, and Alfred H. Scott for the American and English settlers.

Unfortunately, just at this juncture when the unrest was subsiding, he hotheaded Canadian party determined to achieve by force a onclusion of the troubles, although one was well on the way to ttainment through negotiation. A group at the English settlement f Portage la Prairie, incited by the lurid tales of Charles Mair and Thomas Scott, one of Schultz' followers who had escaped from Fort Garry on January 9, determined to make a raid on the fort and escue the other prisoners. A party under the leadership of Major C. A. Boulton descended on Fort Garry during the night of February 4, but, having received a promise of peace from Riel if they disbanded, went off to Kildonan without taking action.[43] A *Métis* named Parisien, who had been picked up by Boulton's party, scaped from them and shot an English settler named Sutherland, vho he thought was pursuing him, at Kildonan the following day. Boulton's party was then rounded up by Lépine and imprisoned at he fort.

Boulton was 'court-martialled' by the provisional government and entenced to be shot, but his life was saved by Smith's intervention in his behalf. Smith was unable to do as much for the troublesome Thomas Scott, who on March 4 came to the end of a stormy career n the West—which had opened with his attempt to murder Snow, he surveyor in charge of the Canadian party to which he was ttached—when he was shot, after a drumhead 'court-martial' presided over by Lépine. His anti-*Métis* activity in December, his scape in January, his role in provoking Boulton's raid and the ubsequent bloodshed, and his rumored physical and verbal assaults on Riel while in prison all affected the verdict.[44] Scott's death has been called 'a judicial murder,'[45] but it seems rather to have been a vigilante execution in the tradition of the West, where people customarily took the law into their own hands in default of established nstitutions of law and order.

Bishop Taché returned to the Red River five days after Scott's death, having been urgently summoned from Rome by the Canadian government, which at last was willing to accept his advice. In nterviews at Ottawa with Macdonald, Cartier, Howe, and the governor-general during February, the Bishop received assurance —at least so he thought—that the insurgents would receive the promised amnesty.[46] Under his influence and the promise of an amnesty the colony quieted down rapidly, although Riel displayed distrust of his lifelong protector and treated him as an agent o the Canadian government.[47] The remaining prisoners were se free by the insurgents on March 16, and two days later Donalc Smith took his departure. The annexation movement collapsed At Bishop Taché's instigation, the Union Jack replaced the pro visional government's flag at Fort Garry on April 23,[48] after Rie had proclaimed peace on April 9. The insurgents continued to govern with the tacit consent of Ottawa until the new governor should arrive.

The execution of Scott, a member of the Orange Order, was used by the expansionist 'Canada First' movement in Ontario to arouse a violent agitation which exploited ethnic and religious hatred Scott's blood was shed on many a platform, and the 'traitor French priests' of the Red River were denounced, although the clergy had been Ottawa's most effective ally in quieting the Red River troubles When Father Ritchot and Alfred Scott arrived in Toronto on their way to Ottawa as delegates of the provisional government, they were arrested on April 11 on a provincial warrant taken out by Thomas Scott's brother, though they were quickly released when the Crown refused to prosecute. The arrest embarrassed the federa and imperial authorities, who were trying to restore calm and feared that a long drawn-out trial would encourage American interven tion.[49] The delegates brought with them a new *Métis* bill of rights whose chief provisions were embodied in the Manitoba Act adopted on May 12 as a result of extended negotiations between the dele gates and Macdonald, Cartier, and the governor-general. Thi act gave Manitoba the same organization of responsible governmen as the old provinces, except that the public lands were reserved to the dominion in exchange for land grants to the *Métis* in extinguish ment of their Indian title. Denominational schools and the existing educational rights and privileges of Protestant and Catholi minorities were given definite safeguards. Both English and French languages were to be used for governmental purposes.[50] In short the Manitoba Act provided for the establishment of a new Quebec in the West.

The long-delayed transfer of title to Canada took effect on July 15, 1870. The new lieutenant-governor, Adams G. Archibald accompanied by a military force under Colonel Garnet Wolseley made up mainly of imperial troops but including a battalion from Quebec and another from Ontario, was to set out from Port Arthur for the Red River on that date. The expedition's purpose, conceived in aroused Ontario as 'suppression' of a 'rebellion' which had already ended, actually was to ensure against another such fiasco as McDougall's inglorious adventure and to prevent any new rising against Canadian authority.[51] The imperial government refused to send troops until reasonable terms had been granted the Red River settlers.[52] Wolseley reached Fort Garry on August 24 without any other difficulty than that provided by the arduous overland route. Wolseley had paved his way with a proclamation of his peaceful objects and assurance that his force represented no party either in religion or politics, and would afford equal protection to the lives and property of all races and creeds.[53] The force occupied Fort Garry without incident, for Riel and the other insurgent leaders, alarmed by Canadian threats of vengeance, fled on its arrival. So calm was the situation that the imperial troops left five days later, in order to return as prearranged to a Canada threatened by Fenian raids before the season closed their path, although the Canadian militia battalions remained.[54]

The Canadian party in the settlements, swollen in numbers by new immigrants, raised an agitation for reprisals which was ignored by Wolseley during his brief stay and later by the new lieutenant-governor, though Donald Smith issued warrants for Riel and some others.[55] This group celebrated the establishment of Canadian rule by a persecution of the French *Métis* which culminated in the killing of Elzéar Goulet, in which two members of the Ontario Rifles were involved. They were not brought to trial.[56] The Ontario Rifles organized an Orange lodge which had 200 members by 1872 and which alienated the English as well as the French *Métis*.[57] Governor Archibald reported to Macdonald on October 8, 1871, that 'many of the French half-breeds have been so beaten and outraged by a small but noisy section of the people that they feel as if they were living in a state of slavery.'[58] He added that the newcomers from Ontario 'seem to feel as if the French half-breeds should be wiped off the face of the globe.' Despite such treatment Riel and Lépine, at the governor's request, raised a force of some 300 *Métis* to meet the threat of Fenian raids from Minnesota in October 1871. This body was publicly reviewed and thanked by Archibald for its loyalty, a proceeding which led Riel and Lépine to assume that Ottawa had decided to overlook their part in organizing the provisional government.[59]

3

After the creation of the new province of Manitoba, the Red River colony passed through a period of rapid transition. The division between old and new settlers prior to the insurrection was replaced by an ethnic and religious division which was a by-product of the rising.[60] The old way of life was destroyed by the advent of newcomers who were interested in agriculture rather than buffalo hunting, and who were inclined to gallophobia, thanks to the agitation aroused by the death of Scott. Though the white settlers did not outnumber the *Métis* for some time after 1870, French political influence in the province was lost by a gerrymander in 1874, which upset Cartier's and Bishop Taché's efforts to maintain a French balance of power, bolstered by such Quebec notables as Joseph Royal, Joseph Dubuc, Marc-A. Girard, Alphonse Larivière, and H. J. H. Clarke,[61] and by the encouragement of immigration from Quebec. Joseph Cauchon became the second lieutenant-governor and Cartier himself sat in the dominion parliament as member for Provencher, after his defeat in Montreal East in 1871, thanks to the resignation of Riel, who had won the seat in the first Manitoba election. Cartier's death in 1873 removed from Ottawa the last strong supporter of French interests in the West, for Hector Langevin's talents were of a lesser and more provincial order than those of his chief.

The swelling Orange agitation over the murder of Thomas Scott led to the arrest of Lépine in 1873 and his condemnation to death the following year, despite an eloquent defence by Adolphe Chapleau, the rising Conservative orator, whose legal fee was paid by Franco-Americans stirred by their compatriot's plight. At the intercession of Bishop Taché, who protested vigorously against the government's repudiation of its promises of a general amnesty,[62] Lépine was reprieved by the governor-general, and his sentence was commuted to two years' imprisonment and the loss of his civil rights. Riel, who like Lépine was paid to take refuge in the States in 1872 by Macdonald and Cartier, acting through Bishop Taché,[63] was re-elected in 1874 to parliament to fill Cartier's Manitoba seat. Risking seizure for the $5,000 reward which had been placed on his head in Ontario, he appeared at Ottawa, hurriedly took the oath and then disappeared. Such a storm arose that he was expelled from the House and later formally declared a fugitive from justice. A Royal Commission appointed in 1875 to investigate the question of whether or not an amnesty had been granted to the insurgents, reported that the execution of Scott was the act of a *de facto* government accepted by the people of the Red River and recognized by the Canadian and imperial authorities; that Bishop Taché and the delegates of the provisional government believed themselves authorized to promise to the insurgents in 1870 a full and complete amnesty, on the strength of the verbal and written promises of Macdonald, Cartier, Langevin, and Howe, made with the knowledge and consent of the governor-general and the imperial government; and that Governor Archibald's appeal to Riel and Lépine in 1871 for aid against the Fenians presupposed that they were not liable to arrest and punishment for their previous actions.[64]

Acting on this report, the government declared a general amnesty for all those who had taken part in the rising, with the provision that Riel, Lépine, and O'Donoghue were to be banished for five years. Lépine, released from prison in 1876, settled at Batoche on the Saskatchewan, where, as also at Duck Lake and Saint-Laurent, many of the *Métis* migrated after being driven from their old homes along the Red River by the tide of Ontario immigration.[65] Riel, who had become mentally unstable and had developed a sense of divine mission, took refuge from the persecution to which he was subjected with the ultramontane leader Alphonse Desjardins in Montreal. Desjardins was forced to put Riel in the Longue Pointe Asylum in 1875 and again in the Longue Pointe and Beauport Asylums from 1876 to 1878 under the names of Louis David and La Rochelle. In 1874 Riel prepared for Desjardins a *Mémoire sur les Causes des Troubles du Nord-Ouest et sur les Négociations qui ont amené leur Règlement aimable*, which was printed by *Le Nouveau Monde*. This account blamed the Canadian government for causing the rising in the first place, and then for failing to fulfil its promises. In the midst of the debate on the amnesty Riel was idolized by the ultramontanes in Montreal, and on two occasions in 1875 and 1876 was encouraged in his sense of mission by Bishop Bourget.[66] He went to the United States, arousing interest in the *Métis* cause in such Franco-American centers as Plattsburg and Keesville, New York, Manchester, and Nashua, New Hampshire, Worcester, Massachusetts, and Woonsocket, Rhode Island. In October 1875 Riel went to Washington to see Major Edmund Mallet, the Franco-American Civil War hero and politician, who had become the unofficial representative of his compatriots. Riel vainly sought a post in the Indian Bureau and proposed a plan for the annexation of Manitoba before succumbing to another period of madness, which led to his return to Canada by friends in February 1876. After his release from Beauport in January 1878, he went to Keesville, New York, and then drifted westward, reaching St. Paul in 1879 and spending a year in the Franco-American community of St. Joseph, Dakota Territory. He finally settled at the Jesuit mission of St. Peter, Montana, after marrying a French *Métis* woman and becoming a school teacher and an American citizen in 1883, though he continued to play *Métis* politics.[67]

4

The North-West Rebellion of 1885 was largely a sequel and repetition of the Red River troubles of 1869–70, though in the second instance the rising was against unquestioned authority. The French and Scottish *Métis*, who made up most of the population west of the new province of Manitoba, began to petition Governor Laird of the North-West Territories and Ottawa as early as 1874, for their semi-nomadic culture was threatened by the westward advance of agricultural civilization and the decline of the buffalo. An 1877 ordinance restricting the buffalo-hunting upon which *Métis* life was based was followed by the rapid disappearance of the beast from the Saskatchewan country, thanks to the ruthless slaughter of the migratory herds by American hunters seeking buffalo robes. As the telegraph and the Canadian Pacific Railway advanced across the plains, bringing settlers in their wake, the buffalo retreated southward over the frontier and the *Métis* were left in sad straits, prey to land speculators who often robbed them of their homes.[68] Their chief grievances—the government's failure to meet their claims for land scrip and to supply aid in making the transition from semi-nomad to agricultural and commercial life—went unheard in an Ottawa which was preoccupied with vast land-grant schemes devised to lessen the heavy financial burden of railroad construction.

Once more Eastern expansionists were little concerned with the rights of Western pioneers; once more trouble arose out of the government's decision to survey lands after the American square section system, without regard for the Quebec-type riverstrip holdings of the *Métis*.[69] One of the North-West missionaries, Father Vegreville of Saint-Louis-de-Langevin, made urgent representations to Ottawa in 1884 about the need to consider existing land divisions.[70] Captain Deville, the Chief Inspector of Surveys, worked out a compromise between the chosen plan of survey and the *Métis* wishes, but this solution of the difficulty was buried, thanks to red tape in the Ministry of the Interior and to the unwillingness of English-speaking land agents in the West to take extra trouble to meet the wishes of the French-speaking pioneers of the country.[71] With the language difficulty increasing the misunderstanding resulting from the inability of the largely uneducated *Métis* to grasp the complexities of surveying and land regulations drawn up in Ottawa by lawyers unacquainted with the country, new unrest developed.

Its growth was fostered by Ottawa's interminable delay in answering *Métis* petitions. Supporting memoranda from Governor Laird, Archbishop Taché, and the Anglican Bishop McLean in 1878–9 finally were answered in 1881.[72] Archbishop Taché visited Ottawa in 1882 to intercede for his people without success. In the following year Father Leduc and one B. Maloney conveyed the settlers' resolutions to Ottawa, where they won a hearing, though no action was taken on the matters complained of. Finally, in the spring of 1884, a committee was formed by the 'people of Saskatchewan,' under the presidency of William Cromartie and the ecretaryship of Louis Schmidt, to take action.[73] A delegation, eaded by Gabriel Dumont and composed of Moise Ouellet, James sbister, and Michel Dumas, was sent 800 miles across the border o seek out Louis Riel in Montana, and to urge him to return to Canada and lead the popular movement.[74] Riel, who was now lreaming of establishing a new half-breed nation in the West, ecided to spend the summer in Canada, urging his own Manioba land claims against the Dominion government, as well as those f the Saskatchewan settlers.

Upon his arrival in the North-West in July, Riel took the lead n agitation for righting of the settlers' wrongs. According to the ccount furnished to Governor Dewdney by Father André of Prince Albert,[75] his proceedings at first were quiet and orderly, and he von the support not only of the *Métis*, among whom his prestige vas great, but also of most of the whites and Indians. Riel advocated ree grants to the *Métis* of the lands they occupied; the erection of he districts of Saskatchewan, Alberta, and Assiniboia into provinces, r at least provision for their representation in parliament; and the mendment of the land laws to further more rapid settlement of the ountry. Father André warned the government against interfering vith Riel as long as he remained quiet, while other informants rged that he should be arrested and the agitation nipped in the ud. Charles Mair, the poetic Canada Firster, who had been a ropagandist for the expansionists in the Red River troubles, came East every six months from 1883 to 1885 to warn the government hat new trouble was brewing and that action should be taken on the ettlers' grievances;[76] but the agitation was nonetheless allowed o run its course.

As Riel became more influential, he displayed aberrations on eligion and politics which led the priests of the North-West to onsider him mad and to bar him from the sacraments.[77] Father André finally became convinced that it would be well to get him out of the country; and was present at negotiations late in December 884 between representatives of the government and Riel, during vhich the *Métis* leader offered to return to the States in exchange or a payment of $35,000 which would cover his personal land laims, while promising that in return he would use his influence o make the *Métis* drop their claims.[78] Until the outbreak of actual ebellion, the government refused to meet the *Métis* demand for and scrip, and contented itself with increasing the North-West Mounted Police force and trying to bribe the *Métis* leaders. Louis Schmidt was made an assistant land agent; Isbister and Dumas vere offered posts as Indian agricultural instructors; and Gabriel Dumont was given a lucrative ferry license.[79] Riel was undoubtedly correct in assuming that the government was willing to bribe him once more, but he seems to have overjudged his market value in th midst of the mounting irresponsibility he displayed in word anc deed during the winter.

During January and February Riel held secret meetings whos tendency was no longer towards constitutional action but rathe towards armed rebellion. When the opposition of the clergy becam more active with this development, he turned against the priests proclaiming that 'the Spirit of God was in him' and that 'Rome hac fallen.'[80] On March 17 a provisional government was established a Saint-Laurent, with Riel as president and Dumont as adjutant general.[81] On the following day Riel seized the church at Batoche overriding the protests of Father Moulin, whom he jestingly dis missed as a fellow 'Protestant,' and took some prisoners.[82] On Marcl 21 he issued an ultimatum to Major Crozier, who commanded th Mounted Police at Carleton and Battleford, requiring him to sur render the police posts and to retire from the country, under threa of 'a war of extermination.'[83] This ultimatum, which was neve delivered but served as the basis of negotiations between representa tives of the insurgents and the authorities, was signed 'Louis "David" Riel, *Exovede*' and issued in the name of 'the Provisional Governmen of the Saskatchewan,' whose council was called the 'Exovedat,' fo Riel insisted that his own and their authority was merely as 'mem bers of the flock.'[84]

Riel's religious mania, the product of his native religiosity, sense of mission, and a persecution complex, had become dominant he proclaimed himself a prophet called to protect the oppresse nationalities of the world, attacked Archbishop Taché and Bisho Grandin of Saint-Albert, and denounced the authority of the Pope.[8 According to his cousin Charles Nolin, who later quarreled with hir and turned state's evidence, Riel had brought from Montana a boo written in buffalo blood which described his mission as 'to destro England and Canada . . . and also to destroy Rome and the Pope.'[8 Riel talked incoherently of dividing the lands of the North-West int sevenths among the pioneer whites, the Indians, the French *Méti* the Church, and Crown lands;[87] on another occasion the Italian Poles, Hungarians, Bavarians, Irish, and Belgians were each to hav a seventh, after Riel had raised support for the *Métis* among thes immigrant groups in the States.[88] He saw the West as the new hom of immigrants of all nationalities from the Old World.[89] As proc of his divine mission to bring about these ends, Riel produced en couraging letters written to him in 1875 and 1876 by Bishop Bourge whom he proposed to make 'Pope of the New World.'[90]

Thus Bishop Bourget's ultramontanism and messianic nationalism the *Métis* concept of themselves as a 'New Nation,' the problems c European nationalism and of large-scale immigration in the State were curiously intermingled in Riel's increasingly troubled mind. He alternated between respect for the clergy and the view that he had a divine right to direct them; he evolved new dogmas and proposed changes in the liturgy; he took to calling himself 'Elias' or 'David.' In the face of such behavior the clergy decided that he was irresponsible in matters of politics and religion; they judged charitably that 'he was insane, otherwise he would have to be too big a criminal.'[91] Both the priests and his followers found that he was excited by opposition, and became even wilder in word and deed when contradicted or checked. The record provides an almost classic case of paranoia, coupled as these symptoms were with a persecution complex, for the proud and sensitive Riel had never forgiven Sir John Macdonald for his banishment from parliament and his exile.[92]

With their religious and ethnic emotions aroused by Riel's ravings, and excited by the rumor that five hundred Mounted Police were being sent into the region, the *Métis* were now ready to take up arms. A party of thirty *Métis* and five Cree Indians on March 6 prevented a party of Prince Albert loyalists from bringing into Carleton some government supplies from Duck Lake. When the loyalists returned with Major Crozier and the police and opened fire on the insurgents, the unarmed Riel rushed about with a crucifix in his hand, urging his followers to reply 'in the name of God the Father, God the Son, and God the Holy Ghost.'[93] The police, no match for Gabriel Dumont and his veteran buffalo hunters in the snow despite their superior numbers, were forced to retire, leaving twelve dead behind them. The North-West Rebellion had begun in grim earnest. Riel sought to win the sympathies of the English settlers, protesting that 'this quarrel was with the Government and the police and the Hudson's Bay Company,' and hinting that American aid would be given to the insurgents.[94] He also promised that he would keep the Indians quiet if the settlers remained neutral. With Custer's massacre by the Sioux fresh in men's minds, it was fear of the Indians joining their half-breed brothers that turned the English settlers of the North-West against Riel and led the government to organize a large military expedition to put down the insurrection. Riel proceeded to recruit his following among the *Métis*, to enter into the endless negotiations required to win Indian support, and to fortify in rough and ready fashion the *Métis* settlement at Batoche. But if, as seems probable, he hoped that the rising would follow the same course as that of 1869–70, and that he would achieve the *Métis*' ends without further bloodshed, he was very much mistaken.[95]

The North-West was no longer isolated from eastern Canada, as it had been fifteen years earlier when eight months passed before Ottawa could support its authority with military force. Thanks to the new telegraph system, which ran as far west as Edmonton and Calgary, the government was kept in close touch with the situation as it unfolded. Major-General Frederick Middleton, the English commander of the Canadian militia, left Ottawa by train on March 23, the day the government ordered the formation of an expeditionary force. He reached Winnipeg, the old Fort Garry, on the morning of the 27th and left that same night with the Winnipeg Rifles (90th Battalion) for Qu'Appelle, almost due south of the disaffected area. The Canadian Pacific Railway had been completed from Winnipeg to Calgary, although there was a hundred miles of unfinished line through the Laurentian Shield north of Lake Superior. Riel had probably gambled on the inability of the government to bring in troops from the East without long delay, and also that no action would be taken while the prairie still lay under the snow and mud of late winter and spring. But thanks to the energy and zeal of the Canadian Pacific officials, headed by William Van Horne, who were anxious to oblige the government so that more public funds might be made available for completion of the line, a force of 3,293 men was carried westward during the last weeks of March and the first few days of April. The men rode in coaches and sometimes in open flat cars where the rails were laid, and were transported in sleighs or marched over the unfinished sections of the line. The troops came chiefly from Ontario and Quebec, although one Nova Scotian battalion made the journey from Halifax to Winnipeg in three weeks, and an additional 1,600 men were drawn from Manitoba and the North-West Territories themselves.[96] It was the first purely Canadian military effort, for no force of British regulars was involved, and great enthusiasm was roused in the young nation by lurid telegraphic accounts of Indian outrages and the movements of the defenders of the country. In Ontario the departing militiamen were hailed as crusaders against the rebel French and Indians; while in Quebec, which supplied a third of the eastern troops, a wave of patriotism swept aside all feeling of kinship with the *Métis* or sympathy for their plight.[97]

The widespread Indian rising whose threat had caused the government to raise so imposing a force failed to materialize, although Big Bear's band of Crees massacred two Catholic missionaries and five officials and traders at Frog Lake on the North Saskatchewan on April 2 and forced the surrender of Fort Pitt on April 15, while Poundmaker's Crees and Stoneys committed isolated outrages at the end of March and besieged Battleford during April. General Middleton's small army, which vastly outnumbered the 600–700 insurgents, was divided into three columns and struck before the *Métis* and Indians had time to complete their organization. During April General Thomas Bland Strange, a retired English fficer who had taken to cattle-ranching near Calgary after training he Canadian artillery, moved north from that point to Edmonton, nd then down the North Saskatchewan to the smoking ruins of 'ort Pitt, where a juncture was made with the eastern columns. The econd column, under Colonel William D. Otter, marched north rom Swift Current to the relief of Battleford, where it was joined by Iiddleton's force coming up the Saskatchewan. Middleton was ccompanied by press correspondents and his well-publicized exloits have unjustifiably overshadowed Strange's remarkable tenlay march through 200 miles of wilderness.

Middleton set out from Qu'Appelle on April 6 against Batoche, he *Métis* stronghold. On April 24 he was halted at Fish Creek on he South Saskatchewan, and lost 10 killed and 40 wounded out f his 350 men to a handful of *Métis* under Gabriel Dumont, who eatly trapped the general in an ambush which made skillful use f folds in the ground.[98] On May 6 Middleton left his camp at Fish Creek after waiting for reinforcements, and with 700 men proceeded gainst Batoche, which he took on May 12 after four days' fighting n which he lost 8 killed and 46 wounded. The *Métis* losses were stimated at 51 killed and 173 wounded.[99] Riel, who had threatened o massacre his prisoners if Middleton shelled the women and hildren in the town, gave himself up on May 15 to two scouts, roducing a note in which Middleton called upon him to surrender nd promised protection until his case was considered by the overnment.[100]

With Riel's surrender—not capture, as the triumphant Middleton elegraphed to Ottawa—the *Métis* resistance subsided. Old buffalo uns were no match for Gatlings and artillery, no matter how skillully used. The remainder of the campaign, which lasted until uly, consisted of the vain pursuit of Big Bear, for Poundmaker urrendered ten days after Riel was reported 'captured.' The ndians and their *Métis* allies vanished like the will-o'-the-wisp efore the cumbersome military columns, which vainly attempted to dapt parade-ground training to campaigning in the bush. General trange was filled with admiration for the Quebec soldiers—'the lucky little French Canadians pulled 9-pr. guns, horses and all, right hrough the muskegs. They are fine little fellows, marching many of hem barefoot, singing their old chansons. There was no flinch about hem in fighting either, they bore the brunt of it such as it was.'[101] But General Middleton infuriated Strange by maintaining that the 'rench-Canadian troops had marched no farther than the other roops—Strange protested 'they have marched four times as far as ny other regiment except Winnipeg Light Infantry of my force lso'—and by praising only the English Canadians who had fought t Batoche.[102]

The North-West Rebellion cost Canada 38 men killed and 11 wounded among soldiers and Mounted Police, while the militar expenses amounted to nearly $4,500,000—two-thirds of which wa incurred after the end of hostilities.[103] The Hudson's Bay Company which had furnished supplies, land transport, and river steamers fo the army, filed a claim for $1,737,032, while the Canadian Pacifi billed the government for $852,231.32.[104] But without the Hudson' Bay Company's knowledge of the country and the railroad' transportation skill, the expedition might have come to grief. Th cost in national unity proved in the event to be incalculable.

5

Ethnic antagonism had largely been latent while French an English troops campaigned together in the North-West, although th *Toronto News* had urged on May 18 that Riel be strangled with th French flag—'the only service which that rag can render in thi country.'[105] But it broke out in the East when Riel was brought t trial for high treason at Regina on July 20, while the returnin troops were receiving tumultuous receptions at Toronto, Montreal and Quebec.

Under the provisions of the North-West Territorial Act of 1880 Riel was tried by an English magistrate with an associated Frenc justice of the peace before a six-man jury of English settlers an merchants.[106] The Crown counsel had received instructions fron the Deputy-Minister of Justice at Ottawa.[107] Only two or thre French Canadians were included in the panel of thirty-six juror selected by the magistrate.[108] The Crown challenged one Irishma and the defence five Englishmen.[109] Christopher Robinson an B. B. Osler of Toronto, and Tom-Chase Casgrain of Quebec wer the leading counsel for the Crown, while F.-X. Lemieux, Charle Fitzpatrick, and J. N. Greenshields were counsel for the prisone The political aspect of the trial was increased by the fact that th prosecution was made up of Conservatives and the defence of Liberal Fitzpatrick first took issue on constitutional grounds with the jurisdic tion of the court, seeking to have Riel tried in Ontario or Britis Columbia, rather than in the aroused Territories. When this ple was rejected, Lemieux and Fitzpatrick obtained an adjournment c a week in order that witnesses for the accused might be obtained During this adjournment Riel's English secretary, William Henr Jackson, was tried, found insane in half an hour, and committe to an asylum, from which he escaped to the States, seemingly wit the connivance of the authorities.[110] Jackson claimed that h shared Riel's responsibility and thus was exposed to the charg of treason.

Among the witnesses called by the defence were Gabriel Dumont, Michel Dumas, and Napoléon Nault—two of the *Métis* leaders who had urged Riel to return and his Montana cousin—and Dr. François Roy of the Beauport Asylum, where Riel had been confined in 1876–8 and which had become a political issue in recent months; Dr. Daniel Clark, superintendent of the Toronto Asylum; and Dr. Arthur Vallée, a leading Quebec physician. Riel's request for the presence of the deputy-minister of the Interior, with official documents and the petitions filed by the *Métis*, was denied, as was his request for his papers, which had been seized at Batoche by General Middleton and which were used with telling effect by the Crown. Among them was his American naturalization certificate. Anticipating a plea by the defence that Riel as an American citizen could not be charged with treason, the Crown had framed its charge of treason on six counts, on three of which he was charged as a British subject, and on three as a resident of Canada, with armed revolt at Duck Lake, Fish Creek, and Batoche.[111]

Driven from its preliminary arguments of unconstitutionality and Riel's American citizenship, the defence devoted most of its attention to proving that Riel was insane. Unfortunately for this contention, Dr. Roy, the only medical witness with any real acquaintance with Riel's mental condition, who pronounced him irresponsible and of unsound mind,[112] became entangled in linguistic difficulties under Osler's ruthless cross-examination, while Dr. Clark of Toronto and Dr. Wallace of Hamilton refused to pronounce Riel incapable of distinguishing between right and wrong, though they thought him of unsound mind.[113] Dr. Jukes, the Mounted Police surgeon, flatly pronounced him sane.[114] Riel himself, who in the early stages of the trial tried to cross-examine the government witnesses and was told that he must either repudiate his counsel or keep silent, in his two remarkable addresses to the court at the end of the trial denied the plea of insanity upon which his defence had rested.

He spoke with remarkable if confused eloquence, calling himself the 'founder of Manitoba' and 'prophet of the New World'[115] and clearly revealing his religious mania as he recapitulated his career and his dream of the West as a haven for the oppressed nationalities of Europe, in which the ancient opposition between Catholics and Protestants would be overcome. He mentioned many things which the government would have wished unsaid, including the details of his dealings with Macdonald and Cartier after the first rising, the provocative role of the Mounted Police in 1885, the failure to give first Manitoba and then the North-West Territories real representation at Ottawa, and the administration's broken promises to the *Métis*.[116] Although he turned against the clergy—even against his lifelong protector Archbishop Taché—and made heretical statements,[117] his deep religiosity was very manifest in a movin plea which is quite as effective despite its imperfect English as Barto lomeo Vanzetti's. He concluded with a request to be tried befor a full jury and to be examined by a medical commission, for th Crown's implication that he was shamming insanity pricked his in tellectual pride. After a seven days' trial, the jury brought in verdict of guilty, with a recommendation of mercy.[118] On August Justice Richardson sentenced Riel to be hanged on September 18 a Regina.

Riel's counsel appealed to the Queen's Bench Court in Manitoba which unanimously confirmed the verdict early in September,[119] an then to the Privy Council, which refused to hear the case on Octobe 22.[120] Meanwhile an agitation arose in Ontario for immediat execution of a double traitor[121] and Quebec was swept by a grea popular movement which demanded that Riel be reprieved as th irresponsible victim of the government's maladministration of th North-West. The Quebec press cited Jackson's easy fate and com pared it with that allotted to Riel, with the observation: 'If madnes is an excuse for an Englishman, it ought to be one for Riel, even i he is a *Métis*.'[122] Riel defence committees had been organized a early as June in Montreal and Quebec. Their sponsor was L.-O David, who considered Riel a spiritual heir of the *Patriotes* of 1837 Thanks to his efforts, protest meetings began to be held throughou the province, with the watchword 'Riel must be saved.'[123]

During July, before the trial began, the Liberal leaders Blake an Laurier had attacked the government. Blake tabled seventy-si *Métis* petitions of grievances, while Laurier accused the governmen of treating the *Métis* as the Russians did the Poles.[124] Althoug Archbishop Taché and most of the Western clergy warned agains mistaken sympathy with Riel, Quebec was won to his cause b Father André's account of the distress of the *Métis* after they ha been ruthlessly pillaged by Middleton's English-Canadian troops.[12] Gradually the question became not one of Riel's guilt or innocence but the execution or pardon of a compatriot. This development o ethnic feeling determined Chapleau's decision not to resign from the federal cabinet and to form a French-Canadian party. He an his French colleagues were denounced by Quebec, while petition rained upon Ottawa from all quarters of French Canada, from Manitoba, the North-West, the United States, and even from England and France.[126] The great majority of them urged mercy although the Ontario Orangemen and the English settlers of Regin recommended that the sentence be executed. While the governmen allowed three successive stays of execution until every avenue o appeal had been exhausted, and appointed a medical commission composed of Dr. Jukes, Dr. F.-X. Valade of Ottawa, and Dr. Lavel of Hamilton, who decided early in November that Riel was not legally insane,[127] the decision had already been made, in the words attributed to Sir John Macdonald, that 'Riel must swing.'[128]

In the last analysis the decision not to show the same mercy to Riel as to the other convicted rebellion prisoners was based upon political necessities. English-Canadian feeling had risen to the explosive point as French pressure for Riel's pardon grew stronger. Even General Strange, an old friend of the French Canadians, was moved to write Henri Joly:

> How sad and silly it all seems—after sending those brave battalions to the front—to start in with this childish twaddle about hanging a cur of a self-interested conspirator who has twice brought this country to rebellion and at last let loose savage Indians to murder White Men and even Priests. The idea that because a criminal is half-French it is to stop the sword of justice is outrageous. I would rather join in a war of extermination between French & English than to submit to live in a Country where such monstrously insolent pretensions were put forward by a part of the population.[129]

Macdonald decided that he could better afford to lose a few seats in Quebec than to have English Canada turn solidly against him. So after the governor-general in council had refused to alter the sentence on November 12, Riel was duly hanged at Regina on November 16.

While in prison and visited daily by priests, he had repeatedly renounced his religious heresies only to relapse into them once more. On August 5 he made a formal abjuration of his errors to his confessor, Father Vital Fourmond, in a moving and revealing document:

To Rev. Father Vital Fourmond, my director of conscience	Jesus, Mary, Joseph, save me	Regina Prison, August 5, 1885. Feast of Our Lady of the Snows

Archbishop Bourget told me: 'God, Who has always directed and assisted you, until the present time will not abandon you in the greatest of your trials for He has given you a mission which you must accomplish in all respects.' My director of conscience tells me that my misfortunes and errors arise from my misunderstanding of my mission. The religious principle which made me have so much confidence in the word of Archbishop Bourget logically leads me to have the same confidence in the interpretation which the approved priest, my director of conscience, gives me of the episcopal word of Archbishop Ignace Bourget of blessed memory.

Renouncing then, all the special interpretations that I have made of my mission which my confessor and director does not approve, I re-enter the bosom of the Catholic, Apostolic, and Roman Church by making the following declaration:

Father, my confessor, my director of conscience, please remit all my sins, all my faults, and all the consequences of my deeds; all my offences and all the consequences of my offences, whether with regard to God and the Faith, whether with regard to society, or my neighbor, or myself.

Witnesses: V. Fourmond, priest
L. Cochin, O.M.I.

Your poor penitent,
Louis Riel, or Louis 'David' Riel[130]

On August 31 Father André, the Oblate superior, in describing Riel's fantastic visions in prison, remarked:

Although his opinions upon religion are greatly erroneous, I do not hold him responsible and do admit him to receive the sacraments. And for all that, he often renews the errors which he has retracted and which he again retracts when I point out to him his heresies as contrary to the dogmas taught by the Holy Catholic Church. On the day following such a retraction, he talks to me more ardently than ever about his revelations and his communications with some angel who honors him with a nocturnal visit.[131]

And in the end, at the instigation of Archbishop Taché, who was convinced that this black sheep of the *Métis* flock was irresponsible, though a criminal, Riel was buried in the shadow of the cathedral of St.-Boniface on December 12, under the guard of *Métis* who carried his coffin six miles from his family home to the church. It was not an unsuitable resting-place for the brilliant and unstable prophet of the West which had begun there and which was there to fulfil some of his fevered dreams.

6

Riel was not allowed to rest in peace. The agitation in Quebec against the execution of a French Canadian summarily condemned by an English judge and jury became a political revolution. The minority group of the assembly, which had in March 1885 censured the federal government for settling by force a disturbance which had been occasioned by its own culpable neglect, became an overpowering majority as Quebec public opinion rose against Sir John Macdonald and the French-Canadian ministers, Sir Hector Langevin, Sir Adolphe Caron, and Adolphe Chapleau, who had refused to break with their leader, though privately they opposed his course in the matter. The ministers were burnt in effigy as Quebec mourned Riel.

On November 22 the greatest mass meeting ever held in the province took place on the Champs de Mars at Montreal, where Conservatives and Liberals alike voiced violent protests and adopted resolutions severely condemning the government. *La Presse* had

Ojibway *Métis*

Photograph by Hine of a typical *Métis* buffalo hunter, posed with his carefully cased gun before a wigwam made of buffalo rugs. (Public Archives of Canada.)

Louis Riel

Drawing from Major Powell's scrapbook. As this contemporary portrait indicates, Riel had little Indian blood and was no wild *Métis* buffalo hunter. (Public Archives of Canada.)

Parliament Building, Quebec

Built 1878–84, after plans by Eugene Taché, a better cartographer than architect. The tradition of exotic imitation,

sounded the warcry on the day after Riel's execution: 'Henceforward there are no more Conservatives nor Liberals nor Castors. There are only PATRIOTS AND TRAITORS.'[132] For once the Quebec press ceased its habitual political axe-grinding and united in a unanimity to which was flatly opposed the equally rare unanimity of the English press, summed up by a Toronto dispatch of November 17 thus: 'A general sentiment of satisfaction prevails.'[133] Three platforms had been raised on the Champs de Mars, around which gathered a crowd of forty or fifty thousand, and from them orator after orator held forth. The three great speeches of this day in which a people voiced its indignation were made by the Liberal Laurier, who with a rare vehemence proclaimed: 'If I had been on the banks of the Saskatchewan, I, too, would have shouldered my musket'; by the ultramontane Trudel, who compared Riel to Christ and Joan of Arc; and by Honoré Mercier who won the leadership of French Canada at this moment of crisis with his opening words:

> Riel, our brother, is dead, victim of his devotion to the cause of the *Métis* of whom he was the leader, victim of fanaticism and treason—of the fanaticism of Sir John and some of his friends, of the treason of three of our people who sold their brother to keep their portfolios.
>
> In killing Riel, Sir John has not only struck a blow at the heart of our race, but above all he struck the cause of justice and humanity, which represented in all languages and sanctified by all religious beliefs, begged mercy for the prisoner of Regina, our poor brother of the North-West.[134]

Mercier called for the formation of a national party, uniting all those who were outraged by Riel's death, to drive Macdonald's government from office and to preserve the French-Canadian solidarity created by this crisis. The crowd enthusiastically adopted the 'Resolutions of the Champs de Mars'[135] which had been previously drafted to embody Mercier's ideas.

The agitation in Quebec, which Macdonald had dismissed as 'a blaze of straw,'[136] spread like a forest fire, with assemblies in each parish adopting resolutions based upon those of the great meeting at Montreal, and with anti-ministerial demonstrations taking place throughout the province. Trudel and others wanted a national movement in which the old party lines would be preserved, except for the Riel matter and national questions; but Mercier succeeded in imposing his doctrine of a racial party founded on the newly made grave of Riel. Quebec rallied like one man to the defence of the outlying minority groups. Riel was enshrined as a national hero and a saint despite his treason and his heresies, and despite the resolute opposition of the Quebec hierarchy, whose attitude had been prompted by Archbishop Taché and who became increasingly alarmed by a movement which began to take on revolutionary tendencies, with public disorders, the burning in effigy of the federal ministers, and the singing of the *Marseillaise.*[137]

As a former missionary in the Red River Country, Bishop Laflèche was sympathetic to the *Métis*. In 1875 he had proposed a protest in Quebec against the federal government's treatment of them, but now he refused to support Mercier's movement. In May 1885 he wrote one of his *curés*:

> The news from the North-West is very sad.
>
> This spark, which would have been so easy to extinguish with a few drops of justice, is going, perhaps, to cause a disastrous conflagration.
>
> For years the *Métis* and savages have been treated in an unworthy manner by brutal agents, and scandalized by a police more immoral than the savages.
>
> The Ontario Orangemen are capable of setting fire to the four corners of the country to satisfy their hatred against Riel and to hang him.
>
> . . . for the *Métis*, the question is clear: they must conquer or die.[138]

But his friend Archbishop Taché assured him during this same month that Riel was a 'miserable madman and a fanatic.'[139] And however strong his sympathy for the *Métis* Laflèche remained convinced that no good could come from Liberal sources and refused to make common cause with his lifelong enemies on the Riel question. He remained silent while the fury at Riel's execution mounted in Quebec and by 1886 Trudel and Tardivel found themselves on the opposite side of the political fence from the bishop who had been so long the guiding spirit of the *Castors*.

While Trudel and Tardivel expressed pious horror that the bishops should support the 'Orange Freemason' Macdonald, Laflèche assured one of his *curés* that the *Parti National* had 'worked great evil' in his diocese, and that the troubles in the North-West were not 'purely a political question.'[140] He reported that he had consulted an Ontario bishop on the respective merits of Macdonald and Blake and of the two parties which they headed, and his conclusion was that 'for us there is no great distinction to be made between one and the other.' At long last Bishop Laflèche had learned the advantages of a united front among the hierarchy, and he stood squarely beside Archbishop Taché and Bishop Grandin on the Riel question as he wrote the federal member for Trois-Rivières in January 1887

> I share entirely the views of Archbishop Taché, which are also those of Bishop Grandin. All the world will agree that these venerable prelates are the most competent judges of the matter. Besides, it seems evident to me that a movement too violently and imprudently aroused by political passions becomes more and more dangerous . . . In this sort of question the bishops can be regarded as the most competent judges

The history of our country shows us that the Canadian people has never had cause for regret in having followed in difficult circumstances the advice of the bishops, but on the contrary the country has gravely suffered when their wise guidance has been rejected.[141]

Party as well as caste loyalty no doubt played some part in Laflèche's attitude toward the Riel agitation, for in traditionally Conservative Trois-Rivières, a marriage between a Conservative and a Liberal was referred to as a 'mixed marriage.'

Under the goad of Mercier's burning eloquence, heard in all regions of the province as he tirelessly sought to break down old party lines and to unite the people under his leadership, the movement was only checked, not halted, by the opposition of the hierarchy, the English Liberals, Chapleau and his friends, and Laurier, who was alarmed at the growing isolation of Quebec from the rest of Canada. At the Champs de Mars meeting the latter had been swept by the wave of public indignation from his lifelong conviction that the formation of a Catholic or French-Canadian party would be suicidal for his people, since it would unite the English Protestants against them and pave the way for a war of religion or race. Once that party began to take form, Laurier withdrew his support from Mercier.

The beginnings of this English reaction which Laurier anticipated had already been produced by the Quebec agitation. On November 23 the *Toronto Mail* published an editorial in which it warned the French Canadians, 'now seeking to compel us to recognize their right to suspend the operation of the law when a representative of their race is in the toils,' that 'rather than to submit to such a yoke, Ontario would smash Confederation into its original fragments, preferring that the dream of a united Canada should be shattered forever, than that unity should be purchased at the price of inequality.'[142] Two days later the *Mail* told Mercier and his friends that 'if the cabinet should fall as a result of the intrigues of French influence, if such is the fruit of Mr. Mercier's programme, in that case, as Britons, we believe that the Conquest will have to be fought over again. Lower Canada may depend upon it, there will be no new treaty of 1763. The victors will not capitulate next time.'[143] To these utterances of the *Mail*, which was considered the chief mouthpiece of the government, but at this moment was running quite as free of political harness as the ministerial organs in Quebec were on the other side of the question, were added the observations of the *Orange Sentinel*: 'Must it be said that the rights and liberties of the English people in this English colony depend upon a foreign race? . . . The day is near when an appeal to arms will be heard in all parts of Canada. Then, certainly, our soldiers, benefiting by the lessons of the past, will have to complete the work they began in the North-West.'[144] Such statements only furthered Mercier's game by increasing the ethnic tension, which was also added to by an English attempt to enforce vaccination to check a severe smallpox epidemic in Montreal, and by the failure of two Channel Island firms, Charles Robin & Co. and LeBoutillier & Brothers, which had monopolized the fisheries and supplying of Gaspé, and whose collapse brought on disorders among the unemployed and starving fishermen, long restive under exploitation by these foreign French-speaking Protestants.

When parliament met at the end of February 1886, the first clash on the Riel question occurred in the Senate, where censure by government supporters of the raising in the press of racial and religious prejudices was opposed by followers of Mercier. In the House early in March the Conservative Philippe Landry offered a motion expressing profound regret at Riel's execution, which had the effect of embarrassing the Liberals, who were divided on this question, although agreed on the government's responsibility for the execution. Archbishop Taché appeared in the visitors' gallery during the debate which followed, and counseled the French-Canadian Conservatives who consulted him not to vote against the government. This well-meant effort to quell the storm was taken in Orange quarters as new proof that Rome was running Canada.

Relief for the ever-growing tension was provided by Laurier's speech in the House on March 16. He denied the *Mail's* charges and forswore Mercier's suicidal policy of forming a French-Canadian party, but he indicted the government for its long neglect of the *Métis'* grievances: 'What is hateful . . . is not rebellion but the despotism which induces that rebellion; what is hateful are not the rebels but the men, who having the enjoyment of power, do not discharge the duties of power.'[145] He did not consider Riel a hero: 'At his worst he was a subject fit for an asylum; at his best he was a religious and political monomaniac.' But he attacked the fairness of the trial and the difference in the treatment of Jackson and Riel. Singling out the root of the Ontario agitation, he observed: 'The death of Scott is the cause of the death of Riel today';[146] and he argued that mercy rather than revenge should have been the guiding principle of the government, as in the United States after the Civil War. He concluded with an eloquent call for mercy to the remaining rebellion prisoners in the name of liberty and justice, which had been won at last for the *Métis* by those who had already suffered martyrdom: 'I say that their country has conquered with their martyrdom, and if we look at that one fact alone, there was cause sufficient, independent of all others, to extend mercy to the one who is dead and to those who live.'[147]

Political friends and foes alike hailed this first great English speech of Laurier. The *Montreal Star*, a Conservative organ, dubbed him the 'silver-tongued Laurier,' while his Liberal colleague Blake ironically referred to his speech as 'the crowning proof of French domination,'[148] since by it Laurier had added the palm for parliamentary eloquence in English to his reputation as the ablest French orator in the House. Blake himself made one of his greatest efforts in this debate, speaking for five hours as he indicted the government for negligence and as he piled up proof of Riel's insanity and precedents against holding madmen responsible for their acts.[149] But in spite of these notable speeches by the leading Liberals and the general weakness of Conservative replies, the government was sustained by a large majority, as Macdonald had foreseen, with losses among the Quebec Conservatives offset by support from Liberals from the English-speaking provinces. The vote gave evidence that the Riel question had become an ethnic rather than a party or a sectional one. It was to ease the ethnic tension that Laurier discussed the question at Toronto the following December, in the same terms that he had used at Ottawa. Quebec, however, turned against its Conservative government, since it placed party loyalty before ethnic considerations. The provincial administration crumbled before Mercier's assault in the October elections, and in January 1887 his *Parti National* took power.

7

A whole generation in Quebec was filled with emotional hatred for all things English by the Riel affair, while the gallophobia and 'no-popery' agitation aroused by it in Ontario were fed by the course of Mercier's administration and sustained by conflicts over the rights of the French language and of separate schools in the West. Mercier, who had won power by invoking the gibbet of Regina at ninety political meetings and had built his government on Riel's grave, did much to further the division between French and English in 1885 and to make it permanent. Faced with the political necessity of maintaining the coalition which the Riel crisis had forged between French-Canadian Liberals and Conservatives, Mercier disregarded the solemn warning which Laurier had given him in the Ottawa debate on Riel's execution:

> It would be simply suicidal for the French Canadians to form a party by themselves. Why, so soon as the French Canadians, who are in the minority in this House and in the country, were to organize as a political party, they would compel the majority to organize as a political party, and the result must be disastrous to themselves. We have only one way of organizing parties. This country must be governed and can be governed only on questions of policy and administration.[150]

But Mercier had discovered how easy it was to organize a party in Quebec on the basis of nationality, and he attempted to govern by using the emotions conjured up by the words 'national,' 'French,' and 'Catholic,' rather than by the reasoned arguments demanded by questions of policy and administration. At the outset of his regime he seemed to take heed of Laurier's warning; speaking at Saint-Hyacinthe at the end of his government's first session, he reaffirmed its character:

> National in its conception, national in its birth, this government was to be national in the basis of its organization, in the affirmation of its ideas and aspirations. The government is truly national; I hasten to add that it must remain national; it is our duty and intention to preserve this character which is its strength and which associates many honest citizens, weary of the ruinous conflicts of the past and anxious not to see them recommence.[151]

But he added: 'The *Parti National* will respect and cause to be respected the rights of the Protestant minority in this province. We wish to live in peace with all races, all creeds. We shall give justice to all, even to those who refuse the like to us.'[152]

Despite such fair words, it was not difficult for Mercier's enemies to use his nationalism to turn the English Canadians against him; and Mercier himself, lacking Laurier's understanding of the English mentality or caring less for its reactions, soon lost caution as power made him domineering. The incorporation in 1887 of the Jesuits, who had educated Mercier at their Collège Sainte-Marie in Montreal, did not cause much comment in the English-speaking world, although some English Quebeckers were disgruntled by the spectacle of the legislature receiving delegates of the Jesuits and of Cardinal Taschereau, who opposed the measure in the interests of Laval, and that of politicians discussing the fine points of theology and canon law. But when Mercier went to New York in search of a loan and there received the honors appropriate to the head of a state; when Mercier summoned an inter-provincial conference—the first held since Confederation—in October 1887 at Quebec and induced the delegates of five provinces (Prince Edward Island and British Columbia abstained from attendance) to reaffirm vigorously the principle of provincial autonomy; and finally when Mercier, unsuccessful in New York, went to Paris to obtain a loan from the Crédit Lyonnais and to Rome to consult the Holy See on the Jesuit Estates question, the English Canadians began to take alarm at this provincial premier whose watchword was 'national' and who acted like the ruler of an independent state. Dark rumors of Mercier's plan to set up a French-Canadian state began to go the rounds.

Mercier's actions did nothing to dispel these suspicions. In New York, on the eve of sailing for France, he had closeted himself in the rectory of the French-Canadian church with Bishop Grandin of Saint-Albert and Gabriel Dumont, the *Métis* 'general' in 1885. In Paris Mercier was given a royal reception and the Legion of Honor, and in his speeches stressed Quebec's ties with France; in Rome he was received in private audience by the Pope. His success abroad in winning popularity and in achieving his commercial and diplomatic ends greatly strengthened his position in Quebec, which felt itself honored through the honor paid to its premier; but Mercier's doings were entirely too French and Catholic for English-Canadian taste.

The vague fears thus aroused were strengthened by Mercier's rigorous opposition to the imperial federalism favored by the new governor-general, Lord Stanley, and the Imperial Federation League, whose English-Canadian nucleus had been active in the suppression of the rebellion and in the persecution of the *Métis*. Mercier attacked imperialism at the Windsor Hotel in Montreal in 1888:

> It is proposed to impose upon us a political regime which through conscription could scatter our sons from the icefields of the North Pole to the burning sands of the Sahara; an odious regime which would condemn us to pay an arbitrary tax of blood and money, and tear our sons from us, in order to cast them into remote and bloody wars which we could neither prevent nor stop.[153]

Having thus stamped himself as 'disloyal' in the minds of the colonial-minded English Canadians of the day, Mercier went on to arouse new opposition by appointing the Curé Labelle deputy-minister of the new Department of Agriculture and Colonization, which he himself headed. It was the first time in America that a priest had held important public office, and the innovation found no favor in the eyes of those who believed in the complete separation of Church and State, as the great majority of English Canadians did. But it was sound Quebec politics, for the Curé Labelle was a popular figure whose devotion to opening up new regions and whose dynamic leadership had made him a hero of his people. The appointment did much to confirm the favor with which Mercier was viewed by the lower clergy after his stand on the Riel question. Only the Bishops of Trois-Rivières, Montreal, and Ottawa remained resolute in their conviction that salvation was only to be found in the Conservative Party.

In June 1888 Mercier announced to the Quebec Legislature that he had come to an agreement with Père Turgeon, representative of the Holy See and the Society of Jesus, for the settlement of the ancier Jesuit Estates question. Since 1831, when the imperial governmer finally turned over the estates to the Canadian government, the revenues had been used for the original purpose, the support of ed cation. With Confederation the estates came into the hands of th Quebec government, which used the revenue for the support of bot Catholic and Protestant institutions. When the Jesuits returned t Canada in 1842 at the invitation of Bishop Bourget, they urged the claim to their ancient property; and as they rose rapidly in influenc they became more insistent about the matter. In 1884 the ultr montane Ross administration had attempted to settle the questio but negotiations had come to nothing in the face of the opposition Archbishop Taschereau and Laval University, who maintained th the proceeds of the estates should be divided among the Cathol schools rather than assigned to the Jesuits, who were active in th agitation to establish a rival university in Montreal. Mercier solve this complicated question by offering $400,000—much less than th value of the estates, which had been placed as high as $2,000,000- in return for the renunciation of further claims. The division of th sum was to be left to the Pope. $60,000 was to be granted to th Protestant schools which had previously received a share of th revenue from the estates. Although two English Protestants raise some objections, they subsequently withdrew them; and the bill w passed unanimously by both houses in the Quebec Legislature. B Mercier's invocation of Papal action—in order to assure a lastin settlement in the face of divided clerical opinion in Quebec—raise the specter of 'papist aggression' in Ontario, which by its deman for federal disallowance of the measure aroused once more the ethni and religious division engendered by the execution of Riel. Th cries of 'no popery' and 'French domination' were sounded by th Equal Rights Association, headed by leading Orangemen.[154]

The storm thus raised, reflected as it was by protests in th *Toronto Globe*, *Mail*, and *World* against 'Roman Catholic aggression could not be ignored by Sir John Macdonald, although he decide after casting a political balance-sheet, to refuse to yield to th Ontario Orangemen, rather than to cement Mercier's hold o Quebec. A debate on the Jesuit Estates Act was held in the Hous at Ottawa in March 1889, when Colonel William E. O'Brien move a resolution for disallowance on the grounds that act was *ultra vire* violated the separation of Church and State, represented 'th usurpation of a right by a foreign authority,' and through i 'endowment of the Society of Jesus, an alien, secret, and politic religious body, the expulsion of which from every Christian com munity wherein it has a foothold has been rendered necessary by i intolerant and mischievous intermeddling with the functions of civ government, is fraught with danger to the civil and religious liberties of the people of Canada.'[155]

The artificial character of the attack on the Jesuit Estates Act was indicated by the fact that it originated in Ontario, which was not affected by the measure, despite acceptance of the act by Quebec Protestants. An editorial in the *Toronto Mail* gives the case for the Ontario crusade:

> If the British and Protestant element in Quebec will not save itself, we must try to save it for our own sakes. That the abandonment of Quebec to the Ultramontane and the Jesuit will be the death of Canadian nationality is clear enough. But Ontario will not be safe. Our eastern gate has already been opened by the perfidious hand of the vote-hunting politician, and French and Roman Catholic invasion is already streaming through. The French priest, it is true, cannot formally import into Ontario his Church establishment and his system of tithes. But this matters little, if he can thrust out the British population and plant in its room a population which will be under his sway, and from which he can wring practically any payments which he thinks fit. The assessor, moreover, will be his creature, and he will be able to distribute the burden of local taxation between the faithful and the heretic pretty much at his pleasure. He will, to all intents and purposes, detach eastern Ontario from the British and Protestant civilization of which it now forms a part, and annex it to the territory of the French race, which is also the dominion of the priest. No distortion of facts by sophistical rhetoric, no hypocritical protests against race feeling will hide from us either the gravity or the imminence of this result.[156]

The most notable speeches in support of the O'Brien motion were those of Clarke Wallace, Grand Master of the Orange Order, and Dalton Macarthy, the head of the Imperial Federation League. The three men, who had founded the Equal Rights Association, covered the same ground according to their varying ability, all protesting that they had no wish to arouse religious antagonism, all making an historical indictment of the Jesuits and of their claim to the Estates, and all viewing the Mercier measure as a threat to the Queen's supremacy and the rights of freeborn Englishmen. But in the face of the statement by C. C. Colby, the oldest English Quebec member, that 'There never was a minority in any country treated with more generosity than the Protestant minority of the Province of Quebec'[157]; of the coldly legal argument by Sir John Thompson, the Catholic Minister of Justice, against disallowance; of Laurier's and Sir William Mulock's deprecation of such invitations to racial division; and of Sir John Macdonald's bland dismissal of the resolution with an anecdote, the Orange onslaught collapsed. The O'Brien resolution found only a handful of supporters—the 'noble thirteen.'

But the agitation raised outside the House by the Equal Rights Association continued unchecked, and brought about a worse state of feeling between French and English than had existed since the height of the Riel affair.

In September 1889 Laurier went to Toronto to speak on the Jesuit Estates question, once more using the same language in Toronto as in Quebec and again pleading for an inclusive rather than a hyphenated Canadianism. This courageous invasion of the citadel of 'no popery' was not without effect, contrasting as it did with the Conservative strategy of being militantly Catholic in Quebec and militantly Protestant in Ontario. Laurier's behavior on these occasions did much to make him a national figure, and played no small part in his elevation to the leadership of the Liberal Party in 1887 and his victory in the elections of 1896.

Mercier, however, took a different course. With the same impetuous energy which he had devoted to settling long-standing provincial questions, he replied on Saint-Jean-Baptiste Day 1889 to attacks from without the province by proudly reaffirming Quebec's French and Catholic tradition:

> As the authorized representative of Quebec . . . with the consciousness of the responsibility attached to my words, I declare in the name of all of us that we have remained and shall remain Catholic and French. Love of the religion and of the nationality of our fathers is stamped upon our hearts, and no one, not even the most potent of tyrants, can take this love from us.
>
> This province of Quebec is Catholic and French, and it will remain Catholic and French.
>
> While protesting our respect and even our friendship for the representatives of other races and other religions, while declaring ourselves ready to give them their legitimate part in everything and everywhere, while offering to share with them as brothers the immense territory and the great resources that Providence has put at our disposition; while desiring to live in the most perfect harmony with them in the shadow of England's flag and under the protection of a sovereign dear to all, we solemnly declare that we shall never renounce the rights which are guaranteed to us by the treaties, the law, and the constitution.
>
> These treaties, this law, this constitution give us the right to remain Catholic and French . . . We are now two million and a half French Canadians in America, proud of our past, strong in our present, and confident in our future; we care little for the threats of our enemies . . .
>
> When we vanish, we shall say to the generation called to succeed us: 'We are Catholic and French, and when you, our successors, vanish in your turn, you must say to the generation which will replace you: "We die Catholic and French!"' This will be our testament and theirs; the supreme last will of an heroic people, transmitted from father to son, from generation to generation, until the end of time.[158]

Mercier, better than any orator French Canada has produced, ould evoke the deepest currents of national feeling. That feeling vas also honestly his, but he played upon it for political purposes. ttacked on the right by Conservatives and on the left by advanced iberals, he followed this declaration of fidelity to the French-anadian tradition with an eloquent appeal for French-Canadian olidarity:

> We are not as strong as we should be, because we are divided. And we re divided because we do not grasp the dangers of the situation. Our nemies are united in their hatred of the French homeland; and we are ivided in our love of this dear homeland.
>
> Why? We do not know. We are divided because the generation which receded us was divided. We are divided because we have inherited the itles of *Rouges* and *Bleus*; because human pride bids us call ourselves iberals or Conservatives; because it is good to have a name and a title n the pretext of having principles; because it is fashionable to defend rinciples, above all when they are attacked.
>
> Let us break with these dangerous traditions; let us sacrifice our hatreds n the altar of the homeland, and on this day of patriotic rejoicing, in he name and for the prosperity of this province of Quebec that we love o well, let us clasp hands like brothers, and let us swear to cease our atricidal strife and unite.
>
> Let your rallying-cry in the future be these words, which will be our trength: 'Let us cease our fratricidal strife and unite!'[159]

Laurier, upon this same occasion—the dedication of the monu-nent to Jacques Cartier and Brébeuf at Quebec—sounded a different ote:

> We are French Canadians, but our country is not confined to the erritory overshadowed by the citadel of Quebec; our country is Canada, is the whole of what is covered by the British flag on the American ontinent, the fertile lands bordered by the Bay of Fundy, the Valley f the St. Lawrence, the region of the Great Lakes, the prairies of the Vest, the Rocky Mountains, the lands washed by the famous ocean vhose breezes are said to be as sweet as the breezes of the Mediterranean. Our fellow-countrymen are not only those in whose veins runs the blood f France. They are all those, whatever their race or whatever their eligion, whom the fortunes of war, the chances of fate, or their own hoice have brought among us, and who acknowledge the sovereignty f the British Crown . . . The first place in my heart is for those in whose eins runs the blood of my own veins. Yet I do not hesitate to say that he rights of my fellow-countrymen of different origins are as dear to me, s sacred to me, as the rights of my own race, and if it unfortunately appened that they were ever attacked, I would defend them with just s much energy and vigor as the rights of my own race . . . What I claim or us is an equal share of the sun, of justice, of liberty; we have that

> share, and have it amply; and what we claim for ourselves we are anxio to grant to others. I do not want French Canadians to domineer ov anyone, nor anyone to domineer over them. Equal justice; equ rights . . . Cannot we believe that in the supreme battle here on t Plains of Abraham, when the fate of arms turned against us, cannot v believe that it entered into the designs of Providence that the two racc enemies up to that time, should henceforth live in peace and harmony Such was the inspiring cause of Confederation.[160]

These two different concepts, which might be called the provinci and the national, or the French-Canadian and the Canadian, we to diverge increasingly in the years to come, and to divide th French Canadians. Their respective popularity has varied with th circumstances of the time. It is one of the tragedies of Canadia national life that in moments of division between the ethn elements, in times of crisis, either political or economic, Frenc Canada is most apt to recoil upon itself, to wrap itself in its di tinctive tradition, and to ease its sense of insecurity by asserting i Frenchness and its Catholicity, thus increasing the resentment c English Canadians that Canada is not a homogeneous nation whos people think and react alike in national emergencies. But th French-Canadian reaction is a natural one in the case of a minorit group whose sense of insecurity leads it to indulge in brash talk t dispel its own fears.

8

Mercier reached the apogee of his career in his Saint-Jear Baptiste Day speech at Quebec in which he voiced the feelings of people scattered over North America. His words read like a declara tion of war to the Ontario Orangemen, who in August established Montreal branch of the Equal Rights Association, the Protestar Protective Association, to 'protect' their brethren of Quebec, an who renewed their attack on the Jesuit Estates Act by calling for i review by the courts. Mercier maddened them still more in Novem ber when he attended the Catholic Congress of Baltimore, where h was the guest of the Jesuits, hobnobbed with the hierarchy, an proclaimed: 'We have returned to the Church, through the Jesuit the possessions of which they were despoiled by the same George II who wished to despoil you of your rights and liberties.'[161] Taillor the leader of the Quebec Conservatives, protested against 'the wa of race and religion inaugurated by M. Mercier,'[162] but the Pro testant Liberal Joly approved the Jesuit Estates Act, despite hi differences with Mercier on the Riel question. Mercier himse sought to reassure the alarmed Protestants by a gift of $10,000 t the University of Toronto, which had suffered in a fire, and b telling Alexander Cameron, the member for Huntingdon, that h ad no intention of replacing the Union Jack on the Quebec citadel y the Tricolor. Mercier also published an English pamphlet, *An nswer to the Equal Rights Association* (Quebec, 1890), containing the orrespondence between himself and the president of the Association, nd also Robert Sellar's 'Disabilities of Protestants in the Province f Quebec' and his own reply to this document. The pamphlet erved as an answer to the Equal Rightists' attacks on the French anadians, and reinforced Mercier's standing with his own people. he latter was also greatly strengthened by the transmission from ome through the Curé Labelle of the Holy See's thanks to Mercier or his services to the Church.

Mercier was returned to office with a larger majority in the rovincial elections of June 1890, despite the opposition's attacks pon himself and his disciples on the basis of the McGreevy and Vhelan graft scandals. He characterized the result as a victory for rovincial autonomy and for his railroad development policy. He nnounced his intention of furthering agriculture and colonization, f attracting foreign capital to develop Quebec's natural resources, f repatriating Franco-Americans, and of seeking commercial eciprocity with the United States. He dreamed of bringing about he downfall of his arch-enemy Sir John, but in the federal elections f 1891 Macdonald was returned to office despite the majority of fteen Liberal seats which Mercier supplied in Quebec to Laurier.

Mercier endorsed a note for $10,000 to pay the expenses of ontesting elections, and then departed for Europe in search of a 10,000,000 French loan. Soon after his departure, several opposiion papers were put under severe pressure by Mercier's aides, amid rotests against 'Caesar Mercier' and 'the Quebec Autocrat.' srael Tarte carried his charges against Thomas McGreevy to Ottawa, where their hearing by the House was interrupted by the leath of Macdonald in June. Meanwhile Mercier was making a oyal progress through Europe, being decorated by the French 'resident, the Belgian King, and Pope Leo XIII, who made him a apal count. His visit to Rome, where he sought the creation of a 'ranco-American bishop for his exiled compatriots, did him no good ither with English Protestants or with the Quebec hierarchy, who esented the presumption of a layman meddling with ecclesiastical natters. The European money market proved tight, but Mercier aised a $4,000,000 loan in Paris and succeeded in interesting French apitalists in Quebec, before his triumphant return to a province vhich had been flattered by his reception in Europe.

But scandal broke out immediately upon his return. Mercier had pproved the transfer of the contract for the Baie des Chaleurs Railway to a new syndicate, which, it was revealed, had paid a comnission of $100,000 to Ernest Pacaud, the Liberal treasurer. And

Pacaud had paid off the $10,000 note endorsed by Mercier and ha supplied him with $5,000 when he ran short of funds in Pari Tarte's charges had also resulted in the resignation of Sir Hect Langevin as Minister of Public Works at Ottawa, and the launchin of a wave of demands for reform. Public opinion dictated that th Lieutenant-Governor of Quebec should first limit Mercier's powe and then appoint a Royal Commission to investigate the Baie d Chaleurs scandal. On the strength of the commission's repor Mercier was dismissed from office on December 16. The lieutenan governor, a Conservative, called upon the Conservative ex-premie Charles de Boucherville, who had been dismissed from office by th Liberal Letellier de Saint-Just in 1878, to form a new governmen Mercier denounced the lieutenant-governor and the Royal Com mission for their political partisanship, and promised to seek new mandate from the people. But the new administration un covered further scandals, and pressed the attack upon the Mercie regime. Laurier showed personal sympathy for Mercier, but re ferred to the Baie des Chaleurs episode as 'an unfortunate trans action which must be condemned without hesitation, which canno be defended.'[163]

In the elections of March 1892, which followed a bitter winte campaign to the cry of '*A bas les voleurs!*' only seventeen partisans o Mercier were elected, and Mercier himself barely retained his ow seat. The press hailed the downfall of the Mercier regime as 'th punishment of a band of brigands who bled the province for fou years.'[164] Mercier saw the verdict as the victory of 'calumny ove the constitution,' and announced his return to private life. At th end of April Mercier and Pacaud were called before the Quebe Assizes on charges of misappropriating public funds, and were hel for trial. Arthur Buies wrote a virtual epitaph for the fallen leader i *La Patrie,* which concluded thus: 'He had in his hands the mos brilliant role which has ever been given to a Canadian statesman he had a whole people behind him and a glorious role to fill; hi vanity, his egotism, and his absolute absence of moral sense los everything.'[165] Mercier was ill, and by June he was bankrupt to th tune of $83,163. At his trial in October he was found not guilty and aroused sympathy by the way in which he had aged unde affliction. During the winter session of the legislature he forced hi enemy Tom-Chase Casgrain to disavow a charge that he had em bezzled $30,000 of public funds.

On April 4, 1893 Mercier addressed a crowd of six thousand at th Parc Sohmer in Montreal on 'The Future of Canada.' This wa rumored to be his political swansong, and his partisans gathered a of old for the occasion. He defended himself against the charges o anglophobia and disloyalty:

I am not an anglophobe. I admire Englishmen and I love Englishwomen, but England leaves me indifferent, nearly cold. I admit that she has done us some good, but I believe that she has done us more harm than good, and that if we, especially we French Canadians, have prospered, it is not her fault. We have contributed much to the fortune of her merchants and manufacturers, as we have always paid generously the governors whom she has sent us. If some of them insulted us, and said that we were an inferior race, we never threw rotten eggs at them, as the English Tories did to Lord Elgin . . .

Thus, all accounts balanced, we owe nothing to England; and we shall separate from her when the majority, regularly consulted, so wishes, without remorse of conscience, without a broken heart, and even without shedding tears. . . .[166]

He weighed the relative merits of the present system, of imperial federation, of annexation to the States, and of independence, observing that Confederation had outlived its time. He blamed Canada's failure to make as much progress as the United States on its false political position. Supporting his position by the statements of Englishmen favorable to colonial emancipation, he came out for independence. With something of his old eloquence he concluded his two-hour speech thus:

Standing as a free man on American soil, I defend the sacred cause of my compatriots, whatever their race or religious belief, and I ask for all colonial emancipation and liberty . . .

In undertaking this considerable task which I have imposed upon myself, I wished to show you what our country could be, this Canada, dear to all our hearts. I have done all that I could to open up new horizons for you, and by making you see them, push you towards the realizations of our natural destinies. You have colonial dependence, I offer you independence; you have shame and misery, I offer you fortune and prosperity; you are only a colony ignored by the entire world, I offer you the opportunity of becoming a great people, recognized and respected among free nations.

Men, women, and children, it is for you to choose; you can remain slaves under colonial status, or become independent and free, among other peoples who invite you to the banquet of nations.[167]

The meeting ended in a triumph for Mercier and for his doctrine of independence, but there was no political aftermath. Mercier had dreamed of raising the people with the cry of independence as he had raised them in the days of the Riel affair.

But that outburst of feeling had exhausted the emotions of French Canada for the time being, and the public mood had changed. There was now more response to Laurier's academic eloquence than to the impassioned melodramatics of Mercier. Laurier's stock was rising steadily, and he was very conscious of being the leader of a party which was both French and English. His watchwords were conciliation and unity, and Mercier's last appeal to the French Canadians was dismissed as a personal one, unsupported by the Liberal Party. So Mercier took his doctrine of independence to the United States, where he aroused much enthusiasm in the Franco-American centers.

In the Quebec legislature that fall, after his administration had undergone many attacks, he improvised despite his failing health a two-hour apologia, which closed thus:

> You have ruined me, you sought to dishonor me, and now you wish to walk on my corpse. Well, here is that corpse! Look at it; look it in the face, for it rises before you to say: You have taken from me all that I possess in the world, even to my library, my beloved books which I amassed during thirty-five years—all has been sold, save my honor. And be assured that I shall defend my honor like a lion, alone against you, were you a hundred or a thousand.[168]

Taillon, who had attacked Mercier bitterly, rose and shook his hand after this speech. During the rest of the session Mercier continued to be the soul of the opposition, but in the summer of 1894 diabetes forced him to give up legal work and to take to his bed. As he lay dying the new Liberal leader Laurier made a triumphant tour to the Pacific Coast, as if to symbolize the triumph of the larger nationalism. But Laurier and many others came to the bedside of the dying Mercier, among the rest his old adversary Chapleau. The end came on October 30. Some twenty-five thousand people paid their respects to the dead leader as he lay in state, and countless thousands attended the funeral, the most impressive seen in Montreal since Cartier's. Notables and rank and file alike did honor to one who, despite all his faults, incarnated the spirit of French Canada, and whose influence was to remain a lasting force in the French-Canadian tradition. Mercier's revival of the old cry of '*Gesta Dei per Francos*' and his messianic pronouncements of the providential mission of the French Canadians were to find echoes in the years to come.

9

Despite his dislike for the 'demagogues' who had won the leadership of the people away from the bishops in the course of the 'Holy War,' Bishop Laflèche shared one great nationalist idea with Honoré Mercier, while he was the new master of Quebec. Laflèche, too, dreamed of the development of a French-Canadian state on the banks of the St. Lawrence, with the French Canadians of Quebec reinforced by the exiled Franco-Americans of New England. In the 1870's, like the other bishops, he had fought the exodus from depressed Quebec, and had encouraged Curé Labelle in his colonization movement with this remarkably foresighted estimate of the resources of Quebec:

The direction that you give your activity in the work of colonization is certainly most patriotic, and the good Lord will lavish His most abundant blessings upon it. The valleys of the Ottawa and of Lake St. John offer a vast field for our surplus population, and it is there that they must be guided. The Saint-Maurice valley offers little advantage for agriculture. Its arid and rocky soil contains few assets for agriculture, and it will be difficult to form prosperous parishes there. By way of compensation, it is rich in minerals and in timber, and the waterpower to work these raw materials is plentiful and powerful. Agriculture and industry, then, join in Providence's plan to make our country prosperous and happy. As industry must follow agriculture, you walk in the paths of Providence by giving the latter all the impetus possible through the colonization of our most fertile lands.[169]

But with Canada racked by the ethnic division of the Riel affair, Bishop Laflèche talked unguardedly to Curé Biron of West Springfield, Massachusetts, who quoted him in the Franco-American press as saying that Confederation was only a house of cards which would soon collapse, and then the 800,000 Franco-Americans of the States must aid the French-Canadians 'to protect ourselves against Anglo-Saxon hatred.'[170] Therefore the exodus from Quebec could no longer be considered a disaster. Bishop Laflèche denied that he had said that Canada would be annexed by the States, as Curé Biron claimed, but declared that on the contrary he had said that part of the United States would annex itself to an independent French state. By guarding their faith and their customs, the Franco-Americans could further this development, which might have been the design of Providence in causing the exodus. This concept of an independent French state, which has ever remained dear to French-Canadian ultranationalists, thus seems to have been the joint idea of Mercier and Laflèche, born of the bitter aftermath of the Riel affair and of the bishop's dismay that Canada was going the way of other nations in which the Church was not dominant over the State.

At this period a wave of anti-Catholicism in New England, aroused by the sudden realization of the great numbers of immigrants of largely Catholic stock, had thrown the Franco-Americans back upon their distinctive traditions. Ferdinand Gagnon, one of their best-known leaders and also the paid repatriation agent of the Canadian government, had aroused much Yankee opposition by his cry of 'Be loyal, yes, but be French always!'[171] Such utterances, combined with national conventions which reunited Franco-Americans and French Canadians, and the constant comings and goings of Canadian mission priests and cultural envoys among the Franco-American colonies of New England, caused alarm among the thinning stock of Yankees. A lingering Puritan prejudice against the faith of some three hundred thousand Franco-Americans was not diminished by aggressive defence of their right to preserve their own language and traditions in their new home. English-Canadian immigrants took a leading role in rousing nativist sentiment. On December 28, 1889 the Boston *British-American Citizen* printed an editorial based upon the fear that a French annexation of New England was being plotted:

Romanism is already a terrible power in our country. It dominates New York, and exercises a considerable influence in many cities and towns of New England. But to this Roman force must be added the French ultramontane power, which we have completely ignored up to now. Reflect, American patriots, the French Jesuits have conceived the project of forming a Catholic nation out of the province of Quebec and New England, and this project of making New England French Catholic has already taken proportions capable of alarming the most optimistic. The French number more than a million in the United States, and in all probability 350,000 in New England. They fill your factories, buy your farms, introduce themselves into your legislatures, and exercise there a powerful influence. The number of their children is unimaginable for Americans. These children are kept away from the public schools, in order to receive an education entirely similar to that they would have received in Quebec. They are told that by learning English they will lose their mother tongue, their nationality, and their religion. They are kept a distinct alien race, subject to the Pope in matters of religion and of politics. Rapidly they acquire the right to vote; in certain places they already have an absolute majority, while in many others they balance their enemies. Soon, united to the Irish, they will govern you, Americans, or rather the Pope will govern you, for these masses recognize him as master.[172]

Thus the religio-political strife of Quebec was echoed in the States, where the Franco-Americans had been awakened to a consciousness of their ethnic origin by the execution of Riel and by the opposition they provoked by insisting upon remaining a people apart. But after a 58 per cent increase of the French-Canadians in the States between 1890 and 1900, the tide of immigration from Quebec dwindled away with the opening of the Canadian West and the industrialization of Quebec. Meanwhile the earlier immigrants had become Americanized, as was witnessed by the decline of the conventions, of the Franco-American press, and of the insistence on maintaining separateness.[173] Those of their sons and grandsons who have returned to Quebec have been among the most bitter opponents of the ultranationalist school which still dreams of that French-Canadian state whose emergence Bishop Laflèche regarded as possibly within the plans of Providence.

10

The political fortunes of the Conservative Party were greatly embarrassed after Macdonald's death in 1891 by the fact that many of those engaged in the struggle for the leadership were also leaders in the Orange crusade against 'French domination'—which was really a crusade, as Dr. Skelton has pointed out, against French-Canadian equality.[174] The anti-French agitation which was aroused by the Riel affair continued with the demand for disallowance of the Jesuit Estates Act in 1889. The Equal Rights Association, formed in June 1889 by the same 'noble thirteen' who had voted for disallowance against an overwhelming majority of both parties, was led by Dalton McCarthy and other leading imperial federalists. The Liberal government of Ontario was attacked for allowing the use of French in the schools of eastern Ontario, but anti-French measures were pressed hardest in the federal House. In February 1890 McCarthy introduced a bill to abolish the use of the French language in the legislature and courts of the North-West Territories, after having made a tour during the previous year through Manitoba and raised an agitation there which revoked the language and scholastic guarantees of the Manitoba Act and raised a question which brought about the downfall of the Conservative regime at Ottawa in 1896.

Meanwhile the nominal leadership of the party changed hands rapidly, with the Catholic and Orange wings of the party alternating in power, and all unity shattered by their bitter differences. No one then or since has been able to repeat Macdonald's feat of reconciling the irreconcilable year in and year out. As in all governments which had held power too long, corruption was rife; and Israel Tarte's revelations of graft in the Public Works Department brought about the downfall of Sir Hector Langevin, who had been slated to succeed Sir John Macdonald as leader. Further Liberal charges of corruption were countered by Conservative revelations of the Baie des Chaleurs Railway scandal in Quebec. With the electors becoming convinced that one party was as crooked as the other, the Conservatives managed to increase their majority from twenty-odd to sixty in the by-elections of 1892, but after that date they steadily lost ground.

Meanwhile Laurier knitted the Liberals together by speaking trips which made him known all over Canada and by a national convention at Ottawa in June 1893, the first ever held by any party. The Liberal program of lower tariffs and reciprocity with the United States gained in popular favor as time went on, and as leader of the opposition Laurier was able to avoid committing himself on the Manitoba school question, which became increasingly embarrassing for the government. The Conservative Party was torn apart by the question, which divided its support from the Catholic hierarchy and the Orange Order. When the government finally decided upon a remedial bill against the Manitoba anti-French legislation, Laurier was able to take his stand as the supporter of the Liberal doctrine of provincial rights, while promising to win better terms for the minority from the Liberal government of Manitoba.

Laurier resisted the intense pressure put upon him by the Catholic hierarchy to support the government measure, and made a moving statement of principle which reassured his English Protestant followers:

> I am here the acknowledged leader of a great party, composed of Roman Catholics and Protestants as well, as Protestants must be in the majority in every party in Canada. Am I to be told, occupying such a position, that I am to be dictated the course I am to take in this House, by reasons that can appeal to the consciences of my fellow-Catholic members, but which do not appeal as well to the consciences of my Protestant colleagues? No. So long as I have a seat in this House, so long as I occupy the position I do now, whenever it shall become my duty to take a stand upon any question whatever, that stand I will take not upon grounds of Roman Catholicism, not upon grounds of Protestantism, but upon grounds which can appeal to the conscience of all men, irrespective of their particular faith, upon grounds which can be occupied by all men who love justice, freedom, and toleration.[175]

Laurier held that the federal government had the power to interfere in Manitoba, but should not do so until all the facts had been investigated and until all means of conciliation had been exhausted. He moved the six months' hoist, and the government defeated that motion by little more than half its normal majority. Sir Charles Tupper's attempt to jam the remedial bill through second reading was met by a filibuster in which rebellious Tories took a leading part. Finally the bill was abandoned. Elections followed in June 1896, with Tupper leading the Conservatives at the head of a cabinet whose ultramontane representation had been strengthened.

The Quebec hierarchy issued a collective pastoral on May 16 which said that the Manitoba school question was primarily a religious one, and while disavowing any intention to side with any political party, ordered that 'all Catholics should vote only for candidates who will formally and solemnly pledge themselves to vote in Parliament in favor of the legislation giving to the Catholics of Manitoba the school laws which are recognized as theirs by the Privy Council in England.'[176] The Vicar-General of Quebec, Mgr. Marois, pronounced it mortal sin to vote Liberal, while Bishop Laflèche condemned Laurier's stand as 'the most categorical affirmation of the liberalism condemned by the Church' and pronounced that 'a Catholic cannot under pain of sinning in a grave matter vote for the chief of a party who has formulated so publicly such an error.'[177] The clergy supported the Conservative candidates even in cases where the Liberals signed the required pledge. Against the solid opposition of the clergy, broken only by the neutrality of Bishop Emard of Valleyfield, Laurier could only rely on Quebec's pride in its native son and in Israel Tarte's organizing ability. Quebec, given the choice of following its bishops or electing the first French-Canadian prime minister of Canada, voted more than three to one for Laurier. It was thanks to this Quebec majority that the Liberals took power and kept it for fifteen years.

Laurier's first task as prime minister was to settle the Manitoba school question. Negotiations between Ottawa and Winnipeg were made easier by the fact that the Liberals held power in both capitals, and that Laurier was pledged to the use of 'sunny ways' rather than the big stick. The Laurier-Greenway Agreement—actually made by Israel Tarte and Clifford Sifton—met with favor in moderate quarters when it was announced on November 19, 1896, though it was denounced by both the Manitoba Orangemen and by Archbishop Langevin, who was supported by most of the Quebec bishops. The days of the 'Holy War' were recalled as the leading Liberal journal of Quebec, *L'Electeur*, was banned in a pastoral letter signed by Archbishop Bégin of Quebec, Bishop Laflèche, Bishop Gravel of Nicolet, Bishop Blais of Rimouski, and Bishop Labrecque of Chicoutimi.[178] The paper was condemned for disrespect to the hierarchy, for criticizing clerical intervention in education, and for reproducing a pamphlet by Laurier's intimate friend L.-O. David, *Le Clergé canadien, Sa Mission, et Son Oeuvre*. In this work David, outraged by the hierarchy's support of the Conservatives on the school question, criticized the policy of the hierarchy from their opposition to the *Patriotes* down to the present day, while professing his faith in a less political Catholicism. The same five bishops sought and won condemnation of the pamphlet at Rome, where it was put on the *Index* in December 1896.

But the Liberals stood firm against this assault on the party in Quebec. They won a contested election involving undue influence in Champlain, where the *curés* had declared it mortal sin to vote for a Liberal; and in the Bonaventure by-election of March 1897 the Liberal candidate, J.-F. Guité, refused to sign the pledge exacted by Bishop Blais to vote against the Laurier-Greenway Agreement. Guité was elected by double the previous Liberal majority, after his statement: 'I am a Catholic, and in all questions of faith and morals I am ready to accept without restriction the decisions of the Church. In all political questions I claim the freedom enjoyed by every British subject . . . I cannot before God and my conscience renounce the freedom of exercising my privilege as a member to the best of my judgment."[179]

In addressing the *Club National* of Montreal in December, Laurier clarified his own position and restrained the anti-clericalism of such inveterate *Rouges* as Honoré Beaugrand, who had proclaimed in *La Patrie* after the banning of *L'Electeur* a struggle to the death between the government and the hierarchy. Laurier spoke thus to the young Liberals:

> Let me give you a word of good counsel. During your career you will have to suffer many things which will appear to you as supreme injustices. Let me say to you that you should never let your religious convictions be affected by the acts of men. Your convictions are immortal. Their foundation is eternal. Let your convictions be always calm, serene, and superior to the inevitable trials of life. Show to the world that Catholicism is compatible with the exercise of liberty in its highest acceptation; show that the Catholics of the country will render to God what is God's, to Caesar what is Caesar's.[180]

And in a personal letter to Beaugrand, who was forced to sell *La Patrie** by clerical pressure, Laurier made a revealing statement of their differences: 'I am a liberal like yourself, but we do not belong to the same school. I am a disciple of Lacordaire.'[181]

Because of the difficult position in which the Quebec Liberals stood after the election of Laurier, an appeal to Rome was launched. Abbé Proulx of Saint-Lin, an old friend of Laurier who had stood by him on the school question, and the Chevalier Drolet of Papal Zouave fame were dispatched to Rome, where Archbishop Langevin likewise hastened to support the hierarchy's stand. Abbé Proulx carried semi-private credentials from Laurier, urging a statement of doctrine from Rome 'which would have the effect of bringing regrettable abuses to an end, maintaining peace and harmony in our country, and reassuring the consciences of Catholics.'[182] In a letter to Drolet at Rome, Laurier regretted the prospect of a war of religion in Canada and the attacks which had been made upon him at Rome, but said that his religious convictions had not been shaken 'by the attacks of those whose mission it is to preach Christian charity.' He added: 'It is a singular thing that these violent acts,

* The paper was purchased by Israel Tarte's sons.

this ignorance of conditions in our own country, this war to which we are going to be exposed, far from estranging me from the Church, draw me closer to it. I feel how superior religion is to all that often is done in the name of religion.'[183]

To support the unofficial envoys went a petition to the Pope from forty-five Catholic Liberal members of Parliament, urging a renewal of Pius IX's prohibition of clerical intervention in politics. But Abbé Proulx found himself outweighed at Rome by the opposition of all the Quebec hierarchy except Bishop Emard, and returned home in December. Meanwhile the bishops prepared a collective pastoral against the Laurier-Greenway Agreement. So Laurier sent his solicitor-general, Charles Fitzpatrick, and Charles Russell, the son of the English chief justice, supplied with letters from Cardinal Vaughan and the Duke of Norfolk and legal opinion from Edward Blake, to Rome to argue the Liberal case and to urge the sending of an apostolic delegate.

The appointment of Mgr. Merry del Val, a thirty-two-year-old confidential chamberlain of the Pope and a schoolmate of Russell, soon followed. Mgr. del Val arrived in Canada in March 1897, and spent several months consulting with the Quebec and Ontario bishops and clergy, and many leading laymen, both Catholic and Protestant. Bishop Laflèche made the mistake of patronizing the young delegate, whose Spanish temperament did not take kindly to the old ultramontane leader's presumption. Laurier soon achieved friendly terms with the delegate, and without any public statement pressure was exerted which ended the 'Holy War.' In May the Liberals swept the provincial elections in Quebec. The bishops had been ordered to suspend all action pending Rome's decision, and Abbé Proulx happily expressed the opinion that 'the number of mortal sins in this country will be diminished by at least one.'[184]

Leo XIII's encyclical *Affari vos*, given at Rome on December 9, 1897 and issued in Canada a month later, justified the hierarchy's protests against the 'unjust' Manitoba law of 1890, which had persecuted Catholic education, and called the Laurier-Greenway Agreement 'defective, imperfect, insufficient.' But it stated that in seeking complete justice, 'the rules of moderation, of meekness, and of brotherly charity were not to be lost sight of,' and meanwhile Catholics were urged that 'wherever the law or the situation or the friendly disposition of individuals offer them some means of lessening the evil and of better averting its dangers, it is altogether becoming and useful that they make use of these means and draw from them the utmost possible advantage.' The provincial plan of improving public instruction was pronounced 'great and noble,' and Catholics were urged to make their schools rival the most flourishing in methods and efficiency.[185] Though the encyclical made neither camp wholly happy, and consequently was twisted to suit the ends of each, it did put a final end to the 'Holy War.' Concessions were duly made on either side, and when the new Liberal premier of Quebec, F.-X. Marchand, sought to achieve the old Liberal goal of putting the schools under government control, he was blocked by the pressure exerted upon Laurier by Archbishop Bruchési of Montreal, who was also an advocate of 'sunny ways.' Liberalism had been restored to good standing in Catholic Quebec, but in the process it was largely purged of its traditional anti-clericalism.

Cartier's dream of another Quebec in the West was doomed forever by the flood of multi-national immigration into that region under the Laurier regime. But Riel's dream came true, as the West became the new home of the poor and oppressed of Europe. The growing dominance of English Canadians in the West, the reaction to the Riel troubles, and the desire to force assimilation, deprived the western French Canadians of the constitutional guarantees for their language and their schools which Cartier had carefully written into the Manitoba Act. The Laurier-Greenway Agreement was the first of a series of compromises in the matter of educational rights in the West which embittered French-Canadian feeling and furthered the development of a provincial nationalism in Quebec.

The French Canadians became convinced that they stood on a basis of equality with their English compatriots only in Quebec, despite their constitutional guarantees, and that their brethren in the West were oppressed by the English majority. The question of the rights of the minority groups in the West has remained a thorn in the flesh of French Canada down to the present day, and the only hope of healing this old wound lies in English-Canadian acceptance of the doctrine that Canada is a bilingual and bicultural nation, and that the rights of the French language are not confined to Quebec. Some evidence that this hope may be realized lies in the growing tendency of English Canadians in the West to regard Riel as a regional hero rather than as a French traitor.

Notes

[1] The *Métis* ('mixed') people were the human result of the French tendency to go native when trade or exploration took them to the Great Lakes or beyond where 'neither *curé* . . . nor Jesuit nor governors existed,' as Denonville put it. M. Giraud, *Le Métis canadien: son rôle dans l'histoire des provinces de l'Ouest* (Paris 1945), 312. Despite the opposition of Church and State and, in the case of some tribes, of the Indians themselves, the number of mixed unions increased and by 1871 the offspring of French and Indians numbered 9,810. The *Métis* supplied much of the personnel of the fur trade in the West. They remained distinct from the French Canadians, unlike the halfbreeds of Quebec, for the children of these western unions were usually assimilated into the mother's family and reared a

savages. But they remained a group apart from both whites and Indians and there was no great unity between the French *Métis* and the smaller number of English or Scottish halfbreeds who originated in the Hudson's Bay Company posts.

[2] A. S. Morton, *A History of the Canadian West to 1870–1* (London, n.d.), 645, 581.

[3] Morton, 802.

[4] *Ibid.*, 651; Giraud, 533–4, 255–6.

[5] Morton, 803–5.

[6] Giraud, 612; Morton, 'The New Nation,' in *TRSC 1939*, 137–45.

[7] Giraud, 920–1. *Métis* unrest, due to poverty and dissatisfaction with the Hudson's Bay Company monopoly, led to risings in 1815–16, and near insurrections in 1826–7. Giraud, 550–93, 727, 742.

[8] Morton, 812; Giraud, 790–1.

[9] Morton, 827–9; T. W. Blegen, 'James Wickes Taylor,' in *Minnesota History Bulletin*, I (Nov. 1915), No. 4, 170–1. In 1856 Colonel C. F. Smith, U.S.A., ordered the *Métis* to stop crossing the border on their annual buffalo hunts, which aroused the Sioux (Morton, 825; Giraud, 828).

[10] Morton, 836–7.

[11] Morton, 844–5.

[12] Morton, 852.

[13] J. W. Taylor, 'Relation between the United States and Northwestern British North America,' *37th Congress, 2nd Session, House Executive Documents*, X, No. 146, Serial 1138; Blegen, 175.

[14] Morton, 854–6.

[15] Kennedy, *Const. Doc.*, 542, Quebec Resolutions, No. 10. This provision became No. 11 of the Westminster Palace Resolutions, and Sec. 146 of the B.N.A. Act, 1867. Kennedy, 611, 633. The Canadian delegates who waited on the colonial secretary on 15 February 1865 declared: 'It appears that nothing deserving the name of "government" exists in the populated portion of the territory known as the "Red River Settlement"' (Morton, 862).

[16] Morton, 863.

[17] G. F. G. Stanley, *The Rise of Western Canada* (London, 1936), 57; Blegen, 179. Taylor proposed the annexation of Western Canada in the absence of a transcontinental Canadian railway and of a Great Lakes seaway. J. W. Taylor, 'Commercial Relations with British America,' 12 June 1866; *39th Congress, 1st Sess., House Ex. Docs.*, No. 128, Serial 1263; Blegen, 178–9.

[18] Morton, 864–5.

[19] *Ibid.*, 866.

[20] *Ibid.*, 870–1.

[21] *Ibid.*, 667.

[22] *Ibid.*, 874.

[23] Blegen, 187–8.

[24] Morton, 880.

[25] *Ibid.*, 881–2.

[26] *The Canadian North-West* (Can. Archives, No. 9, Ottawa, 1915), II, 884–7.

[27] Morton, 882–3.

[28] *Ibid.*, 881, 888–91; *Can. North-West*, II, 881–2, Dennis-McDougall, 27 October 1869.

[29] *Ibid.*, 884–8, 882–3; *Can. North-West*, II, 890–2, Mactavish's proclamation, 16 November 1869.

[30] *Ibid.*, 887.

[31] *Can. North-West*, II, 893–5, McDougall's proclamation, 1 December 1869.

[32] J. Pope, *Memoirs of Sir John A. Macdonald* (Toronto, n.d.), 407–9, Macdonald-McDougal, 20 November 1869.

[33] *Can. North-West*, II, 896–8, Dennis' Commission, 1 December 1869.

[34] *Ibid.*, 891–2.

[35] A. G. Morice, O.M.I., *History of the Catholic Church in Western Canada* (Toronto, 1910), II, 34.

[36] J. Pope (*ed.*), *Correspondence of Sir John A. Macdonald* (Toronto, n.d.) 106–7, Macdonald-J. Rose, 23 November 1869.

[37] Morton, 887.

[38] *Can. North-West*, II, 900–1, royal proclamation, 6 December 1869; 908–13, Howe-McDougall, 24 December 1869.

[39] Morice, II, 13–14, Taché-Gov.-Gen., 23 July 1870, *Northwest Committee Evidence*, 42.

[40] Morton, 896–7.

[41] *Ibid.*, 900–2.

[42] *Ibid.*, 903; Stanley, 96, 108.

[43] Morton, 904.

[44] *Ibid.*, 907–9.

[45] *Ibid.*, 908.

[46] *Ibid.*, 910.

[47] Morice, II, 56.

[48] *Ibid.*, II, 58–9. Cf. Morton, 911.

[49] Morton, 912; Stanley, 117 *n.* 36 and 37.

[50] Kennedy, *Const. Docs.*, 640–4, the Manitoba Act, 1870. Section 22 provided: 'In and for the Province, the said Legislature may exclusively make laws in relation to Education subject and according to the following provisions:

(1) Nothing in any such Law shall prejudicially affect any right or privilege with respect to Denominational Schools which any class of persons have by Law or practice in the Province at the Union:

(2) An appeal shall lie to the Governor-General in Council from any Act or decision of the Legislature of the Province, or of any Provincial Authority, affecting any right or privilege of the Protestant or Roman Catholic minority of the Queen's subjects in relation to Education.

(3) In case any such Provincial Law, as from time to time seems to the Governor-General in Council requisite for the due execution of the provisions of this section, is not made, or in case any decision of the Governor-General in Council on any appeal under this section is not duly executed by the proper Provincial Authority in that behalf, then, and in every such case, as far only as the circumstances of each case require, the Parliament of Canada may make remedial laws for the due execution of the provisions of this section, and of any decision of the Governor-General in Council under this section.'

Section 23 provided: 'Either the English or the French language may be used by any person in the debates of the Houses of Legislature, and both of these languages shall be used in the respective Records and Journals of these Houses: and either of those languages may be used by any person or in any pleading or Process, in or issuing from any Court of Canada established under the British North America Act, 1867, or in or from all or any of the Courts of the Province. The Acts of the Legislature shall be printed and published in both those languages.'

[51] Morton, 916–17; Giraud, 1111 *n.* 3.

[52] Morton, 911–12.

[53] *Ibid.*, 917.

[54] Stanley, 143; C. P. Stacey, *Canada and the British Army, 1846–1871* (London, 1937), 239.

[55] Morton, 919; Giraud, 1112.

[56] Morton, 910–20; Stanley, 165; Giraud, 1111.

[57] Morice, II, 64; Giraud, 1112–13 and *n.* 8.
[58] Morton, 920, Archibald-Macdonald, 9 October 1871.
[59] Morice, II, 72–3.
[60] *CHAR 1940*, 46–7, R. O. MacFarlane, 'Manitoba Politics and Parties after Confederation.'
[61] *Ibid.*, 49–50; Giraud, 1117.
[62] PAC: Macdonald Papers, North-West Rebellion, III, 104, 108; Giraud, 13–15.
[63] *Epitome of Parliamentary Documents in connection with the North-West Rebellion, 1885* (Ottawa, 1886), 221, Riel's testimony.
[64] Mgr. A. Taché, *L'Amnestie* (Montréal, 1874); *Encore l'amnestie* (n.p., 1875).
[65] Stanley, 174.
[66] PAC: Riel Papers, Canada Public, Dept. of Justice, Riel Rebellion, Vol. 61, No. 3, Bourget-Riel, 14 juillet 1875, Bourget-Riel, 2 janvier 1876.
[67] J. A. Jonasson, 'The Background of the Riel Rebellion,' in *Pacific Historical Review*, III (Sept. 1934), 3, 278.

In 1878–9 his friend Father Fabien Barnabé of Keesville, N.Y., sought to find a job for Riel in New York or the West. By June 7, 1879 Riel was planning to leave St. Paul for Dakota or Montana, and Father Barnabé had recommended him to Archbishop Ireland of St. Paul as a founder of Catholic colonies on the frontier. The Jesuits of Fort Benton and St. Peter's Mission, with whom Riel later became on friendly terms, discouraged his political activities, but nonetheless he sought to organize the American *Métis* and vote them in a bloc for the Republican Party in 1882. Riel was indicted for this in 1883, but the case was dropped. J. K. Howard, *Strange Empire* (New York, 1952), 319–22, 334–50.

Riel also interested himself in Indian affairs and was accused of planning an invasion of the North-West Territories to return to the Indians and *Métis* the lands which the whites were occupying (Giraud, 1195).

[68] Giraud, 1163.
[69] *Ibid.*, 1179–94.
[70] *Epitome*, 323–4, V. Vegreville-E. Deville, 19 janvier 1884.
[71] *Ibid.*, 324–5.
[72] Morice, II, 166.
[73] *Ibid.*, 167–8.
[74] *Epitome*, 386–7, 'Report of the Delegates'; 387–8, Riel delegates, 5 June 1884.
[75] *Ibid.*, 383–4, André-Dewdney, 7 July 1884; 388–9, André-Dewdney, 21 July 1884.
[76] G. T. Denison, *Soldiering in Canada* (Toronto, 1906), 262–3.
[77] Morice, II, 172.
[78] *Epitome*, 383, Inspector Howe-C.O., N.W. Police, 24 December 1884; 112, Charles Nolin's evidence; 147, Father André's evidence.
[79] Giraud, 1208.
[80] *Epitome*, 99, George Ness' evidence.
[81] Morice, II, 173.
[82] *Epitome*, 96, George Ness' evidence.
[83] *Ibid.*, 51, Riel-Crozier, 21 March 1885.
[84] *Ibid.*, 197, Riel.
[85] *Ibid.*, 99–100, George Ness; 141, Thomas Sanderson; 149, Philip Garnot.
[86] *Ibid.*, 124, Nolin.
[87] *Ibid.*, 105, Henry Walters.
[88] *Ibid.*, 216, 222–3, Riel; 56, Willoughby; 125, Nolin; 150, Garnot.
[89] *Ibid.*, 193, Riel.
[90] *Epitome*, 149, Garnot; 193, Riel. These letters were in the possession of the Crown at Riel's trial.

PAC: Riel Papers, Canada Public, Dept. of Justice, Riel Rebellion, Nos. and 4, Bourget-Riel, 14 juillet 1875, 2 janvier 1876. The relevant passages are follows:

No. 3—'God, who has always guided and aided you until now, will not abando you in the strongest of your prayers, *for he has given you a mission which y must accomplish in all respects* . . . you will work ceaselessly for the honor of th Faith, for the salvation of souls, and the good of society.' (Italics added

No. 4—'For my part I pray God, who is all good and all merciful, not to abando you and to guide you in all your ways, *so that you shall never wander from t path which Divine Providence has traced out for you for our greatest good and that your country and people.* One must hope and ask that the time of mercy arri for this desolated country and this people afflicted and visited with differe calamities which aggravate its misfortune; but the Faith, which is its on consolation in its hardest tests, will raise it sooner or later from this sta of oppression in order to cover it with honor and good. Be blessed then God and men and have patience in your woes.' (Italics added.)

These are classic examples of the messianic religious dynamic of French Canadian nationalism. They were strong medicine for a disturbed mind.

[91] *Epitome*, 146–8, Father André; 151–3, Father Fourmond.

[92] *Ibid.*, 107, Hillyard Mitchell.

[93] *Ibid.*, 139, Sanderson.

[94] *Ibid.*, 111, Thomas Jackson.

[95] *Ibid.*, 171, Captain Young; 174, General Middleton.

[96] Dept. of Militia and Defence, *Report Upon the Suppression of the Rebellion the North-West Territories, and Matters in Connection Therewith, 1885* (Ottawa, 1886 Frontispiece, 'The North-West Field Forces.'

[97] R. Rumilly, *Histoire*, V, 21.

[98] *Report*, 21.

[99] *Ibid.*, 35–7, 33.

[100] *Ibid.*, 33.

[101] Archives seigneuriales de Lotbinière, T. B. Strange-H.G. Joly, 20 June 188

[102] *Ibid.*, Strange-Joly, July 1885.

[103] *Report*, xi.

[104] *Ibid.*, 68.

[105] *Toronto News*, 18 May 1885; Rumilly, V, 36.

[106] *Epitome*, 4, Memorandum of Minister of Justice, 25 November 1885.

[107] *Ibid.*, 12, Campbell-Robinson, Osler, Burbridge, Casgrain, Scott, 20 Ju 1885.

[108] *Ibid.*, 13, jury list.

[109] *Ibid.*, 48.

[110] Rumilly, V, 63.

[111] *Epitome*, 14–16. The charge against Riel was brought by Alexander Dav Stewart, chief of police of Hamilton, Ontario.

[112] *Ibid.*, 154–5, Dr. Roy.

[113] *Ibid.*, 161, 163, Dr. Clark; 164, Dr. Wallace.

[114] *Ibid.*, 168, Dr. Jukes.

[115] *Ibid.*, 195, 197, Riel.

[116] *Ibid.*, 220–1, 224, 195, 198, 215, 217–19, Riel.

[117] *Ibid.*, 195–7, Riel.

[118] *Ibid.*, 213, verdict.

[119] *The Queen vs. Louis Riel* (Ottawa, 1886), 176–98, Queen's Bench Cou Appeal.

[120] *Ibid.*, 199–202, Privy Council judgment.

[121] Skelton, I, 308.

[122] *La Presse*, 2 août 1885; Rumilly, V, 64.

[123] Rumilly, V, 66.

[124] *Ibid.*, V, 55–6.

[125] *Ibid.*, V, 43, 68–9.

[126] *Epitome*, 235–87, petitions.

[127] Stanley, 450 *n.* 11, gives the full text of the medical reports, not printed in *Epitome*, 1–2.

[128] Skelton, I, 312.

[129] ASL: T. B. Strange-H. G. Joly, 10 decembre 1885.

[130] PAC: Riel Papers, Canada, Miscellaneous Docs., XIV, 1660–1938, 73, Riel-R.P. Vital Fourmond, 5 août 1885.

[131] *Queen vs. Riel*, 204–5, Father André-F. X. Lemieux, 31 August 1885.

[132] *La Presse*, 17 novembre 1885; Rumilly, V, 111.

[133] *Ibid.*, 113.

[134] *Ibid.*, 121, Laurier, Trudel; 123, Mercier.

[135] *Ibid.*, 125–6, Champs de Mars resolutions.

[136] *Ibid.*, 99, Macdonald.

[137] Rumilly, *Laflèche*, 269.

[138] ASTR: Laflèche-Abbé Boucher, 5 mai 1885.

[139] Rumilly, *Laflèche*, 267, Taché-Laflèche, 26 mai 1885.

[140] ASTR: Laflèche-J.-O. Prince, 14 fevrier 1887; *La Minerve*, 14 mars 1887; Rumilly, *Laflèche*, 282.

[141] Rumilly, *Laflèche*, 278–9, Laflèche-H. Montplaisir, 17 janvier 1887.

[142] *Toronto Mail*, 23 November 1885; J. Willison, *Sir Wilfrid Laurier & the Liberal Party* (Toronto, 1903), 450–1 *n.*

[143] *Toronto Mail*, 25 November 1885; Rumilly, V, 119; Skelton, I, 316.

[144] *Orange Sentinel*, Skelton, I, 316–17.

[145] Skelton, I, 321.

[146] *Ibid.*, 322.

[147] *Ibid.*, 323.

[148] *Ibid.*, 323, 325.

[149] *Ibid.*, 326; Rumilly, V, 55–6.

[150] Barthe, Laurier, 256.

[151] Rumilly, *Honoré Mercier* (Montréal, 1936), 325.

[152] *Ibid.*, 326.

[153] *Ibid.*, 339.

[154] *Ibid.*, 353.

[155] *A Complete and Revised Edition of the Debate on the Jesuit Estates Act* (Ottawa, 1889), 3.

[156] *Toronto Mail*, 14 March 1888; *ibid.*, 14.

[157] *Ibid.*, 57.

[158] Rumilly, *Mercier*, 363–4.

[159] *Ibid.*, 365.

[160] Barthe, 527–8. Retranslated in part.

[161] Rumilly, *Mercier*, 375.

[162] *Ibid.*, 377.

[163] *Ibid.*, 467.

[164] *Courier du Canada*, 9 mars 1892; *ibid.*, 479.

[165] *Ibid.*, 489.

[166] *Ibid.*, 518.

[167] *Ibid.*, 519–20.

[168] *Ibid.*, 526.

[169] ASTR: Fonds Laflèche (1848–9, 1862–84), Laflèche-Curé Labelle, 18 novembre 1879.

[170] *La Minerve*, 30 janvier 1889; Rumilly, *Laflèche*, 294.

[171] E. Hamon, *Les Canadiens Français de la Nouvelle-Angleterre* (Québec, 1891), 70

[172] *Ibid.*, 134.

[173] M. Wade, 'The French Parish and *Survivance* in Nineteenth Century New England,' in *Catholic Historical Review*, XXXVI (July 1950) No. 2, 163–89.

[174] Skelton, I, 392.

[175] *Ibid.*, I, 475.

[176] *Mandements de Montréal*, XII, 196, Joint Pastoral, 16 mai 1896; Skelton, I, 482; Rumilly, VIII, 60.

[177] Skelton, I, 483; Rumilly, VIII, 62–3.

[178] Rumilly, VIII, 141.

[179] Skelton, II, 30.

[180] *Ibid.*, 31.

[181] *Ibid.*

[182] Skelton, II, 34.

[183] Skelton, II, 36 *n.*, Laurier-Drolet, 15 December 1896.

[184] Rumilly, VIII, 160.

[185] Skelton, II, 41–2; Rumilly, IX, 37. In most Quebec dioceses the encyclical was read from the pulpit along with a circular on education by Archbishop Bégin, reportedly written by Bishop Bruchési (Rumilly, IX, 42–3).

CHAPTER IX

IMPERIALISM *vs.* NATIONALISM

(1867–1904)

THE BOER WAR split open the cleft between French and English Canadians which had been developing since 1867, and created a deep division between them which has lasted until the present day. Behind this split and behind the internal conflicts which have already been recounted was the interplay of two great, opposed forces, Canadian nationalism and British imperialism. The ethnic division caused by the Riel Rising of 1885 and by the bitter disputes which ensued over the rights of the French language outside Quebec did much to align English Canadians largely in the imperialist camp and French Canadians largely in the nationalist one. But in fact Canadian nationalism in the post-Confederation period was English in origin, and in the last analysis ever since the Conquest the French Canadians have placed a greater reliance on the British connection than their fellow-countrymen, since it affords a certain security to a minority group which has lacked confidence in the goodwill of the majority.

Only in recent years have the French Canadians begun to realize that all English Canadians are not imperialists, and that indeed many of them are as much Canadian nationalists as any French Canadian. As the jingoistic 'Anglo-Saxon' imperialism of the turn of the century gradually lost its compulsive emotional force, the English Canadians have also learned that much was to be said for the French Canadians who fought it tooth and nail. But, as always in time of crisis, the ultraimperialists and the ultranationalists came to represent the ethnic groups of which they were in reality merely the extremist fringes. The conflict between nationalism and imperialism constituted one of the bitterest chapters in Canadian history, and has left lasting wounds which still hinder Canada's national development.

The conflict may well be considered a vicious circle, for as J. A. Hobson pointed out, 'Aggressive Imperialism is an artificial stimulant of nationalism in peoples too foreign to be absorbed and too compact to be permanently crushed.'[1] The 'pan-Anglo-Saxon' idea not only largely swallowed up early English-Canadian nationalism; it stimulated French-Canadian nationalism with its strong tendency toward isolationism, and thus largely defeated the chief purposes of its prophets. Canada was fortunate in being governed during fifteen crucial years of this conflict by a French-Canadian prime minister who possessed an equal devotion to the spirit of British political institutions and to the ideal of Canadian nationhood, and who was able to rally most of his compatriots behind his leadership. Despite the bitterness of the conflict, Laurier held office for a longer consecutive period than any Canadian prime minister had yet done. One of the darkest blots in the record of French and English relations might have been avoided if he had still been in power during the 1917–18 conscription crisis whose roots went back to the Boer War. But he was driven from office in 1911 by a momentary combination of the extreme nationalists and aggressive imperialists, political enemies on either side of the middle path he always favored. For French Canada, with its devotion to the leader principle, the conflict between nationalism and imperialism is largely the story of Laurier and Henri Bourassa, but the ideological background of their long duel has been too much neglected by both French and English Canadians.

I

The ebb and flow of imperialism is one of the remarkable features of nineteenth-century British history. At the outset the old mercantilism which had stimulated the conquest of the first British Empire in the previous century was still firmly in the saddle. Its rigorous application in Canada had much to do with the 1837–8 revolts, though it was already going out of fashion in England. But thanks to the efforts of Durham, Buller, and Wakefield, who were 'the truest Imperialists of their time,'[2] Canada did not go the way of the American colonies. Indeed, their disciple John Stuart Mill largely anticipated the modern view of the Empire as a commonwealth of autonomous nations.[3] The Colonial Reformers' twofold remedy of responsible colonial government and systematic colonization was only half applied to an ailing Canada, for after the great movement of the middle third of the century which populated Ontario, British emigration declined until 1897, while the Canadians had to achieve for themselves the responsible government which Durham had intended should be a primary feature of the new regime. In the face of rapidly rising Little Englandism, the Canadians also gradually acquired many of the powers which Durham had intended should be reserved to the imperial authorities.

Carlyle's cry of 'Why should not London long continue the All-Saxon home?'[4] was not at all typical of English opinion in the 1860's, although his chosen-people complex and his concept of 'Saxondom' were adopted by the imperialists of the '80's and '90's.

'ar more representative were the views of Richard Cobden and ohn Bright, who favored 'this Confed. scheme, because I thought t was a step in the direction of an amical separation'[5] and believed hat 'separation wd. be better for us & better for her,'[6] while from is snug berth in the Post Office Anthony Trollope preached Canadian rebellion and independence.[7] 'Mr. Mothercountry' at he Colonial Office hated to have his leisure disturbed by business rom the colonies; parliament took no interest in colonial debates; nd there was no real English public opinion on Canadian matters ntil indignation arose at the failure of the Canadian Militia Bill of 862, which would have relieved the English taxpayer of some of his olonial burdens. So vast was the prevailing ignorance of colonial natters in England that the London *Times* came out flatly for Montreal as the new Canadian capital, under the impression that t was in 'loyal' Upper Canada.[8] Alexander Galt was able to assert Canada's financial autonomy in 1859 without rebuke from an pathetic Colonial Office,[9] while in 1866 Macdonald almost ucceeded in his effort to have the new Dominion called the 'Kinglom of Canada,' in token of an independent relationship to the Crown which was not finally to win formal recognition until the Balfour Declaration of 1926.[10]

As far as the French Canadians were concerned, the Oxford don Goldwin Smith, then high in favor in political circles, voiced English pinion when he wrote in 1863: 'Our presence in Canada artificilly preserves from absorption the French Canadian element, an ntediluvian relic of old French society with its torpor and bigotry, tterly without value for the purposes of modern civilization.'[11] mith ignored both the existence of a theory of French-Canadian ationality, and Lord Acton's dictum of the previous year that 'at ne present day the theory of nationality is not only the most powerul auxiliary of revolution but its actual substance in the movements f the last three years.'[12] But Smith, like other early prophets of the ew imperialism, was thinking in purely 'Anglo-Saxon' terms, coneniently ignoring the fact that a great part of the British Empire vas not 'Anglo-Saxon.' For him, the dismemberment of the empire night be a step towards 'the moral federation of the whole Englishpeaking race throughout the world.'[13]

This, too, was the vision of Charles Dilke, later under-secretary of ne Foreign Office, who visited and then described the Englishpeaking world in his *Greater Britain* (1869), a book with the revealing ubtitle of 'Saxon Sketches.' In his preface Dilke confessed that his uiding idea was 'a conception, however imperfect, of the grandeur f our race, already girdling the earth, which it is destined, perhaps, ventually to overspread.'[14] He was thrilled by America, for there the peoples of the earth are being fused together, but they are run together into an English mould. . . . Through America, England i speaking to the world.' Dilke's 'Greater Britain' was to consist o America, Australasia, and India. French Canada was an obstacl to his scheme, for 'not only here, but elsewhere, a French "depen dency" is France transported; not a double of the France of today but a mummy of the France of the time of the "colony's" founda tion.'[15] Passing northward into Canada from the United States Dilke was depressed by the 'fog of unenterprise [which] hung ove the land; roads were wanting, houses rude, swamps undrained fields unweeded, plains untilled.'[16] Accustomed to the neat field of a crowded England, Dilke, like the earlier emigrants of the Britis American Land Company and many another traveller, contraste frontier country unfavorably with New England which had bee pioneered a century or two earlier.

Dilke felt that 'in all history there is nothing stranger than th narrowness of mind which has led us to see in Canada a piece c England and in America a hostile country.'[17] He saw a little mor clearly into the North American triangular relationship than thos at home: 'That the Canadians hate the Americans can be no reaso why we should spend blood and treasure in protecting them agair the consequences of their hate. . . . Canada, perhaps, can defen herself, but we most certainly cannot defend her; we provoke muc more than we assist.'[18] But it was to be some years before Canad recovered from her fright at the threats of a militant North to fulf Manifest Destiny by the conquest of its northern neighbor, once th South was subdued; and some years before Canada resentfull realized that English sacrifices of her territory and rights nourishe Anglo-American friendship.

The annexationist *Rouges* might have welcomed Dilke's observa tions on the political future of Canada, but his concluding view tha 'Saxondom will rise triumphant from the doubtful struggle' with th 'cheaper races'[19] would have been gall and wormwood to then The 'Anglo-Saxon' racism of which Dilke was the first popula spokesman nourished the swelling fervor of the imperialist movemer until the Boers humbled English pride of race at the turn of th century. This British chosen-people complex, which steadil acquired more adherents as France lost its European hegemony an Britain filled an ever larger place in the world at large, came int head-on collision with the French-Canadian one nourished by th messianic nationalism of Bishops Bourget and Laflèche, Riel, an Mercier.

About 1870, the long dominant English anti-colonialism began t weaken. It was replaced by a new imperialism which was at fir commercial in outlook, later political and militaristic, and final became international rather than nationalistic in character. Th roots of the new imperialism were many and diverse, but perhaps the most important factors in its evolution were the rise of the newly united Germany and Italy, the emergence of the United States after its Civil War as a world power, and the growing rivalry England began to experience as 'the workshop of the world' as other nations overtook her original lead in the industrial revolution. The powers launched a frenzied competition for colonies and colonial markets which made England value her empire more dearly and made her fear for her commercial supremacy.

The improvements of communications brought the colonies closer to the mother country, and made possible a greater unity of the empire. The new imperialists were among the leading backers of the Atlantic and Australian cables, of an imperial penny-post, of the 'all-red' line of communications which linked England with the East by way of British steamships and the Canadian Pacific Railway. As England's commercial supremacy was challenged by Germany and the United States, the slogan of 'free trade' gave way to that of 'fair trade,' a term which politely covered a reversion to the old mercantilism under a new system of preferential tariffs within the empire. With such factors at work, the rulers of Britain were pleased to discover that Canada's Confederation, hailed in the 1860's as a step towards emancipation, had increased rather than lessened 'a romantic attachment to the mother country.'[20] An overestimate of this sentiment and a neglect of the concurrent development of Canadian nationalism largely accounted for the failure of the Imperial Federalists.

The forerunner of this movement, which became so influential in the 1880's, was the Colonial Society, later known as the Royal Colonial Institute, which was founded in 1868 and began its meetings in the following year. At the outset it was a non-partisan group whose purpose was to overcome Little Englandism. At its inaugural dinner, attended by notables of the Colonial Office, Gladstone spoke of 'the noble tradition of the unity of the English race.'[21] Its spokesmen, under the leadership of Lord Bury, opposed the ideas of Goldwin Smith and other English colonial separatists with the slogan of 'United Empire.' The note of romantic enthusiasm for the imperial idea which was so marked a feature of the movement in its later stages and its true emotional dynamic was first sounded by the Australian P. F. Labilliere in 1869:

> Englishmen at home and their sons in the colonies should not be foreigners to each other . . . My great desire is to show that the idea of dismembering the British Empire should not be entertained for a moment by any good Englishman or by any good colonial; that the union of the Empire is a sentiment or rather a sacred principle, in devoted loyalty to which we should vie with one another . . .

We have, hitherto, only seen England nursing infant nations. I believe, and ardently hope, that she is destined to retain under her mild sway her colonial children, long after they shall attain the maturity and strength of manhood. I am convinced that the existence of such a relation will not only be of vast moral and material advantage both to the parent nation and to the offspring nations, but will constitute an Empire more splendid than any the world has yet seen.[22]

This was the imperial vision which later inspired Kipling and Newbolt, the bards of empire. Fired by it, the Imperial Federalists in 1869 urged the colonial secretary, Lord Granville, to call a conference of colonial representatives to discuss the present unsatisfactory relations with the mother country. This suggestion was coldly rejected by the anti-imperialist Lord Granville, and its sponsors were dismissed as 'presumptuous busybodies'[23] by the colonial press. But they had succeeded at least in arousing English interest in the colonial question, which was brought to the fore by new agitation in favor of state-aided emigration to the colonies, as a remedy for unemployment resulting from the industrial depression of the period. Organized emigration became a favorite theme of the new imperialists and was to remain one, with the twofold object of relieving distress at home and of consolidating the empire.

The new gospel won the adherence of recruits more notable than the founders of the movement. Ruskin held up colonial expansion as the alternative to Mammon-worship for England: 'This is what she must do, or perish; she must found colonies as fast and as far as she is able, formed of her most energetic and worthiest men;—seizing every piece of fruitful waste ground she can set her foot on and there teaching these her colonists that their chief virtue is to be fidelity to their country and that their first aim is to be to advance the power of England by land and sea. . . .'[24] Less eloquent but more influential was the support of the Liberal politician W. E. Forster and of the historian J. A. Froude. Forster soon became one of the chief leaders of the movement, and his address on 'Our Colonial Empire,' delivered at Edinburgh on November 5, 1875, was one of the first statements urging closer imperial union. Froude advocated the imperialist program in 1870 and 1871; then lapsed into the anti-imperialism of the second Disraeli administration; and finally, after 1880, was closely associated with the Imperial Federation League.

Imperial federation was widely publicized by Edward Jenkins, a Radical social reformer, who was the leading spirit of the Westminster Conference on colonial affairs in July 1871. Arguing against the prevailing policy of drift in colonial relations, he concluded his opening address with evangelical fervor:

> It is not necessary that we should dissolve this marvelous Empire, the upgrowth of an energy and sacrifice unrivaled in the history of races. It is not necessary that we should dismiss from our family circle that vast sisterhood of nations which has grown up under our parental care— . . . we must take our stand on the unity of our race, on the unity of our interests, on language, religion, laws, manners, customs, and a citizenship that are one. What God hath joined together let no man put asunder.[25]

Labilliere, who spoke on 'Imperial and Colonial Federalism' on this occasion, proposed that the central government should concern itself with defence and diplomacy, leaving commercial policy to the colonies. Other imperialists were not so wise, and aroused opposition in the colonies by their Anglo-centric ideas, according to which it was the colonist's duty to sacrifice his economic advantage to England's interests without receiving in return anything more than the moral satisfaction of being British.

The movement, which had been attracting more and more support from both Whigs and Tories, was taken under the wing of the Conservative Party in Disraeli's Crystal Palace speech of June 24, 1872. He accused the Liberals of attempting to, and nearly succeeding in bringing about, 'the disintegration of the Empire of England.'[26] Supporting colonial self-government, he nevertheless urged reservations to it:

> But self-government, in my opinion, when it was conceded, ought to have been conceded as part of a great policy of Imperial consolidation. It ought to have been accompanied by an Imperial tariff, by securities for the people of England for the enjoyment of the unappropriated lands which belonged to the Sovereign as their trustee, and by a military code which should have precisely defined the means and responsibilities by which the colonies should be defended, and by which, if necessary, this country should call for aid from the colonies themselves. It ought, further, to have been accompanied by the institution of some representative council in the metropolis, which would have brought the colonies into constant and continuous relations with the Home Government.[27]

These measures—about whose adoption the Canadian imperialists and nationalists were to contend until well after the First World War—had been neglected by the British Liberals because they slighted the 'moral and political considerations which make nations great'[28] in their preoccupation with the financial burden of the colonies. Disraeli rejoiced that the disintegration of the empire had failed to take place, thanks to 'the sympathy of the colonies for the mother country.'[29] Reconstruction of the colonial empire was a policy adopted by Disraeli more in hope of 'dishing the Whigs, however, than from any great personal conviction, for he had long regarded the 'wretched colonies' as 'a mill-stone round our necks.'[30]

Disraeli added little to the doctrine of imperialism, but he did correctly judge its popularity and promote the development of jingoism and of what Seeley called the bombastic school, which gloried in red spaces—no matter how empty—on the map and in an empire on which the sun never set. It was also in 1872 that Tennyson added a new epilogue to the *Idylls of the King* in which he hymned an 'ever-broadening England' and 'one isle that knows not her own greatness.'[31] Ten years later he was hailing imperial unity in the blatant 'Hands All Round,' and in 1886 he vented his imperialist sentiments in such vociferous verse as:

Sons be welded each and all
Into one Imperial whole,
One with Britain heart and soul!
One life, one flag, one fleet, one throne!
Britons, hold your own.[32]

Like many another Englishman of the day, Tennyson was a nationalist who thought he was an imperialist, and it was because of this same confusion that the Imperial Federation movement failed.

The new imperialism fed on the fears aroused by the mounting armaments of Europe. In 1878 a Colonial Defence Committee was appointed, succeeded in the following year by a Royal Commission on defence which after sitting for three years recommended an imperial *Kriegsverein*. While the armament race did not become serious until Germany began to threaten Britain's mastery of the seas, there was recurrent talk about war for the next decade.[33] Renewed British colonial expansion, coupled with rivalry with a Germany and a France now seeking colonies, also served to nourish the imperialist spirit. The scramble for African and Asiatic colonies was on, with France and Germany challenging Britain's place as the great colonial power, and the third British Empire was in the making. The imperialism of the '70's, which had stressed the tightening of internal ties, now became expansionist and jingoistic, while trade rivalry and protective tariffs abroad tended to give an economic basis to proposals for unification of the empire. The cry of 'trade follows the flag' enlisted the support of both manufacturers and working people for the tremendous expansion of British territory which took place in the 1880's and 1890's, despite the fact that England's colonial rivals remained her best customers, while her colonies accounted for only one-third of her trade.[34] Acute depression in England in 1876–9, 1883–6, and 1893, coupled with vigorous competition abroad, created a fearful and panicky state of mind which also supplied an impetus for the new imperialism.

In 1883 John Robert Seeley popularized the new imperialism with his Cambridge lectures, *The Expansion of England*, which when published sold 80,000 copies in two years.[35] Though his ideas were permeated with a pan-'Anglo-Saxonism,' Seeley cared more for the state than for the race, unlike his predecessor Dilke. Thus, instead of accepting without alarm the prospect of the break-up of the empire, Seeley wished to preserve and strengthen its unity. In his study of the creation of the first British Empire in the eighteenth century he found the keynote of English history: a process of expansion of the English state. To him 'in that century the history of England is not in England but in America and Asia.'[36] From this dictum he evolved the principle that the colonial and European policies of England were merely different aspects of the same great national development.[37] He urged a new view of Greater Britain:

> We must cease altogether to say that England is an island off the northwestern coast of Europe, that it has an area of 120,000 square miles and a population of thirty odd millions . . . When we have accustomed ourselves to contemplate the whole Empire together and call it all England, we shall see here too is a United States. Here too is a great homogeneous people, one in blood, language, religion and laws, but dispersed over a boundless space.[38]

This insular view that the empire was 'one in blood, language, religion, and laws,' with its convenient ignoring of the existence of the French Canadians, the Boers, and the native populations of the greater part of the empire, was to arouse much colonial opposition to Imperial Federation when the theory was applied in practical measures for strengthening the bonds of imperial defence and trade. Seeley, like most Englishmen for three decades to come, was ignorant of the existence of colonial nationalism, which blocked imperial federation until the basic concept of the third British Empire, unity in diversity, was evolved and the British Commonwealth of freely associated autonomous nations was made possible. Seeley was not an original thinker, but he gathered together in eloquent and logical form the arguments for closer imperial union and the retention of the colonies. By his emphasis on the importance of colonial expansion, he brought the colonial question to the fore in the public mind and paved the way for the Imperial Federation League which was launched in 1884.

2

Again it was the Australian Labilliere who took the leading role in founding a society for promoting imperial federation in July 1884. He formed a committee including Captain P. H. Colomb, Sir George Baden-Powell, W. E. Westgarth, J. Dennistoun Wood, and Frederick

Young to further the idea. The committee induced the Liberal leader W. E. Forster to preside over a non-partisan inaugural conference at the Westminster Palace Hotel on August 29, 1884, and to become the first chairman of the Imperial Federation League. The meeting was widely attended by English statesmen of both parties and representatives of colonies—among them James Bryce, Albert Grey (later governor-general of Canada), and D'Alton McCarthy—and received the support of many other influential figures, including Seeley. Among the speakers were Forster, W. H. Smith, a former first lord of the Admiralty; Sir Henry Holland, former under-secretary for the Colonies; Lord Rosebery; Edward Stanhope, former parliamentary secretary to the Board of Trade; Sir Charles Tupper, then high commissioner for Canada; Oliver Mowat, premier of Ontario; and W. Gisbourne, a former New Zealand minister. The resolutions prepared by Labilliere's committee went farther than the colonial spokesmen were prepared to go. Tupper refused to support the original resolution, which expressed a belief that federation or separation were the only alternatives for the empire. After much discussion, unanimous support was given a compromise resolution 'that, in order to secure the permanent unity of the Empire, some form of federation is essential,'[39] and that 'a society be formed of men of all classes to advocate and support the principles of federation.'[40]

At a second meeting on November 18, the Imperial Federation League was formally organized, with Forster as chairman, on the basis of the following resolutions:

> That the object of the League be to secure by Federation the permanent unity of the Empire.
>
> That no scheme of Federation should interfere with the existing right of Local Parliaments as regards local affairs.
>
> That any scheme of Imperial Federation should combine on an equitable basis the resources of the Empire for the maintenance of common interests and adequately provide for an organized defence of common rights.[41]

In the large general committee and smaller executive committee which were charged with the management of the organization, English representatives were preponderant, while the main colonial influence was Canadian. The League came into existence on a wave of imperialist sentiment, and the English press hailed its birth by expressing contempt for the school of Goldwin Smith and other Little Englanders.[42] The League embraced many shades of opinion, with some of its members out-and-out federalists, some interested in consolidation of the empire's military resources, some in preferential trade agreements, and some suspicious of any attempt to encroach upon colonial self-government. Forster himself summed up the situation thus:

> My own impression is that, at first, at any rate, we had better aim at concert among the governments rather than at an imperial parliament. Thanks to the steamship and the telegraph, time and space no longer make such concert very difficult; but distance does prevent a member from being fully in touch with his constituents. We must remember that in order to realise federation, we only want (1) an organization for common defence, and (2) a common foreign policy. Practically, great steps have already been made, not merely as regards defence—thanks to Australian aid—but as regards foreign affairs. I do not believe that any colonial secretary will in future venture to disregard any large self-governing colony in negotiating with any foreign government in matters affecting such colony. . . .[43]

Because of the diversity of aims of its members, the League largely confined itself to propaganda for the general concept of imperial unity. When it attempted to produce a definite plan of federation, it broke up, like the later colonial and imperial conferences for which it paved the way.

Though the first branch of the League was formed in Cape Town before the London organization took form, the Canadian branches played a particularly important part. The parent one was formed in Montreal in 1885 by D'Alton McCarthy and George Denison, with the backing of Archbishop O'Brien of Nova Scotia, Sir Leonard Tilley of New Brunswick, Sir John Schultz of Manitoba, and Alexander McNull of Ontario.[44] It was a center of opposition to the depression-born annexation movement; and in its reliance on imperial preference as a means of combating annexationism, it differed from the League in England, which, with its Liberal chairman and many Liberal members committed to free trade, could not adopt such economic views. Other Canadian branches were formed at Ingersoll and Halifax in 1886, and at Peterborough, Victoria, and Ottawa in 1887. Toronto, the center of United Empire Loyalism, only boarded the bandwagon in 1888 when the Liberals favored commercial union to the United States. Brantford, St. Thomas, Port Arthur, and Orillia then followed Toronto's lead. Meanwhile branches were formed in Australia and New Zealand, where the League sent the Canadian Dr. George R. Parkin, a zealous imperial missionary whom Lord Rosebery called the 'bagman of Empire.'[45]

The League's monthly organ, *Imperial Federation*, was launched in January 1886, and a few months later Lord Rosebery succeeded Forster as chairman upon the latter's death. Rosebery took an active part in the League's work, and his moderate and compromising spirit did much to keep its unyoked horses headed towards a common goal. The League was responsible for the Indian and Colonial Exhibition of 1886, which displayed the varied resources of the empire. In July its executive committee, upon a motion of the Canadian Alexander A. McGoun which was supported by Sir Alexander Galt, the Canadian high commissioner in London, resolved that a deputation should call upon the prime minister or colonial secretary and urge the summoning of a conference of 'acredited representatives of the United Kingdom and of each of the self-governing colonies' for the following purposes:

(1) For placing upon a satisfactory basis the defence of the ports and commerce of the Empire in time of war.

(2) For promoting direct intercourse, commercial, postal and telegraphic, between the countries of the Empire in time of peace—and other means for securing the closer federation or union of all parts of the Empire.[46]

Peter Redpath of Montreal was one of the delegation which waited upon Lord Salisbury on August 11 and was favourably received. Some three months later the Colonial Secretary Stanhope, a leading member of the League, issued invitations to the first Colonial Conference, which assembled at London on April 4, 1887, under the chairmanship of Sir Henry Holland, one of the prominent members of the League and Stanhope's successor as colonial secretary.

The conference was epoch-making. For the first time responsible statesmen from the self-governing colonies had an opportunity to join with those of the mother country in common discussion of certain questions important to both. The conference was not merely a piece of pageantry designed to add to the effect of the celebration of Queen Victoria's Golden Jubilee. Such an assembly supplied a precedent which was not likely to be reversed in a land whose law was based upon precedent, and from Salisbury's opening remarks it was evident that the British Government regarded this meeting as 'the parent of a long progeniture.'[47] Stanhope had specifically excluded political federation from the agenda of the conference in his invitations, and Holland as chairman was very cautious in the debates on commercial union which took place at the insistance of Queensland and the Cape Colony.

The colonies were far more eager for closer imperial union than the mother country. The British delegates were reluctant to discuss the topic of imperial preference, because of the political danger attached to departure from the traditional doctrine of free trade; but they sought the assistance of the colonies in imperial defence, a question which had become urgent with the emergence of German and French naval rivalry. On the other hand the spokesmen of the ape, Victoria, and Queensland favoured closer imperial union rough preferential tariffs and had little hesitation in falling in ith the defence proposals of the Admiralty. Canada's representa-ves were scarcely spokesmen of national feeling: Sir Alexander ampbell, the lieutenant-governor of Ontario, called his country a olony and referred to himself as an Englishman, while Sandford leming of the Canadian Pacific was president of the new Ottawa ranch of the Imperial Federation League. Neither, however, ayed a notable part in the proceedings. The Australian Alfred eakin of Victoria was the leading spokesman of colonial nation-ism at the conference, with his request 'that from this time for-ard, Colonial policy will be considered Imperial policy; that olonial interests will be considered and felt to be Imperial terests.'[48]

But such views were hesitantly received by the English. Salis-ury expressed the opinion that neither a *Zollverein* nor a *Kriegs-rein* was yet possible within the British Empire, and brought rward the question of common action for mutual defence as the est field for present discussion and action. The chief feature of the oncrete British proposals was that the Australians should under-ke the local defence of certain points and strengthen the imperial eet in Australian waters by the addition of a local force. The roposals also involved colonial contributions to a common imperial efence fund. Canada, which enjoyed the protection of two navies ithout cost, thanks to the British squadrons based upon Halifax nd Esquimalt and the Monroe Doctrine, stood pat on the arrange-ient made at the time of Confederation whereby Great Britain ssumed the responsibility of naval defence and Canada of that by nd. Much was made of the value for imperial defence purposes of ie Canadian Pacific Railway, completed the previous year. eyond offering to provide men for the naval service from her tlantic fisheries, Canada made no effort to go. J. H. Hofmeyr of ie Cape Colony offered an argument later echoed in Canada when e said that the colonies must be granted some share or influence in ie making of imperial policy before assuming defence responsi-ilities arising out of it: 'So long as no system of federation or govern-ient in which they (i.e., colonial governments) are represented has een hit upon or developed, so long they cannot be expected in duty ound to defend themselves against the European enemies of ngland.'[49]

But all the colonial spokesmen agreed that there was a common urden to be shared, and none declined outright to share it, although iere was disagreement on the manner of doing so. It was Hofmeyr ho most strongly advocated a proposal for a commercial union hich would solve the problem of colonial contribution to imperial defence by means of an imperial customs tariff. The coloni. secretary opposed the passage of a resolution by the conference i favor of this proposal, however, on the grounds that it was beyon the bounds set forth in Stanhope's invitation, and hence of tl instructions supplied to the delegates by their own government For these reasons the Canadians had taken no part in the discussio: Canada also remained silent on the question of the negotiation commercial treaties by the colonies, in which it already enjoyed privileged position, thanks to Galt and Macdonald's efforts in 18 and 1871. Only on the question of inter-imperial communicatio did the Canadian delegates take a notable part, with the result th: the conference endorsed Sandford Fleming's claims for the Canadia Pacific and urged a cable connecting Canada with Australia.

Sir Samuel Griffeth of Queensland, who had raised the propos: of commercial union which Hofmeyr so ably advocated, expounde at the close of the conference his dream for the future: 'I think w may look forward to seeing this sort of informal Council of tl Empire develop until it becomes a legislative body, at any rate consultative body, and some day, perhaps, a legislative body und conditions that we cannot just now foresee; and that, indee meetings such as this will before long be recognized as part of tl general governing machinery of the Empire.'[50]

3

Although in general it was true that in 1887 the colonial spoke men were the most ardent advocates of imperial federation, whi the British authorities were reluctant to consider any change in tl existing order of imperial affairs and displayed a cautious attitu towards the concrete projects advanced by the imperialists, i Canada the situation was reversed. Canadian national feeling ha been awakened at Confederation. Two groups stood apart from tl new Canadianism: the French Canadians, who had only reluctant been won to the support of Confederation; and the United Empi Loyalists, for whom Britain and the empire came before Canad. The Fathers of Confederation did much to foster a sense of nationali with their prophecies of a greater Canada stretching from sea to se and their willingness to sink ancient local differences to make the dream come true. D'Arcy McGee has been credited with havir done more than any single person to establish faith in the possibili of a 'great northern nation' in America, and with having warme into active life a patriotic love for the new nationality.[51]

The degeneration of party politics before Confederation broug a reaction in the form of the Canada First movement, which orig nated in Toronto in 1868, with William A. Foster, George enison, Henry J. Morgan, Charles Mair, and Robert J. Haliburton s its leading spirits. For these men the nation came before party. hey were active expansionists and preached an Ontario crusade to pen up the West. Mair's enthusiastic letters to the *Toronto Globe* om the Red River in 1868 attracted attention and were reprinted oth in Ontario and in the Maritimes. While at Fort Garry, Mair nlisted the support of Dr. John Schultz, who joined the Canada irst group in March 1869.[52] In December of the same year Schultz ormed a Canadian party among the Ontario men at Fort Garry, ut both he and Mair were seized and imprisoned by Riel. Their anada First colleagues took a leading part in arousing the anti-iel agitation in Ontario by exploiting the death of Thomas Scott, nd forced the hand of the government in dealing with the situation. he fiery Colonel Denison disrupted the Manitoba negotiations of artier and Bishop Taché, and raised the war cry: 'Shall French ebels rule our Dominion?'[53] at a Toronto mass meeting on July 22, 870. He and his colleagues formed a North-West Emigration Aid ociety as a front organization for the Canada First group. It was nder the auspices of this society that Foster published his *Canada irst* pamphlet, which strongly evoked national pride and achieved very wide circulation.

After the close of the first Riel affair, and in the midst of the anti-olitical reaction aroused by the Canadian Pacific scandal, the group ounded a political party under the name of the Canadian National ssociation. Its platform, drafted by Foster and adopted in January 874, called for consolidation of the empire and a voice in treaties ffecting Canada; closer trade relations and eventual political con-ection with the British West Indies; an income franchise, secret nd compulsory voting, minority representation; the reorganization f the Senate and the abolition of property qualifications for mem-ers of parliament; the encouragement of immigration and free omesteads; the improvement of the militia system under Canadian fficers; and a tariff designed to encourage native industries. There was a division between the old guard of Canada Firsters and new dherents. Denison and his group were imperial federalists, but Foster and W. H. Howland favored an independent Canada. Howland's speech on December 6, 1873, at the first public meeting of the new party, in which he denounced 'toadyism to English aristocratic usages'[54] and English titles for Canadians, labeled the party as one favoring independence. Some of its members no doubt had that aim, but others sought the achievement of nationality within the empire by rounding out Canadian self-government. Still others were chiefly interested in commercial legislation of the sort later adopted under Macdonald's National Policy, which owed much to the ideas of the Canada Firsters. Most members were moved by anti-annexationist sentiment, and agreed with William Cani that 'the history of the United States was prominently characterize by unswerving efforts to obtain possession of British America.'[55]

Howland took the leading part in the founding of the Nation Association and the National Club, but he could be attacked, as h was by Denison, as the son of an American, and hence hereditaril tainted with disloyalty. For political leadership, therefore, th Canada Firsters looked to Edward Blake and Thomas Moss, whil invoking the name of the martyred D'Arcy McGee as their spiritu father. For two years they possessed a journal of their own in *T Nation*, an independent literary and political journal of high standar founded in 1874. Canada First supported Thomas Moss for electio in West Toronto in 1873, despite the denunciation of the Conservativ press, and with his success at the polls its hopes rose. Edward Blak was undoubtedly affected by the ideals of Canada First in his cel brated Aurora speech of October 1874, when he proclaimed that 'a no distant period the people of Canada would desire that the should have some greater share of control than they now have in th management of foreign affairs. . . . The time will come when tha national spirit which has been spoken of will be truly felt among u when we shall realise that we are four millions of Britons who ar not free.'[56] But the *Globe* and the old-guard Liberals were as hars in condemning Canada First ideas as the Conservative press. I January 1875 Blake set up an independent organ, *The Liberal*, bu in May he re-entered the Mackenzie cabinet which he had qu soon after it took office in 1873, and *The Liberal* ceased pub lication. As minister of justice Blake sought to extend Canada national powers and contributed much to English recognition c her national status. Tentatively he favored imperial federation a an ultimate goal.

Meanwhile Foster had proclaimed the aspirations of the mor ardent members in his February 1875 address to the Nationa Association in which he said:

> We no more advocate Independence than we advocate the Day c Judgment. There are those among us who think, just as Mr. Gladston Mr. Lowe, Mr. Brown, Sir Alexander Galt, Mr. Blake and others think that the relations of Canada to the Empire are proper subjects for dis cussion; that some day or other separation may or must come, and tha now is the time at least to begin to prepare for it. England has bee trying for years to make us stand upon our own feet. The troops hav been withdrawn. We are allowed to legislate as we please and ther is great dislike of interfering with our action. It would rather take u aback if at some early day we were made to strike out for ourselve without any preparation for the event. What must come is either Federa tion of the Empire or Independence.[57]

The regular party organs attacked this statement as treason, with the Grit journals displaying more vigor than the Conservative ones because the unity of the Liberal party was threatened by the popularity of these ideas in its radical wing.

Blake's return to Liberal orthodoxy broke the back of the Canada First movement. Its only other political leader, Moss, soon after quitted parliament for private life. Foster followed suit, for, like Caniff, he became convinced that 'a Canadian political party is an impossibility. No doubt, however, whichever party be in power will hereafter give more prominence to the views originated and urged by the Canadian Association during its brief existence.'[58] Unfortunately, however, neither the Liberals, who had adopted some of Foster's political ideas, nor the Conservatives, who had adopted his economic ones, abandoned the factional use of religious, racial, sectional, and class differences which the Association had decried as barriers to the achievement of national unity.

4

The protective tariff which had been one of the planks of the Canada First platform was put into force in 1879 by the Conservatives under the name of the National Policy. Alexander Mackenzie, as head of the Liberal Government which was defeated in 1878, had opposed protection and maintained the English Liberal tradition of free trade; but his successors in the leadership of the Liberal Party, Blake and Laurier, favored a moderate protective tariff. Laurier personally inclined towards free trade, but the *Parti National* in Quebec, like the Canada Firsters in Ontario, found it politically expedient to favor protection for native industry in the depressed 1870's. But in the 1880's, when Canada became economically stagnant, new economic policies were urged by sections of both parties. Imperial federation and imperial preference found favor in the Tory camp. Although Macdonald was present at the first meeting of the Imperial Federation League in 1884 and expressed sympathy with its aims, in 1888 he formally expressed his belief in the impracticability of anything like an imperial legislature,[59] and characterized as 'an idle dream'[60] the proposal to establish a uniform tariff throughout the empire. However, in 1890 he stated his desire 'that the connection between the mother country and the colonies shall be drawn closer, and that the large groups of colonies shall assume by degrees a position less of dependence and more of alliance.'[61]

Though Macdonald often proclaimed his British loyalty and made political capital of loyalist sentiment, in practice he restrained the enthusiasm of his more imperialist-minded colleagues. In February 1883 he cautioned Galt, then serving as the first Canadian high commissioner in London, against committing himself too much t the 'project of Imperial Federation, which, in my humble opinior can never be worked out.'[62] The instructions given the Canadia delegates to the first Colonial Conference did not authorize suppo of either an imperial tariff or imperial defence. And in 1889, whe Charles Tupper as Canadian high commissioner proposed at London dinner of the Imperial Federation League that a ne colonial conference be called and a policy of mutual preferenti trade be adopted, he was warned by Macdonald to let it be know that he had spoken only for himself and not for Canada.[63] Tuppe somewhat disgruntled, replied to Macdonald that 'although yo and two other members of the Government are on the council the Imperial Federation League, I have stood somewhat aloof. have not disguised the opinion that the difficulties in the way of parliamentary federation were insuperable.'[64]

Macdonald, like the leading English politicians until the adven of Joseph Chamberlain, was content to praise the ideal of imperi federation while opposing any concrete scheme to that end. He wa very much of an opportunist in his attitude towards imperialism Macdonald was in his way a Canadian nationalist, as his fight fo the adoption of the term 'Kingdom of Canada' at Confederation, h share in the Treaty of Washington (1871), his attitude towards th Sudan affair, and his refusal of various imperialist gambits a indicate. It was probably more political necessity than convictio that led him to fight his last election on the cry, 'A British subject was born and a British subject I shall die.'[65] After the Riel affair 1885 had inflamed English-Canadian racial feeling, Macdonald ha to restrain the imperialist hotheads in his own camp who sought holy war against the French Canadians on all fronts, regardless the political necessities which shaped Macdonald's course. Onl after his death did they win sufficient authority in the Conservativ Party to align Quebec against it in a solid Liberal phalanx. Sinc that day the federal Conservative Party has never been a real forc in Quebec.

Since imperial federation and imperial preferential trade foun favor chiefly in Tory quarters, the Liberal party pursued two othe alternatives to the Canadian dilemma. Many Liberals were sym pathetic to the schemes of commercial or customs union with th United States which were advanced in the 1880's and 1890's. Th prophet of this minority group was Goldwin Smith, the brillia Oxford don who first abandoned England for the United State and then the United States for Canada, where from his home i ultra-loyalist Toronto he preached the inevitability of the union English-speaking North America. To him Canada was destined become the Scotland of North America.[66] A larger group of Libera favored independence, which had been preached by Galt and McDougall in the early seventies as the next step in national development after Confederation. In 1878 under Mackenzie and Blake Canada had won the right to self-government in domestic affairs and the right to make her own commercial treaties, and at the outset of his leadership of the Liberal Party Laurier spoke of his hopes for Canadian nationhood: 'The time is coming when the present relations of Great Britain and Cauada must either become closer or be severed altogether. . . . If ever and whenever Canada chooses, to use the language of Lord Palmerston, to stand by herself, the separation will take place not only in peace but in friendship and love . . . But this is not the question of to-day.'[67] In 1889 and 1890 the young Liberals of Toronto favored complete independence, with the support of the *Globe*, which commented in February 1888 in connection with the Atlantic fisheries dispute:

> So long as the Canadian people remain unwilling to assume the responsibility of independent nationality, so long must they expect to be despoiled by the United States with British consent and aid. . . . The truth is that the connection seriously embarrasses England and seriously embarrasses and injures Canada. So long as we insist upon retaining it, we cannot justly complain of suffering for the indulgence in a noble loyalty to a country five-sixths of us never saw.[68]

As an alternative to complete independence, the *Globe* also advocated that the empire should become a league of equal self-governing states under the Crown, thus anticipating the British Commonwealth of Nations born some thirty years later.

With free trade still in the saddle in Britain, Canada had little hope of winning a larger share of that market. Her other and more natural market was the United States, from which she had been largely shut out in 1866 by the termination of the Reciprocity Treaty of 1854 and to which she had since been unable to win greater access, though both Liberal and Conservative administrations had gone more than halfway to meet the Americans. Now, for the first time since the Civil War, the high-tariff Republican party was out of power, while American manufacturers were as anxious for new markets as were the producers of Canadian raw materials.

In 1887 Erastus Wiman, a Canadian who had made his fortune in the States and was interested in Canadian telegraph companies, proposed not mere limited reciprocity but complete free trade between Canada and the United States, with a common tariff against the outside world. Wiman owed the idea to Samuel Ritchie, an American capitalist interested in Ontario railways and the Sudbury ore deposits, and to Hezekiah Butterworth, his legal advisor, who was a member of Congress. Wiman's scheme was supported by Goldwin Smith and found favor in farming, mining, and lumbering circles in Canada. The movement centered in Ontario and received the support of the *Toronto Mail*, then in revolt against 'French domination' as a result of the Riel episode, and of the *Globe*, which thought commercial union would favor the development of national and imperial sentiment. Macdonald and Langevin, with their close ties to the protected manufacturers of Ontario and Quebec, were not interested in Wiman's proposal; but Tupper, hailing from the Maritimes which favored low tariffs, was in a different position. At Wiman's suggestion Tupper visited Washington in 1887 and consulted directly with Secretary of State Bayard, thus short-circuiting the customary triangular negotiations through London. He offered trade reciprocity in exchange for reciprocity of fishing rights. The subsequent Fisheries Treaty was killed in the United States Senate, but a precedent had been established for direct negotiations between Ottawa and Washington.

On the Liberal side, Laurier was not prepared to endorse commercial union, but favored the traditional Liberal program of reciprocity: 'I may say—and it is my actual policy—that the time has come to abandon the policy of retaliation followed thus far by the Canadian government, to show the American people that we are brothers, and to hold out our hands to them, with a due regard for the duties we owe to our mother country.'[69] But his lieutenant Sir Richard Cartwright came out flatly for commercial union, and was joined by David Mills and John Charlton, prominent Ontario Liberals. The sentiment in favor of commercial union was confined largely to Ontario, and at the first Interprovincial Conference at Quebec in October 1887 the delegates unanimously favored unrestricted reciprocity rather than commercial union. Nevertheless the movement for commercial union, supported as it was by some of the wealthiest men in New York, continued to develop. In March 1888 Cartwright proposed in the House a resolution calling for free trade between Canada and the United States in all manufactured and natural products. Laurier declared that he would have liked to make a similar bargain with Britain, but that it was impossible under her free-trade policy. Rejecting the sentimental appeals of the Conservatives for preserving the British connection at all costs, he said that this was a question of duty and not of sentiment: 'If I have to choose between the duty I owe to England and the duty I owe to my native land, I stand by my native land.'[70] Despite the vigorous support of the Liberals, free trade was rejected by the full Conservative majority in an April vote.

Subsequently, the Canadian advocates of commercial union were embarrassed by statements made during the presidential campaign in the United States that fall. Senator Sherman, chairman of the Foreign Affairs Committee, speaking in the Senate on September 18, 1888, favored commercial union as a step toward the political union which seemed to be manifest destiny. On September 26 the *Chicago Tribune* said that if Canada were ready neither for commercial or political union, 'her safety lies in not provoking the United States by unfair or unfriendly dealing, for when the provocation comes, Uncle Sam will reach out and take her in, in order to ensure quiet, and neither she nor her venerable old mother can prevent it.'[71] In December the *New York World* published a map showing Canada included in the United States. W. C. Whitney, Secretary of the Navy, said four armies of 25,000 men each could easily conquer Canada, while Ben Butler described annexation as Canada's fate: 'Peacefully, we hope; forcefully, if we must.'[72] With the defeat of Cleveland in the November 1888 elections, reciprocity became an impossibility in American politics, and the McKinley tariff bill of 1890 bore hardly on Canadian trade.

A group of prominent Republicans then seemingly sought to force political union or annexation by reducing Canada to economic misery. Among the leading members of the Continental Union League which was formed in New York in 1892 were Charles A. Dana, Andrew Carnegie, John Jacob Astor, Ethan Allen, Warner Miller, Edward Lauterbach William C. Whitney, Orlando B. Potter, Horace Porter, John Hay, Theodore Roosevelt, Elihu Root, Cornelius N. Bliss, Chauncey M. Depew, William Walter Phelps, General Henry W. Slocum, General Granville W. Dodge, Charles Francis Adams, Oliver Ames, Seth Low, Bourke Cochrane, Charles L. Tiffany, Nathan Strauss, and many others. In Toronto there was an allied Continental Union Association, with Goldwin Smith as honorary president, John Morrison as president, and T. M. White as secretary.[73] Wiman's most useful Canadian colleague was Edward Farrer, who as chief editorial writer of the *Toronto Mail* in 1887 played a leading role in the creation of commercial union sentiment, and in the summer of 1890 became chief editorial writer for the *Globe*.

Aside from glorification of 'the old man, the old flag, and the old policy,' the Conservative campaign in the 1891 election was based upon the charge that the Liberals were working directly for annexation. Damaging support was given this charge by Macdonald's exposure of a secret pamphlet written by Farrer for American consumption. This document outlined an American policy which would lead Canada to annexation by taxing Nova Scotian fishing vessels, by the suspension of the railroad bonding privilege, and by other preventive measures. Farrer was known to be intimate with Sir Richard Cartwright, and both Cartwright and Honoré Mercier were accused of intriguing with the annexationists in the States.[74] In his manifesto to the electors Macdonald grandly protested: 'A British subject I was born, a British subject I will die. With my utmost strength, with my last breath, will I oppose the "veiled treason" which attempts by sordid means and mercenary proffers to lure our people from their allegiance.'[75] Back of Macdonald stood the business interests of Canada, headed by the Canadian Pacific Railway, which needed the support of its traditional political ally for British loans to cover its extensions into the United States. Macdonald's majority was secured largely thanks to the Canadian Pacific, which returned a Conservative candidate in every constituency but one through which its main line passed.[76]

The Liberals made large gains in both Quebec and Ontario, despite the support won for Macdonald by his own flag-waving and by the drum-beating of such impassioned imperialists as Colonel Denison. But the Liberals' new strength was weakened by division, for the former leader Blake did not approve of the fiscal policy which had been adopted during his absence in England. He issued a manifesto against commercial union to his old constituency of West Durham, which was withheld at Laurier's request until after the election. In it Blake characterized the policy he would have preferred—a moderate tariff with restricted reciprocity—as impossible, an imperial *Zollverein* as outside the realm of practical politics, and commercial union as leading to political union. Though Blake also condemned Tory policy, the net result of his utterance was to give support to Tory charges against the Liberals. But with stagnant trade and continued mass emigration from Canada to the States, public faith in a protective tariff continued to decline, and the advocates of reciprocity and commercial union won more and more adherents.

In consequence the imperialists redoubled their efforts, and the Canadian members of the Imperial Federation League were delighted when the 1894 Ottawa Trade Conference of the self-governing colonies, with a non-participating British representative, passed a strong resolution in favor of imperial preference, coupled with a request to the British government to denounce the Belgian and German trade treaties which extended to those countries any preference Canada might grant to Britain. But the Canadian imperialists had long pressed their case farther than their British colleagues were willing to go, and thanks to the strength of the free trade interests in the parent Imperial Federation League, that body was dissolved in November 1893 without warning to the Canadian members. Those who had been responsible for the dissolution formed the Imperial Federation (Defence) Committee, with a program calling for cash contributions from the colonies to the Army and Navy. The Canadians were still in favor of a *Zollverein* rather than a *Kriegesverein*, and Colonel Denison was dispatched to England to urge that course. He succeeded in rallying enough preferential tariff-minded members of the old League to form a new body, which was inaugurated as the British Empire League in January 1895. At a subsequent meeting in March the Canadian League changed its name and affiliated itself with the new league.

5

The man who became colonial secretary in the new Unionist government of Lord Salisbury in 1895 personified the new imperialism which combined Anglo-Saxon racism, the doctrine of the white man's burden, and the need for new overseas markets. Joseph Chamberlain had begun his political career as a reformer concerned with local government in Birmingham. When he first entered national politics as a Liberal of radical socialist sympathies, he had opposed Disraeli's adventures in imperialism, but found himself hampered by the more conservative elements in the party. When Gladstone set out to repair by Home Rule the Irish economy which had been destroyed by agricultural depression, Chamberlain devloped a passion for the preservation of the empire. The Union was his form of United Empire Loyalism. He broke with Gladstone on Home Rule and gravitated toward the Conservative Party, which had always been the party of imperialism.

Partyless for the time being, he was appointed as head of the British delegation to the fisheries arbitration in Washington. During a holiday recess of the commission, Chamberlain was guest of honor at a dinner given by the Toronto Board of Trade on December 30, 1887. Responding to the toast of 'The Commercial Interests of the Empire,' he spoke of an idea with which he had become obsessed through the influence of Dilke and Seeley:

> The idea is the greatness and importance of the destiny which is reserved for the Anglo-Saxon race—for that proud, persistent, self-asserting, and resolute stock that no change of climate or condition can alter, and which is infallibly destined to be the predominant force in the future history and civilization of the world . . . I am an Englishman. I am proud of the old country from which I come. I am not unmindful of the glorious traditions attached to it, of those institutions moulded by slow centuries of noble endeavour; but I should think that our patriotism was warped and stunted indeed if it did not embrace the Greater Britain beyond the seas—the young and vigorous nations carrying everywhere a knowledge of the English tongue and English love of liberty and law . . . I refuse to make any distinction between the interests

of Englishmen in England, in Canada, and in the United States . . .* Our past is theirs. Their future is ours. You cannot if you would break the invisible bond which binds us together . . . It may yet be that the federation of Canada may be the lamp lighting our path to the federation of the British Empire. If it is a dream—it may be only the imagination of an enthusiast—it is a grand idea. It is one to stimulate the patriotism and statesmanship of every man who loves his country; and whether it be destined or not to perfect realization, at least let us all cherish the sentiment it inspires. Let us do all in our power to promote it and enlarge the relations and goodwill which ought always to exist between sons of England throughout the world and the old folks at home.[77]

Having thus eloquently furthered the work of those in Canada who were engaged in promoting imperial federation and in scotching commercial union, Chamberlain returned to England.

He had become a convert to imperialism, and henceforward devoted most of his attention to imperial affairs. In 1888 he advocated not only the preservation of the empire but its extension in Africa, as essential to further 'the necessary work of colonization and civilization' and 'to justify our position as a nation.'[78] His tour of Egypt in 1889 crystalized his imperialism. Earlier in that year, speaking of imperial federation, he said: 'Although I have never seen my way to any practical scheme of Imperial Federation, yet I do not deem that idea to be altogether beyond the reach of statesmanship. I hold it to be right and proper that we should do nothing to prevent it; that we should do everything in our power to bring it about; and as the first step to any such arrangement I am convinced that the perfection of our means of mutual defence stands in the foreground.'[79] When Colonel Denison visited England in May 1890, he got a pledge from Chamberlain that the latter would examine the policy of imperial preference, which was favored by Canadian imperialists.[80] Chamberlain was already committed to the doctrine that trade follows the flag, and that reducing the empire would reduce British trade. To him, preservation and extension of the empire were matters of economic necessity.[81] But as yet he was unconvinced that Britain ought to sacrifice free trade to the undoubted interest of the colonies in a commercial union of the empire.[82]

Five more years of expanding empire and contracting trade at least partially converted him to the Canadian view that tariff reform was essential to prosperity. Within a few months after taking office as colonial secretary—a hitherto minor post which he chose 'in the hope of furthering closer union between them (the colonies) and the United Kingdom'[83]—Chamberlain sent a circular dispatch to the colonial governors requesting detailed trade surveys:

* This observation was made in the midst of the greatest emigration from Canada to the United States.

> I am impressed with the extreme importance of securing as large a share as possible of the mutual trade of the United Kingdom and the Colonies for British producers and manufacturers, whether located in the Colonies or the United Kingdom . . . I wish to investigate thoroughly the extent to which, in each of the Colonies, foreign imports of any kind have displaced, or are displacing, similar British goods, and the causes of such displacement.
>
> I am further desirous of receiving from you a return of any products of the Colony under your government which might advantageously be exported to the United Kingdom or other parts of the British Empire, but do not at present find a sufficient market there.[84]

This unprecedented inquiry, framed in businesslike terms new to the Colonial Office after Chamberlain had consulted with the Canadian high commissioner and the agents of the unfederated colonies of Australia and Africa, foreshadowed an attempt to realize the dream of imperial federation. It was the first step in that direction by the mother country after the colonies had urged such measures for over a decade,

Chamberlain outlined his scheme for an imperial *Zollverein* on March 25, 1896 at a dinner of the Canada Club in London. He sought to take advantage of the loyalism aroused by Cleveland's militant manifesto on Venezuela, by the Jamieson Raid, and by the Kaiser's telegram to Kruger, coupling imperial defence and imperial trade:

> What is the greatest of common obligations? It is Imperial defence. What is the greatest of our common interests? It is Imperial trade. And these two are very closely connected. It is very difficult to see how you can pretend to deal with the great question of Imperial defence without having first dealt with the question of Imperial trade. . . . My proposition is that a true Zollverein for the Empire, that a free trade established throughout the Empire, although it would involve the imposition of duties against foreign countries, and would be in that respect a derogation from the high principles of free trade, and from the practice of the United Kingdom up to the present time, would still be a proper subject for discussion and might possibly lead to a satisfactory arrangement if the colonies on their part were willing to consider it . . . it would undoubtedly lead to the earliest possible development of their great natural resources, would bring to them population, would open to them the enormous market of the United Kingdom.[85]

Within the empire 'protection must disappear,' and then a council of the empire might be constituted on the basis of the *Zollverein*. Chamberlain declared that he spoke only for himself: 'I want, not to lay down a course of policy which must be followed, but I want to provoke discussion . . . To organize an Empire—one may almost say to create an Empire—greater and more potent for peace and civilization of the world than any that history has ever known—th: is a dream if you like, but a dream of which no man need be ashamed But many in England were as yet unwilling to abandon free trad and the colonies were equally unwilling to abandon protectio Chamberlain urged his scheme upon the Empire Congress of Chan bers of Commerce which met in London in June 1896, but th Canadian delegates attacked free trade, while the British represent: tives characterized tariffs as tabu.

So discouraging was the reaction that Chamberlain abandone his scheme, and even doubted whether it was worthwhile to summo a colonial conference. To him Canada was the bellwether of th colonies, and Canada's new premier was a French Canadian wh stood at the head of a party committed to commercial union wit the United States rather than with Great Britain. There seeme little hope of winning Laurier to a dream of a British *Zollverei* but Chamberlain exerted some pressure. At a meeting in Septemb 1896 with Sir Richard Cartwright, Chamberlain said that recipr city with the United States would be regarded as a great step towar separation, while 'if the Canadian government proposed to reduc their tariff generally, or at least to allow the mother country to sha any reductions which they might make to the United States, the would be nothing but satisfaction on the part of the British Gover ment and people.' Chamberlain backed his position with a threat t halt his plan to subsidize a fast steamship service to Canada.[86]

Meanwhile he invited the premiers of all the self-governing coloni to come to London for Queen Victoria's Diamond Jubilee as sta guests, at the head of picked contingents of colonial troops who we to march in honor of the Queen. All the premiers accepted, an then Chamberlain decided to hold a colonial conference whose pu pose he defined as 'an interchange of ideas about matters of con mon and material interest, about closer commercial union, about th representation of the Colonies, about common defence, abo legislation, about other questions of equal importance, which cann but be productive of the most fruitful results.'[87] This was a ver different attitude from the caution displayed by the British Gover ment in organizing the 1887 Conference.

Meanwhile in Canada, rebuffed in their efforts to win commerci union or tariff concessions from the United States early in 1897, the first budget of the new government the Liberals provided a tar which did not vary greatly from the National Policy which they ha denounced for eighteen years. For the sake of consistency it w called a revenue tariff, but in reality it was protectionist, thoug there was an over-all reduction of about 10 per cent in duties. special feature provided a minimum tariff for British goods, th pleasing both free traders and imperial preference advocates at hon and abroad. The Liberals sought to promote freer trade, particularly with Great Britain and the United States, but reciprocity with the latter country had been doomed first by the McKinley Tariff and then by the still higher Dingley Tariff of 1897.

As Canada emerged from the Great Depression which had afflicted it since the 1870's, with the rise in wholesale prices and the decline in transportation costs, it gained self-confidence. Annexation no longer seemed inevitable, and the unneighborly policy of the United States, carefully made the most of by imperialist spokesmen in Canada, strengthened national and imperial sentiment. In the Venezuela and Yukon incidents, the bumptious imperialism of the United States gravely offended the growing sense of Canadian nationalism. It was easy for this nationalism to take an imperialist channel for the moment, when American markets were barred and English markets stood open, absorbing a 57 per cent increase of Canadian exports in 1896, and when the celebration of the Jubilee in June 1897 served to focus pride of race and pride of empire. The gorgeous pageantry of the Jubilee provided an environment in which Joseph Chamberlain was to find it easy to lead to his way of imperialist thinking the delegates to the Colonial Conference.

Canada's course before the conference met in June, which John Hay characterized as that of 'a married flirt,' changed the whole imperialist movement. Her continuance of protection killed the notion of an imperial *Zollverein* with complete internal free trade. But her provision of a British preference aroused English enthusiasm for Canada. According to the *New York Times* correspondent, Laurier was expected to be 'the most conspicuous and the most popular of all the visiting premiers of the Empire.'[88] The Canadian move suggested to Chamberlain one that might be agreed upon by all the self-governing colonies. As he anticipated, all the colonial premiers supported the Canadian plan which he commended to the conference, and promised to introduce the necessary legislation. But for the rest there was little advance of Chamberlain's ideas, despite the overpowering hospitality which was lavished upon the guests. Laurier wrote home: 'I am not sure whether the British Empire needs a new constitution, but I am certain that every Jubilee guest will need one.'[89] The five sittings of the conference were held at intervals between June 24 and July 8, in the midst of a round of pageants, ceremonies, dinners, luncheons, balls, garden-parties, and country-house weekends.

As chairman of the conference Chamberlain tactfully expressed his desire 'rather to learn your views than to press ours upon you.'[90] The eleven premiers were the heads of their respective states, and were made imperial privy councilors. The assembly thus approximated an imperial cabinet. Chamberlain suggested the possibility of a 'great council of the Empire,' which might grow into a federa council, 'to which we must always look forward as our ultimat ideal.'[91] Laurier, singled out for special honor by being knighte against his will, caught up the idea of colonial representation in a imperial parliament and told the National Liberal Club that 'i would be the proudest moment of my life if I could see a Canadia of French descent affirming the principles of freedom in the parlia ment of Great Britain.'[92] Yet he and other colonial spokesme voiced the view that 'colonies are born to become nations,' 'in a fe years the earth will be encircled by a series of independent nations recognizing, however, the suzerainty of England.' No concrete plan for an imperial council were realized.

In the matter of defence Chamberlain pressed for 'some adequat and regular system of contributions to sea-power'[93] and an interchange of troops between Great Britain and the colonies. Th Australians agreed to continue their naval subsidy for the British squadron defending their home waters, but Canada made no respons to a request from the Admiralty to open similar negotiations. Chamberlain's suggestion of an interchange of troops between Britain and the colonies was not taken up by the colonial spokesmen. Laurier, however, in a public speech observed in an unguarded moment o rhetorical excess: 'Let the watch fires be lit on the hills, and Canada will be the first to respond.'[94]

In the matter of commercial relations, Chamberlain implied that a full imperial *Zollverein* was impracticable for the present. Canada's introduction of the principle of preference had raised an international difficulty. By treaty Germany and Belgium had a right to commercial equality with Britain throughout the empire, and many other countries could claim the same privilege through the most-favored-nation clause. He suggested that the United Kingdom would not hesitate to denounce these treaties if such was the will of conference, and he implied that the other colonies should then follow Canada's example. All the premiers favored the denunciation of the treaties, and agreed to urge the cause of British preference at home. And at the final session the premiers adopted a resolution that conferences should be held at regular intervals, preferably triennially. Chamberlain made the most of this forerunner of a permanent imperial organization: 'That is the beginning of it—the beginning of a Federal conference.'[95] Before July was out, the British Government gave notice of its repudiation of the Belgian and German treaties, and thanks to Canada the empire was launched on a preferential tariff policy.

After his stay in England, Laurier paid a visit to France, Canada's other mother country. Through public speeches and private interviews he endeavored to improve the relations between Britain and

:ance which had been strained by colonial rivalry in Egypt and .e Sudan.[96] Since his statement in England that he was 'British the core,' had aroused criticism in France, he spoke eloquently of anada's double loyalty: 'We are faithful to the great nation which ıve us life, we are faithful to the great nation which has given us berty.'[97] He urged a renewal of the close friendship that had bound rance and Britain together in the Crimean War. He preached the ossibilities of trade between France and Canada. And in a speech efore the British Chamber of Commerce in Paris he clarified his leas on the question of imperial organization:

It may be that this solution will be found in the great principle of nperial representation. The colonies of France are represented in her arliament. Our situation is very different. We have not merely local utonomy, but the most complete legislative independence. If, as the rice of imperial representation, we had to renounce our autonomy, our :gislative independence, we would have none of it. If imperial repre- :ntation is to be the solution, it can only be as the complement and not s the negation of that which exists today.[98]

)nce more he pictured a French Canadian representing Canada at Vestminster. Privately he told French statesmen that Anglo- rench goodwill was essential for the peace of the world and of :anada in particular. Having successfully fulfilled his role of un- fficial ambassador, Sir Wilfrid passed on to Switzerland and Rome, -here he had an interview with the Pope. And then, by way of rance and Ireland he returned home, making a triumphant pro- ress up the St. Lawrence and finding public opinion united in his ıvor. Only a few ultra-imperialists growled at his reference to :anada as a nation and urged more rapid realization of the goal of nperial unity.

6

The bill for Laurier's profession of imperialist sentiments at the ubilee was soon presented. For all his business methods Chamber- ıin was an emotional imperialist who rated sentiment higher than ıterest as a governing factor.[99] His pride of race and sense of the ritish mission drove him onward in the path of expansion until war ı South Africa became inevitable. Meanwhile he had quietly pre- ared the way for Canadian contribution to imperial 'defence' by he appointment in 1898 of Lord Minto as governor-general and of 1ajor-General Edward Hutton as commander of the Canadian nilitia.

The new governor-general, a zealous soldier who was chiefly oted for having broken his neck in the Grand National and living to tell the tale, had as Lord Melgund served as the governor-genera military secretary in Canada from 1883–5. When in August 1884 l friend General Wolseley asked Lansdowne for 300 *voyageurs* to ser under Melgund in the Gordon Relief Expedition to the Sudan,[1] Melgund had declined the command, which went to Major Frederi Denison, but had personally enlisted 367 men, mostly Frenc Canadian raftsmen, but including some English Canadians fro Ontario, and some Caughnawaga Indians, whom Wolseley ha particularly requested.[101] In this task Melgund had the hear co-operation of Adolphe Caron, the minister of militia. The fi officers who served with the *voyageur* contingent included Captain Aumont, the Abbé Bouchard, a former missionary in Egypt, and D Hubert Neilson, John Neilson's grandson who was as much Frenc as he was English.[102]

Later in that same year Melgund served on a Canadian defen committee, and early in 1885 he had prepared a memorandum c preparations to be made against the anticipated Fenian raids c Canada. Before the Sudan campaign came to a close, he was acti in the scheme of raising a Canadian contingent which at Londor suggestion was to serve in Egypt as an imperial force and not Canadian militia.[103] In the Riel Rising of that summer Melgur was General Middleton's chief of staff. Macdonald, who had o posed the Sudan expeditionary force, nonetheless subsequent offered Melgund the post of commandant of the Mounted Polic and when he left Canada in the fall of 1885, told him: 'I shall n live to see it, but some day Canada will welcome you back Governor-General.'[104] Now at Wolseley's instigation Minto w named to the post by Chamberlain, whose imperialism he admire although he abominated Rhodes' 'dirty speculations'[105] in Sou Africa. Laurier judged Minto thus: 'When he came to Canac first, he was absolutely untrained in constitutional practice, kne little but horses and soldiering, but he took his duties to heart, ar became an effective governor, if sometimes very stiff.'[106]

General Hutton was one of the best-known of Wolseley's young disciples, and had organized a co-operative defence plan for tl Australian colonies. As one of the school of soldiers who had bee inspired by Wolseley to work out the problems of imperial defence, l held strong views on the necessity of colonial participation. He ha been at Eton and seen service in Egypt with Minto, who agreed wi the policy that Hutton attempted to inaugurate, but thought it be that he himself 'should not appear too military.'[107] After his fir few months in Canada Minto gave this report of Hutton to Wolsele 'The country itself is very military in feeling, and he has struck right note, with the result that the people and the press general are on his side. . . . He really has put life into everything, is all ov e place organizing and inquiring, and entertains a great deal, ›ding military, political, and civilian society with great judgment, ıd evidently excellent effect.'[108] If anything, Hutton was too ccessful, for his apostolic zeal brought him into conflict with the inisters, whose hand he frequently forced by speeches, interviews, ıd manipulation of the press. These minor difficulties were soon create major ones.

Negotiations concerning Canada's share in a possible South frican war began in March 1899, when the War Office and Adiralty raised through Minto the question of Canadian troops serving ıtside of Canada. In 1885 Sir John Macdonald had interpreted ction 79 of the Militia Act as meaning that Canadian troops uld not be ordered outside of North America, though this interetation was seemingly based upon his reluctance to sacrifice men ıd money 'to get Gladstone and Co. out of the hole they have unged themselves into by their own imbecility.'[109] When Minto nsulted Laurier and his cabinet on the question, they held that e imperial government had the right under the act to order anadian troops anywhere in time of war, but for Laurier the deci-ve point was whether the troops were required for the defence of anada, not whether the war was at home or abroad. In April the outh African League Congress, an organization inspired by Cecil hodes, urged by cable the despatch by the British Empire League Canada of a sympathetic resolution to the imperial government.[110] ut Principal G. M. Grant of Queen's University, a leading figure the League, sympathized with the Boers, as did such divergent anadian public figures as Laurier and Goldwin Smith, and no ction was taken at the time.

In July official and unofficial imperial pressure really began to be xerted on Canada. Chamberlain wrote to Minto on July 3 that ar was probable and asked whether Canadian troops would be ffered: 'Such a proof of the unity of the Empire would have a reat moral effect and might go far to secure a pacific settlement. such an offer probable? If so, it should be made soon, but I do ot desire that it should be the result of external pressure or sugges-on.'[111] Minto promptly urged upon Laurier the adoption of the rinciple of Canadian participation in imperial wars by such an offer. Ieanwhile a representative of the South African League and agent f Rhodes, J. Davis Allen, came to Ottawa in July from England. hrough leading Canadian imperialists he agitated for the passage of resolution expressing sympathy with the imperial government's fforts to obtain justice for British subjects in the Transvaal.[112] On ıly 13 Colonel Sam Hughes, an Ontario Orangeman, fervidly ıpported Canadian intervention in South Africa, citing Queens-ınd's offer of troops.[113] Laurier yielded to pressure and on July 31 moved the requested resolution, which was seconded by Geor Eulas Foster and passed unanimously by a fervid House whi then sang 'God Save the Queen.' This was the only parliamenta action on the question. But Laurier refused to make the offer troops which the British government desired, writing Minto: 'T present case does not seem to be one in which England, if there war, ought to ask us, or even expect us, to take a part; nor do believe that it would add to the strength of the imperial sentiment assert at this juncture that the colonies should assume the burden military expenditure, except—which God forbid!—in the case pressing danger.'[114]

But during August and September, thanks to the activity British agents which found expression in agitation for Canadi participation by Hugh Graham's *Montreal Star* and the Conserv tives under Sir Charles Tupper, public opinion in English Canada- notably in Toronto, where Allen made great play with Milne despatches to Chamberlain[115]—was aroused against the Boe Sam Hughes offered to raise a regiment or brigade for South Afric service, while other militia officers volunteered the services of the battalions. When Hughes' offer was refused by the minister of militi he renewed it directly to Chamberlain. Meanwhile Minto ar Hutton worked out a plan for a Canadian contingent on Septemb 5, offering the command to Major Oscar Pelletier, and turned t project over to the minister of militia. Seemingly, Minto private sympathized as late as September 28 with Laurier:

> From the point of view of a Canadian statesman I don't see why th should commit their country to the expenditure of lives and money f a quarrel not threatening imperial safety and directly contrary to t opinion of a colonial government at the Cape. . . . Sir Wilfred told n the other day that if the question were reconsidered he should call Cabinet Council and ask me to be present. I hope he won't, for I shou be in a nice muddle—my chief at home thirsting for blood, all my frien here ditto, and myself, while recognizing imperial possibilities, al seeing the iniquity of the war, and that the time for colonial support h hardly yet arrived.[116]

Hutton further alienated the cabinet by telling Richard Scott Ontario, who with Israel Tarte of Quebec headed the opposition participation, that if war came, public opinion would force t government to send troops. Then on October 3 the *Canadian Milita Gazette*, an unofficial but authoritative publication, announced th if war began in the Transvaal, the government would offer a for from the militia, and gave the details of Hutton's scheme. Seeming this article was not the work of Hutton himself, but of an ove zealous subordinate who shared his views. Laurier promptly deni the statement as 'pure invention,' and said troops could not be sent without the permission of parliament.[117]

On the same day Chamberlain cabled Minto in the same terms used to the governors of colonies which had already offered contingents, proposing a detailed scheme of organization for Canadian units. The troops were to be integrated with the imperial forces, with no Canadian ranking higher than major. Minto urged Laurier to reconsider the question of an official contingent, thus anticipating Chamberlain's letter of October 4 which informed Minto: 'We do not intend to accept any offer from volunteers. We do not want the men, and the whole point of the offer would be lost unless it was endorsed by the Government of the Colony.'[118] Minto was in New York when the cable arrived, and Hutton in the North-West, while Laurier left Ottawa on October 7 to attend an international gathering in Chicago. After Laurier's return on the 12th—the date hostilities commenced in South Africa—the cabinet weighed its action for two days in the face of the agitation which had been aroused by publication of Chamberlain's cable.

Tupper and the opposition, moved by both imperialist emotion and thirst for office, attacked the government for its delay and its unwillingness to send a Canadian contingent, incidentally arousing anti-French-Canadian sentiment. For Quebec was unmoved by the wave of British feeling which had swept Ontario. *La Patrie*, the organ of Laurier's Quebec organizer Tarte, took its stand on the principle of no share in Britain's wars without a share in Britain's councils. The independent *La Presse* expressed the fundamental French-Canadian attitude toward foreign wars, which was later to cause two more major crises in Canada's national life: 'We French Canadians belong to one country, Canada; Canada is for us the whole world; but the English Canadians have two countries, one here and one across the sea.'[119] A smaller third group would have had no objection to unofficial participation by Canadian volunteers.

On October 13 the government reached a compromise, passing an order-in-council which did not authorize an official contingent but did undertake to equip and transport up to 1,000 volunteers. The order was ingeniously framed to avoid the difficulties with which the government was beset:

The Prime Minister, in view of the well-known desire of a great many Canadians who are ready to take service under such conditions, is of opinion that the moderate expenditure which would thus be involved for the equipment and transportation of such volunteers may readily be undertaken by the Government of Canada without summoning Parliament, especially as such expenditure, under such circumstances, cannot be regarded as a departure from the well-known principles of constitutional government and colonial practice, nor construed as a precedent for future action.[120]

In a letter of October 14 to Chamberlain, Minto thus explained Laurier's position:

. . . though he thoroughly approves the action of the Imperial Government on South Africa and admits the undoubted necessity of war, he has not been inclined to admit the policy of this colony accepting pecuniary liabilities for the old country. He says it is contrary to the traditions of Canadian history. . . . He considers, however, that the acceptance of your offer to contribute to pay and transport of troops so minimizes the expense that the principle of non-acceptance of pecuniary liability is hardly departed from.[121]

Laurier himself publicly defended his course in a speech at Bowmanville, Ontario, on October 17: 'We as a government, and especially I as the head of the government, have in all these matters to think and go slowly and to act formally and with due consideration. For my part, so long as I have the honor to occupy my present post, you shall never see me carried away by passion or prejudice or even enthusiasm. I have to think and consider. I have to look to the right and the wrong. I have to see what will be the effect of any action that we take.'[122]

On the whole the government's course was supported throughout the country. But some Conservatives criticized Canada's unwillingness to shoulder the full burden of sending a contingent, while Henri Bourassa, a promising young Liberal protégé of Laurier from Quebec, resigned in protest from parliament on October 18, after the leading French-Canadian Liberals had abandoned under Laurier's influence the same attitude of non-participation which he held. In caucus, Bourassa asked Laurier whether he took account of Quebec's opinion and Laurier replied: 'My dear Henri, the Province of Quebec has no opinions, it only has sentiments.'[123] Tarte yielded to the party decision and supported the volunteer scheme, after winning the insertion of a no-precedent clause in the order-in-council. He was burnt in effigy at Toronto for maintaining that Canada was not obliged to participate in Britain's wars.

The first contingent, including a French-Canadian company raised with some difficulty at Quebec, sailed from Quebec on October 30, after being addressed by Laurier and Minto. Laurier told the men that they went to fight for the cause of justice, humanity, civil rights, and religious liberty.[124] Minto permitted himself the indiscretion of observing that 'the people of Canada had shown that they had no inclination to discuss the quibbles of colonial responsibility.'[125] The governor-general resented the charge that Chamberlain had attempted to maneuver Canada into the course he desired by accepting in his cable of October 3 an offer which had never been made. Somewhat tortuously, considering the pressure which had been exerted from Britain for months, he now wrote Laurier: 'I have always carefully explained to you that any offer from Canada must be spontaneous.'[126] Laurier for his part made the best of the position into which he had been forced: at his insistance the War Office arranged that the Canadian troops should form a unit, rather than being attached to British regiments as the Australians were.

A week after the first contingent sailed, the government offered to raise a second, but the offer was not accepted until the British disasters of mid-December. Early in the New Year Lord Strathcona (formerly Donald Smith) personally raised three squadrons of mounted infantry, known as Strathcona's Horse. All told, Canada sent some 7,300 men to South Africa, only one-third of whom were in the official contingents.[127] In addition, a battalion was raised in Canada to garrison Halifax and thus to relieve a British regiment, the Leinsters, for active service. The contingents enlisted for a year, and many of the men of the first contingent were unwilling to prolong their service. In money Canadian participation cost the Dominion some $2,800,000.[128]

During the fall and winter the ever-zealous General Hutton proved even more of a thorn in the ministers' flesh than before. Finally he was accused of favoring Conservative interests in purchasing horses for army use. When interviewed by Laurier, he pleaded guilty 'only to have roused the latent military enthusiasm through all ranks of the militia, and having strengthened the innate feeling of patriotism towards the old country and the Empire, which already existed in all parts of the Dominion.' Laurier professed to see 'little difference between inculcating patriotism and arousing military enthusiasm, and party politics;'[129] and asked Minto for the general's recall. Minto defended Hutton, but said he would transmit the request to London with a covering letter expressing his opposition. Laurier said such action might result in the resignation of his government, while Minto advised Chamberlain that he did not 'admit any right on the part of any Government to expect me to refrain from commenting to you adversely on their action.'[130] On February 8, 1900 Hutton was ordered home for South African service, and sent in his resignation as commander in Canada.

In a despatch of April 17, Chamberlain expressed his disappointment 'that Ministers should have found themselves unable to allow General Hutton to complete the work he had begun,' and his own view that 'although the responsibility to Parliament must be maintained, it is desirable that the officer in command of the defensive forces in Canada should have a freer hand in matters essential to the discipline and efficiency of the Militia than would be proper in the case of an ordinary civil servant even of the highest position.'[131] But Laurier had won a victory for the principles of responsible government and Canadian autonomy by resisting an effort to make the English commander in Canada a political agent of the governor-general and of the colonial secretary for whatever colonial program they favored.

When parliament met in February 1900 the war and the coming elections were the dominant issues. The only new legislation increased the British preference from 25 per cent to $33\frac{1}{3}$ per cent and was attacked by the Conservatives on the grounds that the government should have demanded a preference from Britain in return. Sir Charles Tupper led the Conservative attack upon the government for doing too little in the South African War, and doing that little late. One of his lieutenants remarked that Laurier 'had been first in the Jubilee parades, and last in the test of action.'[132] Tarte came under heavy fire in Ontario as the usurper of Bourassa's role and for his own utterances and *La Patrie's* editorials on the theme of 'no taxation without representation' in imperial affairs. The temper of the House grew hot, and there was much name-calling both in parliament and in the press. When Laurier replied to the attacks which had been so freely made upon him, he destroyed the Conservative argument that Canada should have borne all the cost of the Canadian contingents by showing that all the colonies had followed the same policy as Canada, which was that suggested by the British government. He reminded Tupper of the latter's earlier condemnations of imperial federation and imperial war expenses. As to the 'lukewarmness' with which he had been charged by Tupper, he spoke thus:

> Sir, I have no hesitation in admitting that I was not enthusiastic for that war or any war. I have no sympathy for that mad, noisy, dull-witted, and short-sighted throng who clamour for war, who shouted 'On to Pretoria,' who complacently prophesied that General Buller would eat his Christmas dinner in the capital of the Transvaal. . . .
>
> Whilst I cannot admit that Canada should take part in all the wars of Great Britain, neither am I prepared to say that she should not take part in any war at all . . . I claim for Canada this, that in future she shall be at liberty to act or not to act, to interfere or not to interfere, to do just what she pleases.[133]

Meanwhile the cleavage between the races, which Laurier had tried to avoid and which the Conservatives had fostered, bore fruit in Montreal on March 1 when McGill students celebrating the relief of Ladysmith besieged the offices of *La Patrie*, *Le Journal*, and *La Presse* and Laval's building and became involved in riots with the anti-war students of Laval. Rival contingents waved the Union Jack and the Tricolor, and for three or four days there was street fighting. The students were restrained by Archbishop Bruchési and

Principal Peterson of McGill and by the greater part of the press, although *La Patrie* and the *Star* accused one another of responsibility for the 'savage assaults' of the McGill students and the 'insults to the Union Jack' by the Laval students.[134]

It was against this background that on March 13 Bourassa, who had been re-elected by acclamation, made a three-hour speech in the House, proposing that 'parliament insist on its sovereignty and independence, refuse to consider the government's action a precedent for the future, and declare its opposition to any change in the existing relations between Canada and Great Britain, unless decided by parliament and sanctioned by the people of Canada.'[135] To him Canada was now threatened as a result of the government's action with ceaseless wars and unbearable burdens. Why had Canada taken part in this war? Because it was just? The British Liberals did not think so. Because it was necessary? Necessary to aid 40,000,000 to crush 400,000? Because public opinion demanded it? Every French-Canadian journal was opposed. Because of the action of other British colonies? The cable news had been manipulated by the English-Canadian 'yellow press' to make it appear that all the colonies had eagerly offered men, but in several Australian parliaments the issue had been closely contested and in one case carried only by the speaker's vote. The government claimed that no precedent had been created for Canadian participation in imperial wars, but 'the accomplished fact is a precedent,' as Chamberlain had made clear in his reply to the order-in-council authorizing a contingent, in which he hailed 'the desire thus exhibited to share in the risks and burdens of the Empire.'

Chamberlain and his fanatical disciples were leading Canada in a constitutional revolution of which no one could foresee the consequences. Such questions should be submitted to parliament, thoroughly discussed, and settled by plebiscite. Bourassa expressed his own attitude, describing himself as 'a Liberal of the English school,' 'a disciple of Burke, Fox, Gladstone.' No force could impose upon him opinions which were not his. He would support the government's general policy, because he believed it good; but he condemned it in this particular. His constituents had ratified his attitude and charged him to warn the cabinet against any further attempt to mortgage in advance the future of the country without its knowledge and without the consent of the people.[136]

In a reply to Bourassa on March 13 Laurier defended both his deference to public opinion and the justice of the war. He denied that Canada had been forced into the war by England:

> No, we were not forced by England; we were not forced by Mr. Chamberlain or Downing Street to do what we did . . . We acted in the

full independence of our sovereign power. What we did we did of our own free will. . . . My honorable friend says the consequence will be that we shall be called upon to take part in other wars. I have only this to answer, that if it should be the will of the people of Canada at any future period to take part in any war of England, the people of Canada will have to have their own way.[137]

Then he agreed with Bourassa that if it were to be admitted that Canada should take part in all Britain's wars, there would have to be a new constitutional basis; Canada would have to say to Britain, 'If you want us to help you, call us to your councils.'[138] He warned Bourassa of the danger of a cleavage of the races if the government had not followed public opinion: 'A greater calamity could never take place in Canada. My honorable friend knows as well as any man in this House that if there is anything to which I have given my political life, it is to try to promote unity, harmony, and amity between the diverse elements of this country. I shall not deviate a line from the policy that I have traced out for myself.'[139] In conclusion Laurier spoke of the benefits he hoped for from Canadian participation:

The pride of pure patriotism, the pride of consciousness that that day it had been revealed to the world that a new power had arisen in the West. . . . The work of union and harmony between the chief races of this country is not yet complete. We know by the unfortunate occurrences that took place only last week that there is much to do in that way. But there is no bond of union so strong as the bond created by common dangers faced in common. To-day there are men in South Africa representing the two branches of the Canadian family, fighting side by side for the honour of Canada. Already some of them have fallen, giving to their country the last full measure of devotion. Their remains have been laid in the same grave, there to rest to the end of time in that last fraternal embrace. Can we not hope—I ask my honorable friend himself—that in that grave shall be buried the last vestiges of our former antagonism? If such shall be the result, if we can indulge that hope, if we can believe that in that grave shall be buried the former contentions, the sending of the contingents would be the greatest service ever rendered to Canada since Confederation.[140]

Only nine Quebec members, both Liberals and Conservatives, supported Bourassa's resolution that the action of the government created no precedent for future participation in Britain's wars, but his speech had only served to illustrate to English Canadians the difficulties that Laurier faced in Quebec. Three French-Canadian attitudes towards the empire developed during the debate: the colonial-minded, like T.-C. Casgrain, who favored moderate aid when ever Britain demanded it; those who looked forward to independence, like Dominique Monet, and wanted neither colonialism nor imperial entanglements; and the rare imperial federalists, like Tarte, who nevertheless opposed support of military policies which they had no hand in shaping.

Laurier refused to commit himself to any position but guided himself by what seemed best for national unity under the circumstances. When Chamberlain raised the idea of an imperial advisory council in March 1900, Minto discussed the matter with Laurier and reported to Chamberlain:

> Sir Wilfrid's own inclination towards an imperial federation of any sort is, in my opinion, extremely doubtful—in fact, though his recent speeches appear to have been taken in England as enthusiastically imperialist, I am convinced that they guarantee no such opinion. His speech in the House was very eloquent, and the 'call us to your councils' phrase appears to have been accepted as indicating a wish to be called—the very last thing Sir Wilfrid would want, and the speech itself did not justify that interpretation of it. He recognized the strong British devotion to the motherland existent here, and the imperial feeling at home stronger perhaps than here, and got a chance for his great eloquence. But I should say that seriously he is devoid of the British feeling for a united Empire, that it has no sentimental attraction for him, and that a closer connection with the old country he would consider from a utility point of view and nothing more. He recognizes the fact that his Canadian fellow-countrymen must follow the Anglo-Saxon lead, and will do his best to educate them up to it; but I believe it to be much more with the idea of the welding together of a Canadian nation than of forming part of a great Empire . . . and though he has never actually said so to me, I suspect that he dreams of Canadian independence in some future age. He thinks the arrangement of tariff questions far more likely to bring about imperial unity than any joint system of imperial defence; the former may be made to appear magnanimous in an imperial sense, but it would hardly be advocated by a colonial government except in a belief in some practical gain to the colony from it, whilst the latter, upon which the safety of trade must depend, probably appears before the public merely as a direct increase in military expenditure to meet an obscure danger not generally realized.[141]

Minto was singularly apt at reading Laurier's mind, as later developments bore witness. He considered Laurier 'far the biggest man in Canada,' and realized that he expressed the 'strongest feeling of Canadians,' 'a feeling of Canada's national independence,'[142] ready to resent any imperial interference.

In the November 1900 elections Minto's observation was confirmed by the gains which the Laurier government made. British victories in Africa had eased the tension in Canada, but racial appeals were still made by the Conservatives. Ontario accused Quebec of disloyalty, and the *Toronto News* threatened that British Canadians would find means, through the ballot or otherwise, of 'emancipating themselves from the dominance of an inferior people that peculiar circumstances have placed in authority in the Dominion.'[143] Minto wrote home:

> The writing of the leading Opposition papers in Ontario has been positively wicked, simply aiming at stirring up hatred of French Canada. It is perfectly monstrous. . . . I believe myself that the French Canadians are very much maligned as to their disloyalty. French Canada does not wish to be mixed up in imperial wars, and is lukewarm, but at home you do not call a man disloyal if he disapproves of the war. Here, if he is only lukewarm, and is a French Canadian, he must be a rebel.

Later he commented: 'I think pig-headed British assertiveness is much more to be feared than French sympathies.'[144]

In Quebec the Liberals urged French Canadians to stand behind a French and Catholic premier against the Ontario fanatics, while Sir Charles Tupper endeavored to prove in behalf of the Conservatives that Laurier was 'too English for me'[145] and that he himself deserved credit for smashing the Imperial Federation League. Israel Tarte, serving as the Canadian commissioner at the Paris Exposition, made speeches which were interpreted by the press in Ontario as attacks on British policy, and proclamations of independence and of pro-French sentiments, while in Quebec he was represented as advocating imperial federation. But Tupper's attempt to woo Quebec was not successful. Quebec went nearly solidly Liberal, while in Ontario Laurier lost fourteen seats in the larger cities and in the strongly Protestant constituencies which in 1896 had voted against Tupper's 'coercion' of Manitoba. The Maritimes were not distracted by the imperialist cry, which they regarded as an Ontario and Quebec question; they were pleased by the prospects of better British trade under the new preference; while the West, rejoicing in a novel prosperity, strongly supported the government under which it had arrived. But it was still Laurier's majority in Quebec which maintained him in power, and this fact stuck in the imperialists' craw. The *Toronto News* commented: 'It is an intolerable situation for English Canadians to live under French domination. . . . It is infinitely deplorable that the government remains in power by the massive vote of a section of the Canadian people speaking a foreign language and maintaining an ideal foreign to the dominant race in this country.'[146]

In March 1901 there was another flare-up of French-Canadian opposition to the Boer War when Bourassa introduced a resolution requesting the British government to make peace on the basis of independence for South Africa, and opposing any further despatch of Canadian contingents. Canada had the right to make her voice heard, he argued, since Canadian blood and money had been spent in a war not of her making. Laurier expressed his surprise that one who had been so opposed to sending troops should be so ready to send advice. In any case, the question of sending more men was academic, since the war was practically over. It was too late for independence, since the Boer territory had been annexed to the British domain by 'the terrible logic of war.'[147] Laurier looked forward to a South African confederation, 'united together under a federal constitution, under the British flag, and under the sovereignty of England,' and blandly added: 'Mr. Bourassa will agree with me that when they have the British flag over South Africa, they shall have that which has been found everywhere during the last sixty years under the British flag—liberty for all, equality, for all, justice and civil rights for English and Dutch alike.' Bourassa's resolution was defeated with only three votes in its favor, and the House sang 'God Save the King.'

7

The South African War altered the course of Canadian political life by introducing the new ideas of imperialism and nationalism into party strife. This was not a normal process, for as James Bruce observed: 'In Canada ideas are not needed to make parties, for these can live by heredity, and like the Guelfs and the Ghibellines of medieval Italy, by memories of past combats.'[148] But within and without the parties, an influential and determined group demanded closer union of the empire, with Canada having a larger share in the control and responsibilities of imperial policy. The Imperial Federalists and the war itself had aroused pride of race and jingoism in English Canada. There was much waving of the Union Jack in school and press, while the swelling tide of British immigrants, principally to the cities, strengthened the bonds between Canada and England.[149] Almost a billion and a half of British capital poured into Canada between 1900 and 1913, and consciously and unconsciously exerted an imperial influence.[150] Resentment of American economic and political imperialism was increased by the highhandedness of Washington on the tariff question, and in the fur-sealing and Alaska boundary disputes.

On the other hand there was a rapidly developing national consciousness brought about by the opening of the West and the industrial development of the East, which to some extent broke down the old provincialism. Laurier expressed this new nationalism when he called Canada 'the country of the twentieth century,'[151] suggesting that its role would be as great as that of the United States in the nineteenth. Canada's part in the Boer War was exaggerated and served as a stimulant of national pride, while on the other hand friction with English officers and loss of confidence in the War Office and in English military leadership strengthened national consciousness. French Canada, with its instinct for conservatism, on the whole was opposed to Canada's taking a more active role in the empire. A small group, however, headed by Bourassa, had begun to evolve a French-Canadian nationalism in reaction to the imperialist jingoism of English Canada during the Boer War. This nationalism was largely a reiteration of the doctrines of the Canada First movement in French-Canadian terms. Under the brilliant leadership of Bourassa it became an ever more formidable stumbling-block in Laurier's path and finally brought about his downfall.

In the early days of his premiership Laurier inclined towards imperialism, as his statements at the 1897 Jubilee bore witness. This policy was adopted in part to disavow the annexationist sentiments which the Conservatives had long charged against the Liberals; in part because British preference suited Canada's needs after the adoption of the McKinley and Dingley tariffs; and in part because Laurier sought to meet English Canada, then in the full flood of imperialist sentiments, more than halfway, in accordance with his desire to foster national unity. But Quebec's almost unanimous opposition to the South African adventure warned him of the dangers of yielding too much to Ontario's sentiments, and experience with British imperialist pressure cooled his interest in imperial federation. Gradually he evolved the concept of Canada as a nation within the empire, thus reconciling the ideals of nationalism and imperialism, and anticipating the modern concept of the British Commonwealth of Nations.

Preoccupied as he was by the problems of the South African War and of Australian confederation, Chamberlain neglected the development of Laurier's ideas, which was made evident at the Colonial Conference of 1902. With peace in South Africa and the coronation of Edward VII to provide the background of pageantry which had by now become conventional for these gatherings, Chamberlain summoned the premiers of the empire to meet in London in June and July. Judging that 'bloodshed has cemented the British Empire and the sense of unity is stronger than it has ever been before,' Chamberlain felt that 'the time has come when the defence of the Empire, and its military and naval resources, have become the common concern of the whole Empire and not of the Mother Country alone, and that joint action, or at least joint organization with regard to this subject should be organized on a permanent footing.' He proposed the formation of an imperial council, 'acting as an advisory board to enquire into and report to the various governments on the subject of Imperial Defence.'[152]

Laurier, whom Chamberlain had thought of in 1897 as the bell-wether of the colonial statesmen, when sounded out by Minto, thought 'the arrangement of tariff questions far more likely to bring about imperial unity than any joint system of imperial defence.'[153] Chamberlain was reluctant to adopt preferential trade as a means of imperial unity—he still stood for 'free trade under the flag'—but in the face of colonial reluctance to organize an imperial council for defence, he gradually prepared to take his political life in his hands by supporting the plan the colonies favored for closer union of the empire. He was well aware of 'the strong feeling of independence which exists in all the self-governing colonies' and declared that 'I am almost afraid to make suggestions lest I should appear to presume, and I would greatly prefer that the initiative in any further movement towards closer union should be taken by the colonies.'[154]

A debate in the Canadian House in May 1902 on the government's reluctance to discuss political change or imperial defence at the impending conference made clear the new Canadian attitude. Laurier defended the government's position:

> If it be intended simply to discuss what part Canada is prepared to take in her own defence, what share of the burden must fall upon us as being responsible for the safety of the land in which we were born, and to which we owe our allegiance, in which all our hopes and affections are centered, certainly we are always prepared to discuss that subject. Nor do I believe that we need any prompting on that subject, or that our attention should be specially called to it. . . . There is a school abroad, there is a school in England and in Canada, a school which is perhaps represented on the floor of this parliament, a school which wants to bring Canada into the vortex of militarism which is the curse and blight of Europe. I am not prepared to endorse any such policy.[155]

Robert Laird Borden, the new leader of the opposition, who thought that 'the ties that bind self-governing nations of the Empire would probably become closer, but that any change would be slow and gradual,'[156] made a cautious criticism of the government's attitude: 'I am ready to uphold as strongly as anyone the necessity of control by Canada of the expenditure of our public moneys and of the question of imperial defence relating to Canada. But, holding this view, I see no reason why we should not be open to discuss that question with the imperial authorities.'[157]

When the conference finally met, after a delay caused by the King's illness, Chamberlain found no response for his program of an imperial council, of definite pledges of naval and military contributions from every colony, and of union in trade. The conference expressed the opinion that the 'present political relation was generally satisfactory under existing conditions,'[158] and was unmoved by Chamberlain's citation of Laurier's earlier attitude of 'If you want our aid, call us to your councils' and his own statement that 'The weary Titan staggers under the too vast orb of his fate.'[159] A resolution was passed providing that the conference should meet regularly at not greater than four-year intervals, and expressing the desire to keep all parts of the empire in touch, not through a new body exercising direct control over the whole, but through a meeting of governments responsible to their own peoples.[160] Chamberlain's proposal of free trade within the empire found no friends: a resolution affirmed its impracticability, approved the principle of British preference, and recommended reciprocal preference for colonial goods.

Most of the discussion centered on the question of defence, on which the British authorities made a determined effort to take advantage of the imperial loyalty aroused by the South African War and of the precedent established by colonial participation. But the delegates were divided in their reactions to the defence schemes proposed by the War Office and the Admiralty. Canada and Australia jointly repudiated the suggested formation of special colonial forces 'set apart for general imperial service and practically under the absolute control of the imperial government' as 'objectionable in principle, as derogating from the powers of self-government enjoyed by them, and . . . calculated to impede the general improvement in training and organization of their defence forces.'[161] Australia promised a renewal and extension of her contribution to the British Navy, but Canada refused to make any offer of assistance other than its contemplated establishment of a local naval force. The smaller colonies agreed to provide money grants or aid to local naval reserves.

In a private interview Chamberlain, who never appreciated how little Laurier did compared with how much he eloquently said, learned the full measure of the Canadian differences with him on imperial policy. The Englishman expressed his surprise that Canada and Australia did not realize that strength and safety lay in union, and that self-respect did not make them wish to bear a fair share of the imperial burden. Laurier replied that the empire's strength lay in local diversity and freedom. Canada was prepared to bear her just burdens, when the safety of Britain or the whole empire was challenged, but he remarked that what Chamberlain called the empire's interest and the empire's policy were in most cases Britain's interest and Britain's policy. Canada had an immense domain to develop and was far removed from European quarrels; her interests were not those of Britain which constantly sought to extend her domain and to keep open the seaways. Moved by his Anglo-Saxon racism, Chamberlain made evident his impression ıat Laurier was 'a very imperfectly assimilated Englishman.'[162] aurier then suggested that Chamberlain have a private interview ith his English-Canadian colleagues, and Chamberlain found ıat they stood with Laurier: they were Canadians first and believed ıat the empire began at home. Chamberlain was disgruntled by is disappointed hopes and by what he called 'the icy wind from the anadian snows,'[163] and when Lady Minto spoke to him of Laurier 'a very great gentleman,' he replied sourly, 'I would rather do usiness with a cad who knows his mind.'[164]

Laurier had learned how to resist the unofficial blandishments hich were coupled with official pressure in the imperialist camaign, and stood firm. Before the conference he refused a peerage,[165] nd during his stay in England he was led into no such rhetorical xcesses as had characterized his utterances in 1897, to his subsequent nbarrassment. To the Constitutional Club he expounded the text, The British Empire was founded and must be maintained by the rts of peace more than by the arts of war'; at the Guildhall he ıaintained that 'The British Empire is a charter of freedom, united, rosperous; there is no need of organic changes; it would be a fatal ıistake to force events'; at the National Liberal Club he proclaimed ıat 'The devolution of legislative power has been the bond of union f the British Empire.'[166] Though Laurier expressed the Canadian :action to the imperial enthusiasm of the war years, he had not st interest in imperial affairs. Privately he urged a policy of onciliation and self-government for South Africa upon Chamberlain nd other English public men. When his health broke down after summer crowded with public appearances and he sought treatıent in Paris, he preached Anglo-French friendship to President oubet and Foreign Minister Delcassé. Such mediation was needed, r French feeling had been much embittered against Britain by ıe Boer War. Laurier's share in bringing about the subsequent *ntente cordiale* was publicly acknowledged three years later by the rench president.

Laurier returned home, greeted by triumphal receptions at Quebec nd Montreal and finding general support of his stand at the con:rence, although the Conservative press criticized his 'negative' ttitude. Laurier faced, however, a revolt in his own camp, for srael Tarte had taken advantage of his absence and rumored :rious illness to make a bid for power. As minister of public works, 'arte had become the apostle of a new doctrine: 'Outbuild the .mericans in canals, harbours, ships; build a tariff wall as high as ingley's.'[167] As Laurier's lieutenant and as an opponent of Canaian intervention in South Africa, Tarte held Quebec at his comıand; his protectionism now won him friends in the very Ontario ircles which had so enthusiastically condemned his views on the war. Commercial self-interest had a persistent way of outweighi abstract principle in the latter province, where Tarte made triumphant progress in September, delivering more than a hundr ardent protectionist speeches.

The Western Liberals and the official party press repudiat Tarte's campaign, but he was not called to book until Laurie return in October. The prime minister promptly had two intervie with Tarte, demanding his resignation on the grounds that he h advocated revision of the tariff without consultation with his ch or his colleagues. On October 20 Tarte resigned, and when spoke of his resignation, at a National Club dinner given that d in Toronto to Colonel Denison, the leading advocate of imperi preference, the cheering which had greeted him died away.[168] H new Ontario friends had little use for him when he ceased to represe their interests in the government. Tarte retired to the editorsh of *La Patrie*, and within a few months lapsed back into the Co servative camp in which his checkered political life had begun.

The Colonial Conference of 1902 forced Chamberlain to aband temporarily the political and military paths to his goal of Unit Empire. The plan of commercial union through a system of pr ferential tariffs, which the colonies had favored over his imperi *Zollverein*, now seemed the only feasible measure to strengthen t empire immediately. After the conference Canada added to t list of British products which received a preferential treatment 33⅓ per cent; New Zealand granted a preference of 10 per cent manufactures; the Cape Colony and Natal gave a preference 25 per cent; and Australia announced its intention of granting preference.[169] But the English cabinet, whose leaders were st devoted to free trade, made no move to provide in return the pr ferential treatment for colonial products which the conference h requested. After Chamberlain had made a South African tour a had aided in the formation of a customs union of the four coloni there, he returned to England early in 1903 to find that the w tax on grain, which he had hoped would be an entering wed for a system of preferential duties, had been repealed. He could n persuade the cabinet to change its mind, and so in May 19 began his own appeal to the people to support a policy of imperi preferential trade. This, he argued, would protect Britain's i dustries and give her bargaining power against other powers; pr ferential rates on colonial products would be met by preference f her manufactures; and a self-sufficient empire would be bour together so closely that political and military union must necessari follow.

The motives for Chamberlain's decision to press his own progra against the opposition of the cabinet and his party were mixe colonial secretary he had become convinced that imperial union s necessary for the survival of the empire. He had sponsored : resolution of the conference of 1902 in favor of the preferential iff, and he probably felt responsible to the colonies for Britain's ng its share in the program. His long-nourished desire to become me minister also played a part. Until his split with Gladstone Home Rule, he had been expected to succeed the 'Grand Old an.' When Salisbury retired in July 1902, Chamberlain may well ve hoped to replace him, but Balfour took office while Chamber- 1 was out of action as a result of an accident. In any case Cham- ·lain, though the strong man of the cabinet, was unacceptable the Conservative Party as a Liberal Unionist. His best hope w lay in pursuing an independent policy and trying to win pport for it and himself from the public. His decision split the binet, and on September 9 he offered to resign. At first Balfour 1 not accept his resignation, but six days later announced the ignation of two of the most ardent free-trade ministers. The lowing day two more like-minded members of the cabinet resigned, d the next day Balfour announced his acceptance of Chamber- n's resignation. In the reconstructed cabinet his son Austen amberlain became Chancellor of the Exchequer, and a free trader ancial secretary of the Treasury, as Balfour attempted to straddle : issue by proposing a retaliatory tariff program. This policy ased neither Chamberlain nor the free traders.

Chamberlain promptly organized the Tariff Reform League and k to the platform, advocating his policy in every quarter of tain. He spoke as a missionary of empire: fiscal reform was ondary to the need to increase the solidarity of the empire. At asgow he urged:

> . . the realization of the greatest ideal which has ever inspired states- n in any country or any age—the creation of an Empire such as the rld has never seen. We have to cement the union of the states beyond seas; we have to consolidate the British race; we have to meet the sh of competition, commercial now—sometimes in the past it has been erwise—it may be again in the future. Whatever it be, whatever iger threatens, we have to meet it no longer as an isolated country; have to meet it fortified and strengthened and buttressed by all those our kinsmen, all those powerful and continually rising states which ak our common tongue and glory in our common flag.[170]

: appealed to the British public in the name of the eleven million onists who were British in race, religion, and traditions and who nted to unite the empire by commercial union. Contrary to the ts, he contended that the colonies were Britain's best customers, 1 that refusal to adopt the plan they favored would result in unemployment and lowered wages in Great Britain. Witho imperial trade, Great Britain would decline and might become fifth-rate power. The Little Englanders might argue that Britai trade with the colonies was less than with foreign countries, but was willing to lose foreign trade for the sake of an increase in colon trade which would prevent the dominions from drifting away fr the empire. For him the great imperial principle was 'to treat ea other better than we are treated by any one else.'[171] His experien in the Colonial Office had convinced him that free trade was an ar imperial policy and would end in the disruption of the empire. I Chamberlain's attack on free trade only served to unite the Libera while the Conservatives were divided by Balfour's comprom plan of retaliatory duties, which Chamberlain's followers reluctan accepted in March 1905. Balfour was forced to resign in Decemb 1905 and Campbell-Bannerman took over in a Liberal landsli This public verdict marked the defeat of the imperial preferen scheme in England and the last act in Chamberlain's career, for July 1906 he suffered a paralytic stroke which kept him in reti ment until his death in July 1914. French Canadians seldom real that the man who personified imperialism for them never won su port of his views from the British people at the polls.

In Canada his dramatic campaign had won warm support the outset. The Toronto correspondent of the *Morning Post* not on May 17, 1903, after Chamberlain's opening gun at Birmingha that 'Canada has seldom before felt such unanimity over a propos imperial policy, as that which greets the project of Mr. Chamberla for the granting of trade concessions in the markets of Gr Britain.'[172] The Liberal leaders were relieved that those who h criticized them for granting a British preference without exacti an equivalent were now disarmed; but they cautioned that it w for Britain to decide whether she wanted a protective tariff, a that in any subsequent agreements each country must preserve right to change its course or withdraw. The Conservatives ga the proposal warm support, and George Eulas Foster, left witho a seat in the House, went to England to aid Chamberlain in campaign.

Then Canadian enthusiasm gradually waned, as it was realiz that Chamberlain's policy meant a return to the old colonial syste with Canada permanently reduced to the role of producer of r materials and consumer of British manufactures. The difficult soon became apparent of reconciling business with sentiment, p tection of expanding native industries with free trade for Engl manufactures, American reciprocity with preference for the coloni Canada's manufacturers, generally Conservative, soon made evid their conviction that reduction of duties should only be granted goods which Canada did not manufacture; and later they became so imbued with the Liberal faith in Canada's development that they 'were not prepared to admit that there was any article that could not at some point in Canada, and in time, be successfully manufactured.'[173] But the Imperial Federalists under Colonel Denison continued to support Chamberlain's policy, which they had in no small measure succeeded in forcing upon him.

Before the Conservatives lost power in England they made one last attempt at formal federation of the empire. Chamberlain's supporters were anxious to hold another colonial conference to supply proof of colonial support of his policy, while Liberal imperialists of the Asquith-Haldane group likewise favored closer union of the empire. Chamberlain's successor at the Colonial Office, Lyttelton, sent out a circular despatch in April 1905, proposing the establishment of an 'Imperial Council' with the same personnel as before, plus an added permanent commission to prepare agenda and to act on the instructions of the council and of the British and colonial governments. The proposal was welcomed by Australia, New Zealand, Natal, and the Cape, but flatly opposed by Canada. The Canadian ministers maintained that any change of title must originate with the conference itself; they preferred the old terminology, with its traditions of informal consultation, to the new, which indicated 'a formal assembly, possessing an advisory and deliberate character, and, in conjunction with the word imperial, suggested a permanent institution which, endowed with a continuous life, might eventually come to be regarded as an encroachment upon the full measure of autonomous legislative and administrative power now enjoyed by all the self-governing colonies.'[174] In a country where, thanks to massive immigration, 50 per cent of the population was now of non-British descent there were now many besides the French Canadians who disliked the imperial label or were neutral as regards imperial federation.

8

The decisive factor in Laurier's withdrawal from seeming support of imperial centralization was the mushroom growth of the nationalist movement in his own province of Quebec, the Liberal stronghold which assured his majority in the House. The nationalist leader was Henri Bourassa, who by his opposition to Canadian participation in the Boer War personified the French-Canadian reaction to the imperialist movement which had been active in Canada since the 1880's. The movement was also a reaction against the attempt of certain English Canadians since 1885 to make Canada a land of one tongue and one culture, and to treat the French Canadians as foreigners in their own country. Unfortunately for

Canadian national development, many of the leaders of the imperialist movement were also leaders in the anti-French movement; their 'Anglo-Saxon' racism and appeals to British traditions fostered the development of racist feeling in a Quebec which had been aroused by the Riel affair. Attacks on the privileges of the French-Canadian minorities in Manitoba and Ontario fostered a French-Canadian group consciousness, a sense of 'racial and religious separateness.'[175] Clifford Sifton's massive immigration policy brought a steadily increasing flood of New Canadians—Ruthenians and Doukhobors, Germans, Austrians, Americans, and finally a stream of British immigrants, who soon outnumbered the Continental and American newcomers. Few of these immigrants were French-speaking, and even some of those who were, like the Swiss and Belgians, showed a tendency to assimilate to the English Canadians. The French Canadians, remembering Sifton's anti-French record in Manitoba, began to suspect a plot to swamp them in an English-speaking Canada in which Quebec would have little voice and importance.

Thus thrown back upon itself, French Canada began to assert its Frenchness: in literature the Patriotic School of Quebec yielded to the Literary School of Montreal, which found more of its inspiration in France than in Canada; the coming of religious orders banished from France by the anti-clerical laws strengthened the bonds of the French tradition in Quebec; each year the young men in the classical colleges became more intent upon stressing their Frenchness and their Catholicity; even the infant labor movement developed national syndicates as rivals to the American international unions, while opposition arose to the development of Quebec's natural resources by English and American capital under English-Canadian auspices. For some the new sense of separateness involved merely an effort to maintain the faith and culture of French Canada against 'Anglo-Saxon' encroachment, while freely collaborating with English Canadians in building up a nation of dual culture. For a more narrow-minded group, it meant a withdrawal within the shell of an exclusive and isolated French and Catholic province. For them nationalism was really provincialism, but the movement was not provincial in outlook at the start.

The man who became the idolized leader of the nationalist movement was the grandson of Louis-Joseph Papineau, and like his celebrated forebear combined an admiration for British institutions with a passionate devotion to French Canada and a rebellious nature which brooked no restraint of his opinions or actions. Like Papineau, Bourassa was a brilliant orator and a poor politician, able to fire the people with his own intellectual enthusiasm, but unable to work with other men. Laurier once observed: 'Having known Mr.

La Chasse-Gallerie

Oil painting (1906) by Henri Julien, the best known French-Canadian artist of his day. He was famous for his political caricatures, but this illustration for the popular Quebec folk tale is his best-known work. (Quebec Provincial Museum.)

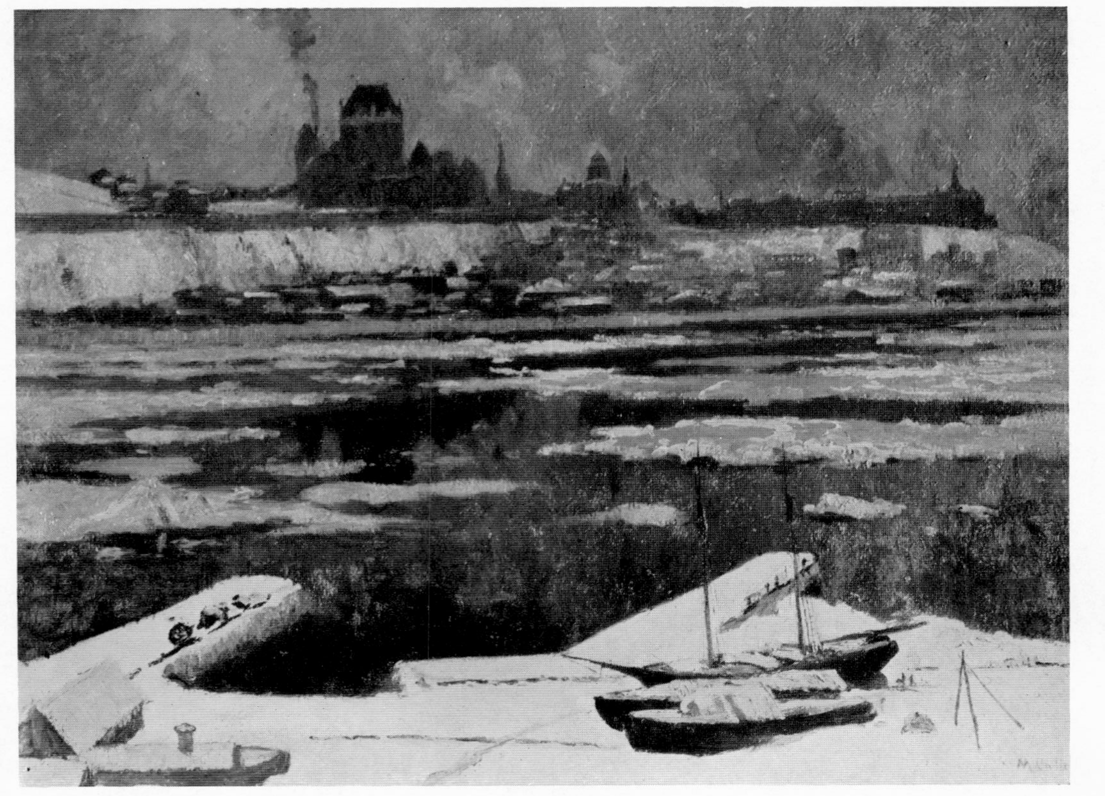

Quebec from Lévis

Oil painting (1920) by Maurice Cullen (1866–1934). This English-Canadian painter, born in Montreal, lived much abroad, but his Montreal and Quebec studies had as much influence in French Canada as the work of the

Papineau, I can in some measure understand Mr. Bourassa; having known Mr. Bourassa, I can in some measure understand Mr. Papineau.'[176] The son of the artist Napoléon Bourassa and Azélie Papineau, Bourassa was born in Montreal in 1868 and privately educated. Before entering parliament in 1896 he spent some years on his grandfather's seigneury of Montebello, the center of the constituency of Labelle which he later represented.

Keenly intelligent, idealistic, widely read in both French and English and a powerful speaker in either tongue, unimpeachable in character, deeply religious, highly cultured, and charming in manner, Bourassa represented the best of the French-Canadian élite and was soon singled out as a promising disciple by Laurier, who thought it well that a politician should be a gentleman. Laurier sent him to Winnipeg in 1896 as an aide to Tarte in the negotiations for the agreement. Then Bourassa accompanied Tarte to the Pacific coast, and gained further first-hand knowledge of the West. It was Bourassa who drafted the petition of the Liberal members to Rome in October 1896, and who urged Mgr. Merry del Val's recommendations on the Manitoba schools in 1897 on the Manitoba authorities. In 1898 Laurier appointed him secretary of the Joint High Commission which met in Quebec in that year and in Washington the following one to discuss the questions outstanding between Canada and the United States. These experiences provided Bourassa with an admirable apprenticeship in domestic politics and in international affairs.

He made dismaying use of this training in the fall of 1899 when he broke with Laurier on the question of Canadian participation in the Boer War. Laurier respected the devotion to principle which motivated Bourassa's resignation from parliament on that issue, however, and bore his '*cher Henri*' no ill will. Their personal relations remained so close that Bourassa went to Laurier at the close of the session with the proposal that the no-precedent clause of the order-in-council should be embodied in a statute. Laurier suggested that Bourassa draft a resolution to this effect, but subsequently refused to propose the one which Bourassa duly prepared and submitted. The prime minister said that Bourassa was free to do so, however, though he himself probably would be forced to speak against it. In March 1900 Laurier did so crushingly, using the occasion to demonstrate to his English-Canadian supporters the difficulties he faced in Quebec which had forced him to take a middle-of-the-road course.[177] In replying to Bourassa's later attacks on the government's war policy Laurier never lost his temper or barred the path to a reconciliation. This reconciliation duly came when Laurier communicated to Bourassa the confidential report of the 1902 Conference which revealed the prime minister's opposition to Chamberlain's pressure for political and military union of the empire.[178]

Meanwhile Bourassa had expounded at length his views on the imperial question in a lecture, 'Great Britain and Canada,' given at the Théâtre National in Montreal on October 20, 1901, and published in both French and English in the following year. In the preface to the printed version Bourassa defined imperialism and gave a classic expression of French Canada's view of it:

British Imperialism—as opposed to British democracy, to British traditions, to British grandeur—is a lust for landgrabbing and military dominion. Born of the overgrowth of British power, bred by that blatant and stupid sense of pride known as *Jingoism*, it delights in high-sounding formulas:—'*Britannia rules the waves*' . . . '*Britons never shall be slaves*' . . . '*Trade Follows the Flag*' . . . '*What we have, we hold!*' . . .; to this last axiom, the Prime-Minister of Ontario has added:—'*and what we don't have, we take*' . . . which is now supplemented by public good sense by: '*when we can.*'

Having undertaken more responsibilities than she is able to stand, surrounded as she is by hostile or indifferent nations, the new Britain of Mr. Chamberlain is in sore need of soldiers and sailors to prop the fabric raised by her frantic ambition. Being actually denuded of troops at home, she turns in distress to her colonies. Realizing as they do that without practicing evasion they cannot possibly achieve their purposes, British rulers of today resort to deceit and bribery with colonial statesmen; they lull the incredulity and inflame the jingo feelings of the people of the colonies. Under miscellaneous names and variegated uniforms—Royal Rifles, Mounted Infantry, Strathcona Horse, Yeomanry,—they extort from us whatever they may get in the shape of human material for their army; even if they have to dangle before our eyes a few paltry advantages to be thrown as a sop to us whenever we get tired of this deadly game.

In short, MILITARY CONTRIBUTIONS FROM THE COLONIES TO GREAT BRITAIN, in men and treasure, but mainly in men, constitute British Imperialism.

. . . In England the taxpayer hears only of the great benefits to be gained by the Mother Country: she is going to be helped with colonial contributions to her army and navy—not only in time of need, but as a permanent military system that will save her from the dread of conscription. In the colonies, we are told that our free and voluntary sacrifices in the cause of the Empire in South Africa are bound to bring us incalculable advantages in trade and industry, in immigration from the British Isles, etc.

In Canada the same double game is carried on by politicians of all shades. In the English-speaking provinces, both parties run for the prize of 'loyalty'—each side claiming the credit of having done the most for Great Britain. Of sole devotion to Canadian interests, we hear no more . . . The only point in real dispute between both parties is which will eat the biggest piece of the jingo pie. All this, of course, does not prevent them from selling Canada wholesale to American railway magnates. In Quebec . . . it is no longer a question of which party has done more for Great Britain, but, the less done, the greater credit claimed. 'The government are selling us to Great Britain,' shout the Conservatives: 'put us back in power and save the country!'—'There is no such thing as imperialism,' retort the Liberals; 'it is an empty dream, kept up by a few eccentrics. We have permitted only a few men to go to Africa; had our opponents been in office, many more men would have gone and more money would have been spent. Keep our illustrious compatriot, Laurier, in power and be safe from Tory imperialism!'[179]

In this double game Bourassa saw a danger of a clash between French and English Canadians and a danger to the British connection, paving the way for ethnic feuds which would lead to annexation to the United States.

In the French edition of his pamphlet Bourassa defined anti-imperialism (which he here significantly called 'counter-imperialism') as 'to denounce these attempts and to fight them—not only between the pear and the cheese of special banquets, but in parliament, in the press, on the platform, everywhere, always, at the risk of one's peace, livelihood, glory, and even popularity. It is to manifest one's thought not only at the moment and the place where profit and applause may be earned, but above all where the adherents of jingoism make their muscles and their lungs felt.'[180] Since imperialism had back of it the majority, money, and influence, its adversaries must preserve their superiority in moral courage, sincerity, and perseverance. Bourassa blamed the popular blindness to the danger on French-Canadian intellectual laziness and on the 'Latin' tendency to refuse to believe in a social development until it was formulated on paper, while the 'Anglo-Saxon,' with less respect for logic and theory, altered constitutions and empires without using paper at all.

In the scholarly manner which characterized all his polemics, using an overpowering wealth of documentation, Bourassa sketched the position of Canada, with a constitution drawn from Britain but modified by certain American elements, and with an industrial life either English or American in its origin and operations. The majority of Canadians were of British stock, who were more English than the French Canadians were French—and occasionally more English than the English, since they were more recent comers and less absorbed into the North American way of life. Since materialism dominated that life, interest rather than sentiment would determine the future of Canada; and if interest drew the English Canadians towards the United States, 'those very same voices would be heard singing the glories of the "Stars and Stripes" which but yesterday were hurraying themselves hoarse over the visit of the heir to the throne of England.'[181] Bourassa deplored French-Canadian ignorance of the history of both 'Great Britain, which holds us, and of the United States, which waits to gobble us up.' He blamed it on Canada's lack of true nationhood since she entrusted her foreign relations to Britain, which admittedly had conducted them wisely until the rise of jingoism. Thus international politics and even British politics had remained unknown to Canadians, who were now ill prepared to direct their own course. Therefore he was led to outline the development of British imperialism.

Expansionism began with the industrial revolution, increased population, and religious controversies, which led the home-loving and insular Englishman to seek new markets and new homes overseas. The British Empire, unlike others of ancient and modern times, was not the fruit of a political or military idea, but was established and grew like the British constitution itself, without a plan, without official aid, and often in opposition to the wishes of government and people. The development of British imperialism within a century was illustrated by the change from official reluctance to take over India from the East India Company and the repudiation of Warren Hastings to the support of Rhodes' African adventure and the whitewashing of his character. Bourassa preferred Pitt to Wellington, and saw in him the 'great man of modern England,' because he governed England in accordance with its national temperament rather than under a policy of military adventure and conquest. The principle of decentralized power which was evolved in the American colonies became the strength of an empire larger and more widely scattered than any ever known. But the expansion of British power in India resulted in the creation of a professional army and civil service, which bred the social evils of militarism and the bureaucratic mind. India led Britain into the Chinese opium wars and the conquest of the Cape Colony, and America into the conquest of New France. To the old Irish question two new racial problems were thus added, 'Than which there are none more irritating, none more fraught with dangers and more difficult to solve.' When England attempted to force the American colonies to share the cost of their defence, they revolted, and their action, hailed by Chatham, checked the progress of imperialism in England.

But Canada was at first denied the privileges of self-government, to whose workings the American Revolution was wrongly imputed by Britain's rulers. Those privileges were finally granted 'with the sole view to safeguarding the interests of the Mother Country.' Bourassa held that to be rightly understood, the relations of Great Britain to the colonies must be studied in the light of the constant fact that the exclusive interest of Great Britain was the mainspring which moved her statesmen, whenever they had to modify the colonial status. After a fifty-year struggle Canada finally won responsible government and provincial autonomy:

To the statesmen who so nobly and manfully struggled, and with such unflinching tenacity, for the triumph of those principles of liberty, decentralization, respect to minorities, which were ever in the past the glory and the strength of Great Britain we do indeed owe—and England and the whole world with us owe—a debt of gratitude . . . What a noble spectacle it was to see this old soldier Wellington . . entering his protest against the bill for the Union of the two Canadas, and thereby constituting himself—unconsciously perhaps—the champion of a weak offspring of the old French parent tree, at which he had struck so many a hard blow!

Yes, indeed, to such men as Gosford, Ellenborough, Brougham, Peel, Grey, Bright, Gladstone—to all those who, few though they be, were, out of a pure love of liberty, instrumental in securing and preserving to us political freedom—our admiration and our gratitude are due without stint.[182]

But the grant of responsible government was due only in part to these men; distance from Britain, their proximity to the United States, and the cost and dangers of military domination were important factors. And now the circumstances which favored Canada sixty years before had changed, while the disciples of her champions had been replaced in power in England by a new school of statesmen, linked to the men like Durham and Colborne who had sought to assimilate the French and to enslave the colony. Bourassa echoed the ancient warning: 'Eternal vigilance is the price of liberty.'

Then he showed how the triumph of free trade under Cobden, who abhorred both military and political imperialism, and distrusted colonial expansion, had favored Canadian liberty by introducing colonial decentralization as a first step towards separation. 'The colonies were given to understand that they were to be self-reliant and self-supporting, and that whensoever they thought fit to sever their connection with the motherland, no obstacle would be put in their way.' But imperialism revived with further expansion in India after the Sepoy Rebellion, resulting in the Afghanistan War, which in turn led to trouble with Russia. Similarly the occupation of Egypt led to the Sudan War and to friction with France. In South Africa were sown the seeds of militarism. The Cape was the sole British colony which had been acquired purely for imperial purposes, as a stronghold on the sea route to India. The attempt to rule it by the sword had caused the Dutch to revolt and to make the Great Trek to the north which resulted in the birth of the two Boer republics. Annexation of the Transvaal in 1879 under the imperialist government of Disraeli aroused hatred and suspicion of the British among the Boers. Then imperialism was momentarily checked by Gladstone's return to power.

But Home Rule split the Liberal party, and Chamberlain led the dissidents into the Tory camp, which was 'instinctively favorable to the autocratic and military government of the Empire.' Debarred from radical reforms at home by his Tory colleagues, Chamberlain stirred up national pride and evoked the prospect of a Cape-to-Cairo African empire. His schemes resulted in 'a war expenditure of half a billion pounds, another prospective expenditure of five hundred millions, seventy thousand men disabled, 200,000 soldiers held in check, the impossibility to find any more recruits, the stupidity of the British staff exhibited to the world, the military prestige of Great Britain destroyed.'

The Englishman was reluctant to tax his own necessities of life, imported from the colonies, in order to secure in return a favorable market for his products, increasingly shut out from the world market by protection and by German and American competition. Thus Chamberlain was unwilling to support publicly commercial imperialism, while the majority of the English people were still inclined to favor imperial decentralization and colonial autonomy. Great Britain now stood isolated from the world by her jingoism, with an army discredited by failure and a navy no longer able to dominate the seas against a rival alliance. Conscription at home spelt political ruin for the government which imposed it. The imperialist solution was an amalgam of military and economic imperialism, with the British taxpayer induced to pay a colonial preference, while in return the colonies were invited to fill up the ranks of the British army and navy. Bourassa concluded that whether or not the British taxpayer could be induced to grant a preference, 'the balance of profit will not be in our favor.' He deplored the growth in England of militarism, of brutal instincts bred by sports, and of a greed for gold which made English youth seek adventure and profit abroad while the moral and intellectual level of parliament declined.

Now, as in 1774, the colonies were to be taxed for the defence of the empire, though the tax was to be self-imposed rather than ordained by the British parliament. Such a program was favored by closer contact with the colonies and the existence of colonists avid for titles and honors; it was threatened by greater colonial freedom and democracy. Chamberlain proposed an imperial *Zollverein*, which was opposed by English taxpayers, in return for colonial military contributions. 'That the whole system rests on the idea of colonial military contributions, it cannot be questioned; all the rest—commercial reciprocity, political representation, judiciary appeal—all are mere accessories tending to secure the adoption of the principle and its permanent development.'

Bourassa paid tribute to Chamberlain's clever showmanship in launching his appeal in the midst of the pageant of the Jubilee in

397, in arranging the Canadian tour of the Duke and Duchess of ork in 1900, and in calling a new conference to meet on the casion of the coronation of Edward VII. 'As at the time of the ıbilee, so upon the occasion of the Coronation, official repre- ntatives from the colonies will gather in London, who may easily : won over and fashioned into docile tools of the powers that be: title to one, a medal to another, an opening in the House of Lords, ssing His Majesty's hand: few virtues are proof against such mptations.' Overcome by such attention, in 1897, Laurier had ıblicly pledged the aid of the colonies in the defence of the mother untry; though Bourassa added: 'to my mind it never occurred the Prime Minister of Canada that in so doing he was going yond a hearty acknowledgment of England's generous hospitality -which was evidenced from his attempted opposition to the sending ıt of Canadian troops to South Africa.' But Bourassa warned that e English were not as fond as the Canadians of 'high-sounding rmulas' and that they 'take words for what they mean.'

Chamberlain made the most of his opening, and sent out to the ılonies governors and military commanders committed to fostering ıperialism: 'Of this class Lord Minto and Col. Hutton are preme types.' Minto disregarded the constitutional tradition tablished by Elgin and followed by all his successors, while Hutton ıade a boast of having smashed a Cabinet in Australia, and in the idst of his petty court of Rideau Club, in Ottawa, he declared at he was ready to repeat the same exploit in Canada.' Bourassa ıarged that 'it was in order to snatch from the Colonies, at a oment when the voice of reason is stifled by pride and passions, e tribute of Blood which until then he had been denied, that Mr. hamberlain forced the South African War.'

He described the way in which the imperialist movement was ganized by Rhodes through the South African League of Rand eculators, which bought the local press and supplied slanted rrespondence to Tory and jingo papers in London. In Canada e *Montreal Star* served the same purpose. The Boers and their ıteresting victims, Cecil Rhodes & Co., were described under ch colors as were best calculated to inflame the indignation of itish subjects throughout the world.' Bourassa did not wonder at the blood of English Canadians had consequently become over- ated. He spoke of the Ottawa mission of Rhodes' emissary Allen, ho 'organized among members of Parliament a Committee of his ague, wherein he introduced a few heads from every herd—I g your pardon!—a few representatives of every political group: rits, Tories, *Rouges*, *Bleus*, Senators, members of the House, past, esent, and future Ministers of the Crown'; and stampeded em into a parliamentary resolution of sympathetic approval of

Chamberlain's policy. He charged that in July 1899 Hutton h: urged Canadian militia officers to prepare for South African servic and that the *Star's* campaign in September for a Canadian conti gent was 'inspired by Lord Minto and managed by General Huttc In well-informed circles, Mr. Graham's trips to Ottawa were an op secret.' Thus the government yielded to 'intrigues and wire-pullin in high and low places.'

Bourassa disposed of the no-precedent question by stating th Chamberlain had boasted after receiving Canada's answer to t call for troops that he had 'at last secured the participation of t Colonies in the Wars of the Empire,' while the Canadian parliame had refused to ratify Bourassa's no-precedent resolution. He argu that 'from the fact of our contributing, whether directly or indirect whether permanently or accidentally, to the imperial exchequer, necessarily follows that we should be represented in the Imper Councils.' He rejected the solution of representation in the imper parliament as out of the question after the experience of Iri members. Canadian democrats and Australian socialists would n be tempted from their principles by admission to the House of Lorc He denounced the suggestion of an imperial consultative council:

From our experience of the influence now exerted from afar by t British authorities over colonial ministers, it may safely be inferred tl for the British Government to keep under the yoke men in close tou with them, and upon whom the whole weight of their favors and sedu tions could be brought to bear, would prove no difficult task. In such issues as involved the interests of both the Mother Country and t colonies, the British government would never fail to secure a major in the council, which would prove easier from the fact that the Unit Kingdom would long be represented by a larger number of delega than the combined colonial representation.[183]

He anticipated that through the periodic '*ad limina*' visits of t colonial premiers and the influence exerted on the resident colon agents, whose offices already had become 'so many branches of t Colonial Office,' the accomplished fact of an imperial organizati would gradually be arrived at without direct action by parliame He laid Lord Strathcona's imperialism to gratitude for his peera and suggested that the Canadian high commissioner in Lond should not be allowed to accept British favors. He denounced tit and decorations as means of political corruption, citing Lo Melbourne's explanation of his refusal of the Garter, 'that he c not see why he should be such a fool as to buy himself, when could buy somebody else with it.'

Though the English middle and educated classes were opposed imperialism, the British Liberal Party was split on the South Afric question and Chamberlain's policy was gaining ground in the absence of strong opposition leadership. Bourassa anticipated that the Australians would prove 'more strenuous opponents of imperialism than we are,' and he discounted New Zealand's loyalism as based upon a temporary need for British capital. He deplored the fact that in the Canadian house the sort of imperialism which had been laughed at, a few years ago, in the speeches of Alexander MacNeill, nicknamed the 'Father of the Empire,' was now cheered when it came from the leaders of both parties. The British Empire League of Dr. Parkin and Colonel Denison was now supported by many ministers and members of parliament. At the last meeting of the League Sir Charles Hibberd Tupper had favored colonial contributions to the imperial army and navy, and had been seconded by the Liberal Dr. Russell. In the summer of 1901 the *Globe* had come out for colonial contributions to imperial defence.

And in the strong Canadian party spirit and in the racial cleavage Bourassa found a two-fold opening for imperialism:

> A mutual regard for racial sympathies on both sides, and a proper discharge of our exclusive duty to this land of ours, such is the only ground upon which it is possible for us to meet, so as to work out our national problems. There are here neither masters nor valets; there are neither conquerors or conquered ones; there are two partners whose partnership was entered into upon fair and well defined lines. We do not ask that our English-speaking fellow-countrymen should help us to draw closer to France; but, on the other hand, they have no right to take advantage of their overwhelming majority to infringe on the treaty of alliance, and induce us to assume, however freely and spontaneously, additional burdens in defence of Great Britain.[184]

He respected the English Canadian's love of his mother country, and expected the same respect for the French Canadian's love for France; 'but the only sure way of obviating fatal misunderstandings lies in a determination that we shall, both of us, French and English alike, look at all constitutional and political questions from a purely Canadian standpoint.'

Until a better understanding was reached between the races, Canada was not ready for independence. Even if it were, there would be danger in independence because of the strength of American imperialism and the threat of annexation. Eventual independence was the most acceptable solution of the Canadian problem for the French Canadian, but imperialism had embittered the relations between the races and under the absolute control of a Canadian parliament, 'our constitution would be exposed to terrible assaults, mainly directed against the French-Canadian minority, whose only refuge, under such circumstances, would be Pan-Americanism.'

Only if imperialism won the upper hand should immediate independence be risked. In conclusion, Bourassa warned against being carried away by enthusiasm or allowing ideals to be debased. He called for a deeper and broader patriotism less given to 'the worship of party leaders than towards the pursuit of principles and lofty ideals.'

9

In this first major public address Bourassa displayed an attitude towards imperialism which was at once Canadian and in accordance with the best traditions of English Liberalism. His ideas were not very different from those of Goldwin Smith, and indeed he was more reluctant to envisage the end of the British connection than the Toronto prophet of annexationism. But Bourassa's opposition to imperialism made him the hero of the young anglophobe French-Canadian students, who envisaged the formation of a new French-Canadian party which would not make concessions to imperialism, as Conservatives and Liberals alike had done. As Laurier's success gradually eclipsed the Conservative party in Quebec, Bourassa became the leader of those French Canadians, particularly the younger generation, who found the Liberal chief too willing to compromise with imperialism and the English Canadians. Bourassa's vanity was too great for him to reject the role that the students thrust upon him, and he did not strongly condemn their anti-English excesses, though these did not express his own position.

A group of young men in Montreal, headed by Louvigny de Montigny and Olivar Asselin, launched in 1900 a weekly paper called *Les Débats*, which made much of Bourassa's skirmishes in the House against war measures, condemned by the press of both old parties. In Quebec Armand Lavergne, the son of Laurier's Arthabaska friends, distributed *Les Débats* and Bourassa's speeches to a circle of Laval students, after the clerical authorities had moderated the tone of the aggressively nationalist *Semaine Religieuse*. At Saint-Jérome, the Nantels launched a weekly, *La Nation*, with a program of seeking independence through constitutional means, and of opposing imperialism and the federal and provincial administrations. Occasionally *Le Pionnier*, formerly of Sherbrooke and now of Montreal, printed articles by the disciples of Bourassa, while the Conservative *Journal* sometimes defended the young Liberal who broke with his leader and his party on the war issue. For Frederick Debartzch Monk, the provincial chief of the Conservatives, son of an English-Canadian father and a French-Canadian mother, and professor of law at Laval University in Montreal, was more French than English in his outlook, and sympathetic to Bourassa's ideas. When in November 1901 the question of a third contingent

›r South Africa arose, Monk condemned imperialism and militar-m in the face of the Ontario Tory press support of the move. aurier followed the same course as before, with an order-in-ouncil authorizing the recruiting of six hundred mounted infantry t the expense of the War Office.

The pamphlet publication of Bourassa's 'Great Britain and anada' early in 1902 stimulated the growth of anti-imperialism n Quebec. When parliament met in February, and the *Toronto Vorld* and the *Montreal Star* urged that Canada should pay the xpenses of the third contingent, Bourassa demanded that corres-ondence between London and Ottawa on the recruiting of Cana-ians for South Africa should be produced in the House. He also ffered an amendment on the speech from the throne, condemning merican control of Canadian railroads, for he was on guard gainst both English military imperialism and American economic mperialism. He yielded to government pressure and withdrew the atter motion, as well as a later one on the Alaska boundary, though n that instance he accused Great Britain of sacrificing Canadian nterests to her desire for American friendship. Again he pressed he government for the production of correspondence relative to the ranting of imperial commissions to Canadian officers, and in doing o attacked the governor-general for interfering in Canadian affairs. aurier and Monk, both realizing that Bourassa was becoming a hreat to their leadership in Quebec, took a stiffer tone towards him. But his ideas continued to gain even wider support in Quebec.

Laurier checked the movement by producing the official corres-ondence in which he had refused to discuss political and military nion of the empire at the forthcoming colonial conference. But Bourassa criticized the grant of a preferential tariff to Britain without eturn—to him, it looked as if imperialism meant that Canada hould give everything and receive nothing—and he urged the government to be guided by Canada's interests in the commercial liscussions to which Laurier had consented. Laurier yielded to mperialist pressure for a fourth contingent, but reassured his Quebec followers by the declaration that nothing but commerce vould be discussed in London: 'Public works, colonization, rail-road construction, and harbor development, there is the field in which our activity must be exercized and it would be criminal to levote a portion of the funds necessary for the accomplishment of these works to the purchase of cannon, rifles, and munitions of war'.[185] Bourassa was now exercising pressure on Laurier, almost to the same extent as Laurier had previously done on him.

Bourassa's lecture on 'Canadian Patriotism' at the Monument National in Montreal on April 27, 1902, was clearly designed to stiffen Laurier's new attitude of resistance to imperialist influence.

The nationalist leader stressed the fact that the French Canadia were first of all Canadian, sympathetic to France but reserving the chief love for Canada. Their resistance to imperialism was not bo of hatred for the English nor of fidelity to France, but of the exclusive devotion to their own country. It would be easy to w applause by denouncing England and everything English, but h refrained from doing so, because he did not believe in arousir racial prejudice and because it would be unjust not to praise th which was good, and there were men in England with just ideas ar generous souls. The French Canadians were bound to Englan and owed her a loyal and suitable fidelity. But they owed her neith bitterness nor gratitude. He urged his hearers to be conciliator tolerant, and generous to their English compatriots, and to exa the same behavior in return. 'Let us be neither servile nor i sulting; let us win their esteem by being proud.'[186] But excite by the enthusiasm which he evoked, Bourassa himself aroused, b the bitter sarcasm to which he was given, the separatism of some his disciples and the fury of English-Canadian Tories.

Unquestionably Bourassa's speech influenced the reply of th French-Canadian Chambre de Commerce of Montreal to th Toronto Chamber's resolution favoring imperialism and defenc contributions. Montreal called for English tariff concessions in re turn for Canada's British preference; it asserted that Canada ha done its part for imperial defence by building the Canadian Pacifi and the Intercolonial, and in the future should reserve its resourc for its own development. Laurier paid heed by his reply to Borde in the House on May 12, denouncing the imperialist school whic wished to plunge Canada into the gulf of European militarism. A the beginning of June the Toronto congress of the Canadian Cham bers of Commerce passed a resolution, originating with the Englisl Canadian Montreal Board of Trade, favorable to imperialism but Laurier replied that the government intended no change i the existing political and military relations with Great Britain.

On June 19, 1902, after Laurier had sailed for London, Napoléo Garceau organized a nationalist manifestation at Drummondvill using Mercier's slogan: 'Let us cease our fratricidal strife an unite!' Of the seven speakers, the only two of the older generation Louis Lavergne and Victor Geoffrion, counselled reliance on Laurie to check imperialism. Dominique Monet proclaimed that imperial ism blocked the progress of Canada to its national destiny b raising obstacles to a single patriotism which would be neithe French nor English. The nationalist movement had been criticize as being impractical and useless, but was it useless to combat th imperialism which imposed upon Canada an annual burden of te to fifteen million dollars for defence of the empire? It had bee ued that Laurier had taken a decided position on the question, considering the great effort of the imperialists to influence the ernment, it was worthwhile to counterbalance this effort. urassa urged all, Liberals and Conservatives alike, to support the ne minister in his resistance to imperialism. Resolutions drawn by Garceau were unanimously approved and cabled to Laurier London. After proclaiming the participants' attachment to their ionality and to its constituent elements, faith, language, laws, and ditions, and their fidelity to the British Crown, the resolutions lared:

r fidelity to Canada, their only fatherland, to its constitution and rties; they declare themselves ready to sacrifice their possessions and r lives to maintain national integrity, as their fathers had done in the t; but they refuse to accept modifications which would diminish the ependence and autonomy of the Canadian people, to draw tighter bonds which united Canada to the British Crown, and to assume ards the Empire obligations more onerous than those imposed by the stitution, with which Great Britain had declared itself satisfied.

'hus this convention approves the attitude that the prime minister taken on this subject at the last session of the federal parliament which he has declared must be maintained at the Colonial Confere soon to meet in London.[187]

is gathering was notable as the first occasion on which a nationalist itical program was presented to a great popular meeting.

Bourassa's ideas received the sanction of Mgr. L.-A. Paquet, the ed theologian and orator of Laval, who in the chief address of 1902 Saint-Jean-Baptiste celebration at Quebec, which celeted simultaneously the fiftieth anniversary of the university and diamond anniversary of the Quebec Saint-Jean-Baptiste Society, nned 'the vocation of the French race in North America':

. . We are not only a civilized race, we are the pioneers of civilization; are not only a religious people, we are the messengers of the religious a; we are not only submissive sons of the Church, we are, we ought be, numbered among its zealots, its defenders, and its apostles. Our sion is less to manipulate capital than to change ideas; it consists less ighting the fire of factories than to maintain and to make shine afar luminous fire of religion and thought.[188]

is sermon of Mgr. Paquet provided a classic example of the ssianic nationalism derived from Bossuet and De Maistre and lely expounded in French Canada, chiefly by the clergy, during last half century. Abbé Casgrain and Louis Fréchette had quently mentioned the providential mission of the French nadians in their writings, and Bishop Laflèche, Judge Routhier, and a host of clerical orators had made it a commonplace of Sa Jean-Baptiste Day sermons and orations.[189] With the renewa close relations with France and the coming of refugees from anti-clerical laws, De Maistre won a new dominance in Fren Canadian thinking. Mgr. Paquet's warning against exces industrialization and his call for the exertion of Quebec's intellect influence outside the province fitted in with Bourassa's progr Canadian priests served in the Franco-American parishes of N England which Bourassa visited early in 1902, and many of th sought to link the expatriates with Quebec. And Quebec it steadily drew more of its culture from France, although there w already those who rebelled against French intellectual influence well as against English political influence and American econo influence.

In June 1902 Bourassa wrote an essay in English, 'The Fre Canadians and the British Empire,' which appeared in the Lon *Monthly Review* and was subsequently published in a French tra lation in *La Nouvelle France*. He wished to explain to the Eng why his compatriots were opposed to British imperialism, and did so in a frank and objective way. He pointed out the importa of the French Canadians as one-third of the population of Cana the most important self-governing dominion, with their domina in Quebec and growing importance in the Maritimes. He sp of their higher birth rate and of the gradual reversal of the f of emigration to the States. He admitted the comparative feriority of the French Canadians in business, but stressed th pioneering and colonizing ability. In intellect and culture they w at least the equals of their 'Anglo-Saxon' neighbors, and they l made notable contributions to constitutional and legal progress Canada. He concluded that they would continue to occupy a s stantial position in Canada, to modify its policy, and gradually augment their influence. They had made British institutions th own and reclaimed their rights with the same pride as all Bri subjects, but they were not ready to follow the British in an evo tion which would lead to new obligations towards the empire.

After reviewing the history of the French Canadians, show how they had struggled to win all the rights they enjoyed and p their debt to Britain by twice preserving Canada for her, Boura outlined their present position. They were not driven by ambit and cupidity in either private or public life. They wished th English compatriots well and often had warm relations with in viduals among them, though no sympathy for the English as a gro They desired no change in Canada's status, but if a change w necessary, they felt it should be in the interest of Canada at lar They were exclusively Canadian, while their English compatri still spoke of England as 'Home.' They did not consider that the English Canadians had the right to make Canada more British than Canadian. Independence seemed to them their inevitable destiny, but they would make no move to break the English connection unless it was sought to tighten it. Recently French Canada had become more French in spirit, as the Americans had become more English, but neither sought reunion with the ancient mother country, and in fact there were more profound differences between the French Canadians and the French of France than between the Americans and the English. The French Canadians' intellectual and moral loyalty to France, their political loyalty to England, were both entirely subordinated to their exclusively Canadian patriotism.

They viewed imperialism not sentimentally but purely logically. For England they felt a reasoned affection, a mixture of esteem and distrust varying according to the time and the circumstances and modified by the education and temperament of each individual and his social milieu. For the empire they had no emotional feeling, since there was no link of blood or pride in imperial power and glory. They considered that they had settled their debt with England and owed nothing to the empire. They did not join the English Canadians in demanding special consideration in commerce, for they judged that for each favor it would be necessary to give compensation. Uncommercial-minded, they were not lured by the prospect of turning the empire into a gigantic business; they preferred to have Canada keep control of its own commercial policy and deal with all nations as its advantage dictated. Bourassa disposed of the argument that Canada owed sacrifices to Great Britain, since it had enjoyed British diplomatic services, by pointing out how costly to Canada this system had been. Since Britain refused to make sacrifices to preserve Canadian interests, why should Canada assume new obligations towards her?

Bourassa declared that the French Canadians had an aversion to militarism. Under British rule Canada had never involved England in a war, but had been twice invaded as a result of British policy. There was no foreseeable prospect of Canada needing the military aid of the empire, and she did not choose to be drawn into foreign conflicts in which she had no interest, such as the South African war. Canada was willing to provide for her own defence, but military imperial federation would offer new dangers without providing any compensation. Canada would be an inevitable victim in an Anglo-American war, and the French Canadians would not be willing to fight the almost equal number of Franco-Americans. He summed up the attitude of the French Canadians thus: 'Indifferent to commercial imperialism, hostile to military imperialism, we desire no organic change in our constitution, ar we reject any project of imperial federation.'[190]

Annexation, though traditionally repugnant to the French Cana dians, might be more popular if their autonomy was lost. Comme cial union with the States offered a better prospect than an imperi *Zollverein*. The American economic invasion of Canada and th prospect of the reunion of the two branches of their race also we weakening the old aversion to annexation. Bourassa conclude that love of the soil and of their nationality had always been chara teristic of robust and growing peoples; while the fever of exaggerate expansion and the thirst for domination had always been signs pr ceding the decadence of nations.

In this article Bourassa adopted the traditional Canadian tact of using annexation as a threat to compel concessions by one maj ethnic group to the other in time of crisis in their relations. In foreword to the French version, he said that he himself was mor opposed than ever to annexation, but he was forced to recogniz that it was increasingly popular with his compatriots, as a result English-Canadian imperialism and jingoism. If forced to choos between imperialism and annexation, he would accept the form without hesitation. But such was not the sentiment of the Frencl Canadian majority, and he foresaw annexation as the inevitabl result of the imperialist movement.[191]

10

Before Laurier returned from London, the Australian delegat to the Colonial Conference passed through Montreal and we given a banquet by the Board of Trade on September 8, 190 Lord Minto was present and spoke on imperial defence, while th Australians confirmed the popular impression that the questio was far from dead. Bourassa, speaking at Labelle a few days late replied to Minto, who had said that Canada would soon have t provide its own army and perhaps cooperate in the defence of th empire, by urging that 'We should keep our sons for ourselves, an before spending millions to make soldiers, ought to mak colonists.'[192] Then he launched into a criticism of the feder government, which imported foreigners of all races to people th West but allowed Quebec to depopulate itself by emigration, an of the provincial government, whose blind policy of granting va timber limits to lumber merchants had aroused the antagonism land-hungry colonists. Bourassa had passed his youth among th pioneers and lumberjacks of his grandfather's seigneury, and h knew them and their needs. He made a moving plea for coloniz tion, in which he took a growing interest as the development of th northern region of the province became more and more of an issue. Bourassa naturally espoused the cause of the colonists, who figured largely among his northern constituents, against the extension of the holdings of American lumber interests in the Témiscamingue country.

Bourassa was privately reconciled with Laurier after reading the confidential report of the 1902 Colonial Conference. Fielding won over other doubters of Laurier's anti-imperialist attitude in London by revealing to the press various documents, in particular a Canadian memorandum presented on August 11 which refused suggested support of the imperial fleet and army. It stated that the delegates' objections were not due to the expense involved, but to the fact that 'acceptance would be considered as an abandonment of the principle of colonial responsible government.' Canada proposed by perfecting its militia system 'to take upon itself, within its territorial limits, some of the functions which until now the imperial government has had to fulfil alone.'[193] Bourassa's reconciliation with Laurier was publicly revealed when at the opening of the session in February 1903 the former refrained from attacking the prime minister while criticizing Great Britain's sacrifice of Canadian interests in the constitution of the Alaska Boundary Tribunal.

Early in 1903 Bourassa published a French translation of Goldwin Smith's *Before the Tribunal of History*. In a foreword he pointed out that the French Canadians, in their almost unanimous condemnation of the Boer War, were supported by the English Liberals and many English Canadians who had commended his anti-war utterances. Despite the check suffered by Chamberlain at the 1902 Conference, aggressive imperialism was still a danger, and 'pan-Anglo-Saxonism' destined no happy lot for minorities and foreign races in the 'United Empire' it desired. He warned that hatred of England might become the common feeling of the French Canadians if England continued to follow an imperialist policy, 'blinded by jingoism and bent under the yoke of Mr. Chamberlain.'[194] But they were reassured by the opposition to imperialism of such men as John Morley, Viscount Bryce, Courtney, and Goldwin Smith himself: 'If we hate Mr. Chamberlain's Empire, we admire and love Gladstone's England.' If England became once more the classic land of liberty and freed Ireland and South Africa, the confidence of the French Canadians would be renewed.

Smith himself pointed out in a preface that the position of the French Canadians was similar to that of the Boers. He warned that the same party which had led Canada into aggression against a people who had never done her wrong would bring on other imperial wars in which Canada, and above all French Canada, had no interest. Forgetting his wonted anti-clericalism, Smith paid tribute to the 'impartial and dignified attitude' of the Catholic clergy, which during the Boer War had not sought popularity nor catered to the passions of the moment like their Protestant colleagues. And he expressed his happiness that his translator was the man who 'had not feared to affirm persistently the thought of his compatriots in the face of a violently hostile parliament.' The pamphlet itself was a vigorous attack on Chamberlain's policy and on the war itself from start to finish, and a demonstration of its uselessness. Smith concluded: 'If the existence and aspirations of a nationality are, as one has always believed, necessary to the well being and progress of men, it is a grave thing to destroy a nation. Those who, having at heart the interest and the honor of their country, wished to prevent the destruction of the South African republics have the satisfaction of feeling that they have not been accomplices in this act.'[195] By publishing a French translation of Smith's pamphlet Bourassa no doubt sought to buttress his own position by English authority, and perhaps to restrain the growing anglophobia of his student followers.

II

The nationalist movement now began to take definite form, as the younger generation rebelled against both the old parties. The group which had cut their teeth since 1900 as editors and contributors to *Les Débats* now founded *La Ligue Nationaliste* at a public meeting in Montreal on March 1, 1903. Its program, which had been submitted to Bourassa, had three main points:

1. For Canada, in its relations with Great Britain, the largest measure of autonomy compatible with the maintenance of the colonial bond.
2. For the Canadian provinces, in their relations with the federal power, the largest measure compatible with the maintenance of the federal bond.
3. Adoption by the federal government and the provincial governments of a policy of Canadian economic and intellectual development.[196]

The autonomy desired for Canada was three-fold: political, commercial, and economic. Under the first head the detailed program called for maintenance of political liberties, opposition to Canadian participation in the imperial parliament or in a periodic or permanent imperial council, consultation of parliament by the government in regard to colonial conferences, freedom to regulate immigration, production of all correspondence between London and Ottawa, restriction of appeals to the Privy Council, and the right of direct representation in international congresses. Under the second head, Canada should have the right to make and revise its commercial treaties with all countries, including Britain and its colonies;

and the privilege of naming commercial agents. The third called for non-participation in imperial wars outside Canada; resistance to all recruiting efforts made by England in Canada; opposition to the establishment of a naval school in Canada, with the aid and for the benefit of the imperial authority; command of the Canadian militia by a Canadian officer named by the Canadian government, and strictly Canadian training for the militia.[197]

This program was drafted by Olivar Asselin, who had been born in the Charlevoix countryside depopulated by emigration to the States. Asselin had been educated at Rimouski, and had then gone to New England at the age of seventeen, dazzled by the prosperity of two Franco-American schoolmates. After working as a grocer's clerk and as a mill foreman, he had embarked on a journalistic career with the Franco-American newspapers of Fall River, Woonsocket, Pawtucket, and Lowell, which was punctuated by military service in the Spanish-American War. Returning to Canada in 1900, he continued his journalistic career on the staffs of *La Patrie*, the *Herald*, *Le Canada*, and *Les Débats*, moving from one paper to another both from a desire to gain varying viewpoints on provincial politics and from temperamental instability. He became the private secretary of Lomer Gouin, the minister of colonization, and was briefly jailed in 1903 for assaulting Louis-Alexandre Taschereau in the Quebec Assembly after being verbally attacked by him.

Asselin then returned to journalism with *Le Journal*, *Le Canada*, and *La Presse*; but devoted much of his time to the new movement of which he was president, with Omer Héroux as secretary, and Armand Lavergne as organizer in the Quebec district. Like his master Bourassa, Asselin admired British institutions, made a distinction between 'imperialist adventurers' like Chamberlain and the 'lovers of liberty' like Campbell-Bannerman and Lloyd George, and sought to defend the French language and French thought in Canada. Endowed with great energy and an eager intelligence which led him to educate himself, by temperament a fighter and gifted with a talent for polemics which often fell into violence and sarcasm but were never dull, he was a notable recruit to the cause of nationalism.[198]

Another group of younger men, at first less politically-minded since they were still in the classical colleges of the Montreal region, had grown up since 1900. They gave their nationalism a more religious bent under the guidance of Abbé Lionel Groulx of Valleyfield, Abbé Emile Chartier of Saint-Hyacinthe, and Père Hermas Lalande, superior of the Jesuit Collège Sainte-Marie. Their 'Catholic Action' groups inspired by Montalembert and the Comte de Mun, were at first religious fraternities, but soon took on nationalist overtones.[199] They rallied around a French-Canadian flag of Catholic character, the so-called '*drapeau Carillon-Sacré Coeur*,' a mythical standard supposedly flown at Ticonderoga in 1758 but actually devised by a romantic abbé at the Seminary of the Quebec under the inspiration of Fréchette's poem and messianic nationalism.[200]

Following a suggestion of Jules-Paul Tardivel of *La Vérité*, Joseph Versailles of the Collège Sainte-Marie summoned a congress of delegates from the chief classical colleges to meet in Montreal on June 24, 1903, on the occasion of the unveiling of a statue of Bishop Bourget.[201] Before that meeting Laurier intervened with Archbishop Bruchési, fearing an Ontario reaction to the inevitable separatist demonstrations; and the Archbishop persuaded the young men to abandon the flag idea and to emphasize Catholic Action rather than nationalism.[202] The delegates agreed to form an *Association Catholique de la Jeunesse canadienne-francaise* (A.C.J.C.), with a permanent central office under the secretary Henri Bernard. The movement steadily grew, and as it grew became more nationalistic.[203] The A.C.J.C. was the nursery of twentieth century French-Canadian nationalism, and its confusion of religion and patriotism was carried into every walk of French-Canadian life by the heady indoctrination which the young élite received as it passed through its ranks.

The existence of the *Ligue Nationaliste*, like that of the A.C.J.C., was at first neither known nor noticed; but it soon came before the public as the imperialist campaign continued, reinforced by the return of the volunteers who had served in South Africa and by the appointment of Lord Dundonald, the hero of Ladysmith, as Canadian commander-in-chief. Dundonald followed the course of Hutton in seeking to stimulate imperialist sentiment in Canada. He found no official support for his pleas for more funds for the militia and for extensive fortifications on the American border, and gradually fell into the habit of publicly criticizing the government. His public speeches at Hamilton and Toronto, proclaiming the necessity of developing Canadian military spirit, caused Bourassa to request in the House that Dundonald be warned that Canada had responsible government, and would form its own policies. An Ontario member, A. H. Clarke, then expressed the opinion that distinguished Englishmen had the right to express their views freely in Canada without being attacked in the House. Laurier supported the right of Bourassa (who expressed an opinion which the prime minister shared but had kept to himself) and of all members of parliament to criticize freely the speeches of public servants.[204] On August 20 Laurier reinforced this anti-imperialist stand at the closing banquet of the Congress of the Empire Chambers of Commerce, which had been held at Montreal at the suggestion of Chamberlain and under the honorary presidency of Lord Strathcona in the hope of influencing Canada into imperialist paths. Senator George Drummond, president of the Montreal Board of Trade, had proposed a resolution asserting the duty of the colonies to participate in wars necessary to the defence of the empire, which was supported by a similar resolution of the Canadian Manufacturers' Association. The French-Canadian delegates, under the leadership of Napoléon Garceau and J.-X. Perrault, raised opposition, but finally adopted the Drummond resolution modified by a clause stating that Canada should itself decide the method and the extent of its participation. In the face of Minto's support of Chamberlain's projects at the dinner, Laurier declared: 'I should not yield an inch of our independence, should the destinies of the Empire be in danger.'[205]

Three days later the *Ligue Nationaliste* proclaimed its existence by holding at the Théâtre National a public protest meeting against the imperialist manifestations of the congress. Bourassa was the chief speaker. He described the congress as the work of Chamberlain, who would use its recognition of the principle of imperial defence as an argument to support his imperialist plans. But Canadian autonomy had been too hardly won and was too dear to be sacrificed to the views of Chamberlain and his Canadian representative, Lord Minto. The French Canadians' first duty was to Canada, to develop their country. To England they owed neither gratitude nor bitterness, since they had done more for her than she had for them. The French Canadians had preserved Canada for England, but they did not wish to be involved in war with all England's enemies. Bourassa urged resistance to imperialism, and 'the silencing of the voice of Rideau Hall, so that the people's voice might be heard.' Too close commercial relations with Britain were dangerous; Laurier's stated principle should be supported. Finally Bourassa said that he desired no break with England, but if there had to be a choice between a break and servile dependence, he favored the break: 'Rather independence than imperialism!'[206] These words brought down the house.

Bourassa's leadership in combating imperialism was praised by the next speaker, L.-A. Chauvin, former member for Terrebonne, who attributed to Bourassa the change in Laurier's attitude in the last three years. Garceau said a few words, and then Dominique Monet hotly proclaimed that the enemy had come within the gates of Montreal to deliberate, so that England might urge Canada to fight the Boers, the Irish, and the French. He urged the French Canadians not to forget that by Confederation they were only bound to defend their own frontiers. He called for the end of party strife and the union of all Canadians in the fight against imperialism. Three M.P.'s, Rodolphe Lemieux, J.-E. Léonard, and Charles Angers, declared by letter their sympathy with the purpose of the meeting and their opposition to political, commercial, and military union of the empire. Unanimously the assembly voted resolutions favoring a reduction of military expenses, a Canadian commander for the militia, Canadian consuls, and free negotiation of treaties; and finally declared:

> . . . the Canadian people has done in the past more than its duty to assure the maintenance of English power in America, refuses to impose upon itself new sacrifices for the organization and defence of the Empire, and affirms that the duty of the colonies in this respect is limited to the defence of their respective territories.[207]

The first effort of the *Ligue* was hailed by the French press as a major event. An account of Bourassa's speech was cabled to London, where according to the shocked *Star* it occasioned 'a certain surprise.'[208] Louvigny de Montigny dispatched to *Le Canada* of Paris an account of the *Ligue* and its meeting, giving its program, which thus was first published in France. Asselin, anticipating political repercussions, resigned as Gouin's secretary and became news editor of *La Presse*.

12

With elections in the offing, Israel Tarte now made a bid for leadership of the Conservative Party in Quebec and took to the platform. Dominique Monet challenged him to an '*assemblée contradictoire*' at La Prairie on September 19, with Monet speaking three-quarters of an hour, Tarte an hour and a half, and Bourassa three-quarters of an hour, with Tarte having ten minutes for rebuttal. Five thousand people came to hear this debate on imperialism between two leading spokesmen of the opposed schools of opinion. Monet attacked Tarte as the champion of economic imperialism, asked him why he returned to the party of the 'brigands and thieves' he had denounced in the days of Langevin, why he had not returned the money lent him by the Liberal Party for the purchase of *La Patrie*, and why he supported the policy of Chamberlain. In reply Tarte defended his departure from the Liberal Party on the grounds that he had the same right to preserve his liberty of thought and action as Monet and Bourassa. He said the tariff was not a Liberal or Conservative question, but a business one, and stressed the importance of the British market which annually absorbed $108,000,000 worth of Canadian agricultural products. Tarte declared that he had purchased *La Patrie*, not with Liberal funds, but with the loans of his own friends; and that he had refused to sell it to the Liberals after his departure from the cabinet. And finally he claimed that the development of the St. Lawrence route and of the port of Montreal was due to his efforts.

Then Bourassa launched a vigorous attack on the man who had ıitiated him into politics. Under an imperial tariff union, Canada ·ould lose the right to make its own commercial treaties. It would e no longer 'Canada for the Canadians,' but 'Canada for England.' Ie pictured Tarte as the creature of Chamberlain, the statesman ·ho had done most to violate colonial liberties and whose ultimate ·iumph would deprive the autonomous peoples of the empire of the ght to govern themselves. Speaking of their collaboration in fighting against participation in the Boer War, he denounced Tarte for ıanging his stand on imperialism because of ambition:

> I voted and spoke against Sir Wilfrid Laurier when, in the fullness of s strength and of his prestige, he seemed to forget his duties to the anadian people and to yield to the current of English imperialism; ıd you, M. Tarte, who condemned the African War as I did, who did ·erything to prevent Canada from participating in it, who were as ınti-British,' as 'disloyal,' as I, you yielded to Laurier when he was in ıe best of health and obeyed the imperialist movement which you ›ndemned. Oh, no; you did not resign then; your conscience permitted ›u to cooperate with a policy that you condemned. But when Laurier, l, but showing himself firmer, more energetic, prouder of the rights of anada than when he was well, you, sir, wishing to regain your popurity in the English provinces and to put yourself in the good graces of ıe great industrialist—while Laurier was in England, sick it is true, ut standing up to Chamberlain—you abandoned him, and knelt before hamberlain . . .
>
> As three years ago I fought Laurier, the partisan of Chamberlain, today fight you, M. Tarte, because you have the sad honor to be the sole artisan of Chamberlain in the Province of Quebec.[209]

'hus the 35-year-old Bourassa crushed the 57-year-old Tarte, who ad made and broken so many political careers and had been called ıe master of Laurier's administration. Tarte found no more effective ınswer to the onslaught than to match Bourassa's prophecy of the ıd of his career with a prophecy of a brilliant one for the young ationalist.

Bourassa, whose sorties against imperialism had been so embarrıssing to Laurier during the Boer War, now justified the prime ıinister's refusal to read him out of the Liberal Party. Acting on his wn account, as always, Bourassa had destroyed Tarte, who had ecome Laurier's most dangerous enemy in Quebec. Later that fall, ·hen the Alaska Boundary Tribunal's award was announced, ourassa used it as an argument in the House that in the future 'anada must conduct her own international negotiations and have er own representative at Washington. This speech paved the way ›r Laurier's declaration that the time had come for the imperial arliament to concede to Canada the right to conclude her own treaties. The press, English and French alike, deplored Englanc concessions at Canada's expense in the Alaska affair, and support the proposed step. Sifton, who had followed the work of the tribun in London, expressed himself even more vigorously than Bourass and upon his return home denounced Chamberlain's mutu preference policy.

Bourassa was invited to speak in Toronto on November 9 on 'T Loyalism of the French Canadians.' Hailed as the spokesman Quebec, he was widely interviewed. Goldwin Smith welcomed hi at his home 'The Grange,' that shrine of maverick Liberalism, whe the pair passed the night in talk. Under the chairmanship of Jam Hughes, the Orangeman brother of Colonel Sam Hughes, Bouras expounded his topic very frankly. He deplored the fact that tl English Canadians did not know the French Canadians as well the latter did the former. His compatriots were not French, b exclusively Canadian in outlook, and hence anti-imperialist. Whi the English Canadian prided himself on loyalty to 'King ar Country,' the French-Canadian's loyalty was to 'Country and King He opposed sending men to fight abroad when they were needed home. Canadians should govern Canada and negotiate Canada treaties. Finally he urged his audience to try and know the Frenc Canadians better. Bourassa, praised in Toronto for his frankne and for having the courage of his convictions, followed up th speech with another at Woodstock, Ontario, on the spirit of tl B.N.A. Act.

Then, upon his return to Montreal, he spoke at a meeting orga nized by the *Ligue Nationaliste* in honor of Charles Ramsay Devlin, former Canadian M.P. for Ottawa, now representative of Galwa in the British Parliament. Devlin spoke of Ireland's martyrdon comparing the position of the Irish and the French Canadians, ar urging them to be united in Canada. Bourassa paid tribute Devlin and urged the solidarity of all the colonies; Canadians ha both the right and the duty to request liberty for Ireland. Bouras was rapidly becoming the man of the hour; he was widely spoken as a possible minister of colonization in a reorganized provinci cabinet. But he aimed still higher, and seemingly expressed Laurier his willingness to enter the provincial field as premier if give a free hand to form a government of his choice.[210] His willingness begin at the top was not gratified.

Bourassa then went to Quebec on December 8 to expound th program of the *Ligue Nationaliste* in the provincial capital. A audience of six thousand gathered at the Ménage Militaire, and tl platform was packed with Liberal senators and M.P.'s. But Erne Roy, who introduced Bourassa, said the meeting was neith Liberal nor Conservative in character. Asselin spoke briefly on tl origins of the *Ligue*, and then Bourassa took the floor. He defined the *Ligue* as neither a revolutionary organization nor a prelude to a racial movement. He was opposed to imperialism as a Canadian, not only as a French Canadian; and he pointed out that his ideas had been applauded in Toronto, where they were shared by some Ontarians. It was not revolutionary to claim for Canada the right to conclude its own treaties and to direct its own foreign policy. 'Every time that a statesman, English or French, Conservative or Liberal, sacrifices Canadian interests to English ones, we shall fight him. Every time that a statesman, French or English, Liberal or Conservative, upholds the country's rights to absolute autonomy, we shall approve him.'[211]

Then Bourassa dealt with three main points: Canada's situation in the empire, the federal organization of Canada, and economic problems with particular reference to Quebec. It was clear that Quebec did not want political or military imperialism, and neither did the majority in Ontario. To the economic imperialism of which Lord Strathcona and Lord Minto had constituted themselves the heralds, he opposed the principle of the absolute autonomy of Great Britain and of each of the colonies in tariff and commercial questions. He urged that the federal subsidy should be divided fairly among the provinces according to their population. The federal government should aid colonization in the old provinces as well as in the West; newcomers in Quebec would replace those who had followed the frontier elsewhere, and they would stimulate by new methods the too traditional agriculture of French Canada. The federal government should vote funds each year for a program of colonization public works prepared by each province. Appeals in cases based upon provincial laws should not be carried beyond the courts of the province; the Supreme Court should decide only the interpretation of federal laws and cases involving citizens of different provinces. He saw colonization as the first and last duty of the Quebec government in the provincial field. He criticized the sales of timber limits as on too great a scale in the first place, and as too often made to speculators who stripped colonization lots of their wood and then abandoned them. He favored a law obliging American lumbermen to convert wood into pulp in Quebec factories. Waterpower rights should be rented rather than sold. This program was less to the taste of the leading provincial Liberals on the platform than Bourassa's anti-imperialism, but it was equally cheered by the students for whom Bourassa was a hero who dared to upset the political applecart in the interest of French Canada.

Laurier was less disturbed by Bourassa's heresies on provincial policy than by the anti-British tendencies of the *Ligue*. He remembered how England had been hooted by the students at the Devlin meeting, and he knew that Armand Lavergne, Bourassa's chief disciple in Quebec, was willing 'to throw the English into the St. Lawrence.'[212] He warned Bourassa of the danger of forming a French party in Quebec which would produce an anti-French-Canadian reaction in Ontario. Bourassa protested that the *Ligue* was purely Canadian and not anti-English, and sent Laurier the *Ligue's* program.[213] When an opening presented itself in Montmagny, Laurier proposed Lavergne as Liberal candidate, probably in hope of restraining him by bringing him under his own influence at Ottawa. Lavergne accepted the nomination after consulting Bourassa, but resisted the Liberal machine's effort to make him sign a pledge to approve all government measures. Laurier refused to be scandalized by such independence, and gave Lavergne the same indulgent leeway as he had long given Bourassa. But he recognized that he had provided himself with 'another thorn in the flesh'[214] by supporting Bourassa's disciple.

At the Théâtre National in Montreal on February 21, 1904, at a meeting called by the *Ligue Nationaliste* to celebrate Lavergne's election, Bourassa repeated the analysis of the *Ligue's* program which he had given in Quebec in December, and renewed the attack he had made three days earlier, before the Colonization Commission, on the existing system. He called for a separation of colonization areas from timber limits, and an end of alienation of the province's natural resourses. With the growing industrial development of the province, it was significant that the nationalists were advancing an economic program as well as a political one.

At this same meeting Asselin announced the forthcoming establishment of a weekly paper, *Le Nationaliste*, which would be the organ of the *Ligue*, and absolutely independent of the old parties. The first number appeared on March 6, 1904, with two articles by Bourassa and others by Asselin, Omer Héroux, Louvigny de Montigny, and the poet Charles Gill. Asselin had the editorial collaboration of Jules Fournier, a brilliant young journalist of A.C.J.C. background whom he had encountered in the office of *La Presse*. The chief backers of the paper were G.-N. Ducharme and Edmond Lepage, whose aid Bourassa had enlisted with the following arguments:

Here are some young men who have talent, character, and ideas. They wish to escape from the sordid slavery that party journalism imposes on its workers. I am a party man—oh, not the most docile one—but I belong to a political party and I freely recognize that the parliamentary regime necessitates the organization and maintenance of two parties. Nevertheless, I believe it good that the parties—mine like the others—should be watched, criticized, and indeed scolded by a free press.

If party spirit here were what it is in England, the necessity of independent journals would be less imperative. In England, party discipline

> lows very great liberty of thought, speech, and even action. Here one ust not only vote with one's party, but one must under threat of major communication write, talk, think, breathe, eat, and sleep according the strict rules of *Rouge* or *Bleu* disciplinary protocol. This regime roduces the moral and intellectual degradation of public men and the emoralization of popular thought and action. . .
>
> Our political parties, less and less divided by principles, dispute the ictory, not to assure the triumph of an idea, but to gather the honors nd profits of power. At bottom, under the cover of bitter battles which volve chiefly men and methods of administration, the two parties gree like thieves at a fair to manage all the great influences. Let the nperial authorities desire to impose upon us some action conformed their wishes—as happened during the war in Africa—they seize pon the minds of the leaders, by seduction or fear; and immediately they ave at their service the orators, the journalists, and the battalions of both arties; and any serious discussion of their projects is stifled. The great nancial interests—railway contractors and directors, manufacturers, ock brokers and speculators, timber merchants, act in the same fashion nd succeed marvelously in having their interests protected under all inistries. If one studies political developments at Ottawa and Quebec, ne observes that this pernicious tendency is growing every day.
>
> It is urgent that a press independent of parties, coteries, and financial yndicates arouse public opinion and put the people on guard against the angers which menace our national integrity and economic stability.[215]

ourassa made clear that he was 'neither founder, proprietor, irector, nor editor of *Le Nationaliste*,' but merely a contributor who ssumed responsibility only for the articles he signed. But it was also lear that he now had an organ and was now more redoubtable an nfluence in Quebec than ever before.

As might have been expected from the dominant influence of ourassa at the start, *Le Nationaliste* was nationalist in a Canadian ense, not merely in a French-Canadian one. It was the first French-Canadian publication to escape from provincialism by adopting his position, and its establishment was welcomed by two of the eading English-Canadian nationalists, Goldwin Smith and John . Ewart. In a letter to the editor dated March 13, 1904, Smith hailed with joy its apparition' and spoke of its important mission f reminding English Canadians that they were not the only in-abitants of a Canada 'which counts today among its citizens, side from your compatriots, representatives of several different aces.' He added: 'One should not expect that the non-British lements of our population should see without protesting their nterests sacrificed to those of a political party in Great Britain whose ends, however glorious they may appear to those who pursue hem, satisfy only British ambition.' Smith judged that the new ournal could contribute to revealing this aspect of imperialism, and that it would introduce into 'the stifling atmosphere of o politics a little of the fresh air of patriotism and of youthful hope.'[2] In the paper Bourassa approved the views of John S. Ewart as thc of the *Ligue* in a more accentuated form: 'The ideal of Mr. Ewa is a federation of sovereign states united by the sole bond of obedien to the same Crown. Mr. Ewart is more radical than I am. I not find the position of Canada as humiliating as he paints it; ar consequently I do not desire, for the moment, as complete a liber tion as that which he calls for.'[217] But Bourassa asserted th Ewart's views were those of the majority of the English Canadiar and he called for the collaboration of English and French in enlargi the Canadian people's field of action.

13

The difference between Bourassa's nationalism and that previous known in Quebec was made evident in an exchange betwee Jules-Paul Tardivel and Bourassa soon after *Le Nationaliste* appeare Tardivel's ultramontanism and anglophobia had developed in separatism, and his apocalyptic novel, *Pour la Patrie* (1895), one the classic texts of the A.C.J.C.,[218] looked forward to the establis ment of a French-Canadian state. In his organ *La Vérité* on April 1904, he distinguished between his nationalism and that of the *Ligu*

> Our own nationalism is French-Canadian nationalism. We hav worked for twenty-three years for the development of French-Canadia national sentiment; what we wish to see flourish is French-Canadia patriotism; for us our compatriots are the French Canadians; for us o fatherland is—we do not say precisely the Province of Quebec—b French Canada; the nation we wish to see founded at the hour marke by Divine Providence is the French-Canadian nation. These gentleme of the *Ligue* appear to take their stand on another point of view. O would say that they wish to work for the development of a Canadia sentiment, independent of all questions of origin, language, and religion.[2]

In reply Bourassa paid tribute to Tardivel's career as a defende of the French-Canadian nationality, but suggested that this strugg had made him too suspicious of those who differed with him. H thus defined the nationalism for which the *Ligue* stood:

> Our own nationalism is a Canadian nationalism founded upon th duality of races and on the particular traditions which this duality i volves. We work for the development of a Canadian patriotism whic is in our eyes the best guaranty of the existence of the two races and the mutual respect they owe each other. For us, as for M. Tardivel, ou compatriots are the French Canadians; but the English Canadians ar

foreigners, and we regard as allies all those among them who respect and who desire like us the maintenance of Canadian autonomy. For the fatherland is all Canada, that is, a federation of distinct races and onomous provinces. The nation that we wish to see develop is the nadian nation, composed of French Canadians and English Canadians, t is of two elements separated by language and religion, and by the al dispositions necessary to the preservation of their respective tradis, but united in a feeling of brotherhood, in a common attachment the common fatherland.[220]

ien Tardivel replied, regretting that Bourassa should write ewhere than in *La Vérité*, since one nationalist journal sufficed, d deploring the fact that *Le Nationaliste* excluded religious sentints from its columns, he provoked a rude rejoinder from the uthful editors, who did not take Tardivel as seriously as Bourassa .[221]

The old politico-religious nationalist school of Tardivel was carried however, by the formal foundation on March 13 of the *Association holique de la Jeunesse canadienne-française* (A.C.J.C.) under the sidency of Joseph Versailles and the guidance of the French uits, with the watchword of 'piety, study, action.' To their ond congress at Montreal in June 1904 they summoned all young nch Canadians 'who believed in Catholicism and in its universal cacy for the good of individuals and societies, in the Frenchnadian race and its providential mission; of all who are aware the dangers which beset our Catholic faith and our Frenchnadian race.'[222] At first the organization had enlisted only the port of classical college students, but their announced purpose study of national problems soon led them into the political field m which Archbishop Bruchési had sought to deflect them at urier's request.

In any case *Le Nationaliste* found an eager audience among their mbers, and Asselin hailed the A.C.J.C.:

The Catholic Association of French-Canadian Youth has bravely cribed on its program the study of the political and social problems ose solution is demanded by the interest of the French-Canadian race; ication, agriculture, colonization, trade and industry, the relations of ital and labor. Our young friends have understood that Catholicism ssentially a social work, and that according to the saying of one of our nch colleagues, those peoples are destined to destruction who choose hour when the enemy beats breaches in their ramparts to discuss ether the light which appeared on Tabor was created or uncreated. mediately after the religious question—we read in the program of the ociation—let us put the national question, studied in the light of the chings of our history; providential mission of the French Canadians; itudes of our race; resources of our soil; our rights to its possession;

the necessity to remain faithful to our tradition and to preserve our d tinct entity; our colonial obligations; our position in regard to other ra and to the Liberal power; our rank among the nations with regard education, commerce, etc.; a purely French-Canadian patriotism, always greater autonomy; resistance to all attempts to absorb us; dang of political partisanship; the Confederation Act; the French langua the religious liberty recognized by the constitution of the country.

There is nothing there that we do not approve wholeheartedly, w the reservation already made by M. Bourassa in his friendly respo to M. Tardivel, to wit: that in our eyes French-Canadian patriotism not incompatible with a larger patriotism extending to all the coun discovered by our fathers.

The Catholic Association, along with the *Ligue Nationaliste* upholds right of minorities to separate schools. [223]

Asselin sought to associate the new movement with the dema raised by the *Ligue d'Enseignement*[224] for reform of primary educati with support of colonization, and with conservation of natu resources—all causes dear to his group—and concluded by observi that the A.C.J.C. was clearly no mere 'pious confraternity,' si it was aware that 'a well-governed state is also one of the fin homages that can be paid to God.'

At the A.C.J.C. Congress in June, Bourassa made the princi address to the 500 delegates, and both the president's speech a the congress' resolutions had a strongly nationalist character. Versailles resigned and was replaced as president by R.-A. Ben The A.C.J.C. launched a monthly bulletin, *Le Semeur*, under editorship of Antonio Perrault. There was some evident distr of exactly what 'action' might be intended by the A.C.J.C.; Ar bishop Bruchési insisted upon the primary purposes of piety a study, but the Rector of Laval made evident his suspicion of organization, which had been joyously hailed by Tardivel.

The new nationalism soon made itself felt at Ottawa. Wh the session opened on March 10, Tom-Chase Casgrain accused government of supporting the *Ligue Nationaliste*, and asked whet its anti-British views had been incorporated in the Liberal progra Had not the Liberals selected Armand Lavergne? Bourassa repl that he was not a member of the *Ligue*, but saw nothing pernici in its doctrine, which was supported by some Conservatives a was anti-imperialist, as Sir John Macdonald and Sir Charles Tup had been on occasion. The *Ligue* members, like Bourassa and Wilfrid Laurier, were Canadians who had only one country, Cana a British land, but Canadian before it was British. The next Bourassa asked why the Union Jack had replaced the Canad flag on the Parliament buildings. The minister of public wo replied that until now a constitutional error had been made

lying the flag of the merchant marine, but the error would be re-
›aired as soon as a new flag was purchased.[226] Bourassa's position
n this matter was scarcely understood by English Canadians, who
lid not see how one could profess to be British and yet object to the
Jnion Jack. The flag question has remained vexed, with one
English school swearing by the Union Jack, the French generally
alling for the '*drapeau fleur-de-lisé*' (now the Quebec provincial
lag) or the '*drapeau Carillon*' or some other distinctively Canadian
lag, and the English generally fancying the Red Ensign. Though
he Red Ensign with the Canadian arms on the fly had long been in
nofficial use as the Canadian flag in 1904, it had not yet been offici-
lly adopted.

14

Imperialism suffered another check when a second Dundonald
ncident arose in June. The acting minister of militia, Sydney
'isher, had crossed off the name of a political opponent from the
st of officers of a new militia regiment raised in the Eastern Town-
hips. General Dundonald, already up in arms at the rejection of his
dvice in the drafting of the new Militia Act, spoke at a military
anquet in Montreal on June 4 of this 'gross instance of political
nterference,'[227] and expressed his desire that 'the militia of Canada
nay be kept free from party politics.' Dundonald had long been
ourting the Conservatives, more sympathetic than the Liberals
› his imperialist views. His conduct was attacked in the House on
une 10 by Fisher and Sir Frederick Borden, and defended by Colonel
am Hughes, who read a statement from Dundonald, and by Robert
aird Borden, the Conservative leader.

Laurier admitted the good motives of Dundonald, but questioned
is discretion and urged him to remember that Canada had re-
ponsible government. In passing he referred to Dundonald as
a foreigner—no . . . he is not a foreigner but he is a stranger,'[228]
naking one of his rare errors in English by using the equivalent of
ne French word '*étranger*,' which has both meanings. The Tories
'axed indignant at a French Canadian describing an Englishman
s a foreigner in Canada. Bourassa intervened in support of Laurier
y stating that it was simply a question of a public servant making
speech in which he had used unjustifiable expressions about a
nember of the cabinet: 'Lord Dundonald and those who preceded
im as commander of the troops never seem to have understood that
ne commander of the militia is a servant of the State . . . If the
ommander of the troops is of the opinion that the system applied
y the Minister of Militia and the Canadian Parliament is defective,
e had only two choices: to submit or to resign . . .'[229] Lord Minto
greed to Dundonald's immediate dismissal, though he disagreed

with the government's support of Fisher, and signed the order-in council of June 14 which relieved Dundonald of his function Dundonald had urged Minto to delay while he sought to appeal public opinion, which he did through Sam Hughes, who got th *Ottawa Citizen* and other Conservative organs in Ontario to espou the general's cause. The *Citizen* declared the country was tired being governed by the Province of Quebec, and called upo Canadian Scots to avenge their distinguished compatriot.

The quarrel, which was really one between Fisher and Dundonal was quickly turned for political purposes into one between Dun donald and Laurier, and thus one in which ethnic feeling coul be aroused. When the question came up again in the Hous Laurier declared firmly: 'So long as there is a Liberal governmen in Canada, the civil power shall rule the military power.'[230] H deplored the press' effort to describe his use of the word 'foreigne as deliberately insulting and indicative of anti-British feeling. H made a statement of his high standards of political controvers and concluded: 'If sixty years of what I believe to be, after al an honourable life, a life which has certainly been one of loy devotion to British institutions, is not a sufficient answer to such a insinuation, I will not attempt to make an answer.'[231] Up to h departure for England late in July Dundonald conducted an im perialist campaign, holding mass meetings in Toronto, Ottawa, an Montreal against the government's action, and urging his auditor 'Keep both hands on the British flag.'[232]

This campaign had its aftermath in the Conservative oppositic to the new Militia Bill, which provided that henceforward th commanding officer should be a Canadian and that the militia cou be put on active service, 'anywhere in Canada and outside Canad for the defence of this last.' A Conservative criticized the 'defen of Canada' clause and asked whether or not Canada was a part the empire. Others saw in it a weakening of the British connectio On August 1 Sam Hughes burst out with the charge that the clau 'was inspired not by the Minister of Militia but by the memb for Labellè.' Bourassa demanded a retraction. When Hughes accordance with the rules of the House was forced to make a ha hearted one, he was interrupted by Armand Lavergne, who observ that 'all our population is faithful to England,' a statement whi Hughes flatly denied.[233]

The Tories also opposed Honoré Gervais' proposal for the found tion in Montreal of a School of Higher Commercial Studies to tra Canadian consular agents, picturing Laurier as being und Bourassa's anti-British influence and yielding to it. In fact Bouras was inclined at this period to retire from politics and to becon postmaster of Montreal. But Laurier thanked him for his servic during the session in reply to Casgrain and Sam Hughes, and urged him to remain in parliament. Laurier wanted an offset to English-Canadian criticism of the guarantee of Catholic minority rights in the two new provinces of Alberta and Saskatchewan, which were to be set up in the North-West Territories after the forthcoming elections.[234] Bourassa promised to stay in politics, and began to prepare himself to argue the case of the minorities.

In Quebec Laurier, hailed as the conqueror of imperialism, had seemingly little to fear in the elections from the Conservatives or the Nationalists. Bourassa and Lavergne ran as Liberals with strong Liberal support, while only Charles Angers in Charlevoix and Asselin in Terrebonne appeared as independent nationalists. Dominique Monet had momentarily withdrawn from politics, hurt at being set aside in favor of Rodolphe Lemieux for the office of solicitor-general. Asselin and Bourassa, both hypercritical by temperament, had drifted apart, and Bourassa ceased to write for *Le Nationaliste*. It was the nationalist organ, however, that on October 16 first published the news of the sale of *La Presse*, previously an influential supporter of Laurier, in an intrigue by Mackenzie and Mann—the promoters of the Canadian Northern—to upset the Laurier government and its plan for the Grand Trunk Pacific, the chief national issue in the election.

Andrew Blair of New Brunswick, who had resigned from the administration after earlier opposition to its railway policy, was enlisted as political chief of the intrigue, which was organized by David Russell, a New Brunswick and Montreal speculator associated with Mackenzie and Mann, and J. N. Greenshields of Montreal, their lawyer. Hugh Graham of the *Star* and Arthur Dansereau of *La Presse* were also involved. The plot called for the purchase of *La Presse* and other Liberal journals, which were to oppose Laurier and reveal scandals in the administration, and the bribing of Liberal candidates in Quebec. Once the revolt was well advanced, the conspirators hoped to be able to dictate the railroad policy of the Conservative government they hoped to put into office.

But the revelations made by *Le Nationaliste* and *La Patrie*—for Tarte found the plot distasteful—indicating that the Mackenzie and Mann interests were involved in the purchase of *La Presse*, upset the scheme. Thomas Côté, Laurier's disciple on *La Presse*, balked at the publication of anti-Laurier articles. Robert Borden, the Conservative leader, refused to have Blair thrust upon him as prospective minister of railways and to have any part of the scheme. Laurier threatened to denounce the sale of *La Presse* to a group of English-speaking speculators, thus destroying its circulation, and party discipline was re-established over the Liberals who had been ready to desert their leader. Edward Farrer, as agent of Laurier, compiled a report on the intrigue and most of the information thus obtained was published in the *Toronto Globe* in December.[23] The conspiracy collapsed, and *La Presse* returned to the Liberal fold.

In the elections of November 3, 1904, the Liberals lost three seats in Quebec and increased their strength in Ontario. Except in Prince Edward Island, they swept the other provinces. Their majority in the House was nearly double that of 1896. If imperialism was to be identified with the Conservative cause, it had suffered a crushing defeat, for even the Conservative leader Borden was overwhelmed at the polls. Laurier had reached the zenith of his power, with his supporters, English and French alike, backing his growing nationalism as prosperity prevailed in the country and the West looked forward to even greater expansion with the construction of a new transcontinental railroad. No one rivaled Laurier in 1904 as the embodiment of the new Canada or matched his hold upon the hearts of Canadians, English and French alike. But in Quebec a groundswell of youthful nationalism was rising which threatened his dominance of his native province. The hero of the young nationalists was Henri Bourassa, not Sir Wilfrid Laurier.

Notes

1 J. A. Hobson, *Imperialism* (New York, 1902), 10.
2 C. A. Bodelsen, *Studies in Mid-Victorian Imperialism* (New York, 1925), 16.
3 *Ibid.*, 19 *n.*
4 *Ibid.*, 26.
5 *Ibid.*, 33-4.
6 *Ibid.*, 34.
7 *Ibid.*, 37.
8 O. D. Skelton, *Life & Times of Sir A. T. Galt* (Toronto, 1920), 232.
9 *Ibid.*, 330-1.
10 The term occurs in all the early drafts of the B.N.A. Act (J. Pope, *Confederation Documents*, 159, 181), and was altered at the instance of Lord Derby (J. Pope, *Macdonald*, 332).
11 Bodelsen, 55.
12 Lord Acton, *History of Freedom & Other Essays* (London, 1907), 276. The essay on 'Nationality' was written in 1862.
13 Bodelsen, 56.
14 C. W. Dilke, *Greater Britain: Saxon Sketches* (New York, 1869), preface.
15 *Ibid.*, 57.
16 *Ibid.*, 59.
17 *Ibid.*, 67.
18 *Ibid.*, 66.
19 *Ibid.*, 346-8.
20 Bodelsen, 80.
21 *Ibid.*, 94.
22 *Ibid.*, 99.
23 *Ibid.*, 103.
24 *Ibid.*, 105 *n.* 2.

[25] *Ibid.*, 115–16.
[26] *Ibid.*, 121.
[27] *Ibid.*
[28] *Ibid.*
[29] *Ibid.*
[30] *Ibid.*, 122.
[31] *Ibid.*, 124–5.
[32] *Ibid.*, 125.
[33] J. E. Tyler, *The Struggle for Imperial Unity 1869–95*, (London, 1938), 31.
[34] *Ibid.*, 36; B. H. Brown, *The Tariff Reform Movement in Great Britain, 1881–1895* (New York, 1943), 87.
[35] Bodelsen, 175.
[36] *Ibid.*, 156.
[37] *Ibid.*, 158.
[38] J. R. Seeley, *The Expansion of England* (London, 1883), 171.
[39] Bodelsen, 206–7.
[40] Tyler, 108.
[41] Bodelsen, 207.
[42] *Ibid.*
[43] Tyler, 110.
[44] Sir J. Willison, *Sir George Parkin* (London, 1929), 44.
[45] *Ibid.*, 85.
[46] Tyler, 113.
[47] *Ibid.*, 115.
[48] *Ibid.*, 120.
[49] Tyler, 126.
[50] *Ibid.*, 135.
[51] W. Caniff, *Canadian Nationality: Its Growth & Development* (Toronto, 1875), 7.
[52] G. T. Denison, *The Struggle for Imperial Unity* (London, 1909), 15.
[53] *Ibid.*, 42.
[54] Caniff, 16.
[55] *Ibid.*, 18.
[56] O. D. Skelton, *Life & Letters of Sir Wilfrid Laurier* (Toronto, 1921), I, 176.
[57] *Canada First: a Memorial of the Late William A. Foster, Q.C.* With an introduction by Goldwin Smith (Toronto, 1890), 80–1.
[58] Caniff, 18.
[59] Sir J. Pope (*ed.*), *Correspondence of Sir John Macdonald* (Toronto, 1921), 422–3, Macdonald-editor of *United Service Gazette*, 18 Sept. 1888.
[60] Sir J. Pope, *Memoirs of Sir John Alexander Macdonald* (Toronto, 1930), 581.
[61] Pope, *Correspondence*, 468, Macdonald-Machin, 4 April 1890.
[62] Skelton, *Galt*, 540.
[63] Pope, *Correspondence*, Macdonald-Tupper, 14 Aug. 1889.
[64] Sir C. Tupper, *Recollections of Sixty Years in Canada* (London, 1914), 249.
[65] Skelton, *Laurier*, I, 415.
[66] G. Smith, *Canada and the Canadian Problem* (London, 1891), 267.
[67] Skelton, *Laurier*, I, 363.
[68] *Ibid.*, 365.
[69] *Ibid.*, 376.
[70] *Ibid.*, 380.
[71] Denison, *Struggle*, 103; *Chicago Tribune*, 26 Sept. 1888.
[72] *Ibid.*, 104–5.
[73] *Ibid.*, 108–9.
[74] *Ibid.*, 110–16.
[75] Skelton, *Laurier*, I, 415.
[76] *Ibid.*, 418.

[77] J. Chamberlain, *Foreign & Colonial Speeches* (London, 1897), 6–13.

[78] *Ibid.*, 200.

[79] J. L. Garvin, *Life of Joseph Chamberlain* (London, 1934), II, 468.

[80] Denison, 146–7.

[81] Chamberlain, *Speeches*, 201–2.

[82] W. L. Strauss, *Joseph Chamberlain* (Washington, 1942), 62.

[83] Garvin, III, 5.

[84] *Ibid.*, III, 23–4.

[85] *Ibid.*, III, 179–81.

[86] *Ibid.*, III, 183–4.

[87] *Ibid.*, III, 185.

[88] Skelton, *Laurier*, II, 58.

[89] *Ibid.*, II, 67.

[90] Garvin, III, 187.

[91] *Ibid.*, 188.

[92] Skelton, *Laurier*, II, 72.

[93] Garvin, III, 188.

[94] R. Rumilly, *Histoire*, VIII, 202.

[95] Garvin, III, 192.

[96] Rumilly, VIII, 203.

[97] Skelton, *Laurier*, II, 81.

[98] *Ibid.*, 82.

[99] Strauss, 82.

[100] PAC: Governor-General's Numbered Files 162 (July-Dec. 1884), Vol. II, Colonial Office-Lansdowne, 20 Aug. 1884.

[101] *Ibid.*, 162-II, Lansdowne-Colonial Office, 21 Aug. 1884; I, Detachment Issue Sheets.

[102] *Ibid.*, 162-I, Lansdowne-Derby, 5 Sept. 1884.

[103] *Ibid.*, 114, Nos. 36–50, 9–19 Feb. 1885. Lansdowne reported to Derby on February 9 and 10 that General J. W. Laurie of Nova Scotia and Lt.-Col. A. T. H. Williams had offered to raise troops 'for active duty in defence of the Empire.' In reply Derby asked whether these offers were sanctioned by the Canadian government. Lansdowne indicated that the offer was probably illegal under Section 61 of the Canadian Militia Act, but that the Canadian government approved recruiting under the Imperial Army Act at British expense. He proposed a contingent of three battalions from the Maritimes, 'Old Canada,' and Manitoba. On February 19 Derby declined the offer for the present because of the delay involved, and suggested New South Wales' offer of men to serve in British units as a model. On February 20 the *Toronto Daily Mail* commented: 'The British Government of course would foot the bill . . . We cannot afford it; moreover there's no necessity for it.' An index of the impact of imperialism on English Canada in the next fifteen years is provided by the fact that such an attitude on the part of the French press in 1899 would have been promptly stamped as 'disloyal.'

[104] J. Buchan, *Lord Minto* (London, 1924), 82, 83.

[105] *Ibid.*, 105.

[106] Skelton, *Laurier*, II, 86 *n.*

[107] Buchan, 129.

[108] *Ibid.*, 130, Minto-Wolseley, 21 April 1899.

[109] Pope, *Correspondence*, 337–8, Macdonald-Tupper, 12 March 1885.

[110] Denison, 258.

[111] Buchan, 133.

[112] W. S. Evans, *The Canadian Contingent & Canadian Imperialism* (Toronto, 1901), 11–12.

[113] *Ibid.*, 13.

[114] Buchan, 134–5, Laurier-Minto, Aug. 1899.
[115] Denison, 260.
[116] Buchan, 136, Minto-Arthur Elliott, 28 Sept. 1899.
[117] *Ibid.*, 137.
[118] Garvin, III, 139.
[119] Skelton, *Laurier*, II, 96.
[120] *Ibid.*, 97.
[121] Buchan, 141, Minto-Chamberlain, 14 Oct. 1899.
[122] Skelton, *Laurier*, II, 98 *n.*
[123] Rumilly, VIII, 120.
[124] *Ibid.*, 139.
[125] Buchan, 143.
[126] Skelton, *Laurier*, II, 99.
[127] The great majority of these men were English Canadians, including many recent immigrants whose ties with the mother country were still close. Some French Canadians laid the foundations of their careers by espousing the unpopular imperial cause: Colonel Oscar Pelletier of Quebec was second in command of the first contingent, and Dr. Eugène Fiset, later deputy-minister of defence and lieutenant-governor of Quebec, was surgeon-major. The Quebec company included four French-Canadian non-commissioned officers and thirty-two privates. Colonel F.-E. Lessard accompanied the second contingent. G. P. Labat, *Le Livre d'or of the Canadian Contingents in South Africa* (Montreal, 1901), 155, 82.
[128] Skelton, *Laurier*, II, 101.
[129] Buchan, 146.
[130] *Ibid.*, 146–7.
[131] *Ibid.*, 148.
[132] Skelton, *Laurier*, II, 104.
[133] *Ibid.*, 104–5.
[134] Evans, 155; Rumilly, IX, 174–81.
[135] Rumilly, IX, 191.
[136] *Ibid.*, IX, 188–92.
[137] Skelton, *Laurier*, II, 106–7.
[138] *Ibid.*, 107.
[139] *Ibid.*
[140] *Ibid.*, 108–9.
[141] Buchan, 159–60, Minto-Chamberlain, March 1900.
[142] *Ibid.*, 158–9.
[143] *Toronto News*, quoted Skelton, II, 113–14.
[144] Buchan, 161–2, Minto-Arthur Elliott, Nov. 1900.
[145] Skelton, II, 114.
[146] *Toronto News*, 8 Nov. 1899; quoted Rumilly, IX, 261–2.
[147] Skelton, II, 110–13; Rumilly, X, 12–21.
[148] Buchan, 153.
[149] Immigration from the United Kingdom, which had averaged 11,000 annually since 1897, reached 50,000 in 1904 and 120,000 in 1908. Although the latter figure was unusually high, the annual total never dropped below 50,000 until 1910, and was over 100,000 for the four following years, reaching 150,000 in 1914. *Canada Year Book 1922–23* (Ottawa, 1924), 206. The total amounted to over a million by 1914.
[150] C. C. Tansill, *Canadian-American Relations, 1875–1911* (New Haven, 1943), 446.
[151] Skelton, *Laurier*, II, 47.
[152] Garvin, III, 129–30.
[153] Buchan, 160.
[154] Garvin, III, 129–30.

155 Skelton, *Laurier*, II, 293.
156 [H. Borden (*ed.*)] *Robert Laird Borden: His Memoirs* (Toronto, 1938), I, 82.
157 *Ibid.*, 87.
158 Buchan, 160.
159 Skelton, *Laurier*, II, 294.
160 *Ibid.*, 295.
161 *Ibid.*, 297.
162 *Ibid.*, 299.
163 Rumilly, X, 125.
164 Buchan, 205.
165 *Ibid.*, 199.
166 Skelton, II, 301.
167 *Ibid.*, 177.
168 Denison, 366–7.
169 Strauss, 106.
170 *Ibid.*, 109.
171 *Ibid.*, 112.
172 Denison, 347.
173 Skelton, *Laurier*, II, 304.
174 *Ibid.*, 305.
175 *Ibid.*, 310.
176 *Ibid.*, 312.
177 Borden, *Memoirs*, I, 62–4.
178 Rumilly, XI, 17.
179 Henri Bourassa, *Great Britain and Canada* (Montreal, 1902), 4–5.
180 H. Bourassa, *Grande-Bretagne et Canada* (Montréal, 1902), 3–4.
181 Bourassa, *Great Britain*, 7.
182 *Ibid.*, 17–18.
183 *Ibid.*, 39.
184 *Ibid.*, 45.
185 Rumilly, X, 106.
186 *Ibid.*, 108.
187 *Ibid.*, 117–18.
188 *Ibid.*, 120–1.
189 *CHAR 1946*, 65–6, J.-C. Bonenfant & J.-C. Falardeau, 'Cultural and Political Implications of French-Canadian Nationalism.' An edition of this sermon for use in the classical colleges was edited by Canon Emile Chartier under the title of *Bréviaire du patriote canadien-français* (Montréal, 1925). *Ibid.*, 66 *n.* 27.
190 H. Bourassa, 'The French Canadians in the British Empire,' London *Monthly Review*, Sept.-Oct. 1902.
191 H. Bourassa, 'Les Canadiens Français et l'Empire britannique,' *La Nouvelle France*, II (Jan. 1903), No. 1, 7–8.
192 Rumilly, X, 149.
193 *Ibid.*, 167–8.
194 G. Smith, *Devant la tribune de l'histoire* (Montréal, 1903), 8.
195 *Ibid.*, 61.
196 J. Gauvreau, *Olivar Asselin: précurseur d'action française* (Montréal, 1937), 24.
197 Rumilly, XI, 14–15.
198 Gauvreau, 14–22.
199 L.-A. Groulx, *Une croisade d'adolescents* (Québec, 1912).
200 *Le Drapeau National des Canadiens Français* (Québec, 1904).
201 *La Croix* (Montréal), 10 May 1903; cited Groulx, *Croisade*, 233.
202 Rumilly, XI, 84.
203 Groulx, *Croisade*, 142–63.
204 Rumilly, XI, 17.

[205] *Ibid.*, 19–21.
[206] *Ibid.*, 23–4.
[207] *Ibid.*, 23–7.
[208] *Ibid.*, 28.
[209] *Ibid.*, 33–44.
[210] *Ibid.*, 73–5.
[211] *Ibid.*, 78–83.
[212] Rumilly, X, 67–8, Laurier-Madame Lavergne, 29 Nov. 1901.
[213] Rumilly, XI, 85–6.
[214] *Ibid.*, 96.
[215] *CHAR 1945*, 70–1, *Le Nationaliste*, 27 March 1904. Abbé Arthur Maheux, 'Le Nationalisme canadien-français à l'aurore du XXe siècle.'
[216] *Ibid.*, 65–6; *Le Nationaliste*, 20 March 1904.
[217] *Ibid.*, 71–2; *Le Nationaliste*, 17 April 1904.
[218] Groulx, *Croisade*, 179. Other favoured authors were Veuillot, Montalembert, Ozanam, Lacordaire, Henri Perreyve. Two books which influenced the movement politically were Père Berthe's life of Garcia Moreno and Nemours Godré's life of Daniel O'Connell.
[219] *CHAR 1945*, 68; *La Vérité*, 2 April 1904.
[220] *Ibid.*, 69; *Le Nationaliste*, 3 April 1904.
[221] *Ibid.*, 69; *Le Nationaliste*, 25 April 1904.
[222] Rumilly, XI, 125.
[223] *CHAR 1945*, 72–3; *Le Nationaliste*, 8 May 1904.
[224] The *Ligue d'enseignement* was founded by Honoré Gervais and Godfroy Langlois in November 1902 for the reform of Quebec's educational system. Under the inspiration of Langlois, who desired to laicize the system, it soon came into conflict with Archbishop Bruchési.
[225] Rumilly, XI, 158–60.
[226] *Ibid.*, 127–8.
[227] Skelton, II, 198–9.
[228] *Ibid.*, 199–200.
[229] Rumilly, XI, 146.
[230] Skelton, II, 201.
[231] *Ibid.*, 202 *n.*
[232] *Ibid.*, 202.
[233] Rumilly, XI, 151–2.
[234] *Ibid.*, 162–3.
[235] Skelton, II, 209–16.

CHAPTER X

NATIONALISM *vs.* IMPERIALISM

(1905–11)

THE YEAR which saw Chamberlain's retirement from politics marked the ebb of the imperialist tide in Canada, and the rise of the nationalist tide in Quebec which had developed in reaction to bumptious jingoism. One appeal to racial solidarity provoked another, and the French Canadians reacted to 'Anglo-Saxonism' by reasserting their French and Catholic heritage with the aggressive spirit which is characteristic of Quebec when it is on the defensive. Two great achievements of Laurier's regime brought about the beginning of its decline. The massive polyglot immigration since 1897 which had peopled the West and added one-third to the nation's population revived French Canada's fears for cultural survival. The rapid development of the West called for the creation of new provinces in the old North-West Territories. This step raised once more the question of minority rights, with its ethnic and religious differences whose power to disrupt Canadian national life Laurier knew only too well. For all his political adroitness and willingness to compromise, he could not avoid a bitter division of the nation and of his following, and with that division the eventual doom of his regime was assured.

I

As early as 1903 the Conservatives demanded the enfranchisement of the Territories, and thenceforward opposition papers began to agitate the school question in order to embarrass the government. During the 1904 campaign Laurier promised to introduce a measure creating new provinces if he were re-elected. Early in that year he wrote John S. Willison, who had declared in the *Toronto News* that the formation of new provinces was being delayed until after the election because the hierarchy demanded separate schools, that he anticipated the outbreak of 'bitter passions on both sides' and that it would be his lot 'to fight extremists and to place and maintain the question where it has been placed by the British North America Act.' Laurier urged Willison to remember that Confederation was a compromise and that the work of effecting union was far from complete: 'The work must be continued in the same spirit in which t was conceived, and I certainly indulge the hope that you and I will always find it easy to stand on that ground.'[1]

On February 21, 1905 Laurier introduced the Autonomy Bills, establishing the provinces of Alberta and Saskatchewan, which had been drafted by Charles Fitzpatrick, the minister of justice, after a conference with the territorial authorities, and after consultation through Bourassa with Mgr. Sbaretti, the apostolic delegate, on the school clause. The bills represented the views of Clifford Sifton, the Western leader in the cabinet, except for the school clause which was drafted after his departure for a rest in Florida. Sifton had already had differences with Laurier as a result of the latter's growing habit of presenting the cabinet with a *fait accompli*, and in particular had been irritated by being passed over for the justice portfolio in favor of Fitzpatrick. In introducing the bills Laurier dealt cautiously with the school question, urging the spirit of tolerance in which Confederation had been achieved. Protection of minority rights was an essential feature of that compact. The principle had been reinforced by Edward Blake's definition of these rights in the North-West Territories Act of 1875, whose educational clause provided that, as in Ontario, the majority should establish such schools as they saw fit, while the minority had the right to organize separate schools and to share in public funds for education. The Act had been opposed by George Brown in the Senate, but had been passed by a large majority of both parties. The new bills provided for the continuation of this tradition. In conclusion Laurier made an appeal for fairness in carrying on the principle embodied in Confederation, whose value he illustrated by contrasting sound conditions in Canada resulting from religious teaching in the schools with the social disorder in the United States where religion was banned in the public schools.[2]

In reply the Conservative leader, R. L. Borden, took the position that the school question and the control of public lands should be left to the people of the new provinces. In fact there was little criticism of the proposals in the West; but the Ontario Conservatives, under the leadership of Sam Hughes, W. F. Maclean, and Dr. Sproule, launched an opposition movement which was supported by the Orange Order. Dr. Carman, General Superintendent of the Methodist Church, called the measure 'reactionary, mad, monstrous, hideous, and oppressive,' while Presbyterian, Baptist, and other Protestant ministerial associations demanded its withdrawal. Goldwin Smith, always an opponent of close relations between Church and State, felt that it bound the new provinces to maintain and propagate Catholicism. Willison's *Toronto News* and the *Toronto Telegram* denounced this 'endowment of clerical privilege,' this 'fastening of the dead hand of denominational control' upon the new provinces.[3]

But the most serious reaction of all was a revolt within the Liberal camp. Sifton hurried back to Ottawa from Florida, and finding that the school clause scrapped all subsequent territorial educational provisions in favor of the 1875 status, promptly resigned as minister of the interior. He had previously advised Laurier that Western public opinion favored continuing the existing school system, which by the ordinances of 1892 and 1901, passed under the influence of Dalton McCarthy, had put crippling restrictions on separate schools and had secularized the educational system. Sifton, the supporter of the Manitoba School Act and the prophet of a West which would be English rather than English and French, could hardly support the administration's policy. In addition he was at swordspoints with Fitzpatrick, and the administration of his department was under fire. His resignation as minister of the interior was announced on March 1, while at the same time it became known that William Fielding, the minister of finance, also disliked the separate school clause and might resign. There were rumors of other prospective cabinet resignations, while the *Toronto Globe* urged that under the Liberal principle of provincial rights the educational clause must be opposed. The *Montreal Herald* and *Witness*, and Sifton's *Manitoba Free Press* also revolted.[4]

Laurier found himself in much the same position as Mackenzie Bowell in 1895 on the Manitoba school question, with his own party split and the opposition making the most of the division. He took a firmer stand in favor of minority rights than he had in 1896, perhaps because of Manitoba's and Ontario's insistence that Quebec should make all the sacrifices demanded for national unity. When Sifton announced his intention of resigning, Laurier replied that this distrust of him as a French Canadian and as a Catholic by Protestant Liberals suggested that he should resign as prime minister.[5] When this threat was ineffective and the agitation against the bill continued to rise both in the House and the press, Laurier called a meeting of the Quebec Liberals, and told them that it was necessary to compromise or lose power—power both to aid the minorities of the West and to enjoy the patronage which maintained their position. Only Bourassa and Lavergne opposed a compromise. Mgr. Sbaretti, bowing to the storm, informed Laurier that he would accept a compromise.[6]

Sifton, who headed the Liberal revolt in parliament, proposed to Laurier a compromise drafted by himself and negotiated with Fitzpatrick by H. M. Howell of Winnipeg as representative of the Western members.[7] The new educational clause, which replaced the original Article 16 when the Autonomy Bills came up for second reading on March 22, applied Section 93 of the British North America Act to the new provinces, as its predecessor had done, but modified by the Territorial Ordinances of 1901. After emphasizing that the minority provision of the British North America Act had been created at the instance of the Protestants of Quebec, Laurier explained the new clause as one avoiding the confusion and litigation which might arise under the original one. But Sifton, in supporting the compromise, flatly characterized the difference between the two clauses as that between a system of complete ecclesiastical control and one of secular control, with religious teaching after school hours. He hailed the new measure as one containing the essential principles of a national school system, free from 'the taint of ecclesiasticism.'[8] Borden confined himself to arguing on the provincial rights issue rather on that of separate schools. He said 'Let the minorities trust the majorities and the result will be the same as in Nova Scotia and New Brunswick,'[9] and moved not to defeat the bill, but for a resolution urging for the new provinces 'full powers of provincial self-government, including power to exclusively make laws in relation to education.'[10] Fielding stated his dislike for the principle of separate schools, but urged that the legal basis now provided did not justify a governmental crisis and a consequent struggle on religious lines.

When Bourassa rose in the House on March 28, fireworks were anticipated; but he contented himself with a statement of the French-Canadian and Catholic position, reserving for the third reading his criticism of the bill and an amendment to it. He spoke, as Rodolphe Lemieux had already done, of the role of French-Canadian priests and colonists in opening up the West to civilization. Their descendants deserved the same treatment that the Protestant minority received in Quebec. But the opposition found it natural to support the suppression of Catholic separate schools in the West, though they would denounce as infamous the suppression of the Protestant separate schools in Quebec. He urged justice to the French Canadians and the two million Catholics who dwelt in Canada. They should not be forced to conclude that their country was limited to Quebec, since they could not obtain justice in the English-speaking provinces.[11] Despite Bourassa's restraint, he did not refrain from referring to Dr. Sproule, Grandmaster of the Orange Order and a leader in the anti-French agitation, as 'chief of the Orange Hierarchy,' and from advising Sam Hughes, who had regretted that unlike most of the French-Canadian members he could not express himself in both languages, to take a course in the separate schools.[12]

The debate dragged on through April, with new fuel added to the fire by the Conservative charge that the government had been influenced by Mgr. Sbaretti. Maclean made rude references to the apostolic delegate and the Pope, and was rebuked by Bourassa, who referred to the 'clerical intervention' of the Protestant ministers of Ontario. The ablest Conservative speaker, George Foster, made a violent attack on the government's inconsistencies; but the influential Conservative Herbert Ames of Montreal supported the bill, while Frederick Monk attacked the myth that the Quebec voter was subjected to any greater clerical influence than his English-speaking fellows. Despite the opposition to the law of Archbishop Langevin of Saint-Boniface and Bishop Cloutier of Trois-Rivières, supported by *Le Nationaliste*, *La Vérité*, *La Semaine religieuse* of Quebec, and *L'Evénement*, which deplored the 'capitulation' of Laurier and urged 'Let us go down like men,' the French Canadians refused to unite against the measure and were gradually won over by the Liberal press.[13] The vote on the second reading on May 3 was carried by 140 to 59. Only one Liberal, a nephew of Dalton McCarthy true to family tradition, voted against it, and ten Quebec Conservatives voted for it. In two Ontario by-elections, where the Conservative cry was to vote against 'Laurier, Sbaretti, and the Pope,' the Liberal candidates were successful; and when Frank Oliver was named to replace Sifton as minister of the interior, he was returned by acclamation in Edmonton, despite Toronto prophecies of revolt in the West.

Bourassa gave a foretaste of his promised future criticism of the bill at a meeting called by the *Ligue Nationaliste* on April 17, 1905 at the Monument National in Montreal. The *Ligue* and the A.C.J.C., now led by Antonio Perrault, were aroused by the issue, and looked to Bourassa for leadership. His disciple Lavergne and Auguste Noel of Edmonton, the fiancé of Lavergne's sister, urged Bourassa to exercise pressure on Laurier. Before speaking on the question, Bourassa studied it thoroughly. His address '*Les Ecoles du Nord-Ouest*,' was a model of scholarly polemic, tracing the historical development of the question and dissolving the fogs of legalism to lay bare the essential points. He began by calling the question 'perhaps the gravest' since Confederation, since it was a matter of providing a constitution for what promised to become half the Canadian nation. The dualism of the British North America Act of 1867 must be applied to the West if it were to become Canadian despite a vast foreign immigration, primarily American and predisposed to commercial union and perhaps even annexation. He asserted the right of the French-Canadian Catholic, whose forefathers had pioneered the West, to enjoy there the same rights which the English-Canadian Protestant enjoyed in Quebec. He announced his intention of analyzing the question justly and impartially, for this was 'one of those hours in which men and parties do not count, since religion, the country, and nationality were in danger.'[14]

Then he traced the development of Canadian educational law from the beginning of the Confederation movement, with Galt as representative of the Quebec English Protestants insisting upon a guarantee of minority rights, which had been interpreted by Lord Carnarvon as putting the Catholic minority of Upper Canada, the Protestant minority of Lower Canada, and the Catholic minority of the Maritimes upon a footing of perfect equality. Thus Section 93 of the British North America Act did not apply, as Borden claimed, only to Ontario and Quebec. This pact had been loyally kept by Quebec; at first it had been violated in the Maritimes but later fulfilled in spirit; and for the last ten years it had been violently attacked in Ontario by the Conservatives, whom Sir Oliver Mowat had firmly resisted. Turning to the North-West Territories, Bourassa pointed out that they were the common property of the whole Canadian people and their development had been brought about at the expense of all Canadian taxpayers. The French Canadians had the moral and legal right to insure the lot of the French and Catholic minority in the West, as that of the Protestant minority in Quebec had been safeguarded by Confederation.

Then Bourassa turned to the constitutional history of the West, paying tribute to Blake for his introduction into the Territorial Act of a guarantee of the minority's right to denominational education. The Senate had disregarded George Brown's objections to separate schools in 1875. Why had that parliament shown itself more broad-minded and superior in national spirit to that of 1905? Was it because of the fact that in 1875 the majority in the North-West was Catholic and the minority Protestant? Today, when the situation was reversed, there was a storm of protest when the government proposed to continue the principle laid down thirty years ago. Before Dalton McCarthy's campaign against the French language and separate schools, the French Canadians of the North-West had enjoyed the same privileges as their compatriots in Quebec. Then the French language had been suppressed in 1891, and the school system secularized in 1892, under a law which Laurier had then said would have been called an 'act of the most infamous tyranny' if it had been directed against the Protestants of Quebec.

It was this very act which the government was now prepared to sanction as an 'honourable compromise.' Faced with such measures, the Catholics of the West had vainly sought justice from Ottawa under Section 93 of the British North America Act. But the government no longer needed the influence of the hierarchy, as it had had in 1869, and no satisfaction was forthcoming. The ordinance of 1901 completed the work of secularizing the separate schools. Bourassa pointed out that the offending territorial ordinances of 1892 and 1901 were illegal, since they violated the underlying

Territorial Act either in letter or spirit. He judged that the government's original bill would have passed without opposition except from Tory Orangemen, if it had not been for Sifton's resignation, which had created a panic in the administration. Laurier had been forced into the path of concession by some of his English colleagues and partisans, while the Quebec members had given him little support. Finally he capitulated and substituted the new clause which Bourassa called the 'Sifton amendment.' But no concession could appease the fanatics who opposed the original clause: 'justice had been betrayed without benefit to the party.'

Bourassa thus characterized the difference between the two clauses thus: 'Article 16 perpetuates the principle of liberty consecrated in 1875. The Sifton amendment ratifies for all time the infringement of this principle made in 1892.' The latter assured the gradual suppression of Catholic and French education. In thirty-three school districts the Catholics, constituting the majority, were forced to establish public schools; in nine districts, where they constituted the minority, they had a right to maintain schools separate only in name. At any time the educational authorities could suppress the teaching of religion and French, yet the Catholics would be bound by compulsory attendance and taxation laws to support these schools. There was little hope of a federal remedial bill, and nothing in the history of the last thirteen years justified the reliance on the benevolence of the majority which the Conservatives urged. Under the regulations of the Department of Public Instruction, French could be taught only between 3 and 4 in the afternoon and religion from 3.30 to 4, while young children could be dismissed at 3. Either health, faith, or nationality had to suffer. Bourassa summed up by saying:

> Such is this regime of liberty, this guarantee of our religious and national rights, that we are urged to accept under the name of an 'honourable compromise!'
>
> In truth, the school system which Lord Kitchener has guaranteed to the Boers of Africa in making peace with them, is more just and liberal than that which it is desired to impose upon us in the West, upon us who have in Canada, and more particularly in these territories, which belong to us as much as to the English and Protestant majority, inalienable rights guaranteed by the treaties and by the constitution.
>
> And because I refuse to accept this iniquity, because I denounce a state of things which so cruelly and odiously infringes the most sacred natural rights of my compatriots and coreligionists, I find myself termed an intransigent, a demagogue, a creator of disorder, a false friend, and a bad citizen.'[15]

He explained that he had not previously spoken against the amendment, because it was not yet formally before the House when he spoke on March 28. He hoped that the administration would keep its pledges and not persist in supporting the amendment when its effect was properly understood. He thus explained his appearance in Montreal:

It was in order that the situation should be clarified and this iniquity not consummated that I have come to demand the moral support of the people of this great city of Montreal—the very heart from which go forth the currents which animate the body of the Canadian nation—of this city where religious liberty reigns so splendidly, where Protestants and Catholics, English and French, you live in such admirable harmony, where each father sees his son grow up in the traditions dear to him, where each Christian mother has the consolation to think, in confiding her child to the public school, that he will find there support for the religious and national ideas she has imparted to him.

I wish that from this hall shall go forth a voice which will penetrate to the floor of the House of Commons and recall the representatives of the people to their duty.[16]

To the argument that Laurier and his colleagues should not be embarrassed, Bourassa replied: 'But it was not in abandoning Laurier to the enemies who surrounded him, more dangerous than his adversaries, that his true friends proved their devotion and affection; on the contrary, by fortifying him with the manifest expression of the desire that they should feel to maintain his individual prestige and his political strength by causing the principles he has himself laid down to triumph.' It was a mistake for the party press to oppose petitions to the House. It was a calumny on the great majority of English Protestants to maintain that the original bill could not be passed because of the fanaticism of the English population and its representatives in Parliament. He had not found the English Canadians fanatics when he spoke in Ontario in time of crisis. He cited the speeches of the Liberal Fisher, and the Conservatives Ames and Pringle, all Protestants, in support of the original bill. He protested against the acceptance of the Sifton amendment as an 'honourable compromise' in the spirit of the conciliation which ought to unite French and English:

Certainly conciliation is good, always and everywhere, and in our country necessary to the existence of our institutions and of our national organization.

But conciliation is never good, it is never possible, between two contrary principles, between truth and error, between justice and iniquity. To search for the union of the two races of Canada, beyond the mutual respect that they owe to their respective rights, is to build the nation on a fragile foundation, to give it as cornerstone an element of ruin and destruction.

To wish to obtain the esteem, the confidence, and the goodwill of our English fellow citizens in sacrificing our incontestable rights, in consenting ourselves to the rupture of the national compact which guarantees these rights and in accepting thefts, infringements, and insults in the same manner as we welcome fair dealing, is to doom ourselves in advance to scorn and slavery.

The Englishman is proud and strong; he scorns baseness and cowardice, but he bows with respect to those who uphold, without insult and provocation, their rights, their honour, and their possessions.

It is in this spirit that Parliament should seek the solution of the problem that must be solved now.

It is in this spirit that the Fathers of Confederation conceived the charter of our liberties and of our autonomy; it will last only as long as our public men and the whole Canadian people conserve its essence and fundamental basis.[17]

In the actual delivery this speech was phrased more strongly than the printed version. Bourassa was always carried away by a crowd, when the crowd was carried away by his eloquence. He could fire a French audience to tumultuous enthusiasm with a closely thought and wrought address which would have left an English audience, less moved by oratory, somewhat cold. On this occasion he spoke as a leader, and created an effect which was not forgotten. He carefully refrained from breaking with Laurier, but he now stood at the head of a growing group which recognized his leadership rather than Laurier's. Laurier recognized the fact, writing to a friend:

I believe I shall pull through this difficulty, but I am not sure that I shall pull through, as you suggest, stronger than at the beginning. Matters are not going too badly at the moment in the English-speaking provinces. . . . But our friend Bourassa has begun, in Quebec, a campaign which may well cause us some trouble. . . .[18]

Laurier steered a middle course between that called for by Bourassa in Quebec and the opposite one urged by John Willison at a mass meeting in Massey Hall in Toronto on the same date. The middle way seldom arouses enthusiasm, and it was Bourassa's extreme position that won the support of French Canada's educated youth, which found his eloquence intoxicating, and of French Canada's clergy, which saw in him a defender of the Church. In the hierarchical society of Quebec such a following was not to be despised.

In the hope that agitation would die down, Laurier delayed the third reading of the Autonomy Bills, but by-elections fed the flames of anti-'papistry' in Ontario, and in turn aroused a French-Canadian reaction. The Conservative Party, because of the excesses of its Ontario champions, lost further ground in Quebec. Monk and

Bergeron sought to rally the *Bleus* with amendments to the bill, providing bilingualism in the legislatures and courts of the new provinces, and a school system similar to Quebec. But it was Bourassa who, in a three-hour speech in the House on June 28, best expressed French Canada's reaction. He repeated his arguments of April 17 in a calmer tone, appealing to the English-Canadian sense of justice and constitutionalism. He concluded by proposing, with the support of Lavergne, an amendment calling for the application of Article 93 of the British North America Act to the new provinces and the equality of public and separate schools in the distribution of public funds. Dr. Sproule replied to Bourassa, and the latter was also criticized by Rodolphe Lemieux for provoking quarrels between French and English. Lemieux compared him to his grandfather Papineau, who had attacked Lafontaine's conciliatory measures just as Bourassa did those of Laurier. After Lavergne had spoken in support of Bourassa, Dr. Sproule crossed the floor to shake hands with Bourassa and his disciple, amid the applause of the House at this gesture of goodwill from one who bitterly opposed their views. The tension of racial feeling was relaxed for the moment.

But Bourassa's amendment was supported only by himself and Lavergne, and five French-Canadian Conservatives, Monk, Bergeron, Léonard, Morin, and Paquet. Monk's and Bergeron's amendments received the same support, with Laurier, Lemieux, and Ernest Lapointe speaking against them. Laurier recognized the value of Bourassa's criticism, and used it as a wedge to obtain support from the Sifton group of an amendment proposed by Lamont of Saskatchewan, which guaranteed a half-hour of religious instruction in a sort of new Laurier-Greenway agreement. The bill then passed. But a new grievance had been added to the indictment of the French Canadians against the federal government, which had failed to uphold their rights in New Brunswick, Manitoba, and now the North-West. In his final speech Bourassa had revealed an emotional French-Canadian patriotism, rather than his former reasoned Canadian one, thus adopting the attitude of the majority of his followers. If a nationalism which was increasingly provincial in outlook gained ground markedly in Quebec after 1905, it was clear what had provoked it.

The excitement aroused in Quebec by the North-West school question died down during the summer. Then, on September 17, Lavergne addressed his electors at Montmagny to explain his stand. Bourbassa supported him, and both refrained largely from blaming Laurier, but rather criticized the failure of his Quebec followers to support his original stand. Paquet, one of the five Conservatives who had backed Bourassa and Lavergne, expressed his pride in having been associated with them. A number of *Bleu* notables of ultramontane stamp attended the meeting, and the Conservative press supported the stand taken by Bourassa and Lavergne. The Liberal press criticized the two young members of parliament for aiding and abetting the Conservatives, and for being unrealistic extremists. There was little popular feeling to add new recruits to the nationalist flock, while the nationalists were divided by differences in principle between the *Ligue Nationaliste*, which put nationalism before religion, and the A.C.J.C., which put religion before nationalism. *La Vérité*, now edited by Omer Héroux, Tardivel's son-in-law who had broken with Asselin, quarreled with *Le Nationaliste*. While division reigned in the nationalist camp, Laurier's prestige was reinforced by overwhelming Liberal victories in the first Alberta and Saskatchewan elections that fall, after a campaign in which the Conservatives urged repeal of the school law as too favorable to Catholics and Archbishop Langevin consequently supported it and the Liberal candidates. Laurier's firm anti-imperialist stand in response to the proposed calling of an imperial council also raised his stock in Quebec.

2

With imperialism seemingly checked, Bourassa now found more frequent occasion to express his French-Canadian patriotism than the larger Canadianism which he had earlier advanced. When during the session of 1906 George Foster sought to discredit the government by attacking Sifton's administration of its immigration policy, Bourassa took the opportunity to criticize a system which peopled the West with a mixture of foreigners, neglecting prospective French and Belgian colonists in favor of Jews from Poland and Russia. The rapid increase of the Jewish population of Montreal had already aroused anti-semitism among the French Canadians,[19] and Bourassa thus gave expression to it. But he was more concerned with voicing Quebec's opposition to an immigration which promised to lessen French Canada's influence by counterbalancing its higher birthrate, and by the national danger which he saw in the new West:

> The East and the West of Canada are separated by a natural barrier which does not exist in the United States . . . Our national unity would be less endangered if there were in the North-West more French and Catholic Canadians, and even separate schools, and fewer of these thousands of strangers who have contributed nothing to the building of the country, who have made no sacrifice for the cause of national unity, and who if we ever had to pass through some fearsome test, would not associate themselves with it.[20]

He warned the government that the Sifton scandals might cause its fall, as other scandals had destroyed the Conservatives.

Again in June, when the government introduced the Sunday Bill desired by the Lord's Day Alliance headed by Dr. Shearer of Toronto, Bourassa criticized the government for yielding to agitators and putting a premium on 'hypocrisy, drunkenness, idleness and the vices that develop in any country where the attempt is made to make people virtuous by law, instead of relying on the individual conscience and the moral quality of the Church.'[21] Laurier took advantage of the opening to proclaim himself once more a follower of the middle path, attacked by extremists on either side; last year he had been accused of being dominated by Mgr. Sbaretti, this year by Dr. Shearer. In fact, the Catholic Fitzpatrick had drafted the bill, and it had been publicly approved by Archbishop Bruchési. But it was a puritanical measure which met with far more approval among the Protestant sects of Ontario and the Maritimes than in Quebec, which habitually enjoyed the freedom of a Continental Sunday after Mass.

The prospect of the extension of the notably cheerless Toronto Sunday to Quebec aroused public feeling. The *Ligue Nationaliste*, quite willing to settle old scores with Ontario fanatics, called a mass meeting in Montreal at the Champs de Mars on June 29, with Bourassa, Lavergne, and labor leaders as speakers. The meeting was intended to reveal public opinion, but the placards announcing it had already taken a stand. They read '*A bas l'hypocrisie!*', '*Vive la liberté!*' Ten thousand workers and small merchants of Montreal attended. Bourassa denounced the bill and a proposed compromise, which gave the provinces the right to make exceptions to it:

> The citizens of Quebec respect the Lord's Day as much as anyone, but protest against a measure derogatory to the ancient customs of the province and infringing the civil rights and social organization which they have enjoyed, both under the French regime and the various constitutions which Great Britain has given them since the Treaty of Paris. . . .[22]

Bourassa concluded by submitting resolutions for the assembly's approval, petitioning parliament to respect provincial rights by submitting the application of the law in each province to the decision of the legislature. He was promised the support of Alphonse Verville, labor member for the Montreal constituency of Maisonneuve, in voting against the bill on its third reading. Bourassa's resolutions were voted by acclamation.

To his student following Bourassa now added that of labor, which was beginning to make itself felt in politics. He was attacked in the Liberal press for setting himself up in opposition to Archbishop

Bruchési as guardian of public morality, and in the House by Camille Piché, representative of the Montreal workers' quarter of Sainte-Marie, who saw in Bourassa's intervention a raid on his political preserves.

On July 6 Bourassa introduced an amendment to the Lord's Day Bill in accordance with the Champs de Mars resolution, and spoke three hours in its favor, heckled by Liberal interruptions. The amendment won the support of fifteen votes, among them those of Lavergne, Verville, Monk, Paquet, Bergeron, and Léonard. The agitation Bourassa had begun continued, with Quebec increasingly indignant at having Ontario's customs thrust upon her, and with the big industrialists joining the opposition to the bill. The latter made their influence felt in the Senate, which imposed amendments to the law embodying Bourassa's suggestions. Thus, while settling old scores with Sifton and the Ontario sectarians, Bourassa increased his political influence. He found himself for the first time in the company of the great English-Canadian interests, which were later to make a brief but effective alliance with him. And he came closer to an open break with Laurier, using his growing popularity in Quebec as a threat in his closing words of personal appeal:

> Despite all that has passed between you and those who think as I do, I appeal to you to remember that the eyes of the Canadian people are fixed upon you tonight.
>
> It is in your hands to decide whether you will give this Bill the stamp which will make it acceptable to the people of this country. You can do that, or you can refuse to do it. But I say again, we are not at present in the same condition that we were on some other questions that have caused so much difficulty in this country. We are not in the same circumstances that we were in the Manitoba school case, or the Northwest school case, or the Boer War, because in those days the government were obliged to adopt and to follow a uniform line of conduct. I think that the government were wrong then, but the people of Canada have judged that they were right. But the position today is not what it was then. Then you were forced as a government to adopt certain legislation and to follow one line of action. But that is not the case at present. You can adopt this legislation and give satisfaction at the same time to Quebec and Ontario. I repeat to the Prime Minister that when it is a question of choosing between Quebec and Ontario, when it becomes necessary to trample upon the feelings of Quebec or the feelings of Ontario, in such a case there must necessarily be a compromise, there must be give and take. On an occasion like this, when you can give to Ontario what it desires and when you can refrain from imposing upon Quebec what she does not desire, I appeal to the best feelings of the Prime Minister, I appeal to the principles he has proclaimed, to the conduct that he has followed ever since he began his career, and I say, do not minimize the authority of the voice that utters these sentiments to you. If anything personal

> has passed between us, let us ignore it; let us trample upon personal feelings. But I repeat to you that my voice tonight is not the echo of a single individual; it is the voice, not only of Quebec, but it is the voice of Ontario as spontaneously expressed in many of their newspaper organs; and it appeals to you that, while giving to Ontario what it wants, you do not impose upon Quebec what it does not want.[23]

This appeal to the people may have been rhetorical, but that fall Bourassa made one in all earnest by supporting an independent Liberal, Lorenzo Robitaille, in a by-election in Quebec County against G.-E. Amyot, the official candidate. The latter, a successful manufacturer, had been imposed by the party upon the constituency; Robitaille was a native son and represented the masses. In the campaign Amyot was supported by the Liberal leaders and the Liberal machine; Robitaille only by Bourassa and a few of his followers, with Asselin exercising his talent for verbal assassination in a little campaign sheet, *La Mitraille*. The culminating point of the campaign was a joint meeting at Beauport on October 20, for which 20,000 people gathered. First Bourassa and Lavergne joined Robitaille in addressing 6,000 of his supporters denouncing the Liberal practice of imposing candidates on the people and turning them into voting machines; while Lemieux and Prévost gave the endorsement of the federal and provincial governments to Amyot before a larger crowd nearby. Then Bourassa invaded Amyot's meeting and attacked him and his supporters for being servile followers of the party to which he himself gave his support—but not blindly.[24]

The election became a test of the leadership of Laurier and that of Bourassa, and the latter's candidate defeated the official Liberal. The Conservative press promptly hailed the beginning of the end of Laurier's supremacy in Quebec, while the Liberal papers denounced Bourassa as a demagogue who concealed personal ambition beneath professions of independence. But other independent candidates appeared, and Bourassa's following grew. The Liberal organs warned that if Quebec adopted Bourassa's strictly French and Catholic point of view, Ontario would follow Dr. Sproule, Sam Hughes, and W. F. MacLean in a strictly English and Protestant policy, with civil war as a result.[25]

In November Bourassa also supported Joseph Ainey, the labor candidate in Sainte-Marie, against Médéric Martin, the official standard-bearer. Bourassa defended the candidate of the international unions against charges of radicalism by expounding Leo XIII's approval of labor organizations and declaring that he had not denounced the international unions. Again he urged a revolt against party discipline in the interest of independent judgment. Carried away by his vehemence, he called his Liberal colleagues 'traitors' and '*vendus*.' The Liberals made the most of the obvious incongruity of the intellectual aristocrat Bourassa supporting the growing labor movement. A coalition of nationalists and 'socialists' appeared too extreme to the electorate, and the official candidate was elected by a large majority.[26] But the Liberals had had a scare at the prospect of the insurgent nationalists being joined in the House by labor members who would doubtless have followed Bourassa's leadership after his intervention in the election.

When parliament met late in November, Bourassa criticized the government policy on immigration, but above all he sought to justify his previous departures from the party's official position and proclaimed his loyalty to true Liberal principles. Late in January Laurier, acting at the instigation of the party regulars who had been outraged by Lavergne's part in managing Robitaille's campaign, expelled his protégé from the party by depriving him of the patronage for his constituency. On February 5, 1906, Lavergne defended his course on the same grounds as Bourassa had done, saying that the people preferred independent men to slaves and voting machines. War between the Liberals and the nationalists was now more or less open. On February 25 Lavergne proposed a bill extending bilingualism to currency and postage stamps. The measure was gently killed by the government forces. Arthur Dansereau wrote condescendingly in *La Presse* that Lavergne was cutting his teeth, to which Lavergne replied that his bibulous critic was still on the bottle. But Lavergne won the support of Senator Philippe Landry, who had called for the use of French in the militia regulations. Bourassa was becoming something of a figure in the House, and when the Conservatives charged that the government members were given to 'wine, women, and graft,' he demanded a parliamentary commission of inquiry into the charge. His holier-than-thou attitude irritated the government's supporters, but he was supported by the Conservatives. Laurier defended the honor of parliament and the motion was rejected by the government majority. But Bourassa continued his attacks, and *Le Nationaliste* published a picture of the cabinet, with a frame suggesting the charges and a large question mark.[27] Laurier's partisans were outraged that he was included, for none of the many scandals engendered by the administration's long stay in office had touched the prime minister.

In April Lavergne and Bourassa launched a new attack on the government's immigration policy. Lavergne pointed out that the newcomers now numbered 37 per cent of the population and in another ten years might well represent half the population. He said Canada needed only English and French immigrants, and called for more of the latter. Bourassa protested against the tendency to swamp the French Canadians, and criticized the railway tariff which made

much more expensive for a French Canadian to reach the West
an for a foreign immigrant. Robitaille joined in with a demand
at the government make the same effort to recruit immigrants in
rance as in England. Bourassa criticized the fact that in the
anadian immigration bureaus he had visited in Europe, all the
terature was devoted to the West. He urged that the East had the
ame right to receive immigrants, and urged Lemieux on his next
isit to France to seek immigrants there and in Belgium. Lemieux
ontented himself with observing that Frenchmen had proved
eluctant to emigrate, despite the efforts made by two Canadian
gents. These criticisms of Bourassa expressed the feeling of his
upporters, who feared that French Canada would lose its influence
s its numbers were dwarfed by immigration, and who felt that
here was a definite attempt to prevent French-Canadian expansion
utside Quebec. Again Bourassa and Lavergne had an opportunity
o pose as the defenders of Quebec when the Fielding resolutions,
roviding for a revision of provincial subsidies according to popula-
ion, every ten years for the old provinces and every five for the
Vest, came before the House. Bourassa protested against the in-
quality, and against the necessary modification of the British North
merica Act by the British parliament. The session closed with the
ationalists having achieved only a nuisance value, but the three-
nan party nonetheless had made itself felt.

Their student followers had been somewhat restrained for the
noment by an article of Antonio Perrault, president of the A.C.J.C.,
n *Le Semeur*, which criticized 'men who believe, wrongly, that they
lone possess, in all things, the monopoly of sound doctrine and of
he good . . . not suffering that anyone think, speak, act differently
rom them, condemning without mercy anyone who does not have
he upright mentality that these gentlemen believe they have.'[28]
This article, written under the inspiration of a visiting French
Dominican, Père Lemarchand, and approved by Archbishop
Bruchési and Bishop Emard, was printed accompanied by reser-
ations to its thesis by the A.C.J.C. chaplain, Père Hermas Lalande,
.J. The Jesuits, more inclined to political action than the Domini-
ans or the bishops, stood firm in the position taken by the chaplain,
lespite pressure from Archbishop Bruchési. Some of the Quebec
nembers of the A.C.J.C. resigned on the advice of Bishop Mathieu,
nd Perrault summoned the annual congress to meet at the Univer-
ity rather than at the Jesuit Collège Sainte-Marie, as usual. Archishop Bruchési attended and supported Perrault's stand. The
ationalism to which many young priests were already given was
ot yet sanctioned by the hierarchy. Archbishop Bruchési and
Bishop Emard also prevailed upon Archbishop Bégin of Quebec to
ostpone the announced establishment of an official Catholic daily

newspaper under the editorship of the crusading Abbé Paul-Eugène Roy and the name of '*L'Action Sociale Catholique*.'

3

Meanwhile Laurier had gone to London for the fifth Colonia Conference, which met in London in April 1907. With Chamber lain, the great showman of empire, no longer at the helm, there was no pageantry or display. Laurier, the only delegate who had taken part in the Conferences of 1897 and 1902, maintained his announced opposition to the setting up of an imperial council. He yielded in the matter of a change of terminology for the gatherings which were henceforward to be called 'imperial' rather thar 'colonial' conferences. Everything associated with colonial status was becoming distasteful to the self-governing dominions, which pressed unsuccessfully for the transfer of their affairs from the colonial secretary's office to that of the prime minister. They won however, official recognition of dominion status and of the equality of the several governments. Laurier declared 'We are all His Majesty's governments,' and his view was adopted in a resolution which described the conferences' business as considering questions 'between His Majesty's Government and His Governments of the self-governing Dominions beyond the Seas.'

Confronted with the Campbell-Bannerman's government's objec tions to imperial preference, the conference could do little bu renew its resolution in favor of that principle. Laurier, however did not renew his 1902 offer of increased preference to Great Britain in exchange for a Canadian preference in British markets. On the question of defence, the Liberal government, hoping for general dis armament as a result of the Second Hague Conference, scheduled for 1908, did not press the dominions. Australia favored creating its own navy rather than cash contribution to the imperial fleet, and Canada refused any defence contribution other than the contem plated establishment of a local naval force. Laurier approved the proposed 'All Red Line' of communication from Great Britain to Australia which had been evolved by Sifton and Strathcona, the Canadian high commissioner in London. This project called for fast steamer services on the Atlantic and Pacific, linked by four-day transcontinental trains, which would cut ten days off the time required to journey from London to New Zealand. The plan demanded an annual subsidy of a million pounds, of which Great Britain was to pay half, and Canada £325,000, with New Zealand and Australia making up the balance. A resolution favorable to the scheme was adopted by the conference, but in the face of the luke-warmness of the British government and the determined opposition f the threatened P. & O. Steamship Line, the project came to othing.[29]

Upon his return from the conference in July, Laurier was faced ith the task of remaking his cabinet, in which the portfolios of ailways and public works were vacant. The former post he had ffered to Sifton while both were in London.[30] The Westerner elayed his answer until his return home, and then sought to bring n three colleagues with him. Laurier wanted Sifton in the cabinet, ut he did not want him as second-in-command and inevitable uccessor. The negotiations fell through. At the same time Laurier ad some thought of appeasing the Quebec wing of the party by ffering a portfolio to Bourassa. The nationalist leader had con-nued to gain in influence during Laurier's absence, and in Quebec e and his followers pressed a bitter attack on Jules Prévost, minister f colonization, and Adélard Turgeon, minister of lands and forests. Discontented Liberals and Conservatives rallied to Bourassa's upport, and there were rumors that he might resign from the ederal parliament and enter the provincial field at the head of an ndependent third party. The Gouin government considered this a eal threat, and Laurier sounded out Bourassa's willingness to enter he federal cabinet through E. W. Thompson and Lavergne.[31] But Bourassa proved unwilling to join a ministry including Sifton. Thus, in both the West and Quebec, Laurier's position became ncreasingly less secure, after failure of these efforts to unite his ivided followers.

Bourassa went his own way, and his path was indicated by the act on August 5 he spoke under the auspices of the *Ligue Nationaliste* t Saint-Roch in Laurier's own county of Quebec. Fifteen thousand eople gathered to hear him, Lavergne, and Robitaille; but the neeting was broken up by a barrage of tomatoes, eggs, and stones om Liberal stalwarts directed by Louis-Alexandre Taschereau. The publicity given this affair did the Liberals no good, and Bourassa romptly began a speaking tour in the country, where various arishes offered a fair hearing. He presented what amounted to a rovincial platform, denouncing the mismanagement of the pro-ince's natural resources and calling for reforms in the administra-on of justice, labor legislation, education, and colonization. Laurier efrained from expelling him from the party, but did make the atement that Bourassa's attitude was not approved by him and aat Bourassa was 'not one of his best political friends.'[32] But Bourassa continued his campaign throughout the province, gaining dherents and larger audiences as he went. Finally, at Trois-Rivières on September 30, he called for the formation of a third arty, 'which ought necessarily absorb the best elements of the two ld parties.'[33] He had already invoked the example of Mercier in following the same course. Under his sustained attack, Prévos Turgeon, and the provincial treasurer resigned early in October.

Prévost then challenged Bourassa to an '*assemblée contradictoire*' a Terrebonne. Speaking before the house of Curé Labelle, Bourass invoked his memory and that of the colonists who had pioneere the North in order to provide for the expansion of the race and th enlargement of the fatherland. He denounced those who sold th natural resources of Quebec to Americans or Belgians for a song and declared: 'I want the people's wealth to be kept for the people Prévost, speaking in his family stronghold, defended himself an called Bourassa's charges lies unworthy of Papineau's grandson. Bu in rebuttal Bourassa evoked the tradition of Papineau and of tru Liberalism as his reason for condemning Prévost, Turgeon, an Gouin: 'If I have undertaken this campaign, it is to save the hono of the Liberal party; it is to snatch the old flag which they hav torn and sullied.' Bourassa was acclaimed in the home town of h opponent.[34]

For his part, Turgeon challenged Bourassa to resign from th federal House, and to run against him in Bellechasse. Bourass promptly accepted the challenge, and said farewell to Laurier, wh dryly remarked: 'I regret your departure. We need a man like yo at Ottawa . . . though I should not want two.'[35] Turgeon wa supported by the Liberal organization; Lavergne improvised on for Bourassa, with the aid of Robitaille, N.-K. Laflamme, Josep Rainville, Alleyn Taschereau, Napoléon Garceau and Ernes Tétreau. Asselin revived *La Mitraille* for the duration of the cam paign; students came from Montreal and Quebec to aid their ido But Bellechasse was a rural constituency, and the farmers remaine attached to Turgeon, a farmer's son, despite the support Bourass received from the clergy. Bourassa was defeated on November 4 b more than 700 votes. Laurier then sought to rally the rebel' followers to the old party, treating their chief not too unkindly:

> No one recognizes Bourassa's talent more than I do. He has on capital defect, he does not know how to keep within bounds. It is impos sible that there should not be differences of opinion among friends, bu he fights his friends with the same violence as his enemies; he become intoxicated with his own words; he grows irritated if contradicted in the end he overshoots his own mark and allows himself to be draw along unconsciously from friendly criticism to open war. Just there the origin of this bitter struggle he is carrying on with the provinci government. . . .[36]

Laurier offered to let Bourassa resume his federal seat withou opposition, while the Conservatives volunteered to support hi ɜainst a Laurier candidate. Bourassa declined both offers, preerring to follow provincial politics. He was in disgrace with the iberals, and coldly treated by those Conservatives who had suported him when he held a federal seat.[37]

4

Bourassa was not left wholly without support, however. On ecember 21, 1907, the first number of *L'Action Sociale* appeared at uebec, with Omer Héroux and Jules Dorion, two of his disciples, mong the editors. The new daily was nominally independent in olitics, but it soon exhibited *Castor* and nationalistic tendencies. n parliament Lavergne upheld the nationalist cause. He objected the imperialist slant being given to plans for the forthcoming elebration of the three hundredth anniversary of the founding of uebec by Champlain. The Prince of Wales and representatives of ll the colonies had been invited; and Lord Grey, the imperialinded governor-general who was one of Cecil Rhodes' executors, ok a lively interest in the preparations. Lavergne protested that hamplain and his work were being lost sight of, and that the elebration was coming to be regarded rather as the apotheosis of Volfe and the English Conquest. He went on to complain that the ghts of the French language were slighted by the railway, telephone, nd telegraph companies. Laurier spoke soothing words, while the rangemen Sam Hughes and MacLean paid tribute to Champlain. avergne, with the aid of Monk, also continued Bourassa's criticism f the government's immigration policy, blaming on it the crime aves and anarchist activity now found in Montreal and other large ities. But Frank Oliver, the new minister of the interior, favored osmopolitan immigration, as his predecessor Sifton had done.

Lavergne's call for bilingualism in the public services was suported by the circulation of petitions to that effect by the A.C.J.C., nd which called a mass meeting at the Monument National on ⁄Iay 8, with Bourassa, Lavergne, and Verville as speakers. The rganization was now in the hands of those who favored political as vell as religious action. Lavergne spoke first, calling for a realization f the constitutional principle of bilingualism. He urged that party pirit should be forgotten in this effort to attain the common good f all French Canadians. Verville, president since 1904 of the anadian Congress of Trades and Labor, supported the bilingual novement. Bourassa was received with wild enthusiasm by the udience, in which young people predominated. He congratulated avergne on his campaign in favor of French, and called it an pportune one, since national consciousness had suffered losses in ecent years. It was only just that companies enjoying public subsidies should give the French language equal rights with Englisl The assembly adopted a resolution urging all public services i Quebec to employ both languages in all their relations with th public, and petitioning parliament to provide penalties for infring ment of this policy. Raoul Dandurand, president of the Senat urged a less aggressive tone, but was howled down by Bourassa tumultuous young followers, who habitually pushed his demands fo equality to the point of provocation. The rising generation wa nationalist almost to a man, to the dismay of Laurier, Gouin, an other prophets of the middle way.

Bourassa believed that the time had come to found a nationali daily, and planned to withdraw from politics for that purpose. Bu nationalists and Conservatives alike urged him to run against Lome Gouin, the provincial premier, in Saint-Jacques. The Conservative promised to help him to acquire a journal if he thus aided the against the Liberal chief. A tacit alliance was arranged whereby th nationalists and Conservatives would conduct separate campaign but the latter would present no rival in constituencies where nationalist candidate was running. Bourassa began his campaign o May 8 at Saint-Lin, Laurier's birthplace, where he attacked the chi Liberal spokesman, Turgeon, and urged the electors not to allo Laurier's mantle to be used 'to wipe the floor of the Legislativ Assembly, soiled by intriguers.' He expounded the nationali program: 'We are going to spread throughout the province th ideas of independence, honesty, and patriotism.'[38] After Gouin an Taschereau, the two leading Liberals, had announced their intentio of each running in two counties, Bourassa declared that he woul contest both Saint-Jacques in Montreal and Saint-Hyacinthe Lavergne resigned from the federal parliament to contest Mon magny. J.-E. Bédard was induced to run in Beauport against th official candidate. These were the most hopeful nationalist candi dacies; Napoléon Garceau in Drummondville, Joseph Rainville i Verchères, and J.-R. Labelle in Iberville admittedly stood littl chance of election.

Bourassa opened his Montreal campaign at the Monumen National on May 25, before a house packed with what the Libera press called 'the choirboys of the new pontiff.'[39] The applause wa so great that three times he tried in vain to begin his speech. Whe finally he was allowed to speak he pointed out how within te months 'two or three young men, supported by men still young having at their disposition neither money, nor papers, nor place nor patronage, but having feeling, thought, and principles, ha succeeded in arousing the province and making it understand tha Confederation was based on two principles: equilibrium betwee the two races and equilibrium between the federal and provinci wers.'[40] He separated provincial and federal affairs, urging his dience not to let Gouin take shelter under Laurier's mantle. Then expounded his provincial program; sale of waterpower rights to e highest bidder, separation of colonization and lumbering areas, ıdy of prospective laws by a legislative commission before debate the assembly, creation of a permanent board for the adjustment differences between employers and labor. In the educational ld he deplored the excessive attention given to secondary and gher education while primary instruction was neglected, and he iticized the establishment of a school of higher commercial studies a province which lacked technical schools for training artisans. ourassa declared that there was nothing in this program to make nglish-Canadians uneasy, though he had been denounced for pealing to racial prejudices. He thus answered his critics:

I have made appeals to my race and I still make them. I make these peals to my race in order that, conscious of its dignity, it may stand straight and proud before others, not as an enemy, but to accept eir hands.

I appeal to my race in order that in this province there shall be no ore question of popular passions but only of honor and dignity, and in der that we may prove to our sister provinces that if we have remained home, alone, without having perhaps as much wealth as others, the tle that we have has sufficed to keep us honest and worthy of those who ave preceded us.

I appeal to my race in order that it may understand that on Canadian il the land is too large for one race to tread on the other and for one ce to fuse with the other.

I appeal to my race in order that it may understand that we are united, atholics and French, English and Protestants, not to fight and crush ch other, but to work with a common mind to enlarge our country.[41]

his peroration brought down the house. Bourassa and his wife ere taken in triumph to their home in a carriage drawn by students, the head of a throng of 1,500 people. The Liberal press belittled e demonstration, but its significance could not be ignored. *L'Action ciale* showed itself well disposed to the nationalist-Conservative alition and assigned Georges Pelletier, a disciple of Bourassa, to ver his campaign at Saint-Hyacinthe.

Bourassa devoted most of his attention, however, to the contest in Iontreal, where a joint Liberal-Conservative committee aided his ld nationalist supporters: Asselin, Fournier, Paul-Emile Lamarche, nd eager troops of students. A meeting on June 2 could not find oom enough in the Théâtre National and paraded through the reets behind Bourassa to St. James' Market. Gouin's gatherings ere not as enthusiastic, and one on June 4 was broken up by followers of Bourassa. On June 5 Bourassa held a special meeti for English voters, and then challenged Gouin to meet him on t following day, the last of the campaign, in an *assemblée contradictoi* Gouin was willing, but the municipal authorities discouraged such meeting, since feeling had risen so high. On the night of the electio when it was learned that Bourassa had defeated the premier by fort three votes, the nationalist leader was met at Bonaventure Stati upon his return from Saint-Hyacinthe and hauled homeward in carriage drawn by students at the head of an impromptu para which interrupted traffic for several hours, as it paused for speech along the way. The triumphant nationalists' cry was 'Saint-Jacqu has avenged Bellechasse.' Bourassa declared that this victory w only the beginning of a great national movement. In Sain Hyacinthe, the result was a tie, subsequently decided in Bourassa favor by a recount which gave him a majority of thirty-eigh Lavergne and twelve Conservatives were also elected, thus doubli the opposition to Gouin's government. The Liberals had done we but Bourassa's prestige was immensely increased by his victory ov Gouin in the latter's home district.

While the nationalist leader took a vacation in Europe, t imperialist forces exerted themselves at the Quebec tercentenar A British naval squadron brought the Prince of Wales and a di tinguished suite including Lord Roberts; a French squadron broug a mission including the Marquis de Lévis and the Comte de Mon calm; an American warship Vice-President Fairbanks. Lauri read an address in English to which the Prince replied in Frenc Quebec was packed with notables drawn from all over Canada an from Newfoundland, Australia, New Zealand, and South Afric. More than 20,000 sailors and soldiers were encamped about t city. For a week the celebrations continued, drawing the attentio of the world to Canada, and particularly to French Canada. A the banquets French Canadians professed their loyalism an Englishmen expressed their sympathy with the French race. T premier of the province and the mayor of Quebec City we knighted; once more Laurier declined the offer of a peerage. B there were rifts in the lute: nationalists quarrelled with the im perialist flavor of the gathering, while imperialists protested at t number of Tricolors in evidence, and the ultramontane pre muttered darkly that the French envoy was a Freemason.

During Bourassa's travels in France and Belgium he gave a interview to *La Gazette de France* in which he expounded the doctrin of the nationalist movement, explaining that one of its princip aims was to develop a more general Canadianism and thus weaken English-Canadian antagonism to French Canada.[42] Mea while at home he was being suggested as chief of the provinci pposition, and Jean Prévost offered him alliance. He returned ome on August 25, and first appeared in public on September 6, hen he spoke with Lavergne at Montmagny. After the exchange f mutual compliments, Bourassa outlined a program in both deral and provincial affairs, stressing the danger of immigration nd calling for a revocation of the colonization laws. He warned gainst the educational reforms preached by Godfroy Langlois nd the *Ligue d'Enseignement.* In France, he said 'I saw a Catholic eople governed by a handful of men without faith or patriotism, ho imposed upon it a dangerous system of education.'[43] He hought such a system would endanger Quebec's Catholicism and hus its nationality.

At Saint-Hyacinthe on September 19 Bourassa announced that e had chosen to represent that county in parliament rather than aint-Jacques. His choice of the less sure seat was admired by his outhful followers. As yet he had said nothing of his attitude in the npending federal elections. Finally he called a meeting at the Ionument National on October 2, barely three weeks before the lections. With the assurance of an established leader he sketched ut his program. He was not content with two or three seats in the rovincial parliament; he was going to conquer the whole province, hose autonomy and proper place in Confederation he wished to ssure. The first step was not to criticize Ontario and the other rovinces, but to bring about reform at home. Once party spirit was eplaced by public spirit, the province could be launched on a rogram of economic, moral, and intellectual development. He alled for the aid of all, Conservatives and Liberals alike. He did ot seek to lead Conservatives to Laurier or Liberals to Borden, nd would remain neutral in the federal elections, except in particular cases.[44] To achieve his purpose he planned to establish a aily newspaper in Montreal and clubs throughout the province, hose dues would be used to meet electoral expenses and those of he paper.

As in 1907, Laurier confined his campaigning to Ontario and Quebec, urging the electors to rally to his 'white plume' on what vas doubtless the last occasion he would appeal to the people. He tood on his record of having raised Canada in twelve years from he status of a colony to that of a great nation, and urged: 'Let me inish my task!'[45] He spoke no word against Bourassa, and Bourassa eturned the compliment. In Quebec the Conservatives were too livided and too unorganized to be effective; elsewhere they charged candals against the government. The Orangemen issued a amphlet, 'The Duty of the Hour,' urging a vote against Laurier s a vote against clerical domination; but this effort did the Conservative cause as much harm as good. When the ballots were counted, Quebec and Ontario showed the same majoriti for Laurier as in 1904, though there were many shifts in ind vidual constituencies and the popular majority in Quebec w: small. The Liberals lost much ground in Manitoba and Britis Columbia, and some in Novia Scotia. Their majority shran from sixty-two to forty-seven, and outside Quebec the party held majority of only four. With British Columbia in revolt again his Japanese policy and Manitoba becoming a Conservative stron hold under Robert Rogers, Laurier could not but be uneasy as th nationalist movement grew ever stronger in Quebec, the backbon of his power.

Bourassa supplied evidence of his growing influence when o February 25, 1909 he drew as large a crowd as Laurier had don on his last appearance at the Monument National to hear a declar: tion announced as 'perhaps one of the turning-points of the politic: history of our province.'[46] The audience was made up largely French-Canadian businessmen and the chairman was J.-A. Vaillar court, head of the Banque d'Hochelaga. Having won the suppo of youth, Bourassa now sought that of older men, particularl businessmen and teachers. The latter were already largely gaine for his cause through the A.C.J.C. and its study groups in th classical colleges. A professor at the Collège Sainte-Marie, fo instance, had formally approved in the classroom one of Bourassa earlier lectures, and had commented that 'perhaps he was destine to change the political face of the country.'[47] At the Monumer National Bourassa spoke in general terms, dismissing his program : familiar enough. He urged the necessity of a third party, now th: the Liberals had lost their idealism and enthusiasm through lon stay in office, and the Conservatives lacked the vigor to goverr Both parties had lost their principles and become mere coterie: 'syndicates of appetites.' A new group, with the life-giving principl of justice and honesty, was needed.

To found such a party, he appealed to men of goodwill in a groups and parties, 'in order that we may unite around the ide: which we believe necessary to the future of our province, around program of economic reforms which we believe necessary to th development of our domain.' A true public opinion must b awakened in the province, like that which existed in England an which permitted English Liberals to vote against the Liberal goverr ment on a question of principle without being called traitors. Th public opinion, once created or regenerated through a new part clubs, and the proposed journal, would permit the establishment of government which would conform to the ideals of the race and th main lines of the British tradition. This strong and honest goverr ment, backed by powerful public opinion, would solve soci:

problems in the best possible fashion and would open more largely the sources of economic development. The English Canadians of Quebec need not fear this program and could collaborate in it. It was not an attempt at fusion or isolation, but one of association. Such was the course which the rising leader of Quebec urged, without sensationalism and without the verbal violence beloved by his younger followers, upon this staider audience. It won him new support, though the Liberal press dismissed it as mere rhetoric and as another proclamation of Bourassa's 'providential mission to regenerate the province of Quebec.'[48]

When the provincial session opened early in March, Tellier, the chief of the Conservative opposition, offered to share his office with Bourassa. The latter made a poor impression with his first speech, which he had neglected to prepare sufficiently, thinking the provincial legislature a small stage after the larger one at Ottawa on which he had already figured prominently. Gouin defended himself successfully and even carried the attack to Bourassa. Then, in support of a Conservative amendment to the speech from the throne, which outlined the opposition's program, Bourassa made a three-hour speech which was a *tour de force* of eloquent polemic. He resumed all his criticisms of the administration and the remedies he proposed. But once more Gouin rose above his diffidence and lack of eloquence to reply adequately to the newcomer who challenged his power. The session went its way, with Bourassa, Lavergne, and their new ally Jean Prévost seizing every possible opportunity to attack the government, and Gouin and Taschereau replying. The galleries were filled in the afternoon with students from the Quebec and Levis seminaries, who came to hear and applaud their hero Bourassa.

In *Le Nationaliste* Olivar Asselin and Jules Fournier pressed their leader's charges of scandal with a vigor that often disregarded the decencies. When one day Taschereau warned Bourassa in parliament that he had about him 'bandits for whom the reputation of a neighbor did not count,' Asselin left the press gallery and struck Taschereau in the face as he left the Chamber. The journalist was promptly arrested and condemned to fifteen days in prison. His plight awakened sympathy among the nationalists, and Omer Héroux of *L'Action Sociale* likened him to one of the '*camelots du roi*' of the *Action française* movement, with their 'necessary violences.'[49] Thus began a long feud between Taschereau and Asselin, and between Taschereau and *L'Action Sociale*. The session closed with the Liberal administration forced into reforms along the lines favored by their opponents, and with a nationalist-Conservative alliance, with clerical backing, wellnigh cemented.

5

Meanwhile the navy question had arisen in the federal House, as a result of a March debate in the British Commons. The armament race in Europe, particularly keen between Britain and Germany since 1900, largely escaped Canadian attention until March 16, 1909, when in a debate at Westminster on the Admiralty estimates it was announced that Germany was speeding up her naval construction and by 1912 would attain equality in dreadnoughts with Britain. The Admiralty, Foreign Secretary Sir Edward Grey, and Asquith and Balfour all spoke of a crucial situation. In March the scare was so pronounced that the Liberal government, instead of reducing the naval estimates, increased them by provision for four more dreadnoughts; and in July, after pressure from the opposition, it added four more. In the first alarm Britain's very safety was pictured as being at stake, and there was an immediate response in Toronto and Winnipeg, where strong demands were made for the gift of a dreadnought by Canada to the British navy. The great Liberal organ, the *Globe*, on March 23 urged Canada 'to fling the smug axioms of commercial prudence to the winds and to do more than her share . . . Within the next two years the Colonies of Britain should be able to place three Dreadnoughts at the disposal of the Motherland, and they should do it. So far as Canada is concerned, such vessels would be under the control of the Canadian government, but that is only another way of saying that they would always be at the call of the Empire in every worthy cause and in every time of danger.'[50] There was an equally prompt anti-imperialist reaction in Quebec, which saw in the situation another imperialist attempt to force Canada's hand, as in 1899.

Nothing had as yet been done to realize the government's announced policy of setting up a Canadian Navy, beyond the taking over in 1905 of the bases at Halifax and Esquimalt when the British fleet was concentrated in home waters. Since the British government held out for a single imperial fleet under its control, while Canada took the position that she should provide for her own naval defence with a force under her control, the situation had remained a stalemate. There had been for some years an imperialist campaign in the English provinces in favor of Canadian contribution to the naval defence of the empire, which had been growing in strength. Early in the session of 1909, before the British scare, George Foster gave notice of a motion calling upon Canada to take action to protect her coastline and seaports. The opposition of Frederick Monk and other members of the Conservative party delayed the proposal, but on March 29 Foster opposed contribution to the British Navy and advocated a Canadian naval force, with an emergency gift of a dreadnought to Britain if the prime minister so desired. Laurier countered with a more specific resolution recognizing Canada's willingness to assume a large share of defence responsibilities, rejecting the policy of contribution, approving 'the organization of a Canadian naval service in co-operation with and close relation to the Imperial navy,' and expressing Canada's belief in the necessity of Britain's naval supremacy and her readiness to co-operate with the Imperial authorities.[51] This resolution was modified to meet Borden's criticisms by not completely ruling out the possibility of contribution in case of an immediate emergency and by approving 'speedy' organization of a Canadian naval force. It was then passed by unanimous vote, for parliament now boasted not a single Quebec nationalist.

The decision was approved by the Liberal press in Quebec, though even *Le Soleil* expressed forebodings at being led by force of events into the armament race. *L'Action Sociale* feared secret imperialism on the part of the government, and *Le Nationaliste* attacked the ministers as having 'sold out to England.'[52] Goldwin Smith wrote to Bourassa, urging him to renew his anti-imperialist campaign of 1899, but Bourassa was too much preoccupied with provincial matters. In June an Imperial Press Conference was held in London, and the British statesmen who addressed the gathering eloquently evoked the immediate danger of Britain's losing its vital mastery of the seas. Sir Hugh Graham of the *Montreal Star*, who had been knighted the previous year and was fuller than ever of imperial zeal, inspired an article which appeared in the *Star* on June 19, denouncing Laurier's naval policy as inadequate, and urging that Canada should follow the example of Australia and New Zealand and make a cash contribution to the British Navy, instead of herself constructing ships which would be 'mere children's toys.' The suggestion was promptly taken up by the Tory press of Ontario.

In July an Imperial Defence Conference was held in London, with Louis-Philippe Brodeur, minister of marine and fisheries, and Sir Frederick Borden, militia minister, as the Canadian delegates. The *Star* and the Tory press urged them to offer dreadnoughts to England; the *Globe* and the Liberal journals of Quebec beseeched them to maintain Laurier's stand; and the nationalist and ultramontane organs warned them to offer no contribution at all. At the conference the Admiralty called for a single imperial navy aided by contributions from the empire, but urged those dominions which insisted upon their own navies to form a 'distinct fleet unit.'[53] Since all the dominions favored separate navies, the Admiralty authorities prepared detailed proposals for the construction and maintenance of such units. The Canadians asked for and received two plans, one calling for an annual expenditure of three million dollars and th other of two millions. The report of the conference was to be kep secret until the government announced its naval proposals, whicl Laurier held off until January 1910.

Meanwhile the nationalist-Conservative alliance in Quebec hac been tightened by the anti-imperialism evoked by the navy question Jules Fournier, Asselin's associate on *Le Nationaliste*, followed him tc jail in June for contempt of court in his comments on the case. Upoı his release Fournier was hailed as a hero by the students, who saw iı him an adversary of imperialism as well as a critic of the provincia government. On June 1 a banquet in honor of Mathias Tellier, th Conservative chief, was given at Joliette; it was attended by Bourassa, Lavergne, Asselin, and other nationalist leaders, as well as b their ex-Liberal ally Jean Prévost. Prévost hailed this 'coalition o the people' against the government's corruption, and Bourass insisted upon its disinterestedness, proclaiming his willingness tc retire from politics when its ideal was realized.[54] Fifteen days earlie Lavergne had attended a Borden banquet at Quebec. Bourassa' aide was unpredictable: to show his opposition to British control o the proposed Canadian Navy, he enlisted in the militia, now completely under Canadian control. The nationalists criticized Lorc Grey's support of the imperialist navy campaign, and urged that th next governor-general should be a Canadian.[55] Ethnic feeling wa already aroused by the divergence of opinion on the navy question the *Quebec Chronicle* protested the flying of the Tricolor on loca yachts, and said that 'if the Red Ensign is good enough for million of British subjects all over the world and on all the seas, it should b good enough for some thousands of Canadians of French extractio scattered in the east of Canada.'[56]

In October the nationalist-Conservative coalition was confirmec by the appearance of Bourassa, Lavergne, Prévost, and Tellier on th same platform at Saint-Hyacinthe. Bourassa proclaimed the disinterestedness of the coalition: 'Above all, comes the general interes of the province of Quebec. We want the right to march in the sam rank as the others in Confederation.'[57] In three by-elections iı November only one nationalist-supported candidate was elected while the candidate chosen by Bourassa to replace him in Saint-Jacques was defeated by the revived Liberal forces. The election wa fought on provincial issues, though the nationalists and *L'Actio Sociale* had already taken a stand on the navy question by adoptin Bourassa's old principle of no obligatory participation in the wars o the empire. As early as June Asselin had published a pamphlet '*La Défense navale de l'empire britannique*,' protesting against th Laurier-Borden naval measure and calling for Canadian autonom or independence. The Quebec Conservatives were as strongly opposec to the government's naval proposal as the nationalists, and the most loyalist of them, Tom-Chase Casgrain, urged Bourassa to campaign against Laurier's plan. Goldwin Smith wrote him: 'It is too bad that you are no longer at Ottawa; but your voice will be heard all the same.'[58]

Frederick Monk, federal leader of the Quebec Conservatives, took his stand against the naval proposal at a banquet at Lachine on November 8. He said a navy would be costly and useless, and that the Canadians, a small and poor people, should concentrate on developing their natural resources before assuming the crushing burden of militarism. The Conservative party was now split wide open, with Borden approving Laurier's position, Roblin of Manitoba calling for a direct contribution to the British Navy, and Monk opposed to both measures. When the federal session opened, the government tabled the blue book containing the official documents on the Imperial Defence Conference, and the naval program was revealed as calling for the immediate construction of three cruisers and four destroyers. Roblin denounced this 'tin-pot navy' and called for cash contributions or the gift of dreadnoughts. The Tory press, led by the *Star*, followed his lead. Borden wavered in his stand, but Sir Charles Tupper supported it. Laurier made a concession to Quebec by declaring that the Canadian fleet would not participate in imperial wars without the consent of the Canadian people.[59] But it was clear that once more public opinion in English Canada was flatly opposed to sentiment in Quebec, and that a political crisis was at hand.

It was in this atmosphere that Bourassa's independent journal *Le Devoir* first appeared, after an eighteen-month campaign for funds. There were some 500 small contributors, and one large one: G.-N. Ducharme, who made an initial investment of $10,000, later increased to $40,000. Some Conservatives, foreseeing a useful ally in the fight against Laurier, subscribed. The board of directors was made up of French-Canadian businessmen without political bias, and Bourassa controlled 51 per cent of the stock, in order to assure the editorial freedom of the paper. He was editor-in-chief, with Omer Héroux and Georges Pelletier leaving *L'Action Sociale* to become his associates. Asselin and the leading writers of *Le Nationaliste*—henceforward a weekly edition of *Le Devoir*—Jules Fournier, Tancrède Marsil, Léon Lorrain, and others made up the staff. Both the ultramontane element, for whom religion came before nationalism, and the liberal one, for whom nationalism came first, were thus included.

Bourassa himself thought of his journal as a center of national rather than Catholic action. In the first number, which appeared on January 10, 1910, he sketched out a program:

Le Devoir will support honest men and denounce rascals.

In provincial politics, we combat the present government because we find in it all the evil tendencies which we want to make disappear from public life: veniality, irresponsibility, cowardice, degrading and narrow party spirit.

We support the opposition because we find in it the opposite tendencies: probity, courage, firm principles, great largeness of views. These principles are admirably united in the personality of its leader, M. Tellier.

On the day when this group no longer follows the inspirations which guide it today, it will find us ready to fight it, as we fight the men now in power.

At Ottawa the situation is less clear.

The two parties are sinking into the same decline in which provincial politics lay some years ago.

Desire for the conquest or conservation of power seems to be their sole motive.

During the last ten years vital questions have demanded attention from our federal parliamentarians: the South African War and imperialism, the constitution of new provinces and minority rights, the construction of the Grand Trunk Pacific and the regulation of railways, foreign immigration and the settlement of the national domain.

By a sort of conspiracy, the two parliamentary groups connived to give each of these problems a solution in which right, justice and national interest have been sacrificed to opportunism, to party intrigues, or still worse to the cupidity of individual interests.

At the very hour that we appear upon the scene, parliament is deliberating a question of the highest importance, which is only a new episode of the imperialist movement: the construction of a Canadian Navy.

Shall we watch a repetition of the comedy of 1899? Will the Canadian people be the dupe of the machinations and miserable intrigues of parties?

The resounding discourse of M. Monk at Lachine gives us the hope that the dangerous and stupefying situation in which we rest will not continue.

The member for Jacques-Cartier can be assured of our support, if he maintains his attitude with firmness, logic, and perseverance.

In order to assure the triumph of ideas over appetites, of the public good over party spirit, there is only one means: to awaken in the people, and above all in the ruling classes, the sentiment of public duty under all its forms: religious duty, national duty, civic duty. Thus the title of this journal, which has astonished some people and caused some colleagues to smile.[60]

Thus from the start *Le Devoir* took an active political role. The expression of sympathy with the Conservatives in the first number was followed the next day by Bourassa's biting reference to the 'golden clouds' in which Laurier 'had veiled the betrayals, weaknesses, and dangers of his policy.'[61] It was clear that open nationalist warfare against Laurier was not far off.

Le Devoir, like *L'Action Sociale* was a journal of opinion addressed to a cultivated audience, not a commercial paper on the new American model addressed to the lowest common denominator of the population, a model increasingly followed by the rest of the French-Canadian press as yellow journalism proved profitable. The founding of *Le Devoir* was warmly hailed by *L'Action Sociale* and *L'Evénement*, which did not fear Montreal competition in the district of Quebec; the Liberal press greeted it sourly. The new paper opposed the Gouin government; it attacked municipal corruption in Montreal; and it espoused the cause of the newly founded Ontario *Association canadienne-française d'éducation*, which under the leadership of Senator Napoléon Belcourt undertook the defence of bilingualism in that province against the Irish clergy under Bishop Fallon. But Bourassa's chief interest at this time was the navy question.

On January 12 Laurier himself introduced the Naval Service Bill, providing for the creation of a permanent force, supplemented by a reserve and by volunteers on the same basis as the militia, with the exception that naval service was to be wholly voluntary. The force was to be under the control of the Canadian government, but in case of war might be placed under imperial control by order-in-council, subject to the approval of parliament, which was to be summoned within fifteen days, if not in session. Five cruisers and six destroyers were to be built, costing \$11,000,000 if constructed in England, and \$15,000,000 if in Canada, as was desired if possible; the annual budget was estimated at \$3,000,000. In response to a question from Dr. Sproule, asking whether 'case of war' referred to war anywhere in the empire or in Canada only, Laurier replied: 'War everywhere. When Britain is at war, Canada is at war; there is no distinction. If Great Britain, to which we are subject, is at war with any nation, Canada is exposed to invasion; hence Canada is at war.'[62] He stressed the fact that there was no liability to service in the navy, as there was under the Militia Act. R. L. Borden approved the proposal, expressing his conviction that Britain would not engage in war without consulting the dominions, but urging that a Defence Committee made up of representatives from both British parties and the self-governing colonies should have some control over the imperial defence organization: 'If we are to take part in the permanent defence of this great empire, we must have some control and some voice in such matters.' He opposed the policy of contribution to the British navy in general, but urged a special emergency contribution under the present circumstances.[63] Monk, like Laurier, belittled the crucial nature of the present situation, which Borden had once more emphasized; and expressed his belief that Canada was unable to build and maintain a suitable navy. He called for a plebiscite on the question.

Bourassa at once attacked the bill and Laurier's declaration that Canada was at war when Britain was at war. In *Le Devoir* for January 17 he pointed out the consequences:

> Let the notion occur to a Chamberlain, a Rhodes, a Beers, to gold-seekers or opium merchants, of causing a conflict in South Africa or India, in the Mediterranean or the Persian Gulf, on the shores of the Baltic or the banks of the Black Sea, on the coasts of Japan or in the China seas, we are involved, always and regardless, with our money and our blood . . .
>
> It is the most complete backward step Canada has made in half a century.
>
> It is the gravest blow our autonomy has suffered since the origin of responsible government.[64]

Bourassa indicted Laurier for his weaknesses and betrayals from 1902 to the present 'national capitulation.' *L'Action Sociale* supported Monk's suggestion of a plebiscite and protested against the creation of a navy without an appeal to the people. In Montreal a lecture by Bourassa on military imperialism and the Navy Bill was announced.

The Monument National on January 20 was packed, with several hundred persons seated on the stage itself. Without oratorical preliminaries, Bourassa plunged into a discussion of the bill. Citing the example of the National Transcontinental Railway, he pointed out that the initial cost of the proposed navy would be dwarfed by later expenses. He criticized the bill for not limiting the navy to the defence of Canada, as the militia was by the law of 1904. He then listed twenty-three wars in which Britain had been engaged since 1812, of which he singled out five as the most serious, and asked when Canada had been threatened with invasion by the Russians, the Sepoys, the Sudanese, the Afghans, or the Boers. If he had a seat in the House, he would ask what possible threat there was to Canada from England's potential enemies, save the United States and Japan. He called Laurier's declaration a reversal of his stand in 1902 and 1907 and a constitutional heresy. If it were sanctioned, Canadian troops could be sent abroad whenever England was at war. It plunged Canada into the very 'whirlpool of militarism' which Laurier had once eloquently denounced.

The bill did not provide, as Laurier had promised, for a Canadian Navy under Canadian control, to be used for the defence of the empire only so far as Canada was concerned; but instead for one placed under imperial authority in all the wars of England. It was not a defence force, but one designed, as the Admiralty had wished, also for offence. No other empire had ever imposed upon its colonies the obligation of constructing a navy. Citing the example of the South African War, Bourassa denounced Borden's assurance that Britain would consult the colonies before making war as impossible under the existing regime. The reservation demanding the approval of parliament was worthless; either parliament would be stampeded, as it had been in 1899, or it would be presented with a *fait accompli*, since the fleet would remain under imperial control until the war's end.

Then Bourassa considered the questions of whether Canada needed a navy, whether England needed aid, and whether that aid was owed by Canada. The projected navy did not augment Canada's security but decreased it, since a young country could stand only so much military expense, and the cost of the militia had doubled within the last five years without providing an army adequate to defend Canada's frontiers. In wartime Canada's maritime commerce could be carried on under a neutral flag without naval protection. Then railroads and canals, built or in prospect, called for the expenditure of 800 millions. Bourassa agreed with Monk that Canada could not bear an additional burden of military and naval expenses. He belittled the German menace, comparing it to the exploded French and Russian menaces of past years, and citing the evidence of Sir William White, long director of British naval construction, in the *Nineteenth Century Review* for April 1909, that there was no real basis for the naval scare. He pictured Britain's present plight as the result of her foreign policy since the end of the Napoleonic Wars, in which the colonies had never been consulted.

Was it Canada's duty to share the burden which Britain had imposed upon herself for her own glory and greatness? 'We Canadians owe all our blood, all our effort, all our consideration to the country that providence has given us. As British subjects, we owe to England only the preservation of that part of the Empire which has fallen to our share, with its inconveniences and its advantages. To depart from this path is to compromise the future of Canada without assuring the security of the Empire.'[65] He recited the long history of Britain's efforts to make Canada assume a larger share in imperial defence, and the stand taken by Mackenzie, Macdonald, Blake, Tupper, and Laurier up to 1907 in favor of local defence and against imperial centralization. Asquith, Dilke, and Lord Charles Beresford were on record to the effect that Britain could not reduce its defence burdens even if Canada left the empire. In the past Canada had been involved in two wars with the United States on Britain's behalf; as for the present and the future he cited Laurier's statement of March 1909: 'Canada has no quarrels with anyone; no desire to expand its territory; it occupies an isolated position; it has only one neighbor, with which it has lived in peace for more than a century.' Britain neither could nor would defend Canada against the United States, her sole possible enemy. Canada enjoyed the protection of the Monroe Doctrine, and if Britain protected the Canadian mer chant marine, she did so because it was essential to her commerce Sure of her supremacy at sea, Britain had rejected the Americai proposal to the Hague Tribunal that the commerce of belligerent should be regarded as neutral.

Canada owed no gratitude for British diplomacy, which had cos her dear, nor for British capital, which had been invested in Canad: because it was profitable. The imperialists argued that Canada owec Britain a debt of gratitude for its liberty and British institutions Bourassa refuted the contention:

> Gentlemen, I highly appreciate this liberty; I love these institution and you love them. But the essential part of British institutions is th preservation of the spirit of liberty and independence. I recognize tha England has admirably governed its colonies, particularly since sh decided to govern them no more. The great English Liberal school more modest and less noisy than the Chamberlains and the Balfours made the British Empire what it is, because it consolidated it in th liberty, independence, and autonomy of its colonies.
>
> Yes, certainly I appreciate the liberty we have enjoyed since Englis Liberal principles triumphed, but, gentlemen, once more, need we den our past?
>
> England accorded us this liberty because those who preceded us i our path, less ardent to seek decorations from His Majesty, carrie the fight for our rights to the foot of the throne.
>
> We obtained this liberty because we knew how to conquer it; not onl we French Canadians, but the patriots of Ontario as well as those c Quebec, the Mackenzies as well as the Papineaus: because we kne how to ask for it during seventy-five years with energy, calm, in the fu awareness of our rights; because we knew how to be a strong people
>
> But we shall preserve this liberty only by guarding intact the traditio of national pride and not, after fifty years of autonomous governmen by putting our flag at the feet of a Chamberlain or a Balfour.[66]

Then Bourassa considered the consequences of the bill, which h summed up as 'disastrous for Canada and fatal to the British Empire. Canada would be drawn into all the wars of England, which ha averaged one every four years in the past century. Canadian arma ment might provoke the United States to fortify the frontier. I would cause the abandonment of the theory that Canada was neutr: in all British wars in which its interests and territory were not in volved. It was absurd to pretend that Canada's entry into the 'whir pool of militarism' was avoided since there would be no nav: conscription—something which no country had adopted. He cite Laurier's denunciation in 1902 of Canada's entry into the Europea armament race as suicidal for the country, and his characterizatio of devoting money needed for public works to armaments as rime. Imperial defence collaboration would lead to an imperial ariff, to an imperial council, to the full realization of Chamberlain's lream, which was impossible because the British Empire was eparated by the seas, diverse in components, and autonomous in its arts. The result of the imperialist policy would be immediate upture of the empire in hatred and conflict of interests, and the lestruction of its ideal. Canadians were not Englishmen; every day hey were becoming more Americanized, though the French Canalians' difference of language was 'the best safeguard of Canadian utonomy and of British institutions.'

There was no racial quarrel involved in this stand. Any of his rguments could have been addressed to an English-speaking Canalian, to a Protestant or a Catholic. The French Canadians were not solated in their anti-imperialism, although there were no doubt nany imperialists among the Anglo-Saxons, captivated by Chamberain's great dream. He defended such rational and sincere imperialsts as Stephen Leacock; such emotional and sincere imperialists s Colonel Denison. But he denounced those who were imperialists n their own financial interest and the snobbish imperialists who ormed a little court about the governor-general at Rideau Hall and ought imperial decorations. He pointed out that there were also English-Canadian anti-imperialists such as Goldwin Smith, Adam Shortt, and the members of the Ontario Grange and of the Manitoba Grain Growers' Association. He denounced the opportunism of Laurier and Borden, and the conspiracy of both parties to sacrifice national interests to party intrigues.

Lord Grey had not caused Laurier's change of attitude by a *oup d'état* such as had been urged upon Minto in the case of General Hutton; but Grey, the disciple of Rhodes in South Africa and his executor, had privately done more for the cause of imperialism in Canada during the last two years than any Canadian politician had ever done. But since the cabinet had failed to remind the governorgeneral that he had no more right to play politics in Canada than the King had in England, the people should raise its voice. Parliament had no right to vote this law without appealing to the people, since t reversed the stand sanctioned at the polls in 1904 and 1908. Not in my name, but in the name of your sons, in the name of those who will bear the weight of this criminal policy, in the name of those who will pay the taxes which will weigh more heavily upon us, in he name of those who perhaps soon will embark upon these vessels to go and perish upon far-off seas, I ask you to unite with me in making known to Lord Grey, Sir Wilfrid Laurier, and Mr. Borden that before starting us on this path, they ought to explain their designs, make them known to the people, and obtain approval of their policy.'[67] Then Bourassa read a resolution, calling upon parliament to defer the bill until a plebiscite had made known the will of the people. He described it as 'neither a declaration of war nor the commencement of a revolution,' but as a resolution already adopted by the Grange of Ontario and the Grain Growers of Manitoba. The resolution was adopted amid vast enthusiasm.

6

Thus began the revolt against Laurier which eventually brought about his downfall. Bourassa's speech was published as a pamphlet '*Le Projet de Loi Navale*,' and widely circulated throughout the province. *Le Devoir* printed a blank petition for a plebiscite, and lawyers, doctors, notaries, and many *curés* sought signatures for these petitions which were forwarded to Monk at Ottawa. The French-Canadian Conservatives generally supported the nationalist campaign. Some Quebec Liberals showed signs of opposing the bill, and Laurier exerted his influence upon them, as he did on those Ontario Liberals who found the measure was not imperialist enough. The Liberal press in Quebec could only argue that the navy would not cost more than the announced figure, and that a plebiscite would set Ontario and Quebec at each other's throats.[68]

When the Navy Bill came up for second reading on February 3, 1910, Laurier defended it in one of his most notable speeches. The measure realized a policy announced to the country in 1902 and reaffirmed in 1907 and 1909. He called it the last link in the long chain since Baldwin and Lafontaine started Canada on the path to nationhood, with its rights and its obligations. He cited Kipling's definition of Canada's position:

Daughter am I in my mother's house,
But Mistress in my own.

The Conservatives were divided in their councils; they had offered no policy of their own, and many of them approved the government's proposal. Of course it had been severely criticized by those ultra imperialists 'who carry abroad upon their foreheads imperial phylacteries, who boldly walk into the temple and there loudly thank the Lord that they are not like other British subjects, that they give tithe of everything they possess, and that in them alone is to be found the true incense of loyalty.'[69] Aside from Monk, who was utterly opposed to any measure of the sort, there were those Conservatives who criticized the government for not going far enough, who wanted an imperial navy supported by colonial contributions, or who wanted the Canadian Navy automatically to pass under imperial control in case of war, or who wanted an emergency contribution in addition to the proposed navy.

To these imperialist solutions Laurier opposed his own, saying that he was 'Canadian first, last, and always,' but that he was a 'British subject by birth, being convinced by tradition and conviction that under favor of British institutions my native land has obtained a measure of security and liberty which it could not have enjoyed under any other regime.'[70] The imperialists thought centralization essential to the maintenance of the empire; he believed that autonomy was. He traced the development of Canadian autonomy from Durham's time, and denounced the contention that it should be abandoned in naval matters. This question had been settled at the last colonial conference, and Australia had adopted Canada's plan of building her own navy. Lord Milner himself, the prophet of imperialism, had supported it in speeches at Vancouver and Toronto in October 1909.

Laurier then discussed the crucial point. He had declared that the 'navy will not go to war unless the parliament of Canada chooses to send it there.' This declaration had been attacked in Quebec, where it was said that Canada ought not to take part in England's wars under any circumstance, and in Ontario where it was said that Canada ought to participate in England's wars under all circumstances. He maintained that it was the function of parliament, which created the navy, to decide when and where it should go to battle. He had declared that 'if England is at war, we are at war,' and had been bitterly criticized in Quebec for thus proclaiming a principle of international law. It did not follow that Canada would always be attacked, nor that Canada should always take part in all the wars of England. That was for parliament to decide, according to the circumstances. England could afford to devote its resources to armament, but Canada had above all to devote herself to the development of the country. He warned the imperialists against compelling the colonies to contribute to England's armaments. Such a course had caused the revolt of the American colonies, and he cited Benjamin Franklin's answer at the bar of the House of Commons, when asked whether the colonies would contribute to the aid of England: 'As long as they are well treated, they will always be ready to defend her to the extent of their feeble means.' Today there was no danger of taxation without representation, but there was the same relationship between the autonomous colonies and Britain.

Laurier defended the provision for immediate mobilization of the fleet without parliament's previous consent on the grounds of the possible necessity of immediate action. Against the dreadnought agitation, he advanced Lord Charles Beresford's opinion that the colonies would do best to provide for the defence of their coasts and their merchant shipping by the construction of cruisers. He belittled the talk of emergency and the possibility of war; but if war should come suddenly, Canada could always aid Britain with funds, as Britain so often had aided her European allies in the past.

The proposal for a Canadian Navy had been before the country since 1902. Since then the population had grown half again as large and the national income had nearly doubled. Canada could afford a navy and needed one, just as Montreal needed a police force. In Quebec it was argued that Canada should not risk a single man or dollar to maintain British supremacy of the seas. But in this measure there was no compulsion to risk one's life for one's King; those who objected could sit at home and 'enjoy the security and comfort procured for them by the self-sacrifice of more generous men.'[71] Canada was a constitutional country and the will of the majority must rule; if parliament decided to mobilize the Navy, the minority must accept the decision. He evoked the military tradition of the French Canadians, and concluded that liberty was worth fighting and dying for. If Britain lost her supremacy, Canada and Quebec would lose their prosperity, so dependent upon British trade. Then he concluded with the argument that Canada could not stand still, and he urged it to go forward in the tradition of union, friendship, and brotherhood established by Lafontaine and Baldwin.

R. L. Borden, influenced by a revolt within his own party against his leadership, criticized Laurier's proposals for not following the recommendations of the Admiralty and for permitting the government to withhold cooperation with England in time of war. The heavy outlay would give no immediate or effective aid to the empire and no satisfactory results in Canada. No permanent policy should be adopted without an appeal to the people, and meanwhile Canada should make an emergency gift sufficient to enable the Admiralty to purchase or construct two dreadnoughts.[72] Monk, clearly inspired by Bourassa's arguments, denounced the bill as a surrender of autonomy, a capitulation to Chamberlainism, an involvement of Canada in the consequences of a policy in which she had little interest and over which she had no control. Parliament had no right to pass such measure, which modified Canada's autonomy, her international relations, her economic security, and perhaps the sacrifice of Canadian lives, without consulting the people. He then proposed an amendment to Borden's resolution, calling for an immediate plebiscite. Lemieux defended Laurier's middle-of-the-road policy, and urged his compatriots of Quebec to abstain from isolationism and to defend the rights granted them by the Quebec Act. The Liberals stood firm behind Laurier's proposal; the Conservatives attacked it on either English loyalist grounds or French-Canadian nationalist ones. Monk's amendment won the support of only 18 votes; Borden's of 74 against the government's 129.

The press sought to increase the division between French and English Canadians on the issue, or to minimize it, according to party affiliation. In *Le Devoir* Bourassa accused Laurier of sacrificing Canada to England; the *Toronto Mail and Empire* accused him of seeking to separate Canada from England. Bourassa hinted at a secret imperialist agreement between Laurier and Borden. *Le Canada* and *La Patrie* opposed a plebiscite as tending to align Quebec against the other eight provinces; *La Presse* straddled the question by organizing a poll, weighted in favor of Laurier, among its readers as to whether they favored Borden's, Monk's, or Laurier's policy. *Le Devoir* continued its petition campaign with clergy and brothers seeking signatures.[73] In a by-election at Drummond, contested by the provincial minister of lands and the nationalist Napoléon Garceau, the Liberal candidate was elected on March 5 by a sharply reduced majority after a campaign marked by much more discussion of the naval question than provincial matters.[74] Anglophobia was aroused in Quebec, while the *Toronto Mail* urged its readers to defend the Union Jack against Laurier and Quebec.[75]

The provincial session opened on March 15, and Bourassa was forced to leave Ottawa, where he had been following the navy debate from the press gallery, for Quebec. Once more he joined Lavergne and Prévost in attacks on the Gouin administration. Prévost introduced the navy question by condemning Taschereau for his loyalist speech at a *bonne entente* dinner in Toronto in December, which gave 'the false impression that the French Canadians were dying with envy to quit the shores of the St. Lawrence to offer their breasts to the enemies of England, to the spears of the Chinese or to the assegais of the Hottentots.' Prévost accused the provincial administration of depopulating Quebec by forcing some of its people into exile in the States or in the West, and of making the rest cannon-fodder.[76] The Orangemen of Ontario, already on the warpath against Quebec to the cry of 'One school, one language, one flag,' were aroused still further by such utterances, and by extracts from Bourassa's and Monk's speeches.

Their attacks increased the division between French and English Conservatives, though Borden defended the loyalty of the French Canadians, and said they merely differed from the English Canadians in their estimate of the situation.[77] Nonetheless Quebec Conservatives revolted against his leadership, while his Ontario followers urged the expulsion of Monk from the party. Borden's concession to the imperialists was sharply criticized in *Le Devoir*, and the Quebec Conservatives affirmed their loyalty to Monk. When they warned Borden that they would not attend the national convention scheduled for June, he cancelled the gathering. In the face of this divided opposition, the Navy Bill was passed on its third reading, April 20, by a vote of 111 to 70. Despite the opposition of the Conservative Landry and the Liberal Choquette, the bill passed through the Senate without much breaking of party lines.

7

The anti-imperialist agitation did not die down in Quebec, however, with the passage of the Navy Act. The Conservatives held a protest meeting on April 24 at Coteau Landing, and published a manifesto in *L'Evénement* threatening a rupture of the coalition with the Ontario Tories which Morin and MacNab had made in 1854. Their program was close to the nationalist one, calling for protection of minority rights, refusal of participation in wars without consultation of the people, the end of 'undesirable' immigration, and respect of provincial autonomy.[78] On May 11 there was a manifestation in honor of Monk at the Monument National, organized by a young lawyer, Paul-Emile Lamarche. Monk maintained his constitutional position:

> I imagine that there are still some Anglo-Saxons in this country, and that they will not tolerate being taxed indefinitely without having a word to say in the making and control of wars to which their taxes are devoted. I have not sought to isolate the province of Quebec, to align it against the other provinces of Confederation . . . but I claim for every group of British subjects, whatever its origin and its importance, the right to say freely, on such a question as this, what it believes to be just and true.[79]

Senator Landry promised Monk the support of all Quebec Conservatives. Bourassa, urging the necessity of forgetting party lines, won the lion's share of applause.

The fight for the rights of the French language was also waged vigorously. Aided by a campaign of the A.C.J.C., Lavergne's proposal of compulsory bilingualism in the public services of Quebec was adopted first by the municipal council of Montreal and then by the provincial legislature. Under the influence of Senator Dandurand, Thomas Shaughnessy, head of the Canadian Pacific, persuaded the Grand Trunk, the Montreal Light, Heat, and Power, the Bell Telephone, and other great English-owned companies to accept the measure rather than to fight it, as they at first proposed to do.

The growing national consciousness of the French Canadians was also reflected by the establishment of the cult of Dollard, the hero of a battle against the Iroquois at the Long Sault 250 years before. The editor of the *Montreal Herald*, John C. Walsh, seems to have been the first to call attention to the anniversary. The artist J.-B. Legacé proposed a ceremony at the Place d'Armes, and a

Evening on the North Shore

il painting (c. 1920) by Clarence Gagnon (1881–1942). This Paris-trained Montreal
ainter had a passion for the simple life and magnificent scenery of the Charlevoix country
between the St. Lawrence and the Saguenay. (Quebec Provincial Museum.)

Sugar-Making

Monotype (c. 1933) from water color by Clarence Gagnon. One of the illustrations to the magnificent Paris edition of Louis Hémon's epic of frontier life, *Maria Chapdelaine*. (I.O.A.P.Q.)

Family Prayers

Monotype (c. 1933) from water color by Clarence Gagnon. Another illustration from *Maria Chapdelaine* which shows the deep piety of the French Canadian and the strong family tradition. (I.O.A.P.Q.)

ommittee consisting of Legacé, the sculptor Philippe Hébert, the Abbé Philippe Perrier, and Emile Vaillancourt, was set up to organize celebration on May 29. The A.C.J.C. anticipated the gathering by congress at the Gésu on May 22, in which tribute was paid to Dollard. The gathering on the 29th was attended by the patriotic ocieties and a detachment of the 65th Militia Battalion. Bourassa vas the chief speaker; he argued that the support given to the celeration by English Canadians foreshadowed better understanding ind that Dollard could become a national hero for Canadians of both aces. Archbishop Bruchési proposed the erection of a monument to he hero, and the A.C.J.C. at once started a fund, to which Lord Grey subscribed $100.[80]

Stimulated by their success, some young members of the A.C.J.C. obtained and published a list of members of the Lodge of Freemasons n Montreal. This exploit was hailed as happily in *Le Devoir*, more ultramontane in tone since Asselin and Fournier had broken with Bourassa and left the staff, as in *L'Action Sociale*. The politico-religious spect of nationalism was increased by the tightening alliance between the A.C.J.C. and the nationalists. The provincial session closed in June, after Lavergne and all members of the Conservative opposition had supported Prévost's motion of censure against Taschereau for his loyalist statement at Toronto.

In this atmosphere the nationalists and Conservatives launched a oint campaign for the repeal of the Navy Act. The Liberals took he agitation so seriously that they published Lemieux's speeches in avor of the act in a pamphlet, to act as a counterweight to Bourassa's *Le Projet de Loi Navale*. The British government extended Lord Grey's erm of office for a year, thus enabling him to continue his imperialst influence. But anti-imperialism in Quebec continued to grow. Monk, Lavergne, and Blondin held a meeting at Beauport on July 0, where Lavergne supplied the first evidence that this was to be a campaign against Laurier as well as one against the Navy Act. On July 17 Bourassa joined in the campaign at a meeting held at Saint-Eustache, before the church which still bore the scars of English bullets fired in 1837. On the previous day *Le Devoir* and *Le Nationaliste* had published resolutions drafted by Bourassa and to be proposed by him at Saint-Eustache. They declared the French Canadians' oyalty and willingness to defend Canada; their opposition to foreign vars without a voice equal to the mother country's in imperial affairs; the rights of the majority to determine Canada's course after deliberation by the people; and censure of Taschereau's declaration, of the federal administration and its supporters, and of Borden and his followers. Monk's course alone was approved.[81]

At Saint-Eustache Monk recounted the rise of imperialism and the decline of opposition to it by the Laurier administration, which now surrendered responsibility to England. Though the Navy Bill ha become law, the people could still have the last word by makin known their opposition to it. Bourassa sketched political histor since 1896, when he had held Laurier to be the 'champion of th tradition of autonomy.' Then in 1899 Laurier had begun to yiel to imperialism by sending a Canadian contingent to Africa. Toda Laurier travelled through the West, 'acclaimed by people wh have done nothing to make our country what it is, while we, descendants of those who thrust back the forest, hunted wild beasts, loyall defended New France, then fought for the English flag against th revolting American colonies, have not the right to say to Laurie and Borden, who have cancelled with a pen stroke all our dearl acquired liberties: "You are only cowards and traitors who do no deserve well of your country."' Bourassa confessed that once he ha loved Laurier, served him to the best of his strength, and believed i him. Then he launched into a denunciation of Laurier for comin to terms with Lord Grey, for betraying his followers, for leading th French Canadians into imperialism, for denying the Catholics c half the country the right to have their children taught the religio and the language of their fathers. 'I say that when a man, whateve his personal qualities, so violates the confidence and the love that people have placed in him by betraying his own kind at one stroke such a man is more dangerous to his religion, to his country, an even to the British Crown than the worst of Orangemen.'[82] Bourass then read the resolutions, to which only three of the crowd of som 8,000 objected. He concluded with a fervent word of thanks: 'No for us, not for M. Monk, not for your humble servant; I thank yo in behalf of your people, your country, your fathers, and above al your sons.'

When the storm of applause died down, Prévost proposed Monk who put his convictions before his ambition, as federal leader in plac of Laurier, the Liberal who had become an imperialist and militarist. Three Conservative speakers and a former Liberal the closed the meeting by promising Monk and Bourassa their support Héroux hailed the Saint-Eustache meeting in *Le Devoir* as th inauguration of a new era. It was so indeed, since Laurier had bee attacked in public without protest or indignation.

The campaign thus launched continued without notable opposition. Laurier spent the whole summer touring the West. Lemieu was abroad; Brodeur was sick; and the provincial Liberals wer reluctant to risk their popularity on a federal issue. The defence o Laurier and the Navy Act was left to the editors of *Le Canada* an *Le Soleil*, whom Bourassa contemptuously dismissed as 'Laurier' domestics.' Meanwhile Bourassa strengthened his hold on th clergy, already sympathetic to him thanks to his opposition t ecular schools and to the proposed nomination of an English-peaking bishop to the see of Ottawa. He took this stand: 'To bind he cause of the Church to that of the French race and tongue in Canada would be an error. To make the Church an instrument of Anglo-Saxon assimilation would be equally absurd and odious.'[83] Abbé Emile Chartier of Saint-Hyacinthe, one of the founders of the A.C.J.C., defended nationalism as being closer in its principles, in he eyes of youth, than any other political doctrine to the ideal and uperior political principles which must be taught to students. With uch views questioned only by faithful Liberals, with *Le Devoir* and *L'Action Sociale* the only newspapers permitted in the classical colleges, the rising generation was thoroughly indoctrinated with nationalist beliefs.

The campaign went on, with meetings at Saint-Henri and Saint-Hyacinthe, at which Bourassa moved the resolutions of Saint-Eustache, and vainly urged opponents of them to express their opposition in the face of almost unanimous support. On August 21 the nationalists held eight simultaneous meetings, while Bourassa journeyed to Halifax to expound before the Canadian Club a program which he wished to be national and not merely provincial. As usual he won the respect of an English-speaking audience by his knowledge of constitutional law, his courage, and his oratorical ability. But he was a little too ready to assume that applause meant agreement. On August 28 eight more meetings were held in Quebec. There was practically no opposition. Again on September 4, at Napierville, Bourassa drew a crowd of 5,000, not one of whom favored the Navy Act. When Laurier returned from the West to attend the Eucharistic Congress at Montreal, the revolt in Quebec against him was well advanced.

8

The Twentieth Eucharistic Congress, the first ever held in North America, assembled in Montreal on September 6, 1910. Present were the Cardinal Legate Vincenze Vanutelli, Archbishop Bourne of Westminster, Archbishop Ireland of St. Paul, all the Canadian hierarchy, and many bishops from Germany, France, Belgium, Holland, Ireland, and Spain, as well as a horde of pilgrims who temporarily doubled the population of the city, which had been specially decorated for the occasion. The provincial government gave a dinner to the legate on September 7, at which Sir Lomer Gouin expressed the eternal attachment of the French Canadians to the Holy See. The Congress divided into two sections, the French one meeting at Notre-Dame Church and the English one at St. Patrick's. Archbishop Bruchési endeavoured to avoid too much emphasis on the division, opposing the plan of the rector of St. Patrick's for a dinner for the English-speaking bishops by suggesting a banquet for all the bishops, at which he and the legate would preside.

Laurier, won over by his friend Bishop Mathieu to participation in the congress despite the risk of arousing Anglo-Protestant feeling made a careful speech on September 9 on religious tolerance, freedom of worship, and legal guarantees, to which no exception could be taken. Remembering political anti-clericalism at home, the French visitors wistfully remarked that Canada was fortunate in having such leaders as Laurier and Gouin. On the afternoon of September 10 the A.C.J.C. assembled 25,000 young people at the Arena, where they were addressed by the legate and Archbishop Langevin, who spoke of his past struggles and future hopes for Catholic and French education in the West. Bourassa congratulated the audience on uniting their patriotism and their faith. After three delegates from France had spoken, Archbishop Langevin stole a march on Archbishop Bruchési by obtaining the legate's blessing for the Carillon–Sacré-Coeur flag, which the Montrealer disapproved as a separatist emblem.

But the great event of the congress was the meeting that same evening at Notre-Dame, from which the Blessed Sacrament was removed so that the church became merely an immense auditorium for the occasion. Archbishop Bourne startled the assemblage by arguing that since Canada was growing and peopling itself with people of different origins but who all spoke English, the Church must not give the impression that Catholicism was linked with the French language, if it were to hold or win the New Canadians. The Church must use the growing influence of the English language in Canada English ought to be the vehicle of the Faith. In the future Catholicism must be linked to the English language. At the conclusion of this address, which clearly implied abandonment of the struggle for the French language outside Quebec, Archbishop Langevin privately urged Bourassa to reply. While Thomas Chapais and Judge Sullivan of New York spoke, Bourassa had an opportunity to consider the language question, which he had barely touched upon in his prepared speech.

When his turn came Bourassa glanced at his text and put it in his pocket, and then improvised an eloquent reply to the English archbishop's address. He promised that in the future as in the past Canadian priests would always supply the consolations of religion to the exiled sons of England and Ireland in the language of their fathers

> But at the same time permit me to claim the same right for my compatriots, for those who speak my language, not only in this province but wherever French groups live in the shadow of the British flag, of the

glorious Stars and Stripes, and above all of the maternal wing of the Catholic Church—the Church of Christ who died for all men and imposed on no one the obligation to deny his race in order to remain faithful to Him.

I do not wish, through a narrow nationalism, to say—that would be the contrary of my thought, and I do not say it, my compatriots—that the Catholic Church ought to be French in Canada. No, but say with me that among three million Catholics, descendants of the first apostles of Christianity in America, the best safeguard of the Faith is the conservation of the idiom in which during three hundred years they have adored Christ.

Yes, when Christ was attacked by the Iroquois, when Christ was denied by the English, when Christ was fought by all the world, we confessed Him, and confessed Him in our language.

The fate of three million Catholics cannot be indifferent, I am certain, to the heart of Pius X, or to the eminent Cardinal who represents him here.

But there is still more to say: Providence has wished that the principal group of this French and Catholic colonization should constitute in America a separate corner of the earth, where the social, religious, and political situation most closely approximates that which the Church teaches us to be the ideal state of society. We do not have union of Church and State in Canada; let us not oppose words. But we have in the Province of Quebec—I might say almost exclusively in the Province of Quebec—peace, good understanding between the civil and religious authorities. From this peace have derived laws which permit us to give the Catholic Church a social and civil organization which she finds in no other province of Canada, and in no other part of the British Empire.

Thanks to these laws, our dioceses are organized, our parishes founded . . . And the Church of Quebec, at peace in legal and material matters, has been able to give the fullness of its efforts to the apostolate; and this effort has been felt far beyond the diocese of St. Paul.

From this Province of Quebec, from this minute French colony, whose language, it is said, is doomed to disappear, have come three-quarters of the clergy of North America, who came to draw from the Seminary of Quebec or Saint-Sulpice the knowledge and virtue which distinguished the clergy of the great American Republic and the English-speaking clergy as well as the French-speaking clergy of Canada.

Your Eminence, you have visited our religious communities, you have gone to seek in the convents, hospitals, and colleges of Montreal the proof of the faith and works of the French-Canadian people. You would have to stay two years in America, to cross five thousand kilometers of country, from Cape Breton to British Columbia, and to visit half the American Republic, to trace the foundations of all sorts—colleges, convents, hospitals, asylums—which are the daughters of these mother institutions that you have visited here . . . Must one conclude that the Roman Catholics have been more zealous, more apostolic than the others? No, but Providence has wished that they should be the apostles of North America.

Let one beware, let one be carefully aware, of extinguishing this fire, with its intense light which has illuminated a whole continent for three centuries . . .

But, it is said, you are only a handful; you are fatally destined to disappear; why persevere in the struggle? We are only a handful, it is true; but in the school of Christ I did not learn to estimate right and moral forces by number and wealth. We are only a handful; but we count for what we are; and we have the right to live . . .

For nineteen centuries there has not been a Hebrew Pope, a Roman Pope, an Italian Pope, a French Pope, but the Pope, father of all the great Catholic family.

Let us go higher, let us go to Calvary; and there on that little hill in Judea, which was not very high in the world, let us learn the lesson of tolerance and of true Christian charity.[84]

There was a hush when Bourassa concluded; then the legate came and shook his hand, a gesture which he had not made in the case of the other speakers. Tumult broke loose. Hats and handkerchiefs were waved, bishops applauded with their feet instead of their hands; within and without the church people embraced one another. The Place d'Armes was filled with dancing, jubilant figures. Bourassa had made himself the hero of the French-Canadian people. The next day, as the procession of 100 prelates, 10,000 priests and religious, and 50,000 lay folk paraded through the streets to close the congress with Benediction at the foot of Mount Royal, the passage of Bourassa provoked demonstrations which dwarfed those aroused by Laurier. Quebec had found a new leader, to whom the Franco-Ontarians now turned for aid in their struggle for a French bishop of Ottawa and for bilingualism in their schools.

9

After the truce of the Eucharistic Congress, the fight against the Navy Act went on with renewed vigor. Bourassa's prestige was much enhanced by his defence of the French language at Notre-Dame, which was published in *Le Devoir* on September 26 as 'Religion, Langue, Nationalité.' At Farnham on September 17, to a largely Liberal audience, Bourassa again denounced Laurier's betrayal of Liberal principles and appealed for support in his campaign in their favor. He conjured up the prospect of future conscription as a result of Laurier's action, and won almost unanimous approval for the Saint-Eustache resolutions. A week later 8,000 people gathered at Grand'Mère to hear Bourassa, who once more warned of the danger of conscription. Meanwhile in *Le Devoir* he supported the Franco-Ontarians.

To an interviewer from the *New York Herald* at this time Bourassa defined nationalism as 'a doctrine and not a political party.' It was based on the familiar American constitutional principle of no taxation without representation. It was not anti-British, since Canada could best serve the empire by devoting herself to her own development. It was not a doctrine for French Canadians alone, but for all Canadians, since it tended to develop national spirit while assuring the French Canadians their right to exercise social and political influence in the country.[85] The *Manitoba Free Press* asked what flag Bourassa would substitute for the British flag. Bourassa replied in *Le Devoir*: 'As a Canadian and a British subject, I recognize only one flag, on which tradition and the sentiment of our era—that since 1867—placed the arms of the Canadian Confederation. This flag is at once the emblem of our allegiance and the mark of our relative autonomy.'[86] He said that he respected, without sharing, the wish of many of his compatriots for a special French-Canadian flag.

On October 10 Laurier himself tried to check the growing agitation in Quebec at a mass meeting at the Monument National under the chairmanship of Sir Lomer Gouin. Gouin hailed Laurier as one of the greatest Canadians; and young Athanase David, son of Laurier's old friend, L.-O. David, assured the prime minister that the youth of Quebec would do its duty under his banner when the time came, though it had been temporarily misled by the campaign against the Navy Act. Then Laurier began his speech, which was a vigorous attack upon the nationalists and a defence of his administration. He began by stressing the disunion of the Conservative party, which in the approaching elections would have as many programs as there were provinces. In British Columbia the government was attacked on the question of Asiatic immigration; in the Prairie Provinces on the tariff question, with a demand for a higher tariff. Also in Ontario the naval policy was attacked on the grounds that it led to the separation of Canada from Britain; while in Quebec it was attacked on the grounds that it would lead to the loss of autonomy and make Canada the slave of Britain.

In Quebec the disintegration of the Conservative party had begun long ago and its saner heads had joined the Liberals, driven out of their party by the violence of the intemperate ones who had seized control:

> This violent section—you know it—comprises the Pharisees of Canadian Catholicism; those who have constituted themselves ostentatiously the defenders of religion, which no one attacked; those who handled the holy water sprinkler like a club; those who have arrogated to themselves a monopoly of orthodoxy; those who excommunicate right and left all whose stature is a little greater than theirs; those who seem to have for motive and instinct only hatred and envy; those who insulted Cardinal Taschereau when he was alive and who since his death have outraged

his memory; those who made life bitter to Chapleau, the most brilliant figure whom the Conservative party has produced; those, finally, whom the people with their picturesque language designated and bedizened under the name of 'Castors.'[87]

To this group had rallied certain young Liberals, who, 'having nothing Liberal in their nature, after some ventures, found their true mentality among the Castors.' Such was the opposition today, which did not even respect the name of nationalist which it had given itself. At Montmagny, Monk and Lavergne had supported a Conservative candidate; at Farnham, Monk had appeared with Bourassa, who declared himself 'the only Liberal left today in the country.' 'They call themselves nationalists, Conservatives, Liberals, according to the character of the audience they address, with the intention of doing the most harm possible to the government and of achieving their goal of destroying the government.'[88]

After thus labeling his opponents *Castors*, Laurier sought to disprove their charges. Monk and Bourassa argued that he had reversed his position since 1902, but the fact was the Navy Act was in full conformity with the policy then announced, which Monk and Bourassa now said they had then approved. The law provided for the creation of a naval service which would remain completely under the control of the Canadian government. It did not provide for a contribution to the British Navy, nor for taking control away from the government, parliament, and people of Canada. In 1907 Laurier had maintained his position that Canada should develop its land and sea defences, but should conserve its autonomy in these matters as in all others. Now he was accused in Quebec of being a traitor to his country, and in Ontario of being a traitor to the empire. But such charges had come his way ever since 1896 for urging moderation upon extremists, who always replied with accusations of treason. He repeated the arguments used in the House as to the necessity of a navy, and refuted Bourassa's argument that Canada was not a nation: 'It is true that we are politically dependent upon England, but we are legislatively independent . . . we have become a nation without breaking the colonial tie.'[89]

He called Bourassa's charge of a Grey-Laurier conspiracy as baseless as that of a Laurier-Borden conspiracy, which Bourassa had abandoned when Borden turned against the Navy Act. Laurier was accused of being influenced by ambition for new honors, but neither the British nor the Canadian government could offer him any reward worth that which he had already received from the Canadian people; when he quit the prime-ministership, either at the will of the people or by his own desire, the only position worthy of his pride would be that of a simple citizen of Canada. He would accept nothing else, no matter what the honor might be. He compared the Navy Act with the Militia Act, which had been accepted without question; and pointed out that naval service was to be purely voluntary. He rebuked Bourassa for misrepresenting this act. He dismissed the argument that the Canadian Navy would be constantly involved in Britain's wars by pointing out that the British Navy had fought no battles since Trafalgar, aside from Navarino, some engagements in the China seas, and the bombardment of Alexandria. And only the Canadian government, parliament, and people could put the Navy at the service of the King. He repeated that Canada was at war when Britain was at war, but that merely meant that 'we shall take part only when we judge it fitting to do so.'[90] Finally, the annual cost of the Navy would amount to only 3 per cent of the annual national revenue.

Once more Laurier promised that no one would be obliged to serve in the Navy who did not desire to do so. The nationalists had no right to forbid those who did wish to serve from doing so, as he had had no right to forbid those who wished to do so from serving in the South African War. His policy then had been approved by Monk. He did not fear the prospect of war; Canada had not had one for nearly a hundred years, and with the rise of democracy war was becoming less frequent, since the poor and humble suffered most from it. He hoped that as Germany became more democratic, it might form an *entente cordiale* with Britain, like that between Britain and France. Canada was not obliged to take part in any war, but if there should be a war in which the empire's naval supremacy was at stake, he himself believed that Canada should aid Britain with all its strength.

Laurier rejected the nationalist policy of forming a party composed exclusively of French Canadians as 'the contradiction of all our traditions. Our duty is to take part in the battles of our country, to defend the rights not only of our province, but also the rights of the other provinces.'[91] In the past, when fighting for their rights, the French Canadians had not rested their case solely on the question of race; they had based it on the principles of truth and justice which appealed to all men's conscience, and thus they received the support without which they could not have succeeded. Papineau had been aided by Neilson and Wolfred Nelson; Lafontaine by Baldwin; Lafontaine and Baldwin by Samuel Blake in the matter of the Rebellion Losses Bill. Lafontaine, the greatest statesman that French Canada had produced, had preached the union of the Reformers of the two provinces in a spirit of peace, union, friendship, and fraternity. Laurier himself had been chosen the leader of a party in which his people were a minority, and when he had hesitated to accept the post, had been told that the Liberal party knew no distinction of race or religion. He had more sympathy for his ow people, but the rights of other races were as sacred to him as th rights of his own.

He was accused of being a traitor to his race because he had per mitted immigration in the West. In that policy Canada had followe the example of the United States in opening their territory to th whole world. For a hundred years the American star had shone i the firmament; he hoped that in the twentieth century the sta towards which all regards would be turned would be the star o Canada. The West had been peopled; he would have liked to see current of emigration from Quebec toward the West, but it had gon to the States instead. But this leakage had been checked by th development of industry in Montreal, thanks to the new market o the West. It was to Montreal and not the States that the surplu agricultural population of Quebec now went, so that Montreal ha doubled in size in ten years. He defended the policy of reciprocit with the States, which would open up a rich market for Canadia goods and provide an inexhaustible source of prosperity. He summe up the results of his fourteen years in power as 'more harmony, mor peace, more prosperity, more well-being, than in any previous epoc of our history.'[92] Whatever the result of the elections, he urged hi auditors to be faithful to the principles of progress, liberty, tolerance and justice which had insured this state of the nation.

This two-hour speech won Laurier an ovation from his audience c loyal Liberals, but cries of '*Vive Bourassa!*' disturbed the overflov meetings held outside the Monument National. The Liberal pres said that the nationalists considered only Canada's interests, th imperialists only the empire's interests; but since Canadians wer British subjects, the two interests should be reconciled as Laurie argued. Liberals of Quebec and Tories of Toronto joined to de nounce Bourassa as an enemy of England and the English. Th *Toronto World* wrote: 'M. Bourassa considers that his mission consist in kicking the English out of Quebec and reconquering Ontario.'[9 *L'Action Sociale* saw a vast plot to confine the French Canadians t Quebec, while Bishop Fallon of London attacked the Quebec nation alist organs for supporting the French-Canadian movement i Ontario. Bourassa took an opportunity to clear himself of the charg of disloyalty by urging the French Canadians to support the pla to erect a statue to Edward VII in Montreal.

A test of power between the followers of Bourassa and those c Laurier was soon provided by a by-election in Drummond-Artha baska, occasioned by the appointment to the Senate of Loui Lavergne, a brother of Laurier's former law partner. His nephev Armand reported to Laurier that he had been asked to be a candi date in the constituency, and promised a fair contest.[94] Laurie imself presided at the Liberal convention which chose the official andidate, J.-E. Perrault, son of an old friend of Laurier, brother of ie A.C.J.C. leader, and in his early days a nationalist, but now the illar of the Arthabaska bar. Arthabaska was Laurier's own ountry, where he maintained a summer home and had many close iends. The constituency was too Liberal for a Conservative to and a chance. The nationalists thought of nominating Armand avergne, who declined in the interests of his profession, and apoléon Garceau, who had the handicap of being at odds with the ergy. In the end they settled upon a young farmer, Arthur Gilbert, hose election would represent a successful protest by the people self. The Conservatives supplied organization and funds, the ationalists orators: Bourassa, Lavergne, Tancrède Marsil, Blondin, nd all the rank and file.

The Arthabaska campaign really began in Montreal, where on)ctober 20 Bourassa and Monk replied to Laurier. The students ame to the meeting at the Ontario Rink in a procession preceded y a band, carrying a great portrait of Bourassa framed by the gend: 'The country before party.' Monk, in analyzing Laurier's eech, gave a stiff warning to Lord Grey: the governor-general ould observe the fundamental constitutional rule that the King or is representative must refrain from political discussions. Bourassa evoted himself to refuting Laurier and sought to show that Laurier ad indeed given ground to the imperialists since 1907. Lavergne ttacked Lemieux and 'Laurier's valets' of *Le Canada*. Albert évigny concluded the evening with a speech which delighted the ounger element of the audience. After the meeting the crowd araded to the Théâtre National, where Lavergne spoke, and then the University, where speeches by Lavergne, Sévigny, and others oncluded an evening which had evoked far more enthusiasm than aurier's meeting.[95]

Throngs of speakers descended upon the peaceful and lovely ountryside of Arthabaska, and *assemblées contradictoires* abounded.)ne of the most notable was at Drummondville on October 27, hen Monk, Bourassa, and Lavergne supported Gilbert, while errault was backed by Brodeur and three Liberal members of arliament. Brodeur and Henri Béland proved a team which could and up to Bourassa and Lavergne. The Liberals maintained aurier's contention that Canada, now become a nation, needed a avy. The nationalists denounced the government's adoption of a olicy hitherto rejected by both parties; ridiculed the notion of anada's having duties to England; and predicted that the Navy ct would lead to involvement in war, which in turn would lead to onscription. Borden's policy of financial contribution was also enounced. The Liberal candidate was reminded that he had approved the nationalist declaration of principles at Drummondvil in 1902. Tancrède Marsil evoked the memory of English outrag at Saint-Eustache in 1837; Pierre Blondin said of the English fla 'Our fathers had to pierce it with bullet holes to breathe the air liberty.'[96] Men in uniform visited the farms and pretended to tak a census of manpower, 'to have the lists ready when the Lauri Naval Act goes into force.'[97] The electors were told that 'To vo for Perrault is to vote for war; to vote for Gilbert is to vote f peace.'[98] The Liberal organizers relied too much on the const tuency's record as a Liberal stronghold. But even Bourassa himse anticipated the election of Perrault and prepared an article for *I Devoir* of November 3 explaining that the Liberal victory was due t 'drunkenness, debauchery, tumult . . . . appeal to the lowe passions . . . under the serene eye and with the tacit and complace connivance of the Right Honorable Sir Wilfrid Laurier, P.C G.C.M.G., K.C., D.C.L., LL.D., etc.'[99]

In fact Gilbert was elected by a majority of 200; the constituenc which had seen Laurier's first defeat in 1878 now gave warning the downfall of his administration. The verdict was taken as victory for Bourassa, who received more congratulations than th successful candidate, and as a defeat for Laurier. The prim minister's prestige suffered not only in Quebec but all over th country, because of the wide attention given to the election by th English-Canadian press. Ontario papers predicted an immedia revolt of the French Canadians against England, not realizin that the verdict represented merely a revolt against Laurier an imperialism.

The nationalist victory was celebrated at a meeting at the Ontari Rink in Montreal on November 9. The gathering was so large th the auditorium, the largest in the city, could not contain the thron and the meeting was adjourned outdoors. The Conservatives ha organized the affair, and aside from Monk and Bourassa all th announced speakers were *Bleus*. But after hearing Monk, the crow called for the nationalists and the list of speakers was hastily r vised.[100] Bourassa stressed the fact that he was not anti-Britis and that he was not conducting a war of races. He insisted: 'The is no more a conquering race nor a conquered race; there is no mo here a right of the stronger and a right of the weaker; there a only the equal rights of two great races.'[101] Bourassa, greeted warmly as ever Laurier had been in his heyday, challenged th prime minister to contest any great city constituency against hin 'to see whether the Canadian people is the slave of a man or wheth it is in the service of a principle.'[102] The crowd paraded to the S James Market, where Bourassa spoke again, and was reinforced l Jean Prévost, Tancrède Marsil, and other nationalists.

The attacks against Laurier now knew no limits; youth had the bit in its teeth and mocked its distinguished elders. Laurier felt obliged to write an article for *La Presse,* explaining once more that the Navy Act provided that parliament should control the fleet, and that conscription was not involved.[103] Lavergne carried the war into Ontario, where he had been invited by the students of the University of Toronto to expound nationalism on November 18. He closed his very restrained exposition with this appeal: 'I want to return to Quebec with a message of peace between the two provinces. I see the two great races working together in the future for the good of the country.' The following day he appeared in uniform as a captain of the Régiment de Montmagny and proclaimed: 'If Canada were attacked, the French Canadians would be the first to rise against the enemy, even if the enemy flew the French flag.'[104]

When the federal session opened on November 16, the Drummond-Arthabaska election had repercussions. Borden had censured the Conservative whip for congratulating Gilbert on his victory, but he himself could not refrain from taunting Laurier with his defeat. Laurier replied: 'There are defeats more honorable than victory. This victory was won not by loyal opposition, but by His Majesty's disloyal opposition.'[105] The Conservatives had joined the nationalists in making the people believe that the government was going to impose conscription. Monk proposed an amendment to the speech to the throne, regretting that it had made no mention of the government's intention to consult the people on its naval policy and on the general question of Canadian contribution to imperial armaments. Borden moved a sub-amendment, supporting the idea of a plebiscite, but stressing Canada's loyalty and willingness to fulfil its imperial responsibilities. Both amendments were defeated by large majorities.[106]

The administration undertook a Quebec campaign in support of the Navy Act. Special attention was given to St. Johns, where a provincial by-election was soon to take place. Despite the effort of the provincial Liberals to avoid the federal issue, the supporters of the opposition candidate succeeded in introducing the navy question. But Bourassa had gone abroad to study international politics, visiting London, Paris, and Rome, where he had a private audience with the Pope. The nationalists were left without a leader and without organization, while the Liberals made up for their overconfidence in Drummond-Arthabaska. The government candidate triumphed by a larger majority than before. The English voters, usually Conservative, supported the Liberal candidate, after his backers had represented Bourassa as an agitator who wished to free Quebec from English rule.

But in Paris Bourassa, interviewed by *La Libre Parole*, said tha separatism was no part of his nationalism. If the tie with Britai were broken, it would be only because of the imposition of a imperialist regime, which would produce a quicker and more violen anti-British reaction among the English Canadians than amon the French Canadians. The Canadian students in Paris, who likene Bourassa's ideas to those of Charles Maurras, and the *Ligue Nation aliste* to the *Ligue d'Action Française*, were contradicted by Bourassa who found the French royalists 'narrow and sectarian.'[107] I Rome, where Bourassa had been preceded by Laurier's friend Curé Côté of Arthabaska, Mgr. Merry del Val judged that 'Arch bishop Bourne and Bishop Fallon had lacked judgment and tact but M. Bourassa is a hothead,' and the Pope dismissed Bourassa' attempt to raise the language question with an assurance that justic would be done.[108]

Bourassa's prestige at home was reinforced by his encounters wit leading figures of the London and Roman worlds, and when h returned to Montreal on January 13, 1911, he was greeted b 2,000 people at the station. When he went to Quebec for th provincial session, which had already opened with mocking regret for his absence from Taschereau, he received an equally warn reception. The first anniversary banquet of *Le Devoir* was attende by 500 guests, headed by Monk, Tellier, and Jean Prévost. Wit the nationalist-Conservative alliance in the Province now firml cemented, Bourassa journeyed to Ottawa to consult with Mon on the possibilities of a national alliance in opposition to the govern- ment's proposal of reciprocity with the United States.

10

The reciprocal tariff agreement with the United States intro- duced in parliament on January 26, 1911, by Fielding, had bee worked out after nearly twelve months of negotiations, initiated a the request of President Taft. The protectionist Payne-Aldric Tariff, enacted in 1909, had proved unpopular at home and source of complications abroad. It carried penalties against thos countries which discriminated against the United States. Canada' recent concessions to France, Germany, Italy, Belgium, and th Netherlands called for the application of the penalty clause agains her, unless concessions were made to the United States. Early i 1910 two American representatives were sent to Ottawa to confe with Laurier and Fielding, and in March Taft met Fielding a Albany. Later Fielding and another Canadian minister went t Washington, and a compromise was worked out, whereby Canad made nominal concessions. With growing sentiment in favor c eciprocity in his own party and with the Democrats clamoring for t, Taft opened negotiations in October for a wider agreement, fter announcing his conviction that 'these two countries, touching ach other for more than three thousand miles, have common nterests in trade and require special arrangements in legislation nd administration.'[109] The negotiations were concluded at Vashington in January 1911, virtually providing for a renewal of he Treaty of 1854. Complete free trade had been offered by the mericans, but refused by the Canadians, who also insisted that he agreement should take effect by concurrent legislation, which ither country might modify at any time, rather than by an inflexible reaty. The reduction given to American imports could be extended o British imports. Essentially the agreement provided for the free ntrance into the United States of all Canadian natural products, vhile American manufacturers benefited by a lower Canadian luty.

The agreement realized the goal of both Canadian political parties ince the revocation of reciprocity in 1866. It met the desires of he farmers of Ontario and the West, who through the Grange nd the Grain Growers' Association had been pressing for lower luties on manufactured goods. In December 1910 900 Western armers had invaded parliament to demand reciprocity. They rged a cause already won, for Laurier was sympathetic to the English Liberal tradition of free trade and Fielding had long avored a measure welcome to the Maritime Provinces, whose atural economic capital lay in New England rather than in central Canada. Reciprocity had offered a distraction from the political-eligious question in 1896, and might once again relieve a menacing ituation in Quebec.

At first the proposal met with general approval, with the Western Conservatives and the *Toronto News* and *Ottawa Journal* backing it. Borden's only criticisms were the possible danger to Canadian in-lustries, the indefinite duration of the agreement and the possi-bility of dislocation of the Canadian economy if it were suddenly erminated, and its threat to the Conservative program of recipro-ity within the empire. The Conservative camp was divided by upport of the proposal in the West and opposition to it from pro-ected Eastern industries. Protests were made from the Montreal nd Toronto Boards of Trade, supported by the industrial, financial, nd railway interests which benefited by an east-west flow of trade, ather than by a north-south one. Clifford Sifton, with the aid of Zebulon Lash, Mackenzie and Mann's lawyer, organized a revolt y eighteen Liberals of Toronto, all eminent in the financial world, vho on February 20 publicly repudiated reciprocity. On the 22nd Sir William Van Horne announced that he was 'out to bust the damn thing,'[110] and most Canadian big business followed the lea of the influential former head of the Canadian Pacific.

Meanwhile the Conservatives had decided to fight the proposa On February 10 Monk, true to form, criticized the haste with whic the measure was being adopted and moved a resolution regrettin that the opinion of the people had not been taken on the questior Borden took a firmer stand, criticizing the radical revision of th Canadian trade structure which had been built up since 1866. Fre trade would lead to commercial union, and the Canadian peopl should not abandon their effort to build up a great nation under th British flag, when the battle was more than half won. But it wa Clifford Sifton who, on February 28, made the strongest attack o reciprocity. He urged that the Liberals, who had abandone reciprocity after the failure of the Joint High Commission in 189 had no mandate to reverse the policy of protection which had sinc been in force. He showed how the agreement would injure suc Canadian industries as meat-packing and milling, while the in dustrial development of Canada by American branch factories an pulp mills would be ended. Canada would become dependen upon the United States, and in the end might lose the America market as well as the British one, which would suffer under thi agreement. In the long run the Canadian wheat growers and cattle men would suffer by American control, while New York woul gain the trade which now passed through Montreal. He oppose the proposal on patriotic grounds, and said it spelled 'retrogressior commercial subordination, the destruction of our national ideal and displacement from our proud position as the rising hope of th British Empire.'[111] Borden soon became involved in negotiation with the dissident Liberals headed by Sifton, who urged a stronge attitude both towards the United States and towards Quebec.[11 These negotiations resulted in another revolt within the Conservativ party against Borden's leadership, and the further alienation c Monk's followers.

Somewhat surprisingly, Bourassa generally supported reciprocit in a series of articles which appeared in *Le Devoir* from January 3 to February 7 and were reprinted in pamphlet form in both Frenc and English.[113] He took the basic position of 'Canada first an Canada for the Canadians,' and then approved reciprocity as foste ing agriculture and not harming Canadian industry. He saw n danger of political union in it, since Canada had attained natior hood under reciprocity from 1854 to 1866; and he expressed th belief that a 'measure of reciprocity, both broad and pruden between the Canada and the United States, is natural; it is i conformity with the political traditions and economic needs c Canada.'[114] Internal east-west trade would be little altered, whil the export trade already enjoyed access to the American routes through the bonding privilege and American railways already drained Canada's wealthiest regions. The development of the Georgian Bay Canal, which Monk desired instead of the creation of a navy, might favor the St. Lawrence route. Bourassa shared Monk's doubts as to whether the agreement was the most advantageous one which Canada could make, with reciprocity steadily growing in favor in the States. He questioned Laurier's trustworthiness and revived the memory of the Liberal annexationist movement in the 1880's and 1890's; but since this agreement was open to termination at any time, he saw no great danger in it. There was no sacrifice of true British interests, but it unquestionably sacrificed imperialist ones by blocking commercial union of the empire. On this ground Borden objected to it, ignoring the fact that Canada had a more natural market in the States than in the empire. The anomaly of the nationalist-Conservative alliance was made evident by the fact that Bourassa favored reciprocity on anti-imperialist grounds, while Borden opposed it on imperialist grounds.

Bourassa made evident his distrust of Laurier, whom he thought had been influenced in favor of reciprocity by the Asquith government and the British Ambassador, James Bryce, at Washington, as he had been influenced in favor of the Navy Act by Lord Grey. At present the West favored reciprocity and Quebec was aroused against imperialism, so Laurier followed an opportunist course, which he might reverse if public opinion changed; therefore the nationalists reserved the right to change their stand. In the Quebec Legislature in March Bourassa also urged the provincial authorities to consider the repercussions of reciprocity upon the paper and lumber industries; but it was clear that he was more interested in what was happening at Ottawa than at Quebec, and that he might once more enter the federal field.

At Ottawa reciprocity made heavy weather against growing Conservative opposition, and Laurier was forced in May to adjourn parliament for two months in order that he might attend the Imperial Conference scheduled for the end of the month. The Conference was chiefly notable for the effort of the Round Table school of imperialists to secure approval of some plan of imperial parliamentary federation. This proposal was made through Sir Joseph Ward of New Zealand, who, in addition to pressing for an imperial council of state, urged the creation of an imperial parliament with power over foreign policy and defence. Laurier rejected the scheme as 'utterly impracticable,'[115] and was joined in his opposition by Asquith of Britain, Fisher of Australia, and Botha of South Africa. Laurier also opposed an alternative scheme suggested by Harcourt, which proposed a standing committee composed of the colonial secretary and his under-secretaries, together with the high commissioners of the dominions. Through the Imperial Defence Committee, in which the dominions did not enjoy the same equality with the British as in the conference, confidential defence information was for the first time given to the colonial representatives.[116] But Laurier objected to an Australian motion that the British government should consult the dominions before signing treaties binding the empire. Giving advice implied backing that advice with armed strength; Laurier was opposed to centralization of policy, as well as centralization of defence. Indeed he won further freedom for Canada to free herself from old commercial treaties made by Britain which impeded her negotiations with the United States. By the end of the 1911 Conference it was evident that imperialism in Chamberlain's sense was dead; the empire was to be a league of equal nations making mutual arrangements by negotiation.

During Laurier's absence his enemies had been busy, both in French and English Canada. While Borden began a campaign in the West against reciprocity, on May 31 the nationalists held a mass meeting in support of Monk at the Ontario Rink in Montreal as the initial step in a new drive against the Navy Act. Taillon read an address to Monk and assured him of support. Monk condemned imperialism, and without discussing the merits of reciprocity criticized the government for adopting that policy and its naval one too quickly, without sufficient study and consultation of the people. Lavergne devoted himself to criticizing the immigration policy, while Paul-Emile Lamarche, a powerful speaker, supported Monk's stand. Bourassa attacked Laurier for his lack of principle, his opportunism, and his betrayals, and predicted the triumph of nationalism. This meeting drew down upon Bourassa and his allies new criticism from the Quebeckers, and the *Quebec Chronicle* announced that no English Conservative could accept an alliance with anti-British Bourassa. Within his own camp Bourassa met with opposition from Asselin and Fournier, who differed with his moderate attitude in the current Franco-Ontarian and Franco-American struggles against assimilation, and criticized his failure to exploit the Drummond-Arthabaska success. In *L'Action*, a little nationalist weekly founded by Fournier in April 1911, Asselin complained that 'M. Bourassa imagined that all parliamentary tactics and all the art of politics consist of speeches.'[117] But the defection of Asselin and Fournier did not check the growth of nationalism, which was now penetrating into Conservative and clerical circles where these hot-headed young men were not in good odor. When Lemieux undertook a speaking tour through Quebec in June in favor of Laurier's policies, the nationalists followed suit with opposition meetings. In early June there were meetings at Joliette, Nicolet orel, and Sainte-Scholastique, where Bourassa and Lavergne were ıpported by Tellier, Monk, and other Conservative orators. .emieux and Bourassa made charges and counter-charges against ach other, and the atmosphere grew bitter.

There was a truce for Saint-Jean-Baptiste Day, when the Montreal aint-Jean-Baptiste Society held a banquet to manifest their sym-athy for the persecuted French Canadians outside Quebec. Asselin avagely attacked Irish bishops who wished to anglicize the French Canadians, and urged his people to support only French-Canadian anks, insurance companies, and businesses, in order to increase heir economic power. Bourassa expressed his sympathy for the ninorities of Maine and Ontario, but counseled moderation:

> Before all and despite all, remain unalterably attached to the Catholic Church. The constituted authorities of the Church can err. The Pope imself can err. Whatever happens, never doubt Rome. At Rome you vill end by finding justice. You will even find there indulgence for the xcesses of word and errors of tactics which may escape you in the course f battle.[118]

And he urged his audience not to make the whole Irish race re-ponsible for the iniquities committed by some of its members. The *Montreal Gazette* took alarm at the boycott of English business pro-posed by Asselin, and Bourassa was credited with his disciple's uggestion, which he himself repudiated. When a rumor came from London that at the conference Laurier had refused the participation of the navy in all Britain's wars, the *Quebec Chronicle* proclaimed: 'It is the voice of Laurier, but the hand of Bourassa.'[119]

The campaign was renewed by both government and opposition forces before Laurier returned to Quebec on July 10. At the ancient capital he claimed that he had adopted the same attitude at the conference as at earlier ones: 'the revindication of our rights and of our policy. This policy has triumphed, and we have succeeded n establishing a solid basis on which the Empire and all the young nations which make it up can grow great: each community, each ociety, each nation ought to govern itself, in taking account of its own public opinion . . . We are loyal subjects of the British Crown, but we shall never consent to being governed from London by Downing Street.'[120] Again at Montreal the following day there was a carefully organized reception for Laurier at the Champs de Mars.[121] But Bourassa was not impressed by these tributes to the old leader and by Laurier's well-worn arguments that he had made Canada a nation, and had followed a middle path which caused him to be attacked by imperialist and nationalist extremists. Bour-assa held that Canada was not a nation since the decisions of its highest court were subject to appeal to the Judicial Committee of the Privy Council; and that Laurier was attacked by both im perialists and nationalists because his policy was neither imperialis nor nationalist. Bourassa concluded his series of articles on Laurie and the Imperial Conference in *Le Devoir*, which were reprinted i pamphlet form, by declaring: 'The power of the man of the golde mean, of the honorable compromises, of false "conciliation solutions, evaporates like morning fog under a hot sun.'[122]

When parliament reassembled on July 18, reciprocity was presse once more by the government. Fielding threatened that if the manu facturers succeeded in defeating the measure, 'then there will ris up in the Western country a storm-cloud no bigger than a man' hand, and the end will be a change in the fiscal policy of the countr which the manufacturers will find much greater than anything the conceived of.'[123] But the opposition had grown stronger in Laurier' absence, and in the face of Conservative obstruction, Laurier ha no recourse but to dissolve parliament and appeal to the country The Conservatives' patriotic argument had gained new strengt from indiscreet statements of President Taft and Speaker Cham Clark in support of the agreement. On two occasions Taft spoke o Canada as 'being at the parting of the ways'[124]—a statement whic was twisted to suit Conservative purposes. On April 27 Taft sai 'no such opportunity will ever again come to the United States The forces which are at work in England and Canada to separat her by a Chinese wall from the United States, and to make her par of an Imperial band reaching from England round the world an back to England again by a system of preferential tariffs would deriv an impetus from the rejection of this treaty.'[125] The president als wrote Theodore Roosevelt, in a letter made public on April 25 that reciprocity 'would made Canada only an adjunct of the Unite States.'[126] Champ Clark, speaking at Chicago, said: 'I hope t see the day when the American flag will float over every square foo of the British North American possessions, clear to the Nort Pole . . . That is the way things are tending now.'[127]

As in 1891, the Liberals found it difficult to convince Canadian whose emotional patriotism was aroused by such statements tha limited reciprocity did not mean annexation, and that the argumen of 'no truck nor trade with the Yankees' came oddly from banker and railroad magnates closely tied to Wall Street and internationa corporations. The old United Empire Loyalist sentiment agains the Yankees was revived, and Canadian national pride found i difficult not to retaliate for years of unfriendly American acts and restrictive tariffs. A Canadian National League was formed unde the auspices of the eighteen rebel Liberals of Toronto; a non-political Anti-Reciprocity League sprang up; and appeals were made to the British-born to keep Canada British. Sifton took an active part in the campaign, and his speech against reciprocity was widely circulated in the West. Upon the dissolution of parliament Sifton issued a manifesto to the people of Canada, restating his arguments against reciprocity.[128]

Laurier's election manifesto insisted that both parties had long sought reciprocity; that the arrangement now made had been criticized in the States as being too favorable to Canada; that the Conservatives had blocked debate in the House upon its merits, and hence had made necessary an appeal to the people. The alleged peril to the British connection was discounted; and it was argued that the arrangement would improve relations between all three countries, and would remove forever the possibility of war between the British Empire and the United States.[129] No mention was made of the naval question.

Borden's first manifesto also ignored the navy question and welcomed the appeal to the people, while condemning the government for the sudden dissolution of parliament. In a second manifesto on August 14, Borden deplored the reversal of Canada's traditional economic policy, and objected to reciprocity on the grounds that it would integrate the Canadian economy with the American one, and lead to commercial union with the United States excluding trade relations with the empire. It threatened the farmer and fisherman, left Canada's natural resources at the mercy of the American trusts, and discouraged Canadian industry. The Conservative platform provided for a reform of extravagant public expenditure, return of their natural resources to the Prairie Provinces, construction of a Hudson Bay railroad, government-controlled grain elevators, encouragement of the meat-packing industry, and other minor reforms. The Conservatives pledged themselves to 'maintain independent and unimpaired the control of our own affairs by the Parliament of Canada; a policy which, while affording no just cause of complaint to any foreign nation, will find its highest ideal in the autonomous development of Canada as a nation within the British Empire.' Borden concluded with a plea 'for the strengthening and not the loosening of the ties which bind this Dominion to the British Empire.'[130] In this manifesto he did not urge Canadian contribution to the British navy, but attacked the Laurier naval policy as costly, inefficient, and likely to result in 'the useless sacrifice of many lives.'

Borden had made a deal with the Quebec Conservatives, whereby the campaign in that province was left to Monk, who was now very much under Bourassa's influence. At a meeting in Montreal on August 1, the Conservative organizer Charles Beaubien achieved the agreement of the very imperialist Herbert B. Ames, the more moderate imperialist C. J. Doherty, the moderate nationalist Monk, and the very nationalist Bourassa to the common objective of defeat ing Laurier. Protectionist and imperialist big business was willin to use the nationalist movement to defeat reciprocity. In Quebe reciprocity was a minor issue, but the nationalists had roused a swel ling and potent agitation against the government on the nav question.

Therefore funds began to flow into the nationalist war ches from Tory sources. One English Conservative from Montreal, wh had violently attacked the nationalists as 'rebels and disloya traitors,' now took out forty subscriptions to *Le Devoir*, and other followed suit.[131] The paper's capital was tripled; and Ernes Lapointe remarked: 'If I were given to the bitterness of the nation alists, I should say that M. Bourassa has opposed reciprocity sinc the capital of his paper has been increased by $200,000; I shoul say that M. Bourassa has been bought.'[132] Rodolphe Forget, whos interests had also been opposed by the Liberals, threw the suppor of his money and influence behind the nationalists. Sir Hug Graham, whose *Montreal Star* had fought reciprocity from the out set, and his imperialist friends now backed them with money an influence. Bourassa stressed that the main issue was imperialism while the Liberals sought to divert public attention from the nav question by concentrating on reciprocity, as a benefit to the farmer of Quebec. Thus Bourassa was soon drawn into criticism of re ciprocity. *Le Devoir* found itself in the same camp as the *Sta Gazette*, *Chronicle*, *La Patrie*, and *L'Evénement*, opposed by *Le Canada La Presse*, the *Herald*, the *Witness*, and *Le Soleil*. Borden's follower chose candidates only for the English seats of Quebec; elsewher a free field was left to Monk and the nationalists.

Bourassa did not contest a seat himself, but in *Le Devoir* and o the platform he acted as leader in the district of Montreal, whil Lavergne directed the campaign in the district of Quebec. Bourass campaigned harder than any candidate, speaking at Fraservill on July 20, at Saint-Hyacinthe on July 30, at Saint-Denis o July 31, at Trois-Rivières on August 6. On August 13 Rodolph Lemieux accepted his challenge to an *assemblée contradictoire* at Saint Hyacinthe, the most memorable of the campaign. Thirty thousan people appeared, three times the normal population of the town Lemieux, aroused by the attacks of *Le Devoir* and *Le Nationaliste* accused the 'independent' Bourassa of having sought the post mastership of Montreal, the Canadian commissionership at Paris and the deputy-speakership of the House; and blamed his hatre of Laurier on the fact that these offices had been refused him Lemieux compared Laurier's work of peace and concord wit Bourassa's work of hatred and envy; supported reciprocity; an once more stressed that the navy would be Canadian, not imperial and that service in it would be voluntary, not compulsory. His final eulogy of Laurier did not arouse the usual storm of applause. Bourassa denied that he had sought the postmastership or the commissionership, and then turned to the political questions. He repeated Monk's criticism of reciprocity, but stressed that the question had been raised to bury the navy issue. But the navy question, the whole imperialist question, was far more important, since reciprocity would be adopted or rejected once for all at the next session, while the imperialist question would remain and rise again. He quoted Fielding to prove that the navy was primarily intended for imperial wars. He traced the history of the Navy Act and of the imperialist movement; and asserted that the law had been passed at the request of the imperial authorities. It did not expressly provide for conscription, but conscription would come when men were needed to man the ships. He concluded:

> The vote you give on September 21 will be a vote for the navy if you vote in favor of Laurier's candidates. It will be a vote against the navy if you vote in favor of independent candidates—whether they call themselves Liberals, Conservatives, or nationalists, provided that they are not tied hand and foot and support M. Monk in the House; M. Monk who has fought and will fight any government, Liberal or Conservative, which refuses to submit these questions to the free judgment of the people.[133]

And then he burst into an attack on Laurier: 'It is time for the people of the province of Quebec to prove to M. Laurier that if they admired him when he served the interests of the country well, today that he has prevaricated, today that he has duped us. . . .'

The rest was lost in a tumult raised by the Liberal followers of T.-D. Bouchard, a local Liberal leader, who were under orders to cover all attacks on Laurier. When Béland attempted to attack Bourassa, by accusing him of abridging his quotation from Fielding and of dishonesty in arguing that conscription would be imposed, another disturbance broke out; for the crowd was divided between partisans of Laurier and partisans of Bourassa. The crowd quieted in order to hear Lavergne, but his attacks on Lemieux were so lively that the latter rose and grappled with him. Then fights broke out in the audience, and the meeting dissolved in disorder. The English-speaking press reported the affair as a nationalist outrage.

Bourassa was defended in the *Gazette* by C. H. Cahan, a leader of the Montreal bar, who said that he had long shared the English prejudice against Bourassa as an enemy of England, but had learned that Bourassa judged Canadian policy from a Canadian point of view, which was just and wise.[134] The journalist John Boyd also published in the Tory *Toronto World* a favorable account of the true Bourassa, 'as eloquent in English as in French, of stainles reputation, of great moral energy, a sincere admirer of Englis institutions which he wishes to preserve while safeguarding Canadia autonomy.'[135] *Le Devoir*, now backed by St. James Street, with a audience made up of the French-Canadian élite and the students o the province, and exercising influence from New England to Wester Canada, had become within a year and a half of its foundation more influential organ than *La Presse* or *La Patrie*, despite thei infinitely greater circulation. And through *Le Devoir* the clergy o Quebec was largely won to the cause of Bourassa. In vain L.-O David protested to Archbishop Bruchési against 'the fatal error made by the clergy in trying to bring about Laurier's downfall.[13]

Laurier did not underestimate the danger in Quebec and mad no less than seven speeches in the province during August. H opened his campaign at Trois-Rivières on August 17, replying t Monk and Bourassa's speeches there ten days before. He urged tha reciprocity would benefit the farmers of Quebec, and defended th navy on the grounds that a greater Canada required its protection as a greater Trois-Rivières needed a police force. He denounce Bourassa's alliance with the Tories and Jingoes of the English speaking provinces, and upheld his own record. Elections wer always as uncertain as a horse race or a cockfight, but 'If I had t bet, I should bet on the old game cock who for fifteen years ha led the Liberal party to victory.'[137] At Sorel, whose shipyard might benefit from the building of a navy, Laurier for once foun little opposition to his naval policy, and moved his old follower by the declaration that he would retire from politics if defeated.[13] At St. Johns he said:

> I am branded in Quebec as a traitor to the French, and in Ontari as a traitor to the English. In Quebec I am branded as a Jingo, an in Ontario as a Separatist. In Quebec I am attacked as an Imperialist and in Ontario as an anti-Imperialist. I am neither. I am a Canadian Canada has been the inspiration of my life. I have had before me as pillar of fire by night and a pillar of cloud by day a policy of true Cana dianism, of moderation, of conciliation. I have followed it consistentl since 1896, and I now appeal with confidence to the whole Canadia people to uphold me in this policy of sound Canadianism which make for the greatness of our country and the Empire.[139]

But he could not arouse the wonted enthusiasm for his cause Bourassa had monopolized the enthusiasm of Quebec, and eve Laurier's long devoted followers could muster only respect for thei old leader.

In Ontario Laurier waged an even more uphill battle. If i Quebec the young nationalists cried that he was betraying Canad

England, in Ontario the Conservatives proclaimed that he was etraying Canada to the United States. It was in vain that he elittled annexation talk by saying that he was willing to meet the mericans in business, but if they wanted to talk politics, they should eep to their side of the line and the Canadians would keep to eirs.[140] A whispering campaign against the French Catholic rime minister was pressed by the Orangemen, who maintained at the papal *Ne Temere* decree of 1907, which annulled marriages ereafter contracted between Catholics before a Protestant minister, validated all marriages not made before a Catholic priest.[141] aurier had nothing to say in this question, which was a purely rovincial one, and the civil code of Quebec had long recognized e impediments to marriage established by the Catholic authorities or Catholics and by the Protestant authorities for Protestants. But he Orangemen proclaimed in a fine frenzy that Canada was overned by the Pope through Laurier and the Province of Quebec, nd backed their argument by citing his appearance and that of ther officials at the Eucharistic Congress. J. S. Ewart's explanation n one of his 'Kingdom Papers'[142] that the *Ne Temere* decree affected nly Catholics appeared too late and reached too few readers to ffset the effect of the campaign. The manufacturers fought Laurier n the reciprocity issue; the imperialists on the navy question; nd the old passionate loyalism of Ontario rose against him in esponse to Kipling's cabled warning, 'It is her own soul that Canada risks today'—despite the fact that Kipling's own soul was eemingly unendangered by the fact that most of his royalties were arned in the States. Throughout Ontario Laurier evoked few heers and found many old friends missing at his meetings.

Bourassa pressed the attack on Laurier relentlessly in Quebec. He spoke on August 21 at Lachine, on the 26th at Joliette, the 29th at Becancour, the 30th at Sainte-Scholastique, the 31st at Saint-Jérome. Borden contented himself with a meeting at Montreal on he 29th in support of the English candidates, and another for the nixed population of Lake Megantic. Asselin, candidate in Saint-Jacques, announced his return to acceptance of Bourassa's leader-hip, and *Le Devoir* wished him well. On September 3 and 4 Bourassa spoke in his old county of Labelle, and on the 5th at Hull, n company with C. H. Cahan, who approved his program. On he 6th he spoke at Sainte-Rose, and on the 8th at the Monument National in Montreal in support of Asselin. On this occasion Cahan coined the slogan 'No Navy made in London; no reciprocity made n Washington,' while John Boyd announced in English that he, oo, was a nationalist.[143] In the face of this effective campaign Laurier privately conceded that the Quebec cities were lost, but he hoped to win back the country districts.[144] The Liberal press began to paint dark pictures of what would result from a defeat Laurier; his compatriots would be humiliated and Borden woul take power:

> Then, instead of an essentially Canadian navy, over which Englar had no rights, we shall see the triumph of jingo imperialism, with pa ticipation in imperial wars and an endless string of dreadnoughts.
>
> Then, instead of the reciprocity which the Canadian farmer ar worker have so long awaited, we shall remain in the *status quo* so keen defended by the trusts.
>
> Then, instead of a French-Canadian prime minister, we shall have prime minister who understands none of our aspirations and who h already promised to the voice of Toronto, i.e., to the voice of fanaticism predominance in the councils of the nation . . . .[145]

But Sir Hugh Graham organized a literary bureau where high paid journalists turned out a stream of articles, advertisement tracts, and pamphlets for the Conservative press. Graham wa reported to have spent more than $250,000 before the campaig was finished. The great industrialists warned their workers tha reciprocity would close the factories. The Liberals derived som comfort from representing an election in which the millionaire William Price and Rodolphe Forget were Conservative candidate as a contest between the trusts and the people.[146] Organs of bot parties embarrassed their opponents by recalling past statement which contradicted present positions: Bourassa was reminded c his support of reciprocity, and both he and Lavergne of thei attacks on the Tories; while Laurier was reproached with aban doning his old autonomist position. William Randolph Hears an advocate of reciprocity, sent articles urging Canadians to suppor Laurier, and the nationalists protested at this foreign interventio in a Canadian election.[147]

At Laprairie on September 9, when the nationalist candidat was greeted by cheers for Laurier, Bourassa rose and said:

> Formerly I also cried hurrah for Laurier. But Laurier has sacrifice his own in the West, Laurier protects the thieves and grafters, Laurie imposes upon us a costly navy, which will serve no purpose except t kill our sons in the wars of England. Laurier forces me today to choos between him and the country; I choose the country.[148]

The campaign grew increasingly bitter, with Asselin and Tancrèd Marsil using ever more violent language. Laurier decided that hi danger was greater in Quebec than in Ontario, and cut short hi tour of the latter province to fight Bourassa. On September 11 h spoke at Victoriaville. On the following day, while Bourassa spok at Verchères, Laurier at Beauceville denounced the insidious an ishonest tactics of the opposition and declared: 'The Imperialists f Toronto and the Nationalists of Quebec will never succeed in eating Laurier.'[149] On the 13th Laurier spoke at Montmagny, vhile Bourassa took the fight into the prime minister's county of oulanges the following day. Meanwhile Laurier held forth in his ld stronghold of Quebec at the Ménage Militaire, promising the ity a new drydock and proclaiming once more that he was neither n imperialist nor an anti-imperialist, but a Canadian. He warned hat the Borden-Bourassa alliance would lead to racial conflict and nternal divisions, while under the Liberal standard, 'which shelters ll races, there is room for all to live in harmony and peace, and to njoy happiness.'[150] On the 15th, while Bourassa spoke against emieux at Marieville, Laurier and Lavergne held rival meetings t Rimouski. The young nationalist did not spare his former patron, nd his violence attracted those who found Laurier too gentle for heir taste. Rival partisans fought in the streets, as they did also at Trois-Rivières on the 17th. On the 16th Bourassa spoke at Acton-ale, while Laurier addressed a meeting at Grand'Mère. On the 17th Bourassa spoke at Victoriaville, and was greeted by the singing of a hymn, 'O Bourassa,' to the air of 'O Canada.' The Conservative leaders of the Eastern Townships provided free subscriptions o *Le Devoir* for all French voters of the region. Rehabilitated in Ontario public opinion through the efforts of the Toronto *World*, Bourassa received numerous invitations to speak there, but agreed nly to abandon the Quebec campaign for a speech at Sudbury, he French center of Northern Ontario, on September 18, where he made two addresses, one in French and one in English.

Bourassa returned to Montreal in haste for a great meeting at the Ontario Rink on the 19th, the principal one of the nationalist campaign. It rivaled that of Laurier at the Parc Sohmer on the eve of his rise to power in 1896. Bourassa was supported by Boyd, Asselin, and Cahan; and his speech won an ovation such as Laurier used to receive. The crowd, too large for the largest hall in the city, would not cease applauding to allow the others to speak. A parade through the streets was improvised. One detachment headed by Asselin encountered Laurier about to take the train at Place Viger Station, and pursued him to his train. Meanwhile Bourassa spoke from a balcony of the Hotel Viger, and was greeted with the singing of 'O Bourassa.' The following day at Saint-Hyacinthe, the outraged partisans of Laurier under the leadership of T.-D. Bouchard stoned Bourassa's meeting and prepared an ambush at the station, which Bourassa avoided by boarding the train at the next stop. Meanwhile Laurier wound up his campaign in Quebec, where he had been attacked in his own district by Lavergne and where a scandal was caused by the sudden withdrawal of the opposition candidate just before the election. As the campaign closed, *L Presse* proclaimed that a vote for Bourassa was a vote for Border and a vote for Borden a vote for extreme imperialism. At Toront the *Globe* reversed the slogan: 'A vote for Borden is a vote fo Bourassa, and a vote for Bourassa is a vote for the break-up of thi country.'[151]

On September 21, 1911, the Laurier regime went down to defea before the united forces of the Conservatives and the nationalists In Quebec the Liberal majority fell from 43 to 11, with one minister Sidney Fisher, losing his seat. In Ontario the Liberals suffered rout, with the Conservatives winning 72 seats and the Liberals onl 14. Three ministers—Graham, Mackenzie King, and Patterson— lost their seats. The Maritimes returned 16 Conservatives and 1 Liberals; Fielding and Sir Frederick Borden were defeated. Britisl Columbia went solidly Conservative and Manitoba strongly so Only Saskatchewan and Alberta returned strong Liberal majorities The majority in the House was exactly reversed, with the Conser vatives now holding 133 seats to the Liberals' 88.

The outcome was hailed in Quebec as a nationalist triumph; i Ontario as an imperialist one. But Borden was escorted to Ottawa under the banner of 'One fleet, one flag, one Throne.'[152] The *Ottawa Citizen* rejoiced that the political center of gravity of Canada had been changed from Quebec to Ontario.

The new Conservative regime rested on the basis of a solid Ontario, just as the old had stood on a solid Quebec. By his fight against Laurier the nationalist Bourassa had delivered Quebec into the hands of an administration committed to imperialist paths and unsympathetic to the French Canadians. Thanks to the unscrupulousness of the campaign on both sides, Canada was already split by bitter ethnic division as one of the great crises of its national life drew near.

Notes

[1] Skelton, *Laurier,* II, 224–5 *n.*
[2] *Ibid.*, 226–8.
[3] *Ibid.*, 229.
[4] Rumilly, XII, 16–17.
[5] J. Dafoe, *Clifford Sifton in Relation to His Times* (Toronto, 1931), 291.
[6] Rumilly, XII, 20–2.
[7] Dafoe, 297.
[8] Skelton, II, 239.
[9] Borden, *Memoirs,* I, 146.
[10] *Ibid.*, 147.
[11] Rumilly, XII, 26–7.
[12] *Ibid.*, 27.
[13] *Ibid.*, 30, 37.

14 H. Bourassa, *Les Ecoles du Nord-Ouest* (Montréal, 1905), 1–3.
15 *Ibid.*, 25.
16 *Ibid.*, 27.
17 *Ibid.*, 28–9.
18 Skelton, II, 247 *n.*, Laurier-J.-B.-A. Casgrain, 20 April 1905.
19 Groulx, *Croisade*, 9.
20 Rumilly, XII, 135.
21 Skelton, II, 248.
22 Rumilly, XII, 151.
23 *Hansard, Commons Debates*, 6 July 1906, IV, 7332–3.
24 Rumilly, XII, 173–6.
25 *Ibid.*, 182.
26 *Ibid.*, 182–6.
27 *Ibid.*, XIII, 33.
28 Rumilly, XIII, 43.
29 Dafoe, *Sifton*, 327–32.
30 *Ibid.*, 332.
31 A. Lavergne, *Trente ans de vie nationale* (Montréal, 1935), 136–7; Rumilly, XIII, 73–5.
32 Rumilly, XIII, 82.
33 *Ibid.*, 92.
34 *Ibid.*, 101–3.
35 *Ibid.*, 105.
36 PAC: Laurier Papers 3233, Laurier-Laflamme, 20 nov. 1907; Skelton, I, 313.
37 Rumilly, XIII, 113–14.
38 *Ibid.*, 139–41.
39 *Ibid.*, 143.
40 *Ibid.*, 144.
41 *Ibid.*, 146–7.
42 *Ibid.*, 163.
43 *Ibid.*, 166.
44 *Ibid.*, 172.
45 Skelton, II, 265, 281.
46 Rumilly, XIV, 17–18.
47 *Ibid.*, 12.
48 *Ibid.*, 20–3.
49 *Ibid.*, 52, 55–6.
50 Skelton, II, 319.
51 Borden, *Memoirs*, I, 246.
52 Rumilly, XIV, 73.
53 Borden, I, 253.
54 Rumilly, XIV, 77–8.
55 *Ibid.*, 81; *La Patrie*, 24 juillet 1909.
56 *Ibid.*, 82; *Quebec Chronicle*, 11 Aug. 1909.
57 *Ibid.*, 85.
58 *Ibid.*, 99, G. Smith-Bourassa.
59 *Ibid.*, 98–100.
60 Rumilly, XIV, 114–18.
61 *Ibid.*, 118.
62 Skelton, II, 327–8; full text in A.-D. DeCelles, *Discours du Sir Wilfrid Laurier de 1889 à 1911* (Montréal, 1920), 113–15.
63 Borden, I, 269–74.
64 Rumilly, XIV, 135, *Le Devoir*, 7 janvier 1909.
65 H. Bourassa, *Le Projet de Loi navale: sa nature, ses conséquences* (Montréal, 1910), 16.

[66] *Ibid.*, 26.
[67] *Ibid.*, 37.
[68] Rumilly, XIV, 138.
[69] Skelton, II, 352–8; DeCelles, 95.
[70] *Ibid.*, 327; DeCelles, 104.
[71] DeCelles, 135.
[72] Borden, I, 280–1.
[73] Rumilly, XIV, 142–7.
[74] *Ibid.*, 149.
[75] *Ibid.*, 150.
[76] Rumilly, XV, 13–14.
[77] *Ibid.*, 17.
[78] *Ibid.*, 25.
[79] *Ibid.*, 28.
[80] *Ibid.*, 52–5.
[81] *Ibid.*, 70–1.
[82] *Ibid.*, 74.
[83] *Ibid.*, 80.
[84] *Ibid.*, 114–16.
[85] *Ibid.*, 136–7, *New York Herald*, 9 Oct. 1910.
[86] *Ibid.*, 137–8.
[87] Skelton, II, 337; DeCelles, 149.
[88] *Ibid.*, 338–9; DeCelles, 151.
[89] DeCelles, 164.
[90] *Ibid.*, 181–2.
[91] *Ibid.*, 192–3.
[92] *Ibid.*, 202.
[93] Rumilly, XV, 14, *Toronto World*.
[94] *Ibid.*, 146.
[95] *Ibid.*, 152–4.
[96] *Ibid.*, 157.
[97] Skelton, II, 339.
[98] Rumilly, XV, 157.
[99] *Ibid.*, 159.
[100] Lavergne, 174–5.
[101] Rumilly, XV, 161.
[102] *Ibid.*, 162.
[103] *Ibid.*, 103, *La Presse*, 7 oct. 1911.
[104] *Ibid.*, 165.
[105] Skelton, II, 339.
[106] Borden, I, 295–7.
[107] Rumilly, XV, 180–2.
[108] *Ibid.*, 183–5.
[109] Skelton, II, 367.
[110] *Ibid.*, 370.
[111] Dafoe, 364–8.
[112] Borden, I, 308.
[113] H. Bourassa, *La Convention Douanière entre le Canada et les Etats-Unis: sa nature, ses conséquences; The Reciprocity Agreement and its Consequences, As viewed from the Nationalist standpoint* (Montréal, 1911).
[114] Bourassa, *Reciprocity*, 12.
[115] Skelton, II, 340.
[116] G. Neuendorf, *Studies in the Evolution of Dominion Status* (London, 1942), 341.
[117] Rumilly, XVI, 57.
[118] Rumilly, XVI, 59–61.

[119] *Ibid.*, 62, *Quebec Chronicle.*
[120] *Ibid.*, 64.
[121] *Ibid.*, 65.
[122] H. Bourassa, *La Conférence impériale et le rôle de M. Laurier* (Montréal, 1911), 5.
[123] Skelton, II, 373.
[124] *Ibid.*, 375.
[125] Dafoe, 370 *n*.
[126] Borden, I, 319.
[127] *Ibid.*, 319–20.
[128] Dafoe, 371–2.
[129] Borden, I, 321–2.
[130] *Ibid.*, 322–5.
[131] Lavergne, 193–4.
[132] Rumilly, XVI, 75. Bourassa denied this charge at the fifth anniversary dinner of *Le Devoir* in 1915, recounting how he had refused to be bought by the Anti-Reciprocity League. *Le 5e Anniversaire du 'Devoir'* (Montréal, 1915), 29.
[133] *Ibid.*, 81–2.
[134] *Ibid.*, 84–5.
[135] *Ibid.*, 86, *Toronto World*, 26 Aug. 1911.
[136] *Ibid.*, 87.
[137] A.-D. DeCelles, *Discours de Sir Wilfrid Laurier de 1911 à 1919* (Montréal, 1920), 7.
[138] Rumilly, XVI, 90.
[139] Skelton, II, 380.
[140] *Ibid.*, 379.
[141] Rumilly, XVI, 105.
[142] J. S. Ewart, *The Kingdom Papers* (Ottawa, 1912), I, 121–32, No. 5, '*Ne Temere Decree.*'
[143] Rumilly, XVI, 97.
[144] Rumilly, XVI, 97.
[145] *Ibid.*, 98–9, *La Presse.*
[146] *Ibid.*, 100.
[147] *Ibid.*, 101.
[148] *Ibid.*, 103–4.
[149] *Ibid.*, 106.
[150] *Ibid.*, 107.
[151] Skelton, II, 379; Rumilly, XVI, 114.
[152] Rumilly, XVI, 118.

CHAPTER XI

STRIFE IN ONTARIO AND WAR IN FRANCE

(1911–16)

IT WAS A new and greater Quebec that in 1911 faced the future i somewhat lonely isolation after bringing about the defeat Canada's first French-Canadian prime minister. Its populatio had increased since 1901 from 1,648,898 to 2,005, 776; a region whic had been nearly two-thirds rural in 1891 was now nearly half urban. These changes were caused largely by the rapid growth of greate Montreal, which now included a quarter of the population of th province. And they reflected the impact of the industrial revolutio upon Quebec, since Montreal's growth was due to the fact that it wa the financial and industrial capital of the Dominion. The city wa the headquarters of eight banks, holding two-thirds of all Canadia bank capital, and of two great railway systems.[2] The great Angu Shops of the Canadian Pacific, the rapidly developing shoe and dres industries, and the port which held an ever-tightening monopoly c the St. Lawrence trade, all combined to make Montreal a magnet fo the surplus rural population. Despite the movement from country t town, farm production doubled from 1895–1910 as agricultura methods improved.[3]

Montreal had become cosmopolitan, rather than more French. It English minority, which controlled most of the great industrial an financial institutions, built the English sub-city of Westmount, wher they could forget that they lived in one of the largest French cities o the world. The French upper-classes abandoned the Place Vige and Saint-Denis districts for the new suburb of Outremont. Th working-class suburbs of Maisonneuve, Verdun, Lachine, and Mon treal-Est expanded or began their rapid development. Meanwhil the older portions of the town became centers for immigrant groups Jews, Poles, Chinese, and Italians. Among the newcomers, only small numbers of French and Belgians assimilated to the French Canadians and hence were welcome; there was growing feeling against the Jews, whose school population had risen from 1,500 in 1901, to 5,900 in 1911,[4] partly because they took over a growing share of the dress industry and of the small business which had been left to the French Canadians by English and American dominance in big business. For by 1907 there were 150 American branch plants established in the province, and much American capital there.[5] Big business, largely integrated into a continental economy regardless of its ownership, tended to give the city an increasingly American air.

Quebec City had not matched Montreal's growth. Its population increased only by 10,000 during the first decade of the century,[6] and its 78,000 would have been lost among Montreal's half million. Its shipbuilding industry was dead. With the improvement of the St. Lawrence channel and of port facilities at Montreal, shipping tended to bypass Quebec in favor of Montreal. Quebec's shoe industry was largely transferred to Montreal, and its cotton industry to Trois-Rivières. G.-E. Amyot's Dominion Corset plant burnt in May 1911, but was replaced before the end of the year by a larger and more modern one, the single exception to the general picture of industrial stagnation. Hull, the industrial capital of the Ottawa and Gatineau Valleys, thrived on its wood industries and increased its population by half in the first decade of the century. Sherbrooke, the industrial center of the Townships, did the same, thanks to its textile factories. Trois-Rivières, largely burnt out in 1908, nevertheless increased its population by a third and became the capital of the rapidly developing Saint-Maurice region. Its pulp and paper industry supplied a notable share of the Canadian contribution of 10 per cent of American newsprint. Prohibition of the export of pulp caused the establishment of paper mills at Trois-Rivières, and a thriving cotton industry also grew up there. Up the Saint-Maurice the ten-year-old industrial town of Grand'Mère, doubled its population, and to its pulp mills added foundries, shirt factories, and woodworking plants. Still farther upstream, the little town of La Tuque was founded. The Lake St. John region, fifty years after its first colonization, was turning towards industry, with great pulp mills at Chicoutimi, and the Dubuc and Price interests struggling for control of the vast water-power resources of the region. The slow-starting colonization of the Abitibi region in the far northwest of the province was stimulated by the discovery of mineral deposits uncovered by the construction of the Canadian Northern from North Bay to Quebec, which opened up this distant and inaccessible region. But colonization activity had lagged behind, the orphan child of a provincial government much more concerned with the rapid industrial development of the province.

At the turn of the century Errol Bouchette had proclaimed the coming of the industrial age in a pamphlet, '*Emparons-nous de l'industrie*,' whose title echoed Ludger Duvernay's outmoded slogan of '*Emparons-nous du sol*.' Bouchette foresaw that industry would become more important than agriculture, which was not 'the exclusive need of our people.'[7] He pointed out that the ground the

French Canadians gained by colonization, they lost in the established centers of the province, where others were founding industries. The new age called for skills acquired through education, and he deplored the fact that there were only 722 French lay university students in the province, out of a population of 1,293,000, while the English students numbered 1,358 out of a population of 196,000. The most serious weakness of the French Canadians was reflected by the fact that there were only 27 students of the applied sciences at Laval, compared to 250 at McGill and Bishop's. He predicted 'foreign control of our industry' unless the provincial government, like the German one, became a patron of science, protected the workers, and financed industries.

Bouchette repeated his warning to the Royal Society in 1901, urging that Quebec stood on the eve of an industrial revolution which would have effects as profound as those of the French Revolution: 'We can approve or disapprove of such movements, but no people can escape them; to dam them out is impossible.'[8] The American trusts, seeking new conquests, would invade Quebec, raising new problems and creating a new industrial population. 'We should welcome the forces which may come from beyond our frontiers, but we should await them in a good strategic position, in order to remain, whatever happens, masters in our house.'[9] He claimed that the French Canadians had the same aptness as any other people for business and industry, though hitherto they had largely followed other paths. He deplored, as Arthur Buies had done many years before, the absence of professional and technical schools, which prevented the French Canadians from making use of their natural dexterity and mechanical ingenuity in industry, in other than subordinate and unskilled positions. The Ecole Polytechnique had few pupils, because primary technical and trade schools were lacking.

Bouchette urged the extension of the cooperative principle, already successful among cheese and butter makers, to industry, to overcome the lack of French-Canadian capital. The colonists of new areas could form such syndicates for the making of pulp, thus avoiding speculative exploitation of the forests by foreigners and making later large-scale agriculture possible. He urged that the French Canadians should become 'an industrial people without ceasing to be an agricultural people,' thus exploiting all their resources:

> A people is never safe when it leaves the resources of its country unexploited. If it does not exploit them itself, others will come to exploit them for it, and thus give themselves a pretext for intervening in its affairs. Or yet again an industrial oligarchy will arise, which is not less to be feared.[10]

But this warning of Bouchette was largely disregarded until Bourassa began his campaign against the Gouin government's administration of natural resources.

Chiefly at the instigation of Honoré Gervais, in 1907 the provincial government added an architectural course at the Polytechnique, and in 1910 a department of decorative arts, forerunner of the Ecole des Beaux-Arts. Then, too, came the opening of the Ecole des Hautes Etudes Commerciales for which Gervais had long agitated, and technical schools in Montreal and Quebec, aided by federal subsidies. The English industrialists of Shawinigan established a technical school there to meet their own need for trained workmen, and the Collège de Sherbrooke opened a two-year industrial course. The new technical schools suffered, however, from criticism on the grounds that they were not under the direction of the Church, and because of this criticism the commercial academies hesitated to introduce the industrial courses for which subsidies were offered by business. The province still lacked trade schools to fill the gap between primary and technical education, and most French Canadians remained unskilled workers, while the more lucrative posts of technicians and managers were filled by non-French Canadians who had the training the natives lacked.

The province's educational system continued to produce too many lawyers, journalists, and would-be politicians, while industrial development went on apace. The result was a dangerous division between English, English-Canadian, or American management and French-Canadian labor, which was soon exploited by the nationalists, who drew their following largely from the economically insecure intellectuals. J.-E.-A. Dubuc of Chicoutimi, Rodolphe Forget of Montreal and Quebec, and G.-E. Amyot of Quebec were almost the only great French-Canadian industrialists and capitalists of a period which saw a tremendous development of industry and finance in Quebec. The cooperative movement founded in 1902 grew slowly, chiefly among farmers, and the Lévis *Caisse Populaire* of Alphonse Desjardins, established in 1901, now mustered a capital of $40,000, with a record of 3,800 loans without a single loss.[11] Desjardins and his disciples, the Abbé Philibert Grondin, the Abbé Joseph Hallé, and Cyrille Vaillancourt, spread the cooperative gospel through the countryside, once they were convinced that the system worked. The fifty *caisses populaires* of 1911 became sixty-five by 1912. Bourassa, Monk, and Lemieux favored the movement; and Desjardins was received at Rideau Hall by Lord Grey, who was an enthusiastic disciple of the cooperative movement.

Intellectually Quebec was also making rapid advances. Its illiteracy rate, the highest in Canada in 1901, dropped during the decade from 17.71 per cent to 12.73 per cent, with the improvement most marked among the younger age groups.[12] In 1901 Quebec had 97 French newspapers for its 1,300,000 inhabitants, and 97 English papers for its 300,000 English inhabitants.[13] During the decade journalism progressed on one hand from pure politics to the discussion of general ideas by such able pens as those of Bourassa, Omer Héroux, Georges Pelletier, Olivar Asselin, and Jules Fournier; on the other it imitated American mass journalism so successfully that *La Presse* possessed the largest circulation of any Canadian daily. Beginning with the Ecole Littéraire de Montréal of 1895 poetry showed notable improvement, abandoning the romantic echoes and patriotic themes of the School of Quebec for more original and artistic expression of emotion.

The most brilliant talent uncovered by the Montreal group's *soirées* at the Château de Ramesay was that of Emile Nelligan, who owed his inspiration to Verlaine and Baudelaire, but achieved an orginal distinction. Unhappily Nelligan's feverish and unstable mind collapsed in 1901, when at 19 he had already produced some of French Canada's best verse.[14] One of the founders of the group, Gonzalve Desaulniers, only published his poems in 1930,[15] but exercised an influence in the tradition of Lamartine upon his contemporaries. The painter and poet Charles Gill's unfinished epic *Le Cap Eternité* was not published until after his death in 1919. The invalid Albert Lozeau published three books of lyrics and three collections of prose poems contributed to the press between 1907 and 1918. Albert Ferland turned from early preoccupation with sentimental themes to the hymning of the Canadian soil and forests in his *Le Canada Chanté* (1908–10). Blanche Lamontagne, Englebert Gallèze, and Alphonse Desilets developed rural themes in the language of the people, as Paul Morin, Guy Delahayne, and René Chopin followed the path of the French symbolists and concentrated on perfection of form.

History, like poetry, showed a marked development, with a more scientific spirit replacing the propagandist patriotism of earlier writers. Thomas Chapais, who also took an active role in politics and journalism, published admirable studies of *Jean Talon* (1904) and *Le Marquis de Montcalm* (1911), and then devoted himself to the history of the English regime from 1760 to 1867, which he taught at Laval and chronicled in eight volumes published from 1919–34. Though a Conservative in politics, Chapais wrote in the spirit of British Liberalism. Using primary source material and much more documentation than earlier writers, he produced an interpretation more favorable to the British. Alfred De Celles, long parliamentary librarian at Ottawa, published a study of the United States, followed by popular lives of Papineau and Cartier in French and English, and of Lafontaine and Laurier in French. A disciple of Laurier, De Celles wrote in the spirit of *bonne entente* between French and English. The Abbé Auguste Gosselin devoted himself to the history of the Church in Canada, while Mgr. Amedée Gosselin produced the first substantial study of education under the French regime. Canon H. A. Scott wrote an excellent history of the parish of *Notre-Dame de Sainte-Foy* (1902). Pierre-Georges Roy, founder of the *Bulletin des recherches historiques* (1895) and later provincial archivist, began his torrent of genealogical and antiquarian publications. Léon Gérin pioneered in the social sciences with his monographs in the tradition of Le Play on *L'Habitant de Saint Justin* (1898) and *Deux familles rurales de la rive sud du Saint-Laurent* (1909.) These admirable studies, produced while Gérin served as a translator at Ottawa, were completed and united with three others in his *Le type économique et social des Canadiens* (1937), when French Canada at last seriously concerned itself with social studies. The novel was a neglected form, with Laure Conan's *L'Oublié* (1902) and Dr. Ernest Choquette's experiments in psychological studies of the rural environment the most notable efforts of the period.

Mgr. Camille Roy established a critical foundation for Canadian literature with his studies published from 1902 onwards in *La Nouvelle France* and *Le Bulletin du Parler Français* and later assembled in book form in *Essais sur la littérature canadienne* (1907), *Nos Origines littéraires* (1909), and *Nouveaux Essais sur la littérature canadienne* (1914). Like Abbé Casgrain, he sought to foster the development of an independent Canadian literature, and in his enthusiasm for the cause erred on the side of leniency in criticizing such efforts as had been made. More critical if equally sympathetic studies of Canadian literature were produced by the Frenchman Charles ab der Halden in his *Etudes* (1904), and *Nouvelles Etudes de Littérature Canadienne Française* (1907), which represented a tightening of the cultural ties between France and Quebec. French newspapers and magazines circulated more widely in Quebec, and more French-Canadian students went abroad to study in Paris. With the French language under attack in Ontario and the West, the defensive *Société du Parler Français au Canada* was founded at Quebec in 1902 by Adjutor Rivard, who devoted his own studies to French-Canadian speech and folklore.

In general Quebec emphasized the Canadian part of the tradition, while more worldly Montreal, in closer contact with Paris and less suspicious of modern anti-clerical France, emphasized the French tradition. Such artists as the illustrator Henri Julien, the painter Suzor Côté, and the sculptors Philippe Hébert and Alfred Laliberté followed the French schools of the period in technique, while using Canadian subject matter. This revival and intensification of the French cultural tradition became dominant as Quebec was separated from the rest of Canada by political and social developments. It played its part in increasing the division between the two chief peoples of Canada.

2

The wedding of the nationalist and Conservative parties, achieved at the point of the electoral gun in 1911, was soon dissolved. Borden called upon Monk to choose the ministers representing Quebec, and Monk consulted with Bourassa, whom he urged to enter the cabinet. Bourassa refused office, both to prove his personal disinterestedness and in fear of Tory influence in the new Borden government; but urged Monk to accept if Borden would agree to a plebiscite on the naval question, relax the immigration policy, and redress the grievances of the minorities in the West. Monk understood that Borden accepted these conditions, and took the portfolio of public works.[16] Lavergne was offered a cabinet post, but declined in favor of Louis-Philippe Pelletier, who became postmaster-general. Lavergne blocked the desire of Rodolphe Forget for a place, and was consulted by Borden[17] on the remaining Quebec nominations: Bruno Nantel, minister of internal revenue; C. J. Doherty, minister of justice; and George Perley, minister without portfolio. None of the French Canadians represented the nationalist movement, and none exercised much influence in the cabinet. Monk, who would have made a good minister of justice, was lost in the post which fell to him; Pelletier was an old style politician who rejoiced in the rich patronage of his post; and Nantel was a staid nonentity. Pierre-Edouard Blondin, named deputy-speaker of the House, was the only nationalist to be rewarded for his part in the campaign which had defeated Laurier. The rest of the cabinet was not of a complection to make Quebec rest easy. Robert Rogers, Sifton's successor in Manitoba, became minister of the interior; Sam Hughes, minister of militia; and George Eulas Foster, minister of trade and commerce. Dr. Sproule, the leader of the Orangemen, became speaker of the House. In Philippe Landry, chosen president of the Senate, the nationalists counted an admirer of Bourassa and a friend of Lavergne, an old ultramontane of *Castor* tendencies. But the Senate, appointed for life, remained Liberal in majority. The need for alliance with the nationalists having passed, Hugh Graham gave orders for the *Star* to cease its support of Bourassa and to launch a new campaign for Canadian participation in the defence of the empire.[18]

In his public appearances after the election Bourassa asserted his independence and his readiness to judge the government by its acts. He called once more for a plebiscite on the naval question. His new friendship with C. H. Cahan, who replaced the late Goldwin Smith as a sympathetic English-Canadian ally, led Bourassa to support Cahan's principle that Canada should make no contribution to imperial defence without a part in the government of the empire. But Bourassa's followers wanted no participation in imperial affairs under any conditions, while Borden's supporters favored contribution without any consideration in exchange. While the candidates supported by Bourassa in the election transferred their allegiance to Borden, the nationalist chief deplored the ruthless use of patronage by the new government. At Saint-Hyacinthe on December 1, 1911, he presented the nationalist program: emancipation from party spirit; no participation in imperial wars but concentration on internal development and defence of Canada; an appeal to the people for approval of any change in this policy. He sketched out a theory of participation in imperial expenses in exchange for a share in imperial government, but aroused no enthusiasm for it. Once more he argued that he was not anti-British, and merely sought to awaken British pride in the French Canadians: 'The ambition of my life, which has sustained and animated me in my battles, when I was isolated, when the *Rouges* did not love me and the *Bleus* mistrusted me, is to make my compatriots understand that they ought to observe in their provinces, with regard to minorities, the great lesson of justice, tolerance, and charity.'[19] Bourassa soon found occasion to assert his independence and his doctrine by attacking Sam Hughes for his imperialist declarations and for purging French Canadians from the militia department. In its final issue of the year *Le Devoir* asserted his independence in regard to the new government.

Questions on which Bourassa, like his grandfather Papineau, might exercise his talent for opposition soon arose in parliament. In a series of articles in *Le Devoir* from February 1 to 21, 1912—reprinted in pamphlet form in English—he discussed imperial problems, calling for a repeal of the Navy Act. He took advantage of Sir Edward Grey's declaration on January 29, urging a policy of non-interference in the imperial ventures of other powers, and of Lord Charles Beresford's arguments in *The Betrayal* against recent naval policies, to support his own stand against the Navy Act and to urge its repeal. The revelation after fifteen years of the Colonial Defence Committee's memorandum of 1896 on imperial defence—it was laid before the House in January 1912—also furnished justification for the nationalist position. He concluded:

Let the Navy Act be repealed.
Let our militia be thoroughly reformed.
Let the defence of our harbours and shores be organized.

Above all, let our system of transportation, by land and by water, be completed without a minute's loss. While we are talking 'Dreadnoughts' and 'Niobes', populations, drawn to Western Canada by alluring advertisements, are clamouring for the means of selling and shipping their wheat. If our politicians lose their time in endeavouring to displace Imperial statesmen and save the British fleet and the motherland in spite of the British people, they may suddenly awaken from their magnificent dreams of Imperialism, and be confronted with serious troubles occasioned in Canada by their neglect to secure Canada's economical safety and national unity.

Let Canada be looked after first. Not only is it the country which Providence has given to all Canadians; it is also *the part of the Empire* committed to our care by the Crown of England and Imperial Parliament. If in order to do other people's work we neglect our own, neither the British nor the Australians will come and help us in setting our house in order.[20]

In the House Sévigny presented a motion for the repeal of the Navy Act, and in the Senate Choquette and another dissident Liberal moved in a similar sense. But Sévigny's motion stood at the end of a long list, with Borden showing no anxiety to consider it.

The government found a more pressing problem in the annexation of the Territory of Keewatin to Manitoba, in fulfilment of an election promise to Robert Rogers. Though there was only a small population in the region, it included Catholics among both whites and Indians, and separate schools existed. Once again the question of the right of the minority to separate schools was raised. The Vicar Apostolic of Keewatin, Mgr. Ovide Charlebois, O.M.I., and Archbishop Langevin of Saint-Boniface insisted that the existence of these schools should be guaranteed. Rogers and Sam Hughes, in the tradition of Sifton, opposed in the cabinet Doherty and Nantel, who supported the schools. Borden yielded to Western pressure and the measure presented by the government on February 19 carried no guarantee of the educational rights of the minority.

Debate on the Keewatin question coincided with that on a bill presented by Edward Arthur Lancaster of Ontario, invalidating any provincial or canonical law against mixed marriages performed by any authorized person. The measure was the fruit of agitation against the application in Quebec of the papal *Ne Temere* decree by annulment of the Hébert-Clouâtre marriage. The Catholic thesis was that the provincial law merely gave civil force to a religious marriage; while the Protestants held that the *Ne Temere* decree had no civil force.[21] The government appealed to the Supreme Court to decide the question. The apostolic delegate conferred in Montreal with the archbishops of Canada and adopted the position that the federal authorities should not interfere with the provincial law in the case of the *Ne Temere* affair. But he decided not to press opposition to the Keewatin decision, to the relief of Quebec members of the government. Meanwhile the Superior Court of Quebec heard the Hébert-Clouâtre case anew, and decided that the *Ne Temere* decree had no force in law, but only on the consciences of Catholics. In the provincial legislature Bourassa protested against federal intervention in the atter, and urged the Quebec government to defend provincial rights hen the case was heard by the Supreme Court. Gouin agreed, and ppointed Aimé Geoffrion, who had served on the Alaska Boundary ommission, and Robert Cooper Smith, like Geoffrion a law pro- ssor at McGill, to represent the province.[22]

While the *Ne Temere* question aroused agitation chiefly in English anada, where John Ewart labored in vain to clarify the question in nother 'Kingdom Paper',[23] the Keewatin question stirred Quebec. he two Western prelates were both natives of the Montreal district, nd Archbishop Langevin was the idol of the A.C.J.C., which aunched petitions in favor of the Keewatin schools. The Quebec embers warned Borden that feeling was aroused in Quebec, but orden refused to hold back a measure urgently desired by the Manitoba government and to reopen the school question, 'which the rench Canadians had settled in 1896, by voting for Mr. Laurier, gainst their own interest.'[24] Lavergne visited Ottawa to muster he opposition, and found only Senator Landry and young P.-E. amarche willing to make a fight against the bill. In the cabinet the uggestion that the four Catholic Quebec ministers might resign on he issue had no great effect, and Borden argued that the Roblin overnment of Manitoba had promised concessions on the order of he Laurier-Greenway agreement. Monk was skeptical, after 1896, f Quebec's real interest in the minorities of the West;[25] Pelletier did ot believe in the effect of a mass resignation and was not willing to e more intransigent than the hierarchy. The apostolic delegate xpressed his willingness to accept the law, accompanied by a written guarantee of concessions.

The Liberals were delighted by the division of their opponents, nd taunted the nationalists with their failure to secure repeal of he Navy Act and separate schools in Keewatin. Choquette's motion n the Senate in favor of repeal of the Navy Act was crushed by the eclaration of the government leader that the administration would ake no action on the question during the session, pending consulta- ion with the Admiralty and maturing of a new proposal. Laurier noved an amendment opposing the 'unjust conditions' of the Kee- vatin bill, and Lamarche pleaded with the French Conservatives o support the amendment. But only five of the rank and file voted gainst the government. Lamarche defended his vote in a moving peech which won admiration from the English members, but Monk nd Pelletier eschewed any revival of the Manitoba school question. The bill was about to enter upon its third reading when Bourassa roke his previous silence upon the question at a meeting at the Monument National in Montreal on March 9. He was supported nly by Lavergne and Garceau, all the nationalist M.P.s having een rallied to support of the government.

Bourassa spoke for three hours, first sketching the history of educational legislation in the North-West and repeating the arguments he had adopted in 1905 in the case of Saskatchewan and Alberta. Then he criticized the government's defenders. Hushing the disapproval expressed by the crowd for Monk, he criticized his friend's stand more in sorrow than in anger, citing the opinions of Blake and C. H. Cahan against Monk's legal stand. With more vigor he disposed of Pelletier's speech in favor of the bill. He emphasized that the Manitoba government had given no written guarantee to protect minority rights, and he expressed his disillusionment with the Laurier-Greenway agreement. He argued on historical grounds that only statutory guarantees had lasting value. As for the argument that the hierarchy had not spoken against the new law he proclaimed: 'It is not the business of bishops and priests to make laws, to support them, and to apply them.'[26] He paid tribute to the bishops and to their authority in religious questions, but quoted Daniel O'Connell's saying, 'I take my theology at Rome, but I take my politics at home.'

Then he evoked the spirit of Confederation: the duality of race and language guaranteed by equality before the law. If Confederation were to be respected, the French Canadians had to fight always and everywhere for the maintenance of their rights and of all minority rights. 'And we should not pursue this fight by invoking the authority of the Church, nor by appealing to the voice of our blood, but in the name and with the strength of our rights as British subjects, of taxpayers of our country.'[27] He warned: 'If the Canadian constitution is to last, if the Canadian Confederation is to be maintained, the narrow attitude towards minorities which increasingly manifests itself in the English provinces must disappear, and we must return to the original spirit of the alliance.' He described the French Canadians as a rampart against annexation to the States or separation from England: 'We are as British as any other race in Canada. We are not British by blood and language, but we are British by reason and tradition.'[28] British institutions were the heritage of the French Canadians from the Norman conquest of England, as well as from the English conquest of Canada:

To these institutions no one is more attached than we; but we are not submissive dogs; we are not valets; and after a hundred and fifty years of good and loyal service to the institutions that we love, to a Crown that we have learned to respect, we deserve better than to be considered like the savages of the old reservations and to be told: 'Remain in Quebec, continue to stagnate in ignorance, you are at home there; but elsewhere you must become English.'

No, we have the right to be French in language; we have the right to be Catholics in faith; we have the right to be free by the constitution.

> We are Canadians before all; and we have the right to be as British as anyone. And we have the right to enjoy these rights throughout the whole expanse of Confederation.[29]

He called upon his audience to invoke these rights and make its voice heard by supporting resolutions calling upon parliament to safeguard the rights of the minority in Keewatin. When a standing vote was taken, the entire audience supported the resolutions, despite Bourassa's plea for respect of difference of opinion.

Seeing Cahan in the hall, Bourassa called upon him to speak. Cahan rebuked the French Canadians for expecting the English to defend French-Canadian rights more vigorously than their own representatives had done, citing the stand taken by Quebec's representatives in 1896 and at the present time. If the French Canadians tried to abolish the English schools of Quebec, the whole English population would protest by acts as well as words. 'But you, people of Quebec, you are content to come and hear fine speeches, and then return to your homes without doing anything, often disposed to belie by your acts the words you have applauded with frenzy . . . If you do not succeed in making yourselves respected, you have only to blame yourselves and your chiefs, in whom you cannot have faith when it is a question of your national interests.'[30] Lavergne thanked Cahan for emphasizing what Bourassa and he himself had preached for seven years: that lack of energy was the worst enemy of the French Canadians. He said that the question of schools was not settled anywhere, and if one day it was necessary to provoke a crisis, 'We shall know how to prove that we are not helots or pariahs in this land which is our own.'[31]

The meeting greatly stimulated the movement of protest against the Keewatin bill. John Boyd appealed to the press of the entire country in favor of the minority, while the *Star* warned the majority against abusing their strength and leaving the minority with the lasting impression that they had been wronged. But the amendment jointly presented by A.-A. Mondou and P.-E. Lamarche, guaranteeing minority rights, was defeated by 160 to 24 votes—seven Conservatives and seventeen Liberals. The bill was passed by the house on March 12. In the Senate the resistance headed by Philippe Landry and John Costigan was quickly overcome. Once more Quebec added another defeat to the long list compiled since 1867. The younger generation, with its newly awakened national pride, did not forget the fact. And Bourassa became more determined than ever to remain free of party ties while undertaking the formation of a new national mentality.[32]

Having outraged Quebec feeling in the matter of Keewatin, the Borden government appeased it by authorizing the annexation of Ungava, once part of Rupert's Land, to the province. This step which nearly doubled Quebec's area and extended its northern limits to Hudson Strait, represented an old dream of Mercier supported by the Gouin government in 1909, and arranged by Gouin and Laurier, though it was carried through by the Borden government. Quebec gained little for the moment, for this New Quebec was a deserted wilderness known only to a few Indians, Eskimos, and fur traders. But it was believed to contain forest, mineral, and water-power resources which might later be developed. The annexation of Ungava chiefly benefited Lomer Gouin, who now appealed to the people on the platform that his government 'had made Quebec richer, better educated, and greater.'[33] Thanks in part to a reaction in favor of Laurier and the Liberals after the nationalist-Conservative alliance had failed to realize its promises, the Gouin government retained it majority of forty-five in the elections of May 15. Lavergne and Jean Prévost were the only nationalists to be re-elected, and Lavergne's majority was considerably reduced. Bourassa had refused to run, and had gone to Europe, where he spent most of his time in France. The Liberal press proclaimed the end of nationalism, and even *Le Devoir* admitted, upon the occasion of a banquet in honor of Laurier at Montreal, that he was still 'the great figure of Canadian politics.'[34]

3

While the Supreme Court decided that the federal government could not supplant the matrimonial legislation of Quebec (though recognizing that the *Ne Temere* decree had no civil effect) and the federal government took an appeal to the Privy Council, the province was preoccupied with preparations for the first Congress of the French Language at Quebec, from June 24 to June 30. This event celebrated the tenth anniversary of the *Société du Parler Français au Canada*, founded by the Abbé Lortie and Adjutor Rivard, who had also collaborated with Bishop Paul-Eugène Roy, the auxiliary of Quebec, in the establishment of *L'Action Sociale*. Bishop Roy's program of Catholic Action included defence of the French language and of national traditions, as well as unionization of the workers, and he wished to assemble in a single organization all the Catholic social movements of the province. But the age-old rivalry of Montreal and Quebec had asserted itself with the foundation of the Ecole Sociale Populaire in Montreal in 1911, under the direction of the Jesuit Père Hudon and Arthur Saint-Pierre. The clergy had shown a growing distrust of the international unions and had become partisans of the Catholic syndicate movement launched at Quebec and Chicoutimi in 1902. The Fédération Ouvrière of Chicoutimi, founded in 1902, took on new life in March 1912 when Bishop

Labrecque recommended that all diocesan social and labor movements should be grouped within it.[35] The congress was to sanction this trend and the campaigns of the A.C.J.C. in favor of the French language, and to consolidate the efforts of the outlying French-Canadian groups in defence of their educational and language rights.

The assembly organized by the Abbé Lortie, Rivard, and Bishop Roy himself was a national gathering. There was a contingent from the West headed by Archbishop Langevin, another from Ontario led by Senator Belcourt and Judge Cousineau; an Acadian group headed by Senator Poirier; and Franco-Americans led by Bishop Guertin. There was a delegate from Louisiana, and a French mission headed by the academician Etienne Lamy. The apostolic delegate and most of the Quebec bishops were on hand. To greet the guests Quebec's notables assembled in force, without distinction of party: Laurier, Gouin, the Lieutenant-Governor Sir François Langelier, Senator Landry, Thomas Chapais, Sir Adolphe Routhier, Boucher de la Bruère, the superintendent of public instruction, and a host of ministers, M.P.'s, and other French-Canadian leaders.

Archbishop Langevin opened the congress with the ringing declaration: 'We do not recognize the right of anyone to stop the French Canadians at the border of Quebec and to say: "Beyond this point you are not at home." We are at home everywhere in Canada.'[36] The French consul, C.-E. Bonin, won an ovation, as did Lamy and the Abbé Thellier de Poncheville, who stressed Quebec's bonds with France. Senator Dandurand and the young Abbé Lionel Groulx differed widely in the ideas they expressed, but Dandurand was sympathetic to Groulx's concluding slogan, '*France quand-même*.' A statue of Mercier by a French sculptor was unveiled, reviving the memory of one who had sought to link Quebec with France once more. The Franco-Ontarian spokesmen won warm applause, although Bishop Roy vetoed Père Charlebois' plan to announce to the congress that the Ontario government had just decided to restrict French teaching to the point of virtual suppression. Senator Belcourt exercized a moderating influence by urging that Quebec's support for the minorities should not draw down reprisals upon them. Mgr. Paquet invoked theological support for the preservation of the mother tongue and identified the French language with the Christian apostolate, thus supporting Bourassa's argument at Notre-Dame in 1910.

Bourassa, just returned from France, spoke at the close of the congress on '*La langue française et l'avenir de notre race*.' He treated not only the role of the French language in the survival of the French Canadians, but also its role in the relations between the French Canadians and the other races of America. Citing the example of the Irish and the Scots, he declared that 'the conservation of the language is absolutely necessary for the conservation of the race its genius, its character and its temperament.'[37] If the French Canadians lost their language, 'we would perhaps be mediocre Englishmen, passable Scots, or bad Irishmen, but we would not be true Canadians.' He maintained the moral right of the French Canadians to use their mother tongue from Halifax to Vancouver because of their defence of Canada in 1775 and 1812, their fight for British rights in 1837, and the work of Lafontaine and the French fathers of Confederation. If the two languages were official in Canada, both had the right to exist in every aspect of Canadian public life. There were two ways to preserve the French language in Canada: through the schools, despite those who betrayed the spirit of Confederation; and through nourishment drawn from the source in France.

Bourassa discounted fear of modern France, and warned that 'if for fear of poison one ceased to eat, one died of hunger, which is just as sure a way of going to the cemetery.'[38] In French literature there was much remedy for poison, as well as the poison itself. Then there was no more danger that the French Canadians would become less Canadian by seeking intellectual stimulation in France than of the Americans becoming English by drawing their culture from England. But he urged that the French Canadian's language should 'give birth to a Canadian literature; it should serve us in writing and reading the history of Canada; it should teach us to draft and plead Canadian laws; and to make us understand the spirit and the letter of the Canadian laws and constitution'—with 'Canadian' understood in the broad sense. 'We should, with the aid of this perfected and living French language, search out the origins of English and American civilization; we should study the history of England and the United States, we should learn to know the English and the Celts better, and to make ourselves better known by them.'[39] He warned of the double danger of isolation from and of fusion with the other races of Canada. French culture held no more dangers to Catholicism than English, the language of Protestantism, of materialism, and of 'the most enthusiastic worshippers of the golden calf.'

Despite Dalton McCarthy's arguments, bilingualism was not a danger to national unity. The French Canadians had been charged with being more French than Catholic, but they believed that their language was the human element most essential to the conservation of their faith. He called the preservation of the French language 'the sole true moral guarantee of the unity of the Canadian Confederation and of the maintenance of British institutions in Canada,'[40] in warning of the penetration of Americanism, articularly in Toronto and Winnipeg. The national school prin-iple was borrowed by the West from the States. If the anglicizers ucceeded in their projects, they would make Americans and not nglishmen of the French Canadians, who then would have no more eason to remain British.[41] French groups in all the Western rovinces would be the best obstacles to Americanization, for they vould not share American ideals.

Mentioning the protest of an Ontario Anglican against the mportation into that province of the 'France of Louis XIV,' Bourassa pointed out that Quebec had adopted the civil code more han fifty years ago, while the English Canadians had remained con-ent with the outmoded laws of England; that Quebec had freedom f religion and worship while England still discussed exempting he non-conformists of Wales from payment of the tithe; that Quebec had abolished seigneurial tenure sixty years ago, while in England a third of the people starved because the great landowners held half the country; that Quebec had enfranchised the Jews before England did the Catholics. While Ontario worried about imaginary perils, English Canada was becoming in habits, language, and mentality more American than if reciprocity had made it an adjunct of the United States.' Knowledge of French was demanded by Canada's growing world trade; its universality would help Canada to the heights of civilization.

In an eloquent peroration Bourassa recalled his recent presence at the beatification of Joan of Arc at Rouen, and urged:

Let us ask of Joan of Arc that she consummate the alliance between he conquered and the conquerors of other days, and that she permit that her tongue, this tongue so beautiful and clear, which enabled her to unknit the subtleties of casuists and repel treason and cowardice, that his French language preserved by us, the French of America, instead of being an element of discord between the two great races should become on the contrary the vehicle of the most beautiful and noble thoughts, generous thoughts, thoughts of union, by which Anglo-Canadians and French Canadians, Saxons and Celts, should cause to triumph in the northern part of the American continent the best traditions of the two great races which have given birth to the nation of Canada.[42]

Though the congress adopted resolutions favouring the mainten-ance and spread of the use of French language in the home, school, commerce, and public life, Bishop Roy discouraged a proposal by a young disciple of Lavergne, supported by Senator Choquette, for a message of sympathy to the Franco-Ontarians in their struggle for their schools. The congress took no significant action, but by rallying the forces of French Canada it supplied evidence of their vitality. It also revealed the important part played by the clergy as national leaders of the French Canadians. An interesting light o the ultramontanism of French-Canadian Catholicism was supplie by criticism of the modernism of the French Abbé Thellier d Poncheville by Paul Tardivel of *Le Vérité* and the Abbé J.-G.-A D'Amours of *L'Action Sociale*.

4

While French Canada mustered its forces at Quebec, Borde had gone to England to consult the imperial authorities on th naval question. He had sought the company of Monk, but the latte refused to go; so the ministerial delegation consisted of Doherty Hazen, and Pelletier. They were subjected to the usual imperialis pressure, and on Borden's first day in London Winston Churchill the First Lord of the Admiralty, warned him of the pressing dange of German aggression. Borden had already been in correspondenc with Churchill, who had offered his assistance in drafting a Canadia naval policy.[43] Borden also conferred with Asquith on the questio of Canada's having a share in imperial policy in exchange for it naval collaboration. He visited the fleet at Spithead and attended meeting of the Defence Committee at which Sir Edward Grey spok on the foreign relations of the empire, and Churchill again stresse the German menace and urged Canadian collaboration.

A series of conferences at the Admiralty then began, which wer interrupted by a brief visit to Paris, where the French governmen besought the Canadians to support the *Entente cordiale*, upon whic France relied for protection against the German menace. Afte Borden's return to England and during his visits to various ship building yards, Churchill prepared a memorandum on the nava emergency, which was revised at Borden's request and finall took form in the dual shape of one secret memorandum for use i the Canadian cabinet and another which could be submitted t the Canadian parliament.[44] Earlier, in exchange for Borden' willingness to commit Canada to a naval program, Asquith modifie his stand of 1911 and spoke in parliament of 'the duty of making suc response as we can to the Dominions' obviously reasonable appea that they should be entitled to be heard in the determination of th policy and the direction of imperial affairs.'[45] Borden conferred wit Asquith, Grey, Harcourt, and Walter Long on how this might b achieved. But though the British pressed for speed in naval contri butions, they urged that imperial representation should not b hurried.

During Borden's extended visit to England, the imperialist pres in Canada, headed by the *Star*, made much of the German menac and urged Canada to save England. *Le Devoir* took a skeptica attitude toward the danger, maintaining that if it were not wholly imaginary, it was exaggerated by the jingoes. Bourassa commented:

> It seems absurd that Canada should and ought to 'save' England and France, preserve the neutrality of Belgium, annihilate the German fleet in the North Sea, and hold Austria and Italy in check in the Mediterranean, when so much remains to be done to put her own house in order, and years of intense effort and the expenditure of fabulous sums are required to complete, on her own territory, the essential works with which England has been provided for centuries.[46]

According to Bourassa, Canada's true danger was from American economic, intellectual, and moral penetration. In a series of articles which appeared in *Le Devoir* from July 16 to 26 and were reprinted in pamphlet form in French and English,[47] he dealt with this danger in reply to the *Star*, which had raised the 'spectre of annexation' by the United States if Britain fell before Germany. He pointed out that the French Canadian, with his rights restricted to Quebec as an Indian's were to his reservation, and with his Church less attacked in the States than in Canada, was now more disposed to favor annexation than ever before. Under the Tenth Amendment of the American Constitution, Quebec would enjoy more autonomy in the American union than under the Canadian constitution. Bourassa stated that this was neither a plea for annexation nor an argument that the French Canadians were ready to accept it. He professed to be 'still more British and less American than the majority of my fellow citizens, either of British or of French origin.'[48] But such was the impression he had formed of a growing sentiment. He recalled Elgin's statement that assimilative efforts might americanize the French Canadians, but would never anglicize them. The French Canadian was still essentially Canadian and profoundly British, but would remain the latter only if the English Canadians put Canada's interests first and treated the French Canadians as equal partners. He pointed out to the English Canadians that they were already American 'by your language, your nasal accent, your common slang, your dress, your daily habits; by the Yankee literature with which your homes and clubs are flooded; by your yellow journals and their rantings; by your loud and intolerant patriotism; by your worship of gold, snobbery and titles.'[49] Most American of all was the principle of the national school. He also deplored adoption of corrupt American political practices, American economic penetration of Canada by both capital and labor, and discrimination against French Canadians in the West and Ontario. To this indictment of the English Canadians he added a confession of partial French-Canadian responsibility for the decline of politics and journalism to a low level and the degradation of public spirit.

The English press promptly accused Bourassa of advocating annexation and illustrated the charge with incomplete quotations from his articles. His friend Cahan protested, in a letter published in the *Montreal Gazette* on August 3, that 'Mr. Bourassa, who is thoroughly Canadian and British in sentiment, and who, of all Canadians, is most antagonistic to those regrettable tendencies which so frequently find expression in the social, political and commercial life of the United States . . . who so frankly expounds and so fearlessly condemns all tendencies which might possibly lead to annexation, should be so falsely and flagrantly misrepresented and so boldly and even brutally censured as an alleged advocate of annexation to the United States.'[50] But Bourassa had been represented as a traitor in New Brunswick, Ontario, Manitoba, and Alberta, while the *Quebec Chronicle* accused him of a desire to drive the English out of Quebec.

Bourassa's habit of mustering in the scholastic tradition the arguments for and against the policy he was discussing lent itself to this sort of misrepresentation, as did his sudden changes of opinion. When asked by the *Canadian Courier* whether he favored imperial federation, to which he had lately seemed to incline, he approved it in theory but denounced its impracticality. And the same Bourassa who insisted upon the necessity of drawing cultural support from France denounced *La Patrie's* campaign for aid to Britain as aid to her ally France: 'The French Canadians are no more ready to exhaust their resources for France than for any other country.'[51] *La Patrie's* campaign, soon taken up by the *Star*, was instigated by Sir Rodolphe Forget, who derived much capital for his enterprises from France and sought a place in the Borden government. But *Le Devoir* assigned it to bribery by armament manufacturers in search of contracts.

When Borden returned from England on September 6, Monk was already under pressure from *Le Devoir* to maintain his stand against a navy or to resign. At a Montreal banquet in honor of the first anniversary of the triumph of 1911, Borden spoke vaguely of calling parliament in November to discuss imperial defence questions, and said that with cooperation in defence must come cooperation in policy.[52] At another banquet in Toronto the following night, he subordinated the theme of Canada's great heritage and future, which he had stressed at Montreal, to that of the greater heritage and future of the empire. He expressed the view that the people of Canada would come as one man to the defence of the empire if the need arose: 'For the preservation of its unity, for the preservation of its power and influence, for the maintenance of its work, the Motherland and the Dominions are one and are indivisible.'[53] Bourassa took alarm at the possibility of the quick passage of an imperialist measure in the midst of the German scare aroused by the press, and warned that its authors would be denounced. Monk was warned that he was obliged 'in honor and conscience, first to demand a plebiscite on any policy of imperial contribution, then to resign from the cabinet and fight against this policy, until the majority of the Canadian people had decided to accept it.'[54] Borden exercized pressure on Monk to remain in the cabinet; but when the latter's insistence on a plebiscite was overruled and the government's proposal of an emergency contribution of £35,000,000 to Britain for naval purposes was announced, Monk resigned on October 18, on the grounds that such a measure, without consultation of the people, violated his electoral promises and went beyond the scope of the constitution. Borden sought to modify the terms of Monk's resignation, and induced him to keep it secret.

Meanwhile Laurier held two meetings in Quebec, minimizing the emergency and taunting the nationalists for their failure to keep their promises. Monk's resignation was promptly rumored in the press. Despite the fact that the young nationalists of Quebec were ready to hail him as a hero, he kept his promise to Borden and went to the States for a rest. Meanwhile the Liberals won a by-election at Sorel on October 24, though by an indecisive margin. Louis Coderre of Montreal was chosen to replace Monk in the cabinet, and the by-election was set for November 19. Borden carefully prepared the ground for his naval proposal, submitting it to a press conference and stressing the emergency as seen by the Admiralty. He passed on the secret Admiralty memorandum to Laurier, and held a special caucus of the Quebec members, most of whom approved the proposal, although some of them declared themselves pledged to vote against it. Laurier decided not to oppose a Liberal to Coderre; but Lavergne and his friends supported an independent candidate. Monk broke his silence to explain to one of the independent's sponsors that he had resigned because the government refused a plebiscite and that he favored an expression of the people's will in this election. This confirmed the suspicions of Bourassa, who opposed Coderre and all those who had accepted a policy contrary to their engagements. But on November 19 Coderre was elected by the solid English vote of Westmount, after winning the three French quarters of the district by a slight majority over his opponent. The death of nationalism was once more proclaimed by *Le Canada*, *Le Soleil*, and *La Patrie*.[55]

Meanwhile the educational situation in Ontario, with its growing French population in the Ottawa Valley, Northern Ontario, and the Windsor-Essex area,[56] had complicated the situation by arousing racial feeling. The Provincial Department of Education had adopted in June 1912 and amended in August 1913 a regulation (Instruction No. 17), which imposed English as the sole language of instruction in the elementary schools, with minor exceptions, an placed the bilingual Catholic schools under English Protestant in spectors. The study of French was confined to an hour a day.[57] Thi step was taken as a result of Dr. F. W. Merchant's highly critica report on the English-French schools of the Province.[58]

The French members of the Ottawa Separate Schools Commission under the leadership of Samuel Genest, immediately protested. *L Devoir*, *L'Action Sociale*, and *Le Soleil* (which had no objection t embarrassing a Conservative government) supported the Franco Ontarians. Senator Landry requested Borden's intervention wit the Ontario government, and raised the question of federal disavowa of the legislation. But no action was taken by the Ontario authoritie to halt enforcement of the new regulations. Bourassa sent a question naire on Regulation 17 to a number of distinguished English Cana dians of Quebec, and their replies, generally recognizing the injustic done to the Franco-Ontarians, were published in *Le Devoir*.[59] Bu Ontario remained determined to realize a program reminiscent o that of the Protestant Protective Association, and feeling mounted s high there that Laurier made a concession to it by not opposin Coderre, lest the ethnic tension be heightened by a campaig against the naval proposal in Quebec.

Before Borden introduced his proposal on December 5, calling fo an emergency contribution of $35,000,000 which would enabl Great Britain to build three dreadnoughts in a situation too grav for the delays demanded to build ships in Canada, A.-A. Mondo moved a resolution, revised by Bourassa,[60] refusing all contributio while Canada was barred from imperial councils. The motio was crushed after Borden and Laurier had made professions o loyalism and the house had sung 'God Save the King'. It was sup ported only by P.-E. Lamarche and two other French-Canadia Conservatives.

Borden argued that he sought to combine cooperation wit autonomy: 'When Great Britain no longer assumes sole responsi bility for defence upon the high seas, she can no longer undertake t assume sole responsibility for and sole control of foreign policy which is closely, vitally and constantly associated in that defence i which the Dominions participate.'[61] This principle had bee accepted by the leaders of both parties in England during his visit The crucial situation called for immediate aid to Britain, but i Canada later established a navy, the three dreadnoughts might b recalled to form part of it. The question of a permanent navy woul be referred to the people. But Borden indicated that he had bee won over by Churchill to the Admiralty policy of outright contri bution by stressing the difficulties and expense of building up Canadian Navy. The Admiralty promised to construct small vessel ı Canada, stimulating the shipbuilding industry and justifying anada's outlay for the dreadnoughts. For the present, the British overnment would welcome the presence of a Canadian minister at .eetings of the Imperial Defence Committee and would consult ith him on important questions of foreign policy. Borden conuded with an evocation of the coming storm in Europe and the eed for immediate action:

> Almost unaided, the Motherland, not for herself alone, but for us as ell, is sustaining the burden of a vital Imperial duty, and confronting an ermastering necessity of national existence. Bringing the best assistance .at we may in the urgency of the moment, we come thus to her aid, in ken of our determination to protect and ensure the safety and integrity this Empire, and of our resolve to defend on sea as well as on land our ıg, our honour and our heritage.[62]

orden won an ovation, and the House adjourned after singing 'God ave the King' and 'Rule Britannia.'

In his reply on December 12 Laurier rejected the idea that ngland was in need of immediate aid. She was rich and not in anger. 'If there were an emergency, if England were in danger—), I shall not use that expression, but simply say if England were ı trial with one or two great European powers, my right honorable iend could come and ask us not for $35,000,000 but twice, three mes, or four times $35,000,000. We should put all the resources Canada at the disposal of England; there would not be a single .ssentient voice.'[63] But the Admiralty's memorandum showed ıere was no immediate or prospective danger, though the armament .ce in Europe had compelled England to concentrate her forces in ome waters. Laurier claimed that everything in the memorandum ıd been discussed four years ago, when it had been agreed that ıe best way for Canada to discharge her duty was not by contri- .ition but by the creation of a Canadian Navy. Borden had oandoned this stand, but the Liberals had not. The Conservatives ıd been forced to take a new position because of their 'unholy liance' with the nationalists. He taunted the Conservatives with .eir willingness to give to England only 'two or three dreadnoughts, be paid for by Canada, but to be equipped, maintained and anned by England,' save for such Canadian officers as might olunteer to serve on those ships:

> Oh, ye Tory jingoes, is that the amount of sacrifice you are prepared to ake? You are ready to furnish admirals, rear-admirals, commodores, .ptains, officers of all grades, plumes, feathers, and gold lace; but you ave it to England to supply the bone and sinews on board those ships. ou say that these ships will bear Canadian names. That will be the

only thing Canadian about them. You hire somebody else to do yo work; in other words, you are ready to do anything except the fightin Is that, sir, the true policy? It is a hybrid policy; it is a cross betwe jingoism and nationalism.[64]

He urged that the Canadian people would not be content witho a contribution of money and men as well, as provided in the Lauri naval plan. He accused Borden of having abandoned the idea of Canadian Navy before he went to England.

Once more Laurier asserted that 'when England is at war, we a at war; but it does not follow, because we are at war, that we a involved in the conflict.' Canada would decide as to whether h forces would take part, if she had her own navy. The governmen proposal settled nothing; it provided no permanent policy, and l foresaw a succession of contributions, which would leave no tra behind them. Borden said that a permanent policy must wait upo a voice in questions of peace or war, but Laurier found objections that plan. Consultation with all the dominions would be unwield and would involve Canada in many questions in which she had interest. To Borden's argument that the empire's existence hu upon the dominions' having a voice in imperial affairs, he oppos his own convictions:

The firm basis of the British Empire, is, next to the British Crown, t local autonomy of the different dependencies; that is to say, their worki out of their own destinies to the central end of Empire. The Crown is t great bond, the cement which binds together the scattered contine over the whole world. The Crown is a purely sentimental bond; but th bond, though purely sentimental, had proven itself stronger than arm or navies; has shown itself to be equal to all occasions. I do not believe t Empire is in danger; I do not believe it can be cemented by the mea suggested by my right honourable friend. I believe the relations of t different parts of the Empire to the Mother country are not perfect, b that essentially they are perfectible. You can discuss problems of improv ment; there is no occasion to discuss problems of existence.[65]

He concluded by moving an amendment in favor of the constructi of two fleet units, to be stationed on the Atlantic and the Pacif rather than a direct contribution of money or ships to Britain. short he stood on the terms of the Navy Act of 1910, and Bord judged that his rival hoped to provoke an appeal to the people the two proposals.[66] On this occasion Laurier displayed his c powers and won an ovation. Again the House sang 'God Save t King.'

Bourassa accused Laurier of wishing to add a human tribute the tribute of gold requested by Borden. He predicted that t principle, 'When England is at war, Canada is at war,' would lead to the sending of a hundred thousand or more young Canadians to die on foreign battlefields. He fought both measures, and published the names of M.P.s elected with nationalist support, challenging them not to support either project without a plebiscite. But party discipline was effective, and Bourassa found himself attacked by both Conservative and Liberal organs. Pressure was even brought to bear on the backers of *Le Devoir*.[67]

Meanwhile the debate continued vigorously in the House until adjournment on December 18. Both parties took advantage of the holiday recess to expound their policies to the people. In Quebec the Borden spokesmen explained that by the contribution of $35,000,000 Canada could avoid the construction of a navy and rid herself of the whole question once and for all; while in Ontario the measure was presented as a temporary one, since in the emergency England could not wait for the creation of a Canadian Navy. Laurier's supporters criticized this 'tribute,' without the promised consultation of the people, as an abdication of autonomy. Lavergne privately urged Monk to resume his seat in parliament, where only Lamarche was left to fight the measure on nationalist grounds. Bourassa deplored the rivalry between the two parties to be 'the most "loyal," the most "jingo," the most "imperialist,"' without regard to Canada's interests.[68] On February 13 Laurier's amendment and that of Alphonse Verville in favor of a plebiscite on the gift to Britain were defeated by straight party votes, with all the Quebec Conservatives siding with the government. Borden's resolution in favor of his proposal were carried by a majority of thirty-two, with seven French Canadians breaking party lines. Once more the House broke into 'Rule Britannia,' 'God Save the King,' and 'O Canada.'

During the debate on the second reading Joseph Guilbault and Lamarche offered an amendment in favor of a plebiscite, while Western Liberals moved for suspension of the debate until redistribution according to the census of 1911, which would give the West fourteen more seats, and until the people had been consulted. Laurier supported the latter amendment but rejected Guilbault's, calling upon Borden to appeal to the people in an election. Guilbault's motion was supported by only eleven votes, and the bill passed its second reading by a vote of 114 to 83. Bourassa prevailed upon Monk to announce that his 'convictions were unchanged';[69] and then made two speeches in Toronto, where he maintained that Canada, having no authority save in her own territory, had no duty to defend anything except that territory. By organizing her own coastal defences and completing the public works necessary to her development, she would contribute to the defence of the empire in better fashion than by giving dreadnoughts. In the future he foresaw a development either towards imperial federation or independence, and favored the latter. In this argument he concurred with John S. Ewart, who had already advanced much the same ideas in *The Kingdom Papers*;[70] and for them he won the support of Ernest Charles Drury, head of the Dominion Grange, who wrote to the *Globe*: 'It is perhaps humiliating for a man who belongs to the same race as Pym and Hampden to admit that it is Frenchmen and not Englishmen who have taken this position. Honor them all the same!'[71]

On third reading the Liberals had resort to obstruction. Their resistance had been stiffened by Borden's revelation of his correspondence with Churchill, in which the latter maintained that the Canadians could not build dreadnoughts nor man cruisers nor maintain an efficient navy, and argued for perpetual use of British shipyards and for permanent Admiralty control. In March Churchill announced in the British Commons an Admiralty plan—on which Borden had been consulted—for the formation of an imperial squadron to be based on Gibraltar and made up of ships supplied by the dominions. This squadron could reach any portion of the empire before an equal force of any European power. The dominions would be consulted about movements of the squadron, in which officers and men from the participating dominions might serve. The dominions were to provide the necessary base facilities and auxiliary craft to enable the squadron to operate in any part of the empire.[72] After two weeks of night and day debate, the House recessed for Easter, and when it reassembled Borden decided to force the bill through by closure, rather than to dissolve parliament and make the appeal to the people which Laurier sought. The bill finally passed on May 15 by a majority of 101 to 68 after the most strenuous parliamentary battle in Canadian history, with five Quebec Conservatives voting against it. Laurier bitterly suggested that the three dreadnoughts should be named the *Pelletier*, *Nantel*, and *Coderre*.[73]

But the bill still had to pass the Senate, controlled by a Liberal majority led by Sir George Ross, an enthusiastic imperialist. Laurier had held a meeting at Toronto on May 5, calling for an appeal to the people and representing himself as the defender of liberty and autonomy. The Conservatives' recourse to closure at the expense of Laurier himself had strengthened the old leader's standing with his Ontario followers, and he received an enthusiastic reception. Borden held a rival meeting at Toronto on May 19, for which imperialist feeling had been carefully stimulated by the Tory organizers. Addressing an audience equipped with small Union Jacks, Borden reviewed his naval policy, emphasized the gravity of England's tuation, and threatened to reform the Senate if it rejected the bill. ourassa, who had already enjoined the Senate to kill the bill, enounced this threat:

It is neither the statesman nor the honest man who has offered this hreat; it is the chief, or rather the instrument, of an arrogant faction noved by jingoism and the gold of the armaments trust. The Senate vould be unworthy of its functions; it would deserve public scorn, if it ielded to this audacious attempt at blackmail.[74]

Meanwhile Lavergne busied himself with influencing Senators andry and Legris against the bill.

The government had already negotiated privately with Sir George Ross about a compromise. Ross objected to a contribution without stablishing a Canadian Navy, and proposed to couple the two plans. But neither the Liberal Senators nor Laurier supported this compromise which Borden would have accepted. The bill was presented y Senator Lougheed on May 20 and attacked by Ross, who stated hat the Naval Act of 1910 was preferable to the present plan. The overnment bill sent only empty ships, not men, to fight; it made no ppeal to national feeling; it would lead to cleavage rather than nity of public opinion. The will of the people should prevail; herefore he proposed in the very words used by Borden in 1910 'that this House is not justified in giving its assent to this bill until t is submitted to the country.'[75] Ross' motion was adopted by a vote of 51 to 27 on May 29, and the Conservative Naval Bill was illed.

But Borden did not give up hope for its eventual passage, either hrough the death of Liberal senators or the creation of additional enatorships under Section 26 of the B.N.A. Act. On June 1 he uggested to Churchill that Britain lay down three ships with the ssurance that Canada would pay for them before completion.[76] Churchill agreed to anticipate the construction of three ships, and Borden proposed to introduce in 1914 a provision for the grant of en or fifteen millions for that purpose. Senator Ross expressed ympathy with such a scheme, but his death in the following March, inancial depression, and the lessened emphasis on dreadnoughts ombined to cause abandonment of the plan. The defeat of Borden's Naval Bill was attributed to the influence of Bourassa by the *Montreal Star* and the press in England. Bourassa did not hesitate to point ut himself his 'moral triumph without precedent'; after four years f agitation the nationalists had succeeded in defeating all imperialist proposals: a Canadian navy, dreadnoughts for Britain, or money contribution.[77]

5

While the naval question dragged on to its inconclusive end, tl educational conflict had grown more bitter and had strengthene Bourassa's role as unofficial leader of French Canada. In Manitol the government's promises of better terms to the Catholic minori were not fulfilled, and Philippe Landry was charged with presentir a petition from the Catholics of the West to the government. A Rome the appeal of the Franco-Americans who had been excom municated by Bishop Walsh was rejected, but they remaine patriots to the French Canadians. In Ontario attempts to enforc Regulation 17 were resisted by the Franco-Ontarians, who no numbered about a tenth of the population and were concentrate in the Ottawa Valley, in the railroad, lumber, and mining cente of the center and northern parts of the province, and aroun Windsor. Under the leadership of Samuel Genest Franco-Ontaria teachers refused to sign the declaration required by the authoritie and students left the schools when the inspectors arrived. A new paper was needed to rally and direct the resistance, and a group priests and civil servants of Ottawa founded *Le Droit* on March 2 1913. The French Canadians of Saskatchewan had already estal lished *Le Patriote de l'Ouest* and those of Winnipeg launched *L Liberté* in May 1913. *Le Droit* followed the pattern of *Le Devoir* an *L'Action Sociale*, and maintained close relations with them and i Western colleagues.

Ontario priests sought support for the venture in Quebec; an Olivar Asselin, now president of the Saint-Jean-Baptiste Society c Montreal, was induced to sponsor a collection for the Ontari schools, actually intended for the support of *Le Droit*. With all hi usual vigor Asselin urged the cause of '*Le Sou de la Pensée Française* and renounced in its favor the customary parade and fireworks c June 24, with some acid remarks about his predecessors. Th Quebec Saint-Jean-Baptiste Society and the Societé du Parle Français, with the usual Quebec distrust of Montreal initiative refused to renounce their customary celebrations but launche collections of their own. Asselin dealt with the opposition whic succeeded in dislodging him as president in an interview in Fournier' *L'Action* of July 26, later reprinted as the third of his '*Feuilles d Combat*,' which were designed 'to serve the truth and make th morons rage.'[78] He pointed out that the celebration of Saint-Jean Baptiste Day was primarily a national rather than a Catholic one that nothing had been done in the past for the cause of Frencl culture on this occasion; and that French culture must be renewe at its source, as Bourassa had advised at the 1912 Congrès de l

Langue Française, regardless of those who feared modern France. He mocked the customary procession of 'ridiculous' historical floats, which cost far more than real contributions to French-Canadian culture, and the choice of a lamb, the '*Bête Nationale*,' as an unfortunate national symbol. Asselin's suppression of the traditional symbol was not anti-religious, as some of his critics had chosen to deduce from Archbishop Bruchési's Saint-Jean-Baptiste sermon on the Lamb of God, nor evidence of a Masonic intrigue. He also defended the right of Gonsalve Desaulniers as a French Canadian to take part in the celebration, though Archbishop Bruchési had barred the poet from the university as a Freemason. The obstacles raised by 'stupid right-thinkers' had reduced the collection to $15,000, although $50,000 was customarily spent on the parade.

A series of articles by Père Joseph-Papin Archambault, S.J. (under the pseudonym of 'Pierre Homier') provoked the organization at Montreal of the Ligue des Droits du Français, a more nationalist version of the Societé du Parler Français. The founders were all friends or disciples of Bourassa: Omer Héroux, Dr. Joseph Gauvreau, Léon Lorrain, Anatole Vanier, A.-G. Casault, Henri Auger, and Père Archambault himself. Their program included the defence and promotion of the French language, insistence on its use in trade and the public services, and an effort to 'give once more to the exterior of our social life an appearance revealing the French soul of our race.'[79] The undertaking was encouraged by Cardinal Bégin, Bishop Roy, and Archbishop Langevin.

At Ottawa on June 22 the Franco-Ontarians held a meeting for a crowd of 7,000. Their spokesman, Senator Belcourt, who a year earlier had counselled moderation, proclaimed: 'Our decision is irrevocable and irreducible. We have resisted and we shall continue to resist the odious attempt to proscribe our mother tongue, despite all threats, at the price of all sacrifices.'[80] Asselin, Adjutor Rivard, and Armand Lavergne promised Quebec's support. Bourassa would have been on hand if he had not begun a tour of the West, during which he had made some twenty speeches at Edmonton, Calgary, Regina, Saskatoon, Winnipeg, St. Norbert, Fort William, Port Arthur, Sault Ste. Marie, and Sudbury, more often in English before Canadian Clubs than in French before audiences of his compatriots. He expounded his views and took advantage of the opportunity to study Western problems, becoming convinced that national sentiment must be developed if the West and East were not to part.

Bourassa's own true nationalism was enhanced by the journey, but his Quebec disciples increasingly tended to narrow down theirs to a provincialism. The A.C.J.C. held its fifth general convention at Trois-Rivières at the end of June. For a year its study groups had considered the educational question, but reached no more startling conclusions than resolutions supporting control of primary education by the Church and parents, and the control of all educational institutions by the Council of Public Instruction. The A.C.J.C. condemned as 'inopportune' all the reforms urged for ten years by the freethinker Godfroy Langlois and other less suspect revisionists. But Abbé Lionel Groulx, in discussing the congress in *La Nouvelle France*, praised the society and proclaimed: 'Those who come after will have only to will it to become the masters of the future.'[81] And to this end Abbé Groulx sought to give a nationalist bent to the teaching of literature and history. Religion and nationalism became curiously intermingled as the clergy took a leading role in the nationalist movement. This development led to such incidents as the differences between the extremist Asselin and the moderate Archbishop Bruchési, and the censuring of Bourassa for his criticism of the apostolic delegate's role in the Keewatin school question. Intervention of the clergy in politics also had unfortunate repercussions among the English Canadians, whose loyalism was further disgruntled by the decision of the A.C.J.C. to celebrate the memory of Dollard des Ormeaux on May 24, long honored as Victoria Day by the English.

Laurier exploited the defeat of Borden's Navy Bill and the growing inflation at a meeting at Saint-Hyacinthe on August 16. He attacked the nationalist movement which had brought Borden to power, and then had become a 'movement toward the manger,'[82] renouncing its pledges in favor of the perquisites of office. He paid tribute to the Liberal Senate which had maintained its independence by defeating the Navy Bill which the nationalists had accepted in the Commons. Bourassa in turn attacked Laurier in a series of four articles. He treated the defeat of Laurier's former minister Sydney Fisher in Chateauguay on October 11 as another repudiation by Quebec of Laurier's leadership. But Laurier continued his campaign to regain Quebec, emphasizing the rising cost of living under the Borden government rather than the naval question, which had been the chief issue in the Chateauguay by-election. The provincial Liberals under Gouin's leadership maintained provincial rights at the Fifth Interprovincial Conference at Ottawa in October, requesting an increase of the federal subsidy since the federal tax receipts had swollen far beyond those of the provinces, thanks to Canada's growth in population and trade. The Borden government proved less friendly to provincial rights than Laurier's, and the question was left unsettled, with Quebec nursing a new grievance against Ottawa.

The Ontario school question grew ever more embroiled. Dr. J. W. Edwards of Toronto, a Conservative Orangeman, urged that the French language be driven out of Ontario. The provincial department of education suppressed its grants to the Ottawa separate schools in October. The Irish of Ottawa largely separated from the French on the school question, and accused them of neo-gallicanism. Senator Landry again sought the intervention of Borden in vain, and Thomas Chapais was advised by Sir James Whitney that Ontario affairs were no concern of *Québecois* when he urged the repeal of Regulation 17.[83] Bourassa took to the platform before three Ontario Canadian Clubs in support of the bilingual schools, and at a St. Andrew's Day banquet found himself at the same speaker's table with Bishop Fallon of London, the leading opponent of the French schools among the Irish clergy, who in 1911 had denounced 'an alleged bi-lingual school system which teaches neither English nor French, encourages incompetency, gives a prize to hypocrisy, and breeds ignorance.'[84] The A.C.J.C. and Saint-Jean-Baptiste Society of Montreal expressed their sympathy with the Franco-Ontarians, and at a protest meeting under the auspices of the latter at the Monument National on December 15 Bourassa insisted upon the presence of an Irish spokesman, J. K. Foran of Ottawa, and urged his audience to support their protests with those from Irish Catholics and English Protestants.

In the middle of January Bourassa spoke at a congress of the Ontario *Association canadienne-française d'Education*, which was torn by political division in its fight against the Conservative government of Ontario. Again he urged the necessity of interesting Irish Catholics and English Protestants in the movement, for after his Western trip he had become convinced that most English-Canadian prejudice against his compatriots could be dissolved by better acquaintance with them. He had already gained the virtual alliance of Ewart, Boyd, Cahan, and J. C. Walsh, and now he sought to generalize the process. His counsel was followed by the Saint-Jean-Baptiste Society of Montreal in a new sympathy meeting at the Monument National on March 6, when the speakers, in addition to Lamarche and Asselin, were Walsh, the Ontario journalist Thomas O'Hagan, and the English Montrealer W. D. Lighthall. Bourassa himself addressed the Irish of Hamilton on St. Patrick's Day[85] and spoke to the Canadian Club of Oshawa the following day, freely criticizing English ignorance of the French language and English injustice to the French Canadians. In January he had conceived the notion of an English page in *Le Devoir* and asked Ewart to collaborate on it.[86]

When the mayoralty campaign in Montreal between G. W. Stephens and Médéric Martin brought an outburst of the ethnic feeling aroused by the Ontario troubles, Bourassa published four articles in English in *Le Devoir* (March 11–14, 1914), which he later brought out in pamphlet form under the title of *French and English Frictions and Misunderstandings*, prefaced by letters from Cahan and

Walsh. For many years it had been the custom in Montreal to elect alternately French and English mayors, despite the fact that the English only constituted a quarter of the population. To this custom there had been three French attitudes: the majority favored it, a minority grumbled about it, and a third group, to which Bourassa belonged, felt that the best man should be elected regardless of race or creed. But the French were becoming disillusioned about English fair play; for the English always claimed their right when it was their turn, and when it was not, the best man always seemed to be English. *Le Devoir* had supported the successful English candidate in 1910 in its effort to reform municipal affairs. But the English papers of Sir Hugh Graham and Lorne McGibbon did not censure political corruption practiced by the great English companies, and were willing to support a corrupt French candidate rather than an honest English one.

Bourassa deplored the lack of contact and understanding between French and English, who seldom met except in politics and business, where they displayed their worst tendencies. He laid the greater blame on the English of Montreal, who in return for the privileges freely granted them made no effort to understand their French fellow-citizens. He exalted the French-Canadian tradition of tolerance of creed and language, and the habit of electing English Protestants to represent communities in majority French and Catholic—a precedent not followed by English majorities. English businessmen had not proved good public men. They had been reluctant to accept the language of the majority in the public services; they regarded the French Canadian as a 'nuisance'; and they refused to learn the language of the majority, internationally recognized as the language of culture and civilization. Only a few English Quebeckers had deplored the Ontario anti-French educational policy, but if Quebec should adopt a similar anti-English one, all English Canada would be up in arms. Yet the educational rights of the English in Quebec rested on the same basis as those of the French in Ontario. He urged equal justice and equal rights for both groups, and recommended that the English should take a more active part in public affairs, instead of 'living in this city and province as a group of isolated Uitlanders, wealthy, self-satisfied, and self-contained, with no care for their French-speaking neighbours—except on such occasions as when French votes are needed to elect an English-speaking mayor.' Bourassa saw in such conduct 'the most active factor in the growing estrangement between the two races.'[87]

In his comment on Bourassa's articles, Cahan made a distinction between the large number of English Montrealers coming from all parts of Canada or outside Canada, who were uninterested in Quebec, and the native English Quebeckers who appreciated the lerance of the French, but had little direct representation or parti-pation in the affairs of the province. He blamed most political rruption on lobbying at Quebec by English business interests hich had no direct political representation. Since they had little litical influence at Ottawa, they allied themselves to their com-ercial colleagues of Ontario and refrained from criticizing their litical actions. Finally he urged that there were many English ontrealers sympathetic with French Canada, but who preferred to eak English rather than to speak bad French to French Canadians ho had mastered both languages. J. C. Walsh deplored the gulf etween English and French Montreal; praised Bourassa for reveal-g the French state of mind; and asserted that 'No Canadian will ssent to seeing another Canadian wronged.'[88] But despite Bour-ssa's support, Stephens was defeated by Martin, backed by the amway interests and Sir Rodolphe Forget. Bourassa deplored the ct that an explosion of racial feeling aroused by the Ontario truggle had resulted in 'the victory of a man of the fifth order, capable of a gesture or action suitable to the revindication of the onor and rights of his race, and the defeat of one of the rare English anadians who had manifested real sympathy for the French anadians.'[89]

Bourassa did not content himself with telling the English where hey were wrong, but also applied himself to attacking French-anadian faults. On April 12 he gave a lecture on '*Nos défauts et os vices nationaux*,' which he called 'an examination of the national onscience.'[90] He censured the capitulation to materialism which ad led a rural people to overcrowd the cities; the loss of the spirit of implicity and economy; and the development of dishonesty with lectoral frauds, political scandals, and unpunished misdeeds. Turning to the clergy who were present, he censured the hierarchy or its tolerance of politicians in exchange for superficial respect and inancial grants to religious institutions. He called upon priests, eachers, and parents to fulfil their responsibilities. This blast, which clearly arraigned Archbishop Bruchési who had made peace with Sir Lomer Gouin, irritated the hierarchy. But a few days later Archbishop Langevin, speaking at a meeting at the Monument National, eulogized Bourassa's 'exemplary Catholicism' and 'con-tagious patriotism,'[91] to vast applause from Bourassa's student followers. Shortly afterward the nationalist leader left for Europe, where he was anxious to study the Irish question, now raised once more by Ulster's resistance to Home Rule, and the minority question in Belgium and Alsace.

With depression at home and a respite in the European war scare, parliament devoted most of its attention to the financially embar-rassed Canadian Northern Railway controlled by Mackenzie and

Mann, and to the proposed Georgian Bay Canal. In the debate o the address, Laurier taunted Borden with the abrupt disappearanc of the 'emergency' of which he had made so much in supportin the Navy Bill, and attacked the government for taking no steps counteract the depression. Borden criticized the Senate's action i killing the Navy Bill as bringing discredit upon Canada and bein detrimental to the empire, but announced his intention of witl holding further action on the naval question until a satisfactor conclusion was possible. A bill abolishing titles failed to win suppo from either party. The Redistribution Act, which increased th Senate's numbers from 72 to 96, was supported by both parties but the Liberals added an amendment that it should not take effec until the termination of the present parliament, thus forestalling an Conservative packing of the Senate in the interests of a nava measure. On the eve of the session Bourassa urged a program c needed public works rather than 'draining the public coffers t enrich the shareholders of Vickers-Maxim, Armstrong-Whitworth Beardmore, and to swell the heritage of the daughter of the Krup dynasty.'[92] On January 14, 1914, Monk, too ill to attend the open ing of parliament, from which he resigned in March, sketched ou in *Le Devoir* a vast program of public works, including the Georgia Bay Canal, favored by Montreal over further development of th Welland Canal and the St. Lawrence route. On February 2 Laurier moved for immediate construction of the Georgian Ba Canal and also the development of the Welland Canal. P.-E Lamarche, in an able speech in which facts and figures were relievec by occasional bursts of eloquence, supported only the Georgian Ba proposal, expressing distrust for joint development of the St. Law rence with the United States, which had always emerged from pas difficulties with Canada with a piece of Canadian territory. Th government promised to study the question, which had always beer blocked, according to Bourassa, by the railways, which thanks t their campaign contributions were more powerful than th government.

Quebec took little interest in the new raids upon the federa treasury by the Canadian Northern and the Grand Trunk Pacific But it did object to a militia budget of $11,000,000, much large than usual because of Sam Hughes' dream of militarizing Canada *Le Canada* deplored 'the frenzy of militarism which deflects so many millions of our money—which we need so much for other purposes— to spend it in purchases of arms, cannons, and munitions,' while *L Soleil* remarked: 'Eleven millions have been sacrificed in the gulf o militarism in order to permit Sam Hughes to play soldier.'[9 Parliament was prorogued on June 12, with a minor cabinet crisis over Sam Hughes' refusal to allow the 65th Battalion of Montrea to take part as usual in the Corpus Christi Day procession. Doherty threatened to resign if the order was not revoked, but Hughes, supported by the Orangemen, remained firm. Finally a compromise was arranged whereby the 65th paraded but without arms. Hughes gained no popularity in Quebec from this incident, or another later in June when he refused to allow the Régiment de Lévis to escort Cardinal Bégin upon his return from consecration in Rome. Quebec buried its political differences to pay honor to the new cardinal, and Laurier, Pelletier, Doherty, Nantel, the lieutenant-governor, the premier, and the chief of the provincial opposition were all on hand for the occasion. Cardinal Bégin's elevation gratified Quebec City's sense of superiority to Montreal, and represented a French-Canadian triumph at the expense of the Irish Catholics, whose role in Ontario heightened the old friction between French and Irish.

For the Ontario school question was now contested on strictly ethnic lines. While Cardinal Bégin was at Rome, urging the cause of the Franco-Ontarians and pleading for a division of mixed parishes, so that the French Canadians might have their own clergy, it was rumored that the Irish bishops intended to issue a pastoral approving Regulation 17.[94] The Irish Catholics of Ottawa were up in arms at the banishment from the French-controlled university of Father James Fallon, who had tried to prevent French Canadians from voting in the election of separate school commissioners. They sought an injunction against payment of teachers opposing Regulation 17. The Ontario government announced that it would take steps not only against the rebelling teachers, but against the parents. Père Charlebois obtained the assistance of Père Roderigue Villeneuve, a young Oblate theologian, in writing editorials for *Le Droit*. He also joined the Montreal *Ligue des Droits du Français*, and kept its members posted on the struggle in Ontario. The Orangemen took up collections to aid Ulster's resistance to Home Rule, and worked off their enthusiasm in attacks on the separate schools. The French Canadians of the West held congresses at Edmonton and Prince Albert, attended by delegates from Quebec. In Montreal the A.C.J.C. met in a congress, at which Abbé Groulx exerted his growing influence. The A.C.J.C. discussed the problems of inflation, immigration, unionization, and unemployment—the latter a novelty in the newly industrialized province. In June the Franco-Ontarians voted against the Conservative government which had introduced Regulation 17; their breaking of party lines aroused English feeling. In Manitoba in July the French Canadians supported the Conservative Roblin government, which by the Coldwell Amendments had shown tolerance to the French minority.

As the First World War drew near, Quebec looked westward to its persecuted compatriots rather than towards Europe. In three of

Canada's nine provinces ethnic feeling had been aroused, and a narrow nationalism predominated in French Canada. These facts played a notable part in the troubled years that lay ahead.

6

War came unexpectedly upon a Canada preoccupied with domestic affairs in 1914, and was met by impromptu measures. Borden, who had been so alarmed by the threat of impending conflict during his European visit of 1912, had attached no great importance to the Sarajevo incident of June 28, and had postponed setting a definite date for Admiral Jellicoe's proposed visit to Canada to discuss naval aid. On July 28, while on vacation at Muskoka, Ontario, he learned that Great Britain would probably be involved if France were attacked.[95] Reassured by his secretary but urged to be ready to return to Ottawa on short notice, he arrived in a virtually deserted capital on August 1. In the absence of the governor-general and most of the cabinet, Borden cabled the British government in Connaught's name a hope for peace and expressed Canada's desire to cooperate in that end, coupled with assurance that 'if unhappily war should ensue, the Canadian people will be united in a common resolve to put forth every effort and to make every sacrifice necessary to ensure the integrity and maintain the honour of our Empire.'[96] On August 2 he asked for advice and suggestions from the imperial naval and military authorities, and offered a considerable Canadian force, to be enlisted as imperial troops to avoid the 'defence of Canada' clause, but to be equipped, paid, and maintained by Canada. In reply, appreciation of the offer was expressed, but the British government postponed 'detailed observations on the proposals put forward pending future developments.'[97]

Meanwhile on August 2 and 3 Borden and the hastily summoned cabinet passed orders-in-council in accordance with the War Book plans drawn up the previous spring by a committee of deputy-ministers and service representatives. Censorship was established; currency regulations adopted to forestall a financial panic; the detainment of enemy ships authorized; and the export of articles useful for war purposes prohibited. The Canadian cruisers *Rainbow* and *Niobe* were ordered manned and put at the disposal of the Admiralty, while two submarines were purchased in hot haste in Seattle and got to sea before they could be detained, in spite of pursuit by U.S. cruisers. The *Rainbow* was ordered south from Esquimalt to escort back two small British craft, the *Shearwater* and *Algerine*, endangered by the presence of German cruisers in the Pacific.

While the cabinet was in session on the evening of August 4, word of England's declaration of war was received. Parliament was promptly summoned to meet on August 18—the two-week limit prescribed by Laurier's Naval Act. The cabinet resisted British pressure to intern German and Austrian reservists in Canada, and granted them protection unless they sought to leave the country. Upon the suggestion of George Perley, who was then in London, on August 6 Canada offered Britain a million bags of flour, a gift which was welcomed by the British government as it steadied prices and relieved distress in England. Sam Hughes, confronted with an opportunity for which his Napoleonic soul had longed, sprang into action. On July 30 he summoned the Militia Council, which decided to send a contingent of 20,000 men if war was declared. A call for volunteers for overseas service was issued on August 3. Mobilization of the First Division was ordered on August 6, when England accepted the offer of troops, by an order-in-council which begged the question of Canada's right to declare war or refrain from it: 'Considering the state of war now existing between the United Kingdom, and the Dominions, colonies, and dependencies of the British Empire on one hand, and Germany on the other . . .'[98] Already many officers had volunteered their own services and those of their units. Sam Hughes ordered the mobilization of two infantry battalions: the 13th, made up of the Royal Highlanders, and 14th, made up of the Grenadier Guards, Victoria Rifles, and Carabiniers de Mont-Royal; and Major Thomas-Louis Tremblay's Field Artillery Battery. A site chosen earlier by Hughes at Valcartier near Quebec was selected as the concentration center, and the first troops arrived there on August 20.

Quebec, with many of its leaders following the growingly popular custom among the bourgeois of European travel, and with its rank and file wholly unconcerned with world events, was taken by surprise by the outbreak of the war. Sir Lomer Gouin was vacationing in Brittany, the speaker of the legislative council was in Berlin, the chief justice and many others in Paris, Dr. Béland in Belgium, and Bourassa in Alsace. Sympathy with threatened France was expressed on August 1 by a crowd which assembled before *La Patrie's* bulletin boards, sang the 'Marseillaise,' and then paraded to the French Consulate under the Union Jack and Tricolor. French and Belgian reservists flocked to their consulates, and were hailed by crowds singing the 'Marseillaise.' Much the same scenes took place at Quebec. Both cities displayed more patriotic enthusiasm than imperialist Toronto.[99] On August 4 the first contingent of French reservists sailed from Montreal, after having been escorted to their ship by an enormous crowd. With the old mother country threatened, French-Canadian suspicion of modern France was disarmed, with the exception of the editors of *La Vérité*, who solemnly warned that France's greatest enemy was not Germany but Freemasonry.[100]

A committee to aid the families of French reservists was organized a Quebec, and later at Montreal. Newspapers carried the intertwine flags of Britain and France at the top of the page, and *La Patri* appeared with a huge headline: '*Vivent la France et l'Angleterre et Die sauve le Roi.*'[101]

Rodolphe Lemieux, a great lover of France, on August 3 urge his people to rally first to the defence of Canada's coasts and then t that of the great empire to which they belonged.[102] Laurier issue a statement on the morning of August 4, expressing a hope for peace but the conviction that 'it is probable and almost certain tha England will have to take her share in the conflict, not only for th protection of her own interests, but for the protection of France an the higher civilization of which these two nations are today th noblest expression.' He proclaimed the Liberal policy of Canada' rendering 'assistance to the full extent of her powers' to the en dangered mother country, and called for a truce to party strife cancelling all his political meetings.[103] Lamarche asserted that i was every Canadian's duty to defend the empire.[104] At Quebe on August 4 Albert Sévigny glorified England for coming to the ai of her allies and evoked British loyalty. Armand Lavergne sounde a discordant note in a following speech, when he stressed that Canad was bound to defend herself, but herself only; and that if the Frenc Canadians were to be called upon to die for their country, they mus first be granted the right to live in their country. 'If we are aske to go and fight for England, we reply: "Let us have our schools!"'[10

Lavergne's utterance was greeted with both approbation an disapproval. *La Presse* on August 5 suggested that French-Canadia volunteers should form distinct battalions and be placed directly a the service of France. In *Le Devoir* the following day Omer Héroux acting as spokesman for the nationalists in Bourassa's absence rejected this proposal and all participation in the war overseas:

> We persist in believing, along with the great statesmen of the pas that the proper duty of Canadian troops is to ensure, along with th defence of our territory for which we are ready to consent to all sacrifice. freedom of communications and the free export of the wheat necessar to the life of the English nation.[106]

The following day Héroux urged the repeal of Regulation 17 an the grant to the Franco-Ontarians of an educational regime such a that enjoyed by the English Protestants of Quebec as 'the mos efficacious fashion in which to promote the necessary rapproche ment between English and French Canadians.' Taken to task b Fernand Rinfret of *Le Canada* for his 'inopportune claims' whe common duty called for united support of the war, Héroux insisted 'Whatever be the gravity of European events and the problems the ıise for us, that does not give us the right to shut our eyes on the ngstanding injustice in Ontario.'[107] But Héroux's voice was lost the general enthusiasm in Quebec. *La Patrie* rebuked him by sking: 'If England were conquered by Germany, would not our nguage and our schools be in danger of being sacrificed?' There as no more hesitation in Quebec to approve Canada's course than mong the members of the Ontario Grange and the Western Grain rowers' Association, reflected in August in the *Ottawa Citizen* and ıe *Winnipeg Free Press*. War enthusiasm was greatest among recent ritish immigrants, but the wave of patriotism soon carried all before it.

Some feeling was aroused in Quebec not against the war, but gainst Sam Hughes, who had issued orders for sentries to shoot to ll. As a consequence a French-Canadian soldier guarding the eaceful dock at Rivière-Ouelle killed a French-Canadian tramp on ugust 9, and an English-Canadian sentry at the Craig Street rsenal in Montreal killed a French reservist on August 14. Mayor édéric Martin protested violently, and some Liberal papers called r Hughes' dismissal. *Le Devoir* did not exploit these incidents, but ith *Le Droit* continued its campaign against Regulation 17. *La ıtrie* deplored it, and *Le Canada* called for the forgetting of all fferences in the pursuit of victory. In the latter paper L.-O. David oquently developed Laurier's theme:

> England being at war, Canada, like all parts of the British Empire, is war. Our destinies are bound to those of England, our duty and our terest command us to aid her to triumph, to protect ourselves and protect France. Loyalty, patriotism, our most sacred interests make it duty for us to contribute in the measure of our strength to the triumph their arms. The defeat of England and France would be a disaster r the world, for Canada, for the province of Quebec especially, for e French Canadians. It would be a mortal blow to our political and ıtional destinies, to our dearest and most sacred interests and senti-ents. . . .[108]

rchbishop Bruchési lent the support of the Church to the cause hen in a sermon on August 9 he declared that it was the duty of the ithful to give the mother country, dragged into the war in spite of rself, the loyal and hearty support demanded by both religion and ıtriotism.[109] He added: 'If troops have to be sent to the other side, ır brave young men will not hesitate to face the ordeal, and I ıow that we will find in them the same heroism which characterized ır forefathers long ago.'[110]

Parliament met for the special war session on August 18, while is mood of enthusiastic national unity was at its height. Clad in ıaki, the governor-general, the soldier Duke of Connaught, de-vered the speech from the throne, which called for approval of the measures already taken by the government and others no proposed. Laurier promptly assured the government of Liber support of all these measures:

> If in what has been done or in what remains to be done there may b anything which in our judgment should not be done or should b differently done, we raise no question, we take no exception, we off no criticism, and we shall offer no criticism so long as there is danger a the front. It is our duty, more pressing upon us than all other dutie on this first day of this extraordinary session of the Canadian parliamen to let Great Britain know, and to let the friends and foes of Great Britai know, that there is in Canada but one mind and heart, and that a Canadians stand behind the mother country, conscious and proud th she has engaged in this war, not from any selfish motive, for any purpo of aggrandizement, but to maintain untarnished the honour of her nam to fulfil her obligations to her allies, to maintain her treaty obligation and to save civilization from the unbridled lust of conquest and powe
>
> We are British subjects, and today we are face to face with the cons quences which are involved in that proud fact. Long have we enjoye the benefit of our British citizenship; today it is our duty to accept i responsibilities and its sacrifices. We have long said that when Gre Britain is at war, we are at war; today we realize that Great Britain at war and that Canada is at war also. Our territory can be attacke and invaded. . . .[111]

He discounted the danger of invasion, but stressed that Canadia ports might be attacked by enemy raiders, which were loose in bot the Atlantic and Pacific. He pointed out, as another proof th Canada was at war when England was at war, that Canadian shi had ceased to sail the Atlantic and Canadian commerce had bee interrupted.

As to the government's decision to send overseas a contingent 20,000 men, Laurier observed:

> I have declared more than once that if England were in danger—ev engaged in a conflict which would test her power—it would be the du of Canada to come to her aid in the full measure of her resources. Tod England is not engaged in an ordinary contest. The war in which she engaged will in all probability—nay, in absolute certainty—stagger t world with its magnitude and horror. But that war is for as noble a cau as ever impelled a nation to risk her all upon the arbitrament of t sword. That question is no longer at issue; the judgment of the wor has already pronounced upon it. I speak not only of those nations whi are engaged in this war, but of the neutral nations. The testimony the ablest men of these nations, without dissenting voice, is that tod the allied nations are fighting for freedom against oppression, for dem cracy against autocracy, for civilization against reversion to that state barbarism in which the supreme law is the law of might.[112]

He spoke of how Canada replied to the call to defend England with a 'ready, aye, ready,'[113] and he made a special appeal to his compatriots:

If my words can be heard beyond the walls of this House in the province from which I come, among the men whose blood flows in my own veins, I should like them to remember that in taking their place today in the ranks of the Canadian army to fight for the cause of the allied nations, a double honour rests upon them. The very cause for which they are called upon to fight is to them doubly sacred.[114]

He paid his respects to the German Canadians and said the war was not one against the German people. He anticipated that as a result of the war 'the German people will decide to put a final end to personal government, so that a single individual nevermore can precipitate millions of human beings into all the horrors of modern war.' He paid tribute to the Belgians for their gallant resistance, and expressed his satisfaction that the Irish troubles had ended in union to fight for King and country. The same spirit of union was to be found in Canada, Australia, New Zealand, and even in South Africa, where English and Boers alike were ready to shed their blood for the common cause. He closed with the hope that 'from this painful war the British Empire will emerge with a new bond of union, the pride of all its citizens, and a living light to all other nations.'[115]

Borden congratulated Laurier upon his patriotism and eloquence. After discussing Britain's efforts to preserve peace, he, too, paid tribute to Canada's half a million Germans and urged regard for their feelings. He warned of trials to come, and said: 'Let us see to it that no heart grows faint and that no courage be found wanting.' After describing the government's measures and reading the dispatches from Britain, he came to an unusually eloquent conclusion:

As to our duty, all are agreed, we stand shoulder to shoulder with Britain and the other British Dominions in this quarrel. Not for love of battle, not for lust of conquest, not for greed of possessions, but for the cause of honour, to maintain solemn pledges, to uphold principles of liberty, to withstand forces that would convert the world into an armed camp; yea, in the very name of the peace that we sought at any cost save that of dishonour, we have entered into this war; and while gravely conscious of the tremendous issues involved and of all the sacrifices that they may entail, we do not shrink from them, but with firm hearts we abide the event.[116]

D.-O. Lesperance spoke in French, professing in the name of Quebec and the French Canadians her loyalty and eagerness 'to defend the integrity of the vast Empire which assures them the greatest amount of liberty and happiness that a people ever enjoyed.'[117] But no

French-Canadian voice was heard in the cabinet, since Pelletier was sick and Nantel and Coderre took no active part. In the four-day session every government proposal was ratified; a war appropriation of $50,000,000 was passed in one minute; the suspension of gold payment and other financial measures were approved; a Canadian Patriotic Fund for the relief of soldier's relatives was incorporated; and the War Measures Act, giving the government broad powers of censorship, deportation, and control over trade and transport, was approved. There was not a question raised nor a hint of party feeling.

When Sir Lomer Gouin returned to Quebec from France on August 17, he summoned his ministers and on August 19 cabled to London an offer of 4,000,000 pounds of cheese as an initial war contribution from Quebec. In the district of Montreal 3,443 volunteers had enlisted; 568 in that of Quebec. Confronted with more numerous enlistments in Ontario and particularly in the West, where many recent English emigrants were established, Omer Héroux in *Le Devoir* foresaw conscription to come when there were not enough volunteers. But upon the return of Bourassa, who had found his way on foot across the German and Belgian borders after being caught in Cologne on August 2, Héroux paid tribute to the French greatness of heart in the moment of danger which Bourassa had observed.[118]

With the exception of *Le Devoir*, the French-Canadian press supported the war effort enthusiastically. There were a few echoes of party spirit, with *L'Evénement* regretting on August 5 that Canada was unprepared thanks to the Liberals, and *La Presse* pointing out on August 6 how the logic of events had justified Laurier's contention that Canada was at war when Britain was at war.[119] On August 11 *La Presse* launched a daily column of army and recruiting news. The country weeklies, which generally published little but local news, began to join in the chorus of approval of Canadian participation. Reservations as to sending men overseas were expressed by the Liberal *L'Avenir du Nord* of Joliette and the ultramontane *Le Bien Public* of Trois-Rivières. But *Le Peuple* of Montmagny, despite Lavergne's influence, from the first espoused wholeheartedly the cause of the war, and approved Pelletier's statement there on August 14 that it was the duty of the French Canadians to observe a political truce and to answer the call of their country.[120]

But French-Canadian recruiting did not match the French-Canadian press' enthusiasm for the war. Thanks to Sam Hughes, the army had been largely anglicized, with preference given to English-Canadian officers. English was the only language of command, and there were few French Canadians among the graduates of the Royal Military College at Kingston, who formed an inner ircle in the army. The highest-ranking Canadian officer, Major-General F.-L. Lessard, a veteran of the North-West Expedition and he South African War who was adjutant-general, was relegated to he post of inspector-general for Eastern Canada instead of receiving he command of the First Division, as his compatriots had hoped. Colonel Eugène Fiset remained deputy-minister of militia, thanks to is South African War record, but had little influence under Hughes' utocratic regime. Only one French-Canadian officer headed a unit n the First Division, Lt.-Col. H.-A. Panet of the Royal Canadian Horse Artillery. Captains Hercule Barré and Emile Ranger of the Carabiniers de Mont-Royal sought to form a separate French-Canadian battalion, but in the face of official opposition had to ontent themselves with raising two French-Canadian companies n the new 14th Battalion. There were also scattered French Canadians in the 13th Battalion. On August 23, 300 French-Canadian volunteers of Montreal were blessed by Archbishop Bruchési as they departed for Valcartier. He said to them:

> The question cannot be discussed. The French-Canadian people has done its duty. We have given England provisions and gold, and we will give her men . . . we shall prove to England that we are not loyal only n words. . . .[121]

t was also Archbishop Bruchési who inspired *Le Soleil* to write:

> Once more, we must grasp all the gravity of the struggle being fought over there, and realize that we must do all that we can, in deeds and not n words, to bring all our aid, under whatever form it may be required, o those who there fight, in the last reckoning, for us and for all ideals hat we hold most dear in the world.[122]

But on the whole the French Canadians had long lost the military pirit. Militia officers were more frequently politicians than soldiers, nd their service had consisted largely of parades and mess dinners. Quebec's growing isolationism since the South African War left few xcept its leaders concerned about world affairs, while the anti-mperialist agitation had revived the traditional folk hatred of England. Quebec's rank and file failed to echo with any real feeling he authentic sympathy for France felt by French-Canadian leaders who knew and loved France. The people had been exposed too long o ecclesiastical warnings against irreligious and anti-clerical modern France, particularly stressed by the French religious orders which had aken refuge in Quebec after the anti-clerical laws of 1900–1. Quebec was more concerned with the struggle in Ontario than that n Europe. With Pelletier incapacitated by illness, French Canada had no real leader at Ottawa. The fervent patriotism of Sévigny and

Blondin in 1914 was contrasted with their violent anti-imperalis of 1911, and so lost effectiveness in moving public opinion. But pe haps the major factor in the poor French-Canadian recruiting recor was the breaking up of the old local militia units and the refusal the authorities to form separate French-Canadian units. Th French Canadian has a strong group consciousness and likes to b among his own people, especially when called upon to venture int the unfamiliar world outside Quebec. For many, the prospect being thrown into an English-speaking environment had mor terrors than the dreadful fates conjured up by patriotic orators as a to befall Quebec if French Canada failed to do its part.

Ottawa did not take advantage of the original enthusiasm i Quebec by authorizing French-Canadian units; and it was not su prising that the First Division numbered only some 1,200 Frenc Canadians out of the 5,733 men furnished by Quebec to the tot of 36,267. Naturally enough, the first to enlist were the English-bor the second those of British stock, the third the French Canadian to whom Canada was the sole fatherland. The First Division me were overwhelmingly British-born, 64 per cent according to th official statistics; 25.6 per cent were non-French-Canadian nativ born; and 3.7 per cent French-Canadian. Aliens contributed 7 pe cent.[123] Most of the British-born came from the Western province most of the Canadian-born from Ontario and Quebec. Quebec mad a poorer showing than Ontario in part because of a higher percentag of rural than urban population, and also because of earlier an heavier family responsibilities. Under the recruiting regulatio of August 17, preference was given to men who had militia experienc or had seen service, and to single men over married men and marrie men with families.

But a certain share in the quick cooling-off of French Canada' enthusiasm for the war must be assigned to Henri Bourassa, wh soon changed his ground on the question. At the Lourdes Eucharisti Congress on July 23 he and Bishop Gauthier, the auxiliary of Montreal, had spoken on the relations between Canada, France, and th Church. Bishop Gauthier had eloquently discussed what the Churc and France had done for Canada, while Bourassa still more eloquently dealt with the theme of what Canada had done for Franc and the Church. He spoke of Canada as 'the oldest son of France established by a patriotic act of faith and preserved as a center intense faith, but become 'the most solid, the most loyal, the mos faithful, support of British dominion in North America.'[124] T France the French-Canadian people owed their mentality, thei temperament, their family spirit, their love of home, their gaiet and endurance, their apostolic zeal, their idealism, the French sou and genius, and the French language in which they were expressed

Canada had scarcely known Jansenism, scarcely been touched by liberalism, and modernism was unknown. French Canada had kept French Catholicism untainted and had prevented the missionary work of the Church from becoming an instrument of a race or a government. It had won for the faith a liberty under the British flag which Catholicism did not enjoy in Catholic countries. As a *quid pro quo* French Canada asked only the right that the Gospel should be preached in the language of the people. Three million French Catholics of Canada bore witness to what the French race had done and what it could do. They had preserved the faith and the French language; they represented France's most lasting mark on North America. France's history was also French Canada's history, and Bourassa pleaded that France's love and aid should be given to Canada.

After the Eucharistic Congress, Bourassa had continued in Alsace the study of the bilingual question which he had already made in Wales and Belgium. He found the Alsatians ready to fight for France. At Lourdes, in Alsace, and in Paris on the eve of the war and during the first hours of mobilization, Bourassa found French courage worthy of all admiration and said as much in the first article he wrote for *Le Devoir* on August 27 after his return. He also reprinted letters from such French Catholic leaders as Cardinal Amette, Mgr. Baudrillart, Maurice Barrès, and Albert de Mun, exalting French courage and France's return to the Faith.

But his critical spirit objected to the wholehearted pro-war enthusiasm which swept Canada, explaining everything in black and white terms, and on August 29 he questioned the theory which assigned blame for the war solely to the Kaiser. On September 8 Bourassa took the stand that Canada as a British colony had no direct reason to intervene in the war and had good reasons for remaining neutral; but that Canada as an 'Anglo-French nation, bound to England and France by a thousand ethnic, social, intellectual and economic ties, had a vital interest in the maintenance of France and England, and of their prestige, power, and world influence.' Consequently: 'It is her national duty to contribute in the measure of her strength and by the means of action proper to her, to the triumph and above all to the *endurance* of the combined efforts of France and England. But to render this contribution effective, Canada should begin by resolutely surveying its real situation, making an exact account of what it can and cannot do and assuring its internal security, before lauding or pursuing an effort which it perhaps will not be able to maintain until the end.'[125]

From September 9 to 14 he published in *Le Devoir* a study of the origins of the war based upon the English *White Book*. This study was immediately republished as *La Politique de l'Angleterre avant et après la guerre*, and early in 1915 in English translation under the title of *The Foreign Policy of Great Britain*. It was a searching and able analysis, which reached the conclusion that Sir Edward Grey had been 'faithful to the highest British traditions, he was, before and above all, the man of his country,' intervening in support of France and Belgium only when his country's interests demanded it. Bourassa drew the inference that 'Canada could not better demonstrate her loyalty to British traditions than by imitating the example of the great nation from which she derived her political institutions.'[126] Self-interest was the true and natural policy of all nations; it was patriotic, and neither hypocritical nor perfidious. Bourassa opposed British policy only when Canadian policy was subordinated to it. He deplored the effort made to convince the French Canadians that they had a 'double obligation' to support the war and only 'half the rights' of other Canadian ethnic groups. He urged Canadian statesmen 'to imitate the example of British statesmen, to unite freely the interests of Canada to those of England when their interests were identical, to oppose Canada's interests to those of England when they were contrary, and to separate them when they were divergent.'[127] His demonstration was treated as disloyal and infamous; the moment was ill chosen for objective, logical analysis.

In the English edition Bourassa supported his study against these charges by reprinting an article of H. N. Brailsford which treated the war as 'a cooperative crime,' and its issue as one 'so barbarous, so remote from any real interest or concern of our daily life in these islands that I can only marvel at the illusions and curse the fatality which have made us belligerents in this struggle.' Bourassa contrasted 'the liberty of appreciation enjoyed and practiced in England even in time of war and under the ban of censure, and the grotesque and stupid intolerance manifested in Canada against everyone who dares think and say that there are many aspects to the struggle in Europe. . . .'[128] He also reprinted from the *Ottawa Citizen* of October 26 a study by John S. Ewart, which named as causes of the war national and racial antipathies, huge alliances, and preparedness for war; and singled out militarism as the real enemy. Bourassa particularly deplored the rousing of racial feeling by invocation of the 'double loyalty' of the French Canadians, since Canada's part should be taken for purely Canadian motives; and in case of the future wars against Russia or France which Brailsford and Ewart anticipated, discord might result from the racial feeling now aroused.[129]

If the English press lavished such epithets as 'pro-German' and 'traitor' upon Bourassa for these articles—*Saturday Night* said: 'Every day in Europe, men who have done no more harm are hung s traitors,'[130]—the French press was equally vigorous. *La Patrie* :lt his articles would justify the federal authorities in accusing him f high treason; *Le Canada* undertook to answer him by a new interretation of the *White Book*; *Le Soleil* accused him of having done more harm to the French Canadian people than its worst enemies ave ever been able to do'; *Le Presse* opposed Archbishop Bruchési's ermon to his articles; *L'Evénement* described him as actuated by hereditary hatred of England.' *L'Action Sociale*, now regarded as the ıspired organ of Cardinal Bégin, then absent at Rome for the election of Benedict XV, and of Mgr. Paul-Eugène Roy, flatly refuted Bourassa's thesis:

We have the duty to grant to the mother country, in just and equitable roportions, the cooperation of which she has need from us . . . We owe er this cooperation as every subject owes it to his sovereign and every itizen to his country when it becomes necessary.

. . . . .

What should be the measure of this cooperation? It should be that emanded by the necessity of conquering. And of this measure, in law nd fact, England is the final judge, since from her derives the authority ecessary to accomplish this great task, along with the burden of defending the Empire.[131]

and on the same day Archbishop Bruchési, speaking in support of he Patriotic Fund at Montreal, confirmed this expression of the ierarchy's views:

England is engaged in a terrible war, which she sought to avoid at all osts. Loyal subjects, recognizing in her the protectress of our liberties, ve owe her our most generous cooperation. Indifference at the present our would be on our part a fault, and also the gravest error. Is it not vident that our fate is bound to the fate of her armies?[132]

Aside from *Le Canada's* articles, Bourassa's thesis was greeted only vith insults, and was misrepresented to such an extent by the English ress that Cahan protested in a letter to the *Gazette*, *Herald*, and other apers on September 15. Even some of Bourassa's closest followers xpressed opposition. Olivar Asselin in *L'Action* on September 16 egretted that Bourassa had 'once more fallen into his customary rror of being erudite when it would have sufficed to have entrenched himself in plain common sense,' while he also objected to Archbishop Bruchési's intervention in the political question of whether Canadian troops should be sent overseas.[133]

But against almost unanimous opposition Bourassa maintained his position that Canada should not refuse to aid England and France, but should do so only under certain conditions and within the limits of Canada's own obligations. On September 23 he pointed out that

Canada's contribution was already greater than that of Britain her self, in proportion to national wealth and population. He called fc the end of persecution of the Franco-Ontarians and censured the lac of discipline and the drunkenness of the troops at Quebec. Sar Hughes had a Winnipeg journalist arrested for criticizing the ac ministration of Valcartier Camp, but he took no steps agains Bourassa. The latter did not hesitate to question the thesis c *L'Action Sociale* that Canada had a moral obligation to suppo England. He also criticized the Belgian mission, brought to Mor treal by the British on September 23 and fêted at the city hall an the Monument National, for not expressing their gratitude to Franc as well as to England.

With Pelletier sick and the two other French-Canadian ministe nonentities, Charles Fitzpatrick, chief justice of the Supreme Cour was much consulted by Borden on the problem of Quebec. Fitz patrick urged that the Quebec bishops should preach a holy wa through a collective *mandement*, in the tradition of their loyalis stands in 1775 and 1812. Doherty was chosen as the government' intermediary, and set to work through his friend Archbishop Bru chési, who was already won to the cause by personal convictior Fitzpatrick also urged the journalists of Quebec to preach a holy wa On September 23 the archbishops and bishops of Quebec, Montrea and Ottawa signed a joint pastoral letter asserting that Englan 'counts on our help with perfect right and this help we are happy t say has been generously offered her in men and money.'[134] Mos of the *mandement*, read in the churches on October 11, was devoted t urging the faithful to subscribe to the Patriotic Fund and to pray for just peace. But the message clearly approved of the war policy an of the sending of troops, and the bishops were thanked by the gover nor-general for their action. For once 'clerical influence' in Quebe was welcomed by English Canadians. But Bourassa wrote at onc to Archbishop Bruchési, asking whether this was a directive bindin in conscience, and was told that he was perfectly free to differ i opinion.[135] Asselin protested in *L'Action* on October 24, when th majority of the French press had taken the attitude that the bishop had spoken and the matter was no longer to be discussed. He sai their action was not interested, and perhaps their hand had bee forced, but he censured them for exalting the imperialist doctrine c the obligation to send troops abroad into an 'untouchable dogma.'[13

While Bourassa was making the transition from approval t criticism of Canada's participation in the War, the movement fo a separate French-Canadian unit gained strength. Dr. Arthu Mignault, something of a French-Canadian Sam Hughes in his fond ness for fancy uniforms and in his blustering militarist enthusiasm won the assistance of L.-T. Maréchal in the cause and beseige

›rden and Hughes. The proposal was supported by J.-M. Tellier, :nator Belcourt, and Rodolphe Lemieux. Laurier wrote Borden in vor of the proposal, pointing out that 'The War Office at all times ıs taken advantage of the force of race sentiment in the formation ' the army.'[137] On September 30 the government authorized the rmation of the Royal 22nd French-Canadian Battalion.

Under the auspices of *La Presse*, a recruiting meeting was held at ıe Parc Sohmer in Montreal on October 15, with Laurier, Gouin, emieux, T.-C. Casgrain, Mathias Tellier, and Belcourt urging ıeir compatriots to enlist. Laurier invoked the memory of Dollard: f there are still a few drops of the blood of Dollard and his com- ınions in the veins of the Canadians who are present at this meeting, ›u will enlist in a body, for this cause is just as sacred as the one for hich Dollard and his companions gave their lives.' He made much f the fact that Canada's aid to Britain was given of her own free ıoice, not as an obligation, and he added: 'If some Canadians were ightened by the monster of conscription in the past, they must now :cognize that this monster was a myth.'[138] Fifteen thousand people ttended the rally, which had been widely publicized by the press, ıd students sang the 'Marseillaise.' The battalion was soon re- cuited to full strength and began training at St. Johns. *La Presse* irtually adopted the 22nd and filled its columns with news of the amp. There was marked popular enthusiasm for 'our regiment,' nd Quebec's support was thus gained for the raising of a Second)ivision, which was decided upon on October 18, three days after ıe First Division landed in England. Borden virtually took charge f military affairs, after convincing the bellicose Duke of Connaught ıat he was only nominally commander-in-chief, and after reluc- ıntly allowing the Napoleonic Hughes to follow the First Division to :ngland.

Bourassa, who had sounded the sole dissenting voice to the Parc ›ohmer meeting by calling it an 'explosion of empty and sterile hauvinism,'[139] gradually was joined by others in his criticism of the overnment as the first enthusiasm wore off. He inveighed against alse patriots who beat their breasts to send other men to war. He riticized the British government for making purchases in the States vhich could have been made in Canada, while the Canadian govern- nent supplied the troops with razors made in Germany. He de- ended Montreal and Trois-Rivières, where unemployment was rife, or their poor showing in contributions to the Patriotic Fund; and he :riticized the snobs who turned over to the Fund their usual gifts to :harity, so that the Montreal Children's Hospital was about to close ts doors for lack of money, while the Patriotic Fund had been given $1,500,000 in a few days. French-Canadian shoe manufacturers ›rotested against British orders being placed in the States. *Le*

Patriote de l'Ouest proclaimed: 'It is not the time to discuss what w the extent of our strict obligations in the circumstances; it is manife that we have exceeded the limits.'[140]

On October 17 Bourassa launched a campaign for a great agricu tural reform, which would establish the unemployed of the East (land in the Prairie Provinces returned to the government by the gre railway companies, which had received excessive grants. He urge that parliament be summoned to adopt this measure. He attacke the government for permitting the continued export to neutr countries of Ontario nickel, which had already gone into the makir of German munitions and arms. He also attacked the proposal of 'khaki election' to which Robert Rogers won Borden in the midd of October, but which was rejected in the face of the opposition of stalwart a Conservative organ as the *Montreal Star*, which termed 'treachery,'[141] and that of the united Liberal press. Borden co tented himself with revising the French representation in the cabine Pelletier retired to the bench because of illness, and Nantel to th Railway Commission, while T.-C. Casgrain, an old-school Tor became postmaster-general and P.-E. Blondin minister of intern revenue. The new ministers were re-elected without either Liberal (nationalist opposition.

On October 22 Bourassa gave a lecture on Belgium at the Mon ment National, under the auspices of the Saint-Jean-Baptiste Societ and for the benefit of the Belgian Relief Fund, the French Red Cros and the St. Vincent de Paul Society. Bourassa cited Belgium's pr war prosperity as a proof that Catholicism was compatible wit modern social organization. But he devoted most of his attention t the Flemings' successful fight for their language and their schoo against the dominant French element. Flemish was now establishe on an equal basis with French, yet Belgian unity had not been er dangered. Whatever might be the military result of the currer struggle, Belgium would live, as Poland, Ireland, and French Canad would live. 'Justice does not die, because God, creator and guardia of justice, does not die.'[142]

Thus Bourassa took the occasion to support indirectly the righ of the Franco-Ontarians, whose struggle continued to enlist mor sympathy in Quebec. *Curés* showed favor for the Ontario caus in the pulpit, and Cardinal Bégin sought support for it at Rome Philippe Landry renewed his efforts to induce Borden to interven with the Ontario government in the interests of a truce during th war. Two members of the Association d'Éducation had an intervie with Doherty and Fitzpatrick on October 15 and got them to inte cede with the Ottawa Irish, who refused to lift the injunction again payment of salaries to the teachers rebelling against Regulation 1 The case of the French-Canadian majority on the Ottawa Separat

School Board was pleaded by Senator Belcourt at Toronto before Judge Lennox, who expressed the view: 'Speak French at home if you like, but not at school.'[143] *Le Devoir* exalted the 'handful of heroes' and said that sympathy for the French and Belgians should not distract Quebec's attention from 'the assassination of a race which is being perpetrated' in Ontario.[144] The French-Canadian clergy followed the question eagerly, but Archbishop Gauthier, the English bishop of Ottawa who bore a French name, considered it a political and not a religious one. The apostolic delegate preserved a discreet silence. Bourassa took to the warpath more openly on November 12 when he gave a lecture on Alsace-Lorraine for the benefit of the French Red Cross and compared the Ontario regime with that of Alsace, showing that the English Ontarians were more Prussian than the Prussians. The whole question was embittered by the stubbornness of both parties, with the French asking for their schools first, and the Ontario loyalists saying 'Enlist first and then we shall see.'[145]

By October 31 Bourassa had so thoroughly swung around to opposition to the government's war policy that he was writing to this effect:

> Instead of spending one hundred to one hundred and fifty millions to enlist and maintain for months, perhaps years, a great number of men badly clad, badly shod, and undisciplined, they could have, with a fifth of this sum, organized a suitable contingent of soldiers, well disciplined and perfectly equipped.
>
> Instead of making a gift, at one swoop, to very wealthy England of millions of bags of flour and great piles of cheese—which rot today on the docks of Liverpool because the English do not know what to do with it, while millions of Belgians starve and thousands of Canadians have scarcely enough to eat,—they could have organized with intelligence and method Canada's economic and agricultural production; they could have controlled vigilantly the operation of transport tariffs; they could have watched with care to prevent any cornering of food supplies; they could have directed the export of Canadian products, and even of charitable gifts, public or private, in such fashion as to meet true needs, to aid true misery, instead of giving all to the rich and nothing to the poor; and above all they could have adopted suitable measures to support to the end the endurance of the effort of the nations whose friends they claim to be.
>
> But no, it was necessary at all costs that Canada's aid should take an inflated, noisy, loud form, worthy of the fat-stomached newly rich who dominate high finance, big business, and the high policy of the Canadian nation. It was necessary also that it should profit above all the boodlers, vampires, the furnishers of bribes and electoral funds, the merchants of boots made of uncured cowhide and razors made in Germany.
>
> Glory to the Empire![146]

This bitter blast was all the more effective, since Sam Hughes awards of contracts to his cronies had already forced Borden to tak the supply question under his supervision late in September and t launch an investigation of contracts in October. But Bourassa' intervention was not relished and he was branded as a traitor. Th *Star* referred to him as 'Von Bourassa.'

On the whole French-Canadian opinion tended to support him, a the early enthusiasm wore off and English-Canadian scorn o Quebec's enlistment record and the Ontario school question ha their effect. But Jules Fournier took objection to Bourassa for no being openly anti-British. Fournier reproduced in *L'Action* all new unfavorable to England and the British Army, thus replying to th English press' habit of making much of the minute B.E.F. in Franc and ignoring the French Army. He compared the German outrage in Belgium to those of the English in South Africa. He aske Bourassa flatly whether or not he favored the sending of the contin- gents, and whether or not he still believed in the principles which h had preached for fifteen years.[147] But the better-publicized Bour- assa alone won the hatred of English Canadians. He was prevente from speaking at Kingston at the invitation of some Queen's Univer- sity professors, thanks to the protest of Dr. J. W. Edwards, who calle Bourassa 'much more dangerous than the Germans or Austrian interned as prisoners of war.[148]

The Franco-Ontarians lost the first step in their long legal battle While Senator Landry sought to interest Casgrain in their plight Père Charlebois appealed to Quebec for funds to continue the battle Fear of charges of disloyalty shut several doors, but the A.C.J.C undertook to raise funds for 'the wounded of Ontario.'[149] This actio aroused the Orangemen, and when Bourassa was invited to spea before the People's Forum of Ottawa on November 22, the clamo raised by the loyalists, with the *Journal* at the head of the agitation resulted in the cancellation of the affair. A committee of nine including three French Canadians, renewed the invitation for Decem- ber 16. While incendiary handbills were circulated in Ottawa calling Bourassa the 'arch traitor of Canada' and urging that 'the skull of rebellion must be smashed,'[150] Bourassa made a lecture tou through the Franco-American centers of New England, where h told the Franco-Americans to be resolutely American, to becom naturalized citizens, and to learn English, but to keep contact with Canada and to preserve their religion, their language, and thei traditions. 'By remaining French and Catholic, you will be bette Americans.'[151] The most notable Franco-American, Governo Aram J. Pothier of Rhode Island, accepted Bourassa's invitation t come to Montreal on December 17. On December 10 a Quebe Dominican priest, Père Pierre Granger, gave a lecture in Ottawa in which he likened the Anglo-Ontarians to the Prussians and paid tribute to *Le Devoir's* 'happy national and religious influence,'[152] and to Bourassa as the soul of the movement in favor of the Franco-Ontarian schools. Bourassa attended a meeting of school commissioners at Hawkesbury on December 15, and learned of the tense feeling in Ottawa from Samuel Genest, Alphonse Charron, and Père Charlebois. A. C. Glennie, the Scottish secretary of the committee sponsoring Bourassa's appearance, was fired from his job, after influence had been brought to bear on his employer.

Police protection had been promised for the meeting at the Russell Theater on December 16, but from the outset songs and catcalls drowned out the voices of the chairman, Dr. Anthony Freeland, and of Bourassa himself. Bourassa nonetheless continued to speak for the benefit of the newspapermen who surrounded him. His speech, printed in 1915 as *The Duty of Canada at the Present Hour*, was made up almost entirely of extracts from his editorials in *Le Devoir* since the outbreak of the War. By giving the context which had been omitted by ultrapatriotic English editors in search of damning extracts, Bourassa hoped to clarify his position. But the speech was not heard except by a few journalists, for the tumult in the auditorium steadily increased. Glennie was manhandled and pushed through the glass entrance door. A sergeant climbed on the platform, handed Bourassa a Union Jack, and ordered him to wave it. The front rows were filled with soldiers ready to support their companion. Bourassa took the flag and laid it on a table, in a momentary hush which allowed the audience to hear his reply: 'I am ready to wave the British flag in liberty, but I shall not do so under threats.'[153] The sergeant repeated his order. Bourassa repeated his reply and eyed him firmly. The audience rose howling to its feet and the soldiers prepared to storm the platform when the curtain was suddenly dropped. Some French Canadians in the audience sang the 'Marseillaise,' while the uproar continued. Bourassa and his party left the theater after the tumult had continued for fifteen minutes, and went to the Chateau Laurier, where he continued the lecture for his friends and the newspapermen.

All Ottawa was up in arms. A French Canadian knocked down an English Canadian who insulted Bourassa in the grill room of the Chateau that evening. The next morning Mrs. Glennie visited the office of the *Journal*, which had played a leading role in arousing the agitation, and horsewhipped the editor. The French Canadians of Ottawa sent her two great bouquets of roses. The *Ottawa Free Press* protested at the part taken by the soldiers at the Russell Theater, and censured the prevalence of drunkenness among the troops camped on the Exposition Grounds. The *Toronto Globe* and *Montreal Star* described the incident as 'regrettable.' Casgrain replied to a suggestion from Landry—that he appeal in behalf of the Franco-Ontarians to the governor-general—with the observation that the invitation to Bourassa to speak in Ottawa was 'a defiance of public opinion' which would injure their cause.[154] *Le Droit* wildly observed that Bourassa had been attacked less as the champion of certain ideas than as champion of the oppressed minority. The party press of Quebec played down the incident, since it gave too much importance to Bourassa.

But at the Montreal reception for Governor Pothier on December 17, at which Coderre represented the federal government, Cyrille Delage the provincial government, Senator Dandurand Laurier, Wilfrid Gariépy the Alberta government, Senator Poirier the Acadians, and Senator Belcourt the Franco-Ontarians, Bourassa was greeted with wild enthusiasm. He warned that 'If we let the French minorities which are our outposts be sacrificed one by one, the day will come when the Province of Quebec itself will undergo assault.'[155] He called for the preservation of French culture against all traps, all denials, and all treasons: 'We have not the right to abdicate by committing suicide, and committing suicide in dishonor.' The following day Lavergne and Lamarche held a meeting in favor of the French language in Montreal. The next day, the A.C.J.C. issued a manifesto for its meeting on December 21, which was to launch the campaign for 'the wounded of Ontario.' In *Le Devoir* Bourassa urged all patriots to attend:

> In the name of religion, liberty, and faithfulness to the British flag, the French Canadians are enjoined to go fight the Prussians of Europe. Shall we let the Prussians of Ontario impose their domination like masters, in the very heart of the Canadian Confederation, under the shelter of the British flag and British institutions?[156]

The meeting was attended unexpectedly by Archbishop Bruchési, as well as by his more nationalist-minded auxiliary Bishop Gauthier, the Jesuit provincial, the rector of the Collège Sainte-Marie, and the secretary of the university. Père Charlebois, Bourassa, and Lavergne sat side by side with Senators Dandurand, Landry, and Belcourt. Party ties were forgotten. Archbishop Bruchési clearly indicated his support of the movement. Senator Landry stressed the importance of the question: 'We wish to have it settled whether Confederation has been for us a pact of honour or an infamous trap.'[157] He appealed to Borden, Laurier, Gouin, Fitzpatrick, and Doherty. Belcourt gave the legal case for the Franco-Ontarians, and Alphonse Charron the history of the movement. Bourassa, not on the program, was called for by the crowd, and once more compared the English Ontarians to the Prussians, to the favor of the latter. Cardinal Bégin later approved Archbishop Bruchési's stand in a letter from Rome: 'If the rial imposed upon our brothers of Ontario must be prolonged, as lease God it may not, it will be the noble duty of the French Pro- ince of Quebec to support with its influence and all its strength those vho fight, until full justice be rendered them.'[158] The A.C.J.C. inder the leadership of Guy Vanier organized meetings, publicity, nd sought subscriptions. Omér Héroux announced in *Le Devoir*: The attention of the public is now fixed on Regulation 17 and we hall try to keep it there.'[159]

7

Quebec entered the year 1915 with far more of its attention and ympathy concentrated on Ontario than on Europe. French Canada till supported generously the numerous appeals for various war unds; but its military enthusiasm cooled as news of illness, mis- nanagement, and poor equipment came from the muddy Canadian amp on Salisbury Plain in England. However, Dr. Mignault roposed to raise a French-Canadian hospital unit, to match that rganized by McGill. Already the bugbear of conscription had been aised. When Borden had assured the Canadian Club of Montreal n December 7 that Canada would send all the men and money ecessary to a triumphal conclusion of a 'terrible and protracted truggle,'[160] Bourassa predicted that this policy would end in con- cription. Speaking at the Montreal Reform Club on December 12, aurier characterized conscription as 'repugnant to the British haracter' and supported the Liberal endorsement of the govern- nent's policy:

> I have no particular love for the government, but I love my country, love the land of my ancestors, France. I love the land of liberty above ll, England, and rather than that I, in my position as leader of the iberal party, should remain passive and quiescent, I would go out of ublic life, and life together.[161]

3ut Bourassa had a firmer hold on Quebec's heart than Laurier at he end of 1914.

The provincial session opened on January 7, 1915 and soon pro- ided evidence that particularist Quebec was being drawn into a vider world. The speech from the throne included an invitation to 3elgian refugees to establish themselves in the province. *L'Action Sociale* and *L'Evénement* had misgivings about thus introducing radicals, Freemasons, and socialists' in a country which wished to reserve 'healthy social and religious ideas.'[162] Tellier endorsed he policy of political truce by approving the government's gifts to England, France, and Belgium, and said that regardless of constitu- ional or civil obligations, he was ready to support any aid that the government proposed to give to England, as a son would fly to th defence of his father's house.[163] But on January 11 Sir Lomer Goui himself anticipated Armand Lavergne, who intended to present resolution in favor of the Franco-Ontarians:

While in Europe English and French rival each other in fighting for th triumph of justice, while on the battlefields French and English generousl shed their blood in order that there may be no more oppression i Europe, why must their brothers of Ontario be divided on the merits c teaching to the children of a minority the language of the discoverers c this nation. . . .

I cannot forget that it was the English Canadians of Ontario and th French Canadians of Quebec who founded the already potent structur which is the Dominion.

Who would wish to pretend that it was not in their minds to give t the two races equal rights in the matter of language, of property, an person, as Sir John Macdonald put it in 1890? And who could preten that it was not under the inspiration of such sentiments that the Britis North America Act was drawn up by the Fathers of Confederation? ..

It is moved by this sentiment, Mr. Speaker, that I wish, before takin my seat, to address in the name of all the population of Quebec—English Scottish, and Irish Canadians as well as French Canadians—an appea to the government and the majority of the Province of Ontario. In th name of the justice and generosity of which England has given so man proofs and which cannot fail to animate every truly British citizen, a well as in the name of the struggles that our fathers waged to open to civi lization the rich domains which are our common heritage, I ask tha justice be done to the French minority of Ontario, and even, if need be that generosity be shown to them.

In the name of the sublime expressions which it has given to huma thought, I ask, for the French tongue, the right to be heard on the lips c the school children of Ontario who wish to learn it and to speak it.[164]

For once Gouin found something of the eloquence and feeling of hi father-in-law Honoré Mercier.

Two days later, at Gouin's instigation, two English-speakin members—W. S. Bullock of Shefford, a former Baptist preacher, an J. T. Finnie of Montreal, born in Scotland—introduced the follow ing motion:

This House, without derogating from the principles of Provincia autonomy and without any intention of advising or intervening in th affairs of other Provinces of the Confederation, views with regret th divisions which seem to exist among the people of the Province of Ontari over the bilingual schools question, and believes that it is in the interest of the Dominion in general that all questions of this sort be considere on broad, generous, and patriotic lines, always remembering that one o the cardinal principles of British liberty throughout the Empire is regar for the rights and privileges of minorities.[165]

Lavergne congratulated Bullock and Finnie, but attacked the tyranny of the Orangemen and Bishop Fallon. He took the opportunity to reaffirm the nationalist principle of no Canadian participation in England's wars, citing Lord Granville's dictum that it was England's duty to defend Canada and not Canada's duty to defend England. Tellier approved the resolution, and deplored Lavergne's irrelevant remarks. Only one English member, C. E. Gault of Montreal, questioned the opportuneness of the gesture. The resolution was passed unanimously. In *Le Devoir* Lavergne stressed the fact that the Liberal government of Quebec had adopted a program which the nationalists had long advanced.

On the following day, January 14, the friends of *Le Devoir* celebrated the paper's fifth anniversary at the Monument National. As chairman, J.-N. Cabana announced that a public meeting had been chosen rather than a private banquet as the means of celebrating the occasion in order that 'examination of conscience'[166] might be made before the public of Montreal. Admission was charged to aid in increasing the circulation of the paper. The chief backer, G.-N. Ducharme, confessed that he had originally supported the paper in the interest of the Conservative Party, but had been converted to Bourassa's view of the necessity of an independent journal to claim and to defend French-Canadian rights. He expressed his perfect confidence in Bourassa and in his disinterestedness. Armand Lavergne retraced the whole history of the nationalist movement and paid tribute to Bourassa, who 'incarnated all the claims of the race.'[167] Bourassa had been accused of treason; so had Lafontaine, Mercier, and Riel. Tomorrow all Quebec and all Canada would thank him, as Quebec's youth did today.

Bourassa himself spoke for more than two hours, giving an account of *Le Devoir's* campaigns and achievements. As for the future:

> In fair or foul weather, with or against all comers, *Le Devoir* will continue to fight for the rights of Canada against the foreigner, and even against the contrary interests of Great Britain and the other countries of the Empire; for the rights of minorities, Catholic or Protestant, French or English, and for the equality of the two races and of the two civilizations in each of the Canadian provinces; for the creation of a true national spirit made up of the best elements of these two civilizations; for the colonization of the land by our citizens and against the invasion of the country by foreigners of all races and countries; for the intellectual, moral, and social progress of the Canadian people; for the economic development of all the resources of the country in the interest of the people who inhabit it; for the honest and intelligent administration of the state and of all its provincial and municipal fractions; for the subordination of particular interests and the cupidity of parties to the higher interests of the nation.[168]

He stressed his belief in the bi-ethnic and bilingual character of Canada, and that a moral agreement between French and English was essential to the formation of Canadian nationality:

We wish both elements to conserve the characteristic traits of their race, their traditions, their language, their literature, and all their aspirations which are compatible with the moral and political unity of the Canadian people. We wish that the one should become more Canadian than French, and the other more Canadian than English. Let each group derive from its country of origin the ideas, advances, and developments necessary to the conservation of its particular patrimony, intellectual or moral; but each must also have enough patriotism, intelligence, and generosity to subordinate its particular tastes or prejudices to the exigencies of national unity.

In other words, we oppose equally French colonialism, in the world of ideas, and English colonialism in the world of politics and facts; we wish that both give place to a Canadian nationalism, both English and French, sharply distinct in the elements proper to the two races and their particular genius, but harmoniously united in the research of a common ideal, made up of Canadian traditions, rooted in the Canadian soil, and having no other object than the moral and material greatness of the Canadian fatherland.[169]

Bourassa explained that *Le Devoir* was a Catholic journal, but not the organ of the hierarchy, the clergy, or any group of monks or priests. He stressed its freedom in all national or political matters, but also its conviction that the French Canadians 'would remain Catholic only on condition of remaining French, and remaining French only on condition of remaining Catholic.'[170] *Le Devoir* would continue independent of party politics. Bourassa opposed the formation of a nationalist party on the grounds that party spirit was already too strong; that third parties were only favored by exceptional circumstances for certain immediate ends, while his program of nationalism was too extensive and too far reaching; and finally that the elements of a superior party were lacking after forty years of degrading party strife. 'Instead of seeking to win elections against one or the other party, or against both, we shall seek more and more to create around the parties a barrier which will contain them, supplying beneath them a solid base which will prevent them from sinking too low, and above them a directing master thought which will force them to work for the good of the nation instead of corrupting its spirit.'[171] Bourassa closed with an appeal for financial aid through subscriptions, printing contracts, and advertising.

In his speech Bourassa had mentioned the possible necessity of forming a third party to combat the ostracism of French in Ontario, if it continued and if both parties refused to remedy it; but in fact he had already rallied almost all of Quebec to the cause of the

Franco-Ontarians. The hierarchy now joined the struggle, subscribing to the A.C.J.C. fund, recommending it to their clergy, and referring to the struggle in Ontario in their pastoral letters. Laval University in Quebec organized a demonstration for January 25, while the campaign in favor of the Franco-Ontarians continued in the press and on the platform. At Quebec the assemblage included Cardinal Bégin, his auxiliary Bishop Roy, Mgr. Amédée Gosselin, rector of Laval, Gouin and four members of his cabinet, Senator Landry, Senator Belcourt, and five or six other senators, the speakers of both houses of the provincial legislature, and Sévigny, the future deputy-speaker of the federal House, the chief justice of Quebec, and a host of other notables.

Only Laurier and Bourassa were missing at what *Le Soleil* called 'the hour of mobilization of the French-Canadian race.'[172] Laurier, who feared the repercussions of the agitation in the other provinces, swept as they were by war hysteria, held himself apart from it. Bourassa spoke on 'The Renaissance of Small Nationalities' at the university in Montreal on January 27 for the benefit of the Franco-Ontarians. He developed the theory of national rights and applied it to the Canadian minorities. He called upon Quebec, the natural protector of all the French of Canada, to make this right respected: 'In the name of our own constitution, of our own dignity, in the name of the conscience of humanity, of which we possess a part which awakens, we have the duty to aid with all our strength the French-Canadian minorities of Canada who fight for the conservation of their rights and their traditions.'[173]

The federal government took alarm at the rising tide of feeling in Quebec, and Borden privately intervened with W. H. Hearst, the premier of Ontario. Afterwards he reported to Fitzpatrick that Hearst desired to do everything possible to remedy injustice, but his efforts were frustrated by interventions from outside the province. In short, if Quebec would quiet down, something might be done by Ontario. Fitzpatrick passed on a copy of Borden's letter to Archbishop Bruchési. But Quebec was now animated by a crusading spirit, and feeling continued to rise in all quarters of the province. In a letter to *Le Devoir* Napoléon Garceau censured the growing tendency to set the re-establishment of the Ontario separate schools as the condition of French-Canadian support of the war. But *Le Devoir* dismissed the old nationalist as merely another 'dissident.' Anti-French-Canadian feeling in Ontario rose as Quebec's feeling against Ontario mounted. Neither side would yield, and the way was paved for the later explosion of ethnic feeling.

Rifts in the political truce appeared during the federal session from February 15 to April 15. The address was moved by an Ontario German and seconded by a former Quebec nationalist,

Honoré Achim. Laurier qualified his pledge of full support of th government by saying that expenditures could not be sanctione without accounting and that such questions as giving 'the Dominio a voice in all questions of peace and war'[174] should be postpone until after the war. He took up the matter of the bad boots supplie to the First Division and urged an investigation, which Borde promised. Borden reported that '31,000 men are today in th British Isles or in France; 1,000 are in Bermuda; and nearly 10,00 are doing garrison duty in Canada.'[175] He also announced tha 50,000 men had been enlisted for the defence of Canada. Laurie taunted Blondin, the new minister of internal revenue, with his pas nationalist statements; 'the honorable gentleman had filled up th holes in the flag and . . . would now breathe the atmosphere o liberty,'[176] as he had taunted Sévigny upon his rise to the deputy speakership by supporting a program contrary to that on whic he had been elected.

In March Laurier criticized the government for extravagance i the budget, which had not been previously submitted to the opposi tion, as was done in England. New taxes, bad boots, profiteerin on war contracts, and a new measure permitting soldiers to vot were debated. The latter was passed, but in the face of the Senate' opposition to immediate application of the Redistribution Act Borden accepted an amendment in that sense. On the final day o the session Borden spoke on the report of the Public Account Committee which had investigated war expenditures, and severel censured the part of two Conservative M.P.'s in profiteering in drug and horses. He announced his intention of appointing a committe to supervise the purchases made under parliament's appropriatio of $100,000,000 for war purposes. This War Purchasing Commission to whose establishment Sir Sam Hughes objected, was made up o Edward Kemp, G. F. Galt, and Hormisdas Laporte on May 8. I eliminated many of the criticisms to which the government had bee exposed by Hughes' favoritism in awarding contracts.

Soon after the prorogation of parliament, Robert Rogers mad a speech in Montreal demanding an immediate election, in orde that the government should not be 'handicapped and crippled an interfered with at every turn, tarrying and disputing with a Opposition that . . . has declared a want of confidence in ou proposals for the carrying on of our part in this great conflict.'[17] A majority of the cabinet favored a dissolution, but Borden decide against it, after the governor-general had deprecated such a cours and adverse public opinion had made itself felt.[178] At Toront on May 15 Laurier declared that he was a party man in time o peace, but 'I do not care, for my part, so long as the war lasts, t open the portals of office with that bloody key.'[179] Oppositio o a wartime election grew as word came across the Atlantic of the remendous casualties suffered by the First Division in the Second 3attle of Ypres.

The Princess Patricia's Canadian Light Infantry had gone into he line in January and by May 7 was down to half strength, and y June only 12 men and one officer, Lieutenant Talbot Papineau, f the original battalion had escaped death or wounds.[180] The 'irst Division reached the front in March. They got their first real aptism of fire in the Battle of Saint-Julien or Langemarck from April 22 to 28. They withstood the first gas attack of the war, osing about 6,000 men in killed, wounded, and missing as they ıeld a gap left in the line by the panic-stricken French Turcos ınd Zouaves against four enemy divisions. Withdrawn from the ront line on May 3–5, they returned to it on May 19 at Festubert ınd Givenchy, losing about half their strength by June 30. Sam Iughes was bitterly critical of British command, and urged the eplacement of the British General E. A. H. Alderson by the Canalian General R. E. W. Turner. The Second Division arrived in England by installments in March, April, and May. It did not go o France until September, though in August it supplied reinforcenents to the First Division. The Canadian Army Corps was then ormed under the command of the British General Alderson, but vith the divisions commanded by the Canadian Generals A. W. Currie and Turner.

The recruiting of 150,000 men was authorized on July 8, 1915 y order-in-council, and in October the limit was raised to 250,000. 3y the end of the year 212,000 men were under arms, of which 80,000 were raised in 1915; and early in the new year an attempt vas made to bring the force up to 500,000 men. The ceaseless lemands for more manpower occasioned by the heavy losses in 'rance resulted in an intensification of the recruiting campaign in Canada. In the House on February 25, 1915 Sam Hughes had oasted that he 'could raise three more contingents in three weeks f necessary.'[181] But he was not given to weighing his words, as ın utterance in Montreal on May 4 gave evidence: 'Canada has ent one contingent, a second is on the way and a third will be going n a week or two. A fourth is almost ready, and if necessary we vill send a fifth, a sixth, a tenth, or a twentieth.'[182] In the face of uch unrealistic enthusiasm a French-Canadian reaction made tself evident. In the Commons on March 9 the Liberal Roch Lanctôt and the Conservative Adélard Bellemare declared their elief that Canada was doing too much and that increased proluction would be Canada's best contribution.[183]

Of the 32,070 men asked for the third contingent, only 22,738 vere raised, according to the Militia Department's figures of March

26, with only one military department (Kingston) enlisting mor than its quota and with all the others short of their goal, gravely s in the Maritimes, British Columbia, Manitoba and Saskatchewar and Quebec.[184] By the end of 1915 only 212,000 had been enliste out of the 250,000 goal set on November 1. The official figures c February 15, 1916 showed that of a total of 249,471 then enlisted 62 per cent were British-born, 30 per cent Canadian-born, other 8 per cent.[185] The increasing difficulties encountered in recruitin were due to the facts that the British-born of military age had largel enlisted in the early days of the war, the unrooted urban populatio had largely been absorbed, native Canadians still showed a reluct ance to fight for 'civilization' or 'the empire' as the recruiting crie went (no specifically Canadian appeal was made), and the rura regions remained apathetic to the war.

Early in 1915 the raising of a second French-Canadian battalion the 41st, was authorized, and Lt.-Col. Louis H. Archambault lef the 22nd to recruit the new unit, based at Quebec but drawn largel from Hull and Montreal. Dr. Mignault was allowed to organiz the French-Canadian hospital unit which he had proposed shoul be put at the service of the French government. But early in th session Hughes returned a vague answer when questioned by Quebec member as to whether the government intended to form th French-Canadian brigade desired by many patriotic *Québecois*. I reply to a whispering campaign against Quebec's enlistment record and to a direct question about the number of French Canadians i the first contingent, Hughes said that Quebec had done its dut and set the number as between 3,000 and 6,000. This statemen encouraged the over-optimistic estimates of French-Canadia patriots, while its vagueness did not quiet English-Canadia detractors. Another French battalion, the 57th, was authorize later in the spring, under the command of Lt.-Col. E.-T. Paquet A fourth, the 69th, was recruited in June by 24-year-old Adolph Dansereau, a wounded veteran of the 14th Battalion and a son o Arthur Dansereau of *La Presse*. By midsummer these units were a full strength, and together with the 22nd, totaled more than 4,00 men, in addition to the French Canadians scattered throughout th forces.

But the group spirit aroused by the formation of exclusivel French-Canadian units was weakened by the refusal to let French Canadian members of the 13th and 14th Battalions transfer to th 22nd, the only French-Canadian unit at the front, and by draft on the 41st and 57th for the reinforcement of English-Canadia units. There were also other developments which dampene enthusiasm. Dr. Mignault's hospital unit, raised for service i France, was ordered to the Dardanelles; but after vigorous protest the order was cancelled and in November the unit was established at Saint-Cloud near Paris as General Hospital No. 8. Colonel J.-P. Landry, a Permanent Force officer, was relieved of the command of the 5th Brigade of the Second Division on the eve of its departure for France in September, and relegated to the post of inspector-general of camps in England. He was replaced by Colonel David Watson of the First Division, a personal friend of Sam Hughes, who was promoted to the rank of brigadier. The highest ranking French Canadian in the whole Canadian Army Corps was Colonel F.-M. Gaudet of the 22nd. The replacement of Colonel Landry, which was considered to be Hughes' revenge on his father Senator Landry for the latter's role in the Ontario school quarrel, confirmed the growing French-Canadian opinion that Hughes kept the higher commands for English Canadians. Recruiting lagged in Quebec, thanks to these factors and to events at home. An English Canadian was appointed chief recruiting officer for Quebec, and the choice was no more popular because of the fact that he was a former Methodist minister. Officers of the French-Canadian units complained that their units were kept too long in Canada, and that it was difficult to maintain discipline when their men were sent home on harvest leave and thus tempted to desert.

But the major factor in the deteriorating war spirit of Quebec was unquestionably the Ontario school question. Most English Canadians did not realize the importance attached to the matter by the French Canadians, and the few sympathetic English-Canadian voices found little hearing in the midst of the concentration of English opinion upon the war. Father M. J. Whalen of Ottawa replied to Cardinal Bégin, Archbishop Bruchési, and Sir Lomer Gouin in an open letter to the *Toronto Mail and Empire* on February 14, in which he blamed the Ontario war of races on a conspiracy on the part of Archbishop Duhamel, the Association d'Education, and *Le Droit* to favor a French invasion of the province. He urged that ecclesiastical provinces should be realigned to coincide with the boundaries of the civil provinces, thus depriving the French clergy of the opportunity to intervene in Ontario. In Manitoba a movement also arose among the Irish clergy in opposition to Archbishop Langevin. Meanwhile in Quebec Héroux supported the Franco-Ontarians in *Le Devoir* and the A.C.J.C. extended its campaign for funds to the classical colleges and primary schools, thus focussing the attention of French-Canadian youth on Ontario rather than on Europe. On March 7 Senator Landry, Thomas Chapais, P.-E. Lamarche, Dr. Baril, and Senator Belcourt took part in a mass meeting of protest against Regulation 17 at the Théâtre Français in Ottawa. The presence of Conservatives, Liberals, and nationalist spokesmen indicated compliance with Landry's injunction: 'Before we are Liberals or Conservatives, let us b French Canadians.'[186]

Three days later Senator L.-O. David presented a motion urging settlement of the school question in accordance with the spirit of the constitution, recalling the aid given to the Irish by French Canadians in the past. An Irish senator, George McHugh, supported the resolution. On the same day the Orange Grand Lodge met, with Sam Hughes in attendance, and called for the suppression of all teaching of French in Ontario. A Conservative M.P., H. B Morphy, proclaimed: 'Never shall we let the French Canadians implant in Ontario the disgusting speech they use.'[187] This utterance was echoed in the Senate, where Senator Choquette called Morphy a 'brutal maniac and ignoramus.'[188] Senator Poirier of New Brunswick urged conciliation and a truce. Senators Béique Dandurand, Legris, and Boyer defended the Franco-Ontarians. Senator Power of Halifax, an eminent Irish Catholic, proposed a sub-amendment which destroyed the force of David's motion. Senator Pope of the Eastern Townships supported Power, and reproached the nationalists with subordinating the French-Canadian military effort to the settlement of the school question. Senator Landry, as speaker, sought to bar Power's amendment on grounds of procedure, but his effort was defeated by an ethnic vote. In the face of the opposition of the English members, Senator Landry ceased to preside over the Senate on April 8 and offered his resignation to Borden, who refused it. Landry resumed his seat for the final session on April 15, after accepting the presidency of the Association d'Education the previous evening. The debate on the David resolution was cut short by the prorogation of parliament, but it had already produced a minor division between French Liberals and Conservatives, both in parliament and in the press.[189]

Quebec continued to grow more aroused about the school question. Père Villeneuve of Ottawa was invited to preside over the March meeting of the Saint-Jean-Baptiste Society of Montreal. On March 19 Bourassa gave a lecture on '*La Langue française au Canada, sa necessité, ses avantages,*' under the auspices of the same society for the benefit of the Franco-Ontarians. At Quebec the *curé* of Saint-Sauveur presided over a protest meeting against the attitude of the Ontario Orangemen.

Bourassa hailed the initial manifesto of Landry, which urged that the school question should not be made a political one. He stressed the overriding importance of the question:

The whole problem of the French language and of French survival is being raised in Ontario. For Canada, for all America, it is not on the battlefields of Europe that this survival will be maintained or extinguished. Let France be victorious or defeated, let her retake Alsace-Lorraine or lose Champagne, it is not the Prussian armies of the Kaiser or German culture which will decide our fate. It is ourselves.

The enemies of the French language, of French civilization in Canada, are not the Boches on the shores of the Spree; but the English-Canadian anglicizers, the Orange intriguers, or Irish priests. Above all they are French Canadians weakened and degraded by the conquest and three centuries of colonial servitude.

Let no mistake be made: if we let the Ontario minority be crushed, it will soon be the turn of other French groups in English Canada.[190]

The French Canadians carried on the war for the defence of their language on many fronts, insisting on the use of French in business and the public services of Quebec.

Ethnic feeling was evident in the hockey games between French and English teams, and also in the sports at military camps. Even the small boys of Montreal, Quebec, and the urban centers of the Townships waged war upon each other on racial lines. The 22nd, transferred to Amherst, New Brunswick, for final training before embarkation, was greeted on arrival by empty streets, closed shops, and cold looks. But thanks to the battalion's contributions to the poor of the town and its good behavior, Amherst declared a holiday to allow the people to escort the troops on their departure, and the mayor accompanied them to Halifax.[191] The news of the Canadians' gallant behavior at Ypres and of the heavy losses brought a momentary lull, with even *Le Devoir* paying homage to the heroic dead; but a reaction soon set in upon the ground that French Canada was not bearing her fair share of the war burden. The loss of one or more sons in the small average English-Canadian family was felt perhaps more strongly than in the larger French-Canadian families.

On May 19 Bourassa delivered at the Monument National an expanded version of his earlier lecture on '*La langue française au Canada, ses droits, sa necessité, ses avantages*,' under the auspices of the A.C.J.C. and for the benefit of the Franco-Ontarians. Senator Landry acted as chairman and assured the large audience that French would continue to be spoken at home and at school in Ontario, since 'we wish it, you wish it, God wishes it.'[192] Senator David appeared on the platform. In a careful constitutional analysis Bourassa reviewed the natural rights of the French Canadians to their language, the rights derived from the capitulations, the Treaty of Paris, the Quebec Act, and the Constitution of 1791. He pointed out that provision was made for a French version of the laws when Upper Canada was established, that Egerton Ryerson had approved of the teaching of both languages in the Ontario schools, and that many French schools were established in Ontario before Confederation and were given government subsidies. He cited Macdonald's interpretation in 1890 of the B.N.A. Act as assuring 'equal rights of every kind, of language, of religion, of property, and of person.'[19] He argued that rights acquired under the federal constitution overrode those acquired under provincial law, and that French Canadians in Ontario had the same rights to their language as English Canadians in Quebec. But he counseled against seeking revenge by reprisals in Quebec.

Bourassa pointed out that the great majority of British subjects were not English-speaking, and that in many quarters of the empire other languages than English enjoyed a larger place than that of French in Canada. He denounced the Prussian and American doctrine that national unity must be based upon one language; he defended bilingualism by citing its success in Wales, Ireland, Belgium, Switzerland, and Alsace, pointing out that the Ontario oppression was worse than that of the Germans in the latter country. The French language was necessary for the preservation of the French Canadians' faith; it was a barrier to Americanization; it was useful in trade and diplomacy; it was the language of superior civilization. He defended Quebec's right to intervene in Ontario, urged contributions to the cause, and the development of a cult for the preservation of the language in its purest form: 'Let us be defenders of the French language, not only against others, but against ourselves.' In a passage omitted from the printed text, he attacked the Irish clergy:

> It is time, high time, that Rome should know that in supporting the cause of the oppressed, our bishops accomplish not only a duty of justice and charity. Inspired by the example of St. Paul, they protect in America the catholicity of the Church against the insidious or declared attempts of those who wish to make religion the weapon of domination of a race. . . .
>
> As to the prelates and priests who unite themselves to the worst enemies of the Church to snatch from the French Canadians the free enjoyment of their natural rights, guaranteed by history, civilization, and the practice of civilized nations, they fail in their double duty of Catholic pastors and British subjects . . . Instead of persecuting the oldest and most faithful people of America, why do they not apply their ardor for fighting to saving the millions of English-speaking Catholics whom mixed marriages, attendance at neutral schools, and Protestant or materialist literature throw each year into the immense army of unbelievers, worshippers of the Golden Calf?
>
> I hope this declaration will scandalize no one. I make it without anger, in the spirit of the father of a Catholic family who knows that God has given him the right and imposed upon him the duty to preserve for his children the unreckonable treasure of the faith and of national traditions . . .

The acts from which we suffer, whatever be the character of their authors—and I do not incriminate the good faith of these authors—do not derive from episcopal authority or the priestly character. These are individual acts, outside their apostolic rule, but which constitute a peril for the faith of a number.

It is time that Rome, mother and protector of all Catholics, should know it clearly.[194]

Bourassa gained prestige by this open appeal to Rome, which no other French-Canadian lay leader had yet dared to make. His audience unanimously ratified resolutions affirming the right of the French Canadians to speak their language and to teach it to their children in all the provinces of Canada; claiming respect for the federal pact and Macdonald's interpretation of it; and expressing the hope that the Ontario minority would receive the support of all Canadians, Catholic or Protestant, French or English, 'desirous of preserving in America the benefits of French civilization and causing to triumph in Canada the precepts and practice of the *entente cordiale* which united England and France on the battlefields of Europe.'[195] These resolutions were reprinted by most of the provincial weeklies. Some days later Archbishop Bruchési and Sir Adolphe Routhier devoted their Royal Society papers to the rights of the French language in Canada.[196] And when Archbishop Langevin died in Montreal on June 15, his funeral was virtually turned into a nationalist demonstration. In every French-Canadian community along the way from Montreal to Winnipeg, troops of kneeling schoolchildren greeted the funeral train as it carried the body of the 'hero of the West' to his last rest.[197]

Bourassa spoke in Montreal again on June 23 for the benefit of the Franco-Ontarians; Lavergne at the Monument National on June 24; and Landry addressed 5,000 people at the Ottawa Arena on the same day, saying that he would appeal to Rome and London after vainly interceding with the Archbishop of Ottawa and the premier of Ontario: 'We shall ask the mother country if our children have no other rights than to go and be killed in the service of the Empire.'[198] *L'Action Sociale*, now known as *L'Action Catholique*, urged a truce, at the instigation of T.-C. Casgrain, who was alarmed by the Ontario reaction to the charges of 'Prussianism.' But Quebec feeling had mounted too high to be calmed. Bourassa replied that 'Mgr. Latulipe was not wrong in considering the proceedings of the Ontario Boches as execrable as those of the Pomeranian Boches.'[199] He warned of the probable extension of the struggle to Saskatchewan and Alberta, where the teaching of French was subjected to new restrictions.[200] After *L'Action Catholique* and Archbishop Bruchési had counseled moderation, *Le Canada*, *La Patrie*, and *La Presse* criticized the turning over to *Le Droit*, which had taken readers from them, of part of the money raised by the A.C.J.C. for the Ontario schools.

On July 12 the Appelate Court of Toronto approved Regulation 17. The Ontario government promptly dissolved the Ottawa Separate School Commission, which was two-thirds French, and replaced it by a new commission of three members, with only one French-Canadian representative. These actions, violently protested by *Le Devoir*, coincided with a new recruiting campaign. Their repercussions were soon evident.

Sam Hughes, now promoted to the rank of general, saw no conflict between further recruiting and the continued expansion of war industry. But 250 factories were now engaged in making munitions in Canada, employing at high wages all the men they could find. Industry thus drained off most of the potential urban recruits, while the farmer remained as attached to his land and as indifferent to the war as ever. Bourassa made much of the 'business as usual' spirit of British industrialists, of British opposition to conscription, and of British labor's unwillingness to speed up the production of munitions urgently needed by the army. Shortage of ammunition had in part accounted for the heavy Canadian losses in April and May. Bourassa hailed the role of John Redmond, the Irish nationalist, in insisting upon Home Rule as a condition of Irish participation in the war, and contrasted it with the servility of Canadian leaders. Aroused by these Irish references, the Duke of Connaught urged Borden to censor *Le Devoir*. But Borden had the wisdom to reply: 'Bourassa would like nothing better. I would not be so foolish. Besides, Campbell Bannerman and Lloyd George were far worse in the South Africa War, and Carson respecting Ulster.'[201] Even *Le Soleil* protested against the attitude of British business and labor, when Canadians were being called upon to make greater sacrifices.

But both the government and the military neglected this new factor in French-Canadian public opinion, as well as that of the Ontario school question, in launching a new recruiting drive. Casgrain made a speaking trip through the lower St. Lawrence region, urging total support of England. Colonel Wilson, commander of the Montreal military district, predicted and hoped for conscription in an interview in the *Star* on July 12. A campaign for the purchase of machine guns was launched, amid objections from the French press that this was hardly a matter for public charity, and open-air recruiting meetings were begun in Montreal. On July 15, two English-Canadian industrialists, C. C. Ballantyne and A. D. Dawson, warned that they would not employ men of military age, who should be at the front.[202] At McGill the following day the ex-nationalist N.-K. Laflamme came out in support of conscription, while a

Protestant minister, clad in uniform, proclaimed that Christ would be at the front, if He were on earth.[203] Napoléon Garceau, who believed in wholehearted support of the war, nevertheless protested in an open letter to the minister of justice against the intimidation practiced by Ballantyne and Dawson:

> If military service should be obligatory, let it be so for all, rich as well as poor, but under laws passed by the parliament of the country, and not because of the authority or power that money may give to certain personages . . .[204]

At a recruiting meeting at the Parc Sohmer on July 22, at which Laflamme, Blondin, and Colonel Paquet spoke, there was heckling. And on the following day at Parc Lafontaine a recruiting meeting was broken up by a crowd of workers, clerks, and students, who then paraded to the Champs de Mars crying 'Down with Conscription!' Recruiting posters were torn down by crowds singing 'O Canada.'[205] *La Patrie* blamed the nationalist papers for denouncing recruiting and preaching sedition, and urged the adoption of censorship. Censorship was indeed established, but not often invoked. Bourassa was careful to use the statements of British public figures to support his charges. *L'Action Catholique* pointed out that the best way for French Canadians to avoid conscription was by enlistment in large numbers, and stressed the moral obligation to aid England and her allies.[206] The young men of the Groupe de l'Arche, headed by Roger Maillet, Ubald Paquin, and Olivar Asselin, made anti-conscriptionist speeches from the steps of the university. On July 26 L.-N.-J. Pagé, a barber with oratorical talent, and other popular figures made violent speeches against recruiting at the Champs de Mars. The speakers' platform was stormed by soldiers, and the police had to intervene.

But this explosive state of feeling, aroused by the threat of conscription, soon quieted down, under assurances from French-Canadian leaders that the government had no thought of conscription. On July 8 Casgrain's organ *L'Evénement* and Blondin's *Semaine* accused the nationalists of frightening the people with an imaginary danger. On July 28 Casgrain issued a statement that 'there will be no conscription,'[207] while Liberal leaders continued to back the recruiting campaign. On August 4 Rodolphe Lemieux proclaimed at Montreal that 'it is, I consider, not only a question of duty, it is a question of honour, for our sons and our brothers to enlist bravely and voluntarily in His Majesty's service.'[208] In spite of ill health the 74-year-old Laurier addressed a crowd of 8,000 at his birthplace, Saint-Lin, on August 7, stressing the double duty of the French Canadians and urging unity with the English Canadians in support of the war:

In Montreal there are to be found men who would prevent recruiting. I claim for my country the supreme honour of bearing arms in this holy cause, and if I support the government, it is because I have the heart to do my duty. . . . The fear of conscription in Canada is as groundless now as it was in 1911. . . . My fellow-countrymen, I envy you your youth and your uniform, but above all your chance to fight for such a cause. If I were a younger man, I would be in the firing line.[209]

Colonel Dansereau claimed that this speech doubled the daily rate of enlistment in his battalion. Again at Sherbrooke on August 12 Laurier urged Canadians of all origins to rally to the armed forces, and speaking particularly to French Canadians he added:

I affirm with all my strength that it is the duty of Canada to give to Great Britain in this war all the assistance that is in the power of Canada. . .

What is the duty of our young men? If I were a young man and had the health which I have today and did not have when I was young, I would not hesitate to take the musket, and to fight for freedom, as so many of our fellow-countrymen are doing. I cannot do that now. But there is one thing I can do; I can use my voice, such as it is, in the great cause in which we all have such a supreme interest. This is the message that I bring to you upon this occasion. The peril is at present great. . . . If we want to win, we must be worthy of freedom, we have to be prepared to fight for freedom.[210]

At Napanee on September 2 he collapsed while addressing a recruiting meeting, and after an operation had to give up public appearances until late in the fall. But other Liberal leaders carried on. At Quebec City on September 8 a recruiting meeting was held under the chairmanship of the mayor, and Sir Lomer Gouin declared his belief that 'the French Canadians should be ready to do all in their power to assist the Allies.'[211] A Citizen's Recruiting League was formed in Montreal on September 17, with a French committee including Senators Dandurand, David, and Béique; Charles Beaubien, L.-T. Maréchal, Hormisdas Laporte, N.-K. Laflamme, Joseph Ainey, and Edouard Fabre-Surveyer, and others. On September 25 at Longueuil Lt.-Col. Hercule Barré, a returned veteran engaged in organizing a new battalion, urged emphatically: 'Don't sit around here and criticize . . . Get out and do something yourself. Remember that Britain is at war, Canada is at war, and you, you are at war.'[212]

Bourassa, who did not let the swelling tide of provincial feeling distract him from international events, took advantage of Pope Benedict XV's appeal for peace, as he had of the sinking of the *Lusitania* to censure England for objecting to the neutrality of merchant ships, and of Italy's entrance into the war to point out that she had acted in her own interest and not out of chivalry. The latter observation cost *Le Devoir* some windows broken by the Montreal Italians, but Bourassa's support of the Pope's plea for peace reinforced his influence with the clergy. *Le Canada* reminded Bourassa that the bishops had supported the contribution of men and money to the war, and asked whether he was trying to censure them. *La Presse* stressed that the war was accepted by the Church and that it was youth's Christian duty to rally to the colors.[213] *L'Action Catholique* began a new series of articles, warning the clergy that they would fail in their duty and injure the Church if they gave 'the least pretext to those who could question their loyalty and their attachment to the British mother country.' It urged Bourassa not 'to anticipate the Pope and the bishops in the defence of Catholic interests' and not 'to admonish those whose advice or orders he ought to take, instead of giving advice and orders to them.'[214] The hierarchy was beginning to take alarm at the evident conversion of the lower clergy to 'Bourassism' and at its silent opposition to conscription, which was beginning to attract attention in Ontario.

Olivar Asselin at once took issue with *L'Action Catholique* in a series of four articles which appeared in *L'Action* from September 11 to October 9 and were reproduced in pamphlet form, like his earlier criticisms of the ecclesiastical organ, as '*Les Evêques et la propagande de l'Action Catholique*'—'a little plea for the freedom of thought of the lower clergy and Catholic laity in political matters.'[215] He accused the 'organ of the Cardinal Archbishop of Quebec'—which fluctuated between being official and unofficial, according to circumstances—with 'seeking to make the French-Canadian bishops popular at London and at Rideau Hall,'[216] by adopting a mild attitude on the Ontario question and censuring Bourassa. Asselin attacked the editor of *L'Action Catholique*, the ex-Jesuit Abbé d'Amours, as 'one of those little jesuitical and Italian abbés such as there were four centuries ago and such as there are, alas, hardly any more left, who wield with equal cleverness the canons of the Church and the pen, and for whom no task is ever too hard, too wicked, or too vile.'[217]

Asselin asserted with his customary vigor that the Cardinal and Bishop Roy had exactly the same authority in politics as his friend Phidime Phidimous of Terrebonne—'and even a little less, since by their cloth they are less free to express their whole thought.'[218] He defended the right of the clergy to their own political opinions, and pointed out that thousands of Protestant ministers had turned their pulpits into political platforms. But he declared that the bishops had gone beyond the loyalist tradition of the Church by approving the sending of men and money overseas in 1914; that their *mandement* was an unjust interference with the rights of citizenship; and that it had paved the way for 'the avalanche of "cretinotheological" bad prose which *L'Action Catholique* had since launched upon the adversaries of the imperialist policy.'[219] He opposed Archbishop Bruchési's support of the Franco-Ontarians to *L'Action Catholique's* lukewarmness in the matter, and denied that the paper was truly the spokesman of all the bishops. He accused Bishop Roy of being its real master, with 'the ex-Jesuit d'Amours, born Damours at Trois-Pistoles'[220] as its Grey Eminence. He ended with a vigorous warning to the bishops that if *L'Action Catholique's* course were approved, they would lose the support of the people and the lower clergy. Asselin followed this attack up with three more articles in *L'Action* on October 24, 30, and November 6. In these he made a detailed analysis of Abbé d'Amours' editorial opinions since the outbreak of the war, and accused him of merely playing politics.

8

Borden spent the summer in Europe, trying to iron out some of the problems raised by friction between Sam Hughes and the British authorities, which had led to complaints from the governor-general. Before his departure from Canada in June the prime minister had launched a further investigation under Sir Charles Piers Davidson of Montreal into war purchases. In the company of R. B. Bennett, he crossed on the *Adriatic*, acting as a courier for the British Ambassador in the United States. In London he conferred with Sir George Perley, a member of the Canadian cabinet who had been acting as high commissioner since the beginning of the war, and New Brunswick-born Max Aitken, who played a growingly important role under the curious title of 'Canadian Eye-Witness'. Borden urged upon Bonar Law that Perley, as a member of the Canadian government, enjoyed a higher status than other dominion high commissioners, and discussed constitutional relations between the United Kingdom and the dominions. Law opposed having dominion ministers resident in London in peacetime, but said Perley's presence had been of advantage during the war. He also warned that a voice in foreign affairs for the dominions might involve higher military and naval expenditure than they cared to make, while Borden argued that population, wealth, and internal needs must be considered in such contributions.

Borden was received by the King, who praised the Canadian troops for having saved the day at Ypres, and expressed the view that the dominions should have a voice in foreign policy. From Kitchener Borden learned that the war was expected to last a long time. He was invited to attend and take part in a cabinet meeting on July 14, the first time that a dominion representative enjoyed that privilege. He had an interview with Sir Edward Grey, and learned from other sources that the coalition government formed in May was shaky. Borden reviewed the Second Division and visited the Canadian wounded as much as possible. Then he went to France late in July, reviewing Canadian troops and visiting hospitals, before returning to England for a Privy Council meeting. He stayed with the King and Queen at Windsor, and was lunched and dined by many groups.

In an interview with Sir James Bryce, who favored giving the dominions a voice in foreign policy, Borden asserted that either they would have it or each would develop a foreign policy of its own. Finally, having vainly sought from various cabinet ministers the information which he desired about Britain's war plans, he warned Bonar Law that he would return to Canada 'with no definite intention of urging my fellow-countrymen to continue in the war work they have begun, or with the extensive preparation which I am sure they are ready to undertake if I inform them that the British Government takes the war seriously, realizes the immensity of the task, is making preparation accordingly, and there is no more cry of "Business as Usual."'[221] Having thus forced a clear picture of the situation out of Bonar Law and Lloyd George, Borden made up his mind that it would be at least eighteen months before the British Empire would be able to throw its whole force and power into the War. He so reported to his colleagues and to Laurier as leader of the opposition when he returned to Ottawa, after receiving a warm welcome at Montreal on September 3.[222]

Upon his return Borden was faced with political problems. George Foster urged a reorganization of the Militia Department so as to deprive Sam Hughes of virtually all authority, while Senator Lougheed, who had administered the department in Hughes' absence abroad, expressed the conviction that Hughes was an incapable administrator. Senator Landry and Alexandre Lacoste, father and brother-in-law of the Colonel Landry so summarily dealt with by Hughes, complained to Borden. But the latter had found Hughes useful in standing up for Canada with the War Office and Max Aitken thought well of him, so for the time being the troublesome general remained in office. Casgrain demanded a reorganization of theFrench section of the cabinet, complaining that Coderre was useless.[223] Consequently Blondin was named secretary of state and Esioff Patenaude minister of internal revenue, with Coderre retiring to the bench. Patenaude was re-elected without opposition, except from the independent Tancrède Marsil, who was disqualified on a technicality.

Patenaude and Casgrain sought vainly to arouse enthusiasm for the war with such statements as Casgrain's 'It is our war; it is my war; it is the war of everyone of us; it is the war of every man who is attached to the free British institutions under which we live.'[224] Blondin and Patenaude multiplied their appeals for wholehearted support of the war during the remainder of the year at Grand' Mère, Valleyfield, Drummondville, and Nicolet, taking the view that Canada's first line of defence was in Belgium and that French Canada should not isolate itself by insisting upon its rights, which would be granted when it had done its part for the defence of the Empire. Charles Beaubien and Napoléon Garceau aided this campaign, but the words of Tories associated with the same party as the Ontario assimilators and of ex-nationalists who had once been violently anti-British had little effect on the people. Casgrain, the only French-Canadian minister who had stood by his lifelong imperialist convictions, was the only one to make the gesture of offering his military services—at the age of 63. The gesture would have had more effect if it had been made by the younger men, Blondin, Patenaude, and Sévigny; and the Liberal and nationalist papers did not hesitate to say so.

The Ontario situation grew more embroiled with the opening of the new school year. Landry had sent two memoranda to the Papal secretary of state, one in the name of the Ottawa Saint-Jean-Baptiste Society, accusing the English bishops of Ontario of persecuting the French population, and the other a personal one, drawn up in even more energetic terms. Archbishop Bruchési and Thomas Chapais accepted Casgrain's view that French intransigence would increase the difficulty of a satisfactory settlement in Ontario. At the call of Landry, the Ontario teachers refused allegiance to the new commission and consequently received no pay. Archbishop Bruchési visited Ottawa at the request of Archbishop Gauthier and urged moderation upon the Franco-Ontarians, while he besought the Ontario premier to avoid taking action against Diane and Beatrice Desloges, teachers at the Ecole Guiges, who had been barred from the school and who had opened classes in a nearby chapel. The striking teachers were aided by contributions from the French parishes of Ottawa and by gifts from Quebec. There were rumors of new restrictions upon French schools in New Brunswick which drew from even *Le Soleil* the observation that the French Canadians could not be expected to fight German tyranny, if the same tyranny was applied in Ontario and New Brunswick. In Quebec there were street rows between students and soldiers and new complaints of prejudice against French Canadians in the public services. With French Canadians everywhere in Canada in an angry mood, the recruiting campaign lagged.

Sam Hughes, who had not spared glowing tributes to the French-Canadian soldiers when he received a civic reception at Quebec n September 14 upon his return from England, decided upon a esture towards Quebec which misfired. In October he offered the ommand of a battalion to Armand Lavergne, who was to raise it imself. Lavergne refused the offer in an open letter to Hughes, rinted in *Le Devoir* on November 2:

. . I have always opposed, in the press and on the platform in the rovinces of Quebec and Ontario, all Canadian participation in foreign ars, save for the defence of our territory.

Since I have been in public life, that has always been the well-known olicy of the nationalist party to which I belong and I have seen the same rinciples shared and defended forcibly by several of your cabinet col- agues, such as M. Monk, who remained faithful to them until his death, nd MM. L.-P. Pelletier, Bruno Nantel, Louis Coderre, and the new Iinister of the Interior, M. Patenaude.

To accept your flattering offer and induce my compatriots to enlist or the present war would be to disavow myself, for which you, with your igh sense of honor, would blame me.

Let me repeat to you here that I consider it unwise and even criminal o put Canada in danger for a war over which we have not had and will ot have any control. I am opposed to, and shall oppose with all my trength, the contribution of a man, a ship, or a dollar until England elieves she must share with us not only the dangers, but also the full ontrol and responsibility of the Empire's affairs. It is not for us to defend ngland, but for England to defend us . . .

I bring you another reason. My compatriots of French origin in ntario, Canadians like you, sir, are now undergoing a regime worse han that imposed by the Prussians in Alsace-Lorraine, because they do ot wish to abandon their mother tongue. Until they have been com- letely freed of this persecution, I cannot consider for an instant the idea f deserting their cause for a somewhat interesting adventure in a foreign ountry. I wish to see the reign of liberty and justice well established and aintained in our country, before imposing it upon other nations . . .[225]

avergne explained his stand at a public meeting on November 7 n Blondin's county of Champlain. It was approved by the nation- lists, cited as clear proof of French disloyalty in Toronto, and ccepted by Hughes as that of 'a man of honor' who 'had the same ight to his opinions as everyone.'[226]

Lavergne himself had written Asselin on November 3 that he xpected conscription, at least for militia officers, within six months, nd 'we then can combine the taste of adventure, our principles, nd *douce France* . . . I have faith that the future and circumstances ill enable me to clear myself of an accusation which may seem ounded until then. If this chance is refused me, I shall still believe hat one owes everything to one's country, even honor.'[227] avergne's gesture focused English-Canadian attention on French

Canada's growing reluctance to support the war effort whole heartedly. As a result patriotic French Canadians redoubled thei efforts in order to clear Quebec's name. It was at this time tha Casgrain offered his military services and that the other French Canadian ministers undertook a speaking campaign in favor c recruiting. One priest, Abbé Tetreau of Drummondville, joined i this campaign, but the great majority of the lower clergy wer opposed to enlistment. They had been converted to anti-imperialism by Bourassa, and they saw a danger to the faith of young men wh left their homes for military camps and foreign service.

During October and November Borden conferred with Laurie about extending the life of parliament, which expired on October 7 1916. He proposed that it should be extended until one year afte the conclusion of peace, to avoid a general election during the wa and to allow time for the men overseas to return home. In the mean time there was to be a suspension of party warfare. As an alternativ to this proposal, Borden suggested an extension of one year. Laurie favored the latter scheme as more definite, but insisted on bein informed about Borden's legislative plans, particularly as regard the railroads. The negotiations broke down because of Laurier' insistence that 'The Canadian Parliament cannot be expected t abdicate its functions.'[228]

During Laurier's illness Rodolphe Lemieux had borne the brun of backing recruiting as the acting Liberal leader; but on December Laurier and the whole Liberal high command appeared before packed audience at the Monument National in support of the wa effort. In war as in peace, Laurier said, the Liberals stood for th cause of the weak and oppressed, for justice and liberty, and i opposition to absolutism. To the extreme attitudes of the im perialists who wanted Canada to fight in all wars and called fo conscription, and of the nationalists who would fight in no war he opposed the Liberal doctrine of voluntary participation in noble cause, reserving Canada's autonomy. He censured th doctrine that Canada should only defend her own soil: 'For noble cause, we must do more than our duty.'[229] He was happ to see France and England united on the battlefield, but the *entent cordiale* was not yet complete in Canada: 'They who have rea patriotism are they who are working for reconciliation, who ar helping to sweep away the old divisions, who are working to restor harmony among the people on a basis acceptable to all.'[230] Afte the war, when the soldiers of both races had mingled their blood o the battlefields, the majority would surely do justice to its com panions in arms.

But Bourassa continued to link persecution in Ontario with th question of participation in the war, and Lavergne's stand, tha

Quebec should not support the latter until the former ceased, found wide favor with French Canadians. On December 16 Bourassa gave a lecture at the Monument National on 'Cartier, Macdonald, and Our Military Obligations,' in which he concluded that Canada had no military obligations outside its territory. Simultaneously he put on sale a book, *Que devons-nous à l'Angleterre ?*, which was an extensive historical and legal development of this thesis. He pointed out how the Fathers of Confederation and the imperial authorities had agreed to limit the new dominion's military obligations to defence of Canadian territory. This agreement had been observed until the development of imperialism at the time of the South African War:

> This was for Canada a very clear backward step. Laurier, chief of the Canadian government, resisted instinctively. Then, under the double pressure from London and Toronto, his resistance weakened. And we had successively the African expedition, the Navy Act of 1910, the 'emergency contribution' of 1912, and participation in the present war as a dependency of England. So many breaches in the established order, so many knife-blows in the treaties concluded between Great Britain and Canada, so many illegal, unconstitutional measures. Until the agreements of 1867 are broken by mutual consent, England has no right to impose such obligations upon us.[231]

Bourassa's book had a rapid sale, but the press protested against his conclusions. *Le Canada* regretted to 'find him in direct rebellion against the religious and civil authorities of his country,' and advanced the thesis that 'to go and attack the enemy where he could be conquered was to defend Canada, and it is ridiculous to pretend that we must wait until he comes to land on our shores.'[232] The *Daily Mail* accused Bourassa of preaching 'treason to the Empire and to the Sovereign.'[233] The Ontario press demanded prosecution of 'Herr Bourassa.' Principal Peterson of McGill did the same, accusing Bourassa of sowing disunion and hindering recruiting.[234] Unquestionably Bourassa did hinder recruiting, for many of his followers drew no other conclusion from his elaborate anti-imperialist arguments than that they should not enlist. Bourassa was not dismayed by the storm of abuse which greeted him; on December 23 he urged the government 'to cease to send Canadians to the butchery so long as the English workers do not decide to yield to the humble plea of the imperial authorities and to furnish the Empire's soldiers with the arms and munitions which they absolutely need to fight under reasonable conditions.'[235]

One of Bourassa's most notable followers, Olivar Asselin, had meanwhile decided to enlist. In his reply to Lavergne, under whom he had offered to serve when he learned of Hughes' offer, Asselin had stated his belief that 'the man who wishes to serve as a soldier France—or England—and who because of his poverty or for other reasons can do so only in the Canadian Expeditionary Force, can very well enlist without thus approving the official participation of Canada in the European conflict in Europe.'[236] He approved Lavergne's stand as reasonable, but said that as for himself, 'If I wish to go, it is because I should rather die than see France conquered and powerless.' He added: 'I sometimes think that the greatest need of our race is still to learn to despise life, when necessary; not to attach itself too much to well-being, to purely material comfort; to be hard on itself, and to be prodigal, on occasion, of its blood. . . . I wish that we were in our manner Spartans, not Nazarenes who turn the other cheek like slaves.'

Three new Quebec battalions, including a French-Canadian one, the 150th, under Lt.-Col. Hercule Barré, wounded veteran of the 14th Battalion, had been authorized in November. Asselin now undertook to raise another, the 163rd, refusing the colonelcy offered by Sam Hughes and contenting himself with the rank of major, while securing the command of the battalion for Henri Desrosiers, a former lieutenant of the 14th. Asselin had no wish to class himself with some of Hughes' honorary colonels whose military exploits were confined to recruiting speeches.

His nationalist friends were at a loss to explain Asselin's action, but at a public meeting at the Monument National on January 21, 1916 he revealed his reasons in a speech which was later printed as *Pourquoi je m'enrôle*. He revealed that as early as October 30, 1914, he had sought through Philippe Roy, the Canadian Commissioner in Paris, to enlist in the French army, and failing that, to secure an administrative job to replace a soldier.[237] In the early spring of 1915 he had tried through Casgrain, Fiset, and Sam Hughes to obtain a post as interpreter with the 22nd Battalion or with any other Canadian, British, or French unit. When Barré sought permission to raise a French-Canadian unit, Asselin had asked to serve as a lieutenant under him. He maintained that while condemning the government's policy, he had always admitted the right of the individual Canadian to serve voluntarily in the war. He took up the question of whether the French Canadians were doing their duty, and cited such heroes as Desrosiers, DeSerres, Roy, and others. He pointed out that 90 per cent of the French Canadians of military age could not hope for advancement in the army because English was the only language of command, and that even in the French-Canadian units the highest ranks would be barred to them. He also pointed out that the French Canadians were more attached to Canada than those who had more recently emigrated from Europe. He criticized the fact that so few decorations had been given to the 8,000 French-Canadian soldiers whose fighting qualities had been praised so highly by Sam Hughes and General Meighan. He did not believe that the Ontario situation would improve if French Canada furnished several more battalions, and he did not withdraw his censure of the pro-war attitude taken by the hierarchy.[238]

But aside from all these considerations, he thought British institutions, Belgium, and France worth fighting for. He, like Péguy, was a man of 1793 and gloried in it, and had not been as shocked by modern France as most of his compatriots. But he asserted that the world could not get along without France, which after the war would be more necessary than ever to humanity. He added that the French of America could remain French only through France. He summed up his reasons for enlisting thus:

> And so we march for British institutions, because by themselves and independently of the half-civilized persons who apply them today in Ontario, they are worth fighting for.
>
> And we march for Belgium, because in this war she incarnates violated justice, the scorned liberty of small peoples.
>
> And we march for France, because her defeat, while marking a regression of the world towards barbarism, would condemn us, her children of America, to drag out henceforward diminished lives.[239]

He called for a rehabilitation of the French Canadians in their own eyes by fighting, after 'the epoch of capitulations' from 1873 to 1911. Asselin's reasons were too personal to convince many of his followers, and those who listened to him quietly prevented Rodolphe Lemieux from speaking by cries of 'Enlist!' Lemieux came equipped with letters endorsing Asselin's effort from Borden, Laurier, and Sam Hughes[240]—strange supporters for a nationalist whose ardor had once surpassed Bourassa's.

Asselin's unit was but one of a number of French-Canadian ones authorized by Hughes in an effort to overcome Quebec's reluctance to enlist. Lt.-Col. Onésime Readman of Lévis was charged with raising the 167th, and Lt.-Col. P.-A. Piuze of the lower St. Lawrence the 189th, Lt.-Col. Tancrède Pagnuelo of Montreal the 206th, and Lt.-Col. René de Salaberry of Hull the 230th. Sir William Price undertook, with the aid of Onésiphore Talbot and Thomas Vien, to raise a mixed French and English battalion, the 171st, in Quebec; while Lt.-Col. L.-J. Gilbert sought to raise the 117th in the Townships, Lt.-Col. A. A. Magee the 148th at Montreal, and Lt.-Col. H. J. Trihey the 199th (Irish Canadian Rangers) at Montreal. But recruiting went slowly, particularly in the rural districts, and none of these battalions reached full strength.

In all, eleven French-Canadian battalions had been authorized. The 22nd was in France, with the 41st acting as its depot battalion in England. The 57th remained at Quebec, but had furnished reinforcements to the 41st. Colonel Dansereau's 69th sailed for England in April, while Colonel Barré's 150th went to Nova Scotia for further training. Colonel Piuze met with fair success in raising the 189th in the lower St. Lawrence region, and Asselin labored valiantly to fill the ranks of the 163rd. Most of the other colonels failed to raise the necessary number of recruits, and their battalions remained skeleton units in which discipline was lacking. French Canada remained more concerned with the battle for cultural survival in Ontario than with the course of the war in Europe.

9

The school question was now indeed a battle. The two Desloges sisters had been reinstalled in their classrooms at the Ecole Guigues in Ottawa by an army of women, who mounted guard over the school with hatpins as weapons, defying all efforts at interference from the authorities. Bourassa came to Ottawa to speak in a parish hall under the auspices of the A.C.J.C. on January 4, 1916, linking conservation of the French language with conservation of Catholicism, and praising the heroism of the Franco-Ontarians. Philippe Landry called upon Quebec to continue its support during the new year. He sought vainly during January to arrange a meeting of the French-Canadian ministers with Doherty, the minister of justice, and Fitzpatrick, the chief justice of the Supreme Court.

Bourassa mentioned the Ontario question at the sixth anniversary dinner of *Le Devoir* on January 12, and predicted the triumph of the minority. Then he turned to the question of imperialism, linking his anti-imperialism with the defence of Catholicism against Anglo-Protestant agnosticism. He asserted his conviction that he was in accord not only with the political tradition, but with the religious tradition of Canada. He pointed out that the French Canadians were the best insurance against the annexation of Canada to the United States, and concluded: 'We love France, we admire England; but we believe that our first duty is to the homeland where God ordained we should be born, where six generations link us to the land.'[241] This utterance followed by a few days another statement by Archbishop Bruchési strongly supporting the Canadian war policy and observing 'There has not been conscription, there is still no question of it in the country, and I hope there never will be question of it.'[242] A student journal, *L'Escholier*, edited by Jean Chauvin, protested strongly:

Monseigneur has said: 'You must enlist, it is your sacred duty to participate in this war.' Monseigneur, we do not believe you. It is not a question of dogma, a truth of religion, an article of morality.[243]

Lavergne also expressed the same attitude at the *Devoir* banquet when he refused to aid the English: 'Not a man, not a penny, not a cannon, until you concede to Canada the right to be represented in the councils of the Empire. . . . If someone wishes to make me undergo a trial for treason, I am ready for it!' And in reply to the threats against Bourassa Lavergne said: 'Let them come and arrest Bourassa if they dare! . . . I have in my county 3,000 farmers ready to protect him with their lives.'[244] Lavergne was just as vigorous the following day in the provincial legislature, asserting that Canada owed nothing to England and the French Canadians had no duty to enlist:

If we must conquer our liberties, it is here we should stay. It is not in the trenches of Flanders that we shall win the right to speak French in Ontario, if we have not been able to obtain it here, we who saved Canada for England when the English merchants of Quebec fled to the Island of Orleans. . . . I say, and I am not afraid to have my words repeated anywhere, that every French Canadian who enlists fails to do his duty. I know that what I say is high treason. I may be thrown into gaol tomorrow, but I don't care. . . . They tell us it is a question of defending liberty and humanity, but that is nothing less than a farce. If the Germans are persecutors, there are worse than Germans at our very gates. I'll go further. I'll say that every cent that is spent in Quebec to aid enlistment of men is money stolen from the minority in Ontario. . . . I am not afraid to become a German subject. I ask myself whether the German regime might not be favorably compared with that of the Boches of Ontario.[245]

Lavergne's outburst was greeted with silence, and followed by a vigorous plea from L.-A. Taschereau that French Canadians should enlist. Tellier called Lavergne a rebel and *Le Soleil* endorsed the Conservative leader's remark. *La Presse* published so hostile an account of the speech that Lavergne brought suit. The English press demanded that Lavergne be cashiered from the militia, and a Toronto minister devoted his sermon the following Sunday to the pious topic: 'Should Armand Lavergne be hung for high treason?'[246] Again on January 17 Lavergne declared that Conservative leaders had in the past expressed nationalist views similar to his, and that monuments had been built to such 'rebels' as Papineau and Lafontaine. Sam Hughes refused to deprive Lavergne of his militia rank, on the ground that militia officers had the right of free speech when not on active service, but the Garrison Club of Quebec did expel him.

When parliament met on January 12, Sévigny replaced Dr. Sproule as speaker. Laurier taunted him with rapid conversion from his extreme nationalist views of 1911, but assured him o support in his new office. Borden defended the increase of the armec forces and announced that the government did not intend to adop conscription. He reported on his English visit, and proposed tha parliament's life should be extended for a year. Laurier agreed t the proposal, and announced that he would support all the govern ment's war measures, but 'to all wrongs, to all frauds, we shall offe determined opposition.'[247] Bourassa protested against this join agreement 'to promote the cooperation of Canada in the defence o the Empire,' and asserted: 'The truth is that Canada, with mor motives to be careful of its strength, has already made more sacrifice than any other country of the Empire, and that apparently thes sacrifices will remain without any compensation.'[248] Both Laurie and Casgrain attacked the nationalists and belittled their signi ficance. Casgrain urged that Quebec should not be judged 'by th dreams and exaggerations of a little group of men who have been lec astray.'[249] Lemieux asserted that Bourassa no more representec popular opinion in Quebec than Bernard Shaw did that of England In the Senate, however, Choquette criticized participation in th war and particularly the stepping-up of recruiting. Belcourt Bolduc, Dandurand, and J.-P.-B. Casgrain censured their colleague while the *Mail and Empire* called for his expulsion from the Senate The *Toronto Telegram* classified all French Canadians as disloyal lumping Bourassa, Lavergne, Choquette, and Laurier together Ernest Lapointe assured the Commons that Choquette did no represent Liberal opinion, and blamed the poor recruiting results i Quebec on the anti-French-Canadian campaign of the Ontari press, rather than on the nationalists.

The ever-mounting indignation of Quebec over the Ontari school question made itself felt both at Ottawa and Quebec. Th French-Canadian *curés* of Ottawa refused to transmit to thei parishes an appeal for the Patriotic Fund, pointing out that thei parishioners' savings were being exhausted to keep the bilingua schools going. At Sainte-Agathe a *curé* interrupted a recruitin meeting by raising the Ontario school question. The A.C.J.C. hel a meeting in honor of the Franco-Ontarians at the Monumen National two days after Asselin's recruiting meeting there. Bourass was unable to be present because of illness, but the presidents o the A.C.J.C. and of the Saint-Jean-Baptiste Society promised t continue their support of the Ontario struggle, and Philippe Landr moved the crowd with his account of Ottawa mothers guarding th doors of the schools in midwinter. On the same day, at a dinner i support of the Patriotic Fund, Archbishop Bruchési thus explaine the Ontario difficulties to an audience largely made up of wealth English Canadians:

What is the basic situation? Two hundred thousand men, proud of their title of British subjects, faithful to their king and country, making it a point of honor to speak English, simply ask to speak also the tongue of their ancestors, the beautiful and sweet French language, and to teach it freely to their children. That is all. The answer belongs to men of goodwill.[250]

On January 25 in the provincial legislature Alexandre Taschereau asserted Quebec's willingness to give her sons and her resources generously to the Allies, but maintained that it was becoming 'profoundly tired and impatient'[251] of the failure of Ontario to pay heed to the message sent last year on the motion of one of its English representatives. Taschereau's observation won long applause. A few days later the *Quebec Chronicle*, owned by General Watson who commanded the brigade which included the 22nd, urged settlement of the Ontario school question in the name of British fair play. Earlier, J. C. Scott, a Quebec contractor, had paid tribute to the French Canadians in a letter to the *Mail and Empire*, which had been reprinted in the *Chronicle* along with another approving it by J. C. Sutherland, the inspector-general of Protestant schools in Quebec.

But Ontario was unmoved by these interventions, particularly since the man in the street had the notion that the French Canadians wished to impose the study of French upon English-speaking students. The new Ottawa School Commission got control of the school funds, and vainly sought to install its own teachers in schools guarded night and day by embattled mothers. On January 31, 3,000 separate school children, presented themselves at the Ottawa City Hall and presented an address to the mayor, petitioning for the payment of their teachers from the school taxes held by the corporation.

Bourassa was accused of being responsible for this demonstration, and in the House Orangemen called for his arrest and the suppression of *Le Devoir*. Dr. Edwards proposed exchanging Bourassa and Lavergne for Dr. Béland, who had been held prisoner in Germany since the outbreak of the war. In an anti-imperialist speech on February 1 Paul-Emile Lamarche defended his compatriots as merely advocating the doctrine that Canada's obligation was confined to the defence of her own territory, a doctrine which had been supported in the past by both parties and was based on the constitution. When interrupted by former nationalists, Lamarche replied to them thus: 'If it is true, Mr. Speaker, that two of my compatriots deserve to be put up against a wall and shot, I ask equal justice for all. It is just that their accomplices should undergo the same punishment.'[252] The 'accomplices' were the twenty Quebec members elected on the nationalist platform in 1911 who provided the government with its majority. Charles Marcil followed him with a plea for English-Canadian generosity towards the Ontario schools if only to help recruiting in Quebec. On February 11 the school children paraded to parliament, then sitting in the Victoria Museum as a result of the fire which had destroyed the Parliament Buildings, and presented petitions to Borden and Laurier. Four M.P.'s, Achim, Boulay, Lamarche, and Paquet, spoke at a meeting in the St. Anne Parish Hall on February 14.

The following day the third congress of the *Association d'Education* opened, with the three French-Canadian bishops of Ontario present. Bishop Beliveau said that the Franco-Ontarians were asking only for their rights, and would continue to do so until the flag of justice flew over the schools. Bishop Latulipe told how he had gone to Rome to explain the school question, and how the Pope and the cardinals had agreed with his views. He denounced Regulation 17 as 'a monument of iniquity and injustice.' Bishop Charlebois called Senator Landry the 'Joffre of Ontario.'[253] Landry, Belcourt, and Genest also spoke, announcing their plans to obtain federal disavowal of the Ontario law and to boycott Ontario products. Bourassa likened the heroic school teachers to Joan of Arc.

Quebec sought new means to aid her compatriots in Ontario. Bishop Blais of Rimouski ordered a special collection in his diocese for the cause. The municipalities wanted to contribute, but could not do so without authority from the provincial legislature. Antonin Galipeault prepared a bill to that effect, while Lavergne intervened in a debate on the Montreal Bill, which permitted that city to contribute to the Patriotic Fund, and urged the substitution of a measure permitting it to contribute to the Ontario schools. Lavergne was censured for his criticism of the Patriotic Fund by Gouin and Taschereau, who announced that Galipeault's bill would permit all municipalities to contribute to the Ontario struggle. The Conservative leader Cousineau objected that the English minority would be irritated by the French majority's voting of public funds for the purpose; and as a result of his intervention, the permission to contribute was transferred from municipalities to school commissions, which were exclusively French-Canadian. The Assembly then approved the bill unanimously. Montreal gave $5,000, and other towns contributed according to their means.

This Quebec development aroused new indignation in Ontario, and Mayor Thomas Church of Toronto observed that Quebec would do better to send more soldiers to the war. In Manitoba and Saskatchewan further restrictions on the teaching of French were urged, with John Dafoe crusading in the *Free Press* for a Manitoba Regulation 17 and with the government withdrawing the privileges of the Laurier-Greenway Agreement. In Manitoba Judge Prendergast headed an organization to defend the French schools, at the request of Bishop Beliveau. *Le Devoir* foresaw 'a grave danger for the future of Confederation,' and asked whether the 'Boches of Ontario and Manitoba would suspend the war they wage on our language' because of the lives sacrificed by the 22nd.[254]

The Ontario situation grew daily more tense. On February 22 no less than five public meetings were held in Ottawa, with French-Canadian M.P.'s from Quebec and the Maritimes as well as Ontario appearing on the platform. Two days later Casgrain and Blondin presented a Franco-Ontarian delegation to Borden, who promised to consider transmitting their petition to the Ontario government. Having avoided an encounter with a delegation of 5,000 persons by insisting upon receiving only a committee of twelve, Borden returned the petition to its sponsors two days later.[255] The A.C.J.C. circulated in Quebec a petition for federal disavowal. Mgr. Paquet of Laval supported the struggle on Thomistic principles. Abbé Groulx, who had inaugurated a new chair of French-Canadian history at Laval of Montreal with a course on '*Nos luttes constitutionnelles*,'[256] tracing the struggle for cultural survival from 1760–1867, drew a large and enthusiastic audience for a lecture on educational liberty, which was attended by Archbishop Bruchési. Bishop Larocque of Sherbrooke issued a circular calling for a special collection in his diocese for the Ontario cause. A Quebec boycott of Ontario manufacturers began to make itself felt, with the great Toronto mail order houses of Eaton's and Simpson's finding their catalogues returned unopened.

Borden managed to postpone a raising of the school question in the House by Charles Marcil, while Laurier contented himself with defending the cause privately among his English-Canadian followers. But in the House Lemieux called for justice and generosity to the Franco-Ontarians, and Roch Lanctôt flatly coupled the question of recruiting and the schools. In answer to the charges of the Ontario press that the French Canadians were not enlisting in sufficient numbers, Lanctôt replied: 'I find that too many of them enlist, considering the treatment which is inflicted upon them in the school question by the majority of this country.'[257] He was supported in this view by Calixte Ethier.

In the face of this united support of the Franco-Ontarians, the *Mail and Empire* denounced French-Canadian 'aggression' at a time when 'all the citizens of Canada should be united against the common enemy.' The *Montreal Star* took issue with its Toronto colleague on the grounds that the French Canadians were assaulted, not aggressors, and added: 'If the Ontario government had not, by the unjust and ungenerous suppression of the educational privileges of the French Canadians, created a profound discontent among the Quebec majority, there would be no cause to complain of recruiting in this province.'[258] Ex-Mayor Andrews of Winnipeg supported this view in a letter to the *Winnipeg Telegram*; while Sir Joseph Pope sent a new letter to the *Ottawa Citizen* criticizing the attitude of the Ontario government as playing into the hands of Bourassa and Lavergne, as did E. R. Cameron, clerk of the Supreme Court. W. H. Moore presented the case for the Franco-Ontarians in the *Canadian Courier*, and J. J. Foran supported it on the platform. But in general the Ontario press, led by the *Toronto News*, continued to refuse any concession to the 'ignorant French,' and proclaimed that Ontario was an English province and would remain so.

On March 2 Bourassa began an important series of six weekly lectures on Canadian policy, which were later published in pamphlet form as '*Hier, aujourd'hui et demain*.' In the first he discussed the principles of the British and Canadian constitutions and pointed out that in the past Canada's political and religious leaders had rejected participation in foreign wars. In the second he discussed the 'imperialist revolution' since the South African War, stressing the fact that his anti-imperialism was a reaction against this development. In the third and fourth he dealt with Canadian participation in the present war, saying that a crusade for France and Belgium could wait until French Canadian rights were won at home. In a later letter to a French correspondent, published in *Le Devoir* on June 23 when his lectures appeared in printed form, Bourassa expressed more clearly his opinion of the official appeal to come to the aid of France:

> We have here a little coterie of Tory and imperialist priests who invoke the interests of religion in order to serve the ends of England and of the Canadian imperialists. These same people also exploit the French-Canadians' love of France, after having denounced her for years as the most impious and corrupt country in the world. It is to this coterie that are particularly addressed the pages devoted to the argument of religion and the episcopal tradition in Canada.[259]

In the fourth lecture Bourassa predicted the dire economic, social, and political consequences to be expected from the war. In the fifth he discussed the possible solutions: independence, imperial federation, or annexation, with independence 'the only true solution of the problem of our destinies.'[260] In the sixth, dealing with Canada's foreign relations, he urged a defensive alliance with the United States as less costly than the British connection. The whole thesis was argued with his customary mastery of historical and legal argument, and his usual eloquence. It offered much food for discussion by the élite; the people gathered from it merely that Bourassa was opposed to enlistment.

During March, while the Canadian troops suffered heavy losses in the Ypres salient, enlistments began to decline. On March 14 Brigadier-General James Mason, a Conservative senator, presented in parliament an analysis of the recruiting situation and called for national registration or conscription. His figures, compiled with the aid of the census and the military authorities, showed that 249,000 men out of a total of 1,500,000 of military age had enlisted. He estimated that 63 per cent of the recruits were British-born, 30 per cent Canadian-born, and the remaining 7 per cent foreign-born. Of the Canadian-born he estimated that 85,000 (28.5 per cent of the total enlisted) were English-speaking, while 12,000 (4.5 per cent of the total enlisted) were French-speaking. The French Canadians, who constituted 40 per cent of the population of military age, had thus supplied only 4.5 per cent of the recruits. But General Mason was careful to point out that the native-born of both races were not doing their full duty, and urged adoption of the English Derby scheme of national registration to determine whether men could best serve the country in the army or in industry, coupled with an urgent appeal for volunteers for active service.[261] He added: 'There can be no question that the additional 250,000 to bring our quota up to 500,000 and the 300,000, if required, annually to keep it at that figure, will not be obtained under the present system of enlistment.'[262] Lord Shaughnessy, head of the Canadian Pacific, had already publicly stated on March 9 in the presence of Sam Hughes that he believed the raising of an army of 500,000 was impracticable when more than 300,000 were already employed in war industry, and many were needed in agriculture to 'help feed the British nation.' He urged: 'We must go slowly about recruiting, and carry out the best plans for the country in a sane, methodical and and business-like way.'[263]

With enlistments particularly heavy among clerical and manual workers, business and industry began to take the attitude that no more of their men could be spared; and through the Canadian Manufacturers' Association they pressed for a plan of national service. These developments tended to confirm French-Canadian belief in Bourassa's view that Canada had already done too much, and henceforward should concentrate on sending supplies rather than men overseas. Recruiting slumped in Quebec, but it also slumped throughout Canada, and only 127,000 men were enlisted between January 1 and June 1, 1916. On a proportional basis, Quebec had raised only one-quarter her share, the Maritimes only one-half and Ontario seven-ninths, while the Western provinces had exceeded their shares. Quebec, of course, had much the lowest proportion of

British-born men of military age.[264] The factors that caused the recruiting decline all over Canada were the exhaustion of the supply of British-born volunteers, and the demands of industry and agriculture for manpower to meet the war boom. In Quebec indignation over the Ontario school question was an added major factor, supplemented by the opposition of the rural clergy to enlistment.

10

Landry and his colleagues now sought publicly to win the concessions which they had previously pursued through private channels. The Ontario government refused a renewed offer of a truce until the Privy Council had rendered its decision on Regulation 17 in the MacBell and Ottawa Separate School Board cases. Landry spoke under the auspices of the A.C.J.C. at meetings organized to gain signatures for the petition for disavowal. Senator Pope censured him for organizing and speaking at 'seditious assemblies.' Choquette defended him, and the wonted calm of the Senate was broken by an angry dispute. Archbishop Bruchési, once so moderate, compared the Franco-Ontario resistance to that of the French on the Marne. Bishop Larocque of Sherbrooke and Bishop Ross of Rimouski supported Landry's appearances in Quebec. A few English Canadians expressed sympathy with the cause. Dr. Finnie urged a peace favorable to the Franco-Ontarians in a Montreal Reform Club speech, while his colleague W. S. Bullock proposed the suspension of Regulation 17. The Canadian Club of Quebec invited Senator Belcourt to expound the bilingual question, and applauded and approved him. John S. Ewart wrote a letter to the *Ottawa Journal* supporting the legal rights of French in Ontario. But on April 2 the Ontario Supreme Court rejected the Franco-Ontarians' appeal, which now went to the Privy Council.

From mid-March to mid-April the seventy-year-old Landry journeyed back and forth between Quebec and Franco-Ontarian centers, pleading his case eloquently despite the rigors of travel at this season which wore out his younger collaborators. He sought the support of the Quebec bishops for the petition in favor of disavowal. But Casgrain and Thomas Chapais persuaded Archbishop Bruchési that the French language had little legal standing outside Quebec and that a disavowal would produce a sharp conflict between the federal government and the Ontario one, with the latter subsequently renewing its stand without a legal basis. Bishop Emard of Valleyfield and Bishop Gauthier, the Montreal auxiliary, followed Archbishop Bruchési in adopting the alternative policy of appealing to the governor-general.

It was known that Paul-Emile Lamarche intended to raise the question in the House. Laurier, who so far had stood officially apart from the question, proposed a conference at the rectory of his Ottawa pastor, the Abbé Myrand, with Belcourt, Lemieux, Lapointe, Lamarche, Patenaude, and Landry on April 6. Laurier foresaw the danger of provoking the English Protestant majority by a request for intervention in provincial affairs, which someday might serve as a precedent for action against the French Catholic minority. He proposed that a resolution should be offered in the House, appealing to the goodwill of the Ontario legislature. The interview was inconclusive. Meanwhile Landry presented to the secretary of state a request for disavowal signed by all the French-Canadian bishops except Archbishop Bruchési, and Bishops Emard and Gauthier. Casgrain, Blondin, and Patenaude put pressure on Borden to intervene with the Ontario government, which replied that any government yielding to the French Canadians would lose power in twenty-four hours. Then, on April 22, the three French-Canadian ministers presented a long request for an examination of the whole language question by the Privy Council, accompanied by a threat not to attend cabinet meetings until satisfaction was obtained. Borden, pressed by the English members of his cabinet, refused the request, and put pressure on the French ministers to remain in office in order to avoid a 'national calamity.'[265] Blondin yielded first, followed by Patenaude, and finally Casgrain, after a week of secret cabinet crisis.

Meanwhile Choquette had set the Senate raging once more by announcing that it was a crime to enlist young farmers, and by reading a letter from Robert Hazelton of Ontario, to the effect that the British-born volunteers were a crowd of undesirables. The Tory journals declared that Choquette expressed Laurier's views, but Laurier replied in the House that he did not share them and that the Senator spoke only for himself. When the *Globe* refused to publish Choquette's corrections of its account, the senator made them in the Senate, renewing his protests against overzealous recruiting. In this troubled atmosphere Landry presented to the government the petition for disavowal, signed by 600,000 persons. Doherty, the minister of justice, decided that the question should be settled by the courts, after the precedents of the New Brunswick school question of 1872, the Manitoba one of 1890, and the North-West ordinances of 1892. His commentaries indicated a preference for the Ontario government's thesis.[266] All the Ottawa bilingual schools were now closed. Senator Belcourt, as a large Ottawa taxpayer, initiated a movement to refuse to pay school taxes to the new commission.

With Quebec on the eve of provincial elections, Bourassa announcing his return to federal politics, and Lavergne resigning from the provincial legislature for the same purpose, the Ontario school question at last came before the House of Commons. Landry had sought to get the French-Canadian ministers to present a resolution and in the face of their refusal had turned to Borden himself, warning that he would have recourse to Laurier if turned down. Borden advised him that Laurier, torn between his English and French followers, would do nothing, nor would he. But on May 8 Laurier warned Borden that Ernest Lapointe would introduce such a resolution, and overrode Borden's objections on the grounds that he himself was alarmed by conditions in Quebec and that he must have 'some sheet anchor with which to fight Nationalists.'[267]

On the following day Lapointe introduced the following resolution:

That this House, especially in this time of universal sacrifices and anxiety, when all energies should be concentrated on the winning of the war, would, while fully recognizing the principle of provincial rights and the necessity of every child being given a thorough knowledge of English education, respectfully suggests to the Legislative Assembly of the province of Ontario the wisdom of making it clear that the privilege of the children of French parentage of being taught in their mother tongue be not interfered with.[268]

He was supported by Emmanuel Devlin, after Borden had sought to avoid debate by invoking a point of order. Laurier refused Borden's appeal:

Let us discuss this question like free men, like British subjects. Out of this discussion will come a more complete knowledge of the situation and of the rights of the minority in this country, and the minority, of which I am a part, will accept the settlement that is proposed, if this settlement is reasonable.[269]

Before the debate opened on May 10, the Conservative and Liberal spokesmen of Ontario affirmed the uselessness of all federal intervention: Regulation 17 was untouchable. Lapointe appealed to Ontario's sense of justice and generosity rather than making a legal or constitutional argument. He closed in the tradition of Laurier:

My greatest desire is that this resolution and that this discussion, instead of dividing more profoundly the two races of this country, should bring them closer together and cement their union for the defence of liberty based upon law. I ask my compatriots to proclaim with Gladstone the equality of the weak and the strong. We ought to try and impregnate Canadian public spirit with high and generous sentiments; we should protect the rights of all citizens, and above all, raise on this Canadian soil a solid wall against the attacks of violence and prejudice. To reach this goal, we should ask our fellow citizens to make concessions, to respec the opinions of others. And I hope that in this fashion we shall succeed in creating the harmony so necessary to the well being of the nation and of the individuals who compose it.[270]

Borden made a constitutional argument against the resolution, quoting Blake and Laurier's statements against federal interference with provincial legislation, and warning Quebec of the danger of encouraging federal interference with education. He thought the resolution would do mischief: 'It can hardly fail to intensify feelings already sufficiently aroused and to strain the relations between the two great races in this country.' He asserted that 'no one is more anxious than I am that these good relations should be maintained and improved,' and in the interests of the country as a whole and particularly of Quebec he called for rejection of the resolution.[271]

Laurier made one of his great speeches in reply, recalling the constitutional rights of the French language but appealing particularly to the spirit of justice, 'not of the justice which clings to the cold letter of the law, but the justice which rests in the heart of every man, whatever his nationality.' He did not question Ontario's right to pass final judgment on the question, and did not propose to advise or admonish that province:

I rise to plead before the people of Ontario, in behalf of His Majesty's subjects of French origin in that province, who complain that by reason of a statute passed by the province they have been deprived of rights in the matter of education which they have enjoyed themselves and their forefathers before them, ever since Canada became a possession of the British Crown. . . .

I know there is in the province of Ontario a sense of irritation at the position taken by some of my fellow-countrymen of French blood in the province of Quebec, who have from the first deprecated the participation of Canada in the present war, and who have exerted their influence to attempt at least to prevent enlistment. Alas, it is true; it is only too true. It is deplorable, and to me as unintelligible as it is deplorable. It is true, alas, that there are in my province men of French origin who, when France is fighting the fight of heroism which stirs the blood of mankind, remain with their blood cold, who tell us: 'No, we will not lift a finger to assist Britain in defending the integrity of France, but we want our wrongs to be righted in Ontario.'

Wrongs or no wrongs, there is a field of honour; there is a call of duty.

Sir, I am not prepared to say that my fellow-countrymen of French origin have no rights in Ontario; but I am prepared to say this, and I want my words to be heard throughout the length and breadth of this land. Whether my countrymen have rights or no rights in Ontario, whether those rights are granted or denied, these considerations are no bar to the duty which the French Canadians owe to themselves and to the honour of their race to come forward in their fullest numbers and take part in the great struggle that is going on to-day in the land of thei[r] ancestors for the cause of freedom, and of the civilization of man kind . . .[272]

He denounced the Toronto theory of 'one language and one languag[e] only' as opposed to the traditions of the Britsh Empire: 'It is becaus[e] British institutions everywhere have carried freedom and respect fo[r] minorities that England is as strong as she is today.'

Then Laurier appealed to the sense of justice and fair play of th[e] people of Ontario, who were determined that every child in that pro vince should have an English education. With that aim he fully agreed

I want every child in the province of Ontario to receive the benefit o[f] an English education. Wherever he may go on this continent I wan[t] him to be able to speak the language of the great majority of the peopl[e] on this continent. I want it, I say, not only because it is the law of th[e] province, but because of merely utilitarian considerations. No man o[n] this continent is equipped for the battle of life unless he has an Englis[h] education. I want every child to have an English education. . . .

When I ask that every child of my own race should receive an Englis[h] education, will you refuse us the privilege of education also in the lan guage of our mothers and our fathers? That is all that I ask to-day; [I] ask nothing more than that. I simply ask you, my fellow-countrymen British subjects like myself, if, when we say that we must have an Englis[h] education, you will say: 'You shall have an English education and nothin[g] else.' There are men who say that in the schools of Ontario and Manitob[a] there should be no other language than the English language. But, sir when I ask that we should also have the benefit of a French education will you refuse us that benefit? Is that an unnatural demand? Is that a[n] obnoxious demand? Will the concession of it do harm to anybody? An[d] will it be said that in the great province of Ontario there is a dispositio[n] to put a bar on knowledge and to stretch every child in the schools o[f] Ontario upon a procrustean bed and say that they shall all be measure[d] alike, that no one shall have the privilege of a second education in a singl[e] language? I do not believe it; and, if we discuss the question with frank ness, as between man and man, in my humble opinion, it can yet b[e] settled by an appeal to the people of Ontario. I do not believe that an[y] man will refuse us the benefit of a French education.[273]

This eloquent appeal was Laurier's swansong. The Quebec an[d] Maritime Liberals backed him, but the Ontario Liberals onl[y] supported the measure after Laurier threatened to resign as leader and the Western Liberals flatly opposed it. John Dafoe, wh[o] criticized the Lapointe motion in the *Manitoba Free Press*, accounte[d] for it on the grounds of Laurier's fear of being supplanted in Quebe[c] by Bourassa and of his desire to become once more in Quebec's eye[s] 'the greatest French Canadian.' But Georges Pelletier of *Le Devoir* no friend of the Liberals, paid homage to Laurier's sincerity in his last great stand.

Casgrain opposed the motion on the ground that it was a Liberal manoeuver to arouse feeling against the Conservatives on the eve of elections in Quebec. Lemieux and Charles Marcil supported it eloquently. Dr. Edwards denounced Quebec as a province peopled by illiterates, and his Orangeman colleague Morphy went farther in abuse. R. B. Bennett called for unity of language in the name of unity of the Empire. Lamarche proclaimed his political independence, and said he was not 'afraid to extend a loyal hand to the public man courageous enough to undertake the defence of his tongue and his race.'[274] Speaking in English, he infused his constitutional argument for liberty based upon respect of law with great eloquence, and in conclusion revealed that J.-P.-O. Guibault, a Conservative then in hospital, had asked to be brought to the House at the risk of his life in order to support the motion. But on May 11 the Lapointe resolution was rejected by a vote of 107 to 60, with eight Quebec Conservatives supporting it.

The *Free Press* rejoiced: 'Let our Quebec friends thoroughly understand the situation. We shall not allow them to impose their will on the rest of Canada.'[275] N. W. Rowell, chief of the Liberal opposition in Ontario, had failed to yield to Laurier's arguments in a long correspondence which ended, as Laurier put it, in 'a line of cleavage which—I so judge from the tone of your letter just received—is final and beyond redemption.'[276] Laurier had urged upon an Ontario Liberal editor that 'We, French Liberals of Quebec, are fighting Bourassa and Lavergne; will the English Liberals in Ontario fight Howard Ferguson and the extreme Orange element?'[277] But in the face of the opposition of the Ontario Liberals to his stand, and the rebellion of the Western ones, he grew discouraged, and suggested to Fielding and Graham that it had been a mistake for a French Canadian to accept the leadership of the party and that it was time he resigned. Outside the House, he was attacked by English Conservatives as an ally of Bourassa and as the man responsible for Quebec's poor recruiting record.

With the bilingual question being raised once more in Manitoba, Laurier gave this discouraged counsel to a French-Canadian leader in Winnipeg:

> We have reached a critical period in the development of Confederation, with regard to the rights of the French language. Unfortunately, the B.N.A. Act contains only one article on this subject, and the rights which are conferred upon us are very restricted alike in letter and spirit . . .
>
> It is a historical fact that without the French population of Quebec the union of the provinces of British North America would have been a

legislative union; the French population of Quebec would never have consented to such a form, since that would mean its disappearance as a distinct element. It is Quebec that suggested the federal form, and it must be accepted with all its consequences. For the French population of Quebec the advantages have been immense; outside Quebec, in face of the positive terms of Section 133, the French tongue has nothing to look for, aside from whatever sentiments the justice of the cause may arouse, and whatever influence may be brought to bear upon the majority.[278]

He did not believe in remedial legislation, and his only hope lay in persuasion and moderation, which might bring in Manitoba and Ontario the regime of tolerance which existed in Nova Scotia and New Brunswick. He had no confidence in the violent methods of Senator Landry, 'whose zeal I respect, but who is of too fiery a temper to be a safe guide.'[279]

The debate on the Lapointe resolution intensified feeling in Quebec. *Le Soleil* spoke of breaking the 'insupportable and odious'[280] tie which bound Quebec to Ontario. *La Patrie* stressed the fact that Western Liberals as well as the Conservatives had defeated the motion, but several Quebec Conservatives gave up the fight and only seven won seats in the provincial elections, three of them English Canadians. The Conservative party in Quebec had been killed by the Ontario school question. Bourassa appealed on May 30 to the provincial government to make a grant to the Franco-Ontarians, to enable them to carry their appeal to the Privy Council and to reopen their schools under the auspices of the Association d'Education. Landry resigned on May 22 as speaker of the Senate in protest 'against a collection of measures which tend to constitute the death sentence of the French race in the Canadian Confederation.' He announced his intention of devoting himself wholly to the Franco-Ontarian cause, and of campaigning against Casgrain, whom he called a devil's advocate, and the other French-Canadian ministers, who had become 'men dangerous to our race and to the rights it wishes to conserve.'[281] When Landry's letter was published on June 2, Bourassa paid tribute to his 'act of courage and honor,' which gave new courage to 'all those who fight for the justice and the respect of "pieces of paper" . . . in Canada.'[282] *Le Soleil* made political capital of Landry's resignation and was rebuked by *L'Action Catholique*, which maintained that the question should remain above parties. But the Abbé d'Amours did not approve the Landry-Bourassa alliance, and waited eleven days before eulogizing the senator for his gesture.

After a triumphal reception from a crowd of 10,000 at the Parc Lafontaine on June 19, Landry and Belcourt went to England, where the latter was to appear before the Privy Council. The Irish bishops of Ontario appealed to Rome in the hope of forcing acceptance of their offer to buy the University of Ottawa from the Oblates, which had been refused and which had aroused great indignation among the Franco-Ontarians. *L'Action Catholique's* attitude led many priests to transfer their subscriptions to *Le Devoir*; it was rumored that Cardinal Bégin and Archbishop Bruchési had become subscribers of the latter organ, to the scandal of the Ontario press.

The usual celebrations of Saint-Jean-Baptiste Day were extended for a week, with all parties making common cause with the Franco-Ontarians. School commissions exhausted their funds in gifts, while school children renounced their prizes that money might be sent to Ottawa. Others supplied prizes for the Franco-Ontarian children, who on their commencement days invoked the aid of Joan of Arc in remaining French. The *Toronto News* informed its readers that the French Canadians wished to impose the supremacy of their language in Canada, as a preliminary to driving out the English;[283] and Robert Sellar brought out a new edition of his *Tragedy of Quebec*, which urged Ontario to stand firm before 'a conspiracy devised by French priests to absorb her soil, violate her laws, and undermine her independence.' For him, the question was 'Whether this Canada of ours is to be British and nothing but British, or whether it is to be a mongrel land with two official languages and ruled by a divided authority? . . . Every Canadian has a deep interest in Ontario's answer, for upon it depends whether our country is to have two official languages fastened upon it and its legislatures pass under the lordship of French clericalism.'[284]

Bourassa had found plenty of ammunition for attacking the government in the charges of munitions profiteering and Conservative favoritism made by William Pugsley, Frank Carvell, and G. W. Kyte, which led to a motion by Laurier on March 7 calling for a parliamentary investigation. With the charges continuing, Borden finally appointed a Royal Commission early in April, and ordered Hughes home from England, since he was personally involved through his close connection with Honorary Colonel J. Wesley Allison, who acted as his 'adviser, counsellor and guide' in munitions purchases. The Commission's report, issued on July 20, cleared the government, the Shell Committee, and Hughes, but censured Allison for conduct which 'could not either be justified or excused.'[285] The investigation shook Hughes' position—Borden administered his department during the inquiry, and subsequently appointed a parliamentary secretary to administer it during Hughes' frequent absences—and left a nasty suspicion in the public mind that many of the most vocal patriots were profiteering on the side. The charges had been brought by Liberals, and the whitewashing report was generally accepted or rejected on Conservative or Liberal grounds. The political truce ended, just as the war entered its most crucial period.

Notes

[1] *Canada Year Book 1922–3*, 145, 170, 171–3.
[2] Rumilly, XVI, 156.
[3] M. Q. Innis, *Econ. Hist.*, 281.
[4] Rumilly, XVI, 159.
[5] Innis, 290.
[6] *Canada Year Book 1922–3*, 171.
[7] E. Bouchette, *Emparons-nous de l'industrie* (Ottawa, 1901), 16.
[8] *RSCT 1901*, Sec. I, 117–44, E. Bouchette, 'L'Evolution économique dans la Province de Québec.'
[9] *Ibid.*, 119.
[10] *Ibid.*, 135.
[11] Rumilly, XVI, 171.
[12] *RSCT 1901*, Sec. I, 169–70, L. Gérin, 'Notre mouvement intellectuelle.'
[13] *Ibid.*, 168.
[14] See L. Dantin, *Emile Nelligan et son oeuvre* (Montréal, 1903).
[15] G. Desaulniers, *Les Bois qui chantent* (Montréal, 1930).
[16] Rumilly, XVI, 123; Lavergne, *Trente ans* 205.
[17] Lavergne, 209.
[18] Rumilly, XVI, 131.
[19] *Ibid.*, 143.
[20] H. Bourassa, *Why the Navy Act Should Be Repealed* (Montreal, 1912), 46.
[21] Rumilly, XVII, 42.
[22] *Ibid.*, 45–8.
[23] J. S. Ewart, *The Kingdom Papers* (Ottawa, 1912), I, 187–93, No. 7, 'Ne Temere Decree.'
[24] Rumilly, XVII, 51.
[25] Lavergne, 213.
[26] H. Bourassa, *Pour la justice* (Montréal, 1912), 30.
[27] *Ibid.*, 32.
[28] *Ibid.*, 33.
[29] *Ibid.*
[30] Rumilly, XVII, 74.
[31] *Ibid.*
[32] Bourassa, *Justice*, 41–2; *Le Devoir*, 14 March 1912.
[33] Rumilly, XVII, 100.
[34] *Ibid.*, 123.
[35] *Ibid.*, 132.
[36] *Ibid.*, 140.
[37] H. Bourassa, *La Langue française et l'avenir de notre race* (Québec, 1913), 4.
[38] *Ibid.*, 11.
[39] *Ibid.*, 12.
[40] *Ibid.*, 15.
[41] *Ibid.*, 18.
[42] *Ibid.*, 22.
[43] *CHR XXVIII* (March 1947), No. 1, 1–30, G. N. Tucker, 'The Naval Policy of Sir Robert Borden, 1912–14.'
[44] Borden, *Memoirs*, I, 365.
[45] *Ibid.*, 361.
[46] Rumilly, XVII, 154.
[47] H. Bourassa, *Le Spectre de l'annexation* (Montréal, 1912); *The Spectre of Annexation and the Real Danger of National Disruption* (Montreal, 1912).

[48] Bourassa, *The Spectre*, 18.
[49] *Ibid.*, 23.
[50] *Ibid.*, vi, Cahan, *Montreal Gazette*, 1 Aug. 1912.
[51] Rumilly, XVII, 163.
[52] Borden, I, 372.
[53] *Ibid.*, 373.
[54] Rumilly, XVII, 163.
[55] *Ibid.*, 180.
[56] The 1911 census figure of 202, 442 French Canadians in Ontario is probably 50,000 short of the mark. C. B. Sissons, *Bilingual Schools in Canada* (Toronto, 1917), 92.
[57] Sissons, 13–5; G. M. Weir, *The Separate School Question in Canada* (Toronto, 1934), 157–8. The full text of Regulation 17 is given in Weir, Ap. VI, 286–9.
[58] F. W. Merchant, *Report on the Condition of English-French Schools in the Province of Ontario* (Toronto, 1912).
[59] Rumilly, XVII, 173.
[60] Rumilly, XVIII, 12.
[61] Borden, I, 404.
[62] *Ibid.*, 409.
[63] Skelton, *Laurier*, II, 398.
[64] *Ibid.*, 401–2.
[65] *Ibid.*, 405.
[66] Borden, I, 410.
[67] Rumilly, XVIII, 16–7, 36–7.
[68] *Ibid.*, 20.
[69] *Ibid.*, 33; *Montreal Gazette*, 3 March 1913.
[70] Ewart, *Kingdom Papers*, I, 243–89, No. 9, 'A Revision of War Relations'; 291–331, No. 10, 'Differences, Dangers, Duty.'
[71] Rumilly, XVIII, 35; *Toronto Globe*, 8 March 1913.
[72] *CHR 1947*, 17–18, Tucker.
[73] Rumilly, XVIII, 45.
[74] *Ibid.*, 46; *Le Devoir*, 22 May 1913.
[75] Skelton, II, 413.
[76] *CHR 1947*, 19, Tucker.
[77] Rumilly, XVIII, 50.
[78] O. Asselin, *Feuilles de Combat III: Le Sou de la pensée française* (Montréal, 1913). According to a typical note, this pamphlet had not been deposited for copyright at the ministry of agriculture, the federal department oddly charged with that function, because 'we are not steers' and in order 'not to deprive *La Croix* and *La Vérité* of the pleasure of copying it without compunction.'
[79] Rumilly, XVIII, 62.
[80] *Ibid.*, 63.
[81] *Ibid.*, 68; *La Nouvelle France* (September 1913), 416.
[82] *Ibid.*, 87.
[83] Rumilly, XVIII, 136–7.
[84] Sissons, 80.
[85] H. Bourassa, *Ireland & Canada* (Montreal, 1914).
[86] Rumilly, XVIII, 167, Bourassa-Ewart, 29 January 1914.
[87] H. Bourassa, *French and English Frictions and Misunderstandings* (Montreal, 1914), 22–3.
[88] *Ibid.*, 7, J. C. Walsh, 15 March 1914.
[89] Rumilly, XVIII, 177.
[90] *Ibid.*, 178.
[91] *Ibid.*, 179.
[92] *Ibid.*, 189.

[93] *Ibid.*, 201.
[94] *Ibid.*, 218.
[95] Borden, I, 451.
[96] *Ibid.*, 452.
[97] *Ibid.*, 452–3.
[98] Rumilly, XIX, 20.
[99] *Canadian Annual Review 1914* (Toronto, 1915), 142–3.
[100] Rumilly, XIX, 14–8.
[101] E. H. Armstrong, *The Crisis of Quebec*, 1914–18 (New York, 1937), 56.
[102] *Can. An. Rev. 1914*, 141.
[103] Skelton, 11, 428.
[104] Armstrong, 57.
[105] Rumilly, XIX, 21.
[106] Rumilly, XIX, 22; *La Presse*, 5 August; *Le Devoir*, 6 August 1914.
[107] *Ibid.*, 23, 27; *Le Devoir*, *Le Canada*; *La Patrie*, August 1914.
[108] *Ibid.*
[109] *Can. An. Rev. 1914*, 287.
[110] Armstrong, 58; *Montreal Gazette*, 8 August 1914.
[111] Skelton, II, 432–3.
[112] Descelles, *Discours*, II, 79–80.
[113] *Ibid.*, 82.
[114] Skelton, II, 434.
[115] Descelles, II, 86. The full text is in Descelles, *Discours*, II, 76–86.
[116] Borden, I, 461.
[117] Rumilly, XIX, 30.
[118] *Ibid.*, 32; *Le Devoir*, 22 August 1914.
[119] Armstrong, 68.
[120] *Ibid.*, 69–75.
[121] Rumilly, XIX, 33.
[122] *Ibid.*, 33.
[123] J. Michel, *La Participation des Canadiens français à la Grande Guerre* (Montréal, 1936), 16.
[124] H. Bourassa, *Le Canada à Loudres* (Montréal, 1914), 16, 27.
[125] H. Bourassa, *Le Devoir et la guerre* (Montréal, 1916), 44–5.
[126] H. Bourassa, *The Foreign Policy of Great Britain* (Montreal, 1915), 26.
[127] H. Bourassa, *La Politique de l'Angleterre avant et après la guerre* (Montréal, 1914), vi, 'Avertissement.'
[128] Bourassa, *Foreign Policy*, 37–47; *Contemporary Review* (September 1914).
[129] *Ibid.*, 2.
[130] Rumilly, XIX, 42.
[131] *Ibid.*, 45; *L'Action Sociale*, 14 September 1914.
[132] *Ibid.*
[133] O. Asselin, '*L'Action Catholique*,' *les evêques et la guerre* (Montréal, 1914), 5–7.
[134] Rumilly, XIX, 62, joint pastoral, 23 September 1914.
[135] *Ibid.*
[136] Asselin, '*L'Action Catholique*,' 8–12.
[137] Skelton, II, 436.
[138] *Ibid.*, 437.
[139] Rumilly, XIX, 64.
[140] *Ibid.*, 64–5.
[141] *Ibid.*, 68–9.
[142] *Ibid.*, 76.
[143] *Ibid.*, 85.
[144] *Ibid.*, 89.
[145] *Ibid.*, 85.

[146] *Ibid.*, 81.
[147] *Ibid.*, 83, *L'Action*, 31 October 1914.
[148] *Ibid.*, 84.
[149] *Ibid.*, 92.
[150] Reproduced in H. Bourassa, *The Duty of Canada at the Present Hour* (Montreal, 1915), [3–4].
[151] Rumilly, XIX, 93.
[152] *Ibid.*, 94.
[153] *Ibid.*, 97–8.
[154] *Ibid.*, 100, Casgrain-Landry, 17 December 1914.
[155] *Ibid.*, 102.
[156] *Ibid.*
[157] *Ibid.*, 103–4.
[158] *Ibid.*, 110, Bégin-Bruchési.
[159] *Ibid.*, 111.
[160] *Ibid.*, 95.
[161] Skelton, II, 438.
[162] Rumilly, XIX, 132.
[163] *Ibid.*
[164] *Ibid.*, 134.
[165] *CAR 1915*, 565.
[166] *Le 5e Anniversaire du Devoir* (Montréal, 1915), 9.
[167] *Ibid.*, 19.
[168] *Ibid.*, 67.
[169] *Ibid.*, 67–8.
[170] *Ibid.*, 69.
[171] *Ibid.*, 72.
[172] Rumilly, XIX, 144.
[173] *Ibid.*, 145.
[174] Skelton, II, 443.
[175] Borden, I, 532.
[176] *Ibid.*, I, 535.
[177] Skelton, II, 445.
[178] Borden, I, 483; *CAR 1915*, 283–6.
[179] Skelton, II, 446.
[180] *Can. An. Rev. 1915*, 366–8.
[181] *Ibid.*, 186.
[182] *Ibid.*, 189.
[183] *Ibid.*, 296.
[184] *Ibid.*, 218.
[185] *Ibid.*, 219.
[186] Rumilly, XX, 22.
[187] *Ibid.*, 28.
[188] *Ibid.*, 29.
[189] *Ibid.*, 28–34, 42–3.
[190] *Ibid.*, 45; *Le Devoir*, 20 April 1915.
[191] *Ibid.*, 24, 62.
[192] *Ibid.*, 57.
[193] H. Bourassa, *La Langue française au Canada* (Montréal, 1915), 28.
[194] Rumilly, XX, 58–9.
[195] *Ibid.*, 60.
[196] *RSCT 1915*, Ap. A, xlvi-xlvii, Mgr. Paul Bruchési, 'Le Dualisme Canadien'; Sec. I, 5–11, A. Routhier, 'Le Problème des races au Canada.'
[197] Rumilly, XX, 66–7.
[198] *Ibid.*, 69.

[199] *Ibid.*, 70, *Le Devoir*, 29 June 1915.

[200] Weir, *Separate School Question*, Ap. III, 268–73, *Saskatoon Daily Star*, 8 and 11 May 1916.

[201] Borden, I, 493.

[202] Rumilly, XX, 81; *Montreal Gazette*, 15 July 1915.

[203] *Ibid.*

[204] *Ibid.*, 82.

[205] Armstrong, 111.

[206] *Ibid.*, *L'Action Catholique*, 26 July 1915.

[207] *Can. An. Rev. 1915*, 258.

[208] *Ibid.*, 291.

[209] *Can. An. Rev. 1915*, 276.

[210] *Ibid.*

[211] *Ibid.*, 291.

[212] *Ibid.*

[213] Rumilly, XX, 95–6; *La Presse*, 21 August 1915.

[214] *Ibid.*, 97–8.

[215] O. Asselin, *Les Evêques et la Propagande de 'l'Action Catholique'* (Montréal, 1915).

[216] *Ibid.*, 13, 20–1.

[217] *Ibid.*, 21.

[218] *Ibid.*, 22.

[219] *Ibid.*, 55, 62.

[220] *Ibid.*, 75.

[221] Borden, I, 508.

[222] *Ibid.*, 496–510.

[223] *Ibid.*, 512.

[224] Rumilly, XX, 109.

[225] *Ibid.*, 117.

[226] *Ibid.*, 118.

[227] O. Asselin, *Pourquoi je m'enrôle* (Montréal, 1916), 9–10, Lavergne-Asselin, 3 November 1915.

[228] Borden, I, 513–21.

[229] Skelton, II, 448–50.

[230] *Ibid.*, 450.

[231] Rumilly, XX, 134.

[232] *Ibid.*, 136–7; *Le Canada*, 17 December 1915.

[233] *Ibid.*, *Daily Mail.*

[234] *Ibid.*, 137; *Montreal Gazette*, 20 December 1915.

[235] *Ibid.*, 138.

[236] Asselin, *Pourquoi*, 10, Asselin-Lavergne, 6 November 1915.

[237] *Ibid.*, 11.

[238] *Ibid.*, 11–12.

[239] *Ibid.*, 39.

[240] *Ibid.*, 48–50. Borden's and Hughes' letters were originally written in French.

[241] H. Bourassa, *Le Devoir et la guerre; le conflit des races* (Montréal, 1916), 40.

[242] Rumilly, XXI, 17.

[243] *Ibid.*, 18.

[244] *Ibid.*, 20.

[245] *Ibid.*, 23; *Can. An. Rev. 1916*, 344.

[246] Rumilly, XXI, 24.

[247] Skelton, II, 455.

[248] Rumilly, XXI, 25.

[249] *Ibid.*

[250] *Ibid.*, 32.
[251] *Ibid.*, 34.
[252] *In Memoriam: Paul-Emile Lamarche* (Montréal, 1919), 117.
[253] Rumilly, XXI, 45.
[254] *Ibid.*, 54.
[255] Borden, II, 573–4.
[256] Abbé Lionel Groulx, *Nos luttes constitutionnelles* (Montréal, 1916).
[257] Rumilly, XXI, 57.
[258] *Ibid.*, 59–60; *Toronto Mail and Empire*, *Montreal Star*, 13 March 1916.
[259] *Ibid.*, 63–4.
[260] H. Bourassa, *Hier, aujourd'hui, demain* (Montréal, 1916), 150.
[261] Armstrong, 121–2.
[262] *Can. An. Rev. 1916*, 312–3.
[263] *Ibid.*, 319; *Montreal Gazette*, 10 March 1916.
[264] *Ibid.*, 303.
[265] Borden, II, 538.
[266] *Parliamentary Documents 1916*, No. 28, Doc. 271a.
[267] Borden, II, 588–9.
[268] *Ibid.*, 589.
[269] Rumilly, XXI, 114.
[270] *Ibid.*, 114–5.
[271] *Ibid.*
[272] Skelton, II, 479–80.
[273] *Ibid.*, 41–2.
[274] Rumilly, XXI, 117.
[275] *Ibid.*, 118.
[276] Skelton, II, 477.
[277] *Ibid.*, 485.
[278] *Ibid.*, 487–8.
[279] *Ibid.*, 490.
[280] Rumilly, XXI, 119.
[281] *Ibid.*, 128–9.
[282] *Ibid.*, 129.
[283] *Ibid.*, 138, *Toronto News*.
[284] R. Sellar, *The Tragedy of Quebec* (Toronto, 1916), 327–8.
[285] Borden, II, 565–6.

CHAPTER XII

THE CONSCRIPTION CRISIS

(1916–19)

IT WAS in a Canada already sharply divided along racial lines by the bilingual school question that the conscription crisis arose. In June 1916 enlistments had dropped to half the April total, and they continued to fall until in December they were only half the June figure.[1] Of the 250,000 additional men sought in 1916 120,000 were raised in the first six months of the year, but only 40,000 in the last.[2] Meanwhile Canadian losses continued to mount. The Canadian Army Corps, composed of three divisions and commanded after May by Sir Julian Byng, lost 2,759 men in the Battle of Saint-Eloi in April, and 8,490 in the Battle of Sanctuary Wood in June. Under these circumstances the training of the Fourth Division was speeded up in England and in Canada reinforcements were embarked.

I

Of the French-Canadian units, Asselin's 163rd, raised only to two-thirds strength despite his tireless efforts, was sent to do garrison duty in Bermuda, to his great disgust. Lieutenant-Colonel Paquet's 57th, which had already supplied several detachments of reinforcements for overseas, sailed for England on June 2nd. Five incomplete French-Canadian battalions were assembled at Valcartier under Major Emile Ranger, the largest units being Lieutenant-Colonel Piuze's 189th and Lieutenant-Colonel Barré's 150th. A demand arose for the organization of a French-Canadian brigade, under the command of General Lessard or Lieutenant-Colonel Leduc, but Sam Hughes opposed the plan. With the demand for reinforcements men were drawn from other battalions to reinforce the 189th and 150th, which were to go overseas in the fall, and in some cases men were transferred from French-Canadian units to English-Canadian ones. These measures destroyed the regional nature of the original battalions, and aroused much ill will, for French-Canadian regionalism is strong. It was one thing to serve with neighbors under their own leaders and another to be thrown into an unfamiliar English-speaking world under officers who knew no French. Desertions increased, while during July there were disturbances in two French-Canadian battalions at Valcartier. When the officers of the 206th were dismissed, Lieutenant-Colonel T. Pagnuelo told his battalion:

> . . . it is a revenge because we are French Canadians and because of small errors here and there. As far as you are concerned, they are shipping you to Bermuda, where you will undergo hardship and suffer misery from the heat. Now, military law prevents me from speaking, but if you are wise enough to read between the lines, you will know what to do. I will give passes to everybody, and be sure that the little money that your friends have subscribed to the Regimental fund will not be used to run after those who will not come back.[3]

Colonel Pagnuelo was later courtmartialed for his extraordinary speech, and sentenced to six months' imprisonment. Officers of the 167th were accused of irregularities and relieved of their commands, though later acquitted. Such incidents did grave harm to recruiting in Quebec, although French-Canadian leaders renewed their appeals for volunteers.

Ontario and English Canadians at large began to call for conscription, which represented a threat to the individualistic French Canadians who could be led to support the war by their own leaders but not driven into it by their hostile compatriots of English speech. Laurier, who assigned Quebec's poor record in enlistment to its small numbers of British-born, its few urban centers (to which recruiting so far had largely been confined), and to the nationalist movement, once more exerted himself to clear Quebec of the charge of disloyalty. At the Monument National on June 3rd he urged an *entente cordiale* between English and French based upon common service, and urged his young compatriots to join those 'brave young men who offer their services—their lives—that France may live again, that Britain may continue her noble and generous rule, and that heroic Belgium may be restored to her standing as a nation.'[4] He maintained that the defence of the French language in Ontario should not interfere with the defence of France at the front.

Le Soleil supported Laurier's contention on June 5: 'It is by enlisting in large numbers and forming good French-Canadian battalions that we shall succeed in resolving in friendly and fruitful fashion the Ontario question.' *L'Evénement* on May 26 had admitted that recruiting in Quebec was a fiasco, and blamed it on the lack of military spirit among the French Canadians and on the antipathy of the bourgeoisie and lower clergy to England. *Le Canada* suggested on July 21 that *L'Evénement* might better blame the ex-nationalist ministers who had preached anti-imperialism in 1911 and were now beating the drum for enlistment. *La Presse* continued, like all the major French-Canadian papers except *Le Devoir*, to support recruiting ardently, urging that the French Canadian position would become worse after the war if they did not do their part in a war which might seem to be solely in British rather than Canadian interests.[5] *L'Action Catholique* on June 5 noted Ferdinand Roy's tribute to France upon his return to Quebec from Europe, and warned: 'If we are proud to be French and British subjects, and we have ample reason to be so, despite the wrongs committed against our race, it is not enough to acclaim France and England; we must, in just and equitable proportions, march with them and not refuse them the testimony of our attachments.'[6] Bourassa mocked *L'Action's* new attachment to France; but at Brome on July 1st, Laurier insisted on the alliance between the 'two mother countries' and replied thus to those who preached against fighting for England until the Ontario question was settled: 'Everywhere where there are rights to enjoy, there are duties to fulfil. Do your duty and you will obtain your rights.' At a Limoilou Saint-Jean-Baptiste dinner the following day, Laurier said that 'the French Canadians are in the Confederation to stay,' to which Armand Lavergne added the reservation in a following speech, 'on condition that they are not dishonoured.'[7] But in Ontario, where a by-election was being contested, the Toronto *News* called for a 'solid Ontario' against a 'solid Quebec' and proclaimed that 'A vote for Laurier is a vote for Bourassa.'[8]

On June 11 Sir Sam Hughes, bound for Valcartier, called upon Cardinal Bégin at Quebec. Ostensibly he sought chaplains for the French-Canadian battalions, but actually he wanted the Cardinal's support for recruiting. It was evident from the communiqué issued by the archbishop's office that this doubtless painful pilgrimage by the Orangeman had been well received. Possibly there was a connection between this visit and the launching on June 17 of a series of weekly anti-Bourassa articles in *La Presse*, under the title of '*Où allons-nous?*', by the Abbé d'Amours writing under the pseudonym of 'Un Patriote.'[9] *L'Action Catholique* had been obliged to suspend its pro-war campaign because of opposition from the lower clergy, but the Abbé d'Amours now rejoiced in the freedom of anonymity and attacked Bourassa savagely.

On the other hand, Arthur Hawkes, an English-born journalist of Toronto, published an intelligent interview with Bourassa in the *Toronto Star* on July 14 and 15, in which he maintained that the nationalist leader was neither a firebrand nor a fool; paid tribute to his knowledge of Canadian and international affairs and his courage; and asserted that Bourassa favored Canadian independence but would accept imperial partnership along the lines suggested by Lionel Curtis and the Round Table group. Hawkes likened the nationalist leader to Lloyd George and anticipated that he would become 'the undisputed champion of the French-Canadian people when the time has fully come.'[10] For many English Canadians, this was the first honest account of Bourassa and his ideas, which had been grossly misrepresented by the English press. Bourassa declared in a letter to Hawkes that he was not anti-British, but anti-imperialist:

> One point I did not make clear in our conversation is the motive of my desire for the disruption of the British Empire. It is not because it is British, but because it is Imperial. All Empires are hateful. They stand in the way of human liberty and true progress, intellectual and moral. They serve nothing but brutal instincts, and national objects: All that is good in British ideals, and there is much of it, would be better served by the free action of several independent British communities than by the common action of a monstrous Empire, built up by force and robbery, and kept together for no other purpose than allowing one race and one nation to dominate one fifth of the human race. But nations have to choose between British ideals and British domination. I stand for ideals against domination. I may be hanged for it in the name of British liberty, but that does not matter.

2

Bourassa figured largely in another role in the summer of 1916. On July 28 most of the Montreal, Quebec, Ottawa, and Toronto papers, both French and English, published an open letter to him from his cousin Captain Talbot Papineau, dated from the front in France on March 21.[11] The letter had been sent to Andrew Ross McMaster of Montreal, Papineau's law partner, who sent it on to Bourassa on July 18 and published it ten days later when no reply was forthcoming in Bourassa's absence from the city. Captain Papineau, like Bourassa, was a grandson of Louis-Joseph Papineau, but belonged to an anglicized branch of the family and had been educated at Oxford and Paris. At the outbreak of the war he had enlisted in the largely English Princess Patricia's Regiment, and was one of the few original members of that unit still surviving. His letter was addressed to his 'dear Cousin Henri,' and was purportedly personal, but was clearly intended as an appeal to the great mass of French-Canadian followers of the nationalist leader, who gained some of his prestige from being Papineau's grandson.

Captain Papineau regretted that he had not had an opportunity to discuss with Bourassa the issues raised by the war before leaving for the front, and paid tribute to the honesty and sincerity of Bourassa's disinterested views, though he deplored them. He was disappointed that events had not modified them: 'Deeply involved as the honour and the very national existence of Canada has become, beautiful but terrible as her sacrifices have been, you and you alone of the leaders of Canadian thought appear to have remained unmoved and your unhappy views unchanged.' He wrote because he feared Bourassa's influence upon a minority of the French Canadians, and because Bourassa's views might be taken as typical of the French Canadians. Then he marshaled the arguments with which he hoped to convert his cousin. As a matter of international law Canada had become involved in the war by Britain's declaration of war upon Germany. Any discussion of the justness of Canada's participation was an 'idle and pernicious' academic discussion. He dismissed the argument that Canada might have remained neutral until it was attacked by saying that if the Allies had been defeated, the unaided strength of Canada could not have prevented German domination. He added: 'By the time you are within fifteen yards of a German army and know yourself to be holding about one yard out of a line of five hundred miles or more, you are liable to be enquiring very anxiously about the presence and power of British and French forces.'

Papineau dismissed the argument of American protection by saying that Canada would have been subdued before the Americans aided her, since the United States had a record of only going to war for a national principle. If the Allies had not been defeated, 'You might still have edited untrammeled your version of *Duty* and Colonel Lavergne might still, publicly and without the restraining fear of death or imprisonment, have spoken seditiously (I mean from the Prussian point of view, of course).' But would nonparticipation have satisfied a nationalist? 'Can a nation's pride or patriotism be built upon the blood and suffering of others or upon the wealth garnered from the coffers of those who in anguish and with blood-sweat are fighting the battles of freedom?' If Bourassa were a true nationalist, he would have felt that 'in the agony of her losses in Belgium and France, Canada was suffering the birth pains of her national life. There, even more than in Canada herself, her citizens are being knit together into a new existence because when men stand side by side and endure a soldier's life and face together a soldier's death, they are united in bonds almost as strong as the closest of blood-ties.' Papineau felt that Canadians had had a call to fight for Canada in Europe, and gave thanks that 'that question had been answered not as you would have had it answered but as those Canadians who have already died or are about to die here in this gallant motherland of France have answered it.'

As a second argument, Papineau exalted the 'spiritual union' of the self-governing portions of the empire, and their civilization and standards, as 'the highest and noblest to which the human race has yet attained and jealously to be protected against destruction.' The uniting bonds might be readjusted, but they must not be broken. He repudiated Canadian nationalism if it meant antagonism to the spirit now uniting the empire. His third argument was a French-Canadian one. 'I may not be, like yourself, "*un pur sang*" [a pure-blooded French Canadian], for I am by birth even more English than French, but I am proud of my French ancestors, I love the French language, and I am as determined as you are that we shall have full liberty to remain French as long as we like.' But in order to preserve this liberty, concessions must be made to the majority, if the latter was to make concessions to the minority. The war had offered the French Canadians an opportunity to demonstrate to the English Canadians 'a common love of our country and a mutual wish that in the future we should unite our distinctive talents and energies to create a proud and happy nation.' But despite the whole-hearted support given by many French-Canadian leaders, and despite the heroism of the French-Canadian battalions, the French Canadians had not rallied to the colors in the same proportion as other Canadians, and the impression had been created that French Canada was not bearing her share of the burden. 'For this fact and this impression you will be held largely responsible.' For the time being, nationalism had been made a stench in English-Canadian nostrils without any furthering of Bourassa's aims, and after the war 'whoever bears a French name in Canada will be an object of suspicion and possibly of hatred.'

Papineau argued that Bourassa should have supported a war for France and French civilization and a fight for the freedom of the world. He closed with a warning of a 'heavy day of reckoning' when the soldiers returned 'for those who, while we fought and suffered here, remained in safety and comfort in Canada and failed to give us encouragement and support, as well as for those who grew fat with the wealth dishonourably gained by political graft and dishonest business methods at our expense.' Finally, he made a plea for Bourassa to play his share in realizing an ideal which he equally shared: 'At this moment, as I write, French and English Canadians are fighting and dying side by side. Is their sacrifice to go for nothing, or will it not cement a foundation for a true Canadian nation, a Canadian nation independent in thought, independent in action, independent even in its political organization—but in spirit united for high international purposes to the two Motherlands of England and France?'

Bourassa replied to McMaster on August 2,[12] casting doubt upon Captain Papineau's authorship of this 'political manifesto' written in English and presented four months after it was written. He minimized the relationship between himself and his cousin, and expressed the opinion that 'the whole thing has the appearance of a political manœuvre executed under the name of a young and gallant officer who has the advantage or inconvenience of being my cousin.' He reviewed his early attitude to the war and termed it analogous to that of his cousin. He summed up the reasons for his change of views: '"free" enlistment is now carried on by means of blackmailing, intimidation and threats of all sorts'; advantage had been taken of war emotion to assert imperial solidarity, and the Liberal leaders had abandoned their nationalist principles, while the Conservative spokesmen who denounced him as a traitor had exploited anti-imperialism to the full in 1911. Captain Papineau had backed his change of opinion by his deeds, but others had not.

Bourassa defended French Canada's recruiting record on the grounds that enlistment throughout Canada was 'in inverse ratio to the enrootment in the soil and the traditional patriotism arising therefrom':

> The simple truth is that the abstention of the French Canadians is no more the result of the present attitude of the Nationalists than the consequence of the Liberal campaign of 1896 or the Conservative appeals of 1911. It relates to deeper causes: hereditary instincts, social and economic conditions, a national tradition of three centuries . . . strengthened by the constant teaching of all our political and social leaders from Lafontaine, Cartier, Macdonald, Mackenzie, to Laurier inclusively.

He maintained that he had always distinguished between support of the war and the school question, but 'to speak of fighting for the preservation of French civilization in Europe while endeavouring to destroy it in America appears to us as an absurd piece of inconsistency.' He said that Captain Papineau was 'utterly unqualified to judge of the feelings of the French Canadians,' since he was separated from them by religion, mother tongue, and upbringing. As for Captain Papineau's threat, 'To propagate systematically national discord by quarrelling with all Canadians, either French or English, who hold different views as to the theory and practice of their national duty would be a misuse of time. Moreover, it would be a singular denial of their professions of faith in liberty and civilization.' He pointed out that the war profiteers were not to be found in the nationalist ranks: 'They are all recruited among the noisiest preachers of the Holy War waged for "civilization" against "barbarity," for the "protection of small nations," for the "honour" of England and the "salvation" of France.' He added an ironical postscript: 'I hope this will reach you before you leave for the front: no doubt you have been the first to respond to the pressing call of your partner.' In reply McMaster denied that he had either written or inspired the letter, and asserted that 'the idea of writing to you and the letter itself are the work of my partner.' He said that he had also striven for national unity, and would not return bitterness for bitterness when 'kindly thoughts and kindly words and kindly deeds should unite all those who call Canada their common duty.'

Whatever the inspiration of Captain Papineau's letter—and that question can scarcely be settled, since Papineau died in France—the propaganda honors of the exchange were won by Bourassa, who focussed national attention on Quebec's dislike of the war and the reasons for it. He had appealed to the instincts of his people and brilliantly analyzed their reasons for dislike of active participation in the war. The exchange of letters attracted more attention than the mass meetings held at Montreal, Quebec, and Sherbrooke on the second anniversary of the declaration of war, with official spokesmen proclaiming Canada's resolution to fight to the end. *La Patrie*, which had first published the Papineau letter, accused Bourassa of going off on a tangent to escape a direct answer. *Le Soleil* charged that he remained entrenched, after two years of a crisis such as humanity had never known, in the position that 'Nothing exists outside the province of Quebec which is worth Quebec's attention from the moment that it requires the least effort or sacrifice on the part of the province of Quebec.' *Le Canada* held that Canadian participation in the war had been decided with the full consent of the people of Canada, and its national liberty remained as intact as individual liberty. Casgrain and Lemieux besought Archbishop Bruchési for an utterance which would deprive Bourassa of the role of interpreter of French-Canadian feeling. On August 8 the archbishop spoke thus:

It is not possible to doubt on which side justice and right are in this terrible war. On one side are our enemies, who have been the aggressors, the violators of treaties and honour, while on our side are the defenders of harmony among nations and the champions of right and justice. It is not men and cannons which will have the last word, but God Almighty, and as God is the God of justice and right, he will ordain that in the end right and justice shall triumph.[13]

The Abbé d'Amours rejoiced at this utterance, and *La Patrie* interpreted it as the refutation of those 'who have openly and laboriously preached the denial of all duties in our province.'

3

In August the Fourth Division landed in France, and recruiting was pressed in Canada. The war factories began to employ women rather than men, in order to promote enlistment. The recruiting sergeants warned that if sufficient volunteers were not forthcoming, conscription would follow. On August 23 L.-N.-J. Pagé broke up a recruiting rally at the Place d'Armes in Montreal by protesting against the insults of the recruiting sergeants of the Irish-Canadian Rangers: 'We shall perhaps allow ourselves to be crushed, but we shall never accept conscription. Our people are insulted every day. French Canadians, it is time to make ourselves respected, and no longer allow ourselves to be crushed as in Ontario.' The recruiting rally turned into an anti-conscription meeting, since the crowd backed Pagé. The following day the French-Canadian crowd forced the soldiers to withdraw from the Place d'Armes. The English press demanded that the hecklers of recruiting rallies be punished, but the *Herald* admitted that the recruiting sergeants had been insulting. *Le Devoir* warned that blows were to be feared if the recruiters behaved like ruffians, though no one would bother them if they behaved honorably. The rallies at the Place d'Armes were given up for the time being.

Laurier, dreading racial differences arising out of the enlistment question, renewed his support for recruiting at an outdoor meeting at Maisonneuve before a crowd of 15,000 on September 21.

There are people who say we will not fight for England; will you then fight for France? I speak to you of French origin; if I were young like you and had the same health that I enjoy to-day. I would join those brave Canadians fighting to-day for the liberation of French territory. I would not have it said that the French Canadians do less for the liberation of France than the citizens of British origin. For my part I want to fight for England and also for France. To those who do not want to fight either for England or for France I say: Will you fight for yourselves?[14]

But Bourassa renewed his warnings that conscription was inevitable, since the raising of 500,000 men by the volunteer system was becoming impossible.[15] At Papineauville on September 3, speaking with Senator Landry in the interest of the Franco-Ontarians, he said that 'England and its Empire, Anglo-Saxon civilization, its guiding principle, its worldwide action, together constitute the most formidable coalition of anti-Catholic forces which exists.'[16] Such statements did more harm to recruiting than the perfervid loyalist speeches of Casgrain, Blondin, and Patenaude did good during the fall.

In September the Canadian Corps saw action again in the Somme. Between September 15 and 18 the Royal 22nd lost a third of its strength in the Battle of Courcelette. The courage shown by the French Canadians, who had led the Canadian attack, was hailed in the French and English press. Again at Regina Trench on October 1, the 22nd lost another third of its strength. Total Canadian casualties for September were 9,051, and even during the uneventful months of July and August had run over 3,000 a month. The problem of reinforcements became serious. Two French-Canadian battalions, Barré's 150th and Piuze's 189th, sailed on September 27 for England, where they became depot battalions for the 22nd. The unruly 206th Battalion was broken up, with its men being sent to Bermuda to fill out the ranks of Asselin's 163rd, which was sent to England later in the fall. Colonel de Salaberry's 230th was transformed into a forestry battalion. All hope of a French-Canadian brigade thus perished.

Faced abroad with the task of supplying reinforcements at an unanticipated rate, and with contradictory demands at home for conscription and for selective enlistment to protect industry, the government decided in August to set up a National Service Board to hold the balance between the manpower needs of army and industry. The director-general, Sir Thomas Tait of Montreal, was not chosen until late in September, however, and the subordinate directors for each of the twelve military districts were not selected until early in October. The board was to be under the direct supervision of the prime minister, not of the minister of militia, and according to Borden its purpose was 'to identify and keep within Canada those who could give better service at home, and to identify and induce to service in the field those who could and ought so to serve.'[17] On October 14 R. B. Bennett was named director-general in place of Sir Thomas Tait, who resigned when the government refused to appoint G. M. Murray, secretary of the Canadian Manufacturers' Association, as secretary of the board. Since the great majority of the directors were Conservatives, Laurier refused to accept Borden's offer to name five Liberal members of a cooperating parliamentary committee of twelve members.

On October 23 Borden issued an appeal to the people of Canada for national service:

> To men of military age I make the appeal that they place themselves at the service of the State for military duty. To all others I make appeal that they place themselves freely at the disposition of their country for such service as they are best fitted to perform.[18]

The government and Director-General Bennett reiterated that conscription was not in question, though Bennett proposed to Borden that the proposed registration card for every male citizen of Canad should carry a question as to conscription, as well as question regarding willingness to change present work for war work, an willingness to move to some other part of Canada to do war work Borden advised against the conscription question.[19] But the Quebe press showed considerable mistrust of the National Service scheme *Le Soleil* congratulated Laurier for refusing to serve in connectio with it, while *Le Bien Public* of Trois-Rivières hinted that it was plan for raising soldiers rather than war workers.[20]

National registration was set for January 1917, and early i December the government began a campaign for full support of it On December 6 in Montreal Borden, accompanied by Casgrain an Doherty, explained the plan to Archbishop Bruchési, who was 'ver friendly and denounced Bourassa.'[21] Then he addressed a mas meeting, which gave him an attentive hearing, but heckled Paten aude and Bennett by cries of 'Why don't you enlist?' and woul hardly allow the former to speak. Students were largely responsibl for the disorder. At Quebec the following day Borden called on Si Lomer Gouin and Cardinal Bégin, who promised their support; an then addressed a mass meeting, backed by Casgrain, Gouin, an Bennett. A group of students cheered Gouin, but called for Bourass and Lavergne when Casgrain was speaking, and left in a body whe Bennett began to speak.[22] On the following day Laurier and Goui spoke at a recruiting meeting in Quebec, while Borden set out west ward to carry his campaign as far as Victoria. Throughout the fal the three French-Canadian ministers had made many speeches i favor of recruiting, while Laurier, Lemieux, and Charles Marcil ha done the same.

But the nationalist opposition had also made itself felt, and wo an ever larger hearing. Paul-Emile Lamarche resigned from parlia ment on September 21, the fifth anniversary of the last elections, i protest over the unprecedented prolongation of its life. On th following Sunday he addressed his electors at Nicolet, supported b Bourassa. Lamarche attacked the government's willingness 'to mortgage the blood of the nation to the amount of 500,000 men, and defended his record, excusing himself for having obtained fo the county few bridges, wharves, and post offices, 'which woul have had to have been bought with pieces of my conscience.'[23] Bourassa took the opportunity to reply to Laurier's Maisonneuv speech of eight days before, blaming on him the initial responsibility of participation in the war, and taunting him with not having gon to the rescue of France in 1870, when he was thirty years old. H ended his attack on Laurier's career since the South African Wa by calling him 'the most nefarious politician of Canada, a traitor to his mission.'[24]

On this same Sunday Armand Lavergne and Tancrède Marsil upported Roch Lanctôt at Napierville, where the latter promised ɔ oppose conscription and denounced the government's policy of xcessive participation in the war, as leading to bankruptcy for vhich the farmer would have to pay. Lavergne refuted the argument f protecting France by enlistment by saying that France was being ttacked in Ontario and it was there that the fight must be won. 'rench was the first language spoken in Canada; it would be the ast, or there would be no more Canada. He invoked the memory f Montcalm, Lévis, the nuns who had sacrificed their lives to eaching, the Jesuit martyrs, and the *Patriote* martyrs of 1837; and alled upon the dead to aid the living in the maintenance of French-Canadian traditions. And on this same Sunday Blondin summoned he people of Batiscan to their prĕdominant duty, to aid France and ngland, since the liberties and even the existence of Canada were t stake. Of all these various declarations Bourassa's attack on aurier excited the most comment in the press. *Le Soleil* announced hat he had 'arrived at the last stage of the brain fever which has een consuming him for some years,' and explained his psychology 1 terms of his phobias for England and for Laurier. *Le Canada* took he same line. Lamarche was accused of pushing nationalism to the oint of anarchy by *L'Evénement*, and others criticized him for etiring from parliament to a well-paid post as counsel of the City f Montreal.[25]

Meanwhile Bourassa criticized Lionel Curtis' recently published *The Problem of the Commonwealth*, in a series of articles in *Le Devoir* rom September 28 to October 9, later reprinted in French and nglish pamphlet form.[26] The Round Table groups, which had een started in 1910 in Canada, Australia, New Zealand, and South frica, and later in the United Kingdom, India, and Newfoundland, ad been studying imperial affairs in a new spirit, with their uarterly, *The Round Table*, serving as a medium of information n imperial questions. Shortly before the war, their study had een concentrated on 'how a British citizen in the Dominions an acquire the same control of foreign policy as one domiciled 1 the British Isles.' A draft drawn up in the fall of 1915 served s the basis of Curtis' book. Curtis saw the war as a struggle or liberty against autocracy, and hence parallel to the Seven 'ears' War in which 'Had France prevailed . . . the principle f self-government would have perished, not merely in America, ut also in the British Isles.'[27] This thesis could not but be triguing to Bourassa, whose interest in control over foreign policy ad grown to such an extent that it alarmed Laurier, who through andurand warned his former disciple that he was 'playing with re.'[28]

But Curtis' veiled 'Anglo-Saxon' racism, with its implication (a people chosen to bear the white man's burden, irritated Bourass: who was beginning to disparage the 'Anglo-Saxon' character:

> To his hereditary pride, which marks his cousinship with the norther German, have come to be added the obtuseness developed by insula isolation and alcoholism, and above all infatuation with his immens wealth and pride of domination over weak peoples. As a result, in spit of his remarkable faculties for government, and the general humanity (his proceedings—when cupidity and the desire of domination do nc push him to brutalities—the Anglo-Saxon does not know how to gai the confidence, much less the affection, of the peoples that he dominat(nor even of those with whom he associates. Now when confidence an love are missing, good understanding is difficult.[29]

Bourassa found himself in complete accord with Curtis, however, o constitutional principles, though he favored dominion independenc rather than equal partnership with the United Kingdom as th solution of the present situation, which Curtis called 'intolerable Bourassa was willing to accept the latter alternative though, if th majority preferred it to independence, since he believed that it woul lead to independence in any case. He reaffirmed his convictio about imperialism as expressed to Arthur Hawkes, and again warne that the anglicizers and the Tory imperialists might drive the Frenc Canadians into the third alternative of annexation to the Unite States. In the English translation of these articles Bourassa develope at greater length his arguments in favor of independence, an removed the indictment of 'Anglo-Saxon' alcoholism. But ther were few English Canadians in the mood for academic analyses (constitutional problems at this period. When Montreal students, o their way to the cathedral for the Mass celebrating the opening (the academic year, tore down recruiting posters and became involve with the police, who made some arrests in the church itself, Bourass was blamed by the press of Ontario and the West. As in the ol song of 1837 which proclaimed '*C'est la faute de Papineau,*' every ur toward incident in Quebec was now blamed on Papineau's granc son Bourassa, whose hanging was called for continually by th English press.

4

With French-English relations growing worse every day, Arthı Hawkes conceived the notion of an exchange of visits betwee representative men of Ontario and Quebec. Two Toronto friend a Methodist lawyer, John Milton Godfrey and Colonel Mulloy, blind veteran of the South African War, helped Hawkes to organiz the project. Bourassa declined Hawkes' request for aid. But earl ı October some fifty leading Ontarians began their goodwill ·ilgrimage through Quebec at a dinner at the Club Saint-Denis in Aontreal. Senator Dandurand asked only that the French Cana- .ians be taken as they were, the most Canadian of all Canadians. 'aul-Emile Lamarche said the French Canadians were Canadian bove all, and that he preferred Canada to the empire. He illus- rated two rival concepts of national unity with two gestures: 'Some vant national unity like that,' laying one hand on top of the other; We wish it like this,' laying one hand beside the other. Charles ≀eaubien protested that it took more courage to urge others to nlist on the platform than to speak thus to English guests. Lam- rche retorted: 'I should not wish to urge others to enlist before ·utting on the uniform myself,' and was greeted with a 'Right you .re' from one of the visitors.[30] With the ice thus broken, the visitors egretted the absence of Bourassa.

The Ontario pilgrims continued on to Trois-Rivières and Quebec, vhere *L'Action Catholique* greeted them in an English article and ırged a permanent *bonne entente* committee. At Sherbrooke Colonel Aulloy received an ovation, and he tried to give Lavergne the .ccolade in the French manner. More impressive in enlightening he visitors about Quebec than the flood of speeches were their 'isits to Montreal's port facilities, the factories of Trois-Rivières, the Quebec Ecole Technique, the asbestos mines of Thetford, and the ›ilingual schools of Sherbrooke. They were also impressed by such listinguished men as Senator Dandurand, Sir Georges Garneau, and Dr. Panteléon Pelletier, Quebec's London agent. Upon his return o Toronto, S. R. Parson, vice-president of the Canadian Manu- acturers' Association, gave an objective lecture on his impressions. But he did not fail to point out that while the bishops supported the var effort, the priests supported Bourassa, which was an index of ›opular feeling. Some of the visitors also persuaded Joseph Flavelle, he head of the Imperial Munitions Board, that two new war actories should be established in Ontario rather than Quebec, since uch a step would 'recompense this population for not having done ts duty toward the Empire, and deprive Ontario whose young men ıave so generously offered and given their lives.'[31]

The Ontario school question continued to set French against English. The Association d'Education opened the bilingual schools n the fall, but was scarcely able to pay the teachers and had no noney to buy coal. A campaign was organized for the latter ›urpose. Abbé Groulx spoke at Ottawa on October 15, and was ntroduced by Landry and thanked by Laurier, who both saw 'ictory as the eventual result of the scholastic struggle. The meeting vas symbolic of Quebec's unity on the question, with a young ıationalist supported by the Conservative and Liberal elder statesmen. There was fresh alarm at the new school regulations ir Manitoba, seemingly inspired by Regulation 17. Bishop Béliveau spoke on the Western situation at Laval in Quebec on October 17 The province was stirred by various benefits and collections for th Ontario schools.

But on October 27 Benedict XV's encyclical '*Commisso divinitus* was published in Canada, leaving the decision of the school questio 'to the bishops, and particularly to those who preside over diocese where the struggle is most ardent.' It added counsels for calm an unity among all Catholics. *La Patrie* hailed it in triumph, callin upon 'the fomenters of discord, the exploiters of race and religion, to give way to 'men of goodwill, to the moderates, to the true friend of progress, peace, and harmony among the different nationalitie which compose our population.'[32] *L'Action Catholique* implied tha the encyclical was a rebuke to the nationalists. *Le Devoir* at firs refrained from all comment. *Le Canada* made common cause witl *L'Evénement* to censure a 'certain politico-religious school' justl reprimanded by the Pope for 'violently pleading a good cause unde the mantle of religion.' *L'Action Catholique* rebuked the journalist who presumed to usurp the bishops' role as interpreters of th Pope's thought.[33] The encyclical at first dismayed the chiefs of th Franco-Ontarian movement. But they drew some comfort from th Privy Council's decision of November 2, which in effect confirme the validity of Regulation 17, but disavowed the new school com mission set up by the Ontario government. Samuel Genest at onc claimed the documents and the funds held by the commission while Mgr. Paquet, Père Rouleau, and Père Villeneuve—two futur cardinals—held a theological consultation at Ottawa on the inter pretation of the encyclical. Mgr. Paquet stopped in press a nev edition of his *Cours de droit public de l'Eglise* to alter his interpretatio of the encyclical. He saw in it an assertion of the principle that th French Canadians had the right, in a province of English majority to have their language taught and to defend it, and that the faithfu also had the right to worship and receive religious teaching in thei mother tongue. He infered an implied condemnation of Regulatio 17, since the encyclical urged that Catholics should work with zea and charity to improve the situation. In an interview in *Le Droit* Mgr. Paquet said that the papal injunction to avoid discord amon the faithful did not preclude efforts to defend the French language.[3] The brash young men of the Arch group in Montreal published tw articles on the encyclical and the Privy Council decision in *L'Escholie* under the headline '*Nous n'irons pas à Canossa.*' In an editoria Jean Chauvin recalled Bourassa's words in the Keewatin affair 'Holy Father, the Catholics of Canada venerate you, but ir matters exclusively political, we, British and Canadian citizens laim from you the liberty the Church has always recognized n these matters for its faithful.'[35] Landry, Belcourt, and Père Charlebois accepted the papal decision, but the young nationalists hus supplied evidence that they had become more French than Catholic. Within a few days, Chauvin renounced his editorial hair and enlisted in the field artillery, giving explanations nore complicated than those of Asselin for his enlistment after ong opposition to the war. A possible conclusive factor may have een the patriotic feeling aroused by the impressive tribute paid to he dead of the Royal 22nd at Notre-Dame on October 26, when ll the regiments of Montreal paraded to the church and Archishop Bruchési told a congregation which included Sam Hughes, Patenaude, Doherty, and many other notables that 'Quebec has one its duty.'[36]

On the day before this service the *Gazette* published a letter from Gustave Lanctot, who had originally been in Asselin's 163rd Battalion, but on being sent to England on a special mission, had ad himself transferred to an English-speaking unit at the front. Writing to a friend in Canada, Lanctot reported that while England nd France lavished praise on the 22nd Battalion, they were stonished at Quebec's indifference to the war and at the fact that ome French-Canadian papers were actually carrying on anti-Allied propaganda. Lanctot wondered whether public opinion in Quebec ad yet awakened to its duty, and appealed to his compatriots to ealize that they were fighting for Canadian liberty and to prevent German domination on the shores of the St. Lawrence.[37] But Lanctot's letter, like Papineau's, came too late to reverse the swelling ide against enlistment in Quebec.

In October *La Presse* began a series of articles, issued as a pamphlet, *Our Volunteer Army*, early in December, which was a defensive nalysis of the recruiting problem, and also an attempt to encourage urther enlistments. It claimed that Quebec did not lag very far behind Ontario in the number of native-born volunteers, with 6,000 or 1 per cent of her eligible male population enlisted as ompared to Ontario's 42,000 or $2\frac{1}{2}$ per cent. It declared that more han 9,000 of Quebec's 16,000 were French Canadians. Quebec's poorer showing was blamed on indignation over the Ontario school question, on English control of the recruiting system, on the lesser hance for French Canadians to win promotion or decorations, and o the breaking up of French-Canadian units. It was pointed out hat Ontario had more unmarried men and a much larger urban population. It was also argued that French Canadians enlisted only in combat battalions, while in Ontario many joined service forces. According to the *Toronto Globe's* figures, that district had ecently supplied only 181 infantry recruits, as compared, to 3,219 enlistments in artillery, engineering, medical, forestry, and oth special branches. On July 17 *Le Canada* had claimed a total of 50,oc French Canadians in the army: 5,000 in the First Contingen 7,200 in the six French battalions subsequently recruited; 7,000 English Quebec units; 1,200 in the 165th Acadian Battalion, wi 3,000 others scattered through other Maritime units; 4,000 Ontario and Western units; 12,000 in hospital, service, pioneer, an forestry units; and 10,000 French and Belgian reservists. O August 21 the *Orange Sentinel* had rejected these figures as gross exaggerated, saying that no more than 5,000 French Canadia had ever enlisted, and also charged that the French-Canadia battalions 'enlist in retail and desert wholesale.' *La Presse* co tented itself with a claim of 16,000 French-Canadian volunteers October. And significantly it admitted, despite its effort to produ patriotic statistics, that Quebec had not done its part and appeale to the French Canadians to equal Ontario's war effort.[38] It w now generally recognized that Quebec's recruiting record was ba but the lack of authoritative figures and the wide disparity of vario claims made the situation worse.

The provincial legislature met on November 7, but was large concerned with local affairs, save for the announcement of the gi of $1,000,000 to the Patriotic Fund by the province, and a Co servative request for the grant of assistance to the Franco-Ontarian Gouin evaded the latter request as inopportune after the encyclica Athanase David, Senator L.-O. David's son, made his maide speech, which revealed the influence of Bourassa even on the so of a staunch Liberal. He defended Quebec against attacks on i enlistment record by urging those who wanted the French Canadia to save France on European battlefields to show the same sympath for France to those in Canada who were attached to the Frenc language. He asserted the rights of the French Canadians and the place in Confederation.[39] Another proof of the growing rift betwee the races was a letter written to Bourassa by John S. Ewart o December 1:

> I am afraid that we view present circumstances from a differe angle and perhaps you will permit me to say that I have very muc regretted the course which you have, I have no doubt, conscientious adopted.
>
> I should not think it at all right, at the time to say anything that woul tend to distract our people during the stress of war. To me, the firs requisite is solidarity and for that purpose necessarily the subordinatio of the many conflicting things and ideas which would effect that solid arity. After the war is over, all those interested not only in its cause o purpose, but in the history of wars in general, will have much to engag their attention and quite possibly I shall not be among the silent one

when the right time arrives. Meanwhile I would hope that we would all contribute to the success of what our country—yours and mine—has almost unanimously agreed to adopt.[40]

With this letter their correspondence was broken off until January 1918, when Ewart sought Bourassa's advice on how the government might mend matters in Quebec. But in December 1916 the division between the races had become so sharply marked that the leading English-Canadian nationalist broke off long existing relations with the leading French-Canadian nationalist.

For most English-speaking Canadians the war came before all else; for the French it was subordinated to certain national interests. The French press devoted more attention to the Ontario question than to the struggle in Europe, and the nationalist agitation had reached into the farthest backwaters of the province, leaving Quebec ill-disposed towards measures for furthering a war effort which it already considered too great. A sharp increase in the cost of living affected more people in Quebec's marginal economy than the high wages paid in war plants. How differently Quebec conceived its duty from the other provinces was revealed by Bourassa's speech on '*Le Devoir National*' on the same night that Borden supported the National Service plan in Montreal. Bourassa thus defined the national duty of the French Canadians: 'Let us be intensely Catholic and French. In default of the superiority of numbers or of wealth which no doubt we shall never have, our faith will insure us a moral superiority, if we know how to live by it; our civilization will insure us an intellectual superiority, provided that we know how not to degrade it.'[41]

The Abbé d'Amours had continued his attacks on Bourassa and his ideas in *La Presse*, and late in 1916 they were reprinted in pamphlet form as *Où allons-nous? Le Nationalisme canadien. Lettres d'un 'Patriote'* and given wide circulation. D'Amours declared that Bourassa's principles were false and that Bourassa was a 'partisan of Kantian subjectivism and of the egotism of the Nietzschian superman.'[42] He asserted that Bourassa had tried to group the French Canadians outside the jurisdiction of the Church and had taught that its opinions on political matters need not necessarily be obeyed, so that the forces of French Canadianism and Catholicism had been divided. D'Amours dismissed independence as being contrary to the will of the majority of Canadians and as leading to the submission of French-Canadian rights to the will of the English majority. Annexation would mean the political and ethnic end of French Canada, as it had that of Louisiana. Belittling Bourassa's fear of imperialism, D'Amours called for the preservation of Confederation and the British connection. The French-Canadian patriot should seek to make friends and allies, rather than to isolate French Canada by a policy of national egoism.

The abbé warned of the dangers of forming a Catholic or nationalist party which would expose French Canada to dangers in a predominantly Protestant country. French Canadians were strongly urged to be loyal to the British Crown and the empire. He denounced as neither legitimate or prudent the nationalist attempt to dispute the decision of the Canadian parliament to participate in the war and Britain's right to be supported by Canada. He condemned Bourassa's views as being contrary to the tradition of the Church in Canada, which had always upheld loyalty to Britain, and which had provided a bulwark against assimilation, Americanization, or contamination by French revolutionary ideas, as well as protection for the Church's teachings on faith and morals. On December 7 Bourassa replied to the abbé with a blast in *Le Devoir* which destroyed him in a few paragraphs.[43] D'Amours' views had long been unpopular, but they had been held to represent the opinion of the hierarchy. But now Archbishop Bruchési criticized him for contributing to a Montreal journal without obtaining the permission necessary for a priest of another diocese. This disavowal by the hierarchy was a highly revealing index of the changing mood of French Canada. Panic-stricken, the abbé excused himself on the grounds of having in the past been encouraged by the archbishop in his opposition, in the interests of the Church and the country, to the 'disastrous campaign of the nationalists,' and of his desire to avoid embarrassing the archbishop.

5

A measure taken by the government in the fall of 1916 removed one ground of nationalist opposition to the war effort, but it came too late to be effective on public opinion in Quebec. Canadian control of the Canadian forces overseas was assured in November by the appointment of Sir George Perley as minister of overseas forces, with Sir Edward Kemp replacing Sam Hughes as minister of militia at home. Hughes had been a constant thorn in Borden's flesh because of his erratic behavior. He had quarrelled with the Duke of Connaught when the latter attempted to be more than nominal commander-in-chief, and he had frequently made trouble with the War Office in London. General Alderson's resignation as commander of the Canadian Corps had come as a direct result of differences with Hughes. The latter had attempted to direct military affairs in the field as well as at home, and his frequent trips to England and France had resulted in poor administration of military affairs in Canada. His connection with the munitions and supply scandals, his notorious favoritism in appointments, and his unwariness in dealing with the sensibilities of Quebec had provided much political embarrassment for Borden. The prime minister allowed his colleague to go his way, however, despite increasing protests both from England and other members of the cabinet, until September 1916, when Hughes set up a Canadian Military Council in London without consultation with the cabinet. Borden at once ordered him home, and announced to him the impending appointment of Perley to the post of minister of overseas troops. Hughes protested violently against Perley's appointment and urged that his friend Sir Max Aitken should have the post.

On November 9 Borden replied to a letter from Hughes, which accused him of making inaccurate statements and referred sarcastically to other 'lovely' commissions appointed by the government, with a demand for Hughes' resignation based upon consultation with his colleagues, among whom Thomas White and George Foster had long favored Hughes' dismissal. Borden referred to Hughes' desire 'to administer your department as if it were a distinct and separate Government in itself' and to his repudiation of the principle of cabinet responsibility.[44] After his resignation had been requested, Hughes made a speech at the Empire Club in Toronto attacking English control of Canadian troops overseas, English rejection of Canadian supplies, and English administration of hospitals. Hughes subsequently intrigued against the government. Lord Birkenhead told Borden of the general's plan to overthrow the administration.[45] Hughes explained his resignation on the grounds of 'interferences and conditions imposed on the administration of this Department' in a farewell speech to his staff on November 15. The English-Canadian press gave him credit for organizing the First Division so rapidly, but spoke freely of his 'weird incompatibility of temperament' and his unwillingness to bear the restraints imposed upon responsible ministers 'with his temperament of a military dictator.'[46]

Hughes had done much to turn French Canada against the war by his Methodist, Orangeman, and Masonic prejudice against French Catholics, by his refusal to appoint French-Canadian officers to high commands, by his unwillingness to exploit fully French Canada's early enthusiasm for the war, and by his association with the war profiteers. During his period in power Hughes kept his opinion of the French Canadians largely to himself, though in laying the cornerstone of the new arsenal which he had secured for his home town of Lindsay, Ontario, on July 15, he had said: 'With all due regard to the Province of Quebec, in this great war it has not done its duty as it should and would if the young manhood of the

Province had been taken in hand by the proper people, who hav benefitted so much from British institutions in days gone by.'[4] In 1918, during the conscription debates, he made far more violen charges against the French Canadians, which probably echoed hi secret opinions while minister of militia. The kindest possible verdic on Hughes' administration as far as Quebec was concerned wa supplied by the recognition of the 'tactless blunders' made durin the First World War in Brigadier Maurice Pope's confidentia study in 1941 of 'The Recruiting Problem in the Province c Quebec.'[48]

T.-Chase Casgrain died on December 29; and Borden addec Albert Sévigny to the cabinet as minister of inland revenue, witl Patenaude receiving the postmaster-generalship. The cabinet thu had no strong French-Canadian representative as it entered th stormy year of 1917, which saw Quebec aligned against the rest c Canada on the question of conscription. Late in December th prime minister, who had earlier assured Cardinal Bégin and Arch bishop Bruchési that there would be no conscription in seeking thei support for the National Service scheme, told labor representatives 'I hope conscription may not be necessary, but if it should prov the only effective method to preserve the existence of the State an of the institutions and liberties which we enjoy, I should conside it necessary and I should not hesitate to act accordingly.'[49] At th same time, however, he issued a public statement that Nationa Service registration was called for in order that there might be n conscription. Relying upon Borden's good faith, Cardinal Bégi and Archbishop Bruchési strongly supported the registration, th former in a circular letter to his clergy on January 4 and the latte in a public statement.[50] But the thesis of the nationalist press tha registration was a prelude to conscription was echoed vaguely i some other journals.

After the January registration was concluded, Director-Genera Bennett announced that 80 per cent of the men between 17 and 4 had replied. Quebec had only 79,700 men classified as militar prospects, compared to Ontario's 186,252, possibly because of th prevalence of early marriage and large families. The classificatio took account of marriage and dependents, as well as employment i war industry.[51] Nothing was done at once with the inventory thu taken, and enlistments continued at a low rate. Throughou Canada opposition to the registration was strongly expressed b labor groups. The farmers of Ontario and the West were also hostil to registration, in so far as they interpreted it as a step toward conscription. There was renewed pressure for conscription fron Tory sources and the recruiting leagues, while the Liberals remaine generally opposed to it.

In January 1917 the *bonne entente* movement renewed its efforts to reconcile Quebec and Ontario, with a French-Canadian group visiting Toronto and Hamilton. Sir Georges Garneau was given an honorary degree by the University of Toronto, and on this occasion paid tribute to the men fighting in France and Flanders and to the British Navy. Sir Lomer Gouin urged unity in Canada, when Frenchmen and Englishmen were fighting for the sacred things common to both, 'mingling their blood on the battlefields of right and justice and for the aid of the defenceless of the community.'[52] The visiting Quebec delegation also included L.-P. Pelletier and Charles Beaubien. But this movement involved only certain leaders of French Canada who were already committed to the Allied cause; it did not affect the rank and file.

The attitude of the latter was revealed in the by-election in Dorchester on January 27 in which the new minister of inland revenue, Albert Sévigny, sought re-election. The Liberals nominated Lucien Cannon, the provincial member for the constituency, and denounced Sévigny for his disloyal and unpatriotic statements in the 1911 campaign and criticized his nomination to the cabinet. At Saint-Prosper on January 19 and at later meetings the two candidates discussed once more the Navy issue, participation in the war, and the possibility of conscription. Sévigny admitted his former opposition to participation in imperial wars, but urged support of the government's war policy, the National Service scheme, and the abandonment of partisan politics. Cannon accused him of betraying his nationalist colleagues of 1911 and his constituents, and declared: 'National Service is preliminary to Conscription, and with the chief of my party I am against Conscription.'[53] Stating that he was not against a participation in the war which would not bankrupt Canada in manpower and wealth, he warned that the election of Sévigny would indicate Quebec's support of conscription and of endless Canadian sacrifices for England. Each candidate claimed the backing of his party chief, but while Patenaude and Blondin energetically supported Sévigny on the platform and with the full resources of the Conservative machine, no Liberal leaders appeared in Cannon's behalf.

The electoral meetings grew violent in tone, with Cannon, who was partially of English descent, telling Sévigny that he would 'rather be a half-breed than a pure French Canadian who had betrayed his people.'[54] The government was attacked for graft and profiteering, and for tolerating the Ontario persecution of French Canadians. Sévigny regretted the Ontario situation, but pointed out that the Liberal government of Manitoba had broken the Laurier-Greenway Agreement. Blondin accused Cannon of wanting to start a revolution by raising the province of Quebec against the other provinces. Sévigny was asked what he had done for recruiting, for the Patriotic Fund, and for the Red Cross, and why he didn't enlist. Cannon said the issue was the record of the government and of Sévigny, and whether the people favored National Service in Canada, when in England it had been followed in six months by conscription. The Conservatives were charged with flooding the constituency with liquor, and the Liberals with conducting a seditious house-to-house campaign. Much was made of the bilinguial question by both sides. The vote gave a majority of 297 for Sévigny, a slight decrease since 1911. *Le Soleil* flatly accused him of having bought the election.[55] This election showed that Quebec opinion had not yet solidified against the government, though the bitterness with which French-Canadian grievances were aired was not encouraging for the future.

6

The long and eventful 1917 session of parliament opened on January 19. Borden announced the government's intention of extending parliament's life for a year to avoid a wartime election, and the British Government's invitation to the dominion prime ministers to attend as members of the British War Cabinet a special Imperial War Conference to be held late in February. J.-H. Rainville was named deputy-speaker in Sévigny's place. Laurier criticised the government's lack of unity of purpose, thought, and action in its war policy, and its belated assertion of Canadian control over the Canadian forces overseas. Privately he agreed to an adjournment of the session so that Borden might attend the Imperial Conference, though he raised a constitutional question as to how Borden could become a member of the War Cabinet without being a member of the British Parliament. Borden defended his government's war record, and listed Canadian casualties to date as 70,263, out of 392,647 enlisted for overseas service and a total manpower contribution of 413,279.[56] He emphasized the need for the extension of parliament's term, but the question was not debated until later in the year, as it promised to be a highly controversial one. The government was unpopular, and Liberal stock was rising. The Liberals now controlled seven of the provinces, with a total of 336 seats to the Conservatives' 180.[57] There was a growing movement for a coalition government in which the Liberals would have a voice, without the strong Quebec representation that would be involved if the Liberals should win outright power at Ottawa.

The Liberal press of Toronto and Winnipeg favored coalition, with the exception of the *Toronto Star* and the *Manitoba Free Press*, while the Conservative press largely opposed it. But J. W. Flavelle,

Conservative chairman of the Imperial Munitions Board, had urged a coalition government in an address to the Ottawa Canadian Club in December, in order to avoid an election fought on a racial basis and to permit postwar revision of the empire by English Canadians, for 'it is inconceivable to me that a government sustained by the vote of a section of this Dominion which, no matter for what reason or conscience, were unwilling to bear their share in this struggle, would be permitted without civil strife to determine what part Canada should take in the Imperial Council which must follow the war.'[58] Borden had sought to prevent Flavelle from making this proposal.[59]. Laurier had had coalition proposed to him by N. W. Rowell and other prominent Liberals, but lacked confidence in that form of government and had faith in a Liberal victory in an election, though he inclined to the belief that the Liberal leader should not be a French Canadian.[60] But pending the Imperial Conference, Laurier agreed to pass the War Appropriation Bill and a portion of the normal estimates, and parliament was adjourned on February 7 until April 19 by joint agreement. On the eve of Borden's departure for England, it was decided to postpone application of the Militia Act for home defence purposes, while Bennett proposed disenfranchising those who had failed to register for national service. The shadow of conscription loomed larger, with enlistments still declining, casualties rising, and a labor shortage in the West.[61]

Accompanied by Douglas Hazen, minister of marine, and Robert Rogers, minister of public works, Borden left Ottawa on February 12 and reached London on the 23rd. Borden at once had a consultation with the colonial secretary, Walter Long, with whom he had corresponded about the conference. He heard the new prime minister, Lloyd George, speak in the Commons, and had an audience with the King. He conferred with Admiral Jellicoe on the problems raised by the intensification of the German submarine campaign, and with the colonial secretary. The opening of the conference was delayed until late in March by the difficulties experienced by the Australian delegation in reaching England, so Borden spent the intervening weeks in visiting the Canadian troops at the front and British and French headquarters, as well as the Canadian base at Shorncliffe in England and many hospitals. On March 2, he attended the first meeting of the War Cabinet set up by Lloyd George, who had acted on Laurier's challenge of 1897, 'If you want our aid, call us to your councils.' For the first time department heads, experts, and other non-members of the cabinet were in attendance, in addition to the dominion representatives.

Borden developed an immediate friendship with the South African representative, General Jan Smuts, and the two evolved a new concept of the imperial relationship which was foreshadowed in their speeches at the Empire Parliamentary Association luncheo on April 2. It was embodied in the mutually drafted Resolutio IX, which Borden moved and Smuts seconded in the conferenc on April 16, calling for the readjustment of the constitutiona structure of the empire at a special Imperial Conference after th war:

> They deem it their duty, however, to place on record their view tha any such readjustment, while thoroughly preserving all existing power of self-government and complete control of domestic affairs, should b based upon a full recognition of the Dominions as autonomous nation of an Imperial Commonwealth, and of India as an important portion o the same, should recognize the right of the Dominions and India to a adequate voice in foreign policy and in foreign relations, and shoul provide effective arrangements for continuous consultation in all importan matters of common Imperial concern, and for such necessary concerte action, founded on consultation, as the several Governments may deter mine.[62]

In his speech in support of this resolution, Borden stressed th importance of the Crown as the tie linking the Dominions with th United Kingdom, and of the acceptance of the general principl by the British Government in establishing the Imperial War Cabinet Smuts stressed that in the future 'the Governments of the Dominion as equal Governments of the King in the British Commonwealt will have to be considered far more fully than that is done today. To him the resolution implied the rejection of the ideas of a imperial parliament and an imperial executive, and favored th development of the empire along the old loose lines with still mor freedom and equality for the constituent parts. The resolution ha been produced in consultation with Australia, New Zealand, an Newfoundland, and was previously approved by the British Wa Cabinet. The inclusion of India was made at the suggestion o Austen Chamberlain, then secretary of state for India.

Resolution IX was passed unanimously by the conference, an the way was thus paved for the establishment of the British Common wealth of Nations in 1926, confirmed by the Statute of Westministe in 1931.

In his public addresses in England and Scotland during th remainder of his stay Borden emphasized the great constitutiona development which had taken place, thanks to the stress of event British flexibility and pragmatism, and the power of the prim minister under the British constitution. Lloyd George was, in fac as Walter Long told Borden, virtually a dictator; and he was dictator who favored Borden's constitutional views and was willin to take his advice on dominion matters. Borden upheld Canada' interests strenuously in the meetings of the Imperial War Cabinet, where matters of common imperial concern were discussed, while the British War Cabinet dealt with day-to-day questions chiefly concerning the United Kingdom. Before the Conference closed on May 2, it unanimously accepted the principle that each part of the empire should give special favorable treatment to the produce and manufactures of other parts of the empire, but this was the only concession to Chamberlain's imperial dream. It was agreed to hold imperial war cabinets regularly, annually or more often. In the new imperial council Great Britain presided, but was merely *primus inter pares* in Borden's favorite formula.

Upon his return to Canada Borden submitted a report to parliament on his English visit, and stressed the importance of this new 'cabinet of governments rather than of ministers.'[63] Laurier put his finger on a major difficulty by pointing out that the imperial cabinet was merely a consultative body, whose conclusions might or might not be adopted by the various parliaments of the empire, each the proper advisor of the Crown in the country in question. In a letter to the editor of the *Manchester Guardian*, who had requested his views on the conference and on future imperial relations, Laurier said that he thought discussion of the subject inopportune during the war, but stated his opinion that since foreign affairs could not be divorced from the domestic policies of the United Kingdom, the dominions could have no real voice in questions of peace and war. To have such a voice, they would have to back it with permanent defence contributions. He was opposed to this on the grounds of Canada's need to devote her wealth to internal development and her unwillingness to participate 'in such a senseless war as the Crimean War.' He regarded imperial federation as impracticable at present, and the present loose connection as 'the safest and the most promising.'[64]

7

But the constitutional questions raised by the Imperial Conference of 1917 were overshadowed by the conscription crisis which arose in Canada at this time. The enlistment figures for the early months of 1917 were dwarfed by the casualty figures:

	Enlistments	*Casualties*
January	9,194	4,396
February	6,809	21,955
March	6,640	6,161
April	5,530	10,894
May	6,407	13,457[65]

The conquest of Vimy Ridge in April had cost the Canadians particularly dear, but with four divisions at the front there were continual losses which threatened to exceed the supply of reinforcements. In March the new militia minister, Sir Edward Kemp, made a last vigorous effort to obtain volunteers. On March 16 he called for the enlistment of 50,000 men as a Canadian Defence Force, so that troops still in Canada might be released for overseas service. It was hoped that the men so enlisted might later be induced to go overseas, though for the time being they were only asked to drill three times a week and to attend a summer camp. Disliked by the army and by conscription enthusiasts, this effort was a recognized failure by May. Meanwhile revolution-torn Russia was virtually out of the war; submarine warfare was proving far more effective than anticipated; and though the United States had declared war, it was felt that it would be a long time before American military strength was exerted in France.

In the same speech on May 18 in which he reported on his London visit, Borden stressed the need for reinforcements and announced his reluctant conviction that the selective conscription of 50,000 to 100,000 men was necessary. The announcement was timed to coincide with the day that the American Select Draft Bill became law at Washington. Previously there had been rumors of considerable numbers of young Canadians crossing the New Brunswick, Quebec, and Ontario borders to the States, in order to avoid pressure to enlist. Laurier reserved comment on the proposal which he had so long dreaded, stating that Canada was in the war to the end, but the method of carrying on the war to the end must be carefully considered before the established policy of the country was set aside. He promised due and fair consideration of the government's proposals, and that his Liberal colleagues would do their duty to the best of their judgment. Privately he stated that he was opposed to conscription by his commitments and by his conviction that, as in England, it would bring in only a tiny number of slackers, since 'the number of men who can be spared from agriculture and industry is infinitesimally small.'[66] To Lomer Gouin he wrote on May 28:

As to conscription, there can equally be no hesitation. After the agitation which has been carried on upon this subject, if we were to hesitate at this moment, we would hand over the province to the extremists; instead of promoting national unity, it would open up a breach, perhaps fatal.

As for myself, the situation is clear, but I doubt whether I will succeed in inducing our friends from the other provinces to accept it. The Eastern provinces will be nearly solid with us; Ontario solid on the other side, and the West perhaps divided; there is some ground for hoping for a fairly solid vote, but I am far from being sure.[67]

The *Montreal Gazette* and the English press in general favored conscription from the start. *La Patrie* and *L'Evénement*, the government organs, accepted it unenthusiastically as a necessity. *Le Canada* on May 21 attacked the government for going back on its promises of no conscription, on May 24 urged a referendum on the question, and on May 26 came out flatly against conscription. On May 28 *La Presse* also urged a referendum, though on May 16 it had asserted that if conscription had been adopted at the beginning of the war 'it would be working well today,' and that if found necessary, 'it will be religiously accepted by the Province of Quebec.'[68] But the rural weeklies at once expressed opposition, and popular feeling in Montreal was indicated by the fact that mobs broke the windows of *La Patrie* on May 23 to the cry of 'Down with conscription!' and again the following night, when *La Presse* also suffered the same attentions. Mass meetings were held on the night of May 23 at the Champs de Mars and at Parc LaFontaine. In Quebec City on May 21, a crowd of 10,000 heard Oscar Drouin say that he would fight conscription to the death, while on May 25 a crowd roused by a fiery speech by Armand Lavergne smashed the windows of the *Chronicle* and *L'Evénement*. On May 29 there was a great anti-conscription meeting at Hull, followed by others in other towns during June. As early as May 28 *Le Devoir* urged the French Canadians to remain calm, and to beware of agents-provocateurs inciting them to violence so as to make them seem rebellious to the laws of the land. They were asked to listen to the voices of their religious leaders and to oppose conscription in a calm, disciplined manner.

But Quebec was in no calm or disciplined mood at the long-expected appearance of conscription, which had so long been used in the province as a political bugaboo. Enthusiasm for the war was at a low ebb. In March Blondin had resigned from the cabinet to raise the 258th Battalion among his compatriots for overseas service, 'deeply convinced that the most imperious duty of the present hour for me is to practice what I have preached to you for the last three years and to devote myself entirely to the rallying of the French Canadians.'[69] Despite support from General Lessard and two returned officers of the 22nd, and an elaborate organization which scheduled fifty-eight meetings throughout Quebec between May 1 and July 15, the Lessard-Blondin effort brought in only 92 recruits. In Montreal on May 7 the crowd refused to listen to any of the political leaders, veterans, or the recruiting officers. An effort was made to invoke the influence of the *curés*, but the recruiting campaign was cancelled on May 20 with the announcement of impending conscription. In April and May troops passing through Quebec were pelted with rotten vegetables, ice, and stones when they taunted

French-Canadian youths with not being in uniform. At the National Unity Convention, which met in Montreal from May 21 to 25, as a development of the *bonne entente* movement, Bishop Gauthier made a passionate defence of French Canada's war efforts, rather than a plea for national unity.

Bourassa was not surprised by the coming of conscription. He had long anticipated it, particularly since the United States declared war in April. For a year he had followed American affairs closely, and from May 7 to 19 he published in *Le Devoir* a series of articles on causes, ends, and consequences of American intervention in the war, which he published in pamphlet form at the end of the month, with a new section on the consequences for Canada.[70] American neutrality had furnished support for French-Canadian nationalism, as it was to do again in the Second World War. Bourassa admired Wilson as a sincere partisan of peace, but blamed his insistance on the right of Americans to travel and trade freely across the seas as compromising his hope for peace. He laid much stress on the influence of German philosophy and educational ideals on both Americans and English Canadians to explain American neutrality, supported by the Irish hatred of England and Jewish hatred of Russia. Sympathy with and against France seemed to him to be about equal in the States, while English legal and financial influences had counteracted pro-German influences. The invasion of Belgium, the heroism of France, the submarine campaign, the swaying of the press by the Morgan interests, and the sinking of the *Lusitania*, cunningly exploited by English and American financial interests deeply committed to the allied cause, had done much to bring about American support of the war. The Russian Revolution had aroused democratic sympathies, as Wilson's peace program became his war program.

Bourassa approved of the immediate adoption of selective conscription in the United States—'the only practical and just means to organize an effective army while reducing to a minimum the dangers of economic disorganization'—as opposed to the so-called voluntary system in Canada, which he characterized as 'enlistment by blackmail, intimidation, seduction, and the grotesque methods of circus advertising, without any regard to the needs of agriculture and industry, as essential to victory as a great number of soldiers.'[71] In Canada there had been 'the triumph of militarism under its most dangerous and stupid form'; in the United States 'the subordination of military organization to the supreme needs of the nation.'[72] The United States had also applied the agricultural measures which Bourassa had long called for vainly in Canada. He cited the difference as that between the concrete applications of nationalism and of colonialism to the solution of vital national problems. The United States was now torn between the immediate contribution of money and supplies, and the eventual contribution of a vast army, with England calling for supplies and France for soldiers. Bourassa indicated his belief that English influence would be the most influential on American policy. He anticipated that the American entry into the war would shorten the conflict; would drain American capital, bring about a postwar depression, and promote a return to the land. He feared permanent militarism and a peace based upon power politics rather than Wilson's 'peace without victory.' In a curiously prophetic passage he foresaw a postwar Anglo-American alliance which would force Japan into an Asia-for-the-Asiatics policy. In considering the consequences for Canada of American intervention, he stressed the fact that Canada was an American country whose future was tied to that of the United States. He foresaw immediate economic advantages, but eventual disadvantages for the weaker partner. American emigration to Canada would be halted, while state socialism, continuing militarism, and eventual absorption of Canada by the United States would be promoted, barring Canadian independence.

Bourassa did not discuss conscription in *Le Devoir* until May 28, when he published a series of articles which ran until June 6, and were immediately printed in pamphlet form in French and later in English.[73] The title-page carried the quoted assurances of both Laurier and Borden on January 17, 1916 that there would be no conscription. Bourassa explained his silence since May 18 on the grounds that calm consideration would have been impossible in the first explosion of popular opposition. His belief since the South African War that Canada had entered upon the road leading to conscription was now justified by events. He called for the signature of the anti-conscription petitions of the *Ligue Patriotique des Intérêts Canadiens*, but warned of the danger of mass meetings which might lead to excesses of language or acts of violence. He argued that now Canada had done enough, though he said he would have favored a policy of selective conscription at the outset of the war. He pointed out that proportionately Canada's military effort was greater than that of England and France, and that proposed by the United States. He warned of the dangers of national bankruptcy, of the labor crisis, and of famine in England; and urged that slackers be conscripted for agricultural service, and that wealth and industry also be conscripted. He supported Laurier's argument of 1916 that conscription would be a bar to postwar immigration.

Bourassa then turned to the racial cleavage created by the war, pointing out that differences were inevitable, but stressing the advantages of racial partnership. He reviewed the nature of French-Canadian patriotism, with its devotion to Canada as the only homeland, with its affection for France and its reasoned sense of duty to

Britain. But this latter view of Canada's obligations to Britain, once held by English Canada, had been transformed by massive British immigration and imperialist propaganda, leaving few unhyphenated Canadians. He stressed the fact that Canada was divided when it entered the war, and had become more so as time went on. Many French-Canadian leaders had sought to win the support of their compatriots for participation by appeals to British loyalty and to duty toward France, and when these efforts failed, sought to prove that French Canadians were supporting the war as vigorously as English Canadians. To Bourassa this second mistake was worse than the first, since it could only end 'in acrimonious explanations, in bitter disillusionment and extremely dangerous reactions'—the present situation. He considered the 'system of mutual deception' practiced by the leaders of both races in recent years the greatest danger to national unity, and called for absolute frankness.[74]

Bourassa stated that the vast majority of French Canadians had long concluded that Canada had gone beyond reasonable limits in its participation in the war. As long as enlistment was voluntary, they had largely kept silent. But when Borden broke the pledges of both himself and his Quebec colleagues, the French-Canadian reaction was first amazement, then anger, and finally determination to oppose conscription by all legitimate means: 'Two million French Canadians are opposed *en masse* to conscription.'[75] He warned that 'everything in the application of compulsory service—however impartial it may appear to be—will tend to irritate the French Canadians, and generally all Canadians who are Canadian before all.'[76] Conscription would bear more heavily upon young French Canadians than upon the English. Bourassa did not mention the main reason: that more young English Canadians had already enlisted; but rather laid the blame on the exodus of young English Canadians to the States. He criticized the presence in Canada of many young Englishmen who had fled conscription at home, and warned that since the large number of unnaturalized aliens could not be conscripted, true Canadian influences at home would be lessened. He censured the government's willingness to exempt from service on religious grounds the Mennonites, Doukhobors, and Quakers, while refusing to recognize the French-Canadian sentiment against military service except in the defence of Canada.

Bourassa warned that the adoption of conscription would 'soon transform the most peaceable, perhaps the most orderly, population of the two Americas into a revolutionary people.'[77] He stated that English-Canadian workers and farmers were anti-conscriptionist, and urged a national referendum to settle the question, 'the only safety valve to prevent a dangerous explosion.'[78] Calling attention to Borden and Laurier's pledges against conscription in 1916, renewed at the National Service registration and in the Dorchester election, he blamed Borden's adoption of conscription on English pressure exerted at the Imperial Conference and on an effort to prevent American draft-dodgers from taking refuge in Canada, as so many British and Canadian slackers had done in the United States before that country entered the war.

He opposed coalition government and the extension of parliament's life: 'To prevent the designs, by no means established, of William the Autocrat, shall we permit Robert the Headstrong—even with the cooperation of Wilfrid the Conciliator—to play with our lives and also with the constitution and the established order?'[79] He saw Borden's program as an effort to avoid the control of the government by the people, and warned that Laurier had no right to lend himself to the manœuvre. He opposed to the analogy with England, which had adopted coalition and conscription, the fact that Canada had neither the right to declare war nor to make overseas service compulsory without the people's consent. Neither Australia nor South Africa had adopted conscription or coalition government. He called for an immediate dissolution of parliament, and a referendum on conscription. He considered that coalition, followed by an election and then conscription if the government were sustained, would, by making anti-conscriptionists run against both parties, be 'a formal and definitive incitement to insurrection.'[80] He claimed that he had done his best to calm the present excitement, would do his best to maintain public order, but would not be responsible for popular anger if this course was followed. Resolutions denouncing conscription and in favor of a referendum were unanimously passed at a meeting organized by Bourassa at the Monument National on June 7.

As feeling mounted in Quebec, Laurier was invited by Borden on May 25 to join a coalition government in which each party would have equal representation, apart from the prime minister. Laurier expressed his opposition to the conscription proposal and warned of the consequences in Quebec if it were adopted without a referendum or an election, the latter course being the one he favored. Borden expressed strong opposition to a wartime election, and Laurier promised to consider the coalition proposal and consult his supporters. On May 29 Borden yielded to Laurier's insistence on an election, and suggested coalition government and passage of the Military Service Act, with the understanding that it should not come into effect until after an election. On June 4 he added his willingness to make the Conservative wing of the coalition government acceptable to Laurier. But on June 6 Laurier declined to enter into coalition, on the grounds that he could not join in carrying out conscription, whose principle had been previously adopted and to which he was opposed. He told Borden that he would be in a stronger position to oppose Bourassa and his propaganda outside the government, and promised his support for the Military Service Act if it should be adopted by parliament. An exchange of letters summarizing the negotiations was published on June 7.[81]

Laurier's private letters of this period indicate that he was opposed to coalition even if conscription were not involved, having no confidence in the stand of some of Borden's colleagues on economic, railway, and other questions.[82] In a letter to Rowell on June 3 he gave his reasons for opposing conscription, which would 'create a line of cleavage in the population, the consequences of which I know too well, and for which I will not be responsible.' He was convinced that there was an undercurrent of opposition to conscription in every other province, as well as Quebec's solid opposition, thanks to the government's repudiation of its no-conscription pledges. Because of his stand on the Navy Bill in 1911, Laurier had been attacked in Quebec as a supporter of conscription and had been led to make many pledges against it. 'Now if I were to waver, to hesitate or to flinch, I would simply hand over the province of Quebec to the extremists. I would lose the respect of the people whom I thus addressed, and would deserve it. I would lose not only their respect, but my own self-respect also.' To him the only solution of the question was an immediate appeal to the people, either by a referendum or an election: 'Let the people decide, and if they decide in favor of conscription, as it seems to me they will, under present circumstances, from the attitude of our friends in Ontario, whatever influence I may have will be employed in pleading to the Quebec people that the question is settled by the verdict of the majority, and that all must loyally accept the issue and submit to the law; and this will be no light task, but a task to which I will devote myself with all my energy.'[83] During this period Clifford Sifton was assuring Borden that he favored coalition, and assuring Laurier that he was opposed to it, but favored an extension of parliament's life. His motive has been variously assigned to a desire for successful prosecution of the war and a desire for assuring an amenable government in the pending crisis of the affairs of the Canadian Northern and Grand Trunk Pacific.

Borden introduced the Military Service Act, which he had previously submitted to Laurier, on June 11. He emphasized the need for reinforcements, and to offset his pledges against conscription quoted his statements of January 1, 1916 ('By the greatness of the need, our future efforts must be measured') and of December 27, when he refused to give labor any assurance against conscription. He denied that conscription was being introduced at the request of the British Government, and maintained that the principle of compulsory service had been embodied in Canadian law for half a century. Instead of the selection by ballot already provided by the Militia Act, he proposed selection according to the country's needs, with exemptions provided for essential war work, serious individual hardship, or conscientious objections. Tribunals were to be set up to deal with exemptions and to hear appeals. He made an eloquent plea for keeping faith with the men overseas, and said he was more concerned about their reaction when they returned home, if the bill were not passed, than about the 'disunion, discord, and strife' foreseen as results of its passage.[84]

Upon second reading on June 18, Laurier moved an amendment providing for a referendum before further consideration. He said that the law of the land had long provided for compulsory military service only for the defence of Canada, and denied Borden's claim that Canada's first line of defence was in France and Flanders. He claimed that there never had been any danger of a German invasion of Canada. He argued that parliament's life would not have been extended in 1916, if the government had announced that it contemplated introduction of conscription; and since parliament no longer represented the people, and labor and the French Canadians were opposed to conscription, he urged a referendum. He blamed the comparative failure of recruiting in Quebec on the fact that the French Canadians were the oldest Canadians, and lacked the close relationship with France which so many English Canadians had with Britain; on the absence of military organization in Quebec since 1760; on Bourassa's attitude since 1903; and on the government's ineptness in dealing with Quebec recruiting. He argued on Colonel Blondin's testimony that the French Canadians would have responded if they had been recruited from the start for French-Canadian battalions by such men as General Lessard, Captain Papineau, and Colonel Barré.[85]

The debate lasted for three weeks, with growing Liberal support for conscription from Ontario, Maritime, and Western members. Hugh Guthrie, George Graham, F. F. Pardee, F. P. Carvell, and Michael Clark led the Liberal revolt against Laurier's stand, while Frank Oliver, Charles Murphy, and all the French-Canadian members except four supported the Liberal leader. Sam Hughes attacked both Laurier and Borden, saying that the latter was responsible for the failure of voluntary responsibility. Solicitor-General Arthur Meighen bitterly told Laurier that the only reason that he believed Canada was not in danger of invasion and could sit safely in his seat was because he knew the Allies would hold the line in France. Laurier was also accused by Dr. Edwards of being responsible for Quebec's anti-British bias by preaching independence and separatism, and his younger followers with interfering with the recruiting campaign in Quebec. J. A. M. Armstrong insisted that the only reason conscription was necessary was because Quebec had failed to do her duty. Patenaude resigned from the cabinet on June 9, leaving Sévigny as the only French-Canadian representative. Deputy-Speaker Rainville and Dr. Paquet, government whip for Quebec, also resigned; while Sévigny said he saw no reason to resign because most French Canadians opposed conscription, and blamed the comparative failure of Quebec's war effort, which he defended, on faulty organization. Conscription was also backed by Dr. J.-L. Chabot of Ottawa and F.-J. Roubidoux of New Brunswick, while a group of nine French Conservatives supported J.-A. Barrette's amendment for the six months' hoist, made on June 20.

A solid bloc of French-Canadian members, with the above exceptions, supported Laurier's stand, and many a Quebec member was heard for the first time. Since most of their speeches were in French, they were neither effective upon the majority of the House at the time, nor did they reach English readers of *Hansard* until some months later, when translations were published in the revised edition. But they expressed French Canada's bitter resentment and foreshadowed the violence which was to come. L.-J. Gauthier warned that 'my people are willing to go to the limit if you impose upon them such a piece of legislation.' Joseph Demers said the sending of 200,000 men would have been sufficient for the needs of the Allies, while Canada should concentrate on the production of food, ships, and munitions. Jacques Bureau resented slanders on the French Canadians: 'We do not want to fight for liberty in Europe and create a condition of slavery in Canada.' Hermenégilde Boulay gave four reasons for French-Canadian opposition to conscription: the traditions, constitution, and colonial status of Canada; the sufficient number of men already sent overseas; the fact that such a step was not justified by the 1911 mandate from the people without a referendum; the lack of fair treatment from the English majority; and opposition to overseas service created in 1896 by the Liberals and in 1911 by the Conservatives.

Alphonse Verville, a Labor Liberal, threatened a general strike. Georges Boivin felt that Canada had done more than the other Allied nations and the other dominions; J.-A.-C. Ethier felt that Canada had done enough and conscription would destroy autonomy, remove liberty, and lead to ruin. Honoré Achim said disruption of the country would not come from Quebec but from Ontario, where capital crushed labor, where manufacturers sought to restrain freedom of trade, and where Jingoes sought to strangle freedom of conscience. Roch Lanctôt said Canada had no trenches to defend in Europe but that the French Canadians must fight the Boches of Ontario and Manitoba. He was not alarmed at the prospect of

Canada's having a third European master. L.-J. Papineau asked whether Canadian troops were sent to the most exposed positions, and warned that many more than 50,000 or 100,000 men would be called for in the future. D.-A. Lafortune said that it was Canada's war only in the mind of the government and its friends: 'They may say that we should give our last cent to save the Empire; as for me, I shall say I have no more to give.' J.-E. Marcile called upon the British Army to display its mettle and relieve the colonial troops of the major burden they had borne since the beginning of the war. Médéric Martin warned of the end of Confederation and civil war, if English and French continued to insult each other and if conscription were adopted. Quebec believed that the best way to aid the empire and the Allies was through supplying food and ammunition. Dr. Paquet supported a referendum but denounced the Liberals for having advocated nationalism, and non-participation in imperial wars before 1909. Major Gustave Boyer expressed lack of confidence in the government, urged that parliament had no mandate from the people, and declared that more men were essential for home production. A.-A. Mondou opposed conscription, although he admitted that the future of the empire was at stake and Britain was fighting for a just cause, and announced his future support of Laurier.[86] At five o'clock on the morning of July 6 Laurier's motion for a referendum was defeated by a majority of 59, and the Military Service Bill was supported by a majority of 63.

The bill came up for third reading on July 19. It was advocated by J. C. Turriff, a Western Liberal, who also supported the proposal made by Hugh Guthrie a month earlier in favour of conscription of wealth. Guthrie and Pardee reiterated their support of the bill. Laurier regretted the estrangement of his former colleagues, but said he had not sought to impose his views upon his followers. He warned that 'We are face to face with a cleavage, which, unless it is checked, may rend and tear this Canada of ours down to the very roots.' He defended his attitude in refusing to join a coalition which had already accepted conscription. He concluded:

> I oppose this Bill because it has in it the seeds of discord and disunion; because it is an obstacle and a bar to that union of heart and soul without which it is impossible to hope that this Confederation will attain the aims and ends that were had in view when Confederation was effected. Sir, all my life I have fought coercion; all my life I have promoted union; and the inspiration which led me to that course shall be my guide at all times, so long as there is a breath left in my body.[87]

Arthur Meighen, who was taking a leading role in the Conservative forces as Borden's health declined, replied to Laurier, pointing out that the bill had been supported on second reading by an overwhelming majority. The bill was carried on July 24 by 102 to 44.

In the Senate the government was sharply criticized by Quebec members, after Cardinal Bégin had opposed the measure for not exempting theological students. Senator Landry accused the authorities of having systematically ignored rural Quebec in recruiting, and stressed resentment of the breaking up of French-Canadian battalions and of the failure to form a French-Canadian brigade. Quebec's indignation over the school issue was frequently assigned as a cause of its poor recruiting record. Senator Dandurand argued that the nationalists had exploited this issue so successfully in 1915 and 1916 that they had brought recruiting to a standstill. He urged organization of agriculture and industry for war purposes. Senator Beaubien admitted the need for reinforcements, but refused to follow his party in supporting conscription, since Quebec feeling was so strong against it. The bill reached second reading in the Senate on August 3. An amendment offered by the Liberal leader, Senator Bostock, that the bill should not come into force until after a general election, was defeated by a vote of 44 to 35, with the Conservative Senators Landry, Beaubien, and Montplaisir supporting it. Senators L'Espérance and Beaubien espoused conscription on the second reading, and were supported by Senators Poirier and Bourque of New Brunswick.

On August 3 General Mason offered in the Senate a summary of recruiting statistics, stating that out of a total of 424,456 men Ontario had supplied 184,545 and Quebec 46,777. He estimated that there were 162,092 British-born volunteers amounting to 49.2 per cent of the men overseas; 132,265 English Canadians constituting 40.2 per cent of the men overseas; and 14,684 French Canadians constituting 4.5 per cent of the men overseas. Laurier questioned the French-Canadian total, expressing the opinion that 20,000 was more nearly correct, while Senator Choquette asserted that the figure ran as high as 25,000 or 30,000. Senators Bourque and Poirier urged their Quebec colleagues to emulate the Acadian example, but told their English colleagues that Quebec would do as well as any other province if she were appealed to in the proper way. The bill passed the Senate by a vote of 54 to 25, with nine English Liberals supporting the government.[88]

On August 9 Borden organized a conference at Government House with Laurier. The governor-general spoke of the dangers of a war-time election and Borden of those of incomplete victory or defeat. Laurier stood firm for an election to clear the air. Lord Shaughnessy and Clifford Sifton proposed postponement of an election. Sir Lomer Gouin backed Laurier and refused to form the government. Borden made a final offer of coalition, with suspension of conscription for six months, extension of parliament for the same period, and a united appeal for recruits; but this offer was refused.[89]

8

The English Canadians gradually united in support of conscription, after the *Toronto Globe* had backed and filled over the question during the first month of discussion. The French-Canadian press, with the exception of *La Patrie* and *L'Evénement*, was almost solidly opposed to conscription. *Le Canada* and *La Presse* at first urged a referendum, and then on July 25 the former said the government had passed the death verdict of 100,000 young Canadians and the latter pressed for an election as the only means to calm racial passions. On July 28 *L'Action Catholique* published an interview with Cardinal Bégin in which the prelate stated that the failure to exempt lay brothers and theological students constituted a grave interference with the rights of the Church and one which should be opposed by all good churchmen. On August 8 Archbishop Bruchési said that racial and religious war was near, since 'incontestable rights have been violated.'[90] After conscription was announced in May, the archbishop had urged his people 'to use their rights as free citizens with calm and moderation,' and on June 6, expressing resentment of the government's change of policy, he explained that he had supported National Service because Borden had assured him that there was no question of conscription and that he was opposed to it.[91] *Le Devoir* continued to oppose conscription, and on June 28 proclaimed that if Canada were to survive enlistment should stop altogether. On July 26 it censured parliament for criminal neglect of the rights of the people and the needs of the nation, saying that Canadian soldiers were fighting for the empire in the same manner as the Senegalese were forced to fight for France.[92]

Ferdinand Roy, a distinguished Quebec lawyer and member of Laval's law faculty, issued a pamphlet, '*L'Appel aux armes et la réponse canadienne-française*,' in which he pleaded with his compatriots to reverse their anti-war stand, to enlist, and to submit gracefully to the Military Service Act when it became law. He appealed for reason, tolerance, and a new view of French Canada's duty lest French Canada be swept away altogether by the mounting tide of racial hatred. He warned of the danger of isolated opposition to Canada's war policy, which he blamed on the school question, the unfortunate policy of the Borden government, the unskilful Liberal maneuvers, nationalist errors, and French anti-clericalism. He insisted that the Allied cause was the cause of civilization, and urged that the French Canadians should not desert a cause which they had espoused in 1914. Stating his own firm opposition to conscription, he urged the French Canadians to cease protesting against a *fait accompli*, a course which could only end in civil war. The time had passed for sterile discussion, which now might only increase the trouble; the French Canadians should sacrifice their opinions, their pacific tastes, and their blood in the interest of the future well-being of their race. Roy censured Bourassa for preaching 'sacred egoism' in a land where compromise between the races was essential, and for saying that French Canada had no call to fight for France, the mother of her civilization.[93] The altered attitude of the hierarchy was reflected by an editorial on Roy's pamphlet in *L'Action Catholique* on July 31, which said the French Canadians' only duty was to safeguard their country, which was now being asked to undertake an effort beyond its strength. Senator Dandurand and Sir Georges Garneau supported Roy's stand, while Armand Lavergne rejected it and said that if a referendum were not granted it would be necessary to call the people to arms to defend democracy in Canada.

The hierarchy's opposition to conscription was made evident by Archbishop Bruchési in an interview with Borden on July 7, when the archbishop expressed his doubts about good results from further recruiting, his opinion that exemption of French Canadians would make them despised, and favored an election. Cardinal Bégin also put pressure on Minister of Justice Doherty at the end of July to modify the act's provisions about clerics.[94] On July 7 the Quebec ecclesiastical weekly *La Vérité* published an article by one 'Louis Romain,' thought to be Mgr. Paquet, the rector of Laval University, which by elaborate theological arguments demonstrated that the bishops' pastoral of 1914 had not made participation an absolute obligation. This utterance by an unofficial spokesman of the hierarchy reflected the shift in the higher clergy's attitude.

Evidence of the lower clergy's views was contained in *Halte là, 'Patriote,'* a pamphlet refuting the Abbé d'Amours and arguing with 'Louis Romain' by one 'Jean Vindex,' thought to be Père Hermas Lalande, S.J. The pamphlet frankly admitted the division of opinion between the pro-war upper clergy of the cities and the anti-war *curés* of the country parishes. It combated the doctrines of the 'New School of Imperialists' to which the hierarchy belonged and defended the nationalists from d'Amours' charges. 'Jean Vindex' accused Abbé d'Amours and the imperialists of misrepresenting the attitude of the hierarchy and twisting the pastoral letter of 1914 to suit their convenience.[95] There can be no doubt that 'Jean Vindex' truthfully expressed the attitude of the lower clergy, whose opposition to the war was completed by the adoption of conscription. The country clergy were in closer touch with the people and less affected by outside influences than the hierarchy and city clergy. They at once reflected public opinion and exercised a strong influence upon it. Through them Bourassa's influence reached into the backwaters of the province. The depth of their anti-war feeling may be judged by the fact that they dared to oppose their superiors' views, despite the strict discipline of the Church.

Feeling soon mounted high in Quebec and continued so. As early as June 15, *La Croix* of Montreal, an ultramontane journal, discussed the possibility of Quebec's secession from Confederation. Lavergne, who had declared in 1915 and 1916 that he would enlist if conscription ever came, announced on May 25 that: 'I will go to jail or be hanged or shot before I will accept it.' At Loretteville on May 27 he urged disobedience to the law if parliament passed it, and evoked the spirit of 1837. To a mass meeting of 15,000 people at Quebec on July 15 he said: 'If the Conscription law is enforced, Canadians have only one choice—to die in Europe or to die in Canada. As far as I am concerned, if my body is to fall in any land, I want it to be on Canadian soil.'[96] Tancrède Marsil, whose anti-war *Le Réveil* had been discontinued in March after a warning from Ottawa, issued the equally violent *La Liberté*, which thought 'revolution a hundred times better than slavery'[97] and was suspended on July 24 after urging a general strike, withdrawal of money from the banks, and revolution if necessary.

Night after night in June, July, and August anti-conscription meetings were held in Montreal, with crowds marching through the streets yelling '*A bas Borden!*' and '*Vive la révolution!*' and breaking windows and shooting off blank cartridges. One Elie Lalumière boasted that he was drilling 500 men for active resistance to conscription. The disturbances came to a head on the nights of August 29 and 30, when the crowds were urged to clean their old guns and to contribute for the purchase of other arms. The police attempted to break up the meetings, with one man shot and four policemen injured as a result.[98] During the conscription debates Borden and his French-Canadian followers also received threatening letters from Quebec.

The verbal violence of the anti-conscription orators produced the first major incident of real violence on August 9 when the Cartierville home of Lord Atholstan (Hugh Graham), whose *Montreal Star* vigorously supported conscription, was dynamited. Lalumière and eleven others were tried for the crime, and the former made a written confession of plots to blow up the offices of the *Star* and *Gazette*, the Mount Royal Club, and Senator Beaubien's home, and to kill Borden and other public men who supported conscription. Paul Lafortune approved the Cartierville crime at a public meeting on August 12, but Bourassa censured it in an editorial on 'Sterile

Violence' on August 11. He warned that the agitators were providing deadly weapons for the foes of French Canada, and deprecated talk of passive resistance. Instead he called for the election of anti-conscriptionist candidates to seek the repeal of the law. He censured acts of violence as illegimate and inexcusable. The rural press, appalled by the violence in Montreal, enthusiastically echoed Bourassa's appeal.[99] But the agitation in Montreal continued with unchecked violence until four of the leaders, Villeneuve, Lafortune, Côté, and Mongeau, were arrested after a public meeting on September 12, in which Villeneuve called for annexation or independence, saying: 'We have had enough of the Union Jack,' while the other speakers condoned the attempt on Atholstan. The agitators were released on bail, and continued their work with less violent words.

9

Meanwhile the government had introduced on July 17 a proposal for the extension of parliament's life for a year, with Borden promising not to act upon it if the opposition opposed it as a party. Laurier did not support the motion, and George Graham moved that consideration of extension should be postponed until conscription of wealth was introduced. This amendment was supported by all the Liberals except Dr. Clark and was defeated only by a majority of seventeen. After Laurier had attacked government administration of the war effort and Dr. Clark had supported Borden, the motion for extension was carried by a vote of twenty. Borden, however, announced that extension would be abandoned, since it had been approved by so small a margin. The British Government had previously indicated that it would provide the necessary imperial legislation to authorize extension only if the proposal received practically unanimous support.

Negotiations for the formation of a coalition government had continued steadily since Laurier's refusal of the proposal on June 6. To facilitate matters, Foster presented Borden with the resignations of all the ministers on June 12. Coalition was made difficult by the division into many different camps of the Liberals as the conscription debates went on. Borden began overtures to the Conscriptionist Liberals of Ontario headed by N. W. Rowell through Sir John Willison. On June 25 he called C. C. Ballantyne of Montreal into conference and received his assurance of support for conscription and coalition. On the following day he discussed coalition with Rowell and Sifton.[100] When Rowell learned that Laurier would not aid the formation of a coalition government under any circumstances, he urged coalition upon the Ontario Conscriptionist Liberals, while Sifton worked upon the Western ones. On July 20 a meeting of

Liberal members and candidates at Toronto supported Laurier's leadership, opposing coalition and the application of conscription until after another voluntary recruiting effort. On July 26 the Liberal editors of Ontario favored coalition on a platform of conscription of men and wealth, though they refused to accept Borden's leadership of such a government.

Meanwhile, on July 3, Sifton had issued a manifesto in favor of union government and conscription, with an extension of parliament if possible. He later called a convention of Western Liberals at Winnipeg on August 7. In a letter to Premier Martin of Saskatchewan, who had assured him that Sifton's alliance with Borden was resented in the West, Laurier expressed approval of the convention, but denounced Sifton's attempt to split the Liberal party along racial and religious lines.[101] In a whirlwind campaign to enlist Western support, Sifton said that an electoral victory under Laurier's leadership would mean that Canada would quit the war. Laurier replied in the House that he was in the war to the end, but on a basis of voluntary enlistment and not of conscription.[102] The convention was a fiasco from Sifton's point of view, since the Alberta and British Columbia Liberals strongly supported Laurier's leadership. Resolutions were passed condemning the Borden government, calling for vigorous support of the war but rejecting an amendment supporting compulsory service, and paying tribute to Laurier as 'the greatest of all Canadians.' Sifton nonetheless continued his efforts for coalition, with the support of the *Manitoba Free Press*, and by August 20 had lined up Western support for a coalition government included his brother Arthur Sifton of Alberta, J. A. Calder of Saskatchewan, and T. A. Crerar of Manitoba. A second Liberal conference at Winnipeg on August 24–5 agreed to coalition, but refused to accept Borden as prime minister, suggesting Sir George Foster, Sir William Mulock, Sir Adam Beck, or F. B. Carvell for the post. A Conservative caucus on August 29 declined to accept Borden's resignation. For the time being coalition efforts were deadlocked.

Meanwhile the government carried on August 29 the Military Voters Act introduced on August 13, which enfranchised all British subjects in the Canadian forces as well as those who had enlisted in certain British forces while in Canada, and made provisions for taking a vote overseas. A further War-Times Election Bill was introduced by Arthur Meighen on September 6 during Borden's illness. This highly controversial measure provided for the enfranchisement of female relatives of soldiers, the disenfranchisement of enemy aliens naturalized since 1902 and of conscientious objectors, and the preparation of new electoral lists upon this basis. Meighen, who had framed the bill, excused the enfranchisement provisions on the grounds that many soldiers could not vote, and the disenfranchisement of aliens on the grounds that they had been barred from enlistment. The majority of the newcomers, however, were Liberals, since they had found prosperity under the Laurier regime. The women were counted upon to support conscription both in gratitude for the privilege of voting and in the interest of their relatives overseas. The measure was obviously a colossal gerrymander, and was attacked by the whole opposition. It was forced through under closure on September 14, with Guthrie as its only Liberal supporter.

This measure broke the back of Western Liberal opposition to coalition on Borden's terms. Rowell conferred with the Western Liberals at Winnipeg on September 20, the day parliament was prorogued, and they resumed negotiations with Borden early in October in Ottawa. Borden had already added several Liberals to his government: Ballantyne as minister of marine, General Mewburn as minister of militia, and Hugh Guthrie as solicitor-general. The Westerners, faced with the prospect of being left out of the government, dropped their objections to Borden's leadership and their insistence on four places in the cabinet; and on October 12 A. L. Sifton was sworn in as minister of customs, Crerar as minister of agriculture, and Calder as minister of immigration and colonization. Rowell was made president of the Privy Council, and later on Carvell was named minister of public works, and G. D. Robertson and A. K. Maclean ministers without portfolio. Sir George Perley was named high commissioner to London—a post he had long coveted—and dropped as a member of the cabinet, which now included thirteen Conservatives and ten Liberals. A ten-man war committee, with equal Conservative and Liberal membership, was set up on October 16, and a reconstruction and development committee, with six Conservative ministers and four Liberals. Blondin and Sévigny were the only French-Canadian ministers, and they were admittedly without influence in Quebec.

Canada now faced a wartime election with Quebec almost completely isolated from the other provinces. An attempt was made early in October by the Conscriptionist Liberals to induce Laurier to resign in favor of an English-Canadian leader, but the party as a whole refused to accept his offer to withdraw. The government made arrangements to avoid Conservative opposition to Liberal-Unionist candidates, and in only two constituencies did the Conservatives rebel and run a candidate against their new allies. Laurier sought to make the government's record of incompetence and corruption the issue, but the government forces insisted that it was a question of going on with the war through conscription or quitting, of supporting the men at the front or deserting them. This plea was all the more effective because of the loss of 30,741 men in

November, in the costly victory of Passchendaele. Losses from July through October had amounted to 38,057, while enlistments had only totalled 18,471.

The first conscripts were summoned under the Military Service Act on October 13 to report in January 1918. But 57 per cent of the men between 20 and 45 who were called had claimed exemption by November 10. The final figures for the year showed that out of 125,750 men registered in Ontario, 118,128 had claimed exemption; while out of 117,104 registered in Quebec, 115,707 had claimed exemption. The Ontario tribunals disallowed 19,148 claims and did not deal with 4,783; the Quebec tribunals disallowed 3,711 claims and did not deal with 22,421. In almost all the provinces a similarly high proportion of men claimed exemption, and in most cases were granted it.[103] In November *La Presse* defended Quebec against the Ontario charge that the local boards in Quebec were exempting men wholesale, and pointed to the general situation throughout the country.[104] The whole conscription question was debated once more during the campaign, and this fact interfered with the effectiveness of the attempt to put the measure into force.

English Canadians, regardless of political affiliation, were loud in their lipservice to conscription, if not much more willing in fact to accept it than the French Canadians, who in overwhelming majority were opposed to it. Of the French press only *L'Evénement* remained faithful to the government, with *La Patrie* wavering in its support. *La Presse* evoked solid French-Canadian support for the old leader Laurier, abandoned by most of his English-Canadian supporters. *Le Canada* made much of a supposed plot to isolate and discredit French Canada. *L'Action Catholique* appealed for calm, but expressed unmitigated opposition to conscription and accused the government of stirring up English Canada against Quebec to win the election. The government had almost the entire English press behind it, as well as the organization of both parties in most of the provinces. A Victory Loan campaign in November, violently opposed by Bourassa as leading to national bankruptcy, fitted in with the government's cause.[105] On the Sunday before the elections of December 17, three out of four Protestant pulpits appealed for support of the government as a sacred duty, in response to a Unionist circular.[106] The soldier ballots provided only for a vote for the government or against it.[107]

Bourassa's decision early in November to urge support of Laurier and the Liberals as the lesser evil for the moment played into the government's hands. He pointed out that there were 4,000,000 men of military age in Britain still not called for service, and argued that Canada had done more than enough without conscription. The press of Ontario and the West conducted a violent campaign against Quebec and Laurier. The *Toronto Mail and Empire* on December 10 announced that Laurier was undoubtedly favored by the Kaiser, and on the following day carried an election advertisement declaring that a united Quebec sought to rule Canada. On election day the *Mail and Empire* called a vote for Laurier and his followers a vote for Bourassa, a vote against the men at the front, the British connection, and the empire; and a vote for Germany, the Kaiser, Hindenburg, von Tirpitz, and the sinker of the *Lusitania*. Laurier was depicted as the hope of Quebec, a menace to Canada, and as satisfactory to the Kaiser. The *Toronto Daily News* printed on December 14 a map of Canada with Quebec in black, under the caption 'The Foul Blot on Canada.' Laurier was represented as having capitulated to Bourassa. On December 7 the *Manitoba Free Press* told its readers that the choice was between union and the war or Laurier and disunion. A Toronto Citizen's Union Committee filled the English press with inflammatory advertisements declaring that 'Quebec must not rule Canada' and that 'a Laurier victory will be the first Canadian defeat.'[108] The Unionist publicity committee under Sir John Willison constantly linked Laurier, Bourassa, and Quebec, and roused ethnic feeling against French Canada.[109] Conservative leaders warned that 'Quebec was the spoiled child of Confederation,' 'the plague-spot of the whole Dominion,' and that if Laurier won the election Bourassa would rule Canada.[110]

In Quebec the government hoped for little beyond the elections of Doherty, Ames, Ballantyne, Sévigny, and Blondin. Sévigny ran in both Dorchester and Westmount, arguing that by refusing to accept coalition, Laurier had brought disgrace upon Quebec and prevented the settlement of the Ontario and Manitoba school questions. But his meetings were systematically obstructed and he was burnt in effigy in Montreal, while his colleagues Blondin and Rainville were coupled with him as the 'triumvirate of traitors.' The meetings of Ballantyne, Doherty, and Ames were also broken up by rioting mobs, as were those of lesser Unionist candidates. Feeling mounted so high that for a time Unionist meetings were abandoned. Sévigny and Joseph Barnard of *L'Evénement* were threatened with lynching. Violence was evident all over the province, in Montreal, Quebec, and Sherbrooke, and in the rural constituencies as well. Reports of it in the English press reacted against the Liberals and Quebec, though Borden was howled down by a crowd at Kitchener, Ontario. Laurier in his election manifesto condemned the coalition government as being purely Conservative in its program, attacked the War-Times Election Act and the government purchase of the railways, and denounced conscription of men without conscription of wealth and without a referendum. He pledged himself to carry out the will of the majority as expressed by a referendum, and to make a strong appeal for voluntary recruiting, which 'especially in Quebec did not get a fair trial.' If called upon to form a government, he would include representatives of business, labor, and agriculture so that the masses would be protected 'against organized privilege, which has heretofore had far too much control over the Government of the country.'[111]

At his first electoral meeting on November 9 at Quebec Laurier said: 'We began with the voluntary system; it is our duty to continue with it,'[112] but called for support of the army with more men. Sir Lomer Gouin denounced the attempt to isolate Quebec, and endorsed Laurier's plea for enlistment. At Ottawa on November 27 Laurier pointed out that conscription had been defeated in Australia, though there was no Quebec or 'racialism' there; stressed his differences with Bourassa; and stated that the way to get men to win the war was 'by appealing to the soul, not to coercion of the conscience.' Leaving Quebec to Lemieux and Gouin, and Ontario to his faithful supporters H. H. Dewart and Sir Allen Aylesworth, Laurier devoted the final weeks of the campaign to the West, where he won a wide hearing but evidently did not influence many votes. Both in the West and in Ontario much agrarian support for Laurier was lost when General Mewburn, minister of militia, promised on November 25 that farmers' sons engaged in the production of food would be exempted from military service. The recruiting leagues, the churches, and the newly enfranchised women threw their support behind the Union government. Labor launched a third party movement, but was not actively hostile to the government. The soldiers were strongly appealed to by the government and the Unionist Liberals, while W. T. R. Preston conducted a one-man campaign for support of Laurier by advertisements in the English papers.[113]

The result was an overwhelming victory for the Union government, with a government majority of seventy-one. Quebec returned only three government supporters, Doherty, Ballantyne, and Ames, in predominantly English Montreal constituencies, while Sévigny was defeated in both Dorchester and Westmount, and Blondin rejected by a huge majority in Champlain and a lesser one in Montreal. In the Maritimes the Liberals won only ten seats, to the government's twenty-one; in Ontario only eight to the government's seventy-four; in the West only two to the government's fifty-five. The soldier vote went twelve to one for the government. Only one French-Canadian supporter of the government was elected, Dr. J.-L. Chabot of Ottawa, who defeated Laurier in that constituency by a majority of over 5,000, though the Liberal leader was returned in Quebec East by the usual triumphant majority. French Canada was left without representation in the government, since Blondin took refuge in senatorship and Sévigny resigned on March 7, paying tribute t Borden's goodwill to French Canadians.[114]

Bourassa described the result of the election as a victory fo independence: 'The French Canadians resisted *en masse* because the are *en masse* and by instinct Nationalist.' He anticipated a postwa breakup of parties, with a new political alignment on the question of settling accounts with England and the readjustment of Canadia economic equilibrium, in which the French Canadians would pla an important role on the nationalist side against imperialism.[11] Arthur Sauvé, the provincial Conservative leader, agreed that th election was a triumph for Bourassa and his ideals, but *L'Evénemen* warned the province that 'Under a leader in whom you have s long placed your confidence, and who has conducted you into s dangerous a position by placing you in opposition to almost al the rest of Confederation, you are now really isolated and alon in your corner, unable to do anything for yourself or for anyon else.' *Le Soleil* assigned Laurier's defeat to fanaticism and the racia cry, but consoled itself with the thought that he would have mor followers in the new parliament than he had had since 1911. *La Presse* said Quebec had been true to its national obligations, but urged a revival of the *bonne entente* movement. The *Montreal Heral* proposed a new invitation to Laurier to enter the cabinet, and wa strongly criticized for it in the Ontario and Western press.[11] Laurier, who felt at first that his lifelong effort for unity had ended in ruin, soon regained confidence in a postwar restoration of a 'fair and respecting partnership.'[117] He blamed his defeat on the gerrymander in the West and on the alliance of press, parsons, and women in Ontario.[118]

10

The isolation of Quebec, admitted by its own press and underlined by the *Toronto Star* and the *Manitoba Free Press* in their comments that 'we in Ontario and the West regard the War as a Canadian question and Quebec does not' and that the only reason for racial cleavage lay in Quebec's refusal to 'walk beside the rest of Canada along the road of national duty and sacrifice,'[119] bore heavily on the French-Canadian mind. The long-heralded cleavage between French and English in Canada, which some had desired and more had dreaded, had at last arrived in all earnest. Sore in heart at being overridden on the conscription question and weary of being the butt of English-Canadian abuse, the province showed much interest in a motion tabled by J.-N. Francoeur before the end of the year in the provincial legislature, that Quebec 'would be disposed to accept the breaking of the Confederation Pact of 1867 if, in the other provinces, it is believed that she is an obstacle to the union, progress, and development of Canada.'[120]

The Francoeur motion was much discussed by the press and public before it came up in the legislature on January 17, 1918. Asserting its belief that Quebec did not wish to secede, *La Presse* said on December 24 that it might be better to terminate an alliance no longer based on the principles upon which it was founded, if the English provinces felt that Quebec was interfering with their freedom of action. But it professed Quebec's loyalty to Britain and her desire to remain under the British flag whatever happened. *La Patrie* on December 22 refused to take the resolution seriously. *Le Canada* on December 24 urged its readers to remain calm and not to be carried away either by English-Canadian jingoes or French-Canadian extremists. *L'Action Catholique* on December 27 admitted that Quebec should not remain in Confederation if the other provinces no longer desired her presence, but opposed secession and characterized the resolution as inopportune. In later articles *L'Action* took the position that Quebec's isolation was not to be dreaded, since the French Canadians were united as never before and Quebec's position was impregnably strong; but it held that the resolution would lead to further persecution by extremist English Canadians. In *Le Devoir* late in December Bourassa also held that isolation was no cause for alarm. There was no possibility of conciliation from the Union government, and no honorable French Canadian could enter the government or co-operate with it. He urged French Canadians to remain aloof and to be the champions of right, truth, and real Canadian interests. The *Courrier de Saint-Hyacinthe* warned the French Canadians against losing their heads because the Liberals had lost the election, while *L'Etoile du Nord* saw no harm in secession if Quebec were not wanted in Confederation. The Montmagny *Peuple* opposed the resolution.[121] Sir Georges Garneau rejected the motion as inopportune and called for support of the *bonne entente* movement. Ferdinand Roy warned in *L'Evénement* that it was dangerous to play with loaded weapons and opposed the resolution.

Meanwhile the eloquent young nationalist leader Abbé Groulx was influencing large audiences by his lectures at Laval University in Montreal on Confederation, in which he made much of the forebodings of the French-Canadian leaders that Confederation spelled danger to their faith and national existence—forebodings which, the abbé made abundantly clear, had been fully realized by 1917. Confederation had resulted in vastly increased parliamentary corruption, the loss of the original ideals of religious liberty and racial equality, and the destruction of the Canadian national soul, torn by racial conflict and menaced by cosmopolitan European immigration.

The abbé later indicated that he was opposed to secession, which would mean abandoning the French Canadians outside Quebec but his argument encouraged separatism and opposition to the Military Service Act.

In introducing his motion, Francoeur said it was demanded by the flood of bitter criticism of Quebec in the last three years. He saw evidence of a conspiracy to ruin the reputation of Quebec quoting defamatory statements from the *Orange Sentinel*, the *Kingston Standard*, the *Toronto News*, and the *Winnipeg Telegram*. He also cited the election propaganda of the Citizen's Union Committee, evoking the 'menace of French-Canadian domination' and accusing Quebec leaders of stabbing Canadian soldiers in the back. He cited the attacks upon Quebec of H. C. Hocken and Isaac Campbell, and threw particular stress upon N. W. Rowell's statement of December that 'There is a Nationalist, clerical, and reactionary movement at work in the Province of Quebec which today dominates the political situation in that province and is using this hour of great national peril to dominate the political situation throughout the Dominion of Canada.'

To all these charges Francoeur replied:

> Her [Quebec's] only crime is that she interpreted the Constitution in a different manner from her fellow-citizens of different origin, that she denounced certain acts which in her opinion not only did not contribute to the success of the war and the safety of the Empire, but rather interfered with the issue of the one and the attainment of the other. It is because her people have shown themselves first of all Canadians, because they believed that the first thing to do was to develop this country in the interest of the Empire itself, that the greater its prosperity is, the greater is the possibility of achieving our destiny, because above all they demanded that the people be consulted before conscription was accepted.[12]

But there were also deeper reasons. Confederation was a compromise, which had not eradicated conflicts arising from differences of language, faith, and tradition. Dorion, Perreault, Taschereau and Joly had foreseen trouble. Quebec had never shrunk from any duty nor evaded any responsibility arising out of Confederation it had gone to 'the extreme limit of conciliation and of concession . . . at the sacrifice of our acquired rights and our race pride. But it had not got credit for it, and was maligned instead of being treated as an equal partner.

The only result could be the breaking of the Confederation pact since 'Nobody can seriously argue that if the spirit of the constitution is not respected, the mere letter of the contract is enough to maintain the association.' The resolution expressed the sentiment of 'the very great majority of our people, who are tired of being treated in this manner, and who think that the time has come to stop these futile struggles or to accept their logical consequences.' Quebec did not want secession, but she would not falter at the prospect if it were thrust upon her. The desire of the French Canadians was to live and let live:

> To live observing not only the letter of the constitution but its spirit more particularly; to live according to our tastes, our temperament, and our mentality; to live as free citizens, conscious of our duties and careful of our responsibilities; to live working for the progress and development of our province, convinced that in this way we are assuring the progress and development of the country; to live preserving our language, our faith, our traditions, our institutions, and our laws; to live, in a word, as loyal Canadians devoted to the British Crown. Let live; to respect among others those things that we demand they respect among us; to recognize the liberty they wished to enjoy in the exercize of their acquired rights; to let them speak and teach their language, retain their faith and their traditions, and even to struggle with them, if it is necessary, for the defense of the heritage which they hold as dear as we . . . It is in this way that we will become in real truth a Canadian nation . . . We will then have not only the outward semblance of a nation whose material interests are its only bonds, but we will form a nation by the true union of hearts and souls.
>
> Why not realize this ideal? While our soldiers on the soil of France are fighting heroically for liberty and civilization, respect of treaties and constitutions, the independence and autonomy of nations, we here should cease to give the spectacle of struggles that have their origin in the negation of these principles. We must be worthy of the supreme sacrifice of these heroes. Their death is the greatest lesson in patriotism. Let us profit by it.[123]

Arthur Sauvé, the Conservative leader, said that all Tories were not anti-French fanatics, and opposed the resolution as inopportune. He blamed the racial feeling on the school question and on anti-conscriptionist feeling. He defended Quebec's record for obeying the law by producing figures which indicated that the province had the lowest percentage of men failing to report when called for military service. He had suggested to Sir Lomer Gouin an amendment to the resolution, petitioning for disallowance of the Military Service Act, but the premier had refused to present it.[124]

Athanase David reviewed the history of Confederation, pointing out that it was necessary from the economic and commercial points of view and at first tended toward the development of a common Canadian mentality. But political-religious problems arose, and with them the specter of French domination, as the imperialist mentality replaced the Canadian one in the English provinces. He defended Quebec's behavior since the outbreak of the war as 'animated purely and simply by a desire to avoid placing in dange the economic future of our country, the national future of our race.'[125] He asserted French Canada's reasoned loyalty to the British flag, but admitted that there was no love for it, and such love could not be evoked by insults. He blamed discord on the introductior of the imperialism of Dilke, Chamberlain, and Milner, who were willing to 'plunge Canada into bankruptcy if necessary to save the Empire.'[126] He asserted that imperialism of any kind, whether German, English, or American, was a danger to the world, and acceptance of it would be a backward step for Canada. He looked forward to full Canadian autonomy and eventual independence Urging that 'only those who believe in the destinies of Canada'[127] should be entrusted with the solution of Canadian problems, he criticised the provisions of the War-Time Election Act.

But David anticipated the day when, the present crisis passed, the relations between the various provinces would once more be re newed in the tradition of Confederation. He believed that even today there was a strong minority of English Canadians who wished tha Canada should remain mistress of her destinies, and that 'the doctrine for which we stand should resume its sway over the Canadiar people.'[128] As in every national crisis in the past, men who did no share the faith and blood of French Canada would arise to join hand with the French Canadians. He had no fear of Quebec's temporary isolation, since it was a market which the English Canadians coulc not neglect. The English Canadians of Quebec would be the greates sufferers from isolation, which might benefit the material and finan cial development of French Canada. He did not regret or fear Que bec's political isolation, since it arose from the refusal to betray ar ideal which sixty-two members of the assembly had received mandate to sustain. Good sense and logic would prevail in the enc over prejudice and fanaticism. He was confident that:

> Our Confederation will arise from this chaos like all the peoples o the world, taught by suffering, enlightened by a new experience, anc finding her pathway, and needing the effort of each group and each race will issue the appeal that will serve to rally all groups and races. Freeing herself then from the grip of the autocracy in which she herself will deen she has remained too long, and understanding the dangers of the futur if she does not consolidate at once all her force, energy, and will, she wil unite in a great ideal of Canadian political democracy all those wh under her aegis wish to continue to live to assure her greatness.[129]

Hector Laferté defended Quebec's loyalty and rejected the insult to which it had been subjected. He thought French Canada was no ready for independence; he was opposed to annexation; but he sup ported the resolution. T.-D. Bouchard opposed the English fea of domination to the French fear of persecution by citing attacks of the Quebec press on the Ontario fanatics, and called for a spirit of brotherhood to ensure the continuance of Confederation. A.-M. Tessier condemned the 'systematic campaign organized against the province of Quebec, accentuated by fanaticism and hatred of everything that is French.' But he did not believe that this represented the opinion of the English-Canadian majority, who in Ontario had given Laurier more support in the last election than in 1911. The fanatics might rave; but 'they cannot prevent the French nationality not only from continuing to exist, but from living, spreading, and increasing its influence in strength and number.' As proof that Quebec could weather this crisis as it had others, he cited history. He condemned the infringement of constitutional rights by the federal government, and he reminded English Canadians of the words of an Ulster leader: 'All we want is fair ground and no favor. We ask for no more and are determined to take no less. We believe you have the same tolerance and the same sanity as we have.'[130]

Lawrence Cannon urged the study of Cartier's career for an understanding of Confederation, and recommended following Laurier's leadership in the solution of the present problem. He rejected the motion because Quebec was the essential center of Confederation and had the right and the duty to remain at the head of Confederation. Louis Letourneau approved the resolution, stressing Quebec's growing industrial self-sufficiency and discounting the dangers of isolation.

Charles Ernest Gault warned that Montreal would secede if Quebec separated from the rest of the dominion, and that tariff barriers would ruin the province. Independence was unthinkable and would be ruinous. Annexation would mean the end of the French language and denominational schools. Gault blamed much of Ontario's bitterness on the feeling that the Catholic Church was not sympathetic to the Allies, and urged that this misapprehension should be cleared up. He paid tribute to the Canadian soldiers, and urged everyone to do something to help them, criticising the number of young men of military age present in the galleries who should be at the front. He blamed the Ontario school question for causing trouble between the provinces, and said it would have been settled fairly if it had not been for the war. He censured extremists in both Ontario and Quebec, and deplored the lack of free speech in the last campaign, which had seen assaults on ministers of the Crown. He regretted that Gouin had refused an invitation to enter the federal government, a step which would have helped to remove the causes of the ethnic trouble. In a fiery speech Dr. Georges Grégoire replied to Gault that Quebec wanted peace, but Ontario seemingly sought to break up Confederation. He opposed French pride of race to British pride of race, and asserted that Quebec had done its part and did no deserve the stigma of cowardice.

Sir Lomer Gouin closed the debate, supporting the motion by citing the precedent of Nova Scotia, which in 1886 had adopted a resolution approving the separation of that province from Confederation and had almost unanimously voted in favor of it at a subsequent election. He asked why Quebec alone should be condemned for voting against conscription, when New Brunswick, Nova Scotia, and Prince Edward Island had also returned a majority against it. He had opposed Sauvé's proposed amendment because it would be ineffective. He expressed his belief in Confederation, which had made possible great development and progress in Quebec, and asked whether it would be in the interest of the half-million French Canadians in the other provinces for Quebec to leave Confederation The school questions in the other provinces would have arisen without Confederation. He pointed out the plight Quebec would be in if it left Confederation, with no winter port, no defences, burdened by a share of the national debt and forced to pay customs duties to other provinces. He cited the example of union provided by the United States and closed with an eloquent appeal to preserve Confederation.[131]

After the premier's speech Francoeur withdrew his motion on January 23, stating that he was satisfied with the results obtained and defending his resolution's opportuneness.[132] Without question the Francoeur Resolution debate had provided a safety valve for Quebec's pent-up resentment at English-Canadian attacks at a crucial moment. It was clear that Quebec had no serious desire to quit Confederation, but had only been driven to consider it by English Canada's intransigent and insulting attitude.

11

Late in December 1917 John S. Ewart reopened his correspondence with Bourassa and sought an interview with him in the hope of improving the strained relations between English and French Canadians. The overture was not particularly welcomed by Bourassa and in several exchanges of letters the two nationalists thrashed out their differences on the war. Ewart thus summed them up in a letter of January 21:

At the commencement we agreed upon the necessity for suppression of home differences with a view to production of war solidarity. Imperialistic war propaganda induced you to change this attitude. To me that change seems illogical. In my view, imperialism is a domestic question and has no relation to our attitude towards Germany. I therefore see in

Sir Robert Borden's excessive imperialism not a reason for alteration of Canada's opposition to her external enemies, but a reason for attack upon the imperialists.[133]

Then he revealed his purpose in seeking an interview with Bourassa.

Profoundly regretting the present political situation, and seeing in it a menace and danger to our political institutions, I have earnestly sought for some method by which our English-speaking and French-speaking peoples can be brought, if not to perfect harmony, at least to the relations which existed before the conscription act. I recognize that bilingual and other questions have always presented difficulties, and have confined myself to the recent acerbation of feeling due to the conscription act. It has occurred to me [to wonder] whether some modification of the statute would not relieve the tension, and I have thought of suggesting that every conscripted man should have the right of choice between service in the army and such other service in Canada as might be assigned to him. I have thought that such an amendment would meet, to a very large extent, the objections which you and your friends have raised against the act, and I desired to ascertain how the suggestion would appeal to you. I have not as yet said anything to Sir Robert Borden or any of his colleagues. It would probably be useless for me to do so without being able to give them some assurance that the proposed amendment would be welcomed in Quebec. May I ask if you will be good enough to let me know whether you think my proposal is practicable? If you should reply in the affirmative, I should then ask you whether I might be permitted to pass on your view to Sir Robert Borden, either in confidence or for such other use as you might think best.

Knowing you as I do, and appreciating your love of Canada, I feel sure that you will lend your assistance to any proposal which, in your judgment, will tend to the creation of sympathetic relations between the provinces.

For some unexplained reason—possibly his wife's illness—Bourassa delayed for two months in answering this request, which was in the great tradition of relations between leaders of the two main Canadian racial groups, and which took considerable courage to make at a time when Bourassa had become the most hated man in Canada. On March 29, 1918 he finally replied:

It is probably too late now for any useful answer to your inquiry, with regard to what might be done to alleviate the hostile feeling in Quebec against the Government and their war policy. I do not wish, however, to leave you under the impression that I had the slightest objection to write you in all open frankness on this or any other matter.

Your suggestion, if honestly and effectively put into execution, would do a great deal to appease the feelings of our people. But I could not leave you under the delusion that it would be sufficient to restore the confidence of the French Canadians either in the Government or, gene ally, in the good faith and fair spirit of the English-speaking majority.

With regard to the Government, the representatives of Quebec in tl Cabinet and Sir Robert Borden himself, have so deceived and disguste the people, that nothing coming from Ottawa would be accepted i confidence. Any announcement such as suggested by you, but comin from the Government, would be taken as a new claptrap, as a new for of deception, soon to be followed, as former assurances were, by measur of coercion. It would take some time and a prolonged application to cor vince the people that the offer was made in good faith; and till the wa is over most people would remain convinced that those conscripts turne on the farm would be liable to war service, the moment the Governme would change their mind on the matter.

As to racial misunderstanding in general, and lack of national uni and spirit, it will take a very long time to convince our people th British fair play is not a mere shibboleth and a pharisaic stock-phrase.

It would take too long a letter to explain fully the reasons and caus of that feeling, and the obstacles to a prompt and decisive reaction. Whe the occasion and the pleasure will be given to me of meeting you, we wi talk these matters over. We will also try to fully dispel the past misunde standing on our respective attitudes on the war. I cannot quite accep your last word upon it.[134]

During the early months of 1918 Bourassa had urged a negotiate peace in *Le Devoir*. On February 22 he described Confederation a 'in fact prejudicial to the French Canadians,' and on March 2 he urged anti-conscriptionist members of parliament to refuse t vote any more money for the war.[135] He also continued his bitt denunciations of British policy.

12

There was much bitter feeling in Quebec early in 1918. Abb Groulx continued to intensify popular indignation about the Ontari school question, and on March 16 the Montreal Saint-Jean-Baptis Society moved a resolution congratulating the Franco-Ontaria 'who had learned to oppose a persistent resistance to iniquito laws.'[136] In response to a query from Toronto as to what Queb wanted, *La Presse* gave this summary on February 20:

1. That the French language, recognized as an official language in th Canadian Parliament, should be similarly treated in all parts of the cou try, because it has rights acquired in virtue of treaties and of the Co stitution.

2. That the Ontario Government, in place of making regulations ostracize the French language and to prevent by the submission of shameful oath the French Canadians from establishing themselves in th

Province, should apply itself to treating our people as brothers: that is to say, as the Anglo-Protestant minority of Quebec is treated by the French.

3. That the Roman Catholic religion should be more respected by the Ontario press.

4. That the treatment of minorities should be based henceforth on justice, fraternity, and the intentions of the Fathers of Confederation, rather than on the very letter of the law.

5. That the other races should not seek a quarrel with us for any cause or no cause; that they should cease to discredit us abroad, because in doing so they discredit the whole of Canada.

6. That there should be an end of the belief that national unity can be secured only by unity of language; that the law of the strongest should no longer be enforced against us.

7. That good understanding between the two great races which predominate in Canada should be established on the basis of a knowledge of the two official languages.[137]

Article 2 referred to the new practice of making French-Canadian settlers in northern Ontario sign an oath to obey Regulation 17, under penalty of losing their land and the money paid for it. This was a measure adopted at the instance of the Orange Order, which on March 13 called upon 'the loyalists of Canada' to secure by changes in legislation the ideal of 'one flag, one school, and one official language from Coast to Coast.'[138]

The enforcement of the Military Service Act aroused difficulties in Quebec, despite *L'Action Catholique's* injunction on January 7 to submit to the law cheerfully and *La Presse's* urging on the same date of 'a courageous and worthy submission to the law.'[139] Exemptions were claimed on a wholesale scale, as they were throughout Canada, with local tribunals in Quebec refusing 4.1 per cent of the claims as compared to a refusal rate of 10.1 per cent in Ontario. But many Quebec cases were appealed by the military authorities, with the result that the total percentage of Quebec claims refused was 9 per cent while in Ontario it was 8.2 per cent.[140] Attention was focused on the operation of the law in Quebec, because of the province's solid opposition to conscription; and it was widely rumored in English Canada that many Quebec defaulters and deserters were seeking refuge in the bush or in the States. When deserters were rounded up in Montreal, the French press asked whether similar zeal was being shown in Ontario.

By the end of February conscription had only put 22,000 men in uniform, of whom 2,000 were from Quebec. Measures were taken to speed up some 30,000 appeals still pending in the province. The resistance of the Western farmers to conscription was also determined, and pressure was brought to bear on the government for the exemption of farmers' sons. An order-in-council of December 31, 1917 provided for the discharge by the militia minister of agricultural draftees whose claims for exemption had been rejected; while on February 8 the militia department issued instructions for special attention to such claims. By the end of March only 31,000 had been ordered to report for duty, with 5,000 of the number defaulting. It was generally agreed that conscription was a failure, as Laurier had maintained it would be. The woods were rumored to be full of armed defaulters ready to resist arrest.

Anti-draft riots were anticipated in Montreal, long a center of violent opposition to conscription, but instead they broke out unexpectedly in Quebec City on the night of March 29, when the federal police arrested a French Canadian named Mercier who was unable to show his exemption papers. After he was able to produce his papers, he was released, but a mob of several thousands gathered and burnt the federal police station. The police appealed to the military for assistance, but were referred to the civil authorities. Mayor Lavigeur sought to get the crowd to disperse, but did not read the Riot Act or call in the troops. The crowd got out of hand, and marched to the tunes of 'O Canada' and the 'Marseillaise' to the offices of the *Chronicle* and *L'Evénement*, which they sacked. On the following evening the crowd gathered after dark and attacked the office of the registrar of the Military Service Act, and burnt it with all its records. The city police were reported to have refused adequate protection to the building and to have looked on passively while it was burnt to the ground.

The commanding officer, Brigadier Landry, asked for reinforcements, which the government tactlessly supplied in the form of a Toronto battalion. On March 30 the troops charged the crowd with fixed bayonets, and aroused a fury which found expression in one continuous riot the following day, March 31, which was Easter Sunday. Cavalry drove back the crowd with improvised bludgeons made of axe-handles, while feeling grew ever uglier. That evening Armand Lavergne addressed the crowds, claiming that he had an agreement with the military authorities that the troops would be withdrawn if the rioters dispersed to their homes. Brigadier Landry at once denied such an agreement. Lavergne then demanded that the troops be withdrawn and that 'reputable men' be used to enforce the Military Service Act; otherwise he promised to put himself at the head of the mob and to fight the authorities without mercy.

On April 1, despite placards posted ubiquitously requiring the citizens to remain at home under orders from General Lessard, who had been sent from Ottawa to take charge, and despite admonitions from Cardinal Bégin and the press for the populace to refrain from violence and to remain at home, the rioters opened fire on the troops from housetops, snowbanks, and other hiding places. After several soldiers had been wounded, they returned the fire with both rifles and machine guns. Cavalry charged the mob with drawn swords, while infantry picked off snipers. Order was restored by one o'clock in the morning of April 2, but five soldiers had been wounded and four civilians killed, with many wounded and fifty-eight arrested. On April 4 the government suspended the *habeas corpus* and provided for the immediate conscription of rioters by order-in-council.[141]

There was much criticism of these actions and of the sending of a Toronto battalion to restore order in Quebec, as well as of the allegedly brutal pursuit of slackers by the military authorities which had aroused the riots. But a Quebec which has always had a deep regard for law and order despite its tendency to verbal violence was horrified by the outbreak; and the Church and press promptly called for the re-establishment of order. The riots were represented as not being typical of public feeling. In a debate in the House on April 5 half-hearted and ineffective enforcement of the Military Service Act in Quebec was sharply criticized by English Canadians, while Laurier blamed the riots upon the men chosen to enforce the Act and upon a secret association drawn from the 'scum of Montreal.' But he joined Borden in calling for submission and obedience to the law. On April 13 a Quebec coroner's jury returned a verdict that 'considering the persons killed on that occasion were innocent of participating in the said riot, which owed its origin to the tactless and grossly unwise fashion in which the Federal police in charge of the Military Service Act did their work, it should be the duty of the Government to reasonably indemnify the families of the victims who have been found innocent and unarmed, and to pay indemnities to all who suffered damages from that riot.'[142]

French Canada blamed the riots on maladministration of the conscription act, while English Canada considered them the outcome of Quebec's resistance to the act. Misled by French-Canadian verbal violence, English Canada overestimated Quebec's rebelliousness, while Quebec made too much of 'Anglo-Saxon brutality' in enforcing conscription and repressing the riots. But since the French press had long been critical of police brutality and tactlessness in enforcing conscription, and had even brought definite charges that notorious criminals and strongarm men were used for the purpose, it seems clear that some blame for the riots must be attached to the way in which the Military Service Act was enforced in Quebec.

Discussion of the Quebec riots in parliament revealed the full extent of racial cleavage. Colonel Currie called for martial law in Quebec, with the internment of Bourassa and Lavergne and the suppression of *Le Devoir*. Borden refused, pointing out that 'a man behind the bars sometimes has more influence than outside the bars.'[143] Sam Hughes, who had often officially professed friendship for French Canada, attacked it savagely. He told of French-Canadian officers who had failed to enlist battalions, and of units which deserted as soon as they were enlisted. He accused the Catholic clergy of opposition to participation in the war, and asserted that Quebec had been perverted by German propaganda. But other English Canadians pointed out that the underlying cause of the riots was that Quebec was no longer under the control of Laurier and the moderates, but rather under that of Bourassa and the more fanatical members of the clergy. Growing opposition to conscription in the farming districts of English Canada led to a more indulgent attitude toward Quebec than during the election, though wholesale exemptions in Quebec were criticized. This criticism was disarmed by an order-in-council of April 19 cancelling exemptions, on the grounds of the emergency presented by the German break-through late in March, which had caused Canadian troops to be sent to reinforce British units. Laurier criticized the measure as a departure from the principles of the Act and of constitutional government, and urged the continued exemption of farmers' sons. General Mewburn declared that urban conscripts would be called first, while farmers would be permitted to finish their planting and would not be called till the last possible moment.

The cancellation of exemptions created intense excitement in Ontario and the West, as well as in Quebec. On May 14 a delegation of 5,000 farmers arrived in Ottawa under the joint leadership of J.-E. Caron, Quebec minister of agriculture, and of the United Farmers of Ontario. The *Toronto Globe* estimated that 3,000 of the delegation came from Ontario.[144] When the delegates were refused permission to wait upon parliament in a body, it was rumored that they were prepared to do so by force. Finally the farmers held a mass meeting at the Russell Theater. Borden addressed the meeting and stood firm by the order-in-council which had been approved by parliament. Protest meetings were held in Ontario and the West and petitions dispatched to Ottawa without effect; and on June 9 the United Farmers of Ontario, meeting for their annual convention at Toronto, censured the government and threatened an appeal to the Privy Council. This action was supported by the United Farmers of Alberta, and later by the Canadian Council of Agriculture meeting at Winnipeg. Criticism of the farmers became as common with ultra-patriots as criticism of the French Canadians. F. B. Carvell admitted in the House on April 19: 'There are thousands and tens of thousands, yes, hundreds of thousands, of people in the rest of Canada who have tried assiduously to evade military service.'[145]

After cancelling exemptions, the government adopted the policy of conciliation rather than coercion of Quebec which Laurier had urged. Bishop Mathieu played a notable role in quieting Quebec feeling, while Gouin was once more urged to join the government. Borden asserted his willingness to support formation of the French-Canadian brigade which was urged by Quebec members, and revealed plans for building up exclusively French-Canadian units by using French-Canadian reinforcements for battalions containing many of their compatriots. But he concluded with the statement that the government was inclined to think the mixing of the races in the army a good thing—which confirmed the fear of some French Canadians that it was sought to anglicize them through the army. General Mewburn visited Montreal and Quebec, and at the latter city on June 5, when welcomed by a formal address from the bench and bar, stated:

> I for one have never for a moment doubted the loyalty of Quebec and its people; and from the wonderful things I have seen during my visit, my firm conviction has been strengthened . . . Permit me to say that I am putting forth every effort that recruited French Canadians be kept together in distinct units, commanded by officers of their own race and tongue.[146]

General Mewburn had also admitted that the recruiting results might have been much better if Sir Sam Hughes had allowed the old militia units to go overseas and to recruit on a territorial basis. Rodolphe Lemieux hailed the government's new policy. Laval University took the lead in the new recruiting effort, as the German threat to the Channel Ports became serious, and by June 21, 9,970 men from Montreal and 2,848 men from Quebec had enrolled. On that day *Le Soleil* urged immediate steps by the authorities to quell disturbances in rural communities blamed on defaulters. Quebec's new willingness to cooperate was noticed even by so long-standing an opponent as the *Toronto Mail and Empire*, which on April 30 commented on the gratifying way in which young men were answering the call to arms under the new order-in-council. The validity of the order-in-council was tested in numerous court cases all over Canada. It was denied by the Alberta Supreme Court, and finally upheld by the Supreme Court of Canada on July 20.

In an effort to make the Military Service Act effective, heavy penalties were provided for defaulting or desertion, and manhunts were held in public places for those without exemption papers. These measures were bitterly resented in Quebec. But on August 2 an amnesty was proclaimed for defaulters if they reported for duty before August 24; and some 10,000 took advantage of it. There were many others who hid out in the Laurentian wilds of Quebec and Ontario, the forests of British Columbia, or fled across the American border. A group of young Nova Scotians sailed away with the fishing fleet in June, while in other provinces men took refuge in remote lumber camps where no questions were asked. In the end conscription yielded a total of 83,355 soldiers actually enlisted, of whom 47,509 actually went overseas, about 11 per cent of the total sent from Canada and the equivalent of two divisions. Quebec provided 19,050 men under the Act, while it had 18,827 defaulters out of the country's total of 27,631, with 40.83 per cent of the men ordered to report failing to do so. Nova Scotia with 16.72 per cent defaulting, Ontario, and Saskatchewan had the next highest percentages of defaulters.[147] At a cost of three and a half millions for administration, conscription provided fewer men per month than the voluntary system, while it bitterly divided the races and provinces and aroused religious feeling. The latter issue was brought to a head in June by a police raid on the Jesuit College at Guelph, Ontario, which the son of the minister of justice had recently entered. The *Orange Sentinel* and the *Toronto Telegram* demanded investigation and action on charges that Catholic students received preferential treatment under the act. Colonel H. A. C. Machin, head of the Military Service Branch of the Department of Justice, denounced the charges with the observation that 'The greatest menace to the Province of Ontario is the Methodist Church, which seems to make us in Ontario the most hypocritical body or class of people in the Dominion of Canada.'[148]

But the triumphs won by the Canadian Corps, in constant action after the Allied break-through at Amiens on August 8 until the Armistice on November 11, at the cost of more than 30,000 casualties, served to unite Canada once more. The Royal 22nd played a notable part in this final struggle, with all its officers casualties at one point, and the fighting qualities of the French Canadians were recognized all over Canada. Two members of the 22nd won Victoria Crosses and two of its commanders became brigadier-generals, F.-M. Gaudet, C.M.G., and T.-L. Tremblay, C.M.G., D.S.O. When the troops came home, French and English alike received a triumphant reception in Quebec and Montreal. About 15,000 French Canadians saw service at the front, 15,000 more were in training in England and Canada, and some 4,000 or 5,000 served in the naval forces.[149] The total of 35,000 thus arrived at represents only the most accurate possible guess, as no official figures were supplied after March 1918, in an effort to let the vexed question of French-Canadian participation die. The fact that the French Canadians contributed only 5 per cent of the Canadian total, as compared to English Canada's contribution of something less than 50 per cent of Canadian-born soldiers,[150] remained to embitter the relations between the races in Canada. English Canada soon lost most of its bitterness against Quebec as time passed, but French

Canada never forgot the troubles of 1917–18, which served to nourish a new nationalist movement which was distinctly provincial and sometimes separatist in outlook.

13

Bourassa seemingly underwent a change of heart after the events of 1917 had split Canada along ethnic lines and made impossible the larger nationalism which he had always professed. He largely abandoned politics for religion. He had little to say about the Francoeur Resolution, and took the attitude that secession had never seriously been contemplated. Late in January 1918 he collected some of his utterances from the beginning of the war and coupled them with the Papal pronouncements on peace in book form, under the title of *Le Pape, arbitre de la paix*, in an effort to prove his adherence to the Papal program throughout. He likened Wilson's attitude to that of the Pope, and urged the presence of the latter at a peace conference which would seek for a Christian peace and thus avoid social revolution. This publication was approved by most of the Quebec bishops, although Archbishop Bruchési dryly observed that some of Bourassa's judgments on men and events were open to discussion, and that he himself would not have dared to make pronouncements on many of the questions with which Bourassa dealt. During the Quebec riots Bourassa's only comment was a strongly worded admonition to the populace to keep cool; and the application of strict censorship in April produced no blast from *Le Devoir*.

Under the auspices of the *Action française* movement launched by Abbé Groulx, Bourassa delivered a lecture on '*La Langue, gardienne de la foi*,' on November 20, 1918 at the Monument National. He rejected the charges that the French Canadians were more French than Catholic, too French and not British enough, and traitors to the empire and ungrateful to France. He asserted that the faith had other safeguards, but the French language, necessary for the preservation of the faith, could only be preserved by vigorous efforts on the part of the French Canadians. He reviewed the principles of social order and natural law which justified the preservation of the mother tongue, and pointed out that the Church had always protected and adopted the language of its adherents. He saw French as the language of Catholicism *par excellence*, and urged his audience to 'fight for our language in order to better preserve our faith.'[151] His second public address of the year was a review of the missionary work of French-Canadian orders, given at the Monument National on December 5 under the patronage of Archbishop Bruchési. This was published in March 1919 in enlarged book form as *Le Canada Apostolique*, with a prefatory appeal for the writing of mission history as 'an excellent manner to react against the singular state of spirit, born of colonial abjection, which leads so many Canadians to remain ignorant c the beauties of their history while according all their admiration t foreign works.'[152]

A pastoral letter, issued by the Pope on June 7 and published i Canada on October 24, had settled the school question with th following injunctions:

The French Canadians may justly appeal to the government for suit able legislation as to the above-mentioned law [Regulation 17], and a the same time desire and seek further concessions. Such are, undoubtedly that the Inspectors of their Separate Schools should be Catholics; tha during the first years of tuition the use of their own language should b granted for the teaching of certain subjects, chiefly and above all, o Christian doctrine; and that Catholics be allowed to establish trainin schools for the education of teachers. But all these advantages and other which may be useful must be invoked and sought for by Catholics withou the least appearance of revolt and without recourse to violent or illegiti mate methods; and let them employ peacefully and moderately all suc means as are legally or by lawful custom permitted to citizens seekin advantages to which they consider themselves entitled. . . .

Thus, while confining themselves within these limits and to thes proceedings, the French Canadians are free to seek for school legislatio the interpretations or changes which they desire. In this matter whic concerns all Catholics, let no one venture, nonetheless, in the futur to appeal to the civil courts or to promote litigation without the know ledge and consent of his Bishop, and in such questions let the latter no decide anything without consultation with other Bishops immediatel interested . . . Let all priests endeavor to acquire the knowledge and us of both languages, English and French, and setting aside all prejudices let them adopt one or the other according to the needs of the faithful.[15

The pastoral included injunctions to the bishops to avoid division b language or race, and to the laity to show charity to one another. I desired that severe warnings should be given to any among th clergy or laity who in the future should dare to nourish or excit 'the animosities which have divided Canadians up to this day. Commentaries on the encyclical by Père Rouleau, Mgr. Paquet, an Père Leduc were published in *Le Droit*, *L'Action Catholique*, and *L Revue Dominicaine*, and reprinted with the text of Bourassa's addres Active and violent agitation of the school question duly came to a end, though not until the adoption of the Merchant Report of 192 was the Ontario policy of coercion abandoned in favor of one c cooperation, with the equal importance of the teaching of Frenc and English in bilingual schools recognized. The bilingual schoc question remained vexed enough throughout Canada for Abb Groulx to make capital of it in 1933, when nationalism regaine strength under the pressure of economic crisis, a condition which, lik a time of war, always favors the development of ethnic feeling in Canada.

The development of English-Canadian nationalism during the war, made evident in the closing months of the conflict and during the peace conference, doubtless had an appeasing effect on French Canada, whose opposition to the government's war policy had been based on the grounds that Canada's interests were subordinated to Britain's. Borden, accompanied by three ministers—Calder, Meighen, and Rowell—sailed for England on May 24, 1918 to attend the second Imperial War Conference. Prompted by Sir Arthur Currie, the first Canadian commander of the Canadian Corps, Borden was frankly critical of the War Office and of the Admiralty, and denounced incompetency, disorganization, and confusion at the front in a meeting of the War Cabinet on June 13. As a result, a sub-committee of the War Cabinet was set up, consisting of the British and dominion prime ministers and thus exemplifying the principles of equal status and autonomy for which Borden had striven. The Imperial War Cabinet remained in almost continuous session during the summer, with Borden and Rowell in attendance, while Meighen and Calder represented Canada in the Imperial War Conference. Borden visited the Canadian troops in France and England in intervals between meetings. He backed the resolution proposed by Hughes of Australia in favor of direct communication between the dominion and British prime ministers, and the right of the dominions to be represented continuously in the Imperial War Cabinet by ministers serving as representatives of the dominion prime ministers. This motion was adopted unanimously, confirming the decline of the authority of the Colonial Office and of the governor-general.

The Imperial War Conference closed on July 26, after dealing with the problems of empire communications, statistics, and news services, in addition to war problems. Ballantyne and Mewburn replaced Calder and Meighen in London, while plans were evolved for a Canadian contingent in the proposed Siberian expedition. Speaking at a luncheon on July 31, Borden made clear that the British government's announcement of the policy of imperial preference was made in behalf of the United Kingdom, while Canada retained the right to control its own fiscal policy. He also rejected the Admiralty's proposal of a single imperial navy under British control in war and peace. Lloyd George suggested that Canada should take over the West Indies and Borden agreed.[154] Borden sailed for Canada on August 17 and on Labor Day at Toronto reported on the work of the conference, emphasizing the fact that no great constitutional changes had been made.

Lloyd George had expressed the desire that Borden should return to England when the war ended, and on October 28 he cabled him to be prepared to start on short notice. It was agreed in cabinet at Ottawa to continue the Union government after peace came; and a Canadian peace mission was formed, composed of Borden, George Foster, and A. L. Sifton, with Doherty to come later, and additional representatives from various government departments, the labor unions, and John Dafoe as press representative. Borden sailed on November 10 and was met in London by Lloyd George and a representative of the King. It was at once proposed that Borden should represent the dominions as one of a five-man British delegation to the peace conference. Borden held that all the dominion prime ministers should have equal status, and agreed to confer with General Smuts. He offered to keep two Canadian divisions overseas during the peace negotiations, but said Canadian public opinion would not permit compulsory service in an army of occupation. In December Borden met General Louis Botha of South Africa for the first time, and like Laurier before him, found that Canada and South Africa held similar imperial ideals and positions. Both believed 'that upon the basis of equal nationhood and adequate voice in external relations the salvation of the Commonwealth could be worked out most surely.'[155] Late in December Borden refused an urgent suggestion from his colleagues that he should return home for the opening of the session in a month's time, as the Union government was under fire and Liberal activity was marked. Borden maintained that his duty lay rather in guarding Canada's interests at the peace conference.

In a meeting of the War Cabinet on December 31 Borden strongly urged that each dominion prime minister should have a turn at representing the empire in the peace conference, and warned that Canada's desire for representation in the making of peace might lead to regrettable consequences if not gratified. Borden was backed by Hughes and Cook of Australia, and Lloyd George agreed. Under the system finally adopted, each dominion was to have the same representation—two delegates—as the smaller Allied nations, and in addition the five representatives of the British empire were to be drawn from a panel including all the dominion prime ministers. This measure caused horror in the Foreign Office, and encountered severe opposition from President Wilson at the first meeting of the Big Four on January 11–12; but was subsequently adopted with the modification that New Zealand only had one representative, while Canada, Australia, South Africa, and India each had two. Borden urged upon Lloyd George a South African proposal drafted by Smuts, limiting the governor-general's status to that of the King in Britain and advocating that governors-general should be chosen from eminent men of the dominion to which they were appointed. Lloyd George rejected the latter suggestion as removing the last link between the dominions and Britain, with Borden replying that 'if the Empire's unity depended upon that link, it was not very secure.'[156] Non-British governors-general were soon appointed in the other dominions, but Canada still waited until 1952 for her first Canadian governor-general.

Borden took so active a role in the peace conference that there were several attempts, seemingly, to kick him upstairs by making him British representative at a proposed meeting of Russian governments at Princes Island in the Sea of Marmora on February 15, or British ambassador to Washington, while the equally independent Botha was named president of the Polish Commission. Disregarding these offers, Borden stood firm, insisting upon the right of dominion representatives to sign the peace treaty as plenipotentiaries, and to be recognized in the League of Nations and in the International Labor Bureau. In the end Borden represented Britain in the Council of Five and also presided over the British Empire delegation, while Canadian representatives took influential parts in committee work. In May Lloyd George urged Borden to delay his return to Canada, which was demanded by the political crisis created by the One Big Union general strike and by differences between Liberal and Conservative cabinet members over tariff matters. But having seen the peace treaty through, Borden was forced to return home to ensure his remaining in power.

14

The general strike in Winnipeg in May, coupled with later strikes in Toronto, Ottawa, Calgary, Vancouver, and elsewhere, was virtually broken late in June 1919, after violence had been suppressed by the use of armed police and soldiers. The Winnipeg disorders were much more severe than the Quebec anti-conscription riots of 1918. Quebec was unaffected by the labor troubles of 1919, since the international unions were not as strong there as in English Canada, and since Quebec labor was moderate in sentiment. Borden took a firm stand, recognizing the rights of labor but refusing to allow interference with public services. Reconstruction of the government became necessary in June as the Unionist Liberals led by Calder, who resigned from the cabinet, supported free trade. The government was unable to pass a measure for setting up a peacetime purchasing commission. Before the session closed on July 7, Borden held a caucus, proposing a continuance of the present government with the formation of a Unionist Party. The caucus adopted a notably vague platform, and authorized Borden to reconstruct the government, from which Sir Thomas White, the finance minister and acting prime minister in Borden's absence, had also now resigned.

Borden was conscious of the necessity of winning Quebec back from its isolation by French-Canadian representation in the cabinet. Early in July he made overtures to Sir Lomer Gouin, the titular leader of French Canada since Laurier's death in February. Gouin suggested that Borden visit Quebec and consult Jacques Bureau, Rodolphe Lemieux, and Ernest Lapointe. Borden did not get far with Bureau at Trois-Rivières, but at Quebec he conferred with Sir Charles Fitzpatrick, the lieutenant-governor, and Cardinal Bégin, stressing his desire that Quebec should take her due share in the government of the country. In a conference with Lapointe at Rivière-du-Loup, Borden offered to resign if that step would ease the situation, but Lapointe held that public opinion in Quebec would prevent French Canadians from taking part in a Union government in any case. He was sympathetic to Borden's ideas, but regarded them as impracticable.[157] At Murray Bay Borden got the same reaction from Gouin and Lemieux, with Gouin urging the prime minister to settle the Ontario school question. In final consultations at Quebec and Montreal Borden found that Fitzpatrick thought Gouin was willing to enter the federal government, but feared he could not be elected; while Lord Atholstan felt that Gouin would be a strong representative of Quebec. In August Borden accompanied the Prince of Wales on his visit to Quebec, and used the French which he had acquired in Paris in conversation with Lady Gouin. But his railway car was stoned at Chaudière Junction when he left for Ottawa.[158]

Under pressure from Borden the British government delayed ratification of the peace treaty until it had been submitted to the Canadian parliament at a special session in September. The treaty was approved on September 12, after a debate in which Fielding contested Borden's theory that Canada's ratification was necessary and proposed a resolution, seconded by Lapointe, to this effect:

> In giving such approval, this House in no way assents to any impairment of the existing autonomous authority of the Dominion, but declares that the question of what part, if any, the forces of Canada shall take in any war, actual or threatened, is one to be determined at all times as occasion may require by the people of Canada through their representatives in Parliament.[159]

There was a sharp conflict over Article X of the League Covenant in parliament. C. G. Power, an English Liberal from Quebec, urged that Canada's policy for the next century should be based upon Washington's principle of 'absolute renunciation of interference in European affairs' and Laurier's doctrine of 'freedom from the vortex of European militarism.' Rodolphe Lemieux declared:

'In military matters we are governed also by and from Ottawa, and not by and from London; and we do not want to be governed by and from Geneva.' L.-T. Pacaud stated that by the adoption of Article X, 'we are placing the Canadian people at the beck and call of a council not responsible to the voters for its actions.' The coalition majority in parliament triumphed, however, over the opposition which came from both parties.[160]

After this final struggle for ratification of the peace treaty, Borden's health began to collapse, but he continued to work until October 3. On that date he forwarded to London a dispatch calling for the appointment of a Canadian minister to Washington to carry on the work of the wartime Canadian mission and to conduct all negotiations between Canada and the United States. This epoch-making proposal was accepted by the British government and announced in 1920, but not carried into effect for seven years.

Borden then went to the States on a vacation recommended by his physicians, though he conferred with his ministers there on several occasions. He sought to aid passage of the peace treaty in the United States Senate by waiving the right of the dominions to vote in the settlement by the League of a dispute in which any part of the British Empire was involved. He returned to Ottawa on November 26, but early in December announced his decision to retire, on grounds of health, to his cabinet colleagues and the governor-general. Under pressure from his colleagues he agreed to defer his resignation until he had sought restoration of his health by a prolonged vacation, which lasted from January 2, 1920, to May 12. Then, on the occasion of prorogation on July 1, he announced his definite decision to resign. After Sir Thomas White had refused to form a government, Arthur Meighen succeeded Borden as prime minister on July 10, with the Unionist Liberals Calder, Guthrie, Ballantyne, and Sifton remaining in the government and with Senator Blondin as the only French-Canadian minister.

In the years that followed Borden came to occupy the position of Canada's elder statesman which Laurier had held after his defeat in 1911. By his lectures and writings on constitutional problems he did much to formulate the new English-Canadian nationalism which he had helped to crystallize in the latter part of a career which had begun in the imperialist camp. In the end he had led in the realization of many of Bourassa's ideals for Canada. With the slow postwar development of English-Canadian nationalism, French Canadians were left less isolated politically, though the chasm between the races remained deep, thanks to the bloodshed in Quebec in 1918.

Laurier, the greatest advocate of unity in Canada, had died in February 1919, and Quebec was left without a federal leader. Laurier's health had failed gradually during 1918; though near the end it revived, and in November and January he made vigorou speeches to Liberal gatherings. In November at London, Ontario, h made a notable plea which summed up his philosophy:

> As for you who stand today on the threshold of life, with a long horizo open before you for a long career of usefulness to your native land, if yo will permit me, after a long life, I shall remind you that already man problems rise before you: problems of race division, problems of cree differences, problems of economic conflict. Problems of national dut and national aspiration. Let me tell you that for the solution of thes problems you have a safe guide, an unfailing light, if you remember tha faith is better than doubt and love is better than hate.
>
> Banish doubt and hate from your life. Let your souls be ever open t the promptings of faith and the gentle influence of brotherly love. B adamant against the haughty, be gentle and kind to the weak. Let you aim and purpose, in good report or ill, in victory or defeat, be so to live so to strive, so to serve as to do your part to raise ever higher the standar of life and living.[161]

Still in harness at seventy-eight, faithful to the end to the politic which he loved and of which he was a great master, Laurier suffere a slight stroke in his office on the eve of the opening of the session i February. Next morning, as he was dressing for church, a secon stroke came, from which he failed to rally. The end came the following day, with the whispered words, '*C'est fini.*'

There was a week of national mourning, with tributes voiced i parliament by Sir Thomas White, the acting prime minister, an Rodolphe Lemieux, Laurier's loyal lieutenant. Borden issued a statement that 'all Canada will mourn his loss and those who differe from him will be profoundly conscious that his death leaves in th public life of our country a blank that cannot be entirely filled.'[16 There was a state funeral at the Basilica in Ottawa, with Bisho Mathieu and Father Burke paying tribute in French and English The King sent his sympathy to Lady Laurier, with assurance of th friendship and esteem he and the Queen had felt for Sir Wilfrid fo seventeen years; and to the governor-general the King expressed hi regret, with the assurance that 'Canada will mourn for one wh dearly loved his country and will remember with pride and gratitud his great powers of administrative genius.' A Canadian friend calle Laurier 'the best man I have ever known. His instinctive honour, his kindliness and forgetfulness of self, that shining out of nobility and distinction of character which men call magnetism, made everyman who entered his presence a better man for it.'[163] Though he was replaced in the leadership of the Liberal Party by his disciple Mackenzie King, who worshipped Laurier's memory and by alliance with Ernest Lapointe sought to remedy his own deficiencies in understanding Quebec, no statesman rose in postwar Canada who, like Laurier, could lead both races in Canada and be equally respected by both.

Notes

[1] *Can. An. Rev. 1916*, 304.
[2] Lucas, II, 31; Armstrong, 121.
[3] *Can. An. Rev. 1916*, 353.
[4] Skelton, II, 468.
[5] Armstrong, 131–3.
[6] Rumilly, XXI, 146.
[7] *Ibid.*
[8] *Ibid.*, 147.
[9] These articles were published in pamphlet form under the title of *Où allons-nous? Le Nationalisme Canadien. Lettres d'un 'Patriote'* (Montréal, 1916), with a note of Cardinal Bégin's observation to the priests of his diocese during their annual retreat in August: 'It is very important that you should not oppose recruiting, and even that you should favor it' (73).
[10] A. Hawkes, *Canadian Nationalism and the War* (Montreal, 1916).
[11] *Montreal Gazette*, 28 July 1916, T. Papineau-Bourassa, 21 March 1916.
[12] *Le Devoir*, 5 août 1916, Bourassa-McMaster, 2 Aug. 1916.
[13] Rumilly, XXI, 155.
[14] Skelton, II, 468.
[15] Armstrong, 141; *Le Devoir*, 18 août, 7 sept. 1916.
[16] Rumilly, XXI, 163.
[17] Borden, *Memoirs*, II, 609.
[18] *Can. An. Rev. 1916*, 329.
[19] Borden, II, 611.
[20] Armstrong, 124; *Le Soleil*, 23 oct. 1916; *Le Bien Public*, 30 nov. 1916.
[21] Borden, II, 613–14.
[22] *Can. An. Rev. 1916*, 330.
[23] Rumilly, XXI, 173.
[24] *Ibid.*, 175.
[25] *Ibid.*, 173–8.
[26] H. Bourassa, *Le Problème de l'Empire: Indépendance ou Association Impériale* (Montréal, 1916); *Independence or Imperial Partnership* (Montreal, 1916).
[27] L. Curtis, *The Problem of the Commonwealth* (London, 1916), 7.
[28] Skelton, II, 467.
[29] Bourassa, *Problème*, 25.
[30] Rumilly, XXI, 181–3.
[31] *Ibid.*, 185; Col. Thomas A. Duff-General Hughes, 19 June 1917.
[32] Sissons, *Bilingual Schools*, Ap. III, 222–7.
[33] Rumilly, XXI, 191.
[34] *Ibid.*, 196–7.
[35] *Ibid.*, 193.
[36] *Ibid.*, 198.
[37] Armstrong, 139–40; *Montreal Gazette*, 25 Oct. 1916.
[38] *Our Volunteer Army* (Montreal, 1916).
[39] Rumilly, XXI, 221–2.
[40] Ewart Papers: J. S. Ewart-Bourassa, 1 Dec. 1916.
[41] Rumilly, XXI, 226–7.
[42] *Où allons-nous?*, 30.
[43] Rumilly, XXI, 231.
[44] Borden, II, 570.

[45] *Ibid.*, 571.

[46] *Can. An. Rev. 1916*, 268.

[47] *Ibid.*, 263.

[48] Rumilly, XXI, 158. See *CHR 1950*, 1–27, D. M. R. Vince, 'The Acting Overseas Sub-Militia Council and the Resignation of Sir Sam Hughes'; *CHAR 1950*, 30–70, S. H. S. Hughes, 'Sir Sam Hughes and the Problem of Imperialism.'

[49] Borden, II, 617.

[50] Armstrong, 163.

[51] *Ibid.*, 162.

[52] *Can. An. Rev. 1916*, 476.

[53] *Ibid.*, 484.

[54] *Ibid.*

[55] Armstrong, 167; *Le Soleil*, 29 Jan. 1917.

[56] Borden, II, 660.

[57] Skelton, II, 492.

[58] *Ibid.*, 498.

[59] Borden, II, 619.

[60] Skelton, II, 497.

[61] Borden, II, 663.

[62] *Ibid.*, 668.

[63] *Ibid.*, 666; Skelton, II, 501.

[64] Skelton, II, 503–4; Laurier-C. P. Scott, 13 Feb. 1917.

[65] *Can. An. Rev. 1917*, 307.

[66] Skelton, II, 509–11; Laurier-Aylesworth, 15 May 1917.

[67] *Ibid.*, 512.

[68] *Can. An. Rev. 1917*, 490.

[69] *Ibid.*, 492.

[70] H. Bourassa, *L'Intervention américaine: ses motifs, son objet, ses conséquences* (Montréal, 1917).

[71] *Ibid.*, 27.

[72] *Ibid.*, 28.

[73] H. Bourassa, *Conscription* (Montreal, 1917).

[74] *Ibid.*, 25.

[75] *Ibid.*, 26.

[76] *Ibid.*

[77] *Ibid.*, 28.

[78] *Ibid.*, 29.

[79] *Ibid.*, 38.

[80] *Ibid.*, 42.

[81] Borden, II, 720–7; Skelton, II, 512–17.

[82] Skelton, II, 514.

[83] *Ibid.*, 515–16; Laurier-Rowell, 3 June 1917.

[84] Borden, II, 701.

[85] Descelles, *Discours*, II, 129–70.

[86] *Can. An. Rev. 1917*, 486–9.

[87] Borden, II, 705.

[88] *Can. An. Rev. 1917*, 347.

[89] Borden, II, 740.

[90] *Can. An. Rev. 1917*, 506.

[91] *Ibid.*, 505–6.

[92] Armstrong, 195–6.

[93] F. Roy, *L'appel aux armes et la réponse canadienne-française* (Québec, 1917).

[94] Borden, II, 733–4.

[95] 'J. Vindex' (R. P. Hermas Lalande, S.J.), *Halte là, 'Patriote'* (Rimouski 1917).

[96] *Can. An. Rev. 1917*, 480–1.
[97] *Ibid.*, 481.
[98] Armstrong, 196–7.
[99] *Ibid.*, 198; *Etoile du Nord*, 16, 30 août; *Le Peuple*, 6 sept. 1917.
[100] Borden, II, 730–1.
[101] Skelton, II, 524.
[102] Dafoe, *Sifton*, 416–17.
[103] *Can. An. Rev. 1917*, 351.
[104] Armstrong, 210; *La Presse*, 23 nov. 1917.
[105] H. Bourassa, *L'Emprunt de la 'Victoire'* (Montréal, 1917).
[106] Skelton, II, 536.
[107] Armstrong, 202.
[108] *Can. An. Rev. 1917*, 610.
[109] *Ibid.*, 610–11.
[110] *Ibid.*, 611.
[111] *Ibid.*, 598–9.
[112] *Ibid.*, 600.
[113] *Ibid.*, 600–1.
[114] Borden, II, 782.
[115] *Can. An. Rev. 1917*, 642–3.
[116] *Ibid.*, 642.
[117] Skelton, II, 543.
[118] *Ibid.*, 544.
[119] Armstrong, 209.
[120] A. Savard & W. E. Playfair (*trans.*), *Quebec & Confederation: A record of the Debate of the Legislative Assembly of Quebec on the Motion proposed by J.-N. Francoeur* (n.p., 1918).
[121] Armstrong, 210–11.
[122] *Quebec & Confed.*, 16–17.
[123] *Ibid.*, 22.
[124] *Ibid.*, 65.
[125] *Ibid.*, 47.
[126] *Ibid.*, 49.
[127] *Ibid.*, 52.
[128] *Ibid.*, 59.
[129] *Ibid.*, 65.
[130] *Ibid.*, 73–4, 80.
[131] *Ibid.*, 117–36.
[132] *Ibid.*, 136.
[133] Ewart Papers: Ewart-Bourassa, 21 Jan. 1918.
[134] *Ibid.*, Bourassa-Ewart, 29 March 1918.
[135] *Can. An. Rev. 1918*, 639.
[136] *Ibid.*, 640.
[137] *Can. An. Rev. 1918*, 641; *La Presse*, 20 feb. 1918.
[138] *Ibid.*, 600.
[139] *Ibid.*, 640–1.
[140] Armstrong, 226 *n.*
[141] *Ibid.*, 227–30; *Can. An. Rev. 1918*, 462–4.
[142] *Can. An. Rev. 1918*, 463–4.
[143] Borden, II, 789.
[144] *Can. An. Rev. 1918*, 411.
[145] *Ibid.*, 466–7.
[146] *Ibid.*, 454.
[147] C. P. Stacey, *The Military Problem of Canada* (Toronto, 1940), 79–80; Armstrong, 238.

[148] *Can. An. Rev. 1918*, 458.
[149] Armstrong, 249.
[150] *Ibid.*, 250.
[151] H. Bourassa, *La Langue, gardienne de la foi* (Montréal, 1918), 51.
[152] H. Bourassa, *Le Canada apostolique* (Montréal, 1918), 9.
[153] *Can. An. Rev. 1918*, 645–6.
[154] Borden, II, 844.
[155] *Ibid.*, 879.
[156] *Ibid.*, 901.
[157] *Ibid.*, 984.
[158] *Ibid.*, 987.
[159] *Ibid.*, 999.
[160] J. B. Brebner, *North Atlantic Triangle* (New Haven, 1945), 280.
[161] Skelton, II, 554–5.
[162] Borden, II, 914–15.
[163] Skelton, II, 588.

CHAPTER XIII

NATIONHOOD AND INTERNATIONALISM

(1920–39)

Quebec's wartime retreat into a narrow provincialism, as a result of its bitter differences with the other provinces over the treatment of their French-Canadian minorities, and as a result of the ethnic cleavage brought about by the conscription crisis, predisposed French Canada toward a more rigid isolationism in the postwar world than otherwise probably would have prevailed. The years between 1920 and 1939 on the national and international scene were characterized by Canada's increasing involvement in international affairs, and by its gradual shift from economic and political dependence upon Britain to a greater economic but lesser political dependence upon the United States as its wartime industrial development continued in the booming 1920's. Both historic processes represented a threat to French-Canadian cultural survival, and hence reinforced Quebec's tendency to turn inward upon itself which did not yield to the new internationalism until the mid-1930's.

French Canada's long conditioning against imperialism resulted in some postwar years of battling against a British political imperialism that was fast dying, while the lack of an economic point of view among most of the humanistically educated élite long blinded French-Canadian spokesmen to the new American economic imperialism, which offered an even greater challenge to a minority determined to maintain its separate way of life. The threat was finally recognized as a result of the simultaneous American cultural penetration of Quebec, which was vigorously fought by the élite and generally welcomed by the masses, to whom industrialization brought a higher standard of living than they had previously known.[1] Towards the end of the period American isolationism reinforced traditional French-Canadian isolationism, as the newer nationalist leaders adopted Henri Bourassa's tactics of quoting British and American public figures to the embarrassment of Canada's own leaders. These leaders were themselves torn between the pull of a new English-Canadian nationalism which went largely unrecognized in a Quebec turned in upon itself, and the sometimes conflicting pressures from London and Washington. Before the vitally important social and cultural developments in Quebec itself can be explained, the national and international political scene against which these developments occurred must be summarized. Henceforward this account must be tentative, like all histories of the recent past, for though facts are here recited, other facts now unknown may upset the interpretation here advanced.

1

Both federal and provincial leaders sought to heal the split between Quebec and the rest of Canada, when Arthur Meighen replaced Sir Robert Borden as head of the Union government and Alexandre Taschereau replaced Sir Lomer Gouin as premier of Quebec in a double changing of the old guard in July 1920. Gouin announced his retirement on July 8, after his return from a tour of France and England, where he was honored by the French president and the King and Queen. Taschereau, long Gouin's chief aide and frequent spokesman, announced that he would follow the same policy as his predecessor had done for fifteen years: continued development of Quebec's natural resources and wealth, and the maintenance of the province as a sanctuary of peace and tolerance. In a speech on July 27 he expressed regret at Quebec's isolation:

> Since Quebec is so necessary to Confederation, is it not deplorable to note its isolation. Some people see good in this isolation; others regret it, and I am of the latter class. . . . We did not enter Confederation to form a band apart, and like new Robinson Crusoes to live alone and separated on our own island . . . Quebec is not the only one to suffer thereby; all the country feels the effects and I shall welcome the day when our Province takes the place in the Canadian household which it deserves by reason of its riches, its geographical position, and all its other elements of greatness.[2]

This same conciliatory attitude was reflected in Taschereau's advice to the students of the Quebec Commercial Academy, whom he urged to learn English well while young, since 'Quebec is not surrounded by a Chinese wall.'[3] The provincial government gave $1,000,000 to both McGill and the new Université de Montréal, which became independent of Laval in this year, with five times as many students as the parent institution. Of the total of $4,000,000 raised to endow the new institution, the Séminaire de Saint-Sulpice supplied $1,000,000, while *bonne entente* sentiment was given substance by gifts of $50,000 by the Canadian Pacific Railway, $20,000 by the Ontario government, and smaller gifts from other English-Canadian sources.[4] The new wealth of French Canada as a result of wartime industrialization was indicated by the ease with which the endowment fund was raised.

The National Liberal and Conservative government formed by Arthur Meighen after Borden's resignation on July 10 included only one French Canadian, Senator Blondin, who was named postmaster-general. His wartime role had left Blondin virtually without support in Quebec, and Meighen's ardent Conservatism made him highly unpopular in Quebec. Only four of the sixteen members of the new government had Liberal antecedents, and it was a coalition government only in name. Bourassa characterized the new prime minister thus in *Le Devoir*: 'Mr. Meighen represents in person and temperament, in his attitudes and in his past declarations, the utmost that Anglo-Saxon jingoism has to offer in the way of brutality, all that is most exclusive, most anti-Canadian.'[5] Yet in his first important speech as prime minister, at Portage la Prairie on August 2, Meighen went out of his way to appeal for French-Canadian support:

> We have two great races. The fundamental institutions of Canada are just as dear to the one race as to the other. The peril of every nation has been a tendency to divide on lines of race, on lines of religion, on lines of social caste—If we do not come together to reach a better understanding and a better unity on things that are vital and essential to the state, there will be a heavy penalty paid.[6]

This plea, echoing Taschereau's recent utterances, was approved by both the *Toronto Globe* and the Montreal *La Presse*, and was taken up by the *Mail and Empire*, which on August 9 urged:

> Quebec ought to be exercising her full and vigorous influence in national affairs. She has everything to lose by remaining in a state of isolation. It cannot but be the wish of the new Premier of the Dominion to have Quebec duly represented in his Cabinet.[7]

In Montreal on September 10 Senator Blondin denounced isolation as suicide for Quebec and called for an end of exploitation of racial and religious prejudices.[8] During that month, after the prime minister had joined Taschereau and Cardinal Bégin in unveiling a statue of Cartier at Quebec, there were rumors of overtures to E.-L. Patenaude and Georges-H. Boivin, and later to L.-J. Gauthier, but Quebec Conservatives and Liberals alike refused to join the new government.

The new leader of the Liberal Party, William Lyon Mackenzie King, fared better than Meighen in wooing Quebec, since he already had some standing there as a favorite disciple of Laurier and was strongly supported by the old leader's lieutenants, Rodolphe Lemieux and Ernest Lapointe, the latter of whom was rising rapidly in influence among the Quebec delegation at Ottawa. During the ssion King conducted a vigorous attack on the government, denouncing the War-Time Election Act as 'one of the most infernal pieces of legislation which was ever perpetrated,'[9] and criticizing the fact that Quebec had no proper share in the administration. Conservative attacks on him for having deserted Canada during the war in favor of the Rockefeller interests—he had been a consultant on industrial relations to the Rockefeller Foundation—did him no harm in Quebec, nor did his denunciation of the government's naval proposals.[10] During the summer King toured Ontario and the West, supported by Quebec members, and in December made two speeches in Montreal, building his political fences for the election made inevitable by Meighen's failure to win backing in French Canada.

The immediate postwar period saw a revival of the old Canadian conflict between imperialism and nationalism, but no longer along ethnic lines. English-Canadian nationalism had developed tremendously during the war years, thanks to pride in Canada's war effort and to friction with colonial-minded Britishers, and tended to grow into an independent nationalism as a result of Borden's struggle for autonomy in the making of the peace treaties. But Britain neglected no means to hold its shaken empire together in the postwar years, and imperialist propaganda was largely concentrated on Canada, the most important dominion. In 1919 the Prince of Wales and Admiral Lord Jellicoe were sent to Canada to strengthen imperial feeling by evoking loyalty to the Royal Family and pride in the Royal Navy. The Prince won wide popularity, but even the most modest of the four alternative schemes which Jellicoe drafted for the postwar Canadian Navy was rejected by the Conservative government.[11] Lord Atholstan, Montreal's leading imperialist, was responsible for the Imperial Press Conference which met at Ottawa on August 5, 1920 and called for an imperial cable service after touching upon other imperial questions. The delegates subsequently toured Canada, spreading the gospel of imperial unity as they went. The Empire Chambers of Commerce also met in congress at Toronto in September 1920, and passed resolutions calling for strengthened imperial commercial ties, organization of imperial resources, an imperial preferential tariff, and the improvement of imperial communications and transportation.

These gatherings were intended to smooth the way for the first postwar Imperial Conference, which was summoned to meet at London in June 1921. Its agenda included preparatory discussion of the constitutional revisions urged at the 1917 Conference, a review of foreign relations, the question of renewal of the Anglo-Japanese Treaty, and discussion of methods of attaining a common understanding on foreign policy affecting all parts of the empire. On February 16 Lloyd George told the Commons that imperial defence should be an imperial concern. He was supported on April 27 by Sir Robert Borden, who argued that: 'We cannot assume or accept the status of nationhood without accepting also its responsibilities . . . whatever the burden may be, I believe it will be less upon this country as a nation of the Empire than if we stood separate as an independent nation.'[12] Mackenzie King replied in the House that the present was no time to settle some of the large questions which had been raised, and proposed a resolution that there should be no change in Canada's relations to the empire and no new expenditure for naval or military purposes. His motion was defeated by 96–64, after Meighen had made a plea for freedom to discuss whatever questions might arise at the conference.

But the strength of the new Canadian nationalism had been made evident. The Canadian correspondent of the *Round Table* reported its program thus:

> . . . separate diplomatic representation for the Dominions at the capitals of all foreign nations; separate navies under national control, abolition of appeals to the Imperial Privy Council, and complete judicial independence; nomination of the Governor-General by the Canadian Cabinet, and the appointment of a Canadian to the office if the Cabinet so wills, and recognition of the Sovereign as the only actual or official link between the Dominions and the Mother Country . . . complete independence under the Crown is natural and inevitable ultimate relation between the overseas British countries and the ancient seat and centre of the Empire.[13]

Meighen subscribed to Borden's view of the future empire as 'based upon equality of nationhood,' with each nation preserving 'its absolute autonomy' but also having 'its voice as to those external relations which involve the issue of peace or war.'[14]

When the conference met in secret session in London on June 20, Mr. Massey of New Zealand was the only dominion spokesman to echo the Chamberlain ideal of imperial federation, with all the others favoring cooperative action on the basis of equality. On June 27 Meighen urged in the tradition of Laurier and Borden that the dominions should be kept informed on all questions of foreign policy concerning the British government directly, while they must be consulted on those concerning the empire as a whole. He argued that no treaties should be entered into by Britain without consultation with the dominions; that such treaties should be subject to approval by the dominion parliaments; and that upon all Canadian-American questions the advice of the Canadian government should be accepted as final.[15] English opinion was sympathetic to the first three points, while the last had long been conceded. On June 29 Meighen, a newcomer to imperial affairs, flatly opposed the demand of the veterans Hughes of Australia and Massey of New Zealand that the Anglo-Japanese Alliance should be renewed, since it was incompatible with the League and opposed by the United States. In the first assertion of Canada's new role as the interpreter between Britain and the United States, Meighen declared that good Anglo-American relations were 'the touchstone of British policy and the hope of the world.' Despite the vigorous objections of Hughes, Lloyd George was won over to Meighen's views and adopted his idea of a Pacific Conference of Britain, the United States, and Japan to determine Pacific policy.[16] On July 6 Meighen expressed regret that all cable news reaching Canada came from New York 'censored from the American standpoint,' and as a result had 'an undesirable influence.' But no steps were taken to create an imperial cable service despite strong representations by Winston Churchill, the colonial secretary, and W. M. Hughes of Australia. As a result of these developments President Harding called the Washington Naval Conference on July 10, in the midst of the London meeting.

The Imperial Conference of 1921 put an end to imperial federation by renouncing the idea of a constitutional revision of imperial relations. It agreed upon a policy of continuous consultation and direct communication between the prime ministers of the United Kingdom and the dominions, with meetings 'annually, or at such longer intervals as may prove feasible.'[17] It supplied the first notable instance of a dominion determining imperial policy, and thanks to Meighen decision upon British Pacific policy was postponed, pending the meeting of the Washington Conference. There is no doubt that Meighen represented a Canadian public opinion which cut across party lines. In a debate in the House on April 27 Lapointe had called for Canada's exclusion from the Anglo-Japanese Treaty, while another French-Canadian member maintained that Canada should be guided by American policy and should form a defensive alliance with the United States. British Columbia also was opposed to renewal of the treaty.[18]

Although the conference had proved inconclusive, upon his return to Canada on August 6 Meighen spoke of the value of such meetings: 'Great Britain is the greatest factor in the world today for preserving peace . . . The influence of British statesmen in the councils of the world is greater because the Dominions and India are within the Empire and because she reflects, or wants to reflect, their views as well as her own . . . We must walk with the nations of the Empire or walk away from them . . . I believe in the British Empire.'[19] But on October 7 Sir Robert Borden observed in his lectures at Toronto: 'The foreign policy of the Empire remains under the same direction and influences as before the War, and that is not what we intended should be the case when we took our stand in 1917; it is nperative that the old conditions should not go on.'[20] There was ttle popular opinion on the question, although Bourassa, John S. :wart, and Lindsay Crawford urged Canada to assert its inde-endence. There was some feeling that a strengthened imperial rganization might conflict with the League of Nations, at the first ıeeting of whose assembly in November 1920 Sir George Foster, :. J. Doherty, and N. W. Rowell had represented Canada. Dr.). D. Skelton had already advanced the opinion that Canadian ationhood was dependent upon 'recognition of the fact that foreign ffairs are not something that can only be discussed abroad, but ıatters, so far as they concern us at all, to be debated first in our wn Parliament or considered in a parliamentary committee.' He lso called for 'clear evidence to the world that the British Empire f other days is now not one state, but many.'[21] Meighen himself ıaintained that Canada had a right to intervene in the Anglo-apanese Treaty, and to press for its abrogation in view of British nd Canadian relations to the United States, which opposed it.

The fact that the invitation to Great Britain to participate in the Vashington Conference had not specified representation of the ominions was a sore point with such pioneers of the new empire as muts and Borden, who protested against the American view that he voice of the empire in world affairs should be that of Britain lone—the same stand taken in connection with the League of Nations. The British government named four dominion represen-atives to its delegation of seven, but at Smuts' insistence the lominion representatives were finally given the same status as at the eace conference. T. A. Crerar, leader of the Western Progressives, leclared that 'we should be represented at Washington in our own ight or not at all,' while on August 11 the *Montreal Star* warned of he responsibilities of the assumption of separate nationhood.[22] Sir Robert Borden served as the Canadian representative on the British lelegation to the Washington Conference, which met on November 2, 1921. Mr. Balfour, the leader of the British delegation, went to Vashington by way of Canada, and upon landing at Quebec paid ribute to Borden and admitted Canada's immediate interest in the 'acific question.[23] Borden took an important part in the conference nd signed the resulting treaty on behalf of Canada. In his report o the Canadian government upon his return Borden traced out the rocedure by which both the diplomatic unity of the empire and the utonomy of the dominions were preserved.[24]

After the Washington Conference the tide of English-Canadian ıationalism continued to rise steadily. It was argued that by repre-entation at the Peace Conference, in the League, and at Washington Canada had given evidence of her growing independence. Inter-ıationalism was set up as the antithesis of imperialism, and much was made of the fact that Canada's interests, particularly in th Pacific, were closer to those of the United States than those c Britain. There were calls for the establishment of a Canadia diplomatic service, the choice of a distinctive Canadian flag, and th replacement of 'God Save the King' by 'O Canada.' John S. Ewar who had come out in favor of a Canadian republic in 1920, joine Lindsay Crawford, the editor of the *Statesman*, in calling for Canadia independence. A Daughters of Canada organization was formed i Toronto as a rival of the Imperial Daughters of the Empire. Arman Lavergne told a Kingston audience on February 5, 1921 that 'S long as we are a colony, until the glorious day when we fulfill th promise made in 1867 of making this country a sovereign and independent country, we must not forget that "eternal vigilance is th price of liberty."' At a Quebec dinner to Lavergne on Decembe 23, Bourassa observed: 'Confederation has lived. I do not know hov long it will continue—perhaps twenty, perhaps thirty years, perhap longer—but it is fatally wounded.' Therefore he held that th nationalists should not fight against Britain, but against 'Anglo Saxonism,' whether British or American.[25]

Abolition of appeals to the Privy Council was generally favore by English-Canadian opinion at this time, with some French Canadian support, although the right of appeal was generall regarded in Quebec as a safeguard against English-Canadia dominance. The appointment of Lord Byng of Vimy, the firs commander of the Canadian Corps in France, as governor-genera was hailed with satisfaction as having been made with the approva of the Canadian government. The Irish troubles provided th French-Canadian nationalists with new allies; and Lavergne Bourassa, and Lucien Cannon took part in the work of the Sel Determination League founded by Lindsay Crawford in 1920. A a meeting in Montreal on May 16 Lavergne called England 'th greatest murderer of small nations,'[26] while Bourassa addressed th national convention of the League in Montreal on November 7 fo three hours on the Irish question, which he claimed to be primaril a religious question and secondarily a minority one, which could b solved if the principle of majority rule were applied. This allianc provided new fuel for Orange hatred of French Canada, and gav new support to the old English-Canadian suspicion of French Canadian loyalty.

2

Upon his return from the Imperial Conference of 1921, Meighe faced the fact that his government must be reorganized and run th risk of election. In September he had added three French Canadian to the cabinet—Louis-de-Gonzague Belley as postmaster-general

Rodolphe Monty as secretary of state, and Dr. Louis-Philippe Normand as president of the Privy Council. These new ministers were undistinguished—only Belley had previously been a member of parliament—and they added little to the strength in French Canada of a government whose leading Quebec member was C. C. Ballantyne, who was unpopular with French Canadians because of his break with Laurier in 1917 and his support of conscription. Later André Fauteux was named solicitor-general, but he shared with his other French-Canadian colleagues a lack of parliamentary and ministerial experience. With the elections set for December 6, Meighen opened the campaign in Montreal in September, supported by Ballantyne, Belley, Monty, and Normand. He held that the protective tariff was the main issue, maintaining that the government's stand on the question was that of Laurier. He made an appeal for racial conciliation and concord, and urged Quebec to bury the past and to vote for the future.

Mackenzie King had also set the tariff as the main issue at Windsor on August 20, calling for revision of it; while Rodolphe Lemieux, the Liberal leader in Quebec, attacked the government's administration of the railroads and supported Lord Shaughnessy's plan for returning them to private ownership. Ernest Lapointe took an active role in the campaign, supporting King in Ontario and the Maritimes, as well as aiding Lemieux in Quebec. The keynote for the campaign in the latter province was sounded at a Montreal banquet to Lemieux on September 21, with Sir Lomer Gouin in the chair and King as the chief speaker, supported by Premier Taschereau, Lapointe, Senator Murphy, and Jacques Bureau. Gouin, who was being urged to enter federal politics, likened the present situation to that of 1896, and called upon Quebec to put its trust in the Liberal party. King echoed the comparison, and declared that Laurier's policy of racial conciliation was bearing fruit in South Africa as well as in Canada. Lemieux came out strongly for Canadian autonomy, saying that 'every interference in the foreign policy of the Empire leads us towards imperialism,' while 'it is here in Canada, not in any distant adventures, that our destiny is fixed.' He wanted no voice in British councils, trusting to the traditional policy of Macdonald, Tupper, and Laurier. King raised the question of autonomy again at Charlottetown on October 5, hailing Laurier as the first Canadian to demand that Canada be recognized as 'a nation within an Empire,' and characterizing Meighen as merely a follower of Laurier in this respect.[27]

On October 20 Gouin accepted the Liberal nomination in Laurier-Outremont, with the declaration: 'I want to go to Ottawa to make Quebec better known, better respected, better loved. I want all the sister provinces of Confederation to treat Quebec as nothing more nor less than their equal.'[28] His decision to enter the federal field was hailed by the Conservative *Montreal Gazette* with the observation that he had 'the respect, the confidence of all classes in Quebec,' and that he was 'solid and steady and sane in matters political.'[29] It was anticipated that a large Quebec delegation would enable Gouin to command the situation at Ottawa. This Conservative support was undoubtedly due to the fact that Sir Lomer had close connections with the financial powers of Montreal, as director of the Bank of Montreal, the Royal Trust Company, and many other leading institutions. Throughout the campaign the traditionally Tory *Montreal Gazette* and *Star* failed to support Meighen chiefly because he favored continued government ownership of railroads.

Lemieux took a leading part in the campaign, accusing the government of betraying public confidence, robbing the soldiers of votes in 1917, trying to establish divorce courts, bankrupting Canada, putting imperialism before Canadianism, and inviting annexation by extravagant policies. He made much of the conscription question, and revealed that Borden had offered Laurier the dominant role in the coalition government if he would accept conscription. Mackenzie King aided his Quebec lieutenant's efforts by charging the government with militarism, stressing certain recent shipments of surplus British munitions to Canada. Meighen defended his foreign policy at Montreal on November 4, arguing that 'matters which appertain to our relations with the world and the Empire should be treated by Canadians as a whole nation, and should not be made the subject of divisions.' He declared that at the Imperial Conference 'this country was committed to nothing whatever beyond what it has always stood committed to, nor was there anything said or done which went a hairsbreadth beyond the pale of what I said to Parliament.'[30] Bourassa, prevented by ill health from running, announced that he and *Le Devoir* would support independent candidates. He found all three parties unsatisfactory and opposed both Meighen and Gouin. Finally he came out in support of the new Quebec United Farmers' Party, founded in the Eastern Townships, which ran twenty-five candidates but found little support. Lavergne ran as a Liberal in Quebec County, proclaiming at Charlesbourg on November 6: 'I am fighting today, as I did in the past, for non-participation in the wars of the Empire,' and declaring his sympathy for 'suffering Ireland crushed under the iron heel of Engand.'[31]

The outcome of the elections was a crushing two-to-one defeat for the government, with Quebec, Nova Scotia, and Prince Edward Island going solidly Liberal, and the three Prairie provinces favoring the National Progressives, the new farmers' party. All the French anadian ministers were defeated, while the Laurier Liberals, Gouin, emieux, Lapointe, Béland, and Bureau won large majorities. *La atrie* held that the government was defeated 'because, being a war overnment, it remained autocratic after peace was restored; ecause, having no mandate, it made no progress towards reconruction; because it was antagonistic to Quebec. The Province of)uebec is splendidly vindicated.' *La Presse* hailed the great Liberal ictory as proof that Qubec could again take her rightful place in ıe government of the country. With the new Liberal government ependent upon Quebec's bloc of sixty-five seats, the *Toronto Mail nd Empire* on December 10 revived an old question by asking: 'Are ve to be governed on Canadian lines or just French-Canadian lines?' 'he *Manitoba Free Press* commented sourly that 'the Montreal istrict went solid for Sir Lomer Gouin, high protection, the right of he Business Interests to control and administer the country, and 'Down with Government ownership of railroads."' The *Orange 'entinel* on December 20 deplored the fact that 'French Canada is n top now, with a vengeance.' On the same day *La Presse* observed: Quebec asks that there be given to her representatives in the 'ederal Parliament their fair share, their whole share, of influence.'[32]

Meighen resigned on December 29, and Mackenzie King was worn in as prime minister, announcing that 'In the formation of he government I have aimed above all else at national unity. This nd I have felt would be served, and the federal spirit of our contitution most acceptably recognized, by according representation n the cabinet, so far as might be possible, to all the Provinces of 'anada.'[33] After her virtual exclusion from the government since 917, Quebec now had a lion's share. Senator Dandurand became he government leader in the Senate, while Lemieux was named peaker of the House. Gouin became minister of justice; Lapointe, ninister of marine and fisheries; Bureau, minister of customs and xcise; Béland, minister of soldiers' re-establishment; and Danurand, minister without portfolio. Quebec thus had five places in cabinet of nineteen members, and its influence was even greater han that fact indicated, thanks to its solid Liberal delegation in the Iouse. But the Liberal government, lacking a working majority, vas dependent upon Progressive support.

3

Canadian nationalism continued to make itself strongly felt, with tendency for withdrawal from European involvements. The new overnment's bent towards autonomy was indicated by Prime Minister King's negotiations in Washington for a definitive reaty confirming the Rush–Bagot Agreement and settling several outstanding Canadian–American questions. When Sir Robert Borde reported to parliament on the Washington Conference, it wa pointed out that the treaties would not be ratified by the King unt approved by the Canadian parliament. The Chanak Crisis in th Near East, precipitated by Kemal's advance on Constantinople i September 1922, brought up once more the old question of Canadia participation in imperial wars. Without any previous warning th dominions were suddenly informed by cable on Friday, Septembe 15, that a crisis existed and were invited to send contingents to ai Britain in resisting Turkish aggression. The press carried the new of the appeal before the official dispatch could be considered by th government. This timing was taken as an English attempt t influence Canadian public opinion and aroused wide oppositio New Zealand and Australia, at whom the appeal was primaril aimed, promptly agreed to supply the desired aid if required; but special meeting of the Canadian cabinet on Monday, September 18 decided that nothing could be done without the sanction of Parlia ment, which was then prorogued, and raised the question of whethe a special session was justified. In response to Conservative attack Mr. King subsequently declared that he had offered to hold dail sessions of the cabinet while the crisis lasted, but had been informe by the British government that there was no need to summon special session of parliament.[34]

In certain English-Canadian circles there was a quick traditiona emotional response to the imperial appeal for Canadian aid, whic was echoed in Protestant pulpits on Sunday, September 17, and b most of the press in Ontario and the West. Mr. Meighen, wh interpreted the despatch as a desire for a declaration of solidarit rather than for the actual sending of a contingent, urged at Toront on September 23: 'When Britain's message came, then Canad should have said: "Ready, aye ready, we stand by you."'[35]

The French press was generally opposed to any Canadian partici pation. *Le Droit* held that 'the duty of Canada in this issue is clear— to reply to England's request by a refusal.' *L'Evénement* observed 'As a party to the League of Nations and a member of the Britis Empire, Canada cannot be indifferent to any danger which ma threaten the Empire on any side, but otherwise the Canadian natio has no interest in a war on Turkey.' *La Patrie* urged the governmen to keep cool and weigh its action carefully, while *La Presse* declare that the matter should be settled by parliament. Bourassa took firm stand in *Le Devoir*: 'The motives for opposing any interventio by Canada in the Near East imbroglio are multiple and peremptory Some that come naturally to mind are: (1) Canada has no interest direct or indirect, in the region concerned; (2) Canada is in no wa morally responsible for the situation which has precipitated thi peril; (3) the European nations have at their disposal ten times the force necessary to crush the Kemalist invasion; (4) why should Canada, with a new outpouring of blood, consummate its ruin so as to expiate faults and obstinacy for which it is not responsible?' On September 29 the Saint-Jean-Baptiste Society of Montreal adopted a resolution that 'Canada, a North American country, should refuse all participation in the Near East.'[36]

Though the *Montreal Star* urged faith in Britain's leaders and the *Quebec Chronicle* held that the government would repudiate Laurier's principle that Canada was at war when Britain was at war if it refused participation, the *Montreal Gazette* was lukewarm about intervention. The *Toronto Star*, the *Manitoba Free Press*, and the *Farmer's Son*, organ of the United Farmers of Ontario, opposed intervention. Prime Minister King, irritated by the British government's failure to respect the new status of the dominions, took advantage of this divided state of public opinion to advance Canadian autonomy. He denied Mr. Meighen's charges of September 22 and 28 that Canada was bound by the Treaty of Sèvres, by pointing out that it had never become operative. The crisis evaporated early in October, but the constitutional issue continued to be discussed in Canada.

John S. Ewart produced a vigorous tract on *Canada and British Wars* which raised the questions:

> Are we to engage when our parliament says so, or merely when requested by a British government? Like bull-terriers, are we to fight when whistled for? Or, like intelligent human beings, are we to investigate and for ourselves determine (1) whether the stated cause is just; (2) whether, from Canadian point of view, it is worth a war; and (3) whether war is unavoidable.[37]

Ewart summed up his constitutional and historical argument with the following conclusions:

> That Canada, without hesitation or investigation, ought to hold herself in readiness to engage in war merely because so requested by the British government, is an assertion unsupported by reason and incompatible with the interests, the self-respect, and the dignity of Canada. . . .
>
> If Canada may, in any true sense, be said to be still a part of the British Empire, the relationship implies protection by the dominant of the subordinate, and not, contrariwise, foreign-war assistance of the dominant by the subordinate. If Canada is not really a part of the British Empire, but a nation enjoying a status equal to that of the United Kingdom, obligation can be created only by treaty. And there is none.
>
> Canada's status with reference to foreign affairs is in process of rapid development. Recent practice indicates that the statement 'When the United Kingdom is at war, Canada is at war' is not now unqualifiedly true.

Canada is situated in the North American continent. Her foreign policy ought to be based upon that indisputable fact. She ought to abstain from engulfment in the affairs—now more than ever perturbed—of Europe and the Near East. She ought to give no pledges with regard to future actions.

While Canadians will refuse to accept this last statement, I trust that there are very few who would agree that our government should have the power to commit Canada to participate in war without the authority of parliament.[38]

Ewart's views were radical in the Canada of that time, but they came to be held by an increasing number of Canadians as the years passed. The effect of Prime Minister King's handling of the Chanak Crisis was to leave the government committed to consultation of parliament before declaring war.

When parliament met in February 1923, the issue was raised again by the Conservatives, who called for the production of all papers dealing with the Chanak affair. Mr. Meighen made a plea against selfish isolationism, while one of his followers called for Canadian representation in the councils of the empire.[39] Prime Minister King blamed his failure to produce the documents on the British government's unwillingness to permit their publication. He explained his actions in the matter, and declared that the British appeal had been primarily intended for Australia and New Zealand. He concluded with a statement of general policy which reaffirmed Laurier's stand on the question.

. . . if the relations between the different parts of the British Empire are to be made of an enduring character, this will be only through a full recognition of the supremacy of Parliament, and this particularly with regard to matters which may involve participation in war. It is for Parliament to decide whether or not we should participate in wars in different parts of the world, and it is neither right nor proper for any individual or for any group of individuals to take any step which might limit the rights of Parliament in a matter which is of such great concern to all the people of the country.[40]

The prime minister's attitude was heartily endorsed by Robert Forke, leader of the National Progressives who held the balance of power in parliament, and by J. S. Woodsworth.[41]

An advance rather than a reassertion of Canadian autonomy characterized the episode of the Halibut Treaty, signed at Washington on March 2, 1923. This treaty dealt with the halibut fisheries of the North Pacific, and thus concerned only Canada and the United States. The Canadian government sought to have it described thus, rather than as a convention between Great Britain and the United States, but failed to win its point. It was successful, however, in having Ernest Lapointe, minister of marine and fisheries, named plenipotentiary with full powers to sign the treaty; and in insisting that he should sign the agreement alone, rather than in association with the British ambassador at Washington, on the grounds that 'The Treaty, being one of concern solely to Canada and the United States, and not affecting, in any particular, any Imperial interest, the signature of the Canadian Minister should be sufficient.' This marked a considerable advance upon the precedent of the Franco-Canadian Commercial Treaty of 1907, which had been signed by a Canadian representative in association with the British ambassador. The United States Senate, however, showed its failure to recognize Canada's new status by ratifying the treaty on March 4, with an added reservation covering the nationals of 'any other part of Great Britain.'[42] This reservation turned a Canadian treaty into an imperial one.

When the treaty came up for ratification in the Canadian parliament on June 27, Meighen objected to the government stand as emphasizing to the world a desire to dissociate Canada from the empire, while Lapointe took the ground that his objection to signature by the British ambassador had been based upon the principle acknowledged at the Peace Conference. The treaty was described as having been 'signed on behalf of His Majesty, acting for Canada, by the plenipotentiary therein named.' Probably because of Meighen's criticism of this formula, it subsequently became 'in behalf of his Majesty in respect of Canada by the plenipotentiary therein named'[43] in the Canada–United States Boundary Treaty of 1925. Prime Minister King's followers held that the treaty had been signed on the advice and responsibility of the Canadian government alone. Bonar Law, the Canadian-born British prime minister, declared that it was on the advice and responsibility of both the British and Canadian governments. Despite criticism from both Conservative sources and older Liberals[44] the treaty was duly ratified, and passed by the United States in its original form in the following year.[45]

Prime Minister King, who had steered such a nationalist course in the Chanak and Halibut Treaty episodes and was following the same line with regard to the Lausanne Treaty, issued a statement reassuring the imperialists before leaving for the Imperial Conference of 1924:

> It is my privilege to go to the Imperial Conference in the name of the people of Canada without a single grievance, to say that our relations with Great Britain and with all parts of the Empire are of the best, and that we have only the most cordial feeling towards all concerned. So long

as this happy condition prevails, friends of Canada and friends of the British Empire need have no concern for the future of either. To make it prevail at all times must be our supreme endeavour.[46]

With the tide of dominion nationalism rising high, there was no question in London of closer imperial union. The precedent afforded by the Halibut Treaty was extended to the whole empire, with the formulation of specific principles for the negotiation, signature, and ratification of treaties relating to the empire.[47] International treaties were to be dealt with on the basis of the Paris and Washington precedents, bilateral treaties affecting more than one part of the empire were to be based upon the fullest possible exchange of views; while bilateral treaties affecting only one part of the empire might be made solely by the government concerned. It was also decided that each dominion should make its own arrangements for defence and such contributions to imperial defence funds as it saw fit.[48] Canada objected to a proposed Imperial Economic Committee, responsible to all the governments involved, and not much was done to foster imperial preference. Sir Lomer Gouin and G. P. Graham, who had accompanied Mr. King to London, also represented Canada at the Geneva Conference of the League of Nations in September, with Gouin pressing for an interpretation of Article X of the Peace Treaty and playing a leading part in the deliberations. Philippe Roy was the Canadian representative at the Fifth International Labor Conference at Geneva in October. This participation by French-Canadians in international affairs helped in some measure to break down Quebec's traditional isolationism.

The question of Canada's national status was again brought up late in March 1924, when J. S. Woodsworth moved that the Canadian parliament 'ought to possess, under the British Crown, the same powers with regard to Canada, its affairs and its people, as the Parliament of Great Britain possesses in regard to Great Britain, its affairs and its people.'[49] The resolution implied that Canada should have the right to amend its constitution, the B.N.A. Act, which as an imperial statute could only be altered by vote of the British parliament. Reform or abolition of the Senate, in which a lingering Conservative majority hampered the carrying through of Liberal or Progressive measures, was also involved. Quebec's reliance upon British support against English-Canadian dominance was once more revealed when Charles Marcil and Thomas Vien reminded the house that Confederation was a compact, and that Quebec and perhaps other provinces would oppose any change in the *status quo* by which provincial rights might suffer from increased federal power.

At this same time the Lausanne episode, which was the third post-war crisis in imperial relations in which Canada took a notably nationalist stand, was coming to a head. On March 24 the Canadian government declined the British invitation to ratify the Lausanne Treaty by refusing to submit it to parliament. In a statement to the House on April 2 Prime Minister King objected to Prime Minister Ramsay Macdonald's assertion on the previous day that Canada had agreed to concur in the outcome of the Lausanne Conference. He took the stand that 'not having been invited, not having been represented directly or indirectly, and not having signed, Canada has no obligations. Therefore we do not feel it necessary to submit the matter to Parliament for approval; nor for that matter, to signify concurrence in ratification to the Treaty.'[50] In his government's correspondence on the matter with the Baldwin and Macdonald governments since October 1922, Mr. King had taken the line that the Canadian parliament would decide the extent to which Canada was bound by the agreements made by the British plenipotentiaries. When pressed for Canadian signature of the agreement, the King government insisted that the four essential features of the Paris and Washington precedents for such action did not exist. Canada had not been directly represented at Lausanne, nor had she signed the treaty, and hence approval by the Canadian parliament and assent by the Canadian government to ratification by the King could not be supplied.[51]

During the debate at Westminster in April and June the British government was censured for not inviting the dominions to confer on the treaty, with Lloyd George characterizing the course followed as 'a very grave departure' and 'a reversal of the whole process by which the unity of the Empire has been advanced during and since the War.'[52] On June 9 Prime Minister King informed the House that the reasons for not inviting the dominions had been given him in confidence—it was subsequently revealed that France had threatened to match a British Empire delegation by a similar one from her own empire—and declared:

> I have been taking my stand from the point of view of Canada a nation within the British Empire, not Canada a Colony, not Canada in any inferior or subordinate position, but Canada a country which has gained and which merits equality of status with other Dominions and with the Mother Country in these inter-Imperial relations.[53]

Mr. King held the view that while Canada would be legally bound by the treaty, it would not be morally bound, as it was by the Treaty of Versailles in whose making it had participated. Meighen criticized him for having acquiesced in a return to colonial status and for his unwillingness to cooperate with the British government.[54] The practical result of the incident was to leave Canada and the other dominions free to decide whether or not they would participate in any British action which might arise under the treaty.

Undoubtedly as a result of the criticism of the Lausanne procedure, the British government proposed on June 24 that a preliminary conference of United Kingdom and dominion representatives be held early in July to decide upon dominion representation at the London Conference on Reparations. In his statement to the House on July 17, Mr. King revealed that the Canadian government had insisted upon the Versailles and Washington Conference precedent being followed, and had requested full powers for Senator Belcourt as Canadian member of the British Empire delegation. He criticized with heat the fact that the press was better informed about how the question of representation was to be settled than he was. On the following day the colonial secretary announced the adoption of a panel system, whereby the British delegation was to consist of two United Kingdom representatives and one from the dominions, the latter to change from day to day. Dominion representatives would also be entitled to be present at the conference on days when they were not serving as active members of the delegation. The plan was characterized as a special one for the purpose of this conference, and not to be taken as a precedent.

Bourassa vigorously denounced the panel plan as absurd, and argued that if the British Empire were several nations, it could not act as one or six or seven at choice. L. M. S. Amery and Lloyd George also censured the plan in the British House, declaring that the world must take the empire as it found it, and that the status of the dominions could not be diminished merely to suit the convenience of other powers.[55] The question was to be discussed at a proposed Imperial Conference in October, but that gathering was indefinitely postponed by the new British government early in December after the dominions had shown reluctance about setting a definite date. With the naming of Colonel Amery to the Colonial Office in the new Baldwin government, a broader concept of imperial relations became dominant in Britain.

4

The concessions made to the free-trade views of the Western Progressives, who remained essential political allies of the King government, played a part in bringing about the resignation in 1924 of two of the most prominent members of the cabinet, Sir Lomer Gouin and W. S. Fielding. Ernest Lapointe succeeded Gouin as minister of justice, and P.-J.-A. Cardin of Sorel took Lapointe's portfolio of marine and fisheries. Though the Liberal-Progressive alliance was strengthened by tariff cuts, higher freight rates lost the government Western support, while Quebec Liberals showed a developing protectionism. The government called elections for October 29, 1925, in an effort to break the increasing political deadlock. The outcome made the situation worse rather than better. The Liberals won 101 seats, with the prime minister and seven of his cabinet colleagues failing of election. The Conservatives took 116 seats, more than doubling their membership in the House, but the balance of power remained with twenty-eight Progressives. Prime Minister King decided against calling another election or turning over the task of forming a ministry to Meighen, on the grounds that the Progressives were more apt to support him than they were the Conservative leader. His course was denounced by Meighen as 'usurpation of power and contempt of the public will.'[56] The defeated ministers resigned, with their colleagues taking temporary charge of their departments until parliament should decide the fate of the government when it reassembled in January 1926.

During the campaign Meighen had sought to woo Quebec by French speeches in favour of protection and development of natural resources. E.-L. Patenaude ran as an independent Conservative, backed by the *Montreal Star* and befriended by the *Gazette*, but criticized by *Le Devoir* for establishing a Quebec party to guard vested English interests. Bourassa returned to political life as an independent with Conservative backing, and was elected for his old constituency of Labelle. Lavergne served as chief lieutenant to Patenaude, but was himself defeated in Montmagny. The wartime curse still hung over the Conservatives in Quebec, and they won only four seats in Quebec, all in English constituencies.

At Hamilton on November 16 Meighen attacked the Liberal tactics in Quebec during the campaign, where he had been branded as a believer in conscription and a supporter of new wars. He declared: 'I believe it would be best, not only that Parliament should be called, but that the decision of the government, which of course would have to be given promptly, should be submitted to the judgment of the people at a general election before troops should leave our shores. This would contribute to the unity of our country in the months to come, and would enable us best to do our duty.'[57] And in the Bagot by-election in Quebec during December Meighen repeated these statements, which were criticized by his fellow Conservative C. H. Cahan and also by the Liberal Cardin, who found it strange that Meighen favored the policy of consultation in time of peace while he had opposed it in time of war. The Liberal candidate was elected, and the *Toronto Globe* pointed out that 'Meighen has bartered his birthright for a mess of pottage,' while the *Winnipeg Tribune* commented that Quebec had not been won by the new Conservative war policy.[58]

When parliament met in January 1926, Lapointe acted as government leader in the house in the absence of Mr. King. A no-confidence motion was defeated on January 15 by a vote of 123–120, with most of the Progressive members joining the labor and independent members in support of the government. In February H. H. Stevens made charges of serious irregularities in the Customs and Excise Department, in connection with the smuggling of liquor into the United States and of various American products into Canada. A parliamentary committee was appointed to investigate the charges. The House adjourned for two weeks early in March for reorganization of the government, and when it met again on March 15 Mr. King was back in his seat, having won a Prince Albert by-election.

On March 18 J. S. Woodsworth introduced a motion, occasioned by the Locarno Pact in which Canada had not participated, that 'Canada should refuse to accept responsibility for complications arising from the foreign policy of the United Kingdom.' Four days later Bourassa made a long review of Canada's imperial relations in support of the Woodsworth motion, which the latter had defended as not anti-British but anti-imperialist. Bourassa maintained that he did not long for secession and that he prized the association with Great Britain, but that he objected to a policy of 'servile worship of everything English':

> On the contrary it is by standing up in the face of Great Britain, not in a defiant attitude, but in an attitude of self-respect and virile admiration, asserting to Great Britain that there are certain matters upon which we can agree with her, and that there are other matters upon which we cannot agree, because they have interests which are not the same as ours and because we have trusts to perform and to hand over to generations still to come with which neither the Englishman nor the Australian can deal for us. We have a duty to perform by Canada; the Australian has a duty to perform by Australia; and the British have a duty to Great Britain, which no other country can perform. If we can only revive these principles, these elementary truths, in the minds of the people of this country or in other portions of the Empire, I am quite sure that this great problem of inter-imperial relations will soon be solved.[59]

Bourassa concluded by announcing that he would not vote for the Woodsworth resolution, which he thought rather narrow in its wording, but that he would not associate himself with those who denounced Woodsworth for raising it. He suggested the formation of a committee, made up of J. S. Ewart, Sir John Willison, Sir Robert Falconer, and Dr. O D. Skelton, to examine the imperial, national, and independent alternatives for Canada's future. He stressed that 'Canada was not bound by any obligation assumed by the government of the United Kingdom in matters of foreign policy, unless and until the government of Canada, duly authorized by Parliament, expresses its adherence thereto.'[60]

The gradual merging of English- and French-Canadian nationalism was revealed by the fact that Bourassa was now able to name four distinguished English Canadians who were at least sympathetic to the views he had long held. In fact he was not very far from the position taken by Mackenzie King at Wiarton, Ontario, during the campaign:

> Just as we have gained self-government in domestic affairs, so in foreign affairs, which are of direct and immediate concern to ourselves, we contend that they should be managed by our own people. In foreign affairs in which we have no immediate or direct interest, we believe these questions should be left to the parts of the Empire concerned. If questions arise which are of a character likely to affect all of us, then we say where our interests come in touch with those of other parts of the Empire, we should take our part in shaping the policy and having our voice heard.[61]

The thinking of both Bourassa and King on these matters had felt the common influence of Laurier upon his bright young men.

This became evident in a second debate on Locarno on June 21, when Prime Minister King announced the government's intention to defer any action on the pact until after the Imperial Conference that fall. He did move, however, that parliamentary approval should be obtained before the government ratified 'any treaties affecting Canada or involving military or economic sanctions.'[62] Bourassa, who had earlier in the session called for the production of the communications between Britain and Canada on Locarno, expressed approval of the prime minister's motion, but said it had already been violated in spirit by the withholding from parliament of these despatches. Arguing that one imperial foreign policy was impossible, he reminded the house that Sir Esmé Howard, Lord Grey, and Lord Fisher had recognized that the Monroe Doctrine must be the basis of Canadian policy, since Canada was British by historical accident but American by geography. Bourassa revived the old slogan of Canada First:

> From a Canadian point of view, or from a British point of view, let us serve notice to the world at large, not in any spirit of animosity toward Great Britain, but in full consciousness of what we owe to our people, that Canada is prepared to uphold morally any real move for peace which may be taken in Europe or anywhere, but that Canada is not prepared to arm her youth and to spend her millions for the sake of any foreign policy with which we are not connected by necessity and from which Canada is disconnected by all the exigencies of her natural situation . . .

> If we are to save Canada from internal dissention, from the turmoil of European politics or from American absorption, it will be by bending our energies . . . to make the different sections of this country one united people for Canada . . . To subscribe to undefined and unlimited engagements, or even defined and limited engagements which go beyond the sphere of our action . . . is wrong. There, I say, British, yes, but Canadian first; if necessary secession from Britain rather than sacrifice of Canada; Canada alongside of Britain so long as it is possible, but Canada first and forever.[63]

This speech was more forthright than the government's expressed attitude, but undoubtedly reflected it. The Western Progressive attitude was even more isolationist.[64]

The question of autonomy on the domestic rather than the international level was raised by King's adroit handling of the Byng incident in the summer of 1926. After several close escapes from votes of no confidence in June, debate on the customs inquiry precipitated the resignation of the King government on June 28. When it became apparent that the Progressives would no longer support the government, Mr. King asked the governor-general to dissolve parliament and call an election. Lord Byng refused to do so, on the grounds that the opposition should be given a chance to form a ministry. Mr. Meighen accepted the task of forming a government, but was faced with the awkward fact that the slender Conservative majority would become non-existent if he and his cabinet colleagues resigned their seats, pending re-election after accepting office under the Crown, according to constitutional custom. Meighen postponed taking the oath of office until he could get guarantees from the Progressives not to oust his government, and appointed a cabinet of six acting ministers to avoid the necessity of re-elections. Mr. King maintained that the government was illegally constituted, and on July 2 the Meighen government was driven from office by a single vote on a want of confidence motion. Meighen promptly sought a dissolution, which was granted by the governor-general, and elections were called for September 14.

The new Meighen government announced on July 13 included only one French Canadian, E.-L. Patenaude, who was named minister of justice, but Eugène Paquet was subsequently named minister of public health and André Fauteux solicitor-general. Meighen sought to wage the campaign on the issue of the customs scandals, and mercilessly exposed the maladministration of the department under Jacques Bureau and Eugène Boivin. King insisted that the unconstitutional conduct of the governor-general in refusing a dissolution to a Liberal government while granting one to a Conservative one was the vital issue, and declared that the election would determine whether Canada would remain a self-governing country or would be reduced to the status of a Crown colony. He denounced Meighen's course as unconstitutional. Both parties trimmed their stand on the tariff to meet sectional sentiment. Meighen was vigorously attacked in Ontario for his efforts to win support in Quebec by his Hamilton and Bagot speeches, and for his refusal to discuss at Toronto the issue of consultation before sending troops abroad.

Bourassa asserted at Papineauville on July 18 that 'either Mr. Meighen has odiously fooled His Excellency or His Excellency has made himself the election agent of Mr. Meighen.'[65] Denouncing his old Conservative allies as the 'Tory-Orange clique,' he later adopted the Liberal view that self-government was at stake: 'It is the slow but gradual conquest of our liberties which is in peril; it is the work of Macdonald and Cartier; it is the very spirit of Confederation in its relation with the metropolis of the empire which is being sapped at the present moment by those who falsely claim for themselves the traditions of the Conservative Party.'[66]

Patenaude supported Meighen vigorously in Quebec, asserting that stable government and a protective tariff could only be achieved through the Conservative Party, and giving his leader credit for reviving the party in Quebec. The Liberal spokesman Lucien Cannon and Raoul Dandurand charged Patenaude with forgetting his pledges and putting too much faith in Meighen's Hamilton speech, which had been repudiated by his lieutenants. Bourassa defended King, who was attacked in the English provinces for not having served in the war, though neither Meighen nor Patenaude had done so either:

> The crime of Mr. King is that he did not work to send our sons to the slaughter. In the eyes of those who consider that it is the duty of Canada to ruin herself for the glory of England, that is perhaps a crime. In the eyes of true Canadians it ought to be a reason for supporting Mr. King, to permit him to carry to the next Imperial Conference in London the expression of our sentiments and to speak there the clear language of the Canadian nation, faithful to the King of England, but faithful also to herself, to her sons, to her future, to her mission as a people in America.[67]

The disintegration of the two-party system was evident in the fact that 528 candidates contested 244 seats, with the Conservatives naming 233, the Liberals 199, the Progressives 20, the Independents 25, Labor 18, the United Farmers of Alberta 12, and the Liberal-Progressives 21. In forty-eight constituencies the Liberals supported Independent, Labor, or Progressive candidates to avoid three-cornered contests.[68]

The elections resulted in a Liberal gain of nineteen seats, a Conservative loss of twenty-six, while the Progressive, Labor, and dependent groups gained six more seats. Though the Conservatives polled practically as many votes as in the last election, Meighen and five members of his cabinet were defeated, including the three French-Canadian ministers. The final results gave the Liberals 118 seats, the Conservatives 91, and the new parties 36. Meighen's defeat was blamed by the Ontario press on his desperate efforts to win the Quebec vote, while *Le Devoir* saw in it 'a decisive, emphatic condemnation of the *coup de force* and abuse of power suggested to Lord Byng by Mr. Meighen or vice versa . . . It will be a long time before another Governor-General will do violence to the constitution and established custom.'[69]

Mackenzie King took office on September 25, with a cabinet which included six French Canadians. Quebec, which had proved the backbone of Liberal strength, had five places: Lapointe as minister of justice, Cardin as minister of marine, Lucien Cannon as solicitor-general, Fernand Rinfret as secretary of state, and Raoul Dandurand as minister of state. An alliance between the Manitoba Progressives and the Liberals was sealed by the inclusion of Robert Forke, the former Progressive leader, in the cabinet. This step broke up the cohesiveness of the Western agricultural bloc which had held the balance of power at Ottawa for five years. Meighen resigned as head of the Conservative Party, with Hugh Guthrie replacing him as House leader until R. B. Bennett was chosen as the new head of the party in the following year.

5

The verdict of the Canadian people on the constitutional issue raised by the Byng episode had an important bearing on the Imperial Conference of 1926, whose meeting had been delayed until October 19 because of the election. On his way to London Mackenzie King, who was accompanied by Ernest Lapointe, issued a statement in which he said that he favored the development of responsible self-government and disapproved of the interpretation of the conference as an imperial cabinet. But he stressed that Canada's course at the conference would be one of goodwill. On the eve of the conference, at a dinner of the Canada Club of London to Lord Byng, whose term as governor-general had just ended, both King and Byng sought to demonstrate that there had been no serious difference of opinion between them on imperial unity.[70] It was General Hertzog of South Africa, reviving the long-standing South African-Canadian alliance in imperial affairs, who raised the question of dominion status early in the conference, calling for 'in principle unrestrained freedom of action to each member of the Commonwealth; in practice, consultation with a view to cooperative action wherever possible.'[71] But it was known that Mr. King and President Cosgrave of the Irish Free State would prove at least as vigorous champions of dominion nationhood. A committee of dominion prime ministers under the chairmanship of Lord Balfour was formed to report on future inter-imperial relations, and the result of their deliberations was a document drafted in the main by Lord Birkenhead, the secretary of state for India.

The Balfour Report[72] was ratified by the conference on November 19. It was noteworthy for its new definition of the relations between Great Britain and the dominions, which has since become classic:

> They are autonomous Communities within the British Empire, equal in status, in no way subordinate to one another in any aspect of their domestic or external affairs, although united by a common allegiance to the Crown, and freely associated as members of the British Commonwealth of Nations.[73]

As a consequence of this definition, the governor-general ceased to be a subordinate of the colonial secretary, and was newly defined as 'the representative of the Crown, holding in all essential respects the same position in relation to the administration of public affairs in the Dominion as is held by His Majesty the King in Great Britain, and . . . he is not the representative or agent of His Majesty's Government in Great Britain or of any Department of that Government.'[74] Communications between Great Britain and the dominions now took place directly between the prime ministers, or between departments of the two governments by way of the new Dominions Office established in 1925 and the governor-general. This latter vestige of the governor's functions as a servant of the imperial government was abolished by the provision that the official channel of communication should be between government and government directly, with the provision that the governor-general should be kept informed and supplied with copies of important documents. No change was made in the method of appointment of the governor-general, already virtually made by the dominion government concerned in consultation with the imperial one. After the conference closed, Mr. King stated in the House at Ottawa that Lord Willingdon had been appointed to Canada after consultation between the British prime minister and himself.[75] This extensive readjustment of the theory of imperial relations, which realized the promise of 1917, was worked out in detail at the 1929 and 1930 Imperial Conferences and given legal force by the Statute of Westminster in 1931, which sanctioned the transformation of the second British Empire into the British Commonwealth of Nations.

This great constitutional development was very largely due to Mackenzie King's insistence that the governor-general should confine himself to the position which Sir Robert Borden had already assumed he occupied.[76] The right of each government to advise the Crown in all matters relating to its own affairs was recognized, while legislation affecting the interests of other self-governing parts of the Commonwealth was to be subject to previous consultation with the parties concerned. As for foreign relations, the principle adopted in 1923 was reaffirmed: each government proposing to make a treaty should give notice to other interested parts of the Commonwealth. Treaties were to be signed in the name of the King, as a symbol of the relationship between the parts of the Commonwealth, while 'it was frankly recognized that in this sphere the conduct of foreign affairs, as in the sphere of defence, the major share of responsibility rests now and must for some time to come, continue to rest, with His Majesty's Government in Great Britain.'[77] Lapointe, whose role at Washington in 1923 had raised so many questions, served as chairman of the subcommittee on treaty procedure. The appointment of Canadian and Irish Free State ministers to Washington was approved, though it was recommended that in the absence of dominion representatives, the foreign relations of the dominions should be carried on through the British representatives.

Canada took a very negative attitude towards defence questions at the conference, while on February 5, 1927 Mr. King rebuked Prime Minister Bruce of Australia for criticizing Canada's stand in speeches at Toronto and elsewhere on his way homeward.[78] Economic relations were hardly touched upon at the conference, thanks to the emphasis on constitutional problems. Mr. King replied to Prime Minister Baldwin's official farewell to the dominion prime ministers at a London dinner on November 27, observing: 'The charter of the liberties we individually and collectively enjoy may, to appearances, have been enlarged. In reality, there has been, as respects British political institutions, natural development along inevitable lines.'[79] And in a press statement upon his return to Ottawa on December 8, Mr. King declared that all doubts as to whether Canada had the proper authority to negotiate and sign treaties and whether or not Canada had a nationhood of her own were at an end. He held that the ties which bound Canada to Great Britain and the empire had been made closer rather than shattered by a larger measure of self-government.[80]

The outcome of the conference aroused mixed comment in Canada. The *Manitoba Free Press* observed:

> The heart of the declaration by the Conference upon the question of status ought to be clear enough to make it evident, even to the most skeptical nationalist on the one hand and the most purblind colonial on the other, that a new system by which the British Empire is to be made over into an alliance of free and equal nations has been established, and that other conceptions of the Commonwealth are out of date. . .[81]

But the *Ottawa Journal* minimized what it regarded as a mere crystalization of advances made since the close of the World War: 'We are no freer today than we were this day last week or this time last year, and for the simple reason that this time last year we were completely unfettered and free.' The *Toronto Globe* commented:

The most cursory glance at the statement made public forces the conviction that no effort whatever has been made to increase the bond of union, while every clause in every article of the Report contributes to rob the Mother Country of any directing power as head and forefront of the Commonwealth. Everywhere it is equality of the Dominions that is stressed, it is the autonomy of these States, not their partnership in a common cause and with common aims that is emphasized.

The *Montreal Gazette* also harked back to an earlier day with its declaration:

It is still the opinion of a great many Canadians that there can be no equality within the Empire without corresponding equality and responsibility expressed in adequate provision for the safety, not of the Empire, but of the Dominion itself. As things are now, Canada's dependence on British seapower is practically as great as it ever was, and that dignified and creditable condition seems likely to continue.[82]

Under their new leader the Conservatives sought to repudiate the Balfour Report. When parliament met in December, Guthrie suggested that the new principle that Canada had 'absolute control in every domestic and external matter' gave the Canadian parliament power to alter the constitution and to abolish bilingualism, 'sweeping away those safeguards which the Fathers of Confederation placed in our constitutional act in 1867.' He suggested that the Report might have to be amended when the government received the opinion of Quebec. He also maintained that equality of status conflicted with the facts: Canada could not declare war without Great Britain doing so, yet she would be involved 'as a belligerent the moment Great Britain made the declaration.' He closed with another warning of the future disaster for minorities involved in the Report.[83] Though Prime Minister King replied to some of Guthrie's points at this time, the main debate on the conference did not take place until March 29, when King reviewed its work. The Conservative leader opposed the government plan to commit the country to approval of the Report by tacit acquiescence, and moved a resolution of formal dissent. Ernest Lapointe discounted Guthrie's reiterated fears for minority rights:

We must rely upon ourselves for the safeguard and protection of those rights, working in cooperation and understanding with our fellow Canadians in this country. It would not be possible to secure the permanent adhesion of any section of the Canadian people to any plan whereby there would be any political force superior to their own government and their own constitution which would, even indirectly, have authority to control their actions.[84]

He added that in his opinion no change in the B.N.A. Act could be made without the consent of the parties to that pact.

Bourassa also discussed the Report, asserting that Britain still claimed the right to initiate and conduct foreign relations, since the dominions were supposed to have acquiesced in all treaties which they did not immediately protest. He criticized British foreign policy, but dissented from the view that 'Imperial partnership is not a fair proposition.' He argued that 'we cannot remain within the Empire and at the same time be a full-fledged independent nation. We might as well attempt to square the circle as to try and carry on a permanent policy at once imperial and national along these lines.' But he agreed with Lapointe as to the absence of danger to minorities:

We are manly enough to be prepared to discuss in the future with our fellow citizens of Canada, whether Protestant or Catholic, whether French or English, whether from the West or the East, every one of those rights which we claim to be ours, not because they are contained in a few articles of law in a printed book, but because we know that in the hearts of all right-thinking Canadians there is a desire to see that justice is done, and if we are to maintain that unity of which the leader of the Opposition has spoken, it is not to be done by declarations of law or the adjudication of a tribunal either in Ottawa or London, but by the desire of all thinking Canadians to maintain the spirit of Confederation and the constitution of Canada.[85]

J. S. Woodsworth, speaking for the labor group, warned of the danger of committing Canada to common action for defence, 'lest we lend ourselves to the manipulations of a group of Imperialists which is largely composed of exploiters.' He cited as an index of inequality Canada's inability to amend its own constitution. The Guthrie motion was lost on April 5 by a vote of 122–78, with the Liberal-Progressive and labor members voting with the government.

The question of abolition of appeals to the Privy Council, which was raised in the debate on the Balfour Report, was brought to the fore by a judgment of March 1, 1927, in which that body settled the long-standing Canada-Newfoundland boundary question in favor of Newfoundland. The decision gave Newfoundland 120,000 square miles of disputed territory in Labrador, including much valuable spruce forest and water-power totaling half that of Quebec. The decision was of particular interest to Quebec, since the territory in question formed an important part of Ungava, the hitherto unexploited northern Quebec region which was becoming of increasing interest as pulp and power interests expanded their operations in the province. The decision provoked some agitation for abolition of appeals to the Privy Council, and a resolution to that effect in the legislature. But the motion was withdrawn after it had been repudiated by Premier Taschereau, who had helped to present Quebec's case in London. The premier held that the Privy Council was an indispensable safeguard of the constitution and of provincial rights in particular. Both he and the leader of the opposition, Arthur Sauvé, expressed the view, in connection with the imperial conference, that the constitution must not be altered without the consent of the Province of Quebec.

6

The celebration of the Diamond Jubilee of Confederation on Dominion Day 1927 centered in Ottawa and did not evoke much enthusiasm in Quebec, which traditionally made more of its own Saint-Jean-Baptiste Day (June 24). The Saint-Jean-Baptiste Day parade in Montreal this year, however, celebrated Confederation and included allegorical floats devoted to episodes of Canadian history. In Ottawa, after the inauguration of the carillon in the Peace Tower of the Parliament Buildings, Sir Lomer Gouin, Thomas Chapais, and Senator Dandurand joined the governor-general, Prime Minister King, L. P. Tilley, Hugh Guthrie, and George Graham in speeches commemorating the anniversary. The Fathers of Confederation were represented by two sons, Chapais and Tilley, and the daughters of Sir George Cartier and W. H. Pope. Speeches were made in both languages, and both French and English music was played. Similar ceremonies were held at the provincial capitals, with Saint-Boniface commemorating the landing of La Vérendrye while Winnipeg on the other side of the Red River celebrated Confederation. Only in Nova Scotia, where one town flew its flags at half-mast and a Halifax newspaper continued its refusal to recognize Dominion Day, was the general enthusiasm lacking. The bicultural status of Canada was recognized in the recommendation that the French and English versions of 'O Canada' should be used in celebrations of the occasion, and by a special issue of bilingual postage stamps.

The Dominion-Provincial Conference which met at Ottawa early in November provided evidence, however, that all was not well with Confederation on its sixtieth anniversary. The conference discussed reform of the Senate, the amendment of the B.N.A. Act, provincial subsidies and representation, immigration, and company law. The result was largely an exchange of views between federal and provincial ministers, with no action taken and no resolutions adopted. Justice Minister Lapointe proposed that Canada, in view of the equality of status she had attained with Britain, should have the power to amend her own constitution after consultation with the provincial legislatures, with majority consent in ordinary cases and unanimous consent in cases affecting provincial and minority rights and questions of race and creed. There was a sharp division of opinion on this proposal, and the King government promised careful consideration of all the views that were expressed. The *Manitoba Free Press* on November 7 approved Lapointe's stand, urging that Canada should not remain 'in the anomalous and humiliating position of being the only country on earth claiming to be a nation, which has to have its constitution patched up for it from time to time by an external parliament.'[86] There were requests from the Western provinces for the return of their natural resources by the federal government and from the Maritimes for special financial treatment, while Ontario protested its heavy share of the financial burden of Confederation and Premier Taschereau of Quebec called for a clearer delimitation of the powers of taxation between federal and provincial authorities.

Public discussion of Canada's national status was renewed by election of Canada to the Council of the League of Nations on September 15, 1927. Senator Dandurand, Canada's representative to the League, who had served as president of the Assembly in 1925, expressed his belief that the election recognized Canada's nationhood in the fullest sense. He decried American comment that Canada was the puppet of Downing Street, and called her 'the spokesman of the North American continent's ideals.'[87] Prime Minister King interpreted the event as definite recognition of Canadian nationhood and an indication of international esteem for Canada. In an address on September 17 Lapointe observed: 'Canada has grown into full nationhood and now takes her place in the international Council of Nations while still proud to retain her position as an autonomous community within the British Empire.' The issue of whether Canada's obligations as a member of the League conflicted with her duties as a member of the Commonwealth continued to be discussed.[88]

When parliament met in January 1928 the question of status was again raised by the government's announcement of its intention to appoint ministers to France and Japan. The Conservatives were reluctant to see Canada assume new international obligations. R. B. Bennett, who had replaced Hugh Guthrie as leader of the opposition in the previous October, decried the doctrine of equality with Britain upon which the appointments were based: 'As long as the

Colonial Laws Validity Act remains on the statute book of Great Britain, we have no equality of status.' Bennett evaded a question from Lapointe as to whether he would join in an effort to secure repeal of this statute, but asserted his willingness 'to use every effort to see to it that this country shall maintain a status of parnership within the British Empire on an equality with other partners in the Commonwealth.'[89] In response to a question from Mr. King, he declared: 'Nationhood . . . involves . . . complete independence. I am not prepared for the complete independence of Canada.'[90] King questioned this interpretation of nationhood, and said: 'The reason that I welcome the equality of status as between the different Dominions of the Empire and Great Britain is that I believe it is the only basis on which the British Empire can continue and endure, and for that reason and not from any desire of independence in the sense to which my honorable friend refers, I am a strong supporter of the recent position of the British Empire as laid down at the Imperial Conference of 1926.'[91]

The two major party leaders continued their debate on Canada's status on the platform during the summer of 1928. At Oshawa on July 22 Bennett asked: 'What port is Mr. King bound for? If he wants to make this an independent country let him say so. Let us have a well-defined expression from Premier King as to where he is heading, what his chart is, and what his port.'[92] On a Western tour Mr. King replied to Bennett at Davidson, Saskatchewan:

> The ship of state is safely anchored in the port of unity, prosperity, and amity. I have designated the port to my anxious friend. Let him no longer be afraid. May I tell him that my chart is the development of the British Constitution throughout the entire course of its history, and my compass is the guiding principle of responsible government.[93]

In August Mr. King went to Paris to sign the Kellogg Peace Pact, and then to Geneva, where he was elected a vice-president of the League of Nations Assembly in September. After the close of the Assembly he returned to Paris, where at a banquet commemorating the opening of the Canadian Legation he expressed the hope that 'a Canadian Legation in France may stand not only today, but always, as a symbol, not to Europe alone but to the world, of that union of French and British minds which has made Canada what she is, and of a never-ending friendship between the two races, alike in the old world and the new.'[94] Later, in London, he indicated Canada's desire for British immigrants. Upon his return to Canada he defined Canada's international role at a Toronto banquet on November 22: 'To do our part in maintaining the unity of the British Commonwealth of Nations and to further to the utmost of our ability friendly relations between the British Empire and the rest of the world, and in particular the three great powers I have mentioned: the United States, France, and Japan.'[95]

During Mr. King's absence abroad Bennett had continued his attacks on the Liberal view of Canada's status and on the Liberal tariff policy. At a Montreal banquet on October 25 Bennett defined the aims of the Conservative Party as 'the maintenance of our integrity as a portion of the British Empire' and 'the safeguarding of our constitution and the rights of minority which are guaranteed thereby.'[96] Arthur Sauvé, the provincial Conservative leader, expressed his agreement with Bennett, while C. H. Cahan blamed the Conservative poor showing in Quebec in recent years on ethnic conflicts in other provinces, which offended the traditions and sentiments of French Canadians. He felt that the recent modifications of separate school regulations in Ontario, New Brunswick, and Nova Scotia had improved the situation.

With an increased American tariff in prospect, Mr. Bennett pressed the tariff question vigorously in 1929. He described the American development as 'a crisis in our economic history' and called for an immediate imperial economic conference. He denounced the fact that the so-called British preference of 1897 had been whittled down by various treaties and had reached a stage in which the average Canadian duties were more favorable to the United States than to the United Kingdom.[97] During the session Prime Minister King repudiated numerous Conservative calls for a retaliatory tariff policy against the United States as a result of Republican high tariff promises during the 1928 campaign, which became law in the Hawley-Smoot Tariff Act of 1930. Dr. R. J. Manion, a rising Conservative leader, called upon parliament to deal in 'a red-blooded Canadian manner'[98] with the American tariff attitude. Mr. King suggested that 'a cool-headed manner' was more appropriate, while Minister of National Revenue Euler deplored talk of 'immediate retaliatory measures.' Ernest Lapointe declared that 'we are going to shape our policies, fiscal and otherwise, at Ottawa' and that Canada would take care of its trade by 'British preference and treaties with other nations of the world.'[99] In reporting to parliament on the Geneva Economic Conference, Lapointe had favored international free trade, and had declared that if the American market were closed, tariff revision would be made 'only in the Canadian interest and not at all as a result of retaliation or tariff war.'[100]

The anti-American agitation aroused by the Conservative Party in its effort to emphasize Canada's British ties took somewhat different grounds in a Quebec whose particularism was irritated by the growing dominance of American industry in the province. Quebec's loss of its potential Labrador resources through the Privy

Council decision in 1927 was offset for the time being by tremendous pulp and power developments in the province, with the investment of over $300,000,000 of English-Canadian and American capital from 1925 to 1927. In fact, the development was so great that expanded facilities and increased competition brought about a decline of prices in 1927 and 1928. The largest single development was that of the Duke-Price and Aluminium Company interests, which spent $100,000,000 in the Lake St. John district. Popular criticism was aroused by the flooding of farmlands caused by the damming of the lake's outlet for the benefit of 'foreign' trusts. Premier Taschereau retorted that the creation of additional power at Lake St. John and at Carillon on the Ottawa would promote industrial development, which would keep Quebec's population at home and might even bring back those who had emigrated. At the opening of the new rayon mills at Drummondville on September 11, 1927, Taschereau stated his power policy:

> The way of success in this province lies in keeping our material resources at home, so that we can develop them here. The key of success is electrical power, so that those who wish to create industries will come here. Such a policy is eminently Canadian and national.[101]

Despite mounting opposition from nationalist sources, the Taschereau government was returned to office in April 1927 with a larger majority, the Conservatives winning only nine seats. In a statement on the result, Taschereau commented that the people had pronounced judgment on the ultramontane press which had opposed him: 'a judgment which should make them understand that the infallibility that they assume is rather slightly acknowledged by the immense majority of the Catholic and French-Canadian element of our province.'[102] The old *Rouge* spirit was not wholly dead, though it was more commonly evident among the young Liberals than in the leaders of the party.

The provincial Conservatives, with their strong tradition of nationalism, continued to charge Taschereau with being subservient to foreign trusts. During the Sainte-Marie by-election in October 1928, the premier replied to the attacks of Camillien Houde thus:

> Yes, there is American money in the province and it is welcome . . . While I and my colleagues are here, we will invite foreign capital to come and help us develop our province. The policy of M. Houde, M. Tremblay, and the others is to close our province, and to say that we will remain like Robinson Crusoe on his island.[103]

Again on December 10 Taschereau told the New York Pilgrims that the North American continent was 'a vast domain open to the spirit

. enterprise of every citizen, whether he be north or south of the 45th parallel.'[104] Houde continued, however, to exploit anti-American feeling among the people successfully by denouncing foreign trusts, and in July 1929 he replaced Sauvé as provincial leader of the Conservative Party. Houde's meteoric rise forced Taschereau to modify his stand in an address to the Quebec convention of the Investment Bankers of America on October 16:

> Americans are welcome here. We need their capital. Let it be well understood that when here, they will receive fair treatment and be placed on the same footing as our own people. But they must cooperate with us . . . public opinion will not accept being dictated to, nor our natural resources being imperiled, even for the benefit of a most lovable neighbor.[105]

Houde asserted both his nationalism and his anti-Americanism in a speech at Morrisburg, Ontario, on October 5, in which he maintained that Canada could not bow to the will of any other nation or of any other part of the empire: 'Canada is called upon to play a great role in the not very distant future in world affairs, and the Canadian people . . . must be prepared to be in the future much more than a mere hyphen between the people of the United States and the rest of the British Empire.'[106] Though the onset of the great depression was felt less in Quebec than in other provinces, unemployment became a problem in Montreal in the winter of 1929, and played its part in the election of Houde, who had become the idol of the masses, to the office of mayor in April 1930. Faced with all the problems that depression brought to Canada's metropolis, where the unemployed tended to congregate to benefit from public works and relief measures, Houde yielded his place as Conservative leader in the provincial legislature to Maurice Duplessis, a clever young lawyer from Trois-Rivières.

The tariff and questions of status continued to dominate federal politics. On November 1, 1929 Prime Minister King announced that an imperial economic conference would probably be held in Canada during the following year. He defended his government's non-provocative course with regard to the proposed upward revision of the American tariff, and justified it by the fact that the special session of Congress had adjourned without taking action on the matter. R. B. Bennett continued his attacks on low duties for American imports, and after the first of the year indicted the government for doing nothing about the rising tide of unemployment which resulted from the market crash of October and November. He coupled the issues at Calgary on January 9, observing: 'Thousands in the United States have been given employment fabricating Canadian goods. They've got the jobs and we've got the soup kitchens.'[107] When parliament met in February, Bennett pressed his attack, protesting against Canada 'being bullied by any power on earth'[108] as to its tariff, and against the government's failure to take steps to meet depression.

In connection with the report of the Conference on Dominion Legislation in London in 1929, he again maintained that there was no true equality of status as long as Canada had to go to Westminster to get its constitution revised. He argued that the constitution could not be changed without the consent of the provinces, and that they should have been represented at the London meeting.[109] Mr. King retorted: 'My honorable friend knows that any time we wish to amend our constitution or to get the power to have the constitution amended of our own right, independently of Westminster altogether, all we have to do is to present an address from both Houses of Parliament to the Parliament at Westminster, and that address will be given effect to in legislation at Westminster.'[110] The budget introduced on May 1 increased the list of British preferences and provided for countervailing duties against countries which raised their rates on Canadian goods. Mr. Bennett criticized the concessions to Britain as meaningless and the countervailing duties as giving control of the Canadian tariff to the United States. On May 6 the prime minister announced a forthcoming general election, in order that the government might have a fresh mandate before the imperial and economic conferences scheduled to take place in the fall. Mr. King's statement in a debate on unemployment on April 3, in which he took the line that it was not a federal problem, and that he 'would not give a single cent to any Tory government for provincial relief'[111] provided much capital for Conservative spokesmen in the ensuing compaign.

The prime minister sought to wage the campaign on the record of his government, the budget, and on representation at the imperial conferences; but unemployment, the St. Lawrence Seaway project on which he had not taken a definite stand, and the so-called 'five-cent speech' were the issues raised by the Conservatives. In Quebec *La Presse* brought up the old bugaboo of conscription, declaring three days before the election that a Conservative victory would encourage the British imperialists to propose conscription in the dominions at the impending imperial conference.[112] Premier Taschereau characterized Mackenzie King as 'a friend of our race' who 'respects our traditions, reverences all that we hold sacred, and merits your support.' He added that 'I have nothing to say against Mr. Bennett, but I must say I don't like his friends.'[113] Mr. Bennett's aides were somewhat too British-minded for Quebec tastes in the first campaign in which radio played a notable part and sectional appeals found a larger audience than was anticipated.

In British Columbia H. H. Stevens appealed for support of the Conservatives in order that Canada might become 'a unit of the Empire' and go to the imperial conference 'in a spirit of cooperation, unity and trust in the Motherland's statesmen.' Dr. Manion attacked the pro-American Liberal tariff policy, and described the elector's choice as one 'between Mr. Bennett, who is a life-long lover of the British Empire, or Mr. King, who suddenly discovers that there is a British Empire and is going out to save it to make us forget the period from 1914 to 1918 when he had business elsewhere.'[114]

At Quebec Mr. Bennett replied to the charges that he was an enemy of French Canadians and that he was an Englishman by declaring that he was a Canadian of nine generations' standing, and that he would not be there accepting hospitality if the former charge were true. He urged Quebec to support the Conservatives in order that its representatives might have a voice in the new government at Ottawa.[115] His platform had planks of strong appeal to Quebec. He pledged the Conservative Party to a protective tariff, the improvement of agriculture, the St. Lawrence Seaway, Hudson Bay and Peace River railways, the fostering of interprovincial and inter-imperial trade, a national old-age pension plan, and federal solution of the unemployment question. On the tariff his slogan was 'Canada first, then the Empire.' Mr. King's defence of the British preference as a solution of unemployment and his denunciation of Bennett's program as mere electoral promises were not enough to stem the influence exercised by Bennett's confident assurance that the Conservatives could check steadily increasing unemployment and his adroit exploitation of Canada's latent dislike for an overbearing United States.

7

In the elections of July 28, 1930 the Conservatives won 138 seats to the Liberals' 87. Under a Western leader who promised effective measures to cope with the disastrous conditions on the Prairies, the Conservatives gained twenty-three seats in that region, largely at the expense of the new farmers' parties. The decisive factor, however, was the unanticipated Conservative capture of 25 seats in Quebec, with the Liberals retaining 39 and Henri Bourassa returned without opposition as an Independent Liberal. The new Bennett government formed on August 9 included only three French Canadians: Arthur Sauvé as postmaster-general, Alfred Duranleau as minister of marine, and Maurice Dupré as solicitor-general. C. H. Cahan of Montreal was named secretary of state, while Senator Blondin replaced Senator Dandurand as speaker of the Senate, to which Rodolphe Lemieux had been named by the King government at the close of the session in June.

A special session of parliament, called to deal with the unemployment emergency, opened on September 8, but adjourned on September 22 in order to permit the new prime minister to attend the imperial conferences in London. In the brief debate on the address, Mackenzie King declared that the Conservative victory was 'much more apparent than real,' since it was based on less than half the popular vote, and criticized Mr. Bennett for combining the posts of minister of finance, secretary of state for external affairs, and president of the council with the prime ministership. J. S. Woodsworth criticized the 'protection craze' as a symptom of 'the postwar recrudescence of nationalism'; while Henri Bourassa declared that Canadian nationalism did not necessarily mean separation from the empire or enmity to Britain. He argued that nationalism was stronger than any party and any man or group of men.[116]

To meet the emergency, the government proposed three measures: $20,000,000 for unemployment relief by public works; a general upward revision of the tariff, with special attention to protecting key Canadian industries; and amendments to the Customs Act which were designed to end dumping in the Canadian market. Mr. King made no objection to the principle of the unemployment relief bill, but objected to giving a blank check to the government, with no time limit to expenditures under the bill. The government amended the bill to meet this objection, setting March 31, 1931 as the terminal date. The tariff measure was criticized as an attempt to coerce the House into passing without discussion the most radical tariff changes in Canadian history. Mr. King protested that increases in the tariff on British goods before the imperial conference were contrary to 'common decency and courtesy' and that such tactics would prove of little avail in winning an empire market. He also warned that the tariff changes would swell the movement of population from rural to urban areas and increase the cost of production and of living.[117] After Mr. Bennett had stated that he did not propose to go to England with this legislation unpassed, the tariff provisions were finally approved on the last day of the special session, with the understanding that discussion might be resumed later. Before his departure the prime minister announced that the office of high commissioner in London, being 'of a political nature,' should be held by a member of the administration; but that the ministers to Paris, Washington, and Tokyo would be regarded as permanent appointees.[118]

The Imperial Conference of 1930, which opened at London on October 1, was called to discuss inter-imperial relations, foreign policy and defence, and economic cooperation, with inter-imperial trade slated to receive major emphasis. The conference was also to consider the report of the 1929 conference on dominion and merchant shipping legislation. Before Mr. Bennett's departure, the premier of Ontario, Howard Ferguson, had urged upon him that the 1929 conference had ignored the fact that Confederation had been brought about by the joint action of the provinces, and that consequently no alteration of the B.N.A. Act could be made without their consent. Ferguson recommended that consideration of the report on dominion legislation should be delayed until the provinces had had an opportunity to discuss it and consult upon it. The conference adopted the report with few modifications, but its embodiment in the Statute of Westminster was delayed until the Canadian provinces had presented their views. The imperial government was eliminated from the appointment of governors-general, who henceforward were to be appointed by the King on the advice of the dominion concerned. The proposed Statute of Westminster repealed the Colonial Laws Validity Act of 1865; provided that Canada might amend or repeal all British laws forming part of Canadian law, with the exception of the B.N.A. Acts; and declared that any future British statute relating to Canada must contain the declaration that Canada had requested it and consented to it. The right of dominion parliaments to make laws having extra-territorial effect was expressly conceded.

But the chief concern of the conference was with economic rather than constitutional problems. Mr. Bennett, who at the opening of the conference had stressed the importance of economic cooperation, on October 8 proposed a policy of inter-imperial tariff preferences, which was approved by practically all the dominions. He opposed empire free trade, declaring that all that was helpful in it might be attained by imperial preference. His plan offered the United Kingdom and all other parts of the empire a preference based upon the addition of 10 per cent to the prevailing general tariffs. The British government, strongly committed to free trade, long delayed an announcement of its policy; but finally rejected Bennett's proposal indirectly in a statement on November 13, which promised not to reduce the existing preferences accorded empire products for three years or pending the outcome of the imperial economic conference which Bennett had proposed. The recent increase in the Canadian tariff on British goods and Bennett's threat of eliminating such preference as remained unless the United Kingdom accepted his scheme did not predispose the Labor government to abandon its free trade doctrine. The British Conservative opposition under Mr. Baldwin favored the Bennett policy, whose origin might be traced to the imperial preference agitation conducted for some years by the Canadian-born Lord Beaverbrook in his newspapers. Mr. Bennett was frequently called upon to act as spokesmen for the dominions at the traditional round of social events and military and naval displays; and on such occasions he emphasized that the dominions were now determined to manufacture their own raw materials, though he made much of the possibilities for British trade in Canada and was optimistic about the future of the empire.[119]

After his return to Canada in December, Mr. Bennett made a speech at Regina on December 30, in which he declared that at the conference he had been actuated by the interest of Canada first and had sought a more stable market for Canadian wheat in the United Kingdom, where Russian wheat was impeding Canadian sales. The British government had refused to alter this situation, but France for the first time had undertaken to purchase a large quantity of Canadian wheat. Late in January Mr. Bennett went to Washington with W. D. Herridge, whose appointment as Canadian minister to the United States was announced some months later. The prime minister conferred with the American president and the secretaries of state and commerce, but no statement was issued as to the result of these conferences. Mr. King avenged a long series of Conservative charges that he was under American influence by asking when parliament would meet, and speculating as to 'what would have been said if, before meeting Parliament at a time of serious economic distress, I had, while in office, found it necessary to go to Washington for an interview with the President of the United States, or indeed for any other reason.'[120]

When parliament met on March 12, 1931, Mr. King launched a vigorous attack upon the government's policy at the imperial conference, and upon its failure to fulfil its election promises of remedying unemployment and agricultural distress. He deplored the government's adoption of 'coercion' towards Britain, which had foredoomed the attempt to find a British market for Canadian wheat and had made Canada an ally of the Conservative opposition in England. He dismissed the imperial preference scheme as an attempt to build a Chinese wall around the British Empire, which would arouse the jealousy of other nations and would end in imposing upon the dominions the burden of naval armaments. He charged that the net result of the conference had been to intensify 'the very serious condition' in Canada.[121] Prime Minister Bennett defended himself against the charge of 'one-man government' which Mr. King had made, and declared that his stand at the conference had been the same as that of Laurier in 1902. His election promises could not be implemented in a mere eight months, but the government was endeavoring to fulfil them.

Bourassa crossed swords with his old aide Lavergne in this debate, with the latter arguing that Laurier had betrayed the Province of Quebec in 1896. Arthur Sauvé praised the prime minister for having put Canada's interests first at the conference, and denounced the view that the Conservative Party was 'the deadly enemy of French-speaking Canadians.' He cited with pride the Ontario premier's statement that Quebec reacted more strongly than other provinces against 'the political and social penetration of Americanism,' and Sir William Mulock's observation that it was equally opposed to 'the penetration of the revolutionary ideas of Communist agents who would induce people to look upon the French as strangers in a country founded and opened up to civilization by them.'[122] Later in the session Solicitor-General Dupré, who had accompanied Mr. Bennett to London, protested against the anti-French laws recently adopted in Saskatchewan and expressed the hope that they would be repealed.

The budget presented by Mr. Bennett on June 1 increased taxation, both direct and indirect, and raised the tariff. The Liberals protested that the taxes would fall most heavily upon those least able to bear them, and that the tariff would curtail consumption and exports. Mr. King observed that 'the promises of yesterday are the taxes of today,' and that the new tariff would build up 'an industrial feudalism' in Canada.[123] He called for a Dominion-Provincial Conference on taxation and a conference of business, labor, and public men on unemployment. Throughout the session the Western members pressed the government for a statement of its unemployment policy, which was refused until the Unemployment and Farm Relief Act was introduced on July 29. This merely provided for the expenditure of such sums as might be advisable under order-in-council, and gave such orders the force of law. Mr. King objected to the bill as a 'complete usurpation of the rights of Parliament'[124] to control expenditure, and finally forced government acceptance of an amendment providing for reports to parliament on expenditure under the Act.

A parliamentary investigation of the Beauharnois power project ended in the revelation that the power company had made campaign contributions amounting to $864,000, largely to the Liberal Party. Mr. King defended his administration's course with regard to the project, and declared that it was no function of a party leader to know who contributed to campaign funds. He professed ignorance of the payments made, and urged an investigation by a royal commission of campaign contributions in the last three elections. Bennett refused to establish such a commission, hinted that the Liberal leader was more deeply involved than he had indicated, and called upon the Senate to judge the actions of its members who were involved in the scandal. Action by a Senate committee of inquiry was suspended until the next session, with the recommendation that provision should be made for penalties against any member found guilty of dishonourable conduct. The federal government took over jurisdiction of the Beauharnois project from Quebec, and authorized the necessary diversion of water from the St. Lawrence.

As an aftermath of the Imperial Conference, a Dominion-Provincial Conference was held at Ottawa on April 8 to consider the report on dominion legislation. It agreed to maintain the *status quo ante* so far as the B.N.A. Act was concerned, while the Colonial Laws Validity Act no longer was to apply to dominion or provincial legislation. A new section to be inserted into the proposed Statute of Westminister was drafted and approved by the conference, but its final acceptance was deferred until the provincial representatives could consult their colleagues about it. Mr. Bennett announced that a future conference would consider how the B.N.A. Act might be amended or modified. On June 30 the prime minister introduced a resolution requesting the enactment of the Statute of Westminster, with the inclusion of the section adopted by the Dominion-Provincial Conference. Mr. Lapointe, who had played a part in drafting the 1929 report, supported the resolution, but urged that all doubts about Canada's right to amend her constitution should be dispelled. The prime minister replied that the provinces had already agreed to deal with the question at a future Dominion-Provincial Conference. Lapointe reiterated his views that 'I do not believe that the rights of the minorities in this country are linked with the legal situation as it exists now' and that Quebec was not the 'last bulwark and safeguard against change and innovation' that it was made out to be. He held that 'Canadians as a whole, in Quebec as well as in the other provinces, would not be satisfied with a condition under which they would be subordinated to another power outside the territory of Canada,' and that 'if Canadians are competent to make their own laws they should be competent to interpret them.'[125]

Armand Lavergne declared that 'equality of status cannot be reached and does not exist—we have to face the facts as they are—until Canada has the right to amend her own constitution.' He suggested that the vexed question of appeals to the Privy Council might be decided by 'having our own privy councillors advise the King on matters of appeal.' Though he reasserted his belief in the doctrine of 'Canada First,' he urged that Canada should recognize its duty 'by taxing ourselves for the maintenance of the king and the royal family.'[126] Henri Bourassa objected to appeals to the Privy Council, which he characterized as 'a semi-political, semi-judicial body,' as 'a brand of inferiority' and as an obstacle to the development of a true national spirit. He declared that 'the time will certainly come when there will be enough wisdom, enough sense of self-respect either in the provinces or the dominion of Canada, to find means of exercising that right of amending our own constitution by cooperation between the Dominion parliament and the provincial legislatures.' He deplored the fact that Canada, which had led the movement for autonomy, now lagged behind Australia and South Africa.[127] The resolution was carried without division, and after the approval of the other dominions had been won, the Statute of Westminster was passed by the British Parliament on December 11, 1931.

The measure shocked many Englishmen who were unaware of the gradual evolution towards autonomy which had been taking place in the empire, and the Labor government was accused of fostering the disintegration of the empire. Winston Churchill, the former colonial secretary, was one of the measure's leading opponents, while L. S. Amery, the dominion secretary who had fathered the measure in the British parliament, declared that the dominions were 'Imperial Nations which have risen gradually to a position and sense of Imperial responsibility like ourselves.'[128] There was a general feeling of regret in the British Parliament that it must abdicate the supreme authority of the empire, but the measure was passed 'to avoid giving offence to our great Dominions,' as Lord Buckmaster observed in the House of Lords.[129] This Magna Carta of the new British Commonwealth of Nations did not result in the disintegration of the empire which pessimists then foresaw, and it was widely hailed in the dominions. For some French-Canadian nationalists like Abbé Groulx, it marked Canada's achievement of independence; and he urged that its date should be commemorated as the national holiday rather than the anniversary of Confederation.[130]

Mr. Bennett, who on the day that the new British National government was elected had issued an invitation to the Commonwealth nations to meet in Ottawa for an economic conference, visited England briefly late in November. Upon his return he declared that the Statute of Westminster marked the passing of the old political empire, and that the forthcoming Ottawa Conference would lay the foundations of 'a new economic Empire in which Canada is destined to play a part of ever-increasing importance.'[131] Mr. King continued his attack on the administration's 'blank-check' legislation and on its shift from a 'Canada First' policy to an 'Empire First' one, which he characterized as a shift from extreme economic nationalism to an economic imperialism or isolationism.[132] Mr. King found fault with the government's failure to give the House an opportunity to discuss the impending imperial economic conference, and suggested that preparations for it had been left in the hands of the Canadian Manufacturers' Association. He gave warning that the Liberals were opposed to any tariff arrangement which would shackle the economic independence of any dominion or of Britain itself in dealing with other countries.

8

Unemployment and farm relief were the main topics of the session which opened on February 4, 1932. The Bennett government sought renewal of its blank-check legislation of the previous year, while the opposition waged a vigorous fight against what it considered a violation of the principle of responsible government by circumventing parliament's right to control expenditure. The prime minister was bluntly told by C. G. Power of Quebec that 'the place for him is in some South American republic where he can be dictator at his will, or better still in Italy or Russia.'[133] The government measure was finally forced through by closure. After an inquiry by a parliamentary committee it was decided to establish a national broadcasting system under the federal government, and a bill setting up the Canadian Broadcasting Company was passed with the approval of all parties on May 24. As early as 1930 Quebec had declared that the provinces had jurisdiction over the radio, and had never abandoned this claim, which was later revived. The Senate's investigation into the connection of Senators McDougald, Haydon, and Raymond with the Beauharnois project ended with the censure of the first two men and the resignation of Senator McDougald. The vote had been on party lines.

The Imperial Economic Conference opened at Ottawa on July 21. Mr. Bennett was elected chairman, and in his opening speech renewed his 1930 proposal, calling upon the United Kingdom to extend its tariff preferences on natural products and promising adjustments of the Canadian tariff in return. He also urged safeguards against unfair state-controlled competition. Stanley Baldwin of Britain urged the clearing of the channels of imperial trade, and favored the lowering of tariff barriers between empire countries rather than the raising of them against other nations. Twelve inter-imperial trade agreements were made during the conference, with Canada concluding pacts with the United Kingdom, South Africa, Southern Rhodesia and the Irish Free State along the lines suggested by Mr. Bennett. The conference passed a resolution endorsing Baldwin's principle as the best means of increasing both imperial and world trade. The conflicting interests of the dominions and of the United Kingdom became apparent, with the dominions seeking preference for their foodstuffs in Britain, and the latter seeking outlets for its manufactures, despite the determination of th dominions to protect their infant industries. No single over-al agreement was thus possible.[134]

At the special session of parliament called in October to conside the Ottawa Trade Agreements, protracted opposition was raise by the Liberal, Labor, and independent members, while the govern ment was also criticized for its failure to find any other remedy fo unemployment than the dole. The prime minister described th agreements as 'the first forward step in a definite scheme of close Empire economic association,'[135] while Mr. King maintained tha they were a complete reversal of the trend of imperial evolution fo the last fifty years.[136] The two leaders clashed repeatedly o whether or not the agreements were in the Canadian tradition Bourassa, who termed the measure 'perhaps the most importan piece of legislation . . . since Confederation,' attacked it as 'device to maintain the principle and practice of protection.'[137] J. S Woodsworth assailed it as 'an arrangement between business-men an those who primarily represented the interests of business-men.'[13 The Ottawa Agreements were finally approved on November 24.

A new political party, born of the depression, was formed at convention of farmer and labor representatives at Calgary on Augus 1, 1932. J. S. Woodsworth was chosen president of this Cooperativ Commonwealth Federation, an unhandy name which soon gav way in general usage to 'C.C.F.' The C.C.F. program, influence by the traditions of Fabian socialism and the British Labor Party called for the establishment of a planned economy, socialization o financial facilities, nationalization of utilities and natural resources encouragement of cooperative enterprises, and a wide range o social legislation. The United Farmers of Ontario affiliated them selves with the new party in December, and C.C.F. study clubs wer formed for those not connected with labor or farm groups. Th new party held that the Conservatives and Liberals were unabl to make fundamental changes in a bankrupt economy, while th Communist Party was pledged to bring about a new social an economic order through violence, bloodshed, and at least a temporar dictatorship. The C.C.F., on the other hand, in the tradition o Fabian socialism, sought to introduce a new order gradually b peaceful and orderly means. It failed in its first electoral effor in an Alberta by-election in January 1933, but came to nationa notice in February, when Mr. Woodsworth introduced a resolutio advocating the setting up of a cooperative commonwealth in Canad as a remedy for the depression.

Despite Woodsworth's emphatic denials of any link with Com munism, the new movement was attacked as Communistic by Con servative spokesmen. Mackenzie King had already deplored th division of anti-Tory forces between the Liberal Party and the C.C.F. in a Toronto speech the previous December, in which he had called for 'humanitarianism' rather than 'selfish nationalism' or 'jingo imperialism.'[139] In the debate on the Woodsworth motion he announced a Liberal program which had clearly been influenced by the growth of the C.C.F. movement. It called for a national unemployment commission, abolition of unwarranted new taxes on imports, promotion of trade with all countries on a reciprocal basis, British preference by reduction rather than increases in the tariff, abolition of artificial price control, regulation of investment, creation of a national central bank, abolition of Section 98 of the Criminal Code which threatened free speech and free association, balancing the budget, and an overhauling of all government costs.[140]

On the eve of the Dominion-Provincial Conference, which had been called to meet at Ottawa on January 17, 1933 to consider economic and constitutional problems, Mr. King attacked the government before a Quebec audience. He charged that there was 'a deliberate manoeuvre to bring about something new in the relations of Canada to the other parts of the Empire,' and declared that 'the real issue is whether we are going to change from the position of national sovereignty into one of imperial sovereignty, with imperial policies instead of national policies governing this country.'[141] Friction between different parts of the empire would follow the adoption of imperial policies. The conference agreed that federal assistance for provincial unemployment relief should be continued. Cooperation in the administration of taxation was agreed upon pending another conference, but no decision was made on the question of unemployment insurance, in the face of opposition from Quebec and Ontario on the grounds of provincial rights.[142]

The session, which resumed on January 30, 1933, gave most of its attention to reorganization of the Canadian National Railways, to the budget, and to redistribution. The government met with vigorous opposition to its stand on unemployment and other matters from the Liberals and the C.C.F., who exploited Western discontent with federal pressure on the Prairie Provinces, which were receiving large loans for relief purposes, to reduce their expenditures. Mr. Bennett indicated that he favored the reviving of Canadian titles, which had not been granted since a vote of the House on May 22, 1919 had opposed them. Quebec members pressed for a bilingual currency, but the debate was without issue.

After conferring with President Roosevelt in Washington in April, Mr. Bennett attended the World Monetary and Economic Conference in London in June. He played an important part in avoiding its breakdown by aligning the dominions with the Scandinavian countries behind the proposals of Cordell Hull, and also induced the British government to abandon its neutrality. He presided over the subsequent World Wheat Conference, and agreed to limit Canada's wheat exports for the ensuing year. Upon his return to Canada he defended his course at both meetings, and declared that Canadians had free entry into the greatest single market in the world, the British Empire. During a fall speaking trip through the West, where Mackenzie King had attacked 'Tory autocracy' during the summer, Mr. Bennett challenged the former to make good his threat to scrap the Ottawa Agreements when he returned to power, declaring that such a step would ruin half of Canadian industry. The prime minister stated that the government had spent $122,552,000 on relief since taking office, and announced a public works program to relieve unemployment. On November 20 he adopted President Roosevelt's practice of announcing government policy in a radio broadcast. He stated that the government's program for the next session would include the public works measure, a proposal for a central bank, and defence of the Wheat Agreement. At a Dominion-Provincial Conference in January 1934, Mr. Bennett vainly sought drastic curtailment of federal contributions to relief, endeavoring to shift the burden to the provinces. Since the provinces found their shrinking revenues inadequate to meet the growing burden, the existing contribution by the dominion of one third of the cost of unemployment relief was continued temporarily. At a second conference in August, federal expenditures for relief were reduced about 20 per cent as the total cost continued to increase.[143]

Mr. King campaigned actively in the three by-elections of 1933, which were all won by Liberals, and continued to attack the high tariff policy and to urge reciprocal trade with the United States. He also opposed the Wheat Agreement and the restoration of titles in Canada. The C.C.F. held its first national convention at Regina in July 1933, and adopted a manifesto calling for the establishment of a socialized economic order, socialized financial machinery, socialization of all industries and services essential to social planning, security of tenure for distressed farmers and the progressive removal of their debts, regulation of external trade, a national labor code, public health, hospital, and medical services; a foreign policy aimed at world peace and international economic cooperation, a new equalized taxation policy; and constitutional changes including the abolition of the Senate, assertion of the rights of freedom of speech and assembly, abolition of the deportation policy, and government responsibility for unemployment and the remedying of it. The Regina Manifesto was drafted by a brains trust of forty, led by six former Rhodes Scholars strongly affected by the ideals of English socialism. The document was denounced as revolutionary and Communistic by spokesmen of the two old parties, and savagely attacked by the press.

The political future of the C.C.F., which had been born of Western depression but was dependent upon Eastern support for national effectiveness, was threatened early in 1934. On February 25 Bishop Georges Gauthier, coadjutor of Montreal, characterized it in a pastoral letter as a dangerous movement, resting 'upon a materialistic conception of the social order which precisely constitutes the anti-Christian character of Socialism.'[144] Mr. Woodsworth, a former Methodist minister, replied a week later in Montreal to this utterance, asking why it was a sin for a Catholic to belong to the C.C.F. in Montreal, but not wrong for one to do so in Alberta and Saskatchewan. He denied that there was anything Communistic about the C.C.F., which guaranteed full religious liberty, autonomy, and minority rights. But for many years to come the C.C.F. remained under a cloud for French-Canadian Catholics, thanks to a confusion of socialism, in the papally condemned revolutionary European sense, with English socialism. Archbishop Villeneuve of Quebec, who was created a cardinal early in 1933 and thus became primate of the Church in Canada, was strongly opposed to the C.C.F., whose centralizing tendencies ran counter to his nationalist ideas. Henri Bourassa, the old nationalist leader who had often made common cause with Woodsworth in the House, had resigned as director of *Le Devoir* in August 1932, and thereafter that influential nationalist organ took a firm stand against the C.C.F. program under Bourassa's conservative and provincialist successor, Georges Pelletier.

From the opening of the session late in January 1934 Mackenzie King waged a vigorous attack upon the government and its measures, declaring that the recent by-elections showed that it had lost the support of the country. He moved a motion of no-confidence as an amendment to the address. The prime minister replied that the people of Canada were opposed to a general election in a time of great problems, and the no-confidence motion was lost after three weeks' debate. The government launched an investigation into Canadian business and economic conditions by creating the Price Spreads and Mass Buying Committee under the chairmanship of H. H. Stevens, minister of trade and commerce. The hearings aroused great public interest and support, and the parliamentary committee was transformed into a royal commission which continued its investigations in 1935. The resignation of Mr. Stevens as chairman and as minister was forced by the prime minister on October 26, after the former had released a pamphlet giving an account of the results of the inquiry up to the end of the session. Differences between the two men had already become widely known. After his resignation Mr. Stevens charged that he hac been thwarted in his efforts to remedy economic abuses by reactionary members of the cabinet.

On April 11 Prime Minister Bennett gave notice of proposals fo revising the B.N.A. Act, under which the provinces would relinquisl their jurisdiction over social problems connected with industry, olc age, illness, working hours and conditions, minimum wages, anc so on. Two days later he alluded to political factors which migh prevent such amendment of the B.N.A. Act, hinting at possibl difficulties with Quebec. The government leader in the Senate Arthur Meighen, referred to the B.N.A. Act as suited to the hors and buggy days of Confederation but no longer adapted to th vastly altered conditions of the present day.[145] At the end o August the prime minister sent a letter to the provincial premier giving a tentative agenda for a Dominion-Provincial Conference lat in the year, which included duplication of taxation and of healtl and agricultural organizations, as well as the already indicatec social problems, and the vital question as to how the B.N.A. Ac should be amended.[146] The proposed meeting was postponed indefinitely, however, after two or three provinces had displayed 'lukewarm if not hostile' attitude.

The 1934 budget called for a reduction of both the tariff and o government expenditures, while laying a heavy tax on gold production. These proposals were criticized by the Liberals as continuing the economic nationalism which had proved disastrous t Canadian trade during the depression. Much attention was devotec during the session to the Natural Products Marketing Bill, whicl conferred wide regulatory powers upon a federal marketing boar and the governor-in-council. The measure was criticized as dictatorial and leading towards regimentation of business, and finall failed when the government refused to accept a Senate amendment The government was supported by the C.C.F. throughout the debat on the question, and this alliance between Tories and radical provided much ammunition for Liberal critics. The unemploymen relief measure was passed after the usual bitter opposition on constitutional grounds, supplemented by criticism of wanton expenditure and irregularities in administration. Farm indebtedness anc credit extension aided the distressed farmers of the West, while $40,000,000 public works act offered further relief for unemployment. A central Bank of Canada was established under privat ownership, despite Liberal and C.C.F. arguments in favor of publi ownership. A government measure to pool the French translator scattered through the various federal departments encounterec violent opposition from French-Canadian members as a scheme t curtail the use of the French language. The opposition was led b

E.-R.-E. Chevrier, with some Quebec Conservatives joining the Liberals in attacking the motion. Bourassa and A. W. Neill led the Progressives, and C.C.F. opposition to the motion. There were stormy scenes in parliament, with the Quebec members singing a French-Canadian folksong and thumping their desks in protest whenever a Quebec Conservative voted for the measure. Alfred Duranleau, minister of marine, aided C. H. Cahan, the sponsor of the bill, in defending it.

Six by-elections in the spring and fall of 1934 resulted in five Liberal victories. Mackenzie King, who had actively engaged in these contests, called upon the government to resign since it was obviously losing the support of the people. Mr. King visited Europe in the fall to get a firsthand knowledge of conditions there in anticipation of a return to office, while Mr. Bennett also went abroad to represent Canada in the League of Nations and to discuss a new trade treaty with France. Upon his return the prime minister again defended the Ottawa Trade Agreements, but indicated a willingness to make a trade treaty with the United States. He also announced that the government would introduce legislation to implement the recommendations of the Price Spreads Commission, declaring that 'the policy of *laissez-faire* is no longer sufficient.'[147] In December Mr. King announced that if he were called upon to form a government, he would seek to increase British preference in the Canadian market and to lower tariffs affecting Canada's external trade. He also called for an empire-wide investigation of armament manufacturers, urging Canada to take the lead in a policy of peace by refusing arms, food, and credits to nations which disturbed the peace of the world. He denounced economic imperialism, which he claimed Canadian nationalism was being made to serve.

With parliament's life due to expire in August 1935, the prospect of elections dominated the new year. Mr. Bennett, a lifelong Conservative and capitalist, suddenly became convinced that the traditional remedies for Canada's economic ills were inadequate, and under the influence of American example, observed at firsthand by his brother-in-law, W. D. Herridge, the Canadian Minister at Washington, he determined to launch a Canadian New Deal. In five radio broadcasts early in January 1935 he announced a program of radical reforms which the government intended to introduce during the session. All involved government control over economic enterprise. He declared that the dole was 'a condemnation of our economic system,' and that 'if we cannot abolish the dole, we should abolish the system.'[148] Denouncing those who had taken advantage of faults in the capitalistic system for unscrupulous or greedy purposes, Mr. Bennett said his government intended to remove these faults in order to make such unfair practices impossible.

He accused the Liberals of becoming Tories, and predicted that a continuance of *laissez-faire* methods would lead to Fascism.

The legislation announced in these broadcasts and later in the speech from the throne on January 17 was designed 'to remedy the social and economic injustices now prevailing and to ensure to all classes and to all parts of the country a greater degree of equality in the distribution of the benefits of the capitalistic system.'[149] Mr. King opened the debate by attacking the prime minister's method of announcing his program on the radio before submitting it to parliament as unconstitutional and akin to Fascist methods. He declared that the proposals only touched 'the fringe of some evils of the system,' and did not go to its heart. He denounced control by capitalists of industrial policy, and argued that labor should be given a share of control. He stated that the Liberal Party intended to follow both the policies of state intervention and *laissez-faire*. He blamed excessive intervention in the free course of trade for existing conditions in Canada, with a million unemployed and 'a network of barbed-wire entanglements' hampering trade. Criticizing private control of the Bank of Canada, he argued that a government which had favored such a scheme could not be sincere in a program of state intervention. The government's much vaunted reform measures had long been a part of Liberal policy.[150] In reply the prime minister defended the record of his administration, which had brought Canada through the worst of the depression 'better than any other country in the world.'[151] He forecast a trade agreement with the United States and refuted Mr. King's charges. J. S. Woodsworth, the C.C.F. leader, criticized the government for waiting so long to launch reform, but expressed the hope that since the Liberals were pledged to it, that the measures would be passed during the session.

The Bennett New Deal was embodied in eight legislative acts which were passed by almost unanimous vote after much wrangling in parliament. They established an eight-hour day and a forty-eight hour week and banned child labor. A minimum wage, an unemployment and social insurance scheme, and a national employment service were set up. The Natural Products Marketing Act and the Farmers' Creditors Act of the previous year were liberalized. A Dominion Trade and Industry Commission was established to regulate and control trusts and monopolies, to check unfair business practices, and to adjust merchandising procedures to new standards of trade and production. The Criminal Code was amended to provide penalties for false advertising, for payment of less than the minimum wage, and for unfair business practices. The Companies Act was amended to eliminate speculative high finance from business and industry. A Canadian Wheat Board was established to control exports and prices. Legislation providing for relief, public works, credit for fishermen, rehabilitation of the Prairie Provinces, and a housing program was also passed. The budget contained slight reductions in the tariff and raised the tax on corporation and individual income in the higher brackets. Finally a National Economic Council, consisting of the prime minister and fifteen unpaid advisers, was set up to deal with social and economic problems.

As a result of the resolution by J. S. Woodsworth, a parliamentary committee was appointed 'to study and report on the best method by which the British North America Act may be amended so that while safeguarding the existing rights of racial and religious minorities and legitimate Provincial claims to autonomy, the Dominion Government may be given adequate power to deal effectively with urgent economic problems which are essentially national in scope.'[152] The provincial attorneys-general refused to offer suggestions to the committee, but many experts testified, and the committee recommended the early holding of a Dominion-Provincial Conference to consider the question.

The constitutionality of much of the Bennett New Deal was criticized by the opposition. The prime minister sought to avoid some of the constitutional difficulties by using the dominion's treaty-making power to ratify the 1928 conventions of the International Labor Office concerning wages, hours, and a labor code. Parliament thus assented to these reforms by resolutions approving the draft conventions of the I.L.O. rather than by specific legislation. Mr. Bennett held that the government was justified in taking emergency measures under the 'peace, order and good government' clause of the B.N.A. Act. His impatient attitude towards the courts under existing emergency conditions was much the same as that of President Roosevelt. Mr. King held that the reforms were *ultra vires* of parliament, but refused to oppose measures which he accepted in principle or to raise an election issue of violated provincial rights. Accusing the government of 'calculated unconstitutionality,' he urged that the constitutional issue be referred to the courts. During the session, from which Mr. Bennett was absent for three months because of illness and attendance at the King's Silver Jubilee, Mr. King exploited the differences between the prime minister and H. H. Stevens, accusing the government of insincerity in its reforms and predicting that most of them would be rejected by the courts.

During the Jubilee celebrations in London Mr. Bennett made an empire-wide broadcast in which he urged greater cooperation between empire nations as a solution of economic difficulties. Upon his return to Canada he denied charges that he had entered upon entangling commitments in England, and that his health would force his resignation from the Conservative leadership in the elections, which were set for October 14. After the appointment of Arthur Sauvé to the Senate and Alfred Duranleau to the Supreme Court of Quebec, L.-H. Gendron was named marine minister and Onésime Gagnon minister without portfolio, while Samuel Gobeil became postmaster-general. Further reorganization of the Bennett cabinet was promised after the elections. In a series of broadcasts the prime minister appealed to the people on the basis of the government's record. He claimed that his promises of 1930 had been fulfilled, and stressed the recent reform measures. Others, designed to correct rather than to destroy capitalism, were promised. During a Western tour he called for a mandate to renew the Ottawa Agreements and to make a trade treaty with the United States. In a final speech at Toronto on October 9 Mr. Bennett urged all members of parliament, regardless of party, to join with him in the task of putting Canada on a firm foundation.

Mr. King denounced this proposal of a National government as another form of dictatorship in a series of campaign speeches on the radio. He urged a repudiation by the electorate of 'the tendencies towards dictatorship manifested during the last five years,' and of all steps in the direction of Hitlerism, Fascism, or Communism.[153] He advanced once more the Liberal platform of 1933, renewed his demand for a national commission on unemployment, and pledged the Liberal Party to an immediate reduction of the tariff rates. After tours through the Western and Eastern provinces, he spoke at Toronto on October 8 with eight of the nine provincial premiers supporting him on a nation-wide radio hook-up. Closing his campaign at Ottawa on October 12, Mr. King denounced an election circular in which three manufacturers appealed for Conservative votes on the grounds that Canadian plants would be shut down if a new government deprived them of protection. He promised that the government would 'run the plants to find out how much tariff protection is needed to safeguard the interests of the workers.'[154]

The C.C.F., entering its first general election, campaigned on a platform which called for extensive socialization and social planning, and appealed for support from farmers, industrial workers, technicians, and professional men. It declared that capitalism could neither be reformed nor restored, and demanded a new social order. Its manifesto closed with the declaration that Canada must not be allowed to drift into another capitalist war and that Canadian neutrality must be rigorously maintained. It disavowed connection with the Communists or any other party. The Social Credit movement, which had swept Alberta in a provincial election in August, entered federal politics, with an active group in Quebec. H. H. Stevens led a Reconstruction Party which called for opportunities for youth, a vast public works scheme, a national housing plan, and fair wages and reasonable hours for all workers. The new party proposed an extensive program of economic reforms based upon the findings of the Price Spreads Commission.

With so many new parties, a total of 894 candidates, the largest number in Canadian history, were nominated, but the bulk of the vote went to the two traditional parties. The Liberals won an overwhelming victory, with a majority of 97 seats over all other parties combined. They held 171 seats, with 56 in Ontario and 55 in Quebec, while the Conservatives only retained 39 seats, with little strength outside Ontario. Social Credit won 17 seats and the C.C.F. 7, while the Reconstruction group only secured 1 seat. Twelve members of the Bennett cabinet were defeated, including all the Quebec members. Mr. Bennett accepted the verdict as an indication that the people wanted a change of government, while Mr. King interpreted it as a response to the Liberal protest against 'all forms of dictatorship' and 'endless and dangerous experimentation in matters of government.'[155] He saw the outcome as a mandate for 'the maintenance of British parliamentary practice and procedure and . . . the end of the superman idea.' The new government which took office on October 23 under Mr. King as prime minister, president of the Privy Council, and secretary of state for external affairs included four French Canadians: Ernest Lapointe as minister of justice, P.-J.-A. Cardin as minister of public works, Fernand Rinfret as secretary of state, and Raoul Dandurand as minister without portfolio. C. G. Power of Quebec was also named minister of pensions and national health.

9

Eight of the Bennett New Deal laws were immediately referred to the Supreme Court of Canada and subsequently to the Privy Council, where only three of them were sustained, the others being rejected as *ultra vires*. New members of the Canadian Wheat Board were appointed, and Vincent Massey was named to replace Howard Ferguson as Canadian high commissioner in London. In November Mr. King went to Washington to discuss the Canadian-United States Trade Treaty, which was signed on November 15. Three large public work projects were cancelled, while the government increased grants to the provinces for direct relief.

The Dominion-Provincial Conference held at Ottawa in December 1935 agreed to a substantial increase of dominion relief grants to the provinces, a census of the unemployed, the establishment of a Dominion Employment Commission, and the seeking of industry's aid in putting more men to work. It rejected a proposal to have the dominion collect and distribute to the provinces mining taxes, and agreed to a new Companies Act, designed to protect the public in new mining stock offers. It agreed that the taxation rights of the provinces should be defined, and that there should be cooperation on taxation between the dominion and the provinces. All governments were to reduce costs and to bring expenditures in line with receipts. It was agreed that Canada should have the right to amend its own constitution, and a continuing committee was to meet later to define a method of doing so. Agriculture was to benefit from dominion farm loans and a reduction of interest. A Trans-Canada Highway was to be built by the dominion and the provinces on a fifty-fifty cost basis. Various measures to promote tourist traffic were proposed, including the establishment of national parks in all provinces lacking them and the improvement of highways.

Parliament met on February 6, 1936 in the midst of mourning for the death of King George V. Pierre-F. Casgrain was named speaker of the House, and Raoul Dandurand government leader in the Senate. The speech from the throne announced that the federal labor camps would be closed as soon as expanding employment permitted, and that inquiries would be launched into the textile and coal industries in the interest of labor and the public. It also announced the government's intention to return to parliament control over taxation and expenditure, to provide for greater parliamentary control over the Canadian National Railways, and to reorganize and consolidate government services. In the debate on the address Mr. Bennett criticized the government's action in repudiating Mr. W. A. Riddell, Canada's representative at Geneva, for his stand in favor of sanctions against Italy. He also attacked its settlement of the Japanese trade dispute and its signing of the Canada-United States Trade Treaty, which his government had refused to sign on the grounds 'that for what we could get we were not prepared to give what was asked.'[156] He protested against immediate and wholesale reference of the reform acts to the courts, and defended the old members of the Wheat Board and their policies. He denied that he had had any thought of a National government in his Toronto broadcast, but maintained that all Canadians must work together to extract Canada from her present situation, which he regarded as 'serious in the extreme.'[157]

The prime minister attacked Mr. Bennett for the use made of the government radio during the campaign, and for burdening the Treasury with obligations amounting to $447,000,000, over the expenditure of which parliament had had no control. He defended the restoration of normal trade between Canada and Japan, and the inquiry into the textile industry. He contrasted the sales record of the new Wheat Board with that of the old one. Both the Japanese and American trade agreements had increased employment in industries and on the railroads. The latter was not a hasty measure, but one which had been arrived at after two years consideration by the experts of both countries. Mr. King declared that Mr. Riddell had exceeded his authority in proposing the addition of oil and certain other commodities during the discussion in a League of Nations committee of sanctions against Italy for its aggression in Ethiopia. He stated that the government had felt it necessary, in view of the critical situation in Europe, to make it clear that the proposal was an individual one and not that of Canada.[158] He declared that Justice Minister Lapointe's statement of December 2 censuring Riddell had been made after consultation with him while he was vacationing in Georgia. J. S. Woodsworth moved an amendment to the address regretting that the government had not indicated any 'definite and immediate steps to end the prevailing poverty and insecurity of the masses by making available to the people of Canada the great actual and potential wealth of the country.'[159]

The United States Trade Agreement was approved by a vote of 175 to 39 after much discussion. Under it Canada lowered her tariff to the 1930 levels on some 700 items, and received concessions on some 200 items which constituted about half her exports to the United States. In general the United States received most-favored-nation treatment in Canada, except for empire preferences, and Canada got the same treatment in the United States. The export of Canadian raw materials and the import of American manufactures was eased by the agreement, which was to last for three years, and was subsequently renewed in more extended form for another three years. The agreement marked an important economic rapprochement. What began as a return to the basis prevailing before the Smoot-Hawley Tariff and the Ottawa Agreements ended as a radical reorientation of the Canadian economy, with American trade displacing British trade.[160]

The Liberal electoral program was soon carried into legislation. The Bank of Canada was nationalized, and a Canadian Broadcasting Corporation, modelled on the B.B.C., was set up with safeguards for political impartiality. Taxes were raised while the tariff was lowered. Finance Minister Dunning called for a halt in the loans which had maintained the four Western provinces in recent years. Under a government-sponsored amendment to the B.N.A. Act, it was proposed to set up a National Financial Council as a permanent forum for the discussion of financial problems, and to establish provincial loan councils to deal with loans and guarantees. The measure was defeated in the Senate. A National Employment Commission was created under the direction of Arthur Purvis. The federal government provided $75,000,000 for unemployment relief, with a corresponding amount to be contributed by the provinces and municipalities. A National Harbors Board was given jurisdiction over the chief ocean ports. Section 98 of the Criminal Code was at last repealed, as was the 1935 Act providing for a National Economic Council. A motion for a joint resolution for amendment of the B.N.A. Act on matters of taxation and guarantees of provincial debts was lost on a straight party vote in the Senate, with its Conservative majority.[161]

For all its overpowering majority in the House, reinforced by by-elections after it came to power, the King government was faced with the same problem as its predecessor in passing emergency economic legislation within the confines of the B.N.A. Act, which had been drawn up before a centralized economy was dreamed of. Justice Minister Lapointe, Opposition Leader Bennett, and C. H. Cahan all took part in a 1937 debate on the question, and all favored amending the act. Lapointe saw 'nothing sacred' in the document, and was opposed to appeals to the Privy Council, which Bennett still favored despite the unfavorable decisions on his New Deal legislation. In 1937 a Royal Commission on Dominion-Provincial Relations was named, charged with drafting proposals for amending the B.N.A. Act, under the chairmanship of the noted constitutional authority N. W. Rowell, with Fernand Rinfret, John Dafoe, R. A. Mackay, and H. F. Angus as members. It began its hearings in November 1937 and concluded them in June 1939, after Joseph Sirois had first replaced Rinfret on the commission and then taken Rowell's place as chairman. Each province was asked to submit briefs of its position.

Quebec called for decentralization of power, and questioned the right of the dominion to investigate provincial finances. Its brief held that 'Confederation was a compact voluntarily entered into and it cannot be modified except with the consent of all parties.'[162] In addition to taking this uncooperative stand, Quebec's new nationalist premier, Maurice Duplessis, opposed a scheme for federal unemployment insurance in 1937, and at Shawinigan Falls on December 16 called for the formation of a bloc of the five eastern provinces, 'not to be run by Ottawa.'[163] He also cemented a virtual alliance with Premier Mitchell Hepburn of Ontario, already at war with Mackenzie King on the power question. Norman Rodgers and C. D. Howe, leading members of the federal cabinet, denounced this 'unnatural' political alliance to oust the King government and to replace it with one controlled by Toronto and Quebec.

The Duplessis régime also won unfavorable notice outside Quebec by its arbitrary Padlock Law, first applied against a Communist paper in Montreal in November 1937, and by its tolerance of Adrien Arcand's *Parti National Social Chrétien*, which held a convention at Kingston on July 3, 1937 and sought to become a national organization under the English leadership of J. C. Farr and William Whittaker. Kurt Ludecke, who had been charged by Rosenberg with representing the political interests of the Nazi Party in the United States, Canada, and Mexico in September 1932, had persuaded Arcand to convert his '*Ordre Patriotique des Goglus*,' which the Nazi agent described as 'a violently anti-Jewish, in the main Catholic folkic movement . . . with three publications, all very demagogic and clever,'[164] into a shirt movement modeled on the Nazi Party. According to Ludecke, Arcand was 'greatly pleased when I gave him an autographed photograph of Hitler. We understood each other perfectly and agreed to cooperate in every way.'[165]

While the C.C.F. sought disallowance by the federal government of the Padlock Law as a violation of civil liberties, thus making new enemies for itself in a Quebec which was eager to crush Communism by any means, the *Toronto Globe and Mail* ran a series of articles on Arcand's group which helped to convince many English Canadians that Quebec was dominated by 'clerical Fascists.' The charges were echoed by the New York *Nation* and other liberal publications.[166] This impression was furthered by the prevalence of pro-Franco sympathies in Quebec, while English Canadians generally sympathized with the Spanish Republicans; and by the prestige of both Mussolini and Franco with the clergy of Quebec, who reserved their highest regard, however, for Salazar, the scholarly dictator of Portugal who had introduced the corporative economic system recommended by the papal encyclicals. These views of the élite had wide backing, as was indicated by the fact that the Liberal *Le Soleil*, the Conservative *La Patrie*, the nationalist *Le Devoir*, and the maverick *La Renaissance* all had opposed sanctions against Italy. Jean-Charles Harvey's *Le Jour* was about the only French paper to adopt the vigorous anti-Fascist line of much of the English press.

Premier Duplessis refused the invitation of Ernest Lapointe to confer on the Padlock Law. The federal minister of justice subsequently made a report on the law, in which he favored neither disallowance nor reference to the Supreme Court of Canada, and observed that most of the protests against it came from outside Quebec. Quebec, which always bitterly resents a bad press outside the province and assigns it to Masonic or Communistic conspiracies, was indignant at this interference in provincial affairs, and also at the publicity given to the Textile Industrial Inquiry, which revealed that wage standards in Quebec were much lower than in the other provinces.[167]

The government did not break its silence on foreign policy until four months after its stand on the Riddell incident had been criticized by both the Conservative and C.C.F. leaders. On June 18, 1936 Prime Minister King made a notable speech[168] on foreign affairs in which he announced the government's decision to end sanctions against Italy—on the same day as Britain took the same step, but as result of an independent decision made earlier. He stressed the need for more discussion of Canada's foreign relations than there had been in the past because of a colonial attitude of mind, relative immunity from the danger of war, internal preoccupations, and 'the unparalleled complexity of our position as a member of the League, a member of the British Commonwealth of Nations and one of the nations of the American continent.' He stated that after the Riddell episode the government had twice instructed its representative at Geneva to vote for the inclusion of oil sanctions if the proposal met general support, but 'collective bluffing cannot bring collective security, and under present conditions most countries have shown they are not prepared to make firm commitments beyond the range of their immediate interest.' As for the future, though Canada was 'fortunate both in its neighbors and in its lack of neighbors' it could not isolate itself from world affairs because international trade was essential to its economy. In view of the League's record, Canada could not make 'binding commitments to use economic force or military force': 'Occasions may arise where military action may become advisable or essential, but so far as Canada is concerned, that would be for the parliament of Canada to decide in the light of all the circumstances at the time.' He warned that 'there is no danger to our national unity and our economic recovery so serious as participation in a prolonged war,' and urged that Canada should continue to work through the League for the ideal of world peace.

J. S. Woodsworth largely agreed with the prime minister's views, but argued that 'we should let Great Britain know now, not later when she may become involved in some war, that she need not count us in.'[169] R. B. Bennett suggested that Canada might have associated herself with South Africa in continuing sanctions; expressed the opinion that the League was a failure; and urged that 'the greatest assurance we have for the maintenance of our peace lies in the strengthening of every tie that binds the commonwealth of nations, the members of the British empire.'[170] Paul Martin, a young Ontario Liberal making his maiden speech, suggested that Canada might participate in the advisory conferences of the Pan-American Union, as well as work to strengthen the League,[171] thus echoing Bourassa's suggestion of April 1, 1935.[172]

Canada's new North American orientation was fostered by events during the summer and fall. Prime Minister King joined Lord Tweedsmuir, the new governor-general, and the provincial authorities in warmly welcoming President Roosevelt to Quebec on July 31. Both Lord Tweedsmuir and Mr. Roosevelt expressed the hope that the friendly relationship between the two countries would serve as a model to the troubled world. It was noteworthy that in his subsequent

Chautauqua speech of August 14, President Roosevelt declared that while the United States desired friendship with all nations, it was prepared if need be to defend itself and its neighbors against aggression.[173]

In September Mr. King represented Canada at the League of Nations Assembly, and in a statement before his departure for Europe called for faith in the League and in the ideal of world peace. He admitted that economic action against aggressors would have to be backed in the last analysis by armed force, but declared that in the latter case, 'that would be for the Parliament of Canada to decide in the light of the circumstances at the time.'[174] He emphasized that Canada desired friendship with all nations. In his address to the plenary session on September 29 Mr. King professed Canada's adherence to the fundamental principles of the League, and to the policy of live and let live as far as doctrines and forms of government were concerned. As for the question of an automatic obligation to use force in international disputes, he cited Canada's attitude in Commonwealth affairs: 'The Canadian Parliament reserves to itself the right to declare in the light of the circumstances existing at the time to what extent, if at all, Canada will participate in conflicts wherein other members of the Commonwealth may be engaged.'[175] He opposed amendment of the League Covenant as neither 'possible nor necessary,' citing the record of broken pledges among League members. After leaving Geneva, the prime minister discussed trade agreements in Paris and London. Upon his return to Ottawa he declared that Canada's greatest contribution to world peace would be to put her own house in order and to maintain friendly relations with other countries. He heartily endorsed on behalf of Canadians President Roosevelt's declaration at the Inter-American Conference at Rio de Janeiro that the United States would oppose any invasion of the New World.

But despite the prime minister's cautious course, Canada was stirred by the darkening European situation. The split between French and English Canadians on the question of sanctions against Italy was widened by the divergence of their views on the Spanish Civil War. Isolationism was generally widespread in both groups, but its basis was very different, as became evident in the foreign policy debate opened by J. S. Woodsworth's neutrality resolution, introduced on January 25, 1937. The English-Canadian isolationists regarded the Abyssinian affair as a clash of rival European imperialisms, in which the League was used merely as windowdressing. They approved Mr. Lapointe's statement on oil sanctions as in accord with true Canadian policy, while they accused John W. Dafoe and N. W. Rowell, the leading advocates of sanctions, of being unconscious 'bell-wethers for British Imperialism.'[176] French-Canadian isolationists dismissed the League as a creation of Freemasons and atheists, dominated by Protestant Britain and anti-clerical France at the expense of Catholic Italy. Italian propagandists, who were active in Montreal, had revived the memory of the South African War, and accused Britain of 'Anglo-Saxon hypocrisy.' According to Jean Bruchési: 'If the Province of Quebec had to make the decision alone she certainly would not have adopted the line of conduct which was actually followed. With practical unanimity our French-Canadian press refused to dissimulate its sympathy with Italy by reason of sanctions; and when Mr. Riddell, at the behest of London we reasonably conclude, demanded severer sanctions against Rome, there arose a veritable storm of protest.'[177] Quebec felt the same sympathy for General Franco's 'crusade' in Spain as it had for Italy; in both instances it saw an alignment of the 'Anglo-Saxon' and Protestant powers against the Latin and Catholic countries with which it felt an increasing bond as a result of the racist views which had dominated the teaching of French-Canadian history since 1917.

Mr. Woodsworth's resolution, which embodied the policy adopted by the C.C.F. at a Toronto convention in August 1936, involved three points:

1. That under existing international relations, in the event of war, Canada should remain strictly neutral regardless of who the belligerents may be.
2. That at no time should Canadian citizens be permitted to make profits out of supplying war munitions or materials.
3. That the Canadian government should make every effort to discover and remove the causes of international friction and social injustice.[178]

The resolution was occasioned by the 70 per cent increase in the defence estimates tabled at the opening of the session. Though the government maintained that increased armament was necessary to protect Canadian neutrality, Mr. Woodsworth feared that Canada might be drawn into another war 'to assist in the defence of the Empire.' He urged that Canada should determine its foreign policy now, rather than await a crisis, since 'the oncoming of a war, which might mean our participation, would split this country from stem to stern.' Since there was very strong sentiment in Quebec against 'being dragged into another war,' he suggested that the French-Canadian members should declare the sentiments of their province and join his party in questioning whether these increased expenditures were being made for Canada's defence or for future participation in a European war. He declared that the League had failed; Canada should have complete control over her foreign policy; and that for defence she could rely for protection upon the United States, since she lived in a fireproof area. The Woodsworth resolution was supported by some Quebec Liberals, headed by Wilfrid Lacroix, Maxime Raymond, and Wilfrid Gariépy.[179]

In his reply Mr. King accepted the third point completely, partially agreed with the second, and totally rejected the first. He declared that the increase in the defence estimates had been made 'only and solely because of what the government believes to be necessary for the defence of Canada, and for Canada alone. The estimates have not been framed with any thought of participation in European wars.'[180] He denied that they had been influenced by the British government. The prime minister objected to the first point on the grounds that 'it binds the hands of Parliament completely.' It was the policy of his government that 'Parliament must be free to decide its attitude in the light of the circumstances as they may exist at the time. Parliament acting for the people is the supreme authority in the state with respect to all matters, and certainly with respect to what is most vital to the nation, namely, the question of whether or not it shall be involved in war . . . in deciding matters of this kind, as the representatives of the people parliament shall be the voice of the nation; parliament shall decide.'[181] In response to Mr. Woodsworth's questions, the prime minister declared that parliament alone could commit Canada to war or authorize the sending of troops out of the country. He expressed the view that most Canadians adhered to a middle way between 'thorough-going imperialism' and 'regardless nationalism': 'They believe in deciding questions relating to defence or foreign policy by reference to what is Canada's interest. Decisions must be made by Canada primarily in the interests of Canada.'[182] He urged the need of national unity, unity with the Commonwealth, and unity among all the English-speaking nations. A declaration of Canadian neutrality at the present time would merely encourage 'those forces that are ready to oppose Canada, to oppose the British commonwealth of nations, to oppose the English-speaking peoples, and that have their hand out against democracy and democratic institutions.'[183]

Miss Agnes MacPhail of the United Farmers of Ontario supported the resolution. She praised the prime minister's Geneva speech, stressed the development of a Canadian national spirit, and regretted that Canada had not attended the Inter-American Conference at Buenos Aires. The prime minister explained that Canada had not been invited. T. C. Douglas of the C.C.F. supported the resolution, criticizing the prime minister's trend towards isolationism and urging collective action against war by economic sanctions. He particularly stressed Canadian sales of nickel to potential aggressors. On February 4 he presented a motion calling for the conscription of finance, industry, transportation, and natural resources in the event of war.[184] Denton Massey, the only Conservative to speak in the debate, opposed both isolation and neutrality, deplored disunity, and speculated as to the price for American protection.[185]

Justice Minister Lapointe opposed the motion because in his opinion it would involve a withdrawal from the League of Nations and the British Commonwealth. He declared that 'Canada should not spend one life or one cent' in support of either Fascism or Communism. But Canada should be ready to defend itself, for 'If international chiefs or gangsters ever come to assail us on a mad impulse—because the world is mad at the present time—we cannot meet them with a declaration of neutrality.'[186] He repeated the statement that he had made during the fight against conscription in 1917: that the French Canadians were 'prepared to do anything for the defence of Canada.' He added: 'But I do not think that our people would like to be involved in a war that might be waged between communism and fascism, because they hate both.' He concluded by stating: 'We are not committed; we shall decide when the time comes whether we shall participate or not, and I trust the circumstances will justify Canada in remaining outside any conflict. But we want to reserve our freedom and our independence as free men should and not be committed by any resolution. . . .'[187]

H.-E. Brunelle (Champlain) seconded Miss MacPhail's proposal that Canadians should cultivate a North American rather than a European mentality. He favored neutrality, if it were compatible 'with our obligations, our honour and our national protection.'[188] He felt that Canada was exposed to attack as part of the empire. Separation would increase the cost of defence. Reliance on the protection of the United States would end in annexation. Canada in any case could not defend herself against serious attack, but 'should have some kind of an army, in the same way that every city needs a police force.'[189] Brunelle was more worried about the danger of Communist revolution at home than aggression from abroad. Vital Mallette (Jacques-Cartier) stressed Quebec's opposition to imperialist wars and her opinion that Canada had never involved England in war but had twice been involved in war by her. He expressed lack of confidence in neutrality or in protection by the United States, and supported the prime minister's policy. In closing he belittled the talk about separatism in Quebec, which was merely the expression of discontent by young men without jobs. He cited recent statements by Premier Duplessis and Agriculture Minister Bona Dussault condemning separatism.[190]

Secretary of State Fernand Rinfret condemned the motion as inopportune, binding for an uncertain future, and futile, since the neutrality of Canada was not within her control. He admitted that 'rench Canadians were not militaristic and not anxious to support)articipation in European wars, but he found that he was 'too good . Britisher' to hold with the language of the resolution. He hinted hat the motion might have been intended to win to the social ideas of the C.C.F. the French Canadians—'a certain class of people they ıave not the least chance of reaching otherwise.'[191] He rejected the irst and second points and favored the third. Mr. Woodsworth in ·eply censured the 'French logic' of the secretary of state, and lefended his own right as an opponent of conscription to appeal to he French Canadians against militarism. He criticized Mr. ..apointe's 'misstatement' of the Spanish situation, and suggested hat the minister either 'had the jitters or wanted to give the jitters o the Canadian people.' In closing he warned that 'We have sown he wind and we are reaping the whirlwind, but we are not going to)revent that whirlwind by sowing more wind.'[192] The prime ninister, by preparing for war, was playing the game of the British mperialists. Mr. Woodsworth urged collective security as an ılternative to travelling 'the road which, throughout the years, nevitably has led to disaster.'[193]

Both the Woodsworth and the Douglas motions failed, but the liscussion of them paved the way for another debate on foreign)olicy when the defence estimates, calling for an increase of ;10,000,000, came before the House on February 15. C. G. Mac-Neil and M. J. Coldwell moved a C.C.F. amendment deploring 'the tartling increases' for armament expenditure in contrast to 'the nadequate provision for the social security of all sections of the Canadian people.'[194] Mr. King maintained that Canada owed t to her 'self-respect as a nation' to see to her defence but calmed he fears of the anti-imperialists by declaring: 'I think it extremely loubtful if any of the British Dominions will ever send another ·xpeditionary force to Europe.'[195] Defence Minister Ian Mackenzie leclared: 'There is no idea whatever of sending a single Canadian oldier overseas in any expeditionary force, and there is not a single :ent providing for that in the estimates . . . They are for the direct lefence of Canada and for the defence of Canadian neutrality.'[196] He stated in reply to Mr. MacNeil's charges that the government had given a blank check to be written in blood 'There are no commit-ments, no understandings, no agreements, open or secret, of any kind.' He stressed that the problem was no longer one of local lefence, but 'the complete responsibility for defence in consequence of Canada's new sovereign status.' He urged upon the nationalists:

The more you believe in, the more you subscribe to doctrines of Cana-dian nationalism, the more you must provide for the defence of the Dominion of Canada. You cannot any longer lean upon the alliances

> or implied alliances of the past; you can no longer lean upon the impli cations of the Monroe Doctrine. If you are going to profess the virtue and the pride of nationalism, you must face your responsibilities and mee your obligations in accordance with the status of sovereignty.[197]

The C.C.F. amendment brought an unusual number of French Canadian members into action, with the same three Quebec Liberal who had supported the Woodsworth resolution backing this motion Maxime Raymond described the question as one of 'the utmos importance, first of all on account of the increase of these estimate over last year, due to war preparations in Europe and following th rather ill-timed statements of some foreign or semi-foreign individual some of whom have no right to interfere in our political discussion and for whom past experience should have been a lesson.'[198] H attacked the suggestions of 'imperialist pilgrims' and approved Mr King's attitude at Geneva. He asked what sudden threat had neces sitated such an increase in defence expenditure, 'apart from the visi of Lord Elibank following the warning of Sir Samuel Hoare.'

> Our boundaries are the same. Our neighbors are the same and are just as peaceful as they were. Our geographical position has not change and we are still separated from Europe and Asia by oceans, that mea almost an absolute security. We have no enemies that we know of. More over, the friction that existed by reason of the sanctions against Ital has disappeared since these sanctions have been removed.
>
> Did the conditions in Europe grow worse? There is not any mor talk about war than there was last June, when the estimates were voted as a matter of fact, there is less talk about it since the Italo-Ethiopia conflict is over. At any rate, our frontiers are not in Europe.[199]

Referring to *L'Action Catholique's* statement on January 14 tha the government had a duty to preserve order in the country, eve by force, and to prevent the enlistment of volunteers for 'the Re army of Spain' in Canada, he favored any necessary increase of th forces to guard against revolution in Canada. But he declared:

> My duty to my electors is to oppose Canada's participation in an war outside of her own territory—the horrors of the last war are sti too vivid,—and I will not vote a single dollar increase that will not b spent "wholly and exclusively" for the defence of Canada, and i Canada only.
>
> Since our dominion is now a sovereign state, the obligation rests upo us to see to our own national defence, and we must protect ourselve against dangers from within and without. For that reason, I am willin to vote any amount shown to be necessary to make this country safe.
>
> But again, I say that our army, our air force and our navy must b called out only in defence of Canada and solely within her territory.[20

ignificantly, Mr. Raymond was applauded by Mr. Lapointe, the overnment leader for Quebec.

Lionel Bertrand (Laurier) agreed that the question was a very mportant one. He declared:

If national defence meant contribution to the future wars of ;urope, then I say undoubtedly I would have to be against national efence. If it meant contribution to European wars, I am sure that the eople of my own province would soon ask themselves the question: Is it orthwhile to stay within the British Empire if we have to go to war ecause South Africa wants its independence recognized, because ;ermany wants its colonies back, or for any other reason.

But if we have to defend Canadian territory and if it means only the efence of our territory, I am going to vote heartily for this measure of efence.[201]

n closing Mr. Bertrand declared that as a French Canadian, he elt he would be belittling his country and his race if he did not favor rovision for proper defence. Deploring the campaign to convince Quebec that national defence meant participation, he cited *Le Devoir's* advocacy of the former in 1914. He declared: 'I am sure hat in my own province the leader of the government, whose ncestors suffered for the autonomy of Canada, is going to be ooked upon as a true Canadian; the province of Quebec will have aith in him and will not have any trouble in voting for these ppropriations.[202]

J.-A. Crète (St. Maurice-Laflèche) wondered whether Bertrand ruly expressed the sentiment of Quebec on the question. He criticized the increase in expenditure as unjustifiable in view of Canada's eographical, political, and economic status. He believed in reliance n the Monroe Doctrine and in Canadian cooperation in the Pan-American Union. Economic stability was a better guarantee against nternal and external conflict than entering the world armament ace. He pointed out that the students of both Quebec and Toronto vere opposed to rearmament.[203] Both he and Liguori Lacombe Laval-Two Mountains) rejected the C.C.F. motion, leaving their ote on the main question undecided. Lacombe opposed Canadian articipation in imperial or European wars. As a 1917 conscript, he enounced Canada's participation in the First World War on both noral and economic grounds. He stressed the Communist danger, nd expressed the view that the defence estimates might be justified s a means to crush it.[204] Joseph Jean (Mercier) deprecated the nportance which had been given to the question. He stressed that ne issue was not Canadian participation in foreign wars, and urged ne responsibilities of nationhood. He saw the organization of a nodest army as a major factor in creating internal peace and developing national unity, if French Canadians were given thei share in its ranks.

Jean-François Pouliot (Témiscouata) supported the estimates, bu criticized the Defence Department for its red tape, for being mor British than Canadian, and for being inefficient. He expresse opposition to federal action against Communism. Oscar-L. Boulange (Bellechasse) supported the government, warning Quebec agains repeating the error of 1911 and maintaining that American im perialism was as bad as British imperialism. He urged Quebec to liv up to its glorious military traditions. Charles Parent (Quebec Wes and South) opposed both the C.C.F. motion and the estimates stressing Canada's geographical isolation and minimizing the dange from without. He did not think that an army was necessary to dea with Communist agitation and labor trouble at home. Mauric Lalonde (Labelle) opposed the C.C.F. amendment and expresse confidence in the Liberal leadership, while opposing Canadia participation in foreign wars. He, too, stressed the Communis menace. Pierre Gauthier (Portneuf) opposed rearmament an stressed the menace of Communism. Alphonse Fournier (Hull pointed out that Canada's unpreparedness had not prevented he participation in the Boer and World Wars. He made a plea for fait in the administration and opposed foreign wars. H.-E. Brunell (Champlain) opposed both the C.C.F. and government motions, bu censured the Quebec press for misrepresenting the administration' attitude. L.-D. Tremblay (Dorchester) opposed the amendmen and expressed full confidence in the government. J.-A. Vervill (Lotbinière) supported the government but condemned the increase expenditure. Wilfrid Lacroix (Quebec-Montmorency) did the sam urging that Canada should join the Pan-American Union. In con trast to the French stand against participation in foreign wars, onl four English members took the same attitude.[205] The C.C. amendment was defeated by 191 to 17, with a few Social Cred members supporting the C.C.F. On the estimates the oppositio mustered 26 votes, with a Manitoba Liberal and a few French Cana dians joining the C.C.F.

For all its sympathy with Franco, French Canada approved th government's embargo on sending men or munitions to Spain. I reply to three questions early in the session as to its attitude abou Canadian volunteers for the Spanish War—one of which wa prompted by Premier Duplessis' statement at Trois-Rivières tha Communist recruiting for Republican Spain had been carried o in Quebec[206]—the government announced its intention of proposin Canadian legislation modelled on the Imperial Foreign Enlistme Act of 1870. On second reading on March 19, Mr. Woodswort criticized the measure for not prohibiting the export of arms an munitions to belligerents, as the United States neutrality law did. This criticism was satisfied by a section in a bill amending the Customs Act which gave the government power to control the export of both arms and provisions.[207] Nationalist and imperialist made common cause in supporting these measures, with the former's distrust of European complications matched by the latter's desire to follow the British policy of non-intervention. Maxime Raymond's comment on the departure of Canadian volunteers for 'the Red army of Spain,' which he hailed as ridding the country of 'undesirable people,' met with applause in the House.[208] There was no reflection in parliament of the sympathy with the Spanish Republicans expressed by a resolution of the Canadian Trades and Labor Congress in the fall of 1937, and by the formation under Communist auspices of a Mackenzie-Papineau Battalion for the Republican Army.[209]

The Conservatives, who had become known as the 'silent party' by their avoidance of involvement in the Liberal–C.C.F. quarrels over foreign policy and defence, broke their silence on March 25 when R. B. Bennett made a plea for close naval cooperation with Britain. He based his argument on speeches made by Laurier before 1914, which tended to confirm the suspicion that Conservative policy was based on the hope of splitting the Liberals on defence, as in 1911. Mr. King replied that the government had always favored the Laurier policy, and evaded his opponent's plea for reaching an understanding with the Admiralty. The Conservative naval plea was echoed in the Senate by Senators Ballantyne, Griesbach, and Macdonell, who urged a policy of 'collective security within the empire.' A French-Canadian senator criticised this 'marathon of flag-waving' by a former marine minister and two generals. Senator Meighen had previously criticized the government's seeming willingness to become 'in fact, if not in law, an adjunct, and a humiliated adjunct, of the American Republic.'[210]

The Imperial Conference of 1937, scheduled to meet in May after the coronation of George VI, was to be devoted to the whole field of imperial policy. Before his departure for London, Mr. King made it clear that no commitments would be made, leaving parliament free to decide on Canadian foreign and defence policy. With Australia and South Africa facing elections and the Irish Free State abstaining from the conference, the gathering served merely the purpose of discussion and review, rather than decision and action, as Mr. King defined its function upon his return.[211] Nevertheless, Neville Chamberlain sought to make capital of the concluding words of Mr. King's speech at the Paris Exposition on July 2 when he said:

> We like to manage our own affairs. We cooperate with other parts of the British Empire in discussing questions of economic interest. The

fact that we have our own representatives in other countries is evidence of that great liberty which above all we prize, and were it imperilled from any source whatsoever, would bring us together in the defence of it.[212]

Mr. King refused to comment on Chamberlain's interpretation, but declared Canada had undertaken no commitments. British disappointment at the conference's inconclusiveness was apparent. Canadian imperialists were still further distressed in October when the governor-general, Lord Tweedsmuir, told the tenth anniversary dinner of the Canadian Institute for International Affairs: 'A Canadian's first duty is not to the British Commonwealth of Nations but to Canada and to Canada's King, and those who deny this are doing, to my mind, a great disservice to the Commonwealth.' This utterance of a distinguished graduate of Milner's 'kindergarten' for young imperialists in South Africa was promptly adopted as a permanent heading for the front page of *Le Devoir*, while C. H. Cahan criticized it in a speech to the Montreal branch of the Royal Empire Society.[213] Conservative criticism and nationalist approval of a governor-general indicated the confusion of public opinion in a Canada divided within herself and uncertain about her role in a world darkened by the shadows of war.

When China, once more invaded by Japan, invoked the League Covenant at the 1937 meeting of the Assembly, Canada continued to follow the 'back-seat' policy it had adopted since the Riddell incident. Senator Dandurand, as Canada's representative on the League's Far Eastern Advisory Committee, refused to vote for resolutions condemning Japan's course until he had received instructions from Ottawa. The Canadian government subsequently declared its approval of the resolutions.[214] Though Canada applied the Foreign Enlistment Act to Spain in August, Senator Dandurand voted in favor of Spain's eligibility for re-election to the League, declaring that 'The sole duty of the Canadian delegation was to think of Spain as an entity, without interfering in its domestic quarrels.'[215] At the Brussels Nine Power Conference in November, Canada followed the American and British lead of merely condemning Japanese aggression and offering to mediate in the Far Eastern struggle. The prime minister subsequently commented on Canada's role: 'It did not think less could be done; it did not urge the great powers represented to do more.'[216] Anti-Japanese feeling was strong in the Canadian West, with an unofficial boycott of Japanese goods, but negligible in Quebec.

For all the discussion of international affairs in 1937, the King government's attention was given primarily to pressing economic questions at home. The economic recovery which began in 193 received a sharp setback from the business recession of 1937 in the States, while successive crop failures on the Prairies increased unemployment. Canada never really rallied from the 1929 collapse until the war boom began in 1939. The successive budgets after 1935 showed decreased deficits, however, and promised tax relief. A new British trade agreement in 1937 and a United States one in 1938, which formed part of the Anglo-American Trade treaty of that year, were important factors in improving Canadian trade, which became increasingly involved in a triangular pattern with Britain and the United States, despite some expansion in Latin America and the British West Indies. It was significant that Mr. King conferred with President Roosevelt and Secretary Hull at Washington in March 1937 before the Imperial Conference in May at which he urged that 'political tension will not lessen without the abatement of economic nationalism and economic imperialism.'[217] Canadian influence played its part in the subsequent Anglo-American Trade Treaty.

Closer Canadian-American and Anglo-American relations were considerably furthered by the visits of Lord Tweedsmuir to Washington and of President Roosevelt to Canada in 1937. The governor-general shattered all precedent by addressing Congress on April 1, telling the House that 'Your nation and mine . . . are the guardians . . of democracy,' and the Senate that 'the future lies in the hands of the English-speaking peoples.' And at Kingston on August 18, when receiving an honorary degree from Queen's University, the President referred to the common democratic inheritance of Canada and the United States, and the new involvement of the Americas in world affairs. He then declared: 'The Dominion of Canada is part of the sisterhood of the British Empire. I give to you assurance that the people of the United States will not stand idly by if domination of Canadian soil is threatened by any other Empire.'[218] Speaking at Woodbridge two days later, Prime Minister King cautiously welcomed Mr. Roosevelt's declaration, describing it as one made with no thought of military alliance, and declaring: 'Canadians know they have their own responsibility for maintaining Canadian soil as a homeland for free men in the Western hemisphere.' He added that Canadians should see to it that 'should the occasion ever arise, enemy forces should not be able to pursue their way by land, sea, or air to the United States across Canadian territory.'[219] Mr. King also stressed that the president's statement did not weaken Canada's relationship to other members of the British Commonwealth.

Mr. King's course of action during the Czechoslovakian crisis of September gave evidence, however, that he was less interested in supporting Britain's European policy than either old-school imperialists or enthusiastic supporters of the League of Nation The government issued no statement until Mr. King telegraphed h congratulations to Mr. Chamberlain after the latter's flight t Berchtesgaden.[220] Despite pressure from the Conservative oppos tion and the Canadian Legion for support of Britain, the goverr ment's statement of September 17 merely declared that it was givin 'unremitting consideration' to the situation and warned agains 'public controversy' as a threat to Canadian peace and Commor wealth unity.[221] The cabinet held an emergency meeting on Sep tember 23, during Mr. Chamberlain's second visit to Germany but no statement was issued, despite growing indignation in Tor and imperialist circles. Finally, after the cabinet had considere Mr. Chamberlain's empire broadcast of September 27, a statemen was made supporting the British prime minister's stand, promisin to summon parliament if war came, and urging the avoidanc of 'controversies or divisions that might seriously impair effectiv and concerted action when Parliament meets.'[222] Upon the new of the Munich settlement Mr. King warmly congratulated M Chamberlain.

The Munich settlement brought a general feeling of relief in Canada which thanks to its growing North Americanism was mor favorable to appeasement than Britain itself. It was significant tha in December 1939 Canada recognized King Victor Emmanuel a Emperor of Abyssinia without debate in parliament.[223] As th falseness of the settlement became evident with time, this first feelin of relief changed to a recognition that the Chamberlain negotiation had destroyed the League of Nations. Consequently, as Professo F. R. Scott pointed out, while 'before the Munich settlement ther were three main groups of opinion in Canada—imperialist, collec tivist, and isolationist or Canadian nationalist—two of whic advocated Canada's participation in external affairs, today ther are only two groups, only one of them willing to intervene i Europe.'[224] There were campaigns for clarification of Canada's righ to neutrality and demands for closer cooperation with the Unitec States and representation in the Pan-American Union. But there wa a general, if reluctant recognition that Canada must in any case in crease its armaments.

The speech from the throne in January 1939 announced that th defence program launched two years earlier would be pursue vigorously—the defence estimates were nearly double the total fo 1938—but that 'While taking the measures necessary to assure th maintenance of our national integrity against the possibility of exter nal aggression, the government have sought in positive ways t strengthen the mutual interests which unite Canada in friendl relations with other countries.'[225] Dr. R. J. Manion, who had wo the Conservative leadership after R. B. Bennett's resignation in a disruptive contest with Arthur Meighen, took the opportunity to declare that Mr. King's lieutenants in Quebec would not find it so difficult to win support there for the present defence program, if they had not spent so much time in the past telling the people that the Conservatives were bloodthirsty militarists, when the latter had merely sought to provide half the defence which now existed.[226] For his part Mr. King sought to reassure Quebec by declaring: 'It might as well be said now, at the beginning of this session, because it will be the attitude of this government for its time, that before this country goes into any war, this parliament will be consulted.' He quoted as the formula of past, present, and future Liberal policy Laurier's declaration in 1910: 'If England is at war we are at war and liable to attack. I do not say that we will always be attacked; neither do I say that we would take part in all the wars of England. That is a matter that must be guided by circumstances, upon which the Canadian parliament will have to pronounce and will have to decide in its own best judgment.'[227]

Nonetheless the Quebec nationalists took alarm, although most of the Liberal members with nationalist leanings were reassured by Mr. King's statement. Liguori Lacombe denied that Canada was necessarily at war because one or more of the equal nations of the Commonwealth was at war:

> Canada being according to the statute of Westminster, a self-governing country as regards England, any declaration contrary to this treaty must be considered, in the event of war, as outmoded and false. I need not repeat that I am irrevocably opposed to any increase in defence appropriations so long as they may serve to involve Canada in a foreign war. I go further. In the name of the country's most cherished interests, no decision should be taken as to Canada's participation in an extra-territorial war without an appeal to the people . . . Should a conflict occur in central Europe, in America or elsewhere, I assert that the Candian people alone would have the right to make a decision in such a serious matter.[228]

He declared that public opinion was opposed to participation, and that 'The supreme folly of another venture in a foreign war would spell the permanent ruin of Canada.' Dr. Pierre Gauthier accepted the necessity of defence measures; hailed King's stand as 'frankly and admirably Canadian;' and warned of the danger of press campaigns for participation and for the defeat of King, which would lead to 'the repetition of what occurred in 1911, 1914, and 1917.' He expressed a basic French-Canadian sentiment with his declaration: 'I stand for Canada above all, for Canada alone, and for Canada forever.'[229] L.-D. Tremblay spelled out the same sentiment in detail:

We, from Quebec, do not claim that Canada should have no defence or armaments; on the contrary, Canada is our only fatherland. We are neither French nor English, we are Canadians, and our only fatherland is Canada. When we are requested to vote for an increase in the estimates of the Department of National Defence for the protection of Canada and the defence of our territory, I say that Quebec is willing to support that, but we do not want to share any longer in foreign adventures . . . Let us think a little more of Canada, our country, than the British Empire.[230]

G.-H. Héon, an able independent Conservative, contrasted Lord Stanley's declaration at Toronto with Mr. King's position. Lord Stanley replied to the question 'Is Canada at war when Britain is at war?' thus: 'Certainly not. Canada has entire responsibility of her own. She is a sovereign state and decides for herself.' Héon declared that the issue of the next election would be 'Colonialism or Canadianism,' and he refused to believe that 'colonialism is the regime under which the overwhelming majority of Canadians want to live today.' He was not opposed to Canadian participation in any war:

What I say is that any war in which we do take part must be a war in which something better than sentiment actuated by prejudiced propaganda is at stake. It must be a war that threatens our very liberty, independence and existence, and the issue of which would be of vital concern immediate to all of us. I say, my country right or wrong, but not fifteen countries.[231]

Héon favored an immediate appeal to the people on the issue.

Wilfrid Lacroix refused to withdraw his resolution for the adoption of the term 'Kingdom of Canada' and for the naming of a Canadian 'Viceroy' with the abolition of the office of dominion secretary. To his mind the best way to protect Canada was 'to create an independent kingdom and officially to proclaim our neutrality, thus placing ourselves on the same footing as the United States as regards any future intervention.'[232] The United States was obliged by the Monroe Doctrine to protect Canada, which should 'keep out of European troubles and complications.'

On March 30, after the German occupation of Czechoslovakia and Mr. Chamberlain's suggestion for consultation by the Commonwealth nations on Hitler's attempt to dominate the world by force, Mr. King again reviewed in parliament international affairs and his government's policies. He reiterated that parliament would decide 'if Canada is faced by the necessity of making a decision on the most serious and momentous issue that can face a nation, whether or not to take part in war.' Echoing Chamberlain's noncommital stand, Mr. King declared:

Speaking as the Prime Minister of Canada, I wish to say that I am not prepared any more than is the Prime Minister of Great Britain to engage his country by new and unspecified commitments operating under conditions which cannot now be foreseen . . .

I cannot accept the view which is being urged in some quarters today, that regardless of what government or party may be in power, regardless of what its policy may be, regardless of what the issue itself may come to be, this country should say here and now that Canada is prepared to support whatever may be proposed by the government at Westminster.[233]

He argued that 'a divided Canada can be of little help to any country, and least of all to itself,' and stressed that 'We are and will remain Canadians, devoted, first and last, to the interests of Canada, but Canadians, I hope, who will be able to take a long range view of what Canada's interests require.' He showed his fundamental sympathy with the French-Canadian nationalists in these words:

. . . we must, to a greater or less extent, choose between keeping our own house in order, and trying to save Europe and Asia. The idea that every twenty years this country should automatically and as a matter of course take part in a war overseas for democracy or self-determination of other small nations, that a country which has all it can do to run itself should feel called upon to save, periodically, a continent that cannot run itself, and to these ends risk the lives of its people, risk bankruptcy and political disunion, seems to many a nightmare and sheer madness.[234]

Mr. King declared that participation in another world war could not be 'passive or formal,' and warned that Canada had to keep its Pacific as well as its Atlantic coast in mind. Altered world conditions had brought a marked decentralization of defence activities within the Commonwealth, and eliminated the need for colonial contingents:

They have brought about a great preoccupation of each part with its own defence, a greater responsibility for that defence, a greater self-containment in the provision of means of defence . . . One strategic fact is clear: the days of the great expeditionary forces of infantry crossing the ocean are not likely to reoccur. Two years ago, I expressed in this house the view that it was extremely doubtful if any of the British dominions would ever send another expeditionary force to Europe.

One political fact is equally clear: in a war to save the liberty of others, and thus our own, we should not sacrifice our own liberty or our own unity . . . The present government believes that conscription of men for overseas service would not be a necessary or an effective step. Let me say that so long as this government may be in power, no such measure will be enacted. We have full faith in the readiness of Canadian men and women to rally for the defence of their country and their liberties, and to resist aggression by any country seeking to dominate the world by force.[235]

Mr. King also pledged that if war came, the government would control war profits and suppress profiteering in general. He amplified his quotation of Laurier on January 16 by saying that he had meant to indicate that an enemy of Britain might force war upon Canada if she chose to do so, but that the Canadian government would not be guided by legalism: 'We would not go into a war merely because of legal uncertainty as to our power to stay out. We would not stay out of a war merely because we had provided technical freedom to do so. Our country's decisions on such vital matters, now or later, will depend on deeper forces, they will depend on the thoughts and feelings of our people.'[236] This clever speech, leaving the way open to neutrality, active belligerency or passive belligerency, offered comfort to isolationist and imperialist alike and deprived the Conservatives and the C.C.F. of any major issue on which to oppose the government.

Dr. Manion, who represented a very different school of Conservatism than Arthur Meighen, and who sought to woo Quebec's sympathies, agreed that Canada should have the right to decide its role in any British war: 'I demand for us in Canada the same right to form and express opinions as is possessed by citizens of the British Isles. I refuse to subscribe to any doctrine of inferiority which would cast us in the role of pawns on the international chess board.'[237] He argued that conscription was dubious in value, since at most only 10,000 Canadians reached the trenches in the First World War as a result of its adoption. Two English Montreal Conservatives, C. H. Cahan and R. S. White, supported their leader by arguing that if Quebec were treated reasonably and courteously she would do her part in any war effort. The C.C.F. and the Social Credit leaders also opposed conscription, though Mr. Woodsworth doubted whether it could be avoided as a war went on and heavy losses occurred in overseas forces.

Justice Minister Lapointe, the recognized Quebec spokesman, won the honors of the debate. First he discussed the legal obstacles to a declaration of neutrality, and concluded that there was no 'possibility of one country being neutral and another a belligerent, when they are not separate sovereignties and when one is linked with the other in respect of its own power of legislation.'[238] A declaration of Canadian neutrality would entail a ban on enlistment by Canadians in the British forces, the closing of the British bases at Halifax and Esquimalt, and the internment of British seamen who sought refuge in Canadian ports. He asked whether anyone seriously believed that these steps could be taken without causing a civil war in Canada.

He quoted with approval the remark of E. J. Tarr that 'the loyalty of French Canadians is concentrated too narrowly, and that of many English Canadians is spread too broadly.' He admitted that bombardment of London would cause a wave of public opinion that would force any Canadian government to intervene, and asked his Quebec colleagues: 'What is the use of closing our eyes to stern realities?' But he also asked English Canadians to pay heed to the sentiments of French Canadians, of whom 'none . . . would say that he is "going home" when he leaves Canada.'[239]

Lapointe ruled out conscription, which he had opposed in 1917, as a frightful blunder whose tragic consequences were still being felt. Even if it had proved effective, 'The best way, the most effective way of helping is not the way that would divide our country and tear it asunder.' Canada was not alone in opposing conscription; Australia, South Africa, and Ireland did so also. He declared solemnly: 'I think I am true to my concept of Canadian unity when I say that I shall always fight against this policy; I would not be a member of a government that would enact it; and not only that, but I say so with all my responsibility to the people of Canada that I would oppose any government that would enforce it.' He agreed with the prime minister that the time for expeditionary forces was past: 'The men will be needed here; and in any event it is parliament which will decide about it.'[240] He closed with a warning against a narrow isolationism by quoting an eloquent editorial of the late Jules Dorion in *L'Action Catholique.*

> We are the masters of our destinies. Agreed. But that does not obliterate the fact that we have a neighbour to the south, icebound solitudes to the north, and, to the east and west, much travelled oceans beyond which dwell populous and active nations with which we cannot avoid having relations—with which we have to deal, to negotiate, to agree or to fight.
>
> This is a reality which we cannot ignore without exposing ourselves to a terrible awakening.
>
> We are our own masters. Agreed. But that does not prevent us from asking ourselves what are to be our relations with England, to wonder whether we can do without her or whether it would not be better for us to remain associated with her.
>
> Canada has become a nation. We must, however, recognize the fact that a nation has other obligations, other duties and other cares than a colony has, and place ourselves in a position to meet them. We must remember that nations evolve, and are sometimes faced with situations not of their own making.[241]

Despite all the assurances given to Quebec by the government leaders and the heads of the other parties, six French Canadians—

Lacombe, Lacroix, Lalonde, A.-J. Lapointe, Tremblay, and Raymond—reiterated their opposition to participation in a European war and to a repetition of the experiences of 1914–8. In April Raymond summed up their position with the greatest force and eloquence:

> Every Canadian citizen has the military obligation of defending the soil of his motherland, and those of the province of Quebec have never shirked that duty, nor shall they ever do so, but no one is entitled to ask them to go and shed their blood in Europe, or in Africa or in Asia for the greater glory or power of any other country, even if that country should be England or France.
>
> And if ever a majority of the people of this country should desire to compel an important minority thereof to take up arms in defence of a foreign land, whichever it may be, that would be the end of confederation.[242]

He concluded by quoting Lapointe's statement at Quebec on December 12, 1938: 'Instead of waging war in a foreign land, we shall remain at home and defend the Canada we love.' In the May debate on the defence estimates as the war clouds darkened, Lacombe, Lacroix, Raymond, Gauthier, Crète, and Gariépy, renewed their protests, which broke the unwonted unity of the House.

The basic isolationism of the King government was in part dictated by a popular mood similar to that in the United States which was responsible for the rejection of collective security and for the adoption of neutrality legislation. In part it was also based upon Mr. King's consciousness of the deep divisions of the Canadian peoples in recent years, their hard-pressed economic position, and his heritage from Laurier of a dread of war setting the two chief peoples of Canada at odds. But it also reflected the growing North Americanism of a Canada which in 1938 had sent 32.3 per cent of her exports to the States and derived 62.7 per cent of her imports thence, as compared with 40.6 per cent of her exports to Britain and 17.6 per cent of her imports from the latter source. This new economic relationship was to grow notably closer after the outbreak of the second World War, despite the barriers of the American Neutrality Act.

This development did not weaken the old sentimental ties with Britain, as was evidenced by the warmth with which the King and Queen were received when they toured Canada in May and June 1939. Anti-imperialist Montreal spent more money on the royal reception than ultra-loyalist Toronto. On the eve of the Second World War some English Canadians deplored the weakening of the British tie and resented the growing paternalism of the United States towards Canada, while French-Canadian nationalists found reinforcement for their isolationism and anti-militarism in the fact that he United States professedly stood ready to defend Canada against aggression. English and French nationalists alike favored the recognition of Canada's new orientation by entrance into the Pan-American Union and hemisphere defence projects.

Notes.

[1] See *Notre Américanisation, enquête de 'La Revue Dominicaine'* (Montréal, 1937) & E. Montpetit, *Reflèts d'Amérique* (Montréal, 1941).

[2] *Can. An. Rev. 1920*, 629. Translation revised.

[3] *Ibid.*, 631.

[4] *Ibid.*, 656.

[5] *Ibid.*, 405.

[6] *Ibid.*, 413.

[7] *Ibid.*, 113–14.

[8] *Ibid.*, 495.

[9] *Ibid.*, 427.

[10] C. P. Stacey, *The Military Problems of Canada* (Toronto, 1940), 90–1.

[11] *Ibid.*, 89–91.

[12] *Can. An. Rev. 1921*, 211.

[13] *The Round Table*, XI, 390–1; cited A. G. Dewey, *The Dominions and Diplomacy* (London, 1929), I, 323.

[14] *Ibid.*

[15] *Can. An. Rev. 1921*, 78.

[16] *Political Science Quarterly*, L (March 1935), 53–5, J. B. Brebner, 'Canada & the Anglo-Japanese Alliance.'

[17] Dewey, I, 328.

[18] *Ibid.*, II, 73; Brebner, 49–50.

[19] *Can. An. Rev. 1921*, 220.

[20] *Ibid.*, 221.

[21] *Ibid.*, 177.

[22] Dewey, II, 83–5.

[23] *Can. An. Rev. 1921*, 113–14.

[24] *Canada, Sessional Papers 1922*, No. 47, 15 March 1922; cited Dewey, II, 86–9.

[25] *Can. An. Rev., 1921*, 171.

[26] *Ibid.*, 309.

[27] *Ibid.*, 482.

[28] *Ibid.*, 486.

[29] *Ibid.*, 485.

[30] *Ibid.*, 489.

[31] *Ibid.*, 488.

[32] *Ibid.*, 518–9.

[33] *Ibid.*, 522.

[34] *Dewey*, II, 116.

[35] *Ibid.*, 122.

[36] *Can. An. Rev. 1922*, 182–3.

[37] J. S. Ewart, *Canada and British Wars* (Ottawa, 1922), 5.

[38] *Ibid.*, 86–8.

[39] Dewey, II, 123–4.

[40] *Ibid.*, 125.

[41] *Ibid.*, 125–6.

[42] *Ibid.*, 141.
[43] *Ibid.*, 140 *n.* 3.
[44] *Can. An. Rev. 1923*, 53.
[45] Dewey, II, 137–47.
[46] *Can. An. Rev. 1923*, 92.
[47] Dewey, II, 169–71.
[48] P. E. Corbett & H. E. Smith, *Canada and World Politics* (London, 1928), Ap. I, 191–4, 'Report of the Imperial Conference of 1923.'
[49] *Can. An. Rev. 1924–5*, 43.
[50] *Ibid.*
[51] Dewey, II, 149–52.
[52] *Ibid.*, 154.
[53] *Canada, Commons Debates 1924*, June 9; cited Dewey, II, 160.
[54] Dewey, II, 161–4.
[55] *Ibid.*, 188.
[56] *Can. An. Rev. 1925–6*, 47.
[57] *Ibid.*, 49.
[58] *Ibid.*, 86.
[59] *Ibid.*, 56.
[60] *Canada, Commons Debates 1926*, 22 March, II, 1806.
[61] C. Wittke, *A History of Canada* (New York, 1941), 349.
[62] Dewey, II, 260–1.
[63] *Ibid.*, 262–3.
[64] *Ibid.*, 264–5.
[65] H. Bourassa, *Le Canada, nation libre* (Montréal, 1926), 18.
[66] *Can. An. Rev. 1926–7*, 40; *Le Devoir*, 10 sept. 1926.
[67] *Ibid.*
[68] Wittke, 366.
[69] *Can. An. Rev. 1926–7*, 55; *Le Devoir*, 16 sept. 1926.
[70] *Ibid.*, 115.
[71] *Ibid.*, 119.
[72] Corbett & Smith, Ap. II, 194–222, 'Report of the Imperial Conference of 1926.'
[73] *Ibid.*, 197–9.
[74] *Ibid.*, 201.
[75] G. Neuendorf, *Studies in the Evolution of Dominion Status* (London, 1942), 23.
[76] R. L. Borden, *Canada in the Commonwealth* (Oxford, 1927), 125–6.
[77] Corbett & Smith, 215.
[78] *Can. An. Rev. 1926–7*, 135.
[79] *Ibid.*, 133.
[80] *Ibid.*, 134–5.
[81] *Ibid.*, 130.
[82] *Ibid.*
[83] *Ibid.*, 62–3.
[84] *Ibid.*, 67–8.
[85] *Ibid.*, 68.
[86] *Can. An. Rev. 1927–8*, 150–1.
[87] *Ibid.*, 140.
[88] Corbett & Smith, 107–30.
[89] *Can. An. Rev. 1927–8*, 55.
[90] *Ibid.*, 56.
[91] *Ibid.*, 56–7.
[92] *Ibid.*, 29.
[93] *Ibid.*, 26.
[94] *Ibid.*, 26.

[95] *Ibid.*, 29.
[96] *Ibid.*, 30.
[97] *Ibid.*, 31.
[98] *Ibid.*, 37.
[99] *Ibid.*, 32.
[100] *Ibid.*, 40.
[101] *Ibid.*, 409.
[102] *Can. An. Rev. 1926–7*, 356.
[103] *Can. An. Rev. 1927–8*, 381–2.
[104] *Ibid.*, 104.
[105] *Ibid.*, 397.
[106] *Ibid.*, 397–8.
[107] *Can. An. Rev. 1929–30*, 30.
[108] *Ibid.*, 32.
[109] *Ibid.*, 31–2.
[110] *Ibid.*, 33.
[111] *Ibid.*, 54.
[112] *Ibid.*, 84; *La Presse*, 25 juillet 1930.
[113] *Ibid.*, 87.
[114] *Ibid.*, 85–6.
[115] *Ibid.*, 100.
[116] *Can. An. Rev. 1930–1*, 32–3.
[117] *Ibid.*, 37.
[118] *Ibid.*, 42.
[119] *Ibid.*, 307–24.
[120] *Ibid.*, 31.
[121] *Ibid.*, 44–6.
[122] *Ibid.*, 47.
[123] *Ibid.*, 46.
[124] *Ibid.*, 731.
[125] *Canada, Commons Debates 1931*, 30 June, 3203–4.
[126] *Ibid.*, 3205–6.
[127] *Ibid.*, 3215–21.
[128] Neuendorf, 292.
[129] *Ibid.*
[130] Abbé L. Groulx, *Directives* (Montréal, 1937), 162–3.
[131] *Can. An. Rev. 1932*, 28.
[132] *Ibid.*, 34–5
[133] *Ibid.*, 57.
[134] *Ibid.*, 319–25.
[135] *Can. An. Rev. 1933*, 43.
[136] *Ibid.*, 51.
[137] *Ibid.*
[138] *Ibid.*, 46.
[139] *Ibid.*, 33.
[140] *Ibid.*, 34–5.
[141] *Ibid.*, 33.
[142] *Ibid.*, 30–3.
[143] *Can. An. Rev. 1934*, 34–5.
[144] *Ibid.*, 53.
[145] *Ibid.*, 35.
[146] *Ibid.*, 36.
[147] *Ibid.*, 33.
[148] *Can. An. Rev. 1935–6*, 2.
[149] *Ibid.*, 11.

[150] *Ibid.*, 12–3.

[151] *Ibid.*, 15.

[152] *Ibid.*, 50.

[154] *Ibid.*, 63.

[154] *Ibid.*, 64–5.

[155] *Ibid.*, 68.

[156] *Ibid.*, 94.

[157] *Ibid.*, 95.

[158] *Ibid.*, 96–7, 93.

[159] *Ibid.*, 97–7.

[160] F. H. Soward, J. F. Parkinson, N. A. M. MacKenzie, T. W. L. MacDermot *Canada in World Affairs: The Pre-War Years* (Toronto, 1941), 198–9.

[161] *Can. An. Rev. 1935–6*, 125–7.

[162] R. Rumilly, *L'Autonomie Provinciale* (Montréal, 1948), 106.

[163] *Can. An. Rev. 1937–8*, 157.

[164] K. G. W. Ludecke, *I Knew Hitler* (New York, 1937), 54.

[165] *Ibid.*

[166] *The Nation, No. 145* (6 Nov. 1937), 497–9, J. McNeil, 'Right Turn in Canada'; *No. 146* (12 Feb. 1938), 176–9, E. S. McLeod, 'Slander over Canada' *No. 148* (26 Feb. 1938) 241–4, D. Martin, 'Adrien Arcand, Fascist.'

[167] *Can. An. Rev. 1937–8*, 92–3.

[168] *Canada, Commons Debates 1936*, 18 June, IV, 3862–73.

[169] *Ibid.*, 3876.

[170] *Ibid.*, 3896.

[171] *Ibid.*, 3384.

[172] *Commons Debates 1935*, 1 April, III, 2287.

[173] Soward, *et al.*, 34.

[174] *Can. An. Rev. 1935–6*, 77.

[175] *Ibid.*, 79.

[176] Soward, *et al.*, 38.

[177] *Ibid.*, 23–4.

[178] *Canada, Commons Debates 1937*, 25 Jan., I, 237.

[179] *Can. An. Rev. 1937–8*, 30.

[180] *Commons Debates 1937*, I, 246.

[181] *Ibid.*, 248.

[182] *Ibid.*, 250–1.

[183] *Ibid.*, 252.

[184] *Ibid.*, 256–61, 564.

[185] *Ibid.*, 261–4.

[186] *Ibid.*, 4 Feb., 550.

[187] *Ibid.*, 551.

[188] *Ibid.*, 552.

[189] *Ibid.*, 554–5.

[190] *Ibid.*, 556–7.

[191] *Ibid.*, 558–9.

[192] *Ibid.*, 563–4.

[193] *Ibid.*, 15 Feb., 876.

[194] *Can. An. Rev. 1937–8*, 32.

[195] *Commons Debates 1937*, 15 Feb., I, 893, 895.

[196] *Ibid.*, 902.

[197] *Ibid.*, 909–10.

[198] *Ibid.*, 911–12.

[199] *Ibid.*, 918.

[200] *Ibid.*, 921.

[201] *Ibid.*, 934–7.

[202] *Ibid.*, 937–40.
[203] Soward, *et al.*, 61 *n.* 4.
[204] *Commons Debates 1937*, 29 Jan., I, 386.
[205] Soward, *et al.*, 64.
[206] *Commons Debates 1937*, 15 Feb., I, 910.
[207] Soward, *et al.*, 64 *n.* 1.
[208] *Ibid.*, 66–8.
[209] *Ibid.*, 70.
[210] *Can. A. Rev. 1937–8*, 4.
[211] Soward, *et al.*, 73 *n.* 1.
[212] *Can. An. Rev. 1937–8*, 5.
[213] Soward, *et al.*, 75–6 & *n.* 1.
[214] *Ibid.*, 76–7.
[215] *Can. An. Rev. 1937–8*, 3.
[218] Soward, *et al.*, 107.
[219] *Ibid.*, 108; *Can. An. Rev. 1937–8*, 32.
[220] *Ibid.*, 114.
[221] *Ibid.*, 114–15.
[222] *Ibid.*, 116.
[223] *Ibid.*, 117.
[224] *Foreign Affairs*, XVII (June 1939), 413; cited Soward, 117–18.
[225] *Commons Debates 1939*, 12 Jan., I, 3.
[226] *Ibid.*, 16 Jan., 23.
[227] *Ibid.*, 53.
[228] *Ibid.*, 23 Jan., 256.
[229] *Ibid.*, 24 Jan., 296–7.
[230] *Ibid.*, 26 Jan., I, 353–4.
[231] *Ibid.*, 30 Jan., I, 472.
[232] *Ibid.*, 473.
[233] *Ibid.*, 30 March, III, 2418.
[234] *Ibid.*, 2419.
[235] *Ibid.*, 2426.
[236] *Ibid.*
[237] *Ibid.*, 2434–40.
[238] *Ibid.*, 31 March, III, 2466.
[239] *Ibid.*, 2468.
[240] *Ibid.*, 2468–9.
[241] *Ibid.*, 2470–1; *L'Action Catholique*, 21 jan. 1939.
[242] *Ibid.*, 3 April, III, 2548.
[243] *Canada Year Book 1945*, 501.

CHAPTER XIV

INDUSTRIALIZATION AND LAURENTIANISM

(1920–39)

It was a new and different Quebec which faced a new and different situation in the postwar Canada of 1920. A region which cherished tradition found itself confronted with drastic political, economic and social changes which were altering the patterns of the past. These changes brought a basic uneasiness which showed itself in many ways. As a result of the bitter feeling and isolation of the school and conscription crises, the French Canadians were inclined to question the advantages of a Confederation in whose government they were virtually without representation and of whose population they now supplied little more than a quarter. Despite a remarkably high birthrate, their proportion of the total population had steadily shrunk instead of growing ever since 1867, thanks to immigration into English Canada, and to the exodus from Quebec to the United States.[1] Quebec's population only increased 17.72 per cent from 1911 to 1921, compared to the Canadian average of 21.95 per cent.[2] Emigration to the States once more took on alarming proportions in the postwar years of agricultural and industrial depression.[3]

Population trends showed a profound change within the province as well as in its position in Confederation. In 1921 for the first time Quebec's population was more urban than rural, and in the following decade the urban population increased 37.13 per cent.[4] Quebec became only slightly less industrialized than Ontario. The agricultural country parishes, the traditional backbone of Quebec society, were sending their sons and daughters to the States or to the cities, where rapid industrialization, brought about by the war and continued in the postwar period, created a vast labor market. Montreal, with its population of 618,506, was the largest city in Canada. One-quarter of Quebec's 10,762 manufacturing establishments were grouped there, representing half the capital invested in industry and employing two-thirds of French-Canadian industrial workers.[5] Though Montreal was the chief magnet for drawing country people, Quebec City's population had increased by one-quarter in the last decade, that of Trois-Rivières had doubled, that of Hull had increased by one-third, that of Sherbrooke by one-half, while Shawinigan had more than doubled in size and Grand'Mère, Chicoutimi, and La Tuque had almost done so. All these towns were industrial centers. Their rapid development was outstripped by the new industrial suburbs of older industrial centers, with Verdun more than doubling its population in the Montreal area and with Cap-de-la Madeleine more than tripling in that of Trois-Rivières.[6]

The wartime industrialization of the province continued in the postwar period at even more rapid a pace, for Quebec felt the depression of 1921 less than any other province of Canada. Though it was affected by the decline of lumber and pulp prices, its leading manufactures—shoes, clothing, cottons, steel, railway rolling stock, tobacco, and refined sugar—found a strong postwar market.[7] This industrial revolution radically altered both Quebec's traditional way of life and the nature of French-Canadian nationalism.[8] It was imposed upon the province largely by English, English-Canadian, and American big business, although a small group of French Canadians proved almost as adroit at exploiting both the natural resources of Quebec and the cheap labor of their compatriots.

Ever since Confederation the provincial government had encouraged the introduction of 'foreign' capital into the province, while only Errol Bouchette at the turn of the century had raised his voice against this process, urging the French Canadians not to neglect industry in their traditional concern with agriculture and colonization.[9] Asselin's and Bourassa's subsequent objections to rapid alienation of Quebec's timber and waterpower resources by the Parent and Gouin regimes had found little popular response, since the French Canadians were not economic-minded, thanks to the neglect of such studies in their traditional educational system and their long exclusion from posts of command in the business world by alien capital and management. The same resources policy, carried on by the Taschereau government from 1920 to 1935, encountered growing opposition as the belated arrival of the industrial revolution upset Quebec's way of life.

With capital and management largely in English-speaking hands, while labor was largely French Canadian, the ethnic feeling aroused by the conscription crisis was heightened by postwar economic developments. The French Canadians were left behind in business and industry, for they lacked both capital and training in economics, engineering, and the physical sciences. They found themselves no longer masters in their own house, and blamed their situation on ethnic discrimination rather than on lack of qualification. The newly industrialized and urbanized *habitant* blamed the trials of his new life not on the industrial system, but on the fact that it was introduced and controlled by aliens.[10] Traditional hatred of *les Anglais*, which had lingered in the folk memory, was thus revived.

This economic invasion of Quebec by cultural aliens produced an economic nationalism. After 1920 the nationalist press came to be characterized more and more by protests against 'foreign exploitation of our natural resources' and agitation in favor of French-Canadian support of French-Canadian business and industry. The old opposition to English Canadians was heightened, while a new anti-Americanism sprang up. During the First World War Canada had become closely integrated into the American economy as Britain was forced to liquidate its holdings in Canada. American capital increasingly replaced English capital, with American management replacing English or English-Canadian management to a lesser extent. In the postwar period this American economic penetration continued until it reached a peak in 1934, with 394 American businesses operating in Quebec, representing one-third of the province's industrial capital.[11] Anti-semitism also became evident as the Jewish population of the province increased sevenfold from 1901 to 1911, largely in the Montreal area where the new forces were most felt,[12] and as the French Canadians were driven by these newcomers from the small industries and small businesses which had been their economic strongholds, since English and American interests largely monopolized finance and big business.

This new economic nationalism led to the formation of exclusively French-Canadian labor unions, credit unions, farmers' and fishermen's cooperatives, and other efforts to make Quebec's economy more self-sufficient and less dependent upon 'foreign' capital and know-how. It was nourished by bitter opposition to the hitherto prevailing principle that Quebec's commercial exploitation should be conducted upon the basis of as much return as possible for master-race management and as little as possible for subject-people labor. The ethnic division between capital and labor was heightened by management's unwillingness to make concessions to the French-Canadian way of life. Company towns were set up and run on English or American lines in remote parts of the province with a blithe disregard of French-Canadian particularism. The old nineteenth-century practice of paying wages in script good only at company stores where high prices prevailed, so that the worker never got out of debt to the company and labor turnover was eliminated, was abandoned; but other practices were adopted which aroused quite as much resentment, such as demanding work on Sundays and other Church holy days. A host of irritations arising from the friction of two very different mentalities served to keep ethnic feeling alive.

As Quebec belatedly felt the full impact of the industrial revolution, the French Canadians found their minority status intensified. They were now arrayed not only against an English-Canadian majority in Canada, which had imposed its will upon the French Canadians during the war years, but also in opposition to the way of life which prevailed in English-speaking North America, and was now invading Quebec. The French Canadians sought to maintain their own 'Latin' way of life against an 'Anglo-Saxon' materialist one which was favored by great odds. The situation furthered development of the racism involved in nationalist theories imported from Europe by such intellectual leaders as Abbé Lionel Groulx, and almost every French Canadian tended to become in some measure a nationalist. The term 'ultranationalist' will henceforward be used to describe the extremists of the Groulx school; though it must be remembered that the term 'nationalism' is a misnomer for the movement after the First World War, which was an intense provincialism complicated by ethnic and religious factors, rather than the true nationalism professed by Henri Bourassa in his early days, and now largely adopted by forward-looking English Canadians.

The period between the two World Wars was characterized by the growth in Quebec of a narrow nationalism which was increasingly economic rather than political, though the dream of a separate French-Canadian state, 'Laurentia,' haunted some hotheaded minds; while on the other hand a group of deeply patriotic French Canadians sought to meet the challenge of the times by modifying their traditional culture to meet the new conditions brought about by the industrialization of Quebec, and to make common cause with English Canadians upon the basis of a broad Canadian nationalism. From 1917 to 1928 Quebec turned in upon itself; from 1932 onwards it looked more abroad, though still deeply isolationist. The great depression of 1929, from which Canada did not recover until the war boom began in 1939, increased the economic emphasis of French-Canadian nationalism and sharpened the ethnic conflict. Depression, like war, has always set French and English Canadians at odds and strained the structure of Confederation.

I

The new nationalism grew directly out of attacks on the French language in 1905 and 1912 and of the rift between French and English during the First World War. Its chief organ, *L'Action française*, began publication in January 1917 under the editorship of Omer Héroux, who had fledged his pen on *L'Action Catholique*. The new magazine, which described itself as 'a doctrinal and *avant-garde* review, which endeavours to present a comprehensive view of the vital problems of French Canada' and which sought the collaboration of 'all free spirits, all right-thinking men,'[13] was launched by the *Ligue des droits de Français*, which had been founded in March 1913 by the Jesuit Père Joseph-Papin Archambault of the Collège Sainte-Marie in Montreal, after consultation with Omer Héroux and Dr. Joseph Gauvreau. The original group consisted of Père Archambault, Dr. Gauvreau, A.-G. Casault, Henri Auger, Léon Lorrain, and Anatole Vanier. Many of the founders had grown up in the A.C.J.C. movement, with its increasing tendency to intermingle political and cultural nationalism with religion, and were disciples of Abbé Groulx, whose zeal surpassed that of their master Henri Bourassa. The group's purpose was to 'assure to the French language the place to which it has a right in the different domains where the French Canadians are active, particularly in commerce and industry.'[14]

Its members bound themselves to use French in business relations, even with English firms, and to give preference to firms which recognized the rights of the French language. Through lectures, pamphlets, a white list of merchants who used French, an editorial and translation service for advertisers, and official protests, the *Ligue* sought to further its end. The founders issued a manifesto:

> The movement which we launch is not a movement of provocation, a declaration of war. Our language has its rights, legal and constitutional. We desire that they shall not remain dead letters; above all we desire that our compatriots shall be the first to respect them. And since their abandonment arises most often from indifference, carelessness, and inertia, it is these plagues that the *Ligue* will first attack.[15]

The translation bureau began activity at once, and in June 1913 the *Ligue* published a pamphlet, '*La Langue française au Canada, Faits et réflexions*,' originally written as a series of articles for *Le Devoir* under the pseudonym of 'Pierre Homier' by Père Archambault, with a preface by Dr. Gauvreau. The *Ligue* also issued monthly lists of correct French expressions in various technical fields, and constantly intervened with government bodies, business, and individuals in the interest of the French language. Mgr. Paul-Eugène Roy gave his enthusiastic sanction to the work in 1914. In the following year Omer Héroux and Père Guillaume Charlebois, the Oblate provincial, joined the directors of the movement, which found shelter in the Monument National thanks to the Saint-Jean-Baptiste Society of Montreal. Later the *Ligue* occupied larger quarters in the Dandurand Building, with Louis Hurtubise assuming direction of its business affairs and Abbé Groulx replacing Léon Lorrain. Abbé Philippe Perrier took the place of Père Charlebois as the latter became preoccupied with the fight for bilingual schools in Ontario. Gradually the *Ligue's* emphasis shifted from its original attempt to 're-Frenchify' Quebec to a generalized intellectual nationalism.

The guiding spirit of the movement soon became Abbé Groulx, who replaced Héroux as editor of *L'Action française* in the fall of 1920, after taking a leading role in the movement since 1917.[16] In its first three years, under the editorship of Héroux, *L'Action française* published only one provocative article, the Jesuit Père Louis Lalande's '*La Revanche des berceaux*,'[17] which in the midst of the bitter feeling of the time expressed the conviction that the French Canadians would avenge the insults directed against them and their inferior position in that period by their eventual dominance in Canada, thanks to their higher birthrate. This 'revenge of the cradle' idea became a perennial bugaboo for racist-minded English Canadians who saw the surplus French-Canadian population steadily overflowing from Quebec into eastern and northern Ontario and into northern New Brunswick, and gradually becoming dominant there, as they already had in the once English Eastern Townships of Quebec. But for the rest *L'Action française* had published scholarly articles on such topics as 'Our national strength' and on such precursors of intellectual nationalism as Errol Bouchette, Edmond de Nevers, and Jules-Paul Tardivel. A new tone at once became evident when Groulx assumed control of the review, with the publication in September 1920 of Emile Bruchési's '*Si la Confédération disparaissait*,' which envisaged a republic of Eastern Canada in which Quebec predominated.[18] In the three following numbers articles were published opposing the teaching of English on a parity with French in the primary schools, the establishment of a *Maison Canadienne* for both English and French students at Paris, and the attempt to put Canadian history 'on a British footing,' as some disciples of the *bonne entente* movement desired.

Abbé Groulx, gifted with a highly charged eloquence as both writer and speaker, espoused a nationalism very different from that of Henri Bourassa, and sought to divide his compatriots sharply from the English Canadians. During his graduate studies at Fribourg in Switzerland and in Paris he had come under the influence of disciples of the Comte de Gobineau, the eminent nineteenth-century French racist whose doctrines so strongly affected Houston Stewart Chamberlain in England and the Nazi racists who derived from him. Groulx was also greatly influenced by the anti-democratic romantic nationalism of Maurice Barrès and Charles Maurras, and from these sources were borrowed many of the ideas, as well as the name, of the Canadian *L'Action française* movement.

This was a much narrower and headier doctrine than the broad traditional nationalism of Bourassa. Among the bases of this integral nationalism were a cult of the homeland and of the French language, folk hero-worship, Catholicism as a national unifying force, a tendency towards Caesarism or monarchism, and corporatism.

As it developed both in France and Quebec, this nationalism was a breeder of hatred of alien influences: Protestant, 'Anglo-Saxon,' Jewish, Masonic, liberal, republican, and socialist. In France the movement even became anti-papal, after its condemnation by Rome in 1927. In Canada the clerical leaders of the movement were too Catholic for this step—which was a not unnatural development, since Maurras was an agnostic himself, though he believed in Catholicism for the masses. But they carried on the movement in the same tradition, which was a logical development from the old *Castor* ultramontane tradition, continuing to be sympathetic to Maurras' doctrine and merely changing the name of their organ to *L'Action canadienne-française* without shunning the ideas condemned by Rome. The myth of 'Latin' cultural dominance was dear to the French-Canadian minority group which was looked down upon by the dominant English-speaking culture of North America; and bitter opposition to the democratic system came naturally to a people which had been born under French absolutism and which had failed to attain equality with the majority under British parliamentary government.

Groulx himself had grown up a young man when the French language and Quebec itself were under constant attack. He was an early follower of Bourassa, Lavergne, Asselin, Omer Héroux, and a leader of the A.C.J.C.; and when he returned from European studies in 1909 the nationalist tide was beginning to sweep Quebec. Supported by Abbé Emile Chartier, Groulx responded to Bourassa's criticism of French-Canadian history-teaching in *Le Devoir* in 1913. In 1915 he became the first professor of Canadian history at the Université de Montréal. It was almost inevitable, considering his background and environment, that he should see Canadian history as a perpetual struggle between the 'races.' The historical views that he evolved during the bitter war years painted the French Canadians as noble martyrs—unless they were *déraciné* traitors to the 'race'—and the English as harsh tyrants, who seemingly devoted themselves to making a mockery of their professed belief in 'British fair play.' He gradually evolved an heroic myth in which the French Canadians—a proud people—could take pride. He painted the days of New France as a golden age, of which the *habitant* and the *coureur de bois* were the folk heroes. He created the cult of Dollard, the hero of the Long Sault fight against the Iroquois, who became the idol of French-Canadian youth. He maintained that a new French race had been evolved in Canada during the seventeenth and eighteenth centuries, with a providential mission to spread the blessing of Catholicism and French culture.

Groulx' history was dominated by the concept of 'race,' not in an anthropological sense, but in the historical ethnological sense.

To him race was 'of all historical elements the most active, the most absolute [*irréductible*]. When thought to have been drowned, it arises after centuries to vindicate its immortal right. It is more powerful than all other influences combined, save the religious one; it transforms without being transformed; and determines the political, economic, social, and intellectual life of a nation.'[19] He constantly stressed the 'racial' factor, for he believed that 'the reality of our national personality, the profound consciousness of our distinct entity, could maintain our racial instincts, could fortify our will to live.'[20] For him French-Canadian particularism was implied by the facts of history: 'history itself shows it, without preconceived design.'[21] Writing as a passionate partisan, he pictured the development of a singularly pure race which had survived despite the errors of French colonial policy and despite the tyranny of the English conquerors. He made much of the just causes of the Papineau Rebellion, of French-Canadian opposition to Confederation, of the persecution of French-Canadian minorities in educational matters, and of British imperialism. He preached a cult of devotion to history and to the traditions of the race, of racial pride and of opposition to anglo-mania and cultural exoticism.[22]

Groulx summed up his doctrine thus in *L'Action française* in January 1921:

Our doctrine can be contained in this brief formula: we wish to reconstitute the fullness of our French life. We wish to re-find, to reconstitute in its integrity, the ethnic type which France left here and which one hundred and fifty years of history has shaped. We wish to remake an inventory of moral and social forces, which in itself will prepare their flowering. We wish to purify this type of foreign growths in order to develop in it intensively the original culture, to attach to it the new virtues acquired since the Conquest, above all to keep it in intimate contact with the vital sources of its past, in order to let it go henceforth its regular and individual way. And it is this rigorously characterized French type, dependent upon history and geography, having ethnical and psychological hereditary traits, which we wish to continue, on which we base the hope of our future; because a people, like all growing things, can develop only what is in itself, only the forces whose living germ it contains.

This germ of a people was one day profoundly strickened in its life; it was constrained, paralysed in its development. The consequences of the Conquest weighed heavily upon it; its laws, its language were hamstrung; its intellectual culture was long hobbled; its system of education, deviated in some of its parts, sacrificed more than was fitting to English culture; its natural domain was invaded, leaving it only partially master of its economic forces; its private and public customs were contaminated by the Protestant and Saxon atmosphere. A distressing make-up has gradually covered the physiognomy of our cities and towns, an implacable sign of the subjection of souls to the law of the conqueror.

This evil of the Conquest was aggravated after 1867 by the evil of federalism. Confederation may have been a political necessity; it may have promoted great material progress; for a time, it may even have given Quebec a greater measure of autonomy. But it could not prevent the system from turning notable influences against us. Our particular situation in the federal alliance, the isolation of our Catholic and French province amidst eight provinces in majority English and Protestant, the imbalance of forces which ensued, sometimes increased by the hostile policy of some rulers, led federal legislation little by little towards principles or acts which endangered our fundamental interests. The political system of our country, such as it is by way of being applied, leads not to unity but straight to uniformity. The dominant ideas at the present time at the seat of the central government tend to restrict from year to year the domain of the French language, to undermine secretly the autonomy of our social, religious, and even political institutions. It suffices to recall the battles so long waged here to maintain respect for the clauses of the federal pact relative to French, the recently projected laws on divorce, the suppression for federal employees of many of our religious holidays, the attempts to make uniform law and education, and finally the multiple assaults directed against our province and denounced by none other than the premier of Quebec, the Honorable Alexandre Taschereau, in his speech of November 22, 1920 at the Hotel Viger. So many symptoms, so many undeniable facts which suffice to explain the regressions of national personality among us and the very large part which *L'Action française* has given and must long give to works of pure defence.[23]

In addition to this negative program, Abbé Groulx proposed to strengthen French-Canadian culture by drawing upon 'the two greatest sources of life,' Rome and France:

For our intellectual élite we ask Roman culture and French culture. The first will give us masters of truth, those who furnish the spiritual rules, which make shine on high the principles without which there is no firm direction, no intangible social basis, no permanent order, no people assured of its goal. In the natural order, the culture of France, the immortal educator of our thoughts, will achieve the perfecting of our minds. And when we speak of French culture, we mean not in the limited sense of literary culture, but in the broad and elevated sense in which the French mind appears to us as an incomparable master of clarity, order, and subtlety, the creator of the sanest and most humane civilization, the highest expression of intellectual health and mental balance. And equally we mean not an initiation which leads to dilettantism or to alienization, but a culture which serves without servility, which safeguards our traditional attitudes before the truth, which become a real and beneficent force, will permit our next élite to apply itself more vigorously to the solution of our problems, to the service of its race, its country, and its faith.[24]

The élite, like the people, would be saved from alienization by mixing with Roman and French sources those nearer sources which embodied 'the substance of our past and our traditions.'

For emphasis upon history was an essential element of Groulx' nationalism:

> By history, which maintains the continuity between the generations, which carries from one to the other, like a river, the accumulated flood of virtues of the race, a people remains in constant and present possession of its moral richness. By history we experience for ourselves, as Charles Maurras says, how 'no living being, no precise reality is worth the activity and latent power of the collective will of our ancestors'; and by it their pressure, their imperious directions, which will push us towards the future. From history we shall learn the aptitudes of our people; it will tell us by the observance of what laws, of what exigencies of the intimate nature of the people, they must today be governed, be initiated to new developments, to evolutions which do not bring ephemeral and false prosperity but which are adapted to life as to teething rings. Finally by history will remain joined to our souls the whole of our traditions, at least those which contain life and are only the prolongment of the soul of our ancestors. Traditions, like language, though less perfectly, are a sign of the race, and by that very fact an element of survival. Must we see there anything except a series of actions by ancestors issuing from their most profound ways of thinking, from their sentimental attitudes before the great objects of life, actions so strongly linked to their intimate and collective soul that they have ended by being established as customs, as permanent gestures? And what is there to say, if not that by history will be restored to us in its fullness the fundamental being of the nationality, which must be sought and which we need to re-find?[25]

As the goal of national action Groulx set the ideal of being 'a Catholic and Latin people, of being absolutely and stubbornly ourselves, the sort of race created by history and desired by God.'[26]

In his watchword of '*rester d'abord nous-mêmes*' ('remaining first of all ourselves'), Groulx found nothing in conflict with the spirit of Confederation. 'The more we preserve our French and Catholic virtues, the more faithful we remain to our history and traditions, the more we remain the element impermeable by the American spirit, the strongest element of order and stability.'[27] But the French Canadians wanted no alliance in which they incurred all the sacrifices and all the dangers, while all the honors and all the profits went to English Canadians. Groulx thought his people should conserve their aspirations, sacred rights, and strength, so that if Confederation broke down or was reconstructed on a new basis, and they had to choose between imperial absorption or annexation to the States, or if a French state arose, they would be able to face their destiny.

There was always a current of separatism in Groulx' thought, despite his repeated denials of the charge. He had been an impressionable adolescent in the day of Mercier and Riel; frequent references in his work to Jules-Paul Tardivel's *Pour la Patrie* (1895) indicate the influence of that exalted separatist novel upon him; and he evolved his views on Canadian history during the bitter war years when Quebec stood opposed to the English-speaking provinces. For him the French Canadians possessed most of the essential attributes of a nation, and their attainment of political independence would be a normal part of their coming of age as a people. In the first postwar years the British Empire seemed to many observers to be breaking up, with the Irish, Egyptian, and Indian troubles and an anti-imperialist Labor government in power for the first time. Meanwhile free-trade Western Canada was at swordpoints with the protectionist East, and the school and conscription questions had arrayed English against French. The breakup of Confederation thus seemed inevitable to Groulx in 1922, when he launched a symposium on '*Notre Avenir National*' ('Our national future') in *L'Action française*, whose conclusion was unmistakably separatist.

The annual symposiums constitute the most valuable and most revealing work of the *Action française* movement, but before turning to them it would be well to examine the early work of the man who inspired them and, amid all the wealth of talent he attracted, remained the dominating influence.

Abbé Lionel Groulx had already made a notable place for himself in French-Canadian life when he became director of *L'Action française* in 1920. He was born at Vaudreuil in 1878 and educated at the Séminaire de Sainte-Thérèse and the Grand Séminaire in Montreal. His ancestors had long lived in the region; his father, who had been a lumberjack and a seasonal worker in New York State, as well as a farmer, died the year he was born, but his mother, thanks to an early remarriage, was able to maintain her family of four. Young Lionel early showed more interest in books than in farming, and was sent to college with the idea of studying for the priesthood.

At college he read widely, becoming an impassioned admirer of Louis Veuillot, Joseph de Maistre, and Montalembert.[28] From Garneau, Ferland, and the *Jesuit Relations* he derived a knowledge of Canadian history, and a patriotism which made him lead a student's revolt against the subject oddly set for competition for the Prince of Wales Prize in 1897: the speech of a Puritan in the General Court of Massachusetts in favor of Shirley's proposed expedition against Louisbourg, 'to promote the interests of the colonies, to humiliate the French name, and above all to combat the hated religion of Papism.'[29]

Torn between the priesthood and the law, the vocations of his idols Lacordaire and Montalembert, the young man decided in favor of the former. His four years at the Grand Séminaire in Montreal were broken by a period as secretary to Bishop Emard of Valleyfield, and by teaching at the Séminaire de Valleyfield, where he first displayed his ability to inspire youth. Maxime Raymond and Jules Fournier were among his pupils in rhetoric. Then in 1906 Groulx went to Rome for further studies, winning his doctorate in philosophy in 1907 and in theology in 1908. His third year abroad he spent studying letters at Fribourg in Switzerland, after passing the summer in Brittany as chaplain to Admiral de Cuverville, who had known Montalembert, Lacordaire, and Veuillot, and was a highly conservative Catholic who thought that Canada should not send its young men to study in a contaminated France.[30]

At Fribourg Groulx acquired an acquaintance with historical techniques from Père Mandonnet, a Dominican church historian, but devoted most of his time to the study of French literature under Pierre-Maurice Masson and to the preparation of a thesis on French-Canadian speech. After a short stay at the Sorbonne and the Institut Catholique in Paris, he returned home, resuming his teaching at Valleyfield in the fall of 1909. There he formed a Catholic Action group, and became known as a radical for his emphasis on lay participation in that movement and for his support of Bourassa. After *Le Devoir* had sharply criticized the teaching of Canadian history, Groulx spent four months at the Ottawa Archives during the winter of 1913–14 with the idea of preparing a new manual of Canadian history.

The following fall he left the diocese of Valleyfield, bailiwick of Laurier's moderate friend Bishop Emard, for that of Montreal, where his nationalist friends sought to secure a post for him in the university's faculty of letters. So far he had published only a tract on social duties, a monograph on Valleyfield (1913), and *Une Croisade d'Adolescents* (1912), an account of the origin of the A.C.J.C. When the lone Frenchman who then constituted the entire faculty of letters at the University was called home by the outbreak of the war, Groulx became professor of history at Montreal, while his friend Abbé Emile Chartier became professor of Canadian literature.

Groulx began his lectures in November 1915 on the topic of '*Nos luttes constitutionnelles,*' the period from 1791 to 1837, winning a wide audience from outside the university thanks to the publicity of *Le Devoir*. He was the first professor of Canadian history in the French universities since the death of Abbé Ferland fifty years before. A supplementary post as professor of history at the Ecole des Hautes Etudes Commerciales led him to attach more importance to economic history than any previous French-Canadian historian had done.

Learning his profession by himself for lack of a master and keeping his researches just ahead of his lectures, he dealt with the constitutional struggle up to 1867 in 1916–17, the Confederation period in 1917–18, the French period in 1918–19 and the immediate post-Conquest period in 1919–20, and that between 1774–91 in 1920–21. His five annual lectures on each topic were published in pamphlet form at the end of each academic year and widely circulated.[31] Their combative tone and stirring eloquence made Groulx the idol of nationalist youth and of many elders who had retreated into nationalism in a Quebec isolated from the rest of Canada by the school and conscription questions.

Olivar Asselin made the first and perhaps the best criticism of Groulx' work in a lecture to students at the Salle Saint-Sulpice in Montreal on February 15, 1923 which was later reprinted as a pamphlet. He singled out the fact that Groulx was the first French-Canadian historian to prefer the French period to the English one, and to exalt its institutions over later British ones. Groulx gave a new emphasis to the well-worn story, seeking in his own words 'to discover, under the pile of facts, the evolution of the young race, the social conditions manifested by it. . . . The least revelations of the old forms of the past, of the *petite histoire* of the ancestors, bring us higher satisfaction than any other discovery.'[32] In '*Les Lendemains de la conquête*,' '*Vers l'émancipation*,' '*Les Luttes constitutionnelles*,' and '*La Confédération*' Groulx subsequently depicted 'the frightful misfortune' which the Conquest had brought upon the French Canadians, destroying education, the *seigneurs*, the system of colonization, and corrupting the system of justice. The English regime, in its partiality for commerce, had neglected agriculture, paving the way for the later exodus to the cities and to the States. In the administration of justice, in legislation, commerce, and industry, a frightful jargon was substituted for French. As the only offsets to these disadvantages the English regime had introduced English criminal law and parliamentary government. The brief period of liberty attained in 1848 was followed by Confederation, which inaugurated an era of abdications and defeats from the point of view of French Catholics.

Asselin criticized Groulx for his unrealistic denial of the charge that the French Canadians had Indian blood, for painting the early French Canadians in too glowing colors, and for his attacks on French policy in the last years of the French regime. Asselin himself held that 'all good that we have we owe to France; all that menaces us comes from Anglo-Saxon societies.'[33] But he defended Groulx' history against Gustave Lanctot's charges of partisanship, preconceived judgments, doctored documents, and faked references. To Groulx historical impartiality was not neutrality:

History is a moral act, consequently not free of the supreme finalities. Our ambition and our right are to write and teach as a Catholic and French Canadian should. The historian ought to work with his whole personality; if he makes it neutral and indifferent, let us say with Bossuet that he abdicates his quality as a man.[34]

Asselin opposed to Groulx' partisan nationalism the serene loyalism of Thomas Chapais. Both historians believed in the intervention of Providence in human affairs, but Providence for Chapais was 'a gentleman who drank ale, ate roastbeef, did much business—a "great, a roaring business"—and occupied his leisure as a good giant by freeing peoples, after teasing them a bit to find out what they were good for.' Chapais had the 'timorous spirit of the men of his generation' in defending his language and his faith, to which he was nonetheless much attached; and since he was the son of one of the Fathers of Confederation, the pact was doubly sacred to him. To Asselin 'the English of Chapais were men we have never seen except in books; those of Groulx, with their Jekyll and Hyde double personality, are those that we have known since our childhood.'[35]

Asselin criticized Groulx for faults of style in the shape of anglicisms and barbarisms, for errors of grammar and spelling, and for echoing French authors, particularly Barrès. But he praised him for emphasizing the anonymous figures of history, for his gift of evoking eloquently the atmosphere and background of past periods. For him Groulx' work was 'the finest element among French-Canadian intellectual assets.'[36] He approved Groulx' view of the Conquest as a great catastrophe rather than as a providential happening, as the loyalist historians saw it; his theory of a French-Canadian defeatist psychology arising from the parasitical role then thrust upon the *seigneurs*; and his repudiation of 'the historical imposture of a liberal and maternal England which treated us as the spoiled children of its empire.'[37] Asselin found valid Groulx' analysis of French-Canadian defeatism, with 'its spontaneous faith in the superiority of the conqueror, his customs, his institutions; . . . its self-distrust, its doubts of its own strength, its scorn of its fellows and of the ethnic genius; . . . its morbid taste for peace without dignity, the easy forgetfulness of injuries which it accepts as the pay of its condition, its valet-like mentality in its own home; instead of the proud movement towards the restorations which efface defeat, the desire to make the defeat complete by total abdication; in short, its likeness to a senseless tree, bent by the storm, which has only the stupid obsession to fall.'[38] To Groulx the French Canadians, alienized by 'political and moral colonialism, reinforced by the dualism of a federated country,'[39] needed to regain consciousness of their racial personality and racial pride.

But he had high hopes for the future:

After a long period of indifference and lethargy, we witness an incomparable awakening of the race . . . Let us leave aside extravagant hopes and fix on solid reality. And the reality is the fact that we are two million French Canadians in the Dominion of Canada. We have an impregnable foothold in the province of Quebec; we occupy a territory with geographical unity, we have all the wealth of the soil, all the channels of communication, all the outlets to the sea, all the resources which assure the strength and independence of a nation. We can, if we wish, if we develop all the powers of our race and our soil, become strong enough to lend vigorous assistance to our dispersed brethren . . . The future and Providence are going to work for us. Joseph de Maistre wrote, on the morrow of the French Revolution, that God made such terrible clean sweeps only to lay bare the bases of the future. Let us believe with firm faith that after the vast disorder of the Great War there will be room for marvellous constructions. We make only this prayer to our leaders and to all the chiefs of our race: know how to foresee and to act. Grant that they may no more abandon the development of our life to improvisation and to incoherent action; that for the vanity of a too largely Canadian patriotism they may not sacrifice us to the dream of an impossible unity; that they may know how to reserve the future; that before concluding and deciding our destinies, they may take account of the premises of our history; and then God will not let perish that which he has conserved by so many miracles.[40]

By his historical work Groulx established himself as an ultranationalist of a radicalism hitherto unknown in Quebec. More realistic and more gifted than Jules-Paul Tardivel, he carried on the ultramontane tradition and gave it a racist, separatist bent. How far this tendency really went was revealed in a novel, *L'Appel de la Race*, which Groulx published in 1922 under the pseudonym of 'Alonie de Lestres.' It was both romantic and written to serve a thesis, and was accused of being a *roman à clef*. It was the story of one Jules de Lantagnac, a bilingual M.P. and ornament of the Ottawa bar, who had become '*déraciné*' thanks to the English atmosphere of Ottawa and to his English-Canadian wife. One of the parliamentary leaders in the fight for the separate schools—while the action takes place from 1914 to 1916, there is no mention of the war, though much of the school conflict—he finally reverts to type, and under the spiritual guidance of an Oblate confessor puts loyalty to his race above loyalty to his family, which he abandons.

The book is a clever tract against anglicization, assimilative influences, and marriages mixed in either blood or religion; as well as a rather good dramatization of the school question in personal terms. It is permeated with intransigent nationalism and racism and with frequent comparisons drawn from the history of other minority peoples. The novel was bitterly attacked by Louvigny de Montigny in *La Revue Moderne*, as spokesmen for the French Canadians of

Ottawa, and by Mgr. Camille Roy in *Le Canada Français*, as spokesman for loyalist Quebec. René du Roure, a Frenchman teaching at McGill, also assailed it in *La Revue Moderne*. But the book was a popular success, and its curious theology was defended in *L'Action française*[41] by none other than the future Cardinal Villeneuve, then a young Oblate theologian who had been Groulx' travelling companion on a trip to Acadia in 1914 and who had taken an active part in the Ottawa school agitation.

Two minor works, *Rapaillages* (1916) and *Chez nos Ancêtres* (1920), were prose poems devoted to hymning the good old pastoral days of French Canada in the manner of the *terroir* school launched by Adjutor Rivard. They were sentimentalizations of a rural life which had no appeal for Groulx himself as a child,[42] but which he, in common with other leaders of the intellectual élite, later idealized as the best life for the masses of French Canada. Groulx' early interest in French Canadianisms led him to dot his text with italicized *patois* expressions, an irritating practice to all but the most narcissistic admirers of French-Canadian culture. As Asselin pointed out, Groulx produced his best regionalist work in the course of his historical writings rather than in these minor efforts.

Finally Groulx exercised a considerable effect by his public lectures on patriotic topics, of which perhaps the most notable in early days were '*Pour L'Action française*' in 1918, '*Si Dollard revenait*' in 1919, and '*Méditation Patriotique*' in 1920.[43] He largely took Bourassa's place as the leading French-Canadian orator on patriotic occasions, and during a year of study in Paris in 1921–2 he won a reputation for eloquence which later gained him an invitation to give a course on the French in Canada at the Sorbonne in 1931. Outraged by French ignorance of Canada, he created a committee in Paris to further relations between the intellectuals of France and French Canada, and gave many lectures on French-Canadian history. The most notable, that of February 2, 1922, was printed as a pamphlet by the French *L'Action française*.[44] Upon his return home, he, like Bourassa before him, undertook oratorical pilgrimages to Franco-American and other outlying French-Canadian minority centers, seeking to promote a reunion of the 'race.'[45]

2

The most solid of the long series of influential annual symposiums conducted in *L'Action française* was the first, that of 1921 on '*Les Problèmes économiques*.' The war, the postwar depression, and the census of that year served to focus French-Canadian nationalist opinion on the economic question for the first time in serious fashion.

Edouard Montpetit, the first thoroughly trained French-Canadian economist, who had pioneered in the inauguration of economi courses at the Ecole des Hautes Etudes Commerciales after hi return from Paris in 1910, opened the discussion with an article o '*L'Indépendence économique des Canadiens-Francais*,' the fruit of his fifteen years study of the question. He singled out the fact that, thank largely to the war, the French Canadians had at last become economic-minded. He argued that it was not a question of sacrificing the intellectual to the material factor. Today the French Canadian had to assure the material basis of a more intense intellectual life it was time to replace the old cries of '*Emparons-nous du sol*' and '*Emparons-nous de l'industrie*,' by that of '*Emparons-nous de la science et de l'art*.'[46] To the old political threats had been added the new menace of commercial imperialism, and French Canada must adapt itself to the new order or die.

Montpetit maintained that French Canada was richer than i believed, but not rich enough for its needs. History and geograph should be taught in the primary schools so as to instill a knowledg of the fundamentals of Quebec's economy. Technical schools should train workers and artisans, while advanced schools produce specialists. These last should give attention to sociology, economics and political science, as well as to history and philosophy. Ther should be a provincial minister of commerce and industry to furthe economic development. In addition to the exploitation of the soil there should be exploitation of waterpower and the forests. Quebe had the manpower, the capital, and the intelligence required fo modern industry. Mines, forests, and waterpower exploitation mus be left to great capitalists; but Quebec could produce much mor of what it consumed in food, clothing, lodging, and meet its highe intellectual, artistic and moral needs. Montpetit urged that French Canadians should buy their own products, their own art. French Canadian credit and financial institutions deserved support, so tha they in turn could favor the development of French-Canadian businesses. In short, 'let us enrich ourselves in order to make ou innate Frenchness shine forth, so that the money question may n longer retard our will and the satisfaction of our noblest ends.'

In March Olivar Asselin pointed out '*Les Lacunes de notre organi zation économique*': the alienation by politicians in the past of water power and timber resources, the need for colonization of new area in Quebec and Ontario, the improvement of agriculture, more credi for industry, emphasis on training industrial chemists, developmen of banks and insurance firms, and above all less defeatism in economi matters. In April Emile Miller, Université de Montréal geographe whose career was cut short by premature death, discussed th natural resources of the province. In June Georges Pelletier of *L*

Devoir traced the history of Quebec's industrial development, emphasizing the extent to which it was due to English Canadians and Americans and calling for the development of French-Canadian industries to meet the needs of the province. In July Léon Lorrain discussed French-Canadian business; in August Beaudry Leman the banking institutions; and in September Henry Laureys commercial and technical education. Omer Héroux dealt with the insurance companies in October, while in November J.-E. Gendreau urged higher scientific education in the French-Canadian universities.

Abbé Groulx summoned up the symposium in December, calling for an economic nationalism:

> It will be the duty of the rising generation, if it wishes to attain the potent fruits of its fortune, to cause it to be admitted that the ethnic being of the Quebec State has been long fixed in irrevocable fashion. A history now three hundred years long, the nearly complete possession of the soil by a determined race, the profound imprint that this race has given it by its original manners and institutions, the special status reserved for it by all the political constitutions since 1791, have made of Quebec a French State that must be recognized in theory as well as in fact. It is this truth which must be replaced on high in order that it may govern the economic order amongst us, as one spontaneously admits it should govern the other functions of our lives. Let us say that we should cease to think like vanquished and conquered people. Together we shall rather raise our thoughts to the reality of the homeland, towards this central idea which will put order and strength into our action. It will give us the noble sentiment of respect that we owe to ourselves; better than all speeches, it will make us prefer the role of architects and builders to that of masons and hired men. And in our own house we shall do otherwise than prepare the lion's share for a rival.[47]

Groulx was never again able to muster so notable a collection of French-Canadian leaders for his annual surveys as in 1921, and younger and more hotheaded writers later replaced some of the distinguished figures who took part in the discussion of '*Les Problèmes économiques*.' The latent nationalism that every French Canadian carries within himself comes to the surface in time of economic or political crisis; in such periods the rampant individualism and backbiting tendencies which are part of the national temperament yield to a 'sacred union,' which temporarily provides a truce in what Mercier called 'our fratricidal conflicts.' In 1921 French Canada was isolated from English Canada by the bitter aftermath of the school and conscription questions, and by a postwar depression which affected French-Canadian labor more deeply than English-Canadian or American capital and management. With the easing of ethnic tension and the rapid improvement of the economic situation,

French-Canadian nationalism once more became a minority radical movement rather than a mass national movement; and Groulx and his followers were criticized by many of the staider leaders of a people which has a fundamental devotion to the golden mean and to moderation as the governing principles of life.

The radical nationalism already implicit in Groulx' earlier work, which found expression in his conclusion to the 1921 symposium, was made clearly evident in *L'Action's* symposium of 1922 on '*Notre Avenir politique*.' In an introduction Groulx stressed that Confederation 'was headed inevitably towards a breakup. . . . The issue appears certain to the most clearsighted minds; only the due date remains still unknown.'[48] Groulx protested that he had no desire to destroy Confederation or to wound anyone's sense of duty. But it was the duty of the French Canadians to prepare for a future announced by 'unmistakable signs.' Then, as a starting point for the symposium, Groulx took Bourassa's prediction of 1901 in *Grande-Bretagne et Canada* that Canada, torn between British and American imperialism, would have to develop sufficient strength to preserve the *status quo*, 'the greatest good fortune for our people,' or be led towards a new destiny, and in any case must be prepared to meet the decisive hour. He carefully defended himself from any charge of desiring to disturb the *status quo*, 'whatever harm colonialism or federalism may do us.'[49] But by all appearances it was going to be shattered in the near future. Europe was declining, while a Pan-American continentalism was developing without Canadian participation. Europe was becoming an economic colony of America. The British Empire, troubled in Ireland, Egypt, and India, was being eclipsed by the United States, whose rivalry with Japan in the Pacific might hasten the breakup of the empire. Groulx asked frankly whether British imperialism was not 'an organization of peoples which has become artificial, an outworn political formula, unable to sustain the shock of approaching realities.'[50]

The Canadian Confederation seemed equally threatened, with free-trade West aligned against protectionist East in the elections of 1921, and racial rivalry, aroused by the war, temporarily subject to a truce dictated by commercial and political interest, and by 'the salutary fear momentarily dictated to yesterday's enemies by the strength of Quebec.'[51] For Groulx the 'saddening truth is that in spite of transitory appeasement, the attitude of the French Canadians to the federal power and the Anglo-Saxon majority remains none the less an attitude of always uneasy and in no way superfluous vigilance.' For twenty years the French language had been treated by the federal government in a fashion which was a most disloyal repudiation of the federal pact, and continued to be so treated despite proclamations of *bonne entente*. In most of the English-

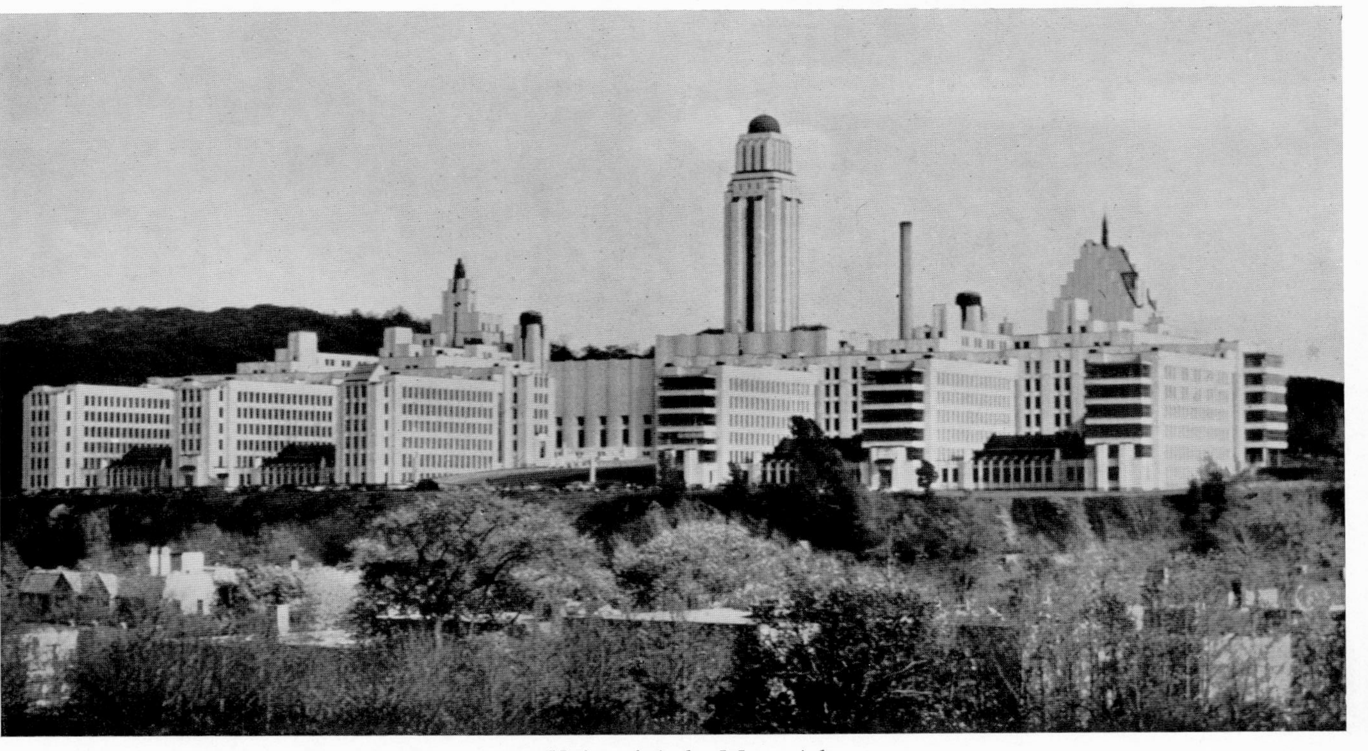

Université de Montréal

The new building on Mount Royal, begun in 1926 and finished in 1941, after plans by Ernest Cormier. The greatest monument of the School of Imitation which began a century before. (I.O.A.P.Q.)

School Yard

Oil painting (1941) by Jean-Charles Faucher (b. 1907). A Brueghel-like study of the recreation period at a Christian Brothers school. (Quebec Provincial Museum.)

Street Scene

Oil painting (c. 1940) by Jean-Charles Faucher. Another study of city life by one of the best Montreal painters. (Quebec Provincial Museum.)

speaking provinces the government had followed the tendency of all federations by encouraging uniformity by all means, including arbitrary force. Not only was there an absolute opposition between the races on the interpretation of the pact of 1867, but the same opposition existed on the relations of Canada with the empire, with the 'Anglo-Saxons' inclined almost unanimously towards imperialism and the French Canadians 'irreducible autonomists.'

Other forces favored the centrifugal action created by the too vast extent of Confederation: lack of geographical continuity, the Americanization of the Canadian West by immigration from the south, tended to create in Canada 'two peoples sharply separated by geography and by ideals, two states of a civilization as diverse as possible.'[52] Edmond de Nevers had foreseen a reorganization of the United States along ethnic lines, while economists foretold that new federative states would arise on the basis of economic unity rather than of such arbitrary geographic divisions as those of Canada. Groulx cited Premier Taschereau's observation on April 17, 1921, that Canada was at the crossroads between preservation of the *status quo* or the breakup of Confederation, annexation to the United States or independence. Nationalization of the railroads which bound Canada together had saved the Western provinces from bankruptcy, but had thrown a burden which threatened to be too heavy upon the old provinces of the East. It was a question to Taschereau whether this was not the first wide breach in the pact of Confederation. Therefore Groulx argued that Quebec must prepare for the future establishment of an Eastern Canada.

He did not believe in economic or geographical determinism; he held that history was determined by the foresight and the will of men in accordance with the plan of Providence. It was 'a people's duty to seek the historic vocation in which it could collaborate most perfectly with God's designs.'[53] The position which the French-Canadian people occupied on a territory which it had made its homeland by three hundred years of effort seemed to indicate for it a separate destiny. Homogeneous in race and faith, grouped by powerful traditions, and possessor of a territory greater than that of many European states, its very situation seemed to offer a separate future designed by Providence. Its providential mission called it to preserve its soul uncontaminated and unfettered in the nationhood to which aspired all nationalities that wished to be absolute masters of their lives. The dream of a French-Canadian nation was an old one which dated back to the Conquest and had ever since 'haunted the spirit of the race.'[54] To Groulx this dream was no artificial creation provoked by an élite of intellectuals and propagandists, but 'the spontaneous manifestation of a national life maintained to a certain degree of perfection, the soul of a history in which the ardent conflict of races had been prolonged in a chronic state.' Nations grew up where human groups were opposed most violently by their family and social institutions, by the geographical diversity of their territories, and above all by their ethnic differences:

> Wherever a human collectivity, conscious of its life and of its moral patrimony, finds itself one day obliged to tremble for the possession or the integrity of its heritage, then a pressing instinct of conservation impels it to put its patrimony out of danger. Of itself, by a force more powerful than its will, it tears itself free from oppressive tutelage, seeks the conditions of existence which will procure its security, organizes itself as a state.[55]

On this reasoning Groulx based his support for the creation of a French state in Eastern Canada if Confederation broke up. He did not invoke the principle of the self-determination of nationalities, but rather the elementary right of a people to prepare a self-chosen destiny with the aid of God. He minimized the danger of such a step for the French Canadians of the other provinces, for whom the *Québecois* felt a solidarity which transcended political bonds. The new state must be based upon political and economic geography; it must safeguard the rights of the ethnic enclaves which would be found within it; much planning and forethought would be necessary. He favored a definitive solution of the problem rather than a transition by way of Canadian independence, American annexation, or adherence to a smaller Confederation. The aspirations of the French-Canadian people must be fixed on the political ideal which was the ultimate goal of its life. 'To be ourselves, absolutely ourselves, to constitute, as soon as Providence wishes it, an independent French state, such should be henceforward the aspiration which should animate our labors, the torch which must no more be extinguished.'[56] Groulx set this goal particularly for French-Canadian youth, 'the architect and worker of great things,' as a principle to guide its action.

Louis Durand saw Canada as a conquered country which had become an autonomous colony, obliged to defend only its own territory and on its way to independence. Then its normal political evolution had been interrupted by Chamberlain's imperialism, which had led it to contribute men and money to the South African War; then to sacrifice legions and millions in the World War; and finally to guarantee the territorial integrity of the empire in the four quarters of the globe. Durand examined in turn the present colonial status of Canada and whether it was worth maintaining; whether the bonds of empire were unbreakable; whether Quebec would be justified in repudiating Confederation if Canada separated from the empire; and what solutions remained for Quebec besides annexation to the States, or the constitution of an independent Eastern Canada with Quebec as the nucleus. He traced out imperial developments since 1910, and found Canada enmeshed in a new imperialism with authority inevitably centralized in London unless the British Empire broke up. But allegiance to the King was now the sole bond of an empire which seemed to be disintegrating at home and abroad, and the 'Anglo-Saxons' of Canada were willing to break that last bond over a simple question of dollars and cents.

Durand was skeptical as to the future of Confederation, in which the new Canadian nationality born at Confederation had been swamped by immigration and crushed by imperialism. French and English were still unable to agree on the interpretation of the basic contract which united them, while the Western provinces were opposed to the Eastern ones on the great questions of free trade, transportation, natural resources, and immigration. A minority constantly on the defensive at Ottawa, which had lost cultural ground decisively in 1872, 1890, 1892, 1896, 1905, and 1912, French Canada had no right to make further sacrifices to prevent the inevitable breakup of Confederation. Annexation and immersion in the American melting-pot were repulsive to 'a people who had three hundred years of existence; its own customs, traditions, language, and religion.'[57] Durand envisaged the formation of an independent Eastern Canada, uniting Quebec and the Maritimes with certain territory to the West, and embracing four or five million inhabitants. This predominantly French state would be linked together by the community of language and faith of the French Canadians and Acadians, and by the tolerance and sincere love of the homeland exhibited by the English Maritimers. It could draw upon the essential resources of wheat, iron, and coal, in addition to its agriculture, fisheries, and timber. All that remained was the task of national organization, defined by Maurras as the ordering of its life and the application of this order to its action.

Abbé Arthur Robert of the Séminaire de Québec provided a theological justification for the '*Aspirations du Canada Français*,' demonstrating that 'a people has the right to the development and the perfecting of its nationality,' and that 'a people has even the right to seek complete autonomy, and if possible, the sovereignty of a State.'[58] The abbé maintained that nationality was based upon origin, language, territory, and government, while unity of blood and language were more essential than unity of territory and government. In the event of a breaking of the British connection through no fault of their own, the French Canadians would be justified in either trying to preserve Confederation, in annexing themselves to the United States, or in founding a French state. The question was a free one, but the abbé concluded that the French Canadians would have a perfect right to found an independent state, 'destined to carry on in America what has so well been called the providential mission of the French race.'

In an article on '*L'Etat Français et les Etats-Unis*' Anatole Vanier urged an alliance of Quebec financiers, merchants, and industrialists with the advocates of a French state. The economic independence of Quebec was a prerequisite of its political independence. The commercial superiority of the United States was due to cheap products; Quebec should seek to produce both cheap and quality goods. The exploitation of Quebec's natural resources by Americans should be prohibited by law; not only exportation of raw materials but their fabrication within the province. With the aid of the government of Quebec, control of its own industry must be won. A new wave of American economic imperialism was threatened by the proposed internationalization of the St. Lawrence, after the inroads already made in the pulp and asbestos industries. He argued that Quebec, with its supply of these raw materials, could obtain an American tariff favoring its agricultural producers, its stock raisers, and its consumers. With its favorable balance of trade, it could maintain favorable foreign commercial relations. The sympathy and racial solidarity of France and Latin America with Quebec would further the development of commercial relations. The establishment of a French state would heighten the prestige of the Franco-Americans, while through cultural relations an old moral alliance could be reasserted for the benefit of French civilization in America. To Vanier the failure of Confederation was complete from the point of view of the French Canadians, and both messianic and economic considerations led him to believe in the eventual establishment of a French state.[59]

Emile Bruchési discussed '*L'Etat Français et l'Amérique Latine*,' taking as a starting point Tardivel's dream in 1895 of the foundation in 1945 of a republic of New France, 'whose mission will be to continue on this American soil the work of Christian civilization which Old France has so long pursued with such glory during such long centuries.'[60] He considered the influence Tardivel assigned to Freemasonry exaggerated, but on the whole he thought Tardivel had seen clearly into a future which was already announced by the breakup of the empire and of Confederation. He pointed out that Alexander Galt had anticipated Canadian independence in 1869, and that hence the French Canadians were free to envisage a French state. Such a state would be welcomed by the United States, which would be glad to see the British flag banished from North America; but against the covetous greed of the 'Giant of the North' French Canada must look for allies in Latin America. In this Latin New World were numerous opponents of the 'Anglo-Saxon' civilization of the United States, 'cousins by blood, by race, by mentality, but unknown cousins who do not know us.'[61] Canada was at last becoming known in Latin America through investments, shipping, and commerce; and thanks to its own industries Quebec could supply manufactured goods which the Latin American countries wanted in exchange for their raw materials. Bruchési urged that cultural and commercial relations with Latin America should be developed by Quebec, which through cultivating its natural allies there could make Tardivel's dream come true.

The Oblate Père Rodrigue Villeneuve considered the problem of the French-Canadian minorities outside Quebec in '*Nos Frères de la Dispersion*,' finding that they had nothing to gain by the continuation of Confederation and that they would remain united by religious and patriotic ties to a French Catholic state, which would be the 'torch of an idealistic and generous civilization in the great whole being shaped by the American future . . . an Israel of the new age in the midst of the Babylon now being formed, an American France, a light and an apostle among nations.'[62]

Georges Pelletier dealt more realistically with '*Les Obstacles économiques à l'indépendence du Canada Français*.' Foreigners of another language and race had taken over most of French Canada's patrimony of natural resources, leaving only agriculture to the natives, who were already deserting their fields to become rootless proletarians in the cities. The English, the Americans, and the Jews prospered in Quebec, while the French Canadians were reduced to serving them. Much of Quebec's forestland was already looted and could not be reforested. Other portions, rented rather than sold outright, might be preserved by regulation of cutting and reforesting. In remote regions there were still unexploited woodlands, which should be preserved for the future rather than disposed of to foreigners. Quebec's asbestos and other mineral deposits should be protected against exportation in the raw state by foreigners, as wood had finally been, and should be rented only for short periods. The resources of New Quebec (Ungava) should be preserved for future generations of French Canadians. Waterpower should be subject to regulation, and in the future leased only to Canadian companies. An inventory of all natural resources should be made in order that they might be sanely developed in the interests of the people.

Pelletier echoed the conclusions of the 1921 symposium on Quebec's industry, stressing the need of self-sufficiency and the industrialization of agriculture and the soil. By creating a class of French-Canadian technicians and by supporting French-Canadian businesses, Quebec could defend itself against the Americanization already threatening Canadian industry. He singled out the danger of the concentration of capital and transport in non-French-Canadian hands. He did not anticipate that foreign capitalists and industrialists would be frightened from Quebec by the establishment of a French state, since Quebec was widely known for its conservatism and its tolerance of foreigners in the midst of a rising tide of socialism among the governments and labor of English-speaking North America. Quebec owned a share of the railways now under government ownership, having helped to build and maintain them, while the Canadian Pacific would scarcely abandon Montreal and Quebec, the principal ports and storage points of Canada. The new state would control the St. Lawrence, the chief artery of an immense hinterland and a source of incalculable waterpower. Pelletier concluded by expressing his conviction that the economic obstacles to a French state could be overcome by effort, hard work, and planning, after a difficult and modest initial period. He preferred the prospect of independence at such a price to that of national annihilation or of a gilded but perpetual servitude.[63]

Joseph Bouchard dealt with the problem of the strangers in Quebec's midst in '*Le Canada Français et les Etrangers*.' He anticipated that this element, reduced to 20 per cent of the population in a predominantly French state and divided into many different groups, could be assimilated or absorbed, while the higher French-Canadian birthrate would gradually reduce the minority's proportion. He called hotly for an end of the old inferiority complex of the French Canadians in economic matters and the indoctrination of a national pride and patriotism which would quickly 're-Frenchify' Quebec. Bilingualism and mixed marriages would henceforward work for the French Canadians rather than against them; and emigration would be halted.[64]

The Dominican Père M.-Ceslas Forest discussed '*La Préparation intellectuelle*', urging the creation of a French-Canadian intellectual life and its defence against foreign influences. He echoed Edouard Montpetit's call in 1917 for the formation of a trained élite of specialists. But the scientific organization of agricultural, commercial, and industrial life was not sufficient; it must be supplemented by the creation of a philosophy, science, literature, and art, in which the French Canadians, thanks to their heritage of French civilization, might surpass their neighbors. Père Forest urged that the culture of Quebec should be French, preferring that the French Canadians should borrow from a suspect but a Latin and Catholic France rather than from Protestant and materialist England and the United States. Some elements of value, nonetheless, could be drawn from 'Anglo-Saxon' civilization, with due caution to preserve an essentially French culture. The culture of Quebec should be Canadian, a French culture purified of modern corruptions and adapted to

North America, and reflecting the Canadian environment. It should be Catholic, since it was based upon the Catholic French and Canadian traditions, and since it must be Catholic to be fruitful and to endure.[65]

Antonio Perrault discussed '*Le Sens national*,' differentiating between patriotism and national feeling. The latter was a higher, more conscious sentiment, disciplining patriotism and guiding it by the light of the spirit. He judged that it already had long existed among the French Canadians, breaking out when attempts had been made to crush French Canada. But it must be further developed. The ethnic type evolved in New France must be purified of 'Anglo-Saxon' and American accretions by emphasizing the French Canadians' historic and traditional particularism, by strengthening their attachment to their own customs, and their love of their own corner of the earth. An élite of intellectuals and men of action must exert itself to instil in the masses a greater love of their faith and language, of their culture and law, their traditions and customs. He favored the nationalization of literature, through emphasis on regionalism and patriotism and repudiation of exoticism and cosmopolitanism. 'In the family and at the school, education and instruction must turn the spirit and heart of the child to fix them always on the soul of its race.'[66] Nationalization of education would awaken a sense of national responsibilities, pride of race, and will to serve the race. Abbé Philippe Perrier dealt with '*L'Etat Français et sa valeur d'idéal pour nous*,' asserting that man had a duty to develop his national personality as well as his moral personality. He called for an end of cultural colonialism, and the development of the unity of blood, language, faith, history, country, customs, and interests which, according to Etienne Lamy, were the attributes of a nation. The ideal of a French state would help to complete the attainment of these attributes.[67]

Abbé Groulx summed up the conclusions of the symposium, once more asserting his unwillingness to shatter the *status quo*, and his desire merely to prepare against the impending rupture of Confederation. The foresight of his introduction to the symposium, written in November 1921, seemed to him to have been realized by the deep antagonisms displayed in the federal elections of December, which had led even Bourassa to envisage the approaching end of Confederation. The breakup of the British Empire seemed still nearer than it had at the outset of the symposium. The conclusions of the participants had supported those of the instigator of the symposium; and Groulx made the most of those conclusions which agreed with his own.

He emphasized the fact that for half a century French Canada had laid more emphasis on survival than on its ideal goal of independence, thanks to 'the mixed marriage contracted by our race in 1841,'[68] which had only been saved from a shattering divorce by the worse error of Confederation. Quebec had abdicated its sense of nationality, its patrimony of national resources, its very traditions and customs. Americanization and anglomania had created havoc, while a large part of the bourgeoisie had betrayed the national ideal. The goal of independence would supply a new orientation: 'the duty of the moment is to relight the old torch and prevent it from ever being extinguished.'[69] This torch would be carried on by youth, to whom Groulx once more made a special appeal. To him it was clear that 'the ideal of a French state was going to correspond more and more among us to a kind of vital impulsion';[70] it was a saving principle which would set the French Canadians free from the chaos of their divisions and of their scattered labors. He warned youth that there were decisive hours which did not come twice in the life of a nation, and said that he was unwilling to be a speculative idealist; he had not promised to act, but had begun to act.

3

The frank separatism of this 1922 symposium caused a division among Abbé Groulx' following, as the French Canadians lost their crisis psychology with the return of Quebec to a large share in the federal government. Confederation held together, as the new Liberal leader Mackenzie King achieved a working alliance with the Western Progressives and followed a course leading to fuller nationhood which was in part dictated by his loyalty to Laurier. The British Empire did not crumble, but in 1926 evolved into the British Commonwealth of Nations, in which the old anglo-centric imperialism gave way to self-determination by the constituent nations. In the development of this third British Empire Canada had taken a leading role, as was pointed out by Alfred Zimmern of Oxford, who further considered that the Constitutional Act of 1791 marked 'a decisive turning point in the history of the British Commonwealth.'[71] On November 23, 1923, Bourassa publicly criticized '*Notre Avenir politique*,' calling its separatism 'a dream neither realizable nor desirable' and commenting that 'the tendencies of immoderate nationalism here or elsewhere, are contrary to real patriotism and true nationalism.'[72]

The conclusions of '*Notre Avenir politique*' were also criticized by middle-of-the-road French Canadians whose faith in the *status quo* was gradually being restored. Edouard Montpetit evolved into a preacher of federalism on the basis of equality between French and English,[73] while devoting his energies to the improvement of economic and social studies at the struggling young Université de

Montréal in which he became a major influence. Henry Laureys continued to foster the growth of the Ecole des Hautes Etudes Commerciales, which long provided the only academic economic training to be had in French Canada. Beaudry Leman became the leading French-Canadian banker, protesting in 1928 in reply to the economic xenophobia of the ultranationalists that 'The most serious menace is not the penetration of money capital, but of the moral and intellectual capital of men better qualified than we to profit from our natural resources.'[74] Léon Lorrain dissociated himself from *L'Action française*. Georges Pelletier succeeded Bourassa in the direction of *Le Devoir* and preached a moderate nationalism. Olivar Asselin became a salesman of stocks and bonds for the two leading French-Canadian brokerage firms, returning to his initial profession of journalism only after the stockmarket crash of 1929, which hit Montreal hard and impoverished some of the religious orders which had large investments. Though he retained his interest in economic nationalism, Asselin was not temperamentally cut out to be a follower of any school of thought except his own, and his devotion to French culture put him at odds with the increasingly provincial nationalism of the Groulx school.

But Antonio Perrault, Anatole Vanier, and Abbé Philippe Perrier remained devoted disciples of Groulx, who also kept his influence in the classical colleges. To this nucleus of veterans were added such young recruits as Jean Bruchési, who had carried on as a student in Paris the work of cementing cultural relations between France and Quebec begun by Groulx in 1921; Esdras Minville, the first Quebec-trained economist, whose nationalism was the more realistic because of the fact that he had risen by his own efforts from a humble fishing family of Gaspé and had never had the classical college training which encouraged a devotion to theory at the expense of awkward facts; Emile Bruchési, Yves Tessier-Lavigne, Harry Bernard, and Hermas Bastien.

In 1923 *L'Action française's* annual symposium was devoted to '*Notre intégrité catholique*,' while the magazine also opposed emigration from the countryside to the cities and to the States, American economic imperialism, and the continued persecution of French in the Ontario schools. In 1924 the symposium dealt with '*L'Ennemi dans la place*,' with denunciations of Quebec's high infant mortality rate, the anticipated decline of the birthrate through urbanization, emigration to the States, American economic imperialism, and American movies. In 1925 there was a return to the original purpose of the movement with a symposium on bilingualism, making the largest possible claims for the rights of the French language and bitterly protesting against violation of the bilingual principle of Confederation. The ebb of nationalist confidence was reflected not only in the renewed insistance on bilingualism, which had been dismissed as impossible in the earlier days when a French state was envisaged, but also in the demand for the establishment of Saint-Jean-Baptiste Day (June 24) as a legal holiday which would unite a race which lacked national independence, a state of its own, its own territory, and its own flag. This new defensive attitude was also reflected by articles supporting the movements for national Catholic unions of workers and farmers. French Canadians were urged to elect only compatriots in the federal elections of October 1925, since their influence in the Commons was steadily declining.

In 1926 there were two chief topics of discussion, '*Défense de notre capital humain*' and '*Doctrines de notre jeunesse*,' with Montpetit, the Jesuit Père Louis Lalande, and Olivar Asselin once more joining the usual contributors in stressing the importance of Quebec's greatest asset, its human capital, threatened despite its strong vitality by infant mortality and tuberculosis, emigration, urbanization, and industrialization. Colonization was as usual advanced as a solution of the social problem, with a new emphasis on public health measures and on the establishment of rural industries. Esdras Minville, Léon Lortie, René Chaloult, Jean Bruchési, Albert Lévesque, and Séraphin Marion responded in the name of the rising generation to the doctrines of *L'Action française*. A symposium on '*La Doctrine de L'Action française*' was launched in 1927, with a new political emphasis. There were attacks on American economic and cultural influences, the Labrador Award of the Privy Council, the fact that Quebec had more Jews than any other province, and approval for measures taken by Mussolini's government.

A special double number in 1927, published on the sixtieth anniversary of Confederation, constituted the most notable symposium since 1922.[75] As might have been expected, no such idyllic view of Confederation was taken as by most English-Canadian spokesmen upon the occasion; but in contrast to 1922 there was a determination to uphold French Canada's rights in Confederation which implied a reluctant belief in its survival. *L'Action française* had always mocked the *bonne entente* movement, but now it justified its freeness and frankness in speaking of Confederation as the only way to prepare a good understanding.

Groulx discussed '*Les Canadiens Français et l'établissement de la Confédération*,' stressing the primary importance of Quebec's role in making Confederation possible by its third of the total proposed population, its political unity, and its geographical situation. He also emphasized the risks Quebec took by merging its destiny with that of four English provinces instead of one. It had to preserve its provincial autonomy and its national and religious rights and those of the French minorities in the other provinces. It was because of French Canada that Confederation took the form of a federal rather than a legislative union. He made much of the misgivings of A.-A. Dorion, Henri Taschereau, and L.-O. David at the time. Cartier and his associates Langevin and Cauchon persuaded Quebec to accept Confederation, 'relying too much on the good faith of their political associates.'[76] Groulx judged that they would not have prevailed without the support of the hierarchy, and stressed the reluctance of Bishop Bourget to back Confederation. He concluded that the good faith of French Canada's political and spiritual leaders had been betrayed by subsequent events, and that 'after more than half a century of existence, the Canadian Confederation still remains an anemic giant, carrying many germs of dissolution. . . .'[77]

He issued a stern warning to the English Canadians:

> All that has been attempted for the last sixty years, and all that will be attempted in the future against the security of the French-Canadian race in this country, has been attempted and will be attempted against its interest in maintaining Confederation. It did not enter into Confederation to die, nor even to let itself be tamed, but to live, to survive as a whole. This is not the hour to subtilize or to restrain the federal spirit; it must be fortified and generalized across Canada as the contact of the two races is further extended. The French-Canadian race is no longer limited to the East of the country; despite the barriers raised against it, it has exported men to all the Western provinces, as far as the shores of the Pacific. The reactions of these French groups, as well as those of the present Quebec, against the denials of justice and administrative meannesses should give warning that, if formerly our adhesion to the federative pact could be traded cheaply, the generation of today does not admit that its chances of living, any more than its right to live worthily, have been sold.[78]

Anatole Vanier protested in a brief note against the immigration policy which made it cheaper for a Britisher or an American to come to Canada and to establish himself in the West than for a French Canadian of Quebec to do likewise. Under such circumstances it was no wonder that French Canadians emigrated to the States, as Vanier suggested the English Canadians desired them to do.[79] Olivar Asselin dealt with the topic of '*Les Canadiens Français et le développement économique du Canada*,' estimating that the French Canadians held about one-seventh of the wealth of Canada, while they represented two-sevenths of its population.[80] He blamed French-Canadian economic inferiority on the Conquest, on a traditional agriculture which impoverished the land, on emigration, on English dominance in trade and industry, on the imposition of the heavy debt of Upper Canada on Lower Canada in 1841, on the favoritism shown to English Canadians in public works and in nominations to administrative posts, and on the development of the West with public funds for the benefit of English Canadians. He concluded that the French Canadians had not been a barrier to the economic development of the country, but had done as much as they could to further it, while Quebec enjoyed the best credit of any Canadian province abroad. Hermas Bastien rehearsed in a brief note the old French-Canadian grievances against the Irish, who had opposed rather than made common cause with their fellow Catholics.[81]

Montpetit discussed '*Les Canadiens Français et le développement intellectuel du Canada*,' giving the history of educational developments under the French regime, which had been interrupted by the Conquest and by the attempt to establish an English system of schools. Gradually the school system had been re-established by the clergy; and granted autonomy in educational matters by Article 93 of the B.N.A. Act, Quebec alone had fully realized the intentions of Macdonald and Cartier with its system of separate Catholic and Protestant schools, numbering 7,000 schools attended by a fifth of the population and fifteen normal schools. Its twenty-one classical colleges had formed an intellectual élite which had influenced the development of English colonial policy, while maintaining the cause of general culture. Two universities had grown up, providing professional and technical training as well as the four fundamental faculties of theology, law, medicine, and arts. Quebec had led the way by establishing the Ecole des Hautes Etudes Commerciales and technical schools. Its government provided scholarships for studies abroad, and more than half the teachers of the universities and colleges had been trained abroad. Since the visit of 'La Capricieuse' in 1855, cultural relations had been renewed with France, enabling Quebec to be the center of French culture in America. By remaining itself French Canada preserved Canada from Americanization and gave a young country the richness of two great civilizations.[82]

Yves Tessier-Lavigne argued in a note on '*Québec, les chemins de fer, et Confédération*,' that Quebec had at least one reason not to celebrate the sixtieth anniversary of Confederation, since the federal government had done little for its railroad development while doing much for the other provinces.[83] Abbé Philippe Perrier discussed '*Les Canadiens Français et la vie morale et sociale du Canada*,' stressing Quebec's contribution to Canadian morality by its Catholicism which maintained the sanctity of the family and of marriage, had given the country a rich 'human capital,' respected the parent's rights in education, insisted on the teaching of morality in the schools, and supplied an answer to the social question.[84] Mgr. Béliveau dealt with '*Les Canadiens Français et le rôle de l'Eglise au Ouest*,' describing the exploration of the West by the Oblate missionaries and their establishment of the first schools in that region.

But Confederation had brought many grievances to the French Canadians of the West, who saw their pact with Ottawa violated again and again. Mgr. Béliveau called for loyalty to the pact of 1867 and a return to its spirit, with equal civil and religious rights for French and English throughout Canada, so that the work of the French Canadian pioneers of the West for their faith and their country might not be wasted.[85]

Louis Durand, in considering '*Les Canadians Français et l'ésprit national*,' emphasized that Confederation had been founded on the basis of absolute respect for the language and the rights of the two contracting nationalities; and that national spirit must find its source and inspiration in the 'high conception which renders to each race and province the justice due to it and which, uniting them in common aspirations and will beyond material prosperity, gives to each the sense of the possibilities, necessities, and duties of a full and fruitful national life.'[86] He maintained that the French Canadian had best respected the fundamental principle of Confederation, and had remained the firmest opponent of the rival dangers which threatened Canada, Americanization and imperialism. He concluded by observing dryly that on the one hundred and twentieth anniversary of Confederation the number of celebrants might be diminished, if others did not remain as faithful to the fundamental principle of the pact, or sought to disorient Canadian patriotism, or were unjust to their national partners.

In a brief note Esdras Minville protested against the Privy Council's 'political' decision in the Labrador boundary case, which had cost Quebec 110,000 square miles of territory in Ungava and access to the Atlantic on the northeast.[87] Antonio Perrault dealt with Quebec's '*Déceptions et griefs*' under Confederation, advancing the nationalist theory that Confederation was a pact between two races and two religious groups on the basis of perfect equality.[88] He blamed the subsequent injustices which the French Canadians had suffered on the failure to fully incorporate the spirit of the pact in its letter, and on the assimilative tendency of the 'Anglo-Saxons.' He asserted that most French Canadians would agree that the Fathers of Confederation deserved to be shot for not making more definite the guarantees provided by the pact. He recalled the violations of the pact in educational matters in 1871, 1877, 1890, 1892, 1905, 1912, 1916, and 1926, without action by the federal government; the refusal to admit that Canada was bilingual; the refusal to give French Canadians their due share of public offices; and the constant insults directed against Quebec and the French Canadians. He asserted that the French Canadians did not believe that either the British Empire or Confederation would survive, but pending the anticipated breakdown they must loyally support

Confederation, though not at the expense of ethnic patriotism. The Canadian union of two nationalities could only be maintained by the maintenance of ethnic duality and provincial diversity. The French Canadians had two duties: 'To express their grievances frankly and to seek to make Confederation conform to its origins and principles.'[89] He regretted that the French-Canadian members had not amended the resolution of the House commemorating the anniversary by adding a wish that Confederation's spirit and letter be better understood in the future. He concluded with the suggestion that Premier Taschereau, as spokesman of French Canada, should express the grief caused the French Canadians by the unjust interpretation of Confederation and their desire to have its rights fairly applied.

Albert Lévesque closed the symposium as the spokesman of youth in '*La Confédération et la Jeunesse Canadienne-Française*.' In contrast to its usual fervent patriotism, French-Canadian youth was apathetic on this anniversary. It was determined, thanks to the nationalist movement since 1900, to make Confederation's spirit effective while developing its own ethnic personality and the prosperity of Quebec. If the English Canadians refused to collaborate, French-Canadian youth would 'organize otherwise its future.'[90]

This symposium of Confederation was practically the swan song of *L'Action française*. The review was stricken by financial difficulties in its later years and survived thanks to the efforts of Albert Lévesque, who developed profitable complementary activities such as the publication of an almanac, books, and pamphlets. Abbé Groulx was at last given a respectable salary by the Université de Montréal, though at first only on the condition that he sign an engagement to respect Confederation and English-Canadian susceptibilities. Groulx refused to sign, but the arrangement was finally concluded on the basis that he would devote all his time to historical work.[91] He retired as editor of *L'Action française* in the spring of 1928. In the following December the directors announced their decison to end publication of the magazine and of the *Almanach de la Langue française*, which had been a sort of annual popular supplement designed to reach the masses, while the magazine sought its smaller audience among the élite.

In January 1928 the title had been changed to *L'Action canadienne-française*, a full year after the condemnation by Rome of Maurras and his movement in France. The change was announced editorially with the observation: 'We have nothing in common with the royalist movement of Paris. . . . For the rest nothing will be changed either in the direction or spirit of the review.'[92] This was a somewhat bland disavowal of an influence more constantly evident than any other in the magazine, with the possible exception of that of Maurice

Barrès; and the hollowness of the repudiation was indicated by the determination not to change the policy of the magazine. This reaction to the condemnation of Maurras was more or less general in French Canada, with many of his admirers continuing to read his paper. But it added to the distrust already felt for the movement by the new school of '*Canadians tous courts*' ('unhyphenated Canadians'), and helped to bring about the end of *L'Action canadienne-française* in December 1928. In its declining years the review devoted itself to what might be called a nationalism of details, rather than its early integral nationalism, with a rather undistinguished list of contributors deploring the decline of the birthrate, the greater attention being given to the study of English, American influences, and preaching a narrow French Canadianism rather than the broad Canadianism then increasingly in vogue in French Canada. That the review now only expressed the views of a segment of the élite was made evident in 1928 by Beaudry Leman's debate with Minville on economic policy and G.-E. Marquis' with Vanier on national unity.

In 1928, at the age of fifty, Abbé Groulx saw the movement to which he had devoted ten years peter out. The boom of the 1920's had made Quebec prosperous; and those French Canadians who had benefited thought politics had nothing to do with business, and that nationalism was bad for it. Quebec had once more become a potent force at Ottawa, with Lomer Gouin and Ernest Lapointe successively taking important roles in the federal cabinet. Mackenzie King had resisted the postwar imperialistic pressures and continued in Laurier's path, seeking fuller nationhood for Canada within the empire. Lapointe had signed the Halibut Treaty of 1923 as the independent representative of Canada, while the first Canadian Minister to the United States took office in 1927, ending the old complaint that the British ambassador at Washington sacrificed Canada's interests to those of Britain. Senator Raoul Dandurand became president of the Assembly of the League of Nations in 1925, and Canada was elected to the League Council in 1927, thus enhancing her nationhood and French Canada's pride. The old sore of the Ontario school question was partially closed in 1927 by the Merchant Report, which recognized the rights of the French language. A final crippling blow to the survival of British control over Canadian policy through the governor-generalship was the outcome of the Byng incident in 1926, when the governor-general refused a dissolution to the King government and granted one to the Meighen government, and the King government was supported by the people in its stand that the governor-general had no right to play politics.

Despite all the social and cultural problems brought by the rapid industrialization of Quebec, largely under American auspices, in this period, the province rejoiced in a prosperity it had never before known. The new economic nationalism was left without a foundation of popular discontent. Except among the élite and the clergy, nationalism was virtually dead on the eve of the great depression which was to revive it and make it almost as potent a force on the eve of the Second World War as it had been at the close of the First.

In the late 1920's Abbé Groulx found his audience at the university reduced to a bare fifty instead of the great crowds which had hailed him ten years before, while he lacked a journal and received few invitations to give public addresses.[93] At the time of the enforced pledge incident he had thought of giving up his work and becoming a *curé*; but he renounced this idea and contented himself with pursuing his historical researches and counselling those young nationalists who sought him out. His influence on youth continued to be strong. French-Canadian youth is naturally nationalist-minded, as American youth is naturally liberal-minded, and this bent was encouraged by the facts that the classical colleges were largely directed by priests sympathetic to nationalism and that history was largely taught in the schools by former pupils of Groulx. Even at the traditionally loyalist Laval University in Quebec Thomas Chapais' interpretation of Canadian history—essentially that of a nineteenth-century British Liberal—seemed pallid and too imperialist to the rising generation by comparison with that of Groulx.

4

Though the *Action française* movement declined rather than gained strength after its triumphant and confident beginning in the post-war period, its influence was widespread among more moderate men than Groulx and his close disciples. Its emphasis on the development of a well-rounded French-Canadian culture furthered a general movement which had begun about 1900. Edouard Montpetit, fortified by three years' study at the Ecole Libre des Sciences Politiques and the Collège des Sciences Sociales in Paris, carried on after 1910 the effort launched by Errol Bouchette and Léon Gérin to study the French-Canadian milieu in economic and sociological terms and to provide French-Canadian training for industry and business. First as professor at the Ecole des Hautes Etudes Commerciales, in whose founding Honoré Gervais had taken the leading role, and after 1920 as secretary-general of the Université de Montréal and director of its Ecole des Sciences Sociales, Montpetit played a notable part in the economic awakening of French Canada. His duties as professor of law, of political economy, public finance, and

The Artist's Family

Oil painting (c. 1940) by Marie Bouchard. A charming primitive by the daughter of a well-known artist. The scene is typical of a country parlor in the French-Canadian taste. (Patrick Morgan Collection.)

Poem of the Earth

Oil painting (1940) by Maurice Raymond. This Montreal-born-and-educated painte reflects the typical French-Canadian intellectual's idealization of rural life. (Quebe Provincial Museum.)

economic politics left him little leisure for the production of original works, but he used his classic French eloquence on many public ocasions to preach the economic approach and to stress Quebec's bonds with French culture.

Marius Barbeau applied his Oxford anthropological training to the study of the Indian and of French-Canadian folklore and artistic history. The Belgian Henry Laureys ably directed the Ecole des Hautes Etudes Commerciales and sought to adapt French economic theories to North American practices. Augustin Frigon sought to broaden the scope of the Ecole Polytechnique, established in 1873 and long devoted to the production of civil engineers, by providing training in the new industrial fields in which non-French Canadians had long supplied the trained leadership. He encountered the resistance of a class-proud élite to any occupation which involved rolling up one's sleeves and getting one's hands dirty—a reluctance born of the strength of the old professional tradition in that class, and not unrelated to the traditional English-Canadian taunt that the French Canadians were a race of hewers of wood and drawers of water.

The secondary schools still failed to provide the scientific training which was the necessary preparation for specialization at the advanced level, but the great work of Frère Marie-Victorin, the founder of Montreal's Botanical Garden, in making French-Canadian youth science-minded and in stressing the importance of observation and experimentation instead of the old tradition of purely dogmatic teaching, helped to make possible the creation at Laval in Quebec of an admirable school of science, under the leadership of Abbé Alexandre Vachon and Adrien Pouliot. This Quebec initiative was soon paralleled at Montreal, and more attention was subsequently given to science in the secondary schools. The teaching standards in a vital and long-neglected field of knowledge were gradually raised to the international level. The provincial government, which underwrote the cost of most of these developments and provided scholarships for graduate study abroad under the intelligent administration of Athanase David, the provincial secretary, also supported agricultural, forestry, and fishery schools associated with the two universities and a wide range of trade, technical, and commercial schools throughout the province.

This intellectual ferment was reflected in literature. Thanks largely to the critical work of Mgr. Camille Roy, many times Rector of Laval University, a French-Canadian literary tradition was firmly established and quickly began to bear fruit in works which were not mere belated echoes of French literary trends. The new literature was largely devoted to glorifying the good old days of the French regime and the obsolescent patriarchal rural world untouched by alien influences, for the privileged clerical and professional élite remained firmly convinced that the national genius was for the hard life of pioneering and tilling the soil, and not for the new industrial life which menaced many of French Canada's traditions and in which the French Canadians were largely left behind by aliens. This *terroir* school, led by Adjutor Rivard with his *Chez nos gens* (1914–19), Frère Marie-Victorin with his *Récits laurentiens* (1919) and *Croquis laurentiens* (1920) and by Blanche Lamontagne with her numerous hymns to Gaspé in both prose and verse, was carried on by the poetry of Emile Coderre and Alfred DesRochers. In 1925 Robert Choquette immediately took first rank among young French-Canadian poets with his *A travers les vents*, whose authentic poetic feeling, eloquence, and precocious power eclipsed earlier work which had suffered from imitativeness of French models, limited themes, and a distrust of realism.

In history, the most popular form of literary expression in French Canada, Thomas Chapais carried on his constitutional study of the period between 1760 and 1867 in volumes published from 1919 to 1934. The Abbé Ivanhoë Caron published a series of scrupulously exact monographs on the colonization of Quebec, based upon the documents provided by the Provincial Archives established in 1920. Aegidius Fauteux and E.-Z. Massicotte carried on tireless archival researches into the past, while Pierre-Georges Roy published a host of antiquarian studies, in addition to supervising the valuable annual reports of the Provincial Archives and the *Bulletin des recherches historiques*. Séraphin Marion, one of the first European-trained historians, published his *Relations des Voyageurs français en Nouvelle France aux XVIIe siècle* in 1923 and a monograph on *Pierre Boucher* in 1927. Gustave Lanctot produced an able critical study of Garneau in 1925 and a notable Sorbonne thesis on *L'Administration de la Nouvelle France* in 1929. The following year saw the publication of Antoine Roy's useful *Les Lettres, les Sciences, et les Arts au Canada sous le Régime français*. A pioneering effort in economic history was Noël Fauteux's *Essai sur l'industrie au Canada sous le Régime français* (1927); while Dr. Arthur Vallée produced an equally novel study in the history of science with his monograph on Michel Sarrazin. The flood of parish histories, evidence of an ancient parochialism undisturbed by new social forces, continued with new vigor. Only Abbé Groulx resisted the general tendency to concentrate attention on the French period and to neglect subsequent history, less glamorous but more significant in its relationship to the present.

The novel first became a popular form of literary expression in this period, after Louis Hémon's *Maria Chapdelaine* (1916), an eloquent picture of pioneer life and French survival in the Lake St. John country, won a notable success first in France and later in Canada.

This young Frenchman was killed in 1913, shortly after finishing his manuscript, but his book had a profound influence on the postwar French-Canadian novel. Harry Bernard carried on the *terroir* tradition under Hémon's influence in a long series of novels of rural life, beginning with *L'Homme tombé* in 1924. His books made use of the popular speech instead of a frozen classical French and were more realistic than earlier novels had been. Robert de Roquebrune published a historical novel, *Les Habits Rouges* (1923), dealing with the events of 1837, and then after a second and unsuccessful effort in this field, turned to the psychological novel in *Les Dames les Marchand* (1937). Léo-Paul Desrosiers renounced an early preoccupation with *terroir* themes, which culminated in *Nord-Sud* (1931), in favor of historical novels, of which *L'Acalmie* (1937) and *Les Engagés du Grand Portage* (1938) are among the best produced in French Canada. Jean-Charles Harvey produced in 1922 a novel, *Marcel Faure*, which mirrored the preoccupation of the time with economic emancipation; and in 1929 with *L'Homme qui va* offered a collection of fantastic and symbolic stories characterized by a fine style, marked realism, and a penchant for melodrama. With *Les Demi-Civilisées* (1934), a sensational novel of Quebec high life and corrupting American influence which is both realistic and fantastic, Harvey caused a small tempest in Quebec which drove him from his editorship of *Le Soleil* to less prudish Montreal. Another collection of short stories, *Sébastien Pierre* (1935), revealed the same qualities and defects as Harvey's earlier work, which remains among the most vital and best-written French-Canadian fiction.

In 1933 Claude-Henri Grignon ('Valdombre') published his *Un homme et son péché*, which has become a French-Canadian classic and serves as the framework of the most popular perennial French-Canadian radio serial. It is a realistic study of *habitant* avarice, tinted by the romanticism of the *terroir* school. There was a return to the older lyrical idealization of the pioneer in Abbé Félix-Antoine Savard's poetic novel, *Menaud, maître-draveur* (1937), and an abler development of 'Valdombre's' realism in Dr. Philippe Panneton's ('Ringuet') *Trente Arpentes* (1938), which deromanticized the *habitant's* life in convincing and moving fashion. Harvey's *Demi-Civilisées* and Ringuet's *Trente Arpentes* were the first French-Canadian novels to be translated and published in English, and the latter attained almost as much fame abroad as *Maria Chapdelaine*. The nationalist tradition in the novel, inaugurated by Tardivel and carried on by Groulx' *L'Appel de la race* was continued by the Jesuit Père Adélard Dugré's *La Campagne canadienne* (1925), Groulx's *Au Cap Blomidon* on the theme of Acadian survival, and Rex Desmarchais' *Le Feu intérieur* and *La Chesnaie*. These are more convincing as illustrations of nationalist theses than as novels.

There was also a notable development of criticism from the traditional log-rolling level. Mgr. Camille Roy remained the leading French-Canadian critic, presiding over Laval's influential review, *Le Canada Français*, and displaying a remarkable tolerance to all writers who sought to realize his goal of a French-Canadian literature. His prewar critical essays were revised and brought out as *Poètes de chez nous* (1934), *Historiens de chez nous* (1935), and *Romanciers de chez nous* (1935). From exile in New England Louis Dantin, who had launched Nelligan's poetry in 1904, kept a sharp critical eye on the development of French-Canadian literature, while writing some verse himself. His *Gloses critiques* (1931, 1935) contain the most searching criticism since the pioneering volumes of Charles ab der Halden in 1904 and 1907 made Europe aware of French-Canadian literature. Jean-Charles Harvey, in his *Pages de Critique* (1926) produced some of the best and frankest critical writing of the period, and acted as a deterrent to the old tradition of log-rolling. Maurice Hébert, a disciple of Mgr. Roy, became the literary critic of *Le Canada Français* and devoted himself to sensitive psychological studies of new books, which were collected in *De Livres en Livres* (1929), *D'un Livre à l'autre* (1932), and *Les Lettres au Canada français* (1936). Marcel Dugas, an exile in Paris until the outbreak of the Second World War, produced more exacting criticism in his *Littérature Canadienne: Aperçus* (1929) and in his study of *Louis Fréchette* (1934). Dugas became the literary prophet of the *anciens de Paris*, the French-Canadian students who returned from Paris convinced that all wisdom and beauty found its source there. Albert Pelletier in *Carquois* and *Egrappages* (1933) displayed ability and unconventionality in judging current books. Claude-Henri Grignon, in his *Ombres et Clameurs* (1933) and in the later pamphlets signed 'Valdombre,' showed a sound judgment which was somewhat outweighed by the violence of his tone as a polemicist.

The analytical tendency of the classical college discipline was reflected in the fact that French Canada produced more critics than creative writers. In the 1930's, as in the 1860's, more ink was spilt over the question of whether a French-Canadian culture existed or was possible than in efforts to advance it. In 1940 and 1941 *L'Action Nationale* was still conducting a symposium on the question as European culture went down before the Nazi assault. The enforced break with France after June 1940 and the unanticipated wartime role of Montreal as one of the two centers of free French culture both emancipated French Canada from its cultural colonialism and furthered the development of an original culture. French Canada at last came of age, after passing through a long imitative period reminiscent of that of American culture before the flowering of New England.

5

French-Canadian nationalism always comes to a head in periods of economic, as well as political, crisis. It was inevitable, considering the economic bent which Abbé Groulx had given to the movement, that it should revive with new intensity in the troubled 1930's, when French Canada felt the effects of the depression more deeply than English Canada, because its lower standard of living afforded less margin for subsistence. Unemployment reached its peak in Quebec in 1932, with 100,000 persons, largely French-Canadians, on relief in Montreal.[94] It was not surprising that January 1933 saw the revival of *L'Action canadienne-française* as *L'Action Nationale*, under the editorship of Harry Bernard. The directors included Esdras Minville, Hermas Bastien, Pierre Homier, Abbé Groulx, Eugène L'Heureux, Abbé Olivier Maurault, Anatole Vanier, Abbé Tessier, Arthur Laurendeau, René Chaloult, Wilfrid Guérin, and Léopold Richer—most of the more extreme elders of the original movement and a group of ultranationalists of the rising generation. The first number affirmed the review's dedication to Catholicism and French-Canadian traditions, and with a foreshadowing of a racism which became more pronounced as time went on, made much of 'our ethnic originality.' Groulx contributed an article calling for aggressive rather than defensive action with regard to French-Canadian rights. It was evident that his nationalism was now more inspired by that of Gonzague du Reynold than by that of Charles Maurras. The editors made an appeal for subscriptions by classical colleges, and it was in these institutions, which usually banned most current periodicals except *L'Action Nationale* and *Le Devoir*, that the new nationalism centered.

It was now primarily a youth movement, for young French-Canadians launched themselves into political action when the depression barred them from normal careers and economic opportunities. The war cry of the new nationalism was sounded at a meeting of university students in Montreal on December 19, 1932, which was presided over by Armand Lavergne, the idol of nationalist youth, and addressed by Esdras Minville. Their manifesto, already published in *Le Quartier Latin* in November, called for scrupulous respect of the rights of each 'race' in Canada, and insisted that the French language should enjoy the same rights as English. It referred to the growing indignation of French Canadians at the denial of their rights, and warned: 'We ask today what we shall exact tomorrow.'[95] It pointed out that the French Canadians constituted a third of the population of Canada, four-fifths of that of Quebec, and three-quarters of that of Montreal; and demanded that French Canadians should have a just share of federal jobs. Observing that the French Canadians were becoming a proletarian people, it insisted that this situation should be remedied. The natural resources of the province were not to be used in a fashion which would compromise or lose the heritage of French Canadians, while 'foreign capitalists' imposed upon them 'the worst of dictatorships' and ostracized their engineers and technicians, leaving open to French Canadians only the roles of laborers and servants. The manifesto closed with an appeal to youth:

> Therefore we appeal to youth, to the whole youth of our race: university youth, the youth of the colleges and schools, the youth of the factories, of the fields, and of the professions. In all domains of national life let the ardent concern awake to reconquer lost positions, to make the future better. It is a vast task: intellectual, literary, artistic, scientific, economic, national to which we, the young, are called by the necessities of our time. Let us remember that we shall be masters in our own house only if we become worthy of being so.[96]

This 'Manifesto of the young generation' was drafted by André Laurendeau, the son of one of the veteran directors of *L'Action* in its various incarnations, and was approved by the twelve or fifteen other members of '*Les Jeune-Canada*,' as the movement soon came to be called. The majority were students at the Université de Montréal, graduates of the Jesuit College Sainte-Marie, and were under the influence of Abbé Groulx.

The movement began with articles in the university paper, *Le Quartier Latin*, and was continued with mass meetings at the Salle Gésu during the winter of 1932–3 and at the Monument National the following winter. It was characterized by Pierre Dansereau in *L'Action Nationale* as a reaction against 'the march of the French-Canadian people towards the abyss.'[97] It sought to transform rather than to revolutionize; to consolidate the effort commenced but abandoned in the past, rather than to destroy. It was impatient with and contemptuous of most of its elders, with the exception of Edouard Montpetit, Abbé Groulx, and Esdras Minville. It was particularly bitter against the politicians, whom it held responsible for the present situation, and whom it considered 'the eternal enemies of our race,'[98] because they promoted party divisions rather than French-Canadian unity. *Les Jeune-Canada* attracted attention by exploiting the growing French-Canadian feeling against the Jews of Montreal, who were becoming politically powerful, as well as driving the French Canadians from the fields of small business which the English-speaking economic overlords of Quebec scorned. And to stimulate national feeling, it organized a pilgrimage on Dollard's anniversary to Carillon, the scene of the folk hero's great fight against the Iroquois, and praised his memory and example at the prompting of Abbé Groulx, who had originated the cult of Dollard. It was also active in the elaborate commemoration of the tercentenary of Jacques Cartier's landing at Gaspé, which was officially celebrated on August 26 in the presence of Prime Minister Bennett, Cardinal Villeneuve, and representatives of France, Britain, and the United States.

L'Action Nationale furthered the *Jeune-Canada* movement while pursuing its own campaigns for 'integral bilingualism,' a back-to-the-land movement, 're-Frenchification' of Quebec, and anti-semitism. In April 1933 it began to attack the capitalist system in Quebec, which it held responsible not only for the depression but also for the condition of the French Canadians. It adhered to the 'Program of Social Restoration' drafted in May by the Jesuits of the Ecole Sociale Populaire which called for state intervention to end the abuses of the 'economic dictatorship,' and urged the adoption of corporatism and the suspension of immigration. The program also called for restoration of agriculture, support of colonization, and promotion of domestic arts and local industries. Its labor policy included wage and hour laws, social insurance, old-age pensions, and collective bargaining. The program also urged a war on the trusts, particularly those of coal, gas, and electricity. The Beauharnois Power Company was to be investigated, and taken over by the state if necessary. The program of financial reforms called for regulation of business and investigation of holding companies. The proposed political reforms included the elimination of graft, the declaration of campaign funds, and the creation of a provincial economic council, with specialists from various professions and classes. The over-all aim was to bring about 'an order more in accord with social justice' and to preserve the country from the 'upsets to which the present situation exposes us.'[99] The signers included Minville, who became the economic prophet of the new nationalists; Dr. Philippe Hamel, the leading crusader against the power trust; Alfred Charpentier, the elder statesman of the Catholic syndicate movement; as well as Albert Rioux, V.-E. Beaupré, Dr. J.-B. Prince, Anatole Vanier, Arthur Laurendeau, Wilfrid Guérin, and René Chaloult.

In 1934 *L'Action Nationale* published a series of articles on '*L'Education nationale*.' Abbé Groulx launched the symposium, calling for a revival of national pride but denying the charge of racism. Jacques Brassier hailed the advent of Dollfuss, with the comment: 'Happy Austria, which has nonetheless found its leader, and with him the way of resurrection . . . What need we also have of a National Front and of a man who, like the young and charming chancellor of Austria, would dare to say these moving words: "I wish to reconstitute my country on the basis of the encyclical *Quadragesimo*

Anno."'[100] This emphasis on the need of a leader ('*chef*') was echoed and re-echoed henceforward, to the tune of citations of Gonzague de Reynold, Barrès, Maurras, and Massis, prophets of the strong-man cult.

In May Arthur Laurendeau repeated Groulx' arguments for the necessity of instilling racial pride, while denying a racism based upon purity of blood: 'We wish to speak of a race refined by a culture, which crossing the Mediterranean, was subsequently transfigured by Christ. It is on the virtue of this civilization that we bolster our defences, and not on a mad pride borrowed from the myths of the Black Forest.'[101] It was the elder Laurendeau who succeeded Bernard as editor in the fall of 1934, and under his direction the review took a more aggressive tone. In an article on 'Language and survival' in September, Abbé Groulx regretted the absence of a national leader, of 'the de Valera, the Mussolini, whose politics are open to discussion, but who in ten years have psychologically remade a new Ireland and a new Italy, as a Dollfuss and a Salazar are re-making a new Austria and a new Portugal.'[102] This '*chefisme*,' re-echoed by Groulx in November in a letter to Jean-Louis Gagnon, director of a new youth magazine called *Vivre*,[103] coupled as it was with a growing anti-semitism, crusades against Communism and the trusts, and impassioned appeals to youth to save the 'race,' was all too reminiscent of the rise of European fascist movements to English-Canadian and American observers.

Under the influence of a depression which weighed far more heavily upon the underprivileged French-Canadians than upon their English-speaking compatriots, the new nationalism became narrowly provincialist and developed the latent tendency to separatism which has always been implicit in French-Canadian nationalism in time of crisis. *L'Action Nationale* was filled with attacks on the English-Canadian and American trusts which controlled the economic life of the province, and upon the constitution and Confederation. In January 1935 the magazine supported Groulx' call for a national leader, a '*chef*' who would guide Quebec in 'the new order which is evolving, in which the theories by which we live today appear perhaps to have expired.'[104] Confronted with the Bennett New Deal, the editors protested against the centralizing tendency of the program and urged either decentralization or the break-up of Confederation.

There was little respect shown to the older leaders of French Canada. In April Thomas Chapais was attacked for his devotion to the Conservative Party; and in May there was a bitter assault upon Bourassa for his 'lamentable' recent lectures, in which he had warned the young nationalists of the dangers of racial pride, ultra-nationalism, and separatism. While admitting the important role

History of Canada

A satirical picture by Robert La Palme, 1945, which was used as the curtain for Gratien Gélinas' revue, *Fridolins-nous*. (Gratien Gélinas Collection.)

Montreal Architecture, 1935

Black-and-white drawings by Jean-Charles Faucher for Oliver Asselin's last journal, *La Renaissance*. The artist interprets the atmosphere of different quarters of Montreal in terms of the distinctive outside stairways.

that Bourassa had played in developing nationalism before 1922, *L'Action Nationale* now formally repudiated his leadership in favor of that of Abbé Groulx, who in February had told the Junior Bar Association of Quebec: 'There is no nationalism in the world more legitimate or more orthodox than French-Canadian nationalism'—a statement sanctioned by the *imprimatur* of Cardinal Villeneuve when the speech appeared in pamphlet form.[105]

Not Bourassa, but Armand Lavergne was the political idol of the new generation of nationalists who found outdated the old nationalist leader's views on the religious and social matters to which he had largely devoted himself since 1920. But just as the Byng episode had roused Bourassa to express his fundamental anti-imperialism, Mr. Bennett's willingness to be guided in foreign affairs by Britain in an increasingly disturbed world provoked an expression of Bourassa's North Americanism, tempered by an international outlook which none of his more provincial disciples had ever equalled. In the House on April 1, 1935 Bourassa made a long speech on the European situation.[106] He moved for re-endorsement of the Kellogg Peace Pact of 1928, urging the government 'to lend its support to all effective measures to ensure the world's peace, either through the League of Nations or otherwise, in cooperation with other governments pledged to the cause of peace.' Bourassa singled out Mr. King—with whom he had a sense of kinship, since they were both grandsons of leaders of the 1837 Rebellion—as 'the Canadian statesman who has done most for peace, not only in words but deeds.' He declared it was Canada's duty to prevent wars or at least to take measures against being engulfed in war. He recommended four 'converging' methods to attain that end: Canada should define its own policy of peace; it should cooperate with Britain if the latter worked for peace; it should cooperate with the peace-loving United States; and it should work for peace through the League.

Bourassa declared that the spirit of Locarno was buried in the tombs of two great men, Briand and Stresemann; and he urged Canada to beware of 'the Locarno of the East': 'Keep aloof, for heaven's sake and for the sake of Canada.' He censured the course adopted towards Russia in 1927 and 1934, a policy 'of kicking and kissing alternately.' As a fundamental principle, he declared: 'There is no great problem of policy, internal or external, which we can solve in Canada without regard to the policy of the United States.' He urged that the government should make it clear to the Americans that Canada stood loyally by Britain as long as Britain stood for peace, and that it should make it equally clear to the British that if the United Kingdom chose war and the United States peace, that Canada also would choose peace. He recalled his conversations in 1914 with Lord Fisher, who found Laurier's and Borden's naval policies 'equally stupid.' The best way to arrange Canada's defence was to go to Washington. In the tradition of his basic anti-militarism and North American isolationism Bourassa urged: 'Let us proclaim to the world that we are disarming, as the best means of defending Canada . . . Why not join the Pan-American Union, in which we would be far more at home than we are in the League of Nations? . . . Canada is a nation in America, and not one in Europe or Asia.' Canada's policy should be based upon its North Americanism. Confidence in the League was now badly shaken, and he deeply regretted that Canada had voted for the admission of Russia into the League.

The extremes to which the new ultranationalism went was witnessed by approving accounts in *L'Action* of the 'Laurentianism' instilled in the young students of the Collège Sainte-Marie by the Jesuit Père Thomas Mignault, who made history, geology, botany, art, literature and economics center upon the concept of a 'Laurentia,' a separate and unique French Canada.[107] In September Arthur Laurendeau supported the manifesto issued by Paul Gouin when he launched his *Action Nationale Libérale*, a political youth movement, and reprinted the document, which called for the creation of a national '*mystique*.'[108] In October Minville nominated Abbé Groulx as the pre-ordained *chef* of French Canada, paraphrasing Gonzague de Reynold's words of approval for the German National Socialist movement as applicable to Groulx and the directors of *L'Action Nationale*. He hailed the formula expounded by Groulx in his book *Orientations*: 'What we wish is a French people in a French country.'[109] In the same number citations from the Popes and from Cardinal Villeneuve and Mgr. Paquet were presented to support the thesis that nationalism was a virtue rather than a sin. While outside critics deplored the rise of 'clerical fascism' in Quebec, André Marois regretted the efforts of certain priests to eliminate political or nationalist tendencies from the Catholic youth movements. Cardinal Villeneuve settled the dispute by his declaration that 'No social, economic, nationalist action can be undertaken for itself by the groups in question [the clerical youth movements], but only as a means to the ends of Catholic Action.' In January 1936 the editors of *L'Action Nationale* interpreted this statement to suit their own ideas, since for them religion and nationalism were inextricably involved.[110] The extent to which these ideas prevailed was revealed by the publication in April 1936 of the Oblate Père Juneau's *Dieu et Patrie*, a sort of nationalist litany written for performance at a classical college.[111]

In March, in renewing their proposal of the previous year for a French-Canadian flag, the editors expressed their desire 'to create, in our province, a French people and a French State.' The proposed flag, the '*drapeau de Carillon*' which bore a white cross and four fleurs-de-lis on a light-blue background, was to serve as a symbol of 'spiritual unanimity.'[112] Writers in the magazine continued to urge economic nationalism by supporting the *achat chez nous* movement, and political nationalism by opposing suggested centralizing reforms of the constitution. The announcement that the annual *Semaine Sociale* in the fall would be devoted to corporatism was highly approved, while the menace of Communism and the 'treason of the élite' was stressed in editorial comments. In September the magazine supported the political course followed by three of its directors, Dr. Hamel, Albert Rioux, and René Chaloult. In December Arthur Laurendeau re-echoed the call for a French-Canadian '*mystique*,' while his son André was becoming aware as a student in Europe of the dangers of Hitlerism and Italian Fascism, which he later reported in the magazine.

The symposium of 1937 was devoted to '*Une Politique Nationale*,' while the doubled defence estimates of the year roused the old anti-imperialism of French Canada, despite Mackenzie King's assurances that 'the Canadian Parliament reserves to itself the right to declare, in the light of the circumstances existing at the time, to what extent, if at all, Canada will participate in conflicts in which other members of the Commonwealth may be engaged.'[113] In May much was made of the fact that in a speech closing a series of six lectures by Groulx at Quebec on 'New France in Champlain's Time,' Cardinal Villeneuve remarked: 'I have come here this evening to manifest the friendship I have for the Abbé Groulx, to express my gratitude to him, at the risk of scandalizing the weak. Abbé Groulx is one of the masters of the hour; he is one of those to whom our race owes much.'[114] In the same number André Marois held that 'our parliamentary gossips could with profit go and take lessons in Italy, Austria, and Portugal'[115] and expressed particular admiration for Mussolini and Salazar.

But *L'Action Nationale's* admiration for the dictators was checked when in September André Laurendeau became director of the review, after two years' study of philosophy and the social sciences in Paris. Fresh from firsthand contact with the rising tide of Fascism and Hitlerism in Europe, Laurendeau was horrified by the amount of racism he found upon his return to Quebec. In a prefatory note to Emile Baas' '*Introduction à la thèse de Rosenberg*,' Laurendeau observed:

> . . . racism, in the strong sense of the word, represents in certain sectors of our intellectual life a menace all the more real because no one yet takes it seriously. In fact the movement, which finds no profound support from us, could not implant itself to a great degree; but it would be already

too much if it infiltrated and contaminated the always shaky 'principles' of our nationalists. Knowing the actual source of the error, one will judge more severely its effects, and the division will be made between the conscious racists and the mass of those who are materialists without knowing it.

. . . . .

To make the National-Socialist doctrine crumble, it suffices to recall that according to modern ethnology there no more exists a pure race in the world, neither Saxon nor Slav nor German. We are confronted with a pseudo-scientific fantasy, whose dynamism must nonetheless not be underestimated. . . .

And to convince oneself that the racists' ideology is essentially anti-Christian, as anti-Christian as Communism for instance, one recalls several major texts of the Gospel and the whole Pauline teaching. Against the predominance of blood, we continue to assert the sovereignty of the spiritual.[116]

And in a long editorial note on the second *Congrès de la Langue française* at Quebec in June 1937, the editors sought to heal the split which had developed between separatists and anti-separatists after Abbé Groulx had on that occasion declared: 'Our sole legitimate and imperative destiny can be only this: to constitute in America in the greatest autonomy possible, this political and spiritual reality . . . a Catholic and French State,' to which he had added: 'Whether or not one wishes it, we shall have our French State.'[117] Bishop Yelle, speaking for the French Canadians of the West, had said on the same occasion: 'When we hear separatism for the Province of Quebec seriously spoken of, we see in it not words of salvation but words of discouragement and defeatism.'

L'Action Nationale hastened to reassure the anti-separatists by quoting earlier pronouncements of Groulx to prove that he referred to a State within Confederation, and that he was not a separatist.[118] But if Groulx was not a separatist at heart—and the whole tendency of his work indicates that he was—many of his followers undoubtedly were, just as Bourassa's followers had gone beyond the limits set by their master. Groulx was severely attacked for his declarations at Quebec, and charged with cultivating a French-Canadian racism. In an editorial note commenting on the papal encyclical '*Mit brennender Sorge*,' which condemned Nazism, André Laurendeau defended Groulx against the charge of racism, while clearly revealing his fear that a racist element had entered French-Canadian nationalism. He observed that 'French Canadians always applaud more willingly anathemas against the extreme left than anathemas against the extreme right. We are too often among those who think, according to the harsh formula of *La Vie intellectuelle*, that God is on the right.'[119] He complained that less publicity than usual had been iven in Quebec to this papal utterance, and warned of the dangerous lliances that might be made in the name of anti-communism. In he same number Gérard Plourde of *Les Jeune-Canada* compared the ecent lectures of Bourassa and Groulx on the 1837 Rebellion and refered Groulx' more extreme thesis.

In the January 1938 number the collaboration of the *Jeune-Canada* roup with *L'Action Nationale* was hailed, while it was announced hat the yearly symposium would be devoted to the problem of corporatist organization. The editors denied the charges that corporaism was a subversive, medieval, fascist system which would mean the nd of parliamentary government; they quoted Cardinal Villeneuve's leclaration of April 17, 1937: 'We have here and there some bits of ocial justice, but these appearances of remedies do not suffice. Ve need more than that: full corporatism.'[120] André Laurendeau elittled Adélard Godbout's anti-fascist crusade against the Duplessis 'adlock Law, as he had previously belittled Duplessis' anti-comnunist stand on the Dominion Textile strike, on the grounds that nti-fascism and anti-communism were mere distractions from the eal problems of Quebec, since only a handful really supported Comnunism or Fascism. The unsuccessful campaign of Paul Bouchard, he editor of the separatist and anti-imperialist *La Nation* in the otbinière federal by-election against J.-N. Francoeur, backed by ustice Minister Ernest Lapointe, was hailed by Roger Duhamel as aving brought before the people the burning issues of militarizaion and centralization. It was significant of the strength of extreme ationalism that the French-Canadian federal leader felt it necessary o take part in this by-election. In February the editors called upon he French Canadians to be on guard against centralization, regardng the period as crucial as that of 1867, while the close defeat of Camilien Houde in the Saint-Henri by-election in Montreal was leplored.

In April André Laurendeau replied to recent articles on Quebec ascism in the London *Daily Herald*, the *New York Post*, the Toronto *Magazine Digest*, and the New York *Nation*. He admitted that ascist organizations existed in Quebec, but maintained that they vere not taken seriously. He blamed their recent activity and their uccess in recruiting on a decreasing lack of popular faith in pariamentary government. He denied that the Church was either at he head of or behind these organizations, but admitted that a few vell-intentioned clerics might have become propagandists for them. He was convinced that the Church would take a stand against 'ascism in Quebec, if the latter ever became important, as it had done lsewhere. He admitted the existence of a 'pre-fascist' mentality vhich might favor the development of Fascism if the political, econonic, and social disorder continued. Archbishop Gauthier's vigorous pastoral in March against Communism also warned that the journa of Adrien Arcand's National Social Christian Party, *Le Fascist Canadien*, advanced a watered German Nazism which minimized it anti-Catholic and Caesarist tendencies. But in Quebec, as elsewhere the Catholic hierarchy was far more voluble about the dangers o Communism than about those of Fascism.

In May two articles in *L'Action Nationale* were concerned with th question of what the proper French-Canadian attitude should be i the face of gathering war clouds in Europe. Léopold Richer, com menting on the debates in the federal House on the rearmamen program, supported the view of Maxime Raymond that Canad should only defend its own territory against aggression, rather tha enter into collective security plans or imperial alliances. In Septem ber, after the Czecho-Slovakian crisis had passed, André Laurendea protested against the passive acceptance of imperialist pressure b the French Canadians, and called for a united stand against in evitable attempts to bring about Canadian intervention at the nex crisis. Roger Duhamel, who in September had begun a new series o monthly political reviews, hailed President Roosevelt's Kingsto declaration as an extension of the Monroe Doctrine to Canada, an suggested that Canada should break its ties with the League o Nations and Britain and fulfil its American destiny.[121] A youn nationalist economist, F.-A. Angers, who was making a name fo himself as Minville's leading disciple, also launched a series o monthly economic commentaries. In December Laurendeau ob served that the principles invoked by Lord Runciman in his repor on Czecho-Slovakia might well be applied in Canada, where Con federation's guarantees to the French Canadians were violated b the ruling race.

The annual symposium was devoted in 1939 to 'Canada in th Commonwealth,' with the editors of *L'Action Nationale* obviousl alarmed at Canada's close escape from being involved in a Europea war the previous fall. Roger Duhamel anticipated that the propose royal visit to Canada would be used to strengthen imperialism, an praised the recent utterance of Professor Percy Corbett of McGill i favor of Canada's joining the Pan-American Union rather tha continuing her association with Great Britain. An editorial not hailed the growing number of English-Canadian anti-imperialist and suggested a 'prudent' alliance with these leftists. Duham regarded the election of Camilien Houde as Mayor of Montreal as sign of popular discontent with the Duplessis *Union Nationale* gover ment which had opposed him strongly. In February an editori called for the return of Labrador to Quebec, since its possession b the Crown colony of Newfoundland might involve Canada in wa and since its rich natural resources could better be exploited b

Quebec than by bankrupt Newfoundland. F.-A. Angers violently opposed the proposed federal scheme of unemployment insurance as an infringement of provincial rights, while Duhamel expressed sympathy for those who had criticized the heavy military expenses announced in the speech from the throne.

Duhamel was alarmed by the divergence of Liberal opinion evident in the statements of Mackenzie King, who maintained Laurier's doctrine 'When Britain is at war, Canada is at war'; of Lapointe, who assured a Quebec public meeting that 'we shall stay at home and protect our country'; and of Senator Dandurand, who suggested a referendum before Canada participated in a war. Duhamel approved Liguori Lacombe's opposition to participation in any conflict which did not endanger Canadian security, but recognized that this was a minority opinion and concluded: 'It will be a happy day for our country when our representatives resolve, while conserving friendly relations with the old mother country, to limit their activity and efforts to the safeguarding of our territorial integrity and of Canadian unity understood in the bilateral sense.'[122] He also warmly supported the program of the federal nationalist party as formulated at its first meeting in Montreal on November 20, 1938 by Paul Bouchard, with the slogan of 'autonomous provinces in a free Canada,' and a program of Canadian neutrality, to be abandoned only after a provincial referendum. Duhamel favored the nomination of a Canadian governor-general to replace Lord Tweedsmuir, after the precedent established in Ireland and Australia.

During the spring of 1939 *L'Action Nationale* continued to discount the promises of King and Lapointe that they would resign rather than vote for conscription in case of war; to describe the royal visit, that of Stanley Baldwin, and the declarations of R. B. Bennett as parts of an imperialist program to assure Canadian support in case of war; and to express sympathy with Maxime Raymond's declaration in the House of French-Canadian opposition to all extra-territorial wars. But in June the editors exulted in the fact that the King and Queen had spoken French and expressed sympathy for the French Canadians; that the King had formally reasserted the 'free and equal' association of the nations of the Commonwealth; and that the Queen had expressed a wish to see the two great races of Canada linked like the Scots and the English by 'the bonds of affection, respect, and a common ideal.' The old monarchist tradition of French Canada responded to the royal visit; the French Canadians were charmed by the King and Queen—particularly by their use of French—and Montreal spent more money on the royal reception than did ultra-loyal Toronto.

But in the same issue Georges Pelletier warned at the close of an exhaustive analysis of imperialist propaganda:

> If we wish to remain Canadians, it is a question of no longer delaying of reacting and finally organizing ourselves. It is already very late. I we do not act, we will no longer be truly Canadians in 1950. At al events, we will no longer be even 'quality niggers.' We will have becom nonentities in the British Empire: propaganda will have melted us by our own fault, into the great imperial whole.[123]

And Roger Duhamel highly commended the opposition to the military estimates shown in parliament by Maxime Raymond Liguori Lacombe, J.-A. Crète, L. Dubois, Pierre Gauthier, Wilfric Gariépy, Wilfrid Lacroix, and Jean-François Pouliot, who had callec for an autonomous Canadian policy, free of all subjection to Britain and had been supported by some English-Canadian M.P.s.

Thus, on the eve of the Second World War French Canada already boasted an anti-war group in the federal House, supportec by an embryo nationalist party in Quebec. The Duplessis administration was anti-war but also anti-nationalist, having broken with it electoral allies of 1936 as the federal Conservatives had broken witl the nationalists after 1911. The Liberals undoubtedly had a strong hold on Quebec's sympathies, thanks to the anti-war and anti-conscription pledges of King and Lapointe, and the reiterated imperialism of such Conservative leaders as Bennett and Arthu Meighen. Ultranationalists admitted that the King governmen would be returned to power if it called elections, but remainec suspicious of its future course. Two generations of the French-Canadian élite had been raised in an atmosphere of hatred for the English who were depicted as eternal enemies of everything French anc Catholic; of distrust for the Americans, who were painted as materialistic slaves of the almighty dollar and ruthless assimilators of othe peoples to their own mediocrity and cultural sterility; and of admiration for the minor prophets of the new cult of the strong mar and of totalitarianism which was to engulf Europe in the greatest o its wars. It was under intellectual leaders with this background, anc with a tradition of passionate preoccupation with French-Canadia problems rather than international ones, that French Canada facec the outbreak of the great conflict that was to last for six years, durin most of which Quebec was cut off from Rome and France, its traditional sources of spiritual strength in the struggle for cultural survival

Notes

[1] 1871: 31.07 per cent; 1881: 30.03 per cent; 1901: 30.70 per cent; 1911: 28.5 per cent; 1921: 27.92 per cent. *Canada Year Book 1922–3*, 159, Table 20.

[2] *Ibid.*, 141, Table 4. Quebec's loss of rural population by emigration wa never less than 50 per cent per decade after 1871. *CJEPS*, IV (1938), 344, E. C Hughes, 'Industry & the Rural System in Quebec.'

[3] 1920–4: 55,352; 1925–30: 36,096; L. E. Truesdale, *The Canadian-Born in the United States* (New Haven, 1943), 92, Table 35.

[4] *Canada Year Book 1945*, 114, Table 23.

[5] *Canada Year Book 1922–3*, 416, Table 1; 739, Table 16.

[6] *Ibid.*, 171–2, Table 32.

[7] *Can. An. Rev. 1921*, 680.

[8] E. C. Hughes, *French Canada in Transition* (Chicago, 1943).

[9] E. Bouchette, *Emparons-nous de l'industrie* (Ottawa, 1901).

[10] Hughes, 'Industry and the Rural System,' 349.

[11] *CHAR 1944*, 31, M. Wade, 'Relations of French Canada & the U.S.' See H. Marshall, F. A. Southard and K. W. Taylor, *Canadian-American Industry* (New Haven, 1936).

[12] *Quebec Statistical Yearbook 1918*, 128; *Canada Year Book 1922–3*, 164.

[13] *L'Action française* (Montréal), I (jan. 1917), 1.

[14] A. Perrault, Abbé L. Groulx, 'P. Homier' (R. P. J.-Papin Archambault), *Soirées de l'Action française* (Montréal, 1926), 14, '*Consignes de Demain.*'

[15] *Ibid.*, 19.

[16] A. Laurendeau, *L'Abbé Lionel Groulx* (Montréal, 1939), 51.

[17] *L'Action française*, II (mars 1918), 3.

[18] *Ibid.*, IV (sept. 1920), 9.

[19] O. Asselin, *L'Oeuvre de l'abbé Groulx* (Montréal, 1923), 87.

[20] Laurendeau, 47–8.

[21] *Ibid.*, 48.

[22] *L'Action française*, V (jan. 1921), 1.

[23] '*Soirées*,' 7–9.

[24] *Ibid.*, 10.

[25] *Ibid.*, 10–11.

[26] *Ibid.*, 12.

[27] *Ibid.*, 13.

[28] Laurendeau, 20.

[29] *Annuaire de l'Université Laval* (Québec, 1897–8), 156; cited Laurendeau, 22.

[30] Laurendeau, 31.

[31] Abbé L. Groulx, *La Naissance d'une Race* (Montréal, 1919), *Lendemains de la Conquête* (1920), *Nos luttes constitutionnelles* (1916), *Les Patriotes de 1837* (1917—not published), *La Confédération canadienne* (1918), *Vers l'Emancipation* (1921).

[32] Asselin, *L'Oeuvre de l'abbé Groulx* (Montréal, 1923).

[33] *Ibid.*, 27–8.

[34] *Ibid.*, 54–5.

[35] *Ibid.*, 62–3.

[36] *Ibid.*, 67.

[37] *Ibid.*, 86.

[38] *Ibid.*, 91.

[39] *Ibid.*, 89.

[40] *Ibid.*, 90.

[41] *Ibid.*, 93.

[42] *L'Action française*, IX (fév. 1923), 2.

[43] Abbé L. Groulx, *Dix ans de l'Action française* (Montréal, 1926); 43–73, '*Pour l'Action française*'; 74–88, '*Méditation patriotique*'; 89–122, '*Si Dollard revenait . . .*'

[44] *L'Action française* [Paris], VII (mars 1922), 3.

[45] Abbé Groulx' speeches have been collected in *Dix ans de l'Action française* (Montréal, 1926), *Orientations* (Montréal, 1935), and *Directives* (Montréal, 1937), as well as published in pamphlet form in most instances.

[46] *L'Action française*, V (jan. 1921), 4–23.

[47] *Ibid.*, VI (déc. 1921), 706.

[48] *Notre Avenir Politique: enquête de l'Action française*, 1922 (Montréal, 1923), 5.
[49] *Ibid.*, 7.
[50] *Ibid.*, 12.
[51] *Ibid.*, 13.
[52] *Ibid.*, 15.
[53] *Ibid.*, 20.
[54] *Ibid.*, 23.
[55] *Ibid.*, 25.
[56] *Ibid.*, 29–30.
[57] *Ibid.*, 50.
[58] *Ibid.*, 71.
[59] *Ibid.*, 84–5.
[60] *Ibid.*, 93.
[61] *Ibid.*, 107.
[62] *Ibid.*, 113.
[63] *Ibid.*, 141–59.
[64] *Ibid.*, 161–78.
[65] *Ibid.*, 179–96.
[66] *Ibid.*, 216.
[67] *Ibid.*, 219–31.
[68] *Ibid.*, 244.
[69] *Ibid.*, 249.
[70] *Ibid.*, 250.
[71] A. Zimmern, *The Third British Empire* (London, 1926), 24.
[72] *L'Action française*, X (déc. 1923), VI, 350.
[73] Cf. E. Montpetit, *D'Azur à trois lys d'or* (Montréal, 1937).
[74] *Revue trimestrielle* (sept. 1928), Beaudry Leman, 'Les Canadiens-français et le milieu américain.'
[75] *Les Canadiens-français et la Confédération canadienne; enquête de* '*L'Action française*' (Montréal, 1927).
[76] *Ibid.*, 12.
[77] *Ibid.*, 20.
[78] *Ibid.*, 20–1.
[79] *Ibid.*, 22–3.
[80] *Ibid.*, 39.
[81] *Ibid.*, 47–8.
[82] *Ibid.*, 49–58.
[83] *Ibid.*, 63.
[84] *Ibid.*, 70.
[85] *Ibid.*, 83–4.
[86] *Ibid.*, 89.
[87] *Ibid.*, 103–4.
[88] *Ibid.*, 107.
[89] *Ibid.*, 120.
[90] *Ibid.*, 142.
[91] Laurendeau, 61.
[92] *L'Action canadienne-française*, XIX (jan. 1928), I, 3.
[93] Laurendeau, 63.
[94] *Can. An. Rev. 1932*, 400.
[95] *L'Action Nationale*, I (fév. 1933), II, 118.
[96] *Ibid.*, 120.
[97] *Ibid.*, I (mai 1933), V, 268.
[98] *Ibid.*, I (juin 1933), VI, 359.
[99] *Ibid.*, II (nov. 1933), III, 210–16.
[100] *Ibid.*, III (jan. 1934), 53–4.

[101] *Ibid.*, III (mai 1934), V, 265.
[102] *Ibid.*, IV (sept. 1934), I, 61.
[103] *Ibid.*, IV (nov. 1934), III, 175–6.
[104] *Ibid.*, V (jan. 1935), I, 4.
[105] Groulx, *Directives*, 52–94.
[106] *Canada, Commons Debates 1935*, April 4, III, 2279–92.
[107] *L'Action Nationale*, V (mai 1935), V, 317; *ibid.*, V (juin 1935), VI, 375.
[108] *Ibid.*, VI (sept. 1935), I, 81.
[109] *Ibid.*, VI (oct. 1935), II, 92–102.
[110] *Ibid.*, VII (jan. 1936), I, 3.
[111] *Ibid.*, VII (avril 1936), IV, 235.
[112] *Ibid.*, VII (mars 1936), III, 129.
[113] *Can. An. Rev. 1935–6*, 79.
[114] *L'Action Nationale*, IX (mai 1937), V, 271.
[115] *Ibid.*, 308.
[116] *Ibid.*, X (sept. 1937), I, 14–15.
[117] Abbé L. Groulx, *Directives* (Montréal, 1937), 234, 242.
[118] *L'Action Nationale*, X (sept. 1937), I, 31–5.
[119] *Ibid.*, X (nov. 1937), III, 181.
[120] *Ibid.*, XI (jan. 1938), I, 25.
[121] *Ibid.*, XII (nov. 1938), III, 262.
[122] *Ibid.*, XIII (fév. 1939), II, 154.
[123] *Ibid.*, XIII (juin 1939), VI, 508.

CHAPTER XV

FRENCH CANADA AND WORLD WAR II

(1939–44)

THE SECOND WORLD WAR came upon a Quebec which had not yet rallied from ten years of economic depression that had gravely shaken its social structure and had also fostered social developments that had made English Canadians and Americans suspicious of French Canada. For some French Canadians, bred in an authoritarian tradition and self-consciously 'Latin' in an 'Anglo-Saxon' North America, felt a certain sympathy for the totalitarian nationalism of Mussolini, Franco, and Salazar which was so antipathetic to English-speaking North Americans. The current of racism which had been running even more strongly in French-Canadian nationalism, thanks to twenty years of Abbé Groulx' teaching and to ten years of being a 'subject people' in a period of economic disorder which did not afflict the 'master race' so sharply, even encouraged a certain sympathy with Hitler in some French-Canadian quarters. It was also difficult for the French Canadians, traditionally anti-imperialists, not to be skeptical of the new anti-imperialism of the English and the Americans as the Germans and Italians sought the empires which the other great powers had long enjoyed.

Preoccupied with its own economic and social troubles, French Canada had not shared the general Western development towards a belief in collective security; and as a world conflagration came ever nearer, French Canada had lapsed more and more into isolationism. The old dream of a separate French Catholic State, a 'Laurentia,' had never been more popular than in the immediate prewar period, thanks to the provincialist trend of Groulx' nationalism and to fears of the outside world. Some French Canadians envisaged such a state within the British Commonwealth of Nations, another Eire enjoying the privileges but none of the responsibilities of membership in the Commonwealth; others favored Canadian neutrality, no matter what happened in Europe; and still others, whose North Americanism was greater than their sense of kinship with France and Rome, even maintained that annexation to the United States would be preferable to endless involvement in Britain's imperial wars.

I

Considering these trends and the fact that much Italian and German money was spent in Quebec with the aim of embarrassing Britain as the Second World War drew close,[1] it was somewhat surprising that French-Canadian opinion so definitely sided with England and France in the final crisis. The Soviet-German Pact produced a general outburst of violent anger in the French-Canadian press,[2] relieved only by *La Presse's* reflection that it was perhaps not regrettable since the democracies thus avoided an unfortunate alliance with godless Russia. *La Patrie*, *Le Soleil*, *Le Canada*, *L'Evénement-Journal*, and *Le Droit* saw in the Pact only the formal alliance of totalitarian regimes which had the same tyrannical and anti-religious conceptions of life, politics, and power, and the same cynical disloyalty to promises and pledges. Louis-Philippe Roy of *L'Action Catholique* considered it an opportunity for Mussolini to disassociate himself from Hitler, while *Le Soleil* anticipated the day when Italy would line up with Germany and Russia. *L'Evénement-Journal* mocked the Italian army and approved *Le Droit's* campaign against the anti-French articles of *Italia Nuova*, the fascist-inspired Italian weekly of Montreal. Both *La Presse* and *L'Action Catholique*, however, suggested that Mussolini might mediate in the tense European situation, though *La Tribune* of Sherbrooke questioned his qualifications for the role. Adrien Arcand's *L'Illustration Nouvelle* maintained that peace could only be preserved by a four-power pact between the United Kingdom, France, Italy and Germany.

Despite the desire of the French-Canadian press for peace, peace at any price was not favored. *La Presse* admitted during the Polish crisis of August that it might not be well to yield to Hitler's demands. *La Patrie* went farther than any other Quebec paper in condemning Hitler's aims and methods. The Liberal papers, particularly *Le Soleil*, were uncompromising in their stand against another Munich. At the end of August *Le Canada* stated that war depended upon the will of one man, Hitler. The nationalist press was less concerned with the current crisis than with the stand Canada should take in case of war in Europe, but *Le Devoir* credited Chamberlain with having avoided war so far and with attempting to limit its scope if it should break out. *L'Evénement-Journal* blamed Chamberlain for his excessive patience and diplomatic weakness, but threw the whole responsibility for the impending war on Hitler. The editor of *L'Action Catholique*, Louis-Philippe Roy, who always sought to follow papal directives, held that Germany and Italy, the have-not nations, were not wrong in complaining of their needs, since the wealth of the world was unjustly distributed; but he blamed the dictators for their violation of treaties and their attempts to plunder weaker countries. Both *L'Action* and *Le Droit* were convinced that Danzig was simply a pretext and that Hitler sought a complete settlement of the Polish question. Poland, as a Catholic country, commanded much sympathy from these papers.

L'Illustration Nouvelle maintained the official Nazi thesis that Danzig was a German city and that Poland had no more right to determine its fate than did England and France. Hitler was pictured as considering war the greatest of plagues, while big business and the international news agencies were accused of supporting war parties in the democracies. *L'Illustration* also bewailed the encirclement of Germany and Polish persecution of the Ukrainians. The Freemasons were blamed for the resistance of the democracies to Hitler. With the exception of this frankly fascist publication, which was also the chief organ of Duplessis' *Union Nationale*, the French-Canadian press favored the democracies against the dictatorships—though there was some lingering sympathy for Mussolini—and held that the war of blackmail must be ended, once and for all.[3] But there was a strange optimism that once more war would be averted, as it had been in the previous year.

It was doubtless because of this state of opinion in Quebec, upon whose support his government rested, that Prime Minister Mackenzie King continued his ambiguity as the time for decision drew near. On August 23 he announced that the government would, if necessary, use the extensive powers granted under the War Measures Act of 1914, in case of war or apprehended war.[4] On August 25 he reiterated that parliament would be summoned if war became inevitable in Europe and that the government would submit its policy to parliament. Mackenzie King also cabled appeals to Hitler, the Polish president, and Stalin, urging them to avoid starting a general war. When Germany invaded Poland on September 1, a proclamation was issued that a state of 'apprehended war exists and has existed as and from the twenty-fifth day of August.'[5] Mr. King then summoned parliament to meet on September 7, and declared that if Britain became involved in war with Germany, his government would seek authority from parliament 'for effective co-operation by Canada at the side of Britain.'[6] When Great Britain formally declared war on September 3, Mr. King stated in a broadcast that the government would recommend to parliament 'the measures which it believes to be the most effective for co-operation and defence.'[7] Meanwhile semi-belligerent measures were taken, with the proclamation of the Defence of Canada Regulations, the placing of the armed forces on a war basis, the internment of enemy aliens, the prohibition of trading with the enemy, and the creation of a Wartime Prices and Trade Board to prevent profiteering.[8]

Although a policy of neutrality was incompatible with such

measures as these, the speech from the throne at the opening of the special session on September 7 still left the government's position vague. Parliament was told it had been summoned 'in order that the government may seek authority for the measures necessary for the defence of Canada, and for co-operation in the determined effort which is being made to resist further aggression, and to prevent the appeal to force instead of to pacific means in the settlement of international disputes.'[9] On September 8, under pressure from Dr. Manion, leader of the opposition, the prime minister refused to disclose his views on an expeditionary force and overseas action, while Maxime Raymond presented a petition signed by thousands of citizens against participation by Canada in any foreign war.[10] In seconding the address, J.-A. Blanchette (Compton) declared: 'I have reason to believe that I am expressing the opinion of the majority of electors in my province, in fact in all provinces, when I say that I am in favor of a reasonable and moderate cooperation, consistent with our interests and resources.' He favored voluntary contribution and was 'completely opposed to conscription.'[11]

On the following day Mr. King committed himself to a declaration of war with his announcement that if the House approved the address in reply to the speech from the throne, proclamation of a state of war between Canada and the German Reich would be issued at once. The address was passed on the evening of September 9, and on September 10 the King gave his formal approval to the proclamation.[12]

Though Mr. King later revealed that since the Munich crisis he himself had thought Canada must be prepared to go to war against Germany,[13] his hesitant course in 1939 was dictated by the desire, as he declared on September 8, 'to let no hasty or premature threat or pronouncement create distrust and divisions between the different elements that compose the population of our vast Dominion, so that when the moment for decision came all should so see the issue itself that our national effort might be marked by unity of purpose, of heart and of endeavour.'[14] He was clearly inspired by the example of Laurier, and by his own recollections of the tragic division of Canada in the First World War. In his speech on the address on September 8 he sought to conciliate both French-Canadian nationalists and the left-wing English-Canadians who were opposed to full participation. He made much of Canada's dual heritage from France and Britain, the need for unity, and the government's primary concern with the defence and security of Canada. He said little about the possibility of an expeditionary force, and emphatically repeated his promise of March 30 that the present government would not introduce conscription for overseas service.[15] He indicated that Canada's role would naturally be concerned with the defence of her own territory and that of Labrador and Newfoundland, and with economic aid to Britain. In short he left the door open for a policy of aggressive neutrality, such as the United States later adopted, in case public opinion blocked more active participation.

But Ernest Lapointe's eloquence supplemented the prime minister's tactics of caution and persuasion in winning French-Canadian support for the government's proposals. The justice minister reviewed the reasons 'Why it is impossible, practically, for Canada to be neutral in a big war in which England is engaged.'[16] He pointed out that Canadian neutrality could not be 'other than a move favorable to the enemies of England and France.'[17] As for an expeditionary force, 'no government could stay in office if it refused to do what the large majority of Canadians wanted it to do.' In reply to Raymond, who had taunted him with his refusal at Quebec the previous December 'to fight in behalf of foreign interests,' he declared: 'For the sake of unity we cannot be neutral in Canada.'[18] But Lapointe made a solemn pledge against conscription for overseas service:

> The whole province of Quebec—and I speak with all the responsibility and all the solemnity I can give to my words—will never agree to accept compulsory service or conscription outside Canada. I will go farther than that: When I say the whole province of Quebec I mean that I personally agree with them. I am authorized by my colleagues in the cabinet from the province of Quebec—the veteran leader of the Senate (Dandurand), my good friend and colleague, the Minister of Public Works (Mr. Cardin), my friend and fellow townsman and colleague, the Minister of Pensions and National Health (Mr. Power)—to say that we will never agree to conscription and will never be members or supporters of a government that will try to enforce it.

He added a warning, which was probably intended for some of his cabinet colleagues as well as for the Tories to whom it was addressed:

> May I add that if my friends and myself from Quebec were forced to leave the government, I question whether anyone would be able to take our place. If my hon. friends in the far corner of the house opposite: if the *Ottawa Citizen*, which just now is waging a campaign for conscription, think they are serving Canada by splitting it at the very outset of the war, then I say they are gravely and seriously wrong.[19]

Mr. Lapointe then appealed to French Canada as he alone could do as Quebec's spokesman at Ottawa:

> Provided these points are understood, we are willing to offer our services without limitation and to devote our best efforts for the success

of the cause we all have at heart. And those in Quebec who say that we will have conscription, in spite of what some of us are saying, are doing the work of disunity, the work of the foe, the work of the enemy. They weaken by their conduct and their words the authority of those who represent them in the government. So far as the insults and abuses of agitators are concerned—I disdain them! They will not deter me from the path of duty as God gives me light to see it. I will protect them against themselves. I believe the majority in my province trusts me; I have never deceived them, and I will not deceive them now. I have been told that my present stand means my political death. Well, at least it would not be a dishonourable end. But let me assure you, Mr. Speaker, that if only I can keep my physical strength, fall I shall not, and my friends shall not fall, either.[20]

With a foresight that was to be borne out by subsequent events, he warned against 'a Balkanized Canada, a plebiscite by provinces,' in reply to Raymond's suggestion that the issue be submitted directly to the people. And then he closed with a deeply emotional and highly effective variation on the Queen's farewell words at Halifax at the conclusion of the royal tour: '*Dieu bénisse le Canada.*'

God bless Canada. God save Canada's honor, Canada's soul, Canada's dignity, Canada's conscience.

God give Canadians the light which will indicate to them where their duty lies in this hour of trial so that our children and our children's children may inherit a land where freedom and peace shall prevail, where our social, political, and religious institutions may be secure and from which the tyrannical doctrines of nazism and communism are forever banished. Yes, God bless Canada, God bless our Queen, God bless our King.[21]

Lapointe's deeply felt evocation of French Canada's love of country and loyalty to the monarchy won the hesitant Quebec members to the government's program. In vain Liguori Lacombe declared that the sacrifice of neutrality was too high a price for national unity, and called for dissolution of parliament and an appeal to the people.[22] Lacombe moved an amendment to the address, which was seconded by Wilfrid Lacroix, 'That this house regrets that the Government did not deem it fitting to advise His Excellency the Governor General that Canada should refrain from participating in war outside Canada.' But the motion found virtually no supporters. Georges Héon's poll of sentiment in his Argenteuil constituency probably provided an accurate picture of popular French-Canadian sentiment: 15 per cent favored conscription to the last man and dollar, 20 per cent favored complete isolation, 65 per cent were for 'cooperation within our means and resources, preferably by the extension of credits, gifts of provisions and foodstuffs, and the manufacture of planes and munitions,' while there was 'a very strong and earnest sentiment against conscription of manpower,' and opposition to an expeditionary force.[23] The government motion received almost unanimous support on an unrecorded vote in which only one member was noted as having risen in opposition.

2

When Britain went to war on September 3, the French-Canadian press was united in the conviction that the conflict was a righteous one into which the democracies had been forced by Hitler. *La Presse* asserted that Canadians endorsed the attitude taken by the King, the British prime minister, and the French president at the outbreak of hostilities. *La Patrie*, *L'Action Catholique*, and *Le Soleil* used the contemptuous word '*Boche*' on all occasions. The dailies were backed up by the weeklies in condemning Hitler for bringing on the war. *L'Action Catholique* considered Hitlerism the chief danger in Europe, particularly since its alliance with Communism; while *Le Droit* blamed the war primarily on Communism. *Le Devoir* devoted little editorial attention to the war during the first two months, although on September 16 its editor, Georges Pelletier, speculated as to why London and Paris had not taken steps against Lenin and Stalin in Russia, and Négrin in Spain, who had long behaved in the same way as Hitler. *L'Illustration Nouvelle* carefully avoided reference to the war.[24]

The French-Canadian press was somewhat less quick to consider the conflict a crusade than the English-Canadian newspapers, which hailed it as a holy war against the enemies of religion and civilization. *Le Canada* questioned this interpretation; but *L'Action Catholique* characterized the Nazis as the 'enemies of Christianity,' *La Patrie* called Hitler 'an Anti-Christ,' and *Le Droit* spoke of 'the truly Catholic character assumed by the Allies in this crusade against an alliance of Hitlerism and Communism.' There was much sympathy for the plight of Catholics in Poland and Germany. *L'Action Catholique* urged a Christian Front against Bolshevism, embracing the Allies, Italy, Spain, and other neutrals, lest it be forgotten that 'the greatest peril of the hour is Bolshevism rather than Hitlerism.' Repressive measures against the Canadian Communists were recommended. There was no sympathy for Hitler's peace proposals after the rapid overrunning of Poland.[25]

While the French press was almost unanimously anti-German and anti-Russian, it was not pro-war, in the sense of favoring Canadian participation. It urged either neutrality or limited participation, in the interests of Canada, national unity, and Canadian freedom of action in foreign affairs. Louis Francoeur, one of Quebec's most popular commentators on world affairs, held that the British government should assume the cost of the war, since 'though it is the duty of every free, responsible man to do his part in the defence of civilization against the aggressor nations and the powers of brute force, Canada as such was not directly interested in the present crisis in Central Europe.'[26] It was pointed out that under the Neutrality Act the United States would be bound to cease supplying Canada once the latter declared war, with results that would be 'very much felt by every friendly belligerent.' Most papers favored American neutrality, and thought it in the interest of internal peace in Canada.

When it became obvious that Canadian public opinion at large favored participation, the French press hailed the policy of limited participation announced by Mackenzie King and Ernest Lapointe when parliament met in special session on September 1. *La Presse* called on September 6 for 'fair and reasonable' aid to Britain:

> The Province of Quebec is ready to lend its most generous aid within the limits set by the speeches of Messrs. King and Lapointe, i.e., putting our national interests first, and adhering to the voluntary principle. Quebec will not associate itself with a policy that would compromise national interests by leading Canada to economic ruin and causing a division of ideas across the country.[27]

Two days later it approved the cautious course announced by the King government in the speech from the throne as sound and constitutional. *La Patrie* on September 10 observed: 'It is fortunate that we have as the Government of Canada men who can reconcile their duty to the British Empire with their duty to their country.'[28]

The Liberal press was markedly reluctant to back participation wholeheartedly. On September 6 *Le Canada* declared that Canada had the right to assert its neutrality, but that complete neutrality was impossible considering the opinion of the English-speaking majority. It criticized anti-participationist agitators for doing a disservice to the French Canadians by presenting the question as a racial issue. Since Canada derived advantages from the Commonwealth in time of peace, it was logical that it should cooperate with Britain in time of war. *Le Canada* saw Lapointe playing a dual role in the cabinet as a defender of Canadian interests and a protector of the link between French Canada and England. In its September 9 editorial on the government's war policy, it called upon Quebec to support this 'intelligent, reasoned participation,' with no conscription for overseas service, no expeditionary force, and reasonable economic aid. It observed: 'If Canada's effective co-operation should mean economic and financial ruin, it would be a disservice to the Commonwealth and disastrous for the Canadian people.' The defence and security of Canada were set up as the first responsibilities of the Canadian people. *La Tribune* of Sherbrooke warned that 90 per cent of French-Canadian electors were opposed to conscription: 'So let no government in this country ever commit the error of passing a law so pregnant with troubles, and which in the past produced nothing but evil.'[29]

Le Soleil during August had demanded that British and French propaganda for Canadian participation should be checked, and had asserted that there was no reason to believe that popular opinion had changed since the King government won power in 1935 on a peace platform. On September 6 it explained its attitude in detail:

> For some years the conflict of ideas and interests has enabled one to foresee the outbreak of a catastrophic European war. *Le Soleil* has strongly urged the Canadian authorities to base their foreign policy on the national interest in relation to the solidarity of the countries of the American continent. It is not our fault if this advice, widely supported by French-Canadian opinion, has not prevailed. But as the majority think otherwise, we would not have the temerity to doubt their patriotism or to encourage any sort of sedition. War is a great calamity, but anarchy is worse.[30]

On the following day it asserted that Canada would stay neutral, following the example of Eire. And on September 9 it noted that Mackenzie King had taken account of the divergences of opinion on the question of participation, and concluded: 'Short of a crisis or a *coup d'état*, the internal peace of Canada will not be disturbed, as in 1917, by a new attempt to raise a levy of Canadian blood for the profit of an imperial power.'[31]

Such independence of attitude in the most widely circulated French Liberal paper indicated the pressure that Quebec brought to bear upon Ottawa at the outbreak of the war. The country weeklies accepted the necessity of participation, since it was favored by the English majority; but they joined the chorus against obligatory service outside Canada. Jean-Charles Harvey of *Le Jour* stood alone on September 2 when he found it 'logical, natural, and right that Canada, a democratic country united to the British Commonwealth by a sort of unwritten treaty, more binding even than the treaties binding France and England to Poland and all the little nations of Europe which wanted to keep their liberty, should join the democratic bloc, participating wisely for the defence and triumph of an ideal which should be that of every man of heart.' But even Harvey favored assistance 'within the measure of our means, for our two nationalities of different origin should remember that the war is not the end of the world and that afterwards we shall have to live side by side, as sons of the same land.'[32]

The nationalist press called for a Canadian foreign policy 'that would take account of geographical realities and our overriding interests.' Canada, as a North American country, should confine its responsibilities to the New World; and since it had no influence on British foreign policy, it was not bound to endorse British commitments. Canada had the right, under the Statute of Westminster, to maintain its neutrality, and should do so; intervention would be a return to colonial status. The example of the United States and the smaller European powers which remained neutral was pointed out, with the comment that they either had greater interests at stake or were closer to the battleground than Canada.

Le Devoir carried on a vigorous campaign against intervention. Omer Héroux saw the crisis as only 'a boundary dispute between Germany and Poland,' into which France and England might be drawn because they promised to stand by Poland. But 'they did not and could not claim to commit Canada,' and Canada had no reason to intervene, either for the survival of Britain, France and Poland, or to restore the balance of power in Europe, or to defend a democracy which for months had sought alliance with Russian autocracy. Georges Pelletier asserted that Canada was not a party to the treaty invoked by the Poles, but that all Canadians were parties to the Confederation pact:

> . . . in which it was agreed among other things that Canadians should defend their common country. Their country is in America. Its frontiers are not in the Rhineland, nor on the shores of the Baltic or banks of the Vistula. They are only on the American continent, between the Atlantic and the Pacific and the Arctic. What has become of the sanctity of that treaty, for it is a treaty bearing the most authoritative signatures? It was violated from 1914 to 1918. They are ready to violate it again in September 1939. And supposedly it is in Europe that treaties are endangered . . . Let us think of our own.[33]

Léopold Richer, *Le Devoir's* Ottawa correspondent, gloomily accepted intervention as foredoomed from the first. He maintained that Mackenzie King's theory that parliament would decide the issue contradicted Laurier's theory that 'when Britain is at war, Canada is at war and exposed to attack.' If the Liberal leaders struck to Laurier's theory, parliament had only to decide the manner and extent of intervention. If the Liberals rejected the idea of Canadian neutrality, it did not mean that Canada had no right to it but that the Liberal government had doubts about it or had decided not to exercise that right. Héroux revived some of Bourassa's old arguments when he proclaimed that 'the people who want to ruin Canada for the sake of the Empire are really the most dangerous promoters of annexation'; and when he argued that intervention now, as in 1899 and in 1914, would constitute a new precedent for later interventions all over the world. He urged that conscription would be the inevitable result of intervention, and 'in any case, whether they fall as conscripts or volunteers, the fallen soldiers are an equal loss to the country, and the costs of war are the same.' As early as August 3 Richer preferred independence to intervention: 'Every Canadian who sincerely wants to save his country the enormous losses of men and money which war requires inevitably, could make no other choice . . . It would be better for the internal peace of the country and for its future to adopt a *modus vivendi* with the nations of the Commonwealth, which would allow us full liberty of action in case of armed conflict in Europe or Asia.' *Le Devoir* saw only two circumstances under which Canada should intervene: if a plebiscite showed that the nation willed it, or if the United States joined the Allies.[34] The nationalists were convinced that a plebiscite would result in a verdict against intervention—a conclusion which seems somewhat dubious.

Le Droit was actively anti-interventionist, asserting that Canadian foreign policy was in the hands of London and that Canada had become a suburb of England. On September 6 it accused Mackenzie King of sabotaging Canadian unity: 'If, supported by the parliamentary majority it counts on, the Federal Government is ready to impose on a part of the Canadian people, by force of numbers, a policy that they do not want, then we have oppression of minorities such as is condemned in Europe by those practising it here.' But on September 8 it admitted that 'the Government would take the attitude which would be least likely to endanger Canadian unity.' Camille L'Heureux seemed to envisage the formation of a French-Canadian party, after he had appealed to French-Canadian members of parliament to put their duty to their electors above party loyalty:

> French Canada has no chance of getting a strictly Canadian foreign policy, to say nothing of respect for the Canadian constitution. In each party our presentation is subjected to the dictatorship of an Anglo-Canadian majority which unites every time it sees fit, to oppose with a united front the legitimate aspirations of the French Canadians . . . In the light of recent events one sees more clearly that there will be no safety for us save outside the present political parties. The present attitude of the Federal Government emphasized this conviction among the French Canadians, and strengthens their determination to break the chains binding them to the present parties and to turn to a strictly Canadian party.[35]

L'Action Catholique argued during August that before rushing into an intervention 'more generous than wise,' it should be considered that 'we are an American nation,' that 'our military assistance could only be relatively diminutive,' that 'the warring nations should count on the production of friendly countries almost exclusively,' that 'civilization needs some corners for refuge during the coming carnage,' that 'as far as we participate with military forces, we take the roles of belligerents and attract reprisals,' that 'prudence compels us to organize some defence for our immense territory,' and that 'our people, crushed by the burden of debt contracted in the last war, are unable to pay the costs of a new war infinitely more disastrous than the last.' On September 2 *L'Action Catholique* set forth its principles for a Canadian foreign policy:

Above all, we still wish the maintenance of peace as far as possible. In principle we refuse to accept the doctrine that Canada is at war just because England is, and in practice we strongly oppose any military participation caused merely by that doctrine. However, if a situation should arise that might really jeopardize one or another of the great interests of humanity, above all the interests of Christianity, the Canadian people would then decide that there was a case for joining with other nations to deal with the peril. Even in that case our participation should be voluntary, and should by no means exceed the rigid limits imposed by our resources. These principles should suit all Canadians, of whatever origin, because they arise from the purest Canadianism and take account of our affection for pacific peoples, and our preoccupation with world welfare.[36]

L'Evénement-Journal on September 7 warned French Canada's representatives at Ottawa that they would be held responsible if they violated the peace pledges they had made in the 1935 elections. And on the following day it expressed the hope that Mackenzie King would not develop the habit of facing the country with *faits accomplis*. *L'Illustration Nouvelle* blended nationalist isolationism with fascist inspiration in its insistence on neutrality, since England and France, in taking up arms against Hitler, 'were waging an aggressive war of intervention.'[37] Self-centered nationalism, with its 'sacred egoism' which put French-Canadian rights and sentiments before the will of the majority, and which for years had sought to build a Chinese Wall about Quebec, found it easy to concentrate on the plight of French Canada in the midst of a world struggle. This isolationism, with its long tradition of anti-imperialism, offered a fertile field of exploitation for Italian and German propagandists, who remained active in Quebec until the outbreak of the war, and whose work was later carried on, in some few instances, by French-Canadian converts to the concept of the 'new order.'

Once parliament had endorsed the government's stand in favor of participation on September 9 and had asserted Canadian sovereignty by declaring war on its own account, not as an automatic consequence of Britain's declaration of war a week before, the French press as a whole preached moderate participation and the maintenance of Canadian interests above those of Britain. *La Presse* envisaged Canada's role as that of principal base of supplies for the Allies. It urged that participation should not be allowed to injure Canadian agricultural, industrial, or economic life, and expressed the hope that the war budget would be confined to necessary expenses. It opposed putting pressure on the unemployed to enlist. *La Patrie* showed somewhat more enthusiasm for recruiting, but in general took the same stand. The Liberal press continued its reserved attitude, with *Le Canada* even likening the sending of an expeditionary force 'to complete participation which would ruin our country.' It stressed the gratitude which French Canadians owed to the King government for persuading the country to adopt a compromise policy, and warned of the dangers of rousing antagonism to French Canada by opposing intervention.[38]

The nationalist papers swallowed the pill of intervention with some bitterness, and urged very moderate participation, except for *Le Devoir*, which remained resolute in its opposition and constantly deplored the cost of participation. *L'Action Catholique* proposed a two-fold program: 'First to spread by all Christian and wise means the spirit of "Canadianism" wherever it is lacking, and secondly, whenever the opportunity occurs, to use our constitutional right to discuss the best manner and extent of participation, while avoiding any appeal to disturbing passions, and always following the line of reasonableness.' Both *Le Droit* and *Le Devoir* suggested in the middle of September that Canada should declare its neutrality at the end of the war, since its declaration of war had established a precedent that it was not automatically at war when Britain was at war. The nationalist press harped on the danger of conscription, 'which could not be accepted or applied in Quebec,' and deplored talk of union government, while continually reminding the present government of its pledges. The French-Canadian press outside Quebec, which had taken little part in the earlier debate as to whether Canada should intervene, now joined its Quebec colleagues in taking a firm stand against conscription.[39]

L'Action Nationale's September number was delayed by the establishment of censorship, which was imposed upon some of its articles, thus lessening its influence at the crucial period of the special session. But the views that were expressed may be taken as typical of the nationalist élite, although doubtless diluted by censorship. The editors took the stand that the government should impose no measure contrary to the will of either interventionists or anti-participationists. They opposed both conscription and war taxes. There should be 'no volunteering organized by the Canadian government at Canadian expense for military operations outside of Canada,' though 'it is well understood that we accept resolutely the principle of true national defence, of a rational nature proportioned to our means.' The editors declared that the French Canadians, to do justice to an 'important portion of English-Canadian opinion,' would accept an embargo on exports to Germany or her co-belligerents, the freedom of individual Canadians to join the British Army or to recruit volunteers for the British Army at their own expense, and the selling to Britain of arms or other needed goods. The keynote of this highly individualistic program was 'Since Canada is divided on this question, let Canadian policy be to leave each individual free to act according to his convictions.'[40] What these convictions were in the case of the editors was made apparent by the hailing of Paul Gouin, René Chaloult, Ligouri Lacombe, Paul Bouchard, and Dr. Philippe Hamel, as well as the leaders of the Catholic syndicates and the Union Catholique des Cultivateurs, for organizing protests against conscription and compromise programs, a course which Lapointe had characterized as 'dishonorable, shameless, ignoble.'[41]

In the face of the *Ottawa Citizen's* campaign for the immediate adoption of conscription, while the *Montreal Star* made much of the demands for it by the Conservative and Social Credit parties and veteran groups, the isolationists of *L'Action Nationale* found comfort both in American belligerent-mindedness and in American isolationism. Roger Duhamel pointed out that President Roosevelt's statement in a September press conference, that the United States would tolerate no domination of Canada by a non-British power, disposed of the argument that Canada would be the prey of the victors if it did not help to crush the Germans.[42] *L'Action Nationale* also quoted with obvious satisfaction Colonel Lindbergh's speech of October 13, which admitted the United States' duty to defend the American nations against invasion, but called for freedom from the 'totalitarian influences of Europe,' and questioned Canada's right to draw the Western Hemisphere into a European war 'for the sole reason that it prefers the Crown of England to American independence.' Lindbergh also urged that the United States 'should not permit any American country to extend the use of its bases to foreign ships of war, or to send its army to fight abroad while remaining safe under our protection.'[43] The isolationists of French Canada, hiding behind their intellectual Chinese Wall, had more in common with the Middle-Western isolationists, insulated by half a continent, than with other dwellers on the Atlantic seaboard who faced the possibility that the war might soon be brought to their doorsteps.

3

The potential opposition and isolation from the rest of Canada latent in this situation was largely dispelled by Quebec's verdict in the provincial elections of October 1939, which were called by Premier Duplessis two weeks after Canada had declared war. He declared that a vote for him would be a vote against conscription and participation, and that the election was 'a battle for the survival of our popular liberties.'[44] But his anti-war, autonomist government was swept from office in an electoral landslide quite as earth-shaking as that which had dislodged the Liberals from office three years before. By its autocratic and extravagant regime which had doubled the debt of the province in three years, *L'Union Nationale* had alienated labor and offended the French-Canadian instinct for the way of moderation. When Ernest Lapointe denounced Duplessis' 'electoral adventure' as 'an act of national sabotage' and threatened that he and his French-Canadian colleagues in the federal cabinet would resign *en masse* unless the province cleaned house and supported the war policy by electing a Liberal government, French Canada responded enthusiastically. The new premier, Adélard Godbout, had declared: 'I pledge myself on my honour to quit my party and even to fight it if a single French Canadian, from now till the end of hostilities, is mobilized against his will under a Liberal regime, or even under a provisional regime in which our present ministers in the King cabinet participate.'[45]

La Presse and *La Patrie* agreed that the electoral verdict indicated that 'Quebec would not allow itself to get into the position of being apart from the other provinces of the Dominion,' though the latter made the reservation that approval of the war policy did not mean approval of obligatory overseas service.[46]

The four federal ministers promised that as long as they held office there would be no conscription for overseas, while the Liberal press interpreted the vote as a ratification of the stand adopted by the French-Canadian ministers and members at Ottawa. In the elections Duplessis was supported by *L'Illustration*, *L'Evénement-Journal*, and somewhat indirectly by *Le Devoir*. On November 4 the latter belittled the result as simply provincial in character, but *L'Illustration* immediately proclaimed that Quebec had pronounced against provincial autonomy. *L'Action Catholique*, which had inclined towards the Liberals before the elections, subsequently expressed fears that Adélard Godbout's victory might be taken as a blank check given to the Federal Government. It interpreted the electoral verdict thus: 'Messieurs the French-Canadian ministers at Ottawa, Quebec accepts the policy you have obtained, and wants you to stay at your posts and vigorously resist any attempt to go beyond the compromise, lest Canada be ruined.'[47]

The English-Canadian press hailed the verdict as a reknitting of the bond of Confederation and a repudiation of an administration which had been associated with the fascist movements in French Canada. Mackenzie King himself observed that 'nothing since Confederation has contributed more to national unity.'[48] English-Canadian confidence in Quebec was still further restored by the federal elections of March 1940, in which the Liberals won all but one of the Quebec seats in a striking endorsement of Mackenzie King's policies, which had been censured by the Hepburn government in Ontario. *Le Soleil* summed up French Canada's attitude by saying that the King government was 'the living symbol of practical cooperation' in the war effort, while *Le Progrès du Saguenay* observed that there could be no doubt that there were fewer dangers for Quebec in the policies of the Liberals.[49] The placid course of the 'phoney war' had disarmed overzealous English Canadians who would have preferred immediate conscription and economic assistance to the last cent from the outbreak of the war, while French Canada was led to play a modest but respectable part in the war effort on the basis of King's moderate, 'pay as you go' policy. A small Canadian expeditionary force of one division landed in England on December 17, without protest from Quebec. Canada faced the real opening of the war in Western Europe in the spring of 1940 far more united that it had been the year before.

4

The *Blitzkreig* which began with the invasion of Norway in early April and closed with the collapse of France in June brought the war very close to Canada. The internment of Adrian Arcand in May for publishing statements prejudicial to the safety of the state was calmly accepted. Quebec saw the France it loved despite all differences brought under the Nazi yoke; English Canada saw Britain left alone to face the conqueror, with only the remains of an army salvaged at Dunkirk. It was fired with enthusiasm by Winston Churchill's statement to the British Commons on June 4:

> We shall go on to the end, we shall fight in France, we shall fight on the seas and oceans, we shall fight with growing confidence and growing strength in the air, we shall defend our Island, whatever the cost may be, we shall fight on the beaches, we shall fight on the landing grounds, we shall fight in the fields and in the streets, we shall fight in the hills; we shall never surrender, and even if, which I do not for a moment believe, this Island or a large part of it were subjugated and starving, then our Empire beyond the seas, armed and guarded by the British fleet,

would carry on the struggle, until, in God's good time, the New World, with all its power and might, steps forth to the rescue and liberation of the old.[50]

The English Canadians were swept by an overpowering desire to rush all possible aid to Britain and to step up Canada's war effort. Loyalism was heightened by the prospect that the royal family might be forced to take refuge in Canada. Feeling rose very high in Ontario, with a mass meeting of 10,000 people in Toronto supporting the *Globe and Mail's* cry of May 24: 'Give us leadership and arms, and Canadians will do the rest.'[51] Mackenzie King's cautious leadership was questioned, and he replied in parliament to the swelling tide of criticism with a warning against hysteria and panic, after recapitulating Canada's war effort to date, which included the sending of 25,000 men to England.

Universal sympathy was expressed by the Quebec press for France after its collapse, which stunned French Canada and produced a certain defeatism. The nationalist *Le Guide* on June 19 observed: 'The heart of New France bleeds for the mother country, but what of our own future? Will it be annexation? Very probably.'[52] And the paper went on to urge the French Canadians to prepare to defend themselves, to bring the Canadian Navy back from Europe to defend Canada, and to enter more fully into the North American orbit. Outrage at the betrayal of France by its own people was also expressed, although *Le Soleil* expressed the general attitude when it observed on June 25: 'Let us not judge too quickly. The least we French Canadians can do for France is to be just.'[53] French Canada felt itself more isolated than ever by the fall of France and by the English-speaking world's attacks on French cowardice and betrayal of the Allied cause. Mackenzie King used the occasion of Saint-Jean-Baptiste Day to declare that 'the tragic fate of France leaves to French Canadians the duty of upholding the traditions of French culture and civilization and the French passion for liberty in the world.'[54]

This message improved French-Canadian morale and helped to make possible acceptance of conscription for the defence of Canada at the end of June. The power given the government under the National Resources Mobilization Act, requiring 'persons to place themselves, their services, and their property' at the disposition of the country 'as may be judged necessary or expedient for securing the public safety, the defence of Canada, the maintenance of public order, or the efficient prosecution of the war,' was carefully limited against requiring 'persons to serve in the military, naval or air forces outside of Canada and the territorial waters thereof.'[55] As a result of this precaution, the limited conscription law was cheerfully accepted in Quebec and the French-Canadian leaders of both Church and State urged their compatriots to comply with it.

With France fallen and Britain beaten to her knees, and with the clear possibility that Canada itself might soon be threatened, the old objections to compulsory service lost most of their force. In vain *Le Devoir* on June 20 headlined its announcement of the measure 'Government "imposes" conscription on the country,' and described it as a repudiation of the free, voluntary, and moderate participation promised by French Canada's leaders at Ottawa.[56] There was little echo of this charge even in the rural regions, where the necessity of compulsory service for the defence of Canada was calmly accepted. An anti-mobilization resolution in the provincial legislature, proposed by René Chaloult and seconded by Camilien Houde, was defeated on June 19 by 56 to 13, despite Chaloult's claim that the resolution represented the opinion of the vast majority of French Canadians, and Maurice Duplessis' statement that he had been right in predicting in 1939 that participation would mean coercion.[57] Maxime Raymond, the most notable of the French-Canadian federal M.P.'s who had opposed participation in September 1939, declared in the House that he would support the mobilization measure, since compulsory service was limited to the defence of Canada on Canadian soil. Liguori Lacombe, however, attacked it as being in flagrant contradiction with the promises of the government, and Wilfrid Lacroix urged that Canadian participation be limited to 'possibilities.'[58] From the outset the Catholic hierarchy approved the measure, with Cardinal Villeneuve instructing his clergy to explain the law from the pulpit in order that the people might fulfil with exactitude and submission a duty which the civil authorities were legitimately requiring of them.[59]

The Cardinal's intervention offset Mayor Houde's advice to the people of Montreal on August 2 not to register as required by the act, lest the law be used to send their sons overseas unwillingly. Houde was promptly interned, and the federal government clumsily sought to suppress news of the incident,[60] but there was no need to do so. A chorus of disapproval for Houde's action broke out, with even *Le Devoir* observing that he had acted like a fool and deserved what he had got, though it maintained his right to appeal against internment. *La Presse* pointed out on August 6 that the French Canadians, who had a profound respect for law and order, were shocked by Houde's defiance of authority. A few days later *L'Action Catholique* told its readers that they could not choose which laws to obey, and added that Cardinal Villeneuve had acted in accordance with the best French-Canadian traditions. A petition for Houde's release was circulated by René Chaloult, Dr. Philippe Hamel, and Paul Bouchard, but it did not attract much support. One rural paper, *L'Eclaireur* of Beauceville, urged that Houde should be released after a short time, lest a reaction in his favor do harm, but it approved the government's action in preventing sabotage of the war effort. The pro-Houde reaction did not come until late in the war, when ethnic feeling had been aroused by a new conscription crisis and he could be exploited as a martyr of the 'race.' Meanwhile the *Winnipeg Free Press* hailed Quebec's repudiation of Houde as an expression of national unity which deserved all Canada's thanks.[61]

On the eve of the national registration, which took place August 15–19, Ernest Lapointe made a broadcast address to his compatriots in which he attacked those who had urged the French Canadians not to register and called attention to Cardinal Villeneuve's stand. He stressed that the purpose of the registration was to obtain an inventory of men and resources for Canada's defence, and that overseas service remained purely voluntary. He reassured his compatriots as to his intention of keeping his promises of no conscription for overseas service.[62] All authorities agreed that Quebec cooperated fully in the registration, and the *Toronto Globe and Mail*, no friend of Quebec or of the Catholic clergy, pointed out with approval that even in remote parishes the *habitants* flocked to register in response to their priests' explanation of the necessity of the measure.[63]

Quebec's acceptance of the National Resources Mobilization Act and her contribution to the war effort in subsequent months led many English Canadians to hold the mistaken idea that the French Canadians would accept conscription for overseas service, which seemed increasingly necessary to the former as time went on. Opposition to such a policy was deeply rooted in the French-Canadian tradition, and had been fostered by the oft-repeated promises of both political parties not to adopt conscription for overseas service. The French Canadian was eager and willing to defend Canada, but he was less concerned with the fate of Britain than his English fellow-citizens and anxious to avoid establishing a precedent for compulsory service in imperial wars. Nationalist spokesmen were not wanting to point out that this was Britain's war and not French Canada's. Among the rank and file in Quebec popular sentiment desired the defeat of Germany, but it was felt that it would do no great harm if *les Anglais* were humbled a bit in the process. There was no popular support for the doctrine that the defence of Canada began in Europe, until the entry of the United States into the war destroyed a prop of French-Canadian isolationism.

When English-Canadian publications proposed conscription or a coalition government which would be free to adopt conscription if necessary, the French-Canadian press repelled both suggestions.

Much use was made of the argument that in the interests of Britain herself, Canada should conserve her manpower, not only to defend her own territory but to maintain the war industries whose products were so badly needed by Britain. Talk of coalition revived the bitter memory of 1917, and *Le Devoir* did not fail to keep that memory alive, while most of the French-Canadian press expressed staunch loyalty to the King government whose policy had been guided by Quebec's sentiments. At the end of February 1941 Ernest Lapointe said that he and his French-Canadian colleagues would resign from the cabinet if a coalition government with a conscription policy was formed. And on June 12 Defence Minister Ralston declared that it was a question of conscription or national unity, and that the wise course was to let well enough alone, since French Canada was giving good support to the voluntary enlistment program.[64]

French Canada's enlistment record in the early years of the Second World War was very different from that of the First War. A French-Canadian unit, the Régiment de Maisonneuve of Montreal, was the first in Canada to fill its ranks with volunteers for overseas service, and General L.-R. Laflèche, the deputy-minister of national defence, estimated that 50,000 French Canadians were in uniform by January 1, 1941.[65] The same authority estimated that 30 per cent of the Royal Canadian Navy was made up of French Canadians, and many French Canadians served in the R.C.A.F., whose famous French-Canadian fighter squadron, '*Les Alouettes*,' was formed in June 1942. Since the Canadian Navy at the outset of the war was largely staffed by British officers and had a strong English tradition, and the R.C.A.F. was at first integrated with the R.A.F., French-Canadian group consciousness favored enlistment in the Army, where French-Canadian regional units were organized at the outset of the war and where a program of bilingual officers' training schools, announced by Lapointe on September 24, 1941, permitted French Canadians to enter all branches of the service and to attain higher ranks. Similar measures were later adopted in the Navy and Air Force, but there remained a popular belief that a French Canadian was handicapped in these services.

At first privately, and later openly, there was much criticism by English Canadians of the fact that there was a higher proportion of French-Canadian enlistments in the Reserve Army units than for overseas service. This criticism neglected the considerations that popular feeling in French Canada was for the defence of Canada rather than for 'overseas adventures,' and that for many a French Canadian who had never been outside of Quebec service in the Maritimes or in British Columbia, and later in Alaska or Greenland, was indeed 'foreign service.' In addition to its military effort,

French Canada made a notable contribution to war industry, which developed much more rapidly in Quebec than it had during the First World War and in the 1920's.

5

After the fall of France the rivalry between the Pétainists and the De Gaullists was a divisive factor in Quebec, although the issue interested a much smaller proportion of the French-Canadian population than English Canadians believed. There was at first much sympathy for the Pétain regime among the élite—particularly among the lower clergy, who were hoodwinked by such pious Vichy slogans as 'Homeland—Work—Family' and by the restoration of religious teaching in the state schools and of the privileges of the religious orders. These measures seemed to indicate a return to the old French values which Quebec cherished and a repudiation of the anti-clerical attitude of French governments since the turn of the century. The De Gaullists were welcomed with intense sympathy by other groups of the élite, who saw in the movement a survival of the French tradition which they cherished, after the capitulation to the Nazis of the Vichy regime. But on the whole the fall of France left Quebec singularly cold, to the astonishment of English-speaking people who had not realized how deep was the isolationism of Quebec and how far its ties with France had been broken. This isolationism was in part a natural result of the long cultivation of a Chinese Wall about the province, so that the French Canadians should not be corrupted either by the surrounding 'Anglo-Saxon' mass or by godless modern France, and in part a parallel of Middle-Western American isolationism.

Both British and De Gaullist propagandists underestimated the new North Americanism of Quebec, and they alienated some of their original sympathizers and the mass of the people by their attempts to pull French-Canadian heartstrings in the interest of the war by invoking Quebec's ties with France. Quebec had not reacted with particular warmth to the French military and cultural missions of the First World War; it was even less pleased by the intellectual refugees and political bagmen of the Second War, who failed to conceal their view that Quebec was a cultural province of France with an unfortunately thin veneer of French culture over its North American barbarism. The fervent de Gaullists in particular alienated sympathy by their view that the French Canadians were un-French, unemancipated, and shockingly unmoved by the tragedy of Europe. On the whole, the De Gaulle-*vs.*-Vichy issue was confined to the press and the élite, while the great mass of the people was unaffected by it.

In July 1940 *La Patrie* asked: 'Why weep over the Third Republic, which confounded liberty with licence?' *L'Action Catholique* and *Le Devoir* displayed strong sympathies for the Pétain regime, with the latter on August 3 commending Pétain for forming the only government possible under the circumstances and defending him against charges of Fascism, and the latter paying tribute on September 10 to his efforts to reorganize French life in the Christian tradition and to suppress Freemasonry. But at the same period *L'Action Catholique* expressed its opinions on the relative merits of Pétain and De Gaulle by explaining that though the Vichy government was the only legitimate government of France and Pétain's reforms were to be commended, naturally Vichy functioned under Nazi surveillance; while De Gaulle was to be approved for continuing the fight at Britain's side and for restoring France's credit with her former allies. There was little reaction in the press to De Gaulle's broadcast appeal of August 2 to French Canada, in which he said: 'The soul of France seeks and calls for your help, French Canadians, because she knows your importance in the British Empire, because in you a branch of the great French stock has become a magnificent tree, and above all because your example restores faith in the future.' As *Le Devoir* later remarked, though the French Canadian has a natural sympathy for France, it is absurd to think that he can be rallied to a cause by sentimental appeals to a French patriotism he has not possessed since Canada became his only country more than 175 years ago.[66]

But *L'Evénement* expressed approval of the Free French movement after the British destruction of the French fleet at Oran on July 4; and as Vichy came more and more under Nazi control and as Britain rallied from the disaster of June, there was a growing realization in the Quebec press that France's future hopes lay in the De Gaullist movement. The organization in Quebec City by Madame André Simard and Père Delos, O.P., of the first Free French group outside of Europe helped to turn the tide of opinion against Vichy. While the bishops' Labor Day message echoed Pétain, on October 25 Ernest Lapointe launched the first of many French-Canadian radio appeals to France, in which he urged the French not to turn against Britain. Declaring that 'we have the same language and with it have inherited a portion of the same soul,' Lapointe said that French Canadians still considered France their ally, for they could not conceive of even a completely defeated France renouncing her century-old ideals. The French Canadians could not believe that their ancient mother country would become the enemy of Britain, to which they were bound not only by community of interests but by a French oath of fidelity. Canada, the offspring of both France and Britain, constituted an indissoluble bond between the two countries. *L'Action Catholique*, in commenting on the Lapointe broadcast, expressed the hope that it would prevent complete French subservience to the Nazis and would show other Canadians what an important role Quebec could play in Franco-British relations.[67]

On October 29 *L'Action*, which had been enthusiastically pro-Pétain, admitted under the headline 'France Betrayed' that Vichy was beginning to play Hitler's game, and expressed the fear that the nazification of France instead of its restoration would be the result. When the De Gaullists sent Commandant Thierry D'Argenlieu, a Carmelite monk with a distinguished war record as a naval officer, to plead their cause in Canada in March 1941, he was given a testimonial dinner in Quebec which was attended by Premier Godbout and Mgr. Camille Roy, the Rector of Laval University. Commandant D'Argenlieu's argument that it was a mere mockery to attempt to erect a Christian state within the Nazi framework, and his careful references to Pétain as a great but misguided Frenchman, made many new friends for De Gaulle's cause. Mackenzie King furthered this gradual evolution of French-Canadian sentiment away from sympathy with Pétain by refusing to break off diplomatic relations with Vichy, despite strong pressure from English-Canadian sources. On October 7 *L'Action Catholique*, still unwilling to condemn the Vichy regime, had warned that such a step would seriously endanger national unity. But it was noteworthy that General Georges Vanier, the Canadian Minister to France who had remained at his post until the armistice of June 1940 and who enjoyed great prestige in Quebec as a hero of the Royal 22nd in the First World War, stated that France's will to resist remained resolute, when he returned to Canada on October 4 after a stay in England.[68]

Another development of the fall of France was a new French-Canadian attitude towards the United States, which loomed larger on Quebec's horizon after contact with Europe was largely cut off. The Ogdensburg Agreement of August 18, 1940 was little short of a Canadian-American military alliance, with its establishment of a Permanent Joint Board to 'consider in the broad sense the defence of the north half of the western hemisphere.'[69] *L'Action Catholique* on August 21 hailed it as an act of immense importance, pointing out that if Germany should defeat Britain, only association with the United States and other American nations could preserve the liberty and national personality of French Canada.

But this relief that the defence of Canada was to be supported by the mighty neighbor to the south was mingled with a certain anxiety lest the United States should swallow up Canada. It was pointed out that after the war Canada would be called upon to choose between the British and the American worlds, and it was hoped that she would not lose her independence. *L'Evénement* on August 20 said that Canadians shared with Americans a common heritage, a common way of life, and a common desire to remain free, which had to be protected in concert with the United States. *Le Devoir* showed no great enthusiasm for joint defence, while on November 7 *L'Action Catholique* argued that Canada should be the partner and not the ward of the United States in the defence of the continent, lest the Americans should be led to annex a neighbor who would not provide for its own defence.[70]

The prospect of close cooperation with the United States raised the old specter of annexation for many French Canadians after the Hyde Park Declaration[71] of April 20, 1941, which provided for economic integration for war purposes; and *L'Action Nationale* was led to devote its June number to a symposium on the subject, which was more widely discussed in private than in the press. The symposium opened with an editorial note, headed 'There'll always be an England, but will there be a Canada?' which expressed the belief that France and England would withstand the catastrophe of war but doubted that Canada, lacking its own culture, geographical unity, and national unity, would survive. It envisaged the hypotheses that Canada might become a colony or protectorate of the United States, or that the provinces as units or groups might be admitted to the Union as new states, or that Quebec might become a state, preserving its frontiers and its autonomy. This latter possibility was studied in its juridical, political, economic, cultural, and religious aspects, with a historical note on annexationism by Abbé Groulx and a note on the American attitude towards French Canada by Burton Ledoux. The editorial foreword urged cautious study of the question, concluding: 'You have a thousand reasons for complaining about the Canadian Confederation; but do not conclude that anything is better than the present situation. An evil is not cured by a greater evil. And before launching oneself in an adventure, one must know where it leads.'[72]

In his historical survey of annexationism up to 1849, Abbé Groulx found 'the resistance of our little people to American continentalism, that is, to any form of imperialism, one of the marvellous facts of the history of this hemisphere.'[73] In a legal study Jacques Perrault expressed his belief that French Canada would enjoy more security for its religion, language, and educational rights under the American states' rights system than under the Canadian constitution.[74] But Edmond Lemieux held that despite the fact that the three main Canadian parties were committed to centralizing policies, the trend of centralization was still stronger in the States, and French Canada would have still less influence at Washington than at Ottawa.[75] In an economic study François-Albert Angers anticipated that under annexation Quebec would lose its industries and become a reserve in which agriculture and extractive industries would flourish, while many French Canadians would be drawn away elsewhere by higher wages. Even if Quebec became more highly industrialized, the need of more labor would swamp the French Canadians with 'foreigners.'[76] Jean Nicolet expressed fears that annexation would mean the end of the French-Canadian ethnic group, with French becoming a dying secondary language. He rehearsed the old arguments against Americanization by movies, radio, and magazines.[77]

The Jesuit Père Jacques Cousineau held that French-Canadian Catholicism had nothing to gain and everything to lose by annexation, since the United States was less Catholic and Christian than Canada.[78] Burton Ledoux evoked the specter of traditional 'Anglo-Saxon' enmity to the 'Gallo-Roman' culture of the French Canadians, who were considered by Americans to be backward, priest-ridden people given to Fascism and anti-semitism. His opinion was that Quebec would have substantially less autonomy after annexation.[79] André Laurendeau summed up the conclusions of the symposium by saying that annexation would lead either to 'death by immersion' or 'death by inanition.' He saw the annexationist movement as a new defeatism, which would diminish the autonomy of French Canada and its influence. He concluded: 'We ought not to desire annexation,' and if it should be imposed, 'We shall live if we are living'—that is, if the French Canadians stimulated their will to live by becoming creative and building up their culture and sense of nationality.[80]

6

From the outset of the war many English and French Canadians labored zealously to prevent the development of the rift between the races which had been such a tragic feature of the First World War. Mackenzie King, inspired by his loyalty to the memory of Laurier and wisely guided by Ernest Lapointe in all matters affecting Quebec, avoided many of the mistakes which Ottawa had made in the First World War. Though some English Canadians grumbled at the government's 'catering to Quebec,' there was a general appreciation of the fact that national unity must not be imperiled. French Canada was largely left to do what it could or would in the war effort, without overzealous loyalism pointing a pistol at its head. Ottawa made no attempt to impose English Canada's ideas of national unity on Quebec, but left the task of stimulating patriotism to French Canada's own lay and clerical leaders. Ernest Lapointe's important role in insuring Quebec's support of the declaration of war, of participation, and of national mobilization has already been mentioned.

Premier Godbout made a pilgrimage to Toronto on December 4, 1940 to discuss 'Canadian Unity'[81] before a joint meeting of the Empire and Canadian Clubs. He recalled the Toronto speeches of Alexandre Taschereau in the 1920's, which had promoted better English-French understanding, and hailed the Franco-Ontarians as 'a living and a necessary bond between us.' Then he launched into an appeal for strengthening Canadian unity by establishing 'a perfect accord in all that has to do with the basic factors of Canadian problems, to be achieved at the expense of neither the one race nor the other, but to the advantage of all.' He assured his audience that 'In no wise are we sparing of our pennies, our pains, our blood when it becomes a question of Canada, human liberty, the democratic ideal, or honor, which are our very soul.' He stressed the historical fact that the French Canadians were the most Canadian of Canadians and had made many contributions to the achievement of Canadian nationhood. He hailed the *bonne entente* efforts of William Henry Moore, Arthur Hawkes, P. F. Morley, Lorne Pierce, Wilfrid Bovey, Howard Ferguson, Harry Stapells, and F. C. A. Jeanneret; and made a plea for bilingualism: 'When the two master languages of the country are in current use from sea to sea, we will have so multiplied the points of contact between our two races that many of our difficulties will have disappeared of themselves, without the necessity of recourse to persuasion, conventions, press campaigns, and the like.' He urged: 'What we ought to safeguard, what we ought to defend, is the privilege of developing ourselves in our own way.' There could be unity in spirit and heart, while each province preserved its own manners, customs, religious practice, and cultural life.

Godbout declared that the French Canadians were a constituent part of Canada, not only as the majority in Quebec, 'but everywhere they are there present; everywhere they make that presence felt; everywhere they contribute to the effort of the country as a whole; everywhere they enrich by their culture, their language, their toil, their devotion, their sacrifices, the patrimony of Canada as a whole.' He maintained that French Canada was doing its duty just as English Canada was, but urged that 'it is high time to accord to our province and our people an adequate share of the national defence, responsible posts in the army, the administration, and the government.' He described French Canada at war, and with a figure of speech drawn from his early career as an agronomist, he asserted: 'In the national hive there is not a French-Canadian bee but brings forth of its honey, beside that of the English-Canadian bee.' He called for 'unity of purpose, unity in fact, unity in general, fair play all along the line, that is to say unity at the cost of no one of our characteristics or respective peculiarities.'

After paying tribute to the heroes of both races and giving an account of the two French-Canadian winners of the Victoria Cross in the First World War, Godbout pledged Quebec's determination not to break faith with its dead. He closed with these eloquent words:

Separatists, gentlemen, we are not, nor could we be. We have made too many sacrifices for Canada. There is not a foot of the soil of the country which has not felt the tread of our people; not a town, not a village but has given birth to a nation-builder, to makers of men, to a hero illustrious or unsung. We will not renounce a single parcel of our patrimony, for it is identified with us as we with it. Moreover you understand us well enough now to know that we will never abandon our brother French Canadians in the other provinces. We only ask that we be respected as we respect others, and that our concept of the indissoluble unity of Canada in war and peace be taken as coming from a heart that is at once fervent and realistic, whose ideal is to serve the nation with all the strength of its being, in order that the opprobrium and the shame of the Nazi yoke be never ours to bear, and that the British Crown may never cease to find in Canada its brightest jewel.

This frank and courageous utterance, coming at the close of a series of such speeches in Quebec, won enthusiastic approval from both the English and French press without regard to party affiliation.

Cardinal Villeneuve, who on June 5, 1940 had declared that 'our allies have the right to count on our sacrifices to ensure their victory,'[82] and had firmly supported the national registration, on November 22 strongly denied rumors that French Canadians were contemplating separatism under his leadership, and asserted that the French Canadians had shown their true loyalty and 'within the last year had struck the greatest blow of a quarter of a century for national unity, at what had seemed unity's darkest hour.'[83] The Cardinal made his greatest contribution to the cause of national unity with his call for the celebration of Masses for victory on February 9, 1941 in every parish of Quebec. He himself officiated at Notre-Dame in Montreal before a congregation which included Ernest Lapointe and almost every high dignitary of Church and State. After urging the people to emulate British steadfastness and to fight for victory against those conquerors whose false ideas must be defeated at any cost, he closed his allocution on this occasion thus: 'We, the Church, the State, and the people of this province, beseech the Lord of Hosts to help us overcome the forces of evil.'[84] This gesture, without precedent in French Canada since the days of the Masses offered for the victory of Britain over Napoleon, made a tremendous impression on English Canadians who had been led to think of the Church as the root of all disloyal evil in Quebec. It also stimulated Canada's war effort by putting the influence of the Church squarely behind the cause.

On numerous occasions the Cardinal stressed national unity, notably in a speech before the Empire Club of Toronto on April 16, 1941. Once more he denied the charges of separatism, clericalism and Fascism that had been leveled at Quebec:

> Never did I wish that Quebec should become either a clerical or a fascist state. The Church does not admit that patriotism should be love of isolation . . . No, patriotism should extend to the whole of Canada. Divine Providence seems to have destined the English and French-speaking Canadians to co-operate in building a nation based on Anglo-Saxon and French civilization.[85]

The Cardinal declared that the French Canadians were the most stable element of the Canadian population and a bulwark against Communism or other subversive doctrines. He urged that the educational rights extended to the English-speaking minority in Quebec should be granted to the French-Canadian minorities in the other provinces, and warned that Quebec would always stand up for the rights of her separated brethren. In conclusion the Cardinal paid tribute to the heroism of the British people, and calling patriotism the highest of virtues, hailed those Canadians who had enlisted in a righteous cause.

From a small group of ultranationalists there continued to come, however, protests against wartime alterations of Quebec's way of life and invasions of its autonomy. When Senator Athanase David warned his compatriots in August 1940 against the tendency of narrow nationalists to consider Quebec the center around which Canada turned, and against their desire to have French Canadians hate their English fellow-citizens, *Le Devoir* deplored David's tendency to address the French Canadians as a refractory people hesitating to obey the law or even sabotaging it. *L'Illustration Nouvelle* said the David speech would not lessen political animosities and was merely the thousandth edition of the anti-conscription promises of King, Lapointe, and their associates. It observed that the Liberal program of half-truths and reticences created doubt in the leaders and even in the cause itself.[86] When the Dominion-Provincial Conference called to take action on the Rowell-Sirois Report collapsed after two days in January 1941, nationalist circles accused Premier Godbout of having failed to defend provincial rights in order not to offend his chiefs, King and Lapointe. Premier Hepburn of Ontario, who played the major part in preventing any action on the recommendations of the Report, accused Godbout of having deserted the other provinces in their fight for provincial autonomy. Henceforward it became a practice in nationalist circles to brand Godbout as a mere creature of Ottawa, sacrificing Quebec's rights to party loyalty. Party loyalty no doubt played its part in Godbout's policy of cooperation with Ottawa, but he was also strongly convinced of the necessity of national unity and of avoidance of the isolation of Quebec in the First World War.

Maxime Raymond, who had become the spokesman at Ottawa of the ultranationalist group by his stand for Canadian neutrality, his vote against participation, and his reluctant acceptance of conscription for home defence, in May 1941 made another attack on government policy. He urged that the government should stop telling the people that Canada was in danger of an invasion which he considered impossible. He said that Canada's strength and resources were not endless, and asked why Canada should ruin itself in the interests of a Britain which after the war might make friends with Germany. He declared that Quebec was unanimously opposed to conscription, and argued that Britain needed munitions and food, not men. He complained that the French-Canadian laborer was asked to work for low wages and under shocking conditions, and yet he was told that he must fight to free Polish or other European workers from slavery. He concluded with an appeal to the government to remember that a Canadian's first loyalty was to his own land, and to consider the future of Canada in its war policy.[87]

Ernest Lapointe replied to Raymond and vehemently denied that he represented anything but a small minority in a Quebec which had repudiated such isolationist and anti-participationist sentiments in the provincial elections of October 1939 and the federal elections of March 1940. *La Presse* commented that Lapointe's disapproval of Raymond's sentiments was shared by the great majority of French Canadians, while the *Montreal Gazette* pointed out that Raymond represented only a small clique of malcontents.[88]

And despite this undercurrent of nationalist opposition, by June 1941 Quebec was playing a large part in Canada's war effort. She had contributed generously to the war loans and had become a leading center of war industry and of vital raw materials. While she lagged somewhat behind other provinces in voluntary enlistments for overseas service, she fully cooperated in the training of home defence forces. Her early sympathy with Vichy had virtually dissolved, and that issue had ceased to divide her from the rest of Canada.

Then the German declaration of war on Russia on June 22 raised the question of what the French-Canadian reaction would be to cooperation with Soviet Russia. Quebec was notoriously anticommunist, as her Padlock Law, her espousal of Franco's cause in Spain, and her sympathy with the anti-communist crusades of the

German and Italian dictators had given evidence. The hierarchy realized that Quebec must be swung into line with the rest of Canada on the Russian alliance if national unity were to be preserved. On June 25 *L'Action Catholique* declared that although Russia enjoyed little or no sympathy in Quebec, it was only right to wish for continued Russian resistance and heavy Nazi losses. Two days later *L'Action* urged French Canada to rejoice at the sight of Germany forced to fight so mighty a foe and to support Russia against the common enemy, although it liked Communism no better than it ever had. Help from any source was to be welcomed when one was in the right and fighting for a just cause. In still another article on July 11 *L'Action* answered the question whether aid to Russia would help Communism by saying that Germany was the common enemy and Canada and Britain were helping Russia in their own interests. There was no question of helping Communism as distinct from the Russian people, unless suppressed Communist organizations were allowed to function again in Canada.[89]

The provincial press generally followed the lead of *L'Action Catholique*, which was thought to have been inspired by Cardinal Villeneuve, accepting Russian help against the Germans as desirable but echoing Quebec's dislike for Communism. There was none of the uncritical acceptance of Russia as a democratic ally which made many idealistic English Canadians innocent dupes of Communism. A traditionally conservative English Canada developed an enthusiasm for all things Russian, under the spell of Russia's gallant resistance and final turning of the Nazi tide of invasion, and among young intellectuals Communist sympathies became as popular as they had been in the States ten years before. This wave of enthusiasm was ruthlessly exploited by Canadian Communists and Russian diplomatic officials to build a spy ring which was only bared after the end of the war.[90] Quebec's reservations about the Russian alliance, which had been branded as 'disloyal,' were then fully justified.

7

French Canada figured largely in the psychological warfare which was waged by shortwave radio. After the fall of France, Radio Paris beamed a program at Quebec which used 'Alouette' as a musical signature. It sought to keep alive the memory of French rule in Canada by making constant allusion to historic ties; to influence French Canada's attitude towards the rest of Canada, fostering separatism and opposition to conscription; to link Pétainist France and Canada, to magnify Canadian cultural differences so as to incite disunity, and to justify collaboration between unoccupied France and Germany. For these ends it used flattery, inculcated persecution and minority complexes, exploited grievances, and cultivated anti-semitism and anti-communism. The Vichy radio also directed broadcasts first to Saint-Pierre and Miquelon, and later to North America as a whole. Its propaganda promoted hostility to Britain, minimized American strength, stressed the virtues of collaboration, attacked De Gaullism, and defended Vichy's policies. Its themes were that France considered the French Canadians to be Frenchmen; that French-Canadian influence in Canada had grown ever stronger since 1763 and would continue to do so; that France was still the mother country of the French Canadians; that the French Canadians were attached to France but not politically disloyal to Canada; that France and French Canada enjoyed a profound cultural identity; that French Canadians were persecuted because of their French views; and that Pétain's France was moving towards the French way of life long cherished in French Canada in the matters of family, land, home, and religious education.[91]

For a year one man took upon himself the task of answering this propaganda barrage. He was Louis Francoeur, a well-known Montreal journalist, who had no love for Germany, having been interned by the Germans from 1914–18 while studying in Belgium as a member of the Benedictine order. His daily radio program, '*La Situation Ce Soir*,' acquired great influence in French Canada and was so highly valued that the texts were printed in bimonthly pamphlets[92] from January 1941 until his death in an automobile accident early in the following summer. Francoeur, with his easy erudition, keen psychological sense, and the outlook of a citizen of the world, did much to guide French-Canadian opinion through the confusions of the Vichy-*vs*.-De Gaulle question and to awaken it to the world-wide and crucial nature of a war which was not merely Britain's, as the nationalists maintained. Francoeur himself was pro-British and a great lover of France and Belgium; he hated Fascism in all its forms but respected differences of opinion on the French question. He protested against the carrying on of France's internecine quarrels in Quebec and against the English-speaking world's confusion of the French Canadians with the French. By his adroit analysis of the news he gradually won French Canada to the cause of De Gaulle.

After his death Mlle. Beatrice Belcourt of the C.B.C. inaugurated a program '*Le Canada Parle à la France*,' which was first shortwaved from Boston and later from Sackville, New Brunswick, when Canada constructed its first shortwave station. This series included broadcasts by Premier Godbout, Cardinal Villeneuve, Archbishop Vachon of Ottawa, General Vanier, General Laflèche, and a host of other French-Canadian notables, who stressed French Canada's sympathy for France but also its enthusiastic loyalty to the Allied cause and its determination to free France from German oppression.[93] These broadcasts unquestionably bolstered French morale under the occupation and likewise met a French-Canadian need for reassurance that France would not die. Since relatively few people in Quebec possessed shortwave receivers, the German and Vichy propaganda had little influence except among a small group of the nationalist élite; while French Canada's messages to France won a much wider audience.

8

The death of Ernest Lapointe late in 1941 deprived French Canada of its only representative in the federal government who thoroughly understood his province, who enjoyed its full confidence, and who was a Canadian first and a French Canadian second. It was then, as the war attained ever greater and graver proportions and the United States was finally forced into all-out participation by Pearl Harbor, that the Canadian government determined to consult the people on the question of freeing it from its promises not to invoke conscription for overseas service. A plebiscite on the question was proposed in the speech from the throne in January 1942. The plebiscite was immediately opposed by Maxime Raymond on February 5, in a speech which also criticized the proposed war effort of the year, including a war budget of three billions and a gift of a billion and a loan of $700,000,000 to Britain, as beyond the means of a 'little people of eleven millions and a half, still in the epoch of development.'[94] Raymond accused a hyperpatriotic Toronto group known as the 'Two Hundred' of a desire to impose their will on the country by 'a campaign of propaganda and intimidation, with the purpose of forcing the government to impose conscription for service overseas, in contempt of the pledge given and the popular will expressed on March 26, 1940.' He ironically compared their enthusiasm for defending democracy and punishing the violators of treaties with their desire to make the government violate its pledges against conscription.

Raymond recalled Lapointe's anti-conscriptionist pledges of September 9, 1939 and the compromise then arrived at of participation without conscription, which had been approved by the country in the elections of March 1940. He maintained that only the anti-conscriptionists, toward whom an obligation had been incurred for their consent to participation, could free the government from its pledge. The need for national unity and the ineffectiveness of conscription were even stronger reasons for avoiding conscription in 1942 than they had been in 1939. Raymond held that Canada's war effort could be compared advantageously with that of any Allied country and should not be stepped up:

It is not at the moment when we are asked to augment agricultural production, which calls for a larger labor supply which is already lacking; it is not at the moment when we are asked to augment industrial production, which calls for more workers to equip and arm the soldiers; it is not at the moment when our defence calls for more soldiers to defend our territory, that we should think of augmenting the number of soldiers for service overseas by means of conscription, with a limited population which represents less than 1 per cent of the total population of the Allied countries.[95]

He saw only one purpose to the plebiscite: to free the government of its anti-conscription pledge and to give it a mandate to impose conscription when and how it saw fit. While he admitted that he preferred to see Mr. King at the head of the government rather than any rival, he preferred to see the prime minister bound by his promise and not given a blank check to be filled out at will. He called for the respect of engagements solemnly undertaken, in the name of national unity both during and after the war:

We are not separatists, but let us not be forced to become separatists. We wish indeed to dwell in the same house, but the house must be habitable for all. We are partisans of national unity, but according to certain equitable conditions, and when our conditions have been fixed in advance, we ask that they be observed.

And I fear that the 'Two Hundred' of Toronto, who agitate in favor of conscription for service overseas in violation of the pact of September 1939, are about to forge the nails which will serve to seal the coffin of national unity, and perhaps of Confederation.[96]

On March 3, when the plebiscite bill was in committee, Raymond renewed his attack upon it, pointing out that the clear purpose of the plebiscite was to enable the government to impose conscription at will, and that in any case the measure should be amended to permit young men between eighteen and twenty-one, who would be conscripted, to vote upon it.

Despite the best efforts of the government to convince Quebec that the issue was not immediate conscription, but the right of the government to consider the question of conscription if it should become necessary, French Canada—perhaps more realistically—saw the plebiscite as an opportunity to vote directly for or against conscription. In vain Mackenzie King broadcast over the French network of the C.B.C. on April 7, appealing for a vote which would give the government complete freedom of action in accomplishing its duty of pursuing the war. He declared that the government had the constitutional and legal power to conduct the war as it saw fit, but that the democratic tradition compelled it to consult the people when it sought to free itself of a solemn promise. He recalled the background of the anti-conscriptionist pledge, and its adoption to preserve national unity, but warned that it now endangered national unity:

You know perfectly well that the preservation of national unity has always been one of my dearest political aspirations. I must say that the situation is no longer the same and that, Canada having played for two years and a half the role in the war that is known, I see no more risk of endangering our unity by making this restriction disappear. On the contrary, I have the firm conviction that in this fashion the germs of irritation and disunity which are being born in our country will be smothered.[97]

As an argument for giving liberty of action to the government, he pointed out that this restriction upon Canada's war effort created misunderstanding in the other countries, which did not realize that 'the fact of not having imposed conscription had in no wise limited our war effort.'

Mr. King explained that the question at stake in the plebiscite was not that of conscription: 'It is a question of establishing whether or not the government should be free to decide the question in terms of all the factors of national interest.' He urged that the government and parliament should have the responsibility of making the decision and judging the question on its merits, since it was essentially a military question and all the necessary information for a wise decision could not be furnished to the public at large. He called for a declaration of confidence in the government by a 'yes' vote. In conclusion he warned that the maintenance of the existence of the nation came before national unity; that the military situation was critical; and that Canada could best defend itself against attack by beating the enemy before he reached her shores. Canada was not fighting to help others, to support some 'egotistical imperial end,' but 'for the preservation of our liberty and national existence, for the defence of our homes and families, against an enemy who ever draws nearer to us,' in the East and in the West.

Two nights later, on April 9, P.-J.-A. Cardin, the veteran minister of transport who was attempting to fill Lapointe's shoes as French Canada's spokesman at Ottawa, also made a broadcast over Radio Canada, calling for a 'yes' vote in the plebiscite. He urged loyalty to King and to his program, and advocated defending Canada by battling overseas, thus warding off an enemy who had quickly overcome other peoples who had waited to defend themselves on their own territory. He also asserted that it was not a question of voting for or against conscription, and that 'Mr. King has on several occasions declared in the House and elsewhere that for the present conscription was not necessary; he has even said that he believed firmly that it would not be necessary to impose it, because voluntary enlistment sufficed and perhaps the present circumstances might change.' He warned that the critics who reproached King with not having at once imposed conscription for overseas service were those who would replace him if the confidence of the majority were not given to him. Cardin reserved his own freedom to decide the question of conscription when it arose, and warned against premature agitation as injurious to the good name of Canada and Quebec in particular.

Cardin said that altered circumstances justified an altered attitude towards conscription, and called for support from all parties of the government which had brought a united Canada almost scatheless through two years of war:

> To my fellow citizens of Quebec, I wish simply to say, without weakness and equally without shame, that it is better not to run the risk of isolating ourselves. We wish that confidence be shown to us; therefore we must show confidence to others. Let us speak not only of rights; let us also sometimes think of the obligations which guarantee them . . .
>
> Be the first to reply 'yes' to the question of the plebiscite. It is in your interest to act thus, first as citizens and then as members of a minority which has need not only of the law and the treaties to develop according to its ideals, but which must count on the goodwill of all and feel its soul surrounded by the respect and comforting friendship of the great majority of the people of the country.[98]

But thanks to the efforts of the *Ligue pour la Défense du Canada*, headed by Jean Drapeau and supported by most ultranationalists, French Canada answered with a resounding 'no' to the question of the plebiscite on April 27, 1942. There was no differentiation of votes by ethnic origin, as there had been no such breakdown of similar enlistment figures; but Quebec as a whole voted 72 per cent 'no,' while all the other provinces voted 80 per cent 'yes.' The old bitter question of conscription had once more isolated Quebec from the rest of Canada. The plebiscite shattered national unity, and henceforward anti-war sentiment grew in French Canada, as it reacted to English-Canadian charges that it was not doing its part.[99]

The government, feeling that it had been freed from its pledge and under pressure from the Conservatives, did not delay in introducing Bill 80, amending the N.R.M.A. Act for eventual conscription for overseas service. In proposing the second reading in June, King declared that conscription 'was not necessary at the present moment and perhaps never will be.'

The prime minister favored consultation with parliament before putting conscription into force, while Colonel Ralston, the defence minister, insisted on acting by order-in-council without reference to parliament, if and when the time came. Two other ministers, T. A. Crerar and Angus MacDonald, also favored this course; and to end a cabinet crisis Mr. King agreed to action by order-in-council, with parliament to be called to approve the action. Ralston subsequently declared in parliament that he was to be the judge of when conscription was required,[100] and described the government's policy as 'not necessarily conscription, but conscription if necessary.'[101] The Quebec Liberals protested strongly against the measure, and P.-J.-A. Cardin resigned from the cabinet in adherence to his pledges.[102]

Maxime Raymond bitterly attacked the bill in June, recalling all the solemn promises of King and Lapointe against conscription. He maintained that Quebec alone could free the government from the obligation which it had incurred in exchange for Quebec's support of participation. He argued that the two motives for the anti-conscription pledge—the necessity of national unity and the ineffectiveness of conscription—were more valid than ever, with the plebiscite showing Canada's profound division on the question, and with an official statement of June 9 showing that 52,615 men had enlisted in the last five months, more than half the quota for the year. He quoted the statements of King, Defence Minister Ralston, Munitions and Supply Minister Howe, Navy Minister Macdonald, and Air Minister Power to prove the excellent results of the voluntary enlistment policy. He belittled King's statements that the law might never be enforced, and criticized the measure for not providing for age limits, exemptions, and appeal tribunals. He warned that after the war the government would enjoy the greatest lack of confidence ever known, having promised no European expeditionary forces before 1939, having promised moderate participation in 1939, having promised conscription for home defence only in 1940 and then used the National Resources Mobilization Act as a system of 'disguised conscription,' having said that the plebiscite was not on the question of conscription and using its result to justify conscription. He complained bitterly: 'The most solemn engagements are violated in the name of the right of the majority, while we are asked to go and fight to defend the rights of minorities.'[103] He declared that Quebec had not forgotten conscription in 1917 and would not forget the 'infinitely more odious and revolting' conscription of 1942.

When the bill came up for third reading, Raymond on July 23 supported Sasseville Roy's motion for the six months' hoist, complaining that 'for a hundred years national unity has always been achieved at the expense of the Province of Quebec' and that 'there must be a limit to sacrifice always at the expense of the Province of Quebec.' To the argument that the will of the majority should prevail, he replied that the majority 'should not abuse its powers and that an engagement made by the majority to the minority is sacred.' He insisted that the plebiscite had not freed the government from its pledge, since the interested party, Quebec, had voted 'no.' He repelled the charge of disloyalty with two questions: 'Since when is it disloyal to insist that engagements be respected? Is not he who seeks to violate them the one who is disloyal?'[104] But the conscription measure was passed on July 23 by a vote of 141 to 45, largely along ethnic lines.

Raymond also expressed during the July debate on the budget another French-Canadian nationalist attitude which was to find ever more support in Quebec as time went on. He quoted the secretary of state's declaration that 'our country, in proportion to population, is doing more for the war than any other of the United Nations.' He protested that war expenses were heavier in Canada than in England, and taxes consequently higher, and he opposed a billion dollar gift to England at a time when that country was lending money at interest to other allied nations. The French Canadian has always shown a very North American reluctance to pay taxes, since he has been emotionally 'agin the government' ever since the early days of New France, when opposition developed between the Canadians and the officials sent out from France. He was willing to contribute to the defence of Canada and proved it by providing notable support for the war loans, which were often oversubscribed in Quebec; but the prospect of pinching himself for the benefit of Britain aroused the same opposition as the early propaganda for Canada to rally to Britain's side, which evoked an emotional loyalty he did not feel. The Hong Kong disaster of December 1941, which cost Canada two battalions (one of which, the Royal Rifles, came from Quebec and was in part French Canadian), had stimulated his latent anti-English feeling. Unfortunately Winston Churchill had then proclaimed that the loss of Hong Kong, which had fallen in less than a month because of inadequate British preparations, was 'a great imperial disaster.' Thus he reinforced the nationalist thesis that the war was an imperialist conflict in which Canada had no real interest.

By the summer of 1942 various incidents and frictions had produced a marked deterioration in French-Canadian enthusiasm for the war. In the previous six months there had been an extraordinary development of anti-British feeling, which was credited to the Nazi propaganda activities of the Vichy consulates. Admiration for Pétain and Vichy France was used to arouse the traditional latent hatred of England, as well as scorn of the British war effort and opposition to the Canadian one. Reaction to the plebiscite played an important role in the change of public opinion. The individualistic French Canadian resented the pressure brought to bear in what was supposed to be a democratic vote. Some voted 'no,' and then promptly volunteered for overseas service. The plebiscite was seen as the last step before conscription, and most French Canadians remained convinced that their leading representatives at Ottawa were right in their earlier declarations that conscription would be deplorable and ineffective. They judged rationally a question which the English Canadians judged emotionally.

It was felt by young men of military age that the recruiting system was unjust in favoring the well-to-do. They could not find employment in business or industry, and unless they had private means they were forced to enlist. There was a general feeling that Canada had neither the manpower nor the means nor the resources to maintain armies to fight everywhere in Europe. Some individuals talked of French Canada being engaged in two wars: the so-called 'holy war' against the Axis, and the traditional war against *les Anglais*. French refugees were welcome in Quebec, but not English ones. The patriotic activities of the hierarchy had led to the development of anti-clericalism on all levels, with Cardinal Villeneuve's zeal winning him the nickname of 'Kid Villeneuve' and 'Newtown, O.H.M.S.' It was felt that he was true neither to his people nor his cloth. The Wartime Information Board showed a singular lack of understanding of the French-Canadian mentality by making appeals to 'Canada at Britain's side' and using the Union Jack on war posters. A basic factor in the situation was the refusal of many English Canadians to recognize that Canada was a bi-ethnic, bicultural, and bilingual country. While there was improvement in mutual understanding among university people, intellectuals, and the younger generation less conditioned by old differences, there remained a fundamental misunderstanding. J.-A. Blanchette (Compton) startled the House in July by proposing to settle it by arranging a golf match between the editors of the *Globe and Mail* and *Le Devoir* and the president of the Saint-Jean-Baptiste Society and the Grand Master of the Orangemen.[105]

9

Quebec's support of the war was momentarily stimulated by the gallant part played by French-Canadian troops in the disastrous Dieppe raid of August 19, 1942. But the growing feeling that Ottawa was betraying French Canada was furthered by the cabinet's decisions of September 4 and September 14 to send home defence conscripts to Alaska, Newfoundland, and Greenland. These steps were taken by order-in-council, without debate in parliament. In October the anti-war *Ligue pour la Défense du Canada* took political form in the *Bloc Populaire Canadien* under the leadership of Maxime Raymond.

This French 'Canada First' party won increasing support as the conviction grew in Quebec that Canada was undertaking too great a war effort which would inevitably lead to application of conscription for overseas service and to national bankruptcy. The *Bloc Populaire* also exploited French Canada's psychological soreness as a result of becoming the target after the plebiscite for all manner of attacks as the home of slackers, traitors, and fascists.

The ill-considered official decision to make it impossible to compare the manpower contributions of French and English gave rise to the freely expressed English-Canadian suspicion that the French-Canadian war record was too bad to be disclosed, while the French Canadians thought it was better than it really was. The result was a passionate clash of unfounded French and English opinion on the question, as in 1917. This intensely irritated a French Canada which was acutely aware, through the maze of family relationships which links people all over the province, that its sons were dying and being wounded in many quarters of the world in a war which it still felt was fundamentally none of its business. Meanwhile Quebec was constantly complimented for its war effort by its own patriotic leaders and by Ottawa spokesmen. English Canada tended to judge war effort exclusively in terms of volunteers for overseas, while French Canada reckoned in service in Canada, its major contribution in war industry, and its notable support of the war loans.

Unfortunately at this difficult period the place of Ernest Lapointe as French Canada's Ottawa leader was not wholly filled, for his successor, Louis St. Laurent, was new to politics and as a successful Quebec corporation lawyer and the son of an Irish mother was popularly considered to be '*anglifié*.' St. Laurent was first elected to parliament in February 1942 in the by-election necessitated by Lapointe's death. He was opposed by Paul Bouchard, who had run against Lapointe in 1940 and on both occasions was supported by the Duplessis machine and various nationalist groups. The newcomer St. Laurent, with all his sincere devotion to French Canada and to the interests of his compatriots, was unable to command the same confidence in his province that the veteran Lapointe had enjoyed.

Quebec rapidly lost faith in the leadership of its Ottawa representatives and turned in upon itself. After three years of war it was gravely disturbed by the shattering of its traditional way of life by mobilization and intensive wartime industrialization, which produced considerable social disorder. Its innate individualism and devotion to provincial rights were irritated by the ever-increasing number of wartime controls ordained by Ottawa; its traditional belief that woman's place was in the home was outraged by efforts to attract young women into the auxiliary army, navy, and air services and into war industry; its national pride was injured by fancied or real grievances as to the lot of French Canadians in the services and in the war agencies. Above all, there was a profound feeling that Canada's real interests were being subordinated to those of Britain and the United States.

Deeply patriotic French and English Canadians labored hard to offset this growing tide of discontent and opposition to the war effort in French Canada. Colonel Dollard Ménard and the Abbé Sabourin, heroes of the Dieppe raid, were brought back to Canada to stimulate French-Canadian pride and support of the war. But Quebec's resentment against the flood of Ottawa propaganda was extended to its own sons who lent themselves to this cause. Abbé Arthur Maheux, the author of a *bonne entente* study of the post-Conquest period who had been slated to become Rector of Laval University, made himself highly unpopular in Quebec by a series of C.B.C. broadcasts from September 1942 to January 1943 on 'Why Are We Divided?'[106] in which he sought to explode the old legends which lay at the base of anti-English feeling in Quebec. But his negative approach to the question of national unity, which denied or minimized certain unpleasant facts, outraged the growing tide of nationalist feeling, which soon made itself felt in personal attacks of a virulence never known before in Quebec in the case of a priest. Abbé Maheux was driven from the lecture platform at Laval, and despite the support of high ecclesiastical authorities he was left in virtual isolation in his own university and among his own people. It was probably an unfortunate decision to delegate a priest to the role of spokesman in the *bonne entente* movement, for his cloth and clerical attitudes—which led him to refer to 'Garibaldi's gangsters' in English-speaking circles which had always idolized Garibaldi—alienated the sympathies of many English Canadians who were vaguely convinced that the Catholic Church was the root of all disloyal and undemocratic evil in 'priest-ridden' Quebec. But Abbé Maheux did succeed in forming an academic axis between Laval and the University of Toronto which enlisted the support of many men of good will on both sides of the ethnic fence and which brought about a better understanding between the élites of French and English Canada, if it failed to have much influence on popular feeling.

F. R. Scott, professor of law at McGill and the son of the beloved Padre Scott of the First World War, made an effort to explain to English Canadians the anti-imperialist and pro-Canadian nature of Quebec's 'no' vote in the plebiscite,[107] which unjustifiably was discounted in the press as an attempt to woo French-Canadian votes for the C.C.F. movement, of which Scott was a national leader. Late in 1942 Emile Vaillancourt published under the title of *Le Canada et les Nations Unies* a collection of his newspaper articles, speeches, radio addresses, and letters to public figures in which he pleaded for respect for France, diplomatic relations with Russia, Canadian support of the United Nations, a second front in Europe, and recognition of Canada's postwar mission as a non-interested country seeking a better world order.[108] General Vanier, who commanded the Quebec military district after his return from Europe in October 1941, continued his exhortations to patriotism until February 1943, when he was named the Canadian representative for negotiations with the DeGaullists and Canadian Minister to the governments in exile in London. General Laflèche, who had taken a leading role in Ottawa since his return from his post as military attaché in France in 1940, campaigned vigorously for election in Outremont when he was named war services minister in November 1942, and succeeded in defeating his opponent Jean Drapeau, the director of the *Ligue pour la Défense du Canada.*

10

French Canada's enthusiasm for the war had sharply diminished by the latter part of 1942. The polls of the Canadian Institute of Public Opinion showed that in August 31 per cent of the French Canadians favored peace if Hitler should offer it on the basis of the *status quo*, while 59 per cent felt that Canada would not be at war if she were completely independent of the British Empire. With 78 per cent of English Canadians favoring conscription, 90 per cent of French Canadians opposed it. While only 44 per cent of the English Canadians felt that Canada was doing all she could to win the war, 89 per cent of French Canadians were so convinced. These sentiments found expression in support of the *Bloc Populaire*, which grew rapidly in strength despite Cardinal Villeneuve's statement of November 10, 1942, reproving the 'impertinence' of Leopold Richer, *Le Devoir's* Ottawa correspondent, in criticizing *L'Action Catholique* for refusing to support the new party. This reproof was based upon the ecclesiastical regulation which requires Catholics to make complaints about institutions under the control of the hierarchy only to the bishops; but it indicated indirectly how the Cardinal viewed the new party. But if the *Bloc Populaire* found little favor with Cardinal Villeneuve and Archbishops Charbonneau and Vachon of Montreal and Ottawa, it was clearly welcomed by the lower clergy. The Jesuits of the Ecole Sociale Populaire had continued their support of the Pétain regime despite the change of popular feeling on that score. They deplored the effects of wartime industrialization upon French-Canadian family life and morals. Their monthly organ *Relations* frequently showed nationalist sympathies, as did their press service carried by many rural weeklies run under clerical auspices. The country *curés* expressed fears as to the corrupting effects of life in the military camps and in the war plants, and winked at attempts to avoid military service.

Fortunately for Canadian unity, the *Bloc Populaire* proved to be anything but a bloc. Its development was beset by differences among its leaders and its history is reminiscent of the shifting combinations which produce the frequent falls of governments in France. The *Bloc* movement, essentially a new phase of nationalist developments since 1933 which had invoked the tradition of Mercier and Bourassa, began with the *Ligue pour la Défense du Canada* in 1941, André Laurendeau's *Bloc Universitaire* of March 1942, and Paul Gouin's call on May 15, 1942 for a French-Canadian congress to channel anti-imperialist and anti-conscriptionist sentiments. Later in May Gouin conferred with Abbé Pierre Gravel, a well-known nationalist orator in Quebec; Emile Latremouille, a collaborator of Paul Bouchard; and Dr. Georges Lambert, a former aide of Adrien Arcand who was seeking to revive the fascist National Unity movement. But it was Maxime Raymond who assumed the leadership of the *Bloc Populaire* when the party took form in October, while André Laurendeau became its secretary-general. Gouin, Dr. Philippe Hamel, and René Chaloult rallied to the new party, but soon fell into disagreement with Raymond over the question whether its field of action should be primarily federal or provincial.

Meanwhile a Gallup poll of April 1943 showed that the *Bloc* was favored by 37 per cent of Quebec voters, as contrasted with 26 per cent in February, while the Liberals were favored by only 39 per cent. The *Bloc* was originally based upon exploitation of the latent nationalist sentiments of French Canada which had been brought to the surface by the conscription question. But it was shattered by division on economic matters; for Gouin, Hamel, and Chaloult were crusaders for corporatism and nationalization, while their trust-busting speeches were opposed by Raymond, a man of large means derived from big business. The adhesion of Edmond Lacroix, a wealthy lumberman, to the *Bloc* resulted in the departure of Chaloult and Hamel, who as a *Québecois* also maintained the ancient tradition that no good could come out of Montreal. The real difficulty of the *Bloc*, however, was that there were too many candidates for the leadership and too little willingness to cooperate.

Paul Gouin made a vigorous bid for provincial leadership of the *Bloc*. *L'Union*, with its Pétainist motto of 'Work-Family-Homeland,' was his personal organ, and his speech of April 28, 1943 at the Monument National was entitled 'What ought we to expect of the *Bloc*?' and was prefaced by a statement that he could speak objectively as he was somewhat outside the bosom of the party. He denounced both the Liberal charge that a French-Canadian bloc would be disastrous and Duplessis' betrayal of the nationalist cause in 1936–9, accusing

Godbout and Duplessis of being 'merely the two faces of the same sinister Janus: the trust.' He expressed his faith in the success of Raymond and his lieutenants, if they avoided admitting a new Duplessis to their ranks and limiting their program too narrowly. As he saw it, the *Bloc* should not limit itself merely to creating an honest government, to maintaining the rights of the French language and of the French Canadians, and to continuing the campaign against conscription. He urged: 'The *Bloc Populaire Canadien* will succeed in being a true French-Canadian bloc only if it advocates, defends, and realizes a complete social and economic program, a pro-French-Canadian policy.' At Ottawa it should claim 'the integral application of the Statute of Westminster which makes of Canada, in right and above all in fact, a free and adult nation, mistress of its destinies like Ireland.' Gouin called for an end to leaving the initiative in time of war to Downing Street, for decentralization, for assurance to French-Canadian minorities in other provinces of the rights enjoyed by the English minority in Quebec, an equitable French-Canadian share of federal offices, and the adoption of 'O Canada' as the national anthem and of a distinctive Canadian flag.

In the provincial field the *Bloc* should work for a French State: 'the absolute control of our land, our natural resources, our economy and our educational system; a French State which will be the loyal application of the whole B.N.A. Act, in letter and spirit, which a young compatriot has summed up in a happy and very just formula: "Autonomous provinces in a free country".' In an echo of Abbé Groulx' celebrated dictum of 1937, he observed: 'This French State is due us, and we shall have it.' The proposed Laurentian state should have a pro-French-Canadian and an anti-trust policy. It should nationalize outright the production of electricity, gas, mines, and chemical fertilizer. It should strictly control the insurance companies and the textile, forest, distilling, refining, and tobacco industries. It should replace the coal, milk, farm implement, butchering and cold storage, fishing, and chain store trusts by co-operatives. It should establish a provincial bank to head the system of credit unions. Agriculture should be aided and the industrial worker given an equal share of the profits of industry, while corporatism should be applied to correct the evils of capitalism. The family should be protected by workmen's compensation; insurance against sickness, unemployment, old age, and death; family allowances; strict regulation of the labor of women and children; and aid to young couples.

Gouin repelled the charge of isolationism, declaring: 'It is not we who isolate ourselves, it is others who wish to isolate us.' The French Canadians wished to collaborate with the English Canadians on a footing of equality. To counter the existing English-Canadian bloc, a French-Canadian bloc must be established. If Quebec had 'a single leader, a true one like Maxime Raymond, who truly spoke in the name of the French Canadians and behind whom the French Canadians were unanimous, the rest of the country would indeed perceive that it was the authorized voice of Quebec which made its claims.' He urged that the *Bloc* should make its program known among the English Canadians by every possible means to overcome the language barrier. He denied the charges of Valmore Bienvenue, Edmond Turcotte, Jean-Charles Harvey, and Fred Rose that the *Bloc* was a fifth-column movement: 'It is . . . because we want our country to be able to continue the War until the end and then to be in condition to win the peace, that we do not wish it to bleed itself white, to ruin itself.' In a moving peroration he concluded:

> The fight for civilization, Christianity, and liberty is not new to us. We have been fighting for just that for three hundred years. We are going to continue this fight until the end, in order that each country may one day know liberty, true liberty, in order that one day Canada may be for the Canadians and French Canada for the French Canadians.
>
> Yes, ladies and gentlemen, the day will come when this Carillon flag that we see this evening, motionless in its strength, motionless in its century-old patience, will fly, flapping in the winds of victory, floating over Quebec, capital of our French State![109]

On this occasion Gouin was introduced by René Chaloult and thanked by Dr. Philippe Hamel. Chaloult assured the audience that he and Hamel would remain at Gouin's side, while Hamel expressed the loyalty of all three to Raymond and discounted talk of dissension in the *Bloc*.

René Chaloult had already become the idol of the ultranationalists for his declaration in May 1942 that 'if the people of Canada ever vote for compulsory military service overseas, let the government face the danger of civil war,' and his subsequent acquittal after trial for violation of the Defence of Canada regulations. As the only *Bloc* leader with a seat in the provincial legislature, Chaloult introduced in February 1943 an anti-conscription motion which no other member would second, and subsequently announced in April that his party stood for nationalization and state ownership. By way of reply to the attacks upon him in the English press, Chaloult brought suit for libel against the *Quebec Chronicle-Telegraph*, the only English paper in the capital, based upon its comments on his role in the fight against conscription the previous year. The trial served to revive the anti-conscriptionist agitation during the end of May and beginning of June, when the *Bloc* was hoping to force a provincial election upon the Liberals. It was exploited in the weekly radio commentaries which *Bloc* orators had been making since April.

French-Canadian public opinion was also aroused at this time by news of a brawl at Sussex Camp in New Brunswick between men of the Voltigeurs de Québec and of the Dufferin and Haldimand Rifles of Ontario, in which fist-fighting led to shooting and the death of one soldier. The commanding officer, Brigadier Topp, denied that the quarrel had been based upon racial or religious prejudices or by animosity between volunteers and conscripts. Nonetheless it was so interpreted by the French press, which was already up in arms at the *Montreal Gazette's* attacks on the conscripts, whom it contemptuously called 'zombies.' The *Gazette* urged that the 'zombies' should be put to work in agriculture and forest industries, since 'under the existing circumstances they will never make good soldiers.'[110] Emile Benoist made a bitter reply in *Le Devoir* on May 20 which admirably expressed the sentiment of French Canada about the home defence forces:

> The regimented conscripts are citizens of whom the State has asked the sacrifice of their liberty, who have submitted to the exigencies of the State, even if they consider that this exigency is not opportune nor justified in the present juncture. As conscripts of the State, the sacrifice to which they have consented is more meritorious since they do not consider it justly motivated, and since this sacrifice which is exacted from them comes in contradiction, even in violation, of the promises that have previously been made to them. And they have the right to the respect of all, even to the respect of those who write in the *Gazette*. Let that organ take what tone it will to speak of these good citizens who conform to the law, the fact none the less remains that the conscripts bear the uniform of His Majesty the King of Canada, that they are soldiers of the King of Canada, and that they are ready to defend at any time the sacred soil of the Canadian homeland quite as well as would the editors of the *Gazette*.
>
> 'Zombies!' Let the old Tory and Ulster gossip of Saint-Antoine Street learn that it was soldiers of this sort, that is to say sons of the Canadian soil and also of our race, who in 1775 undertook to defend the city of Quebec against the Yankee invader, while Quebeckers of another race prudently retired to the tranquil countryside of the Island of Orleans.[111]

English-Canadian contempt for the 'zombies', who were commonly reputed to be predominantly French Canadian, continued to grow as the Canadian forces overseas saw active service and suffered casualties. On the other hand French Canada never lost its sympathy for those who observed the letter of the law by serving in Canada but refused to volunteer for overseas service, despite browbeating by their superior officers and insults from their fellow soldiers and the general public. It is probable that the effort to make the French-Canadian home defence units 'go active' would have had more success if it had been left in the hands of French-Canadian officers who had won honor overseas. At any rate there was a marked increase in volunteering for overseas service after the Quebec camps were put under the command of such officers as Dollard Ménard late in 1944.

It also was probably a mistake to organize a divided army in the first place. It is possible that a policy of imposing conscription for overseas service might have been better accepted in Quebec after some such crisis in the war as Pearl Harbor, which destroyed the American prop of French-Canadian isolationism, than was the gradual extension of conscription by a series of steps, each one of which aroused an increasingly bitter reaction in Quebec. The extensions by order-in-council of 'home defence' service to the outposts of North America in 1942 led P.-J.-A. Cardin to move for suspension of the Mobilization Act in February 1943, and to resign from the cabinet when Mr. King vigorously denounced the proposal.

In continuing his attack upon the government's war policies, which he characterized as being equivalent to Arthur Meighen's 'to the last man, to the last penny,' Maxime Raymond noted on February 10 Churchill's statement that he could not understand how Canada had been able to make such a war effort and observed: 'If Mr. Churchill does not understand it, we understand it: it is by ruining Canada, by sabotaging all our present and future economy.' He also cited Beaudry Leman's comments in the annual report of the Banque Canadienne Nationale on the dangers of attempting simultaneously to be a 'granary, arsenal, and reservoir of man power' and of taking women from the home for war plants. Raymond quoted King's declaration that 'nothing mattered but victory,' but expressing grave fears for the postwar period, he observed: 'Surely we all want victory over the Axis powers, but we do not want to lose the peace.'

Raymond bitterly repelled King's reproaches to him and his handful of followers for having left the Liberal Party and followed a course which did honor neither to themselves, nor their province, nor their country. He remarked: 'In the matter of honor, I would like to make the Prime Minister observe that we do not all have the same notion of honor. In the Province of Quebec, since it is a question of this province, the man of honor is the one who respects his word, his promises, and his obligations; and when the hour comes to present ourselves before our electors and to submit ourselves to the judgment of the province, we shall not fear the result.'[112]

Once more Raymond recalled King's anti-conscription pledges, and added: 'We have parted from the Prime Minister because we no longer have confidence in his declarations and promises, above all since the plebiscite and since the conscription law . . . We have lost confidence because we have been constantly deceived.' He concluded with the declaration that the *Bloc Populaire*, although it had few representatives in the House, represented 'the sentiments of a very great part of the population of Quebec,' and was inspired by truly Canadian interests.[113]

There can be little doubt that Raymond's claim for the *Bloc's* hold on French Canada was true. The war was beginning to weigh heavily upon a Quebec which found its way of life radically altered without its consent, while little attention was paid to its sentiments, which were no longer clearly understood at Ottawa as they had been in Lapointe's day; promises made to it were violated; and outside attacks upon it increased. Particular indignation was aroused by the publication of Fred Rose's pamphlet, *Hitler's Fifth Column in Quebec*, in which the Montreal Communist denounced the secret Order of Jacques Cartier as the mainspring of all nationalist movements and described it as 'anti-Soviet, pro-Vichy, and pro-fascist';[114] and also by an article in *Life*,[115] which depicted Quebec as a backward, medieval region in which fascist youth movements flourished. The gift of a second billion to Britain in 1943, as taxes weighed more heavily upon Canadians, caused *L'Action Catholique* on May 25 to commend as 'true Canadians' those who urged that Britain in return should give up its interest, estimated at $2,900,000,000, in the Canadian economy. By this means it was hoped to end the British economic imperialism which had continued in Canada after the Statute of Westminster had ended British political imperialism. Edouard Laurent concluded his editorial on the question thus: 'Not a Canadian wishes that his country should profit from the present war by acquiring colonies, but there are many who wish that the sacrifices of the present war should be at least in part compensated for by the conquest of our own territory and our economic life.'[116]

The protests made by Quebec members at the end of the federal session in June 1943 against the policy of drafting farm laborers into the army, in defiance of promises to exempt them, were echoed in the provincial legislature when an amendment was proposed on June 9, deploring the shortage of farm labor and the government's failure to fulfil its promises. Duplessis attacked the policy under which 'Farmers and their sons are enlisted, and by virtue of a paradox of the federal administration they are forcibly enlisted voluntarily.'[117] He warned of the danger of a scarcity of food and fuel. Onésime Gagnon declared that farmers' sons were called for military service without regard to their role as essential workers in the war effort, and deplored a published statement that Italian and German prisoners from North Africa would be brought to Canada as farm workers, while young French-Canadian farmers were being conscripted. Premier Godbout explained that farmers' sons were not exempted *ipso facto* from military service, that they must answer when called for service, but would be exempted if they proved that they were essential workers. He admitted that if they failed to report they were made liable for service.

Statistics tabled by Labor Minister Humphrey Mitchell in the federal House on June 23 showed that the Montreal and Quebec districts had the largest number of draft dodgers, 14,932, slightly more than half the national total.[118] John Diefenbaker commented on the figures, and criticized the lenient penalties exacted from defaulters by the courts in Quebec. The manpower question became and remained a political football, with Quebec getting most of the kicks from critics of the government's policies, while French-Canadian nationalists exploited popular dissatisfaction with the regulations. The opposition to the regimentation of men in the armed services and in essential occupations was intensified by the *Winnipeg Free Press's* suggestion on June 10 that women might be drafted into the auxiliary services. On June 18 Omer Héroux pointed out in an editorial in *Le Devoir* that the conscription of women was legally possible and expressed strong opposition to the proposal, while Emile Benoist observed that family life was threatened by the absence of fathers in military service and of mothers working in war plants.

II

Various patriotic French Canadians sought to turn this anti-war and pro-*Bloc* tide of public opinion. In March 1943 Valmore Bienvenue, a member of the Godbout cabinet, told *L'Union Démocratique du Canada Français*:

> It is time, it is more than time, that we said to Canadians in other provinces: 'Do not judge us by the declarations of those whose very existence we deplore.' Before the evil has become irreparable we must put a stop to the work of the wreckers of our country, who discredit us and the prestige of all French Canadians. These demagogues must be stopped from telling the people that our enemies are to be found not in Germany, Italy, and Japan, but in the other provinces of Canada.

He deplored their Utopia: 'a Laurentia surrounded by a very thick, high wall, which will be a French "reservation" into which nothing will enter and out of which nothing will come, a reservation closed to all social and economic progress . . . a sort of museum for lovers of antiques.' Denouncing their charge that Canada was subjugated to England, Bienvenue declared: 'We are the ally of England and not its vassal . . . And if in this struggle unprecedented in history we are at the side of Britain, it is not because we are a colony which blindly espouses London's quarrels, but simply because England, like us, fights on the side of liberty and justice.' He concluded: 'Liberty, like peace, demands solidarity. We cannot keep our liberty in a world in which three-quarters of the population are reduced to slavery. We cannot live alone . . . We cannot alone be free.'[119]

This *Union Démocratique* founded by Jean-Charles Harvey was short-lived, like the earlier *Ligue Pancanadienne*, but the tendency of both groups was carried on by *L'Institut Démocratique* founded by T.-D. Bouchard, provincial minister of roads, on May 8 at a meeting in Montreal. Bouchard was introduced by Senator Léon-Mercier Gouin, who was one of the governors of the new organization, along with Bouchard, Georges Savoy, Dr. Oscar Mercier, and J.-P. Galipault. Bouchard declared that the purpose of the body was 'the progress of French Canadians in all spheres of their public and private activities.' Bouchard described himself as a lifelong disciple of progress, and professed his desire at the close of his political career to establish a society which would permanently group men 'cherishing freedom of thought, believing in science, and having large views on the questions of races and nationalities.' He pointed out that among all peoples two main currents of ideas existed:

> . . . that of men who have faith only in the rules established by the partisans of ancient traditions and antique theories; that of those who have the spirit of research, who believe in evolution towards perfection, and who do not fear to experiment with reforms in all spheres of intellectual, economic, and social activity. . . . These are the two opposed poles of the magnetic field of human society.[120]

He observed that Quebec had until recently been dominated by the former spirit, which had cost it dear. But a change in atmosphere had occurred, with laymen free to preach educational reforms, priests exploding the old legend that the English had mistreated the French Canadians and condemning the instilling of racial hatred, and the majority of the bishops recommending compulsory education.

Bouchard warned of a dangerous reaction to the changing times, of a secret society which sought to establish an independent French and Catholic state on the model of Eire. The *Institut Démocratique* had been formed to oppose such isolationist ideas. It was clad with no religious, charitable, or patriotic mantle; it had no political or commercial interests; and all its activities were to be inspired by a healthy democracy, neither demagogic nor plutocratic. It was limited to French Canadians, so that its enemies might not consider it a tool of the English Canadians. It would be inspired by a progressive patriotism, and would seek to develop public spirit and advance the arts, letters, and the sciences. It would seek to give the younger generation a broader outlook by improving education. It would popularize its ideas by means of the press, radio, lectures, and prize contests. It would launch investigations into public problems of a nature not suited to political bodies and in every fashion would seek to assure the triumph of 'modern progress.'

The foundation of the *Institut Démocratique* was warmly hailed by such Liberal organs as *Le Canada* and *Le Soleil*, and denounced by André Laurendeau in a radio broadcast as the '*Institut Ploutocratique*' and as a Liberal front which returned to the original fanatical *Rouge* ideals of the party. *Le Devoir* took alarm at the growing number of anti-nationalist organizations. It bitterly complained when it learned of the existence of a *Bloc d'Entente Canadienne*, which distributed Abbé Maheux's *Pourquoi Sommes-Nous Divisés?*, which had been published under the auspices of the C.B.C., to all classical college graduates of the year. *Le Devoir* linked Harvey, Bouchard, and Maheux; accused the Wartime Information Board of being responsible for the free distribution of the books; and protested against such one-sided airing of controversial ideas at the expense of the taxpayer.[121]

Quebec's leaders of Church and State, however, continued their efforts to stimulate patriotic feeling. Cardinal Villeneuve ordained a *Te Deum* in his archdiocese on May 16 to celebrate the Allied victory in North Africa. In the June debate on manpower in the legislature, Premier Godbout defended the patriotism of the Quebec farmer and attacked those who had misled the people on the question of military service. On July 14 Godbout sent a Bastille Day message to France, hailing the fact that 'France, represented by her troops in Africa, has retaken her fighting place beside her glorious allies.' He concluded his message thus: 'We, the grandsons of France, French Canadians and Acadians of Quebec and all the provinces of Canada, together with the whole French-speaking population of America, and especially our brothers of the United States, have but one thought—to thank God who gives victory and to extol France and her allies who deserve victory.'[122] A special Bastille Day High Mass—an event which would have curdled Bishop Bourget's blood—was celebrated at Notre-Dame-des-Victoires Church in Quebec, attended by French and French-Canadian members of the R.A.F. and R.C.A.F., who were reviewed by Major-General Thomas-E. Tremblay, inspector-general for Eastern Canada and hero of the First World War.

The federal government simultaneously quieted Quebec's protests that the defence of Canada was being neglected and incited patriotism by organizing Gaspé as a defence area under Brigadier Edmond Blais, the new commander of M.D.5. There had been numerous sinkings of freighters in the lower St. Lawrence and the Gulf by German submarines during the summer of 1942, and a renewal of the campaign was feared. From Ile-Verte on the St. Lawrence to Douglastown on the Baie des Chaleurs the Gaspé peninsula was partially blacked out, to prevent shore lights from silhouetting ships, while army, navy, and air defences were co-ordinated under French-Canadian officers. A civilian defence and warning system was set up with the support of the clergy, while a Reserve Army unit, Les Fusiliers du Bas St. Laurent, under the command of Colonel Joseph Pinault, a Gaspesian hero of the First World War, manned a series of anti-aircraft and defence installations. Gaspé was put on a war footing without arousing anything but French-Canadian pride, thanks to an intelligent choice of leaders, adroit publicity, and the fact that the population, which earned its living from the sea, had had the war brought to its door.

French Canada was further wooed by the holding of the first Quebec Conference in August. For two weeks the ancient capital sheltered the meetings of Roosevelt, Churchill, King, and the British, American, and Canadian general staffs. The streets were thronged with detachments of soldiers, sailors, and marines of the Allied nations; anti-aircraft and radar installations dotted the rocky crest on which Quebec stands; and a squadron of Spitfires maintained guard in the air. The populace lined the streets and the entrances of the Citadel and the Chateau Frontenac for hours in order to catch a glimpse of the civil and military leaders of the United Nations. It was widely rumored and believed that Stalin would attend the conference, and even the prospective presence of the Russian dictator was welcomed by a Quebec which was pleased to find itself momentarily the center of the world. Churchill attended a meeting of the provincial cabinet and was given an ovation when he toured the city in the company of Prime Minister King. Although Roosevelt did not make a formal public appearance, he was easily the most popular statesman present in French-Canadian opinion. His subsequent speech at Ottawa, in which he highly praised Canada's war effort, won him many more Canadian friends.

The joint Canadian-American landing at Kiska in the Aleutians on August 16, which was announced during the conference, lent a culminating touch to French Canada's sense of full participation in the war, since the Régiment de Hull, under Colonel Dollard Ménard, was one of the Canadian units involved. The success of the bloodless Kiska episode took the curse off the further extension by order-in-council of 'home defence' service to Bermuda, the Bahamas, and British Guiana; while the successful conclusion of the Sicilian campaign in thirty-eight days cheered French Canada, which in June had taken a gloomy view of the length of the war.[123] But a poll of the Canadian Institute of Public Opinion in August showed that 66 per cent of the French Canadians still favored keeping the conscripts in Canada, while 56 per cent of the English were in favor of sending them overseas. Relief at the prospect of an early peace was responsible for Quebec's enthusiastic celebration of the surrender of Italy. *Le Canada* hailed it as a judgment on Fascism: 'Fascism's failure is an object lesson for the misguided who maintain that it is possible to exhort people into following a leader blindly.' *Le Soleil* commented more soberly:

> Italy's unconditional surrender should facilitate entry of the United Nations' forces into Germany. It should soon be possible to render practical assistance to Greek and Yugoslav patriots. Even France's early liberation can now be anticipated. Russia, too, may soon have the opportunity of seeing a long-awaited European second front opened up on an extensive scale. The Italian capitulation is, therefore, a most important development of great political value.[124]

12

But once these milestones in the war were passed, Quebec turned back upon itself. The Godbout government had to call an election within a year, and the opposition parties sought to exploit popular dissatisfaction with the administration and the growing social unrest brought about by the war. In two significant federal by-elections in September, the Communist Fred Rose was elected in a Montreal working-class district by a majority of 1,800 over his *Bloc* rival Paul Massé, while Armand Choquette, the *Bloc* candidate, won the agricultural constituency of Stanstead by a 1,300 vote margin over an English Liberal. This radical trend alarmed Liberal leaders, while the press called for a revision of the Electoral Act which permitted the election of candidates who did not win a majority of the votes cast. *Le Devoir*, with its eye on Eire whose neutral status was envied by the nationalists, favored adoption of the Irish electoral system, while *Le Soleil* and *Le Droit* favored that of France. This agitation was in the main produced by fear lest the existing system should permit one of the new political groups to elect an undue number of representatives. Both the old parties were alarmed by the success of the *Bloc*, the C.C.F., and the Labor-Progressive (Communist) parties in exploiting popular unrest.

Rumors that the *Bloc* might join forces with Duplessis' *Union Nationale* were dispelled on September 1 when André Laurendeau, secretary-general of the group, declared:

> We will fight with all our strength against Mackenzie King and Adélard Godbout. We have already given the former a severe jolt; and the latter will not be overlooked. But the first article of our program is not to defeat Mr. So & So. This was the mistake made in 1935 and 1936. True, we succeeded in ridding the province of Taschereau, only to have

him replaced by Duplessis, a great deception. However, the people are frequently deceived. To deceive them again might one day throw them into the arms of Socialism or Communism.[125]

Duplessis returned the compliment by denouncing the *Bloc* on September 19, while on the same occasion one of his chief lieutenants, Antonio Barrette, congratulated P.-J.-A. Cardin for leaving the Liberal Party and thus left the door open for an alliance with the new federal party which Cardin was rumored to be forming among such maverick Liberals as J.-F. Pouliot, Emmanuel D'Anjou, and Wilfrid Lacroix, and the Duplessis Conservatives Frédéric Dorion and Sasseville Roy. This group was to adopt a program similar to that of the *Bloc* and would provide a better federal ally for Duplessis than the Conservative Party, which was handicapped in French Canada's eyes by its imperialist and capitalist traditions.

At the base of the confused political situation in Quebec was the labor problem. Wartime industrialization and unionization had produced a tense situation, with a demand by French-Canadian workers for pay rates equal to those of other provinces. The housing problem was acute, with thousands of new workers jamming the industrial centers. While the C.C.F. and Labor-Progressive parties sought to exploit French-Canadian bitterness about poor pay and working conditions, the *Bloc* blamed these evils on 'foreign' exploitation and called for nationalization of Quebec's natural resources. Even traditionally conservative leaders and newspapers favored reforms of a socialist nature. Cyrille Vaillancourt, a director of the Wartime Prices and Trade Board, told the Junior Chambre de Commerce:

> It appears at the present time that a planned economy will be necessary when peace comes . . . Sound, methodical, progressive planning is required, however, to assure the best possible development of natural resources, industry, and commerce. . . . State intervention will increase in scope as the march of social reforms gains momentum.[126]

Le Soleil and *Le Droit* strongly supported M. Vaillancourt's statement, which was backed by almost all of the Quebec press except the Tory *Montreal Gazette*. Oscar Drouin, the provincial Minister of Commerce was also applauded when he declared:

> As I see it, riches, that is national capital as we understand it, can come from one principal source: the development of our natural resources —hydro-electric energy, mines, forests—through economic planning along national lines, to assure that advantages will accrue to the masses as a whole and not to a few individuals. And above all we must not be

lulled, influenced, or conditioned by arguments and scare stories advanced by the holier-than-thou interests of private enterprise in matters relating to political economy. Practical development of our natural resources must not be impeded by so-called sound private enterprise.[127]

The labor situation was troubled by violent warfare between the so-called 'internationals'—unions affiliated with either the Trades and Labor Congress (A.F.L.) or the Canadian Congress of Labor (C.I.O.)—and the Catholic syndicates. The 'internationals' sought to guard the welfare of their members in English Canada and the United States by organizing French-Canadian labor and achieving equal pay rates, so that Quebec should not become the home of runaway mills and industries. The Catholic syndicates, exploiting French-Canadian group consciousness and nationalist feeling, sought to keep French-Canadian labor under French-Canadian—usually clerical—control, and thus to avoid 'foreign' control of labor as well as of industry. The international unions made the mistakes of not catering to French-Canadian traditional ideals and of advocating violent methods foreign to the tradition of the French-Canadian working class. The syndicates, which had grown up among the old paternalistic small industries, were ill-equipped to bargain on equal terms with national and international industries, since they were generally local and at best only provincial groups. The rivalry between the unions became a serious detriment to Quebec's war effort, first noted when a 1941 strike suspended production of aluminum at Arvida, the world's largest producer of a material which was essential to the Allied war effort.

13

The Lake St. John–Saguenay area of which Arvida is the industrial center provides an admirable social test tube for examining the results of the impact of the industrial revolution upon Quebec and the unrest which resulted. In a little over a century this region passed through the whole cycle of Quebec's economic history. Until well into the nineteenth century the region, which had first been explored by white men in the seventeenth century, remained a preserve for the successive fur-trading empires of the French Crown, the North-Westers, and the Hudson's Bay Company. In 1828, at the instigation of P. Tâché, a former fur-trader, the Quebec Legislature determined to send an expedition to explore the region. The report issued in the following year aroused some interest in the region, but the Hudson's Bay Company, which held a lease on the territory until 1842, managed to discourage any efforts at colonization.

The first settlers in the region came in 1838, and their object was not to clear lands for agriculture—this being forbidden by the fur company—but to cut white pine for William Price of Quebec. Price had come to Canada as an agent of the Admiralty in 1810 to acquire the mast timber which Britain lacked as a result of Napoleon's Continental Blockade, which had cut off the Scandinavian supply. Despite bitter opposition from the Hudson's Bay Company, Price managed to establish two lumber mills on the Saguenay. His river boats brought supplies for the settlers and carried the lumber to Quebec. Price used the same feudal industrial methods as the Channel Island firm of Charles Robin & Co. in Gaspé, paying his labor in script good only at company stores and thus keeping his men constantly in debt to the company. Managers and foremen were English and Scottish, while French-Canadians were never permitted to be anything but hired hands. This exploitation of a subject people and its natural resources by a self-styled 'master race' produced a lasting bitterness against the Price interests, which still exists in Quebec today.

The white pine of the Saguenay was soon gutted by the ruthless lumbering methods of the day and by forest fires, and the industry pushed northward into the Lake St. John region, with its headquarters at Chicoutimi, where the half-breed Peter MacLeod, a former Hudson's Bay employee, had established a mill in 1842. After his death ten years later Price acquired his interests. The region was already sending thirty shiploads of lumber a year to Europe from Chicoutimi, a port at the head of the long fjord of the Saguenay which ocean-going ships could reach with increasing ease as steam came to the aid of sail. Thereafter the lumber industry pushed steadily northward, and by 1868 the Price lumber camps were already ten leagues to the northeast of Lake St. John in the Peribonka country. Overpopulation and soil exhaustion in the old parishes along the St. Lawrence about the middle of the century led to the organization of colonization societies in Charlevoix, Quebec, and Kamouraska, whence colonists were sent to Lake St. John to clear the land and provide the food demanded for man and horse by the expanding lumber industry. Though checked at intervals by the forest fires which accompanied the effort to clear the rich land around the lake in this great natural bowl in the midst of the inhospitable Laurentian Shield, colonization proceeded with extreme rapidity. By 1921 some 250,000 acres had been brought under cultivation and the region had become one of the most prosperous agricultural areas in the province. The original channel of communication by way of the Saguenay, closed for more than five months of the year by ice, was supplemented by three winter roads across the wilderness to the St. Lawrence. A railroad, first proposed in 1854, was finally completed from Quebec to Chambord on the lake in 1888, extended to Chicoutimi in 1893, to Haha Bay at the head of deep-sea navigation on the Saguenay in 1908, and later to Dolbeau, north of Lake St. John.

Meanwhile forest industry had undergone notable changes. By 1871 white pine was beginning to be exhausted and cedar was fast following suit, while the sawmills only occupied some 500 men. Mills on Lake St. John replaced those on the Saguenay, but they lacked the facility and cheapness of transportation which had favored the earlier establishments. After a period of decline from 1880 to 1900, forest industry was rejuvenated by the birth of the pulp industry. In 1897 Alfred Dubuc of Chicoutimi constructed a pulp mill at Chicoutimi, making use of the great waterpower resources of the region and exporting his product to Great Britain and the United States, as well as to English Canada. With the rapid development of this industry the population of Chicoutimi grew fivefold from 1891 to 1921. Many other small mills were established in the region, and it was the pulp industry which established Port Alfred, the new deep-sea port on Haha Bay. But after 1920 the pulp industry suffered from Scandinavian competition, high ocean freight rates, and high railroad rates during the five months when navigation on the Saguenay was closed. Meanwhile another phase of the industry had been launched by Sir William Price, who in 1899 had taken over the tottering forest empire of his grandfather. Benefited by enormous timber limits and large capital resources, he bought the pulp mill at Jonquière, and produced first cardboard and later paper from the pulp it manufactured. Paper was a much more economic product than pulp, since it could be transported easily by rail at all seasons at lower cost. Gradually Price concentrated on supplying the American newsprint market, and his Kénogami-Jonquière establishment became the largest Canadian producer of newsprint.

In 1922 the Price firm controlled nearly three-quarters of the region's 117,000 developed horsepower, but still needed both more power and a more regular supply. Price Brothers then sought American capital and interested the Duke tobacco interests. The Duke-Price Company, which was taken over by Shawinigan Power and the Aluminum Company of America in 1926, began in 1923 to develop the waterpower provided by the outlets of Lake St. John. The level of the lake was raised eighteen feet and eight dams were constructed, while a power-house capable of producing 540,000 horsepower was installed at Ile-Maligne. The village of Saint-Joseph-d'Alma increased its population a hundred-fold in two years, while a new paper mill formed the center of the new company town of Riverbend. This vast program was not carried through without opposition: the farmers of Lake St. John lost land and buildings—15,000 square miles of cultivated land were flooded, while still more was affected—and they complained that the Price company had not compensated them justly; while the importation of workers from Ontario, Finland, Italy, Czechoslovakia, and Poland was resented on nationalist grounds. Port Alfred was linked to the new source of power and became a producer of paper as well as pulp; while a new paper mill at Dolbeau, which had been planned to use local power, was also later connected with Ile-Maligne. Encouraged by this success, a new dam was built at Chute-à-Caron which added 240,000 horsepower to the resources of the region. Plans were already made for developing 800,000 more horsepower at Shipshaw when the 1929 crash brought the project to a halt.

The Aluminum Company of America (later a separate Aluminum Company of Canada was set up) which played the major part in these and later developments, was attracted to the region by the wealth of easily-developed and constant waterpower, the easy access for deep-sea shipping, and by the supply of hardworking, docile, and cheap French-Canadian labor. Cheap power in enormous quantities and cheap labor were the main needs of the aluminum industry, which began work on a great plant and company town at Arvida (named after Arthur Vining Davis, the president of the company) in 1925. It created a great port at Port Alfred, where ocean freighters could bring the vast quantities of bauxite from British Guiana and cryolite from Greenland which were the raw materials of aluminum, and load the finished ingots for transportation to the United States, England, Japan, and the rest of Canada. The Arvida plant had a pre-war capacity of 30,000 tons a year, but plans had already been made for an eventual production of 300,000. The town of Arvida, created out of the wilderness by the company, housed 3,000 people in its individual family houses, each surrounded by lawns and gardens.

With this development the industrial future of the Saguenay-Lake St. John region seemed to be assured of a stability unknown in the forest industries. The lumber mills now employed only a bare hundred workers; while the pulp and paper industry could employ 6,500 when working at full capacity. But the development which had enabled the region in eight years to increase its production of pulp threefold and of paper fourfold, while its power resources were increased eightfold, ended in overproduction before the 1929 crash. Price Brothers began buying and closing down small competing mills in 1927; three years later the company went into bankruptcy itself. In 1932 the region reached the bottom of the depression, with Arvida employing only 300 men in the aluminum industry; Kénogami and Jonquière 1,000 in its pulp and paper plants, Port Alfred 250, and Riverbend half its usual number. Only the small mill at Dolbeau was little affected by the crisis which weighed so heavily upon its giant rivals. Surplus power was used to heat homes and was even transmitted to Quebec. The region rivaled Montreal as that most severely affected by the depression. The agriculture of the region, which was based on supplying food for the industrial centers, was gravely affected by the decline of industry.[128] Public opinion was embittered by the fact that the great 'foreign' industries had revolutionized the life of the region with a high hand, and had left it flat on its back when depression came. Fertile ground was thus provided for the economic nationalism of the 1930's and for leftist schemes of nationalization of industry.

With the coming of the war, however, industrial prosperity returned to a region in which agriculture had already revived, thanks to improved cultivation practices. Lake St. John is one of the few Quebec regions in which large-scale mechanized farming is possible. Arvida soon found itself working at capacity to produce the aluminum so urgently needed by the Allies for airplanes. Its production of aluminum in 1942 equaled the world output in 1939. By 1943 Arvida was employing 15,000 men, while work was carried on night and day on the Shipshaw project, at Ile-Maligne and Chute-à-Caron, and far up the Peribonka at Passe Dangereuse, to increase the developed supply of power, which now amounted to 2,000,000 horsepower—nearly half that of the province as a whole.

This enormous and rapid development had not been accomplished without creating social difficulties. Bad management which disregarded French-Canadian predilections was responsible for the 1941 aluminum strike and for the subsequent struggle between the A.F.L. union and the Catholic syndicate for control of the workers. The aluminum industry became a political football, with the nationalists and Duplessis forces calling for its nationalization, denouncing the Liberals for having sold out to 'foreign' business, and denouncing the Aluminum Company for having ruthlessly undermined the pulp and paper industries of the region. The model industrial city of Arvida was marred by inadequate temporary wartime housing and camps for single men, the latter of which were far superior to the bunkhouses of the lumber trade or to army camp accommodation, but nonetheless introduced into the town a restless and unsettled element. The instinct for the traditional way of life which had forced the company to remodel along traditional French-Canadian lines its original workers' houses designed by an American architect, led many new workers at Arvida to live in the nearby towns of Kénogami, Jonquière, Chicoutimi, and Port Alfred, whose wretched slums were made still worse by this influx. The ever-growing demand for labor drained manpower from the old agricultural centers all around Lake St. John, and even from the lower St. Lawrence region. Husky farmers were favored as potmen, the highest paid laborers, whose job required a strong back, endurance in high temperatures, and a minimum of brains. Veteran workers sought to transfer from this job, particularly in hot weather when breaking up the crust which formed on the pots as aluminum was produced by electro-chemical process became an arduous job, though the men only had to work about half the time they were on duty in the torrid pot rooms. It was on this crucial department of the industry that the A.F.L. centered its organization drive, since a strike there would cripple the whole plant.

The region had almost the longest record of union history of any part of the province. Chicoutimi had been active center of the Catholic syndicate movement since the foundation there in 1907 by Mgr. Eugène Lapointe of the Fédération Ouvrière Mutuelle du Nord. The syndicates' development had been favored by Alfred Dubuc in his pulp mills, but had been opposed by the English-Canadian and American interests. When the pulp syndicates, representing 85 per cent of the workers in the Price Company, sought a collective contract in 1937, their request was refused. In the following year the internationals intensified their organizational work, and in November signed a contract with the company, despite the fact that they only had a minority of members at Kénogami and only a handful at Jonquière and Riverbend. The syndicates protested and sought to be associated with the minority union in any contract, but their demand was refused. Despite intervention by the provincial minister of labor, the company stood firm by its decision not to deal with unions under clerical auspices, and favored the intensive organizing campaign of the International Brotherhood of Paper Makers (A.F.L.).

The Aluminum Company, however, reversed Price Brothers' labor policies and profited thereby. It recognized the emotional force of French-Canadian particularism and the commercial advantages of dealing with a weak local union rather than a strong international one, which someday would insist upon the same wages being paid in Quebec as in the American and English-Canadian plants of the company.

The *Syndicat national catholique de l'Aluminum*, founded in 1937, won a collective contract from its company that same year. Under this contract, renewed from year to year, potmen's wages were raised 20 to 25 per cent, while workers engaged on a weekly basis received a paid vacation of fifteen days, while those engaged on an hourly basis received paid vacations according to their length of service. The contract was extended to all workers in the plant, and negotiations between the syndicate and the company were in process in October 1942 when the A.F.L. sent an organizer, Philip Cutler, to conduct an intensive campaign for the international union. This organizer, denounced as a Jew and a former Communist, promising staggering wage increases to the workers, while warning the company that 'hell would pop if an agreement was not reached on terms satisfactory to the A.F.L.' The international union succeeded in recruiting 3,000 members, and immediately petitioned Prime Minister King to have the federal ministry of labor exercise its influence on the company to sign a contract with the International Union of Aluminum Workers (A.F.L.) as representative of 'the majority of the employees.' This claim was unquestionably false, since the syndicate represented some 4,000 men while the majority of the 15,000 workers were unorganized, being unwilling to pay dues when they were satisfied with wages and working conditions.

An international meeting at Jonquière on December 1, conducted by Cutler, resulted in a resolution requesting the federal minister of labor to name a conciliator and to order a vote among the workers for their bargaining agent. Rose, a federal labor investigator, began work fifteen days later. This dispatch was in sharp contrast with the procedure followed in 1941, when the syndicate representing two-thirds of the pulp and paper workers at Dolbeau requested a federal conciliator and arbitration of labor difficulties there, and intervention was refused after two months' delay had permitted the company to sign a gentleman's agreement with the international union. Rose was immediately denounced by the syndicate as a Jew and as a former counsel for the international unions, and his decision within two days to recommend a vote at Arvida was violently assailed as evidence of his bias. The provincial minister of labor, who was as favorable to the syndicates as the federal minister was to the international unions, was warned in time, thanks to a syndicate-minded stenographer who supplied a carbon of Rose's report, and immediately protested to Ottawa at this decision to regard the existing contract with the syndicate 'as a scrap of paper.' Rose completed his investigation, declaring that he did not take orders from Quebec, and that he would recommend a vote to the federal authorities. But the vote was not ordered, since the international union could not prove that it represented the majority, and because of pressure from Quebec.

The international union then threatened to call a strike, which would have halted production of a vital war material, already hindered by the long drawn-out struggle. While the syndicates urged the international organizers to 'stay at home as we do' and opposed 'enabling these New York bigshots to live on our money,' the international spokesmen attacked the support given by the clergy and provincial officials to the syndicate, and warned that the day of reckoning would come for them. The local clergy and the Jesuit Père Genest fought the international movement vigorously. When the Jewish Philip Cutler was replaced by an Irish Catholic organizer, 'foreign Catholics' were denounced from the pulpit along with the international union. Public opinion was strongly aroused against the internationals as they continued their drive to organize all the war industries of Quebec. Cutler and a colleague, Claude Jodoin, were finally jailed when they launched another organization campaign at Shawinigan.

The Aluminum Company, which feared an attempt to raise the Arvida wage rates to the level prevailing in its American plants, gave the syndicate discreet support. The international's agitation was unsuccessful because the workers recognized that the company had given them wages, working, and living conditions which were scarcely to be matched in Canada; and because the company made a policy of catering to French-Canadian particularism. Not only were 92 per cent of the Arvida workers French Canadians, but the company employed as many French-Canadian technicians and executives as it could find. Its head chemist and its personnel manager were French Canadians, though its general manager at Arvida was an Englishman and most of the chief executives were Americans. The company, an international cartel, was not afflicted with any such narrow nationalist spirit as had caused Price Brothers so much trouble. It could afford to carry no national flag, and its basic loyalty was to the aluminum empire, with its bauxite deposits in British Guiana, its cryolite deposits in Greenland, its processing plants at Galveston, Massena, Toronto, and Kingston; and its English, Italian, and German subsidiaries.

Since Arvida offered admirable manufacturing conditions, thanks to the largest supply of cheap power in the world and easy access by deep-sea shipping, the company strove in every fashion to make good its position in Quebec. It displayed a paternalism which sometimes misfired and irritated French-Canadian individualism. It revised its model housing plans to suit French-Canadian tastes; it rented or sold houses and land at less than cost; it planted trees and encouraged gardens; it established a vast indoor recreation center for the winter months and sports facilities for the summer ones; it provided a newspaper, a hospital, and schools, and contributed heavily to the building of churches. When the politically-minded French Canadians missed the sport of elections, it added an elected town council to the city manager system it had established. In the industry itself it required its English-speaking employees to learn and to use French; it provided safety devices; it instituted the 48-hour week in a region which had grown up on dawn-to-dusk labor; it had labor relations representatives in each division of the plant, to act as buffers between workmen and foremen and to personalize the company to the individual worker. By prizes for useful suggestions it sought to improve industrial practices and to encourage employee loyalty. It favored the *caisse populaire* and co-operative movements sponsored by the syndicates and established its own pension system.

All these measures proved profitable, since after their adoption the Aluminum Company had less labor trouble than any other war industry. Once the management of the Arvida plant had come into the hands of men who understood and respected French-Canadian ideas after the 1941 strike, there was no further serious difficulty. An indication of employee loyalty was supplied when volunteers responded to a call from the company to spend all of Christmas Day 1943 in unloading a shipment of frozen bauxite from open railway cars in order that the plant might keep functioning without interruption.

Under such conditions the international union could make little progress, particularly after the company had delicately suggested that if the union succeeded in raising wages at Arvida to the American level, the Arvida plant might be shut down in order to keep the American plants running. The anti-Aluminum Company agitation raised in Montreal by nationalist organs was curiously unsupported by similar unrest among the workers at Arvida, although there was a small radical group in the plant which distributed anti-English and anti-capitalist propaganda in parody litany form. Despite all the talk of nationalization from nationalists on the one hand and the C.C.F. on the other, the Aluminum Company was not very frightened on that score for the postwar period, putting its faith in French Canada's deep respect for private property and on its own conviction that public ownership would be unwieldy, more expensive, and less efficient than private enterprise in this industry. The company was much more concerned with the problem of converting to peacetime production and finding outlets for the enormous productive facilities built up during the war. But there was a strong feeling that Arvida had become the most economical place in the world to produce aluminum and that it would continue to do so when other war plants were closed, while the enormous power sources might well be put to other industrial uses if a market for aluminum could not be found.[128]

14

The union situation at Arvida was roughly paralleled elsewhere in Quebec. The internationals were strong only in long-established industries in the old urban centers, and even there were under attack as foreign organizations run in American interests. Management in most of the older industries, if forced to accept unions at all, preferred to deal with the English-speaking internationals rather than with the French clerically-influenced syndicates. A few old industries overcame the racist tradition of industry in Quebec and favored the syndicates, which could be used as company unions under cover of favoring French-Canadian ideas. Such was the policy of the Dominion Textile Company at its Magog plant, where the syndicate chaplain, who received a salary as chaplain of the company-supported hospital and whose father enjoyed a company pension, successfully broke up a C.I.O. organizational campaign.

One notable development of the war was the rise of French-Canadian industrialists, such as the Simard brothers of Sorel, who built ships on the Kaiser plan and also made guns. Two old marine railways which had employed 160 men in pre-war days were converted into a bustling shipyard employing 6,000 men at the peak of production. The latest methods of industrial engineering and management were cleverly adapted for use in Quebec, while the paternalistic relationship between French-Canadian *patron* and French-Canadian labor was preserved. The Simards' enterprises were free of the usual bitterness arising from ethnic division between management and labor which provided admirable openings for agitation in other enterprises, such as the Crown company war industries, which were usually directed by men whom the French Canadians regarded as 'foreigners.' Patriotic propaganda helped to avoid labor trouble in such plants, however, while the syndicates loyally adhered to the attitude that strikes were illegal in wartime, though the internationals did not hesitate to threaten to actually call them.

In the face of the announced intention of Trades and Labor Congress spokesman Robert Haddow to organize first the war industries and later all others in Quebec, the syndicates were forced to become more militant than they had ever been before. Alfred Charpentier, president of the Confédération des Travailleurs Catholiques du Canada which claimed a membership of 53,000 Quebec workers, described the American Federation of Labor as 'Our worst enemy, an enemy who is not afraid to use any means at his disposal to further his aim' at the twenty-second annual convention of the syndicates at Granby in 1944. He accounted for the growth of the C.C.L. and C.I.O. unions by their use of illegal strikes and anti-religious propaganda. Bishop Douville of Saint-Hyacinthe, who attended the convention, warned the workers against following the precedent set by the C.C.L. unions in supporting the C.C.F., which he regarded as communistic. He stressed the fact that support of the internationals was detrimental to French-Canadian interests:

> American labor unions, to which certain Quebec workers are affiliated, will logically protect their own before taking care of your welfare. The situation in Quebec must be unique in labor annals, with labor groups here awaiting orders and directives from foreign leaders.[129]

Bishop Douville urged simultaneous development of workers' and employers' syndicates 'as a prelude to the economic corporatism which we consider essential to the future of labor and employers as well.'

The provincial government met this new agitation in clerical and nationalist circles for corporatism by setting up a postwar Economic Council, whose fifteen members included corporatist sympathizers Père Georges-Henri Levesque of Laval, Eugène L'Heureux of *L'Action Catholique*, Esdras Minville of the Ecole des Hautes Etudes Commerciales, and Gérard Picard of the Confédération des Travailleurs Catholiques. The president of the council, however, was Jules Brillant, the able utility magnate of the lower St. Lawrence region. The corporatist movement continued to be strongly supported by the Semaine Sociales, *Le Devoir*, *L'Action Catholique*, and *Le Droit*; while it was bitterly attacked by *Le Jour*, in which Jean-Charles Harvey waged a vigorous campaign in defence of Manchester Liberalism as interpreted by the Canadian Pacific Railway and other big business in the province. It was also violently opposed by the Communists, who regarded it as fascist in inspiration—a view also held by the majority of English-speaking North Americans who had not been inspired by the application of corporatism under Mussolini in Italy and Salazar in Portugal.

Further evidence of the social and economic unrest of French Canada in 1943 was provided by the renewed outbreak of anti-semitism, with a pro-Pétain French Dominican attacking Jacques Maritain in the Quebec press for having been influenced by his Jewish wife,[130] with the Jews of Quebec City being legally blocked from erecting a synagogue on the fashionable Grande Allée, and with the beating up of several Jews at Plage Laval near Montreal in September. The *Bloc* had revived the old nationalist anti-semitic tradition in its campaign against Fred Rose; and Paul Gouin's *L'Union* and the Order of Jacques Cartier's *La Boussole* continued to print anti-semitic propaganda. As Everett Hughes has admirably demonstrated, anti-semitism in French Canada is largely an attempt to find a scapegoat for dissatisfaction with the economic order: 'The symbolic Jew receives the more bitter of the attacks which the French Canadians would like to make upon the English or even upon some of their own leaders and institutions . . . the Jew in Quebec is the physically present small competitor rather than the hidden wirepuller of high finance and big business.'[131]

Anti-semitism fulfils an emotional need for the French Canadian, and is as instinctive as the American Southerner's color prejudice. There was a revealing contrast of the two attitudes, when an American Negro doctor, who had been excluded from the dining-room of the Chateau Frontenac and brought a suit against the hotel, was enthusiastically supported by French-Canadian opinion, which deplored such prejudice, while it objected to the number of New York Jews who frequented the hotel. The *Bloc*, which exploited to the full all the popular emotional attitudes of French Canada, did not fail to use anti-semitism in Montreal, where the Jews have prospered more greatly than the French Canadians in a much shorter time.

The development of the *Bloc* movement continued to be hampered by internal dissension, although its popular appeal was strong, as witnessed by a Canadian Institute of Public Opinion poll in the fall of 1943 which indicated that it was now supported by 33 per cent of the electorate.[132] During Maxime Raymond's illness Edouard Lacroix, the wealthy federal M.P. for the Beauce, took over organization of the movement and alienated the anti-trust radicals. Paul Gouin, Dr. Hamel, Jean Martineau, and René Chaloult conferred together about breaking with the *Bloc*. Hamel and Martineau favoured joining forces with the C.C.F., which had made overtures through Frank Scott's public utterances, while Gouin and Chaloult preferred to revive the *Action Libérale Nationale* movement of the 1930's. On October 16 Dr. Hamel announced in a broadcast the decision of the dissidents to leave the *Bloc*, since it had been taken over by a 'millionaire.' René Chaloult also declared in the legislature: 'We have committed ourselves to fighting the trusts and the financial interests which dominate the lives of French Canadians, and as Mr. Lacroix is himself a millionaire who has made his money by being closely associated with these trusts, we could not in justice to ourselves or to the policy we preach take our place beside him on the hustings.'[133] But there was no hint of the economic reforms dear to the heart of the dissidents, while the Godbout government had already announced its intention of expropriating the Montreal Light, Heat, & Power Co. This step was discounted by Duplessis and the C.C.F. as an electoral measure, but approved by all the French press except *Le Jour*.

No mention of the split within the *Bloc* was made in another radio speech on October 17 in which Raymond outlined the party's provincial program: to champion provincial autonomy, to restore the integrity of the family, and to make Quebec an agricultural province once more. Raymond declared that Quebec must remain French and Catholic, and that the individualism born of the French Revolution must be destroyed. He denounced the injustice of taxes which bore more heavily on large families, and said the *Bloc* would seek to revise the tax laws from a family point of view.[134] Oscar Drouin, leader of the nationalist wing of the Liberal Party, made a bid for support from *Bloc* followers discontented by the defection of the radical nationalists, demanding fair play in the federal civil service for French Canadians and the right for Canada to amend the B.N.A. Act with the consent of the provinces. This utterance, coming after the announcement of the federal plan for family allowances and the provincial plan for nationalization of electricity in Montreal, made evident the Liberal Party's determination to steal the thunder of both the C.C.F. and the *Bloc*.

A bombshell was thrown into the confused political scene by a joint pastoral letter of the Canadian hierarchy in October 1943, which declared the C.C.F. a neutral party for which Catholics were as free to vote as they were for the two old parties. Communism was once more condemned, but the C.C.F. was definitely cleared of the disapproval of the Church. This utterance was a distinct blow to the Liberals and to the nationalists, who sought to belittle its ramifications as much as possible. It was given much fuller attention by the English press than by the French, with the *Canadian Register*, the English Catholic organ of the diocese of Montreal, publishing a lengthy commentary, while *L'Action Catholique* merely printed the text, as did *Le Devoir*, under the disgruntled caption: 'Call it what you like, Communism is still to be condemned.' In an editorial in *Le Devoir* Omer Héroux warned against any 'attempt to read into their statement any more than what it says—neither more nor less.'[135] The Jesuits of the Ecole Sociale Populaire went so far as to distort the clear meaning of the statement in an anti-C.C.F. sense. The Communist spokesman Stanley B. Ryerson deplored the bishops' intervention into politics, while M. J. Coldwell, Frank Scott, and David Lewis welcomed it on behalf of the C.C.F. The utterance cleared from the path of the C.C.F. in Quebec the insuperable barrier of disapproval by the Church.

There remained, however, another major obstacle, the inability of the party to find a representative French-Canadian leader. In the popular mind the party remained 'English,' while the nationalist effort to muddy the clear stream of the bishops' thought offset the original effect of the statement. The semantic confusion of Fabian English socialism with revolutionary and anti-clerical Continental socialism paralleled that of English and Continental liberalism in the previous century, and seemed fated to endure as long. Clarification of the confusion was not facilitated by the subsequent revolutionary utterances of Harold Winch, radical British Columbia chief of the C.C.F., which were duly exploited by the nationalist and clerical opponents of the party in Quebec. In vain Frank Scott and David Lewis sought by statements and speeches to stress the close kinship between the social program of the papal encyclicals and that of the C.C.F., and the party's opposition to imperialism and to racist movements. It was accused by both its French and English opponents of cutting its cloth according to its audience. The newly formed provincial organization of the C.C.F. crumbled as several of its French-Canadian officers resigned under pressure from their compatriots.

The wave of strikes which had afflicted the province in recent months continued, with first the Montreal police and firemen going out, and then the City Hall employees. A similar strike among the municipal employees in Quebec was threatened, while agitation over low wages and consequent poor health and housing conditions mounted ever higher. Faced with general deploring of the situation by the French press and the announced intention of the Communists to profit by it, the Quebec government introduced new labor legislation at the outset of the session in January 1944. The provisions of this bill made it obligatory for employers to recognize any union comprising 60 per cent of their employees and to make collective agreements with them under the supervision of a provincial Labor Relations Board. The bill was based upon the recommendations of the *Conseil Supérieur du Travail*, a provincial body composed of eight representatives of capital, eight of labor, and eight economists. The provincial authorities had hurriedly agreed upon a labor code before Ottawa introduced the proposed federal one. As Premier Godbout stated, the measure would safeguard the autonomy of the province against federal commissions which failed to understand provincial powers under the B.N.A. Act. The first bill was unanimously approved by the legislature. A second bill provided for compulsory arbitration of labor disputes in public service industries, prohibited strikes or lockouts, and denied the right of police or civil servants to join unions. These bills were hailed enthusiastically by the Catholic syndicates. The provincial representatives of the American Federation of Labor, Elphège Beaudoin and Marcel Francq, endorsed the bills, but their endorsement was disowned by officials of the Montreal Trades and Labor Council. The Canadian Congress of Labor which had organized police, firemen, and tramway employees, opposed both measures. The press unanimously approved the legislation.

15

A unanimous reaction such as Quebec had not shown since the plebiscite greeted the Toronto speech of Lord Halifax, British ambassador to the United States, on January 24, 1944, when he proposed a common postwar foreign and defence policy for the Commonwealth. René Chaloult, who had already introduced in the Quebec legislature a resolution deploring Canada's 'excessive' war effort, on January 28 gave notice of the following motion: 'That this House believes it to be its duty to go on record against the new imperialism of Lord Halifax and his dangerous tendencies.' There was a stormy reaction in Quebec, as there was indeed all over Canada, to Halifax's suggestion that a postwar central government for the Commonwealth should be established in London. Godbout and Duplessis followed their federal leaders in keeping silence, but Maxime Raymond echoed M. J. Coldwell's declaration of opposition to the proposal with this statement:

> We are for the independence of Canada. The *Bloc* is of the opinion that Canada has an important role to play in world affairs, but it does not consider the British Commonwealth of Nations as the most appropriate organization to allow it to play such a role.

The French press gave wide publicity to the comments of the *Winnipeg Free Press*, deploring the fact that 'Lord Halifax, a member of the British War Cabinet, should make such a speech on Canadian soil and before consulting the Canadian government,' and of the *Toronto Star* that 'The strength of the Commonwealth rests in autonomous association rather than in centralized authority . . . that the units of the Empire must "necessarily speak as one" is too much to expect, and equally so is it that the Dominion should as a matter of course "take the same point of view as the Mother Country."'

Omer Héroux denounced in *Le Devoir* this new imperial federation movement and asserted that 'Canada, a sovereign nation, will not tamely accept either from Great Britain or the United States or from anywhere else the attitude she must take to world affairs . . . Independence will ensure that Canada, like all great peoples, will order her foreign policy according to her own interests and to her geographical situation.' *Le Droit* warned that 'Empire solidarity has limits inevitably fixed by the national interests of each Dominion, and these cannot be overlooked.' *L'Action Catholique* called Halifax's suggestion 'unacceptable' and observed: 'Far better that we should guard our liberty, not to practice an unwise isolationism in international affairs, but to collaborate with those we wish, in the interests of Canada and world peace, keeping in mind the fact we are an American country.' *La Patrie* declared that Canada 'must first of all consider her own interests, and it must not be forgotten that she is an American country.' *Le Canada* found 'something right and something risky' in the proposal, considering that 'the new relationship proposed by Lord Halifax would undoubtedly be a step forward,' but that on the other hand it would seem to many 'an alliance of lamb with the lion' which might drag Canada 'into a whirlpool of Tory imperialism.' *Le Jour* charged Halifax with indirectly furthering the work of the anti-British element in Quebec and regarded Canada's complete sovereignty as inevitable within fifty years.[136]

The speech from the throne at the opening of the federal session contained an indirect reply to Halifax: 'It is only by the general organization in international affairs of peace-loving nations that dangers of future aggression will be removed, and world peace secured.'[137] In proposing adoption of the speech, Léonard Tremblay (Dorchester) said that Mackenzie King would 'stop the imperialistic intrigues of Halifax, just as Chamberlain's imperialism once received a rebuff from Laurier's Canadianism.'[138] The nationalist press warned that the Liberal Party was just as imperialist at heart as the Conservative, and tended to regard this stand as one taken with future elections in mind, like the proposal of family allowances. The Liberal press naturally hailed both policies with delight, devoting particular attention to explaining how Quebec would specially benefit from the family allowance scheme. In the provincial legislature Liberal support was found for Chaloult's anti-Halifax resolution, with Oscar Drouin denouncing 'a concerted plan' to 'put the machine into reverse and set up an Imperial Federation.' Drouin declared: 'We cannot agree to lose what our fathers before us gained, and what was won at the cost of so much strife . . . Quebec cannot accept the new imperialism of Lord Halifax.'

The *Bloc* held its first general convention from February 3 to 6 in Montreal. Delegates were invited from all French-speaking centers in Canada. English Canada had been made familiar with the new nationalist movement through *Maclean's Magazine's* publication of an interview with Maxime Raymond.[139] His answers to a series of specific questions, which gave him an opportunity to expose the whole platform of the *Bloc*, were summed up in his final answer to the query as to Canada's future status—'Independence.' But Raymond was unable to attend the opening of the convention, while Gouin, Hamel, and Chaloult were notable for their absence, despite Raymond's earlier appeal for unity. André Laurendeau, who had served as secretary-general and radio spokesman of the group for nearly a year and had been named editor of the new weekly organ

Le Bloc, was nominated as provincial leader, a post almost as important as Raymond's since the *Bloc* could only hope to win power in Quebec. It was rumoured that the elderly Raymond would retire from politics because of ill health, leaving the party in Laurendeau's hands. Though it had been anticipated that Laurendeau's nomination might bring back to the fold the dissidents and their young followers, Laurendeau expressed no eagerness for Chaloult's return when he announced that the *Bloc* would run candidates in every Quebec constituency. And in the first issue of *Le Bloc* Laurendeau rejected a suggested merger of the *Bloc* with Duplessis in the provincial field, with the observation that 'Quebec will punish with a single blow both the guilty: Godbout and Duplessis.'[140]

Paul Gouin, Dr. Hamel, and René Chaloult were immediately reported to be planning a new Liberal-nationalist group, since they would not accept Laurendeau's leadership. On February 14 the dissidents issued an anti-*Bloc* statement which declared that their efforts at reconciliation with the *Bloc* had been rejected, and that they had not been given the assurances they required against a repetition of 1936, when they had been repudiated by M. Duplessis after helping to win the election. Maxime Raymond announced on February 26 that he considered the matter 'ended once and for all,' while on the following day Paul Gouin broadcast a reply to Raymond and an explanation of the split in the party. He asserted that Raymond and Laurendeau had rejected all offers of settlement on a fair basis; that the split was not caused by personal differences between the dissidents and Lacroix, but by a matter of basic principle. He denounced Lacroix's financial control over the Quebec district as 'a return to the policy of the old parties, to the policy of dictatorship by those who handed out the party funds.' He added that Lacroix's financial power had compelled Raymond 'to take sides against the unity and interest of the movement which we had entrusted to him.'

René Chaloult, stating that he was the spokesman of Quebec nationalists, echoed Gouin's charges in the legislature and accused the *Bloc* of refusing to nationalize insurance and credit. He declared:

> The only way left to correct the abuses arising from the trusts is to take things over step by step through the agency of expropriation . . . It is only by nationalization that we succeed in delivering ourselves from foreign domination, and once again get control of our own wealth. When our government has once more gained possession of our resources, then it will employ French-Canadian engineers, managers, accountants, chemists, etc., to develop them . . . So long as we continue to let foreign capitalists exploit against our interests our natural resources, the germs of Communism will inevitably continue to multiply.[141]

Paul Gouin continued to wage a vigorous campaign against the *Bloc* over the radio and through his newspaper *L'Union*. On March 5 he declared that followers of Duplessis had been active in the *Bloc* from the beginning and were now planning a formal alliance, with the *Bloc* leaving the provincial field to Duplessis and the latter aiding Raymond in the event of a federal election.

The Godbout government took heart at these developments and at the enthusiastic reception of its nationalization and labor measures. It was considered possible that the Gouin-Hamel-Chaloult group might make common cause with the Liberals, thus severely weakening the *Bloc*; while Maurice Duplessis' refusal to endorse the nationalization of the Montreal Light, Heat & Power and his anti-labor record made him particularly vulnerable in the current state of public opinion. Though the C.C.L. unions promised to throw their support behind the C.C.F., a Communist-inspired effort to create a united labor political front and the continued confusion within the French-Canadian mind of socialism with Communism weakened the strength of the C.C.F. It was considered likely that the provincial elections would be called in June to take advantage of the disintegration of the opposition parties.

The provincial Liberal Party was strengthened by the declaration made by Mr. King before his departure for the Imperial Conference in May:

> Collaboration with the Commonwealth is being carried out and will continue to be carried out, on a footing of the most specific equality. When sometimes great questions determining peace and war come up for discussion, as well as those on matters of prosperity and depression, such a collaboration cannot be exclusive in its aims and methods. Our undertakings, in connection with these great questions, must spring from a general plan, either worldwide or regional in scope. We look forward, in consequence, to a close collaboration in the interests of peace, not only within the Commonwealth, but also with all friendly nations, whether they be great or small.[142]

French Canada found this program more to its taste than that formulated by Conservative leader John Bracken, who declared: 'I look forward in consequence to Canada, acting as an autonomous power, strengthening the bonds which unite the members of the Commonwealth, and with this end in view, I believe that we should draw up in common a plan of permanent consultation in all matters of common interest.' *Le Canada* likened Bracken's position to that expounded by Lord Halifax. *Le Nouvelliste* held that 'an isolationist policy will not be of any more service to Canada than an imperialist policy will be.' *Le Droit* warned that though they might differ on means, all English-speaking politicians sought greater unification of the empire, and that the conference would 'concern itself only with the methods to be used to ensure such coordination.' *L'Action Catholique* declared: 'We are not isolationists. We want Canada to collaborate with the other countries of the world: the United States, the American republics, the Commonwealth nations, etc; but we ask the Prime Minister of Canada not to take on any new obligation which might prevent us from first considering the interests of Canada . . . In international matters let us at last act as a truly autonomous country.' *Le Soleil*, which probably expressed the majority view, urged: 'It is of importance to the British Commonwealth of Nations that their intimate union should be maintained in peacetime as well as during the war. This happy result will be easily obtained by a more generous policy which does not limit in any way the autonomous countries and which encourages the evolution of British Colonies in the democratic framework. Unless she applies this doctrine sincerely, Great Britain will quickly lose the sympathy of free peoples.' *La Presse* lined up with *Le Soleil* in supporting King's insistence on Canadian liberty of action in foreign affairs. *L'Action Catholique* credited Mr. King with 'the idea of playing an important role and with the plan of opposing certain imperialistic policies of Mr. Churchill.' Only *Le Devoir* and *Le Droit* continued to assert that nothing separated King from Bracken, and that once more Canadian sovereignty was 'to be sacrificed on the altar of imperialism.'

Meanwhile the *Bloc* continued to have internal and external troubles. Edouard Lacroix and Dr. Pierre Gauthier were rumored to be on the brink of rupture with Raymond, while in the lower ranks there was a large measure of sympathy for Gouin, Hamel, and Chaloult. Laurendeau's campaign in *Le Bloc* for 'houses before guns' lost some of its effectiveness when the annual May 1 moving day passed without any considerable number of people being left homeless. Duplessis continued to wage violent war on the new movement, while Ernest Grégoire's Social Creditors denounced it as merely one of power-hungry opportunists. The number of *Bloc* public meetings continued to increase, but the question of where electoral funds would come from was raised by Lacroix's prospective departure from the movement. In the Stanstead and Cartier by-elections of the previous year the *Bloc* had sought to exploit the prestige of Henri Bourassa by bringing him out of retirement to speak at its meetings. Bourassa had successfully evoked the old nationalist tradition among the farmers of Stanstead, but carried little weight among the industrial workers of Montreal.

Now, on May 21, Bourassa supported Laurendeau on the platform in his first appearance at a Quebec political meeting since 1907, when he and Lavergne had been stoned at the Marché Saint-Pierre. After making an appeal to the dissidents to rejoin the *Bloc*, he appalled his sponsors by observing: 'In constituencies where there is no *Bloc* candidate at the next federal elections, true Canadians should vote for the C.C.F. candidate.' He also recommended co-operation between French and English on a basis of equality, observing 'that does not mean we have to shine the shoes of Prime Minister Mackenzie King as Premier Godbout does, or to hold Churchill's cigar as Mackenzie King does.' He reiterated his opposition to imperialism of all kinds, and added: 'When they speak of a crusade for Christianity I cannot forget that our first cooperation with British imperialism at the end of the last century contributed to the extermination of a valiant little nation in South Africa.'[143]

Le Bloc omitted the reference to the C.C.F. in its report of 'the Master's' speech, and a week later urged: 'Let us fight against the imperialistic C.C.F., germ of the Communist revolution!' M. J. Coldwell promptly threw cold water on any prospect of an alliance between the *Bloc* and the C.C.F. René Chaloult in a radio speech expressed admiration for Bourassa, but added: 'That does not mean that I agree with his orders in the field of political strategy.' He urged his hearers to vote for the best man, regardless of party, and named some candidates he favored in all camps. Paul Gouin announced his intention to run as an independent, with the support of Chaloult and Hamel. Both dissidents condemned the Liberals, the *Union Nationale*, and the *Bloc* with equal violence.

On the eve of the long-awaited Allied invasion of Europe, French Canada was in an agitated state. Senator Athanase David's proposal in the Senate that a common history textbook be used in all Canadian schools to promote national unity had aroused violent opposition from the nationalists in May.[144] The nationwide unfavorable publicity aroused by the incendiary fire which destroyed the new synagogue in Quebec in May had irritated Quebec, which considered that much less attention was given to a similar incident shortly afterwards in Toronto. There were streetfights in Montreal in May and June between servicemen and slacker 'zootsuiters,' which received unfavorable attention in the English-Canadian and American press. The Duplessis and *Bloc* forces were evoking anti-war and anti-conscription feeling in the rural districts, while urban labor was agitated by the international-*vs.*-syndicate struggle and by Communist and C.C.F. attempts to form a united labor political front. The Liberal government hastily passed several measures at the close of the session which were regarded as electoral ones: government loans to corporations or co-operatives to aid homebuilding, free textbooks for schools, an 18 per cent cut in Montreal electricity rates, and a prospective cut in the cost of chemical fertilizers.

The news of the Normandy landings burst suddenly upon this troubled scene. After Mackenzie King's announcement of the invasion in the federal House, parliament sang the 'Marseillaise' at the suggestion of Maurice Lalonde (Labelle). *Le Canada* hailed the incident 'as an inspired gesture which once again before the whole world affirms the bi-ethnic character of Canada, and which moreover identifies, with an enthusiasm equal to that of all other parts of the Dominion, the Province of Quebec, from which come the majority of French-speaking members, with the glorious volunteers who have been sent as her representatives at the front.' Minister of Fisheries Ernest Bertrand was the first to speak to the people of France by radio in the name of Canada, urging the Resistance forces to follow the instructions sent them by the Allied High Command, and assuring his listeners of the love for France felt by the French Canadians who formed part of the invading armies. Louis St. Laurent spoke of 'the deep emotion that this dawn of June 6 has brought to each household in Canada—especially in our homes of the Province of Quebec where we speak your language and where everything that is French is so dear and familiar to us. As an answer to the misery of the fatal days of June 1940 there rises the exaltation of this daybreak of June 1944.'

Senators David and Bouchard, Valmore Bienvenue, and Major René Garneau were others who broadcast to France on this occasion. Edmond Turcotte of *Le Canada* evoked Normandy, the birthplace of many founders of French Canada. *Le Soleil* hailed the beginning of the campaign of France: 'May it fulfil our dearest wishes, make us forget the disaster of 1940.' *La Patrie* declared that the invaders were not 'coming as conquerors but as liberators' and would be welcomed by an Allied army of civilians, the Résistance. *L'Evénement-Journal* said: 'The French people are rising with a single impulse and rejoicing in the sweetness of their coming liberation. In this decisive hour when the fate of freedom is being sealed, they have heard the moving appeal of that great patriot Charles De Gaulle, who for four long years has embodied the France which fights, which resists, the France which never gives in.' *L'Action Catholique* published Cardinal Villeneuve's message asking for the prayers of the French-Canadian people, and observed that the secret launching of the invasion indicated that the Allies had carried on the war of nerves with the same ability as the Nazis at the beginning of the war. *Le Devoir* and *Le Droit* remained silent, with the former observing: 'The events taking place in Europe must not make us lose sight of what is going on at home.' *Le Canada*, the Liberal organ which under the aggressive editorship of Edmond Turcotte rarely missed an opportunity to attack the nationalists, commented thus on *Le Devoir's* observation:

On the day when the most powerful armies that free men ever assembled in the history of the world for the defence of their liberty were swinging into action for the liberation of the principal home of Western civilization, a continent completely enslaved by a band of criminals without faith or morals, the editor-in-chief of *Le Devoir* is concerned with two Acadian weeklies, the fate of which is no doubt interesting, but nonetheless somewhat less interesting than the fate of the civilized world for several generations to come.[145]

As in 1917, French Canada had reached the crucial stage of a world conflict in a state of mind increasingly pre-occupied with its own domestic concerns, which led it to show a shocking disregard for what English Canadians, Americans, Britishers, and Frenchmen regarded as the vital struggle for the survival of their common way of life. In its revolt against wartime propaganda and against major alterations in its way of life imposed by Ottawa, French Canada discounted the common danger. The prevailing sense of selfish security was expressed by an old *habitant*, reputed to have the traditional stocking well-filled with savings, who when asked by a war bond salesman how he would like to have the Germans running his village, violating his women, and corrupting his children, replied: 'I wouldn't. I'd vote against them.' Cut off by the war from Rome and Paris, in 1944 French Canada was more isolationist than ever. It was in a disgruntled and uncooperative mood as a result of the brickbats which had come its way for not doing more for the war effort than it had, which in its own eyes was already too much. It was deeply involved in a rapid if relatively peaceful social revolution which had shaken the framework of its society and upset its traditional way of life. It was in no state of mind to respond enthusiastically to the stepped-up war program which English Canadians soon came to demand in a mood of emotional hysteria created by the first heavy losses suffered by the Canadian Army overseas. Once more the conscription question opened a deep rift between the people of Canada, and blighted the limited national unity which had been attained through the common sacrifices of men and women of both stocks.

Notes

1 The Casa Italiano in Montreal served as a center for propaganda among both French-Canadians and the considerable Italian population of the city. Though after 1939 the conservative French-Canadian sympathy for Mussolini tended to transfer itself to Franco, it was by no means dead. The German State Railways office in Montreal was an unofficial Nazi propaganda center, and paid subsidies to some ultranationalist publications. Some of the nationalist leaders accompanied their German paymasters to Mexico when war came in 1939. On the eve of the conflict, a German firm sought to buy Anticosti Island, in the

mouth of the St. Lawrence, which would have provided an excellent base for the submarine campaign subsequently waged in those waters. Colin Ross, *Zwischen USA und dem Pol* (Leipzig, 1934), a general study of Canada emphasizing the French-Canadian and New Canadian problems, is interesting for the light it sheds on Nazi policy towards Canada.

[2] Florent Lefevbre, *The French-Canadian Press and the War* (Toronto, 1940), 1–8.

[3] *Ibid.*

[4] *Canada, Commons Debates 1939, Special War Session*, 8 Sept., 28.

[5] *Proceedings and Orders in Council passed under the authority of the War Measures Act* (Ottawa, 1940), I, 19–20.

[6] *Montreal Gazette*, 2 Sept. 1939.

[7] *Ibid.*, 4 Sept. 1939.

[8] R. M. Dawson, *Canada in World Affairs: 1939–41* (Toronto, 1943), 8.

[9] *Commons Debates 1939*, 7 Sept., 1.

[10] *Ibid.*, 8 Sept., 12–41, 6.

[11] *Ibid.*, 12.

[12] Dawson, 285–6. For the first time the King declared war for Canada 'by and with the advice of Our Privy Council for Canada.'

[13] *Montreal Gazette*, 8 July 1941.

[14] *Commons 1939*, 8 Sept., 25.

[15] *Ibid.*, 36.

[16] *Ibid.*, 66.

[17] *Ibid.*, 67.

[18] *Ibid.*, 6.

[19] *Ibid.*, 68.

[20] *Ibid.*, 68–9.

[21] *Ibid.*, 69.

[22] *Ibid.*, 70–1.

[23] *Ibid.*, 82, 88.

[24] Lefevbre, 9–13.

[25] *Ibid.*, 13–14.

[26] *Ibid.*, 18.

[27] *Ibid.*, 19.

[28] *Ibid.*, 18–19.

[29] *Ibid.*, 20–1.

[30] *Ibid.*, 21.

[31] *Ibid.*, 21–2.

[32] *Ibid.*, 23.

[33] *Ibid.*, 25.

[34] *Ibid.*, 24–7.

[35] *Ibid.*, 27–8.

[36] *Ibid.*, 29.

[37] *Ibid.*, 27, 28–9.

[38] *Ibid.*, 31–2.

[39] *Ibid.*, 32–5.

[40] *L'Action nat.*, XIV (sept. 1939), 1, 3.

[41] *Ibid.*, 81–3.

[42] *Ibid.*, XIV (oct. 1939), II, 131–2.

[43] *Ibid.*, 141–2.

[44] Dawson, 17.

[45] *Ibid.*

[46] R. Rumilly, *L'Autonomie provinciale* (Montréal, 1948), 120; *Le Soleil*, 2 oct. 1939.

[47] Lefevbre, 36.

[48] *Le Devoir*, 4 nov. 1939.

[49] E. Armstrong, *French-Canadian Opinion on the War* (Toronto, 1942), 6.
[50] W. Churchill, *Blood, Sweat and Tears* (New York, 1941), 297.
[51] Armstrong, 7.
[52] *Ibid.*, 9.
[53] *Ibid.*
[54] Dawson, 41; *Montreal Gazette*, 24 June 1940.
[55] *Ibid.*, 289, text of National Resources Mobilization Act, 1940.
[56] Armstrong, 16.
[57] *Ibid.*, 18.
[58] *Ibid.*, 17–18.
[59] *Ibid.*, 16.
[60] *Montreal Gazette*, 3, 16 August 1940.
[61] Armstrong, 18–19.
[62] *Ibid.*, 19.
[63] *Ibid.*, 20.
[64] *Ibid.*, 22.
[65] *Montreal Herald*, 30 June 1941, 'The Story of French Canada's War Effort.'
[66] Armstrong, 10–13.
[67] *Ibid.*, 13.
[68] G. Vanier, *Paroles de Guerre* (Montréal, 1944), 15.
[69] Dawson, 310–1, text of Ogdensburg Agreement, 18 Aug. 1941.
[70] Armstrong, 23–4.
[71] Dawson, 321–12, text of Hyde Park Declaration, April 20, 1941.
[72] *L'Act. nat.*, XVII (juin 1941), VI, 441–2.
[73] *Ibid.*, 453–4.
[74] *Ibid.*, 455–72.
[75] *Ibid.*, 473–80.
[76] *Ibid.*, 481–99.
[77] *Ibid.*, 500–7.
[78] *Ibid.*, 508–21.
[79] *Ibid.*, 521–33.
[80] *Ibid.*, 534–7.
[81] A. Godbout, *Canadian Unity* (Québec, 1940).
[82] *Montreal Gazette*, 6 June 1940.
[83] *Ibid.*, 23 Nov. 1940.
[84] *Ibid.*, 10 Feb. 1941.
[85] *Ibid.*, 17 April 1941.
[86] Armstrong, 29–30.
[87] *Commons Debates 1941*, 7 May, III, 2637–43.
[88] *Ibid.*, III, 2651–2; Armstrong, 34–5.
[89] Armstrong, 39.
[90] *Report of the Royal Commission appointed under Order in Council P.C.* 411 . . . (Ottawa, 1946).
[91] A. Shea & E. Estorick, *Canada & the Shortwave War* (Toronto, 1942), 14–16.
[92] L. Francoeur, *La Situation Ce Soir*, 1–10 (Montréal, 1941).
[93] *Le Canada Parle à la France* (Montréal, 1944).
[94] M. Raymond, *Politique en ligne droite* (Montréal, 1943), 183.
[95] *Ibid.*, 192.
[96] *Ibid.*, 194.
[97] *The Plebiscite Question* (Ottawa, 1942).
[98] *La Question du plébiscite* (Ottawa, 1942).
[99] *Canadian Forum* (June 1942), F. R. Scott, 'Quebec & the Plebiscite Vote.'
[100] *Winnipeg Free Press*, 24 May 1948, G. Dexter, 'The Colonel.' See *Commons 1942*, June 23, IV, 3553.
[101] *Commons 1942*, June 10, 3236.

[102] Dawson, 95–6. Cardin's letter of resignation & King's reply, *Commons 1942*, May 11, 2280.

[103] Raymond, 209.

[104] *Ibid.*, 213–16.

[105] *Commons 1942*, July 7, IV, 3994.

[106] Abbé A. Maheux, *Pourquoi Sommes-nous Divisés?* (Montréal, 1943).

[107] See note 99.

[108] E. Vaillancourt, *Le Canada et les Nations Unies* (Montréal, 1942).

[109] *Le Devoir*, 29 avril 1943.

[110] *Montreal Gazette*, 17 April 1943.

[111] *Le Devoir*, 20 mai 1943.

[112] Raymond, 225–31.

[113] *Ibid.*, 236.

[114] F. Rose, *Hitler's Fifth Column in Quebec* (Toronto, 1942).

[115] *Life*, 19 Oct. 1942.

[116] *L'Action Catholique*, 25 mai 1943.

[117] *Ibid.*, 9 juin 1943.

[118] *Montreal Daily Star*, 24 June 1943.

[119] S. Ryerson, *French Canada* (Toronto, 1943), 2–4.

[120] *Montreal Gazette*, 10 May 1943.

[121] *Le Canada*, 11 mai; *Le Soleil*, 12 mai; *Le Devoir*, 26 mai, 19 juin 1943.

[122] *Le Canada*, 17 juillet 1943.

[123] *Le Devoir*, 19 juin 1943, 'Depuis bientôt quatre ans.'

[124] *Le Soleil*, 9 sept. 1943.

[125] *Press Information Bureau*, I, 5.

[126] *Ibid.*, I, 1.

[127] *Ibid.*, I, 6.

[128] R. Blanchard, *L'Est du Canada Français* (Montréal, 1935), II, 61–155; Abbé V. Tremblay, *Histoire du Saguenay* (Chicoutimi, 1938). For wartime labor troubles, see E. Laurent, *Une enquête au pays d'aluminium* (Québec, 1943).

[129] *PIB*, I, 5.

[130] *Le Devoir*, 26 mai, 12 juin 1943.

[131] E. Hughes, *French Canada in Transition* (Chicago, 1944), 217–18.

[132] *PIB*, I, 12.

[133] *Ibid.*, I, 11.

[134] *Ibid.*, I, 13.

[135] *Canadian Register*, 17 Oct. 1943; *Le Devoir*, 20 oct. 1943; *L'Action Catholique*, 21 oct. 1943.

[136] *PIB*, I, 42.

[137] *Commons 1944*, 27 Jan., I, 1.

[138] *Ibid.*, 28 Jan., 12–14.

[139] *Maclean's Magazine* (1 Jan. 1944), 'What does the Bloc Populaire Stand For?'

[140] *Le Bloc*, I (12 fév. 1944), 1.

[141] *PIB*, I, 51.

[142] *Ibid.*, I, 67.

[143] *Ibid.*, I, 75.

[144] *Senate Debates 1944*, 4 May, 147–9.

[145] *PIB*, I, 80.

CHAPTER XVI

THE REINFORCEMENT CRISIS AND ITS AFTERMATH

(1944–5)

THE BEGINNING of the Battle of Europe, with the first heavy losses in the Canadian Army beyond those suffered at Dieppe, opened a rift between English and French Canadians which in the end came perilously near splitting Canada apart on the very eve of victory, after five years of war. Once more, as in 1917, the two main peoples of Canada were opposed by the question of conscription, which meant equality of sacrifice to English Canadians and coercion to serve British and American ends at Canada's cost to the French. All the latent irritations, grievances, and bitterness bred by Canada's effort to maintain a large Army, Navy, and Air Force, as well as to serve as a munition factory, granary, and 'airdrome of democracy,' with a population of only 12,000,000,[1] found expression in the summer and fall of 1944 as the ethnic tension steadily mounted.

I

After the first outburst of enthusiasm at the Normandy landings French Canada's differences with its English-speaking neighbors were once more accentuated. Symptomatic of the long suppressed ill feeling were the street brawls in Montreal between servicemen and 'zoot-suiters.' English Canadians were convinced that the troublemakers were French-Canadian draft-dodgers, who taunted English volunteers, while French Canadians claimed that 'the zoot-suiters are not generally recruited from among French Canadians' and that 'the majority of men in uniform encountered on the streets of Montreal are French-speaking.' The *Montreal Herald* spoke of the threat of mob rule and condemned the lawlessness and racial feeling made evident by the clashes. The incidents produced unfavorable comment in the New York *Newsweek*, and, as always, French-Canadian spokesmen rallied to defend their province from unfavorable outside comment. Justice Minister St. Laurent stated in the House at Ottawa that the Mounted Police were investigating the clashes and that the matter was in no sense a question of racial conflict. Roger Duhamel, president of the Saint-Jean-Baptiste Society of

Montreal, promptly contradicted him in *La Patrie*, but deplored the subsequent clashes between English and French school children with the observation that 'civilized people should have other methods for finding a common ground for their different viewpoints.' In fact, the disturbances seem to have been a natural result of the upsetting social effects of the war upon Montreal's cosmopolitan population.[2]

The Montreal disturbances ceased, but racial feeling had been aroused by them and it continued to grow, particularly among English Canadians as the Canadian forces suffered increasingly heavy losses in Europe. It was generally believed that these losses fell more heavily upon English Canada with its high proportion of volunteers and its small families than upon French Canada. It was impossible to know the facts under the government's policy of avoiding ethnic breakdowns of enlistment figures, and unfounded suspicion probably created a worse atmosphere than the facts would have done.

French Canada's much misunderstood attitude towards France was also once more in question. While no French paper with the exception of *Le Canada* showed as much enthusiasm for the prospective liberation of France as the English press, there was much deploring in the French press of the tension between the Anglo-American high command and the De Gaullist Committee of National Liberation, and relief was felt at the announcement that De Gaulle would visit Washington. *Montréal-Matin*, which with *Le Soleil* and the other Nicol papers had often criticized the State Department, hailed this development with relief and urged that 'a very strong friendship between France and America is indispensable to the maintenance of peace.'[3] Most of the Quebec press made much of the enthusiasm of the liberated people of France for De Gaulle, and deplored American fears of an alliance between Communist Resistance groups in France and Soviet Russia. But *Le Devoir* still failed to smile upon the De Gaullists, and Roger Duhamel in *La Patrie* denounced their 'intransigent' policy. *L'Action Catholique*, however, which had been Pétainist after the fall of France, declared that 'the Algiers group is that most representative of the nation' and urged recognition of the provisional government by London and Washington. For once *L'Action* made common cause with the *Montreal Gazette* and *Le Canada*, both of which came out for recognition of the De Gaullists. Though there had been a brief brush between the French clerical press and the English papers on the eve of the Allied entry into Rome, over the Pope's appeal to the world for a just peace rather than a rigid adherence to the program of 'unconditional surrender,' a June 14 Gallup poll showed that 62 per cent of the French Canadians favored unconditional surrender rather than immediate negotiations for peace with Germany. The liberation of Italy and the establishment of a democratic government there was hailed by *Le Canada*, which had never shared the sympathy felt for Mussolini by French-Canadian nationalists.[4]

2

It was into this troubled atmosphere that Senator T.-D. Bouchard, long a pillar of the Liberal Party in Quebec, dropped a bombshell with his maiden speech in the Senate on June 21, in support of Athanase David's motion for the adoption of a common textbook of Canadian history in the schools of all the provinces. Bouchard opened his speech in French, pointing out that one of the gaps in English-Canadian texts was the failure to note that French was an official language in both the federal and Quebec parliaments. He wished to bring out this fact and to pay tribute to his mother tongue, but he had no desire to impose the study of French upon English Canadians. He declared that 'for their own economic development French-speaking Canadians need to learn a second language more than English-speaking Canadians do,' since English was spoken by 150,000,000 people in North America and French by only 5,000,000.

Then Bouchard repeated his opening remarks and continued his speech in English, since 'it is becoming to speak the language understood by all,' and since he believed that 'speech was given to men to enable them to communicate their ideas to other men rather than to glorify the little corner of the earth where they happened by chance to be born . . . speech is simply the vehicle of thought.' He deplored the fact that he spoke English poorly, because Quebec's teachers had translated Bishop Laflèche's injunction to 'speak English, but speak it badly' into the maxim 'Teach English, but teach it badly.' He strongly supported the basic aim of the David motion—the furthering of Canadian unity—and speculated as to whether all Canadians were as anxious for unity as members of parliament. As a self-made man of no scholarship, he disclaimed any competence to judge the textbooks used in the English provinces, and declared his belief that it would be best for the citizens of each province to criticize the weaknesses of their own teaching of Canadian history.

Then, after deploring the results of history teaching in Quebec, Bouchard launched his bomb, which shattered the customary calm of the Senate and made him a national figure overnight:

> It is by exposing in the open what actually exists in my province, by showing our true history in the making which proceeds from the false history that the past and present generations have been taught in our own schools, that I shall show how urgent it is to make a radical change

in this teaching. Canadian history should not serve as a tool of subversive propaganda in the hands of those who are aiming to disrupt Confederation and overthrow our form of democratic government.

Bouchard declared that he would document his charges by citing excerpts from Quebec history textbooks and by describing the 'subversive tendencies . . . created by the way in which Canadian history is taught in our public schools.' Once more he urged that 'laymen in history,' such as himself, 'should restrict themselves to deploring the deficiencies of history teaching in their own lingual realm.' He believed that the David resolution would help to build up a truly Canadian mentality, since 'a manual of basic facts accepted by each province would necessarily smooth the road to good understanding between us all.' But opposed to the modern and North American mentality of those who favored mutual understanding, despite differences of origin and creed, was the old clannish European mentality of those who wanted 'to rebuild in our country one of the small provincial kingdoms we had in France in days of yore,' while others with a colonial complex refused to recognize that Canada had become a true nation. He admitted that there were major sources of friction between Canadians of French and English descent: 'Differences of religion and language are, though they should not be, fertile fields where the sowers of the seeds of discord work day and night, but mostly in the dark,' forgetting the Christian injunction of brotherhood and the French motto of the British coat of arms.

History teaching was one of the main causes of these frictions, and Bouchard declared that since infancy he had been taught that 'everything the French Canadian has to suffer came from the fact that he was of French and Catholic descent.' Only when he went into business did he learn that 'Canadians of English descent were not all cloven-footed and did not all wear horns, but on the contrary entertained the very same good sentiments as did we of French descent.' From the Christian Brothers' elementary text in Canadian history he cited excerpts such as the following: 'The end pursued by the policy of England in the early times of its administration in Canada was to anglicize the French-Canadian nation, to rob it of its religion, of its language and of its national customs.' Bouchard found such teaching 'intended to prejudice young minds against our compatriots of a different tongue and creed.' He denounced it as 'un-Canadian and even un-Christian,' with the observation that 'the founder of Christianity has never preached that one man should rise against another because of differences of race and language.'

Then Bouchard declared that those who taught Canadian history along such lines 'had now attained their ends to such an extent as to imperil our national peace.' There were some French Canadians like himself who thought that the 'time has come—let us pray God that even now it is not too late—to stop a subversive propaganda, intensified by the state of war which has existed for over four years, which tends to bring us before long to mob rule and perhaps to civil war.' He refused to accept the view of those of higher position that it was better to shut one's eyes to such activities, or to lose his belief that 'a large majority of my compatriots love Canada as it is, constitutionally and otherwise, and do not want any change in their allegiance.' He blamed false history teaching for inspiring the nationalist desire for independence, since only the wrongs and none of the advantages of being under British government were stressed. The secessionists had called the forces of religion, race, and greed to their aid in attempting to win the masses to their dream of a 'Catholic, French, and corporative' state in which 'the Catholic and French toiler would be master of his own religious, social, and economic destinies.'

This revolutionary movement was fostered by a secret society, the *Ordre de Jacques Cartier*, with headquarters in Ottawa, which had been founded about 1928 'with the blessing of the Catholic and French clergy,' despite the Church's ban on secret societies:

Prominent French Canadians were induced to join, the avowed practical end of the society being not revolution, but to permit French Canadians to have their fair share of the jobs in the public service. Later on, when the Jacques Cartier Order decided to expand beyond the capital, the strength of the order was to be applied to restraining what was called foreign investment in local trades, when these trades did not belong to French Canadians. Anti-semitism was also called in to aid in the recruiting of members. Finally, the officers of the highest degree gave, in the utmost secrecy, the watchword to invade the political field and to control patriotic societies, governments, and public administrations of every sort.

The invitation has been well received, and nearly all the St. Jean Baptiste societies, Catholic syndicates, city school commissions, municipal councils, and junior boards of trade are under the direct influence of this secret order. It is due to its secret organization that *L'Union Nationale* went to power in 1936, to give us the poorest and most abusive government in the history of the province . . .

This secret society owns its public and secret newspapers. *La Boussole* is the open organ. *L'Emerillon* is the secret publication.

Bouchard considered that this secret society would not have been tolerated if the teaching of Canadian history in the Quebec schools had not 'prepared our population to receive favorably anything tending to dissociate us from our English fellow-citizens.' He declared his firm belief that at least 75 per cent of the 18,000 members were 'good British citizens who do not suspect where they are being pushed by the fanatics of every description who are the real leaders . . . Imagine the harm that can be done by these active agents of destruction in a more or less passive population such as the one living in my province.' He quoted from a September-October 1937 number of *L'Emerillon*:

> Let us note the interlinking of our groups which threatens to shut in the center of Ontario, and in consequence to choke those who dread, and rightly, our 'French domination' in a more or less near future. Our French masses of the north especially will finally weigh so heavily upon the populations of the center and south of the old Upper Canada that on each side we shall perhaps think of secession, to the end of creating a new province which will be French by a great majority.

Not only did the secret order dream of creating a new French province, but it also proposed to set up an independent Catholic and French state, as the rise of European totalitarianism in the 1930's gave 'a new impetus to that backward movement tending to bring us back to the social and economic status of the Middle Ages.'

It was not only hot-headed young men seeking public recognition who epoused such ideas. Mgr. Mozzoni, chargé d'affaires of the Apostolic Delegation in Canada, had made the following declaration at the 1937 Sémaine Sociale at Saint-Hyacinthe:

> The politicians can talk about the greatness and prosperity of the country under such and such a form of government; this concerns us but indirectly. What we do want, and what we shall work to attain by all our means, is a state completely Catholic, because such a country only can represent the ideal of human progress, and because a Catholic people has the right and duty to organize itself socially and politically according to the tenets of its faith.

Bouchard professed his belief in freedom of thought and of religion, but asserted that the great majority of the French Canadians 'are fully contented with their present governmental institutions and do not ask for a change.' He wanted peace and harmony between people of different origins, and only cited these words to show that 'there is unrest not only among the masses . . . but also among the upper classes, and that we have to keep our eyes opened on the undercurrents producing such apparent eddies on the surface of the troubled waters of our national life.'

The situation had gone from bad to worse since 1937: 'More and more young men have left school with that deformation of the mind proceeding from the bad teaching of Canadian history, and the underground propaganda has increased in intensity.' Calling the *Union Nationale* administration of 1936–9 the 'first governmental offspring of the Jacques Cartier Order,' Bouchard deplored its measures shortening the period of English tuition and giving precedence to the French version of the Quebec statutes. He described his personal experience of the campaign against teaching English, which he blamed on members of the clergy. He declared that 'Preventing French Canadians from learning English by any means, to their utmost detriment, is part of the underground work of our isolationists. They do not want us to meet English Canadians, naturally, because when you talk to somebody preventions (*sic*) inspired by propaganda disappear.'

Bouchard cited instructions of the Jacques Cartier Order to infiltrate patriotic and social organizations and to win leadership in them, so that *bonne-entente* policies might be barred; to avoid adopting English methods in business, and anglicization in general. He described the chain of command whereby the watchwords from the supreme council in Ottawa were handed down through the ranks without question. He denounced the recent raising of the '*Drapeau de Carillon*,' favored by the Order, over the new buildings of the Université de Montreal:

> Three weeks ago, the war being in full swing, the Order also succeeded in persuading the heads of the Montreal University to consecrate this flag as the real Labarum of the non-existing French-Canadian Catholic state by raising it to the mast of the $10,000,000 building erected with government money, that is, money belonging not only to those favoring the secession of our province, but mainly to Canadians true to their political system, and the British Commonwealth of Nations.
>
> This was done on the top of the mountain overlooking the largest city in Canada, in the presence of thousands upon thousands of citizens brought there by the blessing, by an eminent Catholic priest, of the old flag of Louis XV as the national flag of Canadians of French descent. Evidently there are lots of people who play with fire without knowing it.

He deplored the storm of abuse lavished on Abbé Maheux by separatists and isolationists: 'That most respectable priest was banned as a traitor to the race because he spoke the truth.' He denounced the *Jeunes Laurentiens* as 'one of the most active and open organization of the Jacques Cartier Order,' and cited its president's statement in May: 'This revolution that we want will be practical, efficient, calm, and good, because it calls for pure, fundamentally French and Catholic men. It is the revolution of liberated Spain, of organized Portugal, of France under Pétain.'

It seemed obvious to Bouchard that 'a wrong teaching of Canadian history in our province has already done nearly all the harm that could be desired by those who are in favor of disunion in this country between peoples of different languages and creeds.' He charged that 'their ultimate aim is not only to disunite the people on lingual and religious matters, but also to disrupt Confederation, to abandon the more human North American concept of a large nation composed of people of different religious beliefs and racial origins, and to revert to the old European concept of smaller nations of the same religious and racial descent.' The field was already well prepared for an attack on Canadian political institutions. The old Liberal-Conservative Party in Quebec had been destroyed by 'our hidden Fascists.' The *Bloc Populaire* was 'the open political tool of the Jacques Cartier Order.' Bouchard feared that 'if our liberty-loving people do not open their eyes in good time, they will see to what extent underground work has undermined our free institutions.'

Bouchard anticipated criticism for having frankly given his views on the teaching of Canadian history in the Quebec schools and for showing 'what is going on behind the curtain, where the actors are preparing what many believe will be a farce, but which to my mind will eventually turn out to be a national tragedy.' But he preferred to face the coming storm, and not to be caught unaware by it. He made a final plea for the David motion, and expressed the hope that if provincial autonomy prevented official action, that some progressive association would see to it that 'everything tending to disunite the people of this country shall be eliminated from the textbooks of Canadian history and that only the real and proven facts shall be taught to our younger generation.' His closing words were notable:

> We have to build our new generations along different lines from those that have prevailed up to now, and, speaking for my province, I hope the day will come when English and French citizens will realize that they have everything to gain by being at least good neighbors, even if they cannot come up to the evangelical perfection of being good brothers. I must confess that I should like to have painted another picture of the situation in Quebec; but I thought it my duty to present the real situation, being convinced that it has now become dangerous to flatter ourselves regarding things that do not exist. History, past and present, has taught me the hardships of common people during civil wars and revolutions, and it is to preserve my fellow-citizens from their menace that I warn them not to heed the insidious appeals of reactionaries and cheap politicians. Our political institutions and our association with the other nations of the Commonwealth have given us internal peace and prosperity. Let us side with those who are willing to make any sacrifice to preserve them in their integrity. There we shall find safety and happiness [5]

3

Bouchard's speech, made on the same day as a Eucharistic Congress opened in his native town of Saint-Hyacinthe and three days before the national holiday of French Canada, roused such a storm as Canada had not known since the time of the Guibord affair. Maurice Duplessis, leader of the *Union Nationale* which Bouchard had fought in and out of provincial office, on the following day issued a statement calling the speech 'despicable and reprehensible,' denouncing Bouchard's 'anti-Canadian and anti-clerical tendencies,' and demanding his immediate removal from his new office as head of the Quebec Hydro:

It would be inconceivable and intolerable that the government of the Province of Quebec should keep in its employ, particularly in an important post, a public man who knowingly and maliciously becomes guilty of such treason and such vile calumnies. The immense majority of the population of the province demands insistently the immediate destitution of this unworthy politician.

Premier Godbout, long Bouchard's political colleague, repudiated the speech immediately in these terms: 'I consider these accusations as absolutely unjustifiable and damaging, and I affirm that they represent in no way the opinion of a single member of the provincial government.'

Louis St. Laurent, federal leader of the Quebec Liberals, criticized Bouchard's violence and his loose generalizations, and minimized the importance of the Order of Jacques Cartier, which he said represented one-tenth to one-half of one per cent of the population. He remarked that Bouchard was one of those who believed that a spade should be called a spade, but in the excitement of speaking was sometimes led to call it a steam-shovel or a bull-dozer. Maxime Raymond, leader of the *Bloc Populaire*, denounced the speech as a 'tissue of falsities and calumnies,' 'the despicable act of one who denies and tramples upon all that which has permitted his compatriots to survive and to conserve their language and their faith.' He declared that Bouchard was not worthy of the posts of trust which he occupied. Frédéric Dorion referred in the House to 'this Quebec Quisling, who yesterday satisfied his Masonic hatred against the clergy and religious institutions of Quebec by railing for nearly an hour at those he calls his fellow Catholics and fellow-citizens,' and expressed his belief that Bouchard would be forced to resign from the presidency of the Quebec Hydro. Bouchard was also repudiated by his fellow senators from Quebec. P.-A. Choquette, a stormy petrel of Liberalism in an earlier day, denounced the speech as that of 'a dishonest man or a mad man,' and called upon the Godbout government to oust Bouchard from the Quebec Hydro unless it wished to suffer the consequences in the elections. Cyrille Vaillancourt observed that a decent bird does not dirty its own nest, while the Conservative Thomas Chapais, at a loss to understand

Bouchard's action, referred to it as 'a bad deed which can take a tragic turn.'

Quebec at large, as always when under attack, made a common front against Bouchard. The flood of protests which poured in upon the provincial government, demanding repudiation of Bouchard, was overpowering. The officers of Saint-Jean-Baptiste societies, Catholic syndicates, school commissions, municipal councils, and the junior chambers of commerce denounced Bouchard's charges and demanded his ousting from the Hydro with a singular unanimity which suggested that these bodies were in fact under the orders of the Order of Jacques Cartier, as he had charged. But Quebec's indignation at public attacks upon its clergy and the washing at Ottawa of its dirty linen might have been responsible for the tidal wave of protest. Premier Godbout, a former seminarian as well as the leader of a government which had to face the electorate within a few weeks, bowed to the storm.

In a press conference on June 23 Bouchard refused to withdraw his charges, called for proofs rather than insults from those who denied them, and replied to the charge of anti-clericalism made by Duplessis and others with the observation that he hoped that the people of Quebec would soon realize that 'clericalism is the corruption of religion, as nationalism is the rotting of patriotism.' Of Godbout's statement he observed: 'Mr. Godbout is a man of good faith and if he has formed the opinion which he expressed, it is simply because he has not the information which I possess.' An hour later the radio and press services announced that the provincial government had relieved Bouchard of his duties as president of the Hydro by order-in-council, after a brief cabinet session. Informed personally by Premier Godbout of this action, which the premier announced to the press without comment, Bouchard told newspapermen: 'I am satisfied with the turn of events . . . The circumstances show clearly and definitely to what point these people of the Order of Jacques Cartier have influence . . . The fight has only begun.'

On the following morning Bouchard wired Bishop Douville of Saint-Hyacinthe that he would be unable to be present in his role as mayor at the Eucharistic Congress. That evening Cardinal Villeneuve, addressing the 75,000 people gathered for the Congress, made the following statement:

> History has its rights. A shadow was necessary in this resplendent picture which your city offers in these days in which, beside an admirable religious feeling, an old current of anti-clericalism, sometimes open, sometimes latent, betrays itself. And in sharing this evening the piety and pride of the diocese of Saint-Hyacinthe, I feel it is my duty, as one of the spiritual leaders of French Canada, to voice here a solemn protest. Events command it, and you yourselves implore it.

A public man, whom I need not name, has recently before the highest body of the country uttered words as unfair and injurious to our province of Quebec as they are thoughtless and unfounded. They cannot be explained, truly, coming from a man who preaches straightforwardness and justice, and whom for my part I have always tried to understand and interpret with good will. I leave it to others to refute his political and racial accusations. But I openly denounce his insinuations against the Church and the clergy. The words he used carry exactly the same sound and reveal the same corrosive fanaticism as those of another sower of discord whom the great majority of our separated brethren denounce with humiliation. Some time ago, in the House of Commons, the Right Honorable Prime Minister of Canada did not believe it necessary to hide his scorn for such fomenters of national disunity, whom only the grossest ignorance or hereditary madness can excuse. But in the present case the fact that the unfortunate diatribe was made by one of her own sons is what still more enrages and particularly humiliates the people of our province, and with them all those across Canada who share the same blood, the same faith, and the same traditions of Canadian probity and fidelity.

Public opinion will judge this challenge to the national conscience as is fitting.

As for me, I shall avoid committing the episcopate of this province to the movements that our insulter has so little honestly mixed up, in order better to throw his poison. But I ought to reprove publicly this outrage to all that the French-Canadian people holds most dear: its legitimate religious, social, and political aspirations; the authority and mission of its bishops, who are also directly responsible for public education; and finally the teaching of the Sovereign Pontiff and of his very numerous representatives among us. For it is by an unintelligent, not to say perfidious interpretation of the discourse of the secretary of the Apostolic Delegation pronounced in this city in 1937, at the fifteenth session of the Sémaines Sociales, that the orator who at this moment raises such general indignation has wished to throw doubts on the loyalty and diplomatic reserve of this prelate. One can see in the text that in speaking of the integrally Catholic State, the worthy preacher only sought to express the wish that a social doctrine integrally inspired by the Pontifical teachings should be established among us. And who could take umbrage at it, among those who believe in the sincerity and depth of our religious convictions?

And then of what crime must he not accuse the Sovereign Pontiff and the Catholic hierarchy, who wish wholeheartedly that the entire universe become Catholic and under the mandate of Jesus Christ work alertly to that end?

No, truly one is astonished at so much confusion of ideas, so great ignorance about the affirmed facts, and alas so much bitterness in style and word, under cover of independence and high politics.

In the name of my venerated colleagues here present, in the name, I am sure, of all the Catholic hierarchy of the country, in the name of the people that we love and guide, I deny such unworthy denunciations, and

I openly affirm that none of those who follow the teaching of the Church and are faithful to true French-Canadian traditions is no more a danger to Canada than a divisive factor, unlike others who, alas, ignore it.

Repudiated by the highest official of his province and by the highest religious authority, Bouchard issued a statement on Sunday to the press that 'lions are no longer fed upon the flesh of religious reformers, but those who ask only that they be allowed their freedom of opinion on a purely political matter are turned out to die of hunger.' He regretted that Godbout had 'thought it necessary to become the tool of those who dominate our province by exploiting popular prejudice,' but urged support of his government, 'The most progressive by far that we have had since Confederation.' He added: 'It would be national suicide to replace it by the former Duplessis administration or by a reactionary government such as the *Bloc Populaire*.'

Of all the hundred-odd statements[6] from persons of note on the Bouchard speech which appeared in the French press, only two did not denounce him. True to his nineteenth century liberalism Senator Chapais subsequently observed: 'The speech of M. Bouchard is open to criticism, like any other speech delivered in Parliament. Up to a certain point this speech is regrettable, although it has in it certain justifiable elements.' Madame Constance Garneau, president of the League of Woman's Rights, stoutly defended Bouchard:

I should like very much to see an English Canadian denounce his own group in the same way that M. Bouchard has had the courage to do for his. For if we are not deceived, the same thing exists among our English speaking compatriots. As far as we are concerned, it did not befit an English Canadian to put his finger on the sore spot. I should be glad to hear of an English Canadian denouncing those who are anti-French.

The press reaction followed a curious pattern. *Le Devoir* at once reported the speech in full, and represented it as a national tragedy which would bring discredit upon French Canada. Louis-Philippe Roy, acting editor-in-chief of *L'Action Catholique* immediately denounced on the front page of his paper 'the vomitings of T.-D. Bouchard':

Associating himself with Pastor Shields, the Senator has repeated some of the former's hysterical calumnies at a moment of double psychological significance. In St. Hyacinthe, of which city M. Bouchard is still mayor, there is at present being held a great Eucharistic Congress at the opening of which presided His Excellency the Apostolic Delegate. In the Canadian Senate M. Bouchard attacks the Apostolic Delegation and all the Quebec clergy. This reminds us of French Freemasonry at the peak of its anti-Church outbursts under the Third Republic. On Saturday we celebrate the national holiday. Yesterday the Senator attacked our patriotic institutions . . . Could this be a coincidence? One thing is certain: our most fanatical adversaries could never have chosen a more strategic hour to attack us.

Roy went on to demand Bouchard's repudiation by the Liberal Party and his dismissal as president of the Hydro. *L'Action's* Ottawa correspondent, Lorenzo Paré, observed: 'For forty years T.-D. Bouchard has kept on swallowing his anti-clericalism, so that he would not be driven from public life by French Canadians. Yesterday, sure for the rest of his life of senatorial honors, Bouchard spilled forth his spleen, and took a terrible revenge against his compatriots.' And André Roy on the editorial page observed: 'Not content with slinging mud at his compatriots, M. Bouchard used the opportunity of his maiden speech to attack in a most irreverent way the Apostolic Delegation in the person of its secretary, Mgr. Mozzoni.' He added that Bouchard had long served the Liberal Party and done it much harm. If that party did not repudiate Bouchard immediately, it would be eternally ruined in the Catholic and French-Canadian province which it ruled.

The big independent dailies were hesitant in their first reactions, with *La Patrie* preserving a discreet silence and *La Presse* alluding editorially to the speech in a conciliatory way, although it printed many letters of protest. *Le Canada*, the official Liberal organ, kept silent. *Le Soleil* and the other papers of the Liberal Nicol chain published full news stories without editorial comment. *Le Nouvelliste* of Trois-Rivières, however, published on its editorial page *L'Action's* anti-Bouchard blast and the *Montreal Star's* editorial lauding the senator's courage in making the speech. After Godbout's repudiation of Bouchard, *La Presse* observed that the action was 'of a kind to reassure anxious minds and to satisfy the justly indignant French-Canadian and Catholic conscience.' *La Patrie* held that Godbout had given way to popular pressure because the country stood in need of unity among all men of goodwill, and added: 'The action of M. Bouchard could only serve to exaggerate the importance and influence of a society which, to say the least, is an obscure one concerning which nobody among us was much bothered, and to arouse among our English-speaking compatriots unjust suspicions.'

Because of the timing of the speech, the weeklies could not comment on it until the first wave of indignation had calmed down. But Bouchard's action was supported only by his own paper *Le Clairon*, Jean-Charles Harvey's *La Jour*, and *La Victoire*, the French Communist organ. Jean-Charles Harvey devoted two pages of *Le*

Jour to the incident, calling for free men to unite in defence of their threatened liberties. For him Bouchard was the victim of obscurantism and nationalization, and thus the incident aroused his zeal as an apostle of enlightenment and free enterprise: 'The Quebec Hydro, set up on the disastrous socialist principle, is experiencing the worst political interference that could be imagined . . . M. Bouchard is thrown overboard for a purely political reason.' André Bowman, in an article captioned 'The Munich of Quebec,' observed that Bouchard had been sacrificed to clericalism by Godbout as Benes had been sacrificed to fascism by Chamberlain. Emile-Charles Hamel suggested that the time had come for a new party:

> By seeing the Liberals becoming the servile tool of the forces of reaction, we are made to wish for a great party, moderately leftist, which would fight for democratic liberties and assure to us the free functioning of the political institutions which we have inherited from Great Britain, the free expansion of those talents of ours which we owe to France. The Bouchard case raises a question of principle going beyond the personalities and the facts at issue. It is freedom of conscience, freedom of speech, freedom of the press which are at stake. It is a question of discovering whether, because of the occult dictatorship of certain secret societies or certain groups working behind the scenes, a person in government employ can be removed from his post for having expressed ideas or written articles which are not contrary to the laws of our land.

The Communist *La Victoire* supported Bouchard and denounced the Order of Jacques Cartier, calling for an investigation by the minister of justice—a step also favored by the Tory *Montreal Gazette* and several labor unions. *La Victoire*, however, reproached the senator with not having made a distinction 'between the Catholic Church as a whole, and that not very numerous minority of members of the clergy who demean themselves by taking part in Fascist and subversive intrigues.' This valid point was obviously made in view of the special line of the Communist Party in Quebec at that moment, for the editorial went on to observe:

> The great majority of Catholics are opposed to Fascism and are working to bring about its destruction by the United Nations. It is by the united action of Catholics and non-Catholics that a powerful labor movement has been built up in Quebec, the driving force behind the social and economic reforms initiated by the Godbout government. It would be disastrous if controversies of a religious nature were to spread disunion among the democratic, liberal, and labor forces of French Canada.

Le Bloc devoted half its space to the Bouchard affair. While scarcely recognizing the existence of the Order of Jacques Cartier, it accused Bouchard, whom it called a foe of the clergy, of playing the game of enemies of the Church and of French Canada. *L'Action Nationale* denounced Bouchard as a 'public insulter,' and said he had excluded himself from his nationality. It rested its case on Cardinal Villeneuve's statement, but added: 'The revolution of which Bouchard speaks will be the revolt of all upright spirits against a disgraced regime, a peaceful and constitutional revolution, a democratic and Christian revolution. . . .'[7] *Le Progrès du Saguenay*, a clerical-nationalist weekly, defended the Order of Jacques Cartier: 'The enemy is not the Jacques Cartier Order which the Bouchards and the Harveys are denouncing; it is far more Freemasonry, and the senator from the Saint Lawrence Valley is perfectly aware of the fact.' Bouchard's own organ, *Le Clairon* of Saint-Hyacinthe, stressed the fact that the denials of his charges were not supported by facts. It maintained that the senator had not sought to attack the clergy as a whole, but certain facts could not be ignored: 'What is quite certain is that two members of the clergy are directors of the Order, since they themselves signed a document testifying to that effect; what is also incontestable is that each regional command or cell has a spiritual adviser generally belonging to the religious orders, religious communities, or to the secular clergy.'

There was a complete divergence in the attitudes of the English and the French press towards the Bouchard speech. The English press admired his courage in denouncing conditions in his own province before an English audience, while the French press judged it shameful to wash Quebec's dirty linen before a largely English Senate—and in the English language. While the French press howled for and was gratified by Bouchard's dismissal from his \$18,000-a-year post as president of the Hydro, the English press was horrified by this drastic penalty for speaking one's mind. It was not Bouchard's charges which gave Quebec a black eye in English-speaking opinion, but the subsequent breach of the sacred doctrine of free speech. The *Montreal Gazette* made this plain on the day following Godbout's action: 'The plain implication of this series of events is that the fundamental right of free speech, even when exercised on the floor of the Senate of Canada, is denied by the government of Quebec to an appointee on pain of dismissal.' The *Gazette*, which as a Conservative organ associated with big business had bitterly opposed nationalization of the Montreal Light, Heat & Power, went on to observe:

> The most disturbing aspect of the dismissal is that it tears away any pretense of maintaining the Hydro Commission as an entirely non-political and independent body, which was the avowed basis on which it was established. For the Premier's latest move is inherently political,

betraying a panicky weakness in the face of an imminent election and an adverse flurry of reaction to the Senator's speech. It cannot fail but to give the greatest concern to all alive to the full implications of its effects, not only on the Hydro and other provincial government bodies, but upon the plane of political life in this province.

The only French-Canadian reaction of this nature, outside the pages of *Le Jour*, was the announcement on this same day by Hubert Desaulniers, president of the Canadian Civil Liberties Union established in 1937, that the organization was going to resume its activities, which had been suspended at the outbreak of the war.

How little French Canada had ever embraced the doctrine of free speech was revealed not only by the heavy price that Bouchard had to pay for his utterance, but also by two other incidents in June, which saw Tim Buck and other Labor-Progressive leaders prevented from holding a political meeting in Quebec City and escorted out of the city by police, and an assault on the A.F.L. union headquarters in Valleyfield. The *Labor World*, organ of the provincial Federation of Labor, on June 24 observed that 'freedom of speech and of assembly will soon be things of the past in Quebec,' thanks to 'ridiculous and stupid advice given in certain nationalist and ultramontane quarters.'[8] Early in July Bouchard's resignation, 'so as not to cause embarrassment to this association,' as president of the *Institute Démocratique* which he had founded a year earlier was accepted by the governors of the organization, while he also refused to run again as mayor of Saint-Hyacinthe. In the subsequent municipal elections all his followers were defeated.

4

Dominion Day 1944 found French Canada in a mood troubled by the events of recent weeks. *L'Action Catholique* and *Le Droit* used the anniversary to demand more respect for the spirit as well as the letter of the pact by English Canadians, and to urge such a policy as a better way to promote national unity than the proposed revision of Canadian history-teaching. Even the great independent or Liberal dailies displayed a certain soreness about violations of the British traditions of fair play which led the Ottawa government to treat French Canadians like poor relations and the English provinces to disregard French-Canadian rights. These reactions were reflected in the Gallup Poll taken as the provincial campaign opened, which indicated that the Liberal Party was favored by 37 per cent of the electorate, the *Bloc Populaire* by 27 per cent, the *Union Nationale* by 14 per cent, with the remaining 22 per cent scattered among C.C.F., Social Credit, Communist, and undecided voters.[9] The *Bloc* had gained at the expense of both the Liberals and the *Union Nationale*, making violent attacks upon the old parties as tools of the trusts and imperialists, and upon the C.C.F. as espousing a socialism forbidden to Catholics. The *Bloc* missed no opportunity to exploit popular resentment against the Liberal regimes at Quebec and Ottawa: conscription and the regulations requiring employers to report defaulters, the internment of Camilien Houde, the detention of Marc Carrière, the replacement of French-Canadian workers by English-Canadian ones at the Defence Industries plant at Sainte-Thérèse, the profits of the Aluminum Company, the plea in favor of learning English by Edouard Simard, head of the war-booming Marine & Sorel Industries, the agitation in favor of a single manual of Canadian history, the immigration of Jewish refugees and British subjects, the loans and gifts to Britain—all were grist to its mill. It devoted particular attention to the shooting of Georges Guénette, a young deserter, on May 7 at Saint-Lambert near Quebec City by French-Canadian members of the Mounted Police. Though the campaign against Bouchard, with an effort to identify the Godbout government with him, replaced the Guénette affair as the major interest of *Le Bloc* at the end of June, the *Bloc* campaign speakers continued to make much of the incident, which probably had more effect than any argument in favor of the *Bloc* upon the public. French Canada, which has a great devotion to law and order despite its tendency to verbal violence, was shocked by the shedding of blood in the enforcement of the hated conscription which had been introduced bit by bit at the cost of a steadily growing popular bitterness. Though the *Bloc* devoted most of its fire to the Liberals, it was also notably savage in its attacks on Duplessis and his *Union Nationale*.

Godbout and the Liberals waged an uphill fight to regain prestige for their party in these troubled times. A farmer and a textile worker were named to the cabinet in June, in an effort to give the government greater appeal to the restless masses. In an address on June 21 which set August 8 as the election date, Godbout reviewed the progressive record of his government and proclaimed that the Liberal watchword was '*Notre maître, l'avenir*' ('Our master is the future') in contrast to the *Union Nationale* and *Bloc* devotion to the Groulx slogan of '*Notre maître, le passé*' ('The past is our master'). He lumped the two opposition parties together, though it was clear he attached more importance to the Duplessis forces than to the 'hotheads of the *Bloc*.' He warned that if they came to power, with their 'narrow spirit, opportunism, and fanaticism,' there would be 'a methodical and progressive strangulation of the national culture, which has such abundant possibilities.' He declared his unyielding opposition to fanaticism and hatred: 'My conscience, as a man, a citizen, and a political leader thoroughly aware of his responsibilities, imposes upon me the stern duty to say to fanaticism: "You shall not pass, because you are the enemy of my brothers and the destroyer of the nation." '[10] Godbout sought to confine the campaign to provincial issues, urging that his government should be judged on its merits, while the voters would later have a chance to give their verdict on Mr. King's war policy in a federal election. He appointed his most nationalistic and anti-conscriptionist minister, Oscar Drouin, to the Municipal Affairs Commission. But it was already evident that both the *Union Nationale*, with its memories of its 1939 defeat on the federal issue of participation in the war, and the *Bloc*, with its provincial nationalism, would fight the campaign chiefly on the basis of federal issues, with Godbout depicted in the role of a bootlicker of imperialist and centralizing Ottawa.

Godbout's speech was well received by almost the entire French press, which was clearly uneasy over the height to which public feeling had risen in recent weeks. *Le Devoir* had only a few reservations; *L'Action Catholique* argued that partisan passion should not be allowed to suppress reason and urged that 'our political debates should do nothing to raise French Canadians against each other, nor make them lose confidence in authority.' *La Presse* and *La Patrie* showed great sympathy for the speech, while the Liberal press was enthusiastic over it. However, *Le Temps*, organ of the *Union Nationale*, violently denounced Godbout for 'not having spoken a single word about the war, about mobilization, conscription, or autonomy' after having been for five years 'merely the valet, the slave, the marionette of Ottawa.' *Le Bloc* referred to the speech as that of 'one condemned to death' and bitterly denounced Godbout's effort to dissociate himself from Mackenzie King and T.-D. Bouchard, who had been his leaders and political allies since the beginning of his political career in 1935.

Early in July the *Bloc* probably had a good chance to defeat the Godbout government. But its hotheaded young men, drunk on their own eloquence, soon went too far for the moderate French-Canadian masses, angry as they were. The *Bloc* candidate in Maisonneuve, Jacques Sauriol, a thirty-three-year-old journalist with a background of nationalist activity as a supporter of the A.C.J.C. and of Camilien Houde, made an extremely violent speech at Saint-Eustache—with its bitter memories of 1837—on July 2:

> I am for the strong method. The former Mayor of Montreal, Camilien Houde, was unjustly arrested. When we of the *Bloc* are in power at Quebec, we will fix that. Wherever he may be, I, Jacques Sauriol, undertake to go and get him on August 9, if he is still the victim of persecution by the federal police . . .
>
> What is important is not to make bombs to destroy the homes of Poles, Ukrainians, and Frenchmen, it is to provide homes for our own people, to build houses for our workmen which will be available to the

humblest and to the small wage-earner . . . Five years have now gone by in which we have been told repeatedly of the threat of Fascism and Nazism. Have you yet seen Mussolini in Canada? You have not. But you have seen the King and Churchill. . . .

The *Bloc* in Quebec will defend our young men from the iniquitous selective service. At Ottawa, we of the *Bloc* will break conscription just like that . . . If it is desired that Quebec factories do war work, our young men will have to be released so that they can work in the factories. The British Empire is an institution so wicked and so damnable that it has to have a war every twenty years to keep it going. Federal police or no federal police, we of the *Bloc* are against all foreign wars. We will use every means—and I do not say legitimate means—we will use every means necessary to halt this drainage of our young towards the charnel-house of Europe. . . .

I myself have been threatened by selective service because England has need of an iniquitous war every twenty-five years, because the English soldier is the worst in the world, and it is necessary for Canadians to fight England's battles and be killed in the place of the English in the hell of Caen.

Such incendiary statements bred fear of the *Bloc* in many law-abiding French-Canadian circles which feared that violence worse than that of 1917–18 could be the only fruit of such words.

In addition, the *Bloc* suffered the disadvantage that its youthful urban agitators were distrusted in the country districts, while in the cities the *Bloc* lacked the organization and the means to combat the solidly implanted Liberal machine. The *Bloc* was primarily a youth movement and a class movement, drawing its main strength from the élite of nationalist-minded French-Canadian youth. Older French Canadians, who had outgrown the fervent nationalism of their youth as English-speaking people so frequently outgrow youthful radical sympathies, distrusted the *Bloc's* leadership, which was largely young and unknown, with Maxime Raymond ill; Paul Gouin, René Chaloult, and Dr. Hamel still at odds with the group; and Edouard Lacroix not taking an active part in the campaign. The *Bloc's* campaign meetings provided a safety valve for the venting of Quebec's bitterness about all the irritations, grievances, and conflicts which war had brought upon the province; but the rank and file of French Canada were not ready to support so radical a movement.

Maurice Duplessis and his well-organized *Union Nationale* machine played their cards cleverly. Their attack upon the Liberals was nominally based on provincial rights grounds, with the charge that Godbout had betrayed the province to the centralizers at Ottawa. But it exploited French-Canadian anti-semitism and anti-war feeling almost as vigorously as the *Bloc*, while it made overtures to the powerful English Conservative interests who controlled so much of Quebec's economic life. While denouncing the expropriation of the Montreal Light, Heat & Power Company in the English press, it published a violently anti-war and anti-conscriptionist campaign sheet in French which held Godbout responsible for all the blood that had been shed by French Canadians at home and abroad. It lavished its attentions upon the rural districts, whose vote outweighed that of the cities where the Liberal strength was concentrated; and upon the *curés*, who were on the whole as opposed to the war and conscription as in 1917 but unwilling to support the *Bloc* extremists. Duplessis' promise to restore the Padlock Law also helped to win him the support of the clergy and of other conservative elements, which were alarmed at the rise of Communism and social unrest in Quebec; though it deprived him of what little support he might expect from organized labor. The *Union Nationale* provided a middle way for moderate French Canadians who had been antagonized by Liberal support of the war and by the Bouchard affair, and who were unwilling to go as far towards reaction as the *Bloc*, or towards radical revision of society as the C.C.F., Social Credit, or Labor-Progressive parties. And despite the repudiation on July 22 by John Bracken, the national Progressive-Conservative leader, of Bona Arsenault, the provincial Conservative organizer who had called Bouchard a 'Quebec Quisling,' the Duplessis forces held the allegiance of traditionally *Bleu* voters whose chief concern was to oust the hated *Rouges*.

Many French Canadians were reminded during the campaign of the battle in 1911 between Laurier and Bourassa. When André Laurendeau announced that the *Bloc* owed its inspiration to the principles formulated by Henri Bourassa in his younger days, Premier Godbout replied:

> It would be easy for us to preach hate and discord, but we do not want that kind of thing in Quebec. Perhaps the two greatest minds of their generation were Sir Wilfrid Laurier and the nationalist leader Henri Bourassa. But with his principles of kindliness, respect, and cordiality Laurier is today a world figure, while Bourassa has done nothing but promote discord.

Le Devoir, of course, rallied to the defence of its founder, calling Bourassa 'the great interpreter of Canadian thought and particularly of French-Canadian and Catholic thought':

> He has been the champion of educational freedom. He has never sought for discord, but rather for justice, which gives rise to harmony and peace. If he had been listened to in international affairs, our country would not have been dragged, twice in a quarter of a century,

into terrible wars which weigh so heavily upon its life. If he had been listened to in national affairs, there would have been more fair play in Canadian life and therefore more chance of a durable peace.[11]

In Liberal circles there was much re-examination of Laurier's speeches to discover how he had overcome in his day the same combination of the Conservative opposition, the nationalists, and the antipathy of the clergy to the Liberals. There was left-wing Liberal talk of founding a more radical or a more democratic party, if the Liberals were defeated in both the provincial and subsequent federal elections. But though many of the young Liberals were inclined to be sympathetic to the C.C.F., the majority were essentially as conservative as the Conservatives themselves, and as fully committed to the preservation of a hierarchical society in which political leaders served as middle men between the French-Canadian masses and the English-speaking economic overlords of Quebec.

Bourassa had the last notable word in the campaign, when in addressing a *Bloc* meeting in Montreal on August 4 he dropped a bombshell with even greater effect than his advice at Quebec in May to support C.C.F. candidates in the absence of *Bloc* ones. No doubt concerned by the support which Duplessis was winning in clerical circles and by growing anti-clericalism, he observed:

In a country which prides itself on being Christian—(Are we really Christian? I do not know)—and in which there are no scruples about using the influence of bishops to buttress a profane cause, we should at least have a little respect for the principles which Christ came on earth to implant and which we mock in our daily lives. The day is not far off, unfortunately, when those bishops who meddled in politics will be derided, and those who use them today will turn their backs against them, once they have served their purpose. No, they have not served their purpose and we still need their spiritual advice. Yes, we respect you, but safeguard your prestige with the people and do not allow yourselves to be made the tools of conscienceless politicians who exploit you.

No one in French Canada had publicly spoken of the hierarchy in such a tone since Laurier fought them on the Manitoba school issue in 1896. The repercussion of Bourassa's speech was great.

It spoke well for Cardinal Villeneuve's discretion that he delayed until two days after the election publication of the following reply:

In his last address in Montreal Henri Bourassa thought fit, as is his custom, to play his habitual refrain against the bishops. We could, of course, pass this off with a smile, but because there are youths who listen to him, that liberty which he takes upon himself periodically of telling the bishops what he thinks of them compels me to say that he is neither a pontiff nor an authorized doctor of the Church. It has always been observed that he better understands a faraway Pope or a dead Pope than living bishops, who embarrass him. In spite of his claim of respect for the hierarchy, he takes every opportunity to treat the bishops with contempt, to display publicly scandalous examples of presumption and disrespect toward the ecclesiastical authorities.

History will recognize his incontestable qualities and his good public service; but without judging for the moment his doctrinal or historical thesis, history will not confirm his pretense of being a lay theologian. It will not make of him a respectful and obedient son of the episcopate. It is time that this ambiguity should cease, and truly Catholic youth must know it.[12]

It is not surprising that Bourassa returned to retirement after this withering blast. The Cardinal's attitude may have played some part in swaying clerical votes from the *Bloc* to the *Union Nationale*; public revelation of it certainly helped to kill the *Bloc*, which found that its effort to exploit Bourassa had backfired.

For one of several surprises in the election results was the fact that the *Bloc* polled only 15 per cent of the vote, though the Gallup Poll of mid-July had given it 25 per cent and many observers were convinced that it was going to make an even more impressive showing because of Quebec's angry mood. The Liberals polled 37 per cent of the vote but won only thirty-seven seats; while the *Union Nationale*, with 36 per cent of the vote, took forty-five seats. With the *Bloc* securing four seats, the C.C.F. one, and René Chaloult returned as an independent, no party had a true majority. It was a question whether the *Union Nationale* would be able to form a government, since one of their members must be named speaker, while another was absent in Normandy with the Army. The Liberals won their popular majority of 45,000 votes on the Island of Montreal, where the upper-class constituencies of Jacques-Cartier, Notre-Dame-de-Grace, Westmount, Outremont, and St. Anne registered their opposition to the *Bloc* and the *Union Nationale* by crushing majorities. In the working-class quarters of Montreal the election was bitterly fought, with brass knuckles, knives, and even revolvers used by hoodlums seeking to terrorize voters.

While the Liberals carried the cities, the *Union Nationale* swept most of the country districts. Though the urban population constituted two-thirds of the population, it elected only one-third of the legislative assembly under the electoral system, which was much criticized on the morrow of the poll. The new parties did better than the four seats won by the *Bloc* and the one by the C.C.F. indicated, since the *Bloc* polled 172,626 votes (about one-third of the Liberal or *Union Nationale* totals); the C.C.F. 33,158, and the Social Credit, Labor-Progressive, and independent candidates together

65,594. It was clear that the new parties had definite appeal for the Quebec voter, since together they won 275,000 votes (two-thirds of the successful *Union Nationale* total). In particular the growth of nationalist sentiment was indicated by the fact that the *Bloc* polled more than four times the number of votes won by Paul Gouin's *Action Nationale Libérale* in 1936.

Though there was some speculation after election day as to whether Godbout would seek to call new elections, the Liberal chief had confessed defeat in a moving broadcast a few hours after the polls closed:

What interests me most is not power in the province, but the future of the province. Whether as leader of the government or chief of the opposition, I shall try to continue to serve and to help the province. I have attempted to serve my province in a loyal manner and I have tried to be honest, not only in the financial domain, but in intellectual and moral fields as well. I have tried to make the people of the Province of Quebec understand what were our principles—the principles for the salvation of our future. Perhaps I was wrong and possibly I was right. I still believe I was right. But I also believed that the province would definitely appreciate that it should aspire to a constructive future on principles of order and peace based on co-operation.

Mr. Duplessis, addressing a crowd of 25,000 jubilant *Bleus*, promised to regain for Quebec the rights ceded to Ottawa by the Liberals:

We shall fight to the limit, to the final victory, for the restoration and respect of our rights. I consider the election result as a punishment inflicted by the province on those who have abandoned its rights.

André Laurendeau, one of the four successful *Bloc* candidates, was clearly pleased with the results of the election, although the *Bloc* had not rallied '*tout Québec*' as its orators had prophesied:

In the short space of two months the *Bloc Populaire* had to form its ranks. It did so. Its standard-bearers were selected and proved to be faithful. I have never witnessed such hope, confidence and faith in the future as that which tonight marks the arrival at Quebec of the first members of the *Bloc Populaire Canadien*.

R.-J. Lamoureux, provincial leader of the C.C.F., declared that his party had assured itself of a wedge for victory in the next federal election, for which the provincial poll had been a rehearsal. He was clearly counting on a preservation and extension of the united front of Montreal labor which had been attained against the *Union Nationale* and the *Bloc*, with the C.C.L. unions voting C.C.F. and the A.F.L. Liberal.[13]

The unexpected outcome of the election was mirrored in editorial comments. The *Gazette* urged Duplessis to 'distinguish between proper preservation of provincial rights and a return to narrow nationalism,' and rejoiced that the *Bloc Populaire Canadien*, 'which was never Canadian,' had proved not to be popular either. *La Presse* prudently distributed congratulations to Duplessis, Godbout, and Laurendeau, and rejoiced that the people had rejected the socialist C.C.F. *Le Devoir*, which along with *L'Action Catholique* and *Le Droit* had supported the *Bloc*, rejoiced in Laurendeau's victory and forecast new elections in the near future. It took note of the popular revolt against the old parties and observed: 'The political face of the province is in full transition.' *Le Canada*, while pointing out that the Liberals had received the greatest support from the electorate, declared that Mr. Duplessis should be called upon to form a government. It took evident pleasure in the poor showing of the *Bloc*, which 'reveals that the population of Quebec is neither separatist nor isolationist as regards Canada's national policy, nor anti-participationist as regards the war.'[14]

5

There was a lull after the electoral storm in Quebec, for the new Duplessis government did not take office until August 30. French Canada's unity was in some measure restored by a speech on August 9 by George Drew, the Conservative Ontario premier, opposing the federal family allowance scheme as a violation of provincial autonomy and as an electoral bribe to Quebec. It became evident that Duplessis was seeking an anti-Ottawa alliance with the Ontario Conservatives, when an inspired statement pointed out that Drew's speech was 'the strongest backing from outside which Mr. Duplessis has received in his fight for provincial autonomy.'[15] Another portent of a federal election was provided by Mackenzie King's statement that he favored a distinctive national flag and 'O Canada' as a national hymn. This gratified a Quebec which had long favored such symbols of nationhood, while English-Canadian nationalism, developed by the war, was now calling for symbolic recognition of Canada's status. There undoubtedly had been an increase in this sentiment since the Gallup Poll of August 1943 which showed a national flag favored by 51 per cent of the population as a whole, with the French Canadians 82 per cent in favor and those of British origin still 58 per cent in favor of the Union Jack. In *Saturday Night* B. K. Sandwell expressed the opinion that English Canadians would favor the adoption of 'O Canada' if the English words did not reflect 'intrinsically Catholic and French inspiration.'[16] English-Canadian loyalty to the Crown was also reflected in the argument that 'God Save the King' was not merely the national hymn of Great Britain but also of all lands over which the King reigned.

Despite all the campaign talk about Ottawa's invasion of provincial affairs, federal intervention in the Montreal Tramways strike was taken calmly by all camps in Quebec, though the *Gazette* pressed for a return to the open-shop principle which had been embodied in the labor code of the Duplessis government in 1938, though not enforced. The federal government made another step towards appeasing Quebec by releasing Camilien Houde after four years of internment for opposing national registration. Houde declared that he was 'only the victim of a political party and a political organization and nothing else,' and threatened to take political revenge. He was given a triumphant reception in Montreal, where it was evident that his political stock was all the higher for his 'martyrdom.' His release had long been sought by the nationalists, but seemingly came as the result of pressure brought to bear on Ottawa by organized labor in Montreal, with both national syndicates and the international unions making common cause. Both dissident Quebec Liberals and newly politically minded labor sought Houde as a popular leader, and his advent in both the federal and provincial fields was widely rumored. But for the time being he refused to commit himself to any course.

The invasion of southern France on August 15 convinced French Canada that the end of the war was in sight. The Quebec press made much of the role of the *Maquis*, but nothing was said of the Communist share in the Resistance, although *Relations* and *L'Action Catholique* devoted much space in August to denouncing international Communism, and particularly to the use of Soviet embassies as propaganda centers, specifically in Ottawa, Washington, and Mexico City.[17] Soviet sympathizers predicted a revival of the 'Padlock Law' when the Duplessis government took office. French Canada had never regarded the Soviet alliance with confidence, and now that the contest in Europe seemed to be drawing rapidly to a close, it expressed its opposition to postwar commercial and cultural relations with Russia. The liberation of Paris on August 25 by Frenchmen unleashed an outburst of joy in Quebec. Justice Minister St. Laurent spoke by radio to the people of Paris in the name of the Canadian government, as did Mayor Raynault of Montreal. The French flag was flown on the public buildings of Montreal, Trois-Rivières, and Quebec, while the Tricolor decorated private houses everywhere. Madame André Simard, now a delegate to the Algiers Assembly just returned from North Africa, told an enormous crowd in Quebec's Place d'Armes: 'By the grace of God who has allowed this resurrection, the heart of France is again beginning to beat.' Then all joined in the singing of the 'Marseillaise', as did a concert audience at the Chalet on Mount Royal in Montreal. *Te Deums* were chanted in churches throughout the province. The press, French and English alike, hailed the liberation of Paris, with the leading business firms using advertising space to swell the chorus.[18]

The swearing-in of the new Duplessis cabinet on August 30 put an end to rumors that a *Union Nationale–Bloc* alliance would be cemented by the offer of a portfolio to René Chaloult or another nationalist. A previous statement by Duplessis, decrying the postponement of redistribution of federal seats, and urging that it be carried through before the next federal election in order that Quebec might not be deprived of its due influence at Ottawa,[19] indicated that the new government would follow a straight provincial autonomy line, rather than a separatist one. The Duplessis cabinet shattered precedent in two respects: its size, with twenty-one ministers out of forty-three *Union Nationale* members; and the fact that the treasury portfolio, traditionally reserved to an English minister, had been given to a French-Canadian one. Jonathan Robinson, the sole English member of the cabinet, was made minister of mines, while Onésime Gagnon, a former federal minister highly regarded both in Quebec and at Ottawa, took the treasury post.

There was no hint of the government's labor policy in the usual Labor Day messages by the new premier and minister of labor shortly after they took office. Both the Liberals and the C.C.F. were engaged in trying to line up the labor vote for a federal election, while the traditional conflict between the national syndicates and the international unions was once more coming to a head. On August 20, the auxiliary bishop of Rimouski, Mgr. C.-E. Parent, expressed the traditional opposition of the clergy to the internationals when in addressing the National Federation of the Wood Industry he said: 'Have nothing to do with neutral unions, albeit they may have made gains in the great cities. Communism glides in their shadow like a snake. It attempts to fish in troubled waters and tries to turn the workers against the employers, as occurred in the last tramway strike in Montreal. Such unions stir up the workers against the employers, against religion, and against the clergy.'[20] On August 6 the CIO United Steelworkers of America announced an organization campaign among the aluminum workers of Arvida. According to the 1943 vote, only 23 per cent of these workers were organized: 17 per cent in syndicates and 6 per cent with the A.F.L. The CIO maintained that Arvida wages were 40–60 per cent below the level prevailing in the aluminum industry in the States, despite 20–40 per cent cheaper production costs. The Lake St. John district was a stronghold of the Catholic syndicates, and the chaplain of the Arvida syndicate, Abbé Bertrand, had recently declared that 'Catholic workers could not in conscience join non-confessional organizations.'[21]

The holding of the second Quebec Conference (September 11–16), concerned with the war against Japan, as the Allied forces stood ready to break into Germany, once more gratified Quebec's pride. *L'Action Catholique* expressed the popular desire for an opportunity to pay tribute on this occasion to both Churchill and Roosevelt, regretting that at the 1943 conference only the British leader had made a brief public appearance. *L'Action* also called for 'a just and durable peace.' Dissatisfaction was evident in the French-Canadian press that France had not been invited to participate in the conference. *Le Bloc* sought to make capital of a rumored conflict between the United States and Britain over policy in India. Barred from reporting the conference by security regulations, the French press devoted much attention at this time to drawing up a balance sheet of Quebec's war effort on the fifth anniversary of Canada's entrance into the war. The English-Canadian and American press were criticized for their contemptuous attitude towards French Canada's share in the war, which was vigorously defended.

L'Action Catholique gave the fullest statement of the French-Canadian position:

> For a number of English-language newspapers, there has been only one way to further the war effort: enlist for overseas service. Because young French Canadians have not felt bound to do this in numbers as great as English-speaking Canadians, astonishment has been expressed at our rejoicing over recent Allied victories, notably over the liberation of Paris.
>
> When some of our people show themselves hostile to participation as it is being practised, their ideas are eagerly given prominence as if these persons had spoken in the name of the Province of Quebec. On the other hand, if representatives of religious and civil authority issue directives, some little space is given in the English press, but with all due reserve and without comment. Today Church and State are recommending prayer and rejoicing. The people are exulting because the Allies are triumphing and France is liberated. Our colleagues are scandalized and claim that we should be ashamed.
>
> We are proud of the victory of our arms. We salute the success of the land armies of 1944, just as we saluted the success of the R.A.F. in 1940 and of the Navy in 1941 and 1942. We admire the courage of the French 'patriots' in 1944, just as we admired the morale of the British under the bombs of 1940.
>
> We are not ashamed because we are conscious of having contributed to the triumph of the Allies.
>
> No doubt we have had fewer 'volunteers' and fewer draftees, but we have produced proportionally as many ships and foodstuffs. All the War Loans have succeeded very well indeed, and subscriptions to war charities have on every occasion gone over the top.
>
> We have had fewer soldiers of all branches of the service for very sound

reasons: a greater number of men called up have been rejected for health reasons (this will have to be explained one of these days); the land has kept back more men because our agriculture is less industrialized, run more on a family basis; politics has nourished the phobia of overseas conscription for twenty-five years; in the different war services we have been treated as aliens without regard to the antipathy which would thus be engendered against participation; our drafted men were trained in a language which was not their own; the scarcely veiled imperialism of certain clumsy propagandists froze enthusiasm instead of stirring it, etc.

These are some of the causes of the moderate success of voluntary enlistment in Quebec. But, and this has been stated many times by our political leaders as well as by those of England and the United States, the war effort can be effectively supported in other ways than by taking up arms. In the factory and in the fields the French Canadians have fully played their part. They have done it generously despite the mockery, the slanders, the injustices . . . and the official violations of promises of 'voluntary' and 'moderate' participation.

On the other hand Jean-Charles Harvey of *Le Jour*, in a violent denunciation of the 'anti-British element, anti-participationists, isolationists, Fascists, pro-Fascists, *Bloc*-ists, and deserters' who had paid tribute to Camilien Houde upon his release from internment, had earlier pointed out that Quebec's enlistment rate of 22.1 per cent was half that prevailing in the other provinces, and that the fact would always be held against Quebec.[22] The heavy Canadian casualties in the Battle of France had aroused strong emotional feeling in English Canada against Quebec, which continued to grow. *Le Canada* sought to refute charges of 'inequality of sacrifice' by pointing out on the basis of casualty lists that many French Canadians were serving overseas in English-Canadian units, and that Quebec's part should not be judged solely on the basis of the French-Canadian units. *Le Soleil* predicted that Canada would play its due share in bringing the Pacific War to a victorious conclusion, as it had already played its part at Hong Kong, the Aleutians, and in the air and on the sea.[23]

While Prime Minister King took advantage of the Quebec Conference to woo the French-Canadian Liberals to a united front in the next federal election, the Duplessis government through Paul Beaulieu, minister of commerce and industry, and its Quebec organ, *Le Temps*, denounced *Le Devoir*, which was said to have 'done us irreparable harm,' and the nationalists whose motto was '*notre maître, le passé*.' A call was made for the union of all men of good will to maintain the fair name of Quebec and to prepare the way for prosperity in the postwar world. All the Quebec press, with the exception of *Le Devoir* and *Le Bloc*, approved Beaulieu's stand.[24] After the verbal excesses of the provincial campaign, Quebec had swung back to the innate loyalism and moderation of the great majority of its people. In this process unfavorable publicity abroad and the influence of the Quebec Conference and the subsequent U.N.R.R.A. Conference at Montreal had played their parts.

A significant index of Quebec's return to a calmer mood was the re-election of T.-D. Bouchard to the presidency of the *Institut Démocratique*, which had accepted his resignation in the storm which followed his Senate speech. Though virtually deprived of French-Canadian nationality, Bouchard had clung to the ideas he expressed on that occasion, and had re-expressed them in an address at the Couchiching Conference of the Canadian Institute of Public Affairs in August. In his re-acceptance of the presidency, Bouchard said: 'From the testimony you have paid me, I do not infer that you approve the opinions that I uttered in my Senate speech, I simply conclude that you have recognized my right to express them,'[25] and hailed the growth of freedom of opinion and speech in the province.

6

Premier Drew's reflections on Quebec in his August 9 speech against federal family allowances continued to produce bitter reactions in Quebec, which was well aware of the fact that English-Canadian public opinion was mounting against French Canada. There were significant minor incidents which revealed the growing rift. Delegates to an Eastern Ontario Progressive-Conservative meeting at Ottawa protested against the singing of 'O Canada' at the close of a gathering which had been opened with 'God Save the King.' In September Major Connie Smythe, a wounded veteran well known in Toronto hockey circles, charged that half-trained troops were being thrown into the line because of heavy losses and the shortage of reinforcements, which he blamed on Quebec. During October it became common report that there was a shortage of replacements in the Army, while the more popular Navy and the Air Force ceased recruiting, with the latter service discharging men already in training. These men were subject to drafting into the N.R.M.A. home service forces if they did not volunteer for overseas. War correspondents reported that only a small proportion of the troops overseas were prepared to volunteer for service in the Pacific after the European War was over, and that they were bitter about sick and wounded men being sent back into the line, while home defence troops stood idle in Canada. The Conservative press printed anonymous letters to the same effect, allegedly from men at the front. There were calls, chiefly from Conservative sources, for a reopening of the whole manpower question, and the making available of all Canadian troops for service anywhere.

In June, General Stuart, the Army chief of staff in London, had indicated the question would eventually arise of breaking up overseas formations or sending N.R.M.A. conscripts to Europe, in order to meet a heavier call for reinforcements anticipated from October on into 1945. The general informed the government, however, that it could await developments in the war before reaching a decision—he thought there was 'an excellent chance of our being able to finish the war on a voluntary basis'[26]—and he suggested that additional recruiting efforts be made, particularly for infantry. The three defence ministers arranged to slow down Navy and Air Force recruiting for the benefit of the Army. Colonel Ralston brought this situation to the attention of the War Committee of the cabinet in June 1944.[27]

During the first week of August the chief of staff again assured the War Committee of the cabinet that the reinforcement situation was satisfactory.[28] On August 26, however, he reported a shortage of about 3,000 infantrymen in France, which was being met by using men trained for other duties. The estimates for infantry casualties proved too low, however, while those for other branches proved too high. New estimates made in October, when it became apparent that there would be no immediate German collapse and that heavy casualties would continue, indicated a shortage of 2,380 men in the field by the end of the year.

General Stuart then recommended that the trained N.R.M.A. troops should be drawn upon for reinforcements. Defence Minister Ralston concurred after a three-week visit to England and the Canadian fronts in Western Europe and Italy. After warning the prime minister by cable on October 13, Ralston returned to Ottawa with Stuart on October 18, immediately reported to Mr. King, and urged such action at cabinet meetings on the following day and thereafter. When the prime minister showed reluctance to resort to conscription for service overseas, in accordance with his promise in 1942 when Bill 80 was introduced in the House, since it was a step which 'would occasion the most serious controversy that could arise in Canada,' Ralston insisted upon its necessity. He opposed reducing Canada's commitments or breaking up units, and demanded assurance that, if the needed men did not volunteer as a result of a further appeal, N.R.M.A. men would be sent.[29] On October 31 King consulted with General Andrew McNaughton, the man who had built up the Canadian Army and who had retired in December 1943 because of 'ill health,' in which differences with the British were understood to be involved. McNaughton expressed the belief that the necessary recruits could be obtained on a voluntary basis—though only 4,956 men had enlisted for general service during October[30]—and stated his willingness to accept the defence post if Ralston resigned. Confronted with this situation, Ralston resigned at the prime minister's request on October 31, as he had threatened to do since July 1942 if conscription were not adopted if it became necessary.[31] McNaughton was sworn in as minister of defence the following day, while General Montague was appointed to replace General Stuart as chief of staff at Canadian Military Headquarters in London.

One of the most violent political storms in Canada's history then broke loose. It was widely rumored that several other ministers—Navy Minister Angus MacDonald was most frequently named, though Mr. Crerar was seemingly the most conscription-minded minister—would resign in sympathy with Ralston. Conservative forces, the Canadian Legion, army officers, and most English Canadians pressed for all-out conscription, while the French-Canadian press praised Mackenzie King for his faithfulness to his pledge not to invoke conscription, and hailed the shrewdness with which he had replaced a conscriptionist Liberal minister of defence with an anti-conscriptionist Conservative who enjoyed greater personal prestige than any other Canadian. It was evident that many Conservatives sought to make capital of the situation to drive the King government from office. John Bracken, leader of that party, was at odds with the group led by George Drew which was prepared to override Quebec's anti-conscriptionist attitude by force if necessary, although Bracken formally denied any difference of opinion with Drew and that there was an anti-French Canadian group in his party.

A Quebec speech on November 4 by Justice Minister St. Laurent implied that the cabinet had decided against conscription under any circumstances. On November 5, at Arnprior, McNaughton called for no relaxation of effort on the last hard stretch of the war, and urged the public to encourage volunteers. On the following day at Ottawa he repeated these observations to a hostile Canadian Legion meeting, expressing his conviction that the best hope of solving the reinforcement problem was by the voluntary method, and making an appeal for rational rather than emotional thinking.

The nation-wide agitation continued, however, and on November 8 Mackenzie King made a radio address, announcing that there would be no conscription for overseas service and that National Defence officials were working on plans prepared by General McNaughton to increase volunteering. The prime minister declared that: 'The voluntary system has not broken down,' pointing out that more men had volunteered for overseas since D-Day than had been conscripted. He denied that more than a very few men had failed to receive full training before going into action. The N.R.M.A. forces would continue to be maintained for essential home defence duties and as a source of volunteers for overseas. He revealed that the effective strength of the N.R.M.A. troops at present was 60,000 men, of whom only 25,000 were French-speaking and only 23,000 from Quebec. These figures showed, contrary to popular belief, that the draftees who had refused to volunteer for overseas service were not largely French-Canadian, but were divided into three almost equal groups of French Canadians, English Canadians, and New Canadians in proportion to these groups of the population.

Mr. King expressed the belief that 'without any compulsion or intensification of present methods, a considerable number of these draftees would volunteer. We believe many more can be secured by a special appeal.' He then urged young men, both in the Army and outside it, to volunteer at the present time to meet the present need, warning that very grave difficulties might result from substituting conscription for voluntary service. He paid tribute to Colonel Ralston, regretting the difference of opinion which had led to the minister's resignation, and to General McNaughton, who was determined to give full support to the Army. The prime minister characterized the reinforcement situation as 'not an actual shortage now, but a possible shortage in the next few months.' He implied that while the voluntary system was preferred, the question of compulsion might have to be reconsidered in the light of developing circumstances.

On the following day John Bracken issued a statement accusing the prime minister of betraying his trust and deceiving both the Army overseas and the people at home by failing to disclose Colonel Ralston's report and the reasons for the resignation. He summed up the situation in these words: 'Our army overseas is in dire need of trained reinforcements, in dire need of rest and help, and men must be sent to the entire extent available in Canada. This is an immediate national need.' Bracken reasserted the Conservative manpower policy which called for complete conscription, and declared that the situation now transcended partisan politics.

On November 12 Colonel Ralston, who had been away from Ottawa, also issued a statement in reply to the prime minister's radio address, in which he criticized Mr. King's statement of the position as inaccurate and stressed the urgency of the reinforcement problem. He also made it clear that he had resigned at the request of the prime minister, and not on his own initiative.[32]

7

On November 15 the prime minister bowed to the ever-growing storm and summoned the House to meet in special secret session on November 22 to consider the reinforcement question. After a public statement by Senator Ballantyne, the Senate was also called on

November 17. On November 16 the *Montreal Gazette*, which along with the *Toronto Globe and Mail* and the *Toronto Telegram* had been pressing for conscription, reported that the commanders of all the military districts in Canada had advised General McNaughton that compulsion must be used to secure the necessary number of men. This report was denied by the prime minister and General McNaughton. General L.-R. Laflèche, national war services minister, stated on November 19 that he had taken upon himself the task of finding in Quebec the necessary reinforcements for the French-Canadian units overseas. He added that four French-Canadian regiments—Les Fusiliers Mont-Royal, Le Maisonneuve, Le Chateauguay, and Le Joliette—had already promised to find men for reserve battalions; and expressed confidence that the reinforcement problem could be solved by the voluntary method.

When parliament met on November 22, the prime minister read and subsequently tabled the correspondence which had been exchanged between Colonel Ralston and himself concerning the defence minister's resignation and the reasons for it. Though he implied that Colonel Ralston had violated cabinet secrecy in his statement of November 12, Mr. King paid tribute to his former colleague's sincerity, personal integrity, and patriotism. He announced General McNaughton's appointment as defence minister, with the observation that 'from the moment of his appointment as commander of the First Canadian Division on October 5, 1939, the name of no man in Canada has been held in higher esteem or commanded more in the way of confidence in the minds of the citizens of Canada or on the part of members of the Canadian Army and their relatives and friends.'[33] Gordon Graydon, House leader of the opposition, pressed for action on the reinforcement question with a 'minimum of talk,' and called for full application of the N.R.M. Act and the immediate sending overseas of all trained home defence troops. His motion to this effect was ruled out of order. The prime minister, urging 'thoughtful consideration' of 'one of the gravest problems that has ever been before the Canadian Parliament for consideration,' headed off a Conservative proposal that the House should sit 'mornings, afternoons, nights, and Saturdays' until the issue was decided.[34] M. J. Coldwell, the C.C.F. leader, suggested a secret session in order that the House might receive every available bit of information. The Conservative leader opposed the suggestion of a secret session, while Mr. King proposed that General McNaughton should make a statement to the House the following day and answer questions. The House agreed to the prime minister's motion.

At a cabinet meeting on the evening of November 22 Mr. King yielded to pressure from those cabinet members who had been pressing for conscription and who had threatened to appeal to a Liberal caucus. The prime minister said that General McNaughton advised him that the appeal for volunteers could not succeed, and felt it necessary to recommend conscription. Mr. King declared that he had reluctantly decided to support this recommendation. An order-in-council was then approved.[35]

When the House met again on November 23 the prime minister tabled an order-in-council (P.C. 8891), passed that day, which on the recommendation of the defence minister and under the Militia Act (Section 67), the N.R.M. Act, and War Measures Act, authorized the sending overseas of 16,000 N.R.M.A. troops 'for the reinforcement of the Canadian forces fighting in Europe and the Mediterranean.'[36] The order left the way open for the later sending of additional men overseas by further orders-in-council. The figure named represented the number of fully or nearly fully trained infantrymen available, and slightly more than the number required to ensure a reinforcement supply. The leader of the opposition expressed dissatisfaction with this partial surrender on the part of the government, opposed a secret session, and gave notice of a motion of lack of confidence and for immediate application of the full provisions of the N.R.M. Act. The government had called for a vote of confidence, while the prime minister left the question of a secret session to the House.

In his prepared opening statement to parliament General McNaughton declared that he differed only in method and not in purpose with his predecessor. In October Colonel Ralston had held that the forces overseas could no longer be maintained by the voluntary method, while McNaughton thought they could, with proper public support. He argued that a change of method would have been dangerous 'until all measures proper to the existing method had been developed to the full and it had become clear and evident to all that they would not suffice.'[37] He stated his own continuing preference for the voluntary method, but did not exclude compulsion if necessary. He reviewed his efforts in behalf of the voluntary system, revealing that the military district commanders had told him they had little hope of meeting requirements in that way, but had loyally agreed to make another effort.[38] He admitted that the results of the drive for overseas volunteers had not been adequate, and that he had been advised that 'there are very many N.R.M.A. men who will not volunteer under present circumstances but who are quite willing to be sent overseas.' He declared that there was no present overall shortage, but 'a possible prospective shortage of fully trained infantrymen' in late January or early February, 1945. He was also greatly concerned about reinforcements for French-Canadian infantry units, but 'promising results' had already been obtained in meeting this situation, thanks to 'our colleagues from the Province of Quebec and others.'

The crux of General McNaughton's statement came in the following words:

> I want to say, quite definitely, that all anxiety would be removed if we are able to find in December a total, above the numbers now arranged, of 5,000 infantry fully trained or in an advanced state of training, a similar number in January and a further 6,000 in the succeeding months.
>
> Every possible economy in the employment of fit general service personnel in home establishments has now been made or is in process, and the men so made available are included in the figures of planned dispatches.
>
> In consequence the only source from which this additional 16,000 can be secured is from the N.R.M.A.[39]

For the future he anticipated siege warfare in both northwest Europe and in Italy, with conditions approximating those of the later phases of the First World War. An increased production of shells and munitions would be necessary, and in this effort might be used 'large numbers of men who have come into the army in Canada, both general service and N.R.M.A., who can never be employed in battle.'[40] He held that many of the functions performed by N.R.M.A. men at present should not 'be done by soldiers to the prejudice of their proceeding overseas.'

McNaughton announced that N.R.M.A. men who did not volunteer would not be released from the Army 'until they can be demobilised without prejudice to the interests of our men returning from overseas.' Those who volunteered would 'become in all respects an integral part of that great band who served Canada by their own free will and whose pride it is to go where duty calls and needs dictate.' Of those who did not convert to general service, 'all men who are physically fit and deemed likely to make efficient combat soldiers' would be concentrated in N.R.M.A. units 'for potential combat duties.'[41] Those not fit for combat duty would be organized in employment companies 'to discharge any requirements for help on works of national importance to the prosecution of the war.' N.R.M.A. men suitable for neither purpose were to be discharged or placed in industry. In conclusion McNaughton stated that it was absolutely necessary to make available overseas 'a substantial reserve of reinforcements,' and that 'the numbers required to make up the reserve that is necessary are larger than could be provided in time by the volunteer conversion of trained and fit personnel of our N.R.M.A. men to general service.' The order-in-council, extending to the European theaters the service of 16,000 N.R.M.A. men, gave the minister power to fill the gap between the requirements and the number of volunteers. McNaughton added: 'This power will be used only to the extent necessary to make up the numbers of reinforcements required.'[42]

The leader of the opposition deferred to Colonel Ralston in opening the questioning of General McNaughton. Ralston expressed the view that a secret session might be advisable for reasons of security, and declared that McNaughton seemed to have adopted the same view he had always held, 'conscription when necessary.'[43] He pressed for information as to the extent of the shortage of reinforcements—this was refused on grounds of security; as to whether the 16,000 to be sent overseas between December and May would be all N.R.M.A. men; and as to whether they would constitute an adequate supply of reinforcements. McNaughton stated that some general service men might be included in the number, and that the reinforcement supply would be adequate.[44] When questioned further by H. C. Green (Vancouver South), as to the use of N.R.M.A. men, McNaughton stated the government's policy thus: 'As long as there are suitable general service personnel available to fill the requirements, it is our intention to use them. We propose to make good whatever deficiencies there are from N.R.M.A. personnel . . . I have no intention of using compulsion except to meet a deficiency, and having regard to the purpose we have of maintaining the strength of our armies overseas.'[45] He denied Mr. Green's efforts to prove that remustered general service men, inadequately trained for combat, would be sent into action while fully trained N.R.M.A. men remained in Canada.

Mr. Hansell (Macleod) brought the afternoon session to a close with an awkward question 'perhaps more directed to the Prime Minister than to General McNaughton': 'Would Colonel Ralston's resignation have been necessary if this order in council had been passed upon his report to the cabinet after his return from overseas?'[46] Mr. King objected to 'almost continuous cross-examination [of General McNaughton] by members of one particular group,' when the Conservative leader had asked that the general's appearance be confined to one day, and expressed the hope that the C.C.F. and Social Credit members would be given a chance. To Hansell's question he gave this answer in his best inscrutable style:

> There are some things that can be done or which may be necessary at one time which cannot be done or which may become unnecessary at another, and if the government had attempted to do a month or two ago what at that time did not appear necessary or what has been done to-day, I venture to say that its action would have frustrated the ability of the defence department to give to the men fighting on the other side the reinforcements needed at the time they may be needed.[47]

M. J. Coldwell then took over the questioning, and after queries about leaves and the margin of safety for reinforcements, again paved the way for a secret session. In response to a Conservative interruption, he denied that he had discussed his questions with anyone,[48] though it was rumored that he was co-operating with Mr. King.

That evening, in response to further questions by Mr. Coldwell, General McNaughton stated that 16,000 N.R.M.A. were trained as infantry, and that another 26,000 were of an age and medical category suitable for such training. In reply to Mr. Diefenbaker he gave the following general service enlistment figures: June, 6,282; July, 4,860; August, 5,256; September, 5,318; October, 4,710, which ran about 2,000 higher than the monthly discharge figures.[49] Under further questions from the same source he indicated that he had formed 'the definite opinion' that the N.R.M.A. men 'had been pressed rather than led' to volunteer, and that 'with leadership and persuasion and appeal these men will come forward.'[50] The number of N.R.M.A. men who had gone active from November 1 was given as 734, with the weekly rate steadily increasing.[51] To date, however, the monthly rate was about the same as in July, August, and September, and 50 per cent higher than in October.[52] As the Conservative close questioning continued, using General McNaughton as the butt of an attack on the government, the prime minister intervened several times, and finally threatened to resign.[53] At his suggestion it was agreed to continue the questioning on the following day, partially in secret session if the House so desired, with the debate on the vote of confidence to open on Monday, November 27.

Jean-François Pouliot (Témiscouata), stating that he had to make a choice between his constituents and the present government, crossed the floor of the House at the end of Thursday's sitting, while Wilfrid Lacroix (Quebec-Montmorency) likewise left the government's ranks on Friday afternoon. The prime minister then stated that Air Minister C. G. Power had submitted his resignation, as announced by the press, but that thus far it had not been accepted. Pouliot, declaring that 'the province of Quebec is not at all opposed to a well-balanced conscription where the value of the services of every man who is working in an essential industry is recognized as a help to the war effort,' expressed the hope that 'in the future there will be no politics mixed up with this question.' He urged that General McNaughton be given a free hand to reform the defence department.[54]

McNaughton opened his second day's testimony by a written statement which clarified the previous day's discussion, during which, as a soldier without parliamentary experience, he had become confused under ruthless cross-examination by veteran parliamentarians and lawyers:

I expressed a strong preference for our traditional voluntary system, and also my hope that it might not be necessary to use to the full extent the powers given to the Minister of National Defence in the order in council tabled yesterday. In some quarters my remarks have been interpreted as an intention on my part to scrape up men and use our general service men and to use them first even if they are not as well trained as N.R.M.A. men. That is not so. What I desired to convey was that I hoped trained N.R.M.A. men would volunteer for general service soon enough and in large enough numbers that it would not be necessary to send them overseas by compulsion. What I wish to make clear is that if adequately trained men do not volunteer in sufficient numbers the required numbers will be made up from the best-trained men we have. These will be detailed for service overseas under the order in council.

While the order in council extends the locality of service of all N.R.M.A. personnel, the maximum number the Minister of National Defence is authorized by the present order to dispatch overseas is 16,000. This power will be used to the extent that adequately trained men, whether now in the N.R.M.A. or not, do not come forward as volunteers sufficiently rapidly to meet the numbers required. The maximum was fixed at 16,000 in order to provide adequate reserves. In addition to giving the reserves required by the time they are required, these numbers will also enable increased periods of rest for individuals and will provide the increased number needed to compensate for the men given leave to Canada as these proposals develop.[55]

He also revealed that the N.R.M.A. units to provide the 10,000 reinforcements to be sent overseas in December and January had been selected that morning, and would soon be moved to 'concentration areas in eastern Canada.' Men who wished to volunteer would be given every opportunity to do so, but 'the whole units, including those men, would be dispatched on the dates which were then being arranged.'[56]

Total enrollments in the N.R.M.A. from 1941 to September 27, 1944, numbered 150,000. Of these 42,000 had converted to general service, 6,000 had been transferred to other services, and 33,500 had been discharged, leaving a strength of 68,500 of whom 8,500 were on extended leave from their depots for work in the national interest. Those enrolled in 1942, the peak year, provided over a third of the present net strength. The largest number of the 60,000 came from the Quebec military districts (22,800), with 15,000 from the Ontario ones, 13,800 from the Prairies, 4,300 from the Maritimes, and 4,100 from British Columbia.[57] The leaders of the C.C.F. and Social Credit parties expressed opposition to coerced conversion to general service, while Conservative members protested hard cases of remustered men, wounded men returned to service, and men discharged from the Air Force with less than two years' service who were liable to be conscripted for army duty. At the end of the sitting Coldwell again pressed for a secret session, but the House adjourned over the weekend without settling the question.

When parliament met again on Monday afternoon, November 27, the prime minister announced that he had been unable to persuade Air Minister Power to withdraw his resignation and that it had consequently been accepted. In the correspondence which was read and tabled, Mr. Power stated that he was unable to accept the government's policy on the use of N.R.M.A. men:

> I do not believe such a policy to be necessary at this time, nor will it save one single Canadian casualty.
>
> I parted company with Colonel Ralston after the most mature consideration largely on the grounds that the number of troops which he reported as being required was comparatively so small, the means to remedy the situation without placing undue strain on the men at the front so readily available, and the end of the war so imminent that weighing everything in the balance we were not justified in provoking a national scission.
>
> I cannot accept now from a new minister, General McNaughton, a recommendation which I reluctantly felt obliged to reject when made by an old comrade and tried associate Layton Ralston.[58]

In a speech clarifying his stand, Mr. Power paid tribute to Colonel Ralston's sincerity and conscientiousness, but expressed his own conviction that the Army could have lowered its casualty rate and eliminated the reinforcement crisis by taking 'the men out of the line temporarily to refit, to re-equip, to rest, to recuperate and to refill the gaps in their ranks. . . . If the course of systematic recuperation were taken, then the voluntary system which we have been following, which yielded more men last year than was ever estimated, and which in the words of the present Minister of National Defence (Mr. McNaughton) has not failed, would have sufficed at this stage of the war when by the most authoritative accounts victory is certain.'[59] He felt that 'Neither ultimate victory nor national honour requires that Canadian troops should be in action every hour or every day.' He had been unable to change his convictions on conscription 'in a matter of minutes.' Therefore he, 'for opposite reasons to Colonel Ralston, but following his example,' was also leaving the cabinet in accordance with the doctrine of cabinet solidarity.

As the English-speaking Liberal with the best knowledge of Quebec, Power had this to say:

Conscription may be justified in moments of national crisis and in defence of one's country; and in the discussion of Bill 80 of 1942 I said so. It might have been justified at certain periods and phases of this war when we were on the brink of almost certain defeat. It might have been justified if D-day had been a smashing catastrophe instead of a brilliant success. But these days are now past. We have no right to tear this country asunder at this stage, and in this state of the war.

. . . . .

A word as to the consequences of this controversy. Millions of honest, decent people in all parts of Canada and of all shades of opinion are in the process of hating and reviling one another. Reason and sincere conviction have given way to hysteria on both sides. Cleavage between classes and between races has been driven deeper and deeper. The most tragic thing of all is the weakening of faith and confidence in public men—not only by the people of one province, but in all provinces; not only amongst those who hold one view, but in men and women of all sides of this unfortunate debate.

As to the cleavages to which I refer, I cherish and hold fast to the ideas of the chieftain under whose aegis I entered this house, Sir Wilfrid Laurier. He could not and would not believe that as a Canadian he could belong to a party of one province only. With him, I cannot and will not subscribe to a purely isolationist provincial standpoint.

It may be that for some time to come the day has gone when men of similar ideas and principles can meet and join in common action across the Ottawa river.

My hope, my prayer is that there will be no such outcome, and that with the advent of external victory and peace, peace and understanding may come within our own country.[60]

Having lost one cabinet colleague because he refused to adopt conscription, and another because he subsequently did so, the prime minister then moved for a vote of confidence, 'That this House will aid the government in its policy of maintaining a vigorous war effort,' and made a long and moving plea for support of his government. He declared that conscription was the real issue, and that the resignations of Power and Ralston for opposite reasons made clear the difficulties which he faced 'in seeking to carry out what has been, above all else, the purpose of my work in public life; the maintenance of unity as far as that might be possible in the government of this country and in the Dominion of Canada itself.'[61] He reviewed at some length the history of the conscription question since September 1939, when parliament had been of one mind that there should be no conscription for overseas service, and since March 1940, when the government received 'a mandate to carry on the war and to carry it on without resort to conscription.'[62] With the fall of France and the threat of invasion of Canada, the N.R.M.

Act, providing for conscription within Canada, had been passed and accepted by the country. An agitation for conscription for overseas then arose, and the government was freed by the plebiscite from its moral obligation not to invoke its legal power to adopt conscription for overseas. Refuting the view that the plebiscite result was a mandate for conscription, Mr. King described the policy of the government under Bill 80 as 'not necessarily conscription but conscription if necessary . . . and to the extent that it might be necessary.'[63] But no such action had proved necessary until the current situation arose.

Mr. King then reviewed the history of the crisis, declaring that although Colonel Ralston 'for a long time has believed that it might become necessary to resort to conscription for service overseas to provide necessary reinforcements,' no such recommendation had been made until October, when Ralston returned from overseas. The prime minister declared that the shortage of reinforcements then anticipated was not expected to arise until 'the beginning of the new year,' and thus 'while the government has been giving this matter all the mature considerations that its great importance and grave significance necessitate, we have been running no risk so far as our fighting men overseas are concerned,'[64] despite Conservative charges. The cabinet had sought a solution of the problem 'which would not involve a break-up of the government itself in a time of war.' He anticipated that in the future the 'organized propaganda for conscription in Canada,' which had created 'a degree of unrest . . . the like of which has not been seen in the history of Canada before,' would be condemned. The cabinet, feeling that everything had been done that was possible 'to make Canada's war effort a total war effort,'[65] had wondered why it was necessary to run the risk of dividing the country on the eve of certain victory. The prime minister himself had been particularly concerned by the effect upon Canada's postwar role in the world of creating division within the country.

The cabinet had accepted the need for reinforcements, but remained divided on the method of obtaining them. A further appeal for volunteers was agreed upon, but no agreement could be reached as to whether its duration should be limited. Ralston 'had not faith' in the success of this appeal, and threatened to resign unless compulsion was used if necessary. Air Minister Power was ill and unable to take Ralston's place as associate minister of national defence. Other ministers intimated that they would resign if Ralston did.[66] King then called in General McNaughton, who expressed his belief that the required number of men could be found by the voluntary method and agreed to enter the government if a crisis arose. The prime minister then so informed the cabinet, and

Ralston resigned and McNaughton took his place, after Ralston and other ministers had refused to take the responsibility of heading the government and putting through conscription.[67]

The prime minister had decided against an appeal to the people—though he had not the least doubt that he would have been returned with a good majority—since an election would have meant a bitter campaign and a delay in sending reinforcements.[68] He declared that until parliament met on November 22, he had thought that the appeal for volunteers would succeed, but at a cabinet meeting that night McNaughton expressed the view, reached 'in conference with his staff,' that 'it might be taking too great a chance not to act immediately.'[69] The cabinet had then chosen the middle course between all-out conscription and no conscription by adopting the order-in-council which guaranteed the necessary reinforcements. Citing Sir John A. Macdonald's description of the 'deadlock and impending anarchy that hung over us' when Quebec and Ontario could not unite to form a strong government before Confederation, Mr. King declared that 'unless this House of Commons can unite in reasonable measure to support an administration that can carry on at this stage of the war we shall have to face the possibility of anarchy in Canada while our men are fighting overseas, giving their lives that we may maintain our free institutions and that we may have peace and concord through the years to come.'[70]

The step taken by the government in this situation was in accordance with the government's stand on Bill 80, as stated many times by the prime minister in the House. But the government required parliament's support in carrying out now a decision which had been taken in 1942. He clarified the scope of the order-in-council in the following words:

> That order in council P.C. 8891 applies to all personnel who are serving or who may serve in consequence of having been called up under the National Resources Mobilization Act . . . The order in council authorizes the Minister of National Defence to dispatch overseas a maximum of 16,000 N.R.M.A. personnel. In calculating the number of N.R.M.A. men so dispatched of [*sic*] reinforcements men will be counted as N.R.M.A. personnel only if they have embarked on board ship without converting to general service. All N.R.M.A. personnel who convert to general service before embarkation will go overseas as volunteers. The additional numbers estimated to be required total 16,000, regardless of their status on leaving Canada.[71]

Mr. King contended that the government had successfully surmounted two crises, Ralston's resignation and the decision on the order-in-council, in which 'the ministry itself might have been obliged as a whole to resign, with what consequences I leave others to contemplate.' Pleading with the House to back the government and thus avoid another crisis, 'a crisis greater than any other that has ever been on the horizon of Canada,' Mr. King declared that 'it will not help the army to defeat the present government and possibly force a general election.'[72] He reiterated the dangers of a wartime election; stated that he would stand or fall with his own party; and asked whether any of his colleagues in the cabinet, or the leaders of the Conservative, C.C.F., or Social Credit parties were prepared to take on the responsibility of government. 'Unless you are, unless you feel that you can present to the country an alternative government worthy of its support at this time, I think you owe it to this administration to support it.'[73]

Addressing his Quebec supporters, he declared that his public acts had always been 'in the interest of Canada as a whole, not in the interests of any particular province,' although he had been often accused of seeking to appease Quebec or to retain its support at all costs. He had sought, however, 'to have the people of Canada understand the province of Quebec.' The other provinces owed something to Quebec for keeping Canada British in 1775 and 1812, and for playing its part ever since in the development of the Canadian nation. He had defended the people of Quebec from 'ruthless, unprincipled and often brutal attacks' from other parts of the country, not merely in the interest of fair play and justice, but because 'Canada cannot be governed unless the rights of minorities are respected.' He stated that the French Canadians did not fear conscription, to which they had submitted under the N.R.M. Act, but that 'they look upon conscription as a symbol of domination by the majority.' Repelling the charge of appeasement, he pointed out that Quebec had accepted the postponement of redistribution at its expense; it had accepted Bill 80, though 'With that measure began the little rift within the lute of the Liberal party'; and now it was being asked to accept partial conscription. He appealed to his Quebec supporters, 'who have trusted me so firmly through the years that have passed to trust me again on this occasion.'[74]

Quoting Laurier's appeals of 1887 to the French Canadians to be Canadians first, and of 1916 to unite with the English Canadians in offering their services, he added the words spoken in 1939 by Ernest Lapointe, 'the closest, the truest and the most devoted friend I have had in my political life,' that: 'No government could stay in office if it refused to do what the great majority of Canadians wanted it to do.' Mr. King then called for a vote of confidence, not as approval of the order-in-council, not as approval of conscription, not as unlimited approval of government policies, but as an indication of willingness 'to support the government in continuing to carry on Canada's war effort at the present time.' A vote against the motion would be taken by the government as a vote 'to have the present administration resign, and another administration immediately take its place.' He concluded with some words of Laurier spoken in 1900, which he wished to use as his own on this occasion and to have 'remembered of me by my fellow-citizens when I also am gone':

If there is anything to which I have devoted my political life, it is to try to promote unity, harmony and amity between the diverse elements of this country. My friends can desert me, they can remove their confidence from me, they can withdraw the trust they have placed in my hands, but never shall I deviate from that line of policy. Whatever may be the consequences, whether loss of prestige, loss of popularity, or loss of power, I feel that I am in the right, and I know that a time will come when every man will render me full justice on that score.[75]

This speech was one of Mackenzie King's most notable efforts and attained the eloquence and feeling which he so often sacrificed to caution and provision against all future eventualities. While its clear reflections of his own opinion that he was indispensable galled his critics, it provided an unsurpassed proof of his extraordinary ability to steer a course for the nation through troubled waters which made allowances for all the currents of Canadian public opinion. It was the masterpiece of an extraordinary figure, who combined the abilities of an idealistic scholar and a highly practical politician.

That evening Gordon Graydon, as floor leader of the opposition, declared that 'This is peculiarly, I think, a parliament of those who fight for Canada, and indirectly of their dependents as well.' He argued that the government could have met and solved the reinforcement crisis, 'had it taken the courage to do so without allowing it to reach the proportions that it has reached or disturbing and distressing our people, both here and overseas, in the long and tragic process.' He urged that party barriers should be let down in the national interest, and that concern should be shown for national unity, 'with no hatred in our hearts for any single section or part of Canada.'[76] The main issue was winning the war, and the war was not yet won despite cabinet statements to that effect. He argued that the public wanted parliament to clean up the situation once and for all, with no more cabinet crises, and no more delays of reinforcements, and so he protested against the order-in-council restricted to 16,000 men and the possibility of future crises when further orders might have to be passed.

The government seemed half-hearted about its policy of 'controlled conscription,' and Graydon thought that 'the question of confidence in the Prime Minister to carry out properly the terms of that legislation was left more in doubt this afternoon by his words than by anything that might be done over here to throw doubt upon it.'[77] He compared the order-in-council unfavourably with that providing for the sending of N.R.M.A. men to the Alaska-Aleutian theater of war, and stated the Conservative opposition 'to the pulling of punches in this last phase of our struggle in the war.' He pressed for one army and an end of this 'piecemeal and appeasement policy' which had produced confusion in the public mind as the government retreated from trench to trench. He urged emphasis on the maximum rather than the minimum requirements for reinforcements, and pressed the question, 'Are those Canadians now serving in the European field of conflict to be asked to go to fight in the Pacific while men drafted under the N.R.M.A. remain in Canada?' He urged more leave for the men about to spend their sixth Christmas overseas. He criticized the prime minister for setting up the cry of 'King or anarchy in Canada.' Arguing that the opposition wanted total war and had not been getting it from the government, he moved an amendment to the motion of confidence:

> This house is of the opinion that the government has not made certain of adequate and continuous trained reinforcements by requiring all N.R.M.A. personnel whether now or hereafter enrolled to serve in any theatre of war and has failed to assure equality of service and sacrifice.[78]

M. J. Coldwell, leader of the C.C.F., declared that the issue was reinforcements, not conscription, a matter which had been decided in 1940. He regretted that the government had not seen fit to conscript wealth as well as men under the powers given it by the N.R.M. Act, and had never made a thorough inventory of all resources and allocated man-power to agriculture, industry, and the military services. He had urged that parliament should be summoned after Ralston's resignation because he believed that parliament and not the government alone should know the situation in full detail and take responsibility for what was done. The C.C.F. had taken no part in 'the recent discussion throughout the country based on supposition and rumour,' and had not joined 'the hymn of hate against conscripted men who had not volunteered for service overseas.' Some should have volunteered; others were torn 'between their duty to their country and the necessities of their homes, sometimes involving, too, a consideration of the needs of the country in the production of foodstuffs and other supplies.'[79] He pressed for information about the use of Canadian troops in the Pacific, and declared that too many questions remained unanswered, because of Conservative opposition to a secret session.

Criticizing the order-in-council, Coldwell moved a subamendment, which cancelled the Conservative amendment and added the following words to the government motion:

which in the opinion of this house requires the immediate removal of all distinctions between drafted and volunteer personnel, thus making the entire home defence army available for reinforcements overseas, and requires further the total mobilization of all the resources of Canada, material and financial as well as human, to ensure a total war effort, adequate re-establishment of the members of our fighting forces, and full employment after the war.[80]

He felt no confidence in the government's ability to maintain a vigorous war 'when its proposals in all respects fall far short of obvious requirements.' But he also had no confidence in the intentions or ability of the Conservatives, because of the irresponsibility they had shown in this crisis, their 'really shocking display of political manœuvring. . . . Some of their highly placed friends and a section of the press supporting them have done their best to inflame sectional differences and hatreds.' In conclusion he spoke movingly of his recent visit to the Canadian cemetery at Dieppe:

There was no distinction there of race or creed or colour. They were just Canadian lads who had died for their country. Why, oh why cannot we who are left behind in this country, to enjoy the freedom for which they died, live together? Those who in the midst of war engage in the setting of race against race, creed against creed and colour in this land are in my opinion unworthy of the living and the dead.[81]

J. H. Blackmore, leader of the Social Credit group, dismissed the agitation as 'pure politics' and associated himself with Coldwell's views on the Conservatives, before considering economic issues which he considered of far greater importance.

Then the prime minister took the Conservatives unawares by proposing that the House should meet in secret session on the following day, since Mr. Coldwell, Mr. Ralston, and many members desired further information which could only be given under such circumstances. Mr. Graydon's effort not to exclude the press was overridden on the ground of British precedent. The House met in secret session from 3 p.m. to 11 p.m. on Tuesday, November 28, and the only report of its proceedings was issued by the speaker: 'General the Honourable A. G. L. McNaughton, Minister of National Defence, was present and gave information respecting the Canadian forces.'[82]

8

When the House met again in normal fashion on Wednesday, November 29, a Conservative, R. B. Hanson (York-Sunbury), asked what measures the government was taking to meet the 'mutiny among the men of the home army' on the Pacific coast. The prime minister denied that a 'mutiny' existed and declared that the situation was 'being carefully watched and completely controlled.'[83] Further Ontario petitions for an 'all-out war effort' were received. The prime minister denied that Public Works Minister Alphonse Fournier had resigned. Labor Minister Mitchell made a statement that discharged Air Force or Navy men who had either served overseas or for three years in Canada would not be subject to recall for army service. Their plight had been protested by Conservative members. The speaker ruled that the C.C.F. subamendment was out of order, as the debate on the government's war policy was resumed.

J. A. Johnston (London), a Liberal veteran with four years' active service, defended the government's war effort, citing Churchill's tribute in the British Commons the previous day to 'the magnificent character of the Canadian war effort.' He rejected the possibility of a 'hybrid Union government.'[84] W. Earl Rowe (Dufferin-Simcoe), on behalf of the Progressive Conservatives, made 'an offer of co-operation provided the right leadership is found . . . without any request or suggestion of union government':

The Progressive Conservative party, with the full authority of its leader, John Bracken, and with the unanimous voice of its representation in this parliament, hereby declares that in this hour of national crisis, when the fortunes of political parties must be subordinated to the national weal, it stands prepared to co-operate with any government which, under leadership that will ensure equality of service, offers proof of will and determination to send to our soldiers overseas the reinforcements which our war commitments demand.[85]

He criticized the prime minister's record on conscription, and regretted the resignations of 'two of the most important men in the cabinet.' As he continued with kind words for Colonel Ralston and sharp criticism of General McNaughton, he suffered many interruptions from the government benches, where the cry of 'Tory conspiracy' was raised.

Victor Quelch (Acadia) moved a Social Credit amendment, calling upon the government to give:

1. The unqualified assurance to our men on the battle fronts that they will receive at once ample material supplies, and adequate reinforcements; and the use of all persons in any of Canada's armed services in any theatre of war in which they may be required.

2. The unqualified assurance, backed by appropriate action, that:

(a) Upon demobilization the active service men and women in the armed services, together with their families, will be ensured economic security, together with adequate grants and proper opportunities for training to enable them to re-establish themselves in the country's economic life;

(b) Adequate pensions and free medical care will be given to all persons whose health has been impaired during active service in the Canadian forces from any cause whatsoever;

(c) The dependents of all men killed in action or who have died in active service in the Canadian forces will be provided with economic independence for life.

(d) The foregoing will constitute a first charge on the nation.

3. The assurance to the people of Canada, by immediate action to that end, that following the war the abundant productive resources of the country will be used to the full, and that the resulting goods and services will be equitably distributed to ensure every Canadian economic security with full freedom.

4. The assurance that government wartime controls, bureaucratic regimentation and oppressive taxation will be discontinued as rapidly as possible after the war, and that the peace-time economy will be based on a proper democracy free from state domination of the people's lives.

5. Immediate steps to establish the necessary reforms to our financial system without which the foregoing will be impossible.[86]

Liguori Lacombe reviewed his anti-militaristic record and his prophecies since 1939 of 'the present disaster,' declaring that: 'As a result of Canada's participation in the war, the government has spent sixteen billion dollars; agriculture has lost over half a million workers, male and female; families are broken up, while mothers and daughters are toiling in factories, and thousands of our young men are being sacrificed on foreign soil.'[87] He stated that protests against conscription came 'not only from Quebec but from all sections of the country.' He could not find 'words sufficiently scathing to condemn this new reversal of policy by a government which, at the end of its term of office, imposes this evil and anti-national measure,' and declared: 'Never has a government broken so many pledges. Never has it thus sowed doubt and suspicion.' Since 1939 Canada had reverted to colonialism, but he expressed the hope that 'we may forsake this chaotic situation to unfurl at last a Canadian flag in an independent country, mistress of its own destinies . . . Whether we wish it or not, the deep reactions of the postwar period are bound to bring about the independence of Canada.' The government had inevitably been led into conscription by its decision in favor of participation, and he argued that if conscription was a 'tremendous mistake' in 1917, as Ernest Lapointe had said, it was 'doubly wrong today.' He saw this 'blood tax,' on top of 'too heavy a burden of taxes and loans,' as 'the deferred, but dire results of the military and financial imperialism laid down as a creed by the very people who claimed they were opposing it.'[88]

Fred Rose (Cartier), Communist representative of a working class Montreal district, declared that the Labor-Progressive Party included no N.R.M.A. men and had done everything in its power to support volunteering. He stated his belief that if the character of the War had been properly explained to the people of Quebec at the time of the plebiscite, they would have taken a different view of it. Attention should not be distracted from the issue of reinforcements by raising the questions of conscription of wealth and resources. He urged the House to recognize that Canada was 'a two-nation state,' that the French Canadians had reason to be suspicious of wars because of the past and that they had grievances which had not been corrected. He denounced the press campaign in the other eight provinces against 'Quebec and Quebec zombies' as vicious and un-Canadian. He declared that it was a campaign organized by the leaders of the Progressive Conservative party:

> It started a few months ago on the issue of family allowances. At that time Premier Drew of Ontario said: 'Ontario will not pay for Quebec zombies.' Then came a terrific intensification of this sort of thing in which he nearly broke his neck. He then decided to go overseas and to come back with a new issue, the issue of reinforcements. I am not denying the issue of reinforcements, but I do not like how it came to be raised. Premier Drew came back to this country, and at about the same time Major Connie Smyth came back and in a public statement told the country that untrained men were sent to the front. If I understand military law I should think it would have been more proper for the major to take this matter up with the proper authorities than to go into politics, but that was not done. When N.R.M.A. men parade we hear talk of mutiny, but when officers break every rule nobody says anything about mutiny or treason.[89]

French-Canadian isolationism had been nurtured by English-Canadian leaders as well as French-Canadian ones. Rose charged that the Dominion Textile and Aluminum companies had encouraged their workers to join Catholic syndicates, thus isolating them from the rest of Canada and keeping wages lower. Quebec's health and educational levels were lower than in the other provinces; while an English-Canadian always held the pursestrings of the province.

Rose declared that the 'poison spread throughout the country against the province' was 'the work of the same Tory elements who have profited in the past by the isolationism of the people.'[90] The people of Quebec had had 'a bigger dose of fascist propaganda than any other people.' Conservative literature in the 1935 general elections had been edited by 'Hitler's aide in Canada, Adrien Arcand,' while 'The Hon. Sam Gobeil, leader of the Conservative party in Quebec, wrote some of the most open pro-Hitler pamphlets written by any politician in this country.' Paul Bouchard, editor of *La Nation*, 'one of the worst Fascist sheets in our province,' had been financed in his campaign in the 1937 Lotbinière by-election by the federal Conservative leader, Maurice Dupré.[91] The paper had received support from Frédéric Dorion, then a Conservative and now leader of the *Groupement des Indépendants*, which Rose implied was a Conservative front. English Canadians had financed Duplessis' 'anti-war machine' in the last provincial election, which had been supported by the 'same *Montreal Gazette* which is now so loudly demanding conscription.' He did not exempt the Liberal party from blame, but he held the Tories chiefly responsible for Quebec's attitude.

Rose defended the French-Canadian record in the services and in war industry, and declared that if Quebec had a lower recruiting record, its people were 'the victims of certain conditions for which, to a great extent, English-speaking Canadians are responsible.' He favoured General Laflèche's methods of getting French-Canadian volunteers over those of M.P.'s 'who sit here and attack, attack, attack every attempt to induce such men to come forward as volunteers.' He deplored the attacks on General McNaughton and on the campaign for volunteers, declaring that the Tories were 'not interested in reinforcements' but 'in bringing down the government, and in having an election so they could ride to power, not for the good of the men who have gone overseas, but so they could bring us back to the old iron-heel Bennett days.' He supported the order-in-council, which he thought should satisfy everybody, 'that is, if he really wants reinforcements and does not want to force an election on the conscription issue . . . The only ones who would gain from such an election would be those whose interest it is to keep us apart. Whenever the English and French people have stood together, all the people have benefitted; whenever they have been torn apart, every one has suffered with the exception of those who wanted them to be torn apart. There must be greater national unity if our men are to get needed reinforcements, and if the people of Canada are to achieve security and peace in the post-war period.'[92]

That evening Colonel Ralston, who had become the key figure in the crisis and was widely spoken of as the potential prime minister of a coalition government,[93] spoke for over two hours, taking issue with the prime minister's version of the whole affair, and with the implication that he himself had violated cabinet secrecy. He returned the compliment on the latter score, with the observation 'What is all right for the Prime Minister of Canada, I am sure he will admit, ought to be quite all right for a humble ex-minister.' He stated that he had mentioned in the cabinet late in September that 'because of heavier infantry casualties' trained N.R.M.A. men might be needed.[94] Though he had never held that the N.R.M.A. men might not have to be used, he had worked just as hard as he possibly could to support the voluntary method. He now felt that it had failed as 'a dependable source for infantry replacements for the army at this stage of the war,' though he still preferred a voluntary army.[95] His version of the prime minister's offer to resign in favor of any other member of the cabinet was that only he and two others had been asked whether they would accept the office, and that they had all refused, taking the question to be 'purely hypothetical.' Mr. King promptly denied both statements.[96]

Colonel Ralston maintained that he had not proposed a new measure, but one which the government had agreed upon in 1942. He made clear that he had no ambition to become prime minister, and that he had resigned on the basis of the cabinet's refusal to accept his recommendation, and not on the question of a time limit for the appeal to the N.R.M.A. men to volunteer. When the prime minister had spoken of General McNaughton's belief that the 15,000 men Ralston had asked for could be got by voluntary means, and had expressed the view that McNaughton should be asked to take over, mentioning Ralston's unwithdrawn resignation of two years' standing, Ralston had resigned.[97] He contradicted the prime minister's statement about a shortage not arising until the beginning of the new year, declaring that when he resigned 'the figures showed that there would be a considerable shortage by the end of December; I mean a shortage in the strength of the units themselves, with no pools whatever.' For this reason he had pressed for immediate action in October, in order that men might be sent overseas in November, without losing another month.[98]

Ralston made a detailed analysis of the reinforcement situation as he had found it in his trip overseas, and reviewed the failure of previous campaigns to get N.R.M.A. men to volunteer. He criticized the course followed by the government after his resignation. But since action was more important than method, he would support the government's motion, rather than risk further delays through the formation of a new government or a dissolution which would result if the Conservative amendment carried, though he favored the principle of making all N.R.M.A. men subject to overseas service.[99] After a closing tribute to the Canadian Army, he called upon the house to see to it that the gaps in the ranks were filled. Ralston was so clearly the dominant figure in the debate thus far that R. B. Hanson moved adjournment until the following day, in order to let his words sink in, after blaming the prime minister and General McNaughton for the delay of six weeks in taking action on reinforcements, and assigning to them the responsibility for any bloodshed that might occur as a result of that delay.[100]

9

When the House met on Thursday, November 30, Daniel McIvor (Fort William) asked Mr. King whether it was not a waste of time and money to continue the debate since the prime minister, Colonel Ralston, General McNaughton, and the leaders of the opposition had spoken. The prime minister expressed a favorable opinion on the question thus raised, though he said he was unwilling to deprive any member of the liberty to speak. When debate was resumed, the Speaker ruled the Social Credit amendment out of order.

Mr. Hanson, speaking as acting leader of the Progressive Conservatives, declared that the offer made in John Bracken's name by Mr. Rowe the previous day still stood, and that it was not 'a mere political gesture.'[101] He denied that there had been any organized campaign for conscription, except on the part of the Canadian Legion, or that there had been 'a conspiracy simply for the purpose of getting rid of the present prime minister.' 'What public opinion outside of this house has done—and expression has been given to it by the great metropolitan newspapers of Canada—is to focus attention on a critical situation which we now know existed, and which still exists and will not be adequately taken care of by the right-about-face policy of the prime minister and those of his cabinet colleagues who have turned face with him.' Hanson took credit for reshaping the government's policy after Dunkirk by helping to evolve the N.R.M. Act, which he regretted had 'a hamstringing limitation that outraged public opinion in Canada.'[102] He sought to prove that Macdonald, Ralston, Ilsley, and Power had favored all-out conscription after the plebiscite, but had yielded in the interest of cabinet solidarity. He asked what confidence could be felt in King and McNaughton, who reversed their policy overnight and adopted one which they had recently condemned, and expressed regret that Colonel Ralston was not 'carrying through' with his case for immediate conscription of all N.R.M.A. men. He resented the prime minister's implication that no one except himself and the 'eighteen old tired men' of the cabinet could carry on the government of the country. After this effective opening Mr. Hanson lost the sympathy of the House by attacking the cabinet ministers one by one in partisan style. He closed by calling for a vote of no confidence because there remained doubt about 'the mandatory authority of the order in council to take every man that is necessary should the occasion arise, and before it arises, to reinforce our men overseas.'[103] But he refused to answer a question as to whether Manchuria, China, Burma, and India were excluded from the terms of the Conservative amendment, as well as Japan as he had stated.

L.-Philippe Picard (Bellechasse) then made the first notable French-Canadian contribution to the debate. Pointing out that 'sanity and reason are seldom present at the birth of great national or parliamentary crises,' he declared the present situation supplied further proof that 'mass emotional outbursts may develop into a situation such as to cause certain steps to be taken in the governings of the nation which may in turn incite other people to react in a way such as to cause friction and unrest.'[104] He briefly reviewed Canada's achievements in the last five years, and pointed out that they had been possible 'because the country was whole-heartedly behind the methods followed by the government up to now.' As he saw it, 'the trouble in Canada started when the conscriptionist elements in the cabinet yielded to the pressure of the Tory press and forced the government to bring in bill 80.' He declared that 'there was no real urgency in regard to that bill, since two years and four months elapsed after it was passed, over the opposition of myself and quite a number of other hon. members, before further pressure and the threat of a cabinet rupture brought about an order in council applying bill 80.' All wished to bring the war to 'a speedy and successful conclusion.' The divisive issue was conscription, which had 'split the British nation in 1916,' and in the present war still divided public opinion 'in many, if not all of the British dominions . . . The Tory press, the Orange lodges and the technocracy groups cannot blame the French Canadians or Quebec for the situation which exists in other parts of the empire.'

Considering the historic role of the French Canadians in the making of Canada, Picard objected to the English-Canadian habit of using them 'as a sort of national scapegoat on which to blame everything that goes wrong,' and of blaming the isolationist views of a Groulx or a Laurendeau 'on the whole racial group.'[105] Conscription had been opposed in Britain, Northern Ireland, Australia, New Zealand, and South Africa during this war, yet 'In Canada a question which could remain only the subject of discussion as to the merits or demerits of a principle has become the cause of racial disunity and parochial prejudices.'

After citing opinions on conscription in Britain and the other dominions, Picard turned to the development of anti-conscriptionist feeling in Quebec. He pointed out that from 1898 to 1912 'no encouragement was ever given to anybody of French-Canadian origin in Canada to join the army, for fear he might use unwisely some knowledge he would have acquired.'[106] When the South African War broke out, French Canada had little sympathy for it, an attitude now shared by 'a large proportion of broad-minded British people.' Picard saw a parallel between the position then and the position at the start of the present cabinet crisis, and considered that there began the 'break up of unity in the country on military matters':

That is the moment the trouble started. You saw Bourassa going around Quebec, spreading trouble, spreading nationalist sentiment and separatist sentiment. You saw this sentiment growing and growing in the elections of 1904, 1908 and 1911. In 1911 they succeeded in destroying Laurier in that province. Some of our opponents say the Liberals are responsible because in Quebec the people are against conscription. I would ask whether or not the Liberals, by keeping for French Canada a political outlet in following a large national party, have not served the country well. If they had not taken the attitude they took in 1917 the whole of the province of Quebec would have gone nationalist and separatist and we French Canadians would have suffered from it. Canada as a whole would have suffered. But due to the broadmindedness and the understanding of Laurier, who gave them an outlet in a national party, French Canadians were kept in a frame of mind which permitted them to collaborate in confederation, and they carried on for twenty-seven years in that fashion.

We are not responsible for conscription. That has been started by the nationalists, and by those people who believe that there should be two countries in Canada instead of one. But we of the Liberal party have fought against it. Laurier maintained national unity. He felt it was his duty to maintain a political outlet by means of a national party for French Canadians. And because of that attitude we were able afterwards to re-establish and re-unite with the rest of Canada in cordial relations, and to play the part which has been played, under this government, from 1921 to the present.[107]

Though the King government had conducted 'an efficient war effort' for five years, 'a powerful machine has been at work trying to undermine public confidence in the Prime Minister . . . and to convince the country that everything would go wrong unless a union government were formed, or unless a Tory administration were in authority':

A rumour-spreading, lie-whispering, mud-slinging monster has run amok unscrupulously risking to wreck the whole effort of the country . . . No matter how much the welfare of the country would have to suffer, no matter how much the war effort might be hampered, the one question, the only question that was apt to divide public opinion in Canada had to be brought forward and made into a symbol of disunity.[108]

While in English Canada the government was criticized for 'not waging an efficient war effort, and acceding to the views of Quebec in the matter of compulsory service,' in French Canada the same Tory forces, 'masquerading as independents,' accused the government of betraying Quebec.

The Quebec Liberals had backed the war effort wholeheartedly, differing from their colleagues only on Bill 80 and on the order in council sending N.R.M.A. men overseas. Picard declared: 'If I believed that when that order-in-council was passed the security of Canada was at stake unless we sent a few more thousand men overseas, I could have approved it and tried to have it understood in my province. But I cannot believe that, nor can I believe that without these few men the outcome of the war will be changed or even delayed.'[109] He thought 'The whole trouble is that our military experts want to make good the commitments they have made, even if they prove to be too large.' He thought the Canadian forces should have been concentrated on one front, instead of spread out in two theaters, and that thus the reinforcement and recuperation questions would have been simplified. 'If we have taken too large a chunk of the front, let us be sensible and correct our mistake,' since Canada did not have 'the vast reservoirs of men that the Russians or Americans have, and cannot be expected to compete with them.' He urged that Canada, like New Zealand, was justified in relaxing its military war effort if its industrial and agricultural effort were endangered by methods which did not meet with general approval or which would cause more trouble than good. He could not approve of the action of the government in passing the order-in-council.

Picard denounced the 'hysterical panic' which had been 'provoked and kept alive by the Tory press . . . based upon the wrong belief that unless the N.R.M.A. recruits are sent overseas, the sons and relatives of good patriotic Canadians will be incurring more dangers in the battle line.' He sympathized with the government, but believed that it should have given way to another if a change of policy had to be adopted. He made this statement reluctantly, 'because I have more confidence in the Prime Minister than in any other man in public life, and I know that my constituents, except for the passing of Bill 80 and order-in-council 8891, even now have more confidence in the Prime Minister than in any other leader.'[110] He feared that the conduct of a man favorable to the voluntary method but yielding to the pressure of conscriptionist ministers would increase Quebec's distrust of public men, 'while in the rest of the country it will appease but temporarily the worries of those whose attitude on this question has reached a state of hysteria.' He expressed at length his admiration and sympathy for the prime minister, but regretted that Ernest Lapointe was not still associated with him:

His weight in the councils of the nation would have strengthened the will of the Prime Minister to prevent some of the measures which have divided us and at times taken our minds away from Canada's wonderful accomplishments in the war. Never has a man's passing away been so sadly felt, especially when we realize that his presence might have been such an agent of cohesion and of unity.

Picard then moved, seconded by a Western English Canadian, Walter Adam Tucker (Rosthern), an amendment to the amendment: 'That this house will aid in maintaining an efficient war effort but it does not approve of compulsory service overseas.'[111]

Picard's sensible speech failed to sway the aroused conscriptionist English-Canadian members, as was evidenced by Howard Green's (Vancouver South) immediate observation that 'should the amendment be adopted by the House of Commons the effect would be that Canada would be deserting her boys overseas; and neither I nor any other member of the Progressive Conservative party in this house, nor any Tory so-called from coast to coast, has the slightest intention or [of] deserting our lads overseas no matter whatever else may befall.'[112] Green denounced the government measure as 'a political compromise,' and declared that 'this house and the Canadian people must never permit any government to gamble with the lives of our sons.' He called for support of his party's amendment: 'an honest, courageous manpower policy that is in line with the straightforwardness of the Canadian people.'

Walter Tucker, a veteran of both World Wars, criticized the Tories for 'wrapping themselves in the flag' and for breaking their campaign pledges in 1940 against overseas conscription. He supported the Picard motion because 'If we have gone into this war as a partnership on an agreed voluntary basis; if we have done our very best on that basis, and received the support of the whole country on that basis, then nothing short of actual danger to the country's existence, or a loss of the war, would justify our departing from that position.'[113] These conditions did not now exist, with victory assured. Like Picard, he favored solving the reinforcement crisis by the method suggested by Mr. Power, taking the Canadian divisions out of the line for a short time. He thought that the thousands of fully trained aircrew now being discharged could make 'a greater contribution toward the defeat of Germany than two or three times their number of unwilling draftees.'[114] He deplored the attacks upon the French Canadians and upon other Canadians of foreign origin, and cited the situation in his own Saskatchewan riding to prove that under the voluntary policy 'there has been a response from all peoples regardless of their religious beliefs or racial origin.' He condemned Pastor Shield's attacks upon Catholics. Canada's war effort to date could not have been accomplished if disunity had been created at the start by forcing compulsion upon the country.

The campaign for conscription had been started long before the present need for reinforcements arose; it had been intensified at present in an effort to overthrow the government. Tucker suggested that 'the forces of reaction which hate and oppose that great program of social and humanitarian measures which the Prime Minister has laid before Parliament this session saw in this agitation for conscription an opportunity of destroying the greatest Prime Minister Canada has ever seen.'[115] He defended the home defence troops, declaring that they included many Saskatchewan farmers who never should have been called up. Canada faced a troubled world, with the possibility of another situation such as in 1939. He hoped that 'irreparable damage has not been done' to national unity. He considered that conscription in the first war had done more harm than good, and was convinced that history will record once more that 'this attempt at conscription in the present war will have been an equal if not a greater failure.' He closed with a plea for cooperation, 'regardless of racial origin or religious creed, so that we can build up a country worthy of the volunteers who have gone forth to defend us against our enemies.' The speaker then found the Picard amendment out of order.

P.-J.-A. Cardin (Richelieu-Verchères), the veteran minister who had left the cabinet in protest against Bill 80, then spoke, paying tribute to Tucker with this observation: 'It is not very often that we French Canadians hear in this House of Commons an English-speaking voice defending the position that we are taking, expressing views which are similar to those that we entertain and using the same arguments that we ourselves are using in support of our own ideas.'[116] He thanked Tucker for his kindness and frankness in 'an expression of real Canadianism.' He also congratulated Picard, 'who has expressed to a very large extent sentiments which are mine at this time as they were when I debated Bill 80.' The speaker's rulings as to the subamendments also came in for praise, since the effect of these motions was 'purely and simply to becloud the issue and prevent the common people from understanding what is really at stake before parliament.' To Cardin the issue was simply approval or disapproval of the government's policy, which was 'a policy of conscription for service overseas.'[117]

The leaders of Quebec were under attack for creating the present state of mind in that province. He had no apologies to make for his part: 'What I said there was approved by the Prime Minister, with whom I was then associated. What I said there was approved by the leader of the opposition during the last electoral campaign. There was no divergence of view as between Liberals and Conservatives in regard to conscription for overseas service. We all said that this policy was no good for Canada; that it had been a failure in the past and would be a failure in the future.'[118] Laurier, Lapointe, and he himself had been true to their duty: 'We have spoken the truth, and what we have said in the province of Quebec we have repeated on each occasion and at every opportunity that has been given us in other sections of Canada, with the same courage, the same conviction and the same feeling of a real Canadianism.'[119] Lapointe and he had won Quebec to approval of participation in 1939, in the face of agitation against it. Since then Quebec's leaders had faced the situation as they found it and argued with the people, 'and there has been no trouble in my province, even though a certain number of my compatriots felt that they had been unfairly treated, that they had been insulted, that they were being called zombies by people who were irresponsible and who never had the courage to face the electorate in any section of Canada.' This indirect reference to Mr. Bracken, the titular Conservative leader who had never sought a seat in parliament, indicated how strong Cardin's Liberal loyalty was, despite his break with Mr. King. The same was true of many a French Liberal, for party loyalty is deeply engrained in the French-Canadian character.

In reply to the charge that Quebec had not furnished as many soldiers as other sections of Canada, Cardin repeated a statement he had recently made in Montreal:

> We have done more than you English-speaking Canadians of British descent. You have only obeyed the call of blood. You have answered the sentiments of your heart and mind. What we have done could only be done through reasoning, and judging the situation as a judge would do when deciding a case presented to him. It is not a case of reasoning with you; it is a case of sentiment, and I understand you. For a moment, if you wish to understand me and the French Canadians, reverse the picture if you please. Try to imagine Canada as part of a French empire, with the descendants of British citizens in the minority. Can you tell me that if the French empire, of which you would be part, were in danger, you would be as enthusiastic in defending that empire as would be the Canadians of French descent? To any man who would say that he would have the same views and sentiments I would reply that he is not sincere.
>
> Think of the position in which we are placed. Think of the concessions which the French Canadians and their representatives have been making to bring about and maintain unity in this great land of ours. I have no time to enumerate them all, but go over in your minds the concessions that were made by Sir Wilfrid Laurier, by Ernest Lapointe and by myself, at the risk of losing support and, indeed, with the loss of support in certain quarters of my province. We are here in the House of Commons, all friends, and as members of a family capable of understanding the truth. Where are your concessions, you British Canadians, in favour of the French Canadians? What have you ever done to preserve unity between the two great races in Canada? Unity has been maintained

owing to concessions made by French Canadians in this House of Commons and elsewhere. These are strong words, but they are the truth and no one can dispute them. The political history of our country is there to sustain my statement.[120]

Cardin argued that there was no more anti-conscription agitation in Quebec than in British Columbia or Nova Scotia, and maintained that the recent British Columbia demonstrations could not be the work of a handful of French Canadians, 'if the soldiers who are there with them did not have the same views, and if the people watching them did not share their views to a large extent.' He agreed with Mr. Howe that the agitation was mostly political, and he regretted that 'this has now become a political issue on both sides.'[121] The debate had made clear that conscription had been the law of the land and had been applied since 1942. He did not think that the volunteers overseas would ask 'that others be sent to help them, through coercion.'[122] He argued that many of the men overseas did not know what they were fighting for, and he believed that beneath the fine words 'most of the countries making up the allied nations are in the end—it may be a secondary consideration—looking after their own interests.'[123]

Cardin criticized the 'extraordinary situation' of a man resigning from the cabinet, 'leaving behind him three or four men who share his views and who, if necessary, will extend the crisis in which we are at the present time.' He declared that the country was entitled to know 'who precipitated the crisis, who caused the change in policy of the government, who brought about the decision which was given to us on November 23.' The ministers who shared Ralston's views should 'stand up and take their responsibility before this house and before the country.' Cardin discounted Mr. King's fear of a wartime election, since one had recently been held in the United States and another in 1917 in Canada, when Laurier fought for his policy and though defeated, emerged 'even greater than he was before.' Cardin remarked bitterly that the prime minister, who had quoted Laurier and Lapointe to justify conscription, should have quoted their words 'in favour of the voluntary system and denouncing the very stand which two or three ministers have forced him to take and who threatened to resign if conscription were not put into effect.'[124]

The Army, the Air Force, and the Navy had competed for recruits, and Canada 'tried to do too much for a country of our size and population.' That was why a need for reinforcements had arisen. Cardin argued that Canada should have followed Australia's course and reduced its armed forces in order to help civilian and war industries. He pressed for an election: 'The sooner we have one, the sooner the clouded atmosphere in which we are now living and have been living for the past five weeks or more will disappear and the sooner we shall be able to follow a policy that will be in the best interests of Canada as well as in the best interests of the allied nations.' He was not afraid of opposition from the party which had long been his: 'I have not ceased to be a Liberal, but I contend that my party, alas, has been moving toward the other side, towards the imperial and Tory spirit.' He paid tribute to Ralston's speech as that of 'a very sincere and trustworthy man, a man who, whatever his opinions may be, deserves the respect and confidence of every member of this house,' but he criticized as 'a bit weak' the former minister's defence of himself against the prime minister's charge that he had been slow in bringing the gravity of the situation before the cabinet.[125]

As the member who had served longest in the House, Cardin made a final plea for the reconciliation of the conflicting opinions of French Canadians, English Canadians, and New Canadians. He appealed to his compatriots of Quebec, 'whatever may be their sentiments, whatever may be their feelings at the present time, to be calm, to take things easy, to reflect before acting, and to remember that they are not only citizens of the province of Quebec but at the same time citizens of Canada as a whole, who desire to see their country in the not distant future, and with the will of all concerned, become a great and independent country.' They had a right to be firm, to be energetic, to freedom of opinion and speech, but they should be careful not to lose 'the advantage of the friendship which we now enjoy to a greater extent than ever before in the English-speaking provinces of Canada.' He urged that men of good will should get together, 'dispense with the military caste, which is a source of trouble,' and think of Canada first.[126]

In a tumultuous House Maxime Raymond, chief of the *Bloc Populaire*, then declared that a government which violated its most solemn pledges did not deserve a vote of confidence. He quoted the prime minister's words in 1942 that the unhappy state of the world was the result of broken pledges, and then recapitulated his pledges against conscription for overseas service.[127] He argued once more that the plebiscite had not relieved the prime minister from his obligations, since his only mandate was to avoid conscription. He charged that the prime minister 'endorses the principle of self-government in his statements and imperialistic tendencies in his acts.'[128] He traced the development of 'camouflaged' conscription since 1942, and urged an end to 'quibbling and dodging' such as the description of conscription under the November order-in-council as 'conditional voluntary service.' He charged that the war effort was already excessive; and questioned the idealistic argument that Canada had gone to war with Germany because it had invaded Poland, when Canada had allied herself with and aided a Russia which had invaded six countries, including Poland. The government's latest action would increase the existing disunion. He held that 'a nation has the right to compel its citizens to fight for its defence but not for the defence of other countries, especially when that nation has already accomplished a war effort of such magnitude.'[129] Confederation was based on the principles of 'provincial autonomy and respect for the rights of minorities, and from a national standpoint, autonomy of Canada with regard to England.' Those who threatened national unity were the 'people who think as imperialists rather than Canadians.' French Canadians were first of all Canadians. 'Too often has the Prime Minister resorted to the argument in favour of national unity, to find justification now in asking for a vote of confidence on a policy most likely to destroy that unity.'[130]

W. E. Harris (Grey-Bruce), a wounded veteran, denied Cardin's statement that the soldiers overseas did not know what they were fighting for. He opposed the Conservative amendment on the grounds that adequate reinforcements had been provided in the past, and that with Ralston and McNaughton in agreement on the present measure, they would be in the future. He denounced the Ontario campaign to make the home defence army, which included 15,000 Ontario men as well as 22,000 from Quebec, a Quebec problem exclusively. He paid tribute to the French-Canadian units with which he had served in Normandy, and to Quebec's 'very considerable' contribution to the armed forces. He closed with a tribute to the prime minister and the government.[131] G. K. Fraser (Peterborough West), made the typical Conservative charge that the King government had 'played favourites with the French Canadians.'[132] F. G. Hoblitzell (Eglinton) showed sympathy for the position of the Quebec members and favored the Conservative amendment, but announced that he would vote for the government motion because the real issue was 'to see that reinforcements are sent overseas without further delay.'[133]

Emmanuel d'Anjou (Rimouski) charged that Quebec had been betrayed, as Premier Godbout and Justice Minister St. Laurent had declared it would be if conscription for overseas service were ever forced upon the country. He saw the order-in-council of November 23 as 'the logical and unavoidable conclusion of the result of the plebiscite,' but declared that the government had no mandate to impose conscription upon Quebec after that province's refusal to free it from its pledges. The government had 'hatefully and brutally deceived' Quebec, and therefore in view of his own promises to his constituents he had quit the Liberal benches and seated himself with the *Bloc* members, 'because that party's platform embodies the ideas and principles for which I have fought since my entrance into public life and to which I intend to remain faithful.' He denounced war profiteers as the advocates of conscription, called for a Canadian flag, and expressed hope that Canada would become independent in the near future.[134] Opening the debate on Friday, December 1, R. W. Mayhew (Victoria, B.C.), supported the government, declaring that 'Anglo-Saxons' were not in favor of compulsion, but 'We adopt it when we have to—and this is one time when we have to.' He denounced the use of the term 'zombie': 'No Canadian who is good enough to wear the king's uniform should be called a zombie,' and defended both the N.R.M.A. men and the general service men serving in Canada.[135] G. S. White (Hastings-Peterborough), in supporting the Conservative amendment, challenged Cardin to put on record in *Hansard* the concessions which French Canadians had made to English Canadians.[136]

Joseph Jean (Mercier), former secretary of Ernest Lapointe, who had resigned that day as parliamentary assistant to Justice Minister St. Laurent, declared his lifelong opposition to conscription and coercion. He believed that 'there has been lack of good will and lack of competence somewhere in using the voluntary system as it should have been used,' when a reinforcement crisis arose after 750,000 volunteers had been sent overseas. He opened a way for members who wished to support the government without supporting conscription by moving an amendment which was seconded by Gaspard Fauteux (Sainte-Marie), to the Conservative amendment: 'That this house is of the opinion that the government has not made certain of adequate and continuous trained reinforcements *by using to the best advantage the general service personnel in Canada and the volunteers overseas without resorting to conscription for service overseas*.' When a question was raised by the leader of the opposition as to whether Mr. Jean had resigned as a parliamentary assistant before making his motion, he declared that he had. The prime minister stated that though there was no reason why a parliamentary assistant should resign before making a motion, both W. C. Macdonald, assistant to Colonel Ralston, and Jean had done so. He expressed the hope that the latter would reconsider his position later on.[137]

L.-T. Tremblay (Dorchester) opened the debate on Monday, December 4, making much of the popular distrust created by the order-in-council, the opposition to the appeal for volunteers from the profiteers who sought to force conscription, and the insults heaped on Quebec N.R.M.A. men in other provinces. He declared:

> In a democracy, if democracy is to survive, the majority have not the moral right, though they may have the power, to force upon a minority an obligation which they know this minority is unwilling to assume, especially when that majority, through its authorized and constitutional

leaders, have pledged themselves never to impose such an obligation on the minority.[138]

He closed with the question: 'Who has broken the pledge?' Colonel A. J. Brooks (Royal), who had commanded two of the training camps in Canada, made the following statement in reply to Tremblay:

> I have had both French and English Canadians in these camps, and I can say truthfully to this house that I do not know of one instance where there was any difference between these two races. They have played together, worked together, drilled together and slept together, and never has there been any trouble between them . . . I know also that overseas our men feel they are all Canadians and that there is no difficulty of the kind the hon. member has mentioned.[139]

In a vehement speech Brooks maintained that the voluntary system had been a 'failure from the very beginning,' and suggested that thousands of the N.R.M.A. men to be sent overseas would go A.W.O.L. He denounced the government's policy as one which was 'even less than half a measure, and in no way meets the requirements of the men overseas,' and had encouraged 'young men in one part of Canada to tear down the flag and to trample it into the dust, to tear down the flag of a country which for one year stood alone.' He called upon French, British, and Jewish Canadians to answer the call of Canadian blood.[140]

Ralph Maybank (Winnipeg South Centre) urged the French Canadians not to 'nurse a persecution complex.' He agreed that English Canadians should try to understand French Canada better, but thought that the French Canadians should also 'try a little harder also to understand us.' He denied that Pastor Shields and the *Globe and Mail* represented English Canada: 'The one is serving some kind of a financial crowd and the other is a mere bigot.' He did not think that a conspiracy had created the crisis, which had arisen from infantry casualties being 50 per cent over estimates, but he did think that once it had arisen it had been exploited by 'the agents of a cabal that wants a chore-boy union government.' He attacked the Conservative leaders, and compared their strategy to that of the Italian Navy.[141] J. W. Noseworthy (York South) declared that the people of Canada did not want a general election, but that they did want 'legislation or an order in council which beyond all shadow of a doubt will provide adequate reinforcements for the future, as well as the present, and legislation which will mobilize all the resources of the country for the further prosecution of the war.' He added that they also wanted 'a ministry in sympathy with that legislation, one upon which they know they can rely to carry it out.'[142] J. R. MacNicol (Davenport) attacked the C.C.F. for having voted against the Conservative motion for an all-out war effort in 1942, and defended Dr. Shields and the *Globe and Mail* before rehearsing the usual Tory arguments. L. A. Mutch (Winnipeg South), a veteran of both wars, supported the government motion.

Frédéric Dorion (Charlevoix-Saguenay), speaking as one 'independent of all political groups,' declared that he wished to associate himself with Mr. Cardin and to congratulate Messrs. Tucker and Harris, who proved that 'in spite of the malicious campaign of the last few weeks there are still in other provinces men of good will who can understand the sentiments of the French Canadians, together with the fundamental basis of Canadian unity.' Attacking the patriotism of Mr. Rose with a veiled reference to his internment in 1939, he denied that the Montrealer had the right 'to speak for French Canadians in this house.'[143] He charged that the debate was unwarranted after the order-in-council had been passed, and that the discussion had served merely 'to provoke a campaign of abuse towards the province of Quebec.' He argued, indeed, that participation and conscription had been settled since the prime minister had visited Hitler in 1937, with the purpose of making it clear that in case of a war of aggression, nothing would keep Canada from Britain's side. He dismissed all the amendments, and declared that the French-Canadian ministers might have avoided the campaign of abuse and the passage of the order-in-council if they had stuck to their guns. He also thought that if the prime minister had maintained his stand for the voluntary system, he would have been returned to office by an 'even larger majority than he has today.' He concluded with the observations that unity did not mean unification, that the two races had different mentalities, and that there could be understanding if the majority did not 'try to overrule the minority and force it to submit to all its wishes.'[144]

Maurice Lalonde (Labelle) supported the Jean sub-amendment, expressing sympathy for the prime minister but stating that many of his supporters had been placed in an 'unbearable position.'[145] James Sinclair (Vancouver North), an R.C.A.F. officer, declared that he had been converted to total conscription by his experiences in Britain since 1940. He charged that the Army had not made as good use of its manpower as the Air Force, when it had 130,000 general service men and 70,000 conscripts in Canada and a shortage of reinforcements overseas.[146] He had suggested the formation of an R.C.A.F. regiment to serve as infantry, rather than the discharge of surplus airmen. He favored a uniform system of retirement and discharge for all three services, with the use of the whole N.R.M.A. Army on active service, and a 'first-in-first-out' demobilization policy. Though a Liberal, he would vote for the Conservative amendment; if that were defeated, he would support the government motion.

Before the debate continued on Tuesday, December 5, the prime minister in replying to a question stated that in the twenty-six days since November 8, 6,297 men had volunteered for general service, 2,701 from the N.R.M.A. and 3,596 from the general public and the Reserve Army, 'the largest enlistment for a similar period since the outbreak of the war.'[147] J. G. Diefenbaker (Lake Centre) continued the Conservative attack on the order-in-council, arguing that conscription had been the law of the land since Cartier's Militia Act of 1868, and that since 1904, by a provision introduced by Laurier, the militia might be put on active service overseas in case of emergency.[148] He charged that the N.R.M.A. men were being bribed to volunteer. He cited statements of General Laflèche, Justice Minister St. Laurent, Munitions and Supply Minister Howe, Fisheries Minister Bertrand, and General McNaughton, indicating that they favored the voluntary method, as evidence that the government's heart was not in its new policy. He charged that the Jean amendment was designed to allow some members 'to support the government and at the same time remain on friendly terms with their supporters.' He asked whether the prime minister had given any assurance that 16,000 men was the limit, and no further orders would be passed. Mr. King promptly replied that he had 'made no promise to anyone.'[149] Diefenbaker denied that there was any politics in the Conservative amendment. But since reinforcements were on the way, there was no reason why the government should not call an election to see whether or not the people demanded 'equality of service and sacrifice.' A. G. Slaght (Parry Sound) favored the government's course, and charged that the Conservatives were not sincere in moving an amendment in favor of extending the service of N.R.M.A. men to any theater of war, and then excluding Japan as one of those theaters.

Armand Choquette (Stanstead) associated himself with the other *Bloc* members, declaring that their opinions were 'endorsed by the great majority of the Quebec population and by an increasing number of people from other parts of the country.'[150] He charged that political strategy was the cause of the order-in-council: 'The Prime Minister considers himself indispensable and it would seem that, in order to keep him in power, the sacrifice of a few lives and the violation of a few principles are well worth while.'[151] He made an appeal to all Quebec members, from the justice minister down to the lowliest backbencher, to keep their pledges and refuse to support the government policy. He denounced the Jean amendment as inspired by the prime minister. He rejected the idea that the order-in-council was a compromise between two opposing points of view, seeing in it simply an implementation of Bill 80. He defended Canon Groulx and Laurendeau from the charge of isolationism, and associated himself with them in saying that the French Canadians 'do not want to isolate Canada from the rest of the world' or 'to separate Quebec from the other parts of the country':

We are above all Canadians and we wish that Canada as a whole should belong first to its citizens and that it should be the heritage of each and every one of us. We demand complete independence for our country and I do not think that the fact of being supreme masters of our destinies could isolate us from other countries and raise a China wall between ourselves and our neighbours.

Mr. Speaker, those are fables deliberately spread by politicians much more concerned with the unity of their own party than with national unity. We consider the whole of Canada as our motherland . . . It should not be an English or a French Canada, but a Canada where both races would enjoy the same rights, the same privileges and the same opportunities, not only in Quebec but also in the eight other provinces of the dominion.[152]

Lt.-Colonel Hugues Lapointe (Lotbinière), the son of the late minister of justice and a veteran who had returned from the front within the last three weeks, censured the criticism which had been directed at General McNaughton. He stated his belief that 'the voluntary system is the only practical system of recruiting an efficient army in the circumstances in which we find ourselves in this dominion. . . . That system has not been a failure, and it can still bring about adequate results if certain individuals and responsible bodies in this country will use it for the purpose for which it was intended and not as an instrument to overthrow the King government.'[153] Parliament was faced with an accomplished fact, however, and in view of the prime minister's declarations in 1942, that members would have an opportunity to express their approval or disapproval if Bill 80 were put into effect, and the introduction of the present motion of confidence, the Jean subamendment offered 'the only way any hon. member may have of expressing his views on or his approval of the order in council.'

Lapointe had first been elected to the House in 1940, because the people of Lotbinière 'believed that the tradition of the Liberal party of which I was the candidate, and the doctrine which had always been preached, rightly or wrongly, was one of no conscription, and they selected me to follow that doctrine.'[154] He believed that he had 'attended as good a political school as any other hon. member in this house':

I have always been taught that politics was not a game of diplomacy, but that it was the most serious task to which any man could devote his talent and ability, and that to represent one's fellow citizens in the House of Commons was possibly the greatest honour and privilege to be vested in any man. I was also taught that pledges and promises once given had to be kept . . . Personally I cannot go back on the word which I solemnly gave to the people whom I represent in this house, especially when I am not convinced that this order in council was necessary for the winning of the war and the security of Canada. Furthermore, as regards this point, I will not permit any man to doubt my sincerity or impute any political motives to my action. It is purely a question to be settled between myself and my own conscience. It may be considered as a selfish attitude to take, but I would rather withdraw from public life than have it be said by any man who placed his faith in me that I had failed to keep the word I had given.[155]

Lapointe did not believe that the sending of N.R.M.A. men would relieve the pressure on the men at the front, because 'they will be swamped among the men who are already there.' He declared that 'you need a man of determination, of character and courage who will go forward under any conditions, in order to fill the ranks of the infantry.' He did not question the courage of any of the N.R.M.A. men, and declared that he had never heard the term 'zombie' until he returned to Canada. 'There is no monopoly of courage on the battle front—although there seems to be some here in Canada.' He criticized the debate and the countrywide campaign which had been carried on of 'playing on the sentiments and emotions of mothers, sisters and wives.'

I ask those people, and I ask hon. members who may have sons in the infantry in the front line to-night: whom would they rather have to-night in a slit trench along the front line, fighting it out, possibly holding back a counter-attack under the most intense conditions; whom would they rather have, the man who is there because he wanted to go there and who will stay there to fight it out and die, if necessary, or the man who is there simply because order in council P.C. 8891 was passed by this government?[156]

Lapointe doubted that draftees would be welcome in the front line, and he was skeptical that the draftees were 'eager to go overseas, and were just waiting for the government to assume its responsibilities,' as certain commanders in Canada had asserted. But to him the important point was not coercion but the loss of public confidence:

In my mind, what is even more important than that possibly 15,000 Canadians will be sent to serve overseas, against their will, in spite of the pledges made by the government, is the fact that for a long time the people of Canada will have lost some of the faith they usually have in their public men . . . It is not the judgment which the electors may pass now, at a time when the country is going through a period of mob hysteria, that is important; it is the judgment they will pass after the war is over, when they can analyze the facts in their true light, in an atmosphere of peace.

Lapointe did not wish to share the responsibility for undermining the Canadian people's faith and confidence in its public men. He expressed great admiration for the prime minister and deep sympathy for his tragic position, and deeply regretted that 'because of the wording of the motion now before the house I am not able to express to him the confidence I have in his ability to run this country during the difficult times through which we are now passing.' He believed he spoke for the people he represented when he told the prime minister that 'there is no one else whom they want to see as the head of the government of Canada, but on the other hand they cannot forget the breaking of a pledge which to them was sacred.' He expressed the hope that 'once the turmoil of this battle is ended, Canadians will realize at last that they should not be separated from one another, that they should not hate one another because of a mere political issue.'[157] He spoke of how men from Toronto, Regina, and New Brunswick had reinforced his company of the Régiment de la Chaudière in the D-day landing when it lost more than half its strength; and how there had been no national disunity at Carpiquet, Falaise, Calais, and Boulogne; and urged: 'Surely if the men at the front can achieve this national unity and attain this spirit of brotherhood the people back in Canada, and especially hon. members of this house, can fight the war on the home front following the example set for them by our Canadian forces overseas.' Otherwise, he felt, and thought he spoke for many of the men overseas, that 'if here in Canada we cannot achieve a community of spirit; if we cannot learn to understand one another better, then the hardships, the miseries and the losses we shall have suffered during this war may well have been in vain.'[158] Clarence Gillis (Cape Breton South) hailed Lapointe's speech as 'a breath of fresh air,' before expressing grave doubts about the government's policy and restating the C.C.F. stand.

Mr. St. Laurent, speaking on December 6 as the debate drew to a close, indicated that he had been discussing 'the real truths of the matter' with his fellow members from Quebec. He spoke of the needs of total war and reviewed Canada's contribution, with the observation that 'all has to go on and must be kept in full balance until full victory is achieved.'[159] He had believed that object could be attained by the voluntary system until the evening of November 22, but had accepted the change of policy when it was pointed out that the Canadian Army might be paralyzed by the need of infantry, and that inadequate reserves might affect the morale of men in the fighting line. He realized what the reaction in Quebec might be to his action: 'But I came here to do a war job, and because it was felt by the Prime Minister, rightly or wrongly, that I could be of some help, I feel I must still go on, whatever may be the difficulties of the task, so long as it is made apparent to me that these difficulties arise out of facts which have a bearing on the security of the men who are doing so much more for us than anything we can do for them.' He still felt and hoped that compulsion might not be necessary to secure the needed men, but no chance could be taken, and he had decided to 'stand or fall with the Prime Minister.'[160]

Mr. St. Laurent thought the Jean subamendment was apt to be defeated, and he appealed to those who supported it to accept 'that democratic decision in a democratic way':

> I am sure they can do so without accepting the concept of democracy which is sometimes asserted, the concept that it is both a legal right, and a proper exercise of that right, for the majority to assert its will at all times and in all occasions regardless of the feelings and views of the minority and of the reasons for such feelings and views. That is not my concept of the kind of democracy suited to free men; the kind of democracy for which the free nations are waging this war. It is not the kind of democracy which was envisaged by the fathers of confederation; or the kind of democracy which will bring to full fruition the constitution that unites in one nation the various elements which make up our Canadian people.
>
> The will of the majority must be respected and it will prevail. But I trust that, here in Canada, the majority will always, as it is doing in this case, assert that will only after giving due consideration to the feelings and views of the minority and to the reasons for such feelings and views, and then only to the extent to which the minority is sincerely convinced that the general interests of the whole body politic require that it be thus asserted.[161]

He appealed to all members of the House, whether they wished 'to do more or to do less than the order in council provides, to unite and to assert to the men overseas that this nation, from one ocean to the other, stands pledged to a victory that will be decisive and that will endure. . . . Let us neglect nothing that is necessary for victory, but on the other hand let us strive to avoid doing or saying anything that is not really necessary and that might destroy or impair the unity which has made and is still required to make our efforts strong and constant and successful.' Mr. St. Laurent, as titular leader of the Quebec Liberals, rallied many of Mr. King's wavering supporters by his wholehearted and courageous acceptance of the prime minister's decision, which then seemed likely to spell the sudden end of his political career.

10

At the opening of the evening sitting on December 6, the prime minister announced that he had met with the leader of the opposition and the leaders of the C.C.F. and Social Credit groups, and that they had agreed that the debate might be well wound up by the following night, since 'if it were to continue for any length of time it would have an unsettling effect rather than otherwise throughout the country.'[162] It was thereupon agreed to have morning sittings 'until the completion of the current business.'

The Conservative attack on the government motion and the division within the cabinet continued, with H. R. Jackman (Rosedale) pointing out that Mr. St. Laurent was the only minister who had spoken on behalf of the government motion.[163] G. A. Cruickshank (Fraser Valley), a Liberal veteran of the first war, declared that he would vote for the opposition amendment, but if it were defeated would support the main motion, like his colleague Sinclair.[164] Jean-François Pouliot (Témiscouata) explained his departure from the government benches by the observation that the order-in-council was 'the drop of water that made the glass overflow' for him, and that the prime minister had 'since the beginning of the war preferred to take advice from his opponents to taking it from his supporters.'[165] After reviewing his political career, he charged that the Liberal party was dead and the prime minister had killed it.[166] Armand Cloutier (Drummond-Arthabaska) declared that he would vote against the government motion because he was opposed to conscription. He realized that the prime minister was 'the victim of a foul conspiracy hatched by a majority blinded by old prejudices and by new political-military and financial schemes,' and retained confidence in him on other matters than war policy.[167] Similar anti-conscriptionist views, coupled with reluctance to break with their leader, were expressed by other Quebec Liberals. J.-A. Crète (Saint-Maurice-Laflèche), Maurice Bourget (Lévis), and Charles Parent (Quebec West and South), hailed Hugues Lapointe's stand.

On December 7, W. C. Macdonald (Halifax), who had resigned as Ralston's parliamentary assistant, declared he would support the government motion. Colonel Ralston himself for some days past had taken issue with Conservative speakers as the prospect of a coalition under his leadership faded. H.-E. Brunelle (Champlain) bitterly attacked the Conservatives for putting Quebec on trial, and brought out the homely truth that whenever 'there was trouble in our country between the different races it never came from us but because somebody always wanted to interfere with our way of living and our way of thinking.'[168] He saw the current crisis as a repetition of the 1917 one, and quoted the observation of Major David Maclellan of the *Halifax Chronicle*:

As a Canadian with as much British blood as the most energetic flag-waver in the land, it strikes me that English-speaking Canadians may well hang their heads in shame for the stupid, nasty smear campaign against Quebec. Tolerance that has somehow taken root in the Canadian army overseas is, and has been, sadly lacking here. It is a tragedy that many Canadians cannot capture the spirit and resolution which animates their sons and brothers overseas.

Quebec's attitude toward conscription has been no secret for many years, yet, completely ignoring the fact that almost two-thirds of the home defence troops come from other provinces, some Canadians have been vicious enough to pour abuse, all the abuse, on the steadfast, warm-hearted people of Quebec.

For a minority speaking another tongue and subscribing to another faith, the record of cooperation of Quebec residents has been splendid. The record of relations between English and French-speaking Canadians has been blotted repeatedly by the pin pricks, the rude remarks and the stinging insults that have been hurled at Quebec. Regardless of right or wrong, Quebec has every right to be resentful; and the amazing circumstance is that she had not permitted herself to give more forceful evidence of her resentment.

The Canadian voluntary system has worked throughout this war. It can continue to work if given a real chance. One thing is more important than the controversy agitating Canada to-day, and that is the Canadian nation.[169]

Mr. Brunelle retained his confidence in the prime minister but had lost faith in the conscriptionist ministers, and planned to vote against both the Conservative amendment and the government motion.

Sasseville Roy (Gaspé) charged that the debate had been useless, since the prime minister had declared on November 27 in introducing the motion of confidence that it was not a question of approval or disapproval of conscription.[170] He held the Liberal party with its large majority responsible for conscription, and declared that he would vote against both the motion and the amendments. Though he accepted conscription as inevitable, he made a final plea against it: 'If we are Canadians, even if we like England, for God's sake do not let us bring this bitter division into Canada which may do more harm than any good we can ever hope to do by sending a few men overseas.'[171] The prime minister subsequently denied a charge which Mr. Roy had made on the basis of the memoirs of Sir Robert Borden that he had been ready to join the Union Government in the summer of 1917.[172]

Wilfrid Lacroix (Quebec-Montmorency) declared that the Jean subamendment in effect recommended a more vigorous war effort, and asked 'Why we should keep on sacrificing more Canadian lives when Frenchmen, Belgians, and Dutchmen are more than willing to take their revenge?'[173] He called for gradual withdrawal of Canadian troops from the front, and reiterated his opposition to 'every form of participation.' Raymond Eudes (Hochelaga) paid tribute to Canada's war effort, and declared that he would vote against the government motion on anti-conscriptionist grounds, though he backed its policy as a whole and had no wish to favor isolationism, which could 'only bring trouble, worry and misfortune to my fellow-citizens.'[174] Sarto Fournier (Maisonneuve-Rosemont) made a plea for the government to reverse its conscription policy, lest the measure should have the same post-war effects as it had had after the first war.[175] Joseph Lafontaine (Mégantic-Frontenac), the father of three volunteers, favored the Jean subamendment, stating that 'In opposing conscription I am upholding a principle which has inspired all my life; for the French Canadians and for myself what counts above all else is national pride.'[176] D. King Hazen (St. John-Albert), in backing the Conservative amendment in a notably tolerant speech, paid tribute to Mr. St. Laurent's speech as a contribution to national unity, and declared that he had never blamed the French Canadians for their stand. T. V. Grant (Kings), a believer in the voluntary system, favored the government motion as the lesser of two evils. P.-J.-A. Cardin favored the Jean subamendment, despite its 'poor' wording, because it backed the voluntary system and opposed conscription.[177]

The Jean subamendment was lost by a vote of 168 to 43, with 5 English-speaking Quebec members supporting it. The Conservative amendment was lost by a vote of 170 to 44, with George Russell Boucher (Carleton) and Norman Jacques (Wetaskiwin) supporting it.

Stanley Knowles (Winnipeg North Centre), charged that the government motion was admittedly only a vote of confidence in the government 'as a tool to administer a law which is now in effect,' and that it did not present the issue before the country. He moved as an amendment to the main motion the same amendment which M. J. Coldwell had moved as a subamendment on November 27 and which had then been ruled out of order.[178] The speaker again ruled the motion out of order, and the ruling was sustained by a vote of 176 to 20, when Mr. Coldwell appealed it to the House.

Mrs. Dorise Nielsen (North Battleford) opened the debate that evening by endorsing the remarks of Mr. Rose on the position of the Labor-Progressive party, and by agreeing with Leslie Roberts' charge in the *Canadian Mining Reporter* that 'What currently goes on in parliament and press is no political filibuster but sheer political gangsterism, led by men ready to divide and destroy Canada if in the process they can also destroy King.'[179] She declared that the farmers of Saskatchewan sympathized with the French Canadians; that the trades unions supported the government's action; and that the necessity for maintaining unity was generally appreciated throughout Canada. She described the order-in-council as a compromise—'It is more than some French-speaking people feel they should be called upon to support; it is a little less than some English-speaking people feel is necessary'[180]—and called upon all to support it. E. G. Hansell (MacLeod) declared that 90 percent of his constituents whom he had circularized before the special session had favored conscription of the draftees.[181] He was cut off by the speaker before moving a new Social Credit amendment, which was then moved by C. E. Johnston (Bow River):

That this house, while not being requested to support all the policies of the government, will aid the government in sending immediately adequate reinforcements to our men overseas, and will also aid the government at all such times as it wages a vigorous war effort against the totalitarian powers; an effort consistent with Canada's ability and position in the world.[182]

Maxime Raymond challenged Frédéric Dorion's statement that only Liguori Lacombe and Wilfrid Lacroix had voted against participation in the war on September 9, 1939, referring to his own record and that of Mr. Woodsworth. He was contradicted by Mr. Lacombe.[183] The Speaker then ruled the Social Credit amendment out of order, and on appeal to the House was sustained by a division of 165 to 33.

Philippe Picard then moved an amendment in the sense of the rejected Jean subamendment, 'That this house will aid the government in a policy of maintaining an efficient war effort but does not approve of compulsory service overseas,' to clarify the position of those who opposed Bill 80 and the order in council.[184] The Speaker ruled the amendment out of order, despite the protests of its seconder, Mr. Tucker, and Mr. Coldwell, who declared that no opportunity was being given opponents of the government to express their views in motions. The latter then moved that the government motion be amended to read: 'That this house will aid the government in maintaining a vigorous war effort,' so that those in favor of a vigorous war effort but not of government policies could support it. The prime minister declared that the amendment was acceptable to him, since it expressed his meaning.[185] The House agreed to the prime minister's motion not to adjourn at 11 p.m. Cardin charged that all the proposed amendments had beclouded the issue; protested against the change in wording as meaningless; and declared that he would vote against 'the motion of confidence now adorned with a few flowers that have been strewn over it by the leader of the C.C.F. party.'[186]

The leader of the opposition rejected Coldwell's charges that the Conservatives had tricked those who wanted to oppose the government, by revising their motions between November 22 and November 27, and described the Coldwell amendment as 'tantamount to a government amendment moved through the lips of the hon. member.'[187] He accused the C.C.F. group of making common cause with the government. Mr. Knowles reviewed the C.C.F.'s share in the debate. He agreed partially with Mr. Cardin in saying the government motion as amended was no longer a vote of confidence but 'a pious resolution of the house to the effect that we will agree to aid the government in maintaining a vigorous war effort, and then close this session and go home.'[188] He charged the leader of the opposition with reflecting on those who had contributed to the war effort, and declared that the Progressive Conservative party was 'just plain sore' at the failure of their effort to make political capital of the issue. He felt that 'in the government's readiness to accept the amendment we have moved at this last moment we have won, not just for this group but for this parliament and for the people of Canada, a victory over the crisis through which we have passed.'[189] Mr. Picard asked whether the government had again changed its policy, and urged that the C.C.F. amendment should be declared out of order, since the amended motion had the same sense as the subamendment which he had earlier moved, and which had been declared out of order. Mr. Pouliot charged that there had been an understanding between the C.C.F. leader and the prime minister, and Mr. Coldwell denied the charge.[190] Jean-François Pouliot declared that the amended motion was vague, incoherent, and sullied by the C.C.F.[191] Mr. Blackmore, as leader of the Social Credit group, then urged support of the government motion because it provided for reinforcements, which was the main issue. The C.C.F. amendment was accepted by a division of 141 to 70.

The prime minister made a final plea for support of the fighting men overseas, and censured the leader of the opposition for concerning himself 'almost exclusively . . . with matters of petty politics between the different political parties in this country'[192] at such a time. Restating his opinion that the amended resolution conveyed to him the same meaning as the original motion, he thanked Mr. Coldwell for his desire to show that the House was 'united and determined upon having a vigorous war effort in support of our men overseas; a policy of maintaining a vigorous war effort.' He agreed with Messrs.

Coldwell and Knowles that the government was not asking for an unlimited vote of confidence in all its policies, and urged that the motion 'be carried in no uncertain way.' He declared that Mr. Blackmore had touched the 'real note' with his observation that the eyes of the world were upon Canada, and declared that 'No succour could come to the enemy equal to that he will receive from anything that goes to show that a parliament in any part of the British commonwealth is not united in support of its fighting men, and in its determination to do the utmost that can be done in helping to make a great war effort a complete success.'[193] Referring to the words of Lapointe, his 'young friend and gallant soldier, the son of the truest friend I have ever had in this House of Commons,' he held that the men overseas would be either encouraged or dispirited by the result of the vote. He admitted that it might be difficult for some members to explain their support of the government in its course, but that he had 'more faith than some who have spoken in the intelligence of your electors and in their hearts,' if the situation were properly explained.

With a second cryptic reference to the seriousness of the present and future situations, he urged members and the people of Canada to 'beware of doing anything or letting anything be done that may give those enemies or the people of any land cause to believe that the democracies are weakening, that within and between themselves they are becoming divided with the consequence that in their own eyes the power our enemies, present or future, may possess or come to possess may come to loom much greater than anything they behold elsewhere.' He declared that the day had passed 'when local issues or provincial issues—I might almost say the issues in any one country itself—can be separated from the larger question of how this world is going to hold together in the next few years in a way which will enable men to enjoy liberty, and to preserve their lives and their homes.'[194] As to broken pledges and lost faith in public men, he admitted that he, like the leaders of all parties, had in 1939 given anti-conscription pledges 'to the country as a whole, and not to any province or section of the country.' The result of the plebiscite had freed the government and all parties from these pledges; and Bill 80 had provided freedom to introduce overseas conscription if necessary. He had pledged himself to use that power if necessary, and by invoking it, he felt that he was keeping faith with 'this House of Commons, with the people of Canada, and with the fighting men in Canada's army overseas.'[195]

The amended motion was supported on division, a little after 1 a.m. on December 8, by 143 to 70. Though 32 French-Canadian Quebec members voted against the government, Mackenzie King had won an overwhelming and incredible victory over Tory and nationalist opposition. These two poles of Canadian politics were not brought together in 1944 as they had been to defeat Laurier in 1911, largely thanks to Colonel Ralston's loyal refusal to lend himself to a predominantly Conservative coalition government. The support of the C.C.F. and Social Credit groups offset the defection of Quebec Liberals who broke with Mr. King and Mr. St. Laurent. The result of the conscription debate was an index of the enormous development of Canadian national feeling in a third of a century. It was also a tribute to the consummate political skill of the man who had won a victory out of what had generally been regarded as certain defeat when the special session met on November 22.

II

The Senate was belatedly called on November 17 to meet on November 22, after Senator C. C. Ballantyne had expressed the view in the press on November 16 that it, as well as the House, should assemble. When it met, the government leader, J. H. King, promptly proposed adjournment in order that senators might attend the House debate. Senator Ballantyne, as Conservative leader, approved this course, but regretted that the Senate had not been called at the same time as the House 'in one of the greatest crises through which the world has ever passed.' When the Senate met again on November 24, Ballantyne asked whether the government would send the trained N.R.M.A. men overseas first under the order-in-council announced the previous day. With General McNaughton still under cross-examination by the House, Senator King deferred a statement on behalf of the government until November 28, while charging 'a couple of newspapers published in two of our great cities' with printing editorials inspired by 'the idea of embarrassing the government in its war effort.'[196] The Senate met again on November 28 and 29, merely to adjourn while the vote of confidence debate was carried on in the House.

Finally, on November 30 Senator King defended the prime minister and the war effort, and warned of the danger of arousing public opinion. He decried the use of the term 'zombie' and the conscription cry, which he said had had 'a disastrous effect upon one great political party.' He quoted Meighen's Hamilton and Bagot speeches of 1926, and Dr. Manion's pledge against conscription in 1940. Senator Ballantyne replied for the Conservatives, denouncing the government's manpower policy and its creation of 'two armies.' He made much of the fact that at the Winnipeg Convention of December 9–11, 1942, which had chosen John Bracken as leader, the Conservative Party had pledged 'support to the limit of our resources' to the armed services in 'reinforcements, equipment, and munitions of war.' He declared: 'Not only was that our policy in 1942, but it has been our policy ever since, and it is the policy we shall stand on to the end.'[197] Denying Liberal charges that conscription had been ineffective in the last war and asserting that a striking similarity existed between the situation then and at present, Ballantyne cited official army figures showing that while voluntary enlistments in the ten months preceding the application of the Military Service Act in January 1918 had numbered 51,101, a total of 154,560 men were obtained in the following ten months under the Act.[198] During the subsequent debate Senator Ballantyne, a veteran of the Union government, declared that the bitterness stirred up in 1917 was 'nothing compared to the bitterness that prevails today.'[199]

Senator Chapais, the only French Canadian who took a notable part in the Senate discussion of the issue, reiterated his opposition to conscription under Mackenzie King, as under Sir Robert Borden. He expressed the view that conscription might be justifiable for home defence against aggression, but 'conscription or coercion for the purpose of tearing from their homes the pick of our young men, to send them to foreign countries across the oceans and even to the antipodes, to fight on far-removed fields of battle, is an abusive and tyrannical measure.' He described conscription as foreign to the British tradition, and saw no reason for it with victory in sight. He cited with approval C. G. Power's declaration in the House: 'We have no right to tear this country asunder at this stage, and in this state of the war.' He also quoted several statements of the prime minister to bolster his argument that Canada had attempted too great a war effort, and used Ralston's 1941 statement against conscription in the name of national unity in his concluding protest against 'all those excesses in words or actions which we are now witnessing':

> We are going to have conscription, in violation of all pledges and promises. We are going to have that drastic measure which has divided us, which will divide us again, and which we ought to have avoided. . . .[200]

Senator Chapais' eloquence in French was largely wasted on his English-speaking colleagues. It was the only clear-cut expression in the Senate of complete opposition to conscription, although Liberal and Conservative Senators wrangled over the issue largely along party lines, despite the theoretical non-political character of the upper chamber. The most notable speeches made before the Senate adjourned on December 5 were those of J. A. Calder, a Western Liberal and a member of the Union government in 1917, who made a thoughtful and moderate criticism of the government's policy, calling conscription 'a national rather than a purely local issue';[201] and of Major-General W. A. Griesbach, who made an all-out conscriptionist one which expressed the extreme militarist view of his generation of English Canadians. He was the only speaker to oppose English Canada to French Canada:

> We were told that if we wanted national unity, we should have stayed out of this war; and that now we are in it, we should do as little as possible. Honourable senators, that is too high a price to pay for national unity . . . The truth is that a majority of people in this country are fed up with trying to purchase national unity at a price that is too high. We will not pay that price. What we do hope to have in this country is democratic rule by the majority, for a change. We hope that our public men and leaders will have the intestinal fortitude to carry out that policy, let the chips fall where they may.[202]

The Senate served simply as a forum for the expression of the views of the older generation of Canadians during the special session, for it had no official business before it and merely commented on developments in the House.

12

Feeling rose very high in Quebec at the end of November during the early stages of the debate at Ottawa. It was reported that Union Jacks were torn down or burnt at Chicoutimi and Rimouski in response to the slogan launched by Maxime Raymond and echoed by René Chaloult that 'independence is the fitting reply to conscription.' The *Bloc* held mass meetings in Montreal and Quebec and sought to make political capital of the crisis, but the French press of all shades of opinion appealed for calm and minimized the disturbances which were made much of outside the province. Though French Canada was generally united in its opposition to conscription, there was a considerable current of opinion which tacitly or openly favored support of the King government in order 'to avoid a much greater evil.' As feeling rose, the French press turned from defence of Quebec's attitude to attacks on the 'clique of colonels' and on 'St. James Street,' since militarism and big business were thought to be allied in an effort to upset the King government.

In view of the fevered atmosphere, the actual disturbances on November 29 in Montreal and Quebec were somewhat anticlimactic. In Montreal, after a *Bloc Populaire* mass meeting at St. James Market at which André Laurendeau called for 'a united front against conscription' and denounced 'the dictatorship of the majority as being as tyrannical as any Fascism,'[203] a crowd of young men estimated to number 2,000 paraded through the financial district, breaking the windows of the National Selective Service office, *Le Canada*, the Bank of Montreal, the Montreal Trust Company, and other business firms. The *Star* reported that a march against its office and that of the *Gazette* was headed off by the police. On November 30 the *Star* ran a frontpage editorial headed 'This Rioting Must Stop,' which asserted the constitutional right to object to conscription at public meetings, but called for firm repression of outbreaks against law and order. Asserting that 'this country wants no repetition of 1917' and that 'the best elements of Quebec itself want no such repetition,' the *Star* urged 'these young hoodlums . . . to heed the counsel of saner elements who know that Quebec's relationship with the rest of Canada may depend for years to come upon its attitude toward the decisions taken by the people's Government and Parliament.'

Le Devoir, deploring on November 30 the Chicoutimi and Rimouski incidents, recalled its editorial comment on November 27 that 'burning or tearing down flags gets us nowhere, is of no use and can do much harm to the cause it claims to serve,' and added that 'breaking windows is a silly thing to do,' finding both types of demonstration 'equally regrettable.' It cited the *Gazette's* report that 'In the majority of cases, the windows were broken by youngsters out for a lark, who joined the parade as it left the St. James Market Place,' in its protest against giving a false picture of the scenes which had occurred the previous night. In Quebec windows were broken by a mob of young men at the office of the conscriptionist *Chronicle-Telegraph* and at the home of Justice Minister St. Laurent.[204] But after these minor outbursts of popular feeling, which attained no such proportions as the 1917 disturbances, French Canada quickly calmed down and accepted the inevitable with fairly good grace. Fortunately no blood was shed and the demonstrations were wisely put down by local police rather than by troops, although some English Canadians, heedless of the lesson of 1917, had been talking brashly about the advisability of using machine guns to make Quebec accept the will of the rest of Canada.

The reluctant acceptance of a measure abhorrent to the French-Canadian mind was evident in the editorial comments on the vote of confidence in the King government. *Le Soleil* thus expressed the attitude towards Mr. King of the Quebec Liberals, whose federal representatives had mostly voted against the government: 'His former followers of the Province of Quebec are quite willing to believe that the application of a detestable measure will be less cruel under his direction than it would have been under any other government than his; but they feel themselves deceived and wronged by the politician they have trusted for twenty-five years.' *L'Action Catholique*, heading its comment 'A Happy Outcome to a Distressing Crisis,' expressed its continued opposition to conscription and its criticism of King's successive concessions, but added:

We prefer this verdict to an overthrow of the government for three reasons: we like a government that is conscriptionist 'in spite of itself' better than a conscriptionist government angry because compulsion has not been used sooner; we like a government which has reluctantly sacrificed Quebec better than a government which might have sought to sacrifice us still more, if not to be revenged upon us for our anti-conscriptionist stand; we like a government which has approved the recall of French-Canadian recruits to Quebec better than a government which might have cancelled this recall and ordered a repressive discipline very dangerous for peace in military camps and elsewhere.

. . . Just like its representatives in Ottawa, the Quebec electorate prefers the maintenance of the government to an election, but it reproves its policy of compulsion.

La Patrie hailed the vote of confidence as 'a solution which should be acceptable to all those who, opposed to conscription, will stop to reflect what any other alternative would have meant.' It regretted the 'application of a principle which the vast majority of our people reject, as the votes of our members show'; but added: 'It had become evident from the very first hours following the meeting of Parliament that the crisis could not be settled in the absolute way desired by the Province of Quebec, and that it could only end in a compromise.'

Le Canada hailed King's triumph over a 'conspiracy' of Tories and Laurentian nationalists, such as had confronted Laurier a generation before. *Le Devoir* thought Mr. King had won a false if astounding triumph:

He has brought to naught the efforts of all the powerful enemies who were leagued to defeat him . . . The vast plot which was hatched against him brought together the Conservative politicians, almost the whole of the Anglo-Canadian press, numerous conscriptionist elements among the Liberals, the military elements and probably also behind the scenes the big financial interests. The press and the Canadian Legion brilliantly succeeded in arousing public opinion in the English-speaking provinces; the soldiers sabotaged the attempt of General McNaughton to give new life to the voluntary system policy, but those who were chosen as the chief executors of the coup, Colonel Ralston and Conservative Party leaders, failed in ability and decision at the critical moment. Mr. King therefore retains power, but he has won this triumph at the sacrifice of his dignity, at the sacrifice of his friends and those who were faithfully devoted to him, and probably also at the sacrifice of the future of his party and the place it would have been able to occupy in the political history of Canada.[205]

This view of the crisis was generally held in French Canada.

The Montreal mayoralty contest in December between Camilien Houde, campaigning as a victim of arbitrary internment and as an opponent of conscription, and Adhémar Raynault, who proclaimed his belief in order and in full collaboration with the provincial and federal authorities, provided a useful safety valve at this time for pent-up anti-conscriptionist sentiment, which was probably stronger in Montreal than anywhere else in the province. Houde, backed only by *Montréal-Matin*, was re-elected to his old office by a comfortable margin, with French districts voting heavily in his favor and English districts supporting his opponent. When the result was known, *La Presse*, *Le Canada*, and *La Patrie* warned the victor that he had received only a municipal mandate, which was not to be used as a springboard to Quebec or Ottawa.

Premier Duplessis, the other leader likely to exploit Quebec's reaction against Ottawa as a result of the conscription measure, reaffirmed himself a champion of provincial autonomy and of the pact theory of Confederation in an address to the Quebec Saint-Jean-Baptiste Society at this time. Provincial Treasurer Onésime Gagnon, speaking at a Montreal business dinner, made the first statement of the Duplessis government on the expropriation of the Montreal Light, Heat & Power, calling it 'dictatorial,' 'Bolshevist,' and 'a disgrace to our statute books.' He also denounced the C.C.F. Party, likening it to National Socialism, and declared that Quebec would remain as 'a bulwark of security and stability.'[206] Though the Duplessis government had protested officially against the conscription measure, it now seemed evident in the light of these statements that it would be more Tory than nationalist in character. The provincial Liberals, launching their own organ *Le Canadien* to symbolize their break with the federal party on the conscription issue, renewed their bid for labor's support under the influence of the younger members of the party, who sought to halt the gains of the C.C.F. and Labor-Progressive groups at this period when the Quebec masses had largely lost confidence in both of the traditional parties.

The military outcome of the conscription crisis was long shrouded by censorship. The order-in-council of November 23 caused a wave of desertion among the N.R.M.A. soldiers chosen for overseas service when they were moved to eastern camps and given embarkation leave. Wild rumors on this score went unchecked, except by the natural lull after the intense storm of public opinion in November and by the distraction of the Christmas holidays. Finally on January 20, 1945, it was announced that of the 10,000 men warned to report for the sailings of January 3 and 10, 7,800 had been at one time A.W.O.L. or overdue, and that 6,300 were still absent on January 16. There were disturbances in some of the camps, both in Quebec and Ontario, as late as February 24, but absenteeism declined sharply in the case of the third sailing and was nominal in the case of the fourth. Of the total of 14,500 N.R.M.A. men warned for service overseas, 4,082 were still unaccounted for at the end of March, according to the statement of D. C. Abbott, parliamentary assistant to the defence minister on April 5.[207]

The distribution of absentees by military districts of enrollment was then given as follows:

M.D. 1, 2, & 3 (Ontario)	450
M.D. 4 & 5 (Quebec)	2,400
M.D. 6 & 7 (Maritimes)	100
M.D. 10, 12, & 13 (Prairies)	1,000
Pacific Command	150
	4,100

The number of N.R.M.A. men sent overseas by military districts was then given as follows:

M.D. 1, 2, & 3 (Ontario)	3,466
M.D. 4 & 5 (Quebec)	2,391
M.D. 6 & 7 (Maritimes)	888
M.D. 10, 12, & 13 (Prairies)	3,899
Pacific Command	1,192
	11,836

It was also stated at the same time that 10,279 N.R.M.A. men had converted to active service since November 1—about half in November and December—and over 2,400 former N.R.M.A. men had gone overseas as general service men.[208] In all, 12,908 N.R.M.A. men were sent overseas, the balance of the 16,000 provided for under the order-in-council not being needed. Casualties during November, December, and January proved considerably fewer than anticipated by the October estimate, and reinforcements overseas in April were 75 per cent over the estimates of the secret session.[209] From February until the end of hostilities in Europe 'there was no serious difficulty in keeping our battalions in the field up to strength, and no question of disbanding Canadian formations ever arose,' according to the official history of the Canadian Army in World War II.[210]

In other words, Canada had nearly split itself apart in anticipation of a situation which did not materialize. The reinforcement crisis of 1944 was in great measure an artificial one brought on by the unscrupulous efforts of a party long in opposition to win power at any cost. The stake was not military victory in Europe, which was already assured, or the defence of Canada's reputation and honor, which had already been upheld beyond imputation, but control of Canada in a postwar world full of dangers for the conservative-minded.

The 1944 conscription crisis also provided another example of the periodic clashes of two very different Canadian mentalities. While the French Canadian frequently relieves his pent-up emotions, he does not allow emotion to sway him from following a reasonable course of action dictated by logic, although he may nurse bitterness long afterwards. On the other hand the English Canadian is much less given to emotional reactions, but when he does let common sense and reason yield to them, the outbreak is much more serious, though shortlived. The 1944 crisis was fortunately marked by less violence than the 1917–18 one, and hence its aftermath was much milder and shorter than was anticipated at the time. It is probable that the issue of conscription will never again split the peoples of Canada, who have twice learned the cost of trying to ride roughshod over the deepest emotions of French and English.

The collapse of their effort to win power did not prevent the Conservatives from pressing their case against French Canada's military record by close questioning of Mr. Abbott after his statement on April 5. Mr. Diefenbaker cited the statistics given in the February-March issue of *Canada at War* to show that Quebec had the lowest rate of volunteering and of N.R.M.A. call-ups.[211] George Stanley White, an Ontario member, brought out that the Quebec military districts had the largest number of deserters, 7,800 and 3,713, out of a total of 18,943 for all Canada.[212] On the following day Diefenbaker pointed out that over 50 per cent of the Quebec N.R.M.A. men warned for overseas service had deserted. Abbott protested against 'this blazoning of Canada as a nation of deserters' while Jean-François Pouliot pointed out that the Conservative attacks on Quebec were unfortunate 'because we are bound to live together; we are bound to be in the same boat.'[213] But the Conservative attack on the government with regard to military matters centered at this time on the question of Major-General G. R. Pearkes' resignation from the Pacific Command, first offered on November 26, 1944 and finally accepted by the Defence Department on February 14, which had political implications because of the general's known opposition toward the N.R.M.A. policy and his announced candidacy in the impending general election.

13

Quebec's divided mood in 1945 was expressed by two cultural trends of opposed tendencies. At the beginning of the year a French-Canadian Academy, modeled on the French Academy, was established in Montreal. Of its twenty-four members sixteen represented the liberal arts and eight the moral, political, and religious sciences. Its board was headed by Victor Barbeau and included Léo-Paul Desrosiers and Robert Charbonneau, while other members were Marius Barbeau, Roger Brien, Robert Choquette, Marie-Claire Daveluy, Abbé Rodolphe Dubé ('François Hertel'), Guy Frégault, Alain Grandbois, Canon Lionel Groulx, Père Louis Lachance, O.P., Père Gustave Lamarche, O.P., Rina Lasnier, Dr. Philippe Panneton ('Ringuet'), and Robert Rumilly. Eight vacancies were left open to Canadian subjects of either sex, at least twenty-eight years of age, who had produced two published works. The foundation of the Academy was a landmark in the self-conscious development of a French-Canadian culture separate and distinct from that of France. It also was a revolt against the artificial yoking of two distinct colonial cultures in the Royal Society of Canada, whose French-Canadian elder statesmen no longer commanded much respect from the younger generation in Quebec. Many of the members of the new Academy were nationalists who held that French- and English-Canadian cultures were irreconcilable, and that the Royal Society was merely a mutual admiration society of *bonne-ententistes*. French-Canadian art, which had long mirrored the shifting fashions of Paris, returned to native themes while avoiding the sentimentalism of a Henri Julien. Thus a cultural isolationism paralleled Quebec's political isolationism as a result of the reinforcement crisis.

On the other hand, the cartoonist and caricaturist Robert La Palme, a French-Canadian Low, managed to combine the outlook of a citizen of the world with a distinctive French-Canadian spirit. The anonymous *Compagnons de Saint-Laurent* brought new life into the Montreal theater with their stylized productions of Molière, Racine, and Corneille, and modern French, English, and American dramatists. Their director, Père Legault, was a priest who had no use for the Jansenist tradition which had blighted the French-Canadian theater since the days of Bishop Saint-Vallier. 'Fridolin' (Gratien Gélinas), French Canada's beloved dramatic satirist who had espoused the nationalist cause in the early war years, now mocked the *Bloc Populaire* and the Ordre de Jacques Cartier, and resolved the English-French tension by laughter in his annual revue, *Fridolinnous*, which foreshadowed his first full-length play *Tit-Coq* (1948), which gave poignant expression to the conscription question from a French point of view which was basically Canadian. Another index of cultural maturity was supplied by Roger Lemelin's novel, *Au pied de la pente douce* (1944), which satirized nationalism and mirrored the unrest of the urban workers. The appearance of Lemelin's book and of Gabrielle Roy's *Bonheur d'Occasion* in English drew the attention of the rest of North America to the rapid social evolution of French Canada.

Yet despite these evidences of a growing cultural self-sufficiency, which outstripped English Canada's artistic development, French Canada reached out ever more eagerly for cultural support from Latin America. Cut off from France by the war and with its old sympathy for the mother culture divided and weakened by the Pétain-*vs.*-De Gaulle controversy, Quebec suddenly realized that there were other peoples of 'Latin' culture on a continent which, beyond her limits, she had long considered to be exclusively 'Anglo-Saxon'; and proceeded enthusiastically to cultivate relations with them. Such a course had been urged repeatedly since 1915 by Henri Bourassa, who saw a safeguard against United States imperialism in the development of diplomatic and commercial relations with the South American countries, and had proposed a hemispheric alliance against European aggression in 1916.[214] In the House in 1935 he had urged Canada's entrance into the Pan-American Union, 'in which we would be far more at home than we are in the League of Nations,'[215] arguing that Canada would thus meet 'representatives of those states of South America which, in some respects, are in close understanding with the United States, but in others have the same feelings of diffidence that we have and which are natural in small or weak nations toward a very large one, dominating the continent.' *Le Devoir* had always followed the Pan-American line of its founder, while Emile Bruchési, writing in *L'Action française* in 1922, had described the Latin Americans as 'cousins by blood, by race, by mentality' and had evoked visions of a Latin New World counterbalancing the Anglo-Saxon one.[216] But on the whole French Canada showed little interest in Latin America, aside from a tendency to support Pan-Americanism as an offset to British imperialism, until 1940, when it was challenged by Prime Minister King to assume French cultural leadership, as English Canada sought Latin American markets to replace European ones.

In that year the *Union des Latins d'Amérique* was founded in Montreal by Dostaler O'Leary, a prewar advocate of separatism and of the establishment of a free French state on the St. Lawrence which would embody the cultural tradition of Athens, Rome, and Paris.[217] Although it was suggested that O'Leary's enthusiasm for Latin America was stimulated by racism and the hospitality shown to fascist-minded French Canadians who took refuge there when Canada entered the war,[218] the movement received the sanction of the Université de Montréal, whose rector served as honorary president. Membership, which was restricted to French Canadians, amounted to about 1,500 persons, of whom some 250 took up the study of Spanish. Through discussion groups, exhibits, and addresses the *Union* sought to cultivate the cultural unity of the 'Latins' of America in annual Latin-American Days at the university in 1942,

1943, and 1944. Under its auspices 100 French-Canadian students visited Mexico in 1944, while 50 more went there in 1945 under the auspices of the *Cercle Cervantes* of Laval University.

The war also brought to French-Canadian institutions students from Mexico, Central America, and the Antilles who normally would have gone to France. La Tertulia Club of Ottawa and the Canada-Brazil Committee also arranged for the exchange of students and professors between Quebec and Latin America, while Spanish courses were given in the French-Canadian universities, supplemented at the Université de Montréal and the Ecoles des Hautes Études by courses on Latin America.

Sympathy for Latin America was strongest in nationalist circles, though the theory of strong cultural bonds based upon a common Latin and Catholic heritage was troubled by some awkward facts. Latin America prided itself upon its heritage from the French Revolution, which remained to French Canada a curse which it had happily escaped. Spanish-American Catholicism proved very different from that of French Canada, and was far from universal in the Latin-American academic world, with its old freethinking and anti-clerical traditions and its new Marxism. Latin America was proud of its Indian heritage, while French Canada was ashamed of its Indian blood. Over-enthusiastic expressions of brotherhood by Haitian cultural envoys to Quebec produced in certain French-Canadian quarters the reaction that 'after all, we are not North American Negroes.' An unanticipated development of the Latin-American enthusiasm was the discovery that the French Canadians were more North American than 'Latin' in their ways of life and thought, despite the nationalist teaching of the last quarter century. But the Latin-American movement received widespread support from *L'Oeil*, which stressed a common Latinity, and *Le Bloc*, which saw in Canada's entry into the Pan-American Union a means for Latins to unite against Jewish-American finance.[219]

Not racist-minded like the *Union des Latins* and more concerned with the development of commercial than cultural relations with Latin America, the Pan-American League was founded in December 1943, with a head office in Toronto and an active Montreal branch. The latter conducted in 1944 a survey of the teaching of Spanish and Portuguese in seventeen Canadian universities, and in 1945 a survey of Canada's role in the Western Hemisphere. It was at the instigation of Hector C. Boulay, national director of the League, who had previously written the foreign ministers of Chile, Peru, and Uruguay urging such a step, that the Chilean delegation to the Mexico City meeting of the Pan-American Union in February 1945 moved a resolution that Canada be invited to join the Union.

The French press was notably sympathetic to such a step, although it was generally assumed that Canada would not enter the Union because of United States objections that Canada was not a republic and English-Canadian objections that membership in the Union was incompatible with membership in the British Commonwealth. *L'Action Catholique* spoke of the 'passive but powerful hostility of certain Anglo-Saxons who will not admit that something good may emanate from any other place than London.' *Le Soleil* regretted that 'in Pan-American politics Canadians are still considered as British subjects instead of free citizens of a free country.' *L'Evénement-Journal* deplored the fact that Canada was not officially represented at Mexico City, since 'we must realize that we live in America and that the decisions which will be taken in Mexico interest each and every one of us.'

Le Canada was alone in taking the line that entrance into the Pan-American Union would make Canada subject to a 'strong pressure from Washington' which would be incompatible with Canadian autonomy. This statement clearly reflected the desire of Ottawa, torn between Canada's American and British interests, to defer the Pan-American question until that of regional *vs.* world security systems was discussed at the San Francisco Conference. The English-Canadian nationalism developed by the War was reluctant to increase still further Washington's influence on Ottawa, which had waxed as London's waned during the War, while English-Canadian imperialists sought to restore the old order of British dominance of Canadian foreign policy. On the whole French Canadians were more sympathetic than the English Canadians to Canada's participation in inter-American affairs. The declaration of Malcolm Macdonald, British high commissioner to Canada, in a speech at Quebec at this time, that 'You remain masters of your own destinies,' was used by *Le Devoir* to lecture the imperialists on their outmoded colonialism, while *La Patrie* saw a guarantee for the survival of British institutions in the fact that 'the political structure of the Commonwealth and British Empire is in a state of constant evolution and that it has never become crystalized, fossilized, or mummified, which would have meant its destruction.' *La Patrie* saw as the British goal 'the ever-widening expansion of liberty among all the King's subjects, whatever their color, their race, their creed, or the part of the globe they live in.'[220]

Latin America had commercial as well as cultural charms for a Quebec seeking new markets and anxious to offset 'Anglo-Saxon' dominance of its economic life. After the fall of France, Montreal French publishers were quick to see a market for their wares in Latin America, for whose intellectuals French had always been a common tongue. Latin America was eager for Canadian newsprint, whose distribution had been controlled by American agencies for political purposes. Early in January 1945 Provincial Treasurer Gagnon and Minister of Commerce and Industry Beaulieu set out for Mexico and Haiti, in response to invitations extended the previous year by the Mexican ambassador and President Lescaut during state visits to Quebec. *Montréal-Matin*, the Duplessis administration's organ, hailed Quebec as a liaison agent between Latin America and English Canada, praised the work of the *Union des Latins* in making Canada better known abroad, and commented that 'the signing of [trade] agreements would give an impetus to the business and industry of Quebec and place us in a better position to meet the uncertainties of the post-war period.'[221]

14

The storm aroused in Quebec by the conscription crisis died down rapidly, but the province remained in a sore and sensitive mood. Quebec was once more isolated from the rest of Canada, as in 1918, but this time for the most part it turned outward to the international world rather than in upon itself, while it awaited an opportunity to avenge itself upon the King government at the polls. On January 3, 1945, Cardinal Villeneuve renewed in even more vigorous terms the warning he had given against the worldwide menace of Communism upon his return from his trip to Britain and the battlefronts in the fall. *L'Action Catholique* and *Montréal-Matin* warned that the danger existed at home, with the latter journal urging suspicion of 'all those who seek to sow disunion, agitation and revolt.'[222] The selection of the National Catholic Syndicate as the favored bargaining agent of the Arvida aluminum workers, despite a vigorous four months' campaign by the Canadian Congress of Labor (CIO), was hailed as a victory over 'Communists' and 'American racketeers.'[223] The Yalta Conference, which at first only aroused expressions of regret at France's absence from the deliberations, evoked a storm of vigorous protests from *L'Action Catholique*, *Le Devoir*, and *Le Droit* as a 'new Munich' containing the germs of a third world war, when it became known that Poland had been sacrificed to Soviet Russia. *Le Canada* and *Le Soleil* defended the Yalta agreements, but a groundswell of sympathy for the seven million Polish Catholics who came under Soviet control in 'the fifth partition of Poland' swept Quebec and reinforced the skepticism of the nationalists about the principles of the Big Three and their peace plans.[224] The arrival in February of Count Jean de Hautecloque, the first ambassador of France to Canada, was warmly greeted by the French press, which hailed his record in the Resistance and expressed the wish that relations between Canada and France might be drawn closer.[225] But the ambassador had hardly arrived in Ottawa before he received a resolution of protest from the Saint-Jean-Baptiste Society against the imposition of the death penalty on French intellectuals accused of collaboration. A group of French-Canadian intellectuals including Edouard Turcotte, Jean-Charles Harvey, René Garneau, and Lucien Parizeau promptly protested against the action of the society.[226]

The Grey North by-election of February 5, in which General McNaughton was defeated by the Progressive-Conservative candidate, with the C.C.F. candidate credited with splitting the anti-Tory vote, was taken as the inevitable forerunner of a general election. *L'Action Catholique* saw the King government as caught between conscriptionist and anti-conscriptionist forces, with Ontario condemning the prime minister for not applying conscription, while Quebec blamed him for doing so. *Le Devoir* thought no party would be strong enough to form a government in the next parliament, and looked forward happily to the prospect of a Quebec group wielding the balance of power.[227] Sympathy for General McNaughton and condemnation of the anti-Quebec sentiment aroused by Conservative speakers was generally expressed in the French press. But Quebec was less sensitive on the score of conscription than it had been in November, since it had become evident that the disorders and absenteeism among N.R.M.A. men posted for overseas were not confined to French Canadians. General McNaughton's announcement that further coercion would not be necessary as the reinforcement situation was satisfactory also eased the tension in Quebec. Popular feeling against conscription last made itself felt in a Saturday night street brawl at Drummondville on February 24, when Mounted Police and Provost Corps officers sought to round up youths whose military papers were not in order. Regret was expressed by the newspapers that disorder had occurred, but more indignation was expressed that the affair had received undue attention in the English-speaking press. Considerable anti-English-Canadian and anti-American feeling had been aroused by the sensationalism with which Quebec's opposition to conscription had been publicized in recent months.[228]

The ethnic solidarity aroused by the conscription crisis and its aftermath sought political expression in both the provincial and federal fields in the early months of 1945. An independent federal group, headed by Frédéric Dorion, Wilfrid Lacroix, Liguori Lacombe, and Sasseville Roy, was launched in the middle of January. Its first aim was to defeat Mackenzie King, and by exploiting anti-conscription and autonomy feeling to bring together all nationalist and anti-government Quebec members in a party which would seek to wield the balance of power at Ottawa. The independents were strongest in the Quebec district; they obviously sought a working alliance with the *Bloc*, which still commanded nationalist feeling in the Montreal district. Dorion, elected as an independent in 1943, was a recognized follower of the *Union Nationale*; Lacroix had left the Liberal Party on the issue of conscription of N.R.M.A. men; Lacombe had been elected as a Liberal in 1940 but had subsequently established a one-man *Parti Canadien*; while Roy was an independent Conservative who had bolted his party. Efforts were made to induce P.-J.-A. Cardin to bring the nationalist wing of the Quebec Liberals into the fold of the new group. *Le Devoir* and *Le Droit* were enthusiastic in their support of a French-Canadian party.

With revolt widespread within the Liberal fold in Quebec, Mr. King gave the province time to cool off by proroguing parliament when it met on January 31, while leaving the date of a general election unfixed. On February 3 *L'Action Catholique* published a Liberal-inspired story that Mr. King would call an election shortly on a platform calling for nomination of a Canadian governor-general, adoption of a Canadian flag, abolition of appeals to the Privy Council, entrance of Canada into the Pan-American Union, and the independence of Canada.[229] Such a program would at once win many allies for the Liberals from the C.C.F. and from Quebec. The prime minister's statement on the result of the Grey North election, referring to 'the splitting of the vote of those who are opposed to reactionary forces,'[230] strengthened the suspicion which had arisen during the conscription crisis that the Liberals would form a working alliance with the C.C.F. in the coming general elections. While the nationalist elements of the C.C.F. program had strong appeal in Quebec, the party's prospects in Quebec were blighted by its emphasis on further centralization of power at Ottawa and by its socialism, which was taken to be of the Continental revolutionary rather than the English evolutionary sort.

The first session of the Quebec legislature under the new Duplessis government opened on February 6, the morrow of the Grey North election. Four days earlier Premier Duplessis had made public a letter to Mr. King in which the Quebec government claimed that the federal family allowance act was unconstitutional, since it invaded the provinces' 'exclusive rights in the domain of family life, education, and civil law.' The statements of Laurier and Sir Lomer Gouin on the inviolability of provincial rights were cited in support of this view. Quebec Liberals made much of the anomalies of a Duplessis-Drew axis, with Premier Drew of Ontario attacking the family allowance measure as an electoral bribe to Quebec which would burden English-Canadian taxpayers with the support of the large French-Canadian families, while Premier Duplessis atacked it as a federal and hence English-Canadian encroachment on Quebec's rights. The Duplessis government promptly proceeded to introduce a provincial family allowance measure which made more liberal provision than the federal measure for families with more than four children. The speech from the throne also announced that a provincial broadcasting system would be set up.

The general spirit of opposition to Ottawa was indicated by the support given by all parties to a resolution of protest against the imposition of conscription for overseas service introduced by René Chaloult, whose previous anti-war resolutions had met short shrift under the Liberal regime. Early in March the premier gave notice of a bill to prevent appeals to the Supreme Court of Canada in Quebec civil cases, but later opposed a *Bloc* resolution to abolish appeals to the Privy Council. A few days later the legislative assembly by an unanimous vote called for redistribution of electoral seats before the federal elections, so as to do justice to Quebec, whose population had increased more largely than those of the other provinces since the last distribution in 1931. On the same day that the provincial radio bill passed its third reading, the premier introduced a measure annulling the agreement made between Quebec and Ottawa in 1942, whereby the province renounced to the federal government for the duration of the war the right to collect corporation taxes.

The tide of anti-Ottawa motions was turned, however, toward the end of March by the misfiring of Chaloult's charge that the federal government was responsible for the corruption of young girls by forcing them to work in war plants. The Liberal press replied to Mr. Chaloult's charges—that half of the country girls engaged in domestic work in Montreal were unmarried mothers, and that half of the female workers in the Quebec Arsenal were in the same plight—by pointing out that Quebec had the lowest rate of illegitimate births of any province.[231] Quebec labor was also quick to protest against the Chaloult charges. In April the premier introduced a bill amending the Quebec Election Act to make 'Canadian nationality' one of the qualifications for voting, instead of the former requirement of being a British subject, born or naturalized. On March 12, as he departed for a conference in Washington with President Roosevelt, Prime Minister King ended the speculation which had been rife since the prorogation of parliament by announcing that there would be no extension of parliament's life, that the cabinet had been revised, and that the opposition would be invited to form part of Canada's delegation to the San Francisco Conference.

When parliament met on March 19, 1945, the speech from the throne announced the government's acceptance of an invitation to participate in the San Francisco Conference on April 25, and called for a joint resolution assuring the Canadian delegation of 'the widest possible support from Parliament.'[232] It was also pointed out that parliament's term expired on April 17, and that a general election would be held shortly thereafter. Meanwhile the House was asked to make provision for the conduct of the war and for ordinary government expenses until the meeting of a new parliament.

15

The motion on the San Francisco Conference, moved by Mr. King and seconded by Justice Minister St. Laurent on the following day, called for endorsement of the government's decision to participate and for recognition that 'the establishment of an effective international organization for the maintenance of peace and security is of vital importance to Canada, and, indeed, to the future well-being of mankind; and that it is in the interests of Canada that Canada should become a member of such an organization.'[233] It also asked approval of the proposals of the United States, the United Kingdom, the U.S.S.R., and China for the international organization. The charter adopted at San Francisco was to be approved by parliament before ratification by Canada, whose delegates were to use their best endeavors in its preparation.

After outlining the proposals, Mr. King dealt with the difficulties and objections which might arise. While approving the predominant role given to the great powers, he urged clarification of 'the constitutional position within the organization of important secondary countries.' He also admitted that 'the obligation to carry out diplomatic, economic and military sanctions at the request of the Security Council raises another difficult question for Canada and other secondary states,' but suggested that 'if the enforcement of sanctions required active aid from a country not represented on the council, its consent would probably be sought.' He urged broad thinking and taking a long view, since 'the benefits which Canada may hope to gain from full participation are immense.' Aside from prestige, 'no country has a greater interest than ours in the prevention of another general war.' He expressed the belief that 'our part in the shaping of peace may be no less urgent and no less effective' than it had been in the achievement of victory. He urged a willingness to give and take in the coöperative effort to organize world security, pointing out that the development of new weapons made no country immune from sudden aggression, and that 'so long as might is made a substitute for right by any nation there can be no security for this, or the next or any succeeding generation of Canadians.' He closed with the observation that the supreme lesson of five and a half years of war was that 'humanity should no longer be made to serve selfish national ends, whether these ends be world domination or merely isolated self-defence.'[234]

The isolationist tradition of French Canada was clearly challenged by the prospect of Canada's participation in a world organization. Gaspard Fauteux (Sainte-Mary), in backing the resolution, stressed the aim 'of achieving international cooperation in the solution of international economic, social and other humanitarian problems,' and pointed out the benefit to his compatriots of transforming 'a war economy into a peace economy based on the same principles and the same needs.'[235] But Liguori Lacombe (Laval–Two Mountains) protested that the Canadian delegates would lack a mandate, since the San Francisco Conference would be held after the expiration of the life of parliament; and urged an immediate dissolution of parliament, since the people of Canada had lost confidence in the government. He accused the prime minister of 'sacrificing the friends of Canada to those who are not true Canadians'[236] ever since the N.R.M. Act. He asked why Canada should be represented at San Francisco, when the discussions would turn on questions decided at other conferences at which it had not been heard. He characterized Canada's participation in the League of Nations as useless, and expressed skepticism about the proposed charter, in view of the emptiness of the Atlantic Charter and the dismemberment of Poland. 'It is all very well to set up an international organization to maintain world peace and security, but only through having regard to the rights of all martyred peoples to life, justice and liberty can such an organization build something lasting.' He denounced the 'economic dictatorship' which had dominated Canada since the N.R.M. Act; the government's disregard for the supremacy of parliament in now calling for approval of a decision already made; and warned of a day of reckoning at the polls.

Lacombe charged that under the proposals, 'our air, naval and land forces would be requisitioned at any time by the future league of nations to serve anywhere in the world.' He undoubtedly summed up the attitude of many traditional-minded French Canadians when he concluded:

Parliament can not and should not appoint a delegation entrusted with such powers. I refuse to believe that Canada, once the war is over, should mobilize her resources for the protection of world security. I object to the sending of a delegation of members no longer in office to that conference; it would be contrary to our constitution, to custom, and to law. With many others, I wonder if it would not be more appropriate and reasonable to restore order in our own country, to stabilize our finances, and to prepare our youth for careers worthy of their sacrifice. In short, let us put an end to our international commitments. Let us undertake the rebuilding of our economic structure which is crumbling. Let us think first of our own, of the sons and daughters of Canada who will be returning to this country. They shall have the right to work and to positions worthy of their sacrifices. Up to now, the government has found twenty billions for war purposes. We shall need as much, and maybe more for works of peace. Peace and national security for Canada should be our greatest worries. To that noble task we should devote all our energy and our resources. Let us use them for our own people and for our country. I know that my call will not be heard. At least I shall have fulfilled my duty to my country and to my people.[237]

L.-P. Picard (Bellechasse), the former secretary of Ernest Lapointe who had taken an important role in the special session, refuted the Conservative charge that the government had displayed a spineless attitude in the past, and made much of the contributions of both French and English to the development of Canadian nationhood, particularly stressing those of Laurier and Lapointe.[238] It was evident from his remarks that the Quebec Liberals had returned to the government fold. Fred Rose (Cartier) endorsed the resolution on behalf of the Labor-Progressive Party, declaring that both French and English Canadians fully shared the determination of 'the world's peoples' to establish peace and economic collaboration. He denounced 'the suicidal isolationism advocated by the Tory-inspired Nationalists, whose programme is both a denial of the realities of the present day world and a betrayal of the true interests of the great French Canadian community.'[239] He urged that labor should be represented in the Canadian delegation.

Wilfrid Lacroix (Quebec-Montmorency) declared that the decisions already taken at Yalta, which he anticipated would be ratified at San Francisco, 'already include the germs of a new war.'[240] He sharply attacked Yalta as another Munich, with its sacrifice of Poland's right to self-determination, and warned: 'We shall see, after this war, communistic influence permeate the whole of Europe and if Canada approves the purposes and principles set forth in the proposals already framed at Yalta, it means for us a war in which we shall inevitably be involved within ten or fifteen years.' He echoed Lacombe's criticism that the government had no mandate to commit the country to any course at San Francisco. He charged that the prime minister had become 'as much of a Tory as the staunchest of the imperialists who sit opposite him,' and declared that in view of Mr. King's record of broken pledges Quebec had lost faith 'in a man who owes it his present standing.' But there could be felt no confidence in the Progressive-Conservatives, because of 'their imperialistic and reactionary doctrines together with their electioneering methods of continuous mud-slinging against the province of Quebec'; nor in the C.C.F., because 'they have never failed to support the views of the Russian government in the field of international politics.' Anticipating that neither of the three parties would have a working majority after the elections, he thought there would be need for 'a group of members strong enough to force the other parties to follow a truly Canadian policy.' Lacroix charged that the Canadian people were again going to be presented with 'an accomplished fact arranged in London and not in Ottawa,' and protested against 'a policy of internationalism and cooperation in the establishment of a programme of world security dependent upon the good will of Stalin, the dictator, or, which would be still worse, of international high finance.'

On March 22 Frédéric Dorion (Charlevoix-Saguenay) protested against the government's undemocratic procedure in asking ratification of its previous decision to participate at San Francisco, and he warned that the independents would not consider themselves bound by any decisions taken by a Canadian delegation without a mandate.[241] Describing the question as 'participation in any future war in the world,' he called the resolution the most important to come before parliament since September 1939. He urged that 'we must first think of ourselves, rather than the world at large,' and asked whether it was 'a crime to stand for Canada first,' as Roosevelt stood for America first, Churchill for Britain first, and Stalin for Russia first. He charged that little had been done by the government for the benefit of the Canadian people, while everything had been done for other nations, 'under the fallacious pretext that we have to save humanity and civilization.' Canada at present was passing through an internal crisis and suffering from disunity, and the government's first task was 'to see to it that a true and lasting peace be established in our own country, before trying to organize the peace of the whole world.' He held that the proposed conference not only offered no better prospects than earlier peace conferences which had failed to avert war, but, because of the Russian dictatorship's role, offered little hope. He blamed wars on international finance and Communism, and deplored the fact that 'the greatest international power in the world, the Vatican' had been ignored in the proposed conference.[242]

J.-A. Bonnier (Saint-Henri) spoke in favor of participation, but strongly urged the Canadian delegates to look after Poland's interests.[243] J.-Emmanuel d'Anjou (Rimouski) expressed the opinion that there had already been too many conferences, since Poland, for whose sake Canada had gone to war, had already been sacrificed at Yalta for the benefit of Russia. He described the League of Nations as 'a colossal fiasco,' and predicted that the new organization would be an equal failure.[244] He quoted motions made by C. G. Power in 1923 for withdrawal from the League and against participation in foreign wars without the consent of parliament, both of which he had then seconded. He declared that the Canadian delegation would have no mandate for committing Canada to participation, that the conference would inevitably involve Canada in another conflict, and that as in 1923 he still opposed 'participation in empire wars.'[245]

On March 23 Fisheries Minister Ernest Bertrand spoke in favor of an international organization as a necessity in a contracting world. Reversing the words used by the Conservative leader that 'Nothing done by this nation at the coming conference or elsewhere must endanger our close ties with the British commonwealth and empire,' Bertrand urged thinking in Canadian terms by saying 'Nothing done by the British Empire at the coming conference or elsewhere must endanger our relations with the nations of the world with which we are at peace, and we must not be drawn into any conflict where we would not have an immediate interest.' But he condemned the attitude taken by the four Quebec independents in strong terms:

If there is one group of members who should be in favour of creating an organization to settle disputes and prevent wars, it is that group. If they are against war they should be in favour of an organization to prevent it. The class of people to whom these gentlemen are appealing have only one definite article in their programme—the separation of the province of Quebec from the rest of Canada. That is a programme which would bring immediate civil war if Quebec tried to enforce it. The disastrous war that secession brought to the United States would undoubtedly be our lot. So we have a group against all participation in this war although they would sell, and at very profitable prices, our agricultural and industrial products to England. This group is against an organization to prevent war and at the same time it is trying to lead its own province toward a war of secession.[246]

As for the Polish issue raised by the independents, he pointed out that 'We went to war not only to defend Poland but to save our own skins and the skins of twenty-four other nations.' He defended the Polish boundary and the veto, and closed with the declaration that 'the immense majority of the people in Quebec are in favour of establishing an international organization which, while it might not at the start be perfect, could become nearly perfect as the years go by.'[247]

Maurice Lalonde (Labelle) agreed that the four independents did not represent the Quebec majority, and expressed the opinion that 'the efforts of these isolationists who wish that Quebec should become a sort of reserve, shut out from all the great constitutional and economic evolutions of our time' would be repudiated.

It is high time that our nationalistic independents should realize the true situation of our race in Canada . . . We are surrounded by more than 150 million Anglo-Saxons with whom Providence has decreed that we should live, willy-nilly. It will be of no use to moderate independents, such as the hon. member for Charlevoix-Saguenay (Mr. Dorion) or to extremists of the Chaloult type to preach a provoking resistance. It will be of no use to revolutionists of the Shields clan to threaten us with their thunderbolts. Harmony will be the offspring of an acceptable compromise, both to the honour of the parties in the case and for their future in confederation.[248]

He criticized vigorously those who sought through political opportunism or for the sake of political revenge to keep Canada out of the peace conferences.

The independents came under fire from an unexpected quarter on March 27 when Maxime Raymond, federal leader of the *Bloc Populaire*, took Dorion to task for misinterpreting the motion and for reversing the stand which the independent and *Bloc* members had taken in favor of Canada's participation in international conferences in February 1944. After stating that he and his fellow *Bloc* member, J.-A. Choquette, would support the government motion, Raymond refuted Dorion's arguments, pointing out that the Pope in his Christmas allocution had urged the need of an international organization. Raymond renewed the stand he had taken on international relations in an interview published in *Maclean's Magazine* in 1944,[249] and called for 'an enduring peace based on right and not on might.'[250] He opposed the veto and the make-up of the security council, urging that international trade in armaments be prohibited as a cause of war. But Raymond supported international economic and social cooperation, since 'the peace that is to follow the present war must be more than a clever balance of military powers, it must be founded on real efforts to establish international justice.'[251]

Sasseville Roy (Gaspé) replied on behalf of the independents to Raymond and Bertrand, declaring that he opposed the San Francisco Conference because Canada was not aware of the decisions taken at the Atlantic, Casablanca, Teheran, Quebec, and Yalta conferences and of the nature of the peace which the international organization would seek to maintain. He denied that the independents were separatists and declared they favored 'sound collaboration between the two ethnic elements in our country.'[252] He expressed fear that Canada might be committed at San Francisco to maintaining compulsory military service, and that the prime minister might be once more deceiving the country as he had on the question of participation in the war. He concluded with the observation that the independents were 'in favour of such a conference being held, but what we are opposed to is the wrong way in which our government and the great powers are going about it.' He held that the conference was untimely because peace had not yet been made and because the government lacked a mandate to engage Canada's future.

Armand Choquette reiterated Raymond's argument in favor of a democratic world organization, citing the Pope's Christmas allocution. He criticized the proposals for the security council and the veto. He charged that the decisions reached at Yalta were 'based much more on a brutal policy of force than on a policy of sound justice and right,' and urged that the proposed international organization should eliminate such abuses. Though he had opposed the war measures of the government, he favored their peace measures, so long as Canada participated 'as a free and independent nation, due regard being given to our interests.' To him it was more important that Canada should be represented at San Francisco than at Commonwealth Conferences, 'which unfortunately smack of imperialism.'[253]

Closing the debate on March 28, the prime minister appealed to the Quebec independents 'in the interests of Canada as a whole' to reconsider their intention to vote against the motion, so that Canada might speak with one voice. He urged that they would not be representing the feeling of Canada, or of the province of Quebec, or of their constituencies if they voted against the resolution; and he suggested that they might refrain from voting, 'rather than have it broadcast throughout the world that in Canada there were members of her Parliament who felt they were unable to further a great world need.'[254] But Messrs. D'Anjou, Dorion, Lacombe, Lacroix, and Roy remained obdurate, and were the only members to oppose the motion on division. It was noteworthy that the independents did not receive much press support for their stand. *Le Droit* held that Canada must participate in the organization of world peace, while *L'Action Catholique* merely explained the independents' position as the logical consequence of their opposition to Canada's entry into the war.[255] The French press, however, deplored the call for imperial solidarity at San Francisco made by Gordon Graydon, Progressive-Conservative House leader, and denounced 'political colonialism.' *Le Droit* strongly supported Graydon's demand that parliament devote more attention to foreign affairs, and that external affairs should not be a part-time job for 'a very busy Prime Minister.'

Though Mr. King had deplored the concept of the Commonwealth acting as a bloc, the statement made by the prime minister in appealing for Conservative support of the motion, that 'I have done my duty by the British Commonwealth of Nations, by the British Empire, through every hour of the time I have been serving as Prime Minister of this country,' was promptly picked up by Wilfrid Lacroix on April 3 as evidence that Canada would 'continue to be a colony of the empire as heretofore.'[256] On the same occasion Lacroix opposed conscription in any form for the Pacific War on the grounds of cost, of interference with economic reconstruction, and of disregard for the government's promises to Quebec. He also attacked Maxime Raymond's stand on San Francisco and on the N.R.M. Act, though he favored his appointment as a member of the Canadian delegation to the conference.[257] Justice Minister St. Laurent and Senator Lucien Moraud were the only French-Canadian delegates named by the prime minister on April 9, however, while Jean Désy, Ambassador to Brazil, was one of the seven senior advisers who accompanied the delegation. The prime minister's choice was generally approved by the French press, though *Le Droit* regretted that Maxime Raymond and John Blackmore, as leaders of other parliamentary groups, had not been named.[258] On April 11 Philippe Picard urged that French be an official language at the conference. His stand was strongly backed by the whole French press, with *Le Droit* taking the lead, although *La Patrie* feared that the predominance of the United States and Great Britain might cause the elimination of French. The French press was disturbed by the proposal to give several votes to the United States and the U.S.S.R. and its satellites, to offset the six votes of the British commonwealth nations. *Le Devoir* used the occasion to call for 'real independence' as a solution for this international difficulty and the problem of national unity as well.[259]

During the discussion of the war estimates, the independents and *Bloc* members made common cause against continuation of conscription, and particularly against conscription for the Pacific War. The prime minister announced to the House that Canadian participation would be 'strictly limited,' and that only volunteers would go to the Pacific. This stand was approved by the French press, though there was an undercurrent of suspicion which found expression on April 13 when Dorion indicted the government and the Liberal Party for its record of broken promises to Quebec, and moved for repeal of the N.R.M. Act and P.C. 8891.[260] Only nine votes in favor of the amendment were recorded, and with this effort the independent movement, which had sought to create a French-Canadian bloc supplying a balance of power at Ottawa, largely collapsed, though it still talked darkly of the opposition which the prime minister would meet at the polls in Quebec. The last session of the nineteenth parliament closed on April 16, with elections set for June 11.

A Gallup poll early in April indicated that the Liberal Party was barely ahead of the Progressive-Conservatives in the favor of the public, with the prospect of no party commanding an absolute majority.[261] The Quebec Liberals who had planned to take revenge for conscription by voting against Mr. King were faced with the awkward dilemma of thus benefiting either the imperialists in the Tory camp or the socialists of the C.C.F., both anathema to most French Canadians. Anti-King feeling had notably subsided since the previous December, and those who still nourished it were much divided. While the nationalist journals were undecided in their course, *Le Canada*, *Le Soleil*, *Le Nouvelliste*, and *La Tribune* once more lined up squarely behind Mr. King, praising his conduct of the war and his postwar program.[262] A pre-election cabinet shakeup cost the French-Canadians of Quebec one seat, with the retirement of General Laflèche, the Acadians of New Brunswick another, with that of J.-E. Michaud, while the Franco-Ontarians gained two, with the appointment of Paul Martin as secretary of state and Lionel Chevrier as minister of transport. Joseph Jean of Montreal became solicitor-general.

On April 27 P.-J.-A. Cardin announced in a radio speech the formation of the long-rumored anti-King coalition under the name of the National Front. Fréderic Dorion pledged the adherence of his group of independents, while Camilien Houde announced that he had joined forces with the *Bloc Populaire*. *Le Canada* condemned the National Front as having no program other than 'vague grievances,' while *Montréal-Matin* supported it. *Le Droit*, which favored the grouping of all anti-conscriptionists, at first refrained from comment on the new party, as did *Le Devoir* and *L'Action Catholique*.[263] The National Front collapsed within a short time, and those who favored it ran as independents. Alfred Charpentier, president of the Canadian and Catholic Confederation of Labor, supported the non-political tradition of the syndicates in an article in *Le Travail*, though most syndicate members were expected to vote for either the *Bloc* or the National Front. *Labor World*, the provincial A.F.L. organ, came out on May 5 for Mr. King, while the Canadian Congress of Labor was already pledged to the C.C.F. By May 17 there were 294 candidates in Quebec's 65 electoral districts: 72 Independents, 58 Liberals, 29 Progressive-Conservatives, 28 C.C.F., 42 Social Credit, 35 *Bloc Populaire*, and 7 Labor-Progressives.

Le Devoir in a preliminary electoral analysis warned against Conservative candidates disguised as independents; held that the chief issue was Canadian foreign policy; and opposed Canadian intervention in an Anglo-American *vs.* Soviet conflict which it gloomily envisaged as possible within a few years.[264] *Le Droit* continued to regret the absence of a real French-Canadian Front party, while *La Patrie* interpreted the unusual number of candidates as a proof of the vitality of the democratic system and of its complete political freedom. In his opening campaign speech in Montreal Mayor Houde claimed that he had been right in 1938 in warning of a coming conflict and in 1940 in warning of conscription, and predicted that conscription would be invoked again in a new conflict against one of Canada's present allies. He declared that the *Bloc Populaire* favored free enterprise, and defined its position as 'not left of center but right of center.'[265] *Montréal-Matin* also warned of the dangers to Quebec of the demand for the nationalization of its industries, which it termed poor patriotism.[266]

Mr. King's pledge in campaign speeches at Prince Albert and Winnipeg that Canada would have a flag of its own if his government were returned to office was received with great satisfaction by Quebec, where a majority of the French Canadians had long desired such a symbol of Canadian autonomy.[267] Announcement at the end of May by Health Minister Brooke Claxton of a federal health insurance scheme was dismissed by the nationalist press as an electoral maneuver, while *La Presse* urged caution in adopting social legislation which would prove a heavy burden upon the national revenue. *Le Canada* stressed that social measures should be carried out through the cooperation of the federal and provincial governments. Quebec's objections to the family allowance scheme as an invasion of provincial rights had been duly noted by Ottawa.

The Ontario election of June 4, which saw Premier Drew returned to office in a Conservative landslide which cost the C.C.F. twenty-five seats and the Liberals two, made French-Canadian Liberals decide that Toryism was a greater threat than socialism in the federal election scheduled for a week later. Vandalism in the Jewish cemetery at Rivière-des-Prairies, assigned to anti-semitic nationalists, provided unfavorable publicity for the *Bloc Populaire*, already handicapped by inadequate campaign funds and organization. Only two *Bloc* candidates were elected, with Camilien Houde defeated in his stronghold of Montreal-Sainte-Marie. Forty-eight regular Liberals were returned, with six independent Liberals. Only one official Progressive-Conservative candidate was elected, though an independent Conservative also won by a narrow margin. The C.C.F. failed to elect a single candidate in Quebec, while Fred Rose retained the distinction of being the sole Communist member of Parliament. With a political realism which triumphed over appeals to race and class, Quebec remained loyal to the Liberal Party and supplied nearly half its strength at Ottawa.

The Conservative *Montréal-Matin* correctly declared that the King government had been returned to power 'because its policy has been sufficiently elastic to adapt itself to the wishes of the people, while other parties sought to impose their program and doctrines.' It called for a new start in building an opposition party in Quebec. *La Patrie* probably made the most cogent analysis of the electoral verdict:

The variety of groups and the multiplicity of candidates running as independents set a very difficult task in discernment for the electors of our province. There was a serious danger of confusion, which we have been able to avoid. There was likewise the danger of a division of our forces, of the dispersal of French-Canadian representation into irreconcilable groups. Finally, there was the threat of the isolation of Quebec, to which a strong group of the government's opponents invited our province in the name of nationalism, by exhorting the French-Canadian voters to give a negative vote, based on past history. The Province of Quebec has replied to these appeals by a vote which is above all an approval of the doctrine of national unity preached by Mr. Mackenzie King. Our compatriots have understood that they must live united, but that they could not isolate themselves from the majority of the Canadian people and risk stirring up the formation of an anti-French-Canadian parliamentary coalition. After the events of last autumn, the vote which has just been given by our province is an extraordinary demonstration of confidence in the head of the government. The support which Mr. King receives today from French Canadians does not in any way indicate the abandonment of their essential demands; it signifies that our province knows how, as things are, to take account of circumstances and that it wishes, above all, to safeguard the union of the Canadian nation. It has given its approval to a compromise, thus furnishing an example to all Canadians.[268]

Several papers pointed out that Quebec had chosen the middle path between plutocracy and socialism, preferring economic evolution to revolution. Jean-Charles Harvey, who had waged a vigorous campaign against the *Bloc Populaire* in *Le Jour*, proclaimed: 'Our fellow citizens of another language and another faith should know once for all that the Province of Quebec does not march, never has marched, and never will march in the odorous footsteps of the Chaloults, Houdes, Laurendeaus, and Groulx.' For one of the most interesting aspects of the election result was the fact that the *Bloc Populaire* polled only 200,000 votes—some 10,000 more than it had done in the provincial contest of August 1944, and one-seventh of the total—despite the feeling aroused by the imposition of conscription in November and despite the fact that every effort was made to exploit the personal popularity of Camilien Houde and his symbolic value as a 'martyr' in the cause of Quebec's opposition to conscription and to Ottawa's wartime extension of controls over the individualistic French-Canadian way of life.

The federal election of June 1945 extinguished the last hopes of those who sought to unite the French Canadians in an ethnic party which would attempt to play the dangerous game of supplying a balance of power at Ottawa for any national party which would favor its ends. Once more, as in the provincial election of August 1944, French Canada showed its fundamental devotion to the golden mean, after another display of the verbal violence which has so often deceived casual observers, who attach too much importance to the impassioned rhetoric of the nationalist élite and not enough to the inarticulate common sense of the French-Canadian masses. One of the strongest bonds which holds the peoples of Canada together is a fundamental moderation shared by English and French alike. There would be fewer misunderstandings between them if the utterances of extremists on either side of the ethnic fence did not receive so much publicity, in the inevitable emphasis of the popular press on the sensational.

As Quebec repudiated separatism in the postwar election, so English Canada repudiated the Progressive-Conservative effort at the time of the conscription crisis to unite the rest of Canada against Quebec, for only Ontario returned a majority of Conservatives, and a bare forty-eight out of eighty-two at that. Even in that Tory stronghold the Liberals made a notable showing. The C.C.F., the only national group beside the Liberals really accepting Canada's bi-ethnic character, did well only in the Western provinces, long in revolt against the two old parties.

16

The end of the war in Europe on May 8 undoubtedly affected the outcome of the June election. The French press generally agreed that Mussolini met the death he deserved, although *Le Droit* and *Le Devoir* expressed admiration for his early achievements and deplored the summary justice dealt out to him.[269] No such sympathy was expressed at the report of Hitler's death, although *Le Devoir* called him 'one of the principal figures of our time,' and while admitting that he was 'one of the great scourges of mankind,' hailed his achievement in 'embodying the soul of a great country' and 'galvanizing a humiliated people.' *Le Canada* savagely attacked this utterance, as it had *Le Devoir's* editorial on Mussolini. *L'Action Catholique*, in comparing the worldwide sorrow felt at Roosevelt's death with the dishonorable ends of Mussolini and Hitler, stressed the fact that for Hitler: 'Religion, morality, conscience, the Church, God Himself were absolutely nothing outside of the German racial spirit.' *Le Droit* used the occasion to echo Haile Selassie's words when Italy attacked Ethiopia: 'Those nations which seek peace without justice will find neither justice nor peace.'[270]

French Canada hailed the news of Germany's surrender with unrestrained joy. Flag-decked city and village streets alike were filled with happy throngs, while many gave thanks in the churches. Under the headline of '*La Guerre est Finie*' the newspapers expressed relief at the end of six years' war, but all warned that the nation's task was not yet finished, with some drawing attention to the Pacific War and others to the problems of making the peace. *Le Canada*, taking its line from Mr. King's statement at San Francisco, warned that 'we have to conquer fascism and militarism everywhere, as yesterday we conquered it in Germany, and as tomorrow we shall conquer it in Japan. Then, and then only, can we unreservedly rejoice and delight ourselves in a peace which will no longer be threatened.' The Pacific War remained remote from the thinking of most French Canadians, however, and there was more concern for the making of the peace. *La Patrie* urged its readers to 'thank Providence for the great benefit it has accorded us and to ask it to give guidance to the men who are building the peace which is beginning.' *Montréal-Matin* counselled its readers not to forget the men who had given their lives to make victory possible, and *La Presse* said that joy would not be complete until the service men and women returned home 'so that we can celebrate together the victory and the deliverance in ceremonies worthy of their brilliant deeds.' *Le Devoir* alone struck a discordant note in the general rejoicing:

> An illusory victory. Are there many belligerents who can felicitate themselves on the results obtained at the price of incalculable sacrifices? The first of the United Nations went to war to guarantee the integrity of Poland. Poland is today despoiled of nearly half her territory and what remains is subjected to a government imposed from outside. The United Nations went to war especially to prevent a totalitarian régime from establishing its hegemony over Europe and from assuming too big a place in the world. Another totalitarian regime, which relies on populations even more numerous, on natural resources even richer, on sympathies even more efficacious outside its borders, has established its hegemony over all Eastern Europe and threatens to spread to Western Europe. Nazism is dead with Hitler; German imperialism is reduced to impotence; Communism comes out of the conflict stronger than ever. Russian imperialism, supported by the victorious Red Army, is in the process of surrounding itself with a whole string of vassal states and threatens the very independence of the great European nations.[271]

This gloomy view was promptly rebutted by *Le Canada*, which assigned it to *Le Devoir's* disappointment at seeing its fascist idols fall and ultranationalism brought to nought. But once the first reaction to victory in Europe was past, French Canada as a whole faced the postwar world with a greater distrust of Soviet Russia than English Canada, because of its sympathies with Poland, and was less surprised by the subsequent revelations of Soviet espionage operations in Canada under the cloak of a wartime partnership which it had never accepted with good grace.

In the three months that intervened between VE Day and VJ Day, French Canada showed more concern with the making of the peace than with the conclusion of the war. The attitudes it adopted during this period revealed an unsettled mixture of new and old ideas. As in the early 1930's, the provincial government launched a back-to the-land movement, setting aside $16,000,000 to aid the establishment of colonists, in an effort to develop the remote northern districts of the province and to reverse the wartime movement of population towards the cities. The long neglected North had become Quebec's new frontier, with rich mineral resources as well as some colonization and industrial possibilities. The élite was uneasily aware of the stirring of discontent with the old order among the newly industrialized urban masses. Both the provincial government and the clerical authorities sought by promoting colonization to avoid a possible repetition of the social troubles of the 1930's in the period of postwar depression and unemployment which seemed inevitable, with so many of Quebec's industries wartime creations for wartime purposes. They were also concerned with keeping the new northern industrial districts French-Canadian. The Noranda-Rouyn area in the Abitibi, with its rich copper and gold mines, was becoming a frontier of Toronto rather than of Montreal, under English-Canadian and American ownership and management and with a large element of New Canadian workers. The wartime development of the aluminum industry at Arvida had to a considerable extent internationalized the Lake St. John region, in the past a French-Canadian colonization area. Many other northern districts, notably the North Shore on the lower St. Lawrence, were controlled by American and English-Canadian pulp and paper interests, which overwhelmingly dominated Quebec's largest peacetime manufacturing industry. Quebec was torn between its need for foreign capital and know-how, and the old desire to keep its natural resources for itself. Its leading nationalist economist, Esdras Minville, proposed the decentralization of industry and the integration of part-time manufacturing into the traditional regional economies dominated by lumbering, agriculture, and the fisheries; but such a plan ignored Quebec's close integration into a continental economy based upon concentrated mass production.

French Canada's new interest in international affairs continued to be marked. Quebec took pride in the number of French-Canadians appointed to diplomatic posts abroad, and supported the suggestion that the Ministry of External Affairs should be divorced from the prime minister's duties and given to Mr. St. Laurent. It criticized the San Francisco Charter as imperfect because of its failure to give the middle and small powers any role comparable to that of the three great powers, but largely blamed its faults on Russia's unwillingness to cooperate. The Potsdam Agreement was censured for its secrecy and for its concessions to Russia. The Pan-American movement continued to receive much support from the press. Proposals by Lord Beaverbrook that imperial preference be revived were promptly rejected in favor of the multilateral trade policies adopted at Bretton Woods. The appointment as governor-general of Sir Harold Alexander, who had commanded Canadian troops in Italy, was received with good grace, though French Canada had generally favored the appointment of a Canadian to this office. The success of the Labor Party in the British elections aroused Quebec's waning fear of socialism, but the distinction between British evolutionary and Continental revolutionary socialism was generally made by the press, as it had not been when the C.C.F., modeled on the British Labor Party, was regarded as a serious threat to the old Canadian parties.

Dominion Day and the meeting in August of the first Dominion-Provincial Conference since 1941 evoked once more expressions of Quebec's willingness to collaborate with English Canada, so long as the terms of Confederation were respected and not altered to favor centralization of power at Ottawa, which was repugnant to French-Canadian individualism and regarded as a grave danger to the maintenance of Quebec's language, laws, and customs. The avoidance of an anticipated clash between Prime Minister King and Premier Duplessis on this occasion was greeted with pleasure, and while the conference was adjourned until November for study of the federal proposals, a cry was heard for the immediate end of wartime restrictions, conscription, and taxes.

Japan's capitulation brought tributes to those who had won the victory, calls to make the peace more lasting than that of 1918, and sober reflections on an altered world in which Britain was gravely weakened, France had fallen to minor rank, and the United States and Russia had become the dominant world powers. *Le Devoir* gloomily reflected that, though the fighting was over, the world was far from peace, and stressed the division among the conquerors and the injustice of their settlements.

The news of the trial and condemnation to death of Marshal Pétain, which took the edge off joy at the end of the war, was greeted in various fashions by the French press. *Le Canada* saw it as putting an end to an unfortunate difference between French Canadians; to *Le Devoir* it was 'a fearful blow to France's prestige in the world'; to *L'Action Catholique*, Freemasonry, banned by the Marshal, had avenged itself by preventing a fair trial. There was a general call for commutation of the sentence by General De Gaulle, though *Le Jour* defended France's right 'to condemn those who have tried to assassinate her.'[272]

17

It was a new French Canada which faced the postwar world, though many of its old characteristics had survived the changes brought by the conflict. A minority which had long sought cultural enhancement abroad was now emerging from cultural colonialism and learning to be itself instead of a provincial imitation of France. Quebec was more fully and consciously integrated into both North American and international life, though still determined to assert its Frenchness and Catholicity in the midst of what it regarded as an Anglo-Saxon and Protestant civilization. It still dreamed of being, as Cardinal Villeneuve put it, 'a little Paris and a little Rome.' The war had brought the full impact of the industrial revolution to bear upon Quebec, hastening its transition from a rural agricultural society to an urban industrial one. The profound social changes involved in this process were further complicated by the fact that the industries which were altering the face of the province were largely invaders, owned and operated by men who were cultural and sometimes political aliens to French Canada. The war favored a rapid development of the union movement, particularly the internationals, and made the Quebec worker less willing to accept lower wages, poorer working conditions, and longer hours than those of his English-Canadian or American fellows. He was increasingly eager for the same standard of living as they enjoyed, and for fuller educational opportunities than he had had in the past in French Canada's unbalanced social structure.

To some extent the French Canadian was beginning to turn against his traditional leaders, the clergy and the lawyer politicians, who acted as middlemen between the masses and the English-speaking economic and political overlords. New political and social leaders were rising from outside the old hereditary ruling caste of the élite, while some of the clergy displayed a new democratic outlook more appropriate to their origins than to the institutional conservatism arising from their economic isolation from the changing conditions of the life of the people. Lay leadership in Quebec's wide range of Catholic social movements, notably in the Catholic syndicates, was encouraged to check a growing anti-clericalism and to gratify a desire for more democratic ways. Those French Canadians who had served overseas had lost their traditional fear of the unknown, and were inclined to question the old standing order when they returned home. They sought to meet the challenge brought by the breakdown of the old rural parochial system along lines suggested by French and Belgian experience.

In the postwar period there was to be a clash of two mentalities: a Bourbon-like determination on the part of much of the traditional élite to maintain the old closed world, regardless of changed conditions, the attitude of a frozen mind which had learned nothing and forgotten nothing; and on the other hand a widespread desire among the younger intellectuals and the newly emancipated workers, prompted by recognition of worldwide social changes and particularly of French experience, to evolve a new social order incorporating what the outside world had to offer with the best of the French-Canadian tradition. French-Canadian nationalism was still vigorous despite the crumbling of the old self-centered isolationism, but thanks to the tremendous wartime development of Canadian national feeling there was a better possibility of French-Canadian particularism merging with English-Canadian nationalism into that greater Canadianism for which Laurier stood. National unity remained a probably unattainable ideal, for French and English will never be wholly one in Canada; but the prospects for national union were brighter than in the past, thanks to the wartime achievement of a freer and franker relationship between more English and French Canadians than ever before, and a common pride in Canada's wartime achievements. It remained to be seen whether Canada's new international role, as a leader among the minor powers and a middleman between Britain and the United States, would further the development of that union by common effort abroad, or whether differences on external policy would be added to those inevitable on domestic questions.

Notes

[1] F. H. Soward, *Canada in World Affairs: From Normandy to Paris, 1944–1945* (Toronto, 1950), 32. The quoted phrase is President Roosevelt's.

[2] *PIB*, I, 80.

[3] *Ibid.*, 81.

[4] *Ibid.*, 82.

[5] *Senate Debates 1944–5*, 21 June 1944, 210–18; T. D. Bouchard, *The Teaching of Canadian History* (St. Hyacinthe, 1944).

[6] Ecole Sociale Populaire, *Tout un peuple se dresse . . .* (Montréal, 1944).

[7] *L'Action nat.*, XXII (June-July 1944), VI, 490–1.

[8] *PIB*, I, 86.

[9] *Ibid.*, 89.

[10] *Ibid.*, 86.

[11] *Ibid.*, 92.

[12] *Ibid.*

[13] *Ibid*, 97.

[14] *Ibid.*

[15] *Montreal Gazette*, 17 Aug. 1944.

[16] *Saturday Night*, 17 Aug. 1944.

[17] *PIB*, I, 100.

[18] *Ibid.*, 102.

[19] *Ibid.*, 100.

[20] *Ibid.*, 103.
[21] *Ibid.*, II, 1.
[22] *Ibid.*, I, 142.
[23] *Ibid.*, II, 3.
[24] *Ibid.*, 4.
[25] *Ibid.*
[26] C. Stacey, *The Canadian Army 1939–1945* (Ottawa, 1948), 234.
[27] *Commons Debates 1944*, 29 Nov., VI, 6660.
[28] *Ibid.*, 22 Nov., 6508.
[29] Stacey, 233.
[30] *Commons Debates 1944*, 22 Nov., VI, 6505–6.
[31] *Halifax Chronicle-Herald*, 29 Dec. 1949, Angus Macdonald's statement.
[32] *Winnipeg Free Press*, 24 May 1948, G. Dexter, 'The Colonel.'
[33] *Commons Debates 1944*, 22 Nov., 6510.
[34] *Ibid.*, 6513, 6511.
[35] *Ottawa Citizen*, 6 Jan. 1950, G. Dexter, 'In Defence of Ralston.'
[36] *Commons Debates 1944*, 23 Nov., 6516.
[37] *Ibid.*, 6519.
[38] *Ibid.*, 6520.
[39] *Ibid.*, 6521.
[40] *Ibid.*, 6522.
[41] *Ibid.*, 6522–3.
[42] *Ibid.*, 6524.
[43] *Ibid.*
[44] *Ibid.*, 6524–8.
[45] *Ibid.*, 6529.
[46] *Ibid.*, 6537.
[47] *Ibid.*, 6538.
[48] *Ibid.*
[49] *Ibid.*, 6539.
[50] *Ibid.*, 6540.
[51] *Ibid.*, 6541.
[52] *Ibid.*, 6545.
[53] *Ibid.*, 6559.
[54] *Ibid.*, 6566.
[55] *Ibid.*, 24 Nov., 6568.
[56] *Ibid.*, 6579.
[57] *Ibid.*, 6579–80.
[58] *Ibid.*, 27 Nov., 6591.
[59] *Ibid.*, 6593.
[60] *Ibid.*, 6593–4.
[61] *Ibid.*, 6594.
[62] *Ibid.*, 6595.
[63] *Ibid.*, 6597.
[64] *Ibid.*, 6599.
[65] *Ibid.*, 6600.
[66] *Ibid.*, 6602.
[67] *Ibid.*, 6603.
[68] *Ibid.*, 6603–4.
[69] *Ibid.*, 6605.
[70] *Ibid.*, 6606.
[71] *Ibid.*, 6609.
[72] *Ibid.*, 6610.
[73] *Ibid.*, 6614.
[74] *Ibid.*, 6615.

[75] *Ibid.*, 6617.
[76] *Ibid.*, 6618.
[77] *Ibid.*, 6619.
[78] *Ibid.*, 6622.
[79] *Ibid.*, 6623.
[80] *Ibid.*, 6625.
[81] *Ibid.*, 6626.
[82] *Ibid.*, 28 Nov., 6634.
[83] *Ibid.*, 29 Nov., 6635.
[84] *Ibid.*, 6641.
[85] *Ibid.*, 6642.
[86] *Ibid.*, 6652.
[87] *Ibid.*
[88] *Ibid.*
[89] *Ibid.*, 6654.
[90] *Ibid.*
[91] *Ibid.*, 6654–5.
[92] *Ibid.*, 6657.
[93] *Winnipeg Free Press*, 24 May 1948, G. Dexter, 'The Colonel.'
[94] *Commons Debates 1944*, 29 Nov., 6659, 6661–3.
[95] *Ibid.*, 6663.
[96] *Ibid.*, 6663–4.
[97] *Ibid.*, 6666.
[98] *Ibid.*, 6665–6.
[99] *Ibid.*, 6676–7.
[100] *Ibid.*, 6680.
[101] *Ibid.*, 30 Nov., 6682.
[102] *Ibid.*, 6683.
[103] *Ibid.*, 6690.
[104] *Ibid.*, 6691.
[105] *Ibid.*, 6692.
[106] *Ibid.*, 6693.
[107] *Ibid.*, 6694.
[108] *Ibid.*
[109] *Ibid.*, 6695.
[110] *Ibid.*, 6696.
[111] *Ibid.*
[112] *Ibid.*, 6697.
[113] *Ibid.*, 6701–2.
[114] *Ibid.*, 6703.
[115] *Ibid.*, 6704.
[116] *Ibid.*, 6706.
[117] *Ibid.*, 6707.
[118] *Ibid.*, 6707–8.
[119] *Ibid.*, 6708.
[120] *Ibid.*
[121] *Ibid.*, 6708–9.
[122] *Ibid.*, 6709.
[123] *Ibid.*, 6710.
[124] *Ibid.*, 6711.
[125] *Ibid.*, 6711–12.
[126] *Ibid.*, 6712–13.
[127] *Ibid.*, 6713.
[128] *Ibid.*, 6714.
[129] *Ibid.*, 6716.

[130] *Ibid.*
[131] *Ibid.*, 6718.
[132] *Ibid.*, 6722.
[133] *Ibid.*, 6723.
[134] *Ibid.*, 6724–5.
[135] *Ibid.*, 6728.
[136] *Ibid.*, 6734.
[137] *Ibid.*, 6734, 6748–9.
[138] *Ibid.*, 4 Dec., 6756.
[139] *Ibid.*, 6758.
[140] *Ibid.*, 6759–61.
[141] *Ibid.*, 6763.
[142] *Ibid.*, 6768–9.
[143] *Ibid.*, 6771.
[144] *Ibid.*, 6787.
[145] *Ibid.*, 6790.
[146] *Ibid.*, 6791.
[147] *Ibid.*, 5 Dec., 6803.
[148] *Ibid.*, 6806.
[149] *Ibid.*, 6809.
[150] *Ibid.*, 6817.
[151] *Ibid.*, 6818.
[152] *Ibid.*, 6820.
[153] *Ibid.*, 6829.
[154] *Ibid.*, 6829–30.
[155] *Ibid.*, 6830.
[156] *Ibid.*, 6830–1.
[157] *Ibid.*, 6831.
[158] *Ibid.*, 6832.
[159] *Ibid.*, 6 Dec., 6858.
[160] *Ibid.*, 6859.
[161] *Ibid.*, 6860.
[162] *Ibid.*, 6863.
[163] *Ibid.*, 6864.
[164] *Ibid.*, 6869.
[165] *Ibid.*
[166] *Ibid.*, 6872–3.
[167] *Ibid.*, 6874.
[168] *Ibid.*, 7 Dec., 6891.
[169] *Ibid.*, 6893–4.
[170] *Ibid.*, 6895.
[171] *Ibid.*, 6898.
[172] *Ibid.*, 6897, 6901.
[173] *Ibid.*, 6900.
[174] *Ibid.*, 6902.
[175] *Ibid.*, 6907.
[176] *Ibid.*, 6909.
[177] *Ibid.*, 6911.
[178] *Ibid.*, 6914–16.
[179] *Ibid.*, 6918.
[180] *Ibid.*, 6920.
[181] *Ibid.*, 6922.
[182] *Ibid.*, 6926.
[183] *Ibid.*, 6928–30.
[184] *Ibid.*, 6933.

[185] *Ibid.*, 6935.
[186] *Ibid.*, 6939.
[187] *Ibid.*, 6941.
[188] *Ibid.*, 6942.
[189] *Ibid.*, 6943.
[190] *Ibid.*, 6944.
[191] *Ibid.*, 6945.
[192] *Ibid.*, 6949–50.
[193] *Ibid.*, 6950–1.
[194] *Ibid.*, 6951.
[195] *Ibid.*, 6952.
[196] *Senate Debates 1944–5*, 28 Nov., 464–5.
[197] *Ibid.*, 30 Nov., 477.
[198] *Ibid.*, 478.
[199] *Ibid.*, 489.
[200] *Ibid.*, 480–1.
[201] *Ibid.*, 530.
[202] *Ibid.*, 536.
[203] *Montreal Herald*, 30 Nov. 1944.
[204] *PIB*, II, 26.
[205] *Ibid.*, 29.
[206] *Ibid.*, 30.
[207] *Commons Debates 1945*, Sess. I, 5 April, I, 578.
[208] *Ibid.*
[209] *Ibid.*, 577.
[210] Stacey, 235.
[211] *Commons Debates 1945*, Sess. I, 5 April, 584.
[212] *Ibid.*
[213] *Ibid.*, 635.
[214] H. Bourassa, *Hier, aujourd'hui et démain* (Montréal, 1916), 169–70.
[215] *Commons Debates 1935*, 1 April, III, 2287.
[216] *L'Action fran.*, VII (mai 1922), 5, 258–74.
[217] D. O'Leary, *Séparatisme, doctrine constructive* (Montréal, 1937).
[218] *L'Autorite* (Montréal), 19 May 1945.
[219] *Le Bloc*, I (19 Feb. 1944), 2.
[220] *PIB*, II, 50; *International Journal*, III (autumn 1944), 4, 334–48, Iris C. Podea, 'Pan-American Sentiment in French Canada.'
[221] *Ibid.*, 37.
[222] *Ibid.*, 36.
[223] *Ibid.*, 47.
[224] *Ibid.*, 48.
[225] *Ibid.*, 49.
[226] *Ibid.*, 51.
[227] *Ibid.*, 45.
[228] *Ibid.*, 51.
[229] *Ibid.*, 45
[230] *Ibid.*
[231] *Ibid.*, 58.
[232] *Commons Debates 1945*, Sess. I, 19 March, 1.
[233] *Ibid.*, 20 March, 21–2.
[234] *Ibid.*, 29–30.
[235] *Ibid.*, 54–5.
[236] *Ibid.*, 59.
[237] *Ibid.*, 60.
[238] *Ibid.*, 70–6.

[239] *Ibid.*, 100.
[240] *Ibid.*, 101.
[241] *Ibid.*, 25 March, 125.
[242] *Ibid.*, 126.
[243] *Ibid.*, 146.
[244] *Ibid.*
[245] *Ibid.*, 148.
[246] *Ibid.*, 23 March, 159.
[247] *Ibid*, 160.
[248] *Ibid.*, 186.
[249] *Maclean's Magazine* (1 Jan. 1944), M. Raymond, 'What Does the *Bloc Populaire* Stand For?'
[250] *Commons Debates 1945*, Sess. I, 27 March, I, 270.
[251] *Ibid.*, 271.
[252] *Ibid.*, 279.
[253] *Ibid.*, 283–4.
[254] *Ibid.*, 295–6.
[255] *PIB*, II, 58.
[256] *Commons Debates 1945*, Sess. I, 3 April, I, 403.
[257] *Ibid.*, 404.
[258] *PIB*, II, 64.
[259] *Commons Debates 1945*, Sess. I, 11 April, I, 764; *PIB*, II, 61.
[260] *Ibid.*, 13 April, 865–6.
[261] Liberals 36 per cent; Progressive Conservatives 34 per cent; CCF 12 per cent; Independents 12 per cent. *PIB*, II, 62.
[262] *PIB*, II, 65.
[263] *Ibid.*, 68.
[264] *Ibid.*, 73.
[265] *Ibid.*, 74.
[266] *Ibid.*, 76.
[267] *Ibid.*, 79.
[268] *Ibid.*, 1.
[269] *Ibid.*, 69.
[270] *Ibid.*, 70.
[271] *Ibid.*, 71.
[272] *Ibid.*, 100.

INDEX

D

E

G

H

I

U

V

W

PRINTED BY PURNELL AND SONS, LTD.
PAULTON (SOMERSET) AND LONDON